CHAPTER TWELVE:
STANDARD COSTING FOR OVERHEAD

CHAPTER THIRTEEN:
ABSORPTION AND VARIABLE COSTING

CHAPTER FOURTEEN:
COST-VOLUME-PROFIT ANALYSIS

CHAPTER FIFTEEN:
RELEVANT COSTING

MASCO

CHAPTER SIXTEEN:
THE MASTER BUDGET

CHAPTER SEVENTEEN:
COST CONTROL FOR DISCRETIONARY COSTS

CHAPTER EIGHTEEN
CONTROL OF INVENTORY AND PRODUCTION

CHAPTER NINETEEN:
BASICS OF CAPITAL BUDGETING

CHAPTER TWENTY:
ADVANCED CAPITAL BUDGETING TOPICS

Unilever

CHAPTER TWENTY-ONE:
RESPONSIBILITY ACCOUNTING AND TRANSFER
PRICING IN DECENTRALIZED ORGANIZATIONS

CHAPTER TWENTY-TWO:
MEASURING ORGANIZATIONAL PERFORMANCE

CHAPTER TWENTY-THREE:
REWARDING PERFORMANCE

COST ACCOUNTING

TRADITIONS AND INNOVATIONS

SECOND EDITION

ACCOUNTING TEXTBOOKS FROM WEST EDUCATIONAL PUBLISHING

Listed alphabetically by author

Jesse T. Barfield, Cecily A. Raiborn, and Michael R. Kinney: *Cost Accounting: Traditions and Innovations, 2E*

John G. Burch: *Cost and Management Accounting: A Modern Approach*

William H. Hoffman, Jr., William A. Raabe, and James E. Smith: *West's Federal Taxation: Corporations, Partnerships, Estates, and Trusts, 1994 Edition*

William H. Hoffman, Jr., James E. Smith, and Eugene Willis: *West's Federal Taxation: Individual Income Taxes, 1994 Edition*

Michael C. Knapp: *Contemporary Auditing: Issues and Cases*

Michael C. Knapp: *Financial Accounting: Issues and Cases*

Larry F. Konrath: *Auditing Concepts and Applications: A Risk Analysis Approach, 2E*

Joseph G. Louderback, G. Thomas Friedlob, and Franklin J. Plewa: *Survey of Accounting*

Kevin Murphy: *Concepts in Federal Taxation*

William A. Raabe, Gerald E. Whittenburg, and John C. Bost: *West's Federal Tax Research, 3E*

Cecily A. Raiborn, Jesse T. Barfield, and Michael R. Kinney: *Managerial Accounting*

Lanny M. Solomon, Larry M. Walther, and Richard J. Vargo: *Financial Accounting, 3E*

Lanny M. Solomon, Larry M. Walther, Linda Plunkett, and Richard J. Vargo: *Accounting Principles, 4E*

Gerald E. Whittenburg, Ray Whittington, and Martha Altus: *Income Tax Fundamentals, 1994 Edition*

Eugene Willis, William H. Hoffman, Jr., David Maloney, and William A. Raabe: *West's Federal Taxation: Comprehensive Volume, 1994 Edition*

SECOND
EDITION

COST ACCOUNTING

TRADITIONS AND INNOVATIONS

JESSE T. BARFIELD

Loyola University—New Orleans

CECILY A. RAIBORN

Loyola University—New Orleans

MICHAEL R. KINNEY

Texas A & M University

WEST PUBLISHING
COMPANY

Minneapolis/St. Paul
New York
Los Angeles
San Francisco

COPYEDITING   Sheryl Rose
COMPOSITION   G & S Typesetters, Inc.
TEXT DESIGN   Diane Beasley
PAGE LAYOUT   TECHarts/Stephanie Koons and Michelle
  Merrill Betsill
ARTWORK   TECHarts/Brian Betsill
COVER DESIGN   Roslyn Stendahl, Dapper Design
COVER PHOTO   © Arthur Meyerson
ENDSHEET DESIGN   Randy Miyake
Production, Prepress, Printing and Binding by West
  Publishing Company

WEST'S COMMITMENT TO THE ENVIRONMENT

In 1906, West Publishing Company began recycling materials left over from the production of books. This began a tradition of efficient and responsible use of resources. Today, up to 95 percent of our legal books and 70 percent of our college and school texts are printed on recycled, acid-free stock. West also recycles nearly 22 million pounds of scrap paper annually—the equivalent of 181,717 trees. Since the 1960s, West has devised ways to capture and recycle waste inks, solvents, oils, and vapors created in the printing process. We also recycle plastics of all kinds, wood, glass, corrugated cardboard, and batteries, and have eliminated the use of styrofoam book packaging. We at West are proud of the longevity and the scope of our commitment to the environment.

Material from Uniform CPA Examination, Questions and Unofficial Answers, copyright © 1977–1979, 1981–1985, and 1988 by American Institute of Certified Public Accountants, Inc., is reprinted (or adapted) with permission.

Material from Certified Management Accountant Examination, copyright © 1972, 1974, 1976–1988, and 1990–1992 by Institute of Certified Management Accountants, is reprinted (or adapted) with permission.

Photo credits follow index.

COPYRIGHT © 1991   by WEST PUBLISHING
                         COMPANY
COPYRIGHT © 1994   by WEST PUBLISHING
                         COMPANY
                    610 Opperman Drive
                    P.O. Box 64526
                    St. Paul, MN 55164-0526

Printed in the United States of America
01 00 99 98 97 96 95 94   8 7 6 5 4 3 2 1

Library of Congress Cataloging-in-Publication Data

Barfield, Jesse T.
    Cost accounting : traditions and innovations / Jesse T. Barfield, Cecily A. Raiborn, Michael R. Kinney — 2nd ed.
      p. cm.
    Includes indexes.
    ISBN 0-314-02904-4 (student edition)
    ISBN 0-314-02878-1 (annotated instructor's edition)
    1. Cost accounting.   I. Raiborn, Cecily A.
II. Kinney, Michael R.
III. Title.
HF5686.C8B2758   1993
657'.42—dc20   93-41871
                                                     CIP ∞

BRIEF CONTENTS

CONTENTS

PART II

ALLOCATING INDIRECT COSTS   117

CHAPTER

4   DEVELOPING PREDETERMINED OVERHEAD RATES   118

CHAPTER

5

ACTIVITY-BASED COST SYSTEMS FOR MANAGEMENT 164

CHAPTER

6 ADDITIONAL OVERHEAD ALLOCATION CONCEPTS AND ISSUES   212

PART III

PRODUCT COSTING METHODS   253

CHAPTER

7   JOB ORDER COSTING   254

CHAPTER

8

PROCESS COSTING   296

CHAPTER

9

SPECIAL PRODUCTION ISSUES: SPOILED/ DEFECTIVE UNITS AND ACCRETION   344

CHAPTER

10 COST ALLOCATION FOR JOINT PRODUCTS AND BY-PRODUCTS 386

CHAPTER

11

GENERAL CONCEPTS OF STANDARD COSTING; MATERIAL AND LABOR STANDARDS   422

CHAPTER

12 STANDARD COSTING FOR OVERHEAD   474

Learning Objectives   474
Introducing Springfield ReManufacturing Company   475
Flexible Budgets and Standard Overhead Rates   476
Flexible Budgets and Variable Overhead   476
NEWS NOTE Choosing the Capacity   478
Flexible Budgets and Fixed Overhead   478
Combined Overhead Rate Variances   479
One-Variance Approach   480
Two-Variance Approach   480
Three-Variance Approach   483
Four-Variance Approach   485

CHAPTER

13 ABSORPTION AND VARIABLE COSTING 516

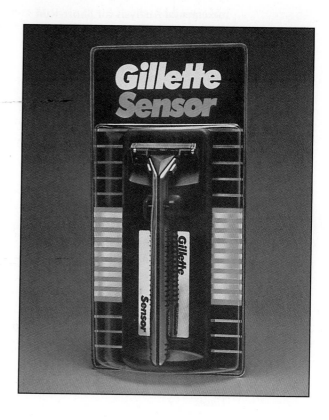

PART IV

COST PLANNING   557

CHAPTER

14   COST-VOLUME-PROFIT ANALYSIS   558

PART V

COST CONTROL   707

CHAPTER

17

COST CONTROL FOR DISCRETIONARY COSTS   708

CHAPTER

**18 CONTROL OF INVENTORY
     AND PRODUCTION   748**

PART VI

DECISION MAKING   797

CHAPTER

19   BASICS OF CAPITAL BUDGETING   798

CHAPTER

20 ADVANCED CAPITAL BUDGETING TOPICS   848

CHAPTER

21 RESPONSIBILITY ACCOUNTING AND TRANSFER PRICING IN DECENTRALIZED ORGANIZATIONS 896

CHAPTER

22 MEASURING ORGANIZATIONAL PERFORMANCE 950

CHAPTER

23 REWARDING PERFORMANCE 998

PREFACE

Cost and management accounting are essential areas of knowledge for an accounting graduate. These areas are interrelated in that both are concerned with internal information. Cost accounting is used to determine the cost of manufacturing products and/or providing services in organizations involved in a conversion process. Conversion can include transforming a raw material into a finished good or an idea into an advertising campaign. Product and service costs are needed both for internal management decisions and for cost of goods sold and inventory valuation on external financial statements. Management accounting involves the provision of accounting information for the managerial functions of planning, controlling, evaluating performance, and making decisions. Thus, management accounting is applicable in all organizations regardless of whether they engage in a conversion process.

The distinction between these two accounting areas is becoming increasingly blurred because of overlapping job functions, growth in information technology, and institution of new production methods that require the availability of more nontraditional information. Therefore, this text addresses both cost and management accounting issues by including coverage of traditional product costing methods as well as innovative topics such as activity-based costing and management, the costs of quality, the accounting effects of a just-in-time philosophy, the use of nonfinancial performance measures, and the process of rewarding performance.

AUDIENCE

This book is written for students endeavoring to become professional accountants and aspiring to obtain professional certifications such as Certified Management Accountant (CMA), Certified Public Accountant (CPA), and/or Certified Internal Auditor (CIA). The text presents the essential issues of cost and management accounting thoroughly but concisely for use in a one- or two-semester course in a college accounting program. Typically, before taking cost accounting, students will have taken a principles of accounting or financial accounting course.

STRUCTURE

The text's chapter sequence reflects both curriculum characteristics and the authors' pedagogical preferences. Since many universities stress product cost computations in the first (or only) cost accounting course, we have grouped the various product costing techniques (job order, process, standard, joint, and absorption/variable) at the beginning of the text in Chapters 7 to 13. In addition, topics such as standard costing and variance analysis are generally covered simultaneously in a cost accounting course even though standard costing is truly a product costing or planning topic and variance analysis is a management control and performance evaluation topic.

Part 1 (Chapters 1 through 3) provides a foundation in both the current business environment (including quality considerations) and management accounting. Part 2 (Chapters 4 through 6) presents a variety of issues related to the allocation of indirect, overhead costs. This section considers the roles of activity-based costing and activity-based management in today's world-class businesses. Part 3 (Chapters 7 through 13) demonstrates the systems and methods of product costing, accounting for product shrinkage and expansion, and treatment of joint process costs. These chapters constitute the traditional cost accounting viewpoint in that the focus is on determining cost for use in valuation on financial statements. Chapters 14 through 23 concentrate on managerial information needs and processes. These chapters are divided into the areas of planning (Chapters 14 to 16), controlling (Chapters 17 and 18), decision making (Chapters 19 and 20), and performance evaluation (Chapters 21–23).

The chapter sequence of the text is only one of many ways that the topics may be covered; other potential sequences are provided in the preface to the Instructor's Manual. Each chapter is written in a fairly stand-alone fashion, assuming that the basic definitions have been covered. Since the end-of-chapter exercises and problems predominantly relate directly to the material within the chapter, an instructor wishing to vary the sequence of chapters should find few difficulties in assigning end-of-chapter material. If a problem in one chapter includes a significant use of another chapter's material, it is so designated in the heading to the problem. (For example, a standard costing problem may also be designated as a process costing problem.)

CHANGES IN THE SECOND EDITION

Because of its innovative topics, student orientation, readability, and inclusion of real-world applications and ethics, the first edition of this text was very well received. The second edition continues these positive features from the first edition; improves upon them by increasing their coverage as well as that of quality issues, multinational businesses, and modern business techniques; and incorporates suggestions from users and reviewers for organizational and pedagogical changes.

The Accounting Education Change Commission (in its "Position Statement Number One: Objectives of Education for Accountants") has also been instrumental in providing guidance on improving and adding to the text's pedagogical features. The AECC has indicated that it is essential for accounting graduates to possess strong communication, intellectual, and interpersonal skills as well as to understand professional ethics and make value-based judgments. Thus, to encourage students to improve their communication and intellectual skills, we have expanded the quantity of essay and "logic" problems in end-of-chapter materials, student study guide, and test bank. The end-of-chapter essay and logic problems directed at developing these skills are presented under the heading Communication Activities. To promote interpersonal skills, the Instructor's Manual provides ideas for group projects that may be assigned for oral or written presentation. And, to improve the process of analyzing and making ethical decisions, we have included more real-world ethics discussion questions in the end-of-chapter materials and a short end-of-text appendix about using these questions.

The following changes to the second edition of *Cost Accounting Traditions and Innovations* increase the text's teachability and real-world focus and enhance the student's comprehension and intellectual skills.

Organization

▪ Chapter 1 begins with a section on changes in the American business environment. This section (included in Chapter 16 of the first edition) has been expanded to discuss differences between companies' traditional short-run perspectives and their emerging long-run perspectives as well as the differences between techniques used by smaller businesses versus those of advanced manufacturing firms. The inclusion of this section helps students to understand the business environment of which they will be a part.

▪ The topics of conversion and stages of production have been moved to Chapter 2 to allow a better flow of macro-ideas in Chapter 1 and to attach the information on conversion more directly to the discussions of direct materials, direct labor, and overhead. Additionally, some definitions have been deleted from this chapter and placed elsewhere in the text to allow a smoother flow of ideas.

■ Chapter 3 is a new chapter on quality considerations in business. This chapter discusses what quality is, why it is demanded, and how it affects the costs and processes of production and service provision as well as pricing issues. Benchmarking, implementation of total quality management, the Malcolm Baldrige Quality Award, and the standards of the International Standards Organization (the ISO 9000 series) are also discussed.

■ Chapter 4 covers the topic of flexible budgets, which was in the first edition's Chapter 10 with standard costs. The discussion of flexible budgets helps students understand why a predetermined fixed overhead application rate changes depending on the volume level chosen and why a variable overhead application rate does not.

■ The use of standard costs in job order and process costing systems has been moved to the appendices of Chapters 7 and 8, respectively. This change allows faculty to include or exclude this material without interrupting the flow of the chapters.

■ The first edition's Chapter 23 on least squares regression analysis has been condensed into a section in Chapter 4 on analyzing mixed costs and the discussion of correlation and dispersion measures is now presented in an appendix to Chapter 4. This reduction in coverage is based on the authors' opinion that a brief discussion of these materials is useful in relation to analyzing mixed costs; however, intense discussion of this topic is more appropriate for a course in either the general education or general business education component of a curriculum. The detailed presentation on scattergraphs in the previous edition has been deleted.

■ The first edition's Chapter 16 on activity-based costing (ABC) and activity-based management (ABM) has been moved to Chapter 5 and expanded in the second edition. This new placement allows the material to be covered with other chapters on overhead allocation and reflects changes in the business environment and the adoption of ABC and ABM by many world-class companies. The theory of constraints has been moved to an appendix and information on critical path has been deleted from this chapter as beyond the scope of the text.

■ The relevant costing chapter has been moved to follow Chapter 14 on cost-volume-profit analysis. In addition, the first edition's Chapter 22 on linear programming has been condensed as an appendix to Chapter 15 on relevant costing. LP is used in making scarce resource decisions and, as such, should be included with this chapter's discussion. Detailed coverage of this topic, however, is more appropriate for a course in the general business education component (such as quantitative methods, production management, or management science).

■ The first edition's Chapter 17 on performance measurement has been divided into two chapters: Chapter 21—Responsibility Accounting and Transfer Pricing in Decentralized Organizations and Chapter 22—Measuring Organizational Performance. Transfer pricing has been combined with responsibility accounting because decentralized units often use transfer prices to convert cost centers into profit centers. Additionally, the business and ethical issues of transfer pricing in multinational organizations is discussed. The new performance measurement chapter provides more insight into the determination and use of nonfinancial performance measures in conjunction with the traditional financial measures of performance. Such measures are increasingly important in today's quality-driven business environment.

■ A new chapter entitled "Rewarding Performance" has been added as an appropriate follow-through to the performance measurement chapter. This chapter discusses basic compensation strategy, the pay-for-performance plans currently being instituted in many organizations, differences between worker and managerial compensation, and a brief overview of the tax implications of various compensation elements. In addition, the chapter addresses the issue of rewarding performance in a multinational enterprise.

Pedagogy

■ All chapters (except Chapters 1 and 23) now include demonstration problems and solutions. These problems are designed to reinforce the student's understanding of chapter concepts before attempting the end-of-chapter materials.

■ Each chapter contains an "Introducing" and "Revisiting" segment about a real organization. Through these chapter openers and closures, students are shown how the topics included in the chapter affect businesses on a daily basis. The opening vignettes have been selected to illustrate both domestic/international, profit/ not-for-profit, large/small, and manufacturing/service organizations. Some organizations that are featured include the Institute of Management Accountants, McIlhenny Company, Marks & Spencer, Merlin Candies, Fresh From Texas, Southwest Airlines, Seton Medical Facilities, and Unilever. While the real organization's data cannot be used in chapter numerical computations (for competitive reasons), comparable data for an illustrative company in the same type of business are used throughout the chapter.

■ To reinforce the real-world perspective and maintain student interest, the chapters contain boxed "News Note" examples from the current business press featuring up-to-date applications of text concepts in real-world situations. These "Notes" are keyed with graphic icons as being primarily related to one of the following areas of interest: behavioral, general business, international, and quality. There are approximately three to five notes per chapter, featuring companies such as Dawson/Berg Corporation, Motorola, L.L. Bean, Mars Co., Boeing, and Toyota.

■ The international and service dimensions of business have been more heavily integrated in the chapters, illustrative examples, and end-of-chapter materials. Such inclusions reflect the ever-increasing global expansion of business enterprises and the diminished quantity of manufacturing in the United States.

■ In addition to the end-of-text glossary, page references for chapter definitions are included for each key term in each chapter.

■ Topics are provided in parentheses for all exercises and problems to indicate the nature of the material included in the end-of-chapter item. These lead-ins make it easier for faculty to select end-of-chapter materials that reinforce chapter objectives or for students to select additional materials to supplement assigned homework.

■ Approximately 25 percent new end-of-chapter items have been added, some of which reflect real-world situations. First edition end-of-chapter materials have been revised or replaced as appropriate; additional problems from current CMA examinations are included. Many of these materials are unstructured thought problems that require students to use their analytical skills to excerpt the relevant information from a set of facts and organize the information into the necessary format. Such end-of-chapter materials are designed to enhance the students' intellectual skills rather than provide a mechanism for rote recalculation of text examples.

■ As mentioned above in response to guidelines of the Accounting Education Change Commission, there is an increased focus in the end-of-chapter materials on written communication skills. Many of these conceptual, essay-type materials require students to analyze facts and exercise judgment in determining their answers. Some of these materials are related to the provision of information to another party (such as management), while others reflect ethics- or quality-based considerations. All materials emphasizing communication skills are found under the heading Communication Activities.

■ End-of-chapter materials now include Quality Discussion questions similar to the Ethics Discussions of the first edition. The quality discussion questions focus on the influence of introducing (or choosing not to introduce) quality techniques on company costs, employee and customer behavior, and the production/service process. These questions provide the dual benefit of indicating that ethical and quality choices are important to an organization's current and future existence as well as providing an additional avenue for written expression and logical thought.

■ The end-of-chapter section "Suggestions for Individual or Class Projects" in the first edition has been moved to the Instructor's Manual. This section provides an expanded list of potential topics that both enhance communication skills and provide the opportunity for students to work in groups to develop the interpersonal skills that are critical in the business world.

■ An end-of-text appendix is included to provide a framework for answering the ethics discussion questions. This appendix briefly discusses two common ethical theories (utilitarianism and categorical imperatives) and the process of making ethical choices. (This information was provided at the beginning of the Solutions Manual of the first edition.)

STYLE

This text is extremely student-oriented and integrates procedural methods with the conceptual and behavioral aspects of information that help students solve real-world problems. The authors have endeavored to make the text highly readable and to provide numerous examples, models, and illustrations of real-world applicability. The coverage is up to date and presents the effects on accounting of phenomena such as just-in-time inventory management, flexible manufacturing systems, and expanded global markets.

Features in the text (such as learning objectives, opening and closing vignettes, news notes, chapter summaries, demonstration problems, and a full range of end-of-chapter materials) have been designed to promote the learning process, provide a high student interest level, and make the text a valuable student resource. The inclusion of quality concepts, international business considerations, discussions of diverse types of organizations, and end-of-chapter materials focusing on actual quality and ethical issues reinforces the applied nature of the text and assists faculty to make the course information more relevant to the students.

INSTRUCTOR SUPPORT MATERIALS

The instructor support package is an innovative response to the growing demand for creative and effective teaching methodologies. The supplements are designed to provide a comprehensive resource package for all faculty adopting this text; the materials used will depend on the faculty member's interest areas, class size, equipment availability, and teaching experience. All supplements not prepared by the authors have been reviewed by the authors for consistency and accuracy with the textual materials.

■ *Annotated Instructor's Edition*   This special edition of the text was prepared by the authors and contains a variety of margin notes to improve and enhance teaching effectiveness and efficiency. The new version of the Annotated Instructor's Edition includes a greater number of annotations per chapter. The margin notes include:

Teaching Notes that provide additional clarification of points or examples that might be used in class

Points to Emphasize that indicate logical "checkpoints" of student clarity on subject matter

Points to Consider that indicate questions to generate student responses which indicate understanding of text material

Teaching Transparency notations that indicate points at which selected transparencies can be used (the transparency masters are included in the Instructor's Manual)

Video Icons that identify points at which videos supplied by West Publishing could be used to enhance or reinforce text material

Check Figures that provide solutions to numerical end-of-chapter materials

■ *Instructor's Manual* This manual (developed by Gregory K. Lowry of Southern State Community College) provides for each chapter a listing of terminology, a thorough lecture outline summary, an assignment classification table (indicating the topical breakdown and level of difficulty of all end-of-chapter questions, exercises, problems, and cases), some CMA exam multiple-choice questions for use as additional test materials or for quizzes, and a selected bibliography of current readings. Masters for over 40 teaching transparencies referenced in the annotated instructor's edition are also included at the end of this volume. These masters are *not* duplicates of textual exhibits, but rather provide additional perspectives on text materials.

■ *Solutions Manual* This volume, prepared by the authors, and independently reviewed and checked for accuracy, contains complete solutions to each question, exercise, problem, and case in the text. Some suggested discussion points or (if from professional exams) complete answers are provided for the ethics and quality questions, but no distinct right-or-wrong answers are given. This volume also contains a copy of the Student Check Figures.

■ *Solution Transparency Acetates* Approximately 250 acetates are provided from the solutions manual for all numerical end-of-chapter materials.

■ *Astound™* This package (prepared by Donna S. Dietz of Concordia College) is a state-of-the-art presentation graphics program for Microsoft Windows™ and the Macintosh. All transparency material is preloaded onto the program, which gives instructors the opportunity to customize transparencies (by editing, adding, or deleting material) so they are specific to classroom needs. Illustrations include additional problems with solutions, definitions, charts, graphs, figures, and other visual support not found in the text. Astound's animation allows for curve editing, scalable type, type manipulation, shape and color blends, rotation and skewing, and variable zoom.

■ *Test Bank* The Test Bank has been prepared by Louis P. Ramsay of Clemson University and contains over one thousand multiple-choice, short exercise, and short discussion questions with related solutions. It has been updated from the first edition to include approximately 40 percent new materials. Two to three additional computational problems have been added for each numerically based chapter. Each question has been categorized according to Bloom's Taxonomy for cognitive complexity. The questions are classified as recall, comprehension, application, and calculation. Furthermore, difficulty rankings allow the instructor to know in advance if students are likely to find a question to be easy, medium, or hard.

■ *WesTest™* This supplement is a computerized version of the hard-copy test bank. WesTest includes edit and word processing features that allow test customization through the addition, deletion, or scrambling of test selections. WesTest is available in DOS, Windows, and Macintosh formats.

■ *Videos* Because the video package accompanying the first edition was so highly praised, additional new videos are available. Many of these videos are directly tied to the companies discussed in the opening vignettes or "Notes" contained in the chapters. There are an average of three to four video segments of various lengths per chapter. In addition to the previously available "On the Road to Manufacturing Excellence" video, two new videos ("We're Getting Closer" and "Managing the Supply Chain") from the Association for Manufacturing Excellence are available to adopters. Many of the in-text examples have been drawn from the video library titled, "Strengthening America's Competitiveness: Resource Management Insights for Small Business Success." This video library was developed by the Blue Chip Enterprise Initiative, sponsored by Connecticut Mutual Life Insurance Company, the U.S. Chamber of Commerce, and *Nation's Business* magazine. The initiative seeks out and recognizes businesses that have demonstrated exceptional management of key resources to meet challenges and emerge stronger. Almost every chapter in the text has one or more videos to accompany it; points of reference for classroom use are fully integrated in the Annotated Instructor's Edition. These tapes are provided free to qualified adopters.

▮ *Video Guide* A video guide has been developed to accompany the video package and provide information on length, alternative points of usage within the text, highlights to address, and some discussion questions to stimulate classroom discussion.

STUDENT SUPPORT MATERIALS

Student supplements are an essential part of providing a quality package for a text and are important in helping students to learn on their own—a factor stressed by the Accounting Education Change Commission. The following items are available for students.

▮ *Student Study Guide* This study guide (developed by Louis P. Ramsay of Clemson University) is a chapter-by-chapter manual that allows students, through independent review and self-examination, to gain additional exposure and reinforce the materials detailed in the text. The study guide contains chapter learning objectives, overviews, detailed chapter notes, and self-test questions. The study guide has been updated to include approximately 40 percent new materials, and two to three additional computational problems have been added for each numerically based chapter. In addition, several projects are included for each chapter that allow students to exercise their written and oral communication and logic skills and, at the same time, develop their interpersonal skills through interaction with other students.

▮ *Student Check Figures* For instructors who wish to provide students with answers to end-of-chapter materials, this list has been prepared by the authors from the solutions contained in the solutions manual. The check figures provide a reference point answer for all numerical end-of-chapter materials, except those for which the provision of a check figure would be inappropriate. Check figures are available free of charge when ordered, to be shrink-wrapped with the textbook.

▮ *Solution Generator and Analyzer for Lotus® 1-2-3®* There are two versions of this package (developed by Ronald J. Grambo of Scranton University) that allow students to solve selected end-of-chapter exercises and problems using Lotus® 1-2-3.® The first, easier version is free to adopters and provides preloaded templates that require the students to input key numbers to obtain the solutions. For more advanced students, a separate, salable version of the package (which includes a disk and workbook) is available that requires students to identify the issues of the problem, program the necessary formulas, and input the data from the exercise or problem. This dual approach to Lotus allows maximum flexibility for use by students at different levels of programming expertise. The second version of the Lotus material also includes comprehensive exercises and problems in addition to those in the text.

■ *Practice Sets*   Two practice sets are available to supplement students' understanding of specific text materials.

Weston Manufacturing: An Activity-Based Costing Case, developed by Mark Bettner of Bucknell University, illustrates activity-based costing using a manufacturing company that produces agricultural irrigation systems and customized commercial irrigation systems. This practice set concentrates on determination of cost drivers and their use in assigning overhead costs to products. It can be used when teaching Chapter 5 or in conjunction with several chapters from the text to show the student the impact of activity-based costing on decision making. A solutions manual is available for instructors.

Laser Logos, Inc. is a computerized practice set that was written by Dana Forgione of The University of Baltimore and L. Murphy Smith of Texas A&M University. It provides students with the opportunity to develop a complete master budget and to use the budgeted information to make managerial decisions. A solutions manual indicates how the practice set can be used in conjunction with Chapter 16 or as a continuing problem for the entire term. The student workbook is available in IBM-compatible format with a disk.

■ *Insights: Readings in Cost Accounting*   A readings book is available for those faculty who wish to supplement text assignments with articles from the current business press. This softcover book contains 20 selections from *FORTUNE, Management Accounting, Journal of Accountancy,* and *Journal of Cost Management* that discuss contemporary issues in cost and management accounting.

Acknowledgements

We would like to thank all the people who have helped us during the revision of this text. The constructive comments and suggestions made by the following reviewers were instrumental in developing, rewriting, and improving the quality, readability, and student orientation of *Cost Accounting Traditions and Innovations.*

C. Rick Aldridge	Western Kentucky University
Jack Bailes	Oregon State University
Larry Bitner	University of Richmond
Sue Borkowski	LaSalle University
James Bullock	New Mexico State University
Judith Cassidy	University of Mississippi
C. Douglas Cloud	Pepperdine University
George Costouros	San Jose State University
David Coy	Adrian College
Karen Cravens	University of Tulsa
Donna Dietz	Concordia College—Moorhead
Janet Dye	Western Carolina University
Elaine Evans	Mississippi University for Women
James A. Fellows	University of Southern Florida—St. Petersburg
David P. Franz	San Francisco State University
Clarence Fries	University of Arkansas
Margaret Gagne	University of Colorado—Colorado Springs
Ronald Grambo	University of Scranton
Kenneth Harper	San Jose State University
Horace Harrell	Georgia Southern University
Jan Heier	Auburn University
Jay Holmen	University of Wisconsin—Eau Claire
Philip Jagolinzer	University of South Maine
Robert Jordan	University of Wisconsin—Superior
Bob Kee	University of Alabama

Randy Kossman	DeVry Institute of Technology
George Letcher	University of Pittsburgh—Johnstown
Paulette Letnes	North Dakota State University
Greg Lowry	Southern State Community College
Bernie Michalek	Larouche University
Robert G. Morgan	East Tennessee State University
Ray Newman	Ramapo College of New Jersey
Fred Nordhauser	University of Texas at San Antonio
Peter Poznanski	Cleveland State University
Joseph Razek	University of New Orleans
Jack M. Ruhl	Louisiana State University
Jeffrey Schatzberg	University of Arizona
Ragnor Seglund	California State University—Sacramento
Douglas Sharp	Wichita State University
Chris Stenberg	Robert Morris College
Phyllis Thomas	Middle Tennessee State University
John Virchick	Chapman University
Beth Walter	Central Michigan University
George Wendelburg	Delaware State College

Special mention must be given to James M. Emig of Villanova University for his hard work as a problem checker and to Joel Ridenour for his arduous task of obtaining all the necessary permissions. In addition, use of materials from the Institute of Management Accountants and American Institute of CPAs, the various periodical publishers, and the featured organizations have contributed significantly to making this revised text a more useful learning tool for the students. Lastly, the authors thank all the people at West Publishing (Rick Leyh, Jessica Evans, Charlene Johnston, Jennifer Ziegler, Jayne Lindesmith, Ann Hillstrom, and Beth Hoeppner) who have helped us on this project and our families and friends for their support and encouragement during this process.

Jesse Barfield
Cecily Raiborn
Mike Kinney

OVERVIEW

THE CONTEMPORARY ENVIRONMENT OF COST AND MANAGEMENT ACCOUNTING

LEARNING OBJECTIVES

After completing this chapter, you should be able to answer these questions:

1. What changes have recently taken place in the business environment?
2. How do management and financial accounting relate to each other?
3. How are cost and management accounting related?
4. What is the scope of management accounting?
5. What is the Certified Management Accountant designation?
6. What standards exist for cost and management accounting?
7. How are ethics integrated into the field of management accounting?
8. (Appendix) How are organizations structured?

INTRODUCING

THE INSTITUTE OF MANAGEMENT ACCOUNTANTS

The Institute of Management Accountants was founded in 1919 as the National Association of Cost Accountants. The 37 charter members believed there was a need for such an organization because of the confusion surrounding the determination of "cost" in cost-plus contracts during and after World War I. There have been two name changes since the organization's start: in 1957, the name was changed to the National Association of Accountants and, in 1991, to the Institute of Management Accountants.

The organization was started to develop individual management accountants technically and professionally. It has succeeded in its function through its continuing education programs, publications (including the *Management Accounting* journal), national and international conferences, and monthly local chapter meetings. Additionally, under the auspices of its Institute of Certified Management Accountants, the IMA offers a professional certification (the CMA) for management accountants and financial executives who pass an examination and meet specified experience requirements.

The IMA seeks to identify and define the management accounting discipline and to call attention to the increasingly dynamic, decision-making responsibilities of the management accountant. In conjunction with bodies such as the Financial Accounting Standards Board, the Securities and Exchange Commission, and the Financial Executives Institute, the IMA addresses a variety of accounting issues.

The **Institute of Management Accountants** (IMA) is one of many professional organizations whose members hold, or are interested in, managerial positions. Effective leadership of any type of organization requires accurate information that can help managers track costs, analyze and solve problems, and reduce uncertainty. Accounting, often referred to as the language of business, provides much of the necessary information. There are two primary "variations" of the accounting language: financial accounting and management accounting. Cost accounting is a mutual subset of financial and management accounting.

Institute of Management Accountants

Financial accounting focuses on the needs of external users (stockholders, creditors, and regulatory agencies) and is dedicated to processing information about historical, monetary transactions. The basic output of the financial accounting process is a set of financial statements that have been prepared using generally accepted accounting principles. On the other hand, **management accounting** focuses on the information needs of an organization's internal managers—needs that are related to their planning, controlling, and decision-making functions. Some management needs are satisfied by historical, monetary information based on generally accepted accounting principles. Other needs require forecasted, qualitative, and frequently nonfinancial information that has been developed and computed for their specific decision purposes.

Management accounting

The environment in which an organization operates affects the information needs of its managers. Thus, this chapter first presents an overview of the contemporary

■ **EXHIBIT 1–1**
Changes in the Business Environment

	"THE OLD DAYS"	"THE NEW AGE"
Major type of business in U.S.*	Manufacturing	Service
Wage rates	Low	High
Major workforce	Human	Machine
View of market	Domestic	International
Performance measurement focus	Production	Consumer
Product variety	Limited	Virtually unlimited
Size of production lots	Large	Limited
Legal environment	Regulated	Deregulated
Social consciousness	Obligatory	Responsive

*In the past, other countries were often primarily involved in service activities or limited manufacturing, choosing to import many of their "hard" goods. Many of these countries have now shifted to manufacturing and exporting activities.

business environment. The chapter then explains the relationships among financial, management, and cost accounting. In addition, the chapter discusses the professional management accounting certification, cost/management accounting standards, and the ethics code for management accountants.

CHANGES IN THE BUSINESS ENVIRONMENT

Because the accounting function reflects the environment in which it takes place, it is first essential to understand how business has changed in the past 50 years. Some of these changes are listed in Exhibit 1–1.

Traditionally, the American economy was heavily manufacturing-based. Since the end of World War II, however, there has been a shift toward more service businesses in the United States and more manufacturing in other countries. Currently in the U.S., jobs in the service sector compose approximately 70 percent of the work force and this percentage is predicted to continue to rise. High wage rates and fringe benefit costs have contributed to the movement of manufacturing to other countries. As indicated in Exhibit 1–2, average hourly wage rates in the United States are significantly higher than, for example, those in its neighbor to the south, Mexico.

Maquiladora

As the cost of labor has increased, some U.S. companies have chosen to establish **maquiladoras** (or *maquilas*) in Mexico. These operations are exempt from duties "charged by Mexico on the inventory and equipment moving into the country from the United States, and the United States charges duties only on the value added to inventory in Mexico when the finished goods are reexported to the United States."[1] Such operations provide lower costs and, therefore, potentially higher profits for the American companies. Other companies looking for lower costs have set up production operations in countries other than Mexico that also have low wage rates. But, as indicated in the News Note "We Want Consumers," some manufacturers are acting in direct contradiction to such alternatives.

American companies not choosing to invest abroad are looking to lower costs and raise quality at home. Many times these changes point directly to automation, which created the change from labor-intensive businesses to machine-intensive businesses. This operational evolution has occurred both in the work area and in the area of information technology. There has been a dramatic increase in the availability of data and in the ability to process information efficiently. Technology has affected all areas of an organization through the use of the low-cost, high-processing capabilities of PCs (personal computers). In engineering, the use of **computer-aided design** (CAD) sys-

Computer-aided design

---

[1] James E. Groff and John P. McCray, "Maquiladoras," *Management Accounting* (January 1991), p. 43.

NEWS NOTE

We Want Consumers, Not Cheap Labor

Less than one-third of the 659 major investments abroad by U.S. manufacturers in 1991 went to countries with low labor rates, according to a new study.

Authors of the study, conducted by Ernst & Young, suggest that U.S. companies use their foreign investments largely to gain access to industrialized countries. The findings contradict a seemingly popular notion that, if given the opportunity, U.S. manufacturers would elect to set up shop where labor is cheapest, such as in Mexico and many South American countries.

[T]he study showed that Mexico and the now-disbanded Soviet Union were the only countries with low hourly wages that were among the top 10 choices of where U.S. manufacturers chose to invest [in 1991]. They came in at fifth and seventh place, respectively. (Low wages were defined as being less than 25% of U.S. wages, as tracked by the U.S. Department of Commerce.)

Jim Searing, director of Ernst & Young's international business services division, said other factors are determining where U.S. manufacturers decide to invest. "Many U.S. companies are first looking to build market share in industrialized countries by accessing customers, technology and skills," Mr. Searing said. Financial incentives and low corporate tax rates also tend to be important factors for first-time investors.

The most popular foreign country for U.S. manufacturers [in 1991] was Canada.

SOURCE: Lucinda Harper, "U.S. Manufacturers in 1991 Invested Largely in Industrialized Countries," *Wall Street Journal* (October 20, 1992), p. A2. Reprinted by permission of the *Wall Street Journal*, © 1992 Dow Jones & Company, Inc. All rights reserved worldwide.

tems have made it easier to visualize and quickly generate prospective product designs. CAD systems contribute to quality processes by making it possible for companies to issue fewer and fewer **engineering change orders** (ECOs) after production is in process. An ECO affects the way in which a product is manufactured by modifying the design, parts, process, or even quality of the product. The current attitude is that planning is critical to a production process; thus, "let's get it right *before* production begins."

Engineering change order

CAD systems are often integrated with **computer-aided manufacturing** (CAM) techniques. CAM refers to using computers to control production processes through the use of numerically controlled (NC) machines, robots, and automated assembly systems. These systems reduce the quantity and cost of labor, produce a high quantity of consistently high-quality goods, and afford management the ability to respond quickly to changes in market needs and demands. Additionally, CAM systems may be used in place of human labor to perform dangerous or boring jobs.

Computer-aided manufacturing

COUNTRY	WAGES PER HOUR
Germany	$21.53
United States	14.77
Japan	12.64
Korea	3.82
Mexico	1.80

SOURCE: U.S. Department of Labor, *International Comparisons of Hourly Compensation Costs for Production Workers* (Bureau of Labor Statistics, November 1991).

■ **EXHIBIT 1–2**

Average Hourly Wages for Manufacturing Workers (1990) (in U.S. dollars)

NEWS NOTE   Automation Equals Big Savings for Carrier

On a pothole-filled road across from a big chicken processor in the remote town of Arkadelphia, Arkansas, sits a Carrier Corporation plant that could be a blueprint for the future of U.S. manufacturing. The plant looks more like an insurance office than a factory, with its sleek, one-story structure, pervasive automation, and lean work force of only 150.

To be competitive, the United Technologies Corp. unit had to make its own compressors. But the big plants it built in the 1970s and 1980s, with their high fixed costs and inflexible production lines, proved to be money-losers, and the company began closing them.

This plant is highly automated. In one work unit, a person places two pieces of metal in a cutting machine, shuts the glass doors and punches a button. Guided by a computer that keeps the cut from straying more than eight millionths of an inch, the machine slices steel like butter.

Carrier makes one part of the compressor—the part requiring the most complex machining—in just over a minute. As a result, the company expects to produce each compressor for $35 less than it now pays to buy them from suppliers, for a saving that could run $26.3 million a year when annual production hits 750,000.

SOURCE: Erle Norton, "Small, Flexible Plants May Play Crucial Role in U.S. Manufacturing," *Wall Street Journal* (January 13, 1992), A1. Reprinted by permission of the *Wall Street Journal,* © 1992 Dow Jones & Company, Inc. All rights reserved worldwide.

Overhead

Because of the increases in automation, a dramatic shift has also taken place in the components of product cost. Less labor and more **overhead** is involved in the production process. Any production cost that cannot be directly traced to the product is considered overhead. For instance, the electricity used by and the depreciation on the automated machinery are overhead costs.

Other overhead costs arise because of the desire of companies to make a large variety of products. Companies have begun offering hundreds of alternative choices in product selection. To accomplish this, manufacturers need to be able to change rapidly from one production run to another and to produce limited quantities of a variety of items. Many Japanese (and some American) companies are installing **flexible manufacturing systems** (FMSs) in which a single factory turns out numerous variations of products through the use of computer-controlled robots. Nissan, a firm believer in flexible manufacturing, "describes its strategy as 'five anys': to make anything in any volume anywhere at any time by anybody."[2] This type of production requires a high level of investment in equipment as well as research and development. Increases in product variety cause many additional costs for ordering and stocking components in a manufacturing company. But even with these additional types of overhead costs, flexible manufacturing systems can cause total costs to decline, as indicated in the News Note on Carrier Corporation.

Flexible manufacturing system

The increased use of computers has also affected the discipline of accounting. Computers can provide less costly and more flexible data analyses. Data can now be easily formatted in a variety of ways to suit managerial, financial, tax, and regulatory needs. The traditional notion of using different figures for different purposes has become more easily achieved.

Technology cost in highly automated companies is becoming quite large and many managers in high-tech firms are taking a longer-run perspective in making decisions. This approach differs from the more prevalent short-run attitude in most organiza-

---

[2] Thomas A. Stewart, "Brace for Japan's Hot New Strategy," *FORTUNE* (September 22, 1992), p. 72.

tions. The changed perspective helps entities achieve a competitive edge by using innovative approaches to production, measuring production costs over a product's entire life, and focusing on product quality and customer service. Concepts involving this innovative perspective and its nontraditional information needs are presented in subsequent chapters. Because all companies are not at the same state-of-the-art development stage, the more traditional cost accounting techniques and information continue to be used in less technologically intense firms.

As technology has developed, the world has essentially become smaller. U.S. companies and consumers have begun to realize that alternative choices exist for the sale and purchase of products and services. The market view has become international rather than domestic. A recent survey of 400 businesses in 20 developed countries by the international accounting firm of Deloitte and Touche provides some information on why companies are becoming more international. "Frequently stated reasons for going international include growth opportunities (84%); less dependence on home economy (39%); customer demand (34%); cost reduction (24%); and the need for information on other markets (17%)."[3] (Multiple answers were permitted so numbers do not add to 100 percent.) Some companies, like Dawn Aeronautics (New Castle, Delaware), have entered foreign markets because home-economy sales of their primary product or service simply "dried up." Dawn, which ran a flight school for U.S. pilots, counteracted a recession and change in V.A. benefits by entering the international market to become one of only seven U.S. flight training programs for foreign pilots.

This international perspective becomes even more apparent as the trade barriers among nations are beginning to diminish. The institution of the North American Free Trade Zone and the European Economic Community are just two examples of how countries are opening their economic doors to "outsiders." Some effects of a North American Free Trade Agreement (NAFTA) are discussed in the News Note "Free-Flowing Trade" on page 8.

Companies have begun emphasizing performance from the standpoint of the consumer rather than quantity of output or ability to meet budget. Choices, especially those of consumers, are made on the bases of quality, access (time of availability), and price rather than on the question of domestic or foreign production. With technological advancements, production quality can be more readily controlled and lead times considerably shortened.

Quality issues are discussed in depth in Chapter 3, but it is essential to recognize that good quality is necessary in both manufacturing and service environments. Additionally, if poor quality occurs, a company should acknowledge its failures and correct them. Consider, for instance, Patrick's Food Service in South Burlington, Vermont. When there was a salmonella outbreak in the company's food products, Josh Patrick contacted customers and the health department about the problem. Because of the disclosure and concern, no customers were lost and product quality was subsequently improved.

In an attempt to generate more reasonable prices and stimulate competition, the government deregulated many previously regulated industries (such as trucking, airlines, and telecommunications). Whether deregulation has worked is debatable, but the action has generally made the prices of these industries' goods more attractive to consumers. Exhibit 1–3 (p. 8) indicates that, at least for the customers of the airline industry, the 1978 deregulation has worked toward the goal of making service better.

Consumers also want integrity, the scope of which encompasses management's social responsibility to consumers, the workforce, the environment, and the community in which the company exists. Consumers are no longer satisfied if companies simply comply with the legal requirements of doing business. Customers expect company managers to adopt an anticipatory or proactive role in social responsibility. Health,

---

[3]"Companies Surveyed on Going International," *Deloitte & Touche Review* (October 5, 1992), p. 1.

NEWS NOTE   **Free-Flowing Trade**

A NAFTA would create a huge North American market with 360 million consumers and a combined GDP of $6 trillion. That compares with 346 million people in the European Community with an annual GDP of $4.7 trillion. By eliminating artificial barriers to trade, investment, and production, an agreement would promote increased exports and allow companies in North America to take advantage of the strengths of each country and to operate more efficiently through greater economies of scale and lower costs.

Canada and Mexico are already the United States' second and fourth largest foreign trading partners respectively (the EC is first, Japan third). In turn, the United States accounts for more than two thirds of Canada's and Mexico's total foreign trade.

The agreement is certain to cover these key areas:

▮ Reduction and ultimate elimination of tariffs.

▮ Reduction or elimination of nontariff barriers to trade in goods. (A nontariff barrier is any law, regulation, or practice that prevents or impedes the importation of goods without reasonable cause. Examples include import licensing requirements, quotas, subsidies, and specifications for levels of domestic content in products being manufactured or sold.)

▮ Removal of barriers to the flow of investment.

▮ Removal of barriers to the flow of services.

▮ Increased protection of intellectual property rights.

▮ Customs issues.

SOURCE: KPMG Peat Marwick, "In Search of One Accord," *World* (No. 1, 1992), p. 12. Reprinted with permission from *World* Magazine, a publication of KPMG Marwick.

▮ **EXHIBIT 1–3**

Relationship of Number of Airline Passengers and Complaints

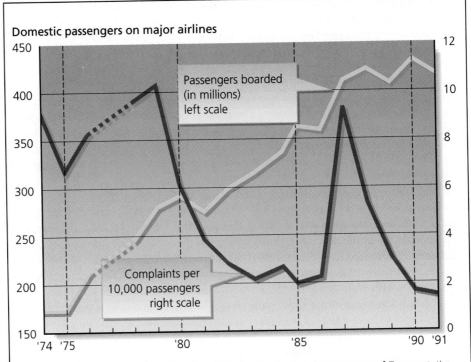

SOURCE: Julian L. Simon, "Freer Skies Gave Us Better Service," and Department of Transportation, "More Passengers, Less Complaining," *Wall Street Journal* (October 14, 1992), p. A16. Reprinted by permission of the *Wall Street Journal*, © 1992 Dow Jones & Company, Inc. All rights reserved.

The owners of Knott's Camp Snoopy at the Mall of America know that there is a maximum price people will pay for entertainment—thus, costs of operation must be kept at a level that will allow a reasonable profit margin.

safety, and environmental issues, as well as corporate ethics, are high priority concerns of all corporate stakeholders, both external and internal and many companies (like Quaker Oats) have introduced codes of ethics as an integral part of the corporate culture.

Each of these changes has affected the production process (or the provision of service), managers' information needs, and the cost of doing business. To remain in business, a company must make a profit on its operating activities. To do so, it must determine which of its products and services are the most attractive to consumers and at what price. At the same time, the company has to be able to produce the product or perform the service at a cost that provides a reasonable profit margin. The selling prices of many goods are set by the marketplace rather than the individual producer. Thus, if companies are to generate reasonable profit margins, they must do so by containing costs and/or enhancing products rather than by raising selling prices. Information about the cost of producing a product or providing a service is determined from, and accounted for, in the company's accounting system.

Accounting information is supposed to address three different functions: (1) provide information to external parties (stockholders, creditors, and various regulatory bodies) for investment and credit decisions; (2) estimate the cost of products produced and services provided by the organization; and (3) provide information useful for making decisions and controlling operations. Financial accounting is designed to meet external information needs and to comply with generally accepted accounting principles. Management accounting attempts to satisfy internal information needs and to provide product costing information for external financial statements. The primary differences between these two accounting disciplines are given in Exhibit 1–4 on page 10.

Financial accounting must comply with the generally accepted accounting principles established by the Financial Accounting Standards Board (FASB), a private-sector body. The information used in financial accounting is typically historical,

RELATIONSHIP OF FINANCIAL AND MANAGEMENT ACCOUNTING

EXHIBIT 1–4
Financial and Management
Accounting Differences

	FINANCIAL	MANAGEMENT
Primary users	External	Internal
Primary organizational focus	Whole	Parts
Information characteristics	Must be:	May be:
	Historical	Forecasted
	Quantitative	Quantitative or qualitative
	Monetary	Monetary or nonmonetary
	Accurate	Should be timely
Overriding criteria	Consistent	Situation-relevant (useful)
	Verifiable	Benefits in excess of cost
	Uniform	Flexible
Recordkeeping	Mandatory	Combination of formal and informal

verifiable, quantifiable, and monetary. These characteristics are essential to the uniformity and consistency needed for external financial statements. Financial accounting information is usually quite aggregated and related to the organization as a whole. In some cases, a regulatory agency such as the Securities and Exchange Commission (SEC) or an industry commission (such as banking or insurance) may mandate financial accounting practices. Financial accounting information is an essential of business because it is necessary for obtaining loans, preparing tax returns, and understanding how well or poorly the business is performing.

By comparison, management accounting provides information for internal users. Managers are often concerned with individual parts or segments of the business rather than the whole organization, so management accounting information commonly addresses such concerns rather than the "big picture" of financial accounting. Management accountants are not required to adhere to generally accepted accounting principles in providing information for managers' internal purposes, but are expected to be flexible in serving management's needs. *A primary criterion for internal information is that it serve management's needs and be useful to managers' functions.* A related criterion is the **cost-benefit** consideration that information should be developed and provided only if the cost of producing that information is less than the benefit of having it. These two criteria, though, must be combined with the financial accounting information criteria of verifiability, uniformity, and consistency because all accounting documents and information (whether internal or external) must be grounded in reality rather than whim.

Cost-benefit analysis

Nonetheless, from a management accounting perspective, it is more important to meet managerial needs than to meet financial accounting requirements; thus, flexibility is the hallmark of modern management accounting. For example, managers are often constrained by time when making decisions. It is often necessary to accept less precise but more timely information for internal decision-making purposes rather than delay a decision until the precise information required for external reporting can be obtained.

Although the objectives and nature of management and financial accounting differ, all accounting information tends to rely on the same basic accounting system and set of accounts. The accounting system provides management with a means by which costs are accumulated from input of materials through the production process until completion and, ultimately, to cost of goods sold. While technology has improved to the point that a company can have different accounting systems designed for different purposes, most companies still rely on a single system to supply the basic accounting information. The single system is typically focused on providing information for financial accounting purposes, but its informational output can be adapted to meet most internal management requirements. As noted in the News Note on accounting

NEWS NOTE

In Russia, Operational Accounting Mirrors Management Accounting

[In the former Soviet Union,] cost accounting and cost analysis are practiced extensively, mostly by administrators [rather than] by accountants, who are engaged solely in financial accounting. [One aspect of these analyses is operational accounting. While] operational accounting has no conceptual accounting basis, certain features can be identified.

- Data are provided rapidly. This feature has given its name to this type of information processing because in Russian the word meaning "operational" derives from the same root word meaning "fast." The speed with which data are provided is considered the principal merit of operational accounting. This feature also distinguishes operational accounting from financial accounting and its strict recording procedures.
- The objectivity of information is not maintained as strictly in operational accounting as it is in financial accounting. Usually, operational accounting requires no documented evidence, and data may be transmitted verbally.
- Approximations can be used for operational accounting data. Rapid estimates often are more important than accurately calculated numbers; that is, speed prevails over accuracy.
- Operational accounting . . . uses ratios, whereas financial accounting deals only with numbers in rubles. Different ratios help in organizing and consolidating substantial data flows for managerial purposes.
- Operational accounting information often deals with events and numbers that are possible rather than certain.
- In operational accounting, data are recorded and reported selectively, based on their relevance to managerial decision making.

Operational accounting is very specialized [and] exists in various forms according to the industry or activity and therefore often merges with the planning and control of operations of a technical and administrative nature. By means of operational accounting, management achieves control over: (1) execution of contracts, (2) the meeting of plan goals, (3) internal reporting, (4) special purpose reporting, and (5) projections.

SOURCE: Adolf J. H. Enthoven, "Accounting in Russia: From Perestroika to Profits," *Management Accounting* (October 1992), pp. 30–31. Reprinted from *Management Accounting.* Copyright by Institute of Management Accountants, Montvale, N.J.

practices in Russia, this concept of "different information for different purposes" is even becoming acceptable in the former Soviet Union's accounting systems.

Account balances in the accounting system are summarizations of many individual details. External financial statements are prepared from account balances and represent past transactions. In reviewing external financial statements, managers find information that is useful for some purposes, but often the information is either outdated or lacking in sufficient detail for other purposes. The information needs of management typically involve day-to-day operational questions; answers to these questions sometimes require the use of details not available in aggregated account balances. Managers may also need information involving estimates of *future* quantities or costs of resources that are not recorded in account balances.

Accounting records provide detail beyond the balances that appear on external financial statements. These records include data that can be formatted and manipulated in numerous ways in response to management's changing needs. Management accountants are often asked to gather and analyze data and make estimates regarding some problem management wishes to solve. For example, management may need information on the estimated cost of producing a new product and whether there is sufficient plant capacity for the additional production. Management accountants would obtain and study the information necessary to make those estimates and present the estimates to management. The basis for the estimates may begin with the historical data recorded in accounting records, but it virtually never ends there.

RELATIONSHIP OF MANAGEMENT AND COST ACCOUNTING

Cost accounting

Management accounting has been defined by the Institute of Management Accountants (IMA)[4] as including almost all manipulations of financial information for use by management in performing their specified organizational functions and, additionally, in assuring the proper use and handling of an entity's resources. The objectives of management accounting (shown in Exhibit 1–5) reflect the comprehensive nature of this area of accounting. The functions of **cost accounting** are focused primarily at the "processes" level in that exhibit. Thus, cost accounting is an integral part of the broader field of management accounting.

Cost accounting is defined as "a technique or method for determining the cost of a project, process, or thing. . . . This cost is determined by direct measurement, arbitrary assignment, or systematic and rational allocation."[5] The appropriate method of determining cost depends on the circumstances that generate the need for information. Various costing methods are illustrated throughout the text.

Although cost information was originally designed for internal managerial use, this purpose was diminished at the time of the 1929 stock market crash when the emphasis shifted to product costing, inventory valuation, and fair and proper financial statement presentation. While financial statement applications of cost information are still important, the current trend is to refocus cost information for managerial use in planning, controlling, performance evaluating, and decision making.

Central to a cost accounting system is the process for tracing various input costs to an organization's outputs (products or services). This process uses the traditional accounting form of recordkeeping—general and subsidiary ledger accounts. Accounts containing cost and management accounting information include those dealing with sales, procurement (materials and plant assets), production and inventory, personnel, payroll, delivery, financing, and funds management.[6] But not all cost information will be reproduced on the financial statements. Correspondingly, not all financial accounting information is useful to managers in performing their daily functions.

Although differences exist between the information provided for management decisions and financial accounting statements, both use a common subset of the same information and share the same physical accounts and records. A well-designed accounting system can be flexible enough to meet management's needs and also provide the basis for preparation of external financial statements. Since two recordkeeping systems might be cumbersome and potentially redundant, cost information is generally kept in the same accounts as financial accounting information and much of the product cost information developed by cost accounting techniques is used in external

---

[4] The IMA's definition of management accounting is "the process of identification, measurement, accumulation, analysis, preparation, interpretation, and communication of financial information used by management to plan, evaluate, and control within an organization and to assure appropriate use of and accountability for its resources." [Institute of Management Accountants (formerly National Association of Accountants), *Statements on Management Accounting: Management Accounting Terminology*, Statement Number 2 (Montvale, N.J.: NAA, now Institute of Management Accountants, June 1, 1983), p. 65.]

[5] Institute of Management Accountants (formerly National Association of Accountants), *Statements on Management Accounting: Management Accounting Terminology*, Statement Number 2 (Montvale, N.J.: NAA, now Institute of Management Accountants, June 1, 1983), p. 25.

[6] With reference to accounts, this text will focus primarily on the set of accounts that depicts the internal flow of costs.

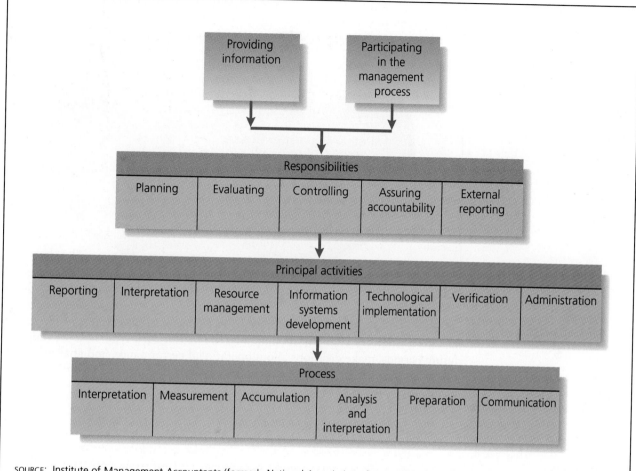

SOURCE: Institute of Management Accountants (formerly National Association of Accountants), *Statements on Management Accounting: Objectives of Management Accounting*, Statement Number 1B (Montvale, N.J.: NAA, now Institute of Management Accountants, June 17, 1982), pp. 8–9.

■ **EXHIBIT 1–5**

Objectives of Management Accounting

financial statement amounts. However, as indicated in the News Note "Design the Information System" on page 15, some professionals have suggested that the use of different accounting systems for different purposes might be justified.

Cost accounting creates an overlap between financial accounting and management accounting. This discipline integrates with financial accounting by providing product costing information for financial statements. Additionally, cost accounting integrates with management accounting by providing some of the quantitative, cost-based information managers need to perform their tasks. Exhibit 1–6 depicts the relationship of cost accounting to the larger systems of financial and management accounting. None of the three areas should be viewed as a separate and exclusive "type" of accounting. The boundaries of each are not clearly and definitively drawn and, because of changing technology and information needs, are becoming increasingly blurred.

The cost accounting overlap causes the financial and management accounting systems to articulate or be joined together to form a complete informational network. Because these two systems articulate, accountants must understand how cost accounting provides costs for financial statements and supports management information needs. Organizations that are not engaged in manufacturing products may not require elaborate *cost accounting systems*. However, even service companies need to understand how much their service costs to provide so that they can determine

■ **EXHIBIT 1–6**

Relationship of Financial, Management, and Cost Accounting

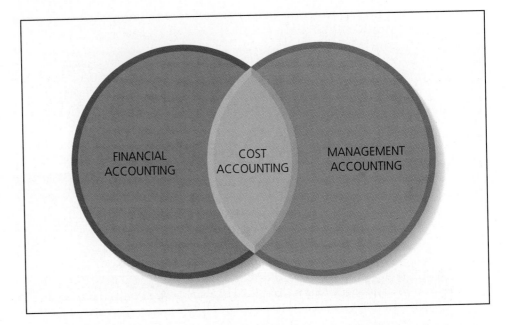

whether it is cost-effective to be engaged in business. But regardless of the need to develop cost information, most companies (no matter what type) need to budget for future periods, make decisions about operational performance, and analyze alternative courses of action. All of these functions require the use of *management accounting* concepts and techniques.

SCOPE OF MANAGEMENT ACCOUNTING

Management accountants should recognize what information is needed by managers, why it is needed, and how to provide it in the best possible form for understandability and in a timely manner so that it is useful in decision making. Managers often want or need information about activities that technically fall outside the production process, but that are related to production. For example, managers need information for making decisions about (1) acquiring and financing production capacity; (2) determining which products to market; (3) pricing jobs, products, or services; (4) determining the best method of delivering finished goods to warehouses; (5) locating the best property for production facilities; and (6) financing the costs of production. To help make such decisions, managers frequently use management accounting information.

Data

Information

Data and information are distinctly different. Whereas **data** are bits of knowledge or facts that have not been summarized and categorized in a manner useful to a decision maker, **information** has been carefully chosen from a body of data and arranged in a meaningful way. Data are not useful in managerial functions. Managers must combine information with experience and judgment to create knowledge that is used in solving problems and making decisions.

The management accountant can help a manager in the decision making process by providing both quantitative and qualitative information. Quantitative information permits managers to view the numerical impact of alternative choices; qualitative information provides facts that help to eliminate some of the inherent uncertainty related to choices. Examples of quantitative information include monetary amounts, number of units of product expected to be sold in the next period, and time needed for a robot to perform a specific production task.

Qualitative information relates to the nature of an item; for instance, the management accountant might provide information on the raw material quality of different suppliers. The purchasing agent can then combine quantitative (price) and qualitative

---

NEWS NOTE

Design the Information System to Meet the Information Needs

Many companies now recognize that their cost systems are inadequate for today's powerful competition. Systems designed mainly to value inventory for financial and tax statements are not giving managers the accurate and timely information they need to promote operating efficiencies and measure product costs.

No single system can adequately answer the demands made by the diverse functions of cost systems. While companies can use one method to capture all their detailed transactions data, the processing of this information for diverse purposes and audiences demands separate, customized development. Companies that try to satisfy all the needs for cost information with a single system have discovered they can't perform important managerial functions adequately. Moreover, systems that work well for one company may fail in a different environment. Each company has to design methods that make sense for its particular products and processes.

SOURCE: Reprinted by permission of *Harvard Business Review*. An excerpt from "One Cost System Isn't Enough," by Robert S. Kaplan (January-February 1988), pp. 61, 66. Copyright © 1988 by the President and Fellows of Harvard College; all rights reserved.

(quality) information to determine the supplier from which to buy raw materials. The supplier offering the lowest materials cost may not provide goods of sufficiently reliable quality to justify purchasing materials from it. (Some information, such as the number of production defects during a period, contains both quantitative and qualitative elements.)

Any single type of information about "cost" may not be useful in performing all management functions. For example, the replacement cost of machinery is useful information for planning because it indicates the amount of insurance to purchase. On the other hand, machinery replacement cost is not useful in controlling operations because current depreciation charges are based on historical cost.

In focusing on the future, managers set goals and objectives. **Goals** are desired results or conditions contemplated in qualitative terms; these are often included in the organization's mission statement. For example, the mission of the Institute of Management Accountants is to:

Goals

▌ Provide to members personal and professional development opportunities through education, association with business professionals, and certification in management accounting skills.

▌ Ensure that the IMA is universally recognized by the financial community as a respected institution influencing the concepts and ethical practices of management accounting.[7]

To implement a mission statement and/or goals, the organization must determine targeted **objectives** that can be expressed in quantitative terms. These objectives should be written so as to be achievable within a preestablished period. Objectives should logically result from goals as shown in the following selected 1992 objectives of the IMA:

Objectives

▌ Education: Increase member participation hours and improve quality and the perception of quality of educational programs. Maintain member continuing professional education hour records as a benefit of membership.

---

[7]Institute of Management Accountants, "Report of the President," *1991 Annual Report*, cover page.

▌ Certification: Maintain required growth rate to reach 80,000 CMAs by the year 2000.

▌ Influence: Establish a presence in Washington, D.C., that would serve as a resource for members, member employers, member institutions, and regulators on management accounting issues.[8]

Role in Planning

Planning

Translating the goals and objectives for a business and developing a strategy for achieving them in a systematic manner is called **planning**. Organizations should develop short-term, intermediate-term, and long-term plans (strategy). Short-term plans, which are prepared in more detail than longer-term plans, are used by managers as a basis for the control and performance evaluation functions.

The planning functions in large and small organizations seem to differ. Large organizations typically have a more established planning process that encompasses all planning horizons, recognizes the organizations' place in the competitive structure, and communicates the plans throughout the organization for a "shared-values" perspective. Small organizations' managers, on the other hand, often plan only for the short run, simply trying to fit into the marketplace, and are either unable or unwilling to communicate, or do not recognize the value of communicating, plans to subordinates. As indicated in the News Note "How Much Planning Is Enough?" researchers do not agree on whether the planning function in a small business should be increased. But, regardless of how much planning is performed, the need for accounting information is critical to success.

In conducting the planning function, managers depend heavily on the management accountant. Long-term plans typically address issues such as share of the market, which is based on projections of costs, prices, volume, quality, and service. Short-term plans may be in the form of budgets for resources such as cash, inventory, and personnel. Budgets are based, in part, on the management accountant's knowledge of operational and financial activities and relationships. The budgeting process results in projected financial statements that allow managers to evaluate the prospective results of their plans before such plans are implemented.

Role in Controlling and Performance Evaluation

Controlling

Standard

Planning is the basis for the management control and performance evaluation functions. **Controlling** is the exertion of managerial influence on operations so that they will conform to plans. Essentially, the control process first involves setting performance **standards** or norms against which actual results are measured. The management accountant helps in determining standards for various quantities, times, and costs in all operating areas. Performance is then measured and compared to the standards on a scheduled basis; the management accountant's role is to provide managers with timely, appropriate, and accurate reports.

Performance evaluation

Using the analyses provided by the management accountant, managers can conduct a **performance evaluation** to determine if operations are proceeding according to plan or if actual results differ significantly from those that were expected. In the latter case, adjustments to operating activities may be needed. After performance is measured during the control process, managers must then evaluate the effectiveness and efficiency of that performance.

Effectiveness
Efficiency

The successful accomplishment of a task reflects **effectiveness**, while performing tasks to produce the stated yield at the lowest cost from the resources used is **efficiency**. For example, it is effective for the production supervisor to lubricate pro-

---

[8]Robert W. Liptak, "Institute of Management Accountants Focus on Mission 1992–93," *Management Accounting* (July 1992), p. 26.

NEWS NOTE

How Much Planning Is Enough?

[I]t seems reasonable to ask whether and/or what kind of planning is of value in a situation where there are no planning specialists, where the orientation is short-run, and where the environment is turbulent and perhaps unpredictable.

Two distinct and very different approaches have emerged in the small business planning literature. The first of these . . . concludes that there is a need for more, and more extensive, planning in the small business environment. Managers are told that they need to become deeply and personally involved in the process, using advisors as necessary to handle specialized functions. Furthermore, they are told that formal planning and control procedures should be developed and incorporated into the everyday management of the organization. In general, this literature stream calls for planning in equal detail and scope as in a large business, and that " . . . executives of small businesses should expect to invest more time than their counterparts in large firms to achieve the same amount and quality of planning output."

The second literature stream . . . suggests that the differences which separate small businesses from large ones are major enough to question the applicability of planning as it is practiced in large business environments. Cohn and Lindberg . . . point out that many small business managers . . . believe that the small firm's susceptibility to rapid market fluctuations make anything beyond short-range, operational planning infeasible. Thurston points out that top managers/owners in small businesses will, in many cases, have a more in-depth, "gut-level" understanding of market conditions, product, and customers than their counterparts in large organizations and that this knowledge can often preclude the need for formal planning. Furthermore, the length of the planning cycle may need to be substantially reduced in the small business. However, more formal approaches to planning may be needed in cases of technological complexity, or where uncertainty is of the type where planning can serve to provide enough data to permit at least partial control over the company's future.

SOURCE: Sandra J. Hartman, Olof Lundberg, and Michael White, "Planning in Small vs. Large Businesses: Do Managers Prefer Different Tools?" *Journal of Small Business Strategy* (February 1990), p. 14.

duction machinery, but it is more efficient to use a lower-paid maintenance worker to perform that task. Efficiency is greatest when the ratio of quality outputs to the related inputs is greatest. The best performance achieves effectiveness and maximizes efficiency.

Role in Decision Making

A manager's ability to manage depends on good **decision making**, that is, choosing the most efficient course of action that will achieve the objective. To make appropriate choices, managers need information related to alternative solutions. Managers, then, are the information users and accountants are the information providers. Accountants must always be aware that the information they produce influences the behavior of individuals and that a clear communication channel must exist between the users and providers of accounting information. For managers to rely on information as a sound basis for making decisions, accountants must understand the uses managers intend to make of the information and ascertain that relevant information is being used appropriately.[9] The quantity of information desired is based, in part, on the

Decision making

---

[9]William J. Vatter, "Tailor-making Cost Data for Specific Uses," from N.A.(C.)A. Bulletin, 1954 Conference Proceedings; reprinted in *Topics in Managerial Accounting* 2nd. ed., L.S. Rosen, editor (McGraw-Hill, 1974), p. 210.

expected consequences of the decision. The more important the decision, the more relevant information it is desirable to have.

Thus, the purpose of management accounting is twofold. First, it must provide the basis for appropriately estimating cost valuations needed for external financial statement presentations (balance sheet inventory values and income statement cost of goods/services sold). Second, it must provide sufficient, useful information to help managers adequately perform their functions of planning, controlling, evaluating performance, and making decisions. The two purposes of the cost/management accountant are separate and distinct. Accomplishing the first does not necessarily or automatically satisfy the second, nor does accomplishing the second automatically accomplish the first. Each of the management functions (planning, controlling, evaluating performance, and making decisions) requires the use of some particular set of cost and management accounting information.

THE CERTIFIED MANAGEMENT ACCOUNTANT DESIGNATION

Common body of knowledge

Because of the many functions that need to be provided by management accountants, management accountants are expected to be versed in a wide variety of topics. The IMA specified the **common body of knowledge** (CBK) presented in Exhibit 1–7 as the minimum set of knowledge needed by a person to function effectively in the field of management accounting. Reviewing the various areas covered by the CBK indicates that management accountants need to be versed in theories and techniques from economics, management, finance, marketing, and statistics in addition to accounting. For example, economics provides a sound base from which to analyze the organization's operating environment and to perform various financial planning functions. The depth of knowledge in any subject area depends on the individual's career level and functional responsibility area.

The common body of knowledge specified for management accountants should not be viewed as being permanently fixed. As changes occur in the business world, the knowledge needed by management accountants will also evolve. Changes most likely will be reflected as expansions, not contractions, in the CBK. Examples of recent changes causing innovations in management accounting include the emergence of robotics and other computerized automation, management strategies developed in post–World War II Japan, and vastly improved information technology. The knowledge needed for a career in management accounting must be gained *both* from class-

EXHIBIT 1–7

Common Body of Knowledge for Management Accountants

CORE OF KNOWLEDGE AREAS		
Information and Decision Processes	**Accounting Principles and Functions**	**Entity Operations**
• Management decision processes • Internal reporting • Financial planning and performance evaluation	• Organizational structure and management • Accounting concepts and principles	• Principal entity operations • Operating environment • Taxation • External reporting • Information systems

SOURCE: Institute of Management Accountants (formerly National Association of Accountants), *Statements on Management Accounting: The Common Body of Knowledge for Management Accountants,* Statement Number 1D (Montvale, N.J.: NAA, now Institute of Management Accountants, June 3, 1986), p. 2.

AGE RANGE	NO CERTIFICATION	CMA CERTIFICATION	CPA CERTIFICATION	CMA, CPA CERTIFICATION
19–29	$30,850	$37,988	$38,454	$36,747
30–39	45,634	53,838	53,871	57,734
40–49	55,409	66,632	72,429	73,293
50–59	61,787	72,675	83,630	78,948

* Data not reported for ages 60 and over because the number of respondents is insufficient to assure individual confidentiality. Data based on IMA membership survey.

SOURCE: David L. Schroeder and Karl E. Reichart, "Salaries 1992," *Management Accounting* (June 1993), p. 29. Published by the Institute of Management Accountants, Montvale, N.J.

EXHIBIT 1–8
Average Salary Differentials Between No Certification and CMA &/or CPA

room courses and from experience—each enhances the other and neither can stand alone.

Even before the issuance of the CBK statement, however, the then-National Association of Accountants began (in 1972) offering a comprehensive examination designed to test an individual's knowledge of technical accounting skills as well as other related business fields. The comprehensive examination related to the field of management accounting is currently administered by the Institute of Certified Management Accountants (ICMA), an IMA affiliate organization. The **Certified Management Accountant** (CMA) designation provides evidence that its holders have professional status, and affords a means for management accountants to demonstrate educational attainment and competency in specific areas of knowledge. In addition to passing the examination, people aspiring to become CMAs must qualify through work experience and must maintain certain continuing education requirements. The work experience and continuing education are reviewed and evaluated by the staff of the ICMA.

Certified Management Accountant

The CMA exam lasts two days and covers topics in all areas important to an upper-level management accountant. There are four sections of the exam: (1) Economics, Finance, and Management; (2) Financial Accounting and Reporting; (3) Management Reporting, Analysis, and Behavioral Issues; and (4) Decision Analysis and Information Systems. Each section of the exam is considered by practicing professionals to be "job pertinent." CMA candidates who have passed the CPA examination are given credit for Part 2.

Although the CMA is a relatively recent designation, many thousands of individuals have obtained certificates. A large number of these people are also CPAs. In fact, a significant proportion of the members of the American Institute of Certified Public Accountants actually work as management accountants rather than as public accountants. A knowledge of management accounting is useful to people in public accounting for two reasons: (1) it helps them to understand client organizations and accounting functions and (2) many public accountants ultimately will choose to work as management accountants.

A major difference between being a CPA and a CMA is that a CPA is granted, by individual states, the right to offer auditing services to the public. The CPA certificate is both a professional designation *and a basis for licensing* by which the states monitor and regulate public accounting. In contrast, the CMA is not a license because CMAs are employed by organizations that do not need to be "protected" by the government. The CMA and CPA do not compete with, but rather complement, each other.

The CMA program will continue to grow and gain recognition from the business community. Rewards for attainment include salary differentials (see Exhibit 1–8) and promotions. In the future, the CMA may be considered a basic credential in the business world for high-level management accounting positions.

COST AND MANAGEMENT ACCOUNTING STANDARDS

Cost Accounting Standards Board

Management accountants can use different costs and different information for different purposes because their discipline does not have to adhere to generally accepted accounting principles when providing information for managers' internal use. Financial accounting standards are established by the Financial Accounting Standards Board (FASB), a private-sector body. No similar board exists to define universal management accounting standards. However, a public-sector board called the **Cost Accounting Standards Board** (CASB) was established in 1970 by the U.S. Congress to promulgate uniform cost accounting standards for defense contractors and federal agencies.

The CASB produced twenty cost accounting standards (of which one has been withdrawn) from its inception until it was terminated in 1980 (see Exhibit 1–9). The CASB was recreated in 1988 as an independent board of the Office of Federal Procurement Policy rather than an agency of Congress. The board's objectives are to:

▌ Increase the degree of uniformity in cost accounting practices among government contractors in like circumstances;

▌ Establish consistency in cost accounting practices in like circumstances by each individual contractor over periods of time; and

▌ Require contractors to disclose their cost accounting practices in writing.[10]

Although CASB standards do not constitute a comprehensive set of rules, compliance is *required* for companies bidding on or pricing cost-related contracts for the federal government.

▌ **EXHIBIT 1–9**
CASB Standards

NUMBER	TOPIC
401	Consistency in estimating, accumulating, and reporting costs
402	Consistency in allocating costs incurred for the same purpose
403	Allocation of home office expenses to segments
404	Capitalization of tangible assets
405	Accounting for unallowable costs
406	Cost accounting period
407	Use of standard costs for direct material and direct labor
408	Accounting for costs of compensated personal absence
409	Depreciation of tangible capital assets
410	Allocation of business unit general and administrative expenses
411	Accounting for acquisition costs of material
412	Composition and measurement of pension cost
413	Adjustment and allocation of pension cost
414	Cost of money as an element of the cost of facilities capital
415	Accounting for the cost of deferred compensation
416	Accounting for insurance costs
417	Cost of money as an element of the cost of capital assets
418	Allocation of direct and indirect costs
419	Not published
420	Accounting for independent research and development costs and bid and proposal costs

SOURCE: Darrel A. Sourwine, "Putting the Pieces Together," *Management Accounting* (July 1991), p. 45. Reprinted from *Management Accounting.* Copyright by Institute of Management Accountants, Montvale, N.J.

[10]Robert B. Hubbard, "Return of the Cost Accounting Standards Board," *Management Accounting* (October 1990), p. 56.

Complaints about its repair services gave Sears an ethical "black eye." Many customers now insist that the phrase "business ethics" is an oxymoron.

In contrast to the CASB, the IMA cannot promulgate legally binding cost accounting standards, but it does produce nonbinding guidelines in the areas of cost and management accounting called **Statements on Management Accounting** (SMAs). These pronouncements are developed by the Management Accounting Practices (MAP) Committee of the IMA after a rigorous developmental and exposure process to ensure their wide support.[11]

Statements on Management Accounting

The first SMAs concentrated on the development of a framework for management accounting and include objectives and terminology. SMA topics such as objectives and the common body of knowledge were introduced earlier in this chapter. Later SMAs addressed management accounting practices and techniques such as determining direct labor cost, computing the cost of capital, and measuring entity performance. These statements are covered at appropriate points throughout the remainder of the text.

Although the CASB and IMA have been instrumental in standards development, much of the body of knowledge and practice in management accounting has been provided by industry practice and economic and finance theory. Thus, while no "official" agency publishes generic management accounting standards for all companies, there is wide acceptance of (and, therefore, authority for) the methods presented in the text. The development of cost and management accounting standards and practices indicates that management accountants are interested and involved in professional recognition. Another indication of this movement is the adoption of an ethics code by the Institute of Management Accountants.

Ethics has become a primary topic of discussion by and for business people. Numerous cases of corporate improprieties (bribery, cover-ups, insider trading, check kiting, and other unsuitable, illegal, or amoral acts) have been documented in recent years.

ETHICS IN BUSINESS

---

[11] An earlier program of the MAP Committee of the National Association of Accountants produced Statements on Management Accounting Practices (SMAPs). These statements also provide guidance in the practice of management accounting. They deal with issues including fixed asset accounting, guidelines for inventory measurement, and criteria for make-or-buy decisions.

The News Note "Sales Downturn" discusses one example of the ramifications of poor business ethics.

Because of the pervasive nature of management accounting and the organizational level at which many management accountants work, the IMA believed it was necessary to issue some guidelines to help its members with ethical dilemmas. Thus, Statement of Management Accounting 1B, *Standards of Ethical Conduct for Management Accountants*, was adopted in June 1982. These standards are in the areas of competence, confidentiality, integrity, and objectivity. The IMA Code of Ethics is reproduced in Exhibit 1–10.

Many items expressed in the code appear to be ideas that would be apparent to any reasonable and moral individual. Reading the standards closely, however, causes

▌ **EXHIBIT 1–10**

Standards of Ethical Conduct for Management Accountants

COMPETENCE
Management accountants have a responsibility to:
 Maintain an appropriate level of professional competence by on-going development of their knowledge and skills.
 Perform their professional duties in accordance with relevant laws, regulations, and technical standards.
 Prepare complete and clear reports and recommendations after appropriate analyses of relevant and reliable information.

CONFIDENTIALITY
Management accountants have a responsibility to:
 Refrain from disclosing confidential information acquired in the course of their work except when authorized, unless legally obligated to do so.
 Inform subordinates as appropriate regarding the confidentiality of information acquired in the course of their work and monitor their activities to assure the maintenance of that confidentiality.
 Refrain from using or appearing to use confidential information acquired in the course of their work for unethical or illegal advantage either personally or through third parties.

INTEGRITY
Management accountants have a responsibility to:
 Avoid actual or apparent conflicts of interest and advise all appropriate parties of any potential conflict.
 Refrain from engaging in any activity that would prejudice their ability to carry out their duties ethically.
 Refuse any gift, favor, or hospitality that would influence or would appear to influence their actions.
 Refrain from either actively or passively subverting the attainment of the organization's legitimate and ethical objectives.
 Recognize and communicate professional limitations or other constraints that would preclude responsible judgment or successful performance of an activity.
 Communicate unfavorable as well as favorable information and professional judgments or opinions.
 Refrain from engaging in or supporting any activity that would discredit the profession.

OBJECTIVITY
Management accountants have a responsibility to:
 Communicate information fairly and objectively.
 Disclose fully all relevant information that could reasonably be expected to influence an intended user's understanding of the reports, comments, and recommendations presented.

SOURCE: Institute of Management Accountants (formerly National Association of Accountants), *Statements on Management Accounting: Objectives of Management Accounting*, Statement No. 1B (New York, N.Y.: NAA, now Institute of Management Accountants, June 17, 1982).

NEWS NOTE   **Sales Downturn Does Not Justify Poor Ethics**

Sears, Roebuck and Co. agreed to settle charges that it cheated customers by doing shoddy or unnecessary work at its auto repair shops. The company said the settlement could affect 933,000 transactions nationwide and cost Sears $15 million after tax adjustments.

Under the agreement, Sears will give coupons worth $50 for Sears merchandise or services to thousands of customers. Those eligible include anyone who had Sears install certain auto parts, including master brake cylinders, idler arms, shock absorbers, brake calipers, or coil springs between August 1, 1990, and January 31, 1992.

The California Department of Consumer Affairs was the first to charge Sears with cheating customers on June 11, 1991, when it moved to revoke or suspend the auto repair licenses of all 72 Sears auto shops in the state.

The department said a yearlong investigation revealed that Sears oversold auto repair work 90 percent of the time, with unneeded repairs averaging $223 per car.

Sears said all its auto repair centers in California will remain open under the settlement.

The company, which has been struggling for years to compete with upstart discount stores, feared that even the perception of dishonesty could further damage its position in the industry. Sears said the scandal cost the company millions of dollars in sales because of lost consumer confidence.

The $50 restitution coupon applies to customers throughout the nation. Sears said that if a customer believes $50 will not cover unfair charges, the company will negotiate individual settlements. The company also said it will hire undercover shoppers to police its auto repair centers nationwide.

SOURCE: The Associated Press, "Sears To Settle Charges Against Auto Repair Shops," *[New Orleans] Times-Picayune* (September 3, 1992), p. C-2.

---

one to wonder how departures will be determined. For example, the confidentiality standards refer to being "legally obligated" to disclose information. Does this refer only to information specifically covered in statutory law or could it also refer to requests for information in a civil lawsuit?[12] Additionally, what if one were morally obligated to disclose information, but not legally obligated to do so? Would disclosure then be a violation of the code of ethics? To provide some increased guidance, the IMA offers the steps listed in Exhibit 1–11 on page 24 as a course of action for resolution of problems.

Accountants have always been regarded as individuals of conviction, trust, and integrity. It seems that the most important of all the standards listed are those designated under the category of integrity. These are statements about honesty of character and embody the essence and intent of U.S. laws and moral codes. Standards of integrity should be foremost in business dealings on an individual, group, and corporate level.

As with all codes of ethics, the IMA Code should be viewed as a goal for professional behavior. Such a code cannot address every potential situation. Moreover, each individual operates under his or her own personal code of ethics; thus, those persons lacking high standards will not be deterred from unethical behavior by either a mandated or a voluntary code. However, the IMA code does provide a benchmark by which management accountants can judge their conduct. If honest business practices are not adhered to voluntarily, laws and regulations will be adopted to mandate such practices.

---

[12] Statutory law is composed of those laws that have been enacted by a legislative body. A civil lawsuit involves one citizen suing another, possibly for breach of contract.

▌EXHIBIT 1–11
Resolution of Ethical Conflict

When faced with significant ethical issues, management accountants should follow the established policies of the organization bearing on the resolution of such conflict. If these policies do not resolve the ethical conflict, management accountants should consider the following course of action:

- ▪ Discuss such problems with the immediate superior except when it appears that the superior is involved, in which case the problem should be presented initially to the next higher managerial level. If satisfactory resolution cannot be achieved when the problem is initially presented, submit the issues to the next higher managerial level.
- ▪ If the immediate superior is the chief executive officer, or equivalent, the acceptable reviewing authority may be a group such as the audit committee, executive committee, board of directors, board of trustees, or owners. Contact with levels above the immediate superior should be initiated only with the superior's knowledge, assuming the superior is not involved.
- ▪ Clarify relevant concepts by confidential discussion with an objective advisor to obtain an understanding of possible courses of action.
- ▪ If the ethical conflict still exists after exhausting all levels of internal review, the management accountant may have no other recourse on significant matters than to resign from the organization and to submit an informative memorandum to an appropriate representative of the organization.

Except where legally prescribed, communication of such problems to authorities or individuals not employed or engaged by the organization is not considered appropriate.

SOURCE: Institute of Management Accountants (formerly National Association of Accountants), *Statements on Management Accounting: Objectives of Management Accounting*, Statement No. 1B (New York, N.Y.: NAA, now Institute of Management Accountants, June 17, 1982).

Foreign Corrupt Practices Act

One example of the government's stand on ethics is the **Foreign Corrupt Practices Act** (FCPA). This law was enacted to prevent bribes from being offered or given (directly or indirectly) to foreign officials to influence those individuals (or to cause them to use their influence) to obtain or retain business. Additionally, the FCPA mandates that a company maintain accurate accounting records and a reasonable system of **internal control**.[13] The intentions of this provision are that internal control systems would prevent or detect foreign bribes and would ensure that all transactions entered into by the firm were properly accounted for and legal. Unfortunately, even the best system of internal control may not prevent or detect circumstances that arise from employee or management collusion or circumvention of the system.

Internal Control

Racketeer Influenced and Corrupt Organizations Act

Another Congressional bill, enacted in 1970, is the **Racketeer Influenced and Corrupt Organizations Act** (RICO). This bill was intended to discourage organized crime from investing profits from illegal activities in legitimate businesses. However, the bill was drafted so broadly that it has been used in extremely diverse cases ranging from divorces and speeding tickets to securities fraud and business failures. RICO cases include civil actions related to industrial espionage, government contracting, labor relations, and insurance fraud. Accountants, brokers, company officers, directors, and managers have been sued under civil RICO.

This discussion simply serves to indicate the effects and complications that other ethics-related laws (rather than voluntary compliance) can produce. Businesses must operate under the established laws of the country in which they are incorporated and of the countries in which they do business. Although laws can institute "roadblocks" to unethical activity, such activity can only be effectively prevented by an ethical code of conduct that has been internalized by company employees. Accountants hold a variety of roles in an organization and "there is no guarantee that [they] can avoid

[13] An internal control is any measure used by management to protect assets, promote the accuracy of records, ensure adherence to company policies, or promote operational efficiency.

some of the pitfalls and problems that engulf our society today, but, clearly, the most important first step is the pursuit of and dedication to high ethical standards."[14]

R E V I S I T I N G

THE INSTITUTE OF MANAGEMENT ACCOUNTANTS

The IMA is an important professional organization with almost 90,000 members in over 300 chapters in the United States and abroad. Student members number around 11,000. Membership is not restricted to persons in a given professional category or with particular certifications. The organization is designed to be broad-based and appeal to anyone with an interest in management accounting or aspiring to management posts.

Because its primary goal is education, the IMA provides authoritative guidance to the business community through its journal, research reports, library services, continuing education programs, and ethics hotline. Association literature is being translated into Italian, Spanish, Portuguese, French, and German.

The IMA will be mentioned throughout this text. Many of its publication items directly affect the manner in which computations are performed or terms are defined; many more provide innovative ideas and fresh ways of thinking about traditional management accounting topics.

CHAPTER SUMMARY

There are two primary variations of the accounting language: financial accounting and managerial accounting. Cost accounting is a mutually shared subset of both financial and management accounting. Cost accounting's role in financial accounting focuses on accumulating production costs to determine valuations for external financial statement presentations. Its role in management accounting is to provide information for managers' planning, controlling, performance evaluation, and decision-making needs.

With changes in business in recent years, management's information needs have significantly expanded in scope and variety. The objectives and common body of knowledge for the management accounting discipline indicate the pervasive nature of the subject matter. Management accountants must be flexible in meeting management's information requirements; this flexibility is thought to be the hallmark of modern management accounting. Management and financial accounting overlap in their uses of the same underlying data and system of accounts, although the focus of each differs (internal and external, respectively). Cost and financial accounting information is primarily monetary in nature, while management accounting information often also includes qualitative and quantitative, nonmonetary information. Management accounting is viewed as encompassing the broader purposes of providing information to assist managers in planning, controlling, evaluating performance, and making decisions. In any case, the primary value of the information is its ability to reduce managers' uncertainty in carrying out their functions effectively and efficiently.

Official, binding cost and management accounting standards do not exist except for pricing cost-related contracts to the federal government. There are, however, nu-

---

[14] Howard L. Siers, "Are We Really a Corporate Conscience?" *Management Accounting* (August 1991), p. 20.

merous guidelines on procedures and practices related to cost and management accounting; most of these have been developed through the efforts of the Institute of Management Accountants. The IMA has instituted a certification program for management accountants that indicates the degree of professionalism the field of cost/management accounting has attained and, additionally, has formulated a code of ethics for the profession. In some cases, where the U.S. Congress believed it necessary, laws and regulations have been enacted to mandate honest business practices.

APPENDIX

Organizational Structure

An organization is a system composed of humans, nonhuman resources, and commitments configured to achieve certain explicit and implicit goals and objectives. This appendix provides some general information regarding organizational structure. The structure or design of an entity normally evolves from its nature, policies, and goals because certain designs are more conducive to certain types of operations. For example, a manufacturer will have an organizational segment known as the production center; a wholesaler will not.

Organization chart

An **organization chart** illustrates the functions, divisions, and positions in a company and how these are related. An important aspect of reviewing an organization chart is the determination of line and staff employees. A **line employee** is directly

Line employee
Staff employee

responsible for achieving the organization's goals and objectives; a **staff employee** is responsible for providing advice, guidance, and service to line personnel. Accountants may be viewed as line or staff personnel depending on their job titles, functions, and the firm's size and structure. Most internal accountants are considered staff employees and are, therefore, responsible for providing line managers with timely, complete, and relevant information to improve decision making and reduce uncertainty.

There is an indication, however, that these traditional classification schemes are fading. More responsibility for financial controls and information is being given to line management and financial personnel are taking on more responsibility for nonfinancial objectives such as quality. Data are being captured on-line with less need for processing and more need for analysis. Thus, the management group begins to operate more as a team and less as actors and advisors.

The organization chart also indicates the lines of authority and responsibility. The right (usually by virtue of position or rank) to use resources to accomplish a task or achieve an objective is called **authority**. This concept differs from **responsibility**,

Authority
Responsibility

which is the obligation to accomplish a task or achieve an objective. Authority can be delegated or assigned to others; ultimate responsibility cannot be delegated.

Although organization charts permit visualization of a company's structure, they do not present all factors necessary to understand how an organization functions. Informal relationships and informal channels of communication (the **grapevine**) that

Grapevine

exist in the organization are not shown on an organization chart. The grapevine is an extremely important factor that influences the way in which things are accomplished in an organization. In addition, at any given level of the organization, it is impossible to discern from the organization chart who wields more power or has more status, authority, and responsibility. Nonetheless, an organization chart does provide a basic diagram of certain official chains of command and channels of communication.

Exhibit 1–12 presents an organization chart for the Lionnel Corporation, which manufactures a variety of equipment. The Lionnel organization chart indicates two positions under the vice president of finance: treasurer and controller. The duties of these two individuals are often confused. The **treasurer** of a corporation generally

Treasurer

handles the actual resources and does not have access to the accounting records. Spe-

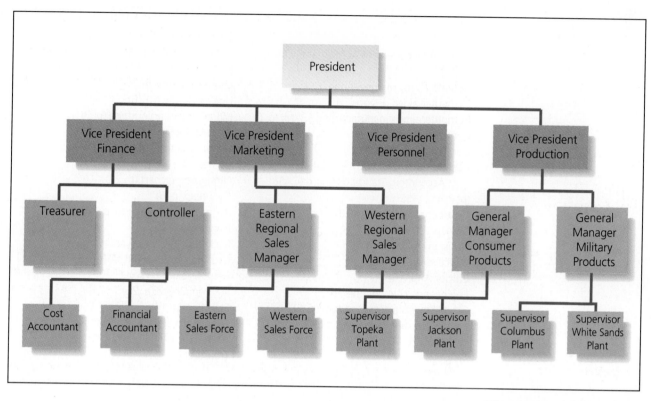

EXHIBIT 1–12

Organization Chart for Lionnel Corporation

Controller

cific duties of the treasurer normally include directing the following: handling cash receipts, disbursements, and balances; managing credit and collections; maintaining bank relations and arranging financing; managing investments; and insuring company assets. These functions are in contrast to those of the **controller** who supervises operations of the accounting system, but does not handle or negotiate changes in actual resources.

In many organizations, the controller is the chief accountant and is responsible for maintaining and reporting on both the cost and financial sets of accounts. The controller should see that the accounting system provides the amount of detail needed for internal and external purposes, while having a minimum amount of redundancy within the accounts. The controller is responsible for designing and maintaining the company's internal control system as well as helping management interpret accounting information. Interpreting accounting information allows the controller to exercise his/her technical abilities by assisting managers in determining the relevance of certain information to a decision, the need for additional accounting data, and the financial consequences of potential actions.

Other internal accounting staff positions may include the cost and financial accountants and their workers. The cost accountant is primarily concerned with internal information relating to the development of product or service cost; the financial accountant is primarily concerned with transactional information necessary to develop external reports. Companies may also have accountants functioning in internal audit and/or tax departments.

In addition to the traditional hierarchal line-staff organization structure just discussed, some companies have adopted **matrix structures**. In these organizational structures, functional departments and project teams exist simultaneously. Thus, an individual reports to two managers (one in the functional area and one in the project team), which provides a dual authority system. This structure is often used in organizations such as R&D companies and consulting firms that require significant coordination of personnel and that must respond to a rapidly changing environment.

Matrix structure

KEY TERMS

Authority (p. 26)
Certified Management Accountant (CMA) (p. 19)
Common body of knowledge (CBK) (p. 18)
Computer-aided design (CAD) (p. 4)
Computer-aided manufacturing (CAM) (p. 5)
Controller (p. 27)
Controlling (p. 16)
Cost accounting (p. 12)
Cost Accounting Standards Board (CASB) (p. 20)
Cost-benefit analysis (p. 10)
Data (p. 14)
Decision making (p. 17)
Effectiveness (p. 16)
Efficiency (p. 16)
Engineering change order (p. 5)
Flexible manufacturing system (p. 6)
Foreign Corrupt Practices Act (FCPA) (p. 24)
Goals (p. 15)
Grapevine (p. 26)

Information (p. 14)
Institute of Management Accountants (IMA) (p. 3)
Internal control (p. 24)
Line employee (p. 26)
Management accounting (p. 3)
Maquiladora (p. 4)
Matrix structure (p. 27)
Objectives (p. 15)
Organization chart (p. 26)
Overhead (p. 6)
Performance evaluation (p. 16)
Planning (p. 16)
Racketeer Influenced and Corrupt Organizations Act (RICO) (p. 24)
Responsibility (p. 26)
Staff employee (p. 26)
Standard (p. 16)
Statements on Management Accounting (SMAs) (p. 21)
Treasurer (p. 26)

QUESTIONS

1. What changes are occurring in the perspectives and information needs of managers as the cost of technology in highly automated companies increases?

2. What are some of the additional information needs of managers as firms advance from domestic to international markets?

3. What is meant by the term *cost*?

4. There are several distinct differences between management and financial accounting. What are they? What are the similarities?

5. Flexibility is said to be the hallmark of modern management accounting while standardization and consistency describe financial accounting. Explain the reason(s) why there is a difference in the focus of these two accounting systems.

6. What are the basic management functions and how might management accounting information help in each of these?

7. Is cost accounting a subset of management accounting or is management accounting a subset of cost accounting? Why?

8. What are the reasons for using a cost accounting system?

9. Define efficiency and effectiveness. What is the relationship of each to performance?

10. Why may the common body of knowledge for management accountants change over a period of time?

11. Why is it important to have a written common body of knowledge for management accountants?

12. Can an individual be both a CMA and a CPA? If so, why is there no conflict between these two professional designations?

13. Do generally accepted cost and management accounting standards exist? If so, indicate how they are or were established.

14. What are ethics? What constitutes ethical behavior?

15. What are the benefits and drawbacks of having ethics mandated as a function of law versus as a function of voluntary compliance?

16. List the four topical areas that comprise the IMA's Code of Ethics. Why do you believe each of these areas was chosen?

17. *(Appendix)* Explain the benefits and limitations of using an organization chart.

18. *(Appendix)* Best Value Realty Company is just starting operations and members of its Board of Directors are discussing the organizational structure. The firm will engage in commercial sales, residential sales, and property management and also maintain leasing services for businesses and individuals. At this time Best will have two branch locations. Using this information and your other knowledge of business operations, prepare a high-level organization chart for Best Value Realty Company.

19. Technological changes have had a major impact on production processes. For example, advances in technology have resulted in the production of fewer defective products, better product designs, and the evolution to machine-based production systems.

    a. What are the major changes that these technological innovations have had on costs?

    b. Why is it important for accountants to be aware of changes in the technology used in their organizations?

COMMUNICATION ACTIVITIES

20. The current trend has been to reduce the barriers to flows of capital, resources, technology, and labor across national borders. Very recently this trend has accelerated with the 1992 initiatives in the European Community (EC) and in North America with the North American Free Trade Agreement.

    a. Discuss how the trend of decreasing national fiscal and physical barriers has created more of a global marketplace.

    b. How has this trend affected management practices in the United States?

21. Accountants in industry are involved in providing relevant financial information to both internal managers and external financial statement users.

    a. Why do internal managers and external users require different sets of information?

    b. What is the role of GAAP (generally accepted accounting principles) in controlling the reporting of internal financial information?

    c. Do most firms have two sets of accounting records, one for internal management and one for external reporting? Explain.

22. In general, the practice of management accounting is less regulated than financial accounting.

    a. Discuss the roles of the FASB, IMA, and the CASB on the practice of management and cost accounting.

    b. Which of these bodies has binding authority over firms' accounting practices? Why or how?

23. Within the last two decades, U.S. businesses moved from an era of minimal regulation to the current environment that includes compliance with numerous social regulations. Businesses no longer have the freedom to design and produce products without regard to social considerations, nor do they have complete control over marketing practices and pricing policies. Social regulations have had an enormous impact on businesses, causing economic and continuity concerns. Despite the fact that there has been criticism against overregulation by the govern-

ment, polls indicate that the majority of Americans continue to support most forms of social regulation.

Listed below are five agencies that have been created for the implementation and administration of social regulations:

- Food and Drug Administration (FDA)
- Consumer Product Safety Commission (CPSC)
- Environmental Protection Agency (EPA)
- Occupational Safety and Health Administration (OSHA)
- Equal Employment Opportunity Commission (EEOC)

a. Discuss the general reasons for the dramatic increase in the social regulation of business during the last two decades.

b. For each of the five areas of social regulation administered by the agencies listed above,
 1. describe the social concerns that gave rise to each area of social regulation.
 2. discuss how each area of social regulation has affected the business community.

(CMA)

24. *(Appendix)* An organization chart illustrates the functions, divisions, and positions in a company and how these are related. In viewing an organization chart,
 a. is it possible to determine the type of business conducted by the firm? Explain.
 b. can one identify all the lines of communication in the firm? Explain.

25. *(Appendix)* Coordination is the organizational integration of tasks and activities. In general, effective coordination can be attained by the proper assignment of responsibility and delegation of authority within the context of the formal organizational structure.
 a. Discuss some basic principles that you think would allow the delegation of authority to be effective.
 b. Identify some actions of a superior that would undermine the effectiveness of the delegation of authority.
 c. Identify some actions of subordinates that would undermine the effectiveness of the delegation of authority.

(CMA adapted)

CASE

26. The Arvee Corporation has manufactured recreational vehicles for nearly 10 years. During this time Arvee bought existing older buildings near the founder's home to expand its facilities as needed. Now, new competition and rapid sales growth to a current annual level of nearly $300 million has made management realize that the company needs to consolidate its locations, reorganize its operations, and modernize its equipment to bring costs into line and to maintain traditional profit margins.

Five existing plant locations service the three operating divisions: Van Division (small motorized travel vans), Home Division (large motorized homes), and Trailer Division (nonmotorized hitch-on trailers). Several warehouses service the various plant locations. The corporate office is at a location separate from the production and warehouse facilities. All buildings are within a five-mile radius. Some plant locations include production facilities for two divisions; the overlap that has developed is creating inefficiencies and additional costs. Corporate management has decided that it should take one of the following two courses of action:

- Alternative 1 is to consolidate the facilities into fewer existing locations.
- Alternative 2 is to consolidate all facilities into one new location.

With either of these two alternatives, each division would have exclusive management, production, and warehouse areas. A central warehouse would house common production materials and components; each division's production locations would house other inventories unique to its vehicle models.

The manufacturing operations at most of the plant locations need to be reorganized for greater production efficiency. Frequently, the planning for the production facilities required to meet the increased sales was not well conceived. This is now adversely affecting the current work activities as well as materials and production flow. Moreover, the technology for this kind of production is changing. Thus, many of the equipment items need to be replaced because they are obsolete or worn out. In general, management has come to realize that a complete plant modernization is needed to survive the emerging market challenges.

Tony Pratt, corporate controller, is charged with the responsibility for presenting a summary report on the proposed plant modernization for an upcoming meeting of the Modernization Committee that will oversee the implementation of the project.

a. Discuss the types of information Tony needs to prepare his report and from what sources such information would be obtained.

b. Design a report format that you think would provide the information to the committee in an understandable and useful way.

(CMA *adapted*)

ETHICS AND QUALITY DISCUSSION

27. Ethics can be viewed in both a moral and a legal sense. Discuss the following:
    a. the similarities and differences that can exist between what is moral and what is legal.
    b. the positive and negative aspects of a corporate code of ethical conduct emphasizing the legal sense of ethics rather than the moral.

28. It has been determined that middle managers and employees often feel pressure to conform to the ethical standards set by upper management, even if this means compromising personal principles. Discuss the following:
    a. why such compromise would occur.
    b. the advantages and disadvantages of such compromises.
    c. ways to avoid making such compromises.

29. The term *whistleblower* is used to describe a person who informs on the wrongdoings of others, especially in a business or government organization. Discuss the following:
    a. why people often do not "blow the whistle" on wrongdoing.
    b. the positive and negative considerations that must be given to the information provided by whistleblowers.
    c. how to encourage whistleblowing.

30. Most airline, hotel, and car rental companies have, or participate in, frequent flyer/stayer/renter programs. Many individuals travel on organizational business.
    a. Are "frequent" programs bribes? Discuss the ethics of companies having such programs.
    b. Discuss the ethics of a person traveling on business who flies/stays/rents solely on the basis of the program advantages rather than on the basis of cost.
    c. The federal government and many companies do not allow their employees to retain the points earned through the use of a "frequent" program. Do you think it is ethical of these organizations to require employees to give the points earned back to the organization for its use? Why or why not?

31. Some U.S. businesses have opted to take advantage of the low wage rates and sometimes lax environmental laws in Mexico by establishing maquiladoras. From a "little-visited, no-man's land," the border area is now "brimming."

> The rapid growth of industry and the numbers of workers have overwhelmed cities from Tijuana to Matamoros, leaving them unable to provide basic services to thousands of inhabitants. Tijuana has grown fivefold, to more than 700,000 in the past 20 years. Juarez has grown from 500,000 to 1.2 million, Nogales from 45,000 to more than 300,000. . . . Nogales is a particularly dire case. One third of its 69 neighborhoods, or colonias, were built in the past 10 years, most of cardboard and scraps from the nearby factories. In some areas, the cardboard is from boxes that once contained toxic polyvinyl chloride, and has a health warning printed on the side. Fully half of the population lives in shanties, and 70 percent have no indoor toilets.
>
> Thirty-five of the 69 colonias have no running water. Subcontractors deliver it three times a week by truck to central areas of the colonias. People pay $1 for a 55-gallon drum's worth, then lug the water back to their houses on the back of a pickup."

[SOURCE: John McQuaid, "Cheap Labor, High Price," *(New Orleans) Times-Picayune,* June 23, 1991, p. A-4.]

   a. Discuss the ethics of operating maquiladoras from the perspective of a United States business.
   b. Discuss the ethics of operating maquiladoras from the perspective of a Mexican worker.
   c. As the manager of a U.S. business, discuss some methods of enhancing the positive impacts of maquiladoras and minimizing the negative impacts. How might the adoption of the North American Free Trade pact affect maquiladoras?

32. Early 1992 was not a good time for Dow Corning. News of the potential hazards of silicone-gel breast implants hit every communication medium in the United States. In addition to the possible problems related to the implant was the release of hundreds of internal company documents that indicated the company knew for over ten years that there were potential rupture problems related to the implants. Immediately after the release of this information, the company's chairman and chief executive officer were replaced. The company, though, had had an ethics program in place for 18 years before the implant scandal.

   a. Investigate and comment on the crisis management program implemented by Dow Corning when the news was released.
   b. Why would a company have allowed the implants to be marketed if there was evidence that pointed to health hazards? Take the position of a high corporate officer in Dow Corning before the scandal became public.
   c. Assume that you or someone close to you has had these implants in the process of *reconstructive* surgery. What issues should be considered?
   d. Do you think the publicity about this matter would have been substantially different had the internal information not existed? Why or why not?

33. *S. Stewart Joslin figured he was being a good citizen when he let the Internal Revenue Service know his bosses weren't forwarding the income taxes they had withheld from employees' paychecks. Instead, Joslin, the operations manager for a defunct New Orleans computer firm, said he is being held liable for the taxes, totaling $69,000. For nearly nine months in 1987 and 1988, Joslin said, he persistently pressed the computer firm's executives to pay [the taxes]. And when that failed he arranged to let the IRS know about the delinquency. Joslin was apparently cited for the tax liability because he had the authority to sign payroll checks.*

   The case against Joslin is not unique. Recently, columnist Jack Anderson wrote about the controller for a landscaping firm in Austin, Texas, who quit and notified the IRS after her boss refused to turn over unpaid withholding taxes. Anderson reported that the IRS still held her liable for the $120,000 tax bill.

   [There is also] a case in which a personnel manager for a San Francisco firm has been held responsible for $600,000 in unpaid taxes after the company declared bankruptcy and its owners left for England.

[SOURCE: Bruce Alpert, "Whistleblowers Get IRS Sting," *(New Orleans) Times-Picayune* (September 25, 1991), p. C1.]

a. Do you believe that it was Joslin's responsibility to see that the taxes were paid? Why or why not?

b. Under the circumstances, do you think Joslin and the others should have blown the whistle? Why or why not?

c. If you found yourself in similar circumstances, knowing what happened to Joslin and the others, would you blow the whistle? Why or why not?

34. The Total Quality Management movement (TQM) has changed the way companies manage. It has shattered the belief that the most effective way to manage an organization is to control and direct employees. Previously held beliefs that only management can make decisions were developed to deal with a poorly educated industrial revolution workforce. But they aren't suited to today's competitive environment, where flexibility, speed, and responsiveness to market demands are required throughout the company. Leading, empowering, coaching, visioning, "walk the talk," and self-directed work teams are some of the popular concepts in TQM companies.

[SOURCE: Paul A. Neblock, "What's a Manager to Do? Coping with TQM," *(Grant Thornton) Benefits & HR Adviser* (Fall 1992), p. 5.]

a. Why do you think the concept of employee "empowerment" would result in higher organizational product or service quality?

b. When is your performance of higher quality: when you are told precisely what to do or when you are given a goal and told to use your own discretion in achieving that goal? Discuss the reasons behind your answer.

c. In an organizational setting, do you think that quality performance can be achieved without communication of a goal? Does that goal have to be the same for everyone in the organization? Discuss.

35. In any profession, there is usually some type of designation of achievement. Accounting has numerous professional designations, two of which are the CMA and CPA.

a. Do you believe that the quality of a person's work can be determined based solely on whether he or she has obtained one or more professional certifications? Why or why not?

b. Do you believe that the attainment of a professional certification is an indicator of the quality of work a person will perform? Why or why not?

c. Discuss possible reasons for the salary differentials shown in Exhibit 1–8 for certified versus noncertified accountants.

36. *Money* magazine publishes a list of cities deemed to have the highest quality of life. Obtain a copy of the most recent listing.

a. Do you agree with the criteria that *Money* used to judge quality of life? Why or why not? What (if any) different elements would you consider in determining quality of life?

b. If you had an opportunity to move (with a job) after you graduated to the city at the top of *Money*'s list, would you do so? Discuss the rationale for your answer, making certain to address quality of life issues.

2 COST TERMINOLOGY AND COST FLOWS

After completing this chapter, you should be able to answer these questions:

1. How are costs classified and why are such classifications useful?
2. What assumptions do accountants make about cost behavior and why are these assumptions necessary?
3. How do product and period costs differ and why is this distinction a critical one?
4. How are cost objects and direct costs related?
5. How does the conversion process occur in manufacturing and service companies?
6. What product cost categories exist and what items compose these categories?
7. How does a manufacturing company calculate cost of goods manufactured?

INTRODUCING

McILHENNY COMPANY

Tabasco brand* sauce, often called "Cajun catsup," has been a success ever since Edmund McIlhenny made gifts of the condiment, packed in ladies' perfume bottles with sprinkler fitments, for family and favorite friends. So enthusiastic were all who tasted the sauce that in 1868 McIlhenny sold his entire inventory of 350 bottles to wholesalers. One year later he received thousands of orders at $1 a bottle, and the sauce was patented in 1870.

Peppers, salt and vinegar—the ingredients in the spicy Tabasco sauce are simple. The ripe pepper pods are picked by hand. A crusher grinds the fresh pods into a mixture of eight pounds of salt to every 100 pounds of Capsicum peppers. The mash is then funneled into 400-pound-capacity Kentucky oak barrels, like those used for wine, for three to four years of aging. The barrels are sealed with wooden lids that are drilled with holes to allow gas to escape; the lids are coated with a thick layer of salt, and the long fermentation period begins.

The aged slurry is mixed with vinegar to stand for another month and is intermittently turned by wooden paddles during every working hour. Each barrel is personally inspected by a McIlhenny for true color, texture and aroma. Only then is the filtered sauce piped to the next building to be bottled and packaged in the familiar red and green box for distribution. The Avery Island factory produces more than 300,000 bottles a day or 78 million of the two-ounce size every year.

SOURCE: Jo Gulledge, *Red Pepper Paradise* (New Orleans: Audubon Park Press, 1986). (The quantities and amounts used in the chapter do not represent McIlhenny Company's data.)

* Tabasco® is a registered trademark of McIlhenny Company, Avery Island, LA 70513.

A s discussed in Chapter 1, every product and service has costs associated with it—the costs of materials, labor, and overhead. **Cost,** a frequently used word in organizations, reflects a monetary measure of the resources given up to attain some objective such as acquiring a good or service. However, like many other words in the English language, the term *cost* must be defined more specifically before "the cost" can be determined. Thus, the term *cost* is seldom used without a preceding adjective to specify the type of cost being considered. Different types of costs are used in different situations. For example, the historical or acquisition cost of an asset is used to prepare a balance sheet, but replacement cost is used to estimate an asset's value for insurance purposes.

Cost

To communicate information effectively to others, accountants must clearly understand the differences among various types of costs, their computations, and their usage. This chapter provides basic terminology that is necessary to understand and communicate cost and management accounting information. The chapter also discusses cost flows and accumulation in a production environment.

COST CATEGORIES

Cost may be defined in a variety of ways depending on the objectives or information desired. In this text, cost classifications are used to define costs in terms of their relationships to the following four items: (1) time of incurrence; (2) reaction to changes in activity; (3) classification on the financial statements; and (4) impact on decision making. Exhibit 2–1 presents these different cost categories and the types of costs included in each. These categories are not mutually exclusive; a cost may be defined in one way at one time and in another way at a different time. The first three classifications of costs are discussed in this chapter. The costs that relate to decision making are covered at various points throughout the text. At this time, it is merely important to understand that "cost" can have many different meanings.

Costs Associated with Time of Incurrence

Costs classified in relationship to the time of incurrence include historical costs, replacement costs, and budgeted costs. **Historical costs** were incurred in the past and are normally used in financial accounting. These costs are objective and verifiable—necessary qualities for income statement and balance sheet valuations. How-

Historical cost

■ **EXHIBIT 2–1**
Cost Classification Categories

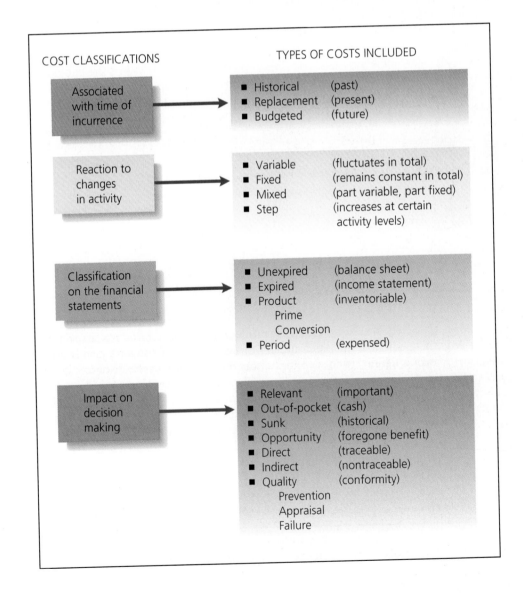

ever, historical costs may not be useful for decision making because conditions may have changed since the costs were incurred.

A **replacement cost** is an amount that a firm would currently have to pay to replace an asset or to buy one that performs functions similar to an asset currently held. Several methods may be used to determine the replacement cost of an item, including referencing supplier catalogs and requesting quotes from established markets that deal in similar assets.

Replacement cost

An asset's replacement cost may be quite different from its original acquisition price for many reasons. Assume that McIlhenny purchased a plot of land for $20,000 in 1965. The $20,000 is the historical cost of the land and represented an equitable exchange price for the property at that time. If the area surrounding the land has been developed and access to the property has been improved, the land's current replacement cost might be $180,000. But if a nuclear power plant or a hazardous material waste disposal facility has since been built next to the McIlhenny land, the land's replacement cost might only be $2,000. If conditions are essentially the same as when the land was purchased (for example, there have been no changes in the surrounding environment, no new access, no improvements, and no inflation), the land's replacement cost may still be $20,000.

Planned future expenditures are called **budgeted costs.** A budgeted cost could be, but is not necessarily, the same amount as the replacement cost. Assume that McIlhenny needs a new bottling machine to replace one that was purchased for $38,000 ten years ago. A similar machine now costs $46,000 (the replacement cost). A new, larger-capacity, more energy-efficient machine is available for $51,000. If McIlhenny plans to buy a machine similar to the one it already has, the budgeted cost is equal to the replacement cost of $46,000. If McIlhenny plans to buy the larger machine, the budgeted cost is $51,000, but the replacement cost of the old machine is still $46,000.

Budgeted cost

The two cost accounting objectives presented in Chapter 1 are to cost products for inventories and other financial accounting purposes and to provide useful information to management. Historical costs are indispensable for the first purpose since financial statement amounts must be objective and verifiable. Replacement, budgeted, and other versions of current costs are normally more appropriate than historical costs for managerial purposes. Current costs provide more up-to-date information and are more relevant to present problems and alternatives than historical costs. However, replacement and budgeted costs are generally not included in the accounting system and typically must be estimated or derived from inference when they are needed.

Cost Reactions to Changes in Activity

In any period, a cost may change in direction and/or in magnitude with corresponding changes in activity levels. Activity measures include sales, production, and/or service volume, machine hours, and number of purchase orders sent. A given cost's behavior pattern is defined according to the way its *total cost* (rather than unit cost) reacts to changes in activity. Every cost will change if activity levels are shifted to extremes and given a long enough span of time. Therefore, to properly identify, analyze, and use cost behavior information, a time frame must be specified to indicate how far into the future a cost should be examined, and a particular range of activity must be assumed. For example, the cost of a gallon of vinegar to make Tabasco might increase by $.05 next year but by $5.00 by the year 2010. The assumed range of activity is referred to as the **relevant range,** which reflects the company's normal operating range. Within the relevant range, the two most common cost behaviors are variable and fixed.

Relevant range

A cost that varies *in total* in direct proportion to changes in activity is a **variable cost.** Examples include the costs of materials, wages, and sales commissions. Variable costs can be extremely important in regard to the total profit picture of a company

Variable cost

EXHIBIT 2–2

Economic Representation
of a Variable Cost

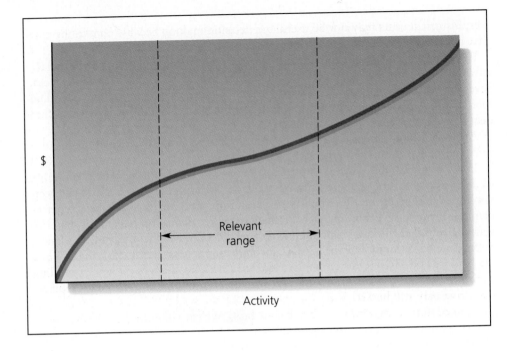

because every time a product is produced and/or sold or a service is rendered and/or sold, a corresponding amount of that variable cost is incurred. Since the total cost varies in direct proportion to the changes in activity levels, a variable cost must be a constant amount *per unit*.

Variable costs are viewed by economists as being curvilinear, as shown in Exhibit 2–2. The cost line slopes upward at a given rate until a range of activity is reached in which the average variable cost rate becomes fairly constant. Within this range, the slope of the cost line becomes less steep because the firm experiences benefits such as discounts on material prices, improved worker skill and productivity, and other operating efficiencies. Beyond this range, the slope becomes quite steep as the entity enters a range of activity in which certain operating factors cause the average variable cost to increase. In this range, the firm finds that costs rise rapidly due to worker crowding, equipment shortages, and other operating inefficiencies.

Fixed cost

On the other hand, a cost that remains constant *in total* within the relevant range of activity is considered a **fixed cost**. Such costs vary inversely on a per unit basis with changes in the level of activity. This means that the *per unit* fixed cost decreases with increases in the activity level, and increases with decreases in the activity level. Fixed costs include supervisors' salaries, depreciation (other than that computed under the units of production method), and insurance. It is important to note that "in the long run all costs are variable at the total business unit level. If you were to stop producing all products, then obviously, all other costs can, in time, be eliminated."[1]

To illustrate the need for a relevant range of activity, assume that McIlhenny has the cost structure for bottles purchased and building depreciation shown in the graphs in Exhibit 2–3. The exhibit indicates that actual variable cost for bottles is curvilinear rather than linear and that, over the long run, several levels of cost exist for building depreciation.

The curves on the cost graph for empty bottles purchased reflect pricing policies by suppliers. If McIlhenny's purchasing agent buys less than 500,000 bottles at a time, the price per empty bottle is $.32. If between 500,000 and 1,200,000 bottles

---

[1] Robert A. Howell and Stephen R. Soucy, "Cost Accounting in the New Manufacturing Environment," *Management Accounting* (August 1987), p. 46.

are purchased, the price is $.30 per bottle. Quantities over 1,200,000 may be purchased for $.28 each. Because the company always buys in quantities of 500,000 to 1,200,000 bottles, this is the relevant range of activity for purchases. The bottle cost is variable because total cost will vary in direct proportion to the quantity purchased within the relevant range. If McIlhenny buys 700,000 bottles, it will pay $210,000 for its purchases; if it buys 950,000 bottles, the cost will be $285,000. In each instance, because both volumes were within the relevant range, the cost remains constant at $.30 per bottle and exemplifies a variable cost that is truly linear over the relevant range.

A decision about the relevant range must also be made for fixed costs. The fixed cost shown in Exhibit 2–3 is for building depreciation. Assume that McIlhenny management has determined that one building, depreciated at the straight-line amount of $3,000 per month, can house enough equipment to produce between 1 and 3,800,000 bottles of Tabasco per month. However, when production exceeds 3,800,000 bottles, additional facilities will be required. If another similar building is acquired, there will be an additional $3,000 of building depreciation per month. While the company purchases bottles in quantities of 600,000 to 1,000,000 at a time, total monthly production is between 4,000,000 and 6,000,000 bottles of Tabasco; thus, multiple empty bottle purchases must be made from the supplier. Production at

■ **EXHIBIT 2–3**

Relevant Range of Activity for McIlhenny

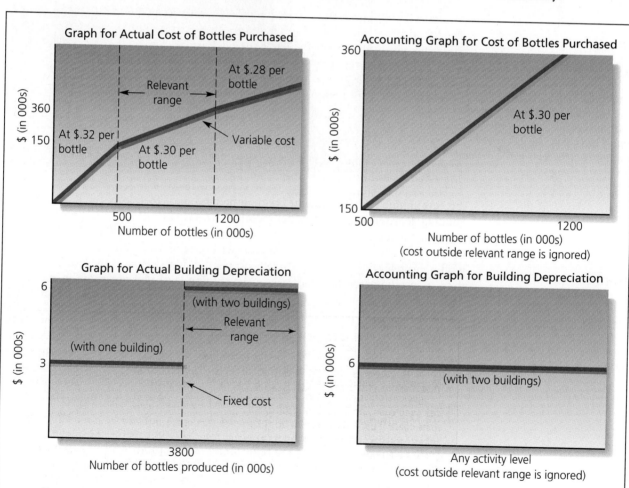

NOTE: The two graphs on the left present the base of activity (bottles purchased and bottles produced) unique to the specific costs being graphed (purchase price for bottles and depreciation, respectively). Once a relevant range of activity is chosen, total variable cost will change at the same rate for all changes in activity and total fixed cost will not change, regardless of changes in activity.

At McIlhenny, the cost of peppers is a variable cost, but labor costs may be variable or fixed. Field and factory workers who are paid on an hourly basis cause the incurrence of a variable cost; supervisors who are paid monthly create a fixed cost.

this level requires that a second building be used and, therefore, the fixed cost for building depreciation is $6,000 per month.

While the total cost of depreciation remains constant at $6,000 per month within the relevant range, the depreciation cost per bottle of sauce produced is not linear within this relevant range. While fixed cost per unit will decline as the level of activity rises, a specific percentage increase in the activity level will not result in the same percentage decrease in unit cost. The depreciation cost per bottle of sauce is illustrated below, assuming 10 percent increases from a base of 4,000,000 bottles:

% Increase in Number of Bottles	Number of Bottles	Depreciation per Bottle	% Decrease in Depreciation per Bottle
	4,000,000	$.0015000	
+10%	4,400,000	.0013636	−9.0933%
+10%	4,840,000	.0012397	−9.0862%
+10%	5,324,000	.0011270	−9.0909%

Mixed cost

Other costs exist that are not strictly variable or fixed. For example, a **mixed cost** has both a variable and a fixed component. On a per unit basis, a mixed cost does not fluctuate in direct proportion with changes in activity nor does it remain constant with changes in activity. An example of a mixed cost is electricity that is computed as a flat charge (the fixed component) for basic service plus a stated rate for each kilowatt hour (kwh) of electricity used (the variable component). Exhibit 2–4 shows a graph for McIlhenny's electricity charge from Louisiana Power & Light, which consists of a flat rate of $500 per month plus $.018 per kwh. If McIlhenny uses 80,000 kwhs of electricity in a month, its total electricity bill is $1,940 [$500 + ($.018 × 80,000)]. If 90,000 kwhs are used, the electricity bill is $2,120.

In some businesses and for some items, variable and fixed costs may be "traded" for one another depending on managerial decisions. For example, McIlhenny could decide to install additional automated equipment (generating an additional fixed cost for depreciation) and eliminate the need for some workers who are paid on an hourly basis (a variable cost). Alternatively, the company could decide to **outsource** some of its production or support functions. (Outsourcing is the process of a company using an external provider of a service or manufacturer of a component.) Almost all large manufacturers—especially automakers—outsource some of their production operations. For example, Pooler Industries (Muncie, Indiana) is a metal-stamping company that makes between five and ten parts for every American car producer as well as selling to other major companies both domestic and international.

By outsourcing a support function such as data processing, a company might be able to trade its own fixed costs of equipment and data processing personnel salaries for a mixed cost. The company providing the data processing service would typically do so for a fixed annual amount plus a charge for the volume of transactions processed. Whether a company exchanges variable for fixed or fixed for mixed costs, shifting costs from one type of cost behavior to another changes the basic cost structure of the company and can have a significant impact on profits, as indicated in the News Note "Trading Cost Behavior."

Another type of cost shifts upward or downward when activity changes by a certain interval or "step." A **step cost** can be variable or fixed. Step variable costs have small steps and step fixed costs have large steps. For example, a water bill computed as $.002 per gallon for 1–1,000 gallons, $.003 per gallon for 1,001–2,000 gallons, $.005 per gallon for 2,001–3,000 gallons, etc. is an example of a step variable cost. Telephone operator salaries, where one operator is paid $2,500 per month and is needed for every 150 calls received per day by the company, is an example of a step fixed cost.

Understanding the types of behavior exhibited by costs is necessary to make valid estimates of total costs at various levels of activity. Although all costs do not conform

Outsource

Step cost

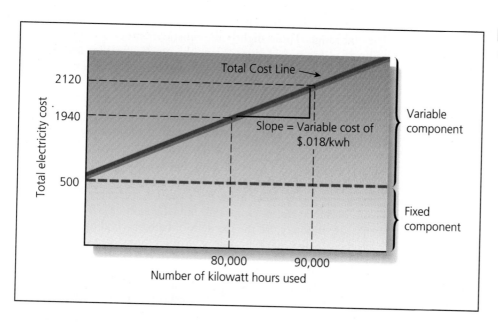

■ **EXHIBIT 2–4**
Graph of a Mixed Cost

NEWS NOTE   Trading Cost Behavior

Computers typically gobble 3% to 5% of an industrial company's operating budget, and often more at service companies. For companies that lay out hundreds of millions of dollars each year for data processing, outsourcing has powerful appeal.

Generally, the [company providing the service] buys a customer's computer hardware and hires all or most of the employees who have been running it. For example, EDS paid Enron some $6 million for its computers, software, and data-transmission network. The Dallas computer services giant also hired some 550 Enron employees—mostly computer operators and programmers—at comparable wages and benefits.

None of the companies FORTUNE spoke with would reveal details of their contracts, but normally an outsourcer charges a fixed annual amount, plus additional fees based on processing volume. Says John McGeachie, an information management consultant for Arthur D. Little: "In an uncertain world, people want to be able to control their costs. That's very hard to do if you own lots of mainframes. Outsourcing lets you pay each time you process a piece of data."

The customer can also save on taxes: While hardware must be depreciated over three to five years, outsourcing fees are deductible as a current business expense. Enron expects to save $200 million in this decade—20% to 24% of total computing costs.

SOURCE: David Kirkpatrick, "Why Not Farm Out Your Computing?" FORTUNE (September 23, 1991), pp. 103–104. © 1991 Time Inc. All rights reserved.

strictly to the above categories, the categories represent the types of cost behavior typically encountered in business. Cost accountants generally separate mixed costs into their variable and fixed components so that behavior of these costs is more readily apparent.[2] This separation allows managers to focus on the two basic types of costs: variable and fixed. When step variable or step fixed costs exist, accountants must choose a specific relevant range of activity that will allow step variable costs to be treated as variable and step fixed costs to be treated as fixed.

By separating mixed costs into their fixed and variable components and by specifying a relevant range for step costs, *accountants force all costs into fixed and variable categories while disregarding economic reality*. A variable cost is *assumed* to be constant per unit within the relevant range, and a fixed cost is *assumed* to be constant in total within the relevant range. These slightly unrealistic treatments of variable and fixed costs can be justified for two reasons. First, the conditions that are assumed approximate reality and, if the company operates only within the relevant range of activity, the cost behaviors selected are the appropriate ones. Second, selection of a constant variable cost per unit and a constant fixed cost in total provides a convenient, stable measurement for use in planning and decision making.

To make these generalizations about variable and fixed costs, accountants need to find a valid predictor for cost changes. A **predictor** is an activity measure that, when changed, is accompanied by consistent, observable changes in a cost item. However, simply because the two items change together does not necessarily prove that the predictor causes the change in the other item. For instance, assume that every time your aunt invites you to dinner, the stock market falls the next day. If this is consistent, observable behavior, you may use the incident of being invited by your aunt to dinner to predict declines in the market—but such invitations do not cause stock market changes!

Predictor

---

[2] A simple method for analyzing a mixed cost is the high-low method discussed in Chapter 4. That chapter also illustrates least squares regression, a more mathematically sophisticated analytical technique.

NEWS NOTE

Find the Driver to Improve the Process

A cost driver is any factor that causes a change in the total cost of an activity. It is, in short, the cause of a cost. Understanding the causal relationship between an activity and its cost enables management to focus improvement efforts on the areas that will produce the best result.

For example, a business process for one company that provides a service to manufacturers that consists of collecting and processing product and demographic information about customers includes the activity of data entry—manually keypunching customer-supplied information into a database. Productivity in this company is measured as a cost per card or the cost per entry of a customer response. Improvement efforts that focused on making data entry clerks (the company's major cost) work better and faster, produced mixed results. [Then] the company instituted a cost driver analysis [which] discovered that, more than any other factor, the design of the card was the root of cost in data entry. Poorly designed cards that were difficult to read slowed the data entry operators. Armed with this information . . . , management focused its improvement efforts on the card design activity, and ultimately achieved performance improvements in the data entry activity.

SOURCE: John A. Miller, "Designing and Implementing a New Cost Management System," *Journal of Cost Management* (Boston: Warren Gorham Lamont, Winter 1992), pp. 44-45.

In contrast to predictors, **cost drivers** are measures of activity that are believed to have a direct cause-effect relationship to a cost. For example, production volume has a direct effect on the total cost of raw material used and can be said to "drive" that cost. Thus, production volume can be used as a valid predictor of that cost. The News Note "Find the Driver" illustrates the concept of a cost driver in a service company activity.

Cost driver

In most situations, the cause-effect relationship is less clear since costs are commonly caused by multiple factors. For example, quality control costs are affected by a variety of factors such as production volume, quality of materials used, skill level of workers, and level of automation. Although it may be difficult to determine which factor actually caused a specific change in quality control cost, any of these factors could be chosen to predict that cost if confidence exists about the factor's relationship with cost changes. To be used as a predictor, it is only necessary that the predictor and the cost change together in a foreseeable manner.

Traditionally, a single cost driver has been used to predict all types of costs. Accountants and managers, however, are realizing that single cost drivers do not necessarily provide the most reasonable predictions. This realization has caused a movement toward activity-based costing, which uses different cost drivers to predict different types of costs. Production volume, for instance, would be a valid cost driver for the cost of Tabasco ingredients, but the number of vendors used might be a more realistic driver for McIlhenny's purchasing department costs.[3]

Cost Classifications on the Financial Statements

Two major financial statements prepared by a company are the balance sheet and income statement. The balance sheet is a statement of **unexpired costs** (assets) and

Unexpired cost

---

[3] Using multiple cost drivers for illustrative purposes in the text would be unwieldy. Therefore, except when topics such as activity-based costing are being discussed, examples will typically make use of a single cost driver.

Expired cost

equities (liabilities and owners' capital); the income statement is a statement of revenues and **expired costs**. The concept of matching revenues and expenses on the income statement is central to financial accounting. The matching concept provides a basis for deciding when an unexpired cost becomes an expired cost and is moved from an asset category (balance sheet) to an expense or loss category (income statement).

The two categories of expired costs (expenses and losses) differ in that expenses are intentionally incurred in the process of generating revenues, and losses are unintentionally incurred. Examples of expired costs that appear as expenses on the income statement include cost of goods sold, selling expenses, and administrative expenses. Examples of losses include costs expiring from conditions such as fire or flood as well as abnormal production waste.

Product cost
Period cost

In addition to being designated as unexpired or expired costs, many costs can also be classified as either product or period costs. **Product costs** are related to the products or services that directly generate the revenues of an entity; **period costs** are related to other business operations (selling, general, and administrative costs).

Inventoriable cost

Product costs are associated with making or acquiring inventory and are also called **inventoriable costs**. These costs include the cost of direct materials, direct labor, and overhead. Any readily identifiable part of a product (such as the wood in a table) is a **direct material**. Direct materials may be purchased raw materials or manufactured subassemblies.[4] **Direct labor** refers to the time spent by individuals who work specifically on manufacturing a product or performing a service. At McIlhenny, the wages paid to the people picking pepper pods and coating the barrels with salt are considered direct labor costs. Any factory or production cost that is **indirect** to the product or service and, accordingly, does not include direct materials and direct labor is **overhead**. This cost element includes all indirect costs incurred in or by the production area, such as factory supervisors' salaries, depreciation on the paddling machines that stir the aged Tabasco slurry, and insurance on the production facilities. Direct materials, direct labor, and overhead are discussed in depth later in the chapter.

Direct material
Direct labor

Indirect cost

Overhead

Period costs are more closely associated with a particular time frame rather than with making or acquiring a product or performing a service. Period costs that have future benefit are classified on the balance sheet as assets, while those deemed to have no future benefit are expensed as incurred. Prepaid insurance on an administration building represents an unexpired period cost; when the premium period passes, the insurance becomes an expired period cost (insurance expense). Salaries paid to the sales force or depreciation on computers in the administrative area are also period costs.

Distribution cost

Mention must be made of one specific type of period cost: distribution. A **distribution cost** is any cost incurred to warehouse, transport, or deliver a product or service. Although distribution costs are expensed as incurred, managers must remember that these costs relate directly to products and services and should not adopt an "out-of-sight, out-of-mind" attitude about these costs simply because they have been expensed for financial accounting purposes. Distribution costs must be planned for in relationship to product/service volume and these costs must be controlled for profitability to result from sales. Thus, even though distribution costs are not technically

Outside processing cost

[4] An additional type of cost that can be considered direct material is **outside processing cost**. For example, if a furniture manufacturer wants its tabletops specially laminated, it may send the tables to another company specializing in this process rather than buying the necessary equipment. The cost would be considered a direct material cost if product cost is defined as consisting of three elements: direct materials, direct labor, and overhead. However, if a significant amount of outside processing is used, the company may want to define product cost as consisting of four components: direct materials, outside processing, direct labor, and overhead.

	COST CLASSIFICATION ON	
	BALANCE SHEET (Unexpired Costs)	INCOME STATEMENT (Expired Costs)

MERCHANDISING COMPANY

Product Costs (Inventoriable)—obtained by purchases of merchandise for resale

Period Costs (Noninventoriable)—obtained by payment or accrual for variety of nonmerchandise-related costs

MANUFACTURING COMPANY

Product Costs (Inventoriable)—obtained by purchase of raw materials; converted through incurrence of direct labor and overhead costs; completed and transferred out of the factory; sold

Period Costs (Noninventoriable)—obtained by payment or accrual for variety of nonproduction-related costs

SERVICE COMPANY

Product Costs (Inventoriable)—converted supplies into service function through direct labor and overhead costs; completed service function; acceptance of service by customers

Period costs (Noninventoriable)—obtained by payment or accrual for variety of nonperformance-related costs

Balance Sheet / Income Statement mapping:

- Merchandise Inventory → Cost of Goods Sold
- Prepaid Expenses → Selling, General, & Administrative (SG&A) Expenses
- Raw Materials, Work in Process, Finished Goods → Cost of Goods Sold
- Prepaid Expenses; Nonproduction Assets → SG&A Expenses
- Supplies, Work in Process, Completed Services* → Cost of Services Rendered
- Prepaid Expenses, Nonproduction Assets → SG&A Expenses

*It is possible for service companies to have WIP and Completed Services on the balance sheet, although most commonly completed services would not appear because they generally cannot be warehoused.

■ EXHIBIT 2–5

Comparison of Product and Period Costs

considered part of product cost, they may have a major impact on managerial decision making,[5] because selling prices must be set high enough to recover such costs.

Retailing, manufacturing, and service companies generally all classify the same basic types of costs as product and period costs, although some of the account titles differ. Exhibit 2–5 compares these costs and account titles.

In a retailing business, typically the only unexpired product cost is the cost of the unsold merchandise that has been purchased for resale (which includes any associated freight charges). In a manufacturer, unexpired product costs are classified as: (1) raw materials; (2) work in process; or (3) finished goods. Each of these costs is maintained in a separate general ledger account. In both retail and manufacturing companies, product costs expire when the goods are sold and the costs are transferred to the cost of goods sold account.

---

[5] The uniform capitalization rules (unicap rules) of the Tax Reform Act of 1986 caused many manufacturers, wholesalers, and retailers to expand the types and amounts of nonproduction-area costs that are treated as product costs for tax purposes. The unicap rules require that distribution costs for warehousing be considered part of product cost, but not distribution costs for marketing and customer delivery. The rationale for such treatment is that such warehousing costs are incident to production or acquisition. See the appendix to Chapter 6 for a more complete discussion on uniform capitalization rules.

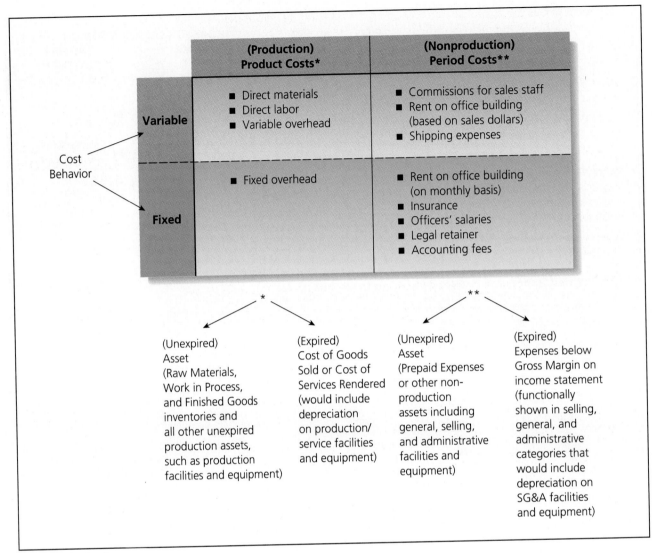

	(Production) Product Costs*	(Nonproduction) Period Costs**
Variable	■ Direct materials ■ Direct labor ■ Variable overhead	■ Commissions for sales staff ■ Rent on office building (based on sales dollars) ■ Shipping expenses
Fixed	■ Fixed overhead	■ Rent on office building (on monthly basis) ■ Insurance ■ Officers' salaries ■ Legal retainer ■ Accounting fees

Cost Behavior

*

(Unexpired)
Asset
(Raw Materials,
Work in Process,
and Finished Goods
inventories and
all other unexpired
production assets,
such as production
facilities and equipment)

(Expired)
Cost of Goods
Sold or Cost of
Services Rendered
(would include
depreciation
on production/
service facilities
and equipment)

**

(Unexpired)
Asset
(Prepaid Expenses
or other non-
production
assets including
general, selling,
and administrative
facilities and
equipment)

(Expired)
Expenses below
Gross Margin on
income statement
(functionally
shown in selling,
general, and
administrative
categories that
would include
depreciation on
SG&A facilities
and equipment)

▌ EXHIBIT 2–6

Cost Classifications for Financial Reporting

In a service company, a work in process inventory account may be maintained to show unexpired costs for projects not yet completed. If necessary, a service company may show a completed services account when projects are finished. However, the latter account is not often shown because most service companies perform services that are transferred to the customer almost immediately upon completion. The total cost of performing the service is sent to the income statement as an expired cost (cost of services rendered) at the time the service is transferred.

Exhibit 2–6 summarizes the classifications of costs for financial reporting and provides some additional examples of period costs. Note that when McIlhenny incurs insurance cost for a manufacturing building, that cost is considered overhead and a type of product cost. On the other hand, the insurance cost for McIlhenny's administrative offices is a period cost. If the insurance were prepaid, the expiration of the insurance cost on the manufacturing building would flow into overhead (a product cost), while the expiration of the insurance on the administrative offices would flow into a period expense. Only when the products were sold would that insurance cost related to the manufacturing building become expired—as part of the cost of goods sold. Thus, the distinction between product and period cost is made primarily on the basis of *where* the cost was incurred rather than the *type* of cost incurred.

The appendix at the end of the chapter presents detailed income statements for each type of business organization. Balance sheets are not shown because the only differences are in the number and titles of inventory accounts.

THE CONVERSION PROCESS

In general, product costs are incurred in the production or conversion area and period costs are incurred in all nonproduction or nonconversion areas.[6] To some extent, all organizations convert (or change) inputs into outputs. Inputs typically consist of materials, labor, and overhead. The outputs of a conversion process include both products and services. Exhibit 2–7 compares the conversion activities of different types of organizations. Note that many service companies engage in a high degree of conversion. Firms of professionals (such as accountants, architects, attorneys, engineers, and surveyors) convert labor and other resource inputs (materials and overhead) into completed jobs (audit reports, building plans, contracts, blueprints, and property survey reports).

Firms that engage in only a low-to-moderate degree of conversion can conveniently expense insignificant costs of labor and overhead related to conversion. The savings in clerical cost of expensing outweighs the value of any slightly improved information that might result from assigning such costs to products or services. For example, when employees in a grocery store open shipping containers and stock individual packages on shelves, a labor cost for conversion is incurred. Grocery stores, however, do not try to attach the stockpeople's wages to inventory; such labor costs are treated as period costs and are expensed as they are incurred.

In contrast, in high-conversion firms, the informational benefits gained from accumulating the materials, labor, and overhead costs of the output produced signifi-

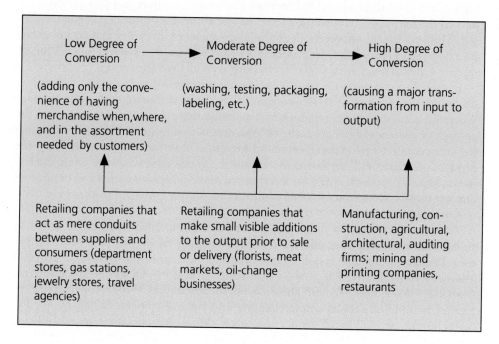

■ **EXHIBIT 2–7**
Degrees of Conversion in Firms

---

[6] It is less common, but possible for a cost physically incurred outside the production area to be in direct support of production and, therefore, considered a product cost. An example of this situation is the salary of a product cost analyst who is based at corporate headquarters; this cost is part of overhead.

cantly exceeds the clerical costs of accumulating these costs. No one would presume to expense the labor costs incurred for workers constructing a bridge; these costs would be treated as product costs and inventoried as part of the cost of the construction job until the bridge was completed for the client.

Manufacturer

For convenience, the term **manufacturer** will be used to refer to any company engaged in a high degree of conversion of raw material input into other tangible output. Manufacturers typically convert raw materials through the use of people and machines to produce large quantities of output that can be physically inspected. The term

Service company

service company will be used to refer to an individual or firm engaged in a high or moderate degree of conversion using a significant amount of labor. The output of a service business may be tangible (an audit report) or intangible (health care) and normally cannot be inspected prior to its use. Service firms may be profit-making businesses or not-for-profit organizations.

Firms engaging in only low-to-moderate degrees of conversion ordinarily have only one inventory account (Merchandise Inventory). In contrast, manufacturers normally use three inventory accounts: (1) Raw Materials; (2) Work in Process (for partially converted goods); and (3) Finished Goods. Service firms will have an inventory account for the supplies used in the conversion process and may have a Work in Process Inventory account, but these firms do not normally have a Finished Goods Inventory account since services typically cannot be warehoused.

Retailers vs. Manufacturers/Service Companies

Retail companies purchase goods in finished or almost finished condition. The goods typically need little, if any, conversion before they are sold to customers. Costs associated with such inventory are usually easy to determine, as are the valuations for financial statement presentation. On the other hand, manufacturers and service companies engage in activities that involve the physical conversion or transformation of inputs into finished products and services. The costs of inputs and conversion of inputs to the output of manufacturers and service companies must be assigned to output. This assignment allows the determination of cost of inventory and cost of goods sold or services rendered. Cost accounting provides the structure and process for assigning material and conversion costs to output products and services.

Exhibit 2–8 compares the basic input/output relationships of a retail company and those of a manufacturing/service company. This exhibit illustrates that the primary difference between retail companies, and manufacturers and service companies is the absence or presence of the area labeled "the production center." This center involves the conversion of raw material inputs to final products. Input factors flow into the production center and are stored there until the goods or services are completed. If the output is a product, it can be warehoused and/or displayed after it is completed until it is sold to a customer. Service outputs are simply provided to the client commissioning the work.

Technically, conversion does occur in merchandising businesses, but it is not as significant in terms of time, effort, or cost as it is in manufacturing or service companies. Merchandising conversion includes tagging merchandise with sales tickets and adding store-name labels to goods, as is often done at stores such as Neiman Marcus, Marshall Field's, and Macy's. The costs of such activities should conceptually be treated as additional costs of merchandise and the department adding these costs could be viewed as a "mini" production center. Most often, however, merchandising companies have no designated "production center."

Exhibit 2–8 reflects an accrual-based accounting system in which costs flow from the various inventory accounts on the balance sheet through (if necessary) the production center. The cost accumulation process begins when raw materials or supplies

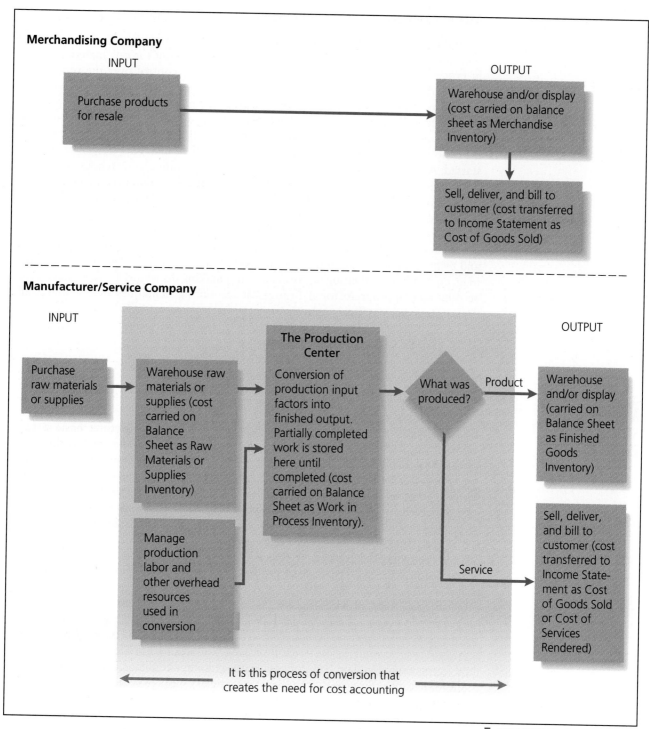

EXHIBIT 2–8

Business Input/Output Relationships

are placed into production. As work progresses on a product or service, costs are accumulated in the firm's accounting records. Accumulating costs in appropriate inventory accounts allows businesses to match the costs of buying or manufacturing a product or providing a service with the revenues generated when the goods or services are sold. At point of sale these product/service costs will flow from an inventory account to cost of goods sold or cost of services rendered on the income statement.

Manufacturers vs. Service Companies

Several differences in accounting for production activities exist between a manufacturer and a service company. A manufacturer must account for raw materials, work in process, and finished goods inventory to maintain control over the production process. An accrual accounting system is essential for such organizations so that the total costs of production can be accumulated as the goods flow through the production process. On the other hand, most service firms need only to keep track of their work in process (incomplete jobs). Such accounting is acceptable because service firms normally have few, if any, materials costs other than supplies for work not started. As mentioned earlier, since services generally cannot be warehoused, costs of finished jobs are transferred immediately to the income statement to be matched against job revenues, rather than being carried on the balance sheet in a finished goods account.

Despite the accounting differences among retailers, manufacturers, and service firms, each type of organization can use cost and management accounting concepts and techniques, although in different degrees. Managers in all firms engage in planning, controlling, evaluating performance, and making decisions. Thus, management accounting is appropriate for all firms. Cost accounting techniques are essential to all firms engaged in significant conversion activities.

STAGES OF PRODUCTION

Production processing or conversion can be viewed as existing in three basic stages: (1) work not started (raw materials); (2) work in process; and (3) finished work. Costs are associated with each processing stage. The stages of production in a manufacturing firm and some costs associated with each stage are illustrated in Exhibit 2-9. In the first stage of processing, the cost incurred reflects the prices paid for purchasing raw materials and/or supplies. As work progresses through the second stage, accrual accounting requires that costs related to the conversion of raw materials or supplies be accumulated and attached to the goods. These costs include the wages paid to people producing the goods as well as overhead charges. The total costs incurred in stages 1 and 2 are equal to the total production cost of goods in the finished goods in stage 3.

Cost accounting provides the means for accumulating the processing costs and allocating the costs to the goods produced. The primary accounts involved in the cost accumulation process are: (1) Raw Materials, (2) Work in Process, and (3) Finished Goods. These accounts relate to the three stages of production shown in Exhibit 2-9 and form a common data base for cost, management, and financial accounting.

Service firms ordinarily do not have the same degree of cost complexity as manufacturers. The work-not-started stage of processing normally consists of the cost of supplies necessary for performing services. Supplies are inventoried until they are placed into a work in process stage. At that point, labor and overhead are added to achieve finished results. Developing the cost of services is extremely important and useful in service-oriented businesses. For instance, cost accounting is very useful in hospitals that need to accumulate the costs incurred by patients during their hospital stays and in architectural firms that need to accumulate the costs incurred for designs and models of individual projects.

The product and/or service costs accumulated in the inventory accounts are composed of three cost components: direct material, direct labor, and overhead. Each of these components is discussed in depth in the next section. Precise classification of some costs into one of these categories may be difficult and judgment may be required in the classification process.

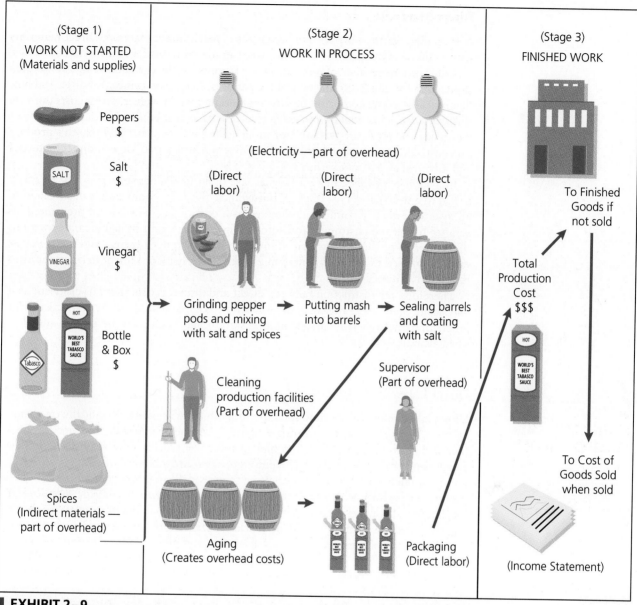

(Stage 1)
WORK NOT STARTED
(Materials and supplies)

Peppers
$

Salt
$

Vinegar
$

Bottle
& Box
$

Spices
(Indirect materials —
part of overhead)

(Stage 2)
WORK IN PROCESS

(Electricity—part of overhead)

(Direct
labor)

(Direct
labor)

(Direct
labor)

Grinding pepper
pods and mixing
with salt and spices → Putting mash
into barrels → Sealing barrels
and coating
with salt

Supervisor
(Part of overhead)

Cleaning
production facilities
(Part of overhead)

Aging
(Creates overhead costs)

Packaging
(Direct labor)

(Stage 3)
FINISHED WORK

To Finished
Goods if
not sold

Total
Production
Cost
$$$

To Cost of
Goods Sold
when sold

(Income Statement)

■ **EXHIBIT 2–9**
Stages and Costs of Production

Product costs are related to the products or services that generate the revenues of an entity. These costs can be separated into three cost components: direct materials, direct labor, and production overhead. To know whether a cost is direct, a **cost object** (anything to which costs attach or are related) must be specified. A cost object can be a product or service, a department, a division, or a territory. Once the cost object is specified, any costs that are distinctly traceable to it are called **direct costs**. Those costs that cannot be traced are called indirect (or common) costs and are **allocated** or assigned to the cost object using one or more appropriate predictors or arbitrarily chosen bases.[7]

COMPONENTS OF PRODUCT COST

Cost object

Direct cost
Allocate

_____

[7]Different cost objects may be designated for different decisions. As the cost object changes, the direct and indirect costs may also change. For instance, if a production division is specified as the cost object, the production division manager's salary is direct. If, instead, the cost object is a sales territory and the production division operates in more than one territory, the production division manager's salary is indirect.

Direct Materials

Any readily identifiable part of a product is called a direct material. Direct materials cost theoretically should include the cost of all materials used in the manufacture of a product or performance of a service. For example, in the production of Tabasco (as depicted in Exhibit 2–9), the cost of the peppers, salt, spices, vinegar, bottle, and box theoretically would comprise the direct materials cost. However, direct costs must be *distinctly and conveniently traceable* to a cost object. It is possible that the costs of the spices are not easily traceable or monetarily significant to the Tabasco's production cost. Thus, these costs could be classified and accounted for as indirect materials and included as part of overhead.

In a service business, direct materials are often insignificant or may not be easily traced to a designated cost object. For instance, the automobile policy department in an insurance agency could be designated as a cost object. The cost of preprinted insurance forms and customer proof-of-insurance cards might be significant enough to trace directly to that department. However, other supplies (pens, paper, envelopes, stationery) used by the department might be relatively inconvenient to trace and thus be treated as overhead.

Therefore, the distinction between direct and indirect costs is not as clear-cut as it may seem. Some costs that may be distinctly traceable would not be conveniently or practically traceable from an accounting standpoint. Such costs are treated and classified as indirect costs.

Direct Labor

Direct labor refers to the time spent by individuals who work specifically on manufacturing a product or performing a service. Another perspective of direct labor is that it directly adds value to the final product or service. The seamstress at Levi Strauss and the nurse at Touro Hospital represent direct labor workers.

Direct labor cost consists of wages or salaries paid to employees who work on a product or perform a service, if that labor transforms raw materials or supplies into finished goods or completed services. Such wages and salaries must also be conveniently traceable to the product or service. Direct labor cost should include basic compensation, production efficiency bonuses, and the employer's share of Social

Ripe peppers are the basic direct material for Tabasco. Other materials such as vinegar and spices may be direct or indirect, depending on whether their costs are considered significant in determining the product cost.

NEWS NOTE

Employee Health Care Costs Are Skyrocketing

Can anyone still doubt that the U.S. health care system is sick and desperately in need of a cure? Costs are so out of control that the nation's medical bills [in 1992 ran] more than $800 billion. That's 14% of all economic output, a sum as big as the combined GDPs of Canada, Norway, and Sweden.

U.S. employers who provided health care coverage in 1991 spend $3,605 per worker, on average—a total of $196 billion. General Motors alone spent $3.4 billion, or $929 for every car it made. The typical company's medical bill equaled 45% of after-tax profits, an enormous handicap in any race against international competitors who bear no such burden.

SOURCE: Lee Smith, "The Right Cure for Health Care," *FORTUNE* (October 19, 1992), pp. 88-89. © 1992 Time Inc. All rights reserved.

Security and Medicare taxes. In addition, if a company's operations are relatively stable, direct labor cost should include all employer-paid insurance costs, holiday and vacation pay, and pension and other retirement benefits.[8]

As with some materials, some labor costs that theoretically should be considered direct are treated as indirect. The first reason for this treatment is that it may be inefficient to specifically trace the particular labor costs to production. For instance, fringe benefit costs should be treated as direct labor cost, but many companies do not have stable work forces that would allow a reasonable estimate of fringe benefit cost to be developed or, alternatively, the time, effort, and cost such an assignment could require might not be worth the additional accuracy it would provide. Thus, the treatment of employee fringe benefits as indirect costs is based on clerical cost inefficiencies. But, when fringe benefit costs are as large as the ones discussed in the News Note "Employee Health Care Costs," tracing them to direct labor may provide extremely useful management information.

Second, treating certain labor costs as direct (in the "theoretically" correct manner) may result in erroneous information about product or service costs. Assume that McIlhenny employs ten workers on the Tabasco sauce bottling line. These workers are paid $7 per hour and time-and-a-half ($10.50) for overtime. One week, the employees worked a total of 1,000 hours or 200 hours of overtime to complete all production orders. If the overtime premium of $3.50 per hour were assigned to the Tabasco sauce produced specifically during the overtime hours, these bottles would appear to have a labor cost 50% greater than items made during regular working hours. Since scheduling is random, the items that *happened* to be completed during overtime hours should not be forced to bear the overtime charges. Therefore, amounts incurred for costs such as overtime or shift premiums are usually considered overhead rather than direct labor cost, and are indirectly allocated to all units. Thus, of the total employee labor payroll of $7,700, only $7,000 (1,000 hours × $7 per hour) would be classified as direct labor cost. The remaining $700 (200 hours × $3.50 per hour) would be considered overhead.

There are occasions, however, when costs such as overtime cannot appropriately be considered overhead. If a customer requests a job to be scheduled during overtime hours or is in a rush and requests overtime to be worked, overtime or shift premiums should be considered direct labor and be attached to the job that created the costs.

---

[8]Institute of Management Accountants (formerly National Association of Accountants), *Statements on Management Accounting: Definition and Measurement of Direct Labor Cost*, Number 4C (Montvale, N.J.: NAA, June 13, 1985), p. 4.

For example, assume that in November, the purchasing agent for Neiman Marcus ordered a shipment of Tabasco to be delivered in three days for a Christmas catalog promotion. This order caused McIlhenny workers to work overtime to bottle the sauce. Neiman Marcus's bill for the Tabasco sauce should reflect the overtime charges.

Because production activity was historically performed by people, direct labor once represented a primary production cost. Now, in the more highly automated work environments, direct labor often comprises less than 10–15 percent of total manufacturing cost. Soon, managers may find that almost all direct labor cost is replaced with a new cost of production—the cost of robots and other fully automated machinery that is used in manufacturing operations. Thus, while labor is an essential element of production, managers should not overstate the importance of labor cost since the proportion of it in products is declining.

Overhead

Overhead is any factory or production cost that is indirect to manufacturing a product or providing a service and, accordingly, does not include direct materials and direct labor. Terms synonymous with overhead are production overhead, factory overhead, and manufacturing overhead.[9] Overhead does include indirect materials and indirect labor as well as any and all other costs incurred in the production area. "The great part of most companies' costs (other than those for purchased materials) typically occur in overhead categories. Even in manufacturing, more than two-thirds of all nonmaterial costs tend to be indirect or overhead expenses."[10]

Overhead costs are categorized as either variable or fixed based on their behavior in response to changes in levels of production volume or some other measure of activity. Variable overhead includes all production costs (other than direct materials and direct labor) that change in direct proportion to changes in activity levels. Variable overhead includes the cost of indirect materials and of indirect labor paid on an hourly basis (such as wages for forklift operators, material handlers, and others who support the production, assembly, and/or service process). Also included in variable overhead is the cost of lubricants used for machine maintenance, floor wax used in the factory lunchroom, and the variable portion of electricity charges (or any other mixed cost) in the factory. Depreciation calculated using the units of production method is a variable overhead cost; this type of depreciation method reflects declines in machine utility based on usage rather than time passage and is very appropriate in an automated plant.

Fixed overhead includes all production costs that remain constant within the company's relevant range of activity. Fixed overhead is comprised of costs such as depreciation (other than units of production depreciation) on factory plant assets, factory license fees, factory insurance and property taxes, and some indirect labor costs. Fixed indirect labor includes salaries for management personnel such as supervisors, shift superintendents, and the plant manager. The fixed portion of mixed costs (such as maintenance and utilities) incurred in the factory is also part of fixed overhead.

An important type of overhead cost is that of quality. Quality is a managerial concern on two general levels. First, the quality of the product or service as it is perceived by the consumer is an important consideration. On another level, managers are concerned about the quality of the production process. Both levels of quality generate

---

[9] Another term used for overhead is *burden*. Although this is the term under which the definition appears in SMA #2, *Management Accounting Terminology*, the authors believe that this term is unacceptable as it connotes costs that are extra, unnecessary, or oppressive. Overhead costs are essential to the conversion process, but simply cannot be traced directly to output.

[10] James Brian Quinn, et al., "Beyond Products: Services-Based Strategy," *Harvard Business Review* (March–April 1990), p. 65.

> ### NEWS NOTE   Understanding Quality Costs
>
>
>
> Managers today understand that unsatisfactory quality means poor use of resources and, thus, higher costs. They also know that good quality can even reduce overall product costs.
>
> An understanding of quality cost can help managers identify those areas in the production of goods or services where corrective action will produce major quality improvements and savings. Cost data can be useful in detecting those products that require further engineering and redesign to reduce scrap and reworking cost. Cost data can help identify defective output before materials and labor are committed (and, thus, before costly disassembly and rework become necessary). Finally, quality cost accounting can redirect quality control priorities. For example, cost data can be used in decisions about whether to eliminate inspections at stations where no problems have occurred.
>
> SOURCE: Lawrence P. Carr and Lawrence A. Poneman, "Managers' Perceptions About Quality Costs," *Journal of Cost Management* (Boston: Warren Gorham Lamont, Spring 1992), pp. 65-67.

costs which often total 20 to 25 percent of sales.[11] There are two basic categories of quality costs: the cost of control and the cost of failure to control.

The cost of control includes prevention and appraisal costs. **Prevention costs** are incurred to improve quality by preventing product defects and dysfunctional processing from occurring. Amounts spent on training programs, researching customer needs, and improved production equipment are considered prevention costs. Amounts incurred for monitoring or inspection are called **appraisal costs**; these costs compensate for mistakes not eliminated through prevention. The second category of quality costs is **failure costs**, which may be internal (such as scrap and rework) or external (such as product returns due to quality problems, warranty costs, and complaint department costs). Expenditures made for prevention will minimize the costs that will be incurred for appraisal and failure.

    Prevention cost

    Appraisal cost

    Failure cost

Airport Security Parking of Little Rock, Arkansas, recognizes the types of and distinction among the various types of quality costs. About one month after opening, the company's parking lot and about 100 customer cars were flooded by the Arkansas River. Although the cause was a natural disaster, Airport Security incurred substantial failure costs in having to notify customers and provide transportation while customer cars were repaired or replaced. Prevention costs were created after the fact to fill and repair the low ground that flooded. Few appraisal costs exist in Airport Security's operations since monitoring of service quality is handled by shuttle drivers who listen to customer comments and suggestions about company services.

In manufacturing, quality costs may be variable in relation to the quantity of defective output, step fixed with increases at specific levels of defective output, or fixed. For example, scrap and rework costs

> approach zero if the quantity of defective output is also nearly zero. However, [these] costs would be extremely high if the number of defective parts produced were high. Training expenditures, on the other hand, would not vary regardless of the quantity of defective output produced in a given time period.[12]

As indicated in the News Note on quality costs, understanding these costs will help

---

[11] *"Measuring the Cost of Quality Takes Creativity," (Grant Thornton) Manufacturing Issues* (Spring 1991), p. 1.

[12] Lawrence A. Poneman, "Accounting for Quality Costs," *Journal of Cost Management* (Fall 1990), p. 46.

managers in their control and decision-making functions. (Implementing a quality program is discussed in depth in Chapter 3.)

The sum of direct materials, direct labor, variable overhead, and fixed overhead costs comprises total product cost.[13] Product costs can also be classified as either prime or conversion costs.

Prime and Conversion Costs

Prime cost

The total cost of direct materials and direct labor is referred to as **prime cost** because these costs are most convincingly associated with and traceable to a specific product. Historically, the term prime cost was equivalent to product cost. There was not a strong consensus on whether to include overhead in the definition of product cost. Since overhead was often difficult to measure, accountants only included direct materials and direct labor cost as part of inventoriable cost; thus, these costs were considered to be of primary or prime importance.

Conversion cost

According to the IMA, **conversion cost** is "the sum of direct labor . . . and factory overhead which is directly or indirectly necessary for transforming raw materials and purchased parts into a salable finished product."[14] In other words, the incurrence of

EXHIBIT 2–10

Components of Product Cost

PRIME COST   Direct Materials

CONVERSION COST   Direct Labor

Factory Overhead
    Variable Overhead Components
        Indirect Materials
        Indirect Labor—Hourly Wages
        Scrap and rework costs
        Variable portion of mixed costs
        Other variable factory
            (including quality) costs
    Fixed Overhead Components
        Rent
        Depreciation
        Indirect Labor—Salaried Employees
        Licenses
        Taxes
        Insurance
        Quality training cost
        Fixed portion of mixed costs
        Other fixed factory
            (including quality) costs

---

[13]This definition of product cost is the traditionally accepted one and is also referred to as absorption costing. Another product costing method, called variable costing, excludes the fixed overhead component. Absorption and variable costing are compared in depth in Chapter 13.

[14]Institute of Management Accountants (formerly National Association of Accountants), *Statements on Management Accounting: Management Accounting Terminology*, Number 2 (Montvale, N.J.: NAA, June 1, 1983), p. 24.

conversion costs causes direct materials to be changed or converted into finished goods. Since direct labor is included as part of both prime cost and conversion cost, prime and conversion costs cannot be added to determine product cost. To do so would be to double count the cost of direct labor.

Exhibit 2–10 shows the typical components of product cost for a manufacturing company. Nevertheless, some companies, such as Allen-Bradley (A-B), view product costs in a slightly different manner. A-B's automated Milwaukee plant, which produces electrical contactors, has virtually no work in process or finished goods inventory. Material cost is the major part of product cost and most other costs are fixed rather than variable. Therefore, "A-B chooses to expense labor and overhead as period costs. For one thing, there is virtually no labor. For another, there is no inventory to attach costs to."[15]

ACCUMULATION OF PRODUCT COSTS

Product costs can be accumulated using either a perpetual or a periodic inventory system. In a perpetual inventory system, all product costs flow through Work in Process to Finished Goods and, ultimately, to Cost of Goods Sold. The perpetual system continuously provides current information for financial statement preparation and for inventory and cost control. Because the costs of maintaining a perpetual system have diminished significantly as computerized production, bar coding, and information processing have become more pervasive, this text will assume that all companies discussed use this inventory method.

The Cajun Hot Stuff Corporation is used to illustrate the flow of product costs in a manufacturing organization. The May 1, 1995, inventory account balances for Cajun Hot Stuff were as follows: Raw Materials Inventory (all direct), $16,500; Work in Process Inventory, $52,500; and Finished Goods Inventory, $23,700. Cajun Hot Stuff uses separate variable and fixed accounts to record the incurrence of overhead. Actual overhead costs are transferred at the end of the month to the Work in Process Inventory account. The following transactions, keyed to the journal entries in Exhibit 2–11 on page 58, represent Cajun Hot Stuff's activity for a month.

During May, Cajun Hot Stuff's purchasing agent bought $120,000 of direct materials on account (entry 1) and the warehouse manager transferred $122,000 of materials into the production area (entry 2). Production wages for the month totaled $225,000, of which $198,000 were for direct labor (entry 3). May salary for the production supervisor was $5,000 (entry 4). May utility cost of $14,000 was accrued; analyzing this cost indicated that $8,000 of this amount was variable and $6,000 was fixed (entry 5). Indirect materials costing $2,600 were removed from the Supplies Inventory and placed into the production process (entry 6). Cajun Hot Stuff also paid $3,500 for May's property taxes on the factory (entry 7), depreciated the factory assets $86,000 (entry 8), and recorded the expiration of $1,500 of prepaid insurance on the factory assets (entry 9). Entry 10 shows the transfer of actual overhead to Work in Process Inventory. During May, $464,100 of goods were completed and transferred to Finished Goods Inventory (entry 11). Sales on account in the amount of $630,000 were recorded during the month (entry 12); the goods that were sold had a total cost of $462,000 (entry 13). An abbreviated presentation of the cost flows is shown in selected T-accounts in Exhibit 2–12 on page 59.

---

[15]Robert A. Howell and Stephen R. Soucy, "Allen-Bradley: Today's Factory of the Future," *Management Accounting* (August 1987), p. 45.

■ EXHIBIT 2–11
Cajun Hot Stuff
Corporation—May 1995
Journal Entries

(1) Raw Materials Inventory	120,000	
Accounts Payable		120,000
To record cost of direct materials purchased on account.		
(2) Work in Process Inventory	122,000	
Raw Materials Inventory		122,000
To record direct materials transferred to production.		
(3) Work in Process Inventory	198,000	
Variable Overhead Control	27,000	
Salaries & Wages Payable		225,000
To accrue factory wages for direct and indirect labor.		
(4) Fixed Overhead Control	5,000	
Salaries & Wages Payable		5,000
To accrue production supervisor's salary.		
(5) Variable Overhead Control	8,000	
Fixed Overhead Control	6,000	
Utilities Payable		14,000
To record mixed utility cost in its variable and fixed proportions.		
(6) Variable Overhead Control	2,600	
Supplies Inventory		2,600
To record indirect materials used.		
(7) Fixed Overhead Control	3,500	
Cash		3,500
To record payments for factory property taxes for the period.		
(8) Fixed Overhead Control	86,000	
Accumulated Depreciation—Equipment		86,000
To record depreciation on factory assets for the period.		
(9) Fixed Overhead Control	1,500	
Prepaid Insurance		1,500
To record expiration of prepaid insurance on factory assets.		
(10) Work in Process Inventory	139,600	
Variable Overhead Control		37,600
Fixed Overhead Control		102,000
To record the transfer of actual overhead costs to Work in Process Inventory.		
(11) Finished Goods Inventory	464,100	
Work in Process Inventory		464,100
To record the transfer of work completed during the period.		
(12) Accounts Receivable	630,000	
Sales		630,000
To record the selling price of goods sold on account during the period.		
(13) Cost of Goods Sold	462,000	
Finished Goods Inventory		462,000
To record cost of goods sold for the period.		

RAW MATERIALS INVENTORY			
Beg. bal.	16,500	(2)	122,000
(1)	120,000		
End. bal.	14,500		

VARIABLE OVERHEAD CONTROL			
(3)	27,000	(10)	37,600
(5)	8,000		
(6)	2,600		

WORK IN PROCESS INVENTORY			
Beg. bal.	52,500	(11)	464,100
(2) DM	122,000		
(3) DL	198,000		
(10) OH	139,600		
End. bal.	48,000		

FIXED OVERHEAD CONTROL			
(4)	5,000	(10)	102,000
(5)	6,000		
(7)	3,500		
(8)	86,000		
(9)	1,500		

FINISHED GOODS INVENTORY			
Beg. bal.	23,700	(13) CGS	462,000
(11) CGM	464,100		
End. bal.	25,800		

COST OF GOODS SOLD			
(13) CGS	462,000		

As can be observed from the T-accounts in Exhibit 2–12, the perpetual inventory system provides detailed information about the cost of materials used, goods transferred from work in process, and goods sold. This information is necessary to prepare formal financial statements. However, such detail would not be readily available to a company using the periodic inventory system. Therefore, a schedule of **cost of goods manufactured** (CGM) would need to be prepared as a preliminary step to the determination of cost of goods sold (CGS).[16] CGM is the total cost of the goods that were completed and transferred to Finished Goods Inventory during the period. Thus, this amount is similar to the cost of net purchases in the cost of goods sold schedule for a retailer. Regardless of the type of inventory method employed, accountants will prepare formal schedules of cost of goods manufactured and cost of goods sold for management. These schedules are used to demonstrate the flow of costs and the calculation (or recalculation in the case of a perpetual system) of important amounts contained on the income statement.

The schedule of cost of goods manufactured starts with the beginning balance of Work in Process (WIP) Inventory and details all product cost components. The cost of materials used in production during the period is equal to the beginning balance of Raw Materials (RM) Inventory plus raw materials purchased minus the ending balance of RM Inventory. If Raw Materials Inventory includes both direct and indirect materials, the cost of direct materials used is assigned to WIP Inventory and the cost of indirect materials used is included in variable overhead. Direct labor cost is added to direct materials used in the schedule of cost of goods manufactured. Since direct labor cannot be warehoused, all charges for direct labor during the period are part of

COST OF GOODS MANUFACTURED AND SOLD

Cost of goods manufactured

---

[16] A service business prepares a schedule of cost of services rendered.

WIP Inventory. Variable and fixed overhead costs are added to direct materials and direct labor to determine total manufacturing costs.

Beginning Work in Process Inventory cost is added to total current period manufacturing costs to obtain a subtotal amount that can be referred to as "total costs to account for." The value of ending WIP Inventory is calculated (through techniques discussed later in the text) and subtracted from the subtotal to provide the cost of goods manufactured during the period. CGM represents the total production cost of the goods that were completed and transferred to Finished Goods (FG) Inventory during the period. This amount does not include the cost of work still in process at the end of the period. The schedule of cost of goods manufactured allows managers to see the relationships among the various production costs and to trace cost flows through the inventory accounts. It is usually prepared only as an internal schedule and is not provided to external parties.

▐ **EXHIBIT 2–13**

Cost of Goods Manufactured and Cost of Goods Sold Schedules

Cajun Hot Stuff Corporation
Schedule of Cost of Goods Manufactured
For Month Ended May 31, 1995

Balance of Work in Process Inventory, 5/1/95			$ 52,500
Manufacturing costs for the period:			
Raw materials (all direct)			
Beginning balance	$ 16,500		
Purchases of materials	120,000		
Raw materials available for use	$136,500		
Ending balance	14,500		
Direct materials used		$122,000	
Direct labor		198,000	
Variable overhead			
Indirect labor	$ 27,000		
Utilities	8,000		
Supplies	2,600	37,600	
Fixed overhead			
Utilities	$ 6,000		
Supervisor's salary	5,000		
Factory property taxes	3,500		
Factory asset depreciation	86,000		
Factory insurance	1,500	102,000	
Total current period manufacturing costs			459,600
Total costs to account for			$512,100
Balance of Work in Process Inventory, 5/31/95			(48,000)
Cost of goods manufactured			$464,100

Cajun Hot Stuff Corporation
Schedule of Cost of Goods Sold
For Month Ended May 31, 1995

Balance of Finished Goods Inventory, 5/1/95	$ 23,700
Cost of Goods Manufactured	464,100
Cost of Goods Available for Sale	$487,800
Balance of Finished Goods Inventory, 5/31/95	(25,800)
Cost of Goods Sold	$462,000

Cost of goods manufactured is added to the beginning balance of FG Inventory to find the cost of goods available for sale during the period. The ending FG Inventory is calculated by multiplying a physical unit count times a unit cost. If a perpetual inventory system is used, the actual amount of ending Finished Goods Inventory can be compared to that which *should* be on hand based on the finished goods account balance recorded at the end of the period. Any differences can be attributed to losses that might have arisen from theft, breakage, evaporation, or accounting errors.

Formal schedules of cost of goods manufactured and cost of goods sold are presented in Exhibit 2–13 using the amounts shown in Exhibits 2–11 and 2–12.

R E V I S I T I N G

McILHENNY COMPANY

McIlhenny Company, like all other organizations, incurs a wide variety of costs. To determine this company's product cost, one would need to gather information on the costs of the following: direct materials costs for peppers, salt, vinegar, bottles, and boxes; direct labor costs for the pickers, barrel sealers, and bottlers; and production overhead costs for items such as plant asset depreciation, supervisors' salaries, and electricity. In addition, McIlhenny incurs period costs (typically expensed when incurred) for advertising and the various costs of the administrative and sales areas.

Some companies can trade one type of cost (such as variable direct labor) for another (a fixed cost for depreciation on automated equipment). For McIlhenny, the direct labor component was reduced when new bottling equipment was installed, but the company found that such a trade was possible only in certain areas of activity. Mechanical pickers were tried, but failed because only humans have the experience needed to determine whether a pepper is ripe enough for the quality of sauce labeled Tabasco.

Since Tabasco is a registered trade name, the McIlhenny company must be very careful about the quality of its product. Training a picker to make the distinction between a "ripe pepper" and a "perfectly ripe pepper" results in the incurrence of a prevention cost of quality. The company is certain that the benefits provided by the money spent on training exceed the failure costs that might result if customers received a bottle of Tabasco that did not meet their taste expectations.

CHAPTER SUMMARY

This chapter presents a variety of ways that the concept of cost is used by accountants and managers and discusses how costs are classified in a company's accounting system. Major categories of costs are: (1) those associated with a particular time of incurrence; (2) those indicating cost behavior; (3) those classified as product or period costs on the financial statements; and (4) those affecting decision making. The first three categories are explained extensively in the chapter; the fourth category is discussed throughout the remainder of the text.

Historical, replacement, and budgeted costs are typically associated with time. Although historical costs are used for external financial statements, replacement and budgeted costs are more often used by managers in conducting their planning, controlling, and decision-making functions.

Variable, fixed, mixed, and step costs describe cost behavior within the context of a relevant range. Total variable costs vary directly and proportionately with changes in an activity measure known as a predictor; these costs are constant on a per unit basis. Costs that remain constant in total, regardless of changes in activity, are fixed. On a per unit basis, fixed costs vary inversely with activity changes. Mixed costs are hybrid costs that contain both a fixed and variable component. For product costing and management's uses, mixed costs are analyzed and separated into their variable and fixed components. (This process is discussed in Chapter 4.) Step costs can be variable or fixed, depending on the size of the "step" change (small or large, respectively) that occurs relative to the change in activity. Accountants select a relevant range that allows step variable costs to be treated as variable and step fixed costs to be treated as fixed.

For financial statement purposes, costs are considered to be unexpired and reported on the balance sheet or expired and reported on the income statement. Costs may also be viewed as product or period costs. Product costs are those that are inventoriable and include direct materials, direct labor, and variable and fixed manufacturing overhead. These costs expire and become cost of goods sold expense when the products are sold. In contrast, period costs are incurred outside the production area and are usually associated with the functions of selling, administrating, and financing. Period costs are related more to the passage of time than to purchasing or manufacturing a product or rendering a service. Expired period costs are shown on the income statement as expenses or losses.

Costs are also said to be direct or indirect relative to a cost object. The direct materials and direct labor costs of production are physically and conveniently traceable to products. These two costs are called prime costs. All other costs incurred in the production area are indirect and are referred to as manufacturing overhead.

The extensive activity required to convert raw materials into finished goods is what distinguishes manufacturers and service companies from retailers. It is this conversion process which necessitates that all factory costs be accumulated and reported under accrual accounting as product costs.

An internal management report, known as the cost of goods manufactured schedule, traces the flow of costs into the production area and through conversion into finished goods. This report provides the necessary information to prepare the cost of goods sold section of a manufacturer's income statement.

APPENDIX

Income Statement Comparisons

The income statements of merchandising, service, and manufacturing businesses are basically the same except for differences in the cost of goods sold section. A merchandising company has only one inventory account and, thus, cost of goods sold reflects only changes within the merchandise inventory account. A service company computes the cost of services rendered instead of cost of goods sold. A manufacturing organization has three inventory accounts and the cost of goods sold section of its income statement depicts the changes in Finished Goods Inventory. A manufacturer supports its cost of goods sold computation with a schedule of cost of goods manufactured for the period. This schedule is not normally presented in the company's external financial statements. Cost of goods manufactured replaces the net purchases amount used by merchandisers. Illustrations of income statements for each type of business follow. Balance sheets are not shown because the only differences are in the number and titles of inventory accounts.

WILSON DEPARTMENT STORE
Income Statement
For the Year Ended December 31, 1995

Net Sales		$2,336,000
Cost of Goods Sold		
Merchandise inventory, 1/1/95	$ 369,000	
Cost of purchases	1,616,000	
Total merchandise available for sale	$1,985,000	
Merchandise inventory, 12/31/95	(360,000)	
Cost of goods sold		(1,625,000)
Gross Margin on Sales		$ 711,000
Operating Expenses		
Selling expenses	$ 359,000	
Administrative expenses	251,000	(610,000)
Income from Operations		$ 101,000
Other Income		
Dividend income	$6,800	
Rental income	2,200	$ 9,000
Other Expenses		
Interest on bonds & notes	(21,000)	(12,000)
Income before Taxes		$ 89,000
Income Taxes		(33,820)
Net Income		$ 55,180
Earnings per share (assume 40,000 shares outstanding)		$1.38

HUNTER ARCHITECTURAL SERVICE
Income Statement
For the Year Ended December 31, 1995

Service Revenue		$1,400,000
Cost of Services Rendered		
Direct labor	$520,000	
Supplies	27,000	
Service department overhead	143,000	(690,000)
Gross Margin on Services		$ 710,000
Operating Expenses		
Selling expenses (similar to items detailed for merchandising company)	$105,000	
Administrative expenses (similar to items detailed for merchandising company)	312,000	(417,000)
Income from Operations		$ 293,000
Interest Expense		(49,200)
Income before Taxes		$ 243,800
Income Taxes		(92,644)
Net Income		$ 151,156
Earnings per share (assume 40,000 shares outstanding)		$3.78

MORA MANUFACTURING COMPANY
Income Statement
For the Year Ended December 31, 1995

Sales			$3,600,000
Cost of Goods Sold			
Beginning inventory of finished goods		$ 72,000	
Cost of goods manufactured (see below)		2,600,000	
Cost of goods available for sale		$2,672,000	
Ending inventory of finished goods		(66,000)	(2,606,000)
Gross Margin on Sales			$ 994,000
Operating Expenses			
Selling expenses (similar to items detailed			
for merchandising company)		$ 360,000	
Administrative expenses (similar to items			
detailed for merchandising company)		216,000	(576,000)
Income from Operations			$ 418,000
Other Expenses			
Interest on notes			(18,000)
Income before Taxes			$ 400,000
Income Taxes			(120,000)
Net Income			$ 280,000
Earnings per share (assume 500,000 shares outstanding)			$.56

MORA MANUFACTURING COMPANY
Schedule of Cost of Goods Manufactured
For the Year Ended December 31, 1995

Beginning balance of Work in			
Process Inventory			$ 240,000
Manufacturing costs for the period:			
Raw materials (all direct)			
Beginning inventory	$ 140,000		
Purchases	1,360,000		
Total materials available	$1,500,000		
Ending inventory	(160,000)		
Direct materials used		$1,340,000	
Direct labor		720,000	
Variable overhead		360,000	
Fixed overhead		140,000	2,560,000
Total costs to account for			$2,800,000
Ending balance of Work in Process			
Inventory			(200,000)
Cost of goods manufactured			$2,600,000

KEY TERMS

Allocate (p. 51)	Conversion cost (p. 56)
Appraisal cost (p. 55)	Cost (p. 35)
Budgeted cost (p. 37)	Cost driver (p. 43)

SOLUTION STRATEGIES

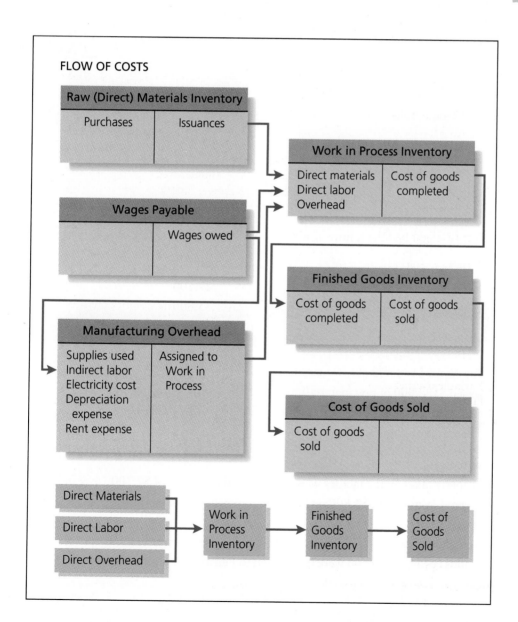

FLOW OF COSTS

Cost of Goods Manufactured

Beginning balance of Work in Process Inventory			XXX
Manufacturing costs for the period:			
Raw materials (all direct)			
Beginning balance		X	
Purchases of materials		+ XX	
Raw materials available for use		XXX	
Ending balance		– XX	
Direct materials used		XXX	
Direct labor		+ XX	
Variable overhead		+ XX	
Fixed overhead		+ XXX	
Total current period manufacturing costs			+ XXXX
Total costs to account for			XXXX
Ending balance of Work in Process Inventory			– XX
Cost of goods manufactured			XXXX ◄

Cost of Goods Sold

Beginning balance of Finished Goods Inventory	XX
Cost of Goods Manufactured	+ XXXX ◄
Cost of Goods Available for Sale	XXXX
Ending balance of Finished Goods Inventory	– X
Cost of Goods Sold	XXXX

DEMONSTRATION PROBLEM

Piquant Delight had the following account balances as of June 1, 1995:

Raw Materials (direct and indirect) Inventory	$18,600
Work in Process Inventory	27,500
Finished Goods Inventory	35,600

During June the company incurred the following factory costs:

▪ Purchased $178,000 of raw materials on account.

▪ Issued $182,000 of raw materials, of which $134,000 were direct materials.

▪ Factory payroll of $88,000 was accrued; $62,000 was for direct labor and the rest was for supervisors.

▪ $8,000 of utility cost was accrued; $6,500 of these costs were variable and $1,500 were fixed.

▪ Property taxes on the factory were accrued in the amount of $2,200.

▪ Prepaid insurance of $1,800 on factory equipment expired in June.

▪ Straight-line depreciation on factory equipment was $40,000.

▪ Actual overhead was transferred to Work in Process Inventory.

▪ Goods costing $340,000 were transferred to Finished Goods Inventory.

▪ Sales on account totaled $700,000.

■ Cost of goods sold was $350,000.

■ Selling, general, and administrative costs were $280,000 (credit "Various accounts").

Required:

a. Journalize the transactions for June.
b. Prepare a schedule of cost of goods manufactured for June.
c. Prepare an income statement, including a detailed schedule of cost of goods sold.

Solution to Demonstration Problem

a. (1) Raw Materials Inventory 178,000
           Accounts Payable 178,000

    (2) Work in Process Inventory 134,000
         Variable Overhead Control 48,000
           Raw Materials Inventory 182,000

    (3) Work in Process Inventory 62,000
         Fixed Overhead Control 26,000
           Salaries and Wages Payable 88,000

    (4) Variable Overhead Control 6,500
         Fixed Overhead Control 1,500
           Utilities Payable 8,000

    (5) Fixed Overhead Control 2,200
           Property Taxes Payable 2,200

    (6) Fixed Overhead Control 1,800
           Prepaid Insurance 1,800

    (7) Fixed Overhead Control 40,000
           Accumulated Depreciation—Factory 40,000

    (8) Work in Process Inventory 126,000
           Variable Overhead Control 54,500
           Fixed Overhead Control 71,500

    (9) Finished Goods Inventory 340,000
           Work in Process Inventory 340,000

   (10) Accounts Receivable 700,000
           Sales 700,000

   (11) Cost of Goods Sold 350,000
           Finished Goods Inventory 350,000

   (12) Selling, General, & Administrative Expense .. 280,000
           Various accounts 280,000

b.
Piquant Delight
Cost of Goods Manufactured Schedule
For Month Ended June 30, 1995

Balance of Work in Process Inventory, 6/1/95		$ 27,500
Manufacturing costs for the period:		
Raw Materials		
Beginning balance	$ 18,600	
Purchases of materials	178,000	
Raw materials available for use	$196,600	
Indirect materials used	$48,000	
Ending balance	14,600	(62,600)
Total direct materials used		$134,000 *(continued)*

Total direct materials used (from previous page)		$134,000
Direct labor		62,000
Variable overhead		
Indirect materials	$48,000	
Utilities	6,500	54,500
Fixed overhead		
Indirect labor	$26,000	
Utilities	1,500	
Factory property taxes	2,200	
Factory insurance	1,800	
Factory asset depreciation	40,000	71,500
Total current period manufacturing costs		322,000
Total costs to account for		$349,500
Balance of Work in Process Inventory, 6/30/95		(9,500)
Cost of goods manufactured		$340,000

c.

Piquant Delight
Income Statement
For Month Ended June 30, 1995

Sales		$700,000
Cost of Goods Sold		
Beginning balance of Finished Goods, 6/1/95	$ 35,600	
Cost of Goods Manufactured	340,000	
Cost of Goods Available for Sale	$375,600	
Ending balance of Finished Goods, 6/30/95	(25,600)	
Cost of Goods Sold		(350,000)
Gross Margin		$350,000
Selling, General, & Administrative Expenses		(280,000)
Income from Operations		$ 70,000

QUESTIONS

1. Distinguish between the cost accounting uses of historical costs and current costs.

2. How does a company determine its relevant range of activity? Of what use to managers is the concept of a relevant range of activity?

3. Why is a cost referred to as variable if it remains constant per unit for all units within the relevant range?

4. What is a mixed cost? How do accountants treat mixed costs in analyzing cost behavior? What information is essential in such a treatment of mixed costs?

5. What is the difference between a variable and a mixed cost, given that each changes in total with changes in activity levels?

6. How do predictors and cost drivers differ? Why is such a distinction important?

7. What is a product cost? What types of costs are included in product costs for merchandising companies, manufacturers, and service companies?

8. What is a period cost? What types of costs are included in period costs for merchandising companies, manufacturers, and service companies?

9. Can you determine whether a cost is a product or period cost if you simply know for what purpose the cost was incurred (for example, depreciation, wages, property taxes, etc.)? If so, indicate how. If not, indicate why not and what other information is needed.

10. Are all product costs unexpired costs and all period costs expired costs? Explain.

11. What is the process of conversion and why does this process create a need for cost accounting?

12. List six types of companies that engage in a high degree of conversion and describe their conversion processes.

13. What are the accounting and reporting implications that accompany the use of a high degree of conversion?

14. How do retailers, manufacturers, and service companies differ in their input/output relationships?

15. What inventory accounts are shown on the balance sheet of a manufacturer and what information is contained in each of these accounts?

16. Why would a service company rarely show a Finished Goods Inventory account on its balance sheet?

17. How is the concept of a direct cost related to that of a cost object?

18. Why are some material and labor costs considered direct and others indirect? Give several examples of costs that would be classified as direct materials and direct labor.

19. "Prime costs and conversion costs compose product cost; therefore, the sum of these two cost categories is equal to product cost." Is this statement true or false? Explain.

20. What is included on the cost of goods manufactured schedule? Why is it said that this schedule shows the flow of costs in a manufacturing company?

21. Why is the amount of cost of goods manufactured different from the amount of cost of goods sold?

22. (Appendix) Describe the differences among service, retail, and manufacturing firms in their respective cost of goods sold accounts.

EXERCISES

23. *(Cost classifications)* Indicate whether each item listed below is a variable (V), fixed (F), or mixed (M) cost and whether it is a product or service (PT) cost or a period (PD) cost. If some items have alternative answers, indicate the alternatives and the reasons for them.
    a. Wages of tractor/trailer operators who move finished goods from a central warehouse to local distribution points.
    b. Hand soap used in factory restrooms.
    c. Property taxes paid on the manufacturing company headquarters.
    d. Drafting paper used in an architectural firm.
    e. Cost of labels attached to shirts made by a company.
    f. Wages of factory maintenance workers.
    g. Insurance premiums on raw materials in a warehouse.
    h. Salaries of secretaries in a CPA firm.
    i. Freight costs of acquiring raw materials from suppliers.
    j. Cost of clay to make pottery.
    k. Cost of radioactive material used to generate power in a nuclear power plant.

23. No check figure.

24. *(Cost behavior)* Roanoke Company produces baseball caps. The company incurred the following costs to produce 2,000 caps last month:

Cardboard for the bills	$ 1,200
Cloth materials	2,000
Plastic for headband straps	1,500
Straight-line depreciation	1,800
Supervisors' salaries	4,800
Utilities	900
Total	$12,200

   a. What did each cap component cost on a per unit basis?
   b. What is the probable type of behavior that each of the costs exhibits?
   c. This month, the company expects to produce 2,500 caps. Would you expect each type of cost to increase or decrease? Why? Why can't the total cost of 2,500 caps be determined?

25. *(Cost behavior)* The Hydraulic Hose Company manufactures high-pressure garden hoses that are used by commercial landscaping firms. Costs incurred in the production process include a rubber material used to make the hoses, steel mesh used in the hoses, depreciation on the factory building, and utilities to run production machinery. Graph the most likely cost behavior for each of these costs and indicate what type of cost behavior is indicated by each cost.

26. *(Total cost determination with mixed cost)* The managers of Jiffy Accounting Service pay $400 per month for a computer maintenance contract. In addition, variable charges average $3 for every tax return the firm prepares.
   a. Determine the total cost and the cost per unit if Jiffy expects to prepare the following number of tax returns in February 1995:
      1. 150
      2. 300
      3. 600
   b. Why does the cost per unit change in each of the three cases above?

27. *(Financial statement classifications)* FastGlider Boating Co. purchased a plastics extruding machine for $200,000 to make boat hulls. During its first operating year, the machine produced 5,000 units and depreciation was calculated to be $25,000 on the machine. The company sold 4,000 of the hulls.
   a. What part of the $200,000 machine cost is expired?
   b. Where would each of the amounts related to this machine appear on the financial statements?

28. *(Product and period cost)* In 1994, Campus Fashions, a firm that produces backpacks, generated sales of $2,000,000 and net income of $300,000. For this same period, the firm's gross margin was $1,200,000.
   a. How much period cost did this firm incur in 1994?
   b. How much product cost did this firm charge against its revenues in 1994?

29. *(Company type, cost type)* For each of the terms listed below, indicate whether the term is associated with a manufacturing (Mfg.) company, a merchandising (Mer.) company, or a service (Ser.) company. There can be more than one correct answer for each term.
   a. Cost of goods sold
   b. Prepaid expenses
   c. Raw materials inventory
   d. Selling, general, and administrative expenses
   e. Merchandise inventory
   f. Work in process
   g. Cost of services rendered

h. Period costs
i. Direct labor

30. (*Degrees of conversion*) For each of the following firm types, indicate whether the firm type is characterized by a high, low, or moderate degree of conversion.
   a. Clothes retailer
   b. Vegetable department of a grocery store
   c. Convenience store
   d. Wheat farm
   e. Bakery
   f. Auto manufacturer
   g. Auto retailer
   h. Custom print shop
   i. Delicatessen
   j. Firm that sells tickets to entertainment events

31. (*Direct vs. indirect costs*) Kitchenware Inc. manufactures silverware and other kitchen utensils. Following are some costs incurred in the factory in 1994:

Material Costs

Stainless steel	$400,000
Equipment oil and grease	8,000
Plastic and fiberglass for handles	15,000
Wooden blocks used for utensil storage	9,200

Labor Costs

Equipment operators	$200,000
Equipment mechanics	50,000
Factory supervisors	118,000

   a. What is the direct materials cost for 1994?
   b. What is the direct labor cost for 1994?
   c. What is the total indirect labor and indirect materials overhead cost for 1994?

32. (*Direct vs. indirect costs*) Big State University's College of Business has five departments: Accounting, Finance, Management, Marketing, and Decision Sciences. Each department chairperson is responsible for the department's budget preparation. Indicate whether each of the following costs incurred in the Management Department is direct or indirect to the department:
   a. Management faculty salaries
   b. Chairperson's salary
   c. Cost of computer time of campus mainframe used by members of the department
   d. Cost of equipment purchased by the department from allocated state funds
   e. Cost of travel by department faculty paid from externally generated funds contributed directly to the department
   f. Cost of secretarial salaries (secretaries are shared by the entire college)
   g. Depreciation allocation of the college building cost for the number of offices used by department faculty
   h. Cost of periodicals/books purchased by the department

33. (*Labor cost classification*) Balboa Sporting Goods Company produces a variety of leisure-use products. The firm operates twenty-four hours per day with three daily work shifts. The first-shift workers receive "regular pay." The second shift receives a 10 percent pay premium and the third shift receives a 20 percent pay premium. In addition, when production is scheduled on weekends, the firm pays an overtime premium of 50 percent (based on the pay rate for first-shift employees). Labor premiums are included in overhead. The December 1994 factory payroll is as follows:

Total wages for December for 15,000 hours	$106,200
Normal hourly wage for Shift #1 employees	$ 6
Total regular hours worked, split evenly among the three shifts	12,000

   a. How many overtime hours were worked in December?

   b. How much of the total labor cost should be charged to direct labor? To overhead?

   c. What amount of overhead was for second- and third-shift premiums? For overtime premiums?

34. (*Prime cost and conversion cost*) Ian Corporation's accounting records showed the following manufacturing costs for the year 1994:

Direct materials	$398,000
Direct labor	671,000
Indirect materials	202,000
Indirect labor	137,000
Factory utilities	114,000
Selling, general, and administrative	229,000

   a. What is prime cost for Ian Corporation for 1994?

   b. What is conversion cost for Ian Corporation for 1994?

   c. What is total product cost for Ian Corporation for 1994?

35. (*Terminology*) Match the terms on the left with the definitions on the right. Definitions may be used more than once.

a. Cost of goods manufactured	1. Sum of direct labor and factory overhead
b. Expired cost	2. A cost outside the conversion area
c. Overhead	3. An inventoriable cost
d. Allocation	4. A cost that has both a variable and fixed component
e. Mixed cost	5. An asset
f. Unexpired cost	6. Sum of direct materials and direct labor
g. Indirect cost	7. A cost that cannot be traced to a particular cost object
h. Product cost	8. A cost that has no future benefit
i. Period cost	9. Total cost of products finished during the period
j. Distribution cost	10. A cost distinctly traceable to a particular object
k. Direct cost	11. The total of all nontraceable costs necessary to make a product or perform a service
l. Prime cost	12. A cost incurred to market a product or promote a service
m. Conversion cost	13. An expense or loss
	14. The process of assigning indirect costs to products or services

36. (*CGM and CGS*) Leather Products Company had the following inventory balances at the beginning and end of May 1995:

	5/1/95	5/31/95
Raw Materials Inventory	$ 6,000	$ 8,000
Work in Process Inventory	34,000	42,000
Finished Goods Inventory	16,000	12,000

All raw materials are direct to the production process. The following information is also available about May manufacturing costs:

Cost of raw materials used	$64,000
Direct labor cost	81,000
Factory overhead	58,000

a. Calculate the cost of goods manufactured for May.
b. Determine the cost of goods sold for May.

37. *(Cost of services rendered)* The following information is related to the Eastside Veterinary Clinic for June 1994, the firm's first month in operation:

Veterinarian salaries for June	$12,000
Assistants' salaries for June	4,200
Medical supplies purchased in June	1,800
Utilities for month (80% related to animal treatment)	900
Office salaries for June (50% related to animal treatment)	2,600
Medical supplies on hand at June 30	800
Depreciation on medical equipment for June	600
Building rental (80% related to animal treatment)	700

Compute the cost of services rendered.

38. *(CGM and CGS)* Cedar Custom Cabinets July 1995 cost of goods sold was $700,000. July 31 work in process was 80% of the July 1 work in process. Overhead was 90% of direct labor cost. During July, $220,000 of direct materials were purchased. Other July information follows:

Inventories	July 1	July 31
Direct materials	$ 54,600	$ 50,000
Work in process	80,000	?
Finished goods	219,000	211,800

a. Prepare a schedule of the cost of goods sold for July.
b. Prepare the July cost of goods manufactured schedule.
c. What was the amount of prime costs incurred in July?
d. What was the amount of conversion costs incurred in July?

COMMUNICATION ACTIVITIES

39. *(Predictors and cost drivers)* To explain or predict the behavior of costs, accountants often use factors that change in a consistent pattern with the costs in question. What are some factors you might select to predict or explain the behavior of the following costs? Would these same factors be considered cost drivers as well as predictors? If not, why not? What other items could be used as cost drivers?
a. Costs of storing raw materials
b. Equipment repair costs
c. Salespersons' travel expenses
d. Factory property insurance costs

40. *(Essay)* A portion of the costs incurred by business organizations is designated as "direct labor costs." As used in practice, the term "direct labor cost" has a wide variety of meanings. Unless the meaning intended in a given context is clear, misunderstanding and confusion are likely to ensue. If a user does not understand the elements included in direct labor cost, erroneous interpretations of the numbers may occur and could result in poor management decisions.

   In addition to understanding the conceptual definition of direct labor cost, management accountants must understand how direct labor cost should be measured.

a. Distinguish between direct labor and indirect labor.

b. Discuss why some nonproductive labor (such as coffee breaks, personal time) can be and often is treated as direct labor, while other nonproductive time (such as downtime, training) is treated as indirect labor.

c. Following are labor cost elements that a company has classified as direct labor, manufacturing overhead, or either direct labor or manufacturing overhead, depending on the situation.

■ Direct labor: Included in the company's direct labor are cost production efficiency bonuses and certain benefits for direct labor workers such as FICA (employer's portion), group life insurance, vacation pay, and workers' compensation insurance.

■ Manufacturing overhead: Included in the company's overhead are costs for wage continuation plans in the event of illness, the company-sponsored cafeteria, the personnel department, and recreational facilities.

■ Direct labor or manufacturing overhead: Included in the "situational" category are maintenance expense, overtime premiums, and shift premiums.

Explain the rationale used by the company in classifying the cost elements in each of the three presented categories.

d. The two aspects of measuring direct labor costs are (1) the quantity of labor effort that is to be included, that is, the types of hours that are to be counted, and (2) the unit price by which each of these quantities is multiplied to arrive at monetary cost. Why are these considered separate and distinct aspects of measuring labor cost?

(CMA adapted)

PROBLEMS

41. *(Cost behavior)* Wordsworth's Custom Stationery manufactures stationery pads. In an average month, the firm produces 200,000 boxes of stationery; each box contains 50 pages of stationery and 40 envelopes. Production costs are incurred for paper, ink, glue, and boxes for packaging. The company produces this product in batches, each of which consists of 500 boxes of a specific stationery design. The following data have been extracted from the company's accounting records for November 1994:

Cost of paper for each batch	$12
Cost of ink and glue per batch	2
Cost of 500 boxes for each batch	31
Direct labor for producing each batch	14
Labor costs for each batch design	40

Overhead charges total $20,400 per month; these are considered fully fixed for purposes of cost estimation.

a. What is the cost per box of stationery based on average production volume?

b. If sales volume increases to 300,000 boxes per month, what will be the cost per box (assuming that cost behavior patterns remain the same as in November)?

c. If sales are 300,000 boxes per month but the firm does not want the cost per box to exceed its current level (based on part a above), what amount can the company pay for labor design costs, assuming all other costs are the same as at November levels?

d. Assume that Wordsworth's Custom Stationery is now able to sell, on average, each box of stationery at a price of $5.00. If the company is able to increase its volume to 300,000 boxes per month, what sales price per box will generate the same gross margin that it is now achieving on 200,000 boxes per month?

e. Would it be possible to lower total costs by producing more boxes per batch, even if the total volume of 200,000 is maintained? Explain.

42. *(Cost behavior)* A company's cost structure may contain numerous different cost behavior patterns. Below are descriptions of several different costs; match these to the appropriate graphs. On each graph, the vertical axis represents cost and the horizontal axis represents level of activity or volume.

Identify, by letter, the graph that illustrates each of the following cost behavior patterns. Graphs may be used more than once.

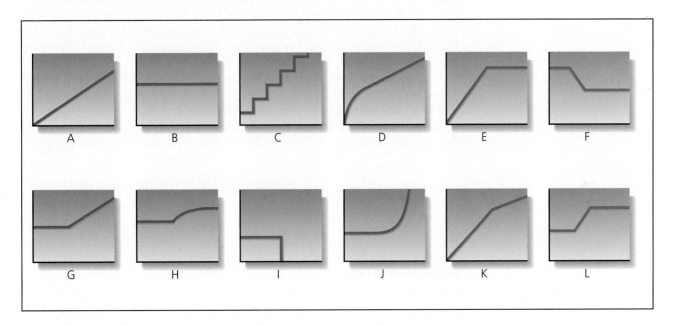

(1) Cost of raw materials, where the cost decreases by 6 cents per unit for each of the first 150 units purchased, after which it remains constant at $2.75 per unit.

(2) City water bill, which is computed as follows:

First 750,000 gallons or less	$1,000 flat fee
Next 15,000 gallons	.002 per gallon used
Next 15,000 gallons	.005 per gallon used
Next 15,000 gallons	.008 per gallon used
Etc.	Etc.

(3) Rent on a factory building donated by the city, where the agreement provides for a fixed-fee payment, unless 250,000 labor hours are worked, in which case no rent needs to be paid.

(4) Cost of raw materials used.

(5) Electricity bill—a flat fixed charge of $250 plus a variable cost after 150,000 kilowatt-hours are used.

(6) Salaries of maintenance workers if one maintenance worker is needed for every 1,000 hours or less of machine time.

(7) Depreciation of equipment using the straight-line method.

(8) Rent on a factory building donated by the county, where the agreement provides for a monthly rental of $100,000 less $1 for each labor hour worked in excess of 200,000 hours. However, a minimum rental payment of $20,000 must be made each month.

(9) Rent on a machine that is billed at $1,000 for up to 500 hours of machine time. After 500 hours of machine time, an additional charge of $1 per hour is paid up to a maximum charge of $2,500 per period.

(AICPA adapted)

43. *(Cost classifications)* Sylvia LeFlore is a painter and incurred the following costs during April 1994 when she painted three houses. She spent $900 on paint, $40 on mineral spirits, and $75 on brushes. She also bought two pair of coveralls for $45 each; she wears coveralls only while she works. During the first week of April, Sylvia placed a $40 ad for her business in the classifieds. She had to hire an assistant for one of the painting jobs; the assistant was paid $12 per hour, and worked 25 hours.

Being a very methodical person, Sylvia kept detailed records of her mileage to and from each painting job. Her average operating cost per mile for her van is $.32. She found a $15 receipt in her van for a Mapsco that she purchased in April. The Mapsco is used as a contact file for referral work and for bids that she has made on potential jobs. She also had $15 in receipts for bridge tolls ($1 per trip) for a painting job she did across the river.

Near the end of April, Sylvia decided to go camping, and she turned down a job on which she had bid $2,800. She called the homeowner long-distance (at a cost of $3.60) to explain her reasons for declining the job.

Using the headings below, indicate how each of the April costs incurred by Sylvia would be classified. Assume that the cost object is a house-painting job.

Type of Cost   Variable   Fixed   Direct   Indirect   Period   Product

44. *(Cost flows)* Alabama Custom Steelworks (ACS) had the following December 1994 inventory balances:

	December 1	December 31
Raw Materials Inventory	$18,100	$20,300
Work in Process Inventory	24,400	22,800
Finished Goods Inventory	20,000	20,500

During December, ACS used $451,000 of raw materials. All raw materials are considered direct materials. Total labor payroll for the month was $70,200. Direct labor employees were paid $9 per hour and worked 6,100 hours in December. Total factory overhead charges for the period were $64,000.

a. How much cost was incurred to purchase raw materials in December?
b. How much conversion cost was added to Work in Process Inventory in December?
c. How much prime cost was added to Work in Process Inventory in December?
d. Determine the cost of goods manufactured in December.
e. Determine the cost of goods sold in December.

45. *(CGM and CGS)* The Electric Wedge Inc. began business in October of last year. The firm makes a log-splitter, a machine that splits logs for more efficient burning in wood stoves and fireplaces. Below are data taken from the firm's accounting records that pertain to its first year operations.

Direct materials purchased on account	$213,000
Direct materials issued to production	192,000
Direct labor payroll accrued	114,000
Indirect labor payroll paid	45,300
Factory insurance expired	2,700
Factory utilities paid	8,900
Factory depreciation recorded	18,700
Ending Work in Process Inventory (48 units)	32,000
Ending Finished Goods Inventory (30 units)	45,600
Sales on account ($1,060 per unit)	212,000

a. How many units did the company sell in its first year? How many units were manufactured in the first year?
b. What was the total cost of goods manufactured?
c. What was the per unit cost of goods manufactured?
d. What was the cost of goods sold in the first year?
e. What was the company's first year gross margin?

46. *(Product and period cost, CGM and CGS)* At the beginning of August 1994, La Siesta Corporation had the following account balances:

Raw Materials Inventory	$4,000
Work in Process Inventory	7,600
Finished Goods Inventory	9,200

During August, the following transactions took place.
1. Raw materials were purchased on account, $30,200.
2. Direct materials ($17,300) and indirect materials ($7,000) were issued to production.
3. Factory payroll consisted of $32,000 for direct labor employees and $9,000 for indirect labor employees.
4. Office salaries totaled $21,100 for the month.
5. Utilities of $6,300 were accrued; 70% of the utilities are for the factory area.
6. Depreciation of $9,000 was recorded on plant assets; 70% of the depreciation is related to factory machinery and equipment.
7. Rent of $12,000 was paid on the building. The factory occupies 60% of the building.
8. At the end of August, the Work in Process Inventory balance was $8,300.
9. At the end of August, the balance in Finished Goods Inventory was $8,900.

a. Determine the total amount of product cost and period cost incurred during August 1994.
b. Compute the cost of goods manufactured for August 1994.
c. Compute the cost of goods sold for August 1994.
d. What level of August sales would have generated net income of $12,200?

47. *(CGM and CGS)* Kinco produces miniature furniture for dollhouses. The company's Raw Materials Inventory account includes the costs of both direct and indirect materials. Account balances for the company at the beginning and end of March 1995 are shown below:

	March 1	March 31
Raw Materials Inventory	$23,300	$17,400
Work in Process Inventory	32,500	29,300
Finished Goods Inventory	18,000	26,200

During the month, Kinco purchased $85,000 of raw materials; direct materials used during the period amounted to $68,000. Factory payroll costs for March were $91,300 of which 85% was related to direct labor. Overhead charges for depreciation, insurance, utilities, and maintenance totaled $81,200 for March.
a. Prepare a schedule of cost of goods manufactured.
b. Prepare a schedule of cost of goods sold.

48. *(CGM; CGS; cost categories)* Cost of goods sold for Lanier Technology Systems for October 1994 was $850,000. Work in Process Inventory at the end of June was 85% of Work in Process Inventory at the beginning of the month. Overhead was 80% of direct labor cost. During October, $205,000 of direct materials were purchased. Other information about the firm's inventories and production follows:

Beginning inventories—October 1		Ending inventories—October 31	
Direct materials	$ 41,400	Direct materials	$ 19,000
Work in process	80,500	Work in process	?
Finished goods	88,300	Finished goods	105,000

a. Prepare a schedule of cost of goods manufactured for October.
b. Prepare a schedule to compute the prime cost incurred during October.

    c. Prepare a schedule to compute the conversion cost charged to work in process during October.

    d. Prepare a schedule of cost of goods sold for October.

49. *(Journal entries)* Dana Clothiers Inc. produces a variety of men's garments. The following data have been extracted from the 1994 company records; it was Dana Clothiers' first year of operations. No Work in Process Inventory existed at the end of 1994.

Direct materials were purchased on account	$110,000
Direct materials were issued to production	98,000
Direct labor payroll was accrued	76,000
Indirect labor payroll was paid	17,300
Factory insurance expired	2,500
Factory utilities were paid	3,800
Factory depreciation was recorded	7,900
Sales made on account	418,000

The company's gross profit for the year was $258,400.

    a. Compute the cost of goods sold for 1994.

    b. What was the total cost of goods manufactured for 1994?

    c. If net income was $12,375, what was the total selling, general, and administrative expense for the year?

    d. Prepare journal entries to record the flow of costs for the year, assuming the company uses a perpetual inventory system.

CASE

50. The Miami Company suffered major losses in a fire on October 23, 1994. In addition to destroying several buildings, the blaze destroyed the company's work in process for an entire product line. Fortunately, the company was insured. However, the company needs to substantiate the amount of the claim. To this end, the company has gathered the following information that pertains to production and sales of the affected product line:

    1. The company's sales for the first 23 days of October amounted to $230,000. Normally, this product line generates a gross profit equal to 30% of sales.

    2. Finished Goods Inventory was $29,000 on October 1 and $42,500 on October 23.

    3. On October 1, work in process inventory was $48,000.

    4. During the first 23 days of October, the company incurred the following costs:

Direct materials used	$76,000
Direct labor	44,000
Manufacturing overhead	42,000

    a. Determine the value of Work in Process Inventory that was destroyed by the fire.

    b. What other information might the insurance company require? How would management determine or estimate this information?

ETHICS AND QUALITY DISCUSSION

51. An extremely important variable cost per employee is health care provided by the employer. In 1990, the average annual cost per employee was $3,161. This figure is expected to continue to rise each year as more and more expensive technology

is used on patients and the costs of that technology must be passed along through the insurance company to the employer. One simple way to reduce these variable costs is to cut back on employee insurance coverage.

   a. Discuss the ethical implications of reducing employee health care coverage to cut back on the variable costs incurred by the employer.

   b. Assume that you are an employer with 500 employees. You are forced to cut back on some insurance benefits. Your coverage currently includes the following items: mental health coverage, long-term disability, convalescent facility care, nonemergency but medically necessary procedures, dependent coverage, and life insurance. Select the two you would eliminate or dramatically reduce and provide reasons for your selections.

   c. Prepare a plan that might allow you to "trade" some of the variable employee health care costs for a fixed or a mixed cost.

52. *General Motors Corp., in a move to improve relations with unhappy customers, said it will fix leaky head gaskets on as many as half a million Quad 4 engines. In addition to paying for future repairs, GM said it will reimburse customers who already have had the gasket—which sits between the engine block and the cylinder head—replaced at their own expense. "GM is doing this in the interest of customer satisfaction," the company said.*

   GM estimates that about 8% of the half million Quad 4 engines sold from 1987 to 1991 will develop leaky head gaskets. At $550 per car, that would put the cost of the repair campaign at $22 million.

   Beginning with the 1992 models, GM switched to a new head gasket in the Quad 4. GM also switched to a new manufacturing procedure to improve head bolt tightening. "We're finding these changes are doubling the life of the head gasket," said a GM spokeswoman.

   [SOURCE: Neal Templin, "GM Will Repair Head Gasket on Engines," *Wall Street Journal* (February 16, 1993), p. A4. Reprinted by permission of the *Wall Street Journal,* © 1993 Dow Jones & Company, Inc. All rights reserved worldwide.]

   a. Discuss items associated with the leaky gasket that would fall under each of the types of quality costs (prevention, appraisal, and failure).

   b. GM quotes a cost of $550 per car to fix the gasket or a total of $22 million. Do you think this estimate reflects the *true* cost of the repairs? Be sure to consider all of the items you mentioned above.

53. *Tabasco pepper sauce is about to turn 125, but it doesn't seem a hot time to celebrate. The brand faces growing competition from Louisiana rivals. At the same time, a slew of new hot sauces, including many Caribbean and Asian varieties, are attracting consumers.*

   "There are a zillion new products out there," says Edward N. Simmons, president of McIlhenny. "We think it's good. It means more competition, but it also helps develop an awareness of the market."

   [SOURCE: Kathleen Deveny, "Rival Hot Sauces Are Breathing Fire at Market Leader Tabasco," *Wall Street Journal* (January 7, 1993), p. B1.]

   a. What do you think Mr. Simmons meant by "competition helps develop an awareness of the market"?

   b. Tabasco is "among the priciest of the hot sauces." Because of this, do you think quality expenditures on prevention, appraisal, or failure would be most important to McIlhenny? Why?

   c. The company has been branching out into alternative products, such as a Bloody Mary mix (quite successful) and a chili base ("still limping along"). Assume you are in charge of developing another new product for McIlhenny. Rank the following categories in order of the size of spending: preproduction costs; direct materials costs; direct labor costs; prevention costs; appraisal costs; postproduction period costs. Discuss what kinds of costs would fall under those categories and why you chose the ranking you did.

CONSIDERING QUALITY IN AN ORGANIZATION

LEARNING OBJECTIVES

After completing this chapter, you should be able to answer these questions:

1. What forces are currently creating a greater worldwide demand for quality?
2. How is quality defined and from whose viewpoint should it be evaluated?
3. Why is total quality management significant and what is necessary to make it work?
4. What basic characteristics comprise product quality?
5. Why do companies engage in benchmarking?
6. What quality costs may a company have and how are they related to each other?
7. Why has the Malcolm Baldrige National Quality Award become so widely sought?
8. Why should a firm be concerned with international quality standards?
9. How can managers instill quality as part of the organizational culture?

INTRODUCING

UNITED SERVICES AUTOMOBILE ASSOCIATION (USAA)

USAA is the nation's fifth largest insurer of privately owned automobiles and homes and is expanding rapidly into the field of financial services. Its 14,000 employees now serve more than 2 million customers and policyholders and manage $2.7 billion in assets. By focusing single-mindedly on service quality—and on its three components: customers, work force, and technology—Robert McDermott has revolutionized USAA's approach to its business and to its customers' financial needs.

USAA has pioneered progressive employment practices like the four-day workweek, spends $19 million annually on employee training (2.7% of its annual budget and double the industry average), and is a leader in integrating minorities into its workforce. The company's 286–acre headquarters complex in San Antonio, Texas includes tennis courts, softball diamonds, jogging trails, three artificial lakes, and 75 classrooms.

At a time when many service companies are discovering that their heavy investments in technology do not translate into productivity gains, USAA has used technology not only to increase productivity but also to improve the quality of service. For example, USAA's state-of-the-art electronic imaging system means that each day some 30,000 pieces of mail never leave the mailroom. Instead, an exact image of the correspondence is placed electronically in the customer's policy service file and, simultaneously, in a sort of electronic in-basket where it will be handled by the first available service representative anywhere in the building.

SOURCE: Reprinted by permission of *Harvard Business Review.* An excerpt from "Service Comes First: An Interview with USAA's Robert F. McDermott," by Thomas Teal (September–October 1991), p. 117. Copyright © 1991 by the President and Fellows of Harvard College; all rights reserved.

The discussion about USAA shows that the company places a high priority on service, both to its customers and to its employees. Such a dedication to service is one aspect of the quality movement in which most domestic and foreign organizations are engaging. Managers have come to recognize that high quality is a fundamental business strategy if businesses are to compete in a global economy.

Regardless of their location, firms are scrambling to attract customers and are able to offer more choices than in the past. Consumers are more aware of the greater variety of choices that are available to satisfy their wants and needs and they often select nondomestic products because of their perceived value. Additionally, consumers perceive the extent of their options with regard to quality, price, service, and lead time. This awareness has stimulated consumer demand that has, in turn, motivated producers to improve quality to benefit from the increased demand. This cycle of successive stimulus-response actions among consumers and producers has caused many firms to adopt a dynamic approach about continuously improving the quality of their products to satisfy consumer demand.

This chapter discusses a variety of quality issues, including total quality management, quality costs, quality standards, and quality culture. Because quality affects costs, it is essential that accountants understand the trade-offs involved between having higher and lower quality. Organizations have come to understand that current expenditures on quality improvement may be more than recouped by future cost reductions and sales volume increases. As the vice president of Video Lottery Consultants (Bozeman, Montana) expressed it after a quality program cut product failures by two-thirds: "We have been paid back many times for the effort and the price that we're willing to pay upfront for our quality."

WHAT IS QUALITY?

To improve its quality, an organization must agree on how it defines the term. Dr. W. Edwards Deming, one of the most famous of the experts on quality control, defines quality as "the pride of workmanship."[1] On a less individualized basis, Philip Crosby (another noted quality expert) defines quality as "conformance to requirements."[2] This definition was also adopted by the American Society for Quality Control and is explained in the News Note "What Is a Requirement?" Joseph M. Juran, a pioneer of quality education in Japan, defines quality as "fitness for use," a customer-based definition.

Quality

A fairly all-inclusive definition of **quality** is all the characteristics of a product or service that make it able to meet the stated or implied needs of the person acquiring it. Thus, quality must always be viewed from the perspective of the user rather than the provider and relates to both performance and value. This perspective was not always held. Originally, after the Industrial Revolution helped manufacturers to increase output and decrease cost, quality was defined as conformity to designated specifications, and making certain that conformity existed (**quality assurance**) was left to inspectors. The extension of the quality definition arose because of more competition, heightened public interest in product safety, and an increase in litigation relative to products and product safety. The responsibility for quality became not simply a production issue, but a company profitability and longevity issue. Thus, there are essentially two related perspectives of quality. The first views quality from the perspective of the process that generates a product or service. The second reflects the consumer's view of the quality of that product or service.

Quality assurance

Production View of Quality

Productivity is measured by the quantity of units of good output generated during a time period. Any factor that either slows down or stops a production process or that causes unnecessary work (redundancy) is an impediment to productivity. **Activity analysis** can be used to highlight such factors. The various repetitive actions performed in making a product or providing a service are detailed and classified value-added (VA) and non-value-added (NVA) categories. **Value-added activities** increase the worth of the product or service to the customer; **non-value-added activities** consume time and costs but add no value for the consumer. Minimizing or eliminating the non-value-added activities increases productivity and reduces costs.

Activity analysis

Value-added activity
Non-value-added activity

One non-value-added activity related to quality—inspecting incoming components—is caused by supplier quality problems. To eliminate this particular NVA activity some companies (such as North Carolina's Alphatronix Inc.) require their suppliers to provide only zero-defect components. Other important internal NVA activities include manufacturing products with defects, having unscheduled production

---

[1] Rafael Aguayo, *Dr. Deming* (New York: Simon & Schuster, 1990), p. xi.
[2] Philip B. Crosby, *Quality Is Free* (New York: New American Library, 1979), p. 15.

NEWS NOTE

What Is a Requirement?

Requirements are merely answers to questions. Whenever two people, departments, entities, etc., are getting together and agreeing to do something, questions will come up. The answers to these questions (where, when, how big, how much, who, etc.) become the agreement between the two parties and, therefore become the requirements for a particular task or undertaking. Requirements may be documented as specifications, product descriptions, procedures, policies, job descriptions, instructions, purchase/service orders, etc., or they may be verbal. Requirements must be measurable or they are not valid. Stating that something must be done "about" 7:00 a.m., for example, cannot be measured. If we say 7:00 a.m. plus or minus 10 minutes, however, it is measurable and when something is done between 6:50 and 7:10, you have conformance. Outside these parameters you have non-conformance.

SOURCE: American Society for Quality Control, *Finance, Accounting, and Quality* (Milwaukee, Wisconsin: ASQC, 1990), p. 3.

interruptions, and experiencing unplanned downtime. Factors causing production redundancy include the need to reprocess, rework, replace, and repair those items that did not conform to specifications. The quality of the production process largely determines the failure rate of the product, its longevity, and whether it is prone to breakage. Further, the amount of waste, rework, and scrap generated by production efforts is related to production process quality. Production technology, worker skill and training, and management programs can, in large part, control the quality of the production process. If the impediments to good production are reduced or eliminated, increases in productivity and higher quality products can be expected. Some techniques that increase productivity and enhance quality include having suppliers preinspect materials for quality, having employees monitor and be responsible for their own output, and fitting machinery for mistake-proof operations.

All attempts to reduce variability and defects in products reflect the implementation of **total quality control** (TQC). TQC places the primary responsibility for the quality of a product or service at the source—the maker or provider. Many companies such as Oregon Cutting Systems (a manufacturer of saws and chains) use **statistical process control** (SPC) techniques to analyze where fluctuations occur in the process. These techniques are based on the theory that a process has natural variations over time, but that "errors," which can be defective goods or poor service, are typically produced at points of uncommon variations. Often these variations are eliminated after the installation of computer-integrated manufacturing systems, which have internal controls to evaluate tolerances and sense production problems.

Total quality control (TQC)

Statistical process control (SPC)

To analyze the process variations, a variety of **control charts** are developed by recording the occurrences of some selected measure(s) of performance. The charts display the results of actual processes on a graph that indicates upper and lower control limits. A process is in or out of control depending on how well results remain within these established limits, as illustrated in Exhibit 3–1 on page 84. It is essential that company personnel who prepare the charts do so consistently and accurately so that an intelligent analysis can be made about the items that are out of control. Although the development of such charts is outside the scope of this text, the management accountant is directly involved in selecting the appropriate performance measures and helping to interpret the charts. The measures selected to prepare control charts would be nonfinancial ones such as number of defective products, errors in tolerance levels, and unexpected work slowdowns or stoppages. Selection of the performance measures to investigate quality is discussed in Chapter 22.

Control chart

■ EXHIBIT 3–1
Control Chart

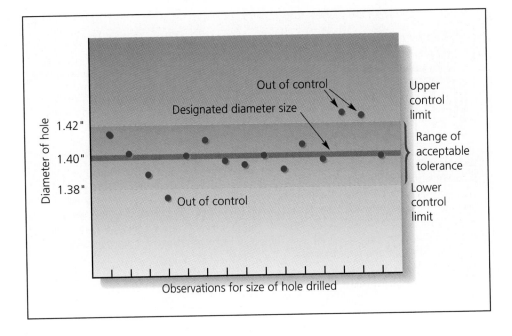

Consumer View of Quality

Every customer who buys a product or service purchases a set of characteristics consisting of features such as range of features, convenience, promptness in delivery, warranty, credit availability, and packaging. The consumer's view of quality encompasses much more than whether the product or service delivers as it was intended, its rate of failure, or the probability of purchasing a defective unit. The customer perceives quality as the ability of a product or service to meet and satisfy all of the specified needs. Businesses entering markets dominated by quality producers must understand customer quality expectations as well as quality standards of competitors. For example, when Cambex Corporation (Waltham, Massachusetts) began selling computers, it focused on the reliability and service effectiveness provided by IBM, its acknowledged lead competitor.

Exhibit 3–2 provides eight basic characteristics that would commonly be included in any customer's definition of product quality. One obvious difference exists among the first six and the last two quality characteristics: the level of objectivity. While the first six product quality characteristics can be reasonably evaluated through objective methods, the last two are strictly subjective judgments. Thus, the first six are significantly more susceptible to control by the organization providing the product than the final two.

Grade

Unfortunately, all customers cannot afford the same **grade** of product or service. Grade refers to the addition or removal of product or service characteristics to satisfy additional needs, especially price. Thus, customers hope to maximize their satisfaction within the context of their willingness and ability to pay. They view a product or service as a **value** when it meets the highest number of their needs at the lowest possible price. Thus, while customers may have a collective vision of what constitutes "high quality," they may choose to accept lower quality for various reasons.

Value

To illustrate the difference between quality and grade, assume that Dana Gibson is in the market for a new car. She needs the car to travel to and from work, run errands, and go on vacation. Thus, she has determined that reliability, gas mileage, and comfort are features that are important to her. She may believe the Rolls Royce to be the highest quality car available, but her additional needs are that the car be within her price range and be manufactured domestically. Thus, she will search for the highest quality product of the grade that maximizes the set of remaining dimensions.

■ EXHIBIT 3–2

Characteristics of Product Quality

1. Performance—relates to a product's primary operating characteristics
2. Features—describes the secondary characteristics that supplement a product's basic function
3. Reliability—addresses the probability of a product's likelihood of performing within a specified period of time
4. Conformance—relates to the degree to which preestablished standards are matched by the product's performance and features
5. Durability—measures a product's economic and technical life
6. Serviceability—measures the ease with which the product is repaired
7. Aesthetics—relates to a product's appeal to the senses
8. Perceived quality—relates to image, brand names, and other indirect measures of quality

SOURCE: David Garvin, "What Does 'Product Quality' Really Mean?" *Sloan Management Review* (Fall 1984), pp. 25–43.

Customers often make quality determinations by comparing a product or service to their ideal level of a characteristic rather than to another product or service of the same type or in the same industry. For example, assume that Joel Ridenour, a USAA policyholder, calls a department store about his bill. Joel may evaluate the various quality dimensions of that store based on his experience with the prompt, efficient service he receives when he calls USAA rather than the service he receives when he calls another department store. It is immaterial to Joel that the department store does not have the same type of computer system that USAA has or that the store's employees may not have had the same level of training that the USAA employees have had. This type of comparison, when formalized in organizations, is called competitive **benchmarking**.

Benchmarking

BENCHMARKING

Benchmarking is the process of investigating, comparing, and evaluating a company's products, processes, and/or services against those of companies believed to be the "best in class." Such comparisons allow a company to understand other production and performance methods, so that the company can identify its strengths and weaknesses. Since each company has its own unique philosophy, products, and people, "copying" is neither appropriate nor feasible. Therefore, the company should attempt to imitate those ideas that are readily transferable, but, more importantly, to upgrade its own effectiveness and efficiency by improving upon methods in use by others.

Although benchmarking against direct competitors is necessary, it also creates the risk of becoming stagnant. To illustrate:

General Motors, Chrysler, and Ford have historically done a lot of competitive benchmarking among themselves. Over time, their processes became similar. But then came the import competition, which had totally different processes and which blew the Big Three away. It was like three club tennis players who all had similar levels of skill and who knew each other's games inside and out—and then Bjorn Borg walked on the court.[3]

For this reason, additional comparisons should be made against companies that are the best in a specific characteristic rather than necessarily the best in a specific industry. Exhibit 3–3 provides some examples of U.S. companies that are recognized as

[3] Beth Enslow, "The Benchmarking Bonanza," *Across the Board* (April 1992), p. 20.

▌EXHIBIT 3–3

Who Are the World-Class Companies?

Benchmarking Methods: AT&T, Digital Equipment, Ford, IBM, Motorola, Texas Instruments, Xerox

Billing & Collection: American Express, MCI, Fidelity Investments

Customer Satisfaction: L.L. Bean, Federal Express, GE Plastics, Xerox

Distribution & Logistics: L.L. Bean, Wal-Mart

Employee Empowerment: Corning, Dow, Milliken, Toledo Scale

Equipment Maintenance: Disney

Flexible Manufacturing: Allen-Bradley, Baldor, Motorola

Health-Care Programs: Allied-Signal, Coors

Marketing: Procter & Gamble

Product Development: Beckman Instruments, Calcamp, Cincinnati Milacron, DEC, Hewlett-Packard, 3M, Motorola, NCR

Quality Methods: AT&T, IBM, Motorola, Westinghouse, Xerox

Quick Shop Floor Changes: Dana, GM Lansing, Johnson Controls

Supplier Management: Bose, Ford, Levi Strauss, 3M, Motorola, Xerox

Worker Training: Disney, General Electric, Federal Express, Ford, Square D

SOURCE: "America's World-Class Champs," *Business Week* (November 30, 1992), pp. 74-75. Reprinted from November 30, 1992 issue of *Business Week* by special permission, copyright © 1992 by McGraw-Hill, Inc.

world-class leaders in certain disciplines. It is against these companies as well as their international counterparts that others should benchmark.

There are two basic types of benchmarking: results and process. In **results benchmarking,** the end product or service is examined and the focus is on product/service specifications and performance results. Results benchmarking helps companies deter-

Results benchmarking

L. L. Bean's distribution center has been hailed as world-class. Stock selection (or "picking") and shipping techniques have been so well defined that a variety of companies have chosen to process benchmark against this facility.

| **NEWS NOTE** | **Benchmark Against the Best— Regardless of the Business** |

 Although a few U.S. corporations have benchmarked for a decade or more, the technique came into widespread use only in the past couple of years. AT&T, DuPont, Ford Motor, IBM, Eastman Kodak, Milliken, Motorola, Xerox, and other leaders in the drive for quality and productivity now use the technique as a standard tool.

In the early Eighties, Robert Camp, Xerox's benchmarking manager, read a magazine article about L.L. Bean, the firm that outfits the outdoor set. Among other virtues, Bean is known for fulfilling orders quickly and accurately. Why, Camp asked himself, should Xerox benchmark only other office equipment companies? Business practices are business practices. Besides, companies that are not direct competitors are more likely to open up.

A mission to Bean's hometown of Freeport, Maine, revealed that warehouse workers there could "pick and pack" items three times as fast as Xerox's. The secret lay not in high technology but in intelligent planning and the right kind of computer software. Items are stored in Bean's warehouse not according to category but according to velocity. The items that sell the fastest are shelved closest to the desk where the pickers get their order sheets, and the slowest-moving items the farthest away. That saves steps. Orders come in randomly, but the software sorts them so that the pickers can combine trips for, say, a whole batch of red flannel shirts ordered during the day. These and other techniques helped Xerox redesign its warehouses—and started a procession of benchmarkers to Freeport that soon became something of a burden to Bean.

SOURCE: Jeremy Main, "How to Steal the Best Ideas Around," *FORTUNE* (October 19, 1992), pp. 102–104. © 1992 Time Inc. All rights reserved.

---

mine which other companies are the "best-in-class" and **process benchmarking** shows how those companies achieved that distinction. Ford used this methodology when designing the Taurus. The company "bought 50 cars from manufacturers around the world and identified the 400 best-in-class features and processes of those cars. It then incorporated 80 percent of them in the design of the Taurus."[4]

Process benchmarking

Focusing on the practices and the ways the best-in-class companies achieved their results is called process benchmarking. It is in process benchmarking that noncompetitor-benchmarking is extremely valuable. For example, after Xerox saw its market being eroded by the Japanese, it found that one of its problem points was its warehousing and shipping functions. After deciding that the catalog company of L.L. Bean performed these functions extremely well, Xerox decided to benchmark against that company as described in the News Note "Benchmark Against the Best."

The process of implementing benchmarking is detailed in Exhibit 3–4. Some companies have more steps, others have fewer, but all have a structured approach. Once the negative gap analysis is made, everyone in the firm is expected to work both toward closing that gap and toward becoming a best-in-class organization.

By benchmarking, companies are working to improve their ability to deliver high-quality products from both the perspective of how they are produced and how they are perceived by the customer. Integrating these two perspectives requires involvement of all members of the organization in the institution of a **total quality management** (TQM) system.

Total quality management (TQM)

---

[4]Gary Plaster, "Benchmarking Helps Companies Remain Competitive," *(Grant Thornton) Tax & Business Adviser* (March/April 1992), p. 5.

1. Determine the specific area in which improvements are desired and/or needed.

5. Have the people who are associated with the specific area being analyzed collect the needed information.

2. Select the characteristic that will be used to measure quality performance.

6. Analyze the "negative gap" between the company's product, process, or service and that of the best-in-class firm.

3. Identify the best-in-class companies based on quality characteristics. Remember that these companies do not have to be industry, product, or service specific.

7. Act on the negative gap analysis and make improvements.

4. Ask for cooperation from the best-in-class companies. This may be handled directly or through a consulting firm. Be prepared to share information and respect requests for confidentiality.

8. Do not become complacent. Strive for continuous improvement.

EXHIBIT 3–4
Steps in Benchmarking

TOTAL QUALITY MANAGEMENT

Total quality management "is a structural system for creating organization-wide participation in planning and implementing a continuous improvement process that exceeds the expectations of the customer/client."[5] Thus, there are three important tenets of TQM:

1. It necessitates an internal managerial system of planning, controlling, and decision making.
2. It requires participation by everyone in the organization.
3. It focuses on improving goods and services from the customer's point of view.

The Quality System

First, the total quality movement requires that a system be implemented to provide information to managers about the quality processes so that they can plan, control, evaluate performance, and make decisions. Consideration of quality historically has not been part of the planning process. More often it involved an after-the-fact measurement of errors because a certain level of defects was simply tolerated as part of the "natural" business process in the United States. Action was not triggered until a predetermined threshold was exceeded.

A total quality system, in contrast, should be designed so that it promotes a re-orientation of thinking from an emphasis on inspection to an emphasis on prevention. It should indicate any existing quality problems so that managers can set goals and

[5] L. Edwin Coate, "Implementing Total Quality Management in a University Setting," *Oregon State University* (July 1990), p. 5.

identify methods for quality improvements. The system should also be capable (possibly through the use of statistical methods) of measuring quality and providing feedback on quality improvements. Last, the system should encourage teamwork in the quality improvement process. In other words, the system should move an organization away from product inspection (finding and correcting problems at the end of the process) to process control (monitoring the process so that problems do not occur).

Employee Involvement

TQM recognizes that all levels of the organization share in the responsibility for product/service quality, and interactions among employee levels are changing the way managers do their jobs. Upper-level management must be involved in the quality process, develop an atmosphere that is conducive to quality improvements, and set an example of commitment to TQM. Positive feedback is essential when improvements are made. Workers should be made to feel as though they are part of the process of success, not the creators of the problems. Encouraging employee suggestions and training workers to handle multiple job functions help improve efficiency and quality. For example, multiskilling is essential at USAA. Each operator is trained to process an insurance application form from start to finish rather than a typical process in which one person takes down the information; another enters the data into the computer; a third retrieves relevant information from files; a fourth assesses the applicant's risk; and a fifth writes the policy.

Product/Service Improvement

Total quality management focuses management attention on the relationship between the internal production/service process and the external customer. This process has designated consumer expectations as the ultimate arbiter of satisfaction. Therefore, TQM requires that companies first know who their customers are. USAA's customers, for instance, are largely active-duty and retired military officers and their families. Robert McDermott characterizes them as "well-educated, affluent, and honest."[6] Recognizing these characteristics allows USAA to take applicants' word and *not* check driving records before issuing a policy, and not to inspect cars when policyholders say that their hubcaps were stolen while they were in a meeting. The company believes that the money it saves by *not* investigating significantly exceeds the potential for losses through misrepresentation.

In analyzing their customers, some companies may want to stop serving some groups of customers in line with cost-benefit analysis. Some customers simply cost more than they add in profits and/or ideas to the organization. The concept that shedding one or more sets of customers would be good for business is difficult to believe at first, but most organizations have some clients who drain, rather than improve, their ability to provide quality products and service.

> Smart businesses pick customers—and learn from them. While some customers consistently add value along several dimensions, other customers are value-subtractors: What they cost in time, money and morale outstrips the prices they pay. Having the courage to identify, and then "fire" low-value customers is a healthy first step. It helps assure that valued customers receive the best possible service and that potential customers recognize that the company cares about quality.[7]

After determining who its value-adding customers are, a company must then understand what they want. The primary characteristics currently desired by customers appear to be quality, value, and "good" service. Good service is an intangible; it

---

[6] Thomas Teal, "Service Comes First: An Interview with USAA's Robert F. McDermott," *Harvard Business Review* (September–October 1991), p. 123.
[7] Michael Schrage, "Fire Your Customers!" *Wall Street Journal* (March 16, 1992), p. A12.

NEWS NOTE

Higher Productivity, Lower Costs at Whirlpool

To each of the 265 employees [at the Benton Harbor, Michigan, Whirlpool plant], improved productivity meant an extra $2,700 of pay in 1991. The gain in productivity—output per hour of work—has also reduced Whirlpool's costs and bolstered its profit. And it has benefited Whirlpool's customers. Aided by productivity advances throughout its operations, the company has been able to hold down prices of its washing machines while improving their quality.

Since 1988, Benton Harbor's productivity has surged more than 19%, to 110.6 parts manufactured per man hour from 92.8. Moreover, the number of parts rejected has sunk to a world-class 10 per million from 837 per million. The pickup in productivity here hasn't been achieved by spending millions of dollars on fancy machines. Instead of building a state-of-the-art plant, Whirlpool overhauled the manufacturing process and taught its workers to improve quality. As a result, from 1989 to 1991, the cost of a washing-machine agitator shaft decreased 13% to $1.95, and a spin pinion fell 24% to $1.65.

Raising quality is important. With less time wasted on making bad parts, productivity increases. The cost of scrapping bad parts drops. And if more parts are made correctly, less inventory has to be kept on hand.

The parts made at Benton Harbor account for only about 5% of a Whirlpool washer—not enough to change its cost. But other Whirlpool factories and some outside suppliers also have raised their productivity and thus lowered costs. For example, Whirlpool's Columbia, S.C., division has raised its productivity nearly 20% since 1990 while cutting costs about 9%.

Whirlpool has been able to funnel its productivity gains into initiatives ranging from research to more effective distribution. But what especially matters to consumers is Whirlpool's ability to keep a lid on prices.

SOURCE: Rick Wartzman, "A Whirlpool Factory Raises Productivity—and Pay of Workers," *Wall Street Journal* (May 4, 1992), pp. A1, A4. Reprinted by permission of the *Wall Street Journal*, © 1992 Dow Jones & Company, Inc. All rights reserved worldwide.

---

means different things to different people. But most customers would agree that it is reflective of the interaction between themselves and organizational employees. "In the broadest sense, customer service is a group of processes that helps [an organization] handle inquiries, orders, complaints, and problems while enhancing the logistical, administrative, and distribution functions of [the] organization."[8]

Frequently, only service quality separates one product from its competition. For instance, all homeowners expect their insurance companies to pay for damages in the event of a disaster. But, after Hurricane Andrew hit south Florida in 1992, "USAA was one of the first insurers to establish an on-site claims location, with cellular phones and laptop computers to facilitate the task of handling thousands of claims."[9] Such customer service is probably a large part of the reason why nearly 99 percent of USAA's policyholders renew their policies every year compared to a renewal rate of about 80 percent for the rest of the insurance industry.[10]

Poor service can be disastrous. Data indicate that "70 percent of customers stop doing business with companies because of perceived rude or indifferent behavior by an employee—over three times the total for price or product quality (20 percent)."[11]

---

[8] Jeffrey M. Margolies, "When Good Service Isn't Good Enough," *(Price Waterhouse) Review* (No. 3, 1988), pp. 25–26.
[9] "How USAA Reacts to a Catastrophe," *(USAA) Aide Magazine* (February 1993), p. 4.
[10] Susan Caminiti, "The Payoff from a Good Reputation," *FORTUNE* (February 10, 1992), p. 76.
[11] Scott J. Simmerman, "Improving Customer Loyalty," *B & E (Business & Economic) Review* (April–June 1992), p. 4.

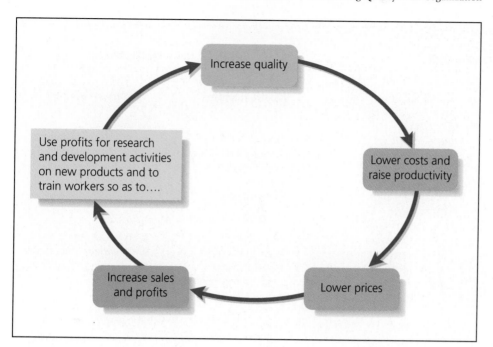

■ EXHIBIT 3–5
Cycle of Quality Benefits

Although instituting "customer service" programs can improve a company's image, such programs should not be taken to the extreme. As noted above, some customers are not cost-beneficial—often those demanding exorbitant service and not willing to pay the related price.

As a company increases its product and service quality, certain costs (those referred to as "failure costs" in Chapter 2) will decrease and other costs will rise ("prevention costs"). The results of TQM indicate that the ultimate net effect of the cost changes is a decline in costs. Also, by eliminating non-value-added activities and installing technologically advanced equipment, productivity will increase, as shown in the News Note on higher productivity at Whirlpool.

Lower costs mean that the company can contain (or reduce) selling prices; and customers, pleased with the higher quality at the same (or lower) price, perceive they have received value and will buy more. These factors create larger profits for the company for reinvesting in research and development activities that will generate new products or services, also of high quality. Alternatively, the profits can be used to train workers to provide even higher quality products and services than are currently available. This cycle of benefit (shown in Exhibit 3–5) will continue in a company that is profitable and secure in its market share—two primary goals of an organization.

QUALITY COSTS

As mentioned in the previous section, the TQM philosophy indicates that total costs will decline, rather than increase, as quality improvements are made in an organization. "Zero defects" means that there is nothing to correct and customers are happy. Thus, total quality management also includes the idea that it is the *lack* of quality, rather than having quality, that is expensive. Understanding the types and causes of quality costs can help managers prioritize improvement projects and provide feedback that supports and justifies improvement efforts.

Chapter 2 indicated that two types of costs comprise the total quality cost of a firm: (1) cost of quality compliance or assurance and (2) cost of noncompliance or quality failure. Costs of compliance equal the sum of prevention and appraisal costs. These costs are incurred with the intention of eliminating the present costs of failure

COSTS OF COMPLIANCE

Prevention Costs

Employees:
- Hiring for quality
- Training and awareness
- Establishing participation programs

Customers:
- Surveying needs
- Researching needs
- Conducting field trials

Machinery:
- Designed to detect defects
- Arranging for efficient flow
- Arranging for monitoring
- Incurring preventive maintenance
- Testing and adjusting equipment
- Fitting machinery for mistake-proof operations

Suppliers:
- Arranging for quality inputs
- Educating suppliers
- Involving suppliers

Product Design:
- Developing specifications
- Engineering and modeling
- Testing and adjusting for: conformity; effective and efficient performance; durability; ease of use; safety; comfort; appeal; and cost

Appraisal Costs

Before Production:
- Receiving inspection

Production Process:
- Monitoring and inspecting
- Keeping the process consistent, stable, and reliable
- Using procedure verification
- Automating

During and After Production:
- Performing quality audits

Information Process:
- Recording and reporting defects
- Measuring performance

Organization:
- Administering quality control department

COSTS OF NONCOMPLIANCE

Internal Failure

Product:
- Reworking defects
- Disposing of waste
- Storing and disposing
- Reinspecting rework

Production Process:
- Reprocessing
- Having unscheduled interruptions
- Experiencing unplanned downtime

External Failure

Organization:
- Staffing complaint departments
- Staffing warranty claims departments

Customers:
- Losing future sales
- Losing reputation
- Losing goodwill

Product:
- Repairing returned parts
- Replacing returned parts
- Reimbursing customers for returns
- Recalling defective units
- Litigating claims

Service:
- Providing unplanned service
- Expediting back orders
- Serving after purchase

▮ EXHIBIT 3–6
Types of Quality Costs

and maintaining that zero level in the future; thus, they are proactive on management's part. Furthermore, effective use of prevention costs can even minimize the costs of appraisal. On the other hand, costs of noncompliance are the results of production imperfections and are equal to internal and external failure costs. Exhibit 3–6 presents specific examples of each of these quality costs.

Information about production quality or lack thereof is contained in inspection reports, SPC control charts, and customer returns or complaints. Information about quality *costs*, on the other hand, is partially contained in the accounting records and supporting documentation. However, since the accounting records are commonly kept with an eye toward financial accounting, other information about such costs must be developed or estimated. The behavior of the costs relative to changes in activity as well as the appropriate drivers for these costs must be considered in making any necessary estimations. The nature of these functions makes it essential that the management accountant be involved in all activities—from system design to cost accumulation—relating to quality costs.

Historically, quality costs have not been given separate recognition in the accounting system. In most instances, the cost of quality is "buried" in a variety of general ledger accounts, including Work in Process and Finished Goods inventories (for rework, scrap, preventive maintenance, and other overhead costs), marketing/advertising expense (to recall products, improve image after poor products were made available to customers, or obtain customer survey information), personnel costs (for training), and engineering department costs (for engineering change orders and redesign).

In trying to determine the cost of quality, actual or estimated costs are identified for each item listed in Exhibit 3–6. If these costs were plotted on a graph, they would appear similar to the cost curves shown in Exhibit 3–7. If the firm spends larger amounts on prevention and appraisal costs, the number of defects is lower and the costs of failure are smaller. If less is spent on prevention and appraisal, the number of defects is greater and failure costs are larger. The external failure costs curve begins moving toward vertical when a certain number of defects are encountered by customers. The ultimate external failure cost is reached when customers will no longer buy a given product or any other products made by that firm because they will not tolerate such poor quality work.

By developing a system in which quality costs are readily available or determin-

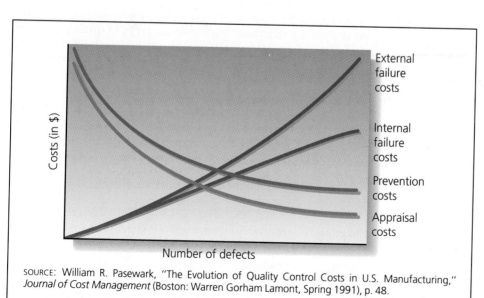

EXHIBIT 3–7
Relationships Among Quality Costs

SOURCE: William R. Pasewark, "The Evolution of Quality Control Costs in U.S. Manufacturing," *Journal of Cost Management* (Boston: Warren Gorham Lamont, Spring 1991), p. 48.

■ **EXHIBIT 3-8**
Time-Phased Model for
Quality Costs

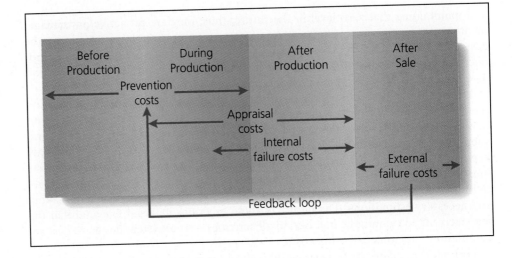

able, the management accountant is able to provide useful information to managers trying to make spending decisions by pinpointing the areas that would provide the highest cost-benefit relationships. Additionally, quality cost information will indicate how a shift in one or more curves will affect the others.

Exhibit 3-8 shows the location in the production-sales cycle where the types of quality costs are usually incurred. Note in this exhibit that an information feedback loop (indicated by the bold line) should be in effect to link the types and causes of failure costs to prevention costs to be subsequently incurred. Alert managers and employees will continuously monitor the nature of failures to discover their causes and will adjust the prevention activities to close the gaps that allowed the failures to occur. These continuous rounds of action, reaction, and action are essential to the continuous improvement initiatives.

■ MEASURING THE COST OF QUALITY

Theoretically, if prevention and appraisal costs were prudently incurred, failure costs would become zero. However, prevention and appraisal costs would still be incurred to achieve zero failure costs. Thus, total quality costs will never be zero. This is not to disregard the knowledge that the benefits of increased sales and greater efficiency should exceed all remaining quality costs. In this sense, the cost of quality is free. It is up to management to analyze the relationships among the types of quality costs and expend money for quality in a manner that will provide the highest level of benefits. Such an analysis requires that the costs of quality be measured to the extent possible and practical and the benefits of those costs estimated.

Pareto analysis

Pareto analysis is one means by which management can decide where to concentrate its quality prevention cost dollars. This technique classifies the causes of variances in a process according to the impact on an objective. For example, a company that makes refrigerators might subclassify its warranty claim costs for the past year according to the type of product failure as follows:

| | **Cost of Type of Failure** | | | | |
Model	Electrical	Motor	Structural	Mechanical	Total Dollars
ZT 100	$14,000	$16,000	$13,000	$ 3,000	$ 46,000
MX 2000	11,000	14,000	7,000	3,000	35,000
All other	6,000	10,000	3,000	4,000	23,000
Total	$31,000	$40,000	$23,000	$10,000	$104,000

Model	Dollars	% of Total	Cumulative % Total
ZT 100	$ 46,000	44%	44%
MX 2000	35,000	34	78
All other	23,000	22	100
Total	$104,000	100%	

Observe that arraying the total costs of failure of all models in descending order of magnitude indicates that models ZT 100 and MX 2000 account for 78 percent of the total warranty cost claims. Furthermore, it is evident that the largest single source of warranty claims cost is caused by problems with the refrigerator motors. Therefore, management has some vital information to focus its efforts on further analysis of what causes these particular models, and the motors on all models, to generate the greatest warranty claims costs. Management can then devote a commensurate portion of its prevention efforts to minimizing or eliminating these problems. This kind of analysis should be conducted sufficiently often that trends can be detected quickly and adjustments made rapidly.

If a company desires to engage in TQM and continuous improvement, it is only reasonable that quality costs be recorded and reported separately so that managers can plan, control, evaluate, and make decisions about the activities that cause those costs. However, just having quality cost information available does not enhance quality. Managers and workers must consistently and aggressively use the information as a basis for creatively and intelligently advancing quality.

The firm's chart of accounts can be expanded to accommodate either separate tracing or allocation of quality costs to new accounts. Exhibit 3–9 lists some suggested additional accounts that can be added to the chart of accounts for this purpose. Opportunity costs are also associated with poor quality and these include foregone future sales and a measure of the reputation of the firm. Although these are real costs and they may be estimated, they are not recorded in the accounting system because they do not result from specific transactions.

If the firm has a data-based management system, the information resulting from an expanded chart of accounts can alternatively be generated by coding transactions representing a quality cost. Coding will permit these transaction types and amounts to be reformatted so that reports detailing the costs of quality can be provided as shown (using assumed numbers) in Exhibit 3–10 on page 96. This report makes two important assumptions: stable production and a monthly reporting system. First, if

PREVENTION COSTS
Quality Training
Quality Circles
Quality Market Research
Quality Technology
Quality Product Design

APPRAISAL COSTS
Quality Inspections
Procedure Verifications
Measurement Equipment
Test Equipment

INTERNAL FAILURE COSTS
Reworking Products
Scrap and Waste
Storing and Disposing of Waste
Reprocessing
Rescheduling and Setup

EXTERNAL FAILURE COSTS
Complaints Handling
Warranty Handling
Repairing and Replacing Returns
Customer Reimbursements
Expediting

EXHIBIT 3–9
New Quality Accounts

	Cost of Current Period	Cost of Prior Period	% Change from Prior Period	Current Period Budget	% Change from Budget
Prevention Costs					
Quality Training	$ 4,700	$ 4,500	+4	$ 5,000	−6
Quality Circles	8,200	8,400	−2	8,000	+3
Quality Market Research	11,000	8,800	+25	12,000	−8
Quality Technology	9,600	10,800	−11	15,000	−36
Quality Product Design	16,600	12,200	+36	16,500	+1
Total	$ 50,100	$ 44,700	+12	$56,500	−11
Appraisal Costs					
Quality Inspections	$ 3,300	$ 3,500	−6	$ 3,000	+10
Procedure Verifications	1,200	1,400	−14	1,500	−20
Measurement Equipment	2,700	3,000	−10	3,200	−16
Test Equipment	1,500	1,200	+25	1,500	0
Total	$ 8,700	$ 9,100	−4	$ 9,200	−5
Internal Failure Costs					
Reworking Products	$ 8,500	$ 8,300	+2	N/A*	
Scrap and Waste	2,200	2,400	−8	N/A	
Storing and Disposing of Waste	4,400	5,700	−23	N/A	
Reprocessing	1,800	1,600	+13	N/A	
Rescheduling and Setup	900	1,200	−25	N/A	
Total	$ 17,800	$ 19,200	−7		
External Failure Costs					
Complaints Handling	$ 5,800	$ 6,200	−6	N/A	
Warranty Handling	10,700	9,300	+15	N/A	
Repairing and Replacing Returns	27,000	29,200	−8	N/A	
Customer Reimbursements	12,000	10,700	+12	N/A	
Expediting	1,100	1,300	−15		
Total	$ 56,600	$ 56,700	+0		
Total Quality Costs	$133,200	$129,700	+3	$65,700	+103

*TQM advocates planning for zero defects; therefore, zero failure costs would be included in the budget.

▍ **EXHIBIT 3–10**

Cost of Quality Report

wide fluctuations in production or service levels occur, period-to-period comparisons of absolute amounts may not be appropriate. Amounts may need to be converted to percentages to have any valid meaning. Second, in some settings (such as a just-in-time environment), a weekly reporting system would be more appropriate because of the need for continuous monitoring.

Exhibit 3–11 provides some formulas for calculating the total cost of quality for an organization, using the basic categories of prevention, appraisal, and failure. Some of the amounts used in these computations are, by necessity, estimates, but it is more important to have reliable estimates than not to perform the calculations because of the lack of verifiable or precise amounts. This situation reflects the idea discussed in Chapter 1 that management accountants are more apt to use estimated figures than financial accountants because of management's need for timely, rather than totally precise, information.

Consider the following July 1995 operating information for the Lee Company:

Defective units (D)	1,000	Units reworked (Y)	600
Profit for good unit (P_1)	$25	Profit for defective unit (P_2)	$15
Cost to rework defective unit (r)	$5	Defective units returned (D_r)	100
Cost of return (w)	$8	Prevention cost (K)	$25,000
Appraisal cost (A)	$4,400		

Substituting these values into the formulas provided in Exhibit 3–11, the following results are determined:

$$Z = (D - Y)(P_1 - P_2) = (1,000 - 600)(\$25 - \$15) = \$4,000$$

$$R = (Y)(r) = (600)(\$5) = \$3,000$$

$$W = (D_r)(w) = (100)(\$8) = \$800$$

$$F = Z + R + W = \$4,000 + \$3,000 + \$800 = \$7,800 \text{ total failure cost}$$

$$T = K + A + F = \$25,000 + \$4,400 + \$7,800$$

$$= \$37,200 \text{ total quality cost}$$

■ **EXHIBIT 3–11**

Formulas for Calculating Total Quality Cost

CALCULATING LOST PROFITS

Profit Lost by Selling Units as Defects = (Total Defective Units − Number of Units Reworked) × (Profit for Good Unit − Profit for Defective Unit)

$$Z = (D - Y)(P_1 - P_2)$$

CALCULATING TOTAL COSTS OF FAILURE

Rework Cost = Number of Units Reworked × Cost to Rework Defective Unit

$$R = (Y)(r)$$

Cost of Processing Customer Returns = Number of Defective Units Returned × Cost of a Return

$$W = (D_r)(w)$$

Total Failure Cost = Profit Lost by Selling Units as Defects + Rework Cost + Cost of Processing Customer Returns

$$F = Z + R + W$$

CALCULATING THE TOTAL QUALITY COST

Total Quality Cost = Defect Control Cost + Failure Cost

$$T = \text{Prevention Cost} + \text{Appraisal Cost} + \text{Failure Cost}$$

$$T = K + A + F$$

Prevention and appraisal costs are total estimated amounts; no formulas are appropriate. As the cost of prevention rises, the number of defective units should decline. Additionally, as the cost of prevention rises, the cost of appraisal should decline; however, appraisal cost can never become zero.

SOURCE: James T. Godfrey and William R. Pasewark, "Controlling Quality Costs," *Management Accounting* (March 1988), p. 50. Reprinted from *Management Accounting.* Copyright by Institute of Management Accountants, Montvale, N.J.

Of the total quality cost of $37,200, Lee Company managers will seek to identify the causes of the $7,800 failure costs and work to eliminate them. The results of the analysis may affect the planned amounts of prevention and appraisal costs for future periods.

High quality affords a company the ability to improve current profits, either through lower costs or, if the market will bear, higher prices. But management is often more interested in business objectives other than short-run profits. An example of an alternative, competing objective is that of increasing the company's market share. Indeed, if increasing market share were the objective, management could combine the strategies of increasing quality while lowering prices to attract a larger share of the market. When quality is increased by giving greater attention to prevention and appraisal activities, overall costs are expected to decline and productivity is expected to increase. Lower costs and greater productivity support lower prices that, in turn, often stimulate demand. The result is greater market share and, perhaps, even greater immediate profits.

THE QUALITY GOAL IN THE UNITED STATES

Any quality program should seek to meet the following three objectives:

■ The organization should achieve and sustain the quality of the product or service produced so as to continuously meet the purchaser's stated or implied needs.

■ The organization should give its own management confidence that the intended quality is being achieved and sustained.

■ The organization should give the purchaser confidence that the intended quality is, or will be, achieved in the delivered product or service. When contractually required, this assurance may involve agreed demonstration requirements.[12]

■ **EXHIBIT 3–12**
Baldrige Quality Award Categories

■ **Leadership**—senior management's success in creating quality values and in building these values into the way the company operates

■ **Information and analysis**—the effectiveness of the company's collection and analysis of information for quality improvement and planning

■ **Strategic quality planning**—the effectiveness of the company's integration of the customers' quality requirements into its business plans

■ **Human resource utilization**—the success of the company's efforts to realize the full potential of the workforce for quality

■ **Quality assurance of products and services**—the effectiveness of the company's systems for assuring quality control of all its operations and in integrating quality control with continuous quality improvement

■ **Quality results**—the company's improvements in quality and demonstration of quality excellence based upon quantitative measures

■ **Customer satisfaction**—the effectiveness of the company's systems to determine customer requirements and a demonstrated success in meeting them

SOURCE: "What's the Baldrige Quality Award, and How Might It Help Your Firm?" *Financial Executive*, p. 30. Reprinted with permission from *Financial Executive*, September/October 1990 by Financial Executives Institute, 10 Madison Avenue, P.O. Box 1938, Morristown, N.J. 07962-1938. (201) 898-4600.

---

[12] A. Faye Borthick and Harold P. Roth, "Will Europeans Buy Your Company's Products?" *Management Accounting* (July 1992), pp. 28–29.

NEWS NOTE   Quality Increases Mean Cost Decreases

[T]he Baldrige has become a standard of excellence for quality-improvement at U.S. firms. Winning it signifies that your products or services are among the world's best—an honor that boosts employee morale and vastly improves a company's reputation among customers and shareholders.

"As the country becomes more quality conscious, we'll be able to do two things: replace foreign imports (with U.S.-made goods) . . . and really build our exports," says Commerce Secretary Robert Mosbacher.

U.S. companies still waste billions of dollars on poor quality: retyping memos, repairing finished goods or reworking products in poorly designed plants. (In 1989, IBM paid $2.4 billion on warranties.) If every U.S. firm mastered quality, the gross national product—[climbing in 1990] at less than 1% a year—would soar 7 percentage points or more, says a study by Armand Feigenbaum, a quality consultant and Baldrige Award overseer. "Those figures don't surprise me at all," says Fred Smith (Federal Express chairman). "Quality is not only extremely important to customers. It's also the best way to lower costs."

SOURCE: John Hillkirk and Micheline Maynard, "Baldrige Sets Standard of Excellence," *USA Today* (October 11, 1990), pp. 1B, 2B. Copyright 1990, *USA TODAY*. Reprinted with permission.

The Malcolm Baldrige National Quality Award has served to raise the quality consciousness of U.S. manufacturing, service, and small businesses, and its standards provide a framework for measuring quality efforts of those businesses.

The embodiment of TQM in the United States is the 1987 Malcolm Baldrige National Quality Improvement Act that established the Malcolm Baldrige Quality Award. The award was named for the late Malcolm Baldrige, U.S. Secretary of Commerce from 1981 to 1987. The Baldrige Award focuses attention on management systems, processes, and consumer satisfaction as the tools required to achieve product and service excellence. There are three categories of entrants: manufacturing, service, and small business. To win the award, applicants must show excellence in the seven categories shown in Exhibit 3–12.

As of 1992, quality results must be demonstrated. Information must be provided by entrants detailing their quality "programs' effects in areas such as reducing waste, speeding products to market, improving employee satisfaction and contributing to 'national and community well-being.'"[13] The News Note "Quality Increases Mean Cost Decreases" provides information on why the Baldrige Award is being embraced by corporate America.

Note that applicants are not judged on financial measures such as profits—in fact, one of the award winners (Wallace Company of Houston, Texas) filed for Chapter 11 bankruptcy after receiving the award. Part of this exclusion of financial measures from consideration is based on the fact that different accounting practices can produce significantly different financial statement results and, therefore, intercompany comparisons may not be appropriate. In addition, because applicants do not have to be publicly held, the same financial information is not available for all.

In 1992, AT&T made history as the first company to win two Baldrige Awards, one for its nonunion Universal Card Services unit in Jacksonville, Florida, and one for its unionized Transmission System unit in Morristown, New Jersey. The AT&T units have a slight advantage over other competitors, however, because there is a companywide internal quality award program based on the Baldrige. About 85 per-

---

[13] Gilbert Fuchsberg, "Baldrige Awards Give More Weight to Results," *Wall Street Journal* (February 24, 1992), p. B1.

cent of AT&T's business units were expected to apply for the internal award during 1993, indicating that the quest for quality is pervasive in that organization.[14]

Japan's equivalent of the Malcolm Baldrige National Quality Award is the Deming Prize. This award, named for W. Edwards Deming, has even more rigorous requirements than those for the Baldrige Award. Globally, the quality movement has progressed to the point that certain quality standards have been set, although these are not considered at the level of those for either the Baldrige Award or the Deming Prize.

INTERNATIONAL QUALITY STANDARDS

Most large companies view their markets on an international, rather than a domestic, basis. To compete effectively in a global environment, companies must recognize and be willing to initiate compliance with a variety of standards outside their domestic borders. Standards are essentially the international language of trade; they are formalized agreements that define the various contractual, functional, and technical requirements that ensure products, services, processes, and/or systems do what they are expected to do.

ISO 9000

A primary international guideline for quality standards is the **ISO 9000** series. In 1987, the Geneva, Switzerland–based International Organization for Standardization developed a comprehensive list of quality standards known as the ISO 9000 series. The series of five standards resulted from discussions among quality standards boards of 91 countries. These directives are written in a general manner and basically prescribe the design, material procurement, production, quality control, and delivery procedures necessary to produce quality products and services.[15] Exhibit 3–13 indicates the coverage of each of the five standards.

EXHIBIT 3–13

Content of ISO 9000 Standards

STANDARD NUMBER	CONTENT
9000	Provides a model for assuring quality in product design and development; covers contracts, organizational structure, purchasing data, processing controls, and production, installation and servicing
9001	Covers requirements for conformance during product design, production, installation, and servicing; applicable to engineering, construction, and manufacturing companies
9002	Provides a model for assuring quality when only production and installation conformance is required; is applicable to companies in which product requirements are stated relative to established designs or specifications (such as chemical, foods, and pharmaceutical companies)
9003	Provides a model for assuring quality when only final inspection and testing conformance is required; is applicable to companies (or internal organizational units) that inspect and test the products they supply (such as laboratories)
9004	Provides guidelines related to a company's internal quality management and developing and implementing a quality system; discusses the technical, administrative, and human factors that affect product and service quality

[14]Peter Coy, "AT&T Smacks a Double," *Business Week* (October 26, 1992), p. 37.
[15]The ISO 9000 standards are equivalent to the American Society for Quality Control (ASQC) Q-90 quality series that was issued in 1987. Companies that currently meet the Q-90 standards also meet the ISO 9000 standards.

NEWS NOTE

Quality Standards Help Assure Competitiveness

"To do business in a global marketplace, manufacturers today need a range of services that comprise what we call 'globalibility,'" says Tom Castino, president of Underwriters Laboratories Inc. "These services include testing for conformance to international standards; certification that this product complies with applicable standards, and—where required—registration of the manufacturer's facilities to the ISO 9000 series quality assessment standards. Finally, confidence must be built in both the products and the associated certification and registration services through appropriate accreditations and mutual recognition arrangements."

"Standards go directly to the heart of the quality issue and quality goes to the heart of the competitiveness issue," says Ed Addison, president and CEO of the Southern Company. In Addison's view, standards are becoming even more critical now in light of the globalization of virtually every major industry: "As the world becomes more interconnected, we must participate in and support a strong system of international standards that will enable the U.S. to manufacture products and provide services with the high level of quality necessary to compete effectively in the global marketplace. Our growth as companies and as a nation depends on our meeting world-class standards."

SOURCE: Jerry Bowles, "International Standardization: The Cornerstone of Global Competitiveness," *FORTUNE* (November 2, 1992), pp. 141–142. © 1992 Time Inc. All rights reserved. Reprinted from a paid advertising section prepared for *FORTUNE* magazine, November 2, 1992 issue.

Beginning in 1993, companies must have an approved quality system in order to sell products in Europe—and the system described in the ISO series is the only one that meets the European Economic Area requirements.[16] Unfortunately, there is no international organization that administers the program. Thus, companies seeking ISO registration have to qualify under an internationally accepted registration program that is administered by a national registrar. Examples of such registrars in the U.S. and Great Britain are, respectively, Underwriters Laboratories and the British Standards Institution. The News Note on Quality Standards stresses the importance of adoption of the ISO standards, regardless of the inconvenience of the process. Additionally, "comparisons show ISO at best meets 40% of the criteria used by the U.S. Baldrige Award. So companies are pressuring the International Standards Organization to upgrade the guidelines by 1996."[17]

If a company decides after an internal review that it can meet the standards, it may apply for ISO registration. To be registered, a company must first submit to a **quality audit** by a third-party reviewer. A quality audit involves a review of product design activities (although not for individual products), manufacturing processes and controls, quality documentation and records, and management quality policy and philosophy. The external audits to determine compliance are quite expensive, costing between $800 to $3,000 per person-day plus expenses. Audit teams usually consist of between two and six people who work up to ten days between the initial review and follow-up. After registration, teams visit the company biannually to monitor compliance.

Quality audit

---

[16] The European Economic Area includes the 12 countries that belong to the European Economic Community (Belgium, Denmark, France, Germany, Greece, Ireland, Italy, Luxembourg, Netherlands, Portugal, Spain, and the United Kingdom) and the 7 countries that belong to the European Free Trade Association (Austria, Finland, Iceland, Liechtenstein, Norway, Sweden, and Switzerland).

[17] Jonathan B. Levine, "Want EC Business? You Have Two Choices," *Business Week* (October 19, 1992), p. 59.

Although the costs are high, companies becoming certified believe the benefits are even higher. Externally, companies certified under ISO 9000 will have an important distinguishing characteristic from their noncertified competitors. Additionally, certified companies are listed in a registry of "approved" suppliers, which should increase business opportunities. Internally, certification will help ensure higher process consistency and quality and should help to reduce costs. The following quote indicates the belief that company executives have in the cost-benefit of ISO registration:

> In direct and indirect costs, we have spent many tens of thousands of dollars. In time, effort, training and documentation, the effort on behalf of our 200 staff has been extraordinary. By the time we gain ISO 9002 accreditation, we will have achieved something that is akin to an organisational PhD. It will make us better managers, better employees, better producers of quality products, more service-oriented and ensure that we have a quality system in the organisation that means we are as good as the best in the world.
>
> The piece of paper that will have ISO 9002 on it will be almost irrelevant, apart from a visual proof that we have aspired to, and met, the highest possible standard for our industry.[18]

The cost-benefit relationships of the quality system must be measured, documented, and reported under ISO 9000—all jobs for management accountants.

The ISO standards are not required to do business in the United States, but should be investigated for possible implementation even by companies that do not sell overseas because of the benefits mentioned above. And, naturally, if a company's competitors are in compliance with and registered under ISO standards, good business sense would indicate the necessity of becoming ISO certified.

The ISO standards are also becoming a part of certain U.S. federal rules and regulations. For example, in revising the 1978 Good Manufacturing Practices, the Food and Drug Administration is currently aligning those standards with ISO 9001 standards by making certain design control and service elements mandatory.

QUALITY AS AN ORGANIZATIONAL CULTURE

Quality must be viewed as a moving target; that is why TQM embodies the concept of continuous improvement. Higher and higher performance standards must be set for everyone (not just the production people) in the organization to provide the sense of working toward a common goal. This philosophy is expressed in the News Note related to Federal-Mogul Corporation.

The behavior of managers and all employees comprise the basis for TQM. Consistent and committed top management leadership is the catalyst for moving the company culture toward an esprit de corps in which all individuals, regardless of rank or position, are obsessed with exceeding customer expectations. Such an attitude should also permeate everything a company does including customer relations, marketing, research and development, product design, production, and information processing.

Management can effectively induce change in its organizational culture by providing an environment in which employees know the company cares and is responsive to their needs and will appreciate and reward excellent results. This knowledge goes a long way toward making the employees feel trusted, respected, and comfortable. Such employees are more likely to treat customers in a similar manner.

The firm must empower employees to participate fully in the quest for excellence in quality by providing the means by which employees gain pride, satisfaction, and substantive involvement. Encouragement, training, job enhancement, and the proper working environment and tools are what managers must provide. Employees should

---

[18] Alan Clarke, CEO Medlah, "Quality Concerns," *Management* (November 1992), p. 29. Reprinted from New Zealand *Management* magazine.

NEWS NOTE

Quality Relates Directly to Our Customers

To remain competitive, every company must find its own distinct ways to add value and deliver fast service around the world. It is the only way to get and keep customers. At Federal-Mogul, this philosophy is expressed in our guiding principles which read, in part: "Our customers are our reason for being. All of our efforts must be directed toward providing them with the best products and services.

Towards this end, we continue to make changes to our processes that give us faster throughput and more flexibility. These improvements make our entire system more responsive to customer needs. But more importantly, they allow our customers to reduce their inventory, improve their profitability, and improve service to their customers."

Federal-Mogul believes that customer response is all inclusive. It involves everything from answering phones quickly, to providing faster customer quotes, faster product development, faster delivery of samples and faster response throughout the organization. We are looking for ways to take redundancy out of our business and our customers' business.

SOURCE: Federal-Mogul Corporation, *1991 Annual Report* (Detroit, Michigan), p. 12.

be recognized with praise and reward for their effective involvement in group problem solving, contributing ideas for improvement, acting as monitors of their own work, and sharing their knowledge and enthusiastic attitudes with their colleagues.

With its focus on process and customers, TQM is founded on one very obvious and simple principle: Do things right the first time. The heart of this principle is zero defects now and in the future. For example, a non-TQM production policy statement might read: "Do not allow defective production to be greater than 1 percent of total production." Total quality management would have the policy statement: "There will be zero defective production." It is then management's responsibility to provide employees with the training, equipment, and quality of materials and other resources to meet this objective.

Exhibit 3–14 depicts the quality continuum along which companies move toward achieving world-class status. This continuum indicates that, at the most basic level of quality assurance, a company simply inspects to find defective products or monitors

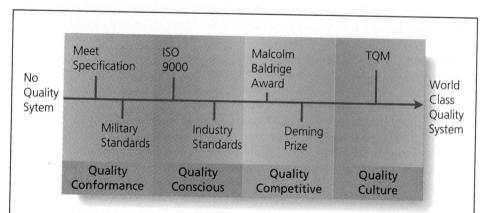

EXHIBIT 3–14
Quality Continuum

SOURCE: Grant Thornton, *Survey of American Manufacturers* (New York, 1992), p. 20. Reprinted with permission from Grant Thornton on *A Survey of American Manufacturers*, 1992.

employees and surveys customers to find poor service. Implementation of a variety of quality control techniques into the system to eliminate the possibilities of defective products or poor service means that the company has become quality conscious. When the company's (or a division of the company's) quality system has progressed to a high level of sophistication, the company (or division) may choose to compete against others for quality honors. Finally, when the concept of quality has become a distinct element of the organizational culture and tolerances for defective products or poor service are set at zero percent, the company has achieved world-class status and can be viewed as the benchmark for others. But achieving world-class status does not mark an ending point. TQM is not a static concept; when one problem has been solved, there is always another one waiting for a solution.

QUALITY IN NOT-FOR-PROFIT ORGANIZATIONS[19]

Although quality improvements allow businesses to raise profits, it is the decreased cost effect of such improvements that primarily benefits not-for-profit (NFP) organizations. These organizations were formed for one of three purposes: to accomplish a task specified by a governmental entity; to provide a public service; or to influence public- or private-sector policy. These organizations are funded either by tax dollars or through contributions, so it is in the public interest that the dollars invested be used in the most effective and efficient manner possible. However, instituting quality improvements in NFPs is slightly more complicated than in for-profits because of four distinctive characteristics.

First, determining the goals and objectives of a not-for-profit may be easier than in a for-profit, but this characteristic may hinder rather than help the quest for quality. For-profit organizations (FPs) typically express their goals in broad, customer-focused terms, which allow expansion into new service areas when opportunities are presented. The not-for-profit typically has a single, directed focus that often hampers its ability to change as the operating environment changes. For example, if the organization's purpose is to find a cure for a specific disease, finding the cure eliminates the need for the organization. Such uncertainty about longevity impedes the NFPs' ability to institute long-range plans for quality improvements because, as Raymond Marlow (president of Marlow Industries, a Dallas, Texas, Baldrige-winning company) says, "'You've got to have patience, because it's going to take time to [implement TQM].' He believes that it takes a couple of years before employees can work together smoothly in problem-solving teams."[20]

Second, determining whether goals and objectives have been achieved (measuring performance) is more difficult in NFPs than in FPs. Many goals and objectives in FPs are measured in quantifiable, often financial, terms. For example, decreasing the cost of producing part X is a common, measurable goal of a for-profit entity. In a NFP, goals may be stated so broadly—to avoid alienating donors—that they may not be measurable at all. Goals such as "to improve the community in which we live" are commendable, but are impossible to measure in any quantifiable way. As noted earlier in the chapter, measurement must be available to know when nonconformance exists. An inability to measure accomplishment obviously makes recognizing achievement significantly more difficult.

Third, judging quality is more difficult in the not-for-profit organization than in the for-profit company. Quality in the FP is deemed to reflect customer satisfaction, which can be measured by repeat business, new customers, and lack of customer complaints. Quality in the NFP must reflect customer/client *and* donor satisfaction and is

[19]The authors are grateful to Dr. Ernest Nordtvedt for his assistance in the preparation of this section.
[20]Michael Barrier, "Small Firms Put Quality First," *Nation's Business* (May 1992), p. 24.

subject to individual interpretation among the organization's several constituencies. In the NFP, customers/clients often do not pay for a service and will avail themselves of it *regardless* of the level of satisfaction. Donors, who pay for providing the service, may not avail themselves of it and may not know or care about its quality. Thus, it is possible for the NFP to satisfy one group without satisfying the other. This situation creates the inevitable conflict: which of the two groups should receive priority in terms of satisfaction? If the customer/client receives priority, the donors may stop supporting and, thus, cause the service to be eliminated. If the donors receive priority, the customers may stop using the service or find alternatives. This situation may eliminate the need for the service or shift responsibility to another organization supported by different donors who may or may not be able to bear the increased financial burden.

Fourth, because of the investment base provided by stockholders (and, to some extent, creditors), for-profit organizations frequently have more time to achieve success than do not-for-profits. FPs can take years to design, test, and produce a new product, but NFPs must meet public needs in the present or they will not exist in the future. As mentioned previously, implementing TQM programs takes substantial time; for instance, H.J. Heinz took eight years to cut its cost of quality by 60 percent. An additional 50 percent reduction is planned for the years 1992–1996.[21] Many NFP donors would not continue their contributions over a twelve-year period unless service results were being achieved currently. Therefore, the planning horizon (like the definition of customer satisfaction) may be ill-defined: even as the NFP provides service in the short-term, it must focus on the longer-term quality issue of customer satisfaction. Attempts to improve quality often require short-run expenditures, leading to requests for increased donations and causing contribution cutbacks because donors believe the organization does not know how to manage its funds—and the downdraft spirals.

These problematic issues should not be used as reasons to justify why TQM cannot be implemented in NFPs. The benefit of reduced costs that is derived from quality improvements should be of equal, if not of more, importance to NFPs than to FPs. Just as the reduced costs allow the FP to hold the line on price increases or to reduce prices, reduced costs in the NFP should provide the donors or taxpayers the advantage of holding the line on increased spending for ongoing programs. For donor-based organizations, this advantage could mean the ability to do more for more people than previously; for the government (the largest not-for-profit in the U.S.), this advantage could mean the ability to begin to manage some out-of-control spending.

R E V I S I T I N G

UNITED SERVICES AUTOMOBILE ASSOCIATION (USAA)

In his 22 years as CEO of USAA, Robert F. McDermott has built a company with a reputation for superb service in an industry infamous for its indifference to the customer. [He says,] "The mission and corporate culture of this company are, in one word, service. As a company objective service comes ahead of either profits or growth. But I submit that it's because service comes first at USAA that profits and growth have been so healthy. We've grown from $200 million to $20.7 billion in to-

---

[21] "Quantifying Quality Improvement Efforts Leads to Reduced Costs, Increased Profits," *(Grant Thornton) Manufacturing Issues* (Spring 1991), p. 2.

tal owned and managed assets in 22 years. Our profits are among the highest in the insurance industry.

"[To increase the types and quality of service, USAA had to install computerized operating systems.] The result was a five-year plan [that] consisted of 81 projects and had a projected price tag of $100 million. In the end, it took us six years and $130 million. But that wasn't bad, considering that along the way we enlarged the scope of the plan [and] made a lot of changes. More important, we achieved our basic goal, to create an AIE—an automated insurance environment—that includes policy writing, service, claims, billing, customer accounting, everything.

"More important yet, it changed the way we think. Now when you want to buy a new car, get it insured, add a driver, and change your coverage and address, you can make one phone call—average time, five minutes—and nothing else is necessary. One-stop, on-line, the policy goes out the door the next morning about 4 a.m. In one five-minute phone call, you and our service representative have done all the work that used to take 55 steps, umpteen people, two weeks, and a lot of money. [Thus,] we don't think of technology as a cost center. It's a strategic weapon. It contributes to service, so cost is not the only or even the primary consideration."

SOURCE: Reprinted by permission of *Harvard Business Review*. An excerpt from "Service Comes First: An Interview with USAA's Robert F. McDermott," by Thomas Teal (September–October 1991), p. 117ff. Copyright © 1991 by the President and Fellows of Harvard College; all rights reserved.

CHAPTER SUMMARY

Continuous quality improvement is essential to survival in the global marketplace. Quality is defined as conformity to requirements. Total quality management is a system involving all company personnel in the pursuit of a continuous improvement process that exceeds customer expectations. The shared planning and decision making among personnel required by TQM is changing the way managers perform their jobs.

If a firm is to succeed in the global marketplace, continuous quality improvement is demanded. World markets are emerging that enlarge the scope and intensity of competition in the quality arena. Enhanced technology in hardware, production processes, and management systems have made the new quality initiatives possible. Consumers are aware of greater variety by type and quality of products, and they discriminate in their purchases with regard to price, quality, service, and lead time. This intensified competition has motivated producers to adopt a more dynamic attitude about quality improvement and has heightened the use of competitive benchmarking to close any performance gaps.

Two broad categories of quality costs are compliance and noncompliance. Compliance costs include costs of prevention and costs of appraisal. Noncompliance costs are separated into internal failure costs and external failure costs. Quality compliance costs are incurred to eliminate the current costs of quality failure and to maintain that zero level in the future.

When sufficient amounts are spent on quality assurance and compliance, the number of product defects and failure costs should be low. If too little is spent on compliance, the number of defects and amount of failure costs become large. If the number of defects becomes excessive, external failure costs skyrocket. The ultimate failure cost results when customers reject a product and this rejection extends to the other products of the firm.

Productivity is measured by the number of good units generated during a period. Improving quality essentially increases productivity because quality improvement works to remove factors that slow down or halt the production process or that require production redundancy. Eliminating non-value-added activities also increases productivity.

Theoretically, quality costs can be said to be free if their benefits exceed their costs. However, management should still measure them if the firm desires to engage in TQM so that managers have specific information by which to plan, control, evaluate, and make decisions in a continuous improvement environment.

The Malcolm Baldrige Quality Award focuses attention on management systems, processes, and consumer satisfaction as the tools to achieve excellence. Competition entrants must demonstrate results and provide evidence of effectiveness in reducing waste, speeding product to market, improving employee satisfaction, and contributing to community and national well-being. Applicants are not judged on financial measures.

To compete internationally in the European market, companies must comply with the ISO 9000 series of quality standards. There are five standards that can serve as guidelines for any company desiring to improve quality. When a company develops quality as a major emphasis in its organizational culture, all personnel are encouraged to become obsessed with exceeding customer expectations.

Assessing quality in a not-for-profit entity is more difficult than in a for-profit firm. Consumers often are not paying for the service and will avail themselves of it regardless of the level of satisfaction. Donors to the NFP may not know of its quality. NFPs must perform satisfactorily in the present or they will not exist in the future. Thus, the NFP planning horizon for quality is shorter than that of the FP.

KEY TERMS

Activity analysis (p. 82)
Benchmarking (p. 85)
Control chart (p. 83)
Grade (p. 84)
ISO 9000 (p. 100)
Non-value-added activity (p. 82)
Pareto analysis (p. 94)
Process benchmarking (p. 87)
Quality (p. 82)

Quality assurance (p. 82)
Quality audit (p. 101)
Results benchmarking (p. 86)
Statistical process control (SPC) (p. 83)
Total quality control (TQC) (p. 83)
Total quality management (TQM) (p. 87)
Value (p. 84)
Value-added activity (p. 82)

SOLUTION STRATEGIES

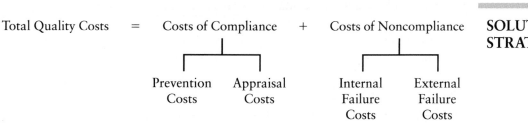

Total Quality Costs = Costs of Compliance + Costs of Noncompliance

Prevention Costs   Appraisal Costs   Internal Failure Costs   External Failure Costs

Costs of noncompliance are inversely related to the costs of compliance. Costs of noncompliance are a direct result of the number of defects.

Dimensions of product quality include:

- Conformity to specifications
- Effective and efficient performance
- Durability
- Ease of use

- Safety
- Comfort of use
- Appeal

TQM leads to greater demand, greater productivity, shorter lead time, lower costs, and greater customer loyalty, which all lead to greater control of pricing.

Cost of Quality Formulas

Profit Lost by Selling Units as Defects = (Total Defective Units—Number of Units Reworked) × (Profit for Good Unit − Profit for Defective Unit)

$$Z = (D - Y)(P_1 - P_2)$$

Rework Cost = Number of Units Reworked × Cost to Rework Defective Unit

$$R = (Y)(r)$$

Cost of Processing Customer Returns = Number of Defective Units Returned × Cost of a Return

$$W = (D_r)(w)$$

Total Failure Cost = Profit Lost by Selling Units as Defects + Rework Cost + Cost of Processing Customer Returns

$$F = Z + R + W$$

Total Quality Cost = Defect Control Cost + Failure Cost

$$T = \text{Prevention Cost} + \text{Appraisal Cost} + \text{Failure Cost}$$

$$T = K + A + F$$

DEMONSTRATION PROBLEM

Foster Company's quality report for April 1995 showed the following information:

Total defective units	1,500
Number of units reworked	900
Number of customer units returned	150
Profit for a good unit	$38
Profit for a defective unit	$22
Cost to rework a defective unit	$ 7
Cost to rework a returned unit	$12
Total prevention cost	$15,000
Total appraisal cost	$ 5,000

Required: Compute the following:

a. Profit lost by selling unreworked defects
b. Total rework cost
c. Cost of processing customer returns
d. Total failure cost
e. Total quality cost

Solution to Demonstration Problem

a. $Z = (D - Y)(P_1 - P_2) = (1,500 - 900)(\$38 - \$22) = \$9,600$
b. $R = (Y)(r) = (900)(\$7) = \$6,300$
c. $W = (D_r)(w) = (150)(\$12) = \$1,800$
d. $F = Z + R + W = \$9,600 + \$6,300 + \$1,800 = \$17,700$
e. $T = K + A + F = \$15,000 + \$5,000 + \$17,700 = \$37,700$

QUESTIONS

1. What is meant by the term *quality*? In defining quality, from what two perspectives may a definition be formulated?

2. In conducting activity analysis, the presence of certain activities is indicative of low quality in the production process. List five of these types of activities.

3. What variables can management manipulate to improve the quality of the production process?

4. How can statistical process control techniques be used to evaluate the quality of a production process?

5. Does a high-quality manufacturing process necessarily guarantee that the consumer of the manufactured product will view it as being of high quality? Explain.

6. Identify the eight characteristics of product quality from the perspective of the consumer.

7. How does benchmarking allow a company to evaluate the quality of its products and services?

8. Describe the eight steps in benchmarking that may be used to improve a specific production process.

9. What is TQM? What are the three important tenets of TQM?

10. When consumers compare alternative products and services, one of the characteristics of each alternative that is evaluated is "customer service." What are some of the important elements of customer service that consumers may examine?

11. What are the two types of costs that comprise the total quality cost of a firm? What are the two subtypes within each type? Given the tradeoffs between the two main types of quality costs, is quality ever free? Explain.

12. What are the sources of information for product quality costs within a firm (both financial and nonfinancial)?

13. In the production–sales cycle, what are the four time phases in which quality costs are incurred?

14. How can Pareto analysis help focus managerial efforts in reducing the costs of quality-related problems?

15. Describe some additional accounts that can be added to financial records to attempt to better capture the costs of quality in the accounting records. Provide some examples of costs contained in the specified accounts.

16. What is the Malcolm Baldrige Award? What are the categories of entrants? What are the award categories?

17. Why do countries establish quality standards? Why is it desirable to have a common set of global quality standards?

18. What role is served by the International Organization for Standardization (ISO)?

19. What are the four stages or levels on the quality continuum? Where is TQM located on the continuum?

20. Why are quality innovations more difficult to implement in governmental and not-for-profit organizations than in profit-oriented firms?

EXERCISES

21. *(Matching)* Match the letter of each of the following terms to the number of the correct definition:

a. Activity analysis		**1.**	Method to rank causes of variation in a process
b. Benchmarking		**2.**	Review of product design, manufacturing processes and controls, quality documentation and records
c. Control chart		**3.**	Technique to identify uncommon variations or errors in a process
d. Grade		**4.**	Process of classifying activities as value-added or non-value-added
e. Pareto analysis		**5.**	Graphical method of documenting when a process is in or out of control
f. Quality		**6.**	Different product or service characteristics to satisfy different customer needs
g. Quality audit		**7.**	Process of investigating how other firms conduct business
h. Statistical process control		**8.**	Effect of meeting customer needs at the lowest possible price
i. Total quality control		**9.**	Product or service characteristic relating to meeting the most customer needs at the lowest price
j. Value		**10.**	Policy and/or practice designed to eliminate poor quality

22. *(True/false)* Mark each of the following statements as true or false and explain why the false statements are incorrect.
   a. Quality is free.
   b. Activity analysis can be used to identify non-value-added activities.
   c. SPC control charts are used to plot the costs of quality over time.
   d. Results benchmarking relies only on comparisons to firms *within* the same industry.
   e. Total quality management has production processes as its focus rather than customer satisfaction.
   f. Higher quality yields lower profits, but higher productivity.
   g. As the number of defective products manufactured rises, internal failure costs also rise, but external failure costs are expected to decline.
   h. Pareto analysis is used to help managers identify areas in which to focus quality-improvement efforts.
   i. Traditional accounting systems have separate accounts to capture quality costs.
   j. The total quality cost is the sum of prevention cost plus failure cost.

23. *(Cost of quality)* Below are selected cost data taken from records of the Milnar Technology Company for 1993 and 1994:

Defect prevention costs	1993	1994
Quality training	$8,000	$9,500
Quality technology	6,000	8,000
Quality production design	4,000	9,000
External failure costs		
Warranty handling	$15,000	$10,000
Customer reimbursements	11,000	7,200
Customer returns handling	7,000	4,000

a. Compute the percentage change in the two quality cost categories from 1993 to 1994.

b. Write a brief explanation for the pattern of change in the two categories.

24. *(Cost of quality)* The Zanadu Corp. is interested in quantifying its costs of quality for May 1994. Accordingly, the company has gathered the following information from records pertaining to May:

Defective units (D)	5,000	Prevention costs (K)	$12,000
Units reworked (Y)	4,500	Profit per good unit produced	
Defective units returned (Dr)	200	and sold (P_1)	$30
Appraisal costs (A)	$8,000	Profit per defective unit sold (P_2)	$10
Cost per unit for rework (r)	$6		
Cost per unit for customer returns (ω)	$12		

For Zanadu in May, compute:

a. lost profits from selling defective work.

b. total costs of failure.

c. total quality cost.

25. *(Cost of quality)* Mile High Bicycle Company has gathered the following information pertaining to quality costs of production for November 1994:

Total defective units (D)	200
Number of units reworked (Y)	140
Number of bicycles returned (Dr)	25
Total prevention cost (K)	$8,000
Total appraisal cost (A)	$9,200
Per unit profit for defective units (P_2)	$12
Per unit profit for good units (P_1)	$30
Cost to rework defective units (r)	$14
Cost to handle returned units (ω)	$18

Using this data, find:

a. total cost to rework.

b. profit lost from not reworking all defective units.

c. cost of processing customer returns.

d. total failure costs.

e. total quality cost.

COMMUNICATION ACTIVITIES

26. *(Cost of quality)* Smithfield Leisure Boats is evaluating its quality control costs for 1993 and preparing plans and budgets for 1994. The 1993 quality costs incurred in the Fishing Rig Division follow:

Prevention	$150,000
Appraisal	50,000
Internal failure costs	200,000
External failure costs	100,000
Total	$500,000

a. Which categories of failure costs would be affected by the decision to spend $150,000 on a new computer-controlled drill press (to replace an old manual drill press)? Explain.

b. Assume that projected external failure costs for 1994 can be reduced 50% (relative to 1993 levels) by either spending $40,000 more on appraisal or $60,000 more on prevention. Why might the firm rationally opt to spend the $60,000 on prevention rather than the $40,000 on appraisal?

27. Summary numbers following have been taken from a quality cost report of Alabama Millworks, Inc. for 1994. The firm manufactures a variety of cast iron products.

Prevention costs	$ 5,000,000
Appraisal costs	4,000,000
Internal failure costs	7,000,000
External failure costs	2,000,000
Total quality costs	$18,000,000

The company is actively seeking to identify ways to reduce total quality costs. The company's current strategy is to increase spending in one or more quality cost categories in hopes of achieving greater spending cuts in other quality cost categories.

a. Which of the spending categories are more susceptible to control by managers?

b. Why is it more logical for the company to increase spending in the prevention cost and appraisal cost categories than in the failure cost categories?

c. Which cost category is the most likely target for spending reductions? Explain.

d. How would the adoption of a TQM philosophy affect the focus in reducing quality costs?

28. Following are data for two firms in the consumer electronics industry. The data pertain to quality costs, by category, as a percentage of sales dollars for 1995. The firms are of similar size in terms of both assets and sales.

	Firm 1	Firm 2
Training and prevention costs	5%	1%
Quality appraisal/evaluation	3%	2%
Internal failure costs	2%	3%
External failure costs	1%	5%
Total	11%	11%

a. Are the two firms equally successful in controlling quality costs?

b. Which firm is more likely to have adopted a TQM philosophy? Explain.

29. Visiting a car dealership in your community are: (1) a 19-year-old college student, (2) a young married couple with two children, and (3) an elderly couple (postretirement age). Each of these three parties is interested in purchasing a new automobile.

a. Do you think each of these three parties would define quality in a vehicle in the same terms? Explain.

b. What vehicle characteristics would be important to all three parties? Which vehicle characteristics would be unique to each of the parties?

30. On February 1, 1993, Xerox paid for a full-page advertisement in the *Wall Street Journal*. The ad did not tout Xerox products nor was it in reference to year-end earnings or a new stock issuance. Instead, the ad was to congratulate "the select group of Xerox suppliers who partnered with us to achieve world-class quality, value, delivery and service through the Total Quality Management philosophy." The ad named each supplier and identified it as located in North America, Europe, or Asia.

a. Why would Xerox want other companies to know what suppliers it uses?

b. Do you think this advertisement had any positive benefit on Xerox itself? Discuss the rationale for your answer.

31. For a benchmark, assume that the typical U.S. firm incurs quality costs in the following proportions:

Prevention	25%
Appraisal	25%
Internal failure	25%
External failure	25%
Total costs	100%

Explain why the following industries might be inclined to have a spending pattern on quality costs that differs from the benchmark:
a. health care profession.
b. lawn fertilizer production.
c. rug and carpet production.
d. used car retailing.

PROBLEMS

32. *(Cost of quality)* Ornamental Lumber Company just completed its first year of operations. The company manufactures hardwood lampposts for the discriminating homeowner. The firm produced 3,000 lampposts during the year: 2,700 were eventually sold through regular market channels; 300 were so defective that they could not be economically reworked and sold through regular channels. At year end, there was no inventory of finished goods. For this first year, the firm spent $30,000 on prevention costs and $15,000 on quality appraisal. There were no customer returns. An income statement for the year follows.

Sales (regular channel)	$270,000	
(scrap)	12,000	$282,000
Cost of Goods Sold		
Original production costs	$150,000	
Rework costs	22,000	
Quality prevention and appraisal	45,000	217,000
Gross margin		$ 65,000
Selling and administrative expenses		90,000
(all fixed)		
Net loss		$ (25,000)

a. Compute the total profits lost by Ornamental Lumber Company in its first year of operations by selling defective units as scrap rather than selling the units through regular channels.
b. Compute the total failure costs for Ornamental Lumber Company in its first year.
c. Compute total quality costs incurred by Ornamental Lumber Company in its first year.
d. What evidence indicates the firm is dedicated to manufacturing and selling high-quality products?

33. *(Cost of quality)* Spandmar Winches manufactures winches used on offshore and coastal cruising sailboats to adjust (called sheeting) sail widths, heights, twists, etc. This is a demanding environment for winches because of the salt water, sun, and physical stress. Even so, the company is a recognized leader in the industry in the quality of its sailboat winches. In recent months, top managers have become more interested in trying to quantify the costs of quality in the company. As an initial effort, the company was able to identify the following 1994 costs, by category, that are associated with quality:

Prevention costs

Quality training	$15,000
Quality technology	50,000
Quality circles	32,000

Appraisal costs

Quality inspections	18,000
Test equipment	14,000
Procedure verifications	9,000

Internal failure costs

| Scrap and waste | 6,500 |
| Waste disposal | 2,100 |

External failure costs

| Warranty handling | 9,500 |
| Customer reimbursements/returns | 7,600 |

Managers were also aware that in 1994, 250 of the 8,000 winches that were produced had to be sold as scrap. These 250 winches were sold for $40 less profit per unit than "good" winches. Also, the company incurred rework costs amounting to $6,000 to sell 200 other winches through regular market channels.

Using the above data, find Spandmar's 1994 expense for:

a. lost profits from scrapping the 250 units.

b. total failure costs.

c. total quality costs.

d. Assume that the company is considering expanding its existing full 5-year warranty to a full 7-year warranty in 1995. How would such a change be reflected in quality costs?

ETHICS AND QUALITY DISCUSSION

34. By building quality into the process, rather than making quality inspections at the end of the process, certain job functions (such as many quality control inspectors) can be eliminated. Additionally, the installation of automated equipment to monitor product processing could eliminate some line worker jobs.

In a nation with fairly high unemployment, would employers attempting to implement valid quality improvements that resulted in employee terminations be appreciated or condemned? Discuss your answer from the standpoint of a variety of concerned constituencies—including the consumers who purchase the company's products.

35. Assume that you are in charge of a social service agency that provides counseling services to welfare families. The agency's costs have been increasing with no corresponding increase in funding. In an effort to implement some cost reductions, you implement the following ideas:

1. Counselors are empowered to make their own decisions about the legitimacy of all welfare claims.

2. To emphasize the concept of "do it right the first time," counselors are told not to review processed claims at a later date.

3. To discourage "out of control" conditions, an upper and lower control limit of 5 minutes is set on a standard 15-minute time for consultations.

Discuss the ethics as well as the positive and negative effects of each of the ideas listed.

36. *The National League of Cities reports that 85% of all U.S. municipalities have raised fees and taxes, or imposed new ones, during 1990. These will amount to another $10 billion annually. Even with all that new cash, 61% of city governments claim they won't have enough money in the kitty to pay their bills during 1991.*

   But state and local governments can be made to work. There are alternatives to the bulimic spend-and-trim cycles that have plagued them for decades. Look behind the headlines about fiscal crises and rising taxes, and you'll find a growing number of officials quietly embracing concepts that have transformed American industry over the past decade—quality, teamwork, outsourcing, and yes, customer service.

   [SOURCE: Ronald Henkoff, "Some Hope for Troubled Cities," *FORTUNE* (September 9, 1991), p. 121. © 1991 Time Inc. All rights reserved.]

   a. How does the concept of civil service for employees mesh with and/or deter the concept of TQM?

   b. What instances have you seen in your city or state in which fees or taxes were increased with no increase in service?

   c. What instances have you seen in your city or state in which fees or taxes were increased with equitable increases in service?

   d. Have there been instances in your city or state in which fees or taxes were reduced because of some governmental program? If so, describe the situation.

   e. What are the differences in the incentives offered to workers in private industry and in government to provide high-quality products and services?

37. *In 1991, Alcoa went through a major reorganization by reducing many senior management positions and splitting the company into more autonomous organizational units. However, while profits are up, so are customer complaints. "Customer rejections at Alcoa's main can-sheet plant are running 25% above [those in 1991], with customer satisfaction at one point falling below 50%. Virtually all of the unit's largest customers have complained of poor quality, and Alcoa has missed deliveries for the first time in years."*

   [SOURCE: Dana Milbank, "Restructured Alcoa Seeks to Juggle Cost and Quality," *Wall Street Journal* (August 24, 1992), p. B4. Reprinted by permission of the *Wall Street Journal*, © 1992 Dow Jones & Company, Inc. All rights reserved worldwide.]

   a. Alcoa has been pointed to as an example of how cost reductions can lower quality. What kinds of costs could be reduced in an organization that would almost automatically lower product/service quality? Why?

   b. If quality improvements create cost reductions, why would cost reductions not create quality improvements?

   c. Are there instances in which cost reductions would create quality improvements?

ALLOCATING INDIRECT COSTS

DEVELOPING PREDETERMINED OVERHEAD RATES

LEARNING OBJECTIVES

After completing this chapter, you should be able to answer these questions:

1. What are predetermined overhead rates and why are they computed?
2. How are the high-low method and least squares regression analysis used in analyzing mixed costs?
3. How are flexible budgets used by managers to set predetermined overhead rates?
4. How is under- or overapplied overhead treated at the end of a period?
5. What causes under- and overapplied overhead?
6. How does the capacity measure chosen to develop a predetermined overhead rate affect product cost?
7. How does activity-based costing differ from traditional overhead application methods?
8. *(Appendix)* Of what significance are the coefficients of correlation and determination and the standard error of the estimate?

INTRODUCING

MARKS & SPENCER

[M]arks & Spencer is to Britain what Wal-Mart is to the United States—one of the] world's great retailers. Like the U.S., Britain has been in the grip of a serious recession, but Marks & Spencer . . . netted 5 cents on the retail dollar, considerably better than Wal-Mart's excellent 4-cents-on-the-dollar net.

What's the formula? Keeping narrowly focused. M&S' 300 European stores carry a relatively limited range of merchandise, so buyers strive to get each offering just right. For instance, the women's department sells separates—blouses, skirts, blazers—allowing shoppers to make their own ensembles. All merchandise is the house St. Michael brand, be it detergent or a silk tie.

How does it cater to affluent customers buying designer-label clothing? Simple. If Armani's designs promise to sell, M&S buyers will order up Armani-esque cuts and sell them at a fraction of Armani prices.

"We're not a department store," explains Brian Godbold, the company's chief design executive, "and I don't intend to offer a lot of choices."

Credit cards? M&S doesn't take [any credit card except] its own, on which it currently levies up to a hefty 30% annual percentage interest rate. It does, however, give instant refunds for returned goods.

But the deeper secret to Marks & Spencer's success is its traditional way of working closely with its suppliers while constantly monitoring the British, and increasingly European and Asian, consumer's changing tastes.

As with apparel, M&S works like a senior partner with its food producers until it finds the right products. Small batches, perhaps 10,000 units, of a new food offering are shipped to M&S' busiest stores. Within a week the results are in. If a new item sells, it's shipped to other stores. If not, it's quickly dropped. M&S tests around 600 items a year this way.

SOURCE: John Marcom Jr., "Blue Blazers and Guacamole," *Forbes* (November 25, 1991), p. 64ff. Reprinted by permission of *FORBES* Magazine. © Forbes Inc., 1991.

In the past, a manufacturing company considered direct materials and direct labor as the prime costs of production; similarly, for a retailer such as Marks & Spencer, the primary costs were for inventory and sales salaries. Overhead was merely an "additional" cost that was necessary, but not exceptionally significant in either amount or treatment. Manufacturing firms, however, have often invested heavily in automation and retailers have been pressured by customers to provide more product variety. Both of these changes have significantly increased the amount of overhead costs incurred. This situation, coupled with the need to sell quality products at competitive prices, makes it necessary for businesses to understand what factors cause costs and to determine a reasonably accurate product cost.

A company must understand what is causing its costs to change in order to control those costs. Companies that are uninformed about the costs they incur to produce a product or perform a service are not likely to be able to make good management decisions. Sir Richard Greenbury, the Marks & Spencer chairman, understands that product variety is a prime contributor to overhead costs. For example, as the variety of product choices increases, more storage space needs to be acquired, more vendors need to be contacted and quality certified, and more people need to be available for restocking. Such reasons underlie why M & S limits the consumer's product choices and sells only house-label brands.

Regardless of the amount, overhead costs must be allocated to an organization's production or service activities for two reasons. First, generally accepted accounting principles require it to determine valuations for financial statements. The allocation of overhead is related to the cost principle, which requires that all costs of acquisition or production attach to the units purchased or produced (or the services rendered). Second and of equal, if not greater, importance, overhead allocation is necessary for managers to efficiently and effectively perform their functions of planning, controlling, and decision making. Traditionally, much of the information generated from satisfying the first purpose was used for the second purpose. It is not imperative that this occur; the focus of each purpose is different and different methods can provide different costs to better satisfy each purpose.

Predetermined overhead rate

Although actual overhead can be assigned to products or services, it is more common for companies to use estimated annual rates called **predetermined overhead rates.** To compute predetermined overhead rates, companies must first select a base on which to apply overhead to the products manufactured or services rendered. The base should be a cost driver that directly causes the incurrence of overhead costs. Since overhead consists of both variable and fixed costs, separate rates can be used for each type or a single overhead rate may be developed. If separate rates are used, the mixed overhead costs must be divided into their variable and fixed components.

This chapter discusses predetermined overhead rates, separation of mixed costs into variable and fixed elements, various capacity measures that can be used to compute predetermined overhead rates, and the use of non-traditional measures of activity for assigning overhead to products or services.

PREDETERMINED OVERHEAD RATES

Actual cost system

The three component elements of product cost incurred by a manufacturer are direct materials, direct labor, and overhead. In an **actual cost system,** actual direct materials and direct labor costs are accumulated in Work in Process Inventory as they are incurred. Actual overhead costs are accumulated separately in the Overhead Control account and are assigned to Work in Process Inventory at the end of a period. In this system, all cost elements are actual costs and no predetermined overhead rate is used.

Actual cost systems are usually less than desirable because they require that all overhead cost information be available before any cost assignment can be made to products or services. Using this type of system would mean that the cost of products and services produced, for example, in May could not be calculated until the May electricity bill was received in June.

Normal cost system

An alternative to an actual costing system is a **normal cost system,** which uses a predetermined overhead (OH) rate or rates to assign overhead cost to Work in Process Inventory. Like an actual cost system, a normal cost system uses actual costs of direct materials and direct labor. A predetermined overhead rate (or overhead application rate) is an estimated and constant charge per unit of activity that is used to assign overhead to the period's production or services quantity. It is calculated by dividing total budgeted overhead costs by a related level of volume or activity.

$$\text{Predetermined OH rate} = \frac{\text{Total budgeted overhead costs}}{\text{Total budgeted level of volume or activity}}$$

Companies should use an activity base that provides a logical relationship between the base and overhead cost incurrence. The activity base that probably first comes to mind is production volume, but this base is reasonable if only one type of product is

NEWS NOTE   ## Distorted Information Breeds Distorted Decisions

Managers in companies selling multiple products are making important decisions about pricing, product mix, and process technology based on distorted cost information. What's worse, alternative information rarely exists to alert these managers that product costs are badly flawed. Most companies detect the problem only after their competitiveness and profitability have deteriorated.

Distorted cost information is the result of sensible accounting choices made decades ago, when most companies manufactured a narrow range of products. Back then, the costs of direct labor and materials, the most important production factors, could be traced easily to individual products. Distortions from allocating factory and corporate overhead by burden rates on direct labor were minor. And the expense of collecting and processing data made it hard to justify more sophisticated allocation of these and other indirect costs.

Today, product lines and marketing channels have proliferated. Direct labor now represents a small fraction of corporate costs, while expenses covering factory support operations, marketing, distribution, engineering, and other overhead functions have exploded. But most companies still allocate these rising overhead and support costs by their diminishing direct labor base or, as with marketing and distribution costs, not at all.

These simplistic approaches are no longer justifiable—especially given the plummeting costs of information technology. They can also be dangerous. Intensified global competition and radically new production technologies have made accurate product cost information crucial to competitive success.

SOURCE: Reprinted by permission of *Harvard Business Review*. An excerpt from "Measure Costs Right: Make the Right Decisions," by Robin Cooper and Robert S. Kaplan (September–October 1988), p. 96. Copyright © 1988 by the President and Fellows of Harvard College; all rights reserved.

manufactured or one type of service is rendered. If multiple products or services exist, a summation cannot be made to determine the activity that occurred because of the heterogeneous nature of the items.

The concept of homogeneity underlies all cost allocation. A measure of activity must be determined that is common to all output to allocate overhead to heterogeneous products. Direct labor hours and direct labor dollars have been the most commonly used measures of activity; however, as discussed in the News Note on distorted information, the flaws in these bases are becoming more apparent as companies become increasingly automated and managers are made more aware of potential product cost distortions. Using direct labor to allocate overhead costs in automated plants results in extremely high overhead rates because the costs are applied over a smaller number of labor hours (or dollars). When automated plants allocate overhead on the basis of labor, managers sometimes conclude that reductions in labor will cause reductions in overhead costs. Such a conclusion is erroneous. The overhead charge is high because labor is low; reducing labor more simply increases the overhead rate! In automated plants, machine hours are probably more appropriate for allocating overhead than either direct labor base.

Other traditional volume measures include number of purchase orders and product-related physical measures such as tons or gallons. Innovative new measures for overhead allocation include activities such as number or time of machine setups, number of parts, material handling time, and quantity of product defects. Use of such nontraditional measures of activity to allocate overhead and the resultant activity-based costs are briefly discussed later in this chapter and more thoroughly in Chapter 5.

Overhead costs and the related activity measure are typically estimated for one year. "An annual period is appropriate for the predetermination of overhead rates unless the production/marketing cycle of the entity is such that the use of a longer or shorter period would clearly provide more useful information."[1] For example, the use of a longer period of time would be appropriate in a company engaged in activities such as constructing ships or high-rise office buildings.

There are three primary reasons for using predetermined overhead rates rather than actual overhead costs for product costing. First, a predetermined overhead rate allows overhead to be assigned to the goods produced or services rendered during the period. If actual overhead is to be assigned to products or services, all indirect production costs must be available before any allocations can be made. The total indirect costs cannot be determined until all overhead transactions of the period have occurred. Thus, use of a predetermined overhead rate increases the availability of timely (though less precise) information for use in planning, controlling, and decision making.

A second reason to use predetermined overhead rates is that they can compensate for fluctuations in actual overhead costs that are unrelated to activity levels. Overhead may vary on a monthly basis because of seasonal or calendar factors. For example, factory utility costs may be higher in the summer than at other times of the year. If production were constant each month and actual overhead were assigned to production, the increase in utilities would cause product cost per unit to be greater during the summer months than in other months.

Assume that Cambridge Cloaks makes woolen garments for Marks & Spencer. The company has total overhead costs of £68,000 per month, excluding maintenance. Maintenance costs for two months (April and July) are £2,000 and £2,600, respectively. Assume that the company has defined activity as units of production and produces 20,000 units in each of these months. The actual overhead cost per unit is calculated below.

	April	**July**
$\dfrac{\text{Actual Overhead}}{\text{Actual Production}}$	$\dfrac{£70,000}{20,000} = £3.50$ per unit	$\dfrac{£70,600}{20,000} = £3.53$ per unit

The £.03 cost differential between these two months is related solely to the £600 difference in the numerators. While this particular difference may not be significant, numerous differences of this type could cause a large distortion in unit cost.

The third reason for using predetermined overhead rates is that they can overcome the problem of fluctuations in activity levels that have no impact on actual fixed overhead costs. Activity may vary because of seasonal or monthly calendar differences, including holiday periods. Even if total overhead costs were equal each period, changes in activity would cause a per unit change in cost because of the fixed cost element of overhead.

Of the £68,000 of total overhead costs for Cambridge Cloaks, £30,000 is fixed. If the company produces 20,000 and 24,000 units in February and March, respectively, actual fixed overhead per unit decreases by £.25 from February to March, as shown below.

	February	**March**
$\dfrac{\text{Actual Fixed Overhead}}{\text{Actual Production}}$	$\dfrac{£30,000}{20,000} = £1.50$ per unit	$\dfrac{£30,000}{24,000} = £1.25$ per unit

Fixed and variable overhead costs behave differently with changes in activity. Fixed overhead cost per unit changes inversely with changes in the level of activity. It is important to realize that *only* fixed overhead creates this fluctuation in cost. Total

---

[1] Institute of Management Accountants (formerly National Association of Accountants), *Statements on Management Accounting: Accounting for Indirect Production Costs*, Number 2G (Montvale, N.J.: NAA, June 1, 1987), p. 11.

variable overhead costs rise in direct proportion to increases in production levels, but the per unit variable cost does not change. Thus, if a company has any mixed costs in its overhead cost structure, the first step in developing a predetermined overhead rate is to separate those costs into their fixed and variable elements.

SEPARATING MIXED COSTS

As discussed in Chapter 2, accountants assume that costs are linear rather than curvilinear. Because of this assumption, the general formula for a straight line can be used to describe any type of cost within a relevant range of activity. The straight line formula is:

$$y = a + bX$$

where y = total cost (dependent variable)
    a = fixed portion of total cost
    b = variable portion of total cost (the rate at which total cost changes in relation to changes in X; when a graph is prepared to depict the straight line, b represents the slope of the line)
    X = activity base to which y is being related (the predictor or independent variable)

The use of this formula for each type of cost behavior is shown in Exhibit 4–1. Since a mixed cost contains amounts for both the fixed and variable values, some method

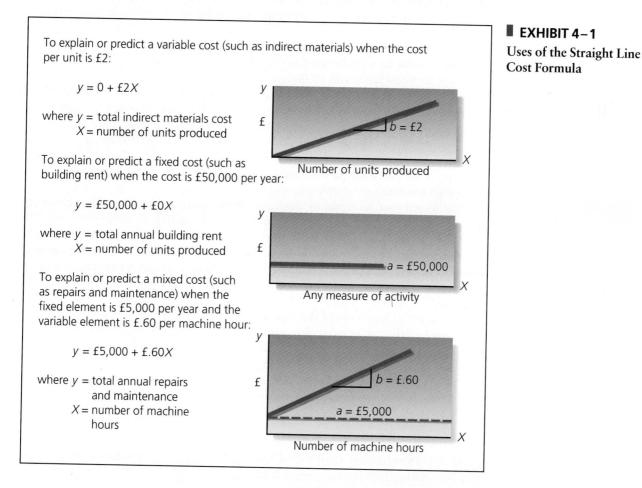

To explain or predict a variable cost (such as indirect materials) when the cost per unit is £2:

$$y = 0 + £2X$$

where y = total indirect materials cost
    X = number of units produced

To explain or predict a fixed cost (such as building rent) when the cost is £50,000 per year:

$$y = £50,000 + £0X$$

where y = total annual building rent
    X = number of units produced

To explain or predict a mixed cost (such as repairs and maintenance) when the fixed element is £5,000 per year and the variable element is £.60 per machine hour:

$$y = £5,000 + £.60X$$

where y = total annual repairs and maintenance
    X = number of machine hours

■ EXHIBIT 4–1

Uses of the Straight Line Cost Formula

must be used to separate the mixed cost into its two component elements. The simplest method to use is the **high-low method**.

High-Low Method

The high-low method is a device for analyzing mixed costs by selecting actual observations of a mixed cost at two levels of activity and calculating the change in both activity and cost. The observations selected are the highest and lowest activity levels *if these levels are within the relevant range*. Since activities cause costs to change rather than the inverse relationship, the selections of "high" and "low" are made on the basis of activity levels rather than costs. The changes in activity and cost are determined by subtracting the low values from the high values. These changes are then used to calculate the b (variable cost) value in the $y = a + bX$ formula as follows:

$$b = \frac{\text{Cost at High Activity Level} - \text{Cost at Low Activity Level}}{\text{High Activity Level} - \text{Low Activity Level}}$$

$$b = \frac{\text{Change in the Total Cost}}{\text{Change in Activity Level}}$$

The b value is the unit variable cost per measure of activity. This value is multiplied by the activity level to determine the amount of total variable cost contained in total cost at either level of activity.

Since total variable cost plus total fixed cost is equal to total mixed cost, the fixed portion of a mixed cost is found by subtracting total variable cost from total cost. This process can be shown as an adaptation of the straight-line formula: $a = y - bX$. Either the high or low level of machine hours can be used to determine the fixed portion of a mixed cost because fixed cost is constant at all activity levels within the relevant range.

These computations are illustrated in Exhibit 4–2 using machine hours and utility cost information for Cambridge Cloaks. The company's normal operating range of activity is between 3,000 and 10,000 machine hours. Occasionally, a company operates at a level of activity outside its relevant range (a rush special order may be taken that requires excess labor or machine time) or there may be distortions of normal cost within the relevant range (a leak in a water pipe goes unnoticed for a period of time). Such nonrepresentative or abnormal observations are called **outliers** and should be disregarded in analyzing a mixed cost. For Cambridge Cloaks, the March observation is an outlier (substantially in excess of normal activity levels) and should not be used in the high-low analysis of utility cost.

Total mixed cost increases or decreases with changes in activity. The change in cost is equal to the change in activity times the unit variable cost; the fixed cost element does not fluctuate because of changes in activity. Therefore, any increase or decrease in total cost is because of the increase or decrease in the independent variable. The variable cost per unit of activity reflects the *average* change in unit cost over the relevant range of activity. For Cambridge Cloaks, this average is £.03 per machine hour used.

One potential weakness of the high-low method is that outliers may be inadvertently used in the calculation. Any estimates of future costs calculated from a line drawn between two such points will not be indicative of actual costs and probably are not good predictors. A second weakness of high-low is that it only considers two data points even after any outliers are eliminated. A more precise method of analyzing mixed costs is **least squares regression analysis**.

Least Squares Regression Analysis

Least squares regression analysis is a statistical technique that analyzes the association (or relationship) between dependent and independent variables. This process is

EXHIBIT 4–2
Cambridge Cloaks'
Analysis of Mixed Cost

The following machine hours and utility cost information is available:

MONTH	LEVEL OF ACTIVITY IN MACHINE HOURS	UTILITY COST
January	4,000	£160
February	9,000	320
March	15,000	420 (Outlier)
April	4,600	175
May	3,000	140
June	8,620	320
July	5,280	210
August	5,000	208

Step 1: Select the highest and lowest levels of activity within the relevant range and obtain the costs associated with those levels. These levels and costs are 9,000 and 3,000 hours and £320 and £140, respectively.

Step 2: Calculate the change in cost compared to the change in activity:

	MACHINE HOURS	ASSOCIATED TOTAL COST
High activity	9,000	£320
Low activity	3,000	140
Changes	6,000	£180

Step 3: Determine the relationship of cost change to activity change to find the variable cost element:

$$b = £180 \div 6,000 \text{ MH} = £.03 \text{ per machine hour}$$

Step 4: Compute total variable cost (TVC) at either level of activity:

High level of activity: TVC = £.03(9,000) = £270
Low level of activity: TVC = £.03(3,000) = £ 90

Step 5: Subtract total variable cost from total cost at either level of activity to determine fixed cost:

High level of activity: a = £320 − £270 = £50
Low level of activity: a = £140 − £ 90 = £50

Step 6: Substitute the fixed and variable cost values in the straight-line formula to get an equation that can be used to estimate total cost at any level of activity within the relevant range:

$$y = £50 + \$.03X$$

where X = machine hours.

used to develop an equation that predicts an unknown value of a **dependent variable** (cost) from the known values of one or more **independent variables** (activity). When multiple independent variables exist, least squares regression also helps to select the independent variable that is the best predictor of the dependent variable. For example, least squares can be used by managers trying to decide if machine hours, direct labor hours, or velocity of throughput best explains and predicts changes in total overhead costs.

Dependent variable
Independent variable

Simple regression
Multiple regression

Regression line

Simple regression analysis uses one independent variable to predict the dependent variable. In **multiple regression**, two or more independent variables are used to predict the dependent variable. All examples in this chapter use simple regression and assume that a linear relationship exists between variables so that each one-unit change in the independent variable produces a constant unit change in the dependent variable.[2]

Observations are made and a technique known as the method of least squares is used to mathematically fit the best possible **regression line** to observed data points. [Technically, a regression line is any line that goes through the means (or averages) of the independent and dependent variables in a set of observations.] Simple linear regression uses the $y = a + bX$ formula for a straight line. For any set of observations, numerous straight lines could be drawn through the data set. However, of the many lines that could be drawn, most would provide a poor fit. The purpose of least squares regression analysis is to find the line of "best fit" for the observed data.

This line is found by predicting the a and b values in a straight line formula using the actual activity and cost values from the observations. (Actual cost values are designated as y values.) The equations necessary to compute b and a values using the method of least squares are as follows:[3]

$$b = \frac{\Sigma xy - n(\bar{x})(\bar{y})}{\Sigma x^2 - n\bar{x}^2}$$

$$a = \bar{y} - b\bar{x}$$

where $\bar{x}$ = mean of the independent variable
$\bar{y}$ = mean of the dependent variable
n = number of observations

Using the Cambridge Cloaks' data, the following calculations can be made:

x	y	xy	x^2
4,000	£ 160	£ 640,000	16,000,000
9,000	320	2,880,000	81,000,000
4,600	175	805,000	21,160,000
3,000	140	420,000	9,000,000
8,620	320	2,758,400	74,304,400
5,280	210	1,108,800	27,878,400
5,000	208	1,040,000	25,000,000
39,500	£1,533	£9,652,200	254,342,800

The mean of x ($\bar{x}$) is 5,642.86 (39,500 ÷ 7) and the mean of y ($\bar{y}$) is £219 (£1,533 ÷ 7). Thus,

$$b = \frac{£9,652,200 - 7(5,642.86)(£219)}{254,342,800 - 7(5,642.86)(5,642.86)}$$

$$= \frac{£1,001,695.62}{31,449,717.14} = £.032$$

$$a = £219 - £.032(5,642.86) = £38.43$$

---

[2] Curvilinear relationships between variables also exist. An example of a curvilinear relationship is that quality defects (dependent variable) tend to increase at an increasing rate in relationship to age of machinery (independent variable). However, since linear relationships are easier to model and more commonly used, this chapter is concerned only with them.
[3] These equations are derived from mathematical computations beyond the scope of this text, but which are found in many statistics books. The symbol Σ means "the summation of."

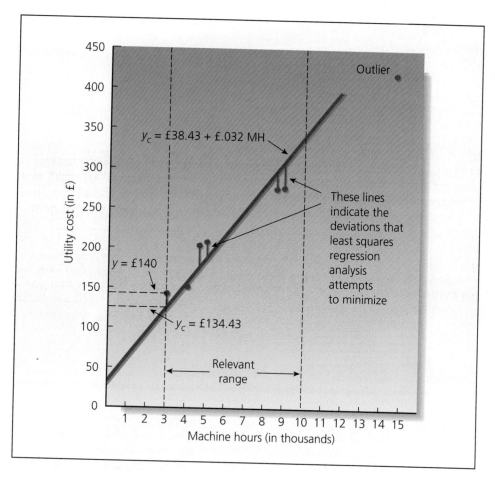

The b (variable cost) and a (fixed cost) values for Cambridge Cloaks' utility costs are £.032 and £38.43, respectively.

Using these a and b values, costs can be predicted for each of the actual activity levels. These computed values are designated as y_c values. The line that is drawn through all of the y_c values will be the line of best fit for the data. Because actual costs do not generally fall directly on the regression line and predicted costs naturally do, there are differences (or deviations) between these two costs at their related activity levels. Although the regression line may not pass through any or all of the actual observation points, this is acceptable because the line has been determined to mathematically "fit" the data.

Exhibit 4–3 illustrates the utility cost and activity level data points for Cambridge Cloaks as they would be plotted on a **scattergraph**. The actual costs (y) are shown as dots on the graph; the predicted costs (y_c) are points on the regression line itself and are therefore not visible. The vertical line segments from the observation points to the regression line in Exhibit 4–3 are deviations between actual and predicted cost amounts. The amount of a deviation is determined by subtracting the y_c value at a specific activity level from the related y value. Deviations above the regression line are positive amounts; deviations below the line are negative. The line of best fit is the least squares regression because it minimizes the sum of the squares of the vertical deviations between the actual observation points and the predicted points on the regression line. Minimizing the sum of the *squared* deviations eliminates the problem of having both positive and negative differences for (y − y_c).

The use of either high-low or regression analysis provides the information needed to separate the variable and fixed cost elements of each mixed cost. Each of these two methods provides a way to predict (within the relevant range) the value of one vari-

Scattergraph

By carrying only a store brand, Marks & Spencer eliminates the numerous overhead costs associated with having a wide selection of products. In addition, Marks & Spencer can make certain that the products stocked are of the quality desired.

able by using values of another variable. Traditional measures of activity include direct labor hours and machine hours; however, some other measures may be more appropriate. Neither high-low nor regression analysis indicates how well the known independent variable is suited to predicting the unknown, dependent variable. Deciding how strongly variables are related requires the use of correlation analysis, which is discussed in the appendix to this chapter.

USING FLEXIBLE BUDGETS IN SETTING PREDETERMINED OVERHEAD RATES

Budget
Flexible budget

Before a predetermined overhead rate can be calculated, estimates are needed for total overhead costs at various levels of activity. Such estimates are usually available in a **budget**, which represents a financial plan for the future. Most budgets are prepared at a single level of activity, but a **flexible budget** is a series of budgets that present costs at different levels of activity. In a flexible budget, all costs are treated as either variable or fixed; thus, this presentation requires that mixed costs be separated into their variable and fixed component elements using one of the previously discussed methods.

Flexible budgets can be prepared for product or period costs and detail the individual cost factors composing the total cost. Cost estimates should consider the potential effects of inflation or other factors that could cause costs to change in the future. The activity levels shown on a flexible budget usually cover management's contemplated range of activity for the budgetary period. If all levels of activity are within the relevant range, costs at each successive level should equal the previous level plus a uniform monetary increment for each variable cost factor. The increment is equal to variable cost per unit of activity times the quantity of additional activity.

In some situations a particular fixed cost component increases as activity increases within the contemplated range. Such an increase may occur because the fixed cost is a step fixed cost, which fluctuates in total with large changes in activity levels. For example, supervision may be a step fixed cost. One supervisor may be able to manage 10 employees who can produce 5,000 units during a month; if 5,001 to 10,000 units need to be produced each month, additional employees would be required, as would an additional supervisor. The increased need for supervisors causes total fixed supervision costs to increase by a "step."

Here we will temporarily depart from the Cambridge Cloaks series of examples to demonstrate two special topics: the use of cost formulas in preparing flexible budgets and the flexible budget effects of changes in step costs. We will use a subsidiary of Cambridge Cloaks, known as Essex Weavers, to demonstrate these topics. The subsidiary's contemplated range is between 8,000 and 14,000 machine hours. Analyzing the individual overhead cost factors has provided the Essex Weavers cost accountant with the information presented in Exhibit 4–4. This exhibit shows all cost factors in terms of the a (fixed) and b (variable) values of the straight-line formula.

Such detail can be summed and restated as a total cost flexible budget formula that would allow computation of total costs at all activity levels within the relevant range. Essex Weavers, though, needs two flexible budget formulas since the analysis indicates the existence of "steps" in the fixed costs. Supervision and machine setup costs both contain "steps" at an activity level of 12,000 machine hours. Supervision costs increase by £2,500 at that level; machine setup costs increase £500. The two flexible budget formulas for Essex Weavers are given at the bottom of Exhibit 4–4.

EXHIBIT 4–4

Essex Weavers Analysis of Manufacturing Overhead Costs

(Formula Presentation Based on Machine Hours)

	a = Total Fixed Cost	b = Variable Cost Per Unit
Purely Variable Costs		
Indirect labor:		
Support workers		£ .22
Idle time		.02
Fringe benefits		.03
Indirect materials		.15
Total purely variable		£ .42
Purely Fixed Costs		
Indirect labor:		
Supervision (X < 12,000 hours)	£5,200*	
Machine setup (X < 12,000 hours)	400**	
Depreciation	350	
Insurance	200	
Total purely fixed (8,000 ≤ X < 12,000)	£6,150	
Mixed***		
Utilities	50	.03
Maintenance	900	.05
Totals for Flexible Budget Formula (for X < 12,000 machine hours)	£7,100	£ .50

* Supervision is expected to be £7,700 when X ≥ 12,000.
** Machine setup is expected to be £900 when X ≥ 12,000.
*** The a and b values may be determined using the high-low method or least squares regression discussed in the previous section.

Flexible Budget Formulas (where y = total manufacturing overhead):

If X < 12,000 MH: y = £ 7,100 + £.50MH
If X ≥ 12,000 MH: y = £10,100 + £.50MH

EXHIBIT 4–5
Essex Weavers' Variable and Fixed Overhead Flexible Budget

	Machine Hours			
	8,000	10,000	12,000	14,000
Variable Costs				
Indirect labor:				
Support workers (@ £.22)	£ 1,760	£ 2,200	£ 2,640	£ 3,080
Idle time (@ £.02)	160	200	240	280
Fringe benefits (@ £.03)	240	300	360	420
Indirect materials (@ £.15)	1,200	1,500	1,800	2,100
Utilities (@ £.03)	240	300	360	420
Maintenance (@ £.05)	400	500	600	700
Total variable cost	£ 4,000	£ 5,000	£ 6,000	£ 7,000
Variable cost per hour	£.50	£.50	£.50	£.50
Fixed Costs				
Indirect labor:				
Supervision	£ 5,200	£ 5,200	£ 7,700	£ 7,700
Machine setup	400	400	900	900
Depreciation	350	350	350	350
Insurance	200	200	200	200
Utilities	50	50	50	50
Maintenance	900	900	900	900
Total fixed costs	£ 7,100	£ 7,100	£10,100	£10,100
Fixed cost per hour	£.89	£.71	£.84	£.72
Total cost	£11,100	£12,100	£16,100	£17,100
Total cost per hour	£1.39	£1.21	£1.34	£1.22

Using the flexible budget formulas in Exhibit 4–4, Essex Weavers' cost accountant has prepared the subsidiary's 1994 flexible budget for overhead costs (Exhibit 4–5). Constructing a flexible budget is a good method of seeing any "steps" that exist for the categories of expected costs. Exhibit 4–5 also illustrates the stable behavior of variable cost per machine hour compared to the irregular behavior of fixed cost per machine hour.

Two factors cause the irregular behavior in the company's fixed cost per hour: a change in activity level and the steps in the fixed costs. As machine hours (the activity base) increase, fixed cost per machine hour (MH) *should* decrease, assuming total fixed cost does not change. However, at Essex Weavers, total fixed cost increases by £3,000 at 12,000 MHs. Such irregular behavior of fixed cost per unit necessitates that one specific level be chosen to calculate a predetermined fixed overhead rate per unit for product costing purposes. The remainder of the chapter returns to using Cambridge Cloaks or departments within that company as a basis for examples and illustrations of the material.

DEVELOPING AND USING PREDETERMINED OVERHEAD RATES

Companies wishing to compute a single predetermined overhead rate in individual departments would begin with the information on total overhead costs shown in the flexible budget. As mentioned above, one particular expected activity level must be specified because of the behavior of fixed, rather than variable, costs. Total budgeted overhead costs at the expected activity level are divided by the expected activity level to derive a single departmental overhead application rate.

A flexible overhead budget for the Finishing Department of Cambridge Cloaks is presented in Exhibit 4–6. Using this information and assuming that management has designated 80,000 machine hours as its expected activity level, the predetermined overhead rate is shown in the exhibit as £3.24 per machine hour. For each machine hour used in 1994, Cambridge Cloaks' Finishing Department Work in Process Inventory account will be charged with £3.24 of overhead. The journal entry to record the incurrence of 1,000 hours of machine time in the Finishing Department is:

Work in Process Inventory (Finishing Department)	3,240	
Manufacturing Overhead (Finishing Department)		3,240

Since most companies produce many different kinds of products, calculation of a plantwide overhead rate generally does not provide useful information. For example, while machine hours may be the most appropriate activity base in a department that is highly automated, direct labor hours (DLH) may be the best basis for assigning overhead in a labor-intensive department. In the quality control area, number of defects may provide the best allocation base. Thus, because there is more likely to be homogeneity within a department than among departments, separate departmental rates are generally thought to provide more useful information than plantwide rates to managers for their various planning, controlling, and decision making needs. Computing departmental rates allows each department to select the most appropriate measure of activity (or cost driver) relative to its operations.

Exhibit 4–7 presents some additional information about Cambridge Cloaks to illustrate the differing results obtained by using departmental and plantwide overhead rates. In addition to the Finishing Department, Cambridge Cloaks has an Assembly

EXHIBIT 4–6
Cambridge Cloaks—Finishing Department 1994 Flexible Budget

	Machine Hours			
	60,000	70,000	80,000	90,000
Variable Costs				
Indirect labor	£ 54,000	£ 63,000	£ 72,000	£ 81,000
Indirect materials	26,400	30,800	35,200	39,600
Variable portion of mixed costs	42,000	49,000	56,000	63,000
Total variable cost	£122,400	£142,800	£163,200	£183,600
Variable cost per hour	£2.04	£2.04	£2.04	£2.04
Fixed Costs				
Rent	£ 12,500	£ 12,500	£ 12,500	£ 12,500
Depreciation	20,000	20,000	20,000	20,000
Supervisor salaries	40,000	40,000	40,000	40,000
Insurance	2,500	2,500	3,500	3,500
Taxes	8,000	8,000	8,000	8,000
Fixed portion of mixed costs	12,000	12,000	12,000	12,000
Total fixed costs	£ 95,000	£ 95,000	£ 96,000	£ 96,000
Fixed cost per hour	£1.58	£1.36	£1.20	£1.07
Total cost	£217,400	£237,800	£259,200	£279,600
Total cost per hour	£3.62	£3.40	£3.24	£3.11

Department in which work is performed by unskilled laborers. Two of the company's products are Cloak #328 and Cloak #576. Cloak #328 requires 5 direct labor hours in Assembly and 2 machine hours in Finishing; Cloak #576 requires 2 direct labor hours in Assembly and 3 machine hours in Finishing. Total budgeted overhead for the Assembly Department is £299,800; Finishing has a £259,200 overhead budget. Departmental and plantwide rate computations are shown in Exhibit 4–7; product overhead application amounts for the two products are also given.

Note the significant difference in the overhead applied to each product using departmental versus plantwide rates. If departmental rates are used, product cost more clearly reflects the different amounts and types of machine/labor work performed on the two products. If a plantwide rate is used, essentially each product only absorbs overhead from a single department—from Assembly if direct labor hours are used and from Finishing if machine hours are used. Use of either plantwide rate ignores the lack of similarity of the work performed in each of the two departments.

Determination of valid unit costs is important because managers must decide whether a "reasonable" profit margin is being made on the goods sold. Although some companies making unique products or having the ability to influence the market can set selling prices, most companies are price takers rather than price makers. Thus, cost may not be a factor in determining selling price, but it is essential in determining profit. If plantwide overhead rates distort product cost, the computed profit on the product may be inaccurate. Assigning too much overhead to a product may make it appear as if the product is not profitable or, perhaps, is less profitable than others. Conversely, assigning too little overhead may make the product appear more profitable than it really is. In either case, using invalid costs may cause management to make invalid decisions.

Assume in the case of Cambridge Cloaks that direct materials and direct labor costs for Cloak #328 are £30 and £11, respectively. Adding these prime costs to the

EXHIBIT 4–7

Cambridge Cloaks'
Departmental versus
Plantwide Overhead Rates

	Assembly	Finishing
Budgeted annual overhead	£299,800	£259,200
Budgeted annual direct labor hours (DLH)	40,000	10,000
Budgeted annual machine hours (MH)	6,000	80,000

Departmental overhead rates:
Assembly (manual):   £299,800 ÷ 40,000 = £7.495 per DLH
Finishing (automated):   259,200 ÷ 80,000 = £3.240 per MH

Total plantwide overhead = £299,800 + £259,200 = £559,000
Plantwide overhead rate (using DLH): (£559,000 ÷ 50,000 = £11.18)
Plantwide overhead rate (using MH): (£559,000 ÷ 86,000 = £6.50)

	To Cloak #328	To Cloak #576
Overhead assigned:		
using departmental rates:		
Assembly	5(£7.495) = £37.48	2(£7.495) = £14.99
Finishing	2(£3.240) = 6.48	3(£3.240) = 9.72
Total	£43.96	£24.71
using plantwide rate:		
based on DLH	5(£11.18) = £55.90	2(£11.18) = £22.36
based on MH	2(£6.50) = £13.00	3(£6.50) = £19.50

	Departmental Rates	Plantwide Rate (DLH)	Plantwide Rate (MH)
Direct materials	£30.00	£30.00	£30.00
Direct labor	11.00	11.00	11.00
Overhead	43.96	55.90	13.00
Total cost	£84.96	£96.90	£54.00
Selling price	£95.00	£95.00	£95.00
Profit (loss)	£10.04	£(1.90)	£41.00
Rate of profit	10.6%	N/A	43.2%

EXHIBIT 4–8

Cambridge Cloaks Total Product Cost and Profits for Cloak #328

overhead computed under each method in Exhibit 4–7 gives total product cost. Exhibit 4–8 provides these product costs and the profit or loss that would be indicated if Cloak #328 has a normal market selling price of £95.

Use of the product costs developed from plantwide rates could cause Cambridge Cloaks' management to make erroneous decisions about Cloak #328. If the cost figure developed from a plantwide direct labor hour basis is used, management may believe that this product should be discontinued because it is generating a loss per unit. If the cost figure developed from a plantwide machine hour basis is used, management may think that this cloak is substantially more successful than it actually is. Such a decision could cause resources to be diverted from other products. Assuming that direct labor hours and machine hours are the best possible allocation bases for Assembly and Finishing, respectively, the only cost that gives management the necessary information upon which to make resource allocation and product development/ elimination decisions is the one produced by using the departmental overhead rates.

Many studies of overhead rates show that companies may not be using the most effective methods to develop those rates. While some companies are still using plantwide overhead application rates, most companies have recognized the benefits of using departmental rates and have begun using them. Even at the departmental level, however, a single total overhead rate tends to reduce the applicability and informational content of the allocations. Therefore, to focus attention on the fact that variable and fixed overhead costs behave differently and generally result from different causal factors, separate application rates for variable and fixed overhead are encouraged.

Either combined or separate overhead rates are effective for the purpose of assigning overhead costs to products. Each method provides a rational and systematic manner of costing products for external financial statement preparation.

Combined overhead accounts and rates are traditional in businesses for three reasons. Combined accounts and rates result in clerical ease, cost savings, and elimination of the need to separate overhead costs by cost behavior. There are two primary disadvantages of combined rates. First, the specific information needed by managers to perform their functions exists only on a limited basis. The lack of detail results in managers having a smaller information base on which to plan operations, control costs, and make decisions. Second, cause and effect relationships between costs and

SEPARATE VARIABLE AND FIXED OVERHEAD APPLICATION RATES

activity are blurred when combined rates are used. This factor may contribute to an inability to reduce costs or improve productivity. Although clerical cost savings may result from the use of a combined rate, we believe that the ultimate cost of poor information is significantly greater than the savings generated. As indicated in the News Note on lack of information, a primary disadvantage of using a single overhead rate is the lack of the ability to understand cost behavior. Thus, separate overhead rates (and the related separate accounts) provide more refined information than does a combined rate for the internal management purposes of planning, controlling, and decision making, in addition to producing better product costs.

The first step in computing separate variable and fixed predetermined overhead rates is to examine the flexible budget for the behavior of each cost item incurred by the department. Costs are either variable, fixed, or mixed. (Exhibit 4–9 illustrates the results of a survey on the types of cost behavior of various categories of costs.) Mixed costs must be separated into their variable and fixed components before separate variable and fixed overhead rates can be calculated using one of the techniques discussed earlier in the chapter.

Variable Overhead Rate

Variable overhead changes in total proportionately with some measure of volume or activity. It includes indirect materials, variable indirect labor costs, and the variable portion of any mixed cost. Separate predetermined overhead rates should be computed for each variable overhead component. Total cost for each element is divided by the level of activity on which the estimate was based. All individual rates are summed to find the total predetermined variable overhead rate.

Since variable overhead is assumed to be constant per unit at any level of activity within the relevant range, the level of activity chosen to estimate total cost is not important. For example, as shown in Exhibit 4–6, Cambridge Cloaks estimates that at a production level of 80,000 machine hours, £35,200 of cost will be incurred for indirect materials in the Finishing Department. This estimate gives a predetermined variable overhead rate for indirect materials of £.44 per hour (£35,200 ÷ 80,000). Correspondingly, if indirect materials cost is truly variable, Cambridge Cloaks would estimate a total cost of £36,080 for 82,000 machine hours or the same £.44 per unit.

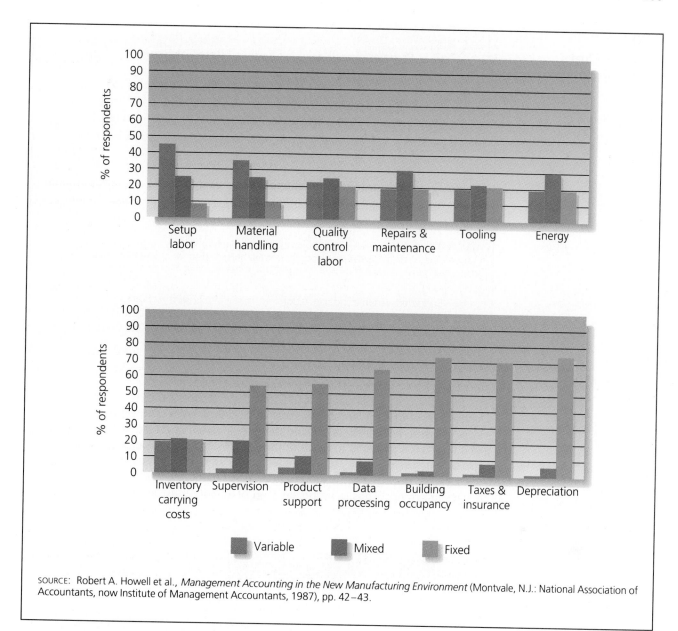

Variable ▪ Mixed ▪ Fixed

SOURCE: Robert A. Howell et al., *Management Accounting in the New Manufacturing Environment* (Montvale, N.J.: National Association of Accountants, now Institute of Management Accountants, 1987), pp. 42–43.

▪ **EXHIBIT 4–9**
Cost Behavior by Category

The predetermined rate is used to apply overhead to Work in Process Inventory based on the actual quantity of the activity base. The variable cost information for Cambridge Cloaks given in Exhibit 4–6 is used in Exhibit 4–10 on page 136 to illustrate the computation of the variable overhead application rate using a machine hour (MH) basis in the Finishing Department. Computation of the predetermined rate is made near the end of 1993, using budgeted variable overhead costs and machine hours for 1994. Predetermined overhead calculations are always made in advance of the year of application.

Fixed Overhead Rate

Fixed overhead is that portion of total overhead that remains constant in total with changes in activity in the relevant range. As indicated in Exhibit 4–6 for the Finishing

---

Predetermined Variable Overhead Rate Calculation

Step 1. Determine budgeted total cost of each component at a selected level of activity. Total these cost components to find total budgeted variable overhead:

Total budgeted variable cost at 80,000 MHs (from Exhibit 4–6): £163,200

Step 2. Divide the total budgeted variable overhead cost by the selected level of activity to find the total predetermined variable overhead rate:

$$\frac{\text{Total budgeted variable overhead cost at 80,000 machine hours}}{80,000 \text{ machine hours}} = \frac{£163,200}{80,000} = £2.04 \text{ per MH}$$

NOTE: While the above computation produces the information necessary for product costing, it does not provide the detail needed by managers. For example, to plan for or control variable overhead costs, managers would need the individual element costs per unit of activity shown below.

Budgeted variable indirect labor	£72,000 ÷ 80,000 = £.90
Budgeted indirect materials	£35,200 ÷ 80,000 = £.44
Budgeted variable portion of mixed costs	£56,000 ÷ 80,000 = £.70

Department of Cambridge Cloaks, fixed overhead includes rent, depreciation, supervisors' salaries, insurance, taxes, and the fixed portion of mixed factory costs. Budgeted figures are gathered for each of the fixed overhead costs and summed to comprise the numerator of the predetermined overhead rate calculation.

Since fixed overhead is constant in total, it varies inversely on a per unit basis with changes in activity. Thus, a particular level of activity must be specified to calculate

Open air markets (such as this one at London's Hyde Park) allow merchants to eliminate the many fixed overhead costs associated with capital facilities—depreciation or rent, utilities, property taxes and so forth.

Predetermined Fixed Overhead Rate Calculation

Budgeted fixed overhead costs for 1994:

Rent	£12,500
Straight-line depreciation on factory	20,000
Supervisor salaries	40,000
Insurance	3,500
Taxes	8,000
Fixed portion of mixed costs	12,000
Total budgeted fixed costs	£96,000

$$\frac{\text{Total budgeted fixed overhead cost at 80,000 machine hours}}{\text{Expected capacity in MHs}} = \frac{£96,000}{80,000}$$

$$= £1.20 \text{ per MH}$$

EXHIBIT 4–11
Cambridge Cloaks'
Finishing Department

the predetermined fixed overhead rate per unit of activity. This activity level is normally the firm's expected annual capacity. **Capacity** refers to a measure of production volume or some other activity base.[4]

To continue the Cambridge Cloaks example, the fixed overhead costs shown in Exhibit 4–6 are used to calculate a predetermined fixed overhead rate for the Finishing Department in Exhibit 4–11. Total budgeted fixed overhead for 1994 is £96,000; expected capacity is 80,000 machine hours. Using these figures, the predetermined fixed overhead rate is £1.20 per machine hour.

Capacity

Once the variable and fixed predetermined overhead rates are calculated, they are used throughout the following year to apply overhead to Work in Process Inventory. Overhead may be applied as production occurs, when goods or services are transferred out of Work in Process Inventory, or at the end of each month. **Applied overhead** is the amount of overhead assigned to Work in Process Inventory as a result of incurring the activity measure that was used to develop the application rate. Application is made using the *predetermined* rates and the *actual* level of activity. And, regardless of whether single or multiple application rates are used, the number of overhead accounts to include in the accounting system must be determined.

The cost accountant can record overhead in the accounting system in two ways: in separate accounts for actual and applied overhead, or in a single account. If actual and applied accounts are separated, the applied account is a contra account to the actual overhead account and is closed against it at the end of the year. The alternative, more convenient, recordkeeping option is to maintain one account in the general ledger that is debited for actual overhead costs and credited for applied overhead. This method is used throughout the text.

A second question facing the accountant relates to the number of overhead accounts to have in the general ledger. All overhead may be recorded in a single, total

APPLYING OVERHEAD TO PRODUCTION

Applied overhead

---

[4] Four production volume–based capacity measures that can be used to compute fixed overhead application rates are discussed later in the chapter.

overhead account or separate accounts can be used for the variable and fixed components. Exhibit 4–12 presents the alternative overhead recording possibilities.

If separate rates are used to apply variable and fixed overhead, the general ledger would most commonly contain separate variable and fixed overhead accounts. When separate variable and fixed accounts are used, a practical problem is created in that mixed costs must be assigned either to the variable or the fixed general ledger account. Rather than arbitrarily assigning these costs to one account or the other, this problem can be overcome by using a predetermined pattern or formula to separate the mixed costs into variable and fixed amounts as they are incurred. Since overhead costs in an automated factory represent an ever larger part of product cost, the benefits of separating costs according to their behavior are thought to be greater than the time and effort expended.

Regardless of the number (combined or separate) or type (plantwide or departmental) of predetermined overhead rates used, actual overhead costs are debited to the appropriate overhead general ledger account(s) and credited to the various sources of overhead costs. Applied overhead is debited to Work in Process Inventory using the predetermined rates and credited to the overhead general ledger accounts. The amount of applied overhead is only indirectly related to the amount of actual overhead incurred by the company. Actual activity causes actual overhead costs to be incurred and causes overhead to be applied to Work in Process Inventory. Thus, actual and applied overhead costs are both related to actual activity and only by actual activity are they related to each other.

Assume that during January 1994, the Finishing Department at Cambridge Cloaks incurs 3,000 actual machine hours. Actual variable and fixed overhead costs for the month were £6,300 and £3,700, respectively. Applied variable overhead for the month is £6,120 (3,000 × £2.04) and applied fixed overhead is £3,600 (3,000 × £1.20). The journal entries to record actual and applied overhead for January 1994 would be:

Variable Manufacturing Overhead	6,300	
Fixed Manufacturing Overhead	3,700	
Various accounts		10,000
To record actual manufacturing overhead.		
Work in Process Inventory	9,720	
Variable Manufacturing Overhead		6,120
Fixed Manufacturing Overhead		3,600
To apply variable and fixed manufacturing overhead to WIP.		

Underapplied overhead
Overapplied overhead

At the end of the period, the amount of actual overhead incurred during a period will not equal applied overhead. This difference is referred to as under- or overapplied overhead. **Underapplied overhead** means that the amount of overhead applied to Work in Process Inventory is less than actual overhead; **overapplied overhead** means that the amount of overhead applied to Work in Process Inventory is greater than actual overhead. Under- or overapplied overhead must be closed at year-end because the time frame used to determine the overhead rates was one year.

Disposition of Under- and Overapplied Overhead

Disposition of under- or overapplied overhead depends on the materiality of the amount involved. If the amount is immaterial, it is closed to the Cost of Goods Sold account. When overhead is underapplied (debit balance), an insufficient amount of

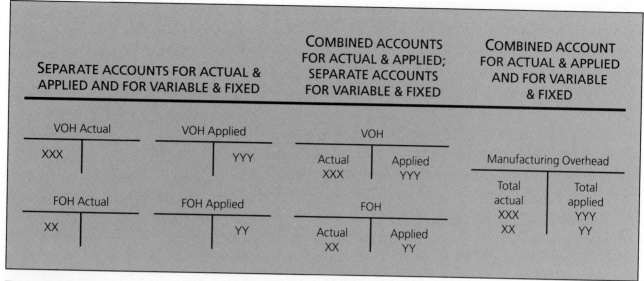

EXHIBIT 4–12

Cost Accounting System Possibilities for Manufacturing Overhead

overhead was applied to production. Thus, closing underapplied overhead causes Cost of Goods Sold to increase. Alternatively, overapplied overhead (credit balance) reflects the fact that too much overhead was applied to production, so closing overapplied overhead causes Cost of Goods Sold to decrease. To illustrate this entry, assume that Cambridge Cloaks has an immaterial overapplied overhead balance at the end of the year of £10,000. If a combined single overhead account is used, the journal entry to close overapplied overhead is:

Manufacturing Overhead	10,000	
Cost of Good Sold		10,000

If the amount of under- or overapplied overhead is significant, it should be allocated among the accounts containing applied overhead. These accounts are Work in Process Inventory, Finished Goods Inventory, and Cost of Goods Sold. A significant amount of under- or overapplied overhead means that the balances in each of these accounts are quite different from what they would have been if actual overhead costs had been assigned to production. The under- or overapplied amount is allocated among the affected accounts to restate their balances to conform more closely with actual historical costs. Such conformity is required for external reporting by generally accepted accounting principles. Exhibit 4–13 on page 140 uses assumed data for Cambridge Cloaks to illustrate the technique of apportioning overapplied overhead among the necessary accounts; had the amount been underapplied, the accounts debited and credited in the journal entry would have been reversed.

Theoretically, under- or overapplied overhead should be allocated based on the amounts of applied overhead contained in each account rather than on total account balances. The logic behind this allocation procedure is that account balances contain direct materials and direct labor costs that are not related to actual or applied overhead. Use of the method shown in the exhibit is more common, however, since (1) the theoretical method is quite complex, requiring detailed account analysis, and (2) overhead tends to lose its identity after leaving Work in Process Inventory, thus making it more difficult to determine in the Finished Goods Inventory and Cost of Goods Sold account balances.

■ **EXHIBIT 4–13**
Proration of Overapplied Overhead

MANUFACTURING OVERHEAD		ACCOUNT BALANCES	
Actual	£580,000	Work in Process Inventory	£116,400
Applied	630,000	Finished Goods Inventory	203,700
		Cost of Goods Sold	649,900
Overapplied	£ 50,000		

1. Add balances of accounts and determine proportional relationships:

	BALANCE	PROPORTION	PERCENTAGE
Work in Process	£116,400	£116,400 ÷ £970,000	12%
Finished Goods	203,700	£203,700 ÷ £970,000	21%
Cost of Goods Sold	649,900	£649,900 ÷ £970,000	67%
Total	£970,000		100%

2. Multiply percentages times overapplied overhead amount to determine the amount of adjustment needed:

	PERCENTAGE	×	OVERAPPLIED OH	=	ADJUSTMENT AMOUNT
Work in Process	12%	×	£50,000	=	£ 6,000
Finished Goods Inventory	21%	×	£50,000	=	£10,500
Cost of Goods Sold	67%	×	£50,000	=	£33,500

3. Prepare journal entry to close manufacturing overhead account and assign adjustment amount to appropriate accounts:

Manufacturing Overhead	50,000	
Work in Process Inventory		6,000
Finished Goods Inventory		10,500
Cost of Goods Sold		33,500

Causes of Under- and Overapplied Overhead

Recognizing that actual and applied overhead will not be equal at the end of the period is easier than determining why that difference occurs. Several factors may give rise to under- or overapplied overhead.

1. *Actual and Budgeted Variable Cost Per Unit Difference.* Variable overhead (VOH) will be under- or overapplied if the actual VOH cost per unit differs from the budgeted VOH cost per unit. If actual VOH unit cost is greater than the budgeted unit cost, variable overhead will be underapplied. If actual VOH unit cost is less than expected, variable overhead will be overapplied. Under- or overapplied VOH is not affected simply by a difference in the actual and budgeted levels of activity. Because the VOH rate is assumed to be constant at all levels of activity within the relevant range, total actual and total applied overhead should be approximately equal at any activity level. Exhibit 4–14 presents a calculation of Cambridge Cloaks' underapplied variable overhead for 1994.

2. *Actual and Budgeted Total Fixed Cost Difference.* A difference between total actual and total budgeted fixed overhead (FOH) cost will cause under- or overapplied fixed overhead. Assume that Cambridge Cloaks' Finishing Department used exactly

Budgeted VOH rate = £2.04 (based on budgeted 80,000 machine hours)
Actual machine hours = 84,000
Applied VOH (84,000 × £2.04) = £171,360

Actual overhead cost   = £173,880

£2,520 underapplied VOH =
84,000 MHs × £.03 differ-
ence in budgeted and
actual VOH rates

Actual VOH rate = £173,880 ÷ 84,000 = £2.07

NOTE: If actual overhead cost had been £171,360 at 84,000 machine hours, no under- or overapplied
overhead would exist since these figures would also represent the original £2.04 rate.

■ EXHIBIT 4–14
Cambridge Cloaks'
Underapplied Variable
Overhead Computation

80,000 machine hours in 1994 (the original estimate) and incurred £97,500 of actual FOH (rather than the budgeted £96,000). This difference would cause £1,500 of underapplied fixed overhead:

Actual fixed overhead	£97,500
Applied fixed overhead (80,000 × £1.20)	96,000
Underapplied fixed overhead	£ 1,500

One possible reason for actual fixed costs differing from expected costs is that costs for individual elements of fixed overhead changed from the original estimates. For example, factory supervisors received an unforeseen raise during the current year.

3. *Actual Activity and Expected Capacity Difference.* Fixed overhead will be under- or overapplied if the actual level of activity differs from the expected level. Under- or overapplied fixed overhead results because one specific capacity level was selected in computing the FOH application rate; if any other activity level had been selected, the predetermined FOH rate would have differed from the one used. Only if the company's actual activity level exactly equals the expected activity level will the total budgeted amount of fixed overhead be applied to production.

Assume that Cambridge Cloaks had £96,000 of actual fixed overhead costs in 1994. This amount is equal to the amount budgeted in the computation of the FOH rate (Exhibit 4–6). During 1994, the company incurred 76,800 machine hours rather than the 80,000 that were budgeted. Fixed overhead would be underapplied by £3,840:

Actual fixed overhead	£96,000
Applied fixed overhead (76,800 × £1.20)	92,160
Underapplied fixed overhead	£ 3,840

Using the above figures for Cambridge Cloaks, the actual FOH rate per machine hour is £1.25 (£96,000 ÷ 76,800). Had 76,800 machine hours been used to calculate the predetermined FOH application rate, there would have been no underapplied overhead.

Overhead is underapplied because the company used fewer machine hours (76,800) than it had anticipated (80,000). Every actual hour of machine time caused Work in Process Inventory to receive £1.20 of FOH cost. Since fewer hours were used than expected, a lesser amount (3,200 × £1.20 = £3,840) of fixed costs was applied than was budgeted. Even though budgeted FOH is equal to actual FOH, too little overhead is applied to production because activity was less than that on which the predetermined fixed overhead rate was based.

In the preceding examples, the two fixed overhead causes (factors 2 and 3 above) of under- and overapplied overhead were assumed to work independently. Usually, factors 2 and 3 work together to create under- or overapplied fixed overhead. Most companies will have both an actual-to-budget cost difference as well as an actual-to-budget activity difference. For example, assume Cambridge Cloaks used 81,000 machine hours in 1994 and incurred actual fixed costs of £97,500. These conditions would react together to cause £300 of underapplied fixed overhead as follows:

Actual fixed overhead	£97,500
Applied fixed overhead (81,000 × £1.20)	97,200
Underapplied fixed overhead	£ 300

This underapplied overhead amount can be explained by the two causal factors:

Actual fixed overhead	£97,500
Budgeted fixed overhead	96,000
= Difference due to underestimation of fixed overhead costs	£ 1,500
− Difference due to underestimation of activity (81,000 − 80,000 = 1,000 machine hours × £1.20 rate)	1,200
= Net difference due to both causes	£ 300

Since the capacity measure selected to compute the fixed overhead application rate (or the combined predetermined application rate) can affect the amount of under- or overapplied overhead, several measures of capacity can be used for this purpose.

ALTERNATIVE CAPACITY MEASURES

Capacity can be defined as any measure of activity. Traditionally, capacity has been thought of in relationship to a measure of production activity such as direct labor hours or machine hours. It is just as appropriate to think of these levels in terms of any measure of activity; for example, the capacity of the purchasing department could be measured by the number of vendors used. Following are discussions of four alternative capacity levels and their appropriateness as the denominator of the predetermined fixed (or combined) overhead application rate.

The estimated maximum potential activity that could occur during a specified time frame is called **theoretical** (or ideal) **capacity.** Such a capacity measure assumes that all factors are operating in a technically and humanly perfect manner. Theoretical capacity disregards realities such as machinery breakdowns and reduced or stopped plant operations on holidays. Because of its fairly unrealistic assumptions, theoretical capacity is normally not considered an acceptable predetermined overhead rate basis because overhead would consistently be underapplied. The underapplied amount might also be consistently large enough to require the type of year-end proration illustrated in Exhibit 4–13.

If, however, a company is attempting to be viewed as a world-class competitor, use of theoretical capacity does have some merit. If a company were totally automated or

NEWS NOTE

Higher Capacity, Lower Costs

Because it has never had a large cushion of crude production to fall back upon when oil prices were rising, Ashland Oil, Inc., has worked hard to make its three-unit refining operation—a big 213,400-barrel-a-day refinery near Ashland, Kentucky, and two much smaller ones in St. Paul Park, Minnesota, and Canton, Ohio—one of the most efficient in the industry. Last year, for example, Ashland converted 62% of its throughput into gasoline and gasoline components, versus about 50% for the industry. Despite the economic slowdown, it operated its refineries at 91% of capacity, seven points higher than the industry average.

"We believe in running a full house," says Ashland Chairman John R. Hall. "It gives us the lowest [unit] cost."

SOURCE: James Cook, "Crude-poor and Happy," *Forbes* (April 13, 1992), p. 102. Reprinted by permission of *FORBES* Magazine. © Forbes Inc., 1992.

if people consistently worked to their fullest potential, such a measure would provide a reasonable overhead application rate. Thus, the underapplied overhead resulting from a difference between theoretical capacity and actual capacity would be an indication of capacity that should be either used or eliminated; it could also indicate human capabilities that have not been fully developed. If a company takes such an attitude, it should view the underapplied overhead as a period cost and close it to a loss account (such as "Loss from Inefficient Operations") on the income statement. Showing the capacity potential and the use of the differential in this manner should attract managerial attention to the inefficient and ineffective use of resources.

Reducing theoretical capacity by ongoing, regular operating interruptions (such as holidays, downtime, and start-up time) provides the **practical capacity** that could be achieved during normal working hours. Although practical capacity is more achievable than theoretical capacity, it is not often used in predetermined overhead rate computations because this level of efficiency in operations is also not often probable. Another pragmatic reason that practical capacity is not used is that the Internal Revenue Service issued regulations under the 1986 Tax Act that prohibit use of this measure in accounting for inventory.[5] The News Note "Higher Capacity, Lower Costs" provides an indication of practical capacity.   **Practical capacity**

Managers may wish to consider historical and estimated future production levels and the cyclical fluctuations. Therefore, they may use a **normal capacity** measure that encompasses the long-run (five to ten years) average activity of the firm. This measure represents a reasonably attainable level of activity, but will not provide costs that are most similar to actual historical costs. Such costs would be generated by defining budgeted activity as **expected annual capacity**.   **Normal capacity**

Expected annual capacity

Expected annual capacity is a short-run concept that represents the anticipated level of activity at which the company expects to be engaged in the upcoming year. If actual results occur close to expected results, this capacity measure should minimize the amount of under- or overapplied overhead for the year. Although expected annual capacity is probably the most commonly used activity measure for calculating predetermined overhead rates, it does nothing to highlight the level of untapped resources of the organization.

---

[5] "IRS Prohibits Use of Practical Capacity Concept for Inventory Cost," *DH&S Review* (September 14, 1987), p. 6.

EXHIBIT 4–15
Relationships Among
Capacity Measures

	BUDGETED FIXED OVERHEAD	CAPACITY LEVEL IN MACHINE HOURS	PREDETERMINED FOH RATE
Theoretical	£992,000	100,000	£ 9.92
Practical	992,000	80,000	12.40
Normal	992,000	70,000	14.17
Expected	992,000	75,000	13.23
	DM, DL, & VOH COST	**APPLIED FOH (RATE × 2 MH)**	**TOTAL PRODUCT COST**
Theoretical	£10.00	£19.84	£29.84
Practical	10.00	24.80	34.80
Normal	10.00	28.34	38.34
Expected	10.00	26.46	36.46

Exhibit 4–15 illustrates predetermined overhead rates and applications under each possible capacity measure. Assuming that direct materials, direct labor, and variable overhead costs total £10 and that each product requires two machine hours, total product cost could range from £29.84 to £38.34! One of the four costs shown in the exhibit is probably fairly close to true product cost. From a short-run perspective, we think that the cost developed using expected capacity is the closest to "truth." From a long-run perspective, we believe that the costs generated from the use of theoretical or normal capacity cost are more reflective of the company's true costs.

ACTIVITY-BASED COSTING

Activity-based costing

This section of the chapter is designed to introduce the concepts of **activity-based costing** (ABC). Activity-based costing is an accounting information and costing system that: (1) identifies the various activities performed in an organization, (2) collects costs on the basis of the underlying nature and extent of those activities, and (3) assigns costs to products and services based on those activities. Many companies allocate production overhead costs using only one or a few traditional measures of activity. In reality, overhead costs are more commonly caused by a variety of activities or cost-drivers that may be related to materials, labor, machines, or support services. Use of a single allocation basis could result in product cost valuations that do not reflect true product costs.

An earlier part of the chapter indicated how product cost distortions could occur if a company uses a plantwide, rather than departmental, rate for overhead application. These same kinds of distortions can arise in a department that has widely varying activities. To illustrate the potential problems, the following discussion provides information on one aspect of Cambridge Cloaks' overhead costs.

According to the flexible budget presented in Exhibit 4–6, insurance costs of £3,500 are incurred at the 80,000 machine hour level in the Finishing Department at Cambridge Cloaks. Using a single activity base such as machine hours to apply insurance costs to products results in all products being assigned the same £.044 (£3,500 ÷ 80,000) amount of insurance costs per machine hour. Such an approach fails to recognize that insurance costs are caused by factors other than machine hours.

Analysis of the insurance cost account reveals that insurance is really comprised of the following components. Each component is presented with its cost, its cause, and a recommended activity base or cost driver.

Component	Cost	Cause	Recommended Driver
Employee disability	£ 800	Risk of injury to employees	# of employees
Fire and casualty	1,600	Potential for loss of value of plant and equipment	Value of plant and equipment
Liability	600	Potential for damage to others	# of products sold
Employee dishonesty coverage	500	Company vulnerability to theft by employees	# of employees considered to be in vulnerable positions
Total	£3,500		

Note that machine hours is several degrees of accuracy removed from the cause of each of the insurance components. Therefore, all of the suggested cost drivers are better measures of causation of their respective components than are machine hours, and these cost drivers will provide more refined bases of allocation of insurance cost to individual products.

Using machine hours as the sole allocation base for all components of overhead in the Finishing Department would lead to product cost distortions. For example, if the largest insurance cost component, fire and casualty, is allocated on the basis of machine hours, the cost per hour is £.02 (£1,600 ÷ 80,000 MH). If the Finishing Department made four types of cloaks in 1994 using the following number of machine hours, the cost allocations of the fire and casualty component would be:

Type of Cloak	Machine Hours Used	×	Cost per Hour	=	Cost Allocated
Men's	20,000		£.02		£400
Women's	40,000		.02		800
Boys'	10,000		.02		200
Girls'	10,000		.02		200

In contrast, consider how the allocation would change if the proportionate values of plant and equipment used to manufacture each product type were used to allocate the £1,600 fire and casualty cost:

Type of Cloak	Value of P&E	% of Total P&E	×	Cost Amount	=	Cost Allocated
Men's	£ 798,000	57%		£1,600		£ 912
Women's	308,000	22		£1,600		352
Boys'	168,000	12		£1,600		192
Girls'	126,000	9		£1,600		144
Total	£1,400,000	100%				£1,600

Activity-based costing requires the use of multiple cost drivers to best reflect the underlying nature of the cost. The cost drivers and total costs in the Cambridge Cloaks Finishing Department example are simplistic and the monetary amounts are insignificant. Consider, however, the benefits to be derived from the use of such an innovative technique in companies such as General Motors and Weyerhaeuser Company, which both utilize activity-based costing. More discussion of this subject appears in Chapter 5.

R E V I S I T I N G

MARKS & SPENCER

In the face of some of the worst economic conditions in recent years, Marks & Spencer reported an increased group profit of 6.2 percent, or about $1.2 billion, during the 1992 fiscal year. In a period when many retailers, particularly those in the United States, are facing difficult times, Marks & Spencer appears to be in robust financial health.

[Julie Ramshan, an analyst at the investment banking firm of Morgan Stanley International, predicts that M&S will have pretax profits of about $1.4 billion in 1993.] During 1992, Sir Richard Greenbury will be hard at work to make that prediction a reality. The corporate staff has already been reduced by 20 percent; workers at the various retail outlets have also been pruned. "We have less people on more footage because we have better operation systems and information services, but a much greater proportion now working on the sales floor serving customers," Greenbury says. "The benefit is the lower costs to operate." [Many of those lower operating costs are in the overhead category because, while Sir Richard is a firm believer in cost control, he still wants M&S to provide the best value to the customer.]

SOURCE: Mike Sheridan, "British Values," *SKY* (October 1992), p. 69ff. This article has been excerpted by permission of the author and through the courtesy of Halsey Publishing Company, publishers of Delta Air Lines' *SKY* magazine.

CHAPTER SUMMARY

This chapter discusses the advantages of using predetermined overhead rates rather than actual overhead charges for product costing. A predetermined overhead rate is calculated in advance of a period using budgeted overhead costs divided by a selected level of a specified activity. Predetermined overhead rates are advantageous because they eliminate the problems caused by time delays in obtaining actual cost data and make the overhead allocation process more effective. Use of an annualized rate allocates uniform amounts of overhead to goods or services based on production efforts associated with those goods or services.

Companies can use different methods of measuring activity or capacity; units of product (output volume) are the best measure only if the company produces a single product. The activity base chosen should be logically related in a predictive sense to changes in costs and be a direct causal factor of that cost (a cost driver). Use of departmental activity bases, rather than a single plantwide base, results in more refined information for product costing and managerial uses.

Separate application rates can be developed for variable and fixed overhead. Because variable cost per unit remains constant within the relevant range of activity, total budgeted variable overhead at any level of activity can be divided by activity to compute the predetermined rate. To compute a fixed overhead rate, however, a specific denominator level of activity must be chosen; most commonly, the level selected is expected annual capacity. Alternative measures include theoretical capacity, practical capacity, and normal capacity. Only if the actual level of activity is the same as the selected activity level, and if budgeted fixed costs are equal to actual fixed costs, will all budgeted fixed overhead be charged to the units produced.

To compute separate variable and fixed overhead rates, mixed costs must be separated into their variable and fixed components. This separation can be accomplished through the use of the high-low method or least squares regression analysis. The high-low method uses two points of actual activity data (the highest and lowest) and determines the change in cost, which reflects the unit variable cost included in the mixed cost. Fixed cost is determined by subtracting total variable cost from total cost at either the high or low level of activity.

Regression analysis uses the method of least squares to mathematically determine a regression equation based on observations of two or more variables. Simple linear regression analysis generates a regression formula for a dependent variable (cost) based on its relationship to a single independent variable (activity).

When a company uses a predetermined overhead rate, under- or overapplied overhead results at the end of the year. This amount (if insignificant) should be closed to Cost of Goods Sold or (if significant) allocated among the Work in Process Inventory, Finished Goods Inventory, and Cost of Goods Sold accounts.

Measures of Correlation and Dispersion

APPENDIX

Regression analysis and the method of least squares provide a means to predict the value of an unknown (dependent) variable by using values of known (independent) variables. These techniques do not, however, indicate how well those known variables are suited to predicting the unknown one. For example, while direct labor hours could be used to estimate maintenance cost, a better cost estimate might be generated by using machine hours, average age of machinery, or number of product change-overs. Deciding how strongly variables are related requires the use of **correlation analysis**. This technique uses statistical measures of **dispersion** (or variability) to reveal the strength of the relationship between variables. (There are no independent and dependent variables in correlation analysis, only interrelated variables.)

Correlation analysis
Dispersion

In regression analysis, dispersion is measured as the distance of an actual point from the estimated regression line. Results are said to be highly correlated when little dispersion exists and poorly correlated when dispersion is large. Thus, the degree of correlation is inversely related to the magnitude of dispersion. One measure of dispersion is the coefficient of correlation.

Coefficient of Correlation

The **coefficient of correlation** (r) shows the strength of relative association between two variables. The coefficient of correlation can be viewed as measuring either (1) the relationship or degree of linearity between two variables or (2) the goodness of fit of data to a regression line. The coefficient of correlation formula is:

Coefficient of correlation

$$r = \frac{\Sigma[(x - \bar{x})(y - \bar{y})]}{\sqrt{\Sigma[(x - \bar{x})^2 \, \Sigma(y - \bar{y})^2]}}$$

The coefficient of correlation can range between -1 and $+1$. A positive coefficient indicates that the two variables move in the same direction. Higher values of one variable are associated with higher values of the other. For example, total variable cost is positively correlated with output volume. A negative r value indicates that the two variables move in opposite directions. Fixed cost expressed on a per unit basis has negative correlation with output.

When all observed points (y values) lie close to the regression line, the unexplained variation in y is small and the correlation coefficient is close to 1 (either positive or negative). As larger deviations of observed values from the regression line occur, the variation becomes larger and the correlation coefficient approaches zero. A coefficient of correlation of +1 or −1 indicates a perfect linear relationship and all actual points lie on the regression line. A coefficient of zero indicates no linear correlation.

Calculations for the coefficient of correlation for the Cambridge Cloaks data given in Exhibit 4–2 are shown below. The values of x̄ and ȳ were computed on page 126 as 5,642.86 and £219, respectively. The r value is found to be .9944, which indicates a high degree of correlation.

x	$(x - \bar{x})$	$(x - \bar{x})^2$	y	$(y - \bar{y})$	$(y - \bar{y})^2$	$[(x - \bar{x})(y - \bar{y})]$
4,000	− 1,642.86	2,698,988.98	£160	£− 59	£ 3,481	£ 96,928.74
9,000	+3,357.14	11,270,388.98	320	+101	10,201	339,071.14
4,600	− 1,042.86	1,087,556.98	175	− 44	1,936	45,885.84
3,000	− 2,642.86	6,984,708.98	140	− 79	6,241	208,785.94
8,620	+2,977.14	8,863,362.58	320	+101	10,201	300,691.14
5,280	− 362.86	131,667.38	210	− 9	81	3,265.74
5,000	− 642.86	413,268.98	208	− 11	121	7,071.46
		31,449,942.86			£32,262	£1,001,700.00

$$r = \frac{£1,001,700}{\sqrt{(31,449,942.86)(£32,262)}} = .9944$$

Coefficient of Determination

The **coefficient of determination** (r^2) measures the "goodness of fit" of the data to the least squares regression line and indicates what proportion of the total variation in y is explained by the regression model. Variation is measured as the sum of the squares of the deviations from the regression line. The coefficient of determination is simply the coefficient of correlation squared. Thus, the coefficient of determination for the Cambridge Cloaks data is .9889, which means that the least squares line for this mixed utility cost explains 98.89 percent of the variation in the utility cost.

Both the coefficients of correlation and determination are helpful in determining the strength of the relationship between two or more variables used in predictive formulas. However, because of the process of squaring, the coefficient of determination gives a more conservative picture about the relationship's strength. For example, assume that a coefficient of correlation were found to be .75. It might be assumed that a significant degree of variation could be explained by the regression formula producing this result. However, the coefficient of determination for the same data set is only .562, meaning that only slightly over half the variation is explained by the regression model.

Standard Error of the Estimate

A common measure of dispersion between predicted and actual data is the **standard error of the estimate** (S_e). This statistic indicates the degree of dispersion (or average difference) of actual observations from estimated values. The standard error of the estimate can be calculated using the a and b values from the regression formula as follows:

$$S_e = \sqrt{\frac{\Sigma y^2 - a(\Sigma y) - b(\Sigma xy)}{n - 2}}$$

where   n = number of observations

If each actual value of the dependent variable fell on the regression line, the standard error of the estimate would be zero, indicating that the regression equation would provide perfect estimations for that data set. As the standard error of the estimate increases, the strength of the relationship between the two variables declines and the regression equation gives progressively less precise predictions of future results.

Using the information from the chapter (page 126) for Cambridge Cloaks, the standard error of the estimate is:

y^2	(from the chapter)
£ 25,600	$a = £38.43$
102,400	$\Sigma y = £1,533$
30,625	$\Sigma xy = £9,652,200$
19,600	$b = £.032$
102,400	$n = 7$
44,100	
43,264	
£367,989	

$$S_e = \sqrt{\frac{£367,989 - (£38.43)(£1,533) - (£.032)(£9,652,200)}{7 - 2}}$$

$$S_e = \sqrt{\frac{£205.41}{5}} = £6.41$$

Thus, the estimates from the regression formula have some variability. At any level of machine hours, a distribution of the differences between the expected and the actual costs of utilities will have a mean of zero and a standard error of the estimate of £6.41.

There is an inverse relationship between the quantitative values measured by the standard error of the estimate and the coefficient of determination. The standard error of the estimate measures size of the deviations of expected values from actual observations, while the coefficient of determination measures the proportion of variation explained by the regression model. Therefore, smaller deviations give a higher proportion of explanation.

KEY TERMS

Activity-based costing (p. 144)
Actual cost system (p. 120)
Applied overhead (p. 137)
Budget (p. 128)
Capacity (p. 137)
Coefficient of correlation (p. 147)
Coefficient of determination (p. 148)
Correlation analysis (p. 147)
Dependent variable (p. 125)
Dispersion (p. 147)
Expected annual capacity (p. 143)
Flexible budget (p. 128)
High-low method (p. 124)
Independent variable (p. 125)

Least squares regression analysis (p. 124)
Multiple regression (p. 126)
Normal capacity (p. 143)
Normal cost system (p. 120)
Outliers (p. 124)
Overapplied overhead (p. 138)
Practical capacity (p. 143)
Predetermined overhead rate (p. 120)
Regression line (p. 126)
Scattergraph (p. 127)
Simple regression (p. 126)
Standard error of the estimate (p. 148)
Theoretical capacity (p. 142)
Underapplied overhead (p. 138)

SOLUTION STRATEGIES

Predetermined Overhead Rate

$$\text{Predetermined OH rate} = \frac{\text{Budgeted Overhead}}{\text{Budgeted Level of Activity}}$$

(Can be separate variable and fixed rates or a combined rate)

High-Low Method
(using assumed amounts)

	(Independent Variable) Activity	(Dependent Variable) Associated Total Cost	=	Total Variable Cost (Rate × Activity)	+	Total Fixed Cost
"High" level	14,000	$18,000	=	$11,200	+	$6,800
"Low" level	9,000	14,000		7,200	+	6,800
Differences	5,000	$ 4,000				

$.80 variable cost per unit of activity

Least-Squares Regression Analysis
The equations necessary to compute b and a values using the method of least squares are as follows:

$$b = \frac{\Sigma xy - n\,(\bar{x})\,(\bar{y})}{\Sigma x^2 - n\bar{x}^2}$$

$$a = \bar{y} - b\bar{x}$$

where $\bar{x}$ = mean of the independent variable
        $\bar{y}$ = mean of the dependent variable
        n = number of observations

Under- and Overapplied Overhead

Manufacturing Overhead	XXX	
Various accounts		XXX

Actual overhead is debited to the overhead general ledger account.

Work in Process Inventory	YYY	
Manufacturing Overhead		YYY

Applied overhead is debited to WIP and credited to the overhead general ledger account.

A debit balance in Manufacturing Overhead at the end of the period is underapplied overhead; a credit balance is overapplied overhead. The under- or overapplied balance in the overhead account is closed at the end of the period to CGS or prorated to WIP, FG, and CGS.

DEMONSTRATION PROBLEM

The South London Tailoring Shop has been able to identify its purely variable overhead costs and its purely fixed overhead costs for 1994 as follows:

Purely Variable Overhead	Rate per Tailor Hour
Indirect labor	£.25
Indirect materials	.12
Employee fringe benefits	.03

Purely Fixed Overhead	Annual Amount
Supervision	£25,000
Insurance	3,000
Depreciation	8,000
Taxes	2,200
Maintenance	1,800

The shop also experienced utilities costs and tailor hours for the past six months as follows:

	Tailor Hours	Utilities
November	720	£682
December	920	730
January	810	708
February	680	673
March	860	721
April	640	660

Required:

a. Using the high-low method, separate utility cost into its fixed and variable components.

b. Using the least squares method, separate utility cost into its fixed and variable components.

c. Prepare an annual flexible overhead budget for the shop for the relevant range from 7,000 to 10,000 tailoring hours at each 1,000 hour interval. For the utility cost component, use your answer to part b. Round the fixed portion of utility cost to the nearest whole British pound sterling.

d. Assuming that expected annual capacity is 8,000 tailor hours, calculate the predetermined variable, fixed, and total overhead rates.

Solution to Demonstration Problem

a.
$$b = \frac{£730 - £660}{920 - 640} = \frac{£70}{280} = £.25$$

$$a = £730 - (£.25)(920) = £500$$

b.

x	y	xy	x^2
720	£ 682	£ 491,040	518,400
920	730	671,600	846,400
810	708	573,480	656,100
680	673	457,640	462,400
860	721	620,060	739,600
640	660	422,400	409,600
4,630	£4,174	£3,236,220	3,632,500

$$\bar{x} = 4,630 \div 6 = 771.67$$

$$\bar{y} = £4,174 \div 6 = £695.67$$

$$b = \frac{£3,236,220 - 6(771.67)(£695.67)}{3,632,500 - 6(771.67)(771.67)} = \frac{£15,253.99}{59,652.47} = £.256$$

$$a = £695.67 - (.256)(771.67) = £498.12 \text{ or } £498 \text{ (rounded)}$$

c.

	Tailor Hours			
	7,000	8,000	9,000	10,000
Variable Overhead				
Indirect labor	£ 1,750	£ 2,000	£ 2,250	£ 2,500
Indirect materials	840	960	1,080	1,200
Employee fringe benefit	210	240	270	300
Utilities—variable portion	1,792	2,048	2,304	2,560
Total VC	£ 4,592	£ 5,248	£ 5,904	£ 6,560
VC per hour	£.656	£.656	£.656	£.656
Fixed Overhead				
Supervision	£25,000	£25,000	£25,000	£25,000
Insurance	3,000	3,000	3,000	3,000
Depreciation	8,000	8,000	8,000	8,000
Taxes	2,200	2,200	2,200	2,200
Maintenance	1,800	1,800	1,800	1,800
Utilities—fixed portion	498	498	498	498
Total FC	£40,498	£40,498	£40,498	£40,498
FC per hour	£5.786	£5.062	£4.500	£4.050
Total Overhead	£45,090	£45,746	£46,402	£47,058
Total OH per hour	£6.442	£5.718	£5.156	£4.706

d. From the 8,000 hour level of the flexible budget:

Predetermined variable rate per hour   £ .656
Predetermined fixed rate per hour   £5.062
Predetermined total rate per hour   £5.718

QUESTIONS

1. What recent changes have occurred in manufacturing and retailing that have driven up overhead costs?

2. Why is it necessary to allocate overhead costs to products and services?

3. Why would a company use a predetermined overhead rate rather than actual overhead for determining product cost?

4. Describe the difference between a normal costing system and an actual costing system. Relative to an actual costing system, what are the advantages associated with the use of a normal costing system? What are the disadvantages?

5. Why is direct labor hours a poor measure of capacity in an automated factory?

6. How would predetermined application rates be determined for variable and fixed overhead?

7. If a company wanted to predict maintenance costs at various levels of activity and knew that maintenance was a mixed cost, how would the company's cost accountant use the high-low method? What alternative methods could the cost accountant use?

8. The high-low method of analyzing mixed costs uses only two observation points: the high and the low points of activity. Are these *always* the best points for prediction purposes? Why or why not?

9. A company might use one of four different measures of capacity to compute its predetermined fixed overhead rate. What are these four capacity measures and what differences exist among them?

10. What is a step fixed cost?

11. What is a flexible budget? How is it used to predict or budget future costs?

12. When a normal costing system is used, how are costs removed from the Manufacturing Overhead account and charged to the Work in Process Inventory account?

13. What are the advantages of using departmental overhead rates relative to plant-wide rates?

14. What causes overhead to be under- or overapplied?

15. If overhead was materially underapplied for a year, how would it be treated at year-end? What might cause this underapplication to occur?

16. How does activity-based costing differ from traditional product costing? How is it similar?

17. (*Appendix*) How can correlation analysis be used to select an overhead allocation base?

18. (*Appendix*) How is the coefficient of determination related to the coefficient of correlation? Can the coefficient of correlation ever be negative? Can the coefficient of determination ever be negative?

19. (*High-low method*) The Materials Receiving Department of Southwood Company experienced the following costs during the first six months of 1994:

EXERCISES

Month	Lbs. of Material Received	Costs	Month	Lbs. of Material Received	Costs
January	5,500	$3,040	April	5,990	$3,088
February	6,040	3,288	May	5,600	3,072
March	7,000	3,340	June	6,400	3,280

a. Using the high-low method, determine the fixed and variable values for the formula $y = a + bX$, where X is pounds of material received.

b. Given your answers to part a, predict July's total departmental costs if expected receipts (in pounds) are 6,700.

20. (*High-low method*) The Marine Hydraulics Corporation wishes to determine variable and fixed portions of its electricity expense (a mixed cost) as measured against machine hours. Information for the first six months of 1994 follows:

Month	Machine Hours	Electricity Expense	Month	Machine Hours	Electricity Expense
January	68,000	$1,220	April	64,000	$1,195
February	62,000	1,172	May	67,500	1,300
March	66,300	1,014	June	62,500	1,150

Use the high-low method to answer the following questions:

a. What is the variable rate per machine hour?
b. What is the fixed cost portion of electricity?
c. Develop the cost (budget) formula for electricity expense.
d. What would be the estimated electricity cost for October 1994 if 65,450 machine hours are projected?

21. *(High-low method)* John Cristal, owner of Cristal's Gymnasium, has determined the following budget formula to account for his monthly costs: Total Cost = $12,000 + $29 per direct labor hour. His only costs are composed of the manager's salary ($4,000), depreciation on the building ($5,000), insurance ($500), labor ($21 per DLH), and utilities.

    a. What is the formula for the utilities cost?

    b. What would John expect total monthly costs to be if the gym is open 30 days per month for 12 hours per day?

    c. During the holidays, the gym remains open longer hours. What are total estimated monthly costs for July, when the gym will be open 31 days for 16 hours per day?

22. *(High-low method)* Micah Franks operates a shop that specializes in building custom crankshafts for high-performance gasoline- and alcohol-powered racing engines. The machinery in the shop is mostly computerized and requires a significant amount of routine maintenance. Micah is wondering if he can use machine hours as a basis for reliably predicting total maintenance costs. To investigate the relationship between machine hours and maintenance costs, Micah has gathered the following weekly data:

Number of Machine Hours	Maintenance Costs
3,000	$980
4,500	690
8,000	510
7,000	600
6,000	550
9,000	440
3,500	840
5,500	600

    a. Using the high-low method, determine the fixed and variable values for maintenance costs using machine hours as the prediction base.

    b. What aspect of the estimated equation is bothersome?

    c. What explanation could account for this result?

    d. Within the relevant range, could the formula you developed be reliably used to predict maintenance costs? Can the parameters of the model you estimated be interpreted as variable and fixed costs?

23. *(Least squares)* Below are data on machine hours and utilities expense for Texas Pneumatic Hose Company for the first seven weeks of 1994:

Machine Hours	Utilities Expense
200	$350
175	325
160	309
140	285
210	370
230	400
240	405

    a. Using the least squares method, develop the equation for predicting weekly utilities expense based on machine hours.

    b. What is the predicted amount of utilities expense for a *month* (assume a month is exactly four weeks) that requires 780 machine hours?

24. *(Least squares, scattergraph)* Billy's Charter Boats operates a fleet of small power boats on Lake Michigan. Billy is interested in developing a model that will reliably predict his labor costs (a mixed cost). To this end, he has gathered the fol-

lowing monthly data from 1994 records on labor costs and two potential predictive bases: number of charters, and gross receipts:

Month	Labor Costs	Number of Charters	Gross Receipts
January	$ 8,000	5	$ 6,000
February	9,200	7	9,000
March	12,000	11	13,000
April	14,200	14	18,000
May	18,500	20	30,000
June	28,000	31	41,000
July	34,000	50	60,000
August	30,000	45	50,000
September	24,000	40	48,000

a. Prepare a scattergraph for labor costs using each of the alternative prediction bases.

b. Using the least squares method, compute the fixed and variable cost elements of labor costs for both prediction bases.

25. *(Flexible budget)* The major overhead cost components of Shreveport Cannery are indirect labor, supplies, and utilities. The company has developed a formula for predicting each of these costs (monthly) using production machine hours:

$$\text{Indirect labor cost} = \$18,000 + \$14X$$
$$\text{Indirect materials cost} = \$ 1,000 + \$30X$$
$$\text{Utilities} = \$ 2,300 + \$17X$$

Prepare a flexible budget for overhead costs of Shreveport Cannery for next month. Use 10,000, 12,000, 14,000, and 15,000 as the potential machine hour levels. Separately identify the fixed and variable cost components.

26. *(Predetermined overhead rate)* The Patman Supply Company manufactures disposable tablecloths for restaurants. The company has decided to use predetermined overhead rates to apply overhead to its products. To set such rates, the company has gathered the following budgeted data:

Variable factory overhead at 12,000 machine hours	$72,000
Variable factory overhead at 14,000 machine hours	84,000
Fixed factory overhead at all levels between 12,000 and 20,000 machine hours	72,000

Practical capacity is 20,000 machine hours; expected capacity is 75% of practical capacity.

a. What is the Patman Supply Company's predetermined variable overhead rate?

b. What is the most common capacity measure used to calculate a predetermined fixed overhead rate? Using this measure, determine the predetermined fixed overhead rate.

c. Use your answers to parts a and b. If the company incurred a total of 13,500 machine hours during a period, what would be the total amount of applied overhead? If actual overhead during the period was $155,000, what was the amount of under- or overapplied overhead?

27. *(Overhead application)* The Millhouse Engineering Company applies overhead at a combined rate for fixed and variable overhead of 175% of professional labor costs. During the first three months of 1994, the following professional labor costs and actual overhead costs were incurred:

Month	Professional Labor Cost	Actual Overhead
January	$180,000	$320,000
February	165,000	285,200
March	170,000	300,000

a. What amount of overhead was applied to the services provided each month by the firm?

b. What was under- or overapplied overhead for each of the three months and for the quarter?

28. *(Under- or overapplied overhead)* The Mexican Salsa Company has an overapplied overhead balance of $10,000 at the end of 1994. The following selected account balances are available at year-end, 1994:

Work in Process Inventory	$ 64,000
Finished Goods Inventory	16,000
Cost of Goods Sold	120,000

a. Prepare the necessary journal entries to close the overapplied overhead balance under two alternative methods.

b. Which method do you feel is more appropriate for the company and why?

29. *(Under- or overapplied overhead)* Assume that Smith Company had the following year-end balances:

Manufacturing Overhead	$ 542,000
Manufacturing Overhead Applied	526,000
Work in Process Inventory	37,766
Finished Goods	16,420
Cost of Goods Sold	1,587,814

The overhead components of the last three accounts are as follows:

Work in Process Inventory	$ 8,610
Finished Goods Inventory	3,444
Cost of Goods Sold	561,946

a. What is the amount of underapplied or overapplied overhead?

b. Prorate the amount you answered in part a based on the relative balances of the appropriate accounts.

c. Prorate the amount you answered in part a based on the relative overhead components of the appropriate account balances.

d. Based on your answer to part b, prepare the journal entry to distribute the under- or overapplied overhead.

30. *(Appendix)* Smithfield Apiaries is trying to identify bases to predict and allocate its honey processing costs. The firm has narrowed down the list of potential bases to two: tons of honey processed and machine hours. The company is now trying to identify the better of these two alternatives. The following data display the historical relationships among these variables for the past 8 years (inflation adjusted).

Year	Honey Processing Costs	Tons of Honey Processed	Machine Hours
1	$18,000	27	1,200
2	21,360	35	1,600
3	20,100	32	1,325
4	22,010	37	1,750
5	19,000	29	1,290
6	20,400	33.5	1,510
7	20,900	34.5	1,580
8	17,100	24.25	1,100

a. Compute the coefficient of correlation and the coefficient of determination between the two candidate bases and honey processing costs.
b. Which base should provide the better predictions? Explain.

31. *(Appendix)* Refer to the information in Exercise 30.

a. Using the least squares method, find the honey processing costs formula for each of the candidate bases.
b. Find the standard error of the estimate for each of the bases.
c. From your answer in part b, which of the bases is a better predictor of honey processing costs?

PROBLEMS

32. *(High low, least squares regression, scattergraph)* Timperly Industries manufactures screens for residential (doors and windows) and commercial (chemical filters) applications. The firm is trying to strengthen its formal budgeting and planning process. The company has encountered a problem in budgeting utilities expense. The expense is apparently a mixed cost and varies most directly with machine hours worked. However, management does not know the exact relationship between machine hours and utilities expense. The following data have been gathered from recent operations and may serve as a basis to describe the relationship.

Month	Machine Hours	Utilities Expense
January	1,400	$ 9,000
February	1,700	9,525
March	2,000	10,900
April	1,900	10,719
May	2,300	11,670
June	2,700	13,154
July	2,500	13,000
August	2,200	11,578

a. In analyzing the data, how do you know that utilities expense is a mixed cost? Prepare a scattergraph. Does the scattergraph indicate utilities expense is a mixed cost?
b. Using the high-low method, estimate utilities expense as a function of machine hours in the form $y = a + bX$.
c. Using least squares regression, estimate utilities expense as a function of machine hours in the form $y = a + bX$.
d. Which of your answers, parts b or c, provides the better estimate of the relationship between utilities expense and machine hours? Why?

33. *(Analyzing Mixed Costs & Predetermined Rates)* Selected overhead accounts are presented below at various levels of activity, although some of the amounts are missing:

Selected Overhead Costs	Machine Hours (X)				
	4,000	5,000	6,000	7,000	8,000
Indirect materials	$1,800			$3,000	
Indirect labor		$18,000			$27,000
Utilities			$ 900	1,000	
Rent	3,000				3,000
Maintenance		1,500	1,700		
Insurance		500		500	

a. Calculate the fixed and variable values for each item above for the formula $y = a + bX$, where X represents machine hours.

b. Determine the total budgeted cost for each overhead item at each budgeted volume level.

c. Assume that 6,000 machine hours is expected capacity for the company and that the above items constitute all overhead. Determine the following:
   1. the predetermined variable overhead application rate
   2. the predetermined fixed overhead application rate
   3. the total predetermined overhead application rate

34. *(Analyzing mixed costs)* The Eastside Horse Stable's predetermined total overhead rate for costing purposes is $3.35 per horse per day (referred to as an "animal day"). Of this, $3.15 is the variable portion. Cost information for two levels of monthly activity within the relevant range are given below:

	4,000 Animal Days	6,000 Animal Days
Overhead Cost:		
Indirect materials	$3,200	$ 4,800
Indirect labor	7,000	10,000
Maintenance	1,300	1,700
Utilities	1,000	1,500
All other	1,900	2,700

a. Determine the fixed and variable values for each of the above overhead items and determine the total overhead cost formula.

b. What is the company's expected capacity volume level, if the predetermined rate is based on expected capacity?

c. Determine expected overhead costs at the expected capacity volume level.

d. If the company decides to revise its expected capacity level to be 3,000 animal days greater than the present level, calculate a new predetermined total overhead rate for product costing.

35. *(Mixed costs and predetermined overhead rates; two bases, flexible budget)* The Cool Pool Company manufactures fiberglass swimming pools for home installations. The firm has two departments: Production and Installation. The Production Department is highly automated and machine hours are used as the basis for allocating departmental overhead. Installation is labor intensive and this department uses direct labor hours to apply overhead. Following is cost information at various activity levels for each department:

	Machine Hours (MHs)			
	3,000	4,000	5,000	6,000
Production Overhead Costs:				
Variable	$ 8,100	$10,800	$13,500	$16,200
Fixed	5,300	5,300	5,300	5,300
Total	$13,400	$16,100	$18,800	$21,500

	Direct Labor Hours (DLHs)			
	1,000	2,000	3,000	4,000
Installation Overhead Costs:				
Variable	$ 9,500	$19,000	$28,500	$38,000
Fixed	4,100	4,100	4,100	4,100
Total	$13,600	$23,100	$32,600	$42,100

Each pool is estimated to require 500 machine hours in Production and 250 hours of direct labor in Installation. Next month, the company plans to produce and install 11 pools, which is 1 pool beyond the company's normal capacity.

a. Compute the fixed and variable values in the formula $y = a + bX$ for each department.
b. Prepare a flexible budget for next month's variable, fixed, and total overhead costs for each department assuming production is 9, 10, 11, or 12 pools.
c. Calculate the predetermined total overhead cost to be applied to each pool scheduled for production in the coming month if normal capacity is used to calculate the predetermined overhead rates.

36. *(Plant vs. dept. OH rates)* Southwest Manufacturing Co. has two departments: Fabrication and Assembly. The Fabrication Department is composed of 1 worker and 15 machines. The Assembly Department has 20 direct laborers and few machines. One product that the company manufactures passes through both departments and uses the following quantities of direct labor and machine time:

	Fabrication	Assembly
Machine hours	8.00	.15
Direct labor hours	.02	2.00

Following are the estimated overhead costs and volumes for each department for the upcoming year:

	Fabrication	Assembly
Estimated overhead	$624,240	$324,000
Estimated machine hours	72,000	9,300
Estimated direct labor hours	4,800	48,000

a. Southwest Manufacturing's accountant computes a plantwide rate for overhead application based on machine hours. What is this rate for the upcoming year?
b. How much overhead would be assigned to each unit under the method currently in use?
c. The company's auditors inform Southwest that the method being used to apply overhead is inappropriate and that machine hours should be used for an application base in Fabrication and direct labor hours in Assembly. What would the rates be for each department? How much overhead would have been assigned to each unit of product using departmental rates?

37. *(Calculation and disposition of predetermined OH rates)* Bill Tooth, an accounting major, was concentrating diligently on his cost accounting homework when his younger sister, Lucy, came in the room. Lucy, a rather advanced 13-year-old, wanted Bill to explain the subject. Bill patiently tried to tell Lucy about predetermined overhead rates and confessed that he was having difficulty grasping the topic. Lucy listened intently, left the room, and came back a few minutes later with the pictures at the right. Explain the analogy that Lucy's picture represents.

38. *(Journal entries)* The Lerner Instruments Company applies overhead at the rate of $5.00 per direct labor hour. The following transactions occurred during May 1994:
   1. Direct materials issued to production, $50,000.
   Cash 2. Direct labor cost paid, 8,300 hours at $16.00 per hour.
   payable 3. Indirect labor cost accrued, 2,500 hours at $9.00 per hour.
   4. Depreciation on factory assets recorded, $12,400.
   cash 5. Supervisor's salary paid, $5,000.
   6. Indirect materials issued to production, $3,000.
   7. Goods costing $125,000 were completed and transferred to finished goods.

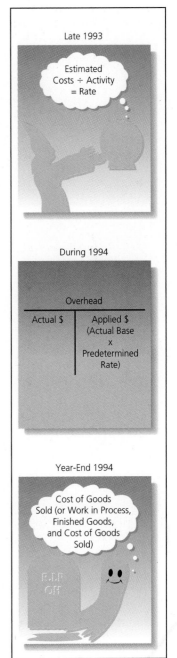

Late 1993

Estimated Costs ÷ Activity = Rate

During 1994

Overhead

Actual $ | Applied $ (Actual Base × Predetermined Rate)

Year-End 1994

Cost of Goods Sold (or Work in Process, Finished Goods, and Cost of Goods Sold)

a. Prepare journal entries for the above transactions using a single overhead account and assuming the Raw Materials Inventory account contains only direct materials.

b. If Work in Process Inventory had a beginning balance of $18,540, what is the ending balance?

c. Was overhead under- or overapplied for the month? By how much?

39. *(Activity-based costing)* Rockaway Sign Co. manufactures bases or stands for roadside advertising. The company produces a stock design base model and occasionally produces custom-designed bases. The company's overhead costs for a month in which no custom bases are produced are shown below:

Purchasing department for raw materials and supplies (10 purchase orders per month)	$ 8,000
Setting up machines for production runs (6 times per month after maintenance checks)	300
Utilities (based on 5,200 machine hours)	5,200
Supervisors (2)	8,000
Machine and building depreciation (fixed)	7,500
Quality control and inspections (performed on randomly selected bases each day; 1 quality control worker)	3,500
Total overhead costs	$32,500

The factory operations are highly automated and the cost accountant is allocating overhead to products based on machine hours. This allocation process has resulted in an overhead allocation rate of $6.25 per machine hour ($32,500 ÷ 5,200 MHs).

In June 1994, six orders were filled for custom-designed bases. The custom order sales prices were based on charges for actual direct materials, actual direct labor, and the $6.25 per machine hour for overhead. During that month, the following costs were incurred for 5,200 hours of machine time:

Purchasing department for raw materials and supplies (22 purchase orders)	$11,600
Setting up machines for production runs (18 times)	900
Utilities (based on 5,200 machine hours)	5,200
Supervisors (2)	8,000
Machine and building depreciation (fixed)	7,500
Quality control and inspections	4,180
Engineering design and specification costs	3,000
Total overhead costs	$40,380

a. What part of the purchasing department cost is variable and what part is fixed? Indicate what types of purchasing department costs would fit into each of these categories.

b. Why might the number of machine setups have increased from 6 to 18 when only 6 custom orders were received?

c. Why might the cost of quality control and inspection have increased?

d. Why were engineering design and specification costs incurred during June, but were not in the original overhead cost listing?

e. If Rockaway were to adopt activity-based costing, what activities should the cost accountant consider to be cost drivers for each of the above items?

f. Do you think the custom orders should have been priced using a rate of $6.25 per machine hour? Indicate the reasoning behind your answer.

40. *(Appendix)* Lion Mfg. uses formal accounting systems in both planning and controlling organizational activities. Historically, indirect labor costs have been dif-

ficult for the company to predict reliably and, hence, to control. The company has been using direct labor hours as a basis to predict indirect labor costs. Management has asked the controller's staff to evaluate machine hours as an alternative prediction base. The controller's staff has assembled data from the latest six months of activity to make the comparison analysis:

Month	Direct Labor Hours	Machine Hours	Indirect Labor Costs
1	425	3,025	$5,049
2	460	2,750	5,921
3	410	2,973	4,968
4	480	3,264	5,297
5	502	4,167	5,410
6	418	2,897	4,998

a. Using least squares regression estimate the fixed and variable values for the formula y = a + bX using direct labor hours.
b. Repeat part a using machine hours as the prediction base.
c. Compute the coefficient of correlation, coefficient of determination, and standard error of the estimate for the equation estimated in part a.
d. Repeat part c using the equation estimated in part b.
e. Based on your computations in parts c and d, is machine hours or direct labor hours the better predictor of indirect labor costs? Explain.

41. *(Appendix)* Stein Company is going to use a predetermined annual factory overhead rate to charge factory overhead to products. To do this, Stein Company must decide whether to use direct labor hours or machine hours as the overhead rate base. Discuss the objectives and criteria that Stein Company should use in selecting the base for its predetermined annual factory overhead rate.
(CPA)

CASES

42. Martin Charity Hospital wishes to budget its expected costs for each month of the upcoming year in its psychiatric ward. The hospital's cost accountant has determined that bed occupancy is the best predictor of cost behavior. The ward has a total of 100 beds, which are generally 70% occupied. At 70% occupancy, the following costs are incurred per patient day:

	Cost per Patient Day	Total per Day Cost	Total Fixed Cost per Month
Variable Costs:			
Linens	$ 4.00	$ 280	
Food	7.50	525	
Drugs	30.00	2,100	
Doctors	60.00	4,200	
Mixed Costs:			
Orderlies (1 full-time)		768	$2,880
Nurses (2 full-time)		2,700	8,000
Maintenance		100	4,000
Fixed Costs:			
Depreciation			1,800
Utilities			960

Except for the 3 full-time employees, nurses and orderlies are hired from a hospital "pool" by the ward; this is the reason their salaries can be computed on a daily basis. One additional full-time nurse and orderly will be necessary if occupancy reaches 85%. Utilities generally cost a fixed fee of $960 per month; this would increase to approximately $1,140 if occupancy reaches 85%. Depreciation charges are computed on a straight-line basis at $1,800 per month. Doctors' charges are entirely variable, based on number of patients and assuming one visit for 30 minutes per day. Variable costs are based on a 30-day month.

a. What costs are expected for the ward for a month at 60%, 80%, and 90% occupancy?

b. What criticisms might be leveled at the above 90% occupancy budget? Or, because of the organizational type, at any of the expected budgets?

43. Rose Bach has recently been hired as controller of Empco Inc., a sheet metal manufacturer. Empco has been in the sheet metal business for many years and is currently investigating ways to modernize its manufacturing process. At the first staff meeting Bach attended, Bob Kelley, the chief engineer, presented a proposal for automating the Drilling Department. Kelley recommended that Empco purchase two robots that would have the capability of replacing the eight direct labor workers in the department.

The cost savings outlined in Kelley's proposal included the elimination of direct labor cost in the Drilling Department plus a reduction of manufacturing overhead cost in the department to zero, because Empco charges manufacturing overhead on the basis of direct labor dollars using a plantwide rate.

The president of Empco was puzzled by Kelley's explanation of cost savings, believing it made no sense. Bach agreed, explaining that as firms become more automated, they should rethink their manufacturing overhead systems. The president then asked Bach to look into the matter and prepare a report for the next staff meeting.

To refresh her knowledge, Bach reviewed articles on manufacturing overhead allocation for an automated factory and discussed the matter with some of her peers. Bach also gathered the historical data presented below on the manufacturing overhead rates experienced by Empco over the years.

Date	Average Annual Direct Labor Cost	Average Annual Manufacturing Overhead Cost	Average Manufacturing Overhead Application Rate
1940s	$1,000,000	$1,000,000	100%
1950s	1,200,000	3,000,000	250%
1960s	2,000,000	7,000,000	350%
1970s	3,000,000	12,000,000	400%
1980s	4,000,000	20,000,000	500%

Bach also wanted to have some departmental data to present at the meeting and, using Empco's accounting records, was able to estimate the following annual averages for each manufacturing department in the 1980s:

	Cutting Department	Grinding Department	Drilling Department
Direct labor	$ 2,000,000	$1,750,000	$ 250,000
Manufacturing overhead	11,000,000	7,000,000	2,000,000

a. Disregarding the proposed use of robots in the Drilling Department, describe the shortcomings of the system for applying overhead that is currently used by Empco Inc.

b. Explain the misconceptions underlying Bob Kelley's statement that manufacturing overhead cost in the Drilling Department would be reduced to zero if the automation proposal was implemented.

c. Recommend ways to improve Empco Inc.'s method for applying overhead by describing how it should revise its overhead accounting system:

1. in the Cutting and Grinding Departments; and

2. to accommodate the automation of the Drilling Department.

(CMA)

44. Haversham Machine Works is bidding on a contract with the government of Bezaire. The contract is a cost-plus situation, with an add-on profit margin of 50%. Direct materials and direct labor are expected to total $15 per unit. Variable overhead is estimated at $4 per unit. Total fixed overhead to produce the 50,000 units needed by the government is $1,400,000. By acquiring the machinery and supervisory support needed to produce the 50,000 units, Haversham will obtain the actual capacity to produce 80,000 units.

   a. Should the price bid by Haversham include a fixed overhead cost of $28 per unit or $17.50? How were these two amounts determined? Which of these two amounts would be more likely to cause Haversham to obtain the contract? Why?

   b. Assume that Haversham set a bid price of $54.75 and obtained the contract. After producing the units, Haversham submitted an invoice to the government of Bezaire for $3,525,000. The minister of finance for the country requests an explanation. Can you provide one?

   c. Haversham uses the excess capacity to produce an additional 30,000 units while making the units for Bezaire. These units are sold to another buyer. Is it ethical to present a $3,525,000 bill to Bezaire? Discuss.

   d. Haversham does not use the excess capacity while making the units for Bezaire. However, several months after that contract was completed, the company begins production of additional units. Was it ethical to present a $3,525,000 bill to Bezaire? Discuss.

   e. Haversham does not use the excess capacity because no other buyer exists for units of this type. Was it ethical to make a bid based on a fixed overhead rate per unit of $54.75? Discuss.

45. *In the course of maintaining its military edge, America contaminated billions of gallons of water and millions of tons of soil with the waste from its bomb-building plants. . . . The Department of Energy, which is responsible for the cleanup effort, initially estimated its cost at between $35 billion and $64 billion. [Between 1988 and 1992], however, the DOE estimate has nearly tripled, and many of those involved now concede that the final bill could go much higher than $200 billion, though just how high no one seems to know.*

   The cost of the job would be daunting enough, but a detailed review of the effort to date indicates . . . billions of dollars of waste, inefficiency and corruption. . . .

   For every $1 budgeted for materials and labor on what is known as "environmental remediation" work in Fernald, Ohio, nearly $2 more goes to administrative costs and other "landlord" activities. The dollars add up. In 1993 at Fernald, the DOE has budgeted $105 million for the cleanup; $203 million will go for contractor overhead and related costs. A review of DOE contracts by the White House Office of Management and Budget (OMB) has found that agency-approved overhead rates were more than twice as high as those on similar contracts let by the Army Corps of Engineers, which also uses commercial contractors for much of its work. According to the OMB review, the DOE's Albuquerque field office could save $51 million and the Savannah River [waste processing] plant $151 million—on overhead alone.

[SOURCE: Douglas Pasternak and Peter Cary, "A $200 Billion Scandal," *U.S. News & World Report* (December 14, 1992), pp. 34, 36.]

   a. What indications can you find that there is some probability of waste and corruption occurring with these contractors?

   b. What can the DOE do to address the problem?

   c. What are some possible implications of the agency-approved overhead rates being more than twice those on similar contracts let by the Army Corps of Engineers?

ETHICS AND QUALITY DISCUSSION

5 ACTIVITY-BASED COST SYSTEMS FOR MANAGEMENT

LEARNING OBJECTIVES

After completing this chapter, you should be able to answer these questions:

1. How do product life cycles affect profitability?
2. What is the focus of activity-based management?
3. Why do non-value-added activities cause costs to increase unnecessarily?
4. How does activity-based costing differ from a traditional cost accounting system?
5. Why must cost drivers be designated in an activity-based costing system?
6. How does the installation of an activity-based costing system affect behavior?
7. *(Appendix)* How can the theory of constraints help in determining production flow?

I N T R O D U C I N G

ELGIN SWEEPER COMPANY

Elgin Sweeper is the leading manufacturer of motorized street sweepers in North America and arguably the world. With $50 million in sales, this 76-year-old manufacturer produces five distinct sweeper models at a single facility in Elgin, Illinois. The production process encompasses numerous facets of manufacturing from the conversion of raw material into components to assembling and painting. This high degree of complexity means that a significant amount of pre- and postproduction planning and support is required, which results in a direct-to-indirect/salaried headcount ratio of approximately one-to-one.

Elgin was the classic case of a one-product domestic company that had evolved into a manufacturer of multiple products for a worldwide market. Overhead had grown in relation to direct labor until the company was allocating more than $4 of overhead for every $1 of direct labor. Elgin used a single allocation basis, standard direct labor hours. Previous management had been enlightened and forward-thinking enough to install a departmental overhead rate system instead of using one shopwide rate, a major plus in that departmental costs and budgets were already in place.

Over the years the chart of accounts had grown so large that there were accounts such as "Administrative Mileage Reimbursement," which would accumulate less than $200 of charges annually. The total chart of accounts contained more than 2,000 accounts [and] expense accounts did not segregate variable and fixed costs.

[To provide better, more useful information], a list of cost "drivers" or factors and actions that prompted a cost was developed. . . . The initial seed of cost management was planted by instilling the idea of "Actions Create Dollars."

SOURCE: John P. Callan, Wesley N. Tredup, and Randy S. Wissinger, "Elgin Sweeper Company's Journey Toward Cost Management," *Management Accounting* (July 1991), p. 24ff. Reprinted from *Management Accounting*. Copyright by Institute of Management Accountants, Montvale, N.J.

Elgin Sweeper Company, like many other American manufacturers, recognized that its traditional overhead allocation system was not providing its managers with the types of information and level of detail needed to make good business decisions in a global economy. The traditional approach is geared to satisfy external reporting requirements, but does a less-than-adequate job of meeting other management needs. Thus, Elgin investigated its cost accounting system and found that some basic changes appeared to be necessary. These changes reflected the observations made in Chapter 4: overhead allocations based on a plantwide rate and a single cost driver often do not provide realistic information for managerial functions.

As mentioned in Chapters 1 and 2, a dramatic shift has taken place in the components of product cost. Less labor and more machines are involved in the production process, causing the overhead portion of product cost to increase immensely. This decrease in direct labor means that the traditional allocation base is less useful for applying overhead. Although machine hours first appeared to be the allocation base of the automation age, more companies are recognizing that the increase in overhead is caused not only by the rise in depreciation charges on the automated equipment, but also by other factors, such as product variety.

This chapter presents topics that are at the forefront of managerial accounting literature and result from the intensely competitive nature of the global economy. First, the chapter discusses the concept of product life cycle costing. Second, the chapter presents the reasons that companies such as Elgin Sweeper now focus on value-added and non-value-added activities, and explains how activities (rather than volume measures) can be used to determine product and service costs and to measure performance. The basics of activity-based costing, as well as some criticisms of this technique, are also discussed and illustrated. Finally, the appendix introduces the theory of constraints to show how it can be applied to production activities.

PRODUCT LIFE CYCLES

Product life cycle

Product profit margins are typically judged on a period-by-period basis without consideration of the **product life cycle**. However, products, like people, go through a series of sequential life cycle stages. The product life cycle is a model depicting the stages through which a product class (not necessarily each product) passes. Those stages are development, introduction, growth, maturity, and decline. Sales in each stage are graphically illustrated in Exhibit 5–1. Companies must be aware of where their products are in their life cycles because, in addition to the sales effects, the life cycle stage may have a tremendous impact on costs and profits. The life cycle impact on each of these items is shown in Exhibit 5–2.

Development Stage and Target Costing

From a cost standpoint, the development stage is an important one that is basically ignored by the traditional financial accounting model. Consider, for example, that MicroGeneSys Inc. (a biopharmaceutical company in Meriden, Connecticut) was started in 1983 and, as of 1992, had not produced any revenues from selling products! Financial accounting requires that development costs be expensed as incurred—even though most studies indicate that decisions made during this stage determine approximately 80 percent to 90 percent of a product's total life cycle costs. That is,

■ EXHIBIT 5–1
Product Life Cycle

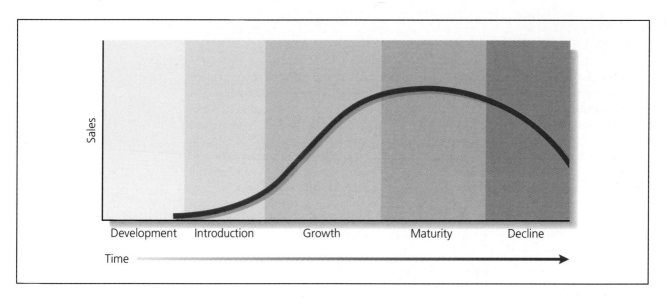

STAGE	COSTS	SALES	PROFITS
Development	No production costs, but R&D costs very high	None	None; large loss on product due to expensing of R&D costs
Introduction	Production cost per unit; probably engineering change costs; high advertising cost	Very low unit sales; selling price may be high (for early profits) or low (for gaining market share)	Typically losses are incurred partially due to expensing of advertising
Growth	Production cost per unit decreases (due to learning curve and spreading fixed overhead over many units)	Rising unit sales; selling price is adjusted to meet competition	High
Maturity	Production cost per unit stable; costs of increasing product mix begin to rise	Peak unit sales; reduced selling price	Falling
Decline	Production cost per unit increases (due to fixed overhead being spread over a lower volume)	Falling unit sales; selling price may be increased in an attempt to raise profits or lowered in an attempt to raise volume	May return to losses

EXHIBIT 5–2

Effects of Product Life Cycles on Costs, Sales, and Profits

the materials and the manufacturing process specifications made during development affect production costs for the rest of the product's life.

Although technology and competition have shortened the development stage time tremendously, effective development efforts are critical to a product's profitability over its entire life cycle. Time spent in the planning and development process can often result "in lower production costs, reduced time from the design to manufacture stage, higher quality, greater flexibility, and lower product life cycle cost."[1] The Japanese are acutely aware of the need to focus attention on the product development stage and the performance measure of "time-to-market" is becoming more critical. "Japan's automakers already can turn out a new model in three years instead of the five [years] Detroit needs. Now they want to cut the cycle to 24 months."[2] The importance of time-to-market is indicated by the following 1987 survey information for the automobile industry: "For each *day* of delay in introducing [a generic $10,000 automobile] to the market, the company will lose about $1 million in profits!"[3] If product delays could create such large profit declines in the late 1980s, imagine what kind of impact long lead times will have in the 1990s!

Once a product or service idea has been formulated, the market is typically researched to determine the features customers desire. Sometimes, however, such product research is foregone for innovative new products. The News Note "We Don't Care What Customers Say" discusses some instances when companies ignore the market and simply develop and introduce products. Because many products can now

[1] James A. Brimson, "How Advanced Manufacturing Technologies Are Reshaping Cost Management," *Management Accounting* (March 1986), p. 26.
[2] Carla Rapoport, "Japan's Capital Spending Spree," *FORTUNE* (April 9, 1990), p. 92.
[3] David Hall and Jerry Jackson, "Speeding Up New Product Development," *Management Accounting* (October 1992), p. 34.

NEWS NOTE

We Don't Care What Customers Say—We Care What They Do!

[H]air styling mousse is now a massive hit. Yet in its initial market tests in the U.S., it flopped. "Goopy and gunky" was what people said about it, and they did not like its feel when it "mooshed" through their hair.

Similarly, when the telephone answering machine was consumer tested, it faced an almost universally negative reaction. Back then, most individuals felt that using a mechanical device to answer a phone was rude and disrespectful. Today, of course, many people regard their answering machines as indispensable.

With customer research not only costly, but often in error, how can a manager determine the innovations customers want? The solution may be design-for-response, a new approach in which a firm uses speed and flexibility to gain customer information instead of, or in addition to, standard customer research.

To illustrate, Sony obtains information from the actual sales of various Walkman models and then quickly adjusts its product mix to conform to those sales patterns.

Similarly, without customer research, every season Seiko "throws" into the market several hundred new models of its watches. Those that the customers buy, it makes more of; the others it drops. Capitalizing on the design-for-response strategy, Seiko has a highly flexible design and production process that lets it quickly and inexpensively introduce new products. [The company's] fast, flexible product design process has slashed the cost of failure.

SOURCE: Willard I. Zangwill, "When Customer Research Is a Lousy Idea," *Wall Street Journal* (March 8, 1993), p. A10. Reprinted by permission of the *Wall Street Journal*, © 1993 Dow Jones & Company, Inc. All rights reserved worldwide.

be built to specifications, companies can further develop the product to meet customer tastes once it is in the market. Alternatively, flexible manufacturing systems allow rapid changeovers to other designs.

After a product is designed, U.S. manufacturers have traditionally determined product costs and set a selling price based, to some extent, on the costs involved. If the market will not bear the resulting selling price (possibly because competitors' prices are lower), the company either does not make as much profit as hoped or it attempts to lower production costs.

In contrast, since the early 1970s, there has been a difference (shown in Exhibit 5–3) in the way the Japanese and Americans have viewed the costing process. The Japanese have used a technique called **target costing** to estimate an "allowable" product cost by using market research to estimate what the market will pay for a product with specific characteristics. Subtracting an acceptable profit margin from the estimated selling price leaves an implied maximum per unit product target cost, which is compared to an expected product cost.

If the expected cost is greater than the target cost, the company has several alternatives. First, the product design and/or production process can be changed to reduce costs. Preparation of **cost tables** help in determining how such adjustments can be made. These tables are data bases that provide information about the impact on product costs of using different input resources, manufacturing processes, and design specifications. Second, a less-than-desired profit margin can be accepted. Third, the company can decide that it does not want to enter this particular product market at the current time because it cannot make the profit margin it desires.

If the company decides to enter the market, the target cost computed at the beginning of the product life cycle does not remain the final focus. Over the life of the product, the target cost is continuously reduced in an effort to spur a process of continuous improvement in actual production cost. These cost reductions are designed

Target costing

Cost tables

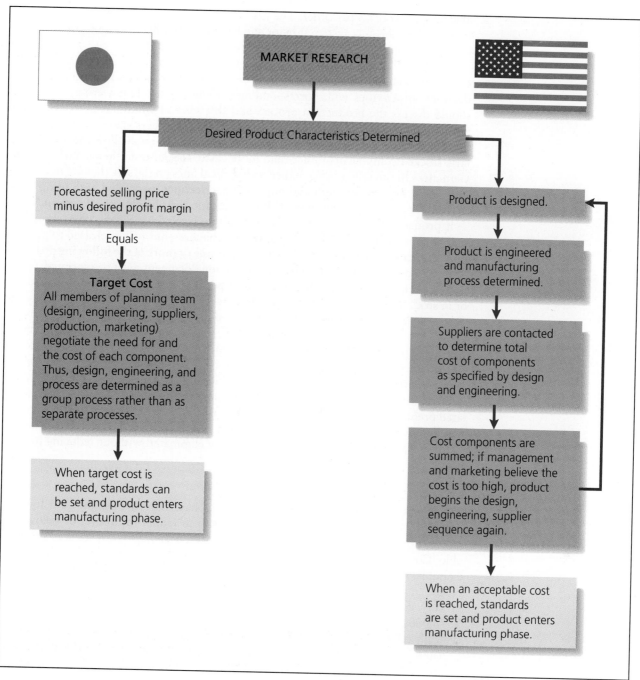

MARKET RESEARCH

Desired Product Characteristics Determined

Forecasted selling price
minus desired profit margin

Equals

Target Cost
All members of planning team
(design, engineering, suppliers,
production, marketing)
negotiate the need for and
the cost of each component.
Thus, design, engineering, and
process are determined as a
group process rather than as
separate processes.

When target cost is
reached, standards can
be set and product enters
manufacturing phase.

Product is designed.

Product is engineered
and manufacturing
process determined.

Suppliers are contacted
to determine total
cost of components
as specified by design
and engineering.

Cost components are
summed; if management
and marketing believe the
cost is too high, product
begins the design,
engineering, supplier
sequence again.

When an acceptable cost
is reached, standards
are set and product enters
manufacturing phase.

▌ **EXHIBIT 5–3**
Developing Product Costs

to keep the profit margin relatively stable as the product price is reduced over the product life cycle.

Target costing can be applied to a service if it is sufficiently uniform to justify the modeling effort required. For example, assume that a supermarket wants to offer a new fax grocery pick-up service. Customers could fax their grocery orders to the store, which will have the merchandise packed (and refrigerated, if needed) and checked out by the time the customers arrive. Without leaving their cars, the customers would pay a clerk as the groceries were loaded. A market survey indicates that customers believe $5 is a reasonable fee for such a service. The store manager believes that a reasonable profit for this service is $2 per order. Thus, the store has an allowable target cost of $3 per order. The manager will invest in the equipment necessary to implement the new system if he or she believes the indicated 2,000-order volume suggested by market research is sufficient to support the effort.

In trying to design a product to meet an allowable cost, engineers and managers can strive to eliminate all inessential activities from the production process. Such reductions in activities will, correspondingly, reduce costs. Engineering and design should discuss the production process and the types of components to be used in recognition of the product quality and cost desired. Suppliers also may participate in the design phase modifications by making suggestions that will allow the use of regularly stocked components rather than more costly special-order items. For example, Germany's Braun sells a coffeemaker with vertical lines on the side that are not simply decorative, but add strength and hide the imperfections associated with using a less expensive plastic. The lines reduced Braun's plastic costs by almost 70 percent.[4]

If products are properly designed during the development stage, they should require only a minimal number of engineering changes after being released to production. Each time an engineering change is made, one or more of the following problems occur and create additional costs: the production document must be reprinted; workers must relearn tasks; machine setups must be changed; and parts currently ordered or in stock may be made obsolete. If costs are to be affected significantly, any design changes must be made early in the process—preferably before production begins.

The use of target costing requires a shift in the way managers think about the relationships among cost, selling price, and profitability. The traditional attitude has been that a product is developed, production cost is identified and measured, a selling price is set (or a market price is met), and profits or losses result. If target costing were adopted, the sequence would be that a product is developed, a selling price and desired profit amount are determined, and maximum allowable costs are calculated. By making costs rely on selling prices rather than the opposite, the incurrence of all costs must be justified. Unnecessary costs should be eliminated without reducing quality.

Other Life Cycle Stages

Substitute good

Product introduction is essentially a "start-up" phase. Sales are usually quite low and selling prices often are set in some relationship to (equal to, above, or below) the market price of similar **substitute goods** or services, if such goods or services are available. Costs, on the other hand, can be substantial during this life cycle stage. For example, in a 1990 survey, a grocery industry task force determined that on the average, "manufacturers paid $5.1 million to get a new product or line extension on grocery store shelves nationwide. The cheapest [product introduction] studied cost $378,000; the most expensive, $21.2 million."[5] Costs incurred during this stage are typically related to product design, market research, advertising, and promotion.

The growth stage begins when the product has been accepted by the market and begins to show a profit. Product quality also may improve during this stage of the life cycle, especially if competitors have improved on original production designs. Prices are fairly stable during the growth stage because many substitutes exist or because consumers have become "attached" to the product and are willing to pay a particular price for it rather than buy a substitute.

In the maturity stage, sales begin to stabilize or slowly decline and firms often compete on the basis of selling price. Costs are often at their lowest level during this period, so profits may be high. Some products (such as Kool-Aid) remain at this stage seemingly forever.

The decline stage reflects waning sales, and prices are often cut dramatically to stimulate business. Production cost per unit can be expected to increase during this stage because fixed overhead is spread over a lower production volume.

---

[4] Brian Dumaine, "Design That Sells and Sells and . . . ," *FORTUNE* (March 11, 1991), p. 90.
[5] Richard Gibson, "Marketing—Pinning Down Costs of Product Introductions," *Wall Street Journal* (November 26, 1990), p. B1.

Life Cycle Costing

Customers are concerned with obtaining a quality product or service for a perceived "reasonable" price. In making such a determination, the consumer views the product from a life cycle perspective. For example, when purchasing a computer, you would investigate not only the original purchase price but also the cost of software and servicing, length of warranty period, frequency and cost of upgrades, and projected obsolescence period. All of these items would enter into your determination of the "total" cost of the computer.

From a manufacturing standpoint, since product selling prices (and sales volumes) change over a product's life cycle, target costing requires that profitability be viewed on a long-range rather than period-by-period basis. Thus, producers of goods and providers of service should be concerned about maximizing profits over a product's or service's life cycle because revenues must be generated in excess of total product (not period) costs for a product to be truly profitable.

For financial statement purposes, costs incurred during the research and development (R&D) stage *must* be expensed in the period. However, the R&D costs that result in marketable products represent a life cycle investment rather than a period expense. Capitalization and product allocation of such costs for managerial purposes would provide better long-range profitability information and a means by which to determine the cost impact of engineering changes on product design and manufacturing process. Thus, companies desiring to focus on life cycle costs and profitability will need to change their *internal* accounting treatments of costs.

Life cycle costing is the "accumulation of costs for activities that occur over the entire life cycle of a product, from inception to abandonment by the manufacturer and consumer."[6] From a manufacturer's viewpoint, life cycle costing expense allocations would be based on an expected number of units to be sold over the product's life. Each period's internal income statement using life cycle costing would present sales revenue on the life to date. This revenue amount would be reduced by total cost of goods sold, total R&D project costs, and total distribution and other types of marketing costs. If life cycle costing were to be used externally, only annual sales and cost of goods sold would be presented in periodic financial statements. But all preproduction costs would be capitalized and a risk reserve could be established "to measure the probability that these deferred product costs will be recovered through related product sales."[7]

Life cycle costing is especially important in industries that face rapid technological or style changes. If substantial amounts of money are spent on development activities, but technology improves faster or customer demand diminishes more rapidly than those monies can be recouped from total sales of the product, was the development investment worthwhile? Using periodic external financial statements may make a product appear to be worthwhile since its development costs are initially expensed. But, in total, the company may not even have recovered its original investment. Thus, over the product or service life cycle, companies need to be aware of and attempt to control the *total* costs of making a product or providing a service. One way of creating awareness is to evaluate all activities related to a product or service as value-added or non-value-added.

Life cycle costing

Product cost determination, although specifically designated as an accounting function, is a major concern of all managers. For example, product costs affect decisions on corporate strategy (is it profitable to be in a particular market?), marketing (how

ACTIVITY-BASED MANAGEMENT

---

[6]Callie Berliner and James A. Brimson (eds.), *Cost Management for Today's Advanced Manufacturing* (Boston: Harvard Business School Press, 1988), p. 241.
[7]Dennis E. Peavy, "It's Time for a Change," *Management Accounting* (February 1990), p. 34.

■ EXHIBIT 5–4
The Activity-Based
Management Umbrella

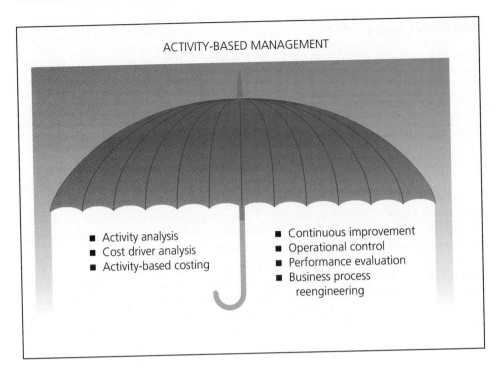

ACTIVITY-BASED MANAGEMENT

- Activity analysis
- Cost driver analysis
- Activity-based costing

- Continuous improvement
- Operational control
- Performance evaluation
- Business process reengineering

much does this product cost and how should it be priced?), and finance (should we invest in additional plant assets to manufacture this product?). In theory, it would not matter what a product or service cost to produce or perform if enough customers were willing to buy that product or service at a price high enough to cover costs and provide a reasonable profit margin. In reality, customers usually only purchase a product or service that provides acceptable value for the price being charged.

Activity-based management

Management, then, should be concerned about whether customers perceive an equal relationship between selling price and value. The concept of **activity-based management** focuses on the activities incurred during the production/performance process as the way to improve the value received by a customer and the resulting profit achieved by providing this value. The concepts covered by activity-based management are shown in Exhibit 5–4 and are discussed in this and other chapters. These concepts help companies to produce more efficiently, determine cost more accurately, and control and evaluate performance more effectively. A primary component of activity-based management is **activity analysis**, which is the process of studying activities to classify them and to devise ways of minimizing or eliminating non-value-added activities.

Activity analysis

Value-Added Versus Non-Value-Added Activities

Activity

In a business context, an **activity** is defined as a repetitive action performed in fulfillment of business functions. If one takes a black-or-white perspective, activities can be said to be value-added or non-value-added. A **value-added activity** (VA) increases the worth of a product or service to a customer and for which the customer is willing to pay. On the other hand, a **non-value-added activity** (NVA) increases the time spent on a product or service but does not increase its worth. Non-value-added activities are unnecessary, which means they create costs that can be eliminated without affecting the market value or quality of the product or service.

Value-added activity

Non-value-added activity

Exhibit 5–5 provides a simplified example of value-added and non-value-added activities in a stage play. While the intermissions spent in changing costumes or props are value-added from the actors' and directors' perspectives, the audience merely sees a drawn curtain on stage. That time is often considered by the audience (the customers) as non-value-added. The two hours spent before and after the play and during intermissions may also be valued-added from certain perspectives such as those persons managing the concession area, but possibly not from some in the audience.

As in a three-act play, businesses also experience a significant amount of non-value-added time and activities. To help in their analysis of activities, managers should prepare a **process map** or a detailed flowchart that indicates every step that goes into making or doing something. It is critical to include all steps, not just the obvious ones. For example, storing newly purchased parts would not be on a typical list of "Steps in Making Product X," but when materials and supplies are purchased, they are commonly warehoused until needed. Such storage uses facilities that cost money and time to move the items in and out. Each process map is unique and based on the results of a management and employee team's study. The News Note "What Steps Are Involved?" on page 175 discusses process mapping at General Electric.

Process map

An illustration of a process flowchart for Brooktree Corporation, which designs, develops, and markets computer chips, is presented in Exhibit 5–6 on page 174. This flowchart relates to the company's wafer commitment process. Wafers contain the die that is the "mind" of a computer chip; they are manufactured by different foundry companies in the United States and Japan. Before analyzing and flowcharting the process, Brooktree found that it often took up to three weeks for foundries to commit to a delivery time for the wafers. Now, the wafer commit times have been reduced by about two-thirds. In a parallel procedure, the wafer chips are started when the work request is received and verified.

Once the process map has been developed, a **value chart** can be constructed that identifies the stages and time spent in those stages from beginning to end of a process. There are four types of time that compose the entire processing time of an entity: production (or performance), inspection, transfer, and idle. The actual time that it takes to perform the functions necessary to manufacture the product or perform the service is the **production (or service) time;** this quantity of time is value-added. Performing quality control results in **inspection time,** while moving products or components from one place to another constitutes **transfer time.** Lastly, storage time and time spent waiting at the production operation for processing is referred to as **idle time.** Inspection time, transfer time, and idle time are all considered non-value-added activities. Thus, the lead or cycle time from the receipt of an order to completion of a

Value chart

Production time
Service time
Inspection time
Transfer time
Idle time

■ **EXHIBIT 5–5**
Value-Added and Non-Value-Added Activities

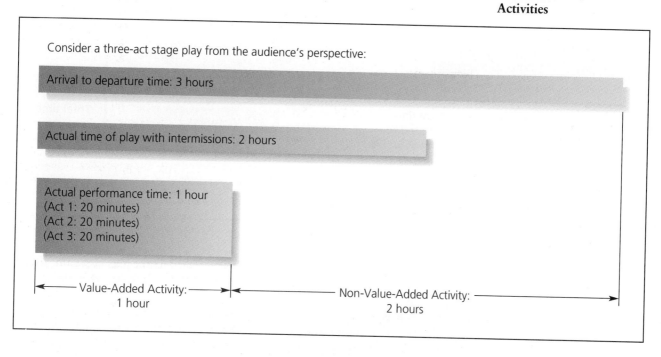

Consider a three-act stage play from the audience's perspective:

Arrival to departure time: 3 hours

Actual time of play with intermissions: 2 hours

Actual performance time: 1 hour
(Act 1: 20 minutes)
(Act 2: 20 minutes)
(Act 3: 20 minutes)

Value-Added Activity: 1 hour   Non-Value-Added Activity: 2 hours

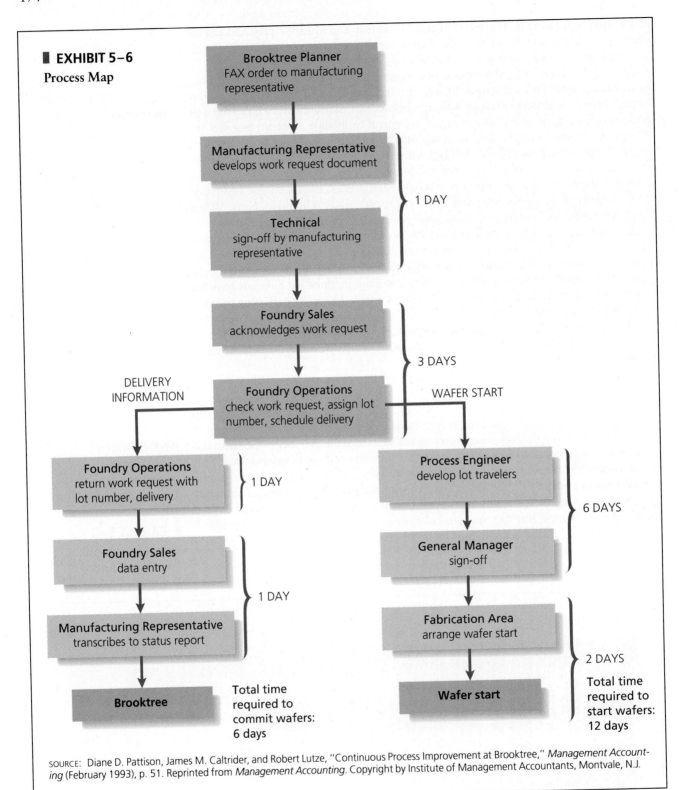

EXHIBIT 5–6
Process Map

Brooktree Planner
FAX order to manufacturing representative

↓

Manufacturing Representative
develops work request document

↓

Technical
sign-off by manufacturing representative

} 1 DAY

↓

Foundry Sales
acknowledges work request

↓

Foundry Operations
check work request, assign lot number, schedule delivery

} 3 DAYS

DELIVERY INFORMATION ←   → WAFER START

Foundry Operations
return work request with lot number, delivery

} 1 DAY

↓

Foundry Sales
data entry

↓

Manufacturing Representative
transcribes to status report

} 1 DAY

↓

Brooktree

Total time required to commit wafers: 6 days

Process Engineer
develop lot travelers

↓

General Manager
sign-off

} 6 DAYS

↓

Fabrication Area
arrange wafer start

↓

Wafer start

} 2 DAYS

Total time required to start wafers: 12 days

SOURCE: Diane D. Pattison, James M. Caltrider, and Robert Lutze, "Continuous Process Improvement at Brooktree," *Management Accounting* (February 1993), p. 51. Reprinted from *Management Accounting*. Copyright by Institute of Management Accountants, Montvale, N.J.

product or performance of a service is equal to production time plus non-value-added time. The News Note about Stevens Graphics on page 175 indicates that eliminating non-value-added time really makes money!

Although it is theoretically correct to view inspection time and transfer time as non-value-added, it is important to realize that few companies can completely eliminate all quality control functions and that it is impossible to eliminate all transfer

NEWS NOTE

What Steps Are Involved?

Elaborate process maps use diamonds, circles, and squares to distinguish work that adds value from work that doesn't, like inspection. These are furbelows, not really necessary. What's essential is that every step be mapped, from the order clerk picking up the phone to the deliveryman getting a signed receipt.

Process mapping sounds simple, but it's not. To do it right, managers, employees, suppliers, and customers must work on the map together to make sure that what the company thinks happens really does. When a team from GE's Evendale, Ohio, plant mapped the process of making turbine shafts for jet engines, the job took more than a month, and the map went all around a conference room.

When a process is mapped, GE has—often for the first time—the ability to manage an operation in a coherent way from start to finish. For example, in pursuit of 100% machine utilization, all rotating parts used to go to a central steam-cleaning facility between operations; now the shaftmakers have their own cleaning booths because the process map revealed that the time saved more than paid for the additional equipment.

SOURCE: Thomas A. Stewart, "GE Keeps Those Ideas Coming," FORTUNE (August 12, 1991), p. 48. © 1991 Time Inc. All rights reserved.

time. Understanding the non-value-added nature of these functions, however, should help managers strive to minimize such activities to the extent possible. Thus, it is more reasonable to view value-added and non-value-added activities as occurring on a continuum and concentrate on attempting to eliminate or minimize those activities that add the most time and cost, and the least value.

Exhibit 5–7 on page 176 illustrates a value chart for a cleaning product made by the Shannen Company. Note the excessive time consumed by simply storing and mov-

NEWS NOTE

For Stevens Graphics, Time Is Literally Money!

Stevens Graphics Corp. has what some say is the next best thing to a license to print money—a government contract to build currency presses. The Bureau of Engraving and Printing gave Stevens the go-ahead to ship the first American-made, web-fed currency press to Washington.

Until Stevens developed its press, U.S. currency was printed in sheets of 32 bills each on German-made presses. "Our press is about four times as efficient as a sheet-fed press," Mr. Stevens (the founder, chairman, and CEO) said.

Using current technology, an individual currency sheet must be run through existing presses twice—once for each side—before it is put into circulation, he said. Bank notes printed by the sheet-fed method must be seasoned for 48 hours between passes stacked in 40-inch stacks waiting for the color of money to set in.

"That requires a lot of inventory waiting for the next operation to take place, where ours goes right through the press and it's dried, finished and off it goes," Mr. Stevens said.

Stevens' "Alexander Hamilton" system prints 490,000 bank notes per hour. That same number of notes would take about four hours to print on each side with 48-hour waiting periods after each printing pass.

SOURCE: Joe Simacher, "Stevens Presses Ahead with Growth," Dallas Morning News (June 2, 1991), p. 1H. Reprinted by permission of the Dallas Morning News.

Assembling									
Operations	Receiving	Quality control	Storage	Move to production	Waiting for use	Setup of machinery	Assembly	Move to inspection	Move to finishing
Average time (days)	2	1	10–15	.5	3	.5	3	.5	.5

Finishing									
Operations	Receiving	Move to production	Waiting for use	Setup of machinery	Finishing	Inspection	Packaging	Move to dockside	Storage	Ship to customer
Average time (days)	.5	.5	5–12	.5	2	.5	.5	.5	1.5	1–4

Total time in assembling: 21.0 – 26.0 days
Total time in finishing: 12.5 – 22.5 days
Total processing time: 33.5 – 48.5 days
–Total value-added time: 05.5 – 5.5 days
Total non-value-added time: 28.0 – 43.0 days

Assembly value-added time: 3.0 days
Finishing value-added time: 2.5 days
Total value-added time: 5.5 days

Non-Value-Added Activities
Value-Added Activities

EXHIBIT 5–7

Value Chart for Shannen Company

ing materials. Value is added to products *only* during the times that production actually occurs; thus, in Shannen Company's entire production sequence, there are only five and one-half days of value-added time.

In some instances, a company may question whether the time spent in packaging is value-added. Packaging is essential for some products but unnecessary for others and, since packaging takes up about a third of the U.S. landfills and creates a substantial amount of cost, companies and consumers are focusing their attention on reducing or eliminating packaging.

Manufacturing Cycle Efficiency

Manufacturing cycle efficiency

Dividing actual production time by total lead time provides a measure of efficiency referred to as **manufacturing cycle efficiency** (MCE). (A service company would compute service cycle efficiency by dividing actual service time by total lead time.) If a company's production time were 3 hours and its total lead time were 24 hours, its manufacturing cycle efficiency would be 12.5 (3 ÷ 24) percent.

While the ultimate goal of 100 percent efficiency can never be achieved,

[t]ypically, value is added to the product only 10% of the time from receipt of the parts until shipment to the customer. Ninety percent of the cycle time is waste. A product is much like a magnet. The longer the cycle time, the more the product attracts and creates cost.[8]

A just-in-time inventory process (discussed in Chapter 18) seeks to achieve substantially higher efficiency by manufacturing components and goods at the precise time

[8]Tom E. Pryor, "Activity Accounting: The Key to Waste Reduction," *Accounting Systems Journal* (Fall 1990), p. 38.

they are needed by either the next production station or the consumer. Another technique to raise MCE is to install and use significant automated technology in flexible manufacturing systems.

In a retail environment, lead time relates to the time from ordering an item to the sale of that item to a customer. Non-value-added activities in retail refer to shipping time from the supplier, receiving delays for counting merchandise, and any storage time between receipt and sale. In a service company, lead time refers to the time between the service order and service completion. All time spent on activities that are not actual service performance or are nonactivities (such as delays in beginning a job) are considered non-value-added for that job.

Non-value-added activities can be attributed to systemic, physical, and human factors. For example, systemic causes could include a system requirement that products be manufactured in large batches to minimize setup cost or that service jobs be taken in order of urgency. Physical factors contribute to non-value-added activities since, in many instances, plant and machine layout do not provide for the most efficient transfer of products. This factor is especially apparent in multistory buildings constructed during the "smokestack" manufacturing period in which receiving and shipping are on the ground floor, but storage and production are on upper floors. People may also be responsible for non-value-added activities because of improper skills or training or the need to be sociable (production workers discussing their weekend activities during production time on Monday morning).

Attempts to reduce non-value-added activities should be directed at all of these causes, but it is imperative that the "Willie Sutton" rule be applied. This rule is named for the bank robber who, when asked why he robbed banks, replied, "That's where the money is." The NVA activities that create the most cost should be the ones that management concentrates its efforts on reducing or eliminating. The system must be changed to reflect a new management philosophy regarding performance measures and determination of product cost. Physical factors must be changed as much as possible to eliminate layout difficulties and machine bottlenecks, and people must accept and work toward total quality control. Automated machines and a "lights-out" factory (run by robots with little or no human intervention) are useful to an extent, but

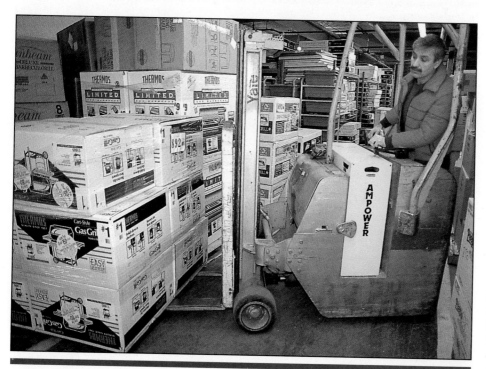

Production in advance of sales demand creates types of NVA time: idle time for storage and transfer time to stack, unstack, and move goods. NVA time creates unnecessary costs.

PART II Allocating Indirect Costs

people are still necessary for businesses—especially service businesses—to continue. Focusing attention on eliminating non-value-added activities should cause product quality to increase and lead time and cost to decrease.

Although constructing a value chart for each product or service could be time-consuming, a few such charts can quickly indicate where a company is losing time and, therefore, money through non-value-added activities. Using amounts such as depreciation on storage facilities, wages for employees who handle warehousing, and the cost of capital on working capital funds tied up in stored inventory can provide an estimate of the amount by which costs could be reduced through the elimination of non-value-added activities.

COST DRIVER ANALYSIS

Companies engage in many activities that consume resources and, thus, cause costs to be incurred. All activities have cost drivers, defined in Chapter 2 as the factors having direct cause-effect relationships to a cost. Many cost drivers may be identified for an individual business unit. For example, cost drivers for factory insurance are number of employees; value of property, plant, and equipment; and number of accidents during some specified prior period of time. Cost drivers affecting the entire plant include inventory size, physical layout, and number of different products produced. Cost drivers are classified as volume-related (such as machine hours) and non-volume-related (such as square feet of operations space).

Usually a greater number of cost drivers can be identified than should be used for cost allocation or activity elimination. Management should limit the cost drivers selected to a reasonable number and ascertain that the cost of measuring the cost driver

NEWS NOTE

Single Cost Pools Are Illogical

Today's competitive environment makes it imperative for manufacturers competing globally to know their costs. They need to understand costs at several levels, the activities that are driving costs, the link between management decisions and subsequent costs incurred, and the areas where improvement opportunities lie.

Simple cost systems are accurate enough for assigning costs that are easily traceable to the production process, such as production material and direct labor, but they don't specifically assign costs such as machine tool energy consumption, setup, machine repair, durable tooling, and manufacturing support activities. Such systems also fail to recognize the product-by-product cost effects of volume, product and process complexity, product design, and the different values of capital assets used in the production process.

A good cost system mirrors the manufacturing process and related support activities and quantifies them product by product. The more complex and inconsistent these processes are the more difficult it is to assign costs to products accurately. Thus, the cost system becomes more complex as it attempts to compensate for the lack of simplicity of the manufacturing processes.

Such considerations led Caterpillar to develop a product costing system . . . [designed] to identify the activities consumed by products and, through a logical, reliable, and consistent process, assign the related costs properly to each.

SOURCE: Lou F. Jones, "Product Costing at Caterpillar," *Management Accounting* (February 1991), pp. 34–35. Reprinted from *Management Accounting.* Copyright by Institute of Management Accountants, Montvale, N.J.

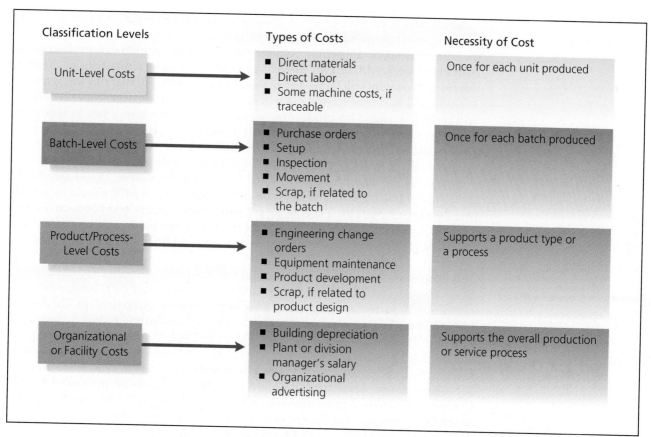

Classification Levels	Types of Costs	Necessity of Cost
Unit-Level Costs	■ Direct materials ■ Direct labor ■ Some machine costs, if traceable	Once for each unit produced
Batch-Level Costs	■ Purchase orders ■ Setup ■ Inspection ■ Movement ■ Scrap, if related to the batch	Once for each batch produced
Product/Process-Level Costs	■ Engineering change orders ■ Equipment maintenance ■ Product development ■ Scrap, if related to product design	Supports a product type or a process
Organizational or Facility Costs	■ Building depreciation ■ Plant or division manager's salary ■ Organizational advertising	Supports the overall production or service process

■ EXHIBIT 5–8
Levels of Costs

does not exceed the benefit of using it. A cost driver should be easy to understand, directly related to the activity being performed, and appropriate for performance measurement.[9]

Costs have traditionally been accumulated into one or two cost pools (total factory overhead or variable and fixed factory overhead) and one or two cost drivers (direct labor hours and/or machine hours) have been used to assign costs to products. These procedures cause few, if any, problems for financial statement preparation. As indicated in the News Note about Caterpillar, however, the use of single cost pools and single cost drivers may produce illogical product or service costs for internal managerial use in complex production (or service) environments.

To reflect the more complex environments, the accounting system must first recognize that costs are created and incurred because their drivers occur at different levels. This realization necessitates using **cost driver analysis**, which investigates, quantifies, and explains the relationships of drivers and their related costs. Traditionally, cost drivers were viewed only at the **unit-level**; for example, how many hours of labor or machine time did it take to produce a product or render a service? These drivers create unit-level costs, meaning that they are caused by the production or acquisition of a single unit of product or the delivery of a single unit of service. Other drivers and their costs are incurred for broader-based categories or levels of activity. These broader-based activity levels have successively wider scopes of influence on products and product types. The categories are classified as batch, product or process, and organizational or facility levels. Examples of the kinds of costs occurring at the various levels are given in Exhibit 5–8.

Cost driver analysis

Unit-level cost

---

[9]The appendix to Chapter 22 provides a detailed list of cost drivers that are appropriate for analyzing cost incurrence as well as performance measures for a variety of areas.

Batch-level cost

Costs that are caused by a group of things being made, handled, or processed at a single time are referred to as **batch-level costs**. A good example of a batch level cost is the cost of setting up a machine. Assume that a machine setup to cast product parts costs Elgin Sweeper $400. Two different parts are to be manufactured during the day; therefore, two setups will be needed at a total cost of $800. The first run will generate 1,000 Type A parts; the second run will generate 200 Type B parts. These quantities are specifically needed for production because the company is on a just-in-time production system. If a unit-based cost driver (volume) were used, the total setup cost of $800 would be divided by 1,200 parts, giving a cost per part of $.67. This method would assign the majority of the cost to Type A parts (1,000 × $.67 = $670). However, because the cost is actually created by a batch-level driver, $400 should be spread over 1,000 Type A parts for a cost of $.40 per part and $400 should be spread over 200 Type B parts for a cost of $2 per part. Using a batch-level perspective indicates the commonality of the cost to the units within the batch and is more indicative of the relationship between the activity (setup) and the driver (different production runs).

Product- or process-level cost

A cost caused by the development, production, or acquisition of different items is called a **product- or process-level cost**. To illustrate this level of cost, assume that the engineering department of Elgin issued five engineering change orders (ECOs) during May. Of these ECOs, four related to Product R, one related to Product S, and none related to Product T. Each ECO costs $3,000 to issue. During May, the company produced 1,000 units of Product R, 1,500 units of Product S, and 5,000 units of Product T. If ECO costs were treated as unit-level costs, the total ECO cost of $15,000 would be spread over the 7,500 units produced at a cost per unit of $2.00. However, this method inappropriately assigns $10,000 of ECO cost to Product T, which had no engineering change orders issued for it! Using a product/process level driver (number of ECOs) for ECO costs would assign $12,000 of costs to Product R and $3,000 to Product S. These amounts would be assigned to R and S, but not simply to the current month's production. The ECO cost should be allocated to all current and future R and S units produced while these ECOs are in effect because the products manufactured using the changed design benefit from the costs of the ECOs.

Organizational-level cost

Certain costs at the **organizational level** are incurred for the singular purpose of supporting continuing facility operations. These costs are common to many different activities and products or services and can be prorated to products only on an arbitrary basis. Although organizational-level costs theoretically should not be assigned to products at all, some companies attach them to goods produced or services rendered because the amounts are insignificant relative to all other costs.

Accountants have traditionally (and incorrectly) assumed that if costs did not vary with changes in production at the unit level, those costs were fixed rather than variable. In reality, batch-, product-, and organizational-level costs are all variable, but these costs vary for reasons other than changes in production volume. Therefore, to determine a valid estimate of product or service cost, costs should be accumulated at each successively higher level of costs. Since unit-, batch-, and product-level costs are all associated with units of products (merely at different levels), these costs can be summed at the product level to match with the revenues generated by product sales. Because organizational-level costs are not product-related, they should only be subtracted in total from net product revenues.

Exhibit 5–9 illustrates how costs collected at the unit, batch, and product levels can be used to generate a total product cost. Each product cost would be multiplied by the number of units sold and that amount of cost of goods sold would be subtracted from total product revenues to obtain a product line profit or loss item. These computations would be performed for each product line and summed to determine net product revenues from which the unassigned organizational level costs would be subtracted to find company profit or loss for internal management use. In this model, the traditional distinction (discussed in Chapter 2) between product and period costs

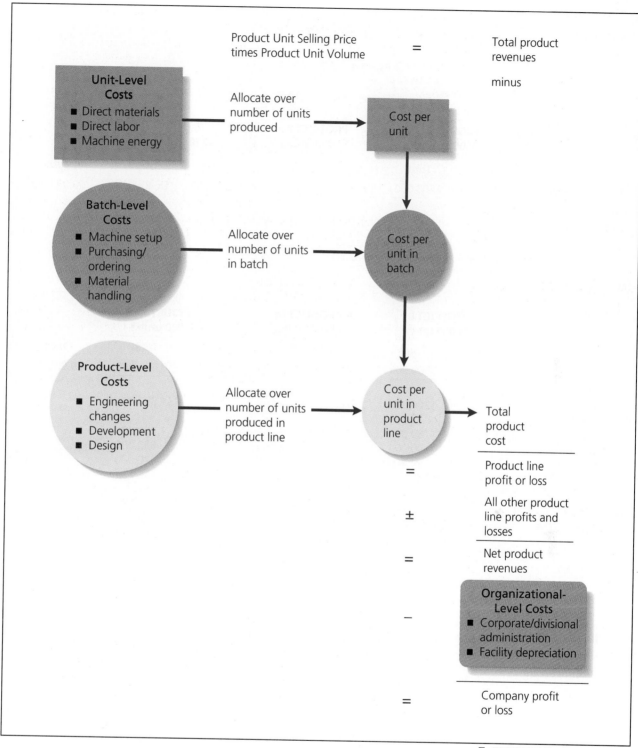

Determining Product Profitability and Company Profit

can be and is ignored. The emphasis is on refining product profitability analysis for internal management purposes, rather than for the external financial statement. Since the product/period cost distinction required by generally accepted accounting principles is not recognized, the model presented in Exhibit 5–9 is not currently acceptable for external reporting.

Bush Manufacturing Company data are presented in Exhibit 5–10 to illustrate the difference in information that would result from recognizing multiple cost levels. Be-

Total OH cost = $3,010,000

Total MHs = 223,000

OH rate per MH = $13.50

	PRODUCT L (10,000 units)		PRODUCT M (3,000 units)		PRODUCT N (210,000 units)		Total
	Unit	Total	Unit	Total	Unit	Total	Total
Product Revenue	$50.00	$500,000	$45.00	$135,000	$40.00	$8,400,000	$9,035,000
Product Costs							
Direct	$20.00	200,000	$20.00	$ 60,000	$ 9.00	$1,890,000	
OH per MH	13.50	135,000	13.50	40,500	13.50	2,835,000	
Total	$33.50	$335,000	$33.50	$100,500	$22.50	$4,725,000	5,160,500
Net Income		$165,000		$ 34,500		$3,675,000	$3,874,500

	PRODUCT L (10,000 units)		PRODUCT M (3,000 units)		PRODUCT N (210,000 units)		Total
	Unit	Total	Unit	Total	Unit	Total	Total
Product Revenue	$50	$500,000	$45	$135,000	$40	$8,400,000	$9,035,000
Product Costs							
Direct	$20	$200,000	$20	$ 60,000	$ 9	$1,890,000	
Overhead							
unit level	8	80,000	12	36,000	6	1,260,000	
batch level	9	90,000	19	57,000	3	630,000	
product level	3	30,000	15	45,000	2	420,000	
Total	$40	$400,000	$66	$198,000	$20	$4,200,000	4,798,000
Product Line Income or (Loss)		$100,000		$ (63,000)		$4,200,000	$4,237,000
Organizational-Level Costs							362,500
Net Income							$3,874,500

▌ **EXHIBIT 5–10**

Profitability Analysis for Bush Manufacturing Company

fore recognizing that some costs were incurred at the batch, product, and organizational level, Bush accumulated its factory overhead costs and allocated them among its three types of products on a machine hour (MH) basis. Each product requires one machine hour, but Product M is a low-volume, special order line. As shown in the first section of Exhibit 5–10, cost information indicated that Product M was a profitable product for Bush Manufacturing. After analyzing its activities, Bush began capturing costs at the different levels and assigning them to products based on appropriate cost drivers. The individual details for this overhead assignment are not shown, but the final assignments and resulting product profitability figures are presented in the second section of Exhibit 5–10. Prior to this analysis, management believed that the company was generating a reasonable profit on Product M. However, this more refined approach to assigning costs shows results contrary to that belief.

It is apparent that costs are incurred because firms engage in a variety of activities and these activities consume company resources. Accountants have traditionally used a transaction basis to accumulate costs and, additionally, they have focused on the cost incurred rather than the source of the cost. However, managers now believe that the "conventional transaction-driven system is costly to administer, fails to control costs, and usually yields erroneous product cost data."[10]

Traditional cost allocation tends to subsidize low-volume specialty products by misallocating overhead to high-volume, standard products. This problem occurs because costs of the extra activities needed to make specialty products are assigned using the one or very few cost drivers of traditional costing—and usually those cost drivers are volume-based. Interestingly, as long ago as 1954, William J. Vatter noted that "[j]ust as soon as cost accounting is found inadequate for the needs it is supposed to meet, just as soon as cost accounting does not provide the data which management must have, cost accounting will either change to meet those needs or it will be replaced with something else."[11] The time has come for cost accounting to change by utilizing new bases on which to collect and assign costs. Those bases are the activities that drive or create the costs.

Recognizing that several levels of costs exist, accumulating costs into related cost pools, and using multiple cost drivers to assign costs to products and services are the three fundamental components of **activity-based costing** (ABC). ABC is a cost accounting system that focuses on the various activities performed in an organization and collects costs on the basis of the underlying nature and extent of those activities. This costing method focuses on attaching costs to products and services based on the activities conducted to produce, perform, distribute, or support those products and services.

As indicated in the opening vignette about Elgin Sweeper and in the News Note about Caterpillar, managers in many American manufacturing companies are concerned about the product costing information being provided by the traditional cost accounting systems (see Exhibit 5–11, page 184). The general consensus seems to be that product costs currently being developed are useful in preparing financial statements, but are of limited use for management decision making. Activity-based costing, on the other hand, is useful in companies having the following characteristics:

1. the production or performance of a wide variety of products or services;
2. high overhead costs that are not proportional to the unit volume of individual products;
3. significant automation that has made it increasingly more difficult to assign overhead to products using the traditional direct labor or machine hour bases;
4. profit margins that are difficult to explain; and
5. hard-to-make products that show big profits and easy-to-make products that show losses.[12]

Companies having the above characteristics may want to reevaluate their cost systems and implement activity-based costing.

ACTIVITY-BASED COSTING
Activity-based costing

---

[10] Richard J. Schonberger, "World-Class Performance Management," *Performance Excellence in Manufacturing and Service Organizations,* Peter B. B. Turney (ed.) (Proceedings of the Third Annual Management Accounting Symposium; Sarasota, FL: American Accounting Association, 1990), p. 1.

[11] William J. Vatter, "Tailor-making Cost Data for Specific Uses," *Topics in Managerial Accounting,* L. S. Rosen, ed. (McGraw-Hill Ryerson Ltd., 1974), p. 194.

[12] Robin Cooper, "You Need a New Cost System When . . . ," *Harvard Business Review* (January–February 1989), pp. 77–82.

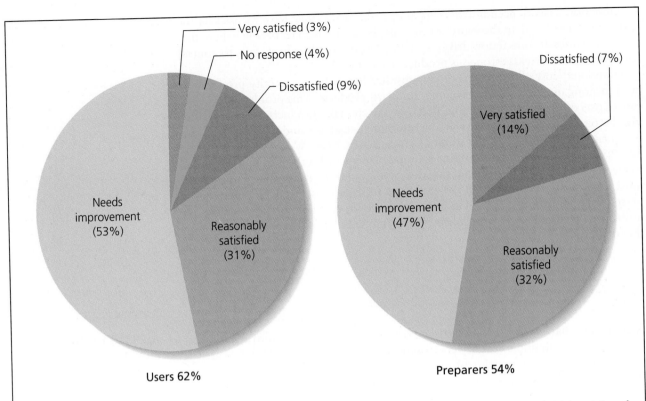

SOURCE: Robert Howell, et al., *Management Accounting in the New Manufacturing Environment* (Montvale, N.J.: National Association of Accountants, now Institute of Management Accountants, 1987), pp. 146, 160.

▌ EXHIBIT 5–11

Level of Dissatisfaction with Product Cost Information

Activity center

Two-Stage Allocation

After being recorded in the general ledger and subledger accounts, costs are accumulated in **activity center** cost pools using first-stage cost drivers that reflect the appropriate level of cost incurrence (unit, batch, or product/process). An activity center is a segment of the production or service process for which management wants to separately report the costs of the activities performed. In identifying these centers, management should consider geographical proximity of equipment, defined centers of managerial responsibility, magnitude of product costs, and the importance of keeping the number of activity centers manageable. If a relationship exists between a cost pool and a cost driver, a decrease in or elimination of the cost driver will cause the associated cost to be decreased or eliminated.

Once costs are accumulated in activity center cost pools, they can be reallocated to products and services using a second-stage cost driver. This second stage allocation is the same as the overhead application process illustrated in Chapter 4. The driver chosen for each cost pool attempts to measure the amount of a specific type of resource required by the product or service. Exhibit 5–12 on page 185 illustrates this two-stage process of tracing costs to products and services in an ABC system.

The exhibit shows that the cost drivers for the collection stage may differ from those for the allocation stage because some activity center costs are not traceable to lower levels of activity. Costs at the lowest (unit) level of activity should be assigned to products using volume-related cost drivers. Costs incurred at higher (batch and product/process) levels should be allocated to products using non-volume-related cost drivers. Costs at these higher levels have been customarily accepted as fixed costs, but activity-based costing systems seldom use the traditional definitions of variable

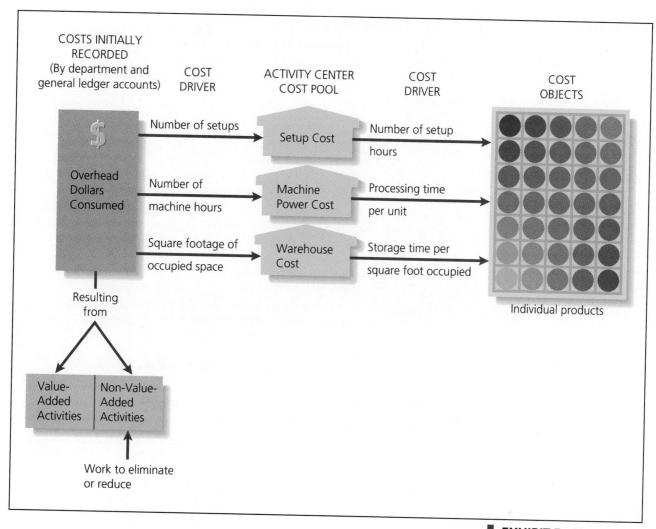

COSTS INITIALLY RECORDED (By department and general ledger accounts)

COST DRIVER

ACTIVITY CENTER COST POOL

COST DRIVER

COST OBJECTS

$

Overhead Dollars Consumed

Number of setups → Setup Cost → Number of setup hours

Number of machine hours → Machine Power Cost → Processing time per unit

Square footage of occupied space → Warehouse Cost → Storage time per square foot occupied

Individual products

Resulting from

Value-Added Activities | Non-Value-Added Activities

Work to eliminate or reduce

EXHIBIT 5–12

Tracing Costs in an Activity-Based Costing System

and fixed costs. An ABC system, instead, refers to costs as being either short-term variable or long-term variable.

Activity-Based Costing Illustrated

An example of activity-based costing is shown in Exhibit 5–13 (page 186). Information is gathered about the activities and costs for this factory maintenance department. Costs are then assigned based on activities to specific products. The department in this illustration has allocated its total personnel cost among the three activities performed in that department based on the number of employees in those areas. This allocation reflects the fact that occurrences of a specific activity, rather than volume of production or service, are indicative of work performed in the department.

One of the products manufactured by this company is Product Z, a rather complex unit that is not in extremely high demand. The cost allocated to Product Z with the activity-based costing system is 132 percent higher than the cost allocated with the traditional allocation system ($1.564 to $.675)!

Although the illustration just given used a cost normally included in product costing, activity-based costing is just as applicable to service department costs. Many companies use an activity-based costing system to allocate corporate overhead costs to their revenue-producing units based on the number of reports, documents, customers, or other reasonable measures of activity. Such techniques are discussed in Chapter 6 on service department allocations.

EXHIBIT 5–13

Illustration of Activity-Based Costing Allocation

Factory Maintenance Department: The company's conventional system assigns the personnel costs of this department to products using direct labor hours (DLHs); the department has 9 employees and incurred $450,000 of personnel costs in the current year

ABC ALLOCATION

Stage 1

Trace costs from general ledger and subsidiary ledger accounts to activity center pools according to number of employees:

- Regular maintenance—uses 5 employees; $250,000 is allocated to this activity; second-stage allocation to be based on machine hours (MHs)

- Preventive maintenance—uses 2 employees; $100,000 is allocated to this activity; second-stage allocation to be based on number of setups

- Repairs—uses 2 employees; $100,000 is allocated to this activity; second-stage allocation is based on number of machine starts

Stage 2

Allocate activity center cost pools to products using cost drivers chosen for each cost pool. 1993 activity of second-stage drivers: 500,000 MHs; 5,000 setups; 100,000 machine starts

Step 1: Allocate costs per unit of activity of second-stage cost drivers
- Regular maintenance—$250,000 ÷ 500,000 MHs = $.50 per MH
- Preventive maintenance—$100,000 ÷ 5,000 setups = $20 per setup
- Repairs—$100,000 ÷ 100,000 machine starts = $1 per machine start

Step 2: Allocate costs to products using quantity of second-stage cost drivers consumed in making these products. The following quantities of activity are relevant to Product Z: 30,000 MHs; 30 setups; 40 machine starts; and 3,000 DLHs out of a total of 200,000 DLHs in 1993. Ten thousand units of Product Z were manufactured during 1993.

ABC Allocation to Product Z = (30,000 × $.50) + (30 × $20) + (40 × $1) = $15,640 for 10,000 units or $1.564 per unit

Traditional Allocation to Product Z = $450,000 ÷ 200,000 DLHs = $2.25 per DLH; (3,000 × $2.25) = $6,750 for 10,000 units or $.675 per unit

Short-Term and Long-Term Variable Costs

Short-term variable costs increase or decrease in correspondence with changes in the volume of activity. Costs that do not move in relation to volume have conventionally been accepted as fixed. "Generally [however], as a business expands, costs tend to be far more variable than they should be, and when it contracts, they are far more fixed than they should be."[13] Professor Robert Kaplan of Harvard University considers the ability of "fixed" costs to change under the "Rule of One," which means that possessing or using more than one unit of a resource is evidence that the resource is variable. Because of this logic, many people have come to view fixed costs as long-term variable costs, for which suitable (usually non-volume-related) cost drivers simply need to be identified.

---

[13]B. Charles Ames and James D. Hlavacek, "Vital Truths About Managing Your Costs," *Harvard Business Review* (January–February 1990), p. 145.

Two significant cost drivers that cause long-term variable costs to change, but which traditionally have been disregarded, are product variety and product complexity. Product variety refers to the number of different types of products made; product complexity refers to the number of components included in a product or the number of processes through which a product flows. Because of the additional overhead support that is needed (such as warehousing, purchasing, setups, and inspections), long-term variable costs tend to increase as the number and types of products increase. Therefore, managers should use these cost drivers in applying ABC when the cost drivers cause significant amounts of overhead.

Horizontal Flow of Activities

ABC permits managers to recognize the horizontal flow of products, services, and activities through an organization. Examining the horizontal flow reveals the many cost impacts that are created by making a product or performing a service. Consider what happens when a plumber, who sets out on a schedule for the day, is contacted and reassigned to an emergency call to a house in which the basement is rapidly filling with water. The office dispatcher has to call other customers either to reschedule the work or, if necessary, assign a substitute plumber. The dispatcher may also have to send materials, parts, or tools to the plumber at the flooding house.

From an organization's vertical perspective, focusing solely on function, all company personnel performed their respective, regular duties and worked a normal eight-hour day. Such a traditionally limited view would fail to identify and measure the additional activities and costs caused by the schedule change. ABC refines the costing process to recognize the historically unheeded additional activities, costs, and cost drivers.

Attribute-Based Costing

Attribute-based costing (ABC II) is an extension of activity-based costing. This system employs detailed cost-benefit analyses relating to information on customer needs (in terms of performance attributes of a product such as reliability, durability, respon-

Attribute-based costing (ABC II)

ABC would identify the cost drivers of purchase order preparation as including the numbers of suppliers and different parts used. Reducing either of these drivers should also reduce the costs associated with the purchasing department.

siveness, and so forth) and the costs of the incremental improvements necessary to obtain these attributes. ABC II employs planned costs rather than past costs since, as discussed earlier, such a high percentage of a product's life cycle costs are locked in during the product's development stage. The approach focuses on satisfying customer needs by searching for the optimum enhancement of customer utility through comparisons of alternatives for attribute enhancements relative to the costs of producing those enhancements.[14]

A vital loss of information may occur in an accounting system that ignores activity and cost relationships. Not every accounting system using direct labor or machine hours as the cost driver is providing inadequate or inaccurate cost information. However, there are some general operating activity clues that may alert managers to the need to review the cost data being provided by their conventional accounting system. Some of these clues are more relevant to manufacturing entities, but others are equally appropriate for both manufacturing and service businesses. The clues are enumerated in the following section.

DETERMINING WHEN AN ABC SYSTEM IS APPROPRIATE

First, if a company's process or product/service line has undergone one or more significant changes, managers and accountants need to determine whether the existing cost system still provides a satisfactory estimate of product or service cost. Many companies have recently experienced large reductions in direct labor because of automation, which in turn create increased overhead charges. Current accounting systems often employ invalid drivers of a company's costs, such as direct labor as an overhead allocation base. If direct labor becomes a small part of total cost, it is unlikely that labor is the primary overhead cost driver. Continuing to use direct labor as the overhead application base will create extraordinarily high application rates, such as those at Elgin Sweeper. Furthermore, products made using automated equipment will tend to be charged an insufficient amount of overhead, while products made using high proportions of direct labor will tend to be overcharged.

Second, many companies now produce a wide variety of products (or perform numerous services) in very small quantities. These companies should review their cost systems carefully because (as indicated in Exhibit 5–14) product or service variety creates additional overhead costs that should ultimately be traced to specific products. Using only one or two overhead pools will cause the overhead related to the specific products to be spread over all products. This process results in increased costs for products that are not responsible for the increased overhead. "If production volumes are fairly similar—say, volume of one product is no more than five times that of any other—product costs will probably be accurate. Accuracy falls off rapidly as the range grows to more than 10 to 1."[15]

Third, a change in the competitive environment in which a company operates may also indicate a need for better cost information. Increased competition may occur because companies have recognized a particular product or service's profit potential, the product or service has become cost-feasible to make or perform, or an industry (such as trucking) has been deregulated. If many new companies are competing for old business, management must more precisely measure the cost to make products or perform services, so that valid profit margins can be determined.

Fourth, changes in management strategy can also indicate a need for a new cost system. For example, if management wants to begin new operations, the cost system should be able to provide information on how costs will change. Accepting costs ac-

---

[14] For additional information, see Mike Walker's "Attribute Based Costing" in the *Australian Accountant* (March 1992), pp. 42–45.
[15] Cooper, p. 80.

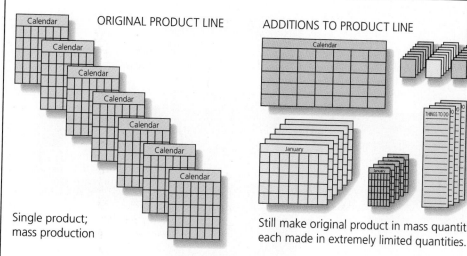

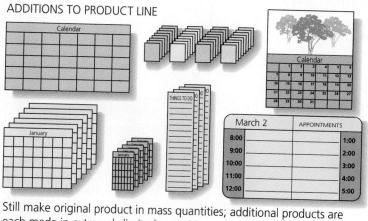

ORIGINAL PRODUCT LINE

Single product;
mass production

ADDITIONS TO PRODUCT LINE

Still make original product in mass quantities; additional products are
each made in extremely limited quantities.

When would the company have more:
- Inventory carrying costs?
- Purchasing costs?
- Scheduling costs?
- Setup and changeover costs?
- Expediting costs?
- Quality control costs?
- Scrap costs?
- Rework costs?

To which products do these increased costs relate?
BUT which product would bear most of the costs under
conventional costing?

▌ **EXHIBIT 5–14**
**Product Variety Creates
Overhead Costs**

cording to the traditional variable and fixed classifications does not allow such information to be developed effectively. Viewing costs as short-term and long-term variable allows managers to focus on cost drivers and the changes the new operations will have on activities and costs.

Another management strategy may involve changing employee behavior. The traditional cost system might not encourage such a change, while an activity-based costing system would. An example of a behavioral change that many companies are currently encouraging is **continuous improvement**, which relates to enhancing employee task performance, the level of product quality, and the level of company service. The continuous improvement concept recognizes the value of eliminating non-value-added activities to reduce lead time, making products (performing services) with zero defects, reducing product costs on an ongoing basis, and simplifying products and processes. Combining these factors with the use of computers and information technology is known as **business process reengineering**.

Irrespective of the reason or reasons supporting a change in costing systems, companies now have the ability to implement ABC systems. In the past, such implementation would have been technologically unfeasible. Introduction of the personal computer, ABC software, numerically controlled (NC) machines, and bar coding allows significantly more information to be more readily available much more cost-effectively.

Continuous improvement

**Business process
reengineering**

Activity-based costing promises many benefits for both production and service organizations. The benefits of activity-based costing are twofold: one is in the area of improving product costs for managerial decision making; the other is in the area of improving the performance measurement process. These two views are illustrated in the model shown in Exhibit 5–15.

**BENEFITS OF
ACTIVITY-BASED
COSTING**

■ **EXHIBIT 5–15**

The Two-Dimensional
ABC Model

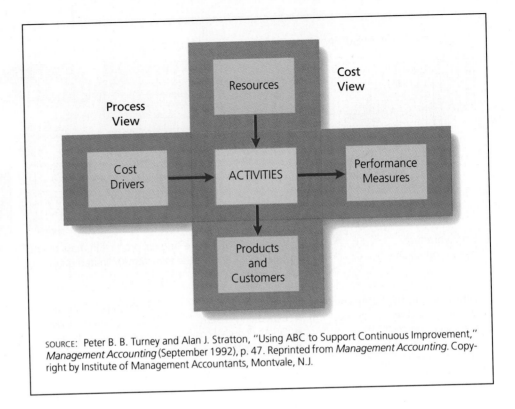

SOURCE: Peter B. B. Turney and Alan J. Stratton, "Using ABC to Support Continuous Improvement," *Management Accounting* (September 1992), p. 47. Reprinted from *Management Accounting*. Copyright by Institute of Management Accountants, Montvale, N.J.

The cost perspective highlights the interrelationships among functional areas since costs incurred in one area are often the result of activities in other areas (for instance, the potential relationship of poor product quality or defects to engineering design). Traditional accounting systems concentrate on controlling cost incurrence, while activity-based costing focuses on controlling the source (activities) of the cost incurrence. Thus, by concentrating control measurements on the cause of costs, costs become more controllable because cost reduction efforts can be directed at specific cost drivers. It is "important to note, however, that a reduction in drivers, which results in a reduced dependency on activities, does not lower costs until the excess resources are reduced or redeployed into more productive areas."[16]

Activity-based costing systems reveal that significant resources are consumed by low-volume products and complex production operations. Activity-based costing typically shifts a substantial amount of overhead costs from the standard, high-volume products where those costs have been assigned under more traditional methods to premium special-order, low-volume products, as shown in Exhibit 5–16. Activity-based costing, in and of itself, does not change the amount of overhead costs incurred; however, it does distribute those costs in a more equitable manner. ABC does not change the cost accumulation process, but it makes that process more realistic about how and why costs are incurred. Finally, activity-based costing provides a more appropriate means of charging overhead costs to products than has been possible under traditional methods.

The process view of activity-based costing allows management to focus on value-added and non-value-added activities in order to reduce or eliminate those activities that are not adding value but are causing costs to be incurred. It provides feedback information related to product design and potential areas for process improvements or waste elimination. This system allows and encourages the use of nonfinancial

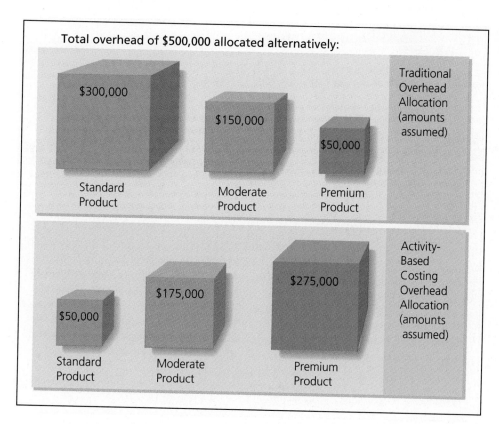

EXHIBIT 5–16
Traditional versus ABC
Overhead Allocations

measures of activity and performance. Managerial decisions may be made, such as raising selling prices or discontinuing production of low-volume, specialty output or products that require complex operations. Or managers may reap the benefits of low-volume or complex production through the implementation of high-technology processes. As indicated in the News Note on page 192 on the benefits of ABC, activity-based costing can even help managers make decisions about instituting quality improvement techniques.

It is always important to assess new models and accounting approaches realistically for what they can help managers accomplish. However, no currently existing accounting technique or system will provide management with exact cost information for every product or with the information needed to make consistently perfect decisions. Activity-based costing, while it typically provides better information than was generated under the traditional overhead allocation process, is not a panacea for all managerial concerns. The following should be noted as some of this method's shortcomings.

First, ABC requires a significant amount of time and, thus, cost to implement. If the implementation process is to be successful, substantial support is needed throughout the firm. An environment for change must be created that requires overcoming a variety of individual, organizational, and environmental barriers. Individual barriers are typically related to fear of (1) the unknown or shift in status quo, (2) the potential loss of status, or (3) the necessity to learn new skills. Organizational barriers are often related to "territorial," hierarchical, or corporate culture issues. Environmental barriers are often built by employee groups (including unions), regulatory agencies, or other stakeholders of interest.

CRITICISMS OF ACTIVITY-BASED COSTING

NEWS NOTE

Benefits of ABC Include a Quality Focus

ABC models can play many different roles to support an organization's operational improvement and customer satisfaction programs. First, ABC can provide an attention-getting mechanism for companies not yet indoctrinated into the religion of the lean production paradigm. ABC collects data on activities and business processes that cut across traditional organizational functional boundaries. Often managers can see, for the first time, the cost of nonconformance, the cost of design activities, the cost of new product launches, and the cost of administrative activities, such as processing customer orders, procurement, and handling special requests. The high cost of these activities can stimulate companies to adopt the TQM, JIT, and business process improvement programs that will produce a leaner and more responsive enterprise. The ABC model also produces, for individual products, services, and customers, the bill of activities that describes the cost buildup for these outputs. Managers can see how much of any unexpectedly higher cost arises from inefficient or unnecessary activities. The bill of activities information will indicate the opportunities for cost reduction and profit enhancement from improving quality or reducing the cost of batch and product- or customer-sustaining activities. The existing cost for these activities can provide the justification for new technology or for launching major process improvements.

SOURCE: Robert S. Kaplan, "In Defense of Activity-Based Cost Management," *Management Accounting* (November 1992), p. 60. Reprinted from *Management Accounting.* Copyright by Institute of Management Accountants, Montvale, N.J.

To overcome these barriers, they first must be recognized as existing; second, their causes need to be investigated; and, third, information about ABC needs to be communicated to all concerned parties. It is absolutely essential that top management be involved with and support the implementation process. Lack of commitment or involvement by top management will make any meaningful progress slow and difficult. Additionally, employees and managers must be educated in some nontraditional techniques that include new terminology, concepts, and performance measurements. Such an education process cannot occur overnight. Assuming that top management supports the changes in the internal accounting system and that employees are educated about the system, additional time will be required to analyze the activities taking place in the activity centers, trace costs to those activities, and determine the cost drivers.

Another problem with ABC is that it does not conform specifically with generally accepted accounting principles. ABC would suggest that some nonproduct costs (such as those in research and development) be allocated to products, while certain other traditionally designated product costs (such as factory building depreciation) not be allocated to products. Therefore, most companies have used ABC for internal reporting, while continuing to maintain their general and subsidiary ledger accounts and prepare their external financial statements on the basis of a more "traditional" system—requiring two product costing systems and causing even more costs to be incurred. It is possible that, as ABC systems become more widely accepted, more companies will choose to refine how ABC and GAAP determine product cost to make those definitions more compatible and, thereby, eliminate the need for two costing systems.

Companies wanting to implement activity-based costing systems must be aware that, while better costs might be provided, ABC systems are not appropriate in all instances. The News Note "ABC Is Only Appropriate IF . . ." discusses the underlying assumptions that must be considered before adopting this system.

NEWS NOTE

ABC Is Only Appropriate IF . . .

Although ABC systems often provide better product cost data than volume-based systems, they are based on a number of assumptions that should be evaluated before ABC costs are considered superior. If the data do not satisfy the assumptions, ABC costs may not be any more reliable than the costs provided by simpler volume-based systems.

Two assumptions underlying activity-based costing are:

1. The costs in each cost pool are driven by homogeneous activities.
2. The costs in each cost pool are strictly proportional to the activity.

The homogeneity assumption will be violated if the costs in a cost pool are driven by two or more not highly correlated activities but only one of the activities is used to assign all costs in the cost pool to products. Under these conditions, some costs are assigned to products on an arbitrary basis. The arbitrarily assigned costs are those caused by an activity or activities not used as the cost driver.

The second assumption, proportionality, . . . will be violated by several conditions, including the presence of nonlinear costs. For example, costs that are subject to the learning curve phenomenon will violate the proportionality assumption. The assumption will also be violated if both fixed and variable costs are included in the same cost pool and they are assigned to products as if they were strictly variable. Finally, joint costs [incurred in making multiple kinds of products at the same time] will violate this assumption when they are not strictly proportional to the activity.

SOURCE: Harold P. Roth and A. Faye Borthick, "Are You Distorting Costs by Violating ABC Assumptions?" *Management Accounting* (November 1991), pp. 39–40. Reprinted from *Management Accounting*. Copyright by Institute of Management Accountants, Montvale, N.J.

One final criticism that has been leveled recently at activity-based costing is that it does not promote total quality management and continuous improvement. Dr. H. Thomas Johnson (the Retzlaff Professor of Quality Management at Portland State University) has issued the following cautions:

> [T]he decade of the 1970s ushered in a new competitive environment—call it the global economy—in which accounting information is not capable of guiding companies toward competitiveness and long-term profitability.
>
> Activity-based prescriptions for improved competitiveness usually entail steps that lead to selling more or doing less of what should not be sold or done in the first place. Indeed, activity-based cost information does nothing to change old remote-control, top-down management behavior. Simply because improved cost information becomes available, a company does not change its commitment to mass-produce output at high speed, to control costs by encouraging people to manipulate processes, and to persuade customers to buy output the company has produced to cover its costs. American businesses will not become long-term global competitors until they change the way managers think. No cost information, not even activity-based cost management information, will do that.[17]

Companies attempting to implement ABC as a cure-all for product failures, volume declines, or financial losses will quickly recognize that Professor Johnson is correct. However, companies can implement ABC and its related management techniques in support of and in conjunction with TQM, JIT, and any other world-class methodologies. Those companies so doing will provide the customer with the best

---

[17]H. Thomas Johnson, "It's Time to Stop Overselling Activity-Based Concepts," *Management Accounting* (September 1992), pp. 31, 33.

variety, price, quality, service, and lead time of which they are capable. Not coincidentally, they should find their businesses booming. Activity-based costing and activity-based management are effective in supporting continuous improvement, short lead times, and flexible manufacturing by helping managers:

▍ identify and monitor significant technology costs;

▍ trace many technology costs directly to products;

▍ promote achievement of market share through use of target costing;

▍ identify the cost drivers that create or influence cost;

▍ identify activities that do not contribute to perceived customer value (i.e., non-value-added activities or waste);

▍ understand the impact of new technologies on all elements of performance;

▍ translate company goals into activity goals;

▍ analyze the performance of activities across business functions;

▍ analyze performance problems; and

▍ promote standards of excellence.

In summary, ABC is an improved cost accounting tool that helps managers know how the score is kept so that they can play the game more competitively.

R E V I S I T I N G

ELGIN SWEEPER COMPANY

Elgin Sweeper developed a new account numbering system that allowed separation of variable and fixed expenses. We recognized that, even in the short term, few departments or expenses are truly either variable or fixed. We decided that if any department/expense combination had a fixed or variable cost behavior characteristic 75% of the time, then it would be satisfactory to classify that combination as either fixed or variable 100% of the time. Once we completed the new numbering and classification structure, our revised chart of accounts had eliminated approximately 75% of the 2,000 numbers.

[The list of cost drivers compiled by Elgin included]: actual labor dollars, actual labor hours, units shipped, units produced, purchase orders, service parts sales dollars, workdays, calendar days, completed engineering change notices, and engineering hours worked. [After analyzing the drivers in relation to the expenses], the major positive result was that the intuition we had used to set up our variable accounts was correct [and] the existing variable accounts were variable to the single driver we already had selected. This exercise made us realize that we needed to go below the surface in our company for the real cost drivers because the usual, readily available drivers did not reflect sufficient positive correlation [or interdependence].

[The company then instituted a reporting system using a two-step allocation process.] The first step was to determine total departmental costs by allocating applicable costs to the responsibility area by various means, such as real estate taxes by square foot. The second step allocated the modified departmental cost to product lines using specific macro drivers, for example: percent of sales, percent of total standard hours, percent of department standard hours, percent of total component pieces sold, manager estimate, engineering product cost system, percent of new business, and staffing. We recognized that this macro driver system might not be absolutely accurate nor would it, in many cases, allow the department manager to better understand the source of costs. We wanted to set up the structure, prove its value to top management, and then move to a superior allocation basis in the future.

Now we have progressed one more step toward cost management: waste elimination for nondirect labor departments. This effort comes under various names (office productivity and quality improvement, to name two), but our goal was to educate our managers to look beyond their own departments and examine the "process stream" their efforts affected. The goal was—and is—to maximize our process effectiveness and improve the efficiency within departments by identifying and eliminating non-value-added costs.

We have made significant progress toward our goal of developing an atmosphere of cost management, but much is yet to be accomplished . . . before the majority of the benefits will be realized.

SOURCE: John P. Callan, Wesley N. Tredup, and Randy S. Wissinger, "Elgin Sweeper Company's Journey Toward Cost Management," *Management Accounting* (July 1991), p. 24ff. Reprinted from *Management Accounting.* Copyright by Institute of Management Accountants, Montvale, N.J.

CHAPTER SUMMARY

Significant changes have taken place in the business environment and these changes have caused concern about the reliability of the cost information generated by a system primarily intended to provide product costs for external financial statements. One suggestion for providing better internal user information is to determine product profitability over the product life cycle rather than on a period-by-period basis. Such a measurement would require a capitalization of product research and development costs and, as such, would not be currently allowable under generally accepted accounting principles for reporting purposes.

Target costing may be combined with life cycle costing to determine an allowable product cost based on an estimated selling price and a desired profit. Because sales volume, costs, and profits fluctuate over the product's life cycle, these items would need to be estimated over the entire life rather than on a periodic basis to determine a target cost.

With the present global competitive environment and the focus of consumers on product price and quality, businesses must find ways to minimize costs in order to make profits. One way to reduce costs without reducing quality is to decrease the number of non-value-added activities performed during the production process. Value is added to products only during the times that production is actually taking place. Inspection time, transfer time, and idle time all add to lead time and cost but not to value. The proportion of lead time spent in value-added processing is referred to as manufacturing cycle efficiency.

A new method of cost assignment, more compatible with the increased high-technology environment in which business operates, is activity-based costing (ABC). ABC assigns costs to products on the basis of the types and quantities of activities that must be performed to create those products. This costing system accumulates costs for activity centers in multiple cost pools at a variety of levels (unit, batch, product, and organizational) and then allocates these costs using multiple cost drivers (both volume- and non-volume-related). Thus, costs are assigned more accurately, and managers can focus on controlling activities that cause costs rather than trying to control the costs that result from the activities. The use of activity-based costing should provide a more realistic picture of actual production cost than has traditionally been available.

Use of activity-based costing and analysis of activities will produce benefits because of the focus on controlling the sources of costs rather than controlling the costs themselves. Eliminating non-value-added activities will affect performance measurements by allowing those measurements to encourage "good" rather than "bad" behavior. The new measurement system will be externally oriented and reflective of the goals of the organization to get a high-quality, low-cost product to a consumer in the shortest lead time possible.

APPENDIX

Theory of constraints

Constraint

Bottleneck

The Theory of Constraints

The **theory of constraints** (TOC) can help management reduce lead time. The theory of constraints indicates that the flow of goods through a production process cannot be at a faster rate than the slowest bottleneck in the process.[18]

Delays in a production environment are caused by **constraints**, some of which are human and some of which are machine. A constraint is anything that confines or limits the ability to perform a project or function. Human constraints can be caused by an inability to understand, react, or perform at some higher rate of speed. These constraints cannot be totally overcome (humans will never be able to work at the speed of an automated machine), but can be reduced through proper hiring and training. Since the labor content contained in products is declining rapidly as automation increases, constraints caused by machines are of more concern than human constraints in reducing lead time.

Machine constraints create **bottlenecks**, which are objects or facilities whose processing levels are sufficiently slow to cause the other processing mechanisms in the network to experience idle time. Bottlenecks cause the processing of an activity to be impeded. Even in a totally automated, "lights out" process, there will always be constraints because all machines do not operate at the same speed nor do they handle the same capacity. Therefore, it is necessary to identify the constraints and work around them. Exhibit 5–17 provides a simplified illustration of a constraint in a production process. While Machine 1 can process 100,000 pounds of raw material in an hour, Machine 2 can only handle 50,000 pounds. Of an input of 80,000 pounds, 30,000 pounds of processed material must wait at the constraining machine at the end of an hour of processing. The effect of the constraint on production is obvious, but the implication is not quite as clear. Managers have a tendency to want to see machines *working*, not sitting idle. Consider what this tendency would mean if the desired output were 500,000 pounds rather than 80,000. If Machine 1 were kept in continual use, all 500,000 pounds would be processed through Machine 1 in 5 hours. However, there would now be a backlog of 250,000 pounds [500,000 − 5(50,000)] of processed material in front of Machine 2! All this material would require storage space and create an additional cost of a non-value-added activity.

Machine constraints also have an implication for quality control. Managers normally choose quality control points to follow the completion of some particular process. When constraint points are known, quality control points should be placed in front of them.

> Make sure the bottleneck works only on good parts by weeding out the ones that are defective. If you scrap a part before it reaches the bottleneck, all you have lost is a scrapped part. But if you scrap the part after it's passed through the bottleneck, you have lost time that cannot be recovered.[19]

---

[18] The theory of constraints was introduced to business environments by Eliyahu Goldratt and Jeff Cox in the book *The Goal* (North River Press, Inc., 1986).
[19] Eliyahu M. Goldratt and Jeff Cox, *The Goal* (North River Press, Inc., 1986). p. 156.

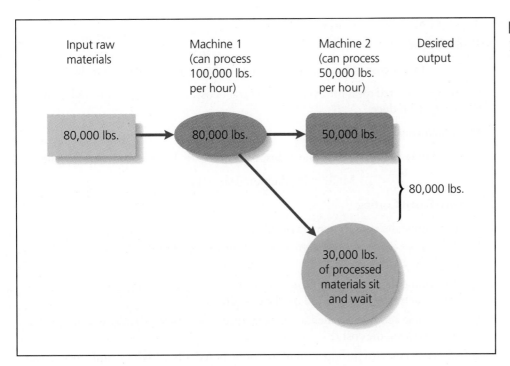

EXHIBIT 5–17
Production Constraint

Once constraints are known, take care to make the best use of the time they provide. Subsequently, "after having made the best use of the existing constraints, the next step is to reduce their limitations on the system's performance."[20] Determine what options are available to reduce those limitations such as adding more machines to perform the functions of the constraint or processing materials through a different machine.

KEY TERMS

---

[20] Robert E. Fox, "The Constraint Theory," *Cost Accounting for the '90s Responding to Technological Change Proceedings* (Montvale, N.J.: National Association of Accountants, 1988), p. 51.

SOLUTION STRATEGIES

Target Costing

Target cost = Expected long-range selling price − Desired profit

Compare predicted total life cycle cost to target cost; if life cycle cost is higher, determine ways to reduce.

Manufacturing Cycle Efficiency

Lead time = Production time + Inspection time + Transfer time + Idle time

MCE = Production time ÷ Lead time

Activity-Based Costing

1. Determine the activity centers of the organization.
2. Determine departmental activities and efforts needed to conduct those activities—the cost drivers.
3. Determine departmental resources consumed in conducting activities and allocate to activity centers based on the cost drivers.
4. Determine activities needed to manufacture products or provide revenue-producing services—the cost drivers.
5. Allocate costs to products and services based on activities and cost drivers involved.

DEMONSTRATION PROBLEM

Pierre Press prepares two versions of gourmet cookbooks: one is paperback and the other is hand-sewn and leather bound. Management is considering publishing only the higher-quality book. The firm assigns its $500,000 of overhead to the two types of books. The overhead is composed of $200,000 of utilities and $300,000 of quality control inspectors' salaries. Some additional data follow:

	Paperback	Leather Bound
Revenues	$1,600,000	$1,400,000
Direct costs	$1,250,000	$ 600,000
Production (units)	500,000	350,000
Machine hours	42,500	7,500
Inspections	2,500	12,500

Required:

a. Compute the overhead cost that should be allocated to each type of cookbook using cost drivers appropriate for each type of overhead cost.

b. The firm has used machine hours to allocate overhead in the past. Should Pierre Press stop producing the paperback cookbooks? Explain why management was considering this action and what their decision should be.

Solution to Demonstration Problem

a.

	Paper-back	Leather Bound	Total
Machine hours	42,500	7,500	50,000
Rate per MH ($200,000 ÷ 50,000)	× $4	× $4	× $4
Utility cost	$170,000	$ 30,000	$200,000

(continued)

Utility cost (from previous page)	$170,000	$ 30,000	$200,000
Number of inspections	2,500	12,500	15,000
Rate per inspection ($300,000 ÷ 15,000)	× $20	× $20	× $20
Quality inspection cost	$ 50,000	$250,000	$300,000
Total traceable overhead costs	$220,000	$280,000	$500,000

b. Income calculation using machine hours to allocate utilities and inspection hours to allocate inspectors' salaries to products.

	Paperback	Leather Bound
Revenue	$1,600,000	$1,400,000
Direct costs	$1,250,000	$ 600,000
Overhead	220,000	280,000
Total costs	$1,470,000	$ 880,000
Margin	$ 130,000	$ 520,000

Using the traditional cost driver (machine hours), the following results had been achieved given a $10 charge ($500,000 ÷ 50,000) per MH:

	Paperback	Leather Bound
Revenue	$1,600,000	$1,400,000
Direct costs	$1,250,000	$ 600,000
Overhead	425,000	75,000
Total costs	$1,675,000	$ 675,000
Margin	$ (75,000)	$ 725,000

The reason that paperbacks were erroneously thought to be unprofitable was caused by the method of allocating overhead. The firm should continue producing paperbacks.

QUESTIONS

1. List several trends in American business that are creating managerial concern and dissatisfaction with traditional product cost information in manufacturing companies.

2. What are the five stages in the product life cycle? Why is each important?

3. What is target costing and how is it useful in assessing a product's total life cycle costs?

4. Does target costing require that profitability be viewed on a period-by-period basis or on a long-term basis? Explain.

5. How would focusing on total life cycle costs call for a different treatment of research and development costs than is made for financial accounting?

6. Define value-added activities and non-value-added activities; compare and give examples of each type.

7. What management opportunity is associated with identifying the non-value-added activities in a production process?

8. How is a process map used to identify opportunities for cost savings?

9. What is manufacturing cycle efficiency (MCE)? What would its value be in an optimized manufacturing environment and why?

10. What is a cost driver and how is it used? Give some examples of cost drivers.

11. Do cost drivers exist in a traditional accounting system? Are they designated as such?

12. What is activity-based costing? How does it differ from traditional product costing approaches?

13. What characteristics of a company would generally indicate that activity-based costing might improve product costing?

14. Describe three general steps in using activity-based costing.

15. Why does activity-based costing require that costs be aggregated at different levels?

16. How, if at all, does the use of cost drivers differ between a traditional accounting system and an activity-based costing system?

17. What are the characteristics of companies that are best suited for adopting an activity-based costing system?

18. List the benefits of activity-based costing. How could these reduce costs?

19. How does attribute-based costing extend the concept of activity-based costing?

20. *(Appendix)* What is meant by the theory of constraints? How is this concept appropriate for manufacturing and service companies?

21. *(Appendix)* Why should quality control inspection points be placed in front of bottleneck operations?

EXERCISES

22. *(Target costing)* Headcrafts has developed a new material that has significant potential in the manufacture of sports caps. This material is both lighter and better ventilated than traditional cap materials. The firm has conducted significant market research and estimated the following pattern for sales of the new caps:

Year	Expected Volume	Expected Price per Unit
1	8,000 units	$7
2	20,000	8
3	35,000	6
4	15,000	5

If the firm desires to net $1.50 per unit in profit, what is the target cost to produce the new caps?

23. *(Terminology)* Match the terms on the left with the concepts and definitions on the right.

a. Life cycle stages
b. Target cost
c. Research & development
d. Value-added activity
e. Manufacturing cycle efficiency
f. Non-value-added activities
g. Cost driver
h. Activity-based costing

1. The process of attaching costs based on activities
2. Expected selling price less desired profit
3. Something that increases worth of a product or service
4. Actual production time divided by total lead time
5. Development, introduction, growth, maturity, decline
6. Part of life cycle costs
7. Idle time, transfer time, and storage time
8. Something that causes or influences costs
9. A costing system that uses multiple cost drivers

24. *(Activity analysis)* Butler Fasteners is investigating the costs of schedule changes in its factory. Following is a list of the activities, estimated times, and average costs required for a single schedule change.

Activity	Estimated Time	Average Cost
Review impact of orders	30 min–2 hrs	$ 300
Reschedule orders	15 min–24 hrs	800
—lost sales		
—unreliable customer service		
Reschedule production orders	15 min–1 hr	75
Contact production supervisor	5 min	5
—stop production and change over		
—generate paperwork to return materials		
Return and locate material (excess inventory)	20 min–6 hrs	1,500
Generate new production paperwork	15 min–4 hrs	500
—change routings		
—change bill of materials		
Change procurement schedule	10 min–8 hrs	2,100
—purchase orders		
—inventory		
Collect paperwork from the floor	15 min	75
Review new line schedule	15 min–30 min	100
Overtime premiums	3 hrs–10 hrs	1,000
Total		$6,455

a. Which of the above, if any, are value-added activities?
b. What is the cost driver in this situation?
c. How can the cost driver be controlled and the activities eliminated?
(Coopers & Lybrand)

25. *(Identifying cost drivers)* MunchaLunch is a fast-food restaurant that is highly automated and relies on sophisticated computer-controlled equipment to prepare and deliver food to customers. Operationally and organizationally, the restaurant operates like the major franchise fast-food restaurants located throughout the United States. For the costs that follow, determine whether the costs are related to the unit level (U), the batch level (B), the product/process level (P), or the organizational or facility level (O).
a. store manager's salary
b. frozen french fries
c. napkins
d. oil for the deep-fat fryer
e. maintenance of the restaurant building
f. wages of employees who clear and clean tables
g. electricity expense for the pizza oven
h. property taxes
i. depreciation on kitchen equipment
j. refrigeration of raw materials

26. *(Identifying cost drivers)* The following costs are incurred in a self-serve photocopy store. In this store, patrons rather than store staff are responsible for operating the store's various machines to make photocopies. For each of the costs listed below, identify a cost driver and defend your choice.
a. maintenance costs of the machinery
b. electricity costs
c. machinery repairs
d. store rent
e. property insurance on equipment

27. (Cost allocation using cost drivers) Sun Products Co. has always maintained an in-house legal department. Recently, the operating costs of this department have been rising dramatically. Management has determined that to control costs, it will institute an activity-based costing system in the legal department and charge the in-house users for its services. The principal expense in the legal department is professional salaries. Activities in the legal department fall into one of three major categories. These categories and the estimated cost of professional salaries associated with each activity follow:

Reviewing supplier or customer contracts	(Contracts)	$400,000
Reviewing regulatory compliance issues	(Regulation)	250,000
Court actions	(Court)	350,000

Management has determined that the appropriate cost allocation base for Contracts is the number of pages in the contract reviewed; for Regulation, the allocation base is the number of reviews; and for Court, the allocation base is professional hours. For 1994, the legal department reviewed 10,000 pages of contracts, responded to 1,000 regulatory review requests, and logged 2,000 professional hours in court.

a. Determine the allocation rate for each activity in the legal department.

b. How much cost would be charged to a producing department that had 1,000 pages of contracts reviewed, made 15 regulatory review requests, and consumed 100 professional hours in court services during the year?

28. (Appendix) Humbel Stationers produces commercial calendars in a two-department operation. Department 1 is labor-intensive; Department 2 is composed of a robot. The average output of Department 1 is 45 units per hour. The units are then transferred to Department 2 where they are finished by the robot. The robot can finish a maximum of 45 units in one hour. Humbel Stationers needs to complete 180 units this afternoon for an order that has been backlogged for 4 months. The production manager has informed the people in Department 1 that they are to work on nothing else except this order from 1 P.M. until 5 P.M.. The foreman in Department 2 has scheduled the same times for the robot to work on the order. Below is the activity of Department 1 for each hour of the afternoon.

| Time | 1:00–2:00 | 2:00–3:00 | 3:00–4:00 | 4:00–4:58 |
| Production | 44 units | 40 units | 49 units | 47 units |

Assume that each unit moves directly from Department 1 to Department 2 with no lag time. Did Humbel Stationers complete the 180 units by 5:00 P.M.? If not, explain and provide detailed computations.

COMMUNICATION ACTIVITIES

29. (Target costing) Clean Energy Options has developed a portable solar power pack that will be marketed as a power source for various electronic devices used by campers. From market research data, the company has determined that the market is willing to pay $75 per unit on a long-range basis for this product. The company's engineers have estimated first-year production costs would amount to $80 per unit. On this type of product, the firm would normally expect to earn $10 per unit in profits. Using the concept of target costing, analyze the prospects for this product and discuss possible considerations. Is it reasonable to believe that long-range costs will be less than $80 per unit? Write a brief memo explaining whether it is.

30. (Activity analysis; MCE) Pioneer Logging Co. constructs a standard type of rustic log cabin vacation home in the Colorado mountains for customers. As the company's consultant, you developed the following value chart:

Operations	Average Number of Days
Receiving materials	1
Storage of materials	3
Measuring and cutting materials	3
Handling materials	5
Setting up and moving scaffolding	5
Assembling materials	7
Building fireplace	6
Pegging logs	4
Cutting and framing doors and windows	3
Sealing joints	4
County inspection	1

a. What are the value-added activities and their total time?

b. What are the non-value-added activities and their total time?

c. Calculate the manufacturing cycle efficiency of the process.

d. Prepare a one-minute presentation explaining the difference between value-added and non-value-added activities.

31. You are the new controller of a small job shop that manufactures special-order company signs. As you review the records, you find that all orders are shipped late; the average process time for any order is 1 month; and the time actually spent in production operations is 3 days. The president of the company has called you in to discuss missed delivery dates.

a. What possible considerations might you suggest to the company president to solve the problems?

b. Discuss how accounting and performance measurement systems could be used to alleviate the problems.

(Coopers & Lybrand)

32. You have been engaged as a consultant to a company in the paint business. The company product line has changed over time from general house paints to specialized industrial coatings. Although some large commodity orders are received, the majority of business is now generated from small lot sizes of products that are designed and produced to meet specifically detailed environmental and technical requirements.

The company has experienced tremendous overhead growth including costs in customer service, production scheduling, inventory control, and laboratory work. Overhead has essentially doubled since the shift in product lines. Management believes that large orders are being penalized and small orders are receiving favorable cost (and, therefore, selling price) treatment.

a. Indicate why the shift in product lines would have caused such major increases in overhead.

b. Is it possible that management is correct in its belief about large and small order costs? If so, why?

c. What would you suggest to management to reflect the change in business?

(Coopers & Lybrand)

33. *(Life cycle costing)* The Products Development Division of Extralite Cuisine has just completed its work on a new microwave entree. The marketing group has decided on a very high original price for the entree, but the selling price will be reduced as competitors appear. Market studies indicate that the following quantities of the product can be sold at the following prices over its life cycle:

PROBLEMS

Year	Quantity	Selling Price	Year	Quantity	Selling Price
1	100,000	$2.50	5	600,000	2.00
2	250,000	2.40	6	450,000	2.00
3	350,000	2.30	7	200,000	1.90
4	500,000	2.10	8	130,000	1.90

Development costs plus other startup costs for this product will total $600,000. Engineering estimates of direct materials and direct labor costs are $0.85 and $0.20 per unit. These costs can be held constant for approximately 4 years and in year 5 will each increase by 10%. Variable overhead per unit is expected to be $.25 and fixed overhead is expected to be $100,000 per year. Extralite Cuisine management likes to earn a 20% gross margin on products of this type.

   a. Prepare an income statement for each year of the product's life, assuming all product costs are inventoried and using 8-year straight-line depreciation of the development and startup costs. What is cost per unit each year? What rate of gross margin will the product generate each year?

   b. Determine the gross margin to be generated by this product over its life. What rate of gross margin is this?

   c. Discuss the differences in the information provided by the analyses in parts a and b.

34. *(Identifying non-value-added activities)* Jenny Gabor is planning to build a patio in back of her home during her annual vacation. She has prepared the following schedule of how her time on the patio project will be allocated:

Purchase materials	2 hrs
Obtain rental equipment	2 hrs
Remove sod and level site	10 hrs
Build forms for concrete	8 hrs
Mix and pour concrete into forms	4 hrs
Level concrete and smooth	1 hr
Remove forms from concrete	1 hr
Return rental tools	1 hr
Clean up	1 hr

   a. Identify the value-added activities. How much total time is value-added?

   b. Identify the non-value-added activities. How much total time is spent performing non-value-added activities?

   c. Calculate the manufacturing cycle efficiency.

35. *(Cost of non-value-added activities)* Refer to the value chart shown in Exhibit 5–7. Harold Rankine, the company president, asked his cost accountant for the following information so that they could try to determine the total cost of non-value-added activities for one lot of the company's product.

Annual salary for receiving clerks	$25,000
Annual salary for quality control personnel	48,000
Annual salary for materials/product handlers	30,000
Annual salary for setup personnel	28,000

    Each unit requires 1 square foot of storage space in a storage building containing 100,000 square feet. Depreciation per year on the building is $125,000 and property taxes and insurance total $35,000. Assume a 365-day year for plant assets and a 240-day year for personnel. Where a range of time is indicated, assume an average. Waiting time can be estimated at $50 per batch per day. Each day of delay in customer receipt is estimated to cost $150 per unit per day. The average production lot size is 500 units.

    Determine the total cost of non-value-added activities per unit per day for each lot.

36. *(Activity-based costing)* Bailey's Leisure Equipment uses a traditional overhead allocation scheme in its manufacturing plant. The company produces three products: umbrellas, sunshades, and lawn chairs. For 1994, the company incurred $1,000,000 of manufacturing overhead costs and produced 100,000 umbrellas, 10,000 sunshades, and 30,000 lawn chairs. The company's overhead application rate was $10 per direct labor hour. Based on this rate, the cost per unit for each product group in 1994 was as follows:

	Umbrellas	Sun-shades	Lawn Chairs
Direct materials	$2.00	$20.00	$ 2.00
Direct labor	3.00	22.50	7.50
Overhead	4.00	30.00	10.00
Total	$9.00	$72.50	$19.50

Because profitability has been lagging and competition has been getting more keen, the company is considering the implementation of an activity-based costing system for 1995. In analyzing the 1994 data, management determined that all $1,000,000 of factory overhead could be assigned to four basic activities: quality control, setups, materials handling, and equipment operation. Data from 1994 on the costs associated with each of the four activities follows:

	Quality Control	Setups	Materials Handling	Equipment Operation	Total
Costs	$50,000	$50,000	$150,000	$750,000	$1,000,000

Management determined that it will use the following allocation bases (number in parentheses indicates total 1994 volume for each allocation base):

Quality control	# of units produced	(140,000)
Setups	# of setups	(500)
Materials handling	lbs. of material used	(1,000,000)
Equipment operation	machine hours	(500,000)

Volume measures for 1994 for each product and each allocation base were as follows:

	Umbrellas	Sunshades	Lawn Chairs
# of units	100,000	10,000	30,000
# of setups	100	200	200
lbs. of material	200,000	500,000	300,000
machine hours	100,000	200,000	200,000

a. For 1994, determine the total amount of overhead allocated to each product group using the traditional allocation based on direct labor hours.

b. For 1994, determine the total overhead that would be allocated to each product group using the activity-based costing allocation measures. Compute the cost per unit for each product group.

c. If the company has a policy of setting selling prices based on product costs, how would the sales prices using activity-based costing differ from those obtained using the traditional overhead allocation?

37. *(Activity-based costing)* The Belden Mfg. Co is attempting to institute an activity-based accounting system to cost products. The purchasing department incurs costs of $623,500 per year and has five people working in it. Because finding the best supplier takes the majority of the effort in the department, most of the costs are allocated to this area.

Activity	Allocation Measure	People	Total Cost
Finding best supplier	# of telephone calls	3	$450,000
Issuing purchase order	# of purchase orders	1	$100,000
Reviewing receiving reports	# of receiving reports	1	$ 73,500

During the year, 150,000 telephone calls are made in the purchasing department, 10,000 purchase orders are issued, and 7,000 shipments are received and reports filed. Many of the purchase orders are received in the same shipment.

A complex product manufactured by the company required the following activities in the purchasing department over the year: 115 telephone calls, 36 purchase orders, and 29 receipts.

a. What amount of purchasing department cost should be assigned to the manufacturing of this product?

b. If 200 units of product are manufactured during the year, what is the purchasing department cost per unit?

38. *(Activity-based costing)* The Stein and Filbrick Company manufactures two products. Following is a production and cost analysis for each product for the year 1994.

Cost Component	Product A	Product B	Both Products	Cost
Units produced	10,000	10,000	20,000	
Raw materials used (units)				
X	50,000	50,000	100,000	$ 800,000
Y		100,000	100,000	$1,200,000
Labor hours used				$ 681,000
Department 1:				
Direct labor ($375,000)	20,000	5,000	25,000	
Indirect labor				
Inspection	2,500	2,500	5,000	
Machine operations	5,000	10,000	15,000	
Setups	200	200	400	
Department 2:				$ 462,000
Direct labor ($200,000)	5,000	5,000	10,000	
Indirect labor				
Inspection	2,500	5,000	7,500	
Machine operations	1,000	4,000	5,000	
Setups	200	400	600	
Machine hours used				
Department 1	5,000	10,000	15,000	$ 400,000
Department 2	5,000	20,000	25,000	$ 800,000
Power used (kw hours)				$ 400,000
Department 1			1,500,000	
Department 2			8,500,000	
Other activity data:				
Building occupancy				$1,000,000
Purchasing—				$ 100,000
# of purchase orders				
Material X			200	
Material Y			300	
Square feet occupied				
Purchasing			10,000	
Power			40,000	
Department 1			200,000	
Department 2			250,000	

Donna Wright, the firm's cost accountant, has just returned from a seminar on activity-based costing. To apply the concepts she has learned, she decides to analyze the costs incurred for Products A and B from an activity basis. In doing so, she specifies the following first and second allocation processes:

First Stage: Allocations to Departments

Cost Pool	Cost Object	Activity Allocation Base
Power	Departments	Kilowatt hours
Purchasing	Materials	# of purchase orders
Building occupancy	Departments	Square feet occupied

Second Stage: Allocations to Products

Cost Pool	Cost Object	Activity Allocation Base
Departments:		
Indirect labor	Products	Hours worked
Power	Products	Machine hours
Machinery-related	Products	Machine hours
Building occupancy	Products	Machine hours
Materials:		
Purchasing	Products	Materials used

a. Determine the total overhead for Stein and Filbrick Company.

b. Determine the plantwide overhead rate for the company, assuming the use of direct labor hours.

c. Determine the cost per unit of Product A and Product B, using the overhead application rate found in part b.

d. Using activity-based costing, determine the cost allocations to departments (first-stage allocations). Allocate in the following order: Building occupancy, Purchasing, and Power.

e. Using the allocations found in part d, determine the cost allocations to products (second-stage allocations).

f. Determine the cost per unit of Product A and Product B, using the overhead allocations found in part e.

[SOURCE: From Harold P. Roth and A. Faye Borthick, "Getting Closer to *Real* Product Costs," *Management Accounting* (May 1989), pp. 28–33. Reprinted from *Management Accounting*. Copyright by Institute of Management Accountants, Montvale, N.J.]

CASES

39. Tektronix, Inc., is a world leader in the production of electronic test and measurement instruments. The company experienced almost uninterrupted growth through the 1970s but, in the 1980s, the low-priced end of the Portables Division product line was challenged by an aggressive low-price strategy of several Japanese competitors. These Japanese companies set prices 25% below Tektronix's prevailing prices. To compete, the division would have to reduce costs and increase customer value by increasing operational efficiency.

Steps were taken to implement just-in-time delivery and scheduling techniques, a total quality control program, and people involvement techniques that moved responsibility for problem solving down to the operating level of the division. The results of these changes were impressive: substantial reductions in cycle time, direct labor hours per unit, and inventory levels as well as increases in output dollars per person per day and operating income. The cost accounting system was providing information, however, that did not seem to support the changes.

Total overhead cost for the division was $10,000,000; of this, part (55%) seemed to be related to materials and the remainder (45%) to conversion. Material-related costs pertain to procurement, receiving, inspection, stockroom personnel, etc. Conversion-related costs pertain to direct labor, supervision, and process-related engineering. All overhead was applied on the basis of direct labor.

The division decided to concentrate efforts on revamping the application system for materials-related overhead. Managers believed the majority of materials overhead (MOH) costs were related to the maintenance and handling of each different part number. Other types of MOH costs were costs due to the value of parts, costs due to the absolute number of parts, and costs due to each use of a different part number.

At this time, the division used 8,000 different parts and in extremely different quantities. For example, annual usage of one part was 35,000 units; usage of another part was only 200 units. The division decided that MOH costs would decrease if a smaller number of different parts were used in the products.

a. Give some reasons that materials overhead (MOH) would decrease if parts were standardized.

b. Using the numbers given above, develop a cost allocation method for MOH to quantify and communicate the strategy of parts standardization.

c. Explain how the use of the method developed in part b would support the strategy of parts standardization.

d. Is any method that applies the entire MOH cost pool on the basis of one cost driver sufficiently accurate for complex products? Explain.

e. Are MOH product costing rates developed for management reporting appropriate for inventory valuation for external reporting? Why or why not?

[SOURCE: Michael A. Robinson, ed., *Cases from Management Accounting Practice*, No. 5 (Montvale, N.J.: National Association of Accountants, 1989), pp. 13–17, adapted. Reprinted by permission of the Institute of Management Accountants.]

40. *(Activity-based costing)* Alaire Corporation manufactures several different types of printed circuit boards; however, two of the boards account for the majority of the company's sales. The first of these boards, a television (TV) circuit board, has been a standard in the industry for several years. The market for this type of board is competitive and, therefore, price-sensitive. Alaire plans to sell 65,000 of the TV circuit boards in 1994 at a price of $150 per unit. The second high-volume product, a personal computer (PC) circuit board, is a recent addition to Alaire's product line. Because the PC board incorporates the latest technology, it can be sold at a premium price; the 1994 plans include the sale of 40,000 PC boards at $300 per unit.

Alaire's management group is meeting to discuss strategies for 1993, and the current topic of conversation is how to spend the sales and promotion dollars for next year. The sales manager believes that the market share for the TV board could be expanded by concentrating Alaire's promotional efforts in this area. In response to this suggestion, the production manager said, "Why don't you go after a bigger market for the PC board? The cost sheets that I get show that the contribution from the PC board is more than double the contribution from the TV board. I know we get a premium price for the PC board; selling it should help overall profitability."

Alaire uses a standard cost system, and the following data apply to the TV and PC boards.

	TV Board	PC Board
Direct material	$80	$140
Direct labor	1.5 hours	4 hours
Machine time	.5 hours	1.5 hours

Variable factory overhead is applied on the basis of direct labor hours. For 1994, variable factory overhead is budgeted at $1,120,000, and direct labor hours are estimated at 280,000. The hourly rates for machine time and direct labor are $10 and $14, respectively. Alaire applies a material handling charge at 10 percent of materials cost; this material handling charge is not included in variable factory overhead. Total 1994 expenditures for materials are budgeted at $10,600,000.

Ed Welch, Alaire's controller, believes that before the management group proceeds with the discussion about allocated sales and promotional dollars to individual products, it might be worthwhile to look at these products on the basis of the activities involved in their production. As Welch explained to the group, "Activity-based costing integrates the cost of all activities, known as cost drivers, into individual product costs rather than including these costs in overhead pools." Welch has prepared the following schedule to help the management group understand this concept.

Budgeted Cost		Cost Driver	Annual Activity for Cost Driver
Material overhead:			
Procurement	$ 400,000	Number of parts	4,000,000 parts
Production scheduling	220,000	Number of boards	110,000 boards
Packaging and shipping	440,000	Number of boards	110,000 boards
	$1,060,000		
Variable overhead:			
Machine setup	$ 446,000	Number of setups	278,750 setups
Hazardous waste disposal	48,000	Pounds of waste	16,000 pounds
Quality control	560,000	Number of inspections	160,000 inspections
General supplies	66,000	Number of boards	110,000 boards
	$1,120,000		
Manufacturing:			
Machine insertion	$1,200,000	Number of parts	3,000,000 parts
Manual insertion	4,000,000	Number of parts	1,000,000 parts
Wave soldering	132,000	Number of boards	110,000 boards
	$5,332,000		

Required per unit	TV board	PC board
Parts	25	55
Machine insertions	24	35
Manual insertions	1	20
Machine setups	2	3
Hazardous waste	.02 lb.	.35 lb.
Inspections	1	2

"Using this information," Welch explained, "we can calculate an activity-based cost for each TV board and each PC board and then compare it to the standard cost we have been using. The only cost that remains the same for both cost methods is the cost of direct materials. The cost drivers will replace the direct labor, machine time, and overhead costs in the standard cost."

a. Identify at least four general advantages that are associated with activity-based costing.
b. On the basis of standard costs, calculate the total contribution expected in 1994 for Alaire Corporation's
   1. TV board.
   2. PC board.
c. On the basis of activity-based costs, calculate the total contribution expected in 1994 for Alaire Corporation's
   1. TV board.
   2. PC board.
d. Explain how the comparison of the results of the two costing methods may impact the decisions made by Alaire Corporation's management group.

(CMA)

41. Miami Valley Architects Inc. provides a wide range of engineering and architectural consulting services through its three branch offices in Columbus, Cincinnati, and Dayton. The company allocates resources and bonuses to the three branches based on the net income reported for the period. The following presents the results of 1994 performance ($ in thousands).

	Columbus	Cincinnati	Dayton	Total
Sales	$1,500	$1,419	$1,067	$3,986
Less: Direct Labor	(382)	(317)	(317)	(1,016)
Direct Materials	(281)	(421)	(185)	(887)
Overhead	(710)	(589)	(589)	(1,888)
Net Income	$ 127	$ 92	$ (24)	$ 195

Overhead items are accumulated in one overhead pool and allocated to the branches based on direct dollars. For 1994, this predetermined overhead rate was $1.859 for every direct labor dollar incurred by an office. The overhead pool includes rent, depreciation, taxes, etc., regardless of which office incurred the expense. This method of accumulating costs forces the offices to absorb a portion of the overhead incurred by other offices.

Management is concerned with the results of the 1994 performance reports. During a review of the overhead, it became apparent that many items of overhead are not correlated to the movement in direct labor dollars as previously assumed. Management decided that applying overhead based on activity-based costing and direct tracing where possible should provide a more accurate picture of the profitability of each branch.

An analysis of the overhead revealed that the following dollars for rent, utilities, depreciation, taxes, etc., could be traced directly to the office that incurred the overhead ($ in thousands).

	Columbus	Cincinnati	Dayton	Total
Direct Overhead	$180	$270	$177	$627

Activity pools and activity drivers were determined form the accounting records and staff surveys as follows:

Activity Pools		Activity Driver	# of Activities by Location		
			Columb.	Cinci.	Dayton
General Administration	$ 409,000	Direct Labor $	382,413	317,086	317,188
Project Costing	48,000	# of Timesheet Entries	6,000	3,800	3,500
Accounts Payable/Receiving	139,000	# of Vendor Invoices	1,020	850	400
Accounts Receivable	47,000	# of Client Invoices	588	444	96
Payroll/Mail Sort & Delivery	30,000	# of Employees	23	26	18
Personnel Recruiting	38,000	# of New Hires	8	4	7
Employee Insurance Processing	14,000	Insurance Claims Filed	230	260	180
Proposals	139,000	# of Proposals	200	250	60
Sales Meetings/Sales Aids	202,000	Contracted Sales	1,824,439	1,399,617	571,208
Shipping	24,000	# of Projects	99	124	30
Ordering	48,000	# of Purchase Orders	135	110	80
Duplicating Costs	46,000	# of Copies Duplicated	162,500	146,250	65,000
Blueprinting	77,000	# of Blueprints	39,000	31,200	16,000
Total	$1,261,000				

a. What overhead costs should be assigned to each branch based on activity-based costing concepts?

b. What is the contribution of each branch before subtracting the results obtained in part b?

c. What is the profitability of each branch office using activity-based costing?
d. Evaluate the concerns of management regarding the traditional costing technique currently used.
(IMA)

42. Cost allocation is a pervasive problem. Nearly every organization must cope with cost allocation in some manner when measuring and reporting costs for purposes such as performance evaluation, product costing, and cost justification or reimbursement. The telecommunications industry has had a cost allocation problem since its inception.

Currently, costs incurred by telecommunications companies may be classified as either *non-traffic-sensitive costs* (NTS costs) or as *traffic-sensitive costs* (TS costs). NTS costs do not fluctuate with traffic volume over a relative range of call volumes and hence have a fixed cost behavior pattern. TS costs are costs of providing telecommunication services that have a direct relationship to the number of messages or volume of traffic handled by the network. TS costs tend to exhibit a "step" cost behavior pattern. NTS costs are substantial in amount and in relation to TS costs.

Most NTS costs for a local exchange company are common to all major services provided by the company. Thus, the allocation of NTS costs will affect local telephone rates and intrastate and interstate toll rates. A large portion of NTS costs can be directly identified with geographic areas and often with specific customers. Despite this fact, regulators generally do not allow telephone companies to vary rates by geographic area or customer by basing rates on recovery of NTS costs that can be directly identified with specific geographic regions or customers.

[SOURCE: From J. Patrick Cardullo and Richard A. Moellenberndt, "The Cost Allocation Problem in a Telecommunications Company," *Management Accounting* (September 1987), pp. 39–44. Published by the Institute of Management Accountants, Montvale, N.J.]

a. Would activity-based costing be useful in a telecommunications company? Would ABC be feasible in the current regulatory environment? Discuss.
b. Is it ethical to spread all charges (even those that can be identified with specific regions and/or customers) among all customers? Take *both* a positive and a negative standpoint and justify each answer.

ETHICS AND QUALITY DISCUSSION

ADDITIONAL OVERHEAD ALLOCATION CONCEPTS AND ISSUES

LEARNING OBJECTIVES

After completing this chapter, you should be able to answer these questions:

1. Why are cost pools necessary in large organizations?
2. How is overhead allocated to products from cost pools?
3. Why are service department costs allocated to producing departments?
4. Why must management be careful in how it uses allocated cost information?
5. How do the three basic methods of allocating service department costs differ?
6. Why is the algebraic method of allocating service department costs thought to be superior to the other methods?
7. Why are only two of the four criteria for choosing an allocation base the most often used?
8. *(Appendix)* How do the uniform capitalization rules affect assignment of service department costs?

INTRODUCING

FEDERAL EXPRESS CORPORATION

In 1965 as a Yale undergraduate, Frederick W. Smith wrote a term paper about the passenger route systems used by most air freight shippers. He viewed this system as economically inadequate and stated that what was needed was a system designed specifically for air freight and a system which could accommodate time-sensitive shipments such as medicines, computer parts and electronics. Mr. Smith received a "C" on this term paper.

Using the ideas from his term paper, Fred Smith started Federal Express Corporation. The company was incorporated in June 1971 and officially began operation on April 17, 1973. Memphis was the most logical location for Federal Express, because the original distribution plan evolved around a "hub and spokes" system and Memphis was the geographical center of the original target market cities for small packages. In addition, the weather in Memphis was excellent in that the airport rarely closed due to the climatic conditions. Additionally, the Memphis International Airport was willing to make the necessary outlay improvements for the operation, with additional hangar space readily available.

FedEx flies into 380 airports, using a transport fleet of 464 Boeing, McDonnell-Douglas, Fokker and Cessna aircraft. More than 30,000 computer and radio equipped vehicles are in service around the globe. Federal Express also maintains a convenience network of over 1,400 staffed facilities and more than 29,500 drop-off locations.

While the concept of picking up and delivering documents and packages is simple, the systems to make it operate quickly and efficiently are innovative, complicated and expensive. The company prides itself on being in the forefront of every industry enhancement to provide customers with better products, faster service, and more attractive pricing.

SOURCES: *Federal Express Corporation Early History* and *Fact Sheet* (August 3, 1993).

To perform the task of delivering approximately 1,500,000 packages per day, Federal Express has invested heavily in people, equipment, and facilities. Revenues are generated primarily by one function—package delivery. Thus, all of the costs of the non-revenue-producing areas must be covered by the package revenue which, for 1992, was $16.08 per express package and $1.16 per pound of airfreight. Such coverage requires the use of **cost allocation** or the assignment of an indirect cost to one or more cost objects using some reasonable basis.[1]

Cost allocation

Much of accounting is based on the process of **allocation**, which means the systematic assignment of an amount to a set of objects. Because of the emphasis in accounting on monetary measurement, the "something" of most concern is cost. For example, in financial accounting, the cost of a building is allocated through periodic

Allocation

---

[1] A cost object is defined in Chapter 2 as anything to which costs attach or are related (such as a product or department).

213

depreciation charges to the time periods benefited by its use. In cost accounting, manufacturing overhead costs can be allocated to products through the use of pre-determined overhead rates.

Cost allocations can be made over several time periods or within a single time period. Depreciation illustrates an allocation over multiple time periods; overhead illustrates an allocation occurring within one time period.

Indirect costs are allocated to cost objects for three reasons: (1) to determine a full cost of the cost object; (2) to motivate the manager in charge of the cost object to manage it efficiently; and (3) to compare alternative courses of action for management decision making.[2] Regardless of the objective, the method and basis of the allocation process should be rational and systematic so that the resulting allocations are useful in product costing and to managers for planning, controlling, and decision making.

Chapter 4, by way of introduction to overhead allocation, made two simplifying assumptions: (1) all factory overhead costs are allocated to products and (2) only *factory* overhead is allocated to products. Chapter 5 eliminated one of these simplified assumptions by introducing the use of multiple cost pools for overhead allocation. This chapter covers the assignment of costs outside the factory to products. Both of these approaches provide more appropriate and accurate costs for managerial uses. Although multiple cost pool allocation techniques can also be used for external reporting purposes, the assignment of nonfactory costs to products is not normally allowed under generally accepted accounting principles. The appendix discusses when nonfactory costs must be assigned to products for tax purposes.

COST ALLOCATION THROUGH COST POOLS

The process of assigning overhead to products is generally not the simple process shown in Chapter 4. In most companies, the process of overhead allocation requires the use of multiple **cost pools** as discussed in Chapter 5. A cost pool is a collection of monetary amounts incurred either for the same purpose or at the same organizational level. The most useful cost pools are those that group costs according to a similarity of purpose.

Cost pool

To illustrate why similar "pools" are the most useful, ignore for the moment the idea of costs. As a student, you are taking five courses of three credit hours each for which you study a total of twenty hours a week; this quantity of time can be considered a "pool." However, twelve hours of that study time is devoted to cost accounting and the remaining eight hours are devoted to your five other classes. While the fact that you study twenty hours a week is important overall, a course grade often reflects the quantity of time spent specifically studying for that course. Even though study time was not spent equally on all courses, to say that you spent an average of four hours on each course would be technically correct.

The same idea holds true in a business environment. While production overhead can be considered as a single mass of costs incurred to generate output, all costs are not necessarily incurred evenly in relationship to a single factor. Consider the cost of a factory machine that is used to make five types of products. In many instances, the depreciation on that machine is simply considered part of general factory overhead and allocated on some basis (in most cases, direct labor or machine hours) to all goods produced by the factory, regardless of whether those goods were processed by that machine. This single-stage allocation system is illustrated in Exhibit 6–1.

Thus, all overhead costs incurred in the factory could, as shown in Chapter 4, be considered one cost pool. However, as discussed in Chapter 5, these costs could be

[2] Institute of Management Accountants (formerly National Association of Accountants), *Statements on Management Accounting: Allocation of Service and Administrative Costs*, Statement Number 4B (Montvale, N.J.: NAA, June 13, 1985), pp. 9–10.

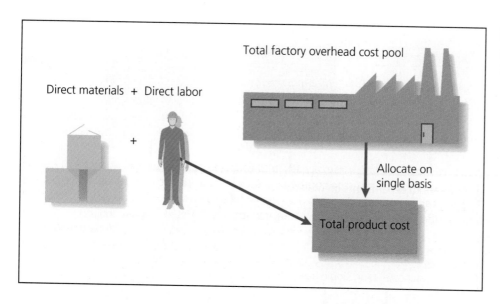

collected in ways that might more accurately reflect the reason for their incurrence. If costs are collected in similar cost pools, their allocation to products is more precise and a more realistic product cost can be calculated and/or managerial decisions can be improved.

Most organizations use cost pools to some extent. Different types of plantwide costs may be gathered in separate pools and then allocated using different bases to departments or product or service lines (cost centers). Plantwide costs include plant depreciation and insurance, utilities, indirect labor such as janitorial and maintenance staff, and material handling costs. These costs can be assigned to cost centers using fairly rational and systematic bases such as the following:

Type of Plantwide Cost	Allocation Base
Plant depreciation and insurance	Square footage
Utilities	Machine hours
Janitorial labor	Square footage
Maintenance	Hours of maintenance time
Material handling	Dollars of material costs

After being pooled in the cost centers, costs are then assigned to products or services or, possibly, to operation processes and then to products. This process is illustrated in Exhibit 6–2 (page 216) for a product flowing through two departments.

To assign product or service cost to reflect a valid cost, multistage systems (such as activity-based costing) can be used. Such a system would require that factory overhead allocation become a process of pooling costs and allocating them into other, successively lower-level pools using numerous cost drivers. Such a system, which would have been virtually impossible twenty years ago, can be managed easily today using spreadsheet software. Departments can be divided into processes and processes can be divided into manufacturing cells or groups of machines that perform similar functions. The cost of each of these layers can then be allocated to lower levels using bases that best reflect the cause of the cost. "Companies must identify drivers for cost centers and cost pools and implement flexible cost management systems to keep allocation bases current and accurate. Understanding the drivers will provide a good basis for monitoring and controlling costs."[3]

Allocating plantwide costs in a more effective manner will help managers better estimate their true product costs. "The most important goal for a product cost system

[3]Callie Berliner and James A. Brimson (eds.), *Cost Management for Today's Advanced Manufacturing* (Boston, MA: Harvard Business School Press, 1988), p. 100.

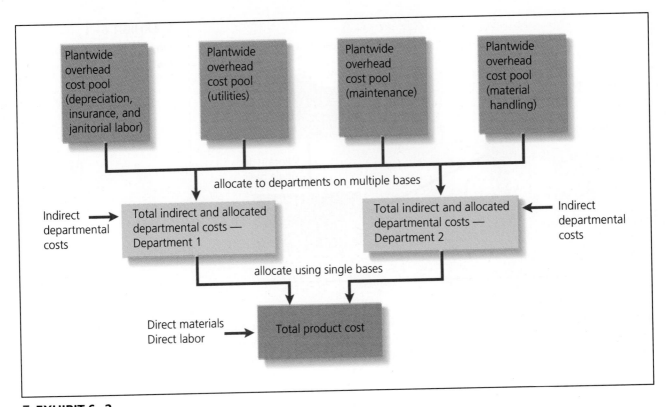

▌ EXHIBIT 6–2
Two-Tier Allocation Pools

is to estimate the long-run costs of producing each product, each salable output, in the company's product line."[4] Use of multiple cost pools for factory overhead allocation will help in reaching this goal. But factory costs are not the only costs incurred in an organization.

ALLOCATION OF SERVICE DEPARTMENT COSTS

Service department

Administrative department

Organizations incur costs for two basic types of activities: those that generate revenue (products and services) and those that do not. Activities that do not generate revenues are conducted to support revenue-producing activities. Typically, as the number of product lines or the quantity of service increases, so does the need for additional support activities. Managers know that the selling prices charged for the organization's goods or services must be high enough to cover the costs of both revenue-generating and support activities before profits can be achieved. However, managers are frequently not certain if, how, or when to allocate the support area costs to the revenue-generating areas and, ultimately, to the output produced by those areas.

An organization's support areas consist of both service and administrative departments. A **service department** is an organizational unit (such as central purchasing, maintenance, engineering, security, central warehousing, or COSMOS—Federal Express' central computer network) that provides one or more specific functional tasks for other internal units. **Administrative departments** perform management activities that benefit the entire organization and include top management personnel, legal, payroll, insurance and organization headquarters. Costs of service and administrative departments are referred to collectively as "service department costs" in this chapter, since corporate administration does service the rest of the company.

[4] H. Thomas Johnson and Robert S. Kaplan, *Relevance Lost: The Rise and Fall of Management Accounting* (Boston, MA: Harvard Business School Press, 1987), p. 234.

To make revenue-producing areas more aware that their activities are responsible for covering all organizational costs, service department costs are often allocated or charged to user departments. This section of the chapter provides reasons for and techniques of service department cost allocation.

Reasons for Service Department Cost Allocations

All service department costs are incurred, in the long run, to support production or service-rendering activities. An organization producing no goods or performing no services has no need to exist; thus, it also would have no need for service departments. Conversely, as long as operating activities occur, there is a need for service department activity. Thus, the conclusion can be drawn that service department costs are simply another form of overhead that must be allocated to revenue-generating departments and, finally, to units of product or service. The three objectives of cost allocation discussed at the beginning of the chapter are full cost computation, managerial motivation, and managerial decision making. Each of these objectives can be met when service department costs are assigned to revenue-producing departments. Such objectives are even met when the revenue-generating (or operating) departments are in the governmental arenas—as indicated in the "Municipal Government" News Note on page 219. Exhibit 6–3 (page 218) presents the reasons for and against allocating service department costs in relationship to each allocation objective; some of the positive points are discussed below.

The full cost of a cost object includes all costs that contribute to its existence. Thus, full cost includes all traceable materials, labor, and overhead costs incurred by the cost object plus a fair share of allocated costs that support the cost object. If the cost object is defined as a revenue-producing department, the full cost of its operations includes all traceable departmental costs plus an allocated amount of service department costs.[5]

To illustrate the idea of full cost, assume that managers at Federal Express are analyzing the addition of ten new routes to South America. The managers must consider not only the increased direct costs of planes, pilots, and landing fees, but also the indirect service costs for computer support, accounting, and insurance. The managers would be more able to make an informed decision if they were aware of the full cost of operating the new routes. This awareness would be heightened by financial reports that indicate the relationships among packages to be sent, direct route costs, and service department costs.

Managers of revenue-producing areas are made more aware of and sensitive to the support provided by the service areas when full costs are used. This increased sensitivity should motivate operations managers to use support areas in the most cost-beneficial manner and to provide recommendations on service department cost control. In addition, assigning service department costs to revenue-producing divisions and segments allows managers to more effectively compare the performance of their units to independent companies that must incur such costs directly.[6]

The third objective of cost allocation is to help provide a basis for comparing alternative courses of action. Including service department costs with the traceable

---

[5]This concept of full cost for revenue-producing departments is recognized to an extent by the Financial Accounting Standards Board in Statement of Financial Accounting Standards No. 14 ("Financial Reporting for Segments of a Business Enterprise"). Based on this Statement, certain indirect costs must be allocated to reportable segments on a benefits-received basis. The Statement does not, however, allow corporate administrative costs to be allocated to segments. In several pronouncements, the Cost Accounting Standards Board also provides guidance on how to include service and administrative costs in full product cost when attempting to determine a "fair" price to charge under government contracts. For example, CAS 403 ("Allocation of Home Office Expenses to Segment") indicates acceptable allocation bases using benefits-provided or causal relationships; CAS 410 ("Allocation of Business Unit General and Administrative Expenses to Final Cost Objectives") also discusses allocation principles.

[6]The use of a full cost that includes allocated service department costs should be restricted to performance comparisons with entities outside the company. This type of full cost should *not* be used for internal performance evaluations by top management since the division or segment manager has no direct control over the allocated costs.

EXHIBIT 6–3

Allocating Service
Department Costs:
Pros and Cons

OBJECTIVE: TO COMPUTE FULL COST

Reasons for:

1. Provides for cost recovery.
2. Instills a consideration of support costs in production managers.
3. Reflects production's "fair share" of costs.
4. Meets regulations in some pricing instances.

Reasons against:

1. Provides costs that are beyond production manager's control.
2. Provides arbitrary costs that are not useful in decision making.
3. Confuses the issues of pricing and costing. Prices should be set high enough for each product to provide a profit margin that should cover all nonproduction costs.

OBJECTIVE: TO MOTIVATE MANAGERS

Reasons for:

1. Instills a consideration of support costs in production managers.
2. Relates individual production unit's profits to total company profits.
3. Reflects usage of services on a fair and equitable basis.
4. Encourages production managers to help service departments control costs.
5. Encourages the usage of certain services.

Reasons against:

1. Distorts production divisions' profit figures since allocations are subjective.
2. Includes costs that are beyond production managers' control.
3. Will not materially affect production divisions' profits.
4. Creates interdivisional ill-will when there is lack of agreement about allocation base or method.
5. Is not cost-beneficial.

OBJECTIVE: TO COMPARE ALTERNATIVE COURSES OF ACTION

Reasons for:

1. Provides relevant information in determining corporatewide profits generated by alternative actions.
2. Provides best available estimate of expected changes in costs due to alternative actions.

Reasons against:

1. Is unnecessary if alternative actions will not cause costs to change.
2. Presents distorted cash flows or profits from alternative actions since allocations are arbitrary.

SOURCE: Adapted from: Institute of Management Accountants (formerly National Association of Accountants), *Statements on Management Accounting: Allocation of Service and Administrative Costs*, Statement Number 4B (Montvale, N.J.: NAA, now Institute of Management Accountants, June 13, 1985), pp. 9–10.

Differential cost

costs of revenue-producing departments gives an indication of the future **differential costs** involved in an activity. (A differential cost is one that differs in amount among the alternatives being considered.) This comparison is especially useful in and relevant to making decisions about capacity utilization.

The Federal Express example used earlier is also applicable to illustrate this objective of cost allocation. If the company is able to fund ten additional routes, it should compare the full cost of establishing those routes in South America with, for instance,

NEWS NOTE

Municipal Government Overhead Cost Allocations

Government reformers have long advocated the more complete costing of services. When a government agency knows the full cost of its services, it gains a number of important advantages. First, unwitting subsidies for fee-supporter services can be eliminated. Second, more informed choices can be made about whether to contract out a service to the private sector. Third, because work output and work quality can be related to true cost, management can better evaluate organizational efficiency. Finally, departments can better justify their budget requests because they can more accurately explain to policy makers how much work can be done at what cost. The result of all these advantages is a much more efficient public organization, better able to meet the needs of its citizens.

[In governmental operations, Internal Service Funds (ISFs) are used to] account for the financing of goods and services provided by one department to other departments on a fee-for-service basis. [However, many] indirect costs cannot be captured by ISFs. Principal among these are organizationwide support services (e.g., personnel, accounting, legal, purchasing, and auditing) provided to operating departments. These services are often called overhead. Several possible mechanisms exist to recover the cost of organizationwide indirect costs. The California League of Cities, in its definitive handbook on indirect cost allocation, describes in detail [the following three] methods: systems of equations (matrix), step down, [and] direct allocation.

[The cities listed below have a complete cost analysis and allocation system and their finance officials indicate their uses for such systems.]

CITY	JUSTIFY BUDGET	CONTRACT FOR SERVICES	PRICE SERVICES	EVALUATE PERFORMANCE
Milwaukee, WI	Yes	Yes	Yes	No
Saginaw, MI	Yes	Yes	Yes	Yes
Baltimore, MD	Yes	Yes	Yes	No
Richfield, MN	Yes	Yes	Yes	No
Winston-Salem, NC	Yes	Yes	Yes	Yes
Austin, TX	No	Yes	Yes	No
Lincoln, NE	Yes	Yes	No	No

SOURCE: Charles K. Coe and Elizabethann O'Sullivan, "Accounting for the Hidden Costs: A National Study of Internal Service Funds and Other Indirect Costing Methods in Municipal Governments," *Public Administration Review* (January/February 1992), pp. 59–63.

placing them in Asia. It is possible that South American routes would cause more insurance costs than would Asian routes; however, the customs clearance costs per package might be lower for packages shipped from South America. The allocation of service department costs to revenue-producing departments, so that full costs can be considered, helps in making the most cost-beneficial decision.

Meeting one allocation objective may, however, preclude the achievement of another. For example, assignment of full cost to a cost object may not, in some situations, motivate the manager of that cost object. Such potential conflicts of objectives may create disagreement as to the propriety of such cost allocations. If service department costs are to be assigned to revenue-producing areas, a rational and systematic means by which to make the assignment must be developed. Numerous types of allocation bases are available.

Allocation Bases

A rational and systematic allocation base for service department costs should reflect the cost accountant's consideration of four criteria. The first criterion is the benefits

Georgia-Pacific's Division Office creates no revenues but does incur costs. If the company is to be profitable, products made and sold by the manufacturing plants must be priced high enough to cover both production costs and all support department costs.

received by the revenue-producing department from the service department; an example of this is the number of computer reports prepared for revenue-producing departments by the computer department. The second criterion is a causal relationship between factors in the revenue-producing department and costs incurred in the service department; the number of pounds of laundry washed for each hospital health-care unit illustrates this type of relationship. The third criterion is the fairness or equity of the allocations between or among revenue-producing departments; the assignment of fire and casualty premiums to the revenue-producing departments on the basis of relative fair market values of assets is an example of this type of allocation. The fourth criterion is the ability of revenue-producing departments to bear the allocated costs; this criterion is being used when the operating costs of the public relations department are assigned to revenue-producing departments on the basis of relative size of revenue dollars.

The benefits received and causal relationships criteria are used most often to select allocation bases because they are reasonably objective and will produce rational allocations. Fairness is a valid theoretical basis for allocation, but its use may cause dissension since everyone does not have the same perception of what is fair or equitable. The ability-to-bear criterion is not normally used to allocate service department costs to revenue-producing departments because it often results in unrealistic or profit-detrimental actions. Managers might manipulate operating data related to the allocation base to minimize service department costs. For example, the manager of a revenue-producing department that is charged a standard maintenance fee per delivery truck mile might manipulate the mileage logs depending on how well the department is otherwise doing.

Applying the two primary criteria (benefits and causes) to the allocation of service department, administrative, and corporate costs can help to specify some acceptable allocation bases. Exhibit 6–4 lists such bases in order of their frequency of use in industry. The allocation base selected should be valid because an improper base will yield improper information regardless of how complex or mathematically precise the allocation process appears to be.

■ EXHIBIT 6-4
Appropriate Service/
Administrative Cost
Allocation Bases

TYPE OF COST	ACCEPTABLE ALLOCATION BASES
Research and development	Estimated time or usage, sales, assets employed, new products developed
Personnel functions	Number of employees, payroll, number of new hires
Accounting functions	Estimated time or usage, sales, assets employed, employment data
Public relations and corporate promotion	Sales
Purchasing function	Dollar value of purchase orders, number of purchase orders, estimated time of usage, percentage of material cost of purchases
Corporate executives' salaries	Sales, assets employed, pretax operating income
Treasurer's functions	Sales, estimated time or usage, assets or liabilities employed
Legal and governmental affairs	Estimated time or usage, sales, assets employed
Tax department	Estimated time or usage, sales, assets employed
Income taxes	Pretax operating income*
Property taxes	Square feet, real estate valuation

*The NAA table lists "net income" as the base of allocation. The authors believe that pretax operating income is more realistic since net income has taxes already deducted.

SOURCE: Institute of Management Accountants (formerly National Association of Accountants), *Statements on Management Accounting: Allocation of Service and Administration Costs*, Statement Number 4B (Montvale, N.J.: NAA, now Institute of Management Accountants, June 13, 1985), p. 8.

EXHIBIT 6-4
Appropriate Service/
Administrative Cost
Allocation Bases

SERVICE DEPARTMENT COST ALLOCATION

The allocation process for service department costs is, like that of revenue-producing areas, a process of pooling, allocating, repooling, and reallocating costs. When service departments are considered in the pooling process, the basic pools are comprised of all costs of both the revenue-producing and service departments. These costs can be gathered and specified in terms of cost behavior (variable and fixed) or in total. Intermediate pools are then developed in the allocation process. There may be one or more layers of intermediate pools; however, the last layer will consist of only revenue-producing departments. The number of layers and the costs shown in the intermediate pools depend on the type of allocation method selected. The costs of the intermediate pools are then distributed to final cost objects (such as products, services, programs, or functional areas).

Exhibit 6–5 depicts this pooling-of-costs process. For simplicity, this exhibit shows only one layer of intermediate cost pools. However, to provide better cost information, a multiple stage system such as those discussed earlier in the chapter should be developed. Costs from the intermediate pools will be allocated to the final cost objects, Products M, N, X, and Y.

In the case illustrated in Exhibit 6–5, one objective of the allocation process is the determination of full product cost. The indirect and allocated costs, respectively, of Departments A and B are combined to comprise the total overhead cost pool. Next, the total related service and production department costs are divided by a specified, rational cost driver allocation base (such as machine hours, machine throughput time, or number of machine setups). Applied overhead is then combined with direct costs of the area so that a full cost of each product can be computed.

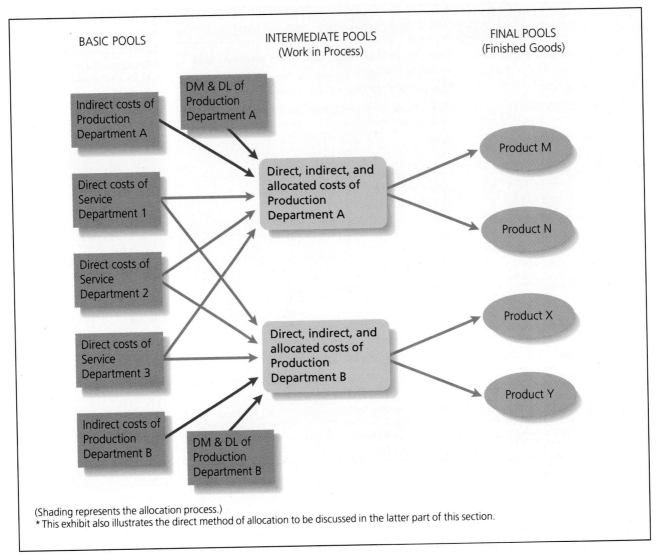

BASIC POOLS

INTERMEDIATE POOLS
(Work in Process)

FINAL POOLS
(Finished Goods)

DM & DL of Production Department A

Indirect costs of Production Department A

Direct costs of Service Department 1

Direct, indirect, and allocated costs of Production Department A

Product M

Product N

Direct costs of Service Department 2

Direct costs of Service Department 3

Direct, indirect, and allocated costs of Production Department B

Product X

Product Y

Indirect costs of Production Department B

DM & DL of Production Department B

(Shading represents the allocation process.)
* This exhibit also illustrates the direct method of allocation to be discussed in the latter part of this section.

▌ EXHIBIT 6–5

**Combined Production and
Service Department
Cost Pools***

Direct method

Step method

Benefits-provided ranking

There are three basic ways to allocate the pooled service department costs to the revenue-producing departments: the direct method, step method, and algebraic method. These methods are listed in order of ease of application, not necessarily in order of soundness of results. The **direct method** assigns service department costs directly to revenue-producing areas with only one set of intermediate cost pools or allocations. This process is the method depicted in Exhibit 6–5. Cost assignment under the direct method is made using one specific cost driver to the intermediate pool; for example, Personnel Department costs are assigned to production departments (the intermediate-level pools) based on the number of people in each production department.

The **step method** of cost allocation assigns indirect costs to cost objects after considering the interrelationships of the service departments. Although a specific base is also used in this method, the step method employs a ranking for the quantity of services provided by each service department to other areas. This **"benefits-provided" ranking** lists service departments in an order that begins with the one providing the most service to all other corporate areas (both nonrevenue and revenue-producing); the ranking ends with the service department providing the least service to all but the revenue-producing areas. After the ranking is developed, service department costs are sequentially allocated down the list until all costs have been assigned to the revenue-producing areas. This ranking sequence allows the step method to partially recognize the reciprocal relationships among the service departments. For example, since Personnel provides services for all company areas, Personnel might be the first department listed in the ranking and all other areas would receive a proportionate allocation of the Personnel Department's costs.

The **algebraic** (or reciprocal) **method** of allocating service department costs considers all departmental interrelationships and reflects these relationships in simultaneous equations. These equations provide for reciprocal allocation of service costs among the service departments as well as to the revenue-producing departments. Thus, no "benefits-provided" ranking is needed and the sequential step approach is not used. The algebraic method is the most complex of all the allocation techniques, but it is also theoretically the most correct and, if relationships are properly formulated, will provide the best allocations.

Algebraic method

SERVICE DEPARTMENT COST ALLOCATION ILLUSTRATION

Data for We D-Liv-R, a local delivery company, are used to illustrate allocation of budgeted service department costs under each of the three allocation methods. We D-Liv-R has two revenue-producing departments: Package Delivery and Floral Delivery. The company's service departments are corporate administration, personnel, and maintenance. Exhibit 6–6 presents the five company areas and their relationships to

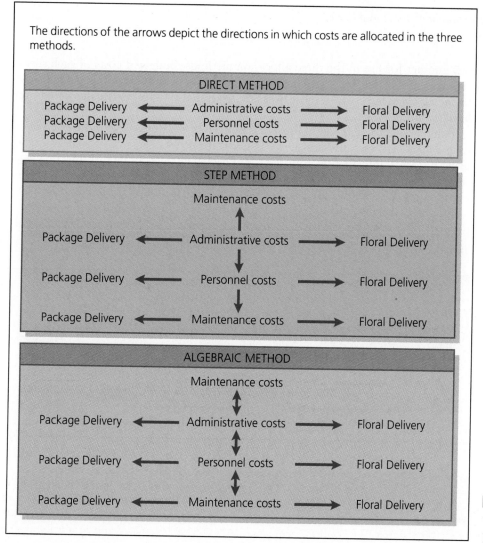

EXHIBIT 6–6

We D-Liv-R Allocation Relationships

	Adminis-tration	Per-sonnel	Mainte-nance	Package	Floral	Total
Direct Costs:						
Materials*	$ 0	$ 0	$ 0	$327,200	$223,200	$ 550,400
Labor	92,000	50,000	120,000	384,000	288,000	934,000
Total	$ 92,000	$50,000	$120,000	$711,200	$511,200	$1,484,400
Departmental Overhead:						
Supplies	$ 6,000	$ 7,200	$ 11,600	$ 26,000	$ 18,000	$ 68,800
Utilities	2,450	2,240	4,400	3,800	2,400	15,290
Utilities	0	0	38,000	58,600	46,200	142,800
Labor	0	8,400	18,800	22,700	17,500	76,600
Depreciation	9,200	5,400	6,600	6,700	5,100	27,550
Other	3,750					
Total	$ 21,400	$23,240	$ 79,400	$117,800	$ 89,200	$ 331,040
Total Initial Dept'l Costs	$113,400	$73,240	$199,400	$829,000	$600,400	$1,815,440

* Materials cost includes fuel charges.

EXHIBIT 6–7
We D-Liv-R Budgeted Departmental and Divisional Costs

one another for use in the three allocation methods. Budgeted costs of each service department are assigned to each revenue-producing area and are then added to the budgeted overhead costs of those areas to determine an appropriate divisional over-head application rate.

Exhibit 6–7 presents an abbreviated budget of the direct and indirect costs for each department and division of We D-Liv-R for 1994. These costs were estimated using historical information adjusted for expected changes in factors affecting costs such as increases or decreases in volume and personnel from prior periods. Budgeted revenues are $1,640,000 for Package Delivery and $1,008,000 for Floral Delivery.

Exhibit 6–8 shows the bases that We D-Liv-R has chosen for allocating its service department costs. The service departments are listed in a "benefits-provided" rank-

EXHIBIT 6–8
We D-Liv-R Allocation Bases

Administration costs—allocated on number of employee hours

Personnel costs—allocated on number of employees

Maintenance costs—allocated on miles driven

	NUMBER OF EMPLOYEE HOURS	NUMBER OF EMPLOYEES	MILES DRIVEN
Administration	4,200	2	0
Personnel	3,840	2	0
Maintenance	11,520	6	0
Package Delivery	28,800	12	960,000
Floral Delivery	22,000	9	672,000

ing. We D-Liv-R feels that Administration provides the most service to all other areas of the company; Personnel provides the majority of its services to the maintenance and the revenue-producing areas; and Maintenance provides its services primarily to Package Delivery and Floral Delivery.

Direct Method Allocation

The direct method of allocation is the easiest of the three methods. Service department costs are assigned directly to the revenue-producing areas using the specified bases for each department. The direct method cost allocation for We D-Liv-R is shown in Exhibit 6–9.

Use of the direct method of service department allocation produces the total budgeted costs for Package Delivery and Floral Delivery shown in Exhibit 6–10 on the next page. If budgeted and actual revenues and budgeted and actual costs were equal, this allocation method would result in Package Delivery showing a profit of $587,435 or 35.8 percent on revenues and Floral Delivery showing a profit of $244,925 or 24.3 percent.

The direct method of allocation for We D-Liv-R does not reflect the revenue-producing departments' "ability to bear" the service department costs. However, the profit margins may reflect the fact that flower deliveries are less important than package deliveries to the company's business. Additionally, the direct method does not reflect the fact that some activities of the service departments are related to other service departments. Ignoring these relationships violates the "fairness" criterion, is an extreme simplification of reality, and can create distorted allocations.

▌ EXHIBIT 6–9

We D-Liv-R Direct Allocation of Service Department Costs

	Base	Proportion of total base	Amount to allocate	Amount allocated
Administration costs (employee hours)				
Package Delivery	28,800	28,800/50,800 = 56.7%	$113,400	$ 64,298
Floral Delivery	22,000	22,000/50,800 = 43.3%	$113,400	49,102
Total	50,800			$113,400
Personnel costs (# of employees)				
Package Delivery	12	12/21 = 57.1%	$ 73,240	$ 41,820
Floral Delivery	9	9/21 = 42.9%	$ 73,240	31,420
Total	21			$ 73,240
Maintenance costs (miles driven—000 omitted)				
Package Delivery	960	960/1,632 = 58.8%	$199,400	$117,247
Floral Delivery	672	672/1,632 = 41.2%	$199,400	82,153
Total	1,632			$199,400

	Package Delivery	Floral Delivery	Total
Direct costs (a)	$ 711,200	$511,200	$1,222,400
Departmental overhead (remaining costs shown in Ex. 6–7) (b)	$ 117,800	$ 89,200	$ 207,000
Allocated overhead			
From administration	$ 64,298	$ 49,102	$ 113,400
From personnel	41,820	31,420	73,240
From maintenance	117,247	82,153	199,400
Subtotal—allocated costs (c)	$ 223,365	$162,675	$ 386,040
Total overhead (for application rate determination) (b + c)	$ 341,165	$251,875	$ 593,040
Total budgeted costs (a + b + c)	$1,052,365	$763,075	$1,815,440

VERIFICATION OF ALLOCATION

To:	Admin.	Personnel	Maintenance	Package	Floral	Total
Initial Costs	$113,400	$73,240	$199,400			$386,040
From: Admin.	(113,400)			$ 64,298	$ 49,102	
Personnel		(73,240)		41,820	31,420	
Maintenance			(199,400)	117,247	82,153	
Totals	$ 0	$ 0	$ 0	$223,365	$162,675	$386,040

■ **EXHIBIT 6–10**
We D-Liv-R Direct Method Allocation to Revenue-Producing Areas

Step Method Allocation

To apply the step method of allocation, a "benefits-provided" ranking needs to be specified. This ranking for We D-Liv-R is shown in Exhibit 6–8. Costs are assigned using an appropriate, specified allocation base to the departments receiving service. Once costs have been assigned from a department, no additional costs are charged back to that department. Step allocation of We D-Liv-R service costs is shown in Exhibit 6–11 on page 227.

In this case, the amount of service department costs assigned to each revenue-producing area differs only slightly between the step and direct methods. However, in many situations, the difference can be substantial. If budgeted and actual revenues and budgeted and actual costs are equal, the step method allocation process will cause Package Delivery and Floral Delivery to show profits of $586,884 and $245,676, respectively, as follows:

	Package Delivery	Floral Delivery
Revenues	$1,640,000	$1,008,000
Departmental costs	(829,000)	(600,400)
Allocated service department costs	(224,116)	(161,924)
Profit	$ 586,884	$ 245,676

These profit figures reflect rates of return on revenues of 35.8 percent and 24.4 percent, respectively.

	Base	Proportion of total base	Amount to allocate	Amount allocated
Administration costs (employee hours)				
Personnel	3,840	3,840/66,160 = 5.8%	$113,400	$ 6,577
Maintenance	11,520	11,520/66,160 = 17.4%	$113,400	19,732
Package	28,800	28,800/66,160 = 43.5%	$113,400	49,329
Floral	22,000	22,000/66,160 = 33.3%	$113,400	37,762
Total	66,160			$113,400
Personnel costs (# of employees)				
Maintenance	6	6/27 = 22.2%	$ 79,817*	$ 17,719
Package	12	12/27 = 44.5%	$ 79,817	35,519
Floral	9	9/27 = 33.3%	$ 79,817	26,579
Total	27			$ 79,817
Maintenance (miles driven)				
Package	960	960/1,632 = 58.8%	$236,851**	$139,268
Floral	672	672/1,632 = 41.2%	$236,851	97,583
Total	1,632			$236,851

* Personnel costs = Original cost + Allocated from administration = $73,240 + $6,577 = $79,817
** Maintenance costs = Original cost + Allocated from administration + Allocated from personnel = $199,400 + $19,732 + $17,719 = $236,851

VERIFICATION OF ALLOCATION

To:	Admin.	Personnel	Maintenance	Package	Floral	Total
Initial Costs	$113,400	$73,240	$199,400			$386,040
From: Admin.	(113,400)	6,577	19,732	$ 49,329	$ 37,762	0
Personnel		(79,817)	17,719	35,519	26,579	0
Maintenance			(236,851)	139,268	97,583	0
Totals	$ 0	$ 0	$ 0	$224,116	$161,924	$386,040

▌ **EXHIBIT 6–11**
We D-Liv-R Step Allocation of Service Department Costs

The step method is a hybrid allocation method between the direct and algebraic methods. This method is more realistic than the direct method in that it partially recognizes relationships among service departments but it does not recognize the dual relationships that may exist. A service department is eliminated from the allocation sequence once its costs have been assigned outward. If a service department further down the ranking sequence provides services to departments that have already been eliminated, these benefits are not recognized by the step method cost allocation process.

Algebraic Method Allocation

The algebraic method of allocation is also called the reciprocal or matrix approach. This method eliminates the two disadvantages of the step method in that all interrelationships among departments are recognized and no decision must be made about a ranking order of service departments. The algebraic method involves setting up si-

Regardless of whether a direct, step, or algebraic allocation method is used, costs of the various service and administration departments at Federal Express must be covered by package shipment and delivery revenues. Thus FedEx's prices must be set after consideration of all direct and indirect company costs as well as prices charged by competitors.

multaneous equations to reflect reciprocal relationships among departments. Solving these equations allows costs to flow both into and out of each department.

The starting point for the algebraic method is a review of the bases used for allocation (shown in Exhibit 6–8) and the respective amounts of those bases for each department. A schedule is created that shows the proportionate usage by each department of the other departments' services. These proportions are then used to develop equations that, when solved simultaneously, will give cost allocations that fully recognize the reciprocal services provided.

The allocation proportions for all departments of We D-Liv-R are shown in Exhibit 6–12. Allocation for the Personnel Department is discussed to illustrate how these proportions were derived. The allocation basis for personnel costs is number of employees; there are twenty-nine employees in the organization *exclusive of* the Personnel Department. The number of employees in Personnel is ignored for allocation proportions since departmental costs are being removed from that department and assigned to other areas. Since Administration has two employees, the proportionate amount of Personnel services used by Administration is 2/29 or 7 percent.

Using the percentages calculated in the exhibit, algebraic equations representing the interdepartmental usage of services can be formulated. The departments are labeled A, P, and M in the equations for Administration, Personnel, and Maintenance, respectively. The initial costs of each service department are shown first in the formulas.

$$
\begin{aligned}
\text{(Administration)} \quad A &= \$113{,}400 + .07P + 0.0M \\
\text{(Personnel)} \quad P &= \$\ 73{,}240 + .06A + 0.0M \\
\text{(Maintenance)} \quad M &= \$199{,}400 + .17A + .21P
\end{aligned}
$$

The above equations are solved simultaneously by substituting one equation into the others, gathering like terms, and reducing the unknowns until only one unknown exists. The value for this unknown is then computed and substituted into the remaining equations. This process is continued until all unknowns have been eliminated, as shown below for the We D-Liv-R example.

EXHIBIT 6–12
We D-Liv-R
Interdepartmental
Relationships

	ADMINISTRATION		PERSONNEL		MAINTENANCE	
	# of Employee Hours		# of Employees		Miles Driven	
	Base	Percent	Base	Percent	Base	Percent
Administration	n/a	n/a	2	7	0	0
Personnel	3,840	6	n/a	n/a	0	0
Maintenance	11,520	17	6	21	n/a	n/a
Package	28,800	44	12	41	960,000	59
Floral	22,000	33	9	31	672,000	41
Total	66,160	100	29	100	1,632,000	100

(NOTE: Percentages have been rounded to the nearest whole number.)

1. Substituting the equation for A into the equations for P and M gives the following:

$$P = \$73,240 + .06(\$113,400 + .07P)$$
$$\text{and } M = \$199,400 + .17(\$113,400 + .07P) + .21P$$
$$\text{or } M = \$199,400 + .17(\$113,400 + .07P)$$
$$+ .21[\$73,240 + .06(\$113,400 + .07P)]$$

2. Multiplying and combining terms produces the following results:

$$P = \$73,240 + \$6,804 + .0042P$$
$$P = \$80,044 + .0042P$$
$$P - .0042P = \$80,044$$
$$.9958P = \$80,044$$
$$P = \$80,382$$

$$M = \$199,400 + .17A + .21P$$
$$M = \$199,400 + .17(\$113,400 + .07P)$$
$$+ .21[\$73,240 + .06(\$113,400 + .07P)]$$
$$M = \$235,487 + .012782P$$
$$M = \$235,487 + .012782(\$80,382)$$
$$M = \$236,514$$

3. The value for P is now substituted in the original formula for the administration area:

$$A = \$113,400 + .07P + 0.0M$$
$$A = \$113,400 + .07(\$80,382)$$
$$A = \$113,400 + \$5,627$$
$$A = \$119,027$$

The amounts provided by these equations are used to reallocate costs among all the departments; then costs will be assigned only to the revenue-producing areas. These allocations are shown in Exhibit 6–13.

The \$119,027 of administration costs derived above are used to illustrate the development of the amounts in Exhibit 6–14. Administration costs are assigned to the other areas based on number of employee hours. Exhibit 6–12 indicated that Personnel has 6 percent of the number of employee hours of We D-Liv-R; thus, costs equal to \$7,142 (6% × \$119,027) are assigned to that area. This same process of proration

EXHIBIT 6–13

We D-Liv-R Allocation of Algebraic Solution of Service Department Costs

Costs are allocated based on percentages computed in Exhibit 6–12.

	ADMINISTRATION		PERSONNEL		MAINTENANCE	
	Percent	Amount	Percent	Amount	Percent	Amount
Administration	n/a	n/a	7	$ 5,627	0	$ 0
Personnel	6	$ 7,142	n/a	n/a	0	0
Maintenance	17	20,234	21	16,880	n/a	n/a
Package	44	52,372	41	32,957	59	139,543
Floral	33	39,279	31	24,918	41	96,971
Total*	100	$119,027	100	$80,382	100	$236,514

*Total costs are the solution results of the set of algebraic equations.

is used for the other departments. Allocations from Exhibit 6–13 are used in Exhibit 6–14 (below) to determine the reallocated costs and finalize the total budgeted overhead of the Package Delivery and Floral Delivery departments.

By allocating costs in this manner, total costs shown for each service department have increased over the amounts originally given. For example, Administration now shows total costs of $119,027 rather than the original amount of $113,400. These added "costs" are double-counted in that they arise from the process of service reciprocity. As shown on the line labeled "Reallocated Costs" in Exhibit 6–14, these additional double-counted costs are not recognized in the revenue-producing areas for purposes of developing an overhead application rate.

When the company has very few departmental interrelationships, the algebraic method can be solved by hand. If a large number of variables are present, this method is too complex to perform without the aid of a computer. Since the use of computers is now prevalent in all but the smallest organizations, the results obtained from the algebraic method are easy to generate and provide the most rational and appropriate means of allocating service department costs. The solution to the demonstration problem at the end of this chapter presents a computer spreadsheet solution to that problem.

EXHIBIT 6–14

We D-Liv-R Final Determination of Revenue-Producing Department Overhead Costs

	TOTAL SERVICE DEPARTMENT COST (FROM EQUATIONS)	ADMINIS-TRATION	PERSONNEL	MAINTENANCE	PACKAGE	FLORAL
Administration	$119,027	$ 0	$7,142	$20,234	$ 52,372	$ 39,279
Personnel	80,382	5,627	0	16,880	32,957	24,918
Maintenance	236,514	0	0	0	139,543	96,971
Total costs	$435,923	$5,627	$7,142	$37,114	$224,872	$161,168
Less Reallo-cated costs	(49,883)	(5,627)	(7,142)	(37,114)		
Budgeted cost	$386,040	$ 0	$ 0	$ 0		
Departmental overhead costs of revenue-producing areas					117,800	89,200
Total budgeted cost for OH application rate determination					$342,672	$250,368

Regardless of the method used to allocate service department costs, the final step is to determine the overhead application rates for the revenue-producing areas. Once service department costs have been assigned to production, they are included as part of production overhead and allocated to products or jobs through normal overhead assignment procedures. Throughout the text, the assignment procedure used (for simplicity) is a predetermined overhead rate based on a single cost driver.

Assume the algebraic method of cost allocation is used by We D-Liv-R. Using the final figures shown in Exhibit 6–14, costs of $342,672 and $250,368 for Package Delivery and Floral Delivery, respectively, are divided by an appropriate allocation base. We D-Liv-R has chosen pounds delivered and number of deliveries as the respective overhead allocation bases. Package Delivery expects to deliver 560,700 pounds in the upcoming year; Floral Delivery expects to make 353,900 deliveries. The overhead cost assigned to each pound delivered by Package Delivery would be $.61 ($342,672 ÷ 560,700). Each floral delivery would carry $.71 of overhead ($250,368 ÷ 353,900).

For simplicity, cost behavior in all departments has been ignored. A more appropriate allocation process would specify different bases in each department for the variable and fixed costs. Costs would then be assigned in a manner more reflective of their behavior. Such differentiation would not change the process of allocation, but would change the results of the three methods (direct, step, or algebraic). Separation of variable and fixed costs would provide better allocations and use of the computer makes this process more practical than it was in the past.

Before attempting an allocation process, make sure that the allocation base is reasonable. Allocations are often based on the easiest available measure, such as number of people or number of documents processed. Use of such measures may distort the allocation process. For example, Bellcore (Bell Communications Research) determined that it had two types of service centers: usage-based and non-usage-based. The word processing department would be considered usage-based; output to users could be determined on a per-page basis. Usage of the library, on the other hand, could not be so easily measured. Bellcore decided to allocate the costs of all non-usage-based service departments by headcount. Exhibit 6–15 shows how unequitable such charges were after analyzing actual usage.

■ **EXHIBIT 6–15**

Bellcore's Analysis of Service Department Charges

The Graphics, Word Processing, Technical Publications, and Secretarial/Clerical Service Centers accounted for 12% of the employment at Bellcore. Thus, these areas in total were charged for 12% of all the following non-usage-based service center costs. Comparing 12% charged to the other percentages used as shown below shows that 12% causes significant misapplications.

NON-USAGE-BASED SERVICES	ACTUAL VERIFIED USAGE
Internal Conference Planning	2%
Mail and Fax Delivery	3%
Stockrooms	3%
Transportation within Bellcore	3%
Travel Planning	1%
Shipping and Moving	2%
External Conference Planning	2%
Purchasing	2%
Records Management	0%
Library	1%
Publications Standards	0%
Service Center Administration	20%

SOURCE: Edward J. Kovac and Henry P. Troy, "Getting Transfer Prices Right: What Bellcore Did," *Harvard Business Review* (September–October 1989), p. 152.

NEWS NOTE

Don't Just Allocate Costs; Charge for Services!

Managers of corporate staff functions typically fight a defensive battle to obtain and maintain their funding levels. Unlike the manufacturing and selling segments of a company, which can demonstrate a bottom-line contribution to profitability, staff groups often are viewed as a necessary evil that is carried on the shoulders of revenue producers. As such, they are constantly challenged to control costs and to be more effective.

A major benefit of identifying and charging users for overhead activities is the clear identification of users with the demand for services. No longer can operating units disassociate themselves from the costs of "overhead" activities they require to serve their customers. A related benefit of such a system is that line and staff groups understand better the nature of the services being provided and their associated costs.

Since 1985, corporate service departments [at Weyerhaeuser] must "charge back" all costs to users. These charge-backs are no mere allocations. They attribute costs to the service departments' use of resources by carefully analyzing the activities that drive the consumption of corporate resources. And they prompt profit-oriented responses because users and suppliers are not free to acquire or sell these corporate services outside the company in the market.

SOURCE: H. Thomas Johnson and Dennis A. Loewe, "How Weyerhaeuser Manages Corporate Overhead Costs," *Management Accounting* (August 1987), p. 21, 24.

When service department cost allocations have been made to revenue-producing areas, income figures derived from the use of these amounts should not be used for manager performance evaluations. Any attempt to evaluate the financial performance of a manager of a revenue-producing department should use an incremental, rather than a full allocation, approach. Although full allocation should not be used for performance evaluations, allocating service department costs to revenue-producing areas does make managers more aware of and responsible for controlling service usage. Chapter 21 discusses this type of responsibility in more depth and also covers the concept of setting transfer prices for the provision of services between organizational units as is briefly discussed in the "Don't Just Allocate" News Note.

R E V I S I T I N G

FEDERAL EXPRESS CORPORATION

Federal Express has ventured beyond the package business by introducing an expanded choice of value-added products and services through its Business Logistics Services division. In 1992, this division signed an agreement with Laura Ashley™ in the United Kingdom to manage the company's worldwide logistics operation. Another important contract was signed with one of the world's largest computer manufacturers to provide an early morning delivery network of repair parts for its field technical staff.

Two international air freight services have been added to complete an array of options for international customers. FedEx IXF (International Expressfreight Service) is a time-definite service designed to appeal to freight agents, forwarders and brokers who can offer their customers single carrier worldwide service. FedEx IP (International Priority Service) provides one- to three-day delivery of documents and packages requiring customs clearance shipped from anywhere in Europe and is also available between the United States and 126 countries.

FedEx has opened an Anchorage facility to serve as a transloading site where large pallets or containers can be transferred from one wide-body aircraft to another. Five "Freight Movement Centers" around the world (Anchorage, Brussels, Chicago, Memphis, and Tokyo) coordinate the movement of all international air cargo traffic.

Federal Express has also developed mechanisms such as its Powership systems to help high volume customers rate and track their own shipments, obtain an invoice, and eliminate the need to reconcile invoices with manifests. Powership Plus is an advanced software program that integrates Federal Express shipping information with the customer's own mainframe.

These diverse revenue-producing services require that Federal Express incur significant costs in the support areas. Determining the appropriate price to charge for package delivery or for any of the logistics services performed by the company necessitates that FedEx understand why the costs of its support departments are generated and how those costs can be allocated to the revenue-producing areas for cost coverage. Such knowledge will make it easier for Federal Express to meet at least one of the items in the company's five-point strategy: that of lowering costs and prices.

SOURCES: *The Federal Express System: How It Works* (Federal Express) and *Federal Express Corporation Five-Point Strategy* (Federal Express: June 10, 1992).

CHAPTER SUMMARY

Costs cannot be allocated effectively through a single cost pool and single base allocation process. Related costs should be grouped together and assigned to consecutively lower levels of responsibility through the use of a multistage, multiple cost driver approach.

Service department costs can be allocated to revenue-producing areas to determine a full cost of making products or performing services, to assign responsibility, and to provide additional information for choosing among alternative courses of action. Like all allocations, service department cost allocations should be made in a rational and systematic manner to be useful for management planning and decision making. The allocation system should use appropriate bases to assign costs.

The three methods of allocating service department costs are the direct method, step method, and algebraic method. The direct method assigns service department costs directly to the revenue-producing departments and does not consider services that may be provided by one service department to another; it is the simplest method of allocation.

The step method of allocation partially recognizes the reciprocal relationships of departments in making cost allocations. It uses a "benefits-provided" ranking that lists the service departments in order, from the one providing the most service to other departments to the one servicing primarily the revenue-producing areas. Costs are assigned, using a proration technique, out of each department in the sequential order of the ranking. Once costs have been assigned from an area, they cannot flow back into that area.

The algebraic method provides full recognition of the interrelationships among all departments through the use of simultaneous equations. This method provides the best allocation information and is readily adaptable to computer computations.

APPENDIX

Uniform Capitalization for Tax Purposes

There are at least three distinct influences on cost allocation systems. An important influence that has been presented in this chapter is internal uses. Two external influences are generally accepted accounting principles (GAAP) and Internal Revenue Service (IRS) rules. GAAP are described in detail in various Financial Accounting Standards Board pronouncements; IRS rules are found in the Internal Revenue Code and other authoritative declarations originating with the IRS.

The Internal Revenue Code has a proliferation of rules that describe how costs must be allocated in determining income tax liabilities. The intent of these rules is to prescribe when a cost must be deducted—that is, in which tax period a cost may be recognized. To achieve this end, **uniform capitalization** (unicap) **rules** determine

Uniform capitalization rules

whether a cost must be capitalized or, alternatively, whether it may be expensed in the period in which it is incurred. The Tax Reform Act of 1986 (TRA '86) caused many manufacturers, wholesalers, and retailers to expand the types and amounts of service department costs that are treated as product costs for tax purposes. The unicap rules require entities to capitalize, as product cost, many costs that previously had been treated as period expenses. The rationale for such capitalization is that such costs are incident to production or acquisition. Exhibit 6–16 presents the costs that are required to be included in or excluded from product cost according to TRA '86 and related IRS regulations.

Superfull absorption costing

The uniform capitalization rules of TRA '86 have also been referred to as **super-full absorption costing** because of the additional costs to be capitalized. Examination of Exhibit 6–16 reveals, for example, that successful bidding costs, distribution costs for warehousing, product development engineering costs, and legal costs related to production are to be treated as product costs. It was estimated that the unicap rules cost manufacturers approximately $35 billion in taxes between 1987 and 1992, since fewer service department costs may initially be written off as period costs for tax purposes.[7] To comply with these regulations, many manufacturers have had to modify their cost accounting systems to identify and accumulate the designated service costs in a way that permits assigning such costs to production.

Costs incurred in the production area and costs outside the production area that are distinctly related to production have always been treated as product costs. TRA '86 requires that indirect costs incurred outside the production area be analyzed and accumulated into two categories: (1) mixed service costs that are to be allocated either as product costs or nonproduction period costs and (2) service costs that are purely nonproduction costs. The diagram in Exhibit 6–17 on page 236 presents the treatment for each of these two categories of service department costs.

To illustrate how the super-full absorption costing rules can affect predetermined overhead rates, assume that Loxley Company estimates the following 1995 budget figures and calculates its overhead rate based on estimated machine hours:

Budgeted overhead for the factory	$ 941,600
Allocation of budgeted costs from the several external service departments	264,000
Total	$1,205,600
Divided by planned machine hours	880,000
Predetermined overhead rate per machine hour	$1.37

---

[7] Joseph V. Richards and James C. Godbout, "GASP—It's Super Full Absorption," (*Ernst & Whinney*) *Ideas* (Fall/Winter 1987–88), p. 2.

Comparison of Full Absorption Regulations and Uniform Capitalization Rules

	FULL ABSORPTION	UNIFORM CAPITALIZATION		FULL ABSORPTION	UNIFORM CAPITALIZATION
Manufacturers	Category I	Category I	**Manufacturers**	Category III	
Direct material	▲	▲	Taxes (other than income)	●	▲
Direct labor	▲	▲	Financial depreciation	●	▲
Repairs	▲	▲	Employee benefits/pensions		
Maintenance	▲	▲	(current service costs)	●	▲
Utilities	▲	▲	Rework, scrap, spoilage	●	▲
Rent	▲	▲	Strike costs	●	■
Indirect labor	▲	▲	Officers' salaries		
Indirect materials	▲	▲	(incident to production)	●	▲
Small tools and equipment	▲	▲	Factory administration	●	▲
Quality control	▲	▲	Insurance		
	Category II		(incident to production)	●	▲
Marketing, advertising, selling	■	■	General and administrative		
Bidding expenses—successful	■	▲	(incident to production):		
Bidding expenses—unsuccessful	■	■	Coordination of projects	●	▲
Distribution	■	▲[1]	Personnel	●	▲
Interest	■	▲[2]	Purchasing	●	▲
Research and experimental	■	■	Materials handling and		
Engineering			warehousing	●	▲
(product development)	■	▲	Accounting	●	▲
Casualty and theft losses	■	■	Data processing	●	▲
Percentage depletion in excess			Security	●	▲
of cost depletion	■	▲	Legal	●	▲
Depreciation and amortization			**Retailers and Wholesalers**		
in excess of financial amounts	■	▲	Purchasing	■	▲
Income taxes	■	■	Offsite storage	■	▲
Pensions (past service costs)	■	▲[3]	Processing and repackaging	■	▲
General and administrative			General and administrative		
(overall activities):			(attributable to above)	■	▲
Overall management	■	■			
Business planning	■	■			
Financial accounting	■	■			
Financial planning	■	■			
Economic analysis	■	■			
Internal audit	■	■			
Public relations	■	■			
Tax department	■	■			
Officers' salaries					
(overall activities)	■	■			

▲ Costs that must be allocated to inventory for tax purposes.

● Costs that were required to be allocated to be inventory if allocated for financial statement purposes.

■ Costs not required to be allocated to inventory.

[1] Distribution costs related to warehousing must be allocated.
Distribution costs related to customer delivery are *not* allocated.

[2] Interest allocated for construction or manufacture of: real property, longlived property, property requiring more than two years to complete, and property costing more than $1 million requiring more than one year to complete

[3] Pension past service costs were not required to be inventoried prior to the 1987 Act (i.e. effective for tax years beginning after 1987).

SOURCE: Joseph V. Richards and James C. Godbout, "Gasp—It's Super Full Absorption," (*Ernst & Whinney*) *Ideas* (Fall/Winter, 1987–88), p. 4. Reprinted with permission of Ernst & Young, formerly Ernst & Whinney.

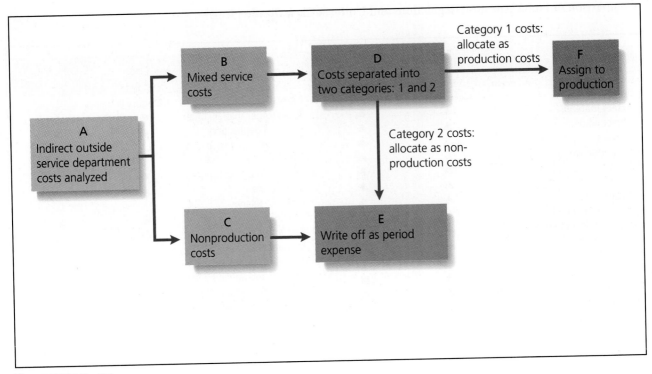

■ EXHIBIT 6–17
Treatment of Service Department Costs (per TRA '86)

If the external service department costs had not been considered in setting the rate, the predetermined overhead rate would have been $1.07 ($941,600 ÷ 880,000). To the extent that the latter rate excludes credible product costs incurred by supporting service departments, ending work in process and finished goods inventories will be understated and expenses will be overstated. To the extent that the latter rate includes questionable product costs, ending work in process and finished goods inventories will be overstated and expenses (other than tax) will be understated.

In analyzing under- or overapplied overhead, actual costs of both factory overhead and allocated actual service department costs must be combined. Managers can then compare individual cost elements to determine which costs were controlled and which were not. If the financial community ultimately accepts the additional service department costs as credible product costs for financial reporting purposes, the IRS Code and Treasury Regulations may, once again, have influenced the evolution of GAAP.

KEY TERMS

Administrative department (p. 216)
Algebraic method (p. 223)
Allocation (p. 213)
Benefits-provided ranking (p. 222)
Cost allocation (p. 213)
Cost pool (p. 214)

Differential cost (p. 218)
Direct method (p. 222)
Service department (p. 216)
Step method (p. 222)
Superfull absorption costing (p. 234)
Uniform capitalization rules (p. 234)

Service Department Cost Allocation

Direct method:

1. Determine rational and systematic allocation bases for each service department.

2. Assign costs from each service department directly to revenue-producing areas using specified allocation bases.

Step method:

1. Determine rational and systematic allocation bases for each service department.

2. List service departments in sequence from the one that provides the most service to all other areas (both revenue- and non-revenue-producing) to the one that only provides service to revenue-producing areas ("benefits-provided" ranking).

3. Beginning with the first service department listed, allocate the costs from that department to all remaining departments; repeat the process until only revenue-producing departments remain.

Algebraic method:

1. Determine rational and systematic allocation bases for each department.

2. Develop algebraic equations representing the services provided by each department to other service departments and to revenue-producing departments using the allocation bases.

3. Solve the simultaneous equations for the service departments to each other either through an iterative process or by computer until all values are known.

4. Allocate costs using allocation bases developed in step 2. Eliminate "reallocated costs" from consideration.

Bodden Publishers has two product divisions (Textbooks and Fiction) and three service departments (Administration, Personnel, and Public Relations). Budgeted costs are as follows:

Administration	$ 900,000
Personnel	420,000
Public Relations	480,000
Textbooks	1,410,000
Fiction	1,688,000

The service departments above are listed in the order of their "benefits-provided" ranking. Selected potential allocation bases are presented below.

	Number of Employee Hours	Number of Employees	$ of Assets Employed
Administration	14,100	7	$570,000
Personnel	9,200	4	210,000
Public Relations	6,600	3	135,000
Textbooks	16,800	8	600,000
Fiction	20,200	10	900,000

Management thinks that administration costs should be allocated on the basis of employee hours, personnel costs on the basis of number of employees, and public relations costs on the basis of dollars of assets employed.

Required:

a. Allocate service department costs using the direct method.

b. Allocate service department costs using the step method.

c. Allocate service department costs using the algebraic method.

Solution to Demonstration Problem

a.

	Base	% of Total Base	Amount to Allocate	Amount Allocated
Administration Costs (employee hours)				
Textbooks	16,800	45.4	$900,000	$ 408,600
Fiction	20,200	54.6	900,000	491,400
Totals	37,000	100.0		$ 900,000
Personnel Costs (# of employees)				
Textbooks	8	44.4	$420,000	$ 186,480
Fiction	10	55.6	420,000	233,520
Totals	18	100.0		$ 420,000
Public Relations Costs ($ of assets employed)				
Textbooks	$ 600,000	40.0	$480,000	$ 192,000
Fiction	900,000	60.0	480,000	288,000
Totals	$1,500,000	100.0		$ 480,000
Grand total of allocated departmental costs:				
Textbooks				$ 787,080
Fiction				1,012,920
Total allocated				$1,800,000

b.

	Base	% of Total Base	Amount to Allocate	Amount Allocated
Administration Costs (employee hours)				
Personnel	9,200	17.4	$900,000	$ 156,600
Public Relations	6,600	12.5	900,000	112,500
Textbooks	16,800	31.8	900,000	286,200
Fiction	20,200	38.3	900,000	344,700
Totals	52,800	100.0		$ 900,000
Personnel Costs (# of employees)				
Public Relations	3	14.3	$576,600[1]	$ 82,454
Textbooks	8	38.1	576,600[1]	219,685
Fiction	10	47.6	576,600[1]	274,461
Totals	21	100.0		$ 576,600
Public Relations Costs ($ of assets employed)				
Textbooks	$ 600,000	40.0	$674,954[2]	$ 269,982
Fiction	900,000	60.0	674,954[2]	404,972
Totals	$1,500,000	100.0		$ 674,954

[1] ($420,000 budgeted for Personnel and $156,600 allocated from Administration costs.)
[2] ($480,000 budgeted for Public Relations and $112,500 allocated from Administration costs.)

Grand total of allocated
departmental costs:
  Textbooks $ 775,867
  Fiction   1,024,133

       Total allocated $1,800,000

c.   Bodden Department Interrelationships

	Administration # of Employee Hours		Personnel # of Employees		Public Relations $ of Assets Employed	
	Base	Percent	Base	Percent	Base	Percent
Administration	n/a	n/a	7	25	570,000	25
Personnel	9,200	17	n/a	n/a	210,000	9
Pub. Relations	6,600	13	3	11	n/a	n/a
Textbooks	16,800	32	8	28	600,000	26
Fiction	20,200	38	10	36	900,000	40
Total	52,800	100	28	100	2,280,000	100

$$A = \$900,000 + .25P + .25R$$
$$P = \$420,000 + .17A + .09R$$
$$R = \$480,000 + .13A + .11P$$

Substituting the first equation into the others:

$$P = \$420,000 + .17(\$900,000 + .25P + .25R) + .09R$$
$$\text{and } R = \$480,000 + .13(\$900,000 + .25P + .25R) + .11P$$

Multiplying and combining terms produces the following results:

$$P = \$420,000 + \$153,000 + .0425P + .0425R + .09R$$
$$P = \$573,000 + .0425P + .1325R$$
$$.9575P = \$573,000 + .1325R$$
$$P = \$598,433 + .1384R$$

$$R = \$480,000 + \$117,000 + .0325P + .0325R + .11P$$
$$R = \$597,000 + .1425P + .0325R$$
$$.9675R = \$597,000 + .1425P$$
$$R = \$617,054 + .1473P$$

$$P = \$598,443 + .1384(\$617,054 + .1473P)$$
$$P = \$598,443 + \$85,400 + .0204P$$
$$.9796P = \$683,843$$
$$P = \$698,084$$

$$R = \$617,054 + .1473(\$698,084)$$
$$R = \$719,882$$

Placing the values of P and R in the original formula, A is calculated as follows:

$$A = \$900,000 + .25(\$698,084) + .25(\$719,882)$$
$$A = \$900,000 + \$174,521 + \$179,971$$
$$A = \$1,254,492$$

These values can now be allocated as follows:

	Administration		Personnel		Public Relations	
	Percent	Amount	Percent	Amount	Percent	Amount
Administration	n/a	n/a	25	$174,521	25	$179,971
Personnel	17	$ 213,264	n/a	n/a	9	64,789
Maintenance	13	163,084	11	76,789	n/a	n/a
Textbooks	32	401,437	28	195,464	26	187,169
Fiction	38	476,707	36	251,310	40	287,953
Total*	100	$1,254,492	100	$698,084	100	$719,882

	Textbooks	Fiction	Total
Administration	$ 401,437	$ 476,707	$ 878,144
Personnel	195,464	251,310	446,774
Public Relations	187,169	287,953	475,122
Total Allocation	$ 784,070	$1,015,970	$1,800,040*
Direct Costs	1,410,000	1,688,000	3,098,000
Total Costs	$2,194,070	$2,703,970	$4,898,040

* Difference due to rounding

The following spreadsheet is the computer solution to the above set of equations. Note that the precision of the computer spreadsheet program is based on six decimal places and, therefore, yields more accurate results than were provided from a manual computation.

Coefficient matrix:

1	0	<0.318182>	<0.285714>	<0.263158>
0	1	<0.382576>	<0.357143>	<0.394737>
0	0	1.000000	<0.250000>	<0.250000>
0	0	<0.174242>	1.000000	<0.092105>
0	0	<0.125000>	<0.010714>	1.000000

Matrix inverse:

1	0	0.447162	0.442040	0.415662
0	1	0.552838	0.557960	0.584338
0	0	1.090723	0.304905	0.300764
0	0	0.204627	1.067169	0.149448
0	0	0.158265	0.152453	1.053608

Calculation of costs:

$$
\begin{bmatrix} P1 \\ P2 \\ S1 \\ S2 \\ S3 \end{bmatrix} = \begin{bmatrix} 1 & 0 & 0.447162 & 0.442040 & 0.415662 \\ 0 & 1 & 0.552838 & 0.557960 & 0.584338 \\ 0 & 0 & 1.090723 & 0.304905 & 0.300764 \\ 0 & 0 & 0.204627 & 1.067169 & 0.149448 \\ 0 & 0 & 0.158265 & 0.152453 & 1.053608 \end{bmatrix} \cdot \begin{bmatrix} \$1,410,000 \\ 1,688,000 \\ 900,000 \\ 420,000 \\ 480,000 \end{bmatrix} = \begin{bmatrix} \$2,197,620.36 \\ 2,700,379.64 \\ 1,254,077.52 \\ 704,110.32 \\ 712,200.60 \end{bmatrix}
$$

Relative distribution of services:

From/To	S1	S2	S3	P1	P2
S1		17.4242%	12.5000%	31.8182%	38.2576%
S2	25.0000%		10.7143%	28.5714%	35.7143%
S3	25.0000%	9.2105%		26.3158%	39.4737%

Distribution of costs:

From/To	S1	S2	S3	P1	P2
Costs	$ 900,000	$ 420,000	$ 480,000	$1,410,000	$1,688,000
Allocation:					
S1	<1,254,078>	218,513	156,760	399,025	479,780
S2	176,028	<704,110>	75,440	201,174	251,468
S3	178,050	65,597	<712,200>	187,421	281,132
Totals	$ -0-	$ -0-	$ -0-	$2,197,620	$2,700,380

QUESTIONS

1. What is cost allocation and why is it necessary in accounting?

2. What is a cost pool? Why are multiple cost pools more effective for overhead allocation than single cost pools?

3. What are the advantages of using a multistage cost allocation system such as activity-based costing?

4. What is a service department? Give examples. How are service departments different from operating departments?

5. Why are service department costs often allocated to revenue-producing departments?

6. How does service department cost allocation create a feeling of cost responsibility among revenue-producing area managers?

7. "There are four criteria to use in selecting an allocation base and all four should be applied equally." Discuss the theoretical and practical merits of this statement.

8. What differences exist among the direct, step, and algebraic methods of allocating service department costs?

9. What are the advantages and disadvantages of each of the following methods of allocating service department costs: (a) direct, (b) step, and (c) algebraic?

10. Why is a "benefits-provided" ranking used in the step method of allocation?

11. When the algebraic method of allocating service department costs is used, total costs for each service department increase from what they were prior to the allocation. Why does this occur and how are the additional costs treated?

12. How has the evolution of computer technology enhanced the feasibility of using the algebraic method of service department cost allocation?

13. What would be some service departments in a hospital and the appropriate methods of allocating their costs to revenue-producing areas? In an accounting firm? In a community theater?

14. *(Appendix)* How would the uniform capitalization rules affect the information-gathering process for accounting purposes?

EXERCISES

15. (*Direct method*) Golden Home Saving Bank has three revenue-generating areas: checking accounts, savings accounts, and loans. The bank also has three service areas: administration, personnel, and accounting. The direct costs per month and the interdepartmental service structure are shown below in a benefits-provided ranking.

| Department | Direct Costs | % of Service Used by ||||||
		Admin.	Pers.	Acctg.	Check.	Sav.	Loans
Administration	$30,000	—	10	10	30	40	10
Personnel	20,000	10	—	10	30	20	30
Accounting	30,000	10	10	—	40	20	20
Checking accounts	30,000						
Savings accounts	25,000						
Loans	50,000						

Compute the total cost for each revenue-generating area using the direct method.

16. *(Step method)* Using the information in Exercise 15, compute the total cost for each revenue-generating area using the step method.

17. *(Algebraic method)* Using the information in Exercise 15, compute the total cost for each revenue-generating area using the algebraic method.

18. *(Cost allocation base)* A service department can express its total operating costs (using the form y = a + bX) as y = $200,000 + $12X, where X represents direct labor hours. For September 1994, the following were the planned and actual hours provided by the service department to the four producing departments:

Department	Planned Hours	Actual Hours
1	2,400	2,400
2	1,800	3,000
3	2,800	4,200
4	3,000	2,400
Total	10,000	12,000

a. Develop a rate that would allow the service department to allocate its costs according to planned activity.

b. Develop a rate that would allow the service department to allocate its costs according to actual activity.

c. Determine how much cost was allocated to Department 1 based on the rate in part a and the rate developed in part b. Is the amount allocated in a and b the same? Explain.

19. *(Direct method)* Elizando Inc. has organized its operations into two service departments, Administration and Maintenance, and two operating departments (revenue-generating departments), Stamping and Assembly. The company uses the direct method to allocate service department costs to operating departments. Information for October 1994 follows:

	Administration	Maintenance
Services provided to other departments:		
Administration		15%
Maintenance	25%	
Stamping	35%	50%
Assembly	40%	35%
Service department costs	$90,000	$30,000

a. What amount of Administration and Maintenance cost should be assigned to each of the operating departments for October?

b. Is the cost allocation affected by the order in which costs are assigned (i.e., Administration costs first and then Maintenance costs, or vice versa)? Explain.

20. *(Cost allocation)* Balmyra Equipment Company is organized into three departments: Administration, Marine, and Commercial. Administration is a service department and the other two are operating departments. Administration costs are allocated to the other departments based on total labor hours. For March 1994,

total costs of Administration were $125,000. Total labor hours worked in each department for March were 15,000, 12,000, and 13,000, respectively, for Administration, Marine, and Commercial.

a. What amount of Administration cost should be allocated to each of the operating departments?

b. Why is it unnecessary to specify an allocation method (such as direct, step, or algebraic) to complete this exercise?

21. *(Algebraic method)* Eastern Science Publications Co. has two divisions: Textbooks and Trade Publications. The company also has two service departments: Administration and Personnel. Direct costs and allocation bases are presented below:

| | | Allocation Bases | |
Department	Direct Costs	# of employees	$ of assets employed
Administration	$ 450,000	10	$ 620,000
Personnel	350,000	5	150,000
Textbooks	2,250,000	50	1,200,000
Trade publications	950,000	30	1,050,000

Administrative costs are best allocated on the basis of dollars of assets employed, while personnel costs are best allocated on the basis of number of employees. Use the algebraic method to allocate the service department costs and determine the final costs of operating the Textbooks and Trade Publications Departments.

22. *(Algebraic method)* The following chart indicates the portion of service department outputs consumed by other departments, where S1, S2, and S3 are the service departments and P1 and P2 are the production departments.

| | Services used | | | | |
Department	S1	S2	S3	P1	P2
S1	—	.2	.3	.4	.1
S2	.3	—	.4	.1	.2
S3	.1	.4	—	.3	.2

The costs accumulated during the period for the service departments were $40,000, $100,000, and $250,000, for S1, S2, and S3, respectively. Allocate the service department costs to the producing departments using the algebraic method.

23. *(Matching)* Match the items on the left with the letter(s) of the items on the right.

1. Benefits received and causal criteria
2. Direct method
3. Step method
4. Algebraic method
5. "Benefits-provided" ranking
6. Objectives of allocating service department costs
7. Uniform capitalization rules
8. Operating department

a. Provides a comparison of alternative courses of action
b. Reflects all the service interrelationships among departments
c. Computes full costs
d. Uses the "benefits-provided" ranking to make allocations
e. Lists relationships most often used to select an allocation basis
f. Lists departments in order of services provided to one another
g. Generates revenue for the organization
h. Assigns indirect costs directly to revenue-producing areas with no intermediate allocations
i. Motivates managers
j. Specifies tax rules for cost allocations

24. *(Appendix)* Navasota Pipe Fitters Inc. experienced the following mixed service department costs during 1994:

	Costs		
	Mixed Service	**Nonproduction**	**Total**
Administrative	$450,000	$225,000	$ 675,000
Personnel	350,000	375,000	725,000
Totals	$800,000	$600,000	$1,400,000

Administrative costs are allocated on the basis of square footage occupied; personnel costs are allocated on the basis of total labor hours. The following statistics were generated for 1994:

	Square footage occupied	Number of labor hours
Administrative	2,000	10,000
Personnel	3,000	25,000
Production Dept. #1	18,000	36,000
Production Dept. #2	9,000	54,000

a. Use the direct method to assign the mixed service department costs to the Production Department.

b. If total overhead of Production Department #2 is $390,000, what is the "super-full absorption" overhead for that department? Assume that all Mixed Service cost should be assigned to Production Departments.

c. How would the total overhead amount for part (b) be used in the department?

COMMUNICATION ACTIVITIES

25. Energy Resources, Inc. is located in West Virginia. The company is comprised of two producing divisions—Mining and Transportation; and two service divisions—Personnel and Information Systems. The corporate president is very much concerned because the services of the Information Systems division is greatly underutilized (presently operating at about 55% of capacity). This is a relatively new division (it has been a separate division for only two years). The costs of operating Information Systems have been charged (allocated) to the producing divisions each month based on their actual usage of Information System services (as measured in computer processing time). For example, in the most recent month, Mining was allocated approximately two-thirds of the cost of the Information Systems Division, because for that month, Mining consumed two-thirds of the actual computer time in the Information Systems division. Also, costs in the Information Systems division are mostly fixed.

a. Identify and discuss explanations for the low capacity utilization in the Information Systems division.

b. Outline a solution for the low level of utilization.

26. Consider the case of the company that is decentrally organized into five operating divisions. The company pays $150,000 annually to subscribe to the Economic Facts and Projections Hotline (EFPH). This hotline is available via a computer link to all five of the division managers and provides sophisticated information about the U.S. and world economies, demand projections for various industries, interest rate forecasts, etc., as requested by clients. The company's contract with EFPH specifies that only one division at a time may maintain a computer link with EFPH. Thus, while one division is using the service, other divisions are precluded from using the service. The entire $150,000 cost to subscribe to the service is fixed; there are no variable costs associated with this contract. Write a memo to the company president discussing what considerations should be taken into account in designing a system to allocate the costs of the EFPH contract to the five operating divisions?

27. *(Multiple cost pools)* The Hydropump Company produces three types of water pumps for automobiles. The company has two operating departments: Machining and Assembly. Most company overhead costs can be directly traced to one department or the other. However, the following companywide overhead costs must be allocated to the two operating departments:

Depreciation and insurance	$2,500,000
Utilities	80,000
Indirect labor	450,000

The above costs are to be allocated to the two departments using square footage, machine hours, and direct labor hours, respectively. The Machining and Assembly departments cover 150,000 and 100,000 square feet, respectively; estimated machine hours in the Machining and Assembly departments are 6,000 and 2,000, respectively; and direct labor hours for the year are 80,000 and 20,000, respectively, in Machining and Assembly.

Overhead costs that may be directly traced to the Machining and Assembly departments are listed below:

	Machining	Assembly
Indirect labor costs	$200,000	$150,000
Depreciation	800,000	450,000
Other	200,000	400,000

All overhead costs (directly traceable and allocated) are applied to products in the Machining Department based on machine hours and in the Assembly Department based on direct labor hours.

Information on the three products produced by the company follows:

	Product 1	Product 2	Product 3
Direct materials—Machining	$15	$14	$18
Direct materials—Assembly	$ 5	$ 3	$ 4
Direct labor hours—Machining	1.2	.8	1.4
Direct labor hours—Assembly	3.0	2.4	4.0
Machine time (hours)—Machining	5.0	6.5	7.0
Machine time (hours)—Assembly	2.5	3.0	3.5
Direct labor wage rate—Machining		$12 per hour	
Direct labor wage rate—Assembly		$10 per hour	

a. Determine how much of the companywide overhead should be allocated to the two departments.
b. Determine the overhead application rate in each department (be sure to include the companywide allocated overhead).
c. Determine the cost to produce one unit of each type of product using the overhead application rates developed in part b and the direct labor and material costs presented.
d. Prepare journal entries to reflect the cost flows for the following:
   1. Assignment of overhead from the Assembly Department to 1,000 units of Product #1.
   2. Assignment of overhead from the Machining Department to 500 units of Product #3.

28. *(Direct method)* Midwest Community Hospital is a small country hospital that wants to determine its full costs of operating its three revenue-producing programs: Surgery, Inpatient Care, and Outpatient Services. The hospital wants to allocate budgeted costs of Administration, Public Relations, and Maintenance to the three revenue-producing programs. The costs budgeted for each service department are: Administration, $1,000,000; Public Relations, $350,000; and Maintenance, $250,000. Total assets employed is chosen as the allocation base for Administration; number of employees is to be used for Public Relations; and number of square feet assigned is used for Maintenance costs. The expected utilization of these activity bases is as follows:

	$ of assets employed	# of employees	Sq. ft. assigned
Administration	$ 740,000	4	2,000
Public relations	450,000	7	2,500
Maintenance	825,000	3	3,500
Surgery	1,975,000	9	4,800
Inpatient care	1,225,000	22	10,600
Outpatient services	525,000	12	5,100

Using the direct method, allocate the expected service department costs to the revenue-producing areas.

29. *(Step method)* Metro Real Estate Company generates revenue through three departments: Commercial Sales, Residential Sales, and Property Management. Warren T. Deed, proprietor, wants to ascertain the total costs (including support department costs) of operating each of these revenue-generating departments. The direct costs of each of the company's departments, along with several allocation bases associated with each, are presented below.

		Available Allocation Bases		
Department	Direct Costs	# Employees/ Sales-persons	$ of Assets Employed	$ of Revenue
Administration	$ 750,000	10	$1,240,000	N/A
Accounting	495,000	5	682,000	N/A
Promotion	360,000	6	360,000	N/A
Commercial Sales	5,245,000	21	500,000	$4,500,000
Residential Sales	4,589,510	101	725,000	9,500,000
Property Management	199,200	13	175,000	500,000

The service departments are listed according to Warren's judgment as to the "benefits-provided" ranking. He has also selected the following allocation bases: number of employees/salespersons for Administration; dollars of assets employed for Accounting; and dollars of revenue for Promotion.

a. Using the step method, allocate the service department costs to the revenue-generating departments.

b. Which department is apparently the most profitable?

 30. *(Comprehensive)* Ohio Structural Engineering Associates has organized its operations into four departments: Administration, Personnel, Commercial, and Residential. Administration and Personnel are service departments and Commercial and Residential are revenue-generating departments. The costs of operating the service departments are allocated to the revenue-generating departments. These costs, in turn, are accumulated with departmental overhead costs in Commercial and Residential and applied to engineering projects. The Personnel allo-

cation base is number of employees, and the Administration allocation base is dollars of assets employed. The following data relate to these two allocation bases and the direct costs of the company's departments:

Department	# of employees	$ of assets employed	Direct costs
Personnel	4	$ 200,000	$ 250,000
Administration	6	225,000	750,000
Residential	20	1,225,000	1,200,000
Commercial	30	1,850,000	1,450,000
Totals	60	$3,500,000	$3,650,000

a. Using the direct method, allocate the service department costs to the revenue-generating departments.
b. Using your answer from part a, what are each of the revenue-generating department's total costs after the allocation?
c. Assume that the company is going to allocate the service department costs using the step method. If the order of the "benefits-provided" ranking is (1) Personnel and (2) Administration, allocate the service department costs.
d. Using your answer from part c, what are each of the revenue-generating department's total costs after the allocation?
e. Using the algebraic method, allocate the service department costs.

31. *(Comprehensive)* Hazelton Mfg. Company's 1995 annual budget for its three service departments (Administration, Legal/Accounting, and Maintenance/Engineering) and its two production departments (Assembly and Finishing) is presented below.

Annual Budget ($000 omitted)

	Admin.	Legal/ Acctg.	Maint./ Eng.	Assem.	Finish.	Total
Direct labor	$ 700	$500	$ 900	$2,800	$2,000	$ 6,900
Material	70	200	90	400	1,200	1,960
Insurance	175	50	75	300	220	820
Depreciation	90	70	80	200	150	590
Miscellaneous	30	20	40	60	30	180
Total	$1,065	$840	$1,185	$3,760	$3,600	$10,450
Sq. ft. of floor space	400	300	300	800	1,000	2,800
# of employees	40	25	30	200	150	445
M & E hours	10	20	15	80	75	200

a. Allocate service department costs to the producing departments using the step method. Assume the "benefits-provided" rankings are as follows: Administration; Legal/Accounting; and Maintenance/Engineering. The bases for allocation of each service department costs are: (1) Administration, number of employees; (2) Legal/Accounting, floor space; and (3) Maintenance/Engineering, M & E hours. Calculate the factory overhead rates using 240 direct labor hours in Assembly and 200 in Finishing.
b. Calculate the overhead allocation rate per service unit using the direct method.
c. Calculate the overhead allocation rate using the algebraic method.

32. *(Direct, step methods)* Amar Supermarkets Corp. operates a chain of three retail stores in a state that permits municipalities to levy an income tax on businesses operating within their respective boundaries. The tax rate is uniform in all of the municipalities that levy the tax, and does not vary according to taxable income. Regulations provide that the tax is to be computed on income earned within the particular taxing municipality, after reasonable and consistent allocation of the corporation's general overhead (including service department costs). Amar's general corporate overhead consists of expenses pertaining to the warehouse, central office, advertising, and delivery.

For the year ended December 31, 1994, operating results for each store, before taxes and allocation of corporation overhead, were as follows:

	Birch	Maple	Spruce	Total
Sales	$500,000	$400,000	$300,000	$1,200,000
Cost of sales	280,000	230,000	190,000	700,000
Gross margin	$220,000	$170,000	$110,000	$ 500,000
Local operating expenses:				
Fixed	$ 70,000	$ 60,000	$ 50,000	$ 180,000
Variable	66,000	73,000	31,000	170,000
Totals	$136,000	$133,000	$ 81,000	$ 350,000
Income before corporate overhead and taxes	$ 84,000	$ 37,000	$ 29,000	$ 150,000

For the year ended December 31, 1994, corporation overhead was as follows:

Warehouse and delivery:		
Warehouse depreciation	$10,000	
Warehouse operations	15,000	
Delivery	35,000	$ 60,000
Central office:		
Advertising	$ 8,000	
Salaries	30,000	
Other	2,000	40,000
Total corporation overhead		$100,000

Delivery expenses vary with distances from the warehouse and number of deliveries to stores. Delivery statistics for 1994 are as follows:

Store	Miles from Warehouse	# of Deliveries	Delivery Miles
Birch	100	150	15,000
Maple	200	50	10,000
Spruce	25	200	5,000

Management has asked the company's cost accountant to evaluate two corporate overhead allocation plans that are being considered, so that operating results under both plans can be compared. In addition, management has decided to expand one of the stores in a plan to increase sales by $80,000. The contemplated expansion is expected to increase local fixed operating costs by $8,000 and to require 10 additional deliveries from the warehouse. The accountant has been asked to furnish management with a recommendation as to which store should be selected for the prospective expansion.

a. Rounding off to the nearest whole percent, compute each store's income that would be subject to the municipal tax under the following two plans:

Plan 1—All corporate overhead costs are allocated directly to the stores, using sales as the basis for allocation.

Plan 2—Central office salaries and other central overhead is allocated equally to warehouse operations and to each store.

Then, allocate the resulting warehouse operations costs, warehouse depreciation, and advertising to each store on the basis of sales. Finally, allocate delivery expenses to each store on the basis of delivery miles.

b. Compute each store's potential increase in relevant expenses, including delivery expenses, but before allocation of other corporation overhead and taxes as a result of the contemplated expansion. Determine which of the three stores should be selected for expansion to maximize corporate net income.

(AICPA adapted)

33. Music Teachers Inc. is an educational association having 20,000 members in 1994. The association operates from a central headquarters but has local membership chapters throughout the United States. Monthly meetings are held by the local chapters to discuss recent developments on topics of interest to music teachers. The association's journal, *Teachers' Forum*, is issued monthly with features about developments in the field. The association also publishes books and reports, and sponsors professional courses that qualify for continuing professional education credit. The Statement of Revenues and Expenses for the current year is presented below.

Music Teachers Inc.
Statement of Revenues and Expenses
For the Year Ended November 30, 1994
($000 omitted)

Revenues		$3,275
Expenses:		
Salaries	$920	
Personnel costs	230	
Occupancy costs	280	
Reimbursement to local chapters	600	
Other membership services	500	
Printing and paper	320	
Postage and shipping	176	
Instructors' fees	80	
General and administrative	38	3,144
Excess of revenues over expenses		$ 131

The Board of Directors of the organization has requested that a segmented statement of operations be prepared showing the contribution of each revenue-generating department (i.e., Membership, Magazine Subscriptions, Books and Reports, Continuing Education). Mike Doyle has been assigned this responsibility and has gathered the following data prior to statement preparation.

Membership dues are $100 per year of which $20 is considered to cover a one-year subscription to the association's journal. Other benefits include membership in the association and chapter affiliation. The portion of the dues covering the magazine subscription should be assigned to the Magazine Subscriptions Center.

Twenty-five hundred one-year subscriptions to *Teachers' Forum* were sold to nonmembers and libraries at $30 each. In addition to subscriptions, the magazine generated $100,000 in advertising revenue. The costs per magazine subscription were $7 for printing and paper and $4 for postage and shipping.

A total of 28,000 technical reports and professional texts were sold by the Books and Reports Department at an average unit selling price of $25. Average costs per publication were $4 for printing and paper and $2 for postage and shipping.

The association offers a variety of continuing education courses to both members and nonmembers. The one-day courses cost $75 each and were attended by 2,400 people in 1994. A total of 1,760 people took two-day courses at a cost of $125 for each course. Outside instructors were paid to teach some of the courses. Salary and occupancy data are as follows:

	Salaries	Square Footage
Membership	$210,000	2,000
Magazine Subscriptions	150,000	2,000
Books and Reports	300,000	3,000
Continuing Education	180,000	2,000
Corporate Staff	80,000	1,000
	$920,000	10,000

The Books and Reports Department also rents warehouse space at an annual cost of $50,000. Personnel costs are 25% of salaries.

Printing and paper costs (other than those discussed above) relate to the Continuing Education Department.

General and administrative expenses include all other costs incurred by the corporate staff to operate the association.

Doyle has decided he will assign to the revenue-generating departments all revenues and expenses that can be (1) traced directly or (2) allocated on a reasonable and logical basis. The expenses that can be traced or assigned to corporate staff as well as any other expenses that cannot be assigned to revenue-generating departments will be grouped with the general and administrative expenses and not allocated to the revenue-generating departments. Doyle believes that allocations often tend to be arbitrary and are not useful for management reporting and analysis. He believes that any further allocation of the general and administrative expenses associated with the operation and administration of the association would be arbitrary.

a. Prepare a segmented Statement of Revenues and Expenses that presents the contribution of each revenue center and includes the common costs of the organization that are not allocated to the revenue-generating departments.

b. If segmented reporting is adopted by the association for continuing usage, discuss the ways the information provided by the report could be utilized by the association.

c. Mike Doyle decided not to allocate some indirect or nontraceable expenses to revenue-generating departments because he believes that allocations tend to be arbitrary.

1. Besides the arbitrariness argument, what reasons could be presented for not allocating indirect or nontraceable expenses to revenue-generating departments?

2. Under what circumstances do you think the allocation of indirect or nontraceable expenses to revenue-generating departments would be accepted?

(CMA adapted)

34. Columbia Company is a regional office supply chain with 26 independent stores. Each store has been responsible for its own credit and collections. The assistant manager in each store is assigned the responsibility for credit activities including the collection of delinquent accounts because the stores do not need a full-time employee assigned to credit activities. The company has experienced a sharp rise in uncollectibles in the last two years. Corporate management has decided to establish a collections department in the home office to be responsible for the

collection function companywide. The home office of Columbia Company will hire the necessary full-time personnel. The size of this department will be based on the historical credit activity of all the stores.

The new centralized collections department was discussed at a recent management meeting. Finding a method to assign the costs of the new department to the stores has been difficult because this type of home office service is somewhat unique. Alternative methods are being reviewed by top management.

The controller favored using a predetermined rate for charging the costs to the stores. The predetermined rate would be based on estimated costs. The vice president of sales had a strong preference for charging actual costs to the stores.

In addition, the basis for the collection charges to the stores was also discussed. The controller identified the following four measures of services or allocation bases that could be used: total dollar sales; average number of past due accounts; number of uncollectible accounts written off; and 1/26 of the cost to each store.

The executive vice president stated he would like the accounting department to prepare a detailed analysis of the two charging methods (predetermined and actual) and the four service allocation bases.

a. Evaluate the two methods that could be used to charge the individual stores the costs of Columbia's new collections department in terms of:
   1. practicality of application and ease of use, and
   2. ability to control costs.
b. For each of the four measures of service allocation bases identified by the controller:
   1. discuss whether the allocation base is appropriate to use in this situation, and
   2. identify some behavioral problems that might arise as a consequence of adopting the allocation base.

(CMA adapted)

---

35. One may view the income tax system in the United States as the largest system of cost allocation in the world because the tax system is used to allocate the cost of the government to the people. Assume that the tax system in the United States is mildly progressive in that people who make more money pay relatively larger portions of their income to the government. As discussed in the text, four criteria may be used to identify a basis for cost allocation: benefits received, causal relationships, fairness or equity, and ability to bear.
    a. Which of the four allocation criteria justifies a progressive form of income tax as a basis to allocate the costs of government to the people?
    b. Identify two alternatives to the income tax system to allocate the costs of government to the people.
    c. Is an income tax an ethical basis to allocate governmental costs?
    d. What ethical dilemmas are created for citizens (who are also taxpayers) when governmental costs are allocated via an income tax?

36. In designing an organization, it may be desirable to establish a separate department to be responsible for maintaining/improving the quality of organizational output. If such a department is established, discuss
    a. advantages associated with allocating the costs of the quality department to producing departments.
    b. disadvantages associated with allocating the costs of the quality department to producing departments.
    c. what would be appropriate bases for allocating costs of the quality department to producing departments.

ETHICS AND QUALITY DISCUSSION

PRODUCT COSTING METHODS

JOB ORDER COSTING

After completing this chapter, you should be able to answer these questions:

1. How do job order and process costing systems and actual, normal, and standard costing valuation methods differ?
2. In what production situations are job order costing systems appropriate and why?
3. What constitutes a "job" from an accounting standpoint?
4. What purposes are served by the basic documents used in a job order costing system?
5. What journal entries are used to accumulate costs in a job order costing system?
6. *(Appendix)* How are standard costs used in a job order costing system?

SALLY INDUSTRIES, INC.

Remember Michelle Pfeiffer's steamy piano number in *The Fabulous Baker Boys?* Well, the lady has some competition from Sally's piano playing and singing—only Sally's a robot. Dressed in a black tuxedo outfit with a white shirt and bow tie, Sally performs around the country on her elegant baby grand or upright console piano. She's the "namesake" of Sally Industries, Inc., and was the company's first animatronic character.

Sally Industries' unlikely start was in 1977 in the garage of one of the founders, dentist John Rob Holland. He conceived the idea of a Sally robot while he was in dentistry school at the University of North Carolina. As part of a class project, he was supposed to explain some complicated dental techniques, so he made a talking head (albeit basic and crude), naming it Sally after a woman patient.

When he returned to Jacksonville (Florida) a few years later, he started a small business to build entertainment robots with two friends. They called their company Sally Industries. The name Sally has remained, even though the expanded company now designs and manufactures a gamut of animatronic characters, props, and shows from Bubba Bear and the Badland Band, a sextet of singing animals; to the "Ghostbusters" dark ride featuring a spooky labyrinth of city streets, a warehouse, cold storage, a laser tunnel, a graveyard, and the fiery depths where the villain Prime Evil lurks; to 54 characters for Seoul Land in Korea.

SOURCE: Kathy Williams, "Let Sally Entertain You," *Management Accounting* (January 1991), p. 31. Reprinted from *Management Accounting.* Copyright by Institute of Management Accountants, Montvale, N.J.

Producing animatronic people and plants is not what could be called mass manufacturing! But, like all others, Sally's production process involves the conversion of raw materials to a finished product through the use of direct labor and overhead. Since each order is substantially different from other orders, estimating a set of common production costs for an order would be impossible. Thus, Sally Industries uses a method of cost accounting called **job order costing** that accumulates the costs of each job separately from all other jobs.

Job order costing

A primary objective of cost accounting is to determine the cost of an organization's products or services. Just as a variety of methods (first in, first out; last in, first out; average; specific identification) exist to determine inventory valuation and cost of goods sold for a retailer, different methods are available to value inventory and calculate product cost in a manufacturing or service environment. The method chosen depends on the nature of the product or service and the company's conversion process. A cost flow assumption is required for processes in which it is not possible to identify and attach costs to specific units of production.

This chapter begins a sequence of chapters presenting various methods of product costing. The chapter first distinguishes between two basic costing systems (job order and process) and then discusses three methods of valuation that can be used within these systems (actual, normal, and standard). The remainder of the chapter focuses on the nature and use of a job order costing system, like that used by Sally Industries.

METHODS OF PRODUCT COSTING

Before products can be costed, a determination must be made about (1) the product costing system and (2) the valuation method to be used. Product costing systems differ markedly and the system used indicates the cost object and the method of assigning costs to production. The valuation method specifies how product costs will be measured. Companies must have both a cost system and a valuation method, meaning that six possible combinations exist (shown in Exhibit 7–1).[1]

Costing Systems

Job order and process costing are the two basic cost systems. Job order costing is used by entities that make or perform relatively small quantities or distinct batches of identifiable, unique products or services. For example, job order costing is appropriate for a publishing company that produces educational textbooks, an accountant who prepares tax returns, and a research firm that performs product development studies. Construction companies such as Gaston & Associates (Juneau, Alaska) and Leevac Shipyards (Jennings, Louisiana) also use job order costing to trace project costs to assure contract compliance and to determine project profit margins. The News Note "Job Order Costing for Paint?" provides another example of a company doing production-to-order work in a traditionally mass production industry. In each instance, the organization produces tailor-made goods or services that conform to specifications designated by the purchaser of those goods or services. Services in general are typically user-specific, so job order costing systems are usually appropriate for such businesses.

The purchaser of the goods or services from a job shop can be external or internal contracting parties. External parties include individuals, other businesses, and the government; internal parties include other organizational units within the producing entity. The following two examples illustrate, respectively, these external and internal possibilities: The U.S. Navy contracted in 1992 with Trinity Marine Group of Gulf-

EXHIBIT 7–1

Costing Systems and Inventory Valuation

COST ACCUMULATION SYSTEM	METHOD OF VALUATION		
	Actual	Normal	Standard
JOB ORDER	Actual DM Actual DL Actual OH (assigned to job after end of period)	Actual DM Actual DL OH applied using predetermined rates at completion of job or end of period (predetermined rates times actual input)	Standard DM and/or Standard DL OH applied using predetermined rates when goods are completed or at end of period (predetermined rates times standard input)
PROCESS	Actual DM Actual DL Actual OH (assigned to job after end of period using FIFO or weighted average cost flow)	Actual DM Actual DL OH applied using predetermined rates (using FIFO or weighted average cost flow)	Standard DM Standard DL Standard OH using predetermined rates (will always be FIFO cost flow)

---

[1] A third and fourth dimension (cost accumulation and cost presentation) are also necessary in this model. These dimensions are related to the use of absorption or variable costing and are covered in Chapter 13.

NEWS NOTE

Job Order Costing for *Paint?*

Los Angeles businessman Robert C. Davidson [is] president of Surface Protection Inc. (SPI), a manufacturer and distributor of paints. The catch is that SPI sells its paints not to the average homeowner putting a second coat on the garage, but to Hollywood studios.

"We don't compete against your Pittsburgh Paints of the world," Davidson says, "because you can't demand the same kind of customer loyalty, your margins aren't as big, and you end up fighting over pennies. In our business, customers are a lot more loyal and willing to pay a higher price for a unique product."

The unique product is the paint used on the production sets in the movie, television and theatrical industries. Customer demand often exceeds the capabilities of more mainstream paint operations (such as paint with a crackled texture so that a building looks as though it was built in the 1930s) and can also be more immediate.

Part of SPI's success can be attributed to the nature of its business. Manufacturing paint requires high levels of both technical expertise and financial resources lacked by many would-be competitors. Providing a difficult-to-copy service is one of the keys to longevity in a niche. "People who want specific products are willing to pay whatever for just the right product, no matter what it is."

SOURCE: Ron Stodghill II, "When Small Is Good," *Black Enterprise* (November 1991), pp. 63, 66. Copyright November 1991 by The Earl G. Graves Publishing Co., Inc., 130 Fifth Avenue, New York, NY 10011.

port, Mississippi, to build an oceanographic research ship and *USA TODAY* Sky Radio uses another Gannett Co., Inc. division (*USA TODAY*) to help in providing airline passengers with live news, business, sports, and lifestyle reports every half-hour. Regardless of whether the relationship is external or internal, the purchasing party specifies details as to what, when, and how many to the selling party.

The other primary product costing system, **process costing**, is used by entities that produce large quantities of homogeneous goods. Process costing is used by companies that mass manufacture products such as bricks, gasoline, detergent, and breakfast cereal. The output of a single process in a company using a process costing system is homogeneous; thus, within a given time frame, one specific unit of output cannot be readily identified with specific input costs. This characteristic of process costing systems makes a cost flow assumption necessary. Cost flow assumptions provide a means for accountants to assign costs to products without regard for the actual physical flow of units. Process costing systems (covered in Chapters 8 and 9) allow the use of either the FIFO or the weighted average cost flow assumption.

Process costing

Valuation Methods

The three basic methods of valuation (shown earlier in Exhibit 7–1) are actual, normal, and standard costing. When a company uses the actual costs of direct materials, direct labor, and overhead to determine the cost of work in process inventory, that company is employing an **actual cost system**. Service businesses, such as some advertising agencies or consulting firms, that have few customers and/or low volume may be able to use an actual cost system. Because of the reasons discussed in Chapter 4, however, many companies modify actual cost systems by using predetermined overhead rates rather than actual overhead costs. This combination of actual direct materials and direct labor costs with predetermined overhead rates is a **normal cost system**. If the predetermined rate is substantially equivalent to what the actual rate would have been for an annual period, its use provides acceptable and useful costs.

Actual cost system

Normal cost system

Standard

Standard cost system

Companies using either job order or process costing may employ **standards** (or predetermined benchmarks) for costs to be incurred and/or quantities to be used. In a **standard cost system**, unit norms or standards are developed for direct material and direct labor quantities and/or costs. Overhead is applied to production using a predetermined rate, which is considered the standard. These standards may then be used to plan for future activities and cost incurrence and to value inventories. Both actual and standard costs are recorded in the accounting records to provide an essential element of cost control—having norms against which actual costs of operations can be compared. A standard cost system allows companies to quickly recognize devia-

Variance

tions or **variances** from normal production costs and to correct problems resulting from excess usage and/or costs. Actual costing systems do not provide this benefit and normal costing systems cannot provide it in relation to materials and labor.

Since the use of predetermined overhead rates is more common than the use of actual overhead costs, this chapter addresses a job order/normal cost system and the appendix briefly describes some possible job order/standard cost combinations.[2]

JOB ORDER COSTING SYSTEM

Job

Product costing is concerned with (1) cost identification, (2) cost measurement, and (3) product cost assignment. In a job order product costing system, costs are accumulated individually on a "per job" basis. A **job** is defined as a single unit[3] or group of like units being produced to distinct customer specifications. Each job is treated as a unique "cost entity" or cost object. Costs of different jobs are maintained in separate subsidiary ledger accounts and are not added together or commingled in those ledger accounts.

The logic of separating costs for individual jobs is shown by the following example. During June, George Petrie, an artist, made drawings and small-scale models of three robots for several amusement parks: a munchkin from Oz, King Kong, and Scarlett O'Hara. When completed, the actual munchkin robot will be 3.5 feet high, King Kong 20 feet, and Scarlett 5.4 feet. Even if all the robots had the same number of moving parts and equal detail, to total all George's business costs for June and divide by three projects would produce a meaningless average cost per robot. This type of average cost per job would be equally meaningless in any other entity that manufactures products or provides services geared to unique customer specifications. Since job results are heterogeneous and distinctive in nature, the costs of those jobs are, logically, not averageable.

Exhibit 7–2 provides the Work in Process Inventory control and subsidiary ledger accounts for Petrie's job order product costing system. The usual production costs of direct materials, direct labor, and overhead are accumulated for each job. Actual direct materials and direct labor costs are combined with an overhead cost that is computed as a predetermined overhead rate multiplied by some actual cost driver (such as direct labor hours, cost or quantity of materials used, or number of materials requisitions). Normal cost valuation is used because, while actual direct material and direct labor costs are fairly easy to identify and associate with a particular job, overhead costs are usually not traceable to specific jobs and must be allocated to production. For example, Petrie's electricity cost during June is related to all jobs worked on during that month. It would be almost impossible to accurately determine which jobs created the need for what amount of electricity.

---

[2] While actual overhead may be assigned to jobs, such an approach would be less customary because total overhead would not be known until the period was over, causing an unwarranted delay in overhead assignment. Activity-based costing can increase the validity of tracing overhead costs to specific products or jobs.
[3] To eliminate the need for repetition, units should be read to mean either products or services since job order costing is applicable to both manufacturing and service companies. For the same reason, *produced* can mean *manufactured* or *performed*.

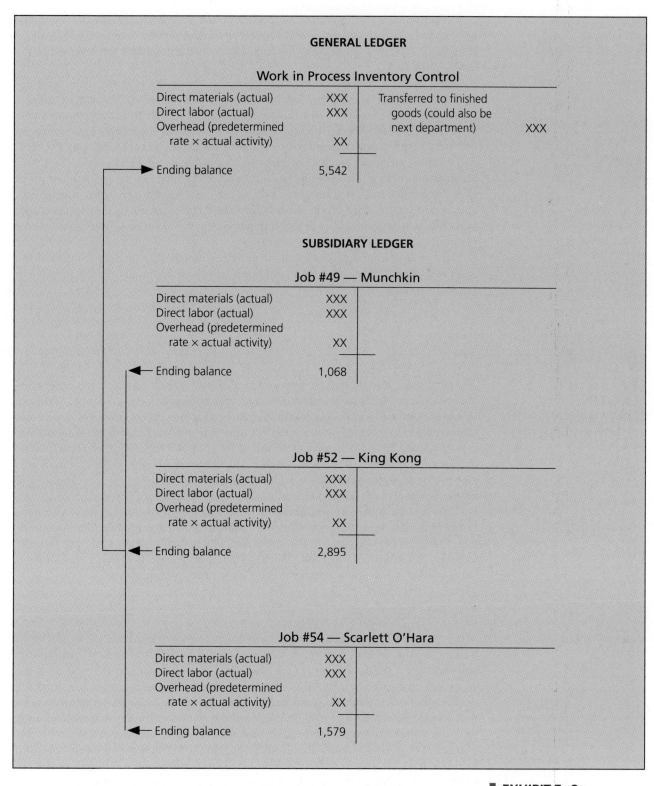

GENERAL LEDGER

Work in Process Inventory Control

Direct materials (actual)	XXX	Transferred to finished	
Direct labor (actual)	XXX	goods (could also be	
Overhead (predetermined		next department)	XXX
rate × actual activity)	XX		
Ending balance	5,542		

SUBSIDIARY LEDGER

Job #49 — Munchkin

Direct materials (actual)	XXX
Direct labor (actual)	XXX
Overhead (predetermined	
rate × actual activity)	XX
Ending balance	1,068

Job #52 — King Kong

Direct materials (actual)	XXX
Direct labor (actual)	XXX
Overhead (predetermined	
rate × actual activity)	XX
Ending balance	2,895

Job #54 — Scarlett O'Hara

Direct materials (actual)	XXX
Direct labor (actual)	XXX
Overhead (predetermined	
rate × actual activity)	XX
Ending balance	1,579

▌ **EXHIBIT 7–2**

Separate Subsidiary Ledger Accounts for Jobs

To help ensure the proper recording of costs, the amounts appearing in the subsidiary ledger accounts are periodically compared and reconciled to the Work in Process Inventory Control account in the general ledger. This reconciliation is indicated by the equality of the assumed ending balances of the subsidiary ledger accounts with the WIP Inventory Control account in Exhibit 7–2.

The output of a given job can be a single unit or multiple similar or dissimilar units. For example, Petrie's output is a clay model of each customer's contracted-for robot. If a job's output is a single unit, the total job costs accumulated are assigned to the individual unit.

When multiple output results, a unit cost may be computed only if the units are similar or if costs can be and are accumulated for each separate unit (such as through an identification number). For example, Conner Peripherals produces compact disk drives for a variety of companies (including Compaq) based on their particular specifications. Conner can determine the cost per disk drive for each company by accumulating the costs per batch of homogeneous products in different production runs and treating each production run as a separate job. In such cases, production costs of each job batch can be commingled because the units are not separately distinguishable. Additionally, since all the units within the batch are similar, the total accumulated job cost is averaged over the number of units produced to determine a cost per unit.

If the output consisted of dissimilar units for which individual cost information was not gathered, no cost per unit could be determined, although it is still possible to know the total job cost.

JOB ORDER COSTING— DETAILS AND DOCUMENTS

The basic facts presented in the previous section about the nature of a job order costing system provide the necessary foundation to account for individual jobs. A job can be categorized by its stage of existence in its production cycle. There are three basic stages of production: (1) contracted for but not yet started, (2) in process, and (3) completed. Since a company using job order costing is making products according to user specifications, jobs might require unique raw materials. Thus, raw materials may not be acquired until a job is under contract and it is known that production will occur. The raw materials acquired, although often separately distinguishable and related to specific jobs, are accounted for in a single general ledger control account (Raw Materials Inventory Control) with subsidiary ledger backup. The materials may, however, be designated in the storeroom (and possibly in the subsidiary records) as being "held for use in Job XX." Such designations should keep the materials from being used on a job other than the one for which they were acquired.

Materials Requisitions

Materials requisition

When materials are needed to begin a job, a **materials requisition** form (shown in Exhibit 7–3) is prepared so that the materials can be released from the warehouse and sent to the production area. This form is a source document that indicates the types and quantities of materials to be placed into production or used to perform a service job. Such documents are usually prenumbered and come in multicopy sets so that completed copies can be maintained in the warehouse, the department, and each job's file. Completed materials requisition forms are important documents in the audit trail of company records because they provide the ability to trace responsibility for materials cost and to verify the flow of materials from the warehouse to the department and job that received the materials. These forms release warehouse personnel from further responsibility for the issued materials and assign responsibility to the department that issued the requisition.

When materials are issued, their costs are released from Raw Materials Inventory and, if the materials are direct to the job, are sent to Work in Process Inventory. If the Raw Materials Inventory account also contains indirect materials, those costs are assigned to Manufacturing Overhead when the indirect materials are issued. Thus, the journal entry will be as follows:

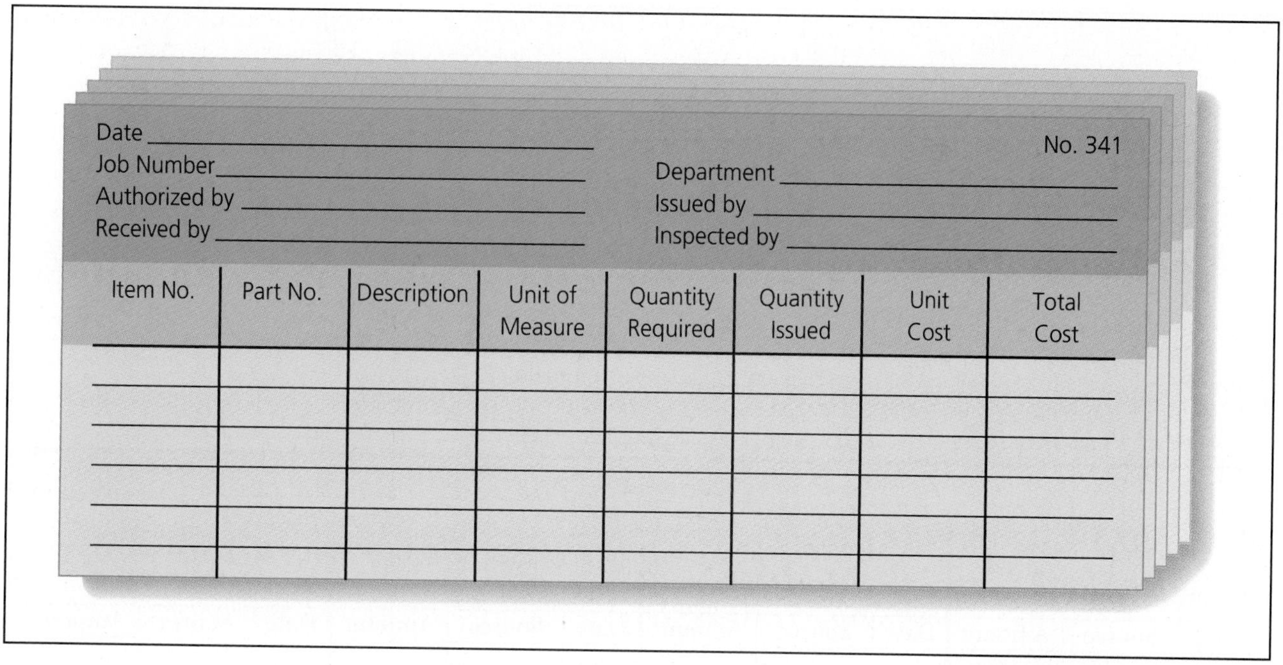

Date ____
Job Number ____
Authorized by ____
Received by ____

No. 341
Department ____
Issued by ____
Inspected by ____

Item No.	Part No.	Description	Unit of Measure	Quantity Required	Quantity Issued	Unit Cost	Total Cost

EXHIBIT 7–3
Materials Requisition Form

Work in Process Inventory (if direct)	XXX	
Manufacturing Overhead (if indirect)	XXX	
Raw Materials Inventory		XXX

When the first direct materials associated with a job are issued to production, that job moves to the second stage of its production cycle—being in process. When a job enters this stage, it is necessary to begin the process of cost accumulation using the primary accounting document in a job order system, the **job order cost sheet** (or job cost record).

Job order cost sheet

Job Order Cost Sheet

The source document that provides virtually all financial information about a particular job is the job order cost sheet. The set of job order cost sheets for all uncompleted jobs makes up the Work in Process Inventory subsidiary ledger. The total costs contained in the job order cost sheets for all uncompleted jobs should reconcile to the Work in Process Inventory Control account balance in the general ledger as shown in Exhibit 7–2.

The top portion of a job order cost sheet includes a job number, a description of the task, customer identification, various scheduling information, delivery instructions, and contract price. The remainder of the form details actual costs for materials and labor and applied overhead costs. The form might also include budgeted cost information, especially if such information was used to estimate the job's selling price. Sally Industries, for instance, operates in a totally fixed-price contract environment; therefore, it is essential that budgeted and actual costs be compared at the end of a job to determine any deviations from estimates.

Exhibit 7–4 illustrates a job cost record for Really Wired, a robotics manufacturer. The company has been contacted to produce one moa robot for the Christchurch (New Zealand) Maori Museum. (The moa is an extinct, flightless bird genetically related to an ostrich.) All of the company's job cost sheets include a section for budgeted data so that budget-to-actual comparisons can be made for planning and control purposes. Direct materials and direct labor costs are assigned to jobs, and the

Job Number ___186___

Customer Name and Address:

Christchurch Maori Museum
8901 Wellingsley Blvd.
Christchurch, New Zealand

Description of Job:

1 Moa; 12 feet high
Weight — approx. 1,500 pounds Include
universal eye, neck and body movement;
500-watt sound system

Contract Agreement Date: ___3/25/94___
Scheduled Starting Date: ___4/5/94___
Agreed Completion Date: ___2/1/95___
Actual Completion Date: _____
Delivery Instructions: ___Crate and deliver to museum___

Contract Price: ___$80,040 (U.S.)___

Department A – Art

Direct Materials (Est. $4,360)			Direct Labor (Est. $1,600)			Overhead based on					
						# of Req. (@ $20) (Est. $440)			# of DLH (@ $3) (Est. $600)		
Date	Source	Amount	Date	Source	Amount	Date	Source	Amount	Date	Source	Amount

Department B – Molding & Covering
(same format as above but with different OH rates)

Department C – Robotics
(same format as above but with different OH rates)

SUMMARY

	Art Dept. Actual	Art Dept. Budget	Molding & Covering Dept. Actual	Molding & Covering Dept. Budget	Robotics Dept. Actual	Robotics Dept. Budget
Direct Materials	___	$4,360	___	$ 9,800	___	$ 7,056
Direct Labor	___	1,600	___	9,648	___	1,324
Overhead (req)	___	440	___	1,922	___	1,176
Overhead (DLH)	___	600	___	1,510	___	584
Totals	___	$7,000	___	$22,880	___	$10,140

Final Costs:		Actual	Budget
	Art Dept.	___	$ 7,000
	Molding & Covering Dept.	___	22,880
	Robotics Dept.	___	10,140
	Total	___	$40,020

■ **EXHIBIT 7–4**
Really Wired Job Order Cost Sheet

amounts are posted to the job order cost sheet as work on the job is performed. Direct materials information is gathered from the materials requisition forms, while direct labor information is found on employee time sheets or employee labor tickets. (Employee time sheets are discussed in the next section.)

EXHIBIT 7–5
Employee Time Sheet

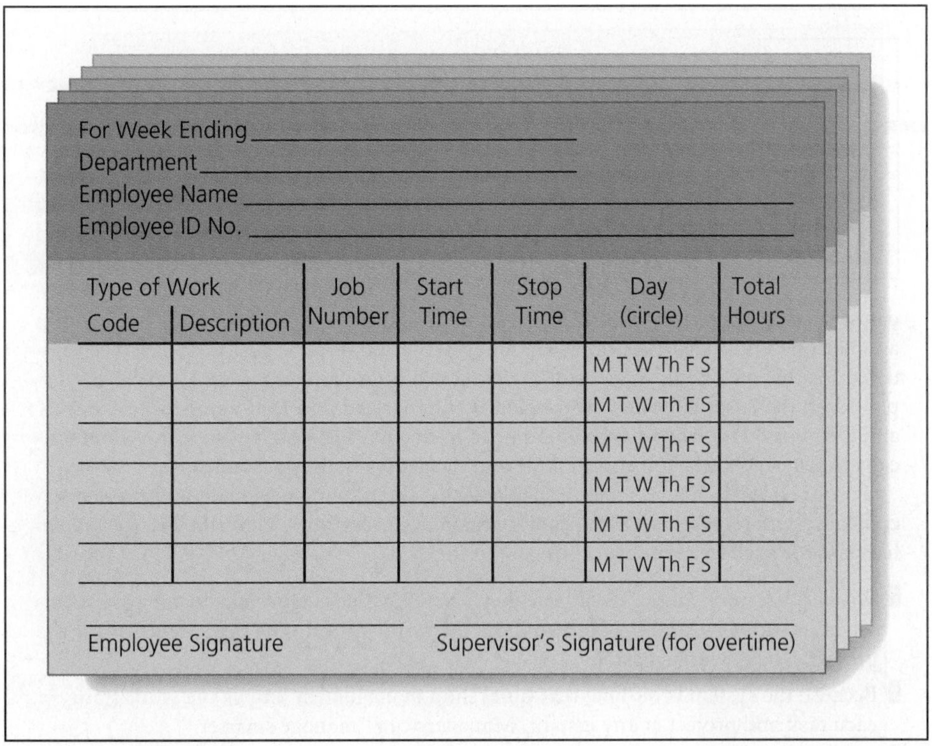

Overhead is applied to production at Really Wired using two predetermined overhead rates.[4] The first rate is based on the number of materials requisitions and the second is based on direct labor hours. Really Wired's management has found that these two activity bases better reflect the incurrence of costs than would a single base. Number of materials requisitions reflects management's determination that numerous parts required by a job create substantially more of some types of overhead support costs, such as warehousing and purchasing. Number of direct labor hours provides a reasonable allocation base for other overhead costs because the production process is highly labor-intensive.

Employee Time Sheets

An **employee time sheet** (Exhibit 7–5) indicates, for each employee, what jobs were worked on during the day and for what amount of time. These time sheets are most reliable if the employee fills them out as the day progresses. As work arrives at an employee station, it is accompanied by a tag specifying its job order number. The employee notes when work was started and stopped on the time sheet.[5] These time sheets should be collected and reviewed by supervisors to ensure that the information is as accurate as possible.

The time sheet shown in Exhibit 7–5 is appropriate if employees are asked to record their time and work manually. But the information that is indicated on the

Employee time sheet

---

[4] If actual overhead is used in product costing, the source column(s) in the overhead section would indicate the general journal page(s) where the entries are made to assign actual overhead to the various jobs. For example, if actual overhead and actual direct labor hours (DLHs) for April were, respectively, $500,000 and 20,000, overhead would be applied to each job at $25 per DLH ($500,000 ÷ 20,000). If one job used 40 DLHs, it would be charged with $1,000 (40 × $25) of overhead.

[5] Alternatives to daily time sheets are job time tickets that supervisors give to employees as they are assigned new jobs and supervisors' records of which employees worked on what jobs for what period of time. The latter alternative is extremely difficult if a supervisor is overseeing a large number of employees or if employees are dispersed through a large section of the plant.

3. In addition to indirect materials and indirect labor, the Art Department incurred other overhead costs during April. Depreciation on the factory building and equipment was recorded for April. Insurance on the factory building for the month had been prepaid and has expired. The bill for factory utility costs for April was received and will be paid during May. Repairs and maintenance costs were paid in cash. Overhead costs were also incurred for some items not detailed (such as supplies used, supervisors' salaries, and so forth); these costs have been credited to various other accounts. The following entry summarizes the accumulation of these other actual overhead costs in the Manufacturing Overhead account:

Manufacturing Overhead—Art Dept.	1,050	
Accumulated Depreciation		330
Prepaid Insurance		60
Utilities Payable		350
Cash		190
Various other accounts		120

To record actual overhead costs of the Art Dept. during April
exclusive of indirect materials and indirect nonsalaried labor.

4. Really Wired prepares financial statements at the end of each month. To do so, Work in Process Inventory must include all production costs—direct materials, direct labor, and overhead. Really Wired allocates overhead to the Art Department Work in Process Inventory based on two predetermined overhead rates: $20 per material requisition and $3 per direct labor hour. In April, materials for Job #186 required 2 materials requisitions and the artists had worked a total of 50 hours. The other jobs worked on during the month received total applied overhead of $1,120 (20 material requisitions × $20, and an assumed 240 DLH × $3).

Work in Process Inventory—Art Dept. (Job #186)	190	
Work in Process Inventory—Art Dept. (other jobs)	1,120	
Manufacturing Overhead—Art Dept.		1,310

To apply overhead to Art Dept. work in process for April
using predetermined application rates.

Notice that the amount of overhead actually incurred during April in the Art Department ($236 + $460 + $1,050 = $1,746) is not equal to the amount of overhead applied to that department's Work in Process Inventory ($1,310). This $436 difference is the underapplied overhead for the month. Because the predetermined rates are based on annual estimates, differences in actual and applied overhead will accumulate during the year. Under- or overapplied overhead will be closed at year-end, as shown in Chapter 4, to either Cost of Goods Sold (if the under- or overapplied amount is immaterial) or to Work in Process Inventory, Finished Goods Inventory, and Cost of Goods Sold (if significant).

The preceding summarizations indicate the types of entries each department of Really Wired Inc. would make. Direct materials and direct labor data are posted to each job order cost sheet on a continuous basis (usually daily); entries are posted to the general ledger control accounts at less frequent intervals (usually monthly).

Job #186 will be worked on by all departments, sometimes concurrently. Similar entries for the moa job are made throughout the production process and Exhibit 7–6 shows the completed cost sheet for Job #186 for Really Wired. Note that direct material requisitions, direct labor cost, and applied overhead shown previously in entries (1), (2) and (4) are posted on the job cost sheet. Other entries are not detailed.

When the job is completed, its costs are transferred to Finished Goods Inventory. The journal entries related to completion and sale are as follows:

Finished Goods Inventory—Job #186	40,048	
Work in Process Inventory—Art Dept.		7,175
Work in Process Inventory—Molding & Covering Dept.		22,728
Work in Process Inventory—Robotics		10,145

Job Number 186

Customer Name and Address:	Description of Job:
Christchurch Maori Museum	1 Moa; 12 feet high
8901 Wellingsley Blvd.	Weight – approx. 1,500 pounds Include
Christchurch, New Zealand	universal eye, neck and body movement;
	500-watt sound system

Contract Agreement Date: 3/25/94
Scheduled Starting Date: 4/5/94
Agreed Completion Date: 2/1/95 Contract Price: $80,040 (U.S.)
Actual Completion Date: 1/26/95
Delivery Instructions: Crate and deliver to museum

Department A – Art

Direct Materials (Est. $4,360)			Direct Labor (Est. $1,600)			Overhead based on # of Req. (@ $20) (Est. $440)			Overhead based on # of DLH (@ $3) (Est. $600)		
Date	Source	Amount	Date	Source	Amount	Date	Source	Amount	Date	Source	Amount
4/5	MR #344	$ 83	4/8	payroll	$147	4/30	2 MRs	$ 40	4/30	50 DLHs	$150
4/18	MR #352	45	4/22	payroll	393						

(other similar entries would be made throughout production)

Department B – Molding & Covering
(same format as above but with different OH rates)

Department C – Robotics
(same format as above but with different OH rates)

SUMMARY

	Art Dept. Actual	Art Dept. Budget	Molding & Covering Dept. Actual	Molding & Covering Dept. Budget	Robotics Dept. Actual	Robotics Dept. Budget
Direct Materials	$4,410	$4,360	$ 9,600	$ 9,800	$ 7,001	$ 7,056
Direct Labor	1,720	1,600	9,620	9,648	1,380	1,324
Overhead (req)	400	440	2,068	1,922	1,152	1,176
Overhead (DLH)	645	600	1,440	1,510	612	584
Totals	$7,175	$7,000	$22,728	$22,880	$10,145	$10,140

Final Costs:	Actual	Budget
Art Dept.	$ 7,175	$ 7,000
Molding & Covering Dept.	22,728	22,880
Robotics Dept.	10,145	10,140
Total	$40,048	$40,020

EXHIBIT 7–6
Really Wired Completed Job Order Cost Sheet

Cost of Goods Sold—Job #186	40,048	
Finished Goods Inventory—Job #186		40,048
Accounts Receivable—Christchurch Museum	80,040	
Sales		80,040

The completed job cost sheet can be used by managers in all departments to determine how well costs were controlled. The Art Department experienced higher direct materials and direct labor costs than budgeted. However, in the Molding & Covering Department, actual direct materials and direct labor costs were slightly below budget. Robotics was very close to budget in all categories. Overall, costs were well controlled on this job, since total actual costs were almost identical to the budgeted ones.

Managers are interested in controlling costs on each job as well as by department for each time period. Actual direct materials, direct labor, and factory overhead costs are accumulated in departmental accounts and are periodically compared to budgets so that managers can respond to significant deviations. Transactions must be recorded in a consistent, complete, and accurate manner to have information on actual costs available for periodic comparisons. Managers may stress different types of cost control in different types of businesses.

The Really Wired example assumed the use of predetermined overhead rates. The journal entries shown on pages 267 and 268 indicate that the Art Department incurred $1,746 ($236 + $460 + $1,050) of actual overhead and $5,570 ($540 + $5,030) of direct labor cost during March. If actual overhead were to be applied to jobs, an application rate of 31.3 percent of direct labor cost ($1,746 ÷ $5,570) would have been used. If Really Wired had used this approach to overhead application, $169.02 ($540 × 31.3%) of overhead would have been applied to Job #186.

Attempting to use actual overhead costs for determination of job cost is often unsatisfactory because of the delayed timing of overhead information and differences in periodic activity levels. The delay in information may be critical when a job is being provided for a customer on a cost-plus basis. Unusual variations in periodic activity could cause management to make incorrect assumptions about the cost per job. A manager might mistakenly determine that a particular job's cost was significantly higher or lower than it would have been in a period of normal activity. In a cost-plus contract, incorrect assumptions about costs could result in overcharging some customers while undercharging others. Such problems are overcome by using predetermined overhead rates.

The major difference in job order costing for a service organization and a manufacturing firm is that a service organization may use an insignificant amount of direct materials on each job. In such cases, direct materials may be treated (for the sake of convenience) as part of overhead rather than accounted for separately. The accountant in the service company may only need to trace direct labor to jobs and allocate all other production costs to jobs. Allocations of these costs may be accomplished most effectively by using a predetermined rate per direct labor hour or, if wage rates are approximately equal throughout the firm, per direct labor dollar. Other alternative cost drivers may also be used as possible overhead allocation bases.

JOB ORDER COSTING TO ASSIST MANAGEMENT

Job order costing is useful to managers in planning, controlling, decision making, and evaluating performance. Knowing the costs of individual jobs will allow managers to better estimate future job costs and establish realistic selling prices. The use of budgets and standards in a job order product costing system provides information against which actual costs can be compared at reasonable time intervals for control purposes. These comparisons can also furnish some performance evaluation information. The following two examples demonstrate the usefulness of job order costing to managers.

Smidley & Smith

Smidley & Smith is a national advertising company with a diversified set of clients and types of jobs. Mr. Smidley, the president of the company, wanted to know which clients were the most profitable and which were the least profitable. To determine this

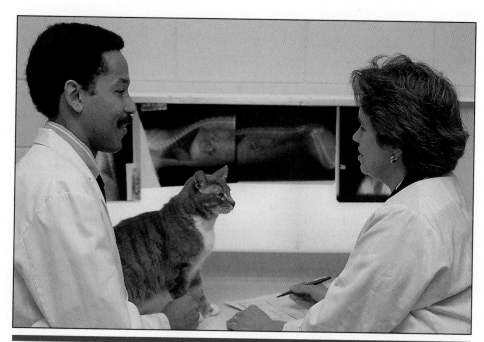

Job order costing is useful in all professional service businesses. For example, accumulating the costs of each animal's tests, x-rays, and direct labor time spent allows a veterinarian to estimate a profit margin on services performed by "patient" and patient-type (cat vs. dog, small vs. large, etc.).

information, he requests a breakdown of profits per job measured on both a percentage and an absolute dollar basis.

Mr. Smidley found that the company did not maintain records of costs per client job. Costs had been accumulated only by type—travel, entertainment, and so forth. Ms. King, the sales manager, was certain that the largest profits came from the company's largest accounts. A careful job cost analysis was performed. It was found that the largest accounts contributed the most revenue to the firm, but the smallest percentage and absolute dollars of incremental profits. Until the president requested this information, no one had totaled all the costs spent on recruiting each client and on the travel, entertainment, and other costs associated with maintaining each client.

When a company has a large number of jobs that vary in size, time or effort, it may be difficult to know which jobs are responsible for disproportionately large amounts of costs. Job order costing can assist in determining which jobs are truly profitable and can help managers to better monitor costs. As a result of the cost analysis, Mr. Smidley changed the company's marketing strategy. The firm began concentrating its efforts on smaller clients who were located closer to the primary office. These efforts caused profits to increase substantially because significantly fewer costs were incurred for travel and entertainment. A job order cost system was implemented to track the per-period and total costs associated with each client. Unprofitable accounts were dropped and account managers felt more responsibility to monitor and control costs related to their particular accounts.

Monkey Business Boat Company

The Monkey Business Boat Company manufactures three types of boats to customer specifications.[7] Before job order costing was instituted, the owner (Swenson Schmidt) had no means of determining the costs associated with the production of each type of boat. When a customer provided boat specifications and asked what the selling price would be, Schmidt merely estimated costs in what he felt was a reasonable manner.

---

[7]This example is based on an article by Leonard A. Robinson and Loudell Ellis Robinson, "Steering a Boat Maker Through Cost Shoals," *Management Accounting* (January 1983), pp. 60–66.

In fact, during the construction process, he did not assign any costs to Work in Process Inventory; all production costs were sent to the Finished Goods Inventory account.

After implementing a job order costing system, Monkey Business Boat Company had better control over its inventory, better inventory valuations for financial statements, and better information with which to prevent part stockouts (not having parts in inventory) and production stoppages. The job order costing system provided Mr. Schmidt with information on what work was currently in process and at what cost. From this information, he was better able to judge whether additional work could be accepted and when current work would be completed. Since job order costing assigns costs to Work in Process Inventory, balance sheet figures were more accurate. As materials were used in the production system, the use of materials requisitions to transfer goods from Raw Materials Inventory to Work in Process Inventory produced inventory records that were more current and reflective of raw materials quantities on hand. Finally, the use of a job order product costing system gave the owner an informed means by which to estimate costs and more adequately price future jobs.

Whether the entity is a manufacturer or a service organization that tailors its output to customer specifications, company management will find that job order costing techniques will help in the managerial functions. This cost system is useful for determining the cost of goods produced or services rendered in companies that are able to attach costs to specific jobs. As product variety becomes wider and the size of production lots for many items shrink, job order costing will be applicable to more companies. Custom-made goods may become the norm rather than the exception in an environment that relies on flexible manufacturing systems and computer-integrated manufacturing.

R E V I S I T I N G

SALLY INDUSTRIES, INC.

Many of Sally's robots begin as standard designs and are modified according to customer specifications. Sally maintains an inventory of raw materials consisting of standard production bushings; bearings; pneumatic cylinders; hoses; prosthetic devices such as hands, arms, and legs; and a large list of other manufacturing materials including resin, plaster, clay, and paint needed in the manufacture of robots and their attendant props and scenery.

Each robot is an exacting mix of latex, wires, tubes, and a distinctive form of artistry that must be nurtured and managed carefully. Entertainment robots are expensive. A simple one with limited movements, off-the-shelf parts, and a standard design may sell for $15,000. More complicated models with custom designs and complex body movements can run as much as $60,000. An entire scripted 10-minute show featuring a sextet of singing robots wearing fancy costumes and performing on a custom-built stage might cost a quarter of a million dollars.

Because of the enormous number of variables per robot character, before pricing a project Sally management carefully estimates the cost of the components through its cost estimation system. The cost Sally's management assigns to its robots is the sum of direct labor (the most important component, so it's estimated first), direct materials, and overhead. Overhead is assigned to products using a predetermined rate with direct labor as the base.

For a small, specialized company like Sally to continue to prosper, it must manage its costs and revenues carefully. Unanticipated cost overruns on a major project such as MCA Universal could be especially damaging. Neither Sally nor any other company can endure without effective management control. The many, many hours that Sally's crew has invested in developing the cost estimation and time management and production control systems pay off every day in that enchanted twinkle in the eye of a singing bear or that exuberant grin on a pint-sized "ghostbuster" scoring a hit on villainous Prime Evil.

SOURCE: Thomas L. Barton and Frederick M. Cole, "Accounting for Magic," *Management Accounting* (January 1991), pp. 27–31. Reprinted from *Management Accounting.* Copyright by Institute of Management Accountants, Montvale, N.J.

CHAPTER SUMMARY

A cost accounting system should be compatible with the manufacturing environment in which it is used. Job order product costing and process costing are two of the traditional cost accounting systems. Job order costing is used in companies that make a limited quantity of products or provide a limited number of services uniquely tailored to customer specifications. Job order costing is especially appropriate and useful for many service businesses, such as advertising, legal, and architectural firms. Process costing is appropriate in production situations in which large quantities of homogeneous products are manufactured on a continuous flow basis.

A job order costing system considers the "job" as the cost object for which costs are accumulated. A job can consist of one or more units of output and job costs are accumulated on a job order cost sheet. Job order cost sheets for uncompleted jobs serve as the Work in Process Inventory subsidiary ledger. Cost sheets for completed jobs not yet delivered to customers constitute the Finished Goods Inventory subsidiary ledger and cost sheets for completed and sold jobs compose the Cost of Goods Sold subsidiary ledger.

In an actual or normal cost job order costing system, direct materials and direct labor are traced specifically (during the period and for each department) to the individual jobs in process. Direct materials and direct labor are traced, respectively, through materials requisition forms and employee time sheets. Service companies may not attempt to trace direct materials to jobs, but consider those costs as part of overhead. Tracing is not considered necessary when the materials cost is insignificant in relation to the job's total cost.

In an actual cost system, actual overhead is assigned to jobs. More commonly, however, a normal costing system is used in which overhead is applied using one or more predetermined overhead rates multiplied by the actual activity base(s) incurred. Overhead is applied to Work in Process Inventory at the end of the month or when the job is complete, whichever is earlier.

Job order costing assists management in planning, controlling, decision making, and evaluating performance. It allows managers to trace costs specifically associated with current jobs to better estimate costs for future jobs. Additionally, managers using job order costing can better control the costs associated with current production, especially if comparisons with budgets or standards are used. Attachment of costs to specific jobs is also necessary to price jobs that are contracted on a cost-plus basis. Lastly, since costs are accumulated by specific jobs, managers can more readily determine which jobs or types of jobs are most profitable to the organization.

Job Order Costing Using Standard Costs

APPENDIX

The Really Wired example in the chapter illustrates the use of actual historical cost data for direct materials and direct labor in a job order product costing system. However, using actual costs for direct materials and direct labor may cause the cost of similar units to fluctuate from period to period or job to job because of changes in component costs. The use of standard costs for direct materials and direct labor can minimize the effects of such cost fluctuations in the same way that predetermined rates do for overhead costs.

A standard costing system determines product cost by using, in the inventory accounts, predetermined estimates for prices and/or quantities of component elements. After production is complete, the standard production cost is compared to the actual production cost to determine the efficiency of the production process. A difference between the actual quantity, price, or rate and its related standard is called a variance.

Standards can be used in a job order system only if a company typically engages in jobs that produce fairly similar products. One type of standard job order product costing system uses standards only for input prices of materials and/or rates for labor. This process is reasonable if all output relies on basically the same kinds of materials and/or labor. If standards are used for price or rate amounts only, the debits to Work in Process Inventory become a combination of actual and standard information: actual quantities at standard prices or rates.

B & B, a house painting company located on the West Coast, is used to illustrate the use of price and rate standards. Management has decided that, because of the climate, one specific brand of paint (costing $27 per gallon) is the best brand of paint to use. Painters employed by B & B are paid $10.50 per hour. These two amounts can be used as price and rate standards for the company. No standards can be set for the quantity of paint that will be used on a job or the amount of time the job will require, because those items will vary with the quantity and texture of wood on the structure being painted.

Assume that B & B paints a house requiring 60 gallons of paint and 48 hours of labor time. The standard paint and labor costs, respectively, are $1,620 (60 × $27) and $504 (48 × $10.50). B & B bought the paint when it was on sale, so the actual price paid was $21 per gallon or a total of $1,260. Comparing this price to the standard results in a $360 favorable material price variance (60 gallons at $6 per gallon). If the actual labor rate paid to painters was $11.25 per hour, there would be a $36 unfavorable (48 hours at $.75 per hour) labor rate variance.

Other job order companies produce output that is homogeneous enough to allow standards to be developed for both quantities and prices for materials and labor. Such companies usually use distinct production runs for numerous similar products. In such circumstances, the output is homogeneous for each run, unlike the heterogeneous output of B & B.

Ventura Company is a job order manufacturer that uses both price and quantity material and labor standards. Ventura manufactures computer housing cases for several computer manufacturers. The cases are contracted for on a job order basis, since there is a tendency by the manufacturers to change style, color, and size with each model year. Ventura produces the cases in distinct production runs each month for each manufacturer. Price and quantity standards for direct materials and direct labor have been established and are used to compare the estimated and actual costs of monthly production runs of the same manufacturer's cases.

The standards set for a computer housing case manufactured for Sigma Corporation by Ventura are as follows:

> 6 square feet of plastic at $1.20 per square foot
> 3 direct labor hours at $8.00 per DLH

In June, 1,000 cases were produced for Sigma. Actual plastic used was 6,125 square feet that was purchased at $1.25 per square foot. Direct labor employees worked 2,800 hours at an average labor rate of $8.10.

From this information, it can be concluded that Ventura used 125 square feet of plastic more than standard for the job [6,125 − (6 × 1,000)]. This usage causes an unfavorable materials quantity variance of $150 at the $1.20 standard price ($1.20 × 125 square feet). The actual plastic used was purchased at $.05 above the standard price per square foot and this results in a $306.25 ($.05 × 6,125) unfavorable materials price variance.

The actual DLHs used were 200 less than standard [(3 hours × 1,000 cases) − 2,800)] and this results in a favorable labor quantity variance of $1,600 ($8 standard rate × 200 hours). The work crew earned $.10 per hour above standard and this translates to a $280 unfavorable labor rate variance ($.10 × 2,800). A summary of variances follows:

Direct materials quantity variance	$ 150.00	unfavorable
Direct materials price variance	306.25	unfavorable
Direct labor quantity variance	1,600.00	favorable
Direct labor rate variance	280.00	unfavorable
Combined net variance	$ 863.75	favorable

From a financial perspective, Ventura controlled its combined materials and labor costs well on the Sigma job.

Variances can be computed for actual-to-standard differences regardless of whether standards have been established for both quantities and prices or only for prices. Standard costs for materials and labor provide the same types of benefits as predetermined overhead rates—more timely information and comparisons against actual amounts.

A predetermined overhead rate is, in essence, a type of standard. It establishes a constant amount of overhead assignable as a component of product cost and eliminates any immediate need for actual overhead information in the calculation of product cost. More is presented on standards and variances in Chapters 11 and 12.

Standard costing job order systems are reasonable substitutes for actual or normal costing systems as long as they provide managers with useful information. Any type of product costing system is acceptable in practice if it is effective and efficient in serving the company's unique production needs, provides the information desired by management, and can be implemented at a cost that is reasonable when compared to the benefits to be received. These criteria apply equally well to both manufacturers and service companies.

KEY TERMS

Actual cost system (p. 257)
Cost-plus contract (p. 265)
Employee time sheet (p. 263)
Job (p. 258)
Job order costing (p. 255)
Job order cost sheet (p. 261)
Materials requisition (p. 260)
Normal cost system (p. 257)
Process costing (p. 257)
Standard (p. 258)
Standard cost system (p. 258)
Variance (p. 258)

SOLUTION STRATEGIES

Basic Journal Entries in a Job Order Costing System

Raw Materials Inventory	XXX	
Accounts Payable		XXX
To record the purchase of raw materials.		
Work in Process Inventory—Dept. (Job #)	XXX	
Manufacturing Overhead	XXX	
Raw Materials Inventory		XXX
To record the issuance of direct and indirect materials requisitioned for a specific job.		

6.	Finished Goods Inventory*		405,804	
	WIP Inventory—Construction			254,000
	WIP Inventory—Finishing			151,804
	To record completion of Job 1.			

Accounts Receivable	605,804	
Sales*		605,804
To record sale of Job 1.		

Cost of Goods Sold	405,804	
Finished Goods Inventory		405,804
To record cost of goods sold for Job 1.		

7. Manufacturing Overhead—Construction	400	
Manufacturing Overhead—Finishing	120	
Cost of Goods Sold		520
To assign overapplied overhead to cost of goods sold.		

b.

	Job 2	Job 3
Direct materials—Construction	$ 48,000	$ 72,000
Direct labor—Construction	40,000	60,000
Manufacturing overhead—Construction	14,080	22,320
Direct materials—Finishing	0	0
Direct labor—Finishing	15,500	0
Manufacturing Overhead—Finishing	43,316	0
Totals	$160,896	$154,320

*Job 1 costs = $120,000 + $100,000 + $40,000 + $34,000 + $111,804 = $405,804; selling price = $405,804 + $200,000 = $605,804

QUESTIONS

1. What production conditions are necessary for a company to use job order costing?

2. What is the alternative to the use of a job order costing system? In what type of an environment would this alternative costing system be found?

3. Identify the three valuation methods discussed in the chapter. What are the differences among these methods?

4. In a job order costing system, what is a job? Why is it necessary to specify the job in a job order costing system?

5. What are the principal documents that are used in a job order costing system?

6. What is a job order cost sheet, and what information does it contain? How do job order cost sheets relate to control accounts for Work in Process Inventory, Finished Goods Inventory, and Cost of Goods Sold?

7. Of what use to management are job order cost sheets?

8. "Since the costs of each job are included in the job order cost sheet, they do not need to be recorded in the general ledger." Is this statement true or false, and why?

9. For most businesses, is an actual overhead application rate better than a predetermined overhead rate? Why or why not?

10. What creates under- or overapplied overhead when applying overhead to jobs?

11. What is the principal difference between service and manufacturing firms in job order costing?

12. The accounting firm of Sims & Co., CPAs, is considering implementing a job order costing system. Briefly discuss how the company would most likely install and use the system.

13. *(Appendix)* What differences exist between job costing based on actual costs and job costing based on standard costs? Why would a company use a standard cost job order system?

14. *(Appendix)* How does a firm use information on "variances" in a standard costing system to control costs?

EXERCISES

15. *(Matching)* For each of the following firms, determine whether it is more likely to use job order or process costing.
    This firm:
    a. manufactures tools and dies to customer specifications.
    b. manufactures household paints.
    c. produces three different types of wine.
    d. is a computer repair shop.
    e. is an architectural firm.
    f. manufactures hairspray and hand lotion.
    g. is a hospital.
    h. cans salmon and tuna.
    i. mass produces two models of bicycles.
    j. provides property management services for a variety of real estate developments.

16. *(Journal entries)* Wessin, Inc., produces custom-made truck hitches, and uses a job order costing system. During June 1994, the company worked on only one job and the following information relates to the month's operations and production:
    a. Direct materials purchased on account, $90,000.
    b. Direct materials issued to jobs, $79,800.
    c. Direct labor hours accrued, 1,800. All direct factory employees are paid $15 per hour.
    d. Actual factory overhead costs incurred for the month totaled $43,600. This overhead consisted of $9,000 of supervisory salaries, $18,000 of depreciation charges, $4,000 of insurance, $8,100 of indirect materials, and $4,500 of utilities. Salaries, insurance, and utilities were paid in cash, and indirect materials were removed from the supplies account.
    e. Overhead is applied to production at the rate of $25.00 per direct labor hour.
    The beginning balances of Direct Materials Inventory and Work in Process Inventory were $5,700 and $16,100, respectively. The ending balance in Work in Process Inventory was $12,300.
    a. Prepare journal entries for the above transactions.
    b. Determine the balances in Direct Materials Inventory at the end of the month.
    c. Determine the cost of goods completed during June. The job consisted of 2,000 similar units. What was the cost per unit?
    d. What amount of under- or overapplied overhead exists at the end of June?

17. *(Journal entries)* The Jackson Corporation custom produces furniture for office buildings in the Atlanta metropolitan area. Jackson incurred the following costs for February 1994:

Direct materials purchased on account		$9,000
Direct materials used for jobs		
Job 107	$1,200	
Job 108	800	
Other jobs	3,400	5,400
Direct labor costs accrued for month		
Job 107	$ 600	
Job 108	500	
Other jobs	900	2,000
Actual overhead costs for February		8,400

The February beginning balance in Work in Process Inventory was $1,400, which consisted of $300 for Job 107 and $1,100 for Job 108.

Actual overhead is applied to jobs on the basis of direct labor cost. Job 108 was completed and transferred to finished goods during February. It was then sold for cash at 150% of cost.

a. Prepare journal entries to record the above information.
b. Determine the February ending balance in Work in Process Inventory, and how much of that balance is related to Job 107.

18. *(Predetermined overhead rate)* Dublin Ironworks began operations on March 1, 1994. Its Work in Process Inventory account on March 31 appeared as follows:

WORK IN PROCESS INVENTORY

Direct materials	$48,600	Cost of completed jobs	?
Direct labor	32,000		
Applied overhead	28,800		

The company applies overhead on the basis of direct labor cost. Only one job was still in process on March 31. That job had $12,200 in direct materials and $10,300 in direct labor cost assigned to it.

a. What was the predetermined overhead application rate?
b. How much cost was transferred out for jobs completed during March?

19. *(Normal versus actual costing)* For fiscal year 1994, the High Tensile Machining Co. estimated it would incur total overhead costs of $300,000 and work 20,000 machine hours. During January 1994, the company worked exclusively on Job 1478. It incurred January costs as follows:

Direct material usage		$48,000
Direct labor (1,400 hours)		28,000
Manufacturing overhead:		
Rent	$1,200	
Utilities	5,200	
Insurance	3,100	
Labor	5,500	
Depreciation	2,700	
Maintenance	1,800	19,500
Machine hours worked in January:	1,400	

a. Assuming the company uses an actual costing system, compute the January costs assigned to Job 1478.
b. Assuming the High Tensile Machining Co. uses a normal costing system, compute the January costs assigned to Job 1478.
c. What is the major factor driving the difference between your answers in parts a and b?

20. *(Cost flows)* Leroy's Custom Trailers is a small firm that manufactures truck trailers for various commercial uses. The firm applies overhead to jobs at a rate of 80% of direct labor cost. On December 31, 1994, a fire destroyed many of the firm's computerized cost records. Only the following information for 1994 was available from the records:

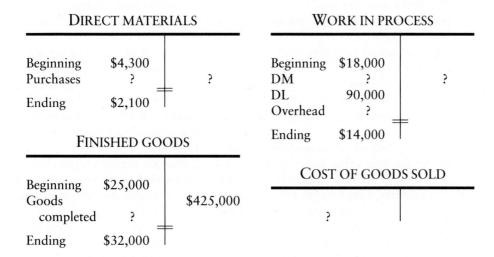

DIRECT MATERIALS			
Beginning	$4,300		
Purchases	?		?
Ending	$2,100		

WORK IN PROCESS			
Beginning	$18,000		
DM	?		?
DL	90,000		
Overhead	?		
Ending	$14,000		

FINISHED GOODS			
Beginning	$25,000		
Goods completed	?	$425,000	
Ending	$32,000		

COST OF GOODS SOLD	
?	

As Leroy's accountant, you have been asked to find the following:
a. Cost of Goods Sold for the year
b. Cost of trailers completed during the year
c. Amount of applied factory overhead
d. Cost of direct materials used
e. Cost of direct materials purchased during the year

21. *(Departmental overhead rates)* The Danforth Modular Construction Company uses a predetermined overhead rate to apply overhead to jobs, and the company employs a job order costing system. Overhead is applied to jobs in the Cutting Department based on the number of machine hours used, while Finishing Department overhead is applied on the basis of direct labor hours. In December 1994, the company estimated the following data for its two departments for the year 1995:

	Cutting Dept.	Finishing Dept.
Direct labor hours	500	2,500
Machine hours	7,500	500
Budgeted overhead cost	$30,000	$25,000

Job #271 was started and completed during March 1995. The job cost sheet shows the following information:

	Cutting Dept.	Finishing Dept.
Direct materials	$2,800	$400
Direct labor cost	$ 60	$525
Direct labor hours	5	40
Machine hours	60	10

a. Compute the predetermined overhead rate that should be used in each department of the Danforth Modular Construction Company.
b. Compute the overhead applied to Job #271 for each department and in total.
c. If the company had computed a companywide rate for overhead rather than departmental rates, do you feel that such a rate would be indicative of the actual overhead charges for each job? Why or why not?

22. *(Job cost and pricing)* Cedric Maxwell is an attorney who employs a job order costing system related to his client engagements. Maxwell is currently working on a case for Ms. Sally Smart. During the first four months of 1994, Maxwell logged 85 hours on the Smart case.

   In addition to direct hours spent by Maxwell, Maxwell's secretary has worked 14 hours typing and copying 126 pages of documents related to the Smart case. Maxwell's secretary works 160 hours per month and is paid a salary of $1,800 per month. The average cost per copy is $.04 for paper, toner, and machine rental. Telephone charges for long-distance calls on the case totaled $165.50. Lastly, Maxwell has estimated that total office overhead for rent, utilities, parking, etc., amount to $7,200 per month, and that during a normal month, he is at the office 120 hours.
   a. Maxwell believes that his time, at a minimum, is worth $40 per hour, and he wishes to cover all direct and allocated indirect costs related to a case. What minimum charge per hour (rounded to the nearest dollar) should Maxwell charge Smart? (*Hint:* include office overhead.)
   b. All the hours that Maxwell spends at the office are not necessarily billable hours. In addition, Maxwell did not take certain other expenses such as license fees, country club dues, and automobile costs into consideration when he determined the amount of overhead per month. Therefore, to cover non-billable time as well as other costs, Maxwell feels that billing each client for direct costs plus allocated indirect costs plus 50% margin on his time and overhead is reasonable. What will Maxwell charge Smart in total per hour for the time spent on her case?

23. *(Under- or overapplied overhead)* For 1994, Engineered Tools Company applies overhead to jobs using a predetermined overhead rate of $5.80 per machine hour. This rate was derived by dividing the company's total budgeted overhead of $139,200 by the 24,000 machine hours anticipated for the year.

   At the end of 1994, the company's manufacturing overhead control account had debits totaling $144,300. Actual machine hours for the year totaled 25,100.
   a. How much overhead should be debited to the Work in Process Inventory account for 1994?
   b. Is overhead under- or overapplied and by how much?
   c. Job #23 consumed 1,400 machine hours during 1994. How much overhead should be assigned to this job for the year?
   d. Describe the disposition of the under- or overapplied overhead determined in part b.

24. *(Assigning costs to jobs)* Seaside Excavation Company uses a job order cost system in which overhead is applied to jobs at a predetermined rate of $1.40 per direct labor dollar. During April 1994, the company spent $3,100 on direct labor related to Job #144. In addition, the company incurred direct materials costs of $1,900 on this job during the month. Budgeted factory overhead for the company for the year is $180,040.
   a. Give the journal entry to apply overhead to all jobs if April's total direct labor cost was $9,800.
   b. How much overhead from part a is assigned to Job #144?
   c. If Job #144 had a balance of $4,150 on April 1, what is the balance on April 30?
   d. Demonstrate how the company arrived at the predetermined overhead rate. Include the amount of budgeted direct labor costs for the year in your answer.

25. *(Assigning costs to jobs, cost flows)* Eastside Custom Drapes uses a job order costing system and applies overhead to jobs using a predetermined rate of 250% of direct labor cost. At the beginning of June 1994, Job #118 was the only job in process. Costs of Job #118 included direct materials of $6,500 and direct labor

of $5,400. During June, Eastside Custom Drapes began work on Jobs #119, #120, and #121 and issued $14,700 of direct materials. Direct labor cost for the month totaled $15,600. Job #120 had not been completed at the end of June, and its direct materials and direct labor charges were $2,700 and $1,900, respectively. All the other jobs were completed in June.

a. What was the total cost of Job #120 as of the end of June 1994?

b. What was the cost of goods manufactured for June 1994?

c. If actual overhead for June was $36,700, was the overhead under- or over-applied for the month? By how much?

26. *(Assigning costs to jobs)* Flash Riprock is an advertising consultant. His account-ant has suggested the use of a job order costing system to simplify costing proce-dures. During September, Flash and his staff worked on jobs for the following companies:

	Lakeland Co.	Balsa Mfg.	Kidstoys Inc.
Direct labor hours	40	125	250
Direct materials cost	$780	$3,100	$6,300
Number of ads designed	4	9	12

Flash is able to trace direct materials to each job since most of his cost associated with materials is related to photography and duplicating. The accountant has told Flash that a reasonable charge for overhead, based on previous information, is $25 per direct labor hour. The normal labor cost per hour is $35.

a. Determine the total cost for each of the advertising accounts for the month.

b. Determine the cost per ad developed for each client if each ad within the job is similar.

c. Flash has been charging $1,700 per ad developed. What was his net income for the month, if normal costs were used? If actual overhead costs of $12,000 were used?

d. Do you have any suggestions for Flash about the way he bills his clients for developing ads?

27. *(Appendix)* Rimfire Electronics Company employs a job order costing system based on standard costs. For one of its products, Part No. 542, the standard costs per unit are as follows:

Direct materials	$11
Direct labor	32
Manufacturing overhead	14

a. Record the journal entry for the transfer of direct materials into production for 375 units of Part. No. 542.

b. Compute the total cost assigned to the 375 units of Part No. 542 and record the journal entry to recognize the completion of the 375 units.

c. Record the journal entries associated with the sale of the 375 units of Part No. 542 on account for $42,800.

28. *(Appendix)* Spudbusters, Inc. uses a job order costing system. During July 1994, the company worked on two production runs of the same product, a tank clutch plate. These units were included in Jobs #144J and #144K. Job #144J consisted of 250 units of the product, and job #144K contained 720 units. The plates are stamped pieces of metal that must be manufactured to rigorous Army specifica-tions. Spudbusters has determined that the standard cost of materials for each plate is $12.50 and the standard direct labor time is five minutes. Direct labor rate per hour is $20.

a. What is the standard prime cost of each tank clutch plate?

b. What was the total material and labor cost assigned to each of the jobs?

　　　c. Total actual cost for Job #144J was $3,167 for direct materials and $435 for direct labor. Compute the variance for direct materials cost and the variance for direct labor cost for Job 144J.

　　　d. Direct materials for Job #144K totaled $8,605, and direct labor was $1,315. Compute the variance for direct materials cost and the variance for direct labor cost for Job 144K.

PROBLEMS

29. *(Journal entries)* Style-o-flex Manufacturing uses a job order costing system based on actual costs. The following transactions relate to a single period when beginning inventory balances were: Raw Materials, $30,000; Work in Process, $45,000; and Finished Goods, $17,000.

　　a. Raw materials purchases on account, $120,000.

　　b. Direct labor cost accrued for the period totaled $97,500 for 15,000 direct labor hours.

　　c. Actual overhead costs were $72,000.

　　d. Actual overhead is applied to production based on direct labor hours.

　　e. The ending inventory of Raw Materials Inventory was $25,000.

　　f. The ending inventory of Work in Process Inventory was $60,000.

　　g. Production orders that cost $129,000 were completed and were sold for $300,000 on account.

Prepare all journal entries for the above transactions and determine the ending balance in the Finished Goods Inventory account.

30. *(Journal entries, assigning costs to jobs)* Bill's Custom Decks uses a job order costing system. On September 1, 1994, Bill's had the following account balances:

Raw Materials (direct and indirect)	$32,400
Work in Process Inventory	56,300
Cost of Goods Sold Inventory	315,000

Work in Process Inventory is the control account for the job cost subsidiary ledger. On September 1, there were three accounts in the job cost ledger with the following balances:

Job #21	$23,200
Job #22	19,800
Job #27	13,300

The following transactions occurred during September:

Sept. 1	Purchased $150,000 of raw materials on account.
Sept. 4	Issued $43,000 of raw materials as follows: Job #21, $13,200; Job #22, $8,200; Job #27, $11,100; Job #28, $6,100; indirect materials, $4,400.
Sept. 15	Prepared and paid the factory payroll for Sept. 1–15 in the amount of $68,700. (Ignore FICA and federal income tax withholding.) Analysis of the payroll for Sept. 1–15 reveals the following information as to where labor effort was devoted:

Job #21	1,430 hrs.	$14,300
Job #22	1,160 hrs.	11,600
Job #27	1,250 hrs.	12,500
Job #28	1,540 hrs.	15,400
Indirect wages		14,900

Sept. 16	Bill's applies manufacturing overhead to jobs at a rate of $6.50 per direct labor hour each time the payroll is made.
Sept. 16	Job #21 was completed and accepted by the customer and billed at a selling price of cost plus 40%.

Sept. 20	Paid the following monthly factory bills: utilities, $7,200; rent, $8,300; and accounts payable (previously accrued), $31,000.
Sept. 25	Issued raw materials as follows: Job #22, $7,400; Job #27, $18,300; Job #28, $12,500; and indirect materials, $7,200.
Sept. 30	Accrued additional factory overhead costs as follows: depreciation, $6,500; expired prepaid insurance, $5,100; and accrued taxes and licenses, $3,000.
Sept. 30	Accrued the gross salaries and wages for the factory payroll for Sept. 16–30 of $57,700. Analysis of the payroll showed the following:

Job #22	1,030 hrs.	$10,300
Job #27	1,640 hrs.	16,400
Job #28	1,980 hrs.	19,800
Indirect wages		11,200

Sept. 30	Applied overhead for the second half of the month to jobs.

a. Prepare journal entries for the transactions for September 1994.
b. Use T-accounts to post the information from the journal entries in part a to the job cost subsidiary accounts and to general ledger accounts.
c. Reconcile the Sept. 30 balances in the subsidiary ledger with the Work in Process Inventory account in the general ledger.
d. Determine the amount of under- or overapplied overhead for the month of September.

31. *(Journal entries, cost flows)* Custom Vans Inc. began 1994 with three jobs in process:

Type of Cost

Job No.	Direct Materials	Direct Labor	Overhead	Total
647	$ 38,600	$ 45,700	$17,366	$101,666
651	88,300	104,900	39,862	233,062
653	72,700	84,800	32,224	189,724
Totals	$199,600	$235,400	$89,452	$524,452

During 1994, the following transactions occurred:
1. The firm purchased and paid for $266,000 of raw materials. The raw materials account contains both direct and indirect materials.
2. Factory payroll records revealed the following:
   Indirect labor accrued was $27,000
   Direct labor accrued was $301,400 and was associated with the jobs as follows:

Job No.	Direct Labor Cost
647	$ 8,700
651	4,400
653	10,500
654	68,300
655	72,500
656	47,300
657	89,700

3. Materials requisition forms issued during the year revealed the following:
   Indirect materials issued totaled $38,000
   Direct materials issued totaled $234,200 and were associated with jobs as follows:

Job No.	Direct Materials Cost
647	$ 7,200
651	3,100
653	8,400
654	51,600
655	59,900
656	36,400
657	67,600

4. Overhead is applied to jobs on the basis of direct labor cost. Management estimated total budgeted overhead of $120,000 and total direct labor cost of $300,000 for 1994. Actual total factory overhead costs (including indirect labor and indirect materials) for the year were $122,200.

5. Jobs #647 through 655 were completed and delivered to customers C.O.D. The revenue on these jobs was $1,132,387.

Required:

a. Prepare journal entries for all of the above events.

b. Determine ending balances for jobs still in process.

c. Determine cost of jobs completed and sold, adjusted for under- or overapplied overhead.

32. *(Simple inventory calculation)* American Billboard Co. manufactures customized billboards for use by advertisers. Production information for the first week in November 1994 follows:

		Work in Process Inventory		Machine Time (Overhead)
	Job No.	Material	Labor	
Nov. 1	101	$750	18 hours	25 hours
	102	310	5 hours	10 hours
Nov. 7	107	425	4 hours	8 hours

Finished Goods Inventory, Nov. 1: $10,300
Finished Goods Inventory, Nov. 7: $ 0

Materials Records

	Inv. 11/1	Purchases	Issuances	Inv. 11/7
Wood	$3,150	$29,150	$19,350	$?
Steel	5,400	3,250	7,100	$?
Hardware	3,900	1,775	2,950	$?

Direct labor hours worked were 240. Labor cost is $15 per direct labor hour. Three hundred machine hours were worked: 75 hours on Job 101; 140 hours on Job 102; 85 hours on Job 107.

Overhead for the first week in November:

Depreciation	$1,500
Supervisory salaries	3,200
Indirect labor	1,175
Insurance	1,400
Utilities	1,125
Total	$8,400

Overhead is charged to production at a rate of $30 per machine hour.

Under- or overapplied overhead is treated as an adjustment to Cost of Goods Sold at year-end. (All company jobs are consecutively numbered, and all work not in ending inventory has been completed and sold.)

a. Calculate the value of beginning Work in Process Inventory.

b. What is the value at the end of November of (1) the three material accounts, (2) Work in Process Inventory, and (3) Cost of Goods Sold?

33. *(Job sheet analysis)* Custom Movers manufactures custom-built conveyor systems for factory and commercial operations. Lisa French is the cost accountant for Custom Movers and she is in the process of educating a new employee, Julie English, about the job order costing system that Custom Movers uses. (The system is based on normal costs; overhead is applied based on direct labor cost and rounded to the next whole dollar.) Lisa gathers the following job order cost records for May:

Job No.	Direct Materials	Direct Labor	Applied OH	Total Cost
667	$ 5,901	$1,730	$ 1,990	$ 9,621
669	18,312	1,810	2,082	22,204
670	406	500	575	1,481
671	51,405	9,500	10,925	71,830
672	9,615	550	633	10,798

To explain the missing job number, Lisa informed Julie that Job #668 had been completed in April. She also told her that Job #667 was the only job in process at the beginning of May. At that time, the job had been assigned $4,300 for direct materials and $900 for direct labor. At the end of May, Job #671 had not been completed; all others had. Lisa asked Julie several questions to determine whether she understood the job order system.

Help Julie answer the following questions:

a. What is the predetermined overhead rate used by Custom Movers?

b. What was the total cost of beginning Work in Process inventory?

c. What was total prime cost incurred for the month of May?

d. What was cost of goods manufactured for May?

34. *(Departmental rates)* The Billings Manufacturing Plant is comprised of two departments: Blending and Finishing. All jobs go through each department, and the company uses a job order costing system. Billings applies overhead to jobs based on machine hours in Blending and on direct labor hours in Finishing. In December 1993, Billings estimated the following production data for 1994 in setting its predetermined overhead rates:

	Blending	Finishing
Machine hours	27,000	6,900
Direct labor hours	4,800	14,600
Departmental overhead	$64,800	$94,900

Two jobs worked on during 1994 were #486 and #493. Information from the job order cost sheets showed the following about these jobs:

	Job #486	Job #493
Direct materials cost	$14,875	$6,300
Direct labor hours—Blending	25	10
Machine hours—Blending	137	68
Direct labor hours—Finishing	241	49
Machine hours—Finishing	12	7

Direct labor workers are paid $6 per hour in the Blending Department and $13 per hour in Finishing.

a. Compute the predetermined overhead rates used in Blending and Finishing for 1994.

b. Compute the direct labor cost associated with each job for both departments.
c. Compute the amount of overhead assigned to each job in each department.
d. Determine the total cost of Jobs #486 and #493.
e. Actual data for 1994 for each department is presented below. What is the amount of under- or overapplied overhead for each department for the year ended Dec. 31, 1994?

	Blending	Finishing
Machine hours	28,100	6,500
Direct labor hours	4,700	14,600
Overhead	$64,000	$96,800

35. *(Comprehensive)* In May 1994, Baldwin Custom Pools was the successful bidder on a contract to build a new municipal swimming pool for a suburb of Atlanta. The firm utilizes a job order costing system and this job was assigned job #315. The contract price for the pool was $150,000. The owners of Baldwin agreed to a completion date of December 15, 1994, for the pool. The firm's engineering and cost accounting departments estimated the following costs for completion of the pool: $40,000 for direct materials, $45,000 for direct labor, and $27,000 for overhead.

The firm began work on the pool in August. During August, direct materials cost assigned to Job #315 was $10,300 and direct labor cost associated with Job #315 was $15,840. The firm uses a predetermined overhead rate of 60% of direct labor cost. Baldwin also worked on several other jobs during August and incurred the following costs:

Direct labor (including Job #315)	$84,000
Indirect labor	9,300
Administrative salaries and wages	6,600
Depreciation on construction equipment	4,800
Depreciation on office equipment	1,300
Client entertainment (on accounts payable)	1,850
Advertising for firm (paid in cash)	1,100
Indirect materials (from "supplies" inventory)	3,100
Miscellaneous expenses (design related; to be paid in the following month)	1,700
Accrued utilities (for office, $300; for construction, $900)	1,200

During August, Baldwin completed several jobs that had been in process before the beginning of the month. These completed jobs generated $104,000 of revenues for the company. The related job cost sheets showed costs associated with those jobs of $71,500. At the beginning of August, Baldwin had Work in Process Inventory of $45,300.

a. Prepare a job order cost record for Job #315, including all job details, and post the appropriate cost information for August.
b. Prepare journal entries for the above information.
c. Prepare a schedule of Cost of Goods Manufactured for August for Baldwin Custom Pools.
d. Assuming the company pays income tax at a 36% rate, prepare an income statement for August.

36. *(Comprehensive)* Clear Lake Protection Corp. custom designs and manufactures protection systems for large retail and commercial buildings. Each order goes through three stages: design, production, and installation. There were three jobs started and completed during the first week in May 1994. There were no jobs in process at the end of April 1994. Information for the three departments for the first week in May follows:

	Department		
Job #2019	**Design**	**Production**	**Installation**
Direct labor hours	50	na	35
Machine hours	na	75	na
Direct labor cost	$ 5,100	$4,250	$ 890
Direct materials cost	1,400	8,550	700
Job #2020	**Design**	**Production**	**Installation**
Direct labor hours	190	410	185
Machine hours	na	180	na
Direct labor cost	$19,300	$ 7,450	$4,700
Direct materials cost	1,025	45,600	1,600
Job #2021	**Design**	**Production**	**Installation**
Direct labor hours	75	350	75
Machine hours	na	145	na
Direct labor cost	$7,600	$ 2,950	$1,900
Direct materials cost	2,000	28,000	400

Overhead is applied using separate rates in each department. Design and Installation use direct labor cost as the base, with rates of 30% and 25%, respectively. Production uses machine hours as the base, with a rate of $15 per hour.

Actual overhead in the Design Department for the month was $10,200. Actual overhead costs for the Production and Installation Departments were $5,750 and $1,780, respectively.

a. Determine the overhead to be applied to each job. By how much is the overhead under- or overapplied in each department? For the company?

b. Assume no journal entries have been made to Work in Process Inventory. Make all necessary entries to both the subsidiary ledger and general ledger accounts.

c. Calculate the total cost for each job.

37. *(Comprehensive; job cost sheet)* The High Road Construction Company builds bridges. For the months of October and November 1994, the firm worked exclusively on a bridge spanning the Trinity River near Dallas, Texas. The firm is organized into two departments. The Precast Department builds structural elements of the bridges in temporary plants which are located near the construction sites. The Construction Department operates at the bridge site and assembles the precast structural elements. Estimated costs for the Trinity River Bridge for the Precast Department were $150,000 for direct labor, $310,500 for direct materials, and $110,000 for overhead. For the Construction Department, estimated costs for the Trinity River Bridge were $160,000 for direct labor, $50,000 for direct materials, and $160,000 for overhead. Overhead is applied on the last day of each month. Overhead application rates for the Precast and Construction Department are $18 per machine hour and 100% of direct labor cost, respectively.

Transactions for October

Oct. 1 $150,000 of materials were purchased (on account) for the Precast Department to begin building structural elements. All of these materials were issued to production; $130,000 were considered direct materials.

Oct. 5   Utilities were installed at the bridge site at a total cost of $15,000.

Oct. 8   Rent was paid for the temporary construction site housing the Precast Department, $4,000.

Oct 15   Bridge support pillars were completed by the Precast Department and transferred to the construction site.

Oct. 20 $30,000 of machine rental expense was incurred by the Construction Department for clearing the bridge site and digging foundations for bridge supports.

Oct. 24   Additional materials costing $285,000 were purchased on account.

Oct. 31   The company paid the following bills for the Precast Department: utilities, $7,000; direct labor, $45,000; insurance, $6,220, supervision and other indirect labor costs, $7,900; and depreciation expense was recorded, $15,200. The company also paid bills for the Construction Department: utilities, $2,300; direct labor, $16,300; indirect labor, $5,700; insurance, $1,900; and depreciation was recorded on equipment, $8,750.

Oct. 31   A check was issued to pay for the materials purchased on October 1 and October 24.

Oct. 31   Overhead was applied to production in each department; 2,000 machine hours were worked in the Precast Department in October.

Transactions for November

Nov. 1   Additional structural elements were transferred from the Precast Department to the construction site. The Construction Department incurred a cash cost of $5,000 to rent a crane.

Nov. 4 $200,000 of materials were issued to the Precast Department. Of this amount, $165,000 was considered direct.

Nov. 8   Rent of $4,000 was paid in cash for the temporary site occupied by the Precast Department.

Nov. 15 $85,000 of materials were issued to the Construction Department. Of this amount, $40,000 was considered direct.

Nov. 18   Additional structural elements were transferred from the Precast Department to the construction site.

Nov. 24   The final batch of structural elements were transferred from the Precast Department to the construction site.

Nov. 29   The bridge was completed.

Nov. 30   The company paid final bills for the month in the Precast Department: utilities $15,000; direct labor, $115,000; insurance, $9,350; supervision and other indirect labor costs, $14,500; and depreciation expense was recorded, $15,200. The company also paid bills for the Construction Department: utilities, $4,900; direct labor, $134,300; indirect labor, $15,200; insurance, $5,400; and depreciation was recorded on equipment, $18,350.

Nov. 30   Overhead was applied in each department; 3,950 machine hours were recorded in November in the Precast Department.

Nov. 30   The company billed the city of Dallas for the completed bridge, at the contract price, $1,550,000.

a. Prepare all necessary journal entries for the problem. For purposes of this problem, it is not necessary to transfer direct materials and direct labor from one department into the other.

b. Post all entries to T-accounts.

c. Prepare a job cost sheet, which includes estimated costs, for the construction of the bridge.

38. *(Appendix)* One of the products made by Tacoma Defense Products is a long-range missile for the military. Since the company has exact specifications for producing the missiles, and because it has substantial experience with such products, a standard costing system is used for missile production. The company has a separate plant which is strictly dedicated to missile production The standard costs to produce a single missile follow:

Direct materials	$ 32,000
Direct labor 1,240 hrs @ $25	31,000
Overhead	80,000
Total standard cost	$143,000

For the 300 missiles produced in 1994, the actual costs were:

Direct materials	$ 9,100,000
Direct labor 360,000 hrs @ $24.90	8,964,000
Overhead	23,400,000
Total actual cost	$41,464,000

a. Compute a separate "variance" between actual and standard cost for direct materials, direct labor, and manufacturing overhead for the missiles produced in 1994.

b. Is the large direct labor variance found in part a driven primarily by the number of hours worked or the cost per hour? Explain.

CASES

39. Riveredge Manufacturing Company realized too late that it had made a mistake locating its controller's office and its electronic data processing system in the basement. Because of the spring thaw, the Mississippi River overflowed on May 2 and flooded the company's basement. Electronic data storage was beyond retrieval, and the company had not provided off-site storage of data. Some of the paper printouts were located but were badly faded and only partially legible. On May 3, when the river subsided, company accountants were able to assemble the following factory-related data from the debris and from discussions with various knowledgeable personnel.

Data about the following accounts were found:
   Raw Materials (includes indirect materials) Inventory: Balance April 1 was $4,800
   Work in Process Inventory: Balance April 1 was $7,700
   Finished Goods Inventory: Balance April 30 was $6,600
   Total company payroll cost for April was $29,200
   Accounts Payable: Balance April 30 was $18,000
   Indirect materials used in April cost $5,800
   Other nonmaterials and nonlabor overhead items for April totaled $2,500

Payroll records, kept at an across-town service center that processes the company's payroll, showed that April's direct labor amounted to $18,200 and represented 4,400 labor hours. Indirect factory labor amounted to $5,400 in April.

The president's office had a file copy of the production budget for the current year. It revealed that the predetermined manufacturing overhead application rate is based on planned annual direct labor hours of 50,400 and expected factory overhead of $151,200.

Discussion with the factory superintendent indicated that only two jobs remained unfinished on April 30. Fortunately, the superintendent also had copies of the job cost sheets on these jobs that showed a combined total of $2,400 of direct materials and $4,500 of direct labor. The direct labor hours on these jobs totaled 1,072. Both of these jobs had been started during the current period.

A badly faded copy of April's Cost of Goods Manufactured and Sold schedule showed Cost of Goods Manufactured was $48,000, and the April 1 Finished Goods Inventory was $8,400.

The treasurer's office files copies of paid invoices chronologically. All invoices are for raw materials purchased on account. Examination of these files revealed that unpaid invoices on April 1 amounted to $6,100; $28,000 of purchases had been made during April; and $18,000 of unpaid invoices existed on April 30.

a. Calculate the direct materials used in April.
b. Calculate the raw materials issued in April.
c. Calculate the April 30 balance of Raw Materials Inventory.
d. Determine the amount of under- or overapplied overhead for April.
e. What is the Cost of Goods Sold for April?

40. *(Comprehensive)* Constructo Inc. is a manufacturer of furnishings for infants and children. The company uses a job order cost system. Constructo's Work in Process Inventory on April 30, 1994, consisted of the following jobs:

Job No.	Items	Units	Accumulated Cost
CBS102	Cribs	20,000	$ 900,000
PLP086	Playpens	15,000	420,000
DRS114	Dressers	25,000	$250,000
			$1,570,000

The company's finished goods inventory, carried on a FIFO basis, consists of five items:

Item	Quantity and Unit Cost	Total Cost
Cribs	7,500 units @ $ 64	$ 480,000
Strollers	13,000 units @ $ 23	299,000
Carriages	11,200 units @ $102	1,142,400
Dressers	21,000 units @ $ 55	1,155,000
Playpens	19,400 units @ $ 35	679,000
		$3,755,400

Constructo applies factory overhead on the basis of direct labor hours. The company's factory overhead budget for the year ending May 31, 1994, totals $4,500,000, and the company plans to expend 600,000 direct labor hours during this period. Through the first eleven months of the year, a total of 555,000 direct labor hours were worked, and total factory overhead amounted to $4,273,500.

At the end of April, the balance in Constructo's Materials Inventory account, which includes both raw materials and purchased parts, was $668,000. Additions to and requisitions from the materials inventory during the month of May included the following:

	Raw Materials	Purchased Parts
Additions	$242,000	$396,000
Requisitions		
Job CBS102	51,000	104,000
Job PLP086	3,000	10,800
Job DRS114	124,000	87,000
Job STR077		
(10,000 strollers)	62,000	81,000
Job CRG098		
(5,000 carriages)	65,000	187,000

During May, Constructo's factory payroll consisted of the following:

Account	Hours	Cost
CBS102	12,000	$122,400
PLP086	4,400	43,200
DRS114	19,500	200,500
STR077	3,500	30,000

CRTG098	14,000	138,000
Indirect	3,000	29,400
Supervision		57,600
		$621,100

Listed below are the jobs that were completed and the unit sales for May:

Job No.	Items	Quantity Completed
CBS102	Cribs	20,000
PLP086	Playpens	15,000
STR077	Strollers	10,000
CRG098	Carriages	5,000

Items	Quantity Shipped
Cribs	17,500
Playpens	21,000
Strollers	14,000
Dressers	18,000
Carriages	6,000

a. Describe when it is appropriate for a company to use a job order costing system.
b. Calculate the dollar balance in Constructo's Work in Process Inventory account as of May 31, 1994.
c. Calculate the dollar amount related to the playpens in Constructo's Finished Goods Inventory as of May 31, 1994.
d. Explain the treatment of under- or overapplied overhead when using a job order costing system.

(CMA *adapted*)

ETHICS AND QUALITY DISCUSSION

41. In March 1989, the Federal Aviation Administration began investigating allegations that some maintenance supervisors for a U.S. airline company had been signing off on maintenance work that actually was not performed on individual aircraft.
    a. Why could an individual airplane be considered a "job" for an airline company?
    b. One of the maintenance tasks that was allegedly not completed was the washing of a cabin heat air exchanger. Assume the following facts: Some of the airline's mechanics are on strike. The task is considered routine; the plane was only one year old and in excellent condition. The plane was scheduled to depart the airport in 30 minutes on a fully booked flight; washing the exchanger would take a minimum of one hour. The airline was currently having problems with on-time departures and arrivals. The plane arrived safely at its destination. Discuss the possible perceptions and thoughts of the maintenance supervisor at the time that this maintenance should be performed.
    c. Discuss the perceptions and thoughts of the passengers at the terminal if the maintenance were performed.
    d. Discuss the ethical issues involved.

42. In job order costing, the costs associated with each job are separately accumulated for each job. The determination of costs are, however, related to the contract between the buyer and seller.

Price Waterhouse (PW) was involved in reviewing the assets of Homefed Bank, a failed San Diego savings and loan, for the Resolution Trust Corporation (RTC). During the process of that review, PW copied more than 10 million documents. According to the Inspector General's Office of the RTC, PW charged government thrift regulators at least 67 cents per page for copying.

Sharon Vander Vennet, an assistant RTC inspector general, said the 67-cents-a-page copying charge covered only labor, and the figure rises if expenses such as machine and paper costs are factored in. Price Waterhouse used temporaries to do the copying and billed the RTC an average of $35 an hour per worker after being billed less than half that amount for the temporary help.

Price Waterhouse said "all copying work done was performed by clerical personnel and was billed to the RTC at the clerical labor rate as defined in the contract."

[SOURCE: John Connor, "Price Waterhouse Copying Charges Stirs RTC Review," *Wall Street Journal* (February 17, 1993), p. A6. Reprinted by permission of the *Wall Street Journal*, © 1993 Dow Jones & Company, Inc. All rights reserved worldwide.]

Price Waterhouse challenges the per-copy cost figure and denies that any of its charges were excessive.
   a. Assuming that Price Waterhouse billed in the manner that was defined in the company's contract with the RTC, should the RTC be concerned about the copying charges? Discuss the rationale for your answer.
   b. Assuming that Price Waterhouse billed in the manner that was defined in the company's contract with the RTC, discuss where the responsibility for "improprieties" (if there were any) should have been placed.
   c. According to an individual in the Inspector General's Office, the "going rate for comparable copying jobs is about 12 to 15 cents a page." Discuss the ethics of charging 67 cents a page for such work. (Consider, in your answer, the situations that created the need for the RTC.)

43. *Cyclemakers Group of Washdyke near Timaru (New Zealand) is lifting its profile locally and overseas in the cycling world through its custom-built bike service.*

While the prospect of sitting astride a 10-speed may not be everyone's idea of relaxation at least now they can dictate their choice of seat—or for that matter, their choice of frame, wheels, gears and the other bits and pieces that Cyclemakers imports from the major branded overseas manufacturers.

The company has built simulators so people can try out a range of configurations to see what measurements suit. They can then choose from an enormous range of components of varying sizes and prices including the colour and style of the paint job.

"We're doing it at a price not much greater than an off-the-peg production bike because we use a computerised system. The idea has proven very successful here and in Australia. It's not a large percentage of business yet but has provided a lot at the top end," says Bryan Jackson, managing director.

[SOURCE: "Boosting Bike Sales," *NZ Business* (November 1992), p. 33. *NZ Business* is published by Minty's Media Ltd., Private Bag 93218, Parnell, Auckland, New Zealand.]

   a. Why would Cyclemakers be able to produce custom-made bicycles for almost the same cost as mass produced ones?
   b. Would you expect the quality of the custom-produced bicycles to be higher or lower than the mass-produced ones? Discuss the rationale for your answer.
   c. Why would the custom-made bicycles "provide a lot at the top end" (show a high profit margin)?

44. Greeting cards are typically mass-produced items. Now, however, there are computer-equipped booths that allow people to make their own greeting cards for $3.50, rather than the normal card price of $1.00 to $1.75. Some of the booths produce fairly sophisticated cards, while others produce cards with drawings that look like doodles.

a. Discuss the effects on direct materials, direct labor, and overhead costs of producing individual cards in a booth rather than in mass quantity.
b. Could such productions be considered a cost-plus job? Why or why not?
c. Are people who create their own cards paying for quality, increased costs, or the personal touch? What other examples can you think of in which people pay more for products of possibly lower quality?

PROCESS COSTING

LEARNING
OBJECTIVES

After completing this chapter, you should be able to answer these questions:

1. How is process costing different from job order costing?
2. Why are equivalent units of production used in process costing?
3. How are equivalent units of production determined using the weighted average and FIFO methods of process costing?
4. How are unit costs determined using the weighted average and FIFO methods of process costing?
5. How are inventory values determined using the weighted average and FIFO methods of process costing?
6. *(Appendix 2)* How can standard costs be used in a process costing system?

INTRODUCING

BIRMINGHAM STEEL CORPORATION

Birmingham Steel Corporation began operations in August 1984 and now operates four (Kankakee, Illinois; Birmingham, Alabama; Jackson, Mississippi; and Seattle, Washington) non-union mini-mills that produce steel and steel products on a low-cost basis. The production process in a mini-mill differs from that of an integrated steel producer, which begins with virgin ore. The raw material of a mini-mill is previously used metal derived from sources that include discarded automobiles, machines and railroad cars.

Mini-mills are typically much more productive than their integrated counterparts. This productivity is gained from the steel-making process employed, which shortens the production time. An integrated steel plant may be able to produce a ton of steel in three to four hours, but it only takes Birmingham Steel approximately one-and-a-half hours per ton.

Because the selling price of recycled steel is less than that of virgin steel, mini-mills strive to control costs—especially in the area of materials and labor. Materials cost less because of the use of recycled scrap metal and labor costs are approximately one-third of that at integrated mills. The mini-mills often have lower base wages and non-union employees, but higher bonus plans.

The number of products is limited and the quantity produced is high—Birmingham Steel produced and shipped almost 1,500,000 tons of steel in 1992. Production of such large quantities of substantially homogeneous products would not require the need to account for processing costs on a job order basis.

SOURCE: Adapted from Birmingham Steel, *1992 Annual Report* (Birmingham, Alabama).

Birmingham Steel produces mass quantities of four basic types of steel products. Because the nature of Birmingham Steel's output differs so dramatically from the nature of the animated robots produced by Sally Industries (discussed in Chapter 7), it seems only reasonable that the two companies' product costing systems would also differ.

Job order costing is appropriate for companies like Sally Industries that make products or provide services in limited quantities, conforming to customer specifications. Birmingham Steel uses **process costing** to accumulate and assign costs to units of production. This costing method is also used by manufacturers of bricks, gasoline, paper, or chocolate chip cookies, among many other types of firms.

Process costing

In a process costing system, as in a job order system, costs are accumulated by cost component in each production department. In a job order costing system, the accumulated departmental costs are assigned to specific jobs. In contrast, a process costing system assigns accumulated departmental costs to all the units produced in that department during the period. Thus, a fundamental characteristic of process costing is the use of an averaging technique when assigning costs to the units produced. If identifiable batches having traceable costs flow through the department, those costs will naturally be assigned only to the units within the identifiable batch. As units are transferred from one department to the next, unit costs in both job order and process costing are also transferred to accumulate a total production cost.

This chapter presents basic process costing procedures and illustrates the two methods (weighted average and FIFO) of calculating unit cost in a process costing system. These methods differ only in the treatment of beginning inventory units and costs. Once unit cost is determined, total costs are assigned to the units transferred out of a department and to that department's ending inventory. Appendix 2 to the chapter illustrates a standard-cost process costing system.

INTRODUCTION TO PROCESS COSTING

Assigning costs to units of production is essentially an averaging process. In general, and in the easiest possible situation, a product's actual unit cost is found by dividing a period's departmental production costs by that period's departmental quantity of production. This average is expressed by the following formula:

$$\text{Unit Cost per Period} = \frac{\text{Sum of Production Costs}}{\text{Quantity of Production}}$$

The Numerator

The formula numerator is obtained by accumulating all departmental costs incurred for a single time period. Since most companies manufacture more than one product, costs must be accumulated by product within each department. For example, Birmingham Steel produces steel reinforcing bar (rebar) used in the construction industry, merchant products (round bars, flats, and strips that are sold to fabricators and others), steel roof support systems used in the underground coal mining industry, and billets (unfinished square or rectangular lengths of steel). The company's production process is illustrated in Exhibit 8–1.

Costs can be accumulated by using different Work in Process Inventory accounts for each product and for each department through which that product passes. Alternatively, costs can be accumulated using a Work in Process Control account for each department (for example, the Melt Shop and the Rolling Mill) with this account being supported by detailed subsidiary ledgers containing specific product information.

Recycled steel is the raw material at the beginning of Birmingham Steel's (and other mini-mill's) manufacturing process. Such materials are the input into a mass production environment of which the end result is a variety of building products for contractors and fabricators.

In the mini-mill, the scrap first passes through the melt shop where it is melted in an electric arc furnace, The molten material is then funnelled through a continuous caster where water-cooled copper molds shape the liquid steel into solid strands. The continuous strands of steel are then cut into billets of a specific length to allow maximum yield during further processing in the rolling mill. After transfer to the rolling mill, the billets are reheated and then rolled into finished steel reinforcing bar or other steel products.

Melt Shop

Ferrous scrap, the primary raw material, is gathered from various sources prior to being recycled in the mini-mill. The scrap is loaded via magnet into a charge bucket for delivery to the melt shop.

The charge bucket drops loads of scrap into the electric arc furnace. The refractory-lined furnace melts the scrap utilizing electricity passing through graphite electrodes.

Once melting is completed, molten steel is poured into a refractory-lined ladle. After quality control standards are met, the liquid is carried by overhead cranes to the continuous caster.

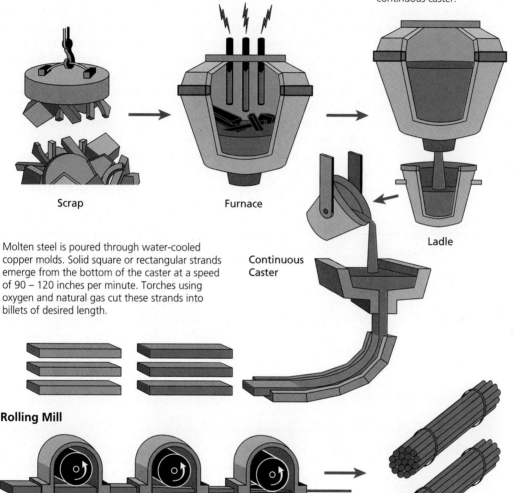

Molten steel is poured through water-cooled copper molds. Solid square or rectangular strands emerge from the bottom of the caster at a speed of 90 – 120 inches per minute. Torches using oxygen and natural gas cut these strands into billets of desired length.

Continuous Caster

Rolling Mill

Finished Product

Semi-finished steel billets are loaded into the reheat furnace where they are heated to approximately 2100 degrees Fahrenheit. Billets are then individually discharged into the rolling mill where each passes through a series of rolls that progressively reduce it to the desired shape — bars, flats, or other merchant shapes.

Finished product is cooled on an automated cooling bed prior to passing through in-line straightening, stacking, and bundling equipment. Once automated bundling is complete, finished product is temporarily stored in inventory and readied for shipment.

SOURCE: Birmingham Steel Corporation, *1991 Annual Report.*

▌ EXHIBIT 8–1
Birmingham Steel's Production Process

In some ways, the cost accumulation in a process costing system is similar to job order costing procedures. The two basic differences are (1) the *quantity* of production for which costs are being accumulated at any one time and (2) the *cost object* to which the costs are assigned. For example, assume that Birmingham Steel custommakes roof support systems only when they are ordered by a specific mine. Birmingham Steel could use a job order costing system for this portion of its business, accumulate the direct materials and direct labor costs associated with production of each roof support job, and assign those costs directly to the individual jobs. After each job was completed, the total material, labor, and overhead costs would be known and cost of the roof support job could be determined.

In contrast, Birmingham Steel mass produces numerous generic products that are used by fabricators in making grating, safety walkways, and ornamental furniture. For these products, Birmingham uses a process costing system. Direct materials and direct labor costs are accumulated during the period for each department and each product. Because the mini-mill can produce a variety of merchant products in its two departments during a period, the costs assignable to each type of product must be individually designated and attached to each production run. These costs are then assigned to the units (whether or not completed) worked on during the period.

Exhibit 8–2 presents the source documents and records used to make an initial cost assignment to production departments during a period. Costs are reassigned at the end of the period (usually each month) from the departments to the units produced. As the goods are transferred from one department to the next, the related departmental production costs are also transferred. When the products are complete, their costs are transferred from Work in Process Inventory to Finished Goods Inventory.

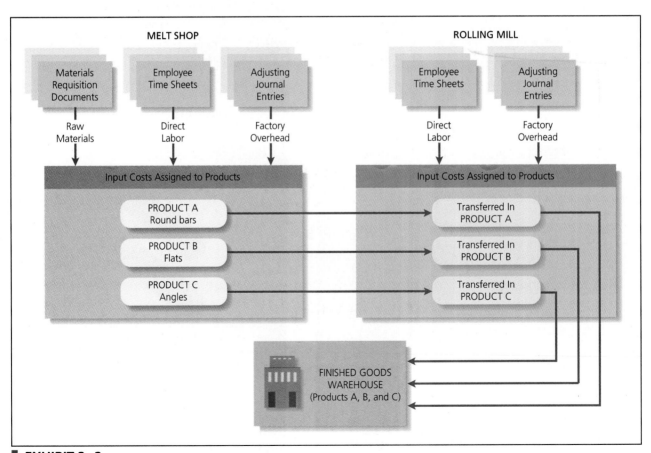

■ **EXHIBIT 8–2**

Cost Flows and Cost Assignment

As was true in job order costing, the direct materials and direct labor components of product cost present relatively few problems for cost accumulation and assignment. Direct materials cost can be measured from the materials requisition slips; direct labor can be determined from the employee time sheets and wage rates for the period.

In contrast, overhead must be assigned to production indirectly. Overhead may be assigned through the use of predetermined application rates, although actual costs are often used for product costing in process costing systems. If total actual overhead costs are relatively constant each period and production volume is relatively steady over time, the use of actual overhead costs will provide a fairly uniform production cost. If such conditions do not exist, application of actual overhead will result in fluctuating product costs and predetermined application rates should be used.

To summarize, the numerator in the fraction to determine average product cost consists of the following: (1) actual direct materials cost; (2) actual direct labor cost; and (3) actual or predetermined overhead cost. These costs are accumulated for an *individual* department and are related to the specific units of product worked on in that department during the period.

The Denominator

The denominator in the unit cost formula represents total departmental production for the period. If all units were 100 percent complete at the end of each accounting period, units could simply be counted to obtain the denominator. But in most production processes, Work in Process (WIP) Inventory at the end of each period typically consists of *partially* completed units. Any partially completed ending inventory of the current period becomes the partially completed beginning inventory of the next period. Process costing assigns costs to *both* fully and partially completed units by mathematically converting partially completed units to equivalent whole units.

Determining actual production for the period requires recognizing two facts. First, the units in beginning WIP Inventory were started last period, but they will be completed during the current period. This two-period production sequence means that some costs related to these units were incurred last period and additional costs will be incurred in the current period. Second, the partially completed units in ending WIP Inventory were started in the current period, but they will not be completed until next period. Therefore, current period production efforts on the units in ending WIP Inventory caused costs to be incurred in this period and will cause additional costs to be incurred next period.

Physical inspection by qualified production personnel is needed to determine the proportion of ending Work in Process Inventory that was completed during the current period. The mathematical complement to this proportion represents the work that needs to be completed next period. The physical inspection performed at the end of last period provides information on the proportion of this period's beginning inventory that needed to be completed during this period.

Equivalent Units of Production

The physical flow of units through a department and the manufacturing effort expended in a department during a period is normally in the following order:

▊ Units started in the previous period and finished in the present period.

▊ Units started in the present period and finished in the present period.

▊ Units started in the present period and not finished in the present period.

Because of these mixed manufacturing efforts, production must be measured by a method *other than* counting whole units. Cost accountants use a concept known as **equivalent units of production** (EUP) to measure the quantity of production achieved during a period.

Equivalent units of production

Equivalent units of production are an approximation of the number of whole units of output that could have been produced during a period from the actual effort expended during that period. Equivalent units of production are calculated by multiplying the number of actual but incomplete units produced by the respective percentage degree of completion. The following simplistic example indicates how equivalent units are calculated. Assume Department 1 had no beginning inventory and, during June, completed 100,000 units and also produced 10,000 units that were 40 percent complete and are in ending work in process. The equivalent units of production for the period are 104,000 [(100,000 × 100%) + (10,000 × 40%)]. This quantity is the denominator of the formula to calculate departmental unit product costs.

WEIGHTED AVERAGE AND FIFO PROCESS COSTING METHODS

There are two alternative methods of accounting for cost flows in process costing: (1) weighted average and (2) FIFO. These methods relate to the manner in which cost flows are assumed to occur in the production process. In a very general way, it is helpful to relate these process costing approaches to the cost flow methods used in financial accounting.

In a retail business, the weighted average method is used to determine an average cost per unit of inventory. This cost is computed by dividing the total cost of goods available by total units available. Total cost and total units are found by adding purchases and beginning inventory. Costs and units of the current period are not distinguished in any way from those of the prior period. The FIFO method of accounting for merchandise inventory separates goods by when they were purchased and at what cost. The cost of beginning inventory is the first cost sent to Cost of Goods Sold; units remaining in the ending inventory are costed at the most recent purchase prices.

Weighted average method (of process costing)

FIFO method (of process costing)

The use of these methods for costing the production of a manufacturing firm is similar to their use in a retailer. The **weighted average method** computes an average cost per unit of prior and current period production; the **FIFO method** separates beginning inventory and current period production and costs. The denominator used in the cost formula to determine unit cost will differ depending on which of the two methods is used.[1]

Operations of Quincy Manufacturing Company for May 1994 are used to illustrate the difference between the weighted average and FIFO methods of process costing. Selected production and cost information for the company is shown in Exhibit 8–3. Assume that materials, labor, and overhead are all added simultaneously in Quincy's production process.

Weighted Average Method

Units started and completed

To determine production quantity for the period, the weighted average (WA) method of computing EUP adds the beginning WIP units, the **units started and completed** during the current period, and the equivalent units in ending inventory. The number of units started and completed equals the total units completed during the current period minus the units in beginning inventory.[2] For Quincy Manufacturing, this num-

---

[1] Note that the term *denominator* is used here rather than equivalent units of production. Based on its definition, EUP are related to current period productive activity. Thus for any given set of production facts, there is only one true measure of equivalent units produced—regardless of the cost flow assumption used—and that measure is the EUP computed under the FIFO method. However, this fact has been obscured over time due to continued references to the "EUP" computation for the weighted average method. Thus, the term "EUP" has taken on a generic use to mean "the denominator used to compute the unit cost of production for a period in a process costing system." We use EUP in this generic manner throughout the discussion of process costing.

[2] Units started and completed can also be computed as the units started during the current period minus the units not finished (or the units in ending inventory).

EXHIBIT 8–3

**Quincy Manufacturing
Company Operating and
Cost Information for
May 1994**

Beginning work in process (60% complete)	5,000 physical units
Units started in May	105,800
Units completed and transferred in May	110,000
Ending work in process (30% complete)	800
Cost of beginning inventory	$ 30,051.20
Cost of the current period	561,937.60

ber is 105,000 (110,000 − 5,000). The calculation of the weighted average equivalent units of production for Quincy Manufacturing Company is:

Beginning inventory units	5,000
Units started and completed in May (105,000 × 100%)	105,000
Work performed on ending inventory during May (800 × 30%)	240
WA equivalent units of production	110,240

This equivalent production quantity is used as the denominator in determining per unit product cost.

Note that the number of units completed (110,000, given in Exhibit 8–3) could have been used rather than the number of units in beginning inventory (5,000) plus the units started and completed (105,000). The WA method is *not* concerned about the quantity of work that was performed in the prior period on the units in beginning inventory. This method focuses only on the units that are *completed* in the current period and the units that remain in ending inventory. Treating these units separately, however, will make the difference between weighted average and FIFO more readily apparent.

Because this method does not distinguish between units in beginning inventory and units worked on only during the current period, the weighted average method also does not differentiate between beginning inventory and current period costs. The numerator of the per unit cost formula for the WA method is composed of the cost of beginning inventory *plus* the cost incurred in the current period:

Beginning inventory cost	$ 30,051.20
Current period cost	561,937.60
Total cost to be accounted for	$591,988.80

The sum of beginning inventory and current period production costs is called **total cost to account for.** Average unit cost is found by dividing the total cost to be accounted for by the total equivalent units of production. Thus, the average unit cost is calculated as follows:

Total cost to account for

$$\text{Average WA Unit Cost} = \frac{\text{BWIP Cost} + \text{Current Period Cost}}{\text{Total WA EUP}}$$

$$= \frac{\$591,988.80}{110,240} = \$5.37$$

Note that under the weighted average method, costs and units (respectively) *from two different periods* are totaled to form the numerator and denominator used to calculate the average unit cost.

FIFO Method

The FIFO method of determining EUP more realistically reflects the way in which goods actually flow through the production system. The FIFO computation of equivalent units of production adds the equivalent units of work performed on beginning inventory units in the current period, the units started and completed during the current period, and the equivalent units in ending inventory. For the Quincy Manufacturing Company, the FIFO equivalent unit computation is as follows:

Equivalent units of work performed on beginning inventory during May (5,000 × 40%*)	2,000
Units started and completed in May (105,000 × 100%)	105,000
Work performed on ending inventory during May (800 × 30%)	240
FIFO equivalent units of production	107,240

*Note that the 40% used in this calculation is the complement to the 60% completed last month.

By ignoring the work performed on the beginning inventory units in the prior period, FIFO focuses specifically on the work performed *during the current period*. The FIFO equivalent units can now be used to compute a per unit cost; however, because the denominator for the FIFO method includes only current period production, the numerator must also reflect only current period cost information. The FIFO average cost per equivalent unit is calculated as follows:

$$\text{Average FIFO Unit Cost} = \frac{\text{Current Period Costs}}{\text{Total FIFO EUP}}$$

$$= \frac{\$561,937.60}{107,240} = \$5.24$$

The Quincy Manufacturing Company example shows a single equivalent unit computation. One computation was sufficient because the assumption was made that materials, labor, and overhead were all introduced to the production process simultaneously. Such an assumption is highly unrealistic. Generally, at a minimum, direct materials are at a different degree of completion than labor and overhead. Materials can be introduced to production at discrete points in processing or on a continual basis. Labor and overhead are typically added on a continual basis. For this reason, the completion percentage must be separately determined *for each cost component* and, therefore, separate EUP calculations must also be made for each cost component.

SEPARATE EUP COMPUTATIONS FOR COST COMPONENTS

In almost all cases, some direct material must be introduced at the start of a production process or there would be no need for labor or overhead to be incurred. For example, to make its various products, Birmingham Steel introduces scrap metal at the start of the process. Any material added at the start of production is 100 percent complete throughout the process *regardless* of the percentage of completion of labor and overhead.

Most production processes require more than one direct material. Additional materials may be added at any point or, possibly, continuously during processing. Materials may even be added at the end of processing. An example of a direct material put into production at the end of processing is a box for a finished product. The product is zero percent complete as to one direct material (the box) at any point in the production process, although other materials and some labor and overhead may have been incurred.

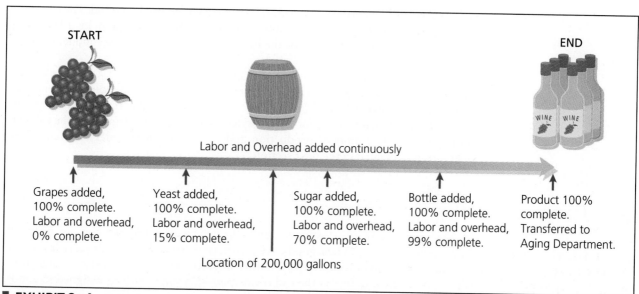

START

Labor and Overhead added continuously

END

Grapes added,
100% complete.
Labor and overhead,
0% complete.

Yeast added,
100% complete.
Labor and overhead,
15% complete.

Sugar added,
100% complete.
Labor and overhead,
70% complete.

Bottle added,
100% complete.
Labor and overhead,
99% complete.

Product 100%
complete.
Transferred to
Aging Department.

Location of 200,000 gallons

▌ EXHIBIT 8–4

Wine Manufacturing Process—Production Department

The production flow of a wine-making process in Exhibit 8–4 visually illustrates the need for separate EUP computations for each cost component. The material "grapes" is 100 percent complete at any point in the process after the start of production; no additional grapes are added later in production. When enough labor and overhead have been added to reach the 15 percent completion point, a second material (yeast) is added. Prior to 15 percent completion, the material "yeast" was zero percent complete; after the 15 percent point, the yeast is 100 percent complete. Sugar is added when production is 70 percent complete. Before this point, sugar is zero percent complete; after this point, it is 100 percent complete. The wine is bottled when processing is 99 percent finished. As far as processing is concerned in the Production Department, the wine is not 100 percent complete until it is bottled. Thus, bottles are zero percent complete throughout production; when the wine is bottled, the product is corked (an indirect material), considered complete, and transferred to the next department for aging.

The 200,000 gallons of wine shown in Exhibit 8–4 are assumed to be 60 percent complete as to labor and overhead at the end of a period. Thus, the product is 100 percent complete as to grapes and yeast and zero percent complete as to sugar and bottles. The EUP calculations would indicate that there are 200,000 EUP for grapes and yeast and zero EUP for sugar and bottles. The labor and overhead (conversion) components of cost would have an equivalency of 120,000 gallons, since the gallons are 60 percent complete and labor and overhead are added continuously during the process.[3]

When overhead is applied on a direct labor basis or when direct labor and overhead are added to the product at the same rate, one percentage of completion estimate can be made and used for both conversion cost components. However, since overhead costs are increasingly caused by cost drivers other than direct labor, single computations for "conversion EUP" will be made less often. For example, the cost driver for the utilities portion of overhead cost may be machine hours; the cost driver for the

---

[3]Although the same number of equivalent units results for grapes and yeast, for sugar and bottles, and for labor and overhead, separate calculations of unit cost may be desirable for each component. These separate calculations would give managers more information for planning and control purposes. Managers must weigh the costs of making separate calculations against the benefits from having the additional information. For illustrative purposes, however, single computations will be made when cost components are at equal percentages of completion.

materials handling portion of overhead cost may be pounds of material. The increased use of multiple cost pools and/or activity-based costing concepts make it less likely that the degrees of completion for the direct labor and overhead component of processing will be equal.

The calculation of equivalent units of production requires that a process costing method be specified. However, as mentioned earlier, there is only one difference between weighted average and FIFO process costing, and that difference lies in the treatment of beginning inventory for EUP calculations. A detailed example of the calculations of equivalent units of production and cost assignment under both cost flow methods is presented in the next section.

EUP CALCULATIONS AND COST ASSIGNMENTS

Total units to account for

A basic purpose of any costing system is to determine a product cost for financial statement purposes. When goods are transferred from Work in Process Inventory to Finished Goods Inventory (or another department), a cost must be assigned to those goods. In addition, at the end of any period, a value must be assigned to goods that are only partially complete and still remain in Work in Process Inventory. Exhibit 8–5 outlines the steps necessary to determine the costs assignable to the units completed and to those still in ending inventory at the end of a period in a process costing system. Each of these steps will be discussed briefly and then a complete example is provided for both weighted average and FIFO costing.

The first step is to calculate the total physical units for which the department is responsible or the **total units to account for**. This amount is equal to the total number of units worked on in the department during the current period—beginning inventory units plus units started.

Second, determine what happened to the units to account for during the period. This step also requires the use of physical units. Units may fit into one of two categories: (1) completed and transferred or (2) partially completed and remaining in ending work in process inventory.[4]

At this point, verify that the total units for which the department was accountable is equal to the total units that were accounted for. If these amounts are not equal, any additional computations will be incorrect.

Third, use either the weighted average or FIFO method to determine the equivalent units of production for each cost component. If all materials are at the same degree of completion, a single materials computation can be made. If multiple materials are used and are placed into production at different points, it may be necessary to make multiple EUP calculations for materials. If overhead is based on direct labor or if these two factors are always at the same degree of completion, a single EUP can be computed for conversion. If neither condition exists, separate EUP schedules must be prepared for labor and overhead.[5]

Fourth, find the total cost to account for, which includes the balance in Work in Process Inventory at the beginning of the period plus all current costs for direct materials, direct labor, and overhead.

Fifth, compute the cost per equivalent unit for each cost component using either the weighted average or FIFO equivalent units of production calculated in Step 3.

---

[4] A third category (spoilage/breakage) does exist. It is assumed at this point that such happenings do not occur. Chapter 9 covers accounting for spoilage in process costing situations.

[5] As discussed in Chapter 5, overhead may be applied to products using a variety of traditional (direct labor hours or machine hours) or nontraditional (such as number of machine setups, pounds of material moved, and/or number of materials requisitions) bases. The number of equivalent unit computations that need to be made result from the number of different cost pools and overhead allocation bases established in a company. It is also possible that some highly automated manufacturers will not have a direct labor category. The quantity of direct labor may be so nominal that it is included in a conversion category and not accounted for separately.

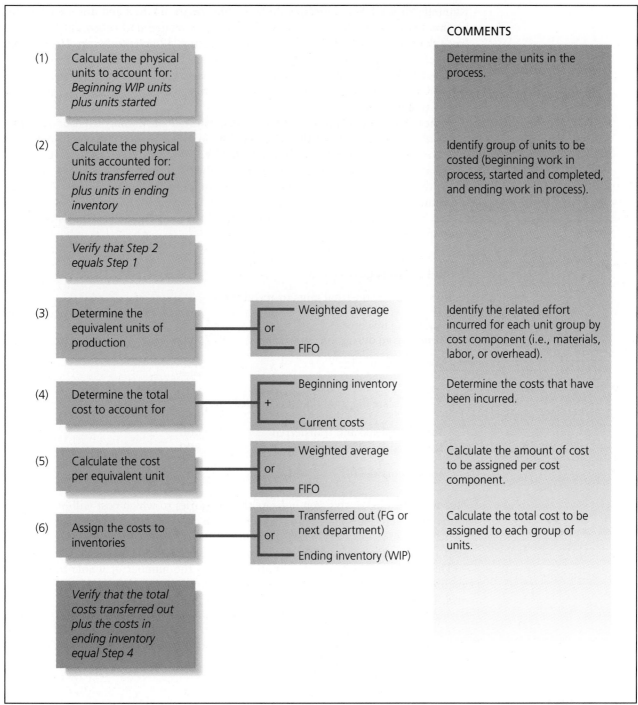

		COMMENTS
(1)	Calculate the physical units to account for: *Beginning WIP units plus units started*	Determine the units in the process.
(2)	Calculate the physical units accounted for: *Units transferred out plus units in ending inventory*	Identify group of units to be costed (beginning work in process, started and completed, and ending work in process).
	Verify that Step 2 equals Step 1	
(3)	Determine the equivalent units of production — or — Weighted average / FIFO	Identify the related effort incurred for each unit group by cost component (i.e., materials, labor, or overhead).
(4)	Determine the total cost to account for — + — Beginning inventory / Current costs	Determine the costs that have been incurred.
(5)	Calculate the cost per equivalent unit — or — Weighted average / FIFO	Calculate the amount of cost to be assigned per cost component.
(6)	Assign the costs to inventories — or — Transferred out (FG or next department) / Ending inventory (WIP)	Calculate the total cost to be assigned to each group of units.
	Verify that the total costs transferred out plus the costs in ending inventory equal Step 4	

EXHIBIT 8–5
Steps in Process Costing

Sixth, use the costs computed in Step 5 to assign costs to the units completed and transferred from the production process and to the units remaining in ending Work in Process Inventory.

Fairmore Steel Company is used to demonstrate the steps involved in the computation of equivalent units of production and cost assignment for both methods of process costing. Fairmore Steel is a mini-mill having the same basic processes as Birmingham Steel. Fairmore Steel views the production process as consisting of a single department rather than the two departments (Melt Shop and Rolling Mill) of

Birmingham Steel. Scrap metal is the only direct material used and it is added at the beginning of the production process. The scrap is melted and rolled into flat bars. Since the material is added at the start of processing, all inventories are 100 percent complete as to material as soon as processing has begun. Labor and overhead are assumed to be added at the same rate throughout the production process. Exhibit 8–6 presents information for the month of November 1994 regarding Fairmore's production inventories and costs.

Although figures are given for both tons transferred and ending inventory, it is not essential to provide both of these figures. The number of tons remaining in ending inventory on November 30 can be calculated by subtracting the tons that were completed and transferred during the period from the total tons to account for. Alternatively, the number of tons transferred can be computed as the total tons to account for minus the tons in ending inventory.

The Fairmore Steel information is used to illustrate each of the steps listed previously in Exhibit 8–5.

Weighted Average Method

Step 1: Calculate the total units to account for.

Beginning inventory	15,000
Tons started during current period	977,800
Tons to account for	992,800

Step 2: Calculate the total units accounted for.

Tons completed and transferred	980,000
Tons in ending WIP inventory	12,800
Tons accounted for	992,800

The items detailed in this step indicate the categories to which cost will be assigned in the final step. The tons accounted for in Step 2 equals the tons to account for in Step 1.

Step 3: Determine the equivalent units of production.

The weighted average EUP computation uses the number of whole tons in beginning inventory and the number of tons started and completed during the period. For Fairmore Steel, the tons started and completed in November are 965,000

■ **EXHIBIT 8–6**

Fairmore Steel Production and Cost Information—November 1994

Beginning inventory (40% complete as to conversion)	15,000 tons
Tons started during current period	977,800
Tons completed and transferred to finished goods	980,000
Ending inventory (80% complete as to conversion)	12,800

Cost of beginning inventory:		
Direct material	$ 988,880	
Direct labor	459,024	
Overhead	435,912	$ 1,883,816

Current period costs:		
Direct material	$90,348,720	
Direct labor	59,054,400	
Overhead	63,385,056	212,788,176

(980,000 − 15,000). Ending inventory is 100 percent complete as to material, since all material is added at the start of production. The ending inventory is 80 percent complete as to labor and overhead (conversion); one EUP computation can be made because these cost elements were assumed to be added at the same rate throughout the production process. The weighted average computation for equivalent units of production is as follows:[6]

	DM	Conversion (Labor and Overhead)
Beginning inventory (whole tons)	15,000	15,000
Tons started and completed	965,000	965,000
Ending inventory (whole tons × % complete)	12,800	10,240
Equivalent units of production	992,800	990,240

Step 4: Determine the total cost to account for.

The total cost to account for equals the costs included in beginning inventory plus current period costs. Note that information is provided in Exhibit 8–6 on the cost for *each element of production*—direct material, direct labor, and overhead. Production costs can be determined from the departmental Work in Process Inventory accounts and their subsidiary details. These costs come from transfers of raw materials from the storeroom, incurrence of direct labor, and either actual or applied overhead amounts. The sum of direct labor and overhead costs is the conversion cost. For Fairmore Steel, the total cost to account for is $214,671,992.

	DM	DL	OH	Total
Beginning inventory cost	$ 988,880	$ 459,024	$ 435,912	$ 1,883,816
Current period costs	90,348,720	59,054,400	63,385,056	212,788,176
to account for	$91,337,600	$59,513,424	$63,820,968	$214,671,992

Total cost is assigned to the goods transferred to the next department (or, alternatively, to Finished Goods Inventory) and to ending Work in Process Inventory in relation to the whole units or equivalent whole units contained in each category.

Step 5: Calculate the cost per equivalent unit of production.

A cost per equivalent unit of production must be computed for each cost component for which a separate calculation of EUP is made. Under the weighted average method, the costs of beginning inventory and the current period are summed for each cost component and averaged over that component's weighted average equivalent units of production. This calculation for unit cost for each cost component at the end of the period is shown below:

$$\text{Unit Cost} = \frac{\text{Beginning Inventory Cost} + \text{Current Period Cost}}{\text{Weighted Average Equivalent Units of Production}}$$

$$= \frac{\text{Total Cost Incurred}}{\text{Total Equivalent Units of Effort}}$$

---

[6] Different approaches exist to compute equivalent units of production and unit costs under the weighted average and FIFO methods. The models presented in this chapter represent the computations that we have found to be the most readily understood and that best assist students in a clear and unambiguous reconciliation of these two methods. However, two other valid and commonly used approaches for computing and reconciling WA and FIFO equivalent units of production and unit costs are presented in Appendix 1 to this chapter.

This computation allows total costs to be divided by total units—the common weighted average approach that produces an average component cost per unit. Fairmore Steel's weighted average calculations for cost per EUP for material, labor, and overhead are shown below:

	Direct Material	Direct Labor	Overhead
Beginning inventory cost	$ 988,880	$ 459,024	$ 435,912
Current period costs	90,348,720	59,054,400	63,385,056
Total cost per component	$91,337,600	$59,513,424	$63,820,968
Divided by EUP (Step 3)	992,800	990,240	990,240
Cost per EUP	$92	$60.10	$64.45

Since labor and overhead are at the same degree of completion, the costs can be combined and shown as a single conversion cost per equivalent unit as follows:

	Direct Labor +	Overhead =	Conversion
Beginning inventory cost	$ 459,024	$ 435,912	$ 894,936
Current period costs	59,054,400	63,385,056	122,439,456
Total cost per component	$59,513,424	$63,820,968	$123,334,392
Divided by EUP (Step 3)	990,240	990,240	990,240
Cost per EUP	$60.10	$64.45	$124.55

The amounts for the three product cost components (materials, labor, and overhead) are summed to find the total production cost for all whole tons completed during November. For Fairmore Steel, this cost is $216.55 ($92 + $60.10 + $64.45). Step 6: Assign costs to inventories.

This step assigns total production costs to units of product. Cost assignment in a department involves determining the cost of (1) the goods completed and transferred during the period and (2) the units in ending work in process inventory.

Using the weighted average method, the cost of goods transferred is found by multiplying the total number of units transferred by a cost per unit that combines all the costs of the components or the total cost per EUP. Since this method is based on an averaging technique that combines both prior and current period work, it does not matter in which period the transferred units were started. All units and all costs have been commingled. The total cost transferred for Fairmore Steel for November is $212,219,000 ($216.55 × 980,000).

Ending WIP Inventory cost is calculated based on the equivalent units of production for each cost component. The equivalent units of production for each component are multiplied by the component cost per unit computed in Step 5. The cost of ending inventory using the weighted average method (using the previously determined equivalent units) is as follows:

Ending inventory	
Direct material (12,800 × $92)	$1,177,600
Direct labor (10,240 × $60.10)	615,424
Overhead (10,240 × $64.45)	659,968
Total cost of ending inventory	$2,452,992

If a conversion cost component were used instead of separate direct labor and overhead categories, the computation would be:

Ending inventory
    Direct material (12,800 × $92) $1,177,600
    Conversion (10,240 × $124.55)   1,275,392

    Total cost of ending inventory $2,452,992

The total costs assigned to units transferred and units in ending inventory must sum to the total cost to account for. For Fairmore Steel, total cost to account for (Step 4) was determined as $214,671,992, which equals transferred cost ($212,219,000) plus cost of ending Work in Process Inventory ($2,452,992).

FIFO Method

Steps 1 and 2 are the same for the FIFO method as for the weighted average method because these two steps involve the use of physical units.
Step 3: Determine the equivalent units of production.
    Under FIFO, the work performed last period is *not* commingled with work of the current period. The EUP schedule for FIFO is:

	DM	Conversion
Beginning inventory		
(EUP completed in the current period)	0	9,000
Tons started and completed	965,000	965,000
Ending inventory (whole tons × % complete)	12,800	10,240
Equivalent units of production	977,800	984,240

Under FIFO, only the work performed on the beginning inventory during the current period is shown in the EUP schedule; this work equals the whole units in beginning inventory times (1 − the percentage of work done in the prior period). No additional material is needed in November to complete the 15,000 tons in the beginning inventory. Since beginning inventory was 40 percent complete as to labor and overhead, the company needs to do 60 percent of the conversion work on the goods in the current period or the equivalent of 9,000 tons (15,000 × 60%).
    Except for the different treatment of units in beginning inventory, the remaining figures in the FIFO EUP schedule are the same as for the weighted average method. Thus, the *only* difference between the FIFO and weighted average EUP computations relates to beginning inventory. The exact difference between the two methods is equal to the number of tons in beginning inventory times the percentage of work performed in the prior period, as shown below:

	Direct Material	Conversion
FIFO EUP	977,800	984,240
Beginning inventory (× % work done in prior period; 100% material, 40% conversion)	15,000	6,000
WA EUP	992,800	990,240

Step 4: Determine the total cost to account for. This step is the same as it was under the weighted average method; the total cost to account for is $214,671,992.
Step 5: Calculate the cost per equivalent unit of production.

Since cost determination is made on the basis of equivalent units of production, different results will be obtained for the weighted average and FIFO methods. The calculations for cost per equivalent unit reflect the difference in quantity that each method uses for beginning inventory. The EUP calculation for FIFO ignores work performed on beginning inventory during the prior period; therefore, the FIFO cost computation per EUP also ignores prior period costs and uses only costs incurred in the current period. The FIFO cost per EUP calculation is:

	Direct Material	Direct Labor	Overhead
Current period costs	$90,348,720	$59,054,400	$63,385,056
Divided by EUP (Step 3)	977,800	984,240	984,240
Cost per EUP	$92.40	$60	$64.40

The production cost for each whole unit produced during November under the FIFO method is $216.80 ($92.40 + $60 + $64.40).

It is useful to recognize the difference between the two total cost computations. The weighted average total cost of $216.55 is the average total cost of each ton completed during November, *regardless of when production was begun*. The FIFO total cost of $216.80 is the total cost of each ton produced (*both started and completed*) during the period. The $.25 difference ($216.55 versus $216.80) is caused by the difference in treatment of beginning work in process costs.

Step 6: Assign costs to inventories.

The FIFO method assumes that the units in beginning inventory are the first units completed during the current period and, thus, are the first units transferred. The remaining units transferred during the period were both started and completed in the current period. The two-step computation needed to determine the cost of goods transferred distinctly presents this FIFO logic.

The first part of the cost assignment for units transferred relates to the units that were in beginning inventory. These units had the cost of material and some labor and overhead costs attached to them at the start of the period. These costs were not included in the cost per EUP calculations in Step 5. The costs to finish these units were incurred in the current period. To determine the total cost of producing the units in beginning inventory, the beginning inventory costs are added to the current period costs needed to complete the goods. Next, the cost of the units started and completed in the current period is computed using current period costs. This cost assignment process is shown for Fairmore Steel, which had a beginning November inventory of 15,000 tons and transferred 980,000 tons during the month.

Transferred		
(1) Beginning inventory (prior period costs)		$ 1,883,816
Completion of beginning inventory:		
Direct material (0 × $92.40)		0
Direct labor (9,000 × $60)		540,000
Overhead (9,000 × $64.40)		579,600
Total cost of beginning inventory transferred		$ 3,003,416
(2) Tons started & completed (965,000 × $216.80)		209,212,000
Total cost transferred		$212,215,416

Since the beginning inventory units were 100 percent complete as to material at the beginning of November, no additional material needs to be added during the period. Conversion at the start of the month was only 40 percent complete, so 60 percent of the labor and overhead work (or 9,000 equivalent units) is added during November at current period costs. The tons started and completed are costed at the total current period FIFO cost of $216.80, since these tons were fully manufactured during the current period.

Calculating the cost of ending Work in Process Inventory is the same under both the FIFO and weighted average methods. Although the cost per ton differs, the number of equivalent units of production is the same under both methods. Ending work in process cost using FIFO is as follows:

Ending inventory
    Direct material (12,800 × $92.40) $1,182,720
    Direct labor (10,240 × $60)   614,400
    Overhead (10,240 × $64.40)   659,456
        Total cost of ending inventory $2,456,576

The total cost of the tons transferred ($212,215,416) plus the cost of the tons in ending inventory ($2,456,576) equals the total cost to be accounted for ($214,671,992).

Because of the two-step process required by the FIFO method in determining the cost of units transferred, a question exists as to how to calculate a per unit cost for the two "groups" of units: those that were in beginning inventory and those that were started and completed in the current period. The resolution of this question is found in the use of either the strict or the modified FIFO method.

Strict versus Modified FIFO

If **strict FIFO** method is used, the beginning inventory units are transferred to the next department or to Finished Goods Inventory at their total completed cost; the units started and completed during the current period are transferred at a separate and distinct current period cost. For Fairmore Steel, use of the strict FIFO method means that the 15,000 tons included in beginning inventory are transferred at a cost per ton of $200.23 ($3,003,416 ÷ 15,000). The tons started and completed in November are transferred at the current period cost of $216.80 (computed in Step 5). If strict FIFO is used, the costs of these two groups should be reported separately and not added together to get a total transferred cost.

Strict FIFO method (of process costing)

However, unless the difference in per unit cost of beginning inventory units and started and completed units is significant, there is no need to maintain the distinction. The costs of the two groups can be combined and averaged over all of the units transferred in a process known as the **modified FIFO** method. For Fairmore Steel, modified FIFO assigns an average cost of $216.55 per ton ($212,215,416 ÷ 980,000) to all tons transferred from the department. The modified FIFO method allows the next department or Finished Goods Inventory to account for all units received during the period at the same cost per unit. This method is useful when products are processed through several departments so that the number of separate unit costs to be accounted for does not become excessive.

Modified FIFO method (of process costing)

The steps discussed in the previous section can be combined into a **cost of production report**. This process costing document details all manufacturing quantities and costs, shows the computation of cost per EUP, and indicates the cost assignment to goods produced during the period. Exhibit 8–7 on page 314 shows Fairmore Steel's cost of production report using the weighted average method information calculated earlier. Exhibit 8–8 on page 315 presents Fairmore Steel's cost of production report prepared using the FIFO method. In both exhibits, the labor and overhead columns are combined into a single conversion column.

Summary journal entries and T-accounts for Fairmore Steel for November follow. It is assumed that 975,000 tons were sold on account for $330 per ton and that a perpetual FIFO inventory system is in use. Assume that Fairmore Steel began Novem-

COST OF PRODUCTION REPORT

Cost of production report

EXHIBIT 8–7

Fairmore Steel Cost of Production Report for Month Ended November 30, 1994

(Weighted Average Method)

PRODUCTION DATA	Whole Units	Equivalent Units of Production	
		Direct Material	Conversion
Beginning inventory	15,000*	15,000	6,000
Tons started	977,800		
Tons to account for	992,800		
Beginning inventory completed	15,000	0	9,000
Started and completed	965,000	965,000	965,000
Tons completed	980,000		
Ending WIP inventory	12,800**	12,800	10,240
Tons accounted for	992,800	992,800	990,240

COST DATA	Total	Direct Material	Conversion
Cost in beginning inventory	$ 1,883,816	$ 988,880	$ 894,936
Current period costs	212,788,176	90,348,720	122,439,456
Total cost to account for	$214,671,992	$91,337,600	$123,334,392
Divided by EUP		992,800	990,240
Cost per EUP	$216.55	$92	$124.55

COST ASSIGNMENT			
Transferred (980,000 × $216.55)			$212,219,000
Ending inventory			
Direct material (12,800 × $92)		$1,177,600	
Conversion (12,800 × 80% × $124.55)		1,275,392	2,452,992
Total cost accounted for			$214,671,992

*Fully complete as to material; 40% complete as to conversion.
**Fully complete as to material; 80% complete as to conversion.

ber with no Finished Goods Inventory. Weighted average amounts are shown where they would differ from FIFO.

1. Work in Process Inventory   90,348,720
        Raw Materials Inventory   90,348,720
    To record current period issuance of
    materials to production (Exhibit 8–6).

2. Work in Process Inventory   59,054,400
        Wages Payable   59,054,400
    To accrue current period wages for di-
    rect labor (Exhibit 8–6).

3. Manufacturing Overhead   63,385,056
        Various accounts   63,385,056
    To record actual overhead costs for
    November (Exhibit 8–6).

■ EXHIBIT 8–8
Fairmore Steel Cost
of Production Report
for Month Ended
November 30, 1994

(FIFO Method)

PRODUCTION DATA	Whole Units	Equivalent Units of Production	
		Direct Material	Conversion
Beginning inventory	15,000*		
Tons started	977,800		
Tons to account for	992,800		
Beginning inventory completed	15,000	0	9,000
Started and completed	965,000	965,000	965,000
Tons completed	980,000		
Ending WIP inventory	12,800**	12,800	10,240
Units accounted for	992,800	977,800	984,240

COST DATA	Total	Direct Material	Conversion
Cost in beginning inventory	$ 1,883,816		
Current period costs	212,788,176	$90,348,720	$122,439,456
Total cost to account for	$214,671,992		
Divided by EUP		977,800	984,240
Cost per EUP	$216.80	$92.40	$124.40

COST ASSIGNMENT

Transferred			
Beginning inventory cost		$1,883,816	
Cost to complete:			
Conversion (9,000 × $124.40)		1,119,600	$ 3,003,416
Started & completed (965,000 × $216.80)			209,212,000
Total cost transferred			$212,215,416
Ending inventory			
Direct material (12,800 × $92.40)		$1,182,720	
Conversion (10,240 × $124.40)		1,273,856	2,456,576
Total cost accounted for			$214,671,992

* Fully complete as to material; 40% complete as to conversion.
** Fully complete as to material; 80% complete as to conversion.

4. Work in Process Inventory 63,385,056
       Manufacturing Overhead 63,385,056
   To apply actual overhead to produc-
   tion in November.

5. Finished Goods Inventory 212,215,416
       Work in Process Inventory 212,215,416
   To transfer cost of completed tons to
   finished goods (Exhibit 8–8). (Entry
   would be for $212,219,000 if weighted
   average were used—Exhibit 8–7.)

6. Cost of Goods Sold   211,131,416
          Finished Goods Inventory   211,131,416
    To transfer cost of goods sold from FG
    Inventory to the appropriate expense
    account, using strict FIFO:

First 15,000 units	$ 3,003,416
Remaining 960,000	
units at $216.80	208,128,000
	$211,131,416

(Entry would be for $211,136,250 if
modified FIFO or weighted average
were used—975,000 × $216.55.)

7. Accounts Receivable   321,750,000
          Sales   321,750,000
    To record November sales on account
    (975,000 tons × $330).

Fairmore Steel T-accounts

WORK IN PROCESS INVENTORY

Beginning balance	1,883,816	Cost of goods	
Direct material	90,348,720	manufactured	212,215,416
Direct labor	59,054,400		
Applied overhead	63,385,056		
Ending balance	2,456,576		

FINISHED GOODS INVENTORY

Beginning balance	0	Cost of goods sold	211,131,416
CGM	212,215,416		
Ending balance	1,084,000		

COST OF GOODS SOLD

November CGS	211,131,416	

Quincy Manufacturing Company and Fairmore Steel both used single production departments. However, most companies (like Birmingham Steel) have multiple rather than single processing facilities. The next section presents the flow of costs in a multi-department manufacturer.

PROCESS COSTING IN A MULTI-DEPARTMENT SETTING

In a multidepartment processing environment, goods are transferred from a predecessor department to a successor department. Costs always follow the physical flow of goods. Therefore, the costs of the completed units of predecessor departments are treated as an input material cost in successor departments. A successor department may add additional raw materials to the units transferred in or may simply provide additional labor with the corresponding incurrence of overhead.

The Fairmore Steel example is continued at this point, with one difference. Fairmore Steel has decided to account for its production costs in two departments: the

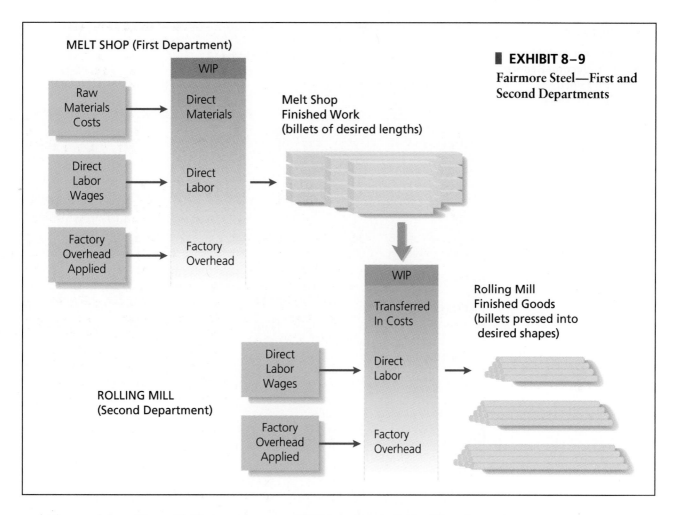

EXHIBIT 8–9
Fairmore Steel—First and Second Departments

melt shop and the rolling mill. The company uses FIFO process costing in all production departments. The flow of input factors from the first department to the second department appears as shown in Exhibit 8–9.

The November 1994 production and cost information shown in Exhibit 8–10 was obtained from records of the Melt Shop of Fairmore Steel. The cost of production

EXHIBIT 8–10
Fairmore Steel Production and Cost Data—Melt Shop

Production Data		
Tons in beginning inventory, fully complete as to material,		
and 40% complete as to conversion		5,000
Tons started during November		977,800
Tons completed during November		978,000
Tons in ending inventory, fully complete as to material,		
and 80% complete as to conversion		4,800
Cost Data		
Beginning inventory cost		
Direct material	$ 1,299,620	
Conversion	300,980	$ 1,600,600
Current period costs		
Direct material	$149,603,400	
Conversion	69,568,640	219,172,040
Total manufacturing costs for November		$220,772,640

EXHIBIT 8–11

Fairmore Steel Melt Shop
Cost of Production Report
for Month Ended
November 30, 1994

(FIFO Method)

PRODUCTION DATA

	Whole Units	Equivalent Units of Production	
		Direct Material	Conversion
Beginning inventory	5,000*		
Units started	977,800		
Units to account for	982,800		
Beginning inventory completed	5,000	0	3,000
Started and completed	973,000	973,000	973,000
Units completed	978,000		
Ending inventory	4,800**	4,800	3,840
Units accounted for	982,800	977,800	979,840

COST DATA

	Total	Direct Material	Conversion
Cost in beginning inventory	$ 1,600,600		
Current period costs	219,172,040	$149,603,640	$69,568,640
Total cost to account for	$220,772,640		
Divided by EUP		977,800	979,840
Cost per EUP	$224	$153	$71

COST ASSIGNMENT

Transferred

Beginning inventory cost	$1,600,600	
Cost to complete		
Direct material (0 × $153)	0	
Conversion (3,000 × $71)	213,000	
Cost of beginning inventory transferred		$ 1,813,600
Started and completed (973,000 × $224)		217,952,000
Total cost transferred (see Exhibit 8–12)		$219,765,600
Ending inventory		
Direct material (4,800 × $153)	$ 734,400	
Conversion (3,840 × $71)	272,640	1,007,040
Total cost accounted for		$220,772,640

*Fully complete as to material; 40% complete as to conversion.
**Fully complete as to material; 80% complete as to conversion.

report for Fairmore Steel shown in Exhibit 8–11 can be prepared using the data shown in Exhibit 8–10. For simplicity, it has been assumed that the beginning and ending inventories of both departments were at the same stage of completion as was indicated in the earlier information.

The Cost Assignment section of Exhibit 8–11 indicates that 978,000 tons of steel with a cost of $219,765,600 are transferred to the Rolling Mill during the month. These same data are also shown as units and cost transferred in on a subsequent presentation of operating statistics for the successor department.

Production Data		
Units in beginning inventory, fully complete as to		
transferred-in costs, and 40% complete as to conversion		10,000
Units transferred-in during November		978,000
Units completed in November		980,000
Units in ending inventory, fully complete as to		
transferred-in costs, and 80% complete as to conversion		8,000
Cost Data		
Beginning inventory cost		
Transferred-in	$ 2,240,000	
Conversion	608,044	$ 2,848,044
Current period costs		
Transferred-in (from Exhibit 8–11)	$219,765,600	
Conversion	63,266,560	283,032,160
Total manufacturing costs for November		$285,880,204

As shown in Exhibit 8–9 the Rolling Mill has three input components and three input costs:

1. transferred-in units from the predecessor department
2. direct labor
3. factory overhead

Since the department has three input components and costs, three equivalent units of production schedules could be prepared. However, because labor and overhead are incurred uniformly in the Rolling Mill, they can be referred to as conversion and can be treated as a single input component.

The transferred-in units and costs are treated as a separate component of the work performed in a successor department. The degree of completion of the transferred-in units is 100 percent because they would not have been transferred from the predecessor department without being fully complete. The November 1994 production and cost data for the Rolling Mill are presented in Exhibit 8–12. Fairmore Steel does not add any additional material in the second department. In other companies, direct material may be added in successor departments. If this is the case, the material is simply treated as another cost component and a separate equivalent unit computation and cost assignment must be made for that component.

The cost of production report (Exhibit 8–13 on page 320) is shown for the Rolling Mill for November 1994. The only difference in this report and the previous reports shown for the company or its Melt Shop is that an additional column is presented for transferred-in units and costs. The steps used in determining the assignment of costs to finished goods transferred and ending inventory units are the same as illustrated earlier. The transferred-in component is always 100 percent complete.

The transferred-in costs for the Rolling Mill reflect the use of the modified FIFO technique discussed earlier in the chapter. The Melt Shop transferred costs associated with two "groups" of inventory—$1,813,600 for the Melt Shop's beginning inventory and $217,952,000 for the tons started and completed during November (see Exhibit 8–11)—to the Rolling Mill. The Rolling Mill added the costs ($219,765,600) and averaged them over the entire 978,000 tons of steel to provide a single unit cost ($224.71) per ton.

■ EXHIBIT 8–13
Fairmore Steel Rolling Mill
Cost of Production Report
for Month Ended
November 30, 1994

(FIFO Method)

PRODUCTION DATA | | **Equivalent Units of Production** |

PRODUCTION DATA	Whole Units	Transferred-In	Conversion
Beginning inventory	10,000*		
Units started	978,000		
Units to account for	988,000		
Beginning inventory completed	10,000	0	6,000
Started and completed	970,000	970,000	970,000
Units completed	980,000		
Ending inventory	8,000**	8,000	6,400
Units accounted for	988,000	978,000	982,400

COST DATA

	Total	Transferred-In	Conversion
Cost in beginning inventory	$ 2,848,044		
Current period costs	283,032,160	$219,765,600	$63,266,560
Total cost to account for	$285,880,204		
Divided by EUP		978,000	982,400
Cost per EUP	$289.11	$224.71	$64.40

COST ASSIGNMENT
Transferred
  Beginning inventory cost $ 2,848,044
  Cost to complete:
    Transferred-in (0 × $224.71)   0
    Conversion (6,000 × $64.40)   386,400

  Cost of beginning inventory transferred $ 3,234,444
  Started and completed (970,000 × $289.11) 280,436,700 $283,671,144

Ending inventory
  Transferred-in (8,000 × $224.71) $ 1,797,680
  Conversion (6,400 × $64.40) 412,160   2,209,840

Total cost accounted for*** $285,880,984

*Fully complete as to transferred-in costs; 40% complete as to conversion costs.
**Fully complete as to transferred-in costs; 80% complete as to conversion costs.
***Difference due to rounding.

HYBRID COSTING SYSTEMS

Hybrid costing system

Many companies are now able to customize what were previously mass-produced items. In such circumstances, neither job order nor process costing techniques are perfectly suited to attach costs to output. Thus, companies may choose to use a **hybrid costing system** that is appropriate for their particular processing situation. A hybrid costing system combines certain characteristics of both a job order and a pro-

Recycled or virgin steel passes through multiple departments during the production process. The cost per ton of steel (or unit of specific product) must be passed along from departments to determine the full production cost when rebar, merchant products, or billets are sent to Finished Goods Inventory.

cess costing system. A hybrid system would be used in a manufacturing environment in which various product lines have different direct materials, but similar processing techniques.

To illustrate the need for hybrid systems, assume you order an automobile with the following options: leather seats, a Bose stereo system and compact disk player, cruise control, and pearlized paint. The cost of all options needs to be traced specifically to your car, but the assembly process for all the cars produced by the plant is similar. The job order costing feature of tracing direct materials is combined with the process costing feature of averaging labor and overhead costs over all homogeneous production to derive the total cost of the automobile you ordered. It would be infeasible to try to use a job order costing system to trace labor (or overhead) cost to your car individually and it would be improper to average the cost of your options over all the cars produced during the period.

A hybrid costing system that is applied to batches of goods having different direct materials but similar processing activity is called an **operation costing system**. This type of system would be appropriate for companies producing items such as furniture, clothing, or jellies and jams. In each instance, numerous kinds of raw materials could be used to create similar output. A table may be made from oak, teak, or pine; a blouse may be made from silk, cotton, or polyester; and jelly may be made from blackberries, strawberries, or jalapeño peppers. The materials cost for a batch run would need to be traced separately, but the production process of the batch is repetitive.

Hybrid costing systems allow accounting systems to portray more accurately the actual type of manufacturing activities in which companies are engaged. Job order costing and process costing are two ends of a continuum and, as is typically the case for any continuum, neither end is the norm. As flexible manufacturing increases, so will hybrid costing systems.

Operation costing system

R E V I S I T I N G

BIRMINGHAM STEEL CORPORATION

Of the almost 1,500,000 tons of steel shipped in fiscal 1992, Birmingham Steel's product mix was as follows: reinforcing bar (rebar) accounted for 60 percent, merchant products for 18 percent, mine roof products for 18 percent, and semi-finished steel billets for 4 percent. The company plans on even higher production capacity for future years, with a higher proportion in the merchant market. Additionally, in the second half of 1991, the Kankakee facility became the first Birmingham Steel location to ship product overseas and the company looks forward to an increase in its export business.

Company management believes that the key to success in today's highly competitive marketplace is to provide the customer with a quality product and a professional level of service, while continually striving to reduce production costs. Conversion costs in the various production locations averaged $117 per ton for the 1992 fiscal year compared to $139 per ton for fiscal 1991.[7] A primary goal of the company is to reduce the cost to convert a ton of steel to $100. Birmingham Steel intends to do this by modernizing production processes and installing new equipment that will enhance efficiency and reduce finished product cost. However, while lowering the overall labor cost per ton, the company is also increasing wages and benefits to individual workers.

New technologies offer opportunities for mini-mills to participate efficiently and effectively in new markets and many of the integrated steel producers have high cost operations that cannot compete with the new equipment and lower production costs of the mini-mills. But regardless of whether a steel producer is a mini-mill or an integrated mill, it will use process costing techniques to account for its production process. These continuous processors will compute equivalent units of production and track their costs through the process from department to department—attaching the costs to each group of products manufactured to ultimately determine a cost per ton of steel product.

SOURCE: Adapted from Birmingham Steel Corporation, *1992 Annual Report.*

CHAPTER SUMMARY

Process costing is an averaging method used to assign costs to output in manufacturing situations producing large quantities of homogeneous products. A process costing system may use either the weighted average or FIFO method to compute equivalent units of production and assign costs. The difference between the two methods lies solely in the treatment of the work performed in the prior period on the beginning work in process inventory.

Under the weighted average method, work performed in the prior period is combined with current period work and the total costs are averaged over all units. Using the FIFO method, work done in the last period on beginning work in process inventory is *not* commingled with current period work nor are costs of beginning work in process added to current period costs to derive unit production cost. With FIFO, current period costs are divided by current period production to generate a unit production cost related entirely to work actually performed in the current period.

Six basic steps are necessary in deriving and assigning product cost under a process costing system.

---

[7] Janet M. Kuntz and R. Wayne Atwell, *Birmingham Steel (BIR): Awaiting the Next Move* (Morgan Stanley Company Analysis; August 11, 1992), p. 1.

1. Calculate the total number of physical units to account for.

2. Calculate the physical units accounted for. This calculation is accomplished by tracing the physical flow of units. This step involves identifying the groups to which costs are to be assigned (transferred or remaining in ending inventory).

3. Determine the number of equivalent units of production, either on the weighted average or FIFO basis, for each cost component. The cost components include transferred-in (if multidepartmental), direct materials, direct labor, and overhead. In cases of multiple materials having different degrees of completion, each material is considered a separate cost component. If overhead is applied on a direct labor basis or is incurred at the same rate as direct labor, labor and overhead may be combined as one cost component and referred to as "conversion."

4. Determine the total cost to account for.

5. Calculate the cost per equivalent unit of production for each cost component.

6. Assign the costs to the units transferred and the units in ending work in process inventory. The method of cost assignment depends on whether weighted average or FIFO costing is used. The total of the costs assigned to units transferred and to units in ending work in process inventory must equal the total cost to account for.

Alternative Calculations of Weighted Average and FIFO Methods

APPENDIX 1

Various methods exist to allow the computation of equivalent units of production under the weighted average and FIFO methods. One of the most common variations is the following EUP calculation for weighted average:

$$
\begin{array}{l}
\text{Units transferred (whole units)} \\
+\ \underline{\text{Ending work in process (equivalent units)}} \\
\\
=\ \underline{\underline{\text{Weighted average EUP}}}
\end{array}
$$

Once the weighted average EUP figure is available, the FIFO equivalent units can be quickly derived by subtracting the equivalent units in beginning work in process inventory that had been produced in the previous period:

$$
\begin{array}{l}
\text{Weighted average EUP} \\
-\ \underline{\text{BWIP equivalent units produced in previous period}} \\
\\
=\ \underline{\underline{\text{FIFO EUP}}}
\end{array}
$$

This computation is appropriate for the following reason: The weighted average method concentrates on the units that were completed during the period as well as the units that were started but not completed during the period. Unlike FIFO, the weighted average method does not exclude the equivalent units that were in beginning inventory. Thus, to convert from weighted average to FIFO, simply remove the equivalent units produced in the previous period from beginning work in process.

Fairmore Steel's November production data presented in the chapter are repeated here to illustrate these alternative calculations for the weighted average and FIFO methods.

Beginning work in process (100% complete as to materials; 40% complete as to conversion costs)	15,000
Tons started during the month	977,800
Tons completed during the month	980,000
Ending work in process (100% complete as to material; 80% complete as to conversion costs)	12,800

Using these data, the EUP are computed as follows:

	DM	Conversion
Tons transferred	980,000	980,000
+ Ending work in process equivalent units (12,800 tons @ 100% and 80% complete)	12,800	10,240
= **Weighted average EUP**	992,800	990,240
− BTWIP equivalent units produced in previous period (15,000 units @ 100% and 40% complete)	(15,000)	(6,000)
= **FIFO EUP**	977,800	984,240

The distinct relationship between the weighted average and FIFO costing models can also be used to derive the equivalent units of production calculations. This method begins with the total number of units to account for in the period. From this amount, the EUP to be completed next period are subtracted to give the weighted average EUP. Next, as in the method shown above, the equivalent units completed in the prior period (the beginning Work in Process Inventory) are deducted to give the FIFO equivalent units of production.

Using the Fairmore Steel data, these computations are:

	DM	Conversion
Total units to account for	992,800	992,800
− EUP to be completed next period (ending inventory × % not completed: 12,800 × 0%; 12,800 × 20%)	0	(2,560)
= **Weighted average EUP**	992,800	990,240
− EUP completed in prior period (beginning inventory × % completed last period: 15,000 × 100%; 15,000 × 40%)	(15,000)	(6,000)
= **FIFO EUP**	977,800	984,240

These alternative calculations can either be used to confirm answers found by using beginning inventory units, units started and completed, and ending inventory units or as a short-cut to initially compute equivalent units of production.

APPENDIX 2

Process Costing with Standard Costs

The examples in the chapter used historical actual costs to assign values to products under either the weighted average or FIFO method. Companies may prefer to use standard rather than actual costs for inventory valuation purposes. Actual costing requires that a new production cost be computed each production period. Standard costing simplifies the costing process because it eliminates such recomputations, although standards do need to be reviewed (and possibly revised) at a minimum of once per year to keep the amounts current.

Calculations for equivalent units of production for standard process costing are identical to those of FIFO process costing. Unlike the weighted average method, the emphasis of both standard costing and FIFO are on the measurement and control of current production and current period costs. The weighted average method com-

(Standard Costing)

Production Data
  Beginning inventory (100%, 40%)   15,000
  Units started   977,800
  Ending inventory (100%, 80%)   12,800

Standard Cost of Production
  Direct materials $ 92
  Direct labor   60
  Overhead   65

  Total $217

Equivalent Units of Production (repeated from Exhibit 8–8):

	DM	Conversion
BI (tons × % not complete at start of period)	0	9,000
Tons started and completed	965,000	965,000
EI (tons × % complete at end of period)	12,800	10,240
Equivalent units of production	977,800	984,240

mingles both units and costs of the prior period with the current period. This commingling reduces the emphasis on current effort that standard costing is intended to represent and measure.

The use of standard costs allows material, labor, and overhead variances to be measured during the period. To show the differences between using actual and standard process costing, the Fairmore Steel example presented in the chapter is used. The company's November production and standard cost information is given in Exhibit 8–14. The beginning inventory cost data have been restated from the original to reflect standard costs and to demonstrate the effect of consistent use of standard costs over successive periods. Beginning inventory consisted of 15,000 units that were fully complete as to the material and 40 percent complete as to conversion. Therefore, the standard cost of beginning inventory is:

Material (15,000 × 100% × $92)	$1,380,000
Labor (15,000 × 40% × $60)	360,000
Overhead (15,000 × 40% × $65)	390,000
Total	$2,130,000

Actual cost information for the month have been repeated from Exhibit 8–6. Exhibit 8–15 on page 326 presents the cost of production report using Fairmore Steel's standard cost information.[8]

When a standard cost system is in effect, inventories are stated at standard rather than actual costs. Summary journal entries for Fairmore Steel's November production, assuming a standard cost FIFO process costing system and amounts from Exhibit 8–15, are as follows.

---

[8]Total material, labor, and overhead variances are shown for Fairmore Steel in Exhibit 8–15. More detailed variances are presented in Chapters 11 and 12 on standard costing. Additionally, variances from actual costs must be closed at the end of a period. If the variances are immaterial, they can be closed to cost of goods sold; otherwise, they should be allocated among the inventory accounts and cost of goods sold.

(Standard Costing)				
COST TO BE ACCOUNTED FOR	**Direct Material**	**Direct Labor**	**Overhead**	**Total**
Total costs				
BWIP (at standard)	$ 1,380,000	$ 360,000	$ 390,000	$ 2,130,000
Current period (actual)	90,348,720	59,054,400	63,385,056	212,788,176
(1) Total	$91,728,720	$59,414,400	$63,775,056	$214,918,176
COST ASSIGNMENT (AT STANDARD)				
Transferred				
BI cost*	$ 1,380,000	$ 360,000	$ 390,000	$ 2,130,000
Cost to complete				
DL (9,000 × $60)		540,000		
OH (9,000 × $65)			585,000	
Total cost to complete				1,125,000
Started and completed				
DM (965,000 × $92)	88,780,000			
DL (965,000 × $60)		57,900,000		
OH (965,000 × $65)			62,725,000	
Total started and completed				209,405,000
Ending inventory				
DM (12,800 × $92)	1,177,600			
DL (10,240 × $60)		614,400		
OH (10,240 × $65)			665,600	
Total WIP ending				2,457,600
(2) Total standard assigned	$91,337,600	$59,414,400	$64,365,600	$215,117,600
Variances from				
actual (1 − 2)*	391,120	0	(590,544)	(199,424)
Total costs accounted for	$91,728,720	$59,414,400	$63,775,056	$214,918,176

NOTE: Favorable variances are shown in parentheses.
*Beginning work in process is carried at standard costs rather than actual. Therefore, no portion of the variance is attributable to BWIP. Any variance that might have been associated with BWIP effort made in the prior period was measured and identified with the prior period.

■ **EXHIBIT 8–15**

Fairmore Steel Cost of Production Report for Month Ended November 30, 1994

1. WIP Inventory is debited for the standard cost ($88,780,000) of material used to complete units that were started in November plus those used to produce ending work in process ($1,177,600). Raw Materials Inventory is credited for the actual cost of the materials withdrawn during November ($90,348,720).

Work in Process Inventory	89,957,600	
Direct Materials Variance	391,120	
Raw Materials Inventory		90,348,720

To record issuance of materials at standard and variance from standard.

2. WIP Inventory is debited for the standard cost of labor allowed based on the equivalent units produced in November. The EUP for the month reflect the production necessary to complete the beginning inventory tons (9,000) plus the tons started and completed (965,000) plus the work performed on the ending inventory tons (10,240) or a total of 984,240 EUP. Multiplying this equivalent production by the standard labor cost per ton of $60 gives a total of $59,054,400.

Work in Process Inventory   59,054,400
    Wages Payable   59,054,400
  To accrue direct labor cost and assign it to
  WIP Inventory at standard. Labor variance
  from standard did not occur.

3. Actual factory overhead incurred in November is $63,385,056.

Manufacturing Overhead   63,385,056
    Various accounts   63,385,056
  To record actual overhead cost for
  November.

4. WIP Inventory is debited for the standard cost of overhead based on the EUP produced in November. Since labor and overhead are performed at the same rate, equivalent production is the same as in entry 2: 984,240 EUP. Multiplying the EUP by the standard overhead application rate of $65 per ton gives $63,975,600.

Work in Process Inventory   63,975,600
    Manufacturing Overhead   63,385,056
    Manufacturing Overhead Variance   590,544
  To apply overhead to WIP Inventory.

5. Finished Goods Inventory is debited for the standard cost ($212,660,000) of all units completed during the month (15,000 + 965,000) or a total of 980,000 tons.

Finished Goods Inventory   212,660,000
    Work in Process Inventory   212,660,000
  To transfer standard cost of completed tons
  to finished goods.

KEY TERMS

Steps in Process Costing Computations

**SOLUTION
STRATEGIES**

1. Compute the total units to account for (in physical units):
    Beginning inventory in physical units
    + Units started (or transferred in) during period

2. Compute units accounted for (in physical units):
    Units completed and transferred
    + Ending inventory in physical units

3. Compute equivalent units of production per cost component:
   a. Weighted average
         Beginning inventory in physical units
       + Units started and completed*
       + (Ending inventory × % complete)
   b. FIFO
         (Beginning inventory × % *not* complete at start of period)
       + Units started and completed*
       + (Ending inventory × % complete)
   * Units started and completed = (Units transferred − Units in beginning inventory)

4. Compute total cost to account for:
         Costs in beginning inventory
       + Costs of current period

5. Compute cost per equivalent unit per cost component:
   a. Weighted average
         Cost of component in beginning inventory
       + Cost of component for current period
       = Total cost of component
       ÷ EUP for component
   b. FIFO
         Cost of component for current period
       ÷ EUP for component

6. Assign costs to inventories:
   a. Weighted average
      (1) Transferred:
          Units transferred × (Total cost per EUP for all components)
      (2) Ending inventory:
          EUP for each component × Cost per EUP for each component
   b. FIFO
      (1) Transferred:
            Beginning inventory costs
          + (Beginning inventory × % *not* complete at beginning of period for each component × Cost per EUP for each component)
          + (Units started and completed × Total cost per EUP for all components)
      (2) Ending inventory:
          EUP for each component × Cost per EUP for each component

DEMONSTRATION PROBLEM

The LaGuardia Company manufactures briefcases. During April, the following production data and costs have been gathered:

Units

Beginning work in process (100% complete for materials; 40% complete for conversion)	250
Units started	8,800
Ending work in process (100% complete for materials; 50% complete for conversion)	400

Costs

	Materials	Direct Labor	Overhead	Total
Beginning inventory	$ 3,755	$ 1,585	$ 1,185	$ 6,525
Current costs incurred	100,320	61,250	26,250	187,820
Totals	$104,075	$62,835	$27,435	$194,345

Required:

a. Calculate equivalent units of production under FIFO.

b. Determine FIFO unit costs.

c. Account for the costs under FIFO.

d. Calculate equivalent units of production under weighted average.

e. Determine weighted average unit costs.

f. Account for the costs under weighted average.

g. Reconcile your answers to parts a and d.

Solution to Demonstration Problem

	Whole Units	Direct Materials	Direct Labor	Overhead
		Equivalent Units of Production		
Beginning inventory	250			
Units started	8,800			
Units to account for	9,050			
Beginning inventory	250	0	150	150
Started and completed	8,400	8,400	8,400	8,400
Units completed	8,650			
Ending inventory	400	400	200	200
Units accounted for	9,050			
(a) FIFO EUP		8,800	8,750	8,750

	Total			
Current period costs	$187,820	$100,320	$61,250	$26,250
Divided by EUP		8,800	8,750	8,750
(b) Cost per EUP	$21.40	$11.40	$7.00	$3.00

(c) Cost Assignment
Transferred

Beginning inventory cost	$ 6,525	
Cost to complete		
Direct labor (150 × $7.00)	1,050	
Overhead (150 × $3.00)	450	
Cost of beginning inventory transferred	$ 8,025	
Started and completed (8,400 × $21.40)	179,760	$187,785
Ending inventory		
Direct materials (400 × $11.40)	$ 4,560	
Direct labor (200 × $7.00)	1,400	
Overhead (200 × $3.00)	600	6,560
Total cost accounted for		$194,345

	Whole Units	Equivalent Units of Production		
		Direct Materials	Direct Labor	Overhead
Beginning inventory	250	250	100	100
Units started	8,800			
Units to account for	9,050			
Beginning inventory	250	0	150	150
Started and completed	8,400	8,400	8,400	8,400
Units completed	8,650			
Ending inventory	400	400	200	200
Units accounted for	9,050			
(d) Weighted average EUP		9,050	8,850	8,850

	Total			
BWIP costs	$ 6,525	$ 3,755	$ 1,585	$ 1,185
Current period costs	187,820	100,320	61,250	26,250
Total costs	$194,345	$104,075	$62,835	$27,435
Divided by EUP		9,050	8,850	8,850
(e) Cost per EUP	$21.70	$11.50	$7.10	$3.10

(f) Cost Assignment
Transferred (8,650 × $21.70) $187,705
Ending inventory
   Direct materials (400 × $11.50) $4,600
   Direct labor (200 × $7.10)   1,420
   Overhead (200 × $3.10)   620   6,640

Total cost accounted for $194,345

(g) Reconciliation:

	Direct Materials	Direct Labor	Overhead
FIFO EUP	8,800	8,750	8,750
+ Beginning WIP from last period	250	100	100
WA EUP	9,050	8,850	8,850

QUESTIONS

1. What are the typical characteristics of a company that should employ a process costing system?

2. How are job order and process costing different? How are they similar?

3. Why is the process of assigning costs to products essentially an averaging process?

4. What is the difference between weighted average and FIFO equivalent units of production? Which more accurately portrays the actual flow of units through a manufacturing process and why?

5. Why is it necessary to prepare separate equivalent units of production schedules for each cost component of a product? Are there times when separate EUP schedules would not be necessary and, if so, why?

6. How are units "started and completed" in the current period calculated? Is this figure used in both weighted average and FIFO cost assignment? Why or why not?

7. In which of the six basic steps used in inventory valuation are physical units used and in which are equivalent units of production used?

8. How are the unit costs for each cost component assigned to the units produced during the current period under (a) the weighted average method and (b) the FIFO method?

9. How does process costing differ in a multidepartmental manufacturing environment from a single department manufacturing environment? Why does this difference exist?

10. What is a hybrid costing system? Under what circumstances is the use of such a system appropriate?

11. *(Appendix 2)* Why are the EUP calculations made for standard process costing the same as the EUP calculations for FIFO process costing?

12. *(Appendix 2)* Standard process costing may often give rise to variances during the period. Why is this true and how are such variances handled at the end of the period?

EXERCISES

13. *(EUP; weighted average)* La Chaca Pasta uses a weighted average process costing system. All materials are added at the start of the production process and direct labor and overhead are added at the same rate throughout the process. La Chaca records indicate the following production for February 1994:

Beginning inventory (70% complete as to conversion)   2,000 units
Started during February   7,000 units
Completed during February   6,000 units

Ending inventory for February is 20 percent complete as to conversion.
a. What are the equivalent units of production for direct materials?
b. What are the equivalent units of production for labor and overhead?

14. *(EUP; FIFO)* Assume that La Chaca Pasta in Exercise 13 uses the FIFO method of process costing.
a. What are the equivalent units of production for direct materials?
b. What are the equivalent units of production for labor and overhead?

15. *(Cost per EUP; weighted average)* Rawhide Inc. manufactures cologne in a mass production process. In March 1994, company production is 13,400 equivalent units (bottles) for direct materials, 12,200 equivalent units for labor, and 10,500 equivalent units for overhead. During March, direct materials and conversion costs incurred are as follows:

Direct materials $ 78,880
Conversion   122,400
Overhead   42,600

Beginning inventory costs for March were $14,920 for direct materials, $36,200 for labor, and $9,900 for overhead. What is the weighted average cost per equivalent unit for the cost components for March?

16. *(Cost per EUP; FIFO)* Assume that Rawhide Inc. in Exercise 15 had 1,800 EUP for direct materials in March's beginning inventory, 2,000 EUP for direct labor, and 1,980 EUP for overhead. What was the FIFO cost per equivalent unit for direct materials, labor, and overhead for March?

17. *(Cost assignment; weighted average)* The California Cannery operates a food processing plant. One of its products is canned ripe olives. During June 1995, the company had the following production and cost information:

Cans of completed products	440,000 lbs.
Cans in process at end of month	31,000 lbs.

(100% complete as to olives; 70% complete
as to direct labor; 80% complete as to overhead;
0% complete as to can)

Cost data:

Olives	$.25 per equivalent pound of production
Direct labor	.29 per equivalent pound of production
Overhead	.12 per equivalent pound of production
Can	.04 per can

Each can contains 1 pound of olives.

a. What is the cost of the completed production for June 1995?

b. What is the cost of the ending Work in Process Inventory for June 1995?

18. *(EUP for weighted average & FIFO; reconciliation)* Lectrocharge manufactures 60-month car batteries in its plant in Pittsburgh. On August 1, 1995, the company had 8,000 units in its beginning Work in Process Inventory. Each unit was 100 percent complete as to material and 85 percent complete as to conversion costs. During August, the company started 100,000 additional units, and completed and transferred 84,000 units to its finished goods warehouse. Units in ending Work in Process Inventory were 100 percent complete as to material and 60 percent complete as to conversion costs.

a. Calculate the weighted average equivalent units of production.

b. Calculate the FIFO equivalent units of production.

c. Reconcile the calculations of weighted average and FIFO equivalent units of production.

19. *(EUP for weighted average)* Vermont's Finest produces maple syrup in a continuous flow production process. The company uses process costing based on the weighted average method to assign production costs to products. All material is added at the beginning of the process; direct labor costs are incurred evenly throughout the process. The following information is available on the direct labor costs and physical unit activity for January 1995:

	Gallons of Syrup	Direct Labor Costs
Beginning inventory	25,000	$ 8,715
Completed this period	80,000	41,000
Ending inventory	15,000	

The beginning and ending inventories for January are, respectively, 80 percent and 10 percent complete as to direct labor costs.

a. Determine the equivalent units of production for direct labor in January.

b. Determine the cost per equivalent unit of production for direct labor in January.

20. *(EUP; weighted average & FIFO)* MegaBlaster Inc. manufactures canisters of mace that are sold through a variety of retail stores. On October 1, 1994, the company had 1,600 units in beginning Work in Process Inventory that were 100 percent complete as to canisters, 60 percent complete as to other materials, 10 percent complete as to direct labor, and 20 percent complete as to overhead. During October, the company started 7,500 units into the manufacturing process. The ending Work in Process Inventory included 1,200 units that were 100 percent complete as to canisters, 30 percent complete as to other materials, 15 percent complete as to direct labor, and 30 percent complete as to overhead. Prepare a schedule showing MegaBlaster Inc.'s October 1994 computation of both weighted average and FIFO equivalent units of production.

21. *(EUP; weighted average & FIFO)* The New Wave Board Co. makes sailboards. The company began November with 500 boards in process that were 70 percent complete as to materials and 85 percent complete as to conversion costs. During the month, 1,900 additional boards were started. On November 30, 400 boards

were still in process (60 percent complete as to materials and 70 percent complete as to conversion costs).
  a. Present the physical flow of units.
  b. Calculate EUP using the weighted average method.
  c. Calculate EUP using the FIFO method.
  d. *(Appendix 1)* Verify answers to parts b and c using an alternative method.

22. *(Cost per EUP for weighted average)* The Boston Beanery produces baked beans and employs a process costing system based on the weighted average method to assign costs to production. Various materials are added at discrete stages in the production process while direct labor and factory overhead are incurred evenly throughout the process. For the first week in June 1995, the company experienced the following results:

Gallons of beans in beginning inventory	4,000
Gallons of beans started	30,000
Gallons of beans completed	24,000

For the same week, relevant costs were as follows:

	Direct Labor	Factory Overhead
Beginning inventory	$ 1,200	$ 1,425
Costs of the current week	10,000	11,400

Also for this week, the beginning inventory was 25 percent complete as to direct labor and 40 percent complete as to overhead. The ending inventory was 40 percent complete as to direct labor and 45 percent complete as to overhead.
  a. Compute equivalent units of production for direct labor and overhead.
  b. For direct labor and overhead, compute the cost per equivalent unit of production.
  c. For direct labor and overhead, determine the cost of the ending inventory and the cost transferred to finished goods.

23. *(Cost per EUP for FIFO)* Little Rock Chemical Company uses a FIFO costing system. Some summary information for September 1994 regarding direct labor costs follows:

Beginning WIP inventory (80% complete as to labor)	3,000,000 drums
Units started	15,000,000 drums
Ending WIP inventory (30% complete as to labor)	5,000,000 drums
Direct labor cost per equivalent unit	$0.85
Direct labor costs transferred	$9,116,000

Compute the cost of:
  a. direct labor in the beginning Work in Process Inventory for September.
  b. direct labor assigned to the ending Work in Process Inventory.

24. *(EUP; cost per EUP; cost assignment; FIFO & weighted average)* The Hi Fidelity Sound Co. mass produces miniature speakers to attach to portable cassette players. The following T-account presents the firm's production information for February 1994:

WORK IN PROCESS INVENTORY

2/1 Balance of direct materials	$ 1,027	
2/1 Balance of conversion costs	588	
DM issued to production	11,682	
DL applied to production	2,513	
OH applied to production	1,257	

The company had 800 units in process on February 1. These units were 40 percent complete as to materials and 30 percent complete as to conversion cost. During February, the firm started 3,000 units and ended the month with 300 units still in process. The units in ending WIP Inventory were 20 percent complete

Standard Cost of 1 Unit

Direct materials	$ 4.50
Conversion costs	12.50
Total manufacturing cost	$17.00

Beginning WIP inventory	10,000 units (100% DM; 70% Conversion)
Started in July	180,000 units
Completed in July	160,000 units
Ending WIP inventory	? units (100% DM; 60% Conversion)

Actual costs for July

Direct materials	$ 781,000
Conversion	2,045,000
Total actual cost	$2,826,000

a. Prepare a FIFO equivalent units of production schedule.
b. Prepare a cost of production report and assign costs to inventories.
c. Label the variances that exist and charge them to Cost of Goods Sold.

CASE

44. Kristina Company, which manufactures quality paint sold at premium prices, uses a single production department. Production begins with the blending of various chemicals, which are added at the beginning of the process, and ends with the canning of the paint. Canning occurs when the mixture reaches the 90 percent stage of completion. The gallon cans are then transferred to the Shipping Department for crating and shipment. Labor and overhead are added continuously throughout the process. Factory overhead is applied on the basis of direct labor hours at the rate of $3 per hour.

Prior to May, when a change in the process was implemented, work in process inventories were insignificant. The change in process enables greater production but results in material amounts of work in process for the first time. The company has always used the weighted average method to determine equivalent production and unit costs. Now, production management is considering changing from the weighted average method to the first in, first out method.

The following data relate to actual production during the month of May:

Costs for May

Work in process inventory, May 1
(4,000 gallons 25% complete)

Direct materials—chemicals	$ 45,600
Direct labor ($10 per hour)	6,250
Factory overhead	1,875

May costs added

Direct materials—chemicals	228,400
Direct materials—cans	7,000
Direct labor ($10 per hour)	35,000
Factory overhead	10,500

Units for May (Gallons)

Work in process inventory, May 1 (25% complete)	4,000
Sent to Shipping Department	20,000
Started in May	21,000
Work in process inventory, May 31 (80% complete)	5,000

a. Prepare a schedule of equivalent units for each cost element for the month of May using the
   1. weighted average method.   2. FIFO method.

b. Calculate the cost (to the nearest cent) per equivalent unit for each element for the month of May using the
   1. weighted average method.   2. FIFO method.
c. Discuss the advantages and disadvantages of using the weighted average method versus the FIFO method, and explain under what circumstances each method should be used.

(CMA)

ETHICS AND QUALITY DISCUSSION

45. Pharmaceutical companies make most drugs in mass production processes after the products are cleared for sale by the Food and Drug Administration. Additionally, they spend huge amounts of money on research and development; the estimated cost of bringing a drug to market is almost $200 million. However, a study by the Office of Technology Assessment said:

the pharmaceutical industry earns at least $36 million more than development costs on each new drug and is able to raise prices for brand name drugs even after they lose patent protection. The surplus return amounts to about 4.3% of the price of each drug over its product life, and the profit margin is two to three percentage points higher than in other industries.

[SOURCE: "Drug Profits Said to Outstrip R&D Costs," *Wall Street Journal* (February 26, 1993), p. B6.]

a. Which of the following types of costs do you think would be the highest for manufacturing pharmaceuticals: materials, labor, or overhead? (Remember that past R&D costs cannot currently be included in overhead because they were expensed when incurred.) What kind of costing system would be most applicable to the pharmaceutical industry and why?
b. Is the pharmaceutical industry engaging in life-cycle costing as discussed in Chapter 5? If so, how?
c. President Clinton has called drug prices "shocking." Do you believe that pharmaceutical companies should be allowed to earn a significantly higher rate of return than companies in other industries? Why or why not?
d. Is it ethical to charge high prices for drugs that are life-essential for users? For drugs that are non-life-essential? Discuss the rationale for your answer(s).

46. *Quantex makes high-quality steel for specialized applications like ball bearings, camshafts, and tank treads. Most of the armor of Desert Storm rode to victory on Quantex steel.*

The company keeps almost no inventory—a lesson learned from the days when steel produced for the oil patch rusted on its lots. At the company's Fort Smith, Arkansas, facility, every batch of steel is a custom-recipe, sold before it's even cooked in the pot. When cool, it is bar-coded with the owner's name and address.

Mill workers get a bonus based on the amount of steel shipped, minus any defective steel that comes back. That gives them an incentive to make defect-free steel using as few people as possible. Quantex takes about 1.9 man-hours to produce a ton of steel, vs. about four hours for a big integrated mill. Other mini-mill companies are about as efficient as Quantex, but their commodity-grade reinforcing bars sell for roughly $300 a ton, while Quantex specialty steel fetches around $500.

[SOURCE: Peter Nulty, "The Less-Is-More Strategy," *FORTUNE* (December 2, 1991), pp. 102–103. © 1991 Time Inc. All rights reserved.]

a. Discuss the applicability of use to Quantex of a traditional process costing system, a standard process costing system, and a hybrid costing system.
b. What two reasons can be given for such a wide selling price differential for rebars between Quantex and the other mini-mills? Which of these do you think has more influence on the high selling price and why?
c. Why is quality an extremely important issue for steel producers?

SPECIAL PRODUCTION ISSUES: SPOILED/DEFECTIVE UNITS AND ACCRETION

LEARNING OBJECTIVES

After completing this chapter, you should be able to answer these questions:

1. Why do lost units occur in manufacturing processes?
2. What is the difference between normal and abnormal spoilage?
3. How is each type of spoilage treated in the EUP schedule?
4. How are the costs of each type of spoilage assigned?
5. How is spoilage handled in a job order costing system?
6. How does accretion of units affect the EUP schedule and costs per unit?
7. How are rework costs of defective units treated?
8. What is the cost of quality products?

INTRODUCING

SENCO PRODUCTS

A privately held company headquartered in Cincinnati, Senco Products, is the world's largest manufacturer of industrial fastening systems. These include pneumatic staple guns of all sizes as well as the staples and nails they use. These guns and fasteners are used in many industries. They fasten wood and panels in such items as furniture, mobile homes, cars, and trucks.

Senco's product quality has always been good, [but the company wanted to make it even better.] Senco had to change its corporate culture to become obsessive about quality. Then the company had to implement its quality goals in production.

"Our first step in changing our culture was to develop a quality policy," says William Been, director of fastener manufacturing. "We decided that our policy was to meet customer requirements with defect-free products and excellence as the standard." This sounds innocuous enough, but a careful look at the components of this policy unearth some important assumptions.

"Defect-free products" means just that. It is common in manufacturing for companies to judge their quality performance on something called an "accepted quality level" (AQL). If the percentage of defective products falls below its AQL, the company considers it has met its quality goals.

At Senco, the AQL is zero. Every product must meet requirements.

SOURCE: "Quality Equals Perfection at Cincinnati Fastener Systems Company," [Grant Thornton] Manufacturing Issues (Winter 1990), p. 8. Reprinted by permission from Grant Thornton's Manufacturing Issues. © Grant Thornton 1990.

P roducing goods with zero defects is a laudable goal and one toward which domestic and foreign companies are striving. The situations shown in Chapter 8 are based on the assumption that all units to be accounted for have either been transferred or are in ending work in process; however, almost every process produces some units that are spoiled or do not meet production specifications. It is also possible that phenomena in the production process may cause the total number of units accounted for to be less than the total number of units to account for. In other situations (unrelated to spoiled units), the addition or expansion of materials after the start of the process may cause the number of units accounted for to be greater than those to be accounted for originally or in a previous department.

This chapter covers some of these more complex issues of process costing. Spoiled and defective units, reworking of defective units, and accretion require adjustments to the equivalent units of production schedule shown in the previous chapter. The cost assignments made at the end of a period must be modified because of these special occurrences. The last section of the chapter discusses the concept of controlling quality so that there is only minimal production of inferior goods.

LOSS OF UNITS

Spoilage

Economically reworked

Defective unit
Spoiled unit

Normal loss

Abnormal loss

There are few, if any, processes that combine materials, labor, and overhead with no loss of units. Any occurrence in the production process that causes units to be rejected at an inspection point for failure to meet the appropriate standard of quality or the designated product specifications creates **spoilage**. Whether units are defective or truly spoiled depends on their ability to be economically reworked to a sufficient level to be salable through normal distribution channels. **Economically reworked** means that the incremental revenue from the sale of reworked units is greater than the incremental rework cost. A **defective unit** can be economically reworked, but a **spoiled unit** is one in which the degree of unacceptability is so great that it cannot be reworked at all or cannot be economically reworked to be brought up to standard. This differentiation is determined by an inspector in the producing company.

To illustrate the difference between defective and spoiled units, assume that you go into a restaurant and order a medium-rare steak. You are now the control inspector. If the steak brought to you is rare, it is a defective unit since the chef can cook it longer to bring it up to "product specifications." The incremental revenue is the selling price of the steak; the incremental cost is a few moments of the chef's time. However, if the steak brought to you is well-done, it is a spoiled unit since it cannot be reworked. Therefore, a newly cooked steak would have to be provided.

A **normal loss** of units falls within a tolerance level expected during production. The range of tolerance specified by management creates what is referred to in the opening vignette as the accepted quality level (AQL). If Senco had set its quality goal as 98 percent of goods produced, the company would have been expecting a normal loss of 2 percent. Any loss in excess of the AQL is an **abnormal loss**. Thus, the difference between normal and abnormal loss is merely one of degree and is determined by management.

A variety of methods may be used to account for units lost during production. Selection of the most appropriate method depends on two factors: (1) the cause of the decrease and (2) management expectations regarding lost units. Understanding why units decreased during production requires detailed knowledge of the manufacturing process. Management's expectations are important to determine the acceptable loss quantities from defects, spoilage, or shrinkage as well as the revenue and cost considerations of defective and spoiled units. This chapter presents a general approach for the treatment of all types of lost units. Accounting for spoiled units is emphasized in the chapter to minimize any redundant treatment.

TYPES OF SPOILAGE

Normal spoilage

In developing the product design, manufacturing process, and product quality, management selects a combination of materials, labor, and overhead from the wide resource spectrum available. This combination is chosen to provide the lowest long-run cost per unit *and* to achieve the designated product specifications—including those for quality. In making this resource combination choice, managers recognize that, for most combinations, some degree of production error will occur that will result in spoiled units. Given the resource choices made by management, the amount of spoilage to be generated in a given period or production run should be reasonably estimable. This estimate is called **normal spoilage** because it is planned for and expected. Normal spoilage is usually calculated on the basis of good output or actual input. It may be estimated in absolute quantities of units or in percentage terms.

Some companies may estimate the spoilage quantity to be quite high because the lowest cost material, labor, or overhead support is chosen. For example, assume that Poore Manufacturing Corp. chooses to install the least advanced, lowest cost machinery for production purposes because its workers do not have the educational or technological skills to handle the more advanced equipment. The installed equipment may have fewer quality checks and, thus, produce more spoiled units than the more advanced equipment. Poore's managers have made the choice that the costs of up-grading worker skills were greater than the cost of spoiled units. Such a decision would be in total contrast to the one made by the managers at Delta Wire in Clarks-dale, Mississippi. Rather than allow the low education of workers to raise spoilage levels, the company decided to raise the employees' educational levels and reduce spoilage, as described in the News Note "Increased Education" on page 348.

Another reason for high estimated spoilage relates not to the resources chosen, but to a problem inherent in the design or production process. For instance, the entire first batch of product manufactured by Prolight in Holland, Michigan was defective because of a design flaw. In other cases, based on cost-benefit analysis, managers may find that a problem would cost more to eliminate than to tolerate. For example, as-sume a machine malfunctions once every 100 runs and improperly blends ingredients. The machine processes 50,000 runs each year and the ingredients in each run cost $10. Correcting the problem has been estimated to cost $20,000 per year. Spoilage cost is $5,000 per year (500 spoiled batches × $10 worth of ingredients) plus a mini-mal amount of overhead costs. If company personnel is aware of the malfunction and catches every improperly blended run, it is less expensive to accept the spoilage than to correct the problem.

If, on the other hand, the spoiled runs are allowed to leave the plant, they may create substantial quality failure costs in the form of dissatisfied customers and/or salespeople who might receive the spoiled product. Exhibit 9–1 provides estimates of the cost of unhappy customers. In making their cost-benefit analysis, managers must be certain to quantify *all* the costs (both direct and indirect) involved in spoilage problems.

Abnormal spoilage is spoilage in excess of the normal, predicted tolerance limits. Thus, when abnormal spoilage occurs, so does normal spoilage (unless zero defects have been set as the AQL). Abnormal spoilage generally arises because of human or machine error during the production process. For example, if the tolerances on one of Senco's machines were set incorrectly, a significant quantity of incorrect-sized fas-teners might be produced before the error was noticed. Abnormal spoilage is more likely to be preventable than some types of normal spoilage.

Abnormal spoilage

While spoilage during a production process realistically takes place at a specific point, accounting for spoilage requires that it be specified as being either continuous

EXHIBIT 9–1

The Cost of Unhappy Customers

Potential Annual Revenue Loss from Dissatisfied Buyers

IF YOU LOSE	1 customer per day	5 customers per day	10 customers per day
spending $5 weekly	$ 94,900	$ 474,500	$ 949,000
spending $10 weekly	$ 189,800	$ 949,000	$ 1,898,000
spending $50 weekly	$ 949,000	$4,745,000	$ 9,490,000
spending $100 weekly	$1,898,000	$9,490,000	$18,980,000

SOURCE: Customer Service Institute, "The Unhappy Customer," *Black Enterprise* (June 1991), p. 234. The Earl Graves Publishing Co., Inc., copyright June 1991.

Increased Education Causes Reduced Spoilage

Delta Wire Corporation is a manufacturer of high carbon specialty steel wire for global markets. Delta Wire found itself caught in a potentially disastrous bind. Foreign competition was a growing threat to its market position and industry quality requirements were moving higher year by year. Delta knew it must meet the challenge of adhering to these standards.

To counter these negative conditions, which were beyond its control, Delta vigorously attacked the one area within its reach—employee education.

In 1990, the company began working with the training programs developed by the State of Mississippi and the local community college to set up its own school. There, employees were introduced to such sophisticated topics as advanced statistical process control and other quality assurance techniques.

[Company president George Walker is quite pleased with the results, saying that productivity, measured in the amount of usable production compared to spoiled production, has jumped 20 percent since the education program was begun.]

SOURCE: The Blue Chip Enterprise Initiative, *Strengthening America's Competitiveness* (U.S.A.: Connecticut Mutual, 1991), p. 87.

Continuous spoilage

Shrinkage

Discrete spoilage

or discrete. For example, the relatively continual breakage of fragile glass Christmas tree ornaments could be considered **continuous spoilage** because it occurs fairly uniformly throughout the production process. Another continuous reduction in units often arises from **shrinkage** caused by an inherent characteristic of the production process, such as evaporation, leakage, or oxidation. It may be difficult, impossible, or simply not cost-beneficial to modify the production process to reduce or eliminate the causes of shrinkage. (Because shrinkage causes the same type of unit reduction as continuous spoilage, these two occurrences will be jointly considered as continuous spoilage although, technically, they differ.)

Discrete spoilage is assumed to occur precisely at an inspection point, although it may actually take place at any point before inspection. Examples of discrete spoilage include adding the wrong amount of dye to a vat or sewing a collar on a garment backwards. Each of these occurrences might not be noticed until some quality check is made. Thus, the units past the inspection point should be good units, while the units prior to this point may be good or may be spoiled.

Regardless of when the spoilage occurs, it is normally detected only at quality control points. Control points can be either built into the system or performed by inspectors. The former requires investments in prevention costs; the latter results in appraisal costs. Both are effective, but prevention is often more efficient. This statement is based on the fact that acceptable quality cannot be inspected into a product; it must be a part of the production process. Investments to prevent defects and spoilage may relate to either people or machines, as indicated in the following News Note "Invest in Quality," and both should provide high benefits.

In determining how many quality control (or inspection) points to have (machine or human), management must weigh the costs of having more inspections against the savings resulting from: (1) not applying additional materials, labor, and overhead to products that are already spoiled (direct savings) and (2) the reduction or elimination of internal and external failure costs (indirect savings). As mentioned in the appendix to Chapter 5, quality control points should always be placed before any bottlenecks in the system. Additionally, continuous spoilage requires a quality control point at the end of production, because otherwise some spoiled units would not be found and would be sent to customers.

ACCOUNTING FOR SPOILAGE

The traditional method of accounting for normal spoilage is simple. Normal spoilage cost is considered a product cost and is included as part of the cost of the *good* units resulting from the process. Thus, the cost of spoilage is inventoried in Work in Process and Finished Goods Inventories and expensed only when the good units are sold. This treatment is considered appropriate because normal spoilage has traditionally been viewed as an unavoidable cost in the production of good units. In today's world-class environments, however, many companies like Senco are instituting zero-defect policies that indicate there should be no "normal" spoilage. *All* spoilage would be outside the tolerance specifications for acceptable quality.

The cost of abnormal spoilage should be accumulated and treated as a loss in the period in which it occurred. This treatment is justified by the cost principle discussed in financial accounting. The cost principle allows only costs that are necessary to acquire or produce inventory to attach to it. All unnecessary costs are written off in the period in which they are incurred. Since abnormal spoilage is not necessary to the production of good units and its cost is avoidable in the future, the cost of abnormal spoilage is regarded as a period cost. The cost of abnormal spoilage should be brought to the attention of the manager responsible for production. The manager should investigate the causes of the spoilage to determine how to prevent future similar occurrences.

Treating normal spoilage cost as a product cost and abnormal spoilage as a period cost is appropriate regardless of whether the spoilage is continuous or discrete. However, it is necessary to understand the point at which the spoilage occurred to properly determine the amount and assignment of the spoilage cost.

Exhibit 9–2 on page 350 indicates how the costs of continuous and discrete spoilage are treated. The cost of normal, continuous spoilage is handled through the **method of neglect,** which simply excludes the spoiled units in the equivalent units schedule. Ignoring the spoilage results in a smaller number of equivalent units of production (EUP) and, by default, raises the cost per equivalent unit. Thus, the cost of the spoiled units is spread proportionately over the good units transferred and those remaining in Work in Process Inventory.

Method of neglect

Type	Assumed to Occur	May Be	Cost Handled How?	Cost Assigned To?
Continuous	Uniformly throughout process	Normal	Absorbed by all units in ending inventory and transferred out on an EUP basis	Product
		or		
		Abnormal	Written off as a loss on an EUP basis	Period
Discrete	At inspection point or at end of process	Normal	Absorbed by all units past inspection point on an EUP basis	Product
		or		
		Abnormal	Written off as a loss on an EUP basis	Period

■ EXHIBIT 9–2

Continuous versus Discrete Spoilage

The cost of normal, discrete spoilage is assigned only to the good units that have passed the inspection point. Normal, discrete spoilage is assumed to occur precisely at the inspection point; therefore, the units past this point should be good units, while the units prior to this point may be good or may be spoiled. It is improper to assign spoilage costs to units that may themselves be spoiled. If the units in ending Work in Process Inventory have passed the inspection point, they are assigned a pro rata share of the spoilage cost. If ending inventory units have not passed the inspection point, no spoilage cost is assigned to them. All units transferred out of the department are assigned some spoilage cost since they were inspected and found to be good units.

Regardless of whether spoilage occurs in a continuous or discrete fashion, the cost of abnormal spoilage is *always* accounted for on an equivalent unit basis and is assigned to a loss account during the period in which the spoilage occurred.

ILLUSTRATIONS OF SPOILAGE

To best understand how to account for a process that creates spoiled goods, it is helpful to know the answers to the following questions:

1. What is the flow of the process?
2. Where is material added during the process?
3. How are labor and overhead applied? (Usually continuously, but not necessarily at the same rate)
4. At what stage of completion was the beginning, and is the ending, inventory?
5. Where are the quality control inspection points?
6. How does spoilage occur? (Continuous or discrete?)

Senco's production line has been designed to minimize the number of units spoiled during processing. Investments in mechanical control devices reduce the need for human inspection.

So Tacky Inc. is used to illustrate several alternative situations regarding the handling of spoilage in a process costing environment. So Tacky manufactures a variety of adhesives, including Glue-All, in a single department. All materials are added at the start of the Glue-All production process. Conversion costs are applied uniformly throughout the process. Containers are provided by buyers and, therefore, are not a cost of So Tacky Inc. The company uses the FIFO method of calculating equivalent units.

Situation 1—Normal Shrinkage Only; Shrinkage Occurs Throughout Production Process (Continuous)

Glue-All is mechanically blended during processing and there is a normal loss from shinkage because ingredients adhere to the mixing machine and harden. Any decrease of less than 10 percent of the gallons placed into production for the period is considered normal. The June 1994 data for So Tacky Inc. is given below:

Gallons

Beginning inventory (60% complete)	2,000
Started during month	15,000
Gallons completed and transferred	13,200
Ending inventory (75% complete)	2,500
Lost gallons (normal)	1,300

Costs

Beginning inventory:		
Material	$15,000	
Conversion	1,620	$ 16,620
Current period:		
Material	$102,750	
Conversion	19,425	122,175
Total costs		$138,795

To visualize the manufacturing process for So Tacky, a flow diagram can be constructed. Such a diagram provides distinct, definitive answers to all of the questions asked at the beginning of this section.

Flow Diagram

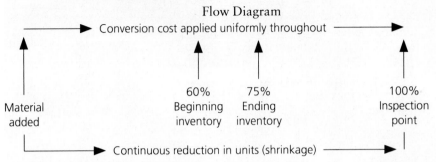

The steps discussed in Chapter 8 on process costing are followed to determine the units accountable for, units accounted for, equivalent units of production, costs accountable for, cost per equivalent unit, and cost assignment. These steps are presented in the cost of production report shown in Exhibit 9–3.

EXHIBIT 9–3

So Tacky Inc. Cost of Production Report for Month Ended June 30, 1994 (FIFO method) (Normal continuous shrinkage)

PRODUCTION DATA		EQUIVALENT UNITS	
	Whole Units	**Materials**	**Conversion**
Beginning inventory (60%)	2,000		
+ Gallons started	15,000		
= Gallons to account for	17,000		
Beginning inventory (completed)	2,000	0	800
+ Gallons started and completed	11,200	11,200	11,200
= Total gallons completed	13,200		
+ Ending inventory (75%)	2,500	2,500	1,875
+ Normal loss	1,300		
= Gallons accounted for	17,000	13,700	13,875

COST DATA			
	Total	**Materials**	**Conversion**
Beginning inventory costs	$ 16,620		
Current costs	122,175	$102,750	$19,425
Total costs	$138,795		
Divided by EUP		13,700	13,875
Cost per FIFO EUP	$8.90	$7.50	$1.40

COST ASSIGNMENT

Transferred:			
From beginning inventory	$16,620		
Cost to complete: Conversion (800 × $1.40)	1,120		
Total cost of beginning inventory	$17,740		
Started and completed (11,200 × $8.90)	99,680		
Total cost of gallons transferred			$117,420
Ending Inventory:			
Material (2,500 × $7.50)	$18,750		
Conversion (1,875 × $1.40)	2,625		21,375
Total costs accounted for			$138,795

The department is accountable for 17,000 gallons of Glue-All: 2,000 gallons in beginning inventory plus 15,000 gallons started into processing during June. Only 15,700 gallons (13,200 completed and 2,500 in ending inventory) are accounted for prior to considering the processing loss. The 1,300 lost gallons are included in the schedule of gallons accounted for in order to account for the total 17,000 gallons, but these gallons are not extended into the computation of equivalent units of production. By allowing these gallons to simply "disappear" in the EUP schedule (using the method of neglect), the cost per equivalent gallon of the remaining good production of the period is higher for each cost component.

Had these lost gallons been used in the denominator of the cost per EUP computation, the cost per EUP would have been smaller than otherwise. For example, if the 1,300 gallons had been included in the calculation of EUP, the materials cost per unit would have been $6.85 ($102,750 ÷ 15,000). Since the lost units do not appear in the Cost Assignment section because their costs must be assigned only to good production, the use of the lower cost per EUP would not allow all of the costs to be accounted for in Exhibit 9–3.

Accounting for normal, continuous shrinkage (or spoilage) is the easiest of all the spoilage computations. There is, however, a theoretical problem with this computation when a company uses weighted average process costing. The units in ending Work in Process Inventory have spoilage cost assigned to them in the current period and will have spoilage assigned *again* in the next period. But, even with this flaw, this method provides a reasonable measure of unit cost if the rate of spoilage is consistent from period to period.

Situation 2—Normal Spoilage Only; Spoilage Determined at Final Inspection Point in Production Process (Discrete)

This example uses the same basic cost and unit information given above for So Tacky Inc. except there are no machine malfunctions. Instead, the Glue-All compound is inspected at the end of the production process. Any spoiled gallons are removed and discarded at inspection; spoilage is usually caused by an improper blending of a batch of compound. Any spoilage of 10 percent or less of the gallons placed into production during the period is considered normal. A production flow diagram is shown below.

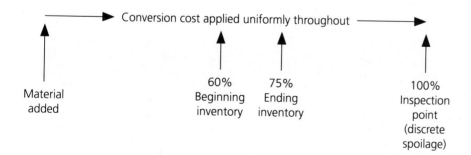

In this situation, the gallons of product that are spoiled *are* included in the equivalent unit schedule. Since the inspection point is at 100 percent completion, all work has been performed on the spoiled gallons and all costs have been incurred to produce those gallons. By including the spoiled gallons at 100 percent completion in the EUP schedule, cost per gallon reflects the cost that *would have been incurred* had all production been good production.

Cost of the spoiled gallons is assigned solely to the completed units. Since ending Work in Process Inventory has not yet passed the inspection point, this inventory may contain its own normal spoilage that will be detected next period. The cost of production report for Situation 2 is shown in Exhibit 9–4.

EXHIBIT 9–4
So Tacky Inc. Cost of
Production Report for
Month Ended June 30,
1994 (FIFO method)
(Normal discrete spoilage)

PRODUCTION DATA		EQUIVALENT UNITS	
	Whole Units	Materials	Conversion
Beginning inventory (60%)	2,000		
+ Gallons started	15,000		
= Gallons to account for	17,000		
Beginning inventory (completed)	2,000	0	800
+ Gallons started and completed	11,200	11,200	11,200
= Total gallons completed	13,200		
+ Ending inventory (75%)	2,500	2,500	1,875
+ Normal spoilage	1,300	1,300	1,300
= Gallons accounted for	17,000	15,000	15,175

COST DATA			
	Total	Materials	Conversion
Beginning inventory costs	$ 16,620		
Current costs	122,175	$102,750	$19,425
Total costs	$138,795		
Divided by EUP		15,000	15,175
Cost per FIFO EUP	$8.13	$6.85	$1.28

COST ASSIGNMENT

Transferred:			
From beginning inventory		$ 16,620	
Cost to complete: Conversion (800 × $1.28)		1,024	
Total cost of beginning inventory		$ 17,644	
Started and completed (11,200 × $8.13)		91,056	
Normal spoilage (1,300 × $8.13)*		10,569	
Total cost of gallons transferred (13,200 × $9.04)**			$119,269
Ending Inventory:			
Material (2,500 × $6.85)		$ 17,125	
Conversion (1,875 × $1.28)		2,400	19,525
Total costs accounted for (off due to rounding)			$138,794

*NOTE: All spoilage cost is assigned to the units transferred.
**For convenience and clerical efficiency, modified FIFO (described in the previous chapter) is used. Otherwise, spoilage would have to be allocated to beginning WIP and units started and completed. Notice that the $9.04 figure is also computed as the sum of the $8.24 cost [($17,644 + $91,056) ÷ 13,200] per good EUP plus another $.80. This $.80 is simply the cost of spoilage ($10,569) divided by the 13,200 good units transferred.

Situation 3—Normal Spoilage Only; Spoilage Determined During Production Process (Discrete)

In this example, So Tacky Inc. inspects Glue-All when the process is 50 percent complete as to labor and overhead. The only difference between this example and the previous one is that, for June, the ending Work in Process Inventory has passed the inspection point. Because of this difference, spoilage cost must be allocated both to the gallons transferred and to the gallons in ending inventory. Although it is possible that the ending inventory could become spoiled during the remainder of processing, it is either highly unlikely or the cost is so minimal that SoTacky Inc. cannot justify the need for an end-of-process inspection. The flow diagram for this situation is:

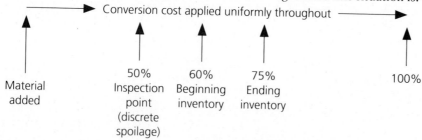

Using the same basic data as in the two previous situations, the cost per gallon and cost assignment for this situation are shown in Exhibit 9–5. Spoiled gallons are extended in the EUP schedule at the inspection point degree of completion (100% for material and 50% for conversion) and cause an effect on the cost per gallon. As in Situation 2, the resulting cost per gallon reflects what the cost *would have been* had all the gallons produced been good output. Total cost of the spoiled goods is calculated by multiplying the component cost per gallon by the EUP for each cost component. Total spoilage cost is then prorated based on the EUP for each cost component between gallons transferred and gallons in ending inventory.

PRODUCTION DATA		EQUIVALENT UNITS	
	Whole Units	Materials	Conversion
Beginning inventory (60%)	2,000		
+ Gallons started	15,000		
= Gallons to account for	17,000		
Beginning inventory (completed)	2,000	0	800
+ Gallons started and completed	11,200	11,200	11,200
= Total gallons completed	13,200		
+ Ending inventory (75%)	2,500	2,500	1,875
+ Normal spoilage (50%)	1,300	1,300	650
= Gallons accounted for	17,000	15,000	14,525

COST DATA	Total	Materials	Conversion
Beginning inventory costs	$ 16,620		
Current costs	122,175	$102,750	$19,425
Total costs	$138,795		
Divided by EUP		15,000	14,525
Cost per FIFO EUP	$8.19	$6.85	$1.34

COST ASSIGNMENT
Transferred:

From beginning inventory	$ 16,620	
Cost to complete: Conversion (800 × $1.34)	1,072	
Total cost of beginning inventory	$ 17,692	
Started and completed (11,200 × $8.19)	91,728	
Cost prior to proration of spoilage	$109,420	
Normal spoilage*	8,051	
Total cost of gallons transferred		$117,471

(continued)

■ EXHIBIT 9–5
So Tacky Inc. Cost of Production Report for Month Ended June 30, 1994 (FIFO method) (Normal discrete shrinkage)

■ **EXHIBIT 9–5 (cont.)**

Total cost of gallons transferred (from previous page)		$117,471
Ending Inventory:		
Material (2,500 × $6.85)	$ 17,125	
Conversion (1,875 × $1.34)	2,513	
Cost prior to proration of spoilage	$ 19,638	
Normal spoilage*	1,725	
Total cost of ending inventory		21,363
Total costs accounted for (off due to rounding)		$138,834

*Proration of normal spoilage is as follows:

	Material EUP	Material %	Conver-sion EUP	Conver-sion %
Gallons started and completed**	11,200	82	11,200	86
Ending work in process	2,500	18	1,875	14
	13,700	100	13,075	100

Given the above relative EUP percentages, proration of spoilage costs is:

Material (1,300 × $6.85)	$8,905
Conversion (650 × $1.34)	871
Cost of normal spoilage to be prorated	$9,776

	Materials	Conversion	Total
Gallons started and completed:			
.82 × $8,905	$7,302		
.86 × $ 871		$749	$8,051
Ending work in process:			
.18 × $8,905	1,603		
.14 × $ 871		122	1,725
Total allocations	$8,905	$871	$9,776

**The gallons in beginning Work in Process were not included in this calculation because beginning WIP was already 100% complete as to materials and 60% complete as to conversion when the year began. This inventory, therefore, was beyond the inspection point (50%) and no spoilage cost should be assigned to it.

Situation 4—Abnormal Shrinkage (Continuous or Discrete); Some Normal Shrinkage (Continuous)

The final example of So Tacky Inc. assumes that normal spoilage cannot exceed 5 percent of the gallons placed into production. Additionally, as in Situation 1, the unit reduction is assumed to occur because the ingredients adhere to the sides of the mixing machine and harden during the production process. The quality control inspection point is at the end of processing. Since 15,000 gallons were started in June, the maximum allowable normal shrinkage is 750 gallons (15,000 × 5%). Since the total reduction in units in June was 1,300 gallons, 550 gallons are considered abnormal shrinkage. Exhibit 9–6 presents the cost of production report for Situation 4.

There is one inequity in the approach presented for Situation 4. This approach automatically allocates a portion of the normal shrinkage to abnormal shrinkage. This allocation occurs because the calculation of EUP allows for the "disappearance" of the normal shrinkage. Then cost per gallon is computed based on the equivalent units of production. This approach is justified on the basis of expediency as long as the amount of the allocation of normal shrinkage to abnormal shrinkage is not considered significant.

PRODUCTION DATA		EQUIVALENT UNITS	
	Whole Units	Materials	Conversion
Beginning inventory (60%)	2,000		
+ Gallons started	15,000		
= Gallons to account for	17,000		
Beginning inventory (completed)	2,000	0	800
+ Gallons started and completed	11,200	11,200	11,200
= Total gallons completed	13,200		
+ Ending inventory (75%)	2,500	2,500	1,875
+ Normal spoilage	750		
+ Abnormal spoilage (100%)	550	550	550
= Gallons accounted for	17,000	14,250	14,425

COST DATA

	Total	Materials	Conversion
Beginning inventory costs	$ 16,620		
Current costs	122,175	$102,750	$19,425
Total costs	$138,795		
Divided by EUP		14,250	14,425
Cost per FIFO EUP	$8.56	$7.21	$1.35

COST ASSIGNMENT

Transferred:

From beginning inventory	$16,620	
Cost to complete: Conversion (800 × $1.35)	1,080	
Total cost of beginning inventory	$17,700	
Started and completed (11,200 × $8.56)	95,872	
Total cost of gallons transferred		$113,572

Ending Inventory:

Material (2,500 × $7.21)	$18,025	
Conversion (1,875 × $1.35)	2,531	20,556
Abnormal loss (550 × $8.56)		4,708
Total costs accounted for (off due to rounding)		$138,836

EXHIBIT 9–6

So Tacky Inc. Cost of Production Report for Month Ended June 30, 1994 (FIFO method) (Abnormal shrinkage; normal continuous shrinkage)

Situation 4 is used to illustrate the journal entries necessary to account for shrinkage or spoilage. These entries are:

Work in Process Inventory	122,175	
Raw Materials Inventory		102,750
Wages Payable (and/or other appropriate accounts)		19,425
To record current period costs.		
Finished Goods Inventory	113,572	
Work in Process Inventory		113,572
To record cost transferred from the department.		
Loss from Abnormal Spoilage	4,708	
Work in Process Inventory		4,708
To remove cost of abnormal spoilage from Work in Process Inventory.		

EXHIBIT 9–7

EXHIBIT 9–7

So Tacky Inc. Cost of Production Report for Month Ended June 30, 1994 (Weighted average method) (Abnormal shrinkage; normal continuous shrinkage)

PRODUCTION DATA		EQUIVALENT UNITS	
	Whole Units	**Materials**	**Conversion**
Beginning inventory (60%)	2,000		
+ Gallons started	15,000		
= Gallons to account for	17,000		
Beginning inventory (completed)	2,000	2,000	2,000
+ Gallons started and completed	11,200	11,200	11,200
= Total gallons completed	13,200		
+ Ending inventory (75%)	2,500	2,500	1,875
+ Normal spoilage	750		
+ Abnormal spoilage (100%)	550	550	550
= Gallons accounted for	17,000	16,250	15,625

COST DATA			
	Total	**Materials**	**Conversion**
Beginning inventory costs	$ 16,620	$ 15,000	$ 1,620
Current costs	122,175	102,750	19,425
Total costs	$138,795	$117,750	$21,045
Divided by EUP		16,250	15,625
Cost per FIFO EUP	$8.60	$7.25	$1.35

COST ASSIGNMENT			
Transferred (13,200 × $8.60)			$113,520
Ending Inventory:			
Material (2,500 × $7.25)		$18,125	
Conversion (1,875 × $1.35)		2,531	20,656
Abnormal loss (550 × $8.60)			4,730
Total costs accounted for (off due to rounding)			$138,906

The accounts debited and credited in the first journal entry would be the same for Situations 1, 2, and 3. The dollar amount of the second entry would change for each of Situations 1, 2, and 3 to reflect the appropriate "cost transferred" figure shown in the respective cost of production report. The third journal entry above is made only when abnormal spoilage occurs.

All illustrations to this point have used FIFO process costing. If the weighted average method were used, the difference would appear (as discussed in Chapter 8) only in the treatment of beginning inventory and its related costs. Spoilage would be handled as illustrated in each exhibit shown for Situations 1 through 4. Exhibit 9–7 illustrates the weighted average method for the data used in Exhibit 9–6.

A summary of the treatment of various types of spoilage in a process costing system is shown in Exhibit 9–8.

DEFECTIVE UNITS

The preceding examples have all been based on the presumption that the lost units were valueless. However, some goods that do not meet quality specifications can be reworked. They are called defective units or "reworks." Such units are either repro-

	NORMAL	ABNORMAL
Continuous	Do not include equivalent spoiled units in EUP schedule. Units effectively "disappear"; unit costs of good production are increased.	Must include equivalent spoiled units in EUP schedule. Assign cost to spoiled units and charge to period.
Discrete	Must include equivalent spoiled units in EUP schedule. Assign cost to spoiled units. Determine point of ending work in process: a. If before inspection point, assign cost of spoiled units only to units transferred. b. If after inspection point, prorate cost of spoiled units between units transferred and units in ending inventory.*	Must include equivalent spoiled units in EUP schedule. Assign cost to spoiled units and charge to period.

▌EXHIBIT 9–8

Summary of Handling Spoilage in a Process Costing System

cessed to meet product specifications or are sold as irregulars. Rework cost is a product or period cost depending on whether the rework is considered to be normal or abnormal.

If the rework is normal and actual costing is used, the rework cost is added to the current period's work in process costs for good units and assigned to all units completed. In companies using predetermined overhead application rates, normal rework cost should be estimated and be included as part of the estimated factory overhead cost used in computing the overhead application rates. In this way, the overhead application rate will be large enough to cover rework costs. When actual rework costs are incurred, they are assigned to the Manufacturing Overhead account.

If rework is abnormal, the costs should be accumulated and assigned to a loss account. The units will be included in the EUP schedule for the period and only actual production (not rework) costs will be considered in determining unit cost.[1]

Reworked units may be irregular and have to be sold at less than the normal selling price. Production cost of irregular items should be transferred to a special inventory account and should not be commingled with the production costs of good units. If the net realizable value (selling price minus cost to rework and sell) is less than total cost, the difference is referred to as a deficiency. This amount should be treated as part of the production cost of good units, if the number of defective units is normal. If some proportion of the defective units is considered abnormal spoilage, that same proportion of the deficiency should be written off as a period cost.

Accounting for defective units is illustrated by the August 1994 manufacturing data of So Tacky Inc. During August, the company produced 17,900 good gallons and 100 defective gallons of Glue-All. The 100 gallons were considered defective because the traditional pink coloration of the product was, instead, red. Total production costs other than rework were $160,200. The 100 defective gallons can be re-

[1] If the company is using a standard costing system, then standard costs will be considered in determining unit cost.

worked at a total cost of $140 (or $1.40 per gallon) by mixing the defective gallons with a chemical lightening additive. The cost of the additive itself is only $.05 per gallon, so all rework costs are assumed to be related to direct labor. The chemical additive is also gaseous and will cause no increase in the number of gallons of Glue-All. Entries for defective units are shown in Exhibit 9–9. This exhibit uses the basic information and shows a variety of circumstances involving defective goods.

EXHIBIT 9–9

So Tacky Entries for Defective Units

Good production: 17,900 gallons
Defects: 100 gallons
Cost of production other than rework: $160,200
Cost of rework: $140 or $1.40 per gallon

1. Rework is normal; actual costing is used; reworks can be sold at normal selling price.

Work in Process Inventory	140	
Wages Payable		140

   Cost per acceptable gallon = $8.91 ($160,340 ÷ 18,000)

2. Rework is normal; predetermined OH rate is used (rework estimated); reworks can be sold at normal selling price.

Manufacturing Overhead	140	
Wages Payable		140

   Cost per acceptable gallon = $8.90 ($160,200 ÷ 18,000)

3. Rework is abnormal; reworks can be sold at normal selling price.

Loss from Defects.	140	
Wages Payable		140

   Cost per acceptable gallon = $8.90 ($160,200 ÷ 18,000)

4. Reworks are irregular; can only be sold for $7; actual costing is used.

Normal production cost ($8.90 × 100)	$ 890
Cost of rework	140
Total cost of defective units	$1,030
Total sales value of defective units (100 × $7)	700
Total deficiency	$ 330

   If defects are normal:

Work in Process Inventory	140	
Inventory—Defects	700	
Wages Payable		140
Work in Process Inventory		700

   The amount of the deficiency ($330) remains with the good units; cost assigned as a product cost; cost per acceptable gallon is $8.92 [($160,200 + $140 − $700) ÷ 17,900]

   If defects are abnormal:

Inventory—Defects	700	
Loss from Defects	330	
Wages Payable		140
Work in Process Inventory		890

   The amount of the deficiency is assigned as a period loss; cost per acceptable gallon is $8.90 [($160,200 − $890) ÷ 17,900]

The previous examples are related to spoilage issues in a process costing environment. In a job order situation, the accounting treatment of spoilage depends on two issues: (1) Is spoilage generally incurred for most jobs or is it specifically identified with a particular job? (2) Is the spoilage normal or abnormal?

SPOILAGE IN JOB ORDER COSTING

Spoilage Generally Anticipated on All Jobs

If normal spoilage is anticipated on all jobs, the predetermined overhead application rate should include an amount for the **net cost of normal spoilage**, which is equal to the cost of spoiled work less the estimated disposal value of that work. This approach assumes that spoilage is naturally inherent and unavoidable in the production of good jobs and its estimated cost should, therefore, be proportionately assigned among the good jobs produced.

Net cost of normal spoilage

Assume that So Tacky produces a line of custom-manufactured adhesives for several wallpaper manufacturers. Each production run is considered a separate job because each manufacturer indicates the particular adhesive specifications it requires. Regardless of the job, there is always some spoilage because of the mixing process. In computing the predetermined overhead rate related to the custom adhesives product line, the following estimates are made:

Overhead costs other than spoilage		$121,500
Estimated spoilage cost	$10,300	
Sales of improperly mixed adhesive to discount do-it-yourself stores	4,300	6,000
Total estimated overhead		$127,500
Estimated gallons of production during the year		150,000
Predetermined rate per gallon		$.85

During the year, So Tacky Inc. accepted a job (#73) for Precious Papers to manufacture 495 gallons of adhesive. The direct materials cost for this job was $4,660, direct labor cost totaled $640, and applied overhead was $425, giving a total cost for the job of $5,725. So Tacky Inc. put 500 gallons of adhesive into production. Five gallons (or 1 percent) of the adhesive were spoiled during the production process when a worker knocked some dye meant for another job into a container of the adhesive. The actual cost of the spoiled mixture was $57.25 (.01 × $5,725) and it can be sold for $14. The entry below is made to account for the actual spoilage cost:

Disposal Value of Spoiled Work	14.00	
Manufacturing Overhead	43.25	
Department Work in Process Inventory—Job 73		57.25
To record disposal value of spoiled work incurred on Job 73 for Precious Papers.		

The estimated cost of spoilage was originally included in determining the predetermined overhead rate. Therefore, as actual spoilage occurs, the disposal value of the spoiled work is included in an inventory account (if it is salable) and the net cost of the normal spoilage is charged to the Manufacturing Overhead account as is any other actual overhead cost.

Spoilage Specifically Identified with a Particular Job

If spoilage is not generally anticipated, but is occasionally experienced on specific jobs *because of job-related characteristics*, its estimated cost should *not* be included in setting the predetermined overhead application rate. Since the cost of spoilage attaches to the job, the disposal value of any spoiled goods is used to reduce the cost of the specific job that caused the spoilage. If no disposal value exists for the spoiled goods, the spoilage cost remains with the job that caused the spoilage.

Assume that in the above information for So Tacky, the company did not typically experience spoilage. The company's predetermined overhead would have been calculated as $.81 per gallon ($121,500 ÷ 150,000). Thus, the total cost for the Precious Papers job would have been $5,705 [$4,660 + $640 + ($.81 × 500)]. Five gallons of the batch were dyed yellow at the request of Precious Papers. After checking the color, Precious Papers rejected the five gallons and changed the tinting formula slightly. The disposal value of the five gallons would be used to reduce the cost of the Precious Papers job as shown in the following entry:

Disposal Value of Spoiled Work	14	
Department Work in Process Inventory—Job 73		14
To record disposal value of spoiled work incurred on Job 73 for Precious Papers.		

The production cost of any new mixture will be assigned a new job number.

Abnormal Spoilage

The cost of abnormal spoilage (net of any disposal value) should be written off as a period loss. The following entry assumes that So Tacky normally anticipates some spoilage on its custom orders and the estimated cost of that spoilage was included in the development of a predetermined overhead application rate. Assume that on Job 286, the cost of units spoiled was $395, but there was $35 of disposal value associated with those spoiled units. Of the remaining $360 of spoilage cost, $240 was determined to be normal and $120 was determined to be abnormal.

Disposal Value of Spoiled Work	35	
Manufacturing Overhead	240	
Loss from Abnormal Spoilage	120	
Department Work in Process Inventory—Job 286		395
To record reassignment of cost of spoiled work on Job 286.		

The first debit represents the spoilage's disposal value; the debit to Manufacturing Overhead is for the net cost of the normal spoilage. The debit to Loss from Abnormal Spoilage is for that portion of the net cost of spoilage that was not anticipated in setting the predetermined application rate and is, therefore, considered abnormal.

ACCRETION

Accretion

Accretion refers to an increase in units or volume because of the addition of material in successor departments or to factors (such as heat) that are inherent in the production process.[2] For example, adding filler to beef in preparing packages of ground meat causes the pounds of product to increase just as cooking pasta increases the volume of product.

---

[2] Not all additions of material in successor departments cause an increase in units. Adding bindings to books in a second department does not increase the number of books printed and transferred from the prior department. When the material added in a successor department does not increase the number of units, it is accounted for as shown in Chapter 8.

If materials are added in a single department, the number of equivalent units computed for that department already compensates for this increase from the beginning to the end of processing. When accretion occurs in successor departments in a multi-department process, the number of units transferred into the department and the related cost per unit must be adjusted. For instance, assume that one complex adhesive made by So Tacky Inc. for an automobile manufacturer requires processing in two departments. Department Two adds a heavy-duty compound to increase the holding properties of the mixture produced in Department One. The gallons of compound added increase the total gallons of mixture that were transferred out of Department One and decrease the transferred-in cost per unit.

The automotive adhesive produced by So Tacky is used to illustrate the accounting for accretion of units in a successor department. Department One mixes the basic adhesive ingredients in large vats. The mixture is then sent to Department Two, which adds the heavy-duty compound and remixes the adhesive. The adhesive is poured into 50-gallon containers that are shipped to the automobile manufacturer. Spoilage occurs in Department Two when too much compound is added to the adhesive mixture. The spoilage is detected when the mixture is transferred from the vats to the containers. Spoilage is never containerized. Spoilage is considered normal as long as it does not exceed 1 percent of the gallons transferred into Department Two from Department One.

October production information for Department Two is given below. For this product, assume that So Tacky Inc. uses weighted average process costing. The units in beginning inventory were 100 percent complete as to the compound, zero percent complete as to the container, and 25 percent complete as to labor and overhead costs. The ending inventory units are 100 percent complete as to the compound, zero percent complete as to the container, and 70 percent complete as to labor and overhead.

Gallons in beginning inventory	1,000
Gallons transferred in	21,000
Gallons of compound added	5,000
Gallons in ending inventory	1,200
Units completed (50-gallon containers)	512

Note that the measure for completed production is containers rather than gallons. Since each container represents 50 gallons, the actual gallons completed are 25,600 (50 × 512). To handle this change in measuring units, either the incoming gallons must be reported as containers or the completed containers must be reported as gallons. The cost of production report for October (Exhibit 9–10 on page 364) is prepared using gallons as the measurement unit and assumed cost information is supplied in the exhibit.

Several items need to be noted about this exhibit. First, the number of spoiled gallons was determined by subtracting the total gallons completed plus the gallons in ending inventory from the total gallons for which the department was responsible. Since spoilage was less than 1 percent of the gallons transferred into Department Two, it was all considered normal. Second, the $197,100 cost transferred from Department One was related to 22,000 gallons of mixture: the gallons in beginning inventory plus those transferred during the period. Thus, the original cost of each gallon was approximately $8.96 ($197,100 ÷ 22,000). With the addition of the compound in Department Two, the transferred-in cost per gallon declined to $7.30. Third, spoilage is assignable only to the completed units because the ending inventory has not yet reached the discrete point of inspection (transference to containers). Finally, the average cost of each 50-gallon container completed is approximately $643.48 ($329,460 ÷ 512).

PRODUCTION DATA

	Whole Units	EQUIVALENT UNITS			
		Trans.-In	Compound	Container	Conversion
Beginning inventory (25%)	1,000	1,000	1,000	0	250
+ Transferred-in	21,000				
+ Compound added	5,000				
= Gallons to account for	27,000				
Beginning inventory (completed)	1,000	0	0	1,000	750
+ Started and completed	24,600	24,600	24,600	24,600	24,600
= Total gallons completed	25,600				
+ Ending inventory (70%)	1,200	1,200	1,200	0	840
+ Normal spoilage (100%)	200	200	200	0	200
= Gallons accounted for	27,000	27,000	27,000	25,600	26,640

COST DATA

	Total	Trans.-In	Compound	Container	Conversion
Beginning inventory costs	$ 8,415	$ 7,385	$ 840	$ 0	$ 190
Current costs	331,455	189,715	22,110	99,840	19,790
Total costs	$339,870	$197,100	$22,950	$99,840	$19,980
Divided by EUP		27,000	27,000	25,600	26,640
Cost per EUP	$12.80	$7.30	$.85	$3.90	$.75

COST ASSIGNMENT

Transferred:
    Cost of good units (25,600 × $12.80) $327,680
    Cost of spoilage:
      Transferred-in (200 × $7.30)   1,460
      Compound (200 × $.85)   170
      Conversion (200 × $.75)   150

        Total cost transferred $329,460

Ending Inventory:
    Transferred-in (1,200 × $7.30) $ 8,760
    Compound (1,200 × $.85)   1,020
    Conversion (840 × $.75)   630   10,410

Total costs accounted for $339,870

▌ EXHIBIT 9–10
So Tacky Inc. (Department 2) Cost of Production Report for the Month Ended
October 31, 1994 (Weighted average method)

Up to this point, the chapter has focused on the ways to account for improper production. The fact is, if there were no improper production, there would be no need to account for it. The control aspect in quality control requires knowledge of three questions in addition to the six questions posed earlier in the chapter. These three questions are:

1. What does the spoilage actually cost?
2. Why does the spoilage occur?
3. How can the spoilage be controlled?

Many companies find it difficult, if not impossible, to answer the question of what spoilage (or lack of quality) costs. A direct cause of part of this difficulty is the use of the traditional method of assigning the cost of normal spoilage to the good units produced. By excluding the spoiled units from the extensions in the equivalent units in a process costing situation, the cost of those units is effectively "buried" and hidden in magnitude from managers. In a job order costing environment, if the cost of spoilage is included in calculating the predetermined overhead rate, that cost is also being hidden and ignored. In service organizations, the cost of "spoilage" may be even more difficult to determine because spoilage is, from a customer viewpoint, poor service; the customer simply may not do business with the organization again. Such an opportunity cost is not processed by the accounting system. Thus, in all instances, a potentially significant dollar amount is unavailable for investigation as to its planning, controlling, and decision-making ramifications.

As to the second question, managers may be able to pinpoint the reasons for spoilage or poor service but may also have two perspectives of those reasons that instinctively allow for a lack of control. First, the managers may believe that the cause creates only a "minimal" amount of spoilage; such an attitude creates the allowance of an "accepted quality level" with some tolerance for error. These error tolerances are built into the system and they become justifications for problems. Production is "graded on a curve" that allows for a less-than-perfect result.

Incorporating such error tolerances into the production/performance system and combining such tolerances with the method of neglect discussed earlier results in managers not being provided with the information necessary to determine how much spoilage cost is incurred by the company. Therefore, while believing that the quantity and cost of spoiled goods are "minimal," the managers do not have historical or even estimated accounting amounts on which to base such a conclusion. If managers were aware of the cost, they could make more informed decisions about whether to ignore it or try to correct its causes.

In other instances, managers may believe that spoilage is uncontrollable. In some cases, this belief is accurate. For example, when a printing press converts from one job to the next, some number of pages are consistently misprinted. The number is not large and process analysis has proven that the cost of attempting to correct this production defect would be significantly greater than the savings resulting from the correction. But in most production situations and almost every service situation, the cause of spoiled goods or poor service is controllable. It is only necessary to determine the cause of the problem and institute corrective action.

Spoilage was originally controlled through a process of inspecting goods or, in the case of service organizations, surveying customers. Now companies are deciding that if quality is *built* into the process, there will be less need for inspections or surveys because spoilage and poor service will be minimized. The goal is, then, process *control* rather than output *inspection or observation*.

As discussed in Chapter 3, companies implementing quality programs to minimize defects or poor service often employ a tool called statistical process control (SPC) to

NEWS NOTE

SPC Lets You Determine the Causes of Process Problems

SPC theory is based on the postulate that process performance is dynamic—that natural up-and-down variation is the rule, rather than the exception. Accordingly, performance measurements fluctuate over time, and a single measurement by itself is not meaningful. Proper assessments of process performance require correct interpretations of performance variation over time.

SPC relies on the use of graphic aids or control charts to understand and reduce fluctuations in processes until they are in a state of control (stable). A stable process is subject only to common fluctuations, which result from causes of variation natural to the process. An unstable process is subject to uncommon fluctuations as well as common fluctuations. Uncommon fluctuations result from special causes of variation.

The performance of a stable production process can be improved only by making fundamental changes in the process itself. An unstable production process can be stabilized by locating and eliminating the special causes of uncommon fluctuations. Once the causes of uncommon fluctuations are eliminated, the overall performance of the process can be improved.

SOURCE: David E. Keys and Kurt F. Reding, "Statistical Process Control: What Management Accountants Need to Know," *Management Accounting* (January 1992), pp. 26–27. Reprinted from *Management Accounting*. Copyright by Institute of Management Accountants, Montvale, N.J.

analyze their processes for situations that are "out of control." This technique uses graphs and/or control charts to understand and reduce fluctuations in processes until they are under control. As discussed in the accompanying News Note, SPC requires that persons or machines involved in problem areas select a relevant measure of performance and track that performance measurement over time. The resulting control chart provides information on the circumstances existing when a problem arises. Analyzing this chart in relation to the benchmark or standard and to the amount of variation expected in a stable (controlled) process provides process control information that lets the company improve its performance.

SPC allows the individuals involved with the process to become the quality control points and helps to eliminate the need for quality inspections. Thus, the "accepted quality level" can be raised, and the defects reduced, significantly. Motorola, for example, wants "a reduction of defects to within 'six sigma' (no more than 3.4 defects per million—or 99.9997% perfect)."[3] Additionally, company chairman George Fisher is even concentrating on quality standards for areas such as research and development and "meetings." Senco Products' goal of zero defects is not that unusual for companies competing in global, world-class environments.

The development, implementation, and interpretation of an SPC system requires a firm grasp on statistics and is well beyond the scope of this text. However, it is essential that cost and management accountants recognize the usefulness of such a tool in determining why problems occur. Such knowledge allows cost and managerial accountants to better track the costs flowing into the problem areas, estimate the opportunity costs associated with the problems, and make a more informed cost-benefit analysis about problem correction.

In conclusion, the important managerial concern regarding spoilage is in *controlling* it rather than *accounting for* spoilage costs. Quality control programs can be implemented to develop ideas on product redesign for quality, determine where quality control problems exist, decide how to measure the costs associated with those

---

[3]Graham Sharman, "When Quality Control Gets in the Way of Quality," *Wall Street Journal* (February 24, 1992), p. A14.

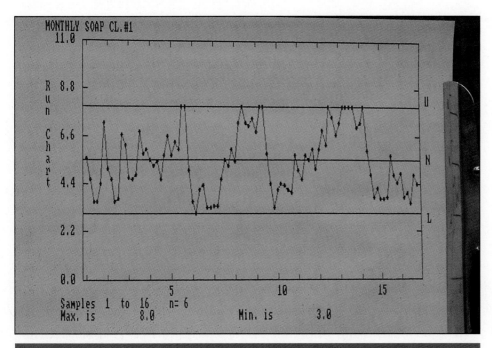

SPC charts are important tools in a total quality environment. They indicate the variations in the process, so that unacceptable deviations can be noted and corrective action taken.

problems, and decide how to correct the problems. If quality is defined in an organization as zero defects, all spoilage will be accounted for as an abnormal cost of production or service. Such accounting would mean that spoilage costs would no longer be hidden from managerial eyes through the use of the method of neglect discussed earlier in the chapter.

R E V I S I T I N G

SENCO PRODUCTS

In committing Senco to defect-free, customer-sensitive manufacturing, management had to do some deep thinking. For starters, they needed to define what quality actually was. At Senco, "quality" is the art of making a product so that it conforms to the customer's requirements. To insure quality, the company tries to prevent mistakes and defects from happening, not wait until they happen and then try to fix them.

The performance standard for quality is zero defects. "This goal is really an attitude," says Been. "We're manufacturing products knowing that if 99 out of 100 products are correct, we're falling short. That 100th customer is out of luck. We refuse to think like that. Anything short of meeting [customer] product requirements is unacceptable."

Through aggressive prevention of mistakes, defects can be whittled down, Been says. He cites the case of Japanese companies where defects are now measured in parts per million.

The commitment to quality pays off, Been says. Senco has seen its defect rates plunge, customer satisfaction climb, and employee morale improve. On average, scrap and rework costs have been reduced more than 40 percent.

Devotion to total quality works.

SOURCE: "Quality Equals Perfection at Cincinnati Fastener Systems Company," *[Grant Thornton] Manufacturing Issues* (Winter 1990), p. 8. Reprinted by permission from Grant Thornton's *Manufacturing Issues.* © Grant Thornton 1990.

CHAPTER SUMMARY

This chapter covers the accounting treatment for spoilage/shrinkage, defective units, and accretion of units in a process costing system. If the loss of units is anticipated, management will specify a certain level of spoilage that will be tolerated as normal; if spoilage exceeds expectations, the excess loss is considered abnormal. Normal losses are product costs and abnormal losses are period costs.

To account for spoilage costs, the point at which the spoilage is deemed to occur in the manufacturing process must be known. If the spoilage is normal and continuous, the period's good production absorbs the cost of the spoilage. This treatment is handled in the cost of production report by not extending the spoiled units to the equivalent units columns. If the loss is normal and discrete, the spoiled units are included in the EUP schedule at their unit equivalency at the quality control point. If ending inventory has reached the inspection point, the cost of spoiled units is allocated to both units transferred from the department and units in ending inventory. If ending inventory has not yet reached the quality control inspection point, spoilage cost attaches only to the units transferred. If the spoilage is abnormal, the units are included in the EUP schedule at their unit equivalency at the quality control point. Cost is assigned to the abnormal spoilage and that amount is considered a period loss.

In a job order costing system, the cost of anticipated spoilage is estimated and included in setting the predetermined overhead rate. This approach allows expected spoilage cost to be assigned to all jobs. When spoilage occurs, any disposal value of spoiled work is carried in a separate inventory account; the net cost of spoilage is debited to Manufacturing Overhead. If spoilage is not generally incurred in a job order system, any normal spoilage associated with a specific job is carried as part of that job's cost; any disposal value of the spoilage reduces the cost of the specific job. Abnormal spoilage is treated as a loss of the period.

Adding material to partially completed units may increase the number of units. If the material addition occurs in a successor department, a new transferred-in cost per unit must be calculated using the increased number of units. If units of measure change between the start and end of production, a consistent measuring unit must be used in the cost of production report to properly reflect production of the period.

The treatment of the rework cost for defective units depends on whether the rework is normal or abnormal. If the rework is normal, the cost is considered to be a product cost and either (1) increases actual costs in the cost schedule or (2) is considered in setting an overhead application rate and charged to overhead when incurred. If rework is abnormal, the cost is assigned to the period as a loss.

Accounting for spoiled and defective units is essential when total quality does not exist. The traditional methods of accounting for spoilage often "bury" the cost of poor quality by spreading that cost over good output. Managers should attempt to compute the costs of spoiled or defective units and search for ways to improve product quality, reduce product cost, and increase the company's competitive market position.

KEY TERMS

Abnormal loss (p. 346)
Abnormal spoilage (p. 347)
Accretion (p. 362)
Continuous spoilage (p. 348)
Defective unit (p. 346)
Discrete spoilage (p. 348)
Economically reworked (p. 346)

Method of neglect (p. 349)
Net cost of normal spoilage (p. 361)
Normal loss (p. 346)
Normal spoilage (p. 346)
Shrinkage (p. 348)
Spoilage (p. 346)
Spoiled unit (p. 346)

Spoiled units are *always* shown with other whole units under "Units accounted for" in the cost of production report.

Continuous normal spoilage

1. Spoiled units are *not* extended to EUP schedule.
2. All good production (both fully and partially completed) absorb the spoilage cost through higher per unit costs.

Continuous abnormal spoilage

1. All units are appropriately extended to EUP schedule.
2. Cost of spoiled units is assigned as period loss.

Discrete normal spoilage

1. Normal spoilage is appropriately extended to the EUP schedule.
2. Determine if ending inventory has passed inspection point.
    a. If no, cost of spoiled units is assigned only to the good production that was transferred.
    b. If yes, cost of spoiled units is prorated between units in ending WIP Inventory and units transferred out based on
       (1) (weighted average) total costs contained in each category prior to proration or
       (2) (FIFO) current costs contained in each category prior to proration.

Discrete abnormal spoilage

1. Abnormal spoilage is appropriately extended to the EUP schedule.
2. Cost of spoiled units is assigned as period loss.

Normal rework

1. *(Actual cost system)* Add rework costs to original materials, labor, and overhead costs and spread over all production.
2. *(Normal and standard cost systems)* Include cost of rework in estimated overhead when determining standard application rate. Assign actual rework costs to Manufacturing Overhead.

Abnormal rework
Accumulate rework costs separately and assign as period loss.

Accretion in successor departments
An increase in units requires that the per unit transferred-in cost be reduced in the successor department based on the new, larger number of units.

Linda Newmann Enterprises incurs spoilage continuously throughout the manufacturing process. All materials are added at the beginning of the process and the inspection point is at the end of the production process. June 1994 operating statistics are as follows:

Pounds

Beginning inventory (75% complete)	1,000
Started in June	10,000
Completed and transferred	8,000
Ending inventory (60% complete)	1,000
Normal spoilage	1,000
Abnormal spoilage	?

Costs
   Beginning inventory
     Materials $ 58,000
     Conversion   22,026 $ 80,026

   Current period
     Materials $540,000
     Conversion   309,750   849,750

      Total costs $929,776

Required:

a. Prepare a cost of production report using the weighted average method.
b. Prepare a cost of production report using the FIFO method.
c. Using the information from part b, prepare the journal entry to recognize the abnormal loss from spoilage.

Solution to Demonstration Problem

a.   Linda Newmann Cost of Production Report
(Continuous spoilage—normal and abnormal; weighted average method)
For the Month Ended June 30, 1994

PRODUCTION DATA	Whole Units	Materials	Conversion
Beginning inventory (75%)	1,000	1,000	750
+ Pounds started	10,000		
= Pounds to account for	11,000		
Beginning inventory (completed)	1,000	0	250
+ Pounds started and completed	7,000	7,000	7,000
= Total pounds completed	8,000		
+ Ending inventory (60%)	1,000	1,000	600
+ Normal spoilage	1,000		
+ Abnormal spoilage	1,000	1,000	1,000
= Pounds accounted for	11,000	10,000	9,600

COST DATA	Total	Materials	Conversion
Beginning inventory costs	$ 80,026	$ 58,000	$ 22,026
Current costs	849,750	540,000	309,750
Total costs	$929,776	$598,000	$331,776
Divided by EUP		10,000	9,600
Cost per WA EUP	$94.36	$59.80	$34.56

COST ASSIGNMENT
Transferred (8,000 × $94.36) $754,880
Ending Inventory:
   Material (1,000 × $59.80) $59,800
   Conversion (600 × $34.56)   20,736   80,536
Abnormal Loss (1,000 × $94.36)   94,360
Total costs accounted for $929,776

b.

Linda Newmann Cost of Production Report
(Continuous spoilage—normal and abnormal; FIFO method)
For the Month Ended June 30, 1994

PRODUCTION DATA	Whole Units	Materials	Conversion
Beginning inventory (75%)	1,000		
+ Pounds started	10,000		
= Pounds to account for	11,000		
Beginning inventory (completed)	1,000	0	250
+ Pounds started and completed	7,000	7,000	7,000
= Total pounds completed	8,000		
+ Ending inventory (60%)	1,000	1,000	600
+ Normal spoilage	1,000		
+ Abnormal spoilage	1,000	1,000	1,000
= Pounds accounted for	11,000	9,000	8,850

COST DATA	Total	Materials	Conversion
Beginning inventory costs	$ 80,026		
Current costs	849,750	$540,000	$309,750
Total costs	$929,776		
Divided by EUP		9,000	8,850
Cost per FIFO EUP	$95	$60	$35

COST ASSIGNMENT

Transferred:
From beginning inventory — $ 80,026
Cost to complete: Conversion (250 × $35) — 8,750

Total cost of beginning inventory — $ 88,776
Started and completed (7,000 × $95) — 665,000

Total cost of pounds transferred — $753,776
Ending Inventory:
Material (1,000 × $60) — $ 60,000
Conversion (600 × $35) — 21,000 — 81,000

Abnormal Loss (1,000 × $95) — 95,000

Total costs accounted for — $929,776

c. Loss from Abnormal Spoilage — 95,000
  Work in Process Inventory — 95,000
  To remove cost of abnormal spoilage from Work in Process Inventory account.

QUESTIONS

1. What are the differences between spoiled units, defective units, scrap, and waste?
2. What is the difference between "normal" and "abnormal" spoilage or loss?
3. Why do managers provide for the incurrence of production losses in their plans?
4. How is continuous spoilage differentiated from discrete spoilage?
5. Does "discrete" spoilage actually occur just prior to the inspection point? Explain.
6. Why is the cost of abnormal spoilage considered a period cost? How is the cost of abnormal spoilage removed from the Work in Process Inventory?
7. How is normal spoilage determined at an inspection point accounted for? What is meant by the term "method of neglect"?
8. Why are normal, spoiled units resulting from a continuous process not extended to the equivalent units of production schedule? How does this treatment affect the cost of the good production of the period?
9. In a job order costing system, spoilage may be incurred in general for all jobs or it may be related to a specific job. What differences do these circumstances make in the treatment of spoilage?
10. In a production process what is accretion? How does it affect the volume of the product?
11. The Mixing Department of MJH Enterprises transferred 45,000 pounds of material into the Baking Department during July. The cost per pound shown on the cost of production report for Mixing was $2.50. On the cost of production report for Baking for the same period, the cost per pound for material transferred in was $2.00. Why might the cost have changed?
12. How are costs of reworking defective units treated if the defects are considered normal? Abnormal?
13. Why should management attempt to measure the cost of producing spoiled and defective goods when costs from normal spoilage are simply included as part of the cost of good production?
14. How do statistical process control techniques contribute to the control of spoilage costs?

EXERCISES

15. *(Normal vs. abnormal spoilage)* Information regarding Simington Cannery operations in June follow. The firm uses a process costing system. All material is added at the beginning of production.

Beginning inventory (10% complete—conversion)	7,000 units
Started during June	60,000 units
Completed during June	50,000 units
Spoilage	7,000 units
Ending inventory (60% complete—conversion)	10,000 units

The firm's management has specified that normal spoilage cannot exceed 9% of the units started in a period. Spoilage occurs on a continuous basis. The company uses a weighted average process costing system.
a. How many total units are there to account for?
b. How many units should be treated as normal spoilage?
c. How many units should be treated as abnormal spoilage?
d. What are the equivalent units of production for direct materials? For conversion?

16. *(EUP computation, normal and abnormal spoilage)* Southern Textiles manufactures drapery material in a continuous, mass production process. All material is added at the beginning of the process. The material is inspected at the end of production for gaps and tears. Normally, spoilage is treated as continuous. The March production data are shown below:

Beginning work in process (85% complete)	50,000 yds.
Started during the month	425,000 yds.
Ending work in process (25% complete)	10,000 yds.
Normal spoilage	1,000 yds.
Abnormal spoilage	18,000 yds.

   During March, a machine malfunctioned and "chewed up" 18,000 yards of material (abnormal spoilage quantity). These units had all been started during March. The malfunction occurred when 70% of the labor and overhead had been completed on those yards of product. The remaining spoilage was detected at the inspection point and considered well within reasonable limits.

   a. Determine the number of equivalent units for direct materials assuming a FIFO cost flow.
   b. Determine the number of equivalent units for conversion assuming a FIFO cost flow.
   c. If the costs per equivalent unit are $4.50 and $3.50 for direct materials and conversion, respectively, what is the cost of ending inventory?
   d. What is the cost of abnormal spoilage? How is this cost treated in March?

17. *(EUP computation, normal and abnormal spoilage)* The Buzzwizer Co. employs a process costing system (based on FIFO assumptions) in its root beer plant. In this plant, root beer is packaged in 16-gallon kegs. Materials are added at the beginning of the process. When the soda is 50% complete (with respect to conversion), it is quality inspected. Based on the production technology, it is expected that normal spoilage will be equal to 10% of all good units inspected. Unit information for July 1994 follows:

Beginning WIP inventory	1,200 kegs (30% complete)
Units started	5,000 kegs
Units transferred	4,500 kegs
Ending WIP inventory	800 kegs (80% complete)

   a. Determine the number of units to account for.
   b. Compute: the total number of units spoiled, normal spoilage, and abnormal spoilage.

18. *(EUP computation, normal and abnormal spoilage, cost per EUP)* Bright Lights Candle Company manufactures votive candles. Costs are accounted for with a process costing system. Spoilage occurs continuously throughout production because wax is formed in imperfect shapes in the molds. Spoilage of less than 8% of the pounds of wax placed in production is considered normal. All wax is entered at the beginning of the process. November 1994 data are as follows:

Beginning inventory (30% complete)	3,000 pounds
Started during month	10,000 pounds
Transferred	10,500 pounds
(105,000 candles; there are 10 wax candles obtained from a pound of wax)	
Ending inventory (20% complete)	1,800 pounds
Spoiled	? pounds

   a. Prepare the production data segment of the cost of production report for the company for November 1994 using the FIFO method.
   b. Assume the following costs are associated with November production:

Beginning inventory:

Material	$1,200	
Conversion	900	$2,100

Current period:

Material	$3,069	
Conversion	2,690	5,759
Total costs		$7,859

Prepare the cost determination and assignment sections of a cost of production report for the company for November 1994.

19. *(EUP computations, normal and abnormal spoilage)* The Houston factory of the Midland Chemical Company produces a liquid fuel that is used by campers for lanterns and portable stoves. The fuel is packaged in one gallon containers. Company management considers normal spoilage to be no more than 0.5% of gallons of material placed into production. Spoilage is assumed to take place on a continuous basis. The following operating statistics are available for September 1994:

Beginning inventory (20% complete as to materials; 30% complete as to conversion)	4,000 gallons
Started during September	90,000 gallons
Ending inventory (60% complete as to materials; 70% complete as to conversion)	2,000 gallons
Spoiled gallons	700 gallons

a. How many gallons were transferred out?
b. How much normal spoilage occurred?
c. How much abnormal spoilage occurred?
d. What are the FIFO equivalent units of production for materials? For conversion costs?
e. How are costs associated with the abnormal spoilage handled?
f. How are costs associated with the normal spoilage handled?

 20. *(Cost assignment)* The Auto Suspension Company manufactures coil springs in a single production process. For every 100 units of good output, there are usually 5 units that are spoiled and must be discarded. The determination of spoilage (discrete) is made through inspection at the end of the process. All material is added at the beginning of the process. Assume the following data:

Beginning inventory	8,000 units (60% complete)
Units started	40,000 units
Ending inventory	6,000 units (30% complete)
Good units completed	40,000 units

	Materials	Conversion	Total
Beginning inventory	$ 24,984	$ 19,854	$ 44,838
Current period	225,096	126,000	351,096
Total costs	$250,080	$145,854	$395,934

a. Prepare an EUP schedule using the weighted average method.
b. Determine the cost of the normal spoilage and allocate that cost to the appropriate inventory.

 21. *(Cost assignment)* Data below summarize the operations of AgriCo's Herbicide Production Department. Units are five-gallon containers of the herbicide product. All material is obtained from other operating subunits of AgriCo and is added at the beginning of the process.

Costs	Material	Conversion	Total
Beginning inventory	$ 7,500	$ 900	$ 8,400
Current period	221,280	83,772	305,052
Total costs	$228,780	$84,672	$313,452

Units

Beginning inventory	1,500 units	(30% complete—conversion)
Started	45,000 units	
Completed	38,000 units	
Ending inventory	5,000 units	(70% complete—conversion)
Normal spoilage	1,200 units	

Spoilage is detected at inspection when the units are 50% complete.
a. Prepare an EUP schedule using the weighted average method.
b. Determine the cost of goods transferred out, ending inventory, and abnormal spoilage.

22. *(Cost assignment)* The Patio Umbrella Co. of New Jersey employs a process costing system. One of the company's products (a small umbrella that attaches to floating pool chairs) passes through three departments (molding, assembly, and finishing) before it is completed. The following activity took place in the Finishing Department during May 1994:

Units in beginning inventory	1,400
Units transferred in from Assembly	14,000
Units spoiled	700
Good units transferred out	11,200

Raw material is added at the beginning of processing in Finishing without changing the number of units being processed. Work in process inventory was 70% complete as to conversion on May 1 and 40% complete as to conversion on May 31. All spoilage was discovered at final inspection before the units were transferred to finished goods. Five hundred sixty of the units spoiled were within the limit considered normal.

The company uses the weighted average costing method. The equivalent units and the costs per equivalent unit of production for each cost factor are as follows:

Cost per EUP

Cost of prior departments	$5.00
Raw materials	1.00
Conversion	3.00
	$9.00

a. Calculate the equivalent units of production.
b. Determine the cost of units transferred out of Finishing.
c. Determine the cost of ending Work in Process Inventory.
d. The portion of the total transferred in cost associated with beginning Work in Process Inventory amounted to $6,300. What is the current period cost that was transferred in from Assembly to Finishing?
e. Determine the cost associated with abnormal spoilage for the month. How would this amount be accounted for?
(CMA adapted)

23. *(Rework)* Final Finish Inc. manufactures a single product, a two-gallon tub of professional car wax. The company uses a process costing system based on actual costs. At the end of the production process, inspection takes place and defective units are identified for reworking. All material is added at the beginning of pro-

duction; labor and overhead are incurred evenly throughout the process. The following information with regard to production is for February 1994:

Beginning inventory (30% complete as to conversion)	500 units
Started during month	11,500
Completed during month	10,000
Defective units (100% complete as to conversion)	1,200
Ending inventory (70% complete as to conversion)	800

Production costs, other than for reworking, were $84,000 for the month for direct materials and $27,048 for conversion (these figures include beginning inventory costs). The cost of reworking the 1,200 units to bring them up to specifications was $2,100 for material and $882 for labor and overhead.

a. Determine the equivalent units of production using the FIFO method.
b. Determine the equivalent units of production using the weighted average method.
c. Using the weighted average EUP and assuming that the rework is normal, determine the cost per unit for direct materials and conversion cost for the good units.
d. Using the weighted average EUP and assuming that the rework is abnormal, determine the cost per unit for direct materials and conversion cost for the good units. How are the rework cost recorded for financial statement purposes?
e. Assuming that the rework is normal, how would rework costs be handled if a normal costing system is used?

**COMMUNICATION
ACTIVITY**

24. *(Normal discrete spoilage, weighted average)* The Potato Division of Global Foods Company processes potatoes. In the process, raw potatoes are sequentially cleaned, skinned, cooked, and canned. Spoilage amounting to less than 12% of the total pounds of potatoes that are introduced to the cleaning operation is considered normal (in this case, normal spoilage is to include the weight of the potato peels). Inspection occurs when the products are 50% complete. Information that follows pertains to operations in the Potato Division for the month of January 1994:

Beginning WIP inventory	500,000 lbs. (30% complete)
Started	13,500,000 lbs.
Transferred	11,400,000 lbs.
Ending WIP inventory	750,000 lbs. (40% complete)

a. Compute the amount of spoilage in January. How much of the spoilage was normal?
b. Compute the equivalent units of production assuming the weighted average method is used.
c. Prepare a one-minute presentation explaining why you might expect some accretion in the canning operation.
d. Write a brief memo explaining why you might expect some shrinkage other than the weight of the peels in one or more of the operations?

25. *(Normal discrete spoilage; FIFO)* Bean Crushers Ltd. operates a soybean "crusher" to produce soybean oil. Spoilage amounting to less than 5% of the gallons of good soybean oil produced is considered normal. Spoiled gallons are removed and discarded at the inspection point. All materials (mainly soybeans) are added at the beginning of the production process. During May 1994, the following operating statistics were compiled:

Operating Statistics	Gallons
Beginning inventory (50% complete)	6,000
Started in May	50,000
Completed and transferred out	44,000
Ending inventory (40% complete)	10,500
Spoiled	1,500

Costs		
Beginning inventory:		
Material	$ 18,000	
Conversion	1,500	$ 19,500
Current period:		
Material	$150,000	
Conversion	23,817	173,817
Total costs		$193,317

Prepare a cost of production report for May 1994, using FIFO and assuming that the discrete inspection point is at 100% completion.

26. *(Normal and abnormal discrete spoilage; FIFO)* The Golden Gate Co. manufactures several varieties of gates for use in chain-link fences. The Hinge Department of the company produces a standard gate hinge that is used with all models of gates produced by the firm. Materials for the Hinge Department are obtained internally from the Fabrication Department. Completed units from the Hinge Department are transferred to another internal unit, the Assembly Department.

Completed hinges are inspected in the Hinge Department just prior to being transferred to the Assembly Department. For every 100 units that pass inspection, 2 fail and are discarded as normal spoilage. Any spoilage in excess of 2% of the completed units should be considered abnormal. Other than the materials received from the Fabrication Department, materials are added evenly throughout the process in the Hinge Department. Likewise, labor and overhead are incurred evenly throughout the process.

The following data are available for the Hinge Department for August 1994:

Beginning inventory	5,600	(50% complete)
Transferred in	74,400	
Good units completed	70,000	
Ending inventory	7,500	(⅓ complete)

Costs for the month in the Hinge Department were:

	Transferred In	Material	Conversion	Total
Beginning inventory	$ 6,400	$ 2,582	$ 1,232	$ 10,214
Current period	74,400	85,918	31,768	192,086
Total	$80,800	$88,500	$33,000	$202,300

For the Hinge Department, calculate the equivalent units schedule, prepare the FIFO cost of production report, and assign all costs.

27. *(Normal and abnormal discrete spoilage; weighted average)* Use the same data as given in Problem 26. Prepare a cost of production report for the Hinge Department using the weighted average method.

28. *(Normal and abnormal discrete spoilage; weighted average)* The Old Town Bakery produces a 16-inch cake that is sold to four different wholesale grocers. The product is customized to a limited extent in that a different label is added to the package for each of the four grocers. Old Town produces the cakes in a two-department process. A separate work in process account is maintained for each department. The first department is Mixing; the second is Baking. At the end of the production process in the Baking Department, the packaging and label are added to the product after the quality inspection is made. Overhead in the Baking Department is applied based on machine hours. Production and cost data for the Baking Department for February 1994 follow:

Production data:

Beginning inventory (labor, 30% complete)	4,000 units
(overhead, 40% complete)	
Transferred in from Mixing	99,600 units
Normal spoilage (discrete–found at the end of processing during quality control)	1,300 units
Abnormal spoilage (found at end of processing during quality control; caused by a malfunctioning oven)	700 units
Ending inventory (labor, 40% complete)	3,600 units
(overhead, 65% complete)	
Transferred to finished goods	? units

Cost data:

Beginning inventory:		
Transferred in	$ 12,100	
Materials (label and package)	0	
Direct labor	650	
Overhead	1,500	$ 14,250
Current period:		
Transferred in	$298,700	
Materials (label and package)	23,520	
Direct labor	47,534	
Overhead	101,863	471,617
Total cost to account for		$485,867

a. Determine the number of units transferred out during February.
b. Prepare a cost of production report using the weighted average method for the Baking Department for February.
c. Prepare the journal entry to dispose of the cost of abnormal spoilage.

29. *(Normal and abnormal spoilage; weighted average)* The Pine Furniture Co. produces wooden chairs in a two-department process. The first Department is Cutting/Assembly and the second department is Lamination. In the Lamination Department, varnish is added when the goods are 60% complete as to overhead. The units that are spoiled during processing are found upon inspection at the end of production. Spoilage is considered discrete.

Production Data for March 1994

Beginning inventory (80% complete as to labor, 70% complete as to overhead)	1,000 units
Transferred-in during month	7,450 units
Ending inventory (40% complete as to labor, 20% complete as to overhead)	1,500 units
Normal spoilage (found during final quality inspection)	100 units

Abnormal spoilage—found at 30% completion of direct labor
    and 15% of conversion; the sanding machine was misaligned
    and scarred the chairs   200 units

All other units were transferred to finished goods

Cost Data for March 1994
Beginning Work in Process Inventory:

Prior department costs	$ 7,510	
Varnish	950	
Direct labor	2,194	
Overhead	5,522	$ 16,176

Current period costs:

Prior department costs	$68,540	
Varnish	7,015	
Direct labor	23,000	
Overhead	56,782	155,337
Total costs to account for		$171,513

Determine the proper disposition of the March costs for the Laminating Department using the weighted average method; include journal entries.

30. *(Normal and abnormal discrete spoilage; FIFO method)* Use the Pine Furniture Co. information from Problem 29. Determine the proper disposition of the costs of the Laminating Department for March using the FIFO method; include journal entries.

31. *(Comprehensive; weighted average)* In a two-step production process, the Clean Sweep Co. produces straw brooms. The Cutting Department cuts raw materials (straw) into appropriate lengths for brooms; the Assembly Department adds a handle and assembles each broom. The straw is added at the start of production in the Cutting Department and the handle is added at the end of production in the Assembly Department.

    Spoilage occurs in each department. Normal losses in Cutting should not exceed 5% of the units started; loss occurs when the cutting machine or its operator "misfires." Such losses are determined at the end of the production process when the straw "bunches" (a bunch is the quantity of straw required to make one broom) are inspected. Normal losses in Assembly occur when the strands of straw are sewn together. Allowable loss in Assembly is 10% of the straw bunches transferred in; the losses are found approximately 70% of the way through the production process. Any losses in excess of the normal or allowed rates are considered abnormal.

    The following production and cost data are available for June 1994.

**Production Record
(in Units)**

	Cutting	Assembly
Beginning inventory	2,000	1,000
Started or transferred in	50,000	?
Ending inventory	6,000	5,000
Spoiled units	3,000	2,000
Transferred out	?	37,000

Cost Record

Beginning inventory:		
Preceding department	n/a	$ 2,230
Materials	$ 1,000	-0-
Conversion	778	168

Current costs:		
Preceding department	n/a	76,970*
Materials	12,000	740
Conversion	69,654	17,640

*This is **not** the amount derived from your calculations. Use this amount so that you do not carry forward any possible cost errors from the Cutting Department.

The beginning and ending inventory units in Cutting are 10% and 60% complete as to conversion, respectively. In Assembly, the beginning and ending units are 40% and 80% complete as to conversion.

Using the weighted average method, determine the value of the units transferred out, the ending inventories, and any abnormal loss in each department.

32. *(Comprehensive; FIFO method)* Use the information for Clean Sweep Co. from Problem 31. Based on the FIFO method, determine the value of the units transferred out, the ending inventories, and any abnormal loss in each department.

33. *(Comprehensive; weighted average and FIFO)* The Kansas Salt Co. operates a salt mine in central Kansas. Approximately 30% of the salt that is mined is further processed into table salt. For the table salt operation, the company uses a process costing system; processing is split into two departments. Department 1 uses FIFO costing and Department 2 uses weighted average. The processed salt transferred to Department 2 is costed on a modified FIFO approach.

Salt is introduced into the process in Department 1 (this is the only material added in Department 1). Spoilage occurs continuously through the department and normal spoilage should not exceed 10% of the units (a unit is 50 pounds of salt) started.

Department 2 adds material (packaging) at the 75% completion point; this material does not cause an increase in the number of units being processed. A quality control inspection takes place when the goods are 80% complete. Spoilage should not exceed 5% of the units transferred in from Department 1.

The following production and cost data are applicable to Kansas Salt's table salt operations for May 1994:

Department 1 Production Data

Beginning inventory (65% complete)	1,000
Units started	25,000
Units completed	22,000
Units in ending inventory (40% complete)	2,800

Department 1 Cost Data

Beginning inventory:		
Material	$ 1,550	
Conversion	2,300	$ 3,850

Current period:		
Material	$38,080	
Conversion	78,645	116,725
Total costs to account for		$120,575

Department 2 Production Data

Beginning inventory (90% complete)	8,000
Units transferred in	22,000
Units completed	24,000
Units in ending inventory (20% complete)	4,500

Department 2 Cost Data
Beginning inventory:

Transferred in	$ 40,800	
Material	24,000	
Conversion	4,320	$ 69,120

Current period:

Transferred in	$113,700*	
Material	53,775	
Conversion	11,079	178,554
Total costs to account for		$247,674

*This may not be the same amount determined for Department 1; ignore any difference and use this figure.

   a. Compute the equivalent units of production in each department.
   b. Determine the cost per equivalent unit in each department and compute the cost transferred out, the cost in ending inventory, and the cost of spoilage (if necessary).

34. *(Defective units and rework)* In a simple process, Aluminco produces aluminum, vinyl-clad rain gutters for use in residential construction. The company uses a weighted average process costing system. All material is added at the beginning of the production process. In setting its predetermined overhead rate for the year 1994, Aluminco made the following estimates:

Estimated overhead other than rework	$850,000
Estimated rework costs	75,000
Total estimated overhead	$925,000
Expected machine hours for 1994	100,000

During 1994, the following production and cost data were accumulated:

Production

Total good production completed	4,000,000 feet of gutter
Total defects	80,000 feet of gutter
Ending inventory (35% complete)	150,000 feet of gutter

Costs (including beginning inventory costs)

Total cost of direct materials	$ 7,500,000
Total cost of conversion	$11,300,000
Additional cost of reworking defects	$ 75,500

On average, the company expects to sell its output at the rate of $3.50 per foot of gutter.

   a. Determine the overhead application rate for 1994.
   b. Determine the cost per gutter-foot for production in 1994.
   c. Assume that the rework is normal and that the reworked units can be sold for the regular selling price. How is the rework cost of $75,500 accounted for?
   d. Assume that the rework is normal, but the reworked gutter is irregular and can only be sold for $2.50 per foot. Prepare the journal entry to establish the inventory account for the reworked gutter. What is the total cost per unit for the good output completed?
   e. Assume that 20% of the rework is abnormal and that all reworked output is irregular and can only be sold for $2.50 per foot. Prepare the journal entry to establish the inventory account for the reworked gutter. What is the total cost per foot for the good output completed during 1994?

35. *(Job order costing, rework)* Johnson Custom Rigging manufactures pulley systems to the specifications of its customers. It accounts for production costs using a job order system. One recent job entailed the production of 5,000 pulleys for Einmahr Window Systems. Einmahr ordered the pulleys to be used in a counter-

weight system to reduce the amount of lift required to open its larger windows. This job was assigned number 417EWS. The job cost sheet for 417EWS revealed the following:

WIP–Job 417EWS

Direct materials	$10,200
Direct labor	12,300
Overhead	9,200
Total	$31,700

Upon final inspection of the lot of 5,000 pulleys, it was discovered that 115 of the pulleys were defective. In correcting the defects, an additional $475 of cost was incurred ($125 for direct materials, $350 for direct labor). After the defects were cured, the pulleys were included with the nondefective units and shipped to the customer.

a. Assuming the rework costs are normal but specific to this job, show the journal entry to record incurrence of the rework costs.

b. Assuming the company has a predetermined overhead rate that includes normal rework costs, show the journal entry to record incurrence of the rework costs.

c. Assuming the rework costs are abnormal, show the journal entry to record incurrence of the rework costs.

CASE

36. *(Normal and abnormal spoilage; weighted average method)* APCO Company manufactures various lines of bicycles. Because of the high volume of each type of product, the company employs a process cost system using the weighted average method to determine unit costs. Bicycle parts are manufactured in the Molding Department and transferred to the Assembly Department where they are partially assembled. After assembly, the bicycle is sent to the Packing Department.

Cost per unit data for the 20-inch dirt bike has been completed through the Molding Department. Annual cost and production figures for the Assembly Department are presented below.

Production Data:

Beginning inventory	3,000 units	(100% complete as to transferred-in; 100% complete as to assembly material; 80% complete as to conversion)
Transferred-in during the year	45,000 units	(100% complete as to transferred-in)
Transferred to Packing	40,000 units	
Ending inventory	4,000 units	(100% complete as to transferred-in; 50% complete as to assembly material; 20% complete as to conversion)

Cost Data:	Transferred-In	Direct Materials	Conversion
Beginning inventory	$ 82,200	$ 6,660	$ 11,930
Current period	1,237,800	96,840	236,590
Totals	$1,320,000	$103,500	$248,520

Damaged bicycles are identified upon inspection when the assembly process is 70% complete; all assembly material has been added at this point of the process.

The normal rejection rate for damaged bicycles is 5% of the bicycles reaching the inspection point. Any damaged bicycles above the 5% quota are considered to be abnormal. All damaged bikes are removed from the production process and destroyed.

a. Compute the number of damaged bikes that are considered to be
   1. a normal quantity of damaged bikes.
   2. an abnormal quantity of damaged bikes.
b. Compute the weighted average equivalent units of production for the year for
   1. bicycles transferred-in from the Molding Department.
   2. bicycles produced with regard to assembly material.
   3. bicycles produced with regard to assembly conversion.
c. Compute the cost per equivalent unit for the fully assembled dirt bike.
d. Compute the amount of the total production cost of $1,672,020 that will be associated with the following items:
   1. normal damaged units.
   2. abnormal damaged units.
   3. good units completed in the Assembly Department.
   4. ending Work in Process Inventory in the Assembly Department.
e. Describe how the applicable dollar amounts for the following items would be presented in the financial statements:
   1. normal damaged units.
   2. abnormal damaged units.
   3. completed units transferred to the Packing Department.
   4. ending Work in Process Inventory in the Assembly Department.
f. Determine the cost to APCO Company of normal spoilage. Discuss some potential reasons for spoilage to occur in this company. Which of these reasons would you consider important enough to correct and why? How might you attempt to correct these problems?

(CMA adapted)

---

37. FulRange Inc. produces complex printed circuits for stereo amplifiers. The circuits are sold primarily to major component manufacturers, and any production overruns are sold to small manufacturers at a substantial discount. The small manufacturer segment appears to be very profitable because the basic operating budget assigns all fixed expenses to production for the major manufacturers, the only predictable market.

ETHICS AND
QUALITY
DISCUSSION

A common product defect that occurs in production is a "drift," caused by failure to maintain precise heat levels during the production process. Rejects from the 100% testing program can be reworked to acceptable levels if the defect is drift. However, in a recent analysis of customer complaints, George Wilson, the cost accountant, and the quality control engineer have ascertained that normal rework does not bring the circuits up to standard. Sampling shows that about one-half of the reworked circuits fail after extended, high-volume amplifier operation. The incidence of failure in the reworked circuits is projected to be about 10% over one to five years' operation.

Unfortunately, there is no way to determine which reworked circuits will fail because testing does not detect this problem. The rework process could be changed to correct the problem, but the cost-benefit analysis for the suggested change in the rework process indicates that it is not practicable. FulRange's marketing analyst feels that this problem will have a significant impact on the company's reputation and customer satisfaction if it is not corrected. Consequently, the board of directors would interpret this problem as having serious negative implications for the company's profitability.

Wilson has included the circuit failure and rework problem in his report for the upcoming quarterly meeting of the board of directors. Due to the potential adverse economic impact, Wilson has followed a longstanding practice of highlighting this information.

After reviewing the reports to be presented, the plant manager and her staff were upset and indicated to the controller that he should control his people better. "We can't upset the board with this kind of material. Tell Wilson to tone that down. Maybe we can get it by this meeting and have some time to work on it. People who buy those cheap systems and play them that loud shouldn't expect them to last forever."

The controller called Wilson into his office and said, "George, you'll have to bury this one. The probable failure of reworks can be referred to briefly in the oral presentation, but it should not be mentioned or highlighted in the advance material mailed to the board."

Wilson feels strongly that the board will be misinformed on a potentially serious loss of income if he follows the controller's orders. Wilson discussed the problem with the quality control engineer, who simply remarked, "That's your problem, George."

a. Discuss the ethical considerations that George Wilson should recognize in deciding how to proceed in this matter.
b. Explain what ethical responsibilities should be accepted in this situation by
1. the controller.
2. the quality control engineer.
3. the plant manager and her staff.
c. What should George Wilson do in this situation? Explain your answer.

(CMA)

38. *Quality management guru Philip Crosby [provides the following] "absolutes" of total quality management.*
    a. Quality is defined as conformity to requirements.
    b. Quality is achieved through prevention, not inspection.
    c. The quality performance standard is zero defects.
    d. Quality is measured by the price of non-conformity.
    [In a 1992 keynote address to Louisiana Quality Symposium, Crosby said that the] price of non-conformity was immeasurable in the Challenger *disaster. "One of the requirements was not to shoot* Challenger *off if the temperature was below 38 degrees," he said. "NASA decided to override that requirement and launched in 26-degree weather. And we all know what happened."*

    [SOURCE: Sharon Drain, "Crosby Calls for Corporate Culture Change," *BIC U.S.* (November/December 1992), p. 38.]

    a. A faulty seal has also been discussed in relation to the *Challenger* disaster. Discuss your feelings as to whether such seemingly minor factors (lack of conformity to requirements and spoiled goods) truly could have been the "cause(s)" of such a major disaster.
    b. Do you think that ethical considerations about overriding the weather requirement or installing a flawed seal were even deliberated before the disaster? After the disaster?
    c. Most decisions to override process requirements do not result in disasters of the magnitude of the *Challenger*. Choose two requirements either for your job or one of your classes. Discuss the conditions under which you would make a decision to override the requirements that had been specified.

39. *Federal regulators asked a federal judge to order generic drug maker Barr Laboratories Inc. to stop making and selling 15 pharmaceutical products and improve its production of 45 other drugs.*
    In inspections of Barr's plants in Northvale, N.Y., the Food and Drug Administration said it found hundreds of cases in which drugs failed quality tests. Assistant U.S. Attor-

ney Beth Kaswan called Barr "among the worst violators" of FDA manufacturing guidelines.

"They routinely release products that have failed to meet their specifications," Kaswan said. "Barr really needs to go back to the drawing board and fix their manufacturing processes." In June 1992, Barr agreed to stop making 15 drugs.

Bruce Downey, Barr's lead attorney, told U.S. District Judge Alfred Wolin that no one has ever been injured by a Barr product. Downey accused the FDA of constantly changing the standards that Barr was to meet.

The FDA has charged Barr with mixing foreign substances into its drugs, using contaminated water in processing antibiotics, distributing mislabeled drugs, and repackaging and reselling drugs that had been returned as defective.

Barr recorded a large number of what the FDA calls "failures"—instances where a pill's strength or ability to be absorbed by the body do not meet standards, said David Mulligan, a compliance officer for the FDA's Newark office. Barr recorded 205 failures of batches in 1991 and 1992, Mulligan said. "I have never been at a firm which had so many in-process and finished product violations as Barr," he said. Mulligan said he found at least a dozen cases of product mix-up—instances where the wrong drug was packaged in lots or bottles. The mix-ups happened because Barr failed to fully clean manufacturing equipment, Mulligan said. He also stated that pills or capsules lodged in the equipment would end up in the next batch of drugs.

[SOURCE: Associated Press, "FDA Attacks Quality of Generic Maker's Drugs," *(New Orleans) Times-Picayune* (August 18, 1992), p. D-2.]

a. In the health care industry, why does the matter of quality control involve ethical considerations as well as cost considerations?

b. For this company, are the standards of quality set internally or externally? Explain.

c. Why do you think Barr has been slow to improve its quality control procedures?

d. If Barr tracks spoilage costs, do you think its recorded costs of spoiled products would be higher or lower than those of the most quality-conscious drug makers? Explain.

e. If operating in such a manner is profitable for Barr, what does this suggest about the penalties for poor quality control in the generic drug industry?

10

COST ALLOCATION FOR JOINT PRODUCTS AND BY-PRODUCTS

LEARNING OBJECTIVES

After completing this chapter, you should be able to answer these questions:

1. How are the outputs of a joint process classified?
2. At what point in a joint process are joint products identifiable?
3. What management decisions must be made before a joint process is begun?
4. How are joint costs allocated to products?
5. How are by-products treated in job order costing?
6. How should nonprofit organizations account for joint costs?

INTRODUCING

TYSON FOODS INC.

While Tyson Foods processes beef, pork, and fish, most people think of chicken in relation to the company. This relationship could possibly have something to do with the fact that Tyson is the world's largest chicken processor—processing 1.4 billion chickens a year. By controlling the system from breeding to marketing and turning the simple chicken into more than 300 products with fixed prices, Tyson shielded it-self from the historical volatility in prices of plain fresh chickens. Those now account for just 15 percent of the firm's sales. More than half its customers are restaurant chains—it has one plant devoted to Kentucky Fried Chicken's new "crispy" chicken, another to McDonald's restaurants—and institutional customers such as colleges and the military. Profit margins from chicken products are about double those from whole chickens.

Tyson Foods and its competitors—many of which it later bought—created the breeding, feeding, slaughtering, marketing, and other systems that today move chickens from hatchery to slaughterhouse in as little as 28 days. It used to take three to four months. Other changes in the industry are just as dramatic. It takes eight minutes' labor to produce 100 pounds of chicken today, versus five hours in 1949. And in just the last decade, prices have been driven down 40 percent in real terms.

Tyson sells chicken products to markets nationally and internationally. It offers a full line of raw and fully cooked chicken products under a variety of product line names including Tyson, Holly Farms, Tastybird, and Healthy Portion™ Meals. To use as much of the raw material input as possible, the company also sells protein by-products that are used in pet foods and animal feed.

SOURCES: Tyson Foods Inc., *1991 Annual Report*, and Donald Woutat, "Ruler of the Roost," *Dallas Morning News* (February 1, 1993), p. 4D.

Almost every company produces and sells more than one type of product. While companies may engage in multiple production processes to manufacture a variety of products, it is possible for a single process to simultaneously generate various different outputs such as those at Tyson Foods (chicken parts). In a like manner, the refining of crude oil may produce gasoline, motor oil, heating oil, and kerosene. A single process in which one product cannot be manufactured without producing others is known as a **joint process**. Such processes are common in the extractive, agricultural, food, and chemical industries. The costs incurred for materials, labor, and overhead during a joint process are referred to as the **joint cost** of the production process.

Joint process
Joint cost

This chapter discusses joint processes, their related product outputs, and the accounting treatment of joint cost. Outputs of a joint process are classified based on their revenue-generating ability and joint cost is allocated, using either a physical or monetary measure, only to the primary products of a joint process. Although joint cost allocations are necessary to determine financial statement valuations, such allocations should *not* be used in internal decision making.

Joint costs may also be incurred in service businesses and not-for-profit organizations. Such costs in these organizations are often for advertisements that publicize different product lines or locations, or ads for different purposes, such as public service information and requests for donations. Joint costs of not-for-profit firms are covered in the last section of this chapter.

OUTPUTS OF A JOINT PROCESS
Joint products

A joint process simultaneously produces more than one product line. The product lines resulting from a joint process and having a sales value are referred to as (1) joint products, (2) by-products, and (3) scrap. **Joint products** are the *primary* outputs of a joint process; each joint product individually has substantial revenue-generating ability. Joint products are the primary reason management undertakes the production process yielding them. These products are also called primary products, main products, or co-products.

Joint products do not necessarily have to be totally different products; the definition of joint products has been extended to include similar products of differing quality that result from the same process. For example, when computer memory chips are fabricated, the output will all have the same design, but some will be usable while others are not and some will have more memory density than others.

By-products
Scrap

Waste

In contrast, **by-products** and **scrap** are *incidental* outputs of a joint process. Both are salable, but their sales values alone would not be sufficient for management to justify undertaking the joint process. By-products are viewed as having a higher sales value than scrap. A final output from a joint process is **waste**, which is a residual output that has no sales value. A normal amount of waste may be a production cost that cannot be avoided in some industries. On the other hand, many companies have learned either to minimize their production waste by changing their processing techniques or, alternatively, to reclassify waste as a by-product or scrap item used to generate some minimal amount of revenue.

It is not unusual for a product classification to be changed by a company over time because of changes in technology, consumer demand, or ecological factors. Some products originally classified as by-products are reclassified as joint products, while some joint products are reduced to by-product category. Even products originally viewed as scrap or waste may be upgraded to a joint product status. Years ago, for example, the sawdust and chips produced in a lumber mill were considered waste and discarded. These items are now processed further to produce particle board used in making inexpensive furniture. Therefore, depending on the company, sawdust and chips may be considered a joint product or a by-product. The News Note on waste provides an unusual example of innovative waste usage.

NEWS NOTE   Waste Is Not Wasted

After months of talks with the post office, Britain's Chester Zoo is offering a Christmas gift with a difference for gardeners whose roses need special pampering—tubs of mail-order elephant dung.

Chester's seven industrious Asian elephants produce up to five tons a week of the "miracle" fertilizer and the zoo's gardens, where it is applied liberally, won the Britain in Bloom best flower award four times in six years.

The Christmas packages of "zoo poo" are carefully sealed so as not to upset the post office, which was initially concerned about sending elephant dung through its system, and come with a certificate of authenticity from the head keeper.

"Because elephants are vegetarian animals, the poo is actually quite dry and odourless," said Ms. Pat Cade, a spokeswoman at the zoo. "We've had requests for tiger dung, but we can't possibly provide that because it's really unpleasant to pick up and handle."

SOURCE: "Zoo Offers Ideal Gift for Keen Gardeners," *The (Christchurch, New Zealand) Press* (November 25, 1992), p. 10.

The variety of chicken pieces available at Kentucky Fried Chicken constitutes the output of Tyson Foods joint process. One joint product (chicken breasts) may be processed further to obtain deboned meat needed for "popcorn chicken."

Classification of joint process output is based on the judgment of company managers, normally after considering the relative sales values of the outputs. Classifications are unique to each company engaged in the joint process. For example, Aldo Company and Sequin Inc. each engage in the same joint production process that produces three chemicals: X, Y, and Z. Aldo Company classifies all three chemicals as joint products, whereas Sequin Inc. classifies Chemicals Y and Z as joint products and Chemical X as a by-product. These classifications could have resulted from the fact that Aldo has the facilities to refine Chemical X beyond the joint process, but Sequin does not have such facilities. Further refining provides Chemical X with a substantially higher sales value per unit than selling the chemical as it exits the joint process.

THE JOINT PROCESS

Joint products are typically produced in companies using mass production processes and, thus, a process costing accounting method.[1] The outputs of a corn processing plant, for example, may include corn-on-the-cob and whole-kernel corn (joint products), corn kernels (by-products) used for corn meal and grits, inferior kernels (scrap) for sale to producers of animal food, and husks, corn silk, and cobs (waste) that are discarded. Exhibit 10–1 on page 390 illustrates the output of such a joint process.

The point at which joint process outputs are first identifiable as individual products is called the **split-off point.** A joint process may have one or more split-off points, depending on the number and types of output produced. Output may be sold at the split-off point, if a market exists for products in that condition. Alternatively, some or all of the products may be processed further after exiting the joint process.

Split-off point

Joint cost includes all costs incurred up to the split-off point for direct materials, direct labor, and overhead. Joint cost is allocated, at the split-off point, to *only* the joint products because these products are the reason that management undertook the production process. Allocation is necessary because of the cost principle. Joint cost is a necessary and reasonable cost of producing the joint products and, therefore,

---

[1] For simplicity, Chapters 8 and 9 on process costing included examples only of single product processes.

■ EXHIBIT 10-1
Illustration of Joint Process
Output

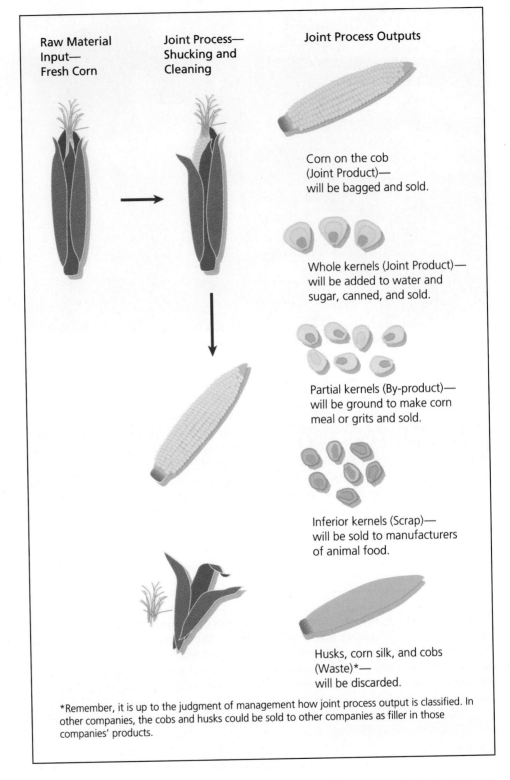

Raw Material
Input—
Fresh Corn

Joint Process—
Shucking and
Cleaning

Joint Process Outputs

Corn on the cob
(Joint Product)—
will be bagged and sold.

Whole kernels (Joint Product)—
will be added to water and
sugar, canned, and sold.

Partial kernels (By-product)—
will be ground to make corn
meal or grits and sold.

Inferior kernels (Scrap)—
will be sold to manufacturers
of animal food.

Husks, corn silk, and cobs
(Waste)*—
will be discarded.

*Remember, it is up to the judgment of management how joint process output is classified. In
other companies, the cobs and husks could be sold to other companies as filler in those
companies' products.

should be attached to them. But while necessary for valuation purposes, *the joint cost
allocation to joint products is not relevant to decision making*. Once the split-off
point is reached, the joint cost has already been incurred and is a **sunk cost** that cannot be changed no matter what future course of action is taken.

If any of the joint process outputs are processed further, additional costs after split-
off will be incurred. Any costs after split-off are assigned to the separate products for
which those costs are incurred. Exhibit 10-2 depicts a joint process with multiple

Sunk cost

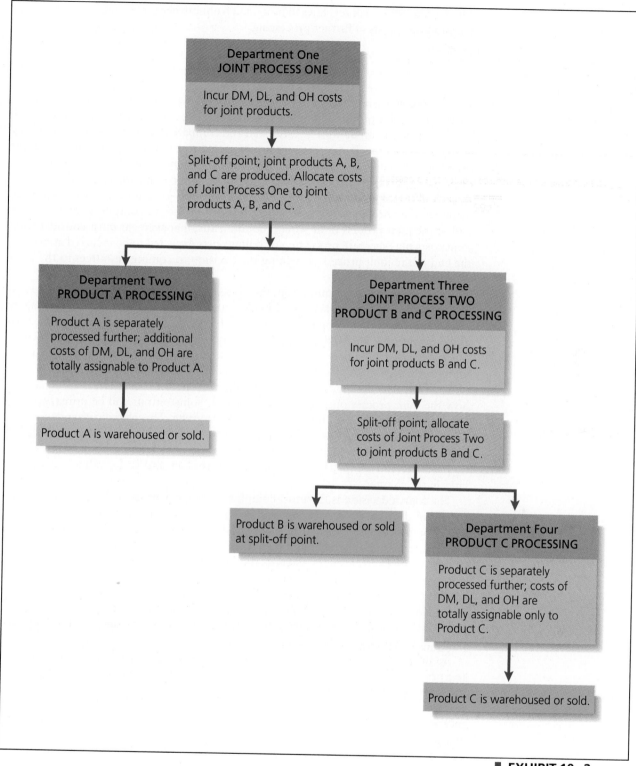

split-off points and the allocation of costs to products. For simplicity, all the output of this joint process is primary output; there are no by-products, scrap, or waste. Note that some of the output of Joint Process One (joint products B and C) becomes part of the direct material for Joint Process Two. The joint cost allocations will follow products B and C into Joint Process Two for accounting purposes, but these allocated costs should not be used in making decisions about further processing in that department or in Department 4. Such decisions should be made after considering only whether the additional revenues to be gained from further processing are greater than the additional costs of further processing.

MANAGEMENT DECISIONS REGARDING JOINT PROCESSES

Certain decisions need to be made by company managers before committing resources to a joint production process. First, total expected revenues from the sale of the joint process output must be estimated and compared to total expected processing costs of the output. If the revenues are expected to exceed the costs, management must then consider other potential costs. Since the joint process results in a "basket" of products, managers must be aware that some of the joint process output may require additional processing to make it salable. Once joint process costs have been incurred, they become sunk costs *regardless* of whether the output is salable at the end of the joint process or at what amount. Thus, management must consider total joint costs plus separate processing or selling costs expected to be incurred at or after the end of the joint process in making the decision to commit resources to the joint process.

If total anticipated revenues from the "basket" of products exceed the anticipated joint and separate costs, the second management decision must be made. Managers must compare the net income from this use of resources to that which would be provided by all other alternative uses of company resources. If joint process net income is greater than would be provided by other uses, management would decide that this joint production process is the best use of capacity and would begin production.

The next two decisions are made at split-off. The third decision is to determine how the joint process output is to be classified. Some output will be primary; other output will be considered by-product, scrap, or waste. This classification decision is necessary for the joint cost to be allocated since *joint cost is only assigned to joint products.* However, before allocation, joint cost may be reduced by the value of the by-products and scrap. Determination of by-product and scrap value is discussed later in the chapter.

The fourth decision is the most complex. Management must decide whether any (or all) of the joint process output will be sold (if marketable) at split-off or whether it will be processed further. If primary products are marketable at split-off, further processing should only be undertaken if the value added to the product, as reflected by the incremental revenues, exceeds the incremental costs. If a primary product is not marketable at split-off, additional costs *must* be incurred to make that product marketable. For nonprimary output, management must also estimate whether the incremental revenues from additional processing will exceed additional processing costs. If there is no net incremental benefit, the nonmarketable output should be disposed of without further processing after the split-off point.

To illustrate a further-processing decision, assume that a whole chicken has a selling price of $.15 per pound at split-off, but the minimum selling price for chicken parts after further processing is $.19 per pound. If the additional processing costs are less than $.04 per pound, the $.04 incremental revenue ($.19 − $.15) exceeds the incremental costs and additional processing should occur. Note that the joint cost is *not* used in this decision process. The joint cost is a sunk cost after it has been incurred, and the only relevant items in the decision to process further are the incremental revenues and incremental costs.

Exhibit 10–3 presents the four management decision points in a joint production process. In making decisions at any potential point of sale, managers must have a valid estimate of the selling price of each type of joint process output. Expected selling prices should be based on both cost and market factors. In the long run, assuming demand exists, the selling prices and volumes of products must be sufficient to cover their total costs. However, immediate economic influences on setting selling prices, such as competitors' prices and consumers' sensitivity to price changes, cannot be ignored in estimating selling prices and forecasting revenues.

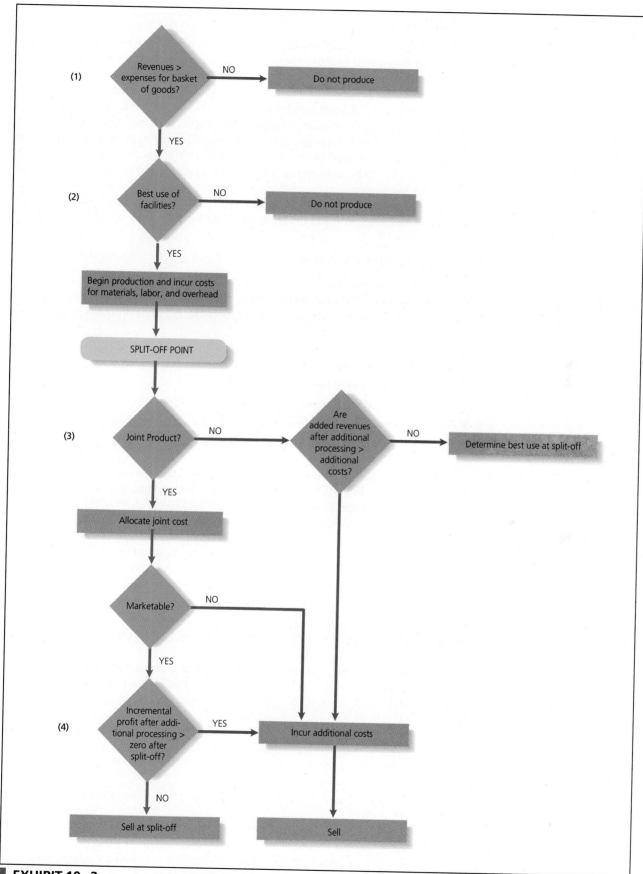

EXHIBIT 10–3

Decision Points in a Joint Production Process

ALLOCATION OF JOINT COSTS

The Cluck-Cluck Company is used to demonstrate alternative methods of allocating joint processing costs. Because the profit margins are higher for chicken parts than for whole chickens, Cluck-Cluck processes chickens into three distinct primary products during a joint process: breasts, legs, and thighs. (The remaining parts are considered by-products.) All joint products may be sold at split-off. Alternatively, each chicken product may be processed further, which will create additional separate costs for the products. Chicken breasts may be processed further to produce sandwich patties; legs can be processed further to make children's meals; and thigh meat can be processed further to be used as part of a stir-fry mixture. Certain marketing and disposal costs for advertising, commissions, and transportation are incurred regardless of when the products are sold. Assumed information on Cluck-Cluck's processing operations and joint products for September 1994 is presented in Exhibit 10−4.

Physical Measure Allocation

Physical measurement allocation

An easy, objective way to prorate joint cost at the split-off point is through the use of a physical measure. **Physical measurement allocation** uses a common physical characteristic of the joint products as the proration base. All joint products must be measurable by the same characteristic, such as:

■ tons of ore in the mining industry

■ linear board feet in the lumber milling industry

■ barrels of oil in the petroleum refining industry

■ pounds of meat, bone, and hide in the meat packing or processing industry

■ number of computer chips in the semiconductor industry

Using physical measurement allocation, Cluck-Cluck Company's $3,800,000 of joint cost is assigned as shown in Exhibit 10−5. For Cluck-Cluck, physical measurement allocation would assign a cost of approximately $851.06 ($3,800,000 ÷ 4,465 tons) per ton of chicken, regardless of type of part.

Physical measurement allocation treats each unit of measure as equally desirable and assigns the same per unit cost to each. Also, unlike monetary measures, physical measures provide an unchanging yardstick of output. A ton of output produced from a process five years ago is the same measurement as a ton produced from that process

■ EXHIBIT 10−4
Cluck-Cluck Company Basic Joint Cost Information

Joint processing cost for period: $3,800,000

(1) Joint Products	(2) Tons of Production	(3) Sales Price per Ton at Split-Off	(4) Cost per Ton if Sold at Split-Off*	(5) Separate Costs per Ton if Processed Further	(6) Final Sales Price per Ton
Breasts	1,860	$1,900	$150	$190	$2,500
Legs	1,215	1,120	60	100	1,200
Thighs	1,390	784	40	60	1,000
	4,465				

*These costs will also be incurred if product is processed further.

$$\text{Cost per Physical Measure} = \frac{\text{Total Joint Cost}}{\text{Total Units of Physical Measurement}}$$

$$= \frac{\$3,800,000}{4,465 \text{ tons}} = \approx\$851.06 \text{ per ton}$$

JOINT PRODUCT	TONS	COST PER TON	TOTAL ALLOCATED COST
Breasts	1,860	$851.06	$1,582,972
Legs	1,215	$851.06	1,034,038
Thighs	1,390	$851.06	1,182,973
Total	4,465		$3,799,983*

*Off due to rounding of cost per ton.

EXHIBIT 10–5

Cluck-Cluck Company Joint Cost Allocation Based on Physical Measurement

today. Physical measures are useful in allocating joint cost to products that have extremely unstable selling prices. These measures are also necessary in rate-regulated industries that use cost to determine selling prices. For example, assume that a rate-regulated company has the right to set selling price at 15 percent above cost. It is circular logic to allocate joint cost based on selling prices that were set based on cost to produce the output.

A major disadvantage of allocating joint costs based on a physical measure is that the revenue-generating ability of individual joint products is ignored. Products that weigh the most or that are produced in the largest quantity will receive the highest proportion of joint cost allocation—regardless of their ability to bear that cost when they are sold. In the case of Cluck-Cluck, each ton of thighs has been assigned a cost of $851.06. However, the selling price per ton of these parts at split-off is only $784. Using this method of joint cost allocation, each ton of thighs sold at split-off will result in an *apparent* significant loss relative to the sales price per ton at that point.

Monetary Measure Allocation

All commonly used allocation methods employ a process of proration. Because of the simplicity of the physical measure allocation process, a detailed proration scheme was unnecessary. However, the following steps can be used to prorate joint cost to joint products in the more complex monetary measure allocations:

1. Choose a monetary allocation base.
2. List the values that comprise the base for each joint product.
3. Sum the values in step 2 to obtain a total value for the list.
4. Divide each individual value in step 2 by the total in step 3 to obtain a numerical proportion for each value. The sum of these proportions should total to 1.00 or 100%.[2]
5. Multiply the joint cost by each proportion to obtain the amount to be allocated to each product.
6. Divide the prorated joint cost for each product by the number of equivalent units of production for each product to obtain a cost per EUP for valuation purposes.

---

[2] Decimal fractions rounded to two places are used throughout the chapter for presentation purposes and to highlight the proportion of the total joint cost allocated to each joint product. Greater precision may be obtained by simply dividing each step 2 value by the step 3 value, leaving the result in the calculator, and multiplying that resulting value by the total joint cost.

Three of the many monetary measures that can be used to allocate joint costs to primary output are presented in this text. These measures are sales value at split-off, net realizable value at split-off, and approximated net realizable value at split-off. The primary benefit of monetary measure allocations over physical measure allocations is that the former recognize the relative ability of each product to generate a profit at sale. A problem with monetary measure allocations is that the basis used is not constant or unchanging. Because of fluctuations in the general and specific price levels, a dollar's worth of output today is different from a dollar's worth of output from the same process five years ago. However, accountants customarily ignore price level fluctuations when recording or processing data, so this particular flaw of monetary measures is not usually viewed as significant.

Sales value at split-off allocation

1. Sales Value at Split-Off The **sales value at split-off allocation** assigns joint cost to joint products based solely on relative sales values of the products at the split-off point. Thus, to use this method, all joint products must be marketable at split-off. Exhibit 10–6 shows how Cluck-Cluck's joint cost is assigned to production using the sales value at split-off allocation method. Under this method, the low selling price per ton of thighs, relative to the other chicken parts, results in a lower allocated cost per ton than resulted from the physical measure allocation technique. This process uses a weighting technique based both on quantity produced and selling price of production.

Net realizable value at split-off allocation

2. Net Realizable Value at Split-Off The **net realizable value at split-off allocation** method assigns joint cost based on the joint products' proportional net realizable values at the point of split-off. Net realizable value is equal to product sales revenue at split-off minus any costs necessary to prepare and dispose of the product. This method also requires that all joint products be marketable at the split-off point, but it considers the additional costs that must be incurred at split-off to realize the estimated sales revenue. The costs at split-off point for Cluck-Cluck's products are shown in the fourth column of Exhibit 10–4. The net realizable value of each product is computed by subtracting the costs at split-off from the selling price at split-off. The $3,800,000 joint cost is then assigned based on each product's relative proportion of total net realizable value (Exhibit 10–7). This method provides an allocated product cost that considers the disposal costs which would be necessitated if the product were to be sold at split-off.

3. Approximated Net Realizable Value at Split-Off Often, some or all of the joint products are not salable at the split-off point. For these products to be sold, additional processing must take place after split-off, causing additional costs to be incurred. Because of this lack of marketability at split-off, neither the sales value nor the net realizable value

▌ EXHIBIT 10–6

Cluck-Cluck Company
Joint Cost Allocation Based on Sales Value at Split-Off

JOINT PRODUCT	TONS	SELLING PRICE	REVENUES	DECIMAL FRACTION	AMOUNT ALLOCATED	COST PER TON
Breasts	1,860	$1,900	$3,534,000	.59	$2,242,000	$1,205.38
Legs	1,215	1,120	1,360,800	.23	874,000	719.34
Thighs	1,390	784	1,089,760	.18	684,000	492.09
Total	4,465		$5,984,560	1.00	$3,800,000	

JOINT PRODUCT	TONS	UNIT NET REALIZABLE VALUES	TOTAL NET REALIZABLE VALUES	DECIMAL FRACTION	AMOUNT ALLOCATED	COST PER TON
Breasts	1,860	$1,750	$3,255,000	.58	$2,204,000	$1,184.95
Legs	1,215	1,060	1,287,900	.23	874,000	719.34
Thighs	1,390	744	1,034,160	.19	722,000	519.42
Total	4,465		$5,577,060	1.00	$3,800,000	

▌ EXHIBIT 10–7

Cluck-Cluck Company Joint Cost Allocation Based on Net Realizable Value at Split-Off

approach can be used. **Approximated net realizable value at split-off allocation** requires that a simulated net realizable value at the split-off point be calculated. This approximated value is computed on a per product basis as final sales price minus incremental separate costs. **Incremental separate costs** refer to all costs that are incurred between the split-off point and the point of sale. The approximated net realizable values are then used to proportionately distribute joint cost. An underlying assumption in this method is that the incremental revenue from further processing is equal to or greater than the incremental cost of further processing and selling. Using the information in Exhibit 10–4, approximated net realizable values at split-off are determined for each product processed by Cluck-Cluck:

Approximated net realizable value at split-off allocation

Incremental separate costs

Joint Products	Per Ton Final Selling Price	Per Ton Separate Costs after Split-Off	Approximated Net Realizable Value at Split-Off
Breasts	$2,500	$340	$2,160
Legs	1,200	160	1,040
Thighs	1,000	100	900

Further processing should be undertaken only if the incremental revenues will exceed the incremental costs. These computations are shown as follows:

Joint Product	Final Sales Price	Sales Price at Split-off	Cost per Ton at Split-off	Cost per Ton after Split-off
Breasts	$2,500	$1,900	$150	$340
Legs	1,200	1,120	60	160
Thighs	1,000	784	40	100

Joint Product	Incremental Revenue	Incremental Cost	Difference
Breasts	$600	$190	$410
Legs	80	100	(20)
Thighs	216	60	156

The previous information shows that Cluck-Cluck would be $20 worse off per ton if legs were processed further than if they were sold at split-off. For breasts and thighs, however, the incremental revenues from further processing exceed the incremental costs beyond split-off, so Cluck-Cluck's management should process these two products further. The same conclusion can be reached by comparing the net realizable values at split-off with the approximated net realizable values at split-off as follows:

Joint Product	Net Realizable Value at Split-Off	Approximated Net Realizable Value at Split-Off	Difference
Breasts	$1,750	$2,160	$410
Legs	1,060	1,040	(20)
Thighs	744	900	156

The decisions made about further processing affect the values used to allocate joint costs in the approximated net realizable sales value method. When one or more products will not be processed further because it is uneconomical to do so, the value base used for allocation of joint cost will be a mixture of actual and approximated net realizable values at split-off. Products that will not be processed further will be valued at their actual net realizable values at split-off; products that will be processed further are valued at approximated net realizable values at split-off. Using this mixture of values, Cluck-Cluck's $3,800,000 joint cost is allocated among the products as shown in Exhibit 10–8.

Each of the above physical and monetary measures allocates a different amount of joint cost to product and results in a different per unit cost for each product. Each method has advantages and disadvantages. For most companies, approximated net realizable value at split-off provides the best joint cost assignment. This method is the most flexible in that no requirements exist about similar measurement bases (pounds, tons, and so forth) or actual marketability at split-off. It is, however, more complex than the other methods, because estimations must be made about additional processing costs and potential future sales values.

The values obtained from the approximated net realizable value at split-off allocation method are used to illustrate cost flows in a joint cost environment. Cluck-Cluck has three production departments: (1) Chicken Processing; (2) Sandwich Patty Production (using chicken breasts); and (3) Stir-Fry Production (using chicken thighs). Work performed in the second and third departments creates the finished, further-processed products. Legs are transferred directly from Chicken Processing to Finished Goods Inventory since these parts are not processed beyond split-off. Cluck-Cluck uses FIFO costing and had the following finished goods inventories at the beginning of September:

Sandwich Patties	190 tons @ $1,450	$275,500
Legs	120 tons @ $ 620	74,400
Stir-Fry	140 tons @ $ 584	81,760

During September, the company incurred separable costs for chicken breasts and thighs of $353,400 and $83,400, respectively. All the chicken that was started into pro-

■ EXHIBIT 10–8

Cluck-Cluck Company Joint Cost Allocation Based on Approximated Net Realizable Value at Split-Off

JOINT PRODUCTS	TONS	APPROXIMATED NET REALIZABLE VALUE PER TON	TOTAL APPROXIMATED NET REALIZABLE VALUE	DECIMAL FRACTION	AMOUNT ALLOCATED	COST PER TON
Breasts	1,860	$2,160	$4,017,600	.61	$2,318,000	$1,246.24
Legs	1,215	1,060*	1,287,900	.20	760,000	625.51
Thighs	1,390	900	1,251,000	.19	722,000	519.42
Total	4,465		$6,556,500	1.00	$3,800,000	

*Note that this is *actual* net realizable value at split-off.

cessing in September was also completed during that month. The company sold the following quantities of chicken in September:

Product	Quantity	Sales Price Per Ton	Total Sales Price (Cash)
Sandwich Patties	1,886 tons	$2,500	$4,715,000
Legs	1,220 tons	1,120	1,366,400
Stir-Fry	1,410 tons	1,000	1,410,000

The September 1994 journal entries for Cluck-Cluck Company are shown in Exhibit 10–9.

■ EXHIBIT 10–9

Cluck-Cluck Company Journal Entries for September 1994

(1) Work in Process Inventory—Chicken Processing	3,800,000	
Supplies Inventory		135,714
Payroll Summary		2,850,000
Manufacturing Overhead		814,286
To record joint process costs incurred in September 1994; credit amounts are assumed.		
(2) Finished Goods Inventory—Legs	760,000	
Work in Process Inventory—Patty Production	2,318,000	
Work in Process Inventory—Stir-Fry Production	722,000	
Work in Process Inventory—Chicken Processing		3,800,000
To allocate the joint cost incurred in Chicken Processing to the joint products.		
(3) Work in Process Inventory—Patty Production	353,400	
Work in Process Inventory—Stir-Fry Production	83,400	
Various accounts		436,800
To record separate costs for further processing incurred in the Patty and Stir-Fry Production Departments. (Actual costs are assumed to equal estimated separate costs shown in Exhibit 10–4.)		
(4) Finished Goods Inventory—Sandwich Patties	2,671,400	
Finished Goods Inventory—Stir-Fry	805,400	
Work in Process Inventory—Patty Production		2,671,400
Work in Process Inventory—Stir-Fry Production		805,400
To transfer 1,860 tons of sandwich patties and 1,500 tons of Stir-Fry to Finished Goods Inventory (cost per ton: Patties, $1,436.24; Stir-Fry, $536.93). The tonnage increased in the Stir-Fry Department due to the addition of other ingredients.		
(5) Cash	7,491,400	
Sales		7,491,400
To record cash sales: Sandwich Patties, $4,715,000; Legs, $1,366,400; Stir-Fry, $1,410,000.		
(6) Cost of Goods Sold	4,237,485	
Finished Goods Inventory—Sandwich Patties		2,711,363
Finished Goods Inventory—Legs		762,461
Finished Goods Inventory—Stir-Fry		763,661
To record cost of goods sold on a FIFO basis: Sandwich Patties (190 tons × $1,450) + (1,696 tons × $1,436.24) Legs (120 tons × $620) + (1,100 tons × $625.51) Stir-Fry (140 tons × $584) + (1,270 tons × $536.93)		
(7) Selling Expenses	412,500	
Cash		412,500
To record selling expenses ($150 × 1,886) + ($60 × 1,220) + ($40 × 1,410). (Actual costs are assumed to equal estimated costs shown in Exhibit 10–4.)		

The ending balances of Cluck-Cluck's three finished goods accounts are computed as follows:

| | Tons | | |
	Sandwich Patties	Legs	Stir-Fry
Beginning inventory (p. 398)	190	120	140
Tons completed (Exhibit 10–8)	1,860	1,215	1,500[a]
Tons available	2,050	1,335	1,640
Tons sold (p. 399)	1,886	1,220	1,410
Ending inventory	164	115	230
Times FIFO unit costs	$1,436.24[b]	$625.51[c]	$536.93[d]
EI valued at FIFO costs	$235,543.36	$71,933.65	$123,493.90

[a] As per entry (4) in Exhibit 10–9, the tonnage of Stir-Fry increased due to adding ingredients.
[b] ($2,318,000 + $353,400) ÷ 1,860 tons = $1,436.24
[c] From Exhibit 10–8
[d] ($722,000 + $83,400) ÷ 1,500 tons = $536.93

These ending inventory unit values represent *approximate* actual costs of production.

Prorating joint costs provides necessary inventory valuations for manufacturing companies. However, the allocation process may be influenced by the net realizable values of the other possible output of a joint process—by-products and scrap.

ACCOUNTING FOR BY-PRODUCTS AND SCRAP

Because the distinction between by-products and scrap is one of degree, we have chosen to discuss them together by presenting several of the many treatments found in practice. The appropriate choice of method depends on the magnitude of the net realizable value of the by-products/scrap and the need for additional processing after split-off. As the sales value of the by-product/scrap increases, so does the need for inventory recognition. Sales value of the by-products/scrap is generally recorded under either the (1) net realizable value or (2) realized value approach. These approaches are discussed in the following sections using additional data for Cluck-Cluck Company, which considers chicken wings as a by-product. Data for November 1994 is shown in Exhibit 10–10.

Net Realizable Value Approach

Net realizable value approach

Use of the **net realizable value** (or offset) **approach** requires that the net realizable value of the by-products/scrap be treated as a reduction in the joint cost of manufacturing primary products. This method is normally used when the net realizable value of the by-product or scrap is expected to be significant.

Under the net realizable value approach, an inventory value is recorded that equals the selling price of the by-product/scrap produced minus the related processing, storing, and disposing costs. Any income remaining after covering these costs is used to reduce the joint cost of the main products. Any loss generated by the by-products/scrap is added to the cost of the main products. The credit for this Work in Process Inventory debit may be to one of two accounts. First, under the indirect method, Cost of Goods Sold for the joint products is reduced when the by-products/scrap are generated and joint products are sold:

■ EXHIBIT 10–10
**Cluck-Cluck Company
November 1994 Data**

Total purchases for month: 5,000 tons of chickens

Chicken wings (by-product) included in purchases: 250 tons
Selling price of chicken wings: $200 per ton
Processing costs per ton of chicken wings: $20 for labor and $5 for overhead
Net realizable value per ton of chicken: $175

Work in Process Inventory—Chicken Wings	43,750	
Cost of Goods Sold—Main Products		43,750

When additional costs are incurred:

Work in Process Inventory—Chicken Wings	6,250	
Various accounts		6,250

When by-product is completed:

Finished Goods Inventory—Chicken Wings	50,000	
Work in Process Inventory—Chicken Wings		50,000

When by-product is sold:

Cash (or Accounts Receivable)	50,000	
Finished Goods Inventory—Chicken Wings		50,000

This technique may result in a slight mismatching of costs if by-products are created in a different period than joint products are sold. Also, inventory values for the main products will be slightly overstated.

Alternatively, under the direct method, the work in process (WIP) joint cost of the primary products is reduced by the net realizable value of the by-product/scrap produced. Reducing WIP joint cost causes the costs of the primary products to be lowered for both cost of goods sold and inventory purposes. Thus, the only change in the above journal entries would be on the date the by-product was generated. The direct approach journal entry at that time is:

Work in Process Inventory—Chicken Wings	43,750	
Work in Process Inventory—Main Products		43,750

The major advantage of the direct approach is timing. The reduction in main products' joint cost is accomplished simultaneously with production of the main products. The disadvantage of this approach is that it is less conservative than waiting to record revenues until the by-product or scrap is actually sold, as does the realized value approach presented in the next section.

By-products and scrap may have sales potential beyond that currently known to management. Although reducing joint costs by the net realizable value of by-products/scrap is the traditional method of accounting for these goods, it is not necessarily the best method for managerial decision making, as indicated in the News Note on page 402 about by-product accounting. The net realizable value method does not indicate the sales dollars, expenses, or profits from the by-products/scrap and, thus, does not provide sufficient information to induce management to maximize the inflows from by-products/scrap disposal.

Realized Value Approach

Realized value approach

Under the **realized value** (or other income) **approach,** no value is recognized for the by-products/scrap until they are sold. This method is the simplest approach to accounting for by-products/scrap. Several reporting techniques can be used with the realized value approach. One form of presentation shows total sales price of the by-product/scrap on the income statement under an "other revenue" caption. Costs of additional processing or disposal of the by-product/scrap are included with the cost of producing the main products. This presentation provides little useful information to management since the cost of producing the by-products/scrap is not matched with the revenues generated by those items.

For the Cluck-Cluck Company, the entries under the "other revenue" method are as follows. When labor and overhead costs are incurred:

Work in Process Inventory—Joint Products	5,000	
Manufacturing Overhead	1,250	
Various accounts		6,250

To record the labor cost of cleaning (to WIP Inventory) and overhead charges for chicken wings (all included in the cost of joint products).

At point of sale:

Cash (or Accounts Receivable)	50,000	
Other Revenue		50,000

To record sale of chicken wings.

Another presentation shows by-product/scrap revenue on the income statement net of additional costs of processing and disposal. This method presents the net by-product revenue as an enhancement of net income in the period of sale under an "other income" caption. Such a presentation allows management to recognize the dollar benefit added to company income by managing the costs and revenues related to the by-products/scrap. The entries for the processing and sale of the by-products/scrap under this method for the Cluck-Cluck Company are as follows. When labor and overhead costs are incurred:

Work in Process Inventory—Chicken Wings	6,250	
Various accounts		6,250
To record the labor cost of cleaning and overhead charges for chicken wings; this assumes that overhead charges are applied to WIP (with a corresponding credit to Manufacturing Overhead included in the various accounts).		

At point of sale:

Cash (or Accounts Receivable)	50,000	
Work in Process Inventory—		
Chicken Wings		6,250
Miscellaneous Income		43,750
To record sale of chicken wings net of processing/disposal costs.		

Because the "other income" method matches by-products/scrap revenue with related storage, further processing, transportation, and disposal costs, this method provides detailed information on financial responsibility and accountability for disposition, provides better control, and may improve performance. Managers are more apt to look for new or expanded sales potential since the net benefits of doing so are shown directly on the income statement.

Other alternative presentations include showing the realized value from the sale of the by-product or scrap as (1) an addition to gross margin, (2) a reduction of the cost of goods manufactured, or (3) a reduction of the cost of goods sold. The major advantage of these simplistic approaches is that of clerical efficiency.

Regardless of whether a company uses the net realizable value or the realized value approach, the specific method used to account for by-products/scrap should be established *before* the joint costs are allocated to the primary products. Exhibit 10–11 on page 404 presents four comparative income statements using different methods of accounting for by-product income for the Cluck-Cluck Company. Some assumed amounts have been included to provide complete income statements.

By-products, scrap, and waste are created in all types of businesses, not just manufacturing. Managers may not see the need to determine the cost of these secondary types of products. However, as discussed in Chapters 3 and 9 in relation to the cost of quality, the importance of this cost information is only recently being recognized.

> Scrap material represents a source of revenue that has not been fully exploited. Unless companies can establish the value of their scrap, they will be indecisive about expending the capital (time and effort) needed to recover the revenue.[3]

The following three examples illustrate organizations that have made the utmost of their scrap/waste. A florist began selling bouquets of dead flowers to customers who wanted to send prank gifts.[4] At almost $40 per bouquet, sales of what had been

---

[3] Donald Rogoff, "Scrap into Profits: How to Fully Exploit Scrap as a Revenue Source," *Journal of Accountancy* (February 1987), p. 113.
[4] Andrea Rothman, "Roses Are Brown, Lilies Are Gray, Here's Wishing You a Terrible Day," *Wall Street Journal* (Feb. 10, 1987), p. 41.

(a)
Net Realizable Approach: Reduce CGS

Sales		$7,200,000
Cost of Goods Sold		
Beginning FG	$ 400,000	
CGM	3,600,000	
CGA	$4,000,000	
Ending FG	380,000	
Unadjusted CGS	$3,620,000	
NRV of By-Product	43,750	3,576,250
Gross Margin		$3,623,750
Operating Expenses		2,600,000
Income from Principal Operations		$1,023,750
Other Income		
Commissions		80,000
Income before Income Taxes		$1,103,750

(b)
Net Realizable Approach: Reduce CGM

Sales		$7,200,000
Cost of Goods Sold		
Beginning FG	$ 400,000	
CGM ($3,600,000–		
$43,750 NRV)	3,556,250	
CGA	$3,956,250	
Ending FG [assumed		
to be smaller than		
under (a)]	375,380	3,580,870
Gross Margin		$3,619,130
Operating Expenses		2,600,000
Income from Principal Operations		$1,019,130
Other Income		
Commissions		80,000
Income before Income Taxes		$1,099,130

(c)
Net Realized Value Approach: Increase Revenue

Sales		$7,200,000
Other Revenue		
Sale of By-Product		50,000
Total Revenue		$7,250,000
Cost of Goods Sold		
Beginning FG	$ 400,000	
CGS (Main Products)	3,600,000	
CGS (Processing		
By-Product)	6,250	
CGA	$4,006,250	
Ending FG	380,000	3,626,250
Gross Margin		$3,623,750
Operating Expenses		2,600,000
Income from Principal Operations		$1,023,750
Other Income		
Commissions		80,000
Income before Income Taxes		$1,103,750

(d)
Net Realized Value Approach: Present as Other Income

Sales		$7,200,000
Cost of Goods Sold		
Beginning FG	$ 400,000	
CGM	3,600,000	
CGA	$4,000,000	
Ending FG	380,000	3,620,000
Gross Margin		$3,580,000
Operating Expenses		2,600,000
Income from Principal Operations		$ 980,000
Other Income		
Commissions	$ 80,000	
By-Products Sale		
(NRV)	43,750	123,750
Income before Income Taxes		$1,103,750

▌ EXHIBIT 10–11

Comparative Income Statement By-Product Presentations for Cluck-Cluck Company

waste is becoming a large source of revenue! Arizona Record Destruction pulverizes confidential documents such as payroll records, credit card receipts, and legal briefs for customers. The remains are then sold for $50 per 1,000-pound bale to ranchers and horse trainers, who use the material as bedding for horse stalls. It has been a good source of extra revenue for Arizona Record and using the shredded documents is more environmentally conscious than using similarly priced wood shavings.[5] Many

---

[5] Anthony J. Michels, "Animals Do Their Bit for Recycling, the Olympics, and Alternative Energy," *FORTUNE* (July 27, 1992), p. 14.

plastics producers routinely recycle their own plant scrap by grinding it up and compressing the flakes into pellets that work almost as well as original plastic. GE even buys back scrap from plants that purchase GE products. This buy-back plan allows GE to know the quality of the p' .stic being purchased that is then recycled into new products for GE to sell.[6]

BY-PRODUCTS OR SCRAP IN JOB ORDER COSTING

Although joint products normally are not associated with job order costing systems, it is possible for these systems to have by-products or scrap. Either the realized value approach or the net realizable value approach can be used with regard to the timing of recognition of the value of by-products/scrap.

The value of by-products/scrap in a job order system is appropriately credited to either manufacturing overhead or to the specific jobs in process. The former account is credited if by-product/scrap value is generally created by a significant proportion of all jobs undertaken. In contrast, if only a few or specific jobs generate a disproportionate amount of by-products/scrap, then individual jobs should be credited with the value since they directly generated the by-product/scrap.

To illustrate, assume that Cluck-Cluck occasionally prepares special chicken-based foods for several large institutional clients. Recently, the company received an order for 20,000 chicken potpies for the Brian Wood Elementary School. As the potpies are prepared, some scrap meat and vegetables are generated. During October 1994, Cluck-Cluck sold $200 of scraps to the Min Catfood Corporation. The entry to record the sale, using the realized value approach, is:

Cash	200	
Manufacturing Overhead		200

In contrast, assume that Cluck-Cluck Company seldom has salable scrap on its jobs. However, during October 1994, Cluck-Cluck contracted with the Lillian Correctional Facility to prepare 100,000 frozen salmon croquettes. Specific raw materials had to be acquired for the job because Cluck-Cluck normally does not process fish. Thus, all raw materials costs will be charged directly to the Lillian Correctional Facility. As the salmon is filleted for the order, some fish scraps are generated that can be sold to the Min Catfood Corporation for $450. Because the cost of the materials is directly related to this job, the sale of the scrap from those raw materials also relates to the specific job. Under these circumstances, the production of the scrap is recorded (using the net realizable value approach) as follows:

Scrap Inventory—Salmon	450	
Work in Process Inventory—		
Lillian Correctional Facility		450

In this case, the net realizable value approach is preferred because of the timing of recognition. To affect the specific job cost that caused an unusual incidence and amount of scrap, it may be necessary to recognize the by-product/scrap upon production; otherwise, the job may be completed before a sale of the by-product/scrap can be made.

It is common to think of manufacturing processes as creating the need to allocate costs. However, some costs incurred in service businesses and not-for-profit organizations may be allocated among product lines, organizational locations, or types of activities performed by the organizations.

---

[6]Stratford P. Sherman, "Trashing a $150 Billion Business," *FORTUNE* (August 28, 1989), p. 94.

The process of obtaining sides of beef from cattle requires the incurrence of many joint costs. These costs should be allocated to the primary output produced, such as steaks, ground beef, and roasts.

JOINT COSTS IN SERVICE AND NOT-FOR-PROFIT ORGANIZATIONS

Service and not-for-profit organizations may incur joint costs for advertising multiple products, printing multipurpose documents, or holding multipurpose events. For example, not-for-profits often issue brochures containing information about the organization, its purposes, and its programs; simultaneously, these documents make an appeal for funds.

If a service business decides to allocate joint costs, either a physical or monetary allocation base can be chosen. Joint costs in a service business often relate to advertisements rather than to a process. For example, a local carpet cleaning store may advertise a sale and list all store locations in a single newspaper ad. The ad cost could be allocated equally to all the locations or be based on sales volume for each location during the period of the sale. Alternatively, a laundry service may wash several customers' clothes in the same load. The cost of the load could be allocated based on the number of pieces or the pounds of clothes washed for each customer.

Service businesses may decide it is not necessary to allocate joint costs. Not-for-profit organizations, however, are *required* under AICPA Statement of Position (SOP) 78–10 to categorize their expenses as either "program" or "support" costs.[7] Program

---

[7] AICPA Accounting Standards Division, *Statement of Position 78-10: Accounting Principles and Reporting Practices for Certain Nonprofit Organizations* (December 31, 1978), p. 29, para. 86.

costs are necessary for the accomplishment of the organization's specific objectives. Support costs arise from purposes other than the charitable objective; such costs include administrative and fund-raising expenses.

Since regulations exist as to the classification of nonprofit expenses, any joint cost of multipurpose communications must be allocated between the program and support activities. A valid multipurpose communication is one that clearly demonstrates that a non-fund-raising purpose has been enhanced by the communication in addition to the request for funds. If a communication does not qualify, the cost is not eligible for allocation between program and support activities.

The AICPA did not provide definitive guidelines on how to allocate joint costs of multipurpose communications in SOP 87–2.[8] This statement indicated that cost accounting techniques are available to assist in such a process. For example, the directors of the nonprofit, as well as the auditors associated with it, may decide that an allocation can be made based on the proportional amount of space or time in the communication that is devoted to program activities compared to fund-raising activities. Regardless of the allocation method used, the SOP requires a footnote disclosure be made that indicates the total amount of the allocated cost and the amounts assigned to each category. This disclosure allows external users to recalculate the allocation in another manner should they choose to do so. The requirement for such disclosure implies that users have different attitudes about costs incurred in not-for-profits as compared to for-profit businesses. In for-profit businesses, external users of financial statements are typically unconcerned as to how joint costs are allocated.

R E V I S I T I N G

TYSON FOODS INC.

Chickens are still raised on Tyson Foods' headquarters grounds in the Ozark foothills of northwestern Arkansas. [But] in the more than three decades that Don Tyson has headed the company, it has both initiated and successfully reacted to numerous changes in the marketplace and in the poultry industry itself. Over the years, Tyson has seen consumer acceptance of chicken grow significantly. He sees no irreconcilable clash between taste and nutrition. "We've gotten around that by finding ways to keep the flavor profile up while lowering the sodium levels," Tyson says.

Along with this has come a trend toward what Tyson calls "value-enhanced products"—chicken-based processed products like patties. These products are in great demand as timesavers in both the supermarket and the fast-food business, two disparate industries that have traditionally comprised a near-equal share of Tyson Foods' U.S. sales.

Make no mistake about it—the food business is one of the more highly competitive fields in the world of commerce. Not only are the tastes of consumers susceptible to sudden change, but the outlets in which most of Tyson's products are sold compete with one another. For these and other reasons, Don Tyson decided several years ago that his company would not live by chicken alone. [In June 1992], Don Tyson approved the latest company acquisition, Seattle-based Arctic Alaska Fisheries Corp., which is a major player in the worlds of crab and pollock processing.

---

[8] AICPA Accounting Standards Division, *Statement of Position 87-2: Accounting for Joint Costs of Informational Materials and Activities of Not-for-Profit Organizations that Include a Fund-Raising Appeal* (August 21, 1987).

[At Tyson, joint cost allocations would be used to prepare product line financial statements. Such allocations should not, however, be used for internal decision making about the profitability of products resulting from a joint process. When company managers analyze whether to sell chicken breasts as fresh poultry products or to make that meat into processed chicken patties, that analysis is performed using incremental revenues and costs. Whole chickens command a lower sales price than further-processed and value-enhanced products. Thus, Tyson is moving toward additional processing activities. Such further processing also creates more tonnage of by-products that are marketed to the animal and pet food industry.]

SOURCE: Russell Shaw, "A Taste of Tyson," *SKY* (December 1992), pp. 53–61 and Tyson Foods Inc., *1991 Annual Report*, p. 29. Russell Shaw is an Atlanta-based journalist. This article has been excerpted by permission of the author and through Halsey Publishing Company, publishers of Delta Air Lines' *SKY* magazine.

CHAPTER SUMMARY

Multiple products from a joint process are defined (based on market value) as joint products, by-products, and scrap. A residual product that has no market value is called waste. Joint process cost is allocated only to joint products. However, before the allocation is made, the joint cost may be reduced by the net realizable value of by-products and/or scrap. Costs incurred after the split-off point(s) are traced directly to the products with which they are associated.

There are three decision points in a multiple product setting: (1) before the joint process is started; (2) at a split-off point; and (3) after a split-off point. At any of these points, management should consider further processing only if it believes that the incremental revenues from proceeding will exceed the incremental costs of proceeding. How joint cost was allocated is irrelevant to these decisions because the joint cost is considered sunk and, therefore, unrecoverable.

All of the commonly used techniques for allocating joint process cost to the joint products use proration. Allocation bases are classified as either physical or monetary. Physical measures provide an unchanging yardstick of output over time and treat each unit of product as equally desirable. Monetary measures, because of inflation, are a changing yardstick of output over time, but these measures consider the different market values of the individual joint products.

The realized value approach to accounting for by-products and scrap ignores the value of such output until it is sold. At that time, either revenue is recorded or the selling price is used to reduce the joint cost of production. Alternatively, when by-products or scrap are generated, the net realizable value of the by-products/scrap at the split-off point can be recorded in a special inventory account and the production costs of the primary products can be reduced. Additional processing costs for the by-products/scrap are debited to the special inventory account. Regardless of the approach used, if joint cost is to be reduced by the value of the by-product/scrap, the method and value to be used must be determined before allocating the net joint processing cost to the primary products.

Joint costs are also incurred in service businesses and not-for-profit organizations for some types of processes or for things such as communications instruments (brochures, media advertisements) that serve multiple purposes. Service businesses may allocate joint costs if they so desire. Not-for-profits must allocate all expenses between program and support activities based on some reasonable measure, such as percentage of space or time.

SOLUTION STRATEGIES

Allocation of Joint Cost

Joint costs are allocated only to joint products; however, joint costs may be reduced by the value of by-products/scrap before the allocation process begins.

For physical measure allocation: Divide joint cost by the products' total physical measurements to obtain a cost per unit of physical measure.

For monetary measure allocation:

1. Choose an allocation base.
2. List the values that comprise the allocation base for each joint process.
3. Sum the values in step 2.
4. Calculate the decimal fraction of value of the base to the total of all values in the base. The decimal fractions so derived should add to 100% or 1.00.
5. Multiply the total joint process cost to be allocated by each of the decimal fractions to separate the total cost into prorated parts.

Allocation bases, measured at the split-off point, by which joint costs are prorated to the joint products include the following:

Type of Measure	Allocation Base
Physical output	Physical measurement of units of output (e.g., tons, feet, barrels, liters, etc.)
Monetary:	Currency units of value:
Sales value	Revenues of the several products
Net realizable value	Net realizable value of the several joint products
Approximated net realizable value	Approximated net realizable value of the several joint products (may be a hybrid measure)

DEMONSTRATION PROBLEM

Rockwell Quarries, Inc. incurred $260,000 in 1994 in a joint process to extract two joint products, X and Z. The following are data related to 1994 operations:

(1) Joint Products	(2) Tons of Production	(3) Sales Price Per Ton at Split-off	(4) Per Ton Separate Costs if Sold at Split-off	(5) Per Ton Separate Costs if Processed Further	(6) Per Ton Final Sales Price
X	48	$1,200	$ 20	$170	$1,550
Z	20	1,600	150	200	2,000

Required:

a. Allocate the joint process cost to X and Z using tons as the allocation base.

b. Allocate the joint process cost to X and Z using the sales value at split-off.

c. Allocate the joint process cost to X and Z using the net realizable value at split-off.

d. Allocate the joint process cost to X and Z using the approximated net realizable value at split-off.

Solution to Demonstration Problem

a. $260,000 ÷ 68 tons = ≈$3,824 per ton

Product	Tons of Production	Cost per Ton	Allocation of Joint Cost	
X	48	$3,824	$183,552	
Z	20	3,824	76,480	
Total	68		$260,032	(off due to rounding)

b.

Product	Tons of Production	Sales Price at Split-off	Sales Value	Decimal Fraction	Allocation of Joint Cost
X	48	$1,200	$57,600	.64	$166,400
Z	20	1,600	32,000	.36	93,600
Total	68		$89,600	1.00	$260,000

c.

Product	Tons of Production	Per Ton NRV at Split-off	Total NRV at Split-off	Decimal Fraction	Allocation of Joint Cost
X	48	$1,180	$56,640	.66	$171,600
Z	20	1,450	29,000	.34	88,400
Total	68		$85,640	1.00	$260,000

d.

Product	Tons of Production	Per Ton Approximate NRV	Total Approximate NRV	Decimal Fraction	Allocation of Joint Cost
X	48	$1,380	$ 66,240	.65	$169,000
Z	20	1,800	36,000	.35	91,000
Total	68		$102,240	1.00	$260,000

QUESTIONS

1. What is a joint production process? Give several examples of joint processes.

2. What are joint products, by-products, and scrap? How do they differ? Which of these product categories provides the greatest incentive or justification to produce?

3. How does management determine into which category to classify each type of output from a joint process?

4. When do the multiple products of a joint process gain separate identity?

5. How are separate costs distinguished from joint costs?

6. To which types of joint process output are joint costs allocated? Why?

7. What are the decision points associated with multiple products? By what criteria would management assess whether to proceed at each point?

8. What is cost allocation and why is it necessary in a joint process?

9. What are the two primary methods used to allocate joint costs to joint products? Compare the advantages and disadvantages of each.

10. Why is it sometimes necessary to use an approximated rather than actual net realizable value at split-off to allocate joint costs? How is this approximated value calculated?

11. Describe two common approaches used to account for by-products.

12. When are by-product or scrap costs considered in setting a predetermined overhead rate in a job order costing system? When are they not considered?

13. Why must not-for-profits allocate joint costs of multipurpose documents or events between "program" and "support" costs?

EXERCISES

14. *(Physical measure allocation)* U.S. Chemical Company uses a joint process to manufacture two chemicals. During October 1994, the company incurred $100,000,000 of joint production costs in producing 12,000 tons (ton = 2,000 pounds) of Chemical A and 8,000 tons of Chemical B. Joint costs incurred by the company are allocated on the basis of tons of chemicals produced. U.S. Chemical is able to sell Chemical A at the split-off point for $.50 per pound or it can be processed further at a cost of $1,500 per ton and can then be sold for $1.25 per pound. There is no opportunity for the company to further process Chemical B.
   a. What amount of joint cost is allocated to Chemical A and Chemical B?
   b. If Chemical A is processed further and then sold, what is the incremental effect on U.S. Chemical Company's net income? Should the additional processing be performed?

15. *(Monetary measure allocation)* Metro Realty is comprised of two operating divisions: Leasing and Sales. In March 1994, the firm spent $150,000 for general company promotions (as opposed to advertisements promoting specific properties). Sara Burnery, the corporate controller, is now faced with the task of fairly allocating the promotion costs to the two operating divisions.

    Sara has reduced the potential bases for allocating the promotion costs to two alternatives: the expected revenue to be generated for each division from the promotion, or the expected profit to be generated in each division from the promotion.

    The promotions are expected to have the following effects on the two divisions:

	Leasing	Sales
Increase in revenue	$400,000	$800,000
Increase in net income		
before allocated promotion costs	150,000	100,000

   a. Allocate the total promotion costs to the two divisions using change in revenue.
   b. Allocate the total promotion costs to the two divisions using change in net income before joint cost allocation.
   c. Which of the two approaches is most appropriate? Explain.

16. *(Net realizable value allocation)* Carbon Mining Company had the following gem output during October 1994: 1 diamond, 1 carat; multiple rubies, 10 carats; and multiple opals, 20 carats. This production was determined at the split-off point and the output had to be processed further before the company could sell

it. The joint cost amounted to $16,000 and the total additional costs after split-off and the final per-carat selling prices are as follows:

	Additional Processing Cost	Final Selling Price
Diamond	$15,000	$43,000
Rubies	5,000	8,000
Opals	1,000	2,000

Using the approximated net realizable value at split-off method, allocate the joint cost to the joint products.

 17. *(Sales value allocation)* Country Dairy produces milk and sour cream from a joint process. During February, the company produced 120,000 quarts of milk and 160,000 pints of sour cream. Sales value at split-off point was $50,000 for the milk and $110,000 for the sour cream. The milk was assigned $21,600 of the joint cost.

   a. Using the sales value at split-off approach, what was the total joint cost for February?

   b. Assume, instead, that the joint cost was allocated based on units (quarts) produced. What was the total joint cost incurred in February?

18. *(Sell or process further)* A certain joint process yields two joint products, A and B. The joint cost for June 1994 is $80,000 and the sales value of the output at split-off is $120,000 for Product A and $100,000 for Product B. Management is trying to decide whether to process the products further. If the products are processed beyond split-off, the final sales value will be $180,000 for Product A and $140,000 for Product B. The additional costs of processing are expected to be $70,000 for A and $34,000 for B.

   a. Should management process the products further? Show computations.

   b. Were there any revenues and/or costs that are not relevant to the decision? If so, what are they?

19. *(By-products and cost allocation)* Southwest Petroleum has a joint process that yields three products: A, B, and C. The company allocates the joint process costs to the products on the basis of pounds of output. A particular joint process run cost $125,000 and yielded the following output by weight:

Product	Weight in lbs.
A	4,800
B	13,000
C	4,200

The run also produced by-products, the net realizable value of which was $15,000. The company recognizes by-product inventory at the time of production. Allocate the joint cost to the joint products.

20. *(Sell or process further)* North American Textiles produces three products (precut fabrics for Hats, Shirts, and Pants) from a joint process. Joint cost is allocated on the basis of relative sales value at the split-off. Rather than sell the products at the split-off, the company has the option to complete each of the products. Information related to these products is shown below:

	Hats	Shirts	Pants	Total
# of units produced	5,000	8,000	3,000	16,000
Joint cost allocated	$ 87,000	?	?	$180,000
Sales value at split-off point	?	?	$ 40,000	$300,000
Additional costs of processing further	$ 13,000	$ 10,000	$ 39,000	$ 62,000
Sales value after all processing	$150,000	$134,000	$105,000	$389,000

a. What amount of joint cost should be allocated to the shirts and pants products?

b. What are the sales values at split-off for hats and shirts?

c. Which products should be processed further? Show computations.

d. If 4,000 shirts are processed further and sold for $67,000, what is gross profit on the sale?

21. *(By-products and cost allocation)* Tinsel Town Productions produced two movies (joint products) in 1994 in its Hollywood facilities. The company also generated revenue from admissions paid by fans touring the movie production sets. Tinsel Town regards the net income from tours as a by-product of movie production. The firm accounts for this income as a reduction in the joint cost before that joint cost is allocated to movies. The following information pertains to the two movies:

Products	Total receipts	Separate costs
Movie 1	$ 4,000,000	$ 2,400,000
Movie 2	27,000,000	18,600,000
Tours	300,000	140,000

The joint cost incurred to produce the two movies was $8,000,000. Joint costs are allocated based on net realizable value.

a. How much of the joint cost is allocated to each movie?

b. How much profit was generated by each movie?

22. *(Accounting for by-products)* East Texas Timber Company manufactures various wood products that yield sawdust as a by-product. The only costs associated with the sawdust are selling costs of $5 per ton sold. The company accounts for sales of sawdust by deducting sawdust's net realizable value from the major product's cost of goods sold. Sawdust sales in 1994 were 12,000 tons at $40.00 each. If East Texas Timber changes its method of accounting for sawdust sales to showing the net realizable value as other revenue (presented at the bottom of the income statement), how would its gross margin be affected?

23. *(Accounting for by-products)* A by-product, produced from processing the joint products of frozen potato patties and potatoes for dehydration, is potato skins. These potato skins can be frozen and sold to restaurants for use in preparing appetizers. The additional processing and disposal costs associated with such by-product sales are $0.30 per pound of skins. During May 1994, the Bassett Potato Plant produced and sold 45,000 pounds of potato skins for $23,850. In addition, joint costs for its dehydrated potatoes and frozen potato patties totaled $60,000 and 80% of all joint production was sold for $79,000. Nonfactory operating expenses for May were $7,600.

a. Prepare an income statement for Bassett Potato Plant if sales of the by-product are shown as other revenue and its selling costs are shown as additional cost of goods sold of the joint products.

b. Prepare an income statement for Bassett Potato Plant if the net realizable value of the by-product is shown as other income.

c. Prepare an income statement for Bassett Potato Plant if the net realizable value of the by-product is subtracted from the joint production costs of the main products.

d. Which of the above presentations do you think would be most helpful to managers and why?

24. *(Accounting for by-products)* Tri-Cities Data Processing provides computing services for its commercial clients. Records for clients are maintained on both computer files and paper files. After seven years, the paper records are sold for recycling material. The net value of the recycled paper is treated as a reduction to operating overhead. Data pertaining to operations for 1994 follow:

Estimated operating overhead	$400,500
Estimated CPU time (hours)	35,000
Estimated net realizable value of recycled paper	$ 20,400

During 1994, the following actual data were recorded:

Operating overhead	$399,500
Actual CPU time	34,200
Net realizable value of recycled paper	$ 21,500

a. What was the company's estimated predetermined overhead rate?
b. What journal entry should the company make to record the sale of the recycled paper?
c. What was the company's under- or overapplied overhead for 1994?

25. *(Accounting for scrap)* Classic Windows restores antique stained glass windows. Regardless of the job, there is always some breakage or improper cuts. This scrap can be sold to amateur stained glass hobbyists. The following estimates are made in setting the predetermined overhead rate for 1994:

Overhead costs other than breakage		$124,100
Estimated cost of scrap	$8,800	
Estimated sales value of scrap	2,400	6,400
Total estimated overhead		$130,500

Classic Windows expects to incur approximately 15,000 direct labor hours during 1994.

One job that Anne Friedland worked on during 1994 was a stained glass window of a rose; the job took 63 hours. Direct materials cost $420; direct labor is costed at $20 per hour. The actual cost of the scrap on this job was $55 and this scrap was sold for $18.

a. What predetermined overhead rate was set for 1994?
b. What was the cost of the rose stained glass window?
c. What journal entry is made to record the cost and selling value of the scrap from the rose stained glass window?

26. *(Scrap, job order costing)* Arkansas Architects offers a variety of architectural services for its commercial construction clients. For each major job, architectural models of the completed structures are built for use in presentations to clients. The firm tracks all costs using a job order costing system. At the completion of the job, the architectural models can be sold to an arts and crafts retailer. The firm uses the realized value method of accounting for the sale of the models. The sales value of each model is credited to the cost of the specific job for which the model was built. During 1994, the model for the Hightower Building was sold for $2,750.

a. Using the realized value approach, give the entry to record the sale.
b. Independent of your answer to part a, assume instead that the sales value of the models is not credited to specific jobs. Give the entry to account for the sale of the Hightower Building model.

27. *(Net realizable value versus realized value)* Indicate whether each item listed below is associated with the (1) realized value approach or (2) the net realizable value approach.

a. Ignores value of by-product/scrap until it is sold.
b. Is simplest.
c. Has the advantage of better timing.
d. Is used to reduce the cost of main products when by-products are produced.
e. Presents proceeds from sale of by-product as other revenue or other income.
f. Is appropriate if by-product's net realizable value is small.
g. Credits either cost of goods sold of main products or the joint process cost when the by-product inventory is recorded.
h. Is less conservative.
i. Is the most clerically efficient.
j. Should be used when the by-product's net realizable value is large.

28. *(Matching)* Match the items labeled a–k with the number of the appropriate definitions (1–11).

   a. Monetary measure allocation
   b. Joint cost
   c. Joint product
   d. By-product
   e. Split-off point
   f. Joint process
   g. Physical measure allocation
   h. Waste
   i. Sales value at split-off
   j. Proration
   k. Scrap

   1. Incidental result of a joint process; has little sales value
   2. Point when output is first identified as individual products
   3. Proration of joint cost on basis of dollar values
   4. Has significant sales value but such value would not, by itself, be sufficient to justify joint process
   5. Employed by all commonly used allocation methods
   6. Proration of joint cost on the basis of relative sales values of joint products at split-off
   7. Proration of joint cost on nonmonetary basis
   8. The primary or main output of a joint process
   9. Cost incurred to produce several products at the same time in one process
   10. A single production process that yields more than one product
   11. Residual output with no sales value

29. *(Not-for-profit, program, and support cost allocation)* The Greater Atlanta Opera Company is preparing a small pamphlet that will provide information on the types of opera, opera terminology, and storylines of some of the more well-known operas. In addition, there will be a request for funds to support the Opera Company at the end of the brochure. The company has tax-exempt status and operates on a not-for-profit basis.

   The cost of designing and printing 200,000 copies of the pamphlet is $780,000. One page out of twelve is devoted to soliciting funding; however, 98% of the time spent in the design stage was on developing and writing the opera information.

   a. If space is used as the allocation measure, how much of the pamphlet's cost should be assigned to program activities? To support activities?
   b. If design time is used as the allocation measure, how much of the pamphlet's cost should be assigned to program activities? To support activities?

COMMUNICATION ACTIVITIES

30. *(Net realizable value allocation)* Nitro Broadcasting Company is a regional TV network. The firm has three service groups: Sports, News, and Entertainment. Joint production costs (costs incurred for facilities, administration, etc.) for August 1994 were $24,000,000. The revenues and separate production costs of each group for August follow:

	Sports	News	Entertainment
Revenues	$18,000,000	$15,000,000	$95,000,000
Separate costs	17,000,000	8,000,000	55,000,000

   a. What amounts of joint cost are allocated to each service group using the net realizable value approach? Compute the profit for each group after the allocation.
   b. What amount of cost is allocated to each service group if the allocation is based on revenues? Compute the profit for each group after the allocation.
   c. Assume you are head of the Sports group. Would the difference in allocation bases create significant problems for you when you report to Nitro's Board of Directors? Develop a short presentation to make to the Board if the allocation base in part b is used to determine group relative profitability. Be certain to discuss important differences in revenues and cost figures between the Sports and Entertainment groups.

c. further processed and transferred to finished goods, with joint cost being allocated between wheat and straw based on relative sales value at the split-off point.

(CPA *adapted*)

CASE

39. Hawney Meat Packers experienced the operating statistics in the table below for its joint meat cutting process during June 1994, its first month of operations. The costs of the joint process were: direct materials, $24,400; direct labor, $8,200; and overhead, $4,100. Products X, Y, and Z are main products; B is a by-product. The company's policy is to recognize the net realizable value of any by-product inventory at split-off and reduce the total joint cost by that amount. Neither the main products nor the by-product *require* any additional processing or disposal costs although management may consider additional processing.

Products	Weight in Pounds	Sales Value at Split-Off	Units Produced	Units Sold
X	4,300	$66,000	3,220	2,720
Y	6,700	43,000	8,370	7,070
Z	5,400	11,200	4,320	3,800
B	2,300	2,300	4,600	4,000

a. Calculate the ending inventory values of each joint product based on (1) relative sales value and (2) pounds.
b. Discuss the advantages and disadvantages of each allocation base for (1) financial statement purposes and (2) decisions about the desirability of processing the joint products beyond the split-off point.

ETHICS AND QUALITY DISCUSSION

40. *Some waste, scrap, or by-product materials have little value. In fact many such materials represent liabilities for companies in that the materials require companies to incur significant disposal costs. Alternatively, some companies have historically found "cheap" ways to dispose of such materials. For example, on Friday, April 2, 1993 residents of Brazos County, Texas stumbled across 19 cans of industrial waste that were scattered along the banks of the Navasota River. The cans were labeled "lacquer thinner," but the actual contents which were leaking into the ground and the river, were not immediately known. The cans appeared to have been thrown from a vehicle traveling over a nearby road. Some cans were heavily dented, some were capped with rags, and all of them appeared to be scattered in a random pattern. State and county officials worked most of Saturday, April 3, cleaning up the site.*

[SOURCE: Chuck Squatriglia, "Solvent Cans Dumped near Navasota River," *Bryan/College Station Eagle* (April 4, 1993), p. A9. Courtesy: *Bryan/College Station Eagle*.]

a. Comment on whether this method of disposing of industrial waste is a "cheap" alternative.
b. Discuss the ethical and legal implications of disposing of industrial waste in this manner.
c. What actions can people take to reduce these kinds of incidents?
d. Ethically, what obligation does the vendor/manufacturer of these industrial materials have to the industrial consumer of the materials?

41. Gypsum waste is created from manufacturing phosphorous fertilizer. Pure gypsum is better known as the wallboard used in interior walls of buildings; gypsum waste is contaminated with low levels of potentially toxic heavy metals and some radioactive

elements. Freeport-McMoRan owns two fertilizer plants producing the waste material. Early in 1990, the company completed a $6 million experimental plant to recycle gypsum waste into an environmentally safe, synthetic aggregate that could be used in building materials. The waste from the recycling plant is a rocklike cinder that the company hopes to use as an additive to concrete and in roadbeds.

[SOURCE: Based on James O'Byrne, "Protests inspired $6 million plant to Recycle Gypsum," *(New Orleans) Times-Picayune* (March 4, 1990), p. B1.]

a. Which of the methods of accounting for by-products/scrap discussed in the chapter would allow Freeport-McMoRan to know whether recycling gypsum waste is cost-beneficial? Why is this information available from this particular method?

b. Discuss the ethics of the recycling plan begun by the company.

c. Discuss the potential profitability of the recycling plan.

d. The gypsum waste cannot be dumped into the Mississippi River. Currently there are stacks of gypsum waste more than a mile long and 80 feet high. If the waste were not recycled, how would you suggest eliminating it? How would you estimate the costs and benefits of your plan compare to the costs and benefits of the recycling plan?

42. *In the late 1980's two unlikely organizations, the Environmental Protection Agency and Amoco, agreed to form a joint venture to produce two unlikely joint products, regulation and cost savings. The substance of the joint venture was a study of pollution at the Yorktown, Virginia, oil refinery of Amoco. Initially, communication between employees of the two groups was stiff and cautious, and miscommunication frequently resulted from differing definitions of words such as "risk." After a time, the two groups learned to work together and (perhaps) grudgingly became more appreciative of the other's problems and concerns.*

Ultimately, it appears the project will be very fruitful for both parties. The EPA has learned that many of the requirements it has placed on oil refineries do little to protect the environment and much to increase the costs of operating the refinery. For example, it had required Amoco to build a $41 million enclosed canal to control benzene vapors. In the testing that was conducted in the joint project, it was discovered that the benzene vapors in this part of the operation were 20 times smaller than expected. Also, the EPA has identified areas of the oil refinery operation that produce substantial amounts of pollution that the EPA has historically ignored. For example, at the loading docks in Yorktown, the team estimated that 1.6 million pounds of pollutants are pumped into the atmosphere annually. No EPA rules address this area of the operation. Perhaps the greatest lesson learned by the EPA is that it should refocus its efforts on identifying and controlling pollution rather than mandating the type and extent of equipment that must be used by industry.

[SOURCE: Caleb Solomon, "What Really Pollutes? Study of a Refinery Proves an Eye-Opener," *Wall Street Journal* (March 29, 1993), pp. A1, A6. Reprinted by permission of the *Wall Street Journal*, © 1993 Dow Jones & Company, Inc. All rights reserved worldwide.]

a. Potentially, how will the quality of Amoco's operations be affected by the joint venture?

b. Potentially, how will the quality of the EPA's operations be affected by the joint venture?

c. Why would the EPA have been reluctant to participate in the joint venture?

d. Comment on the ethical considerations in a joint venture that involves a regulator and one of its regulated groups.

GENERAL CONCEPTS OF STANDARD COSTING: MATERIAL AND LABOR STANDARDS

LEARNING OBJECTIVES

After completing this chapter, you should be able to answer these questions:

1. Why are standard cost systems used?
2. How are standards for materials and labor set?
3. What documents are associated with standard cost systems and what information do they provide?
4. How are material and labor variances calculated and recorded?
5. How can variance analysis be used for control and performance evaluation purposes?
6. *(Appendix 1)* How do multiple material and labor categories affect variances?
7. *(Appendix 2)* What effects do learning curves have on the setting of labor standards?

MERLIN CANDIES, INC.

Running a company that, as a matter of routine, has a negative cash flow for nine months of the year may sound a little hairy. But that's life in the chocolate bunny business.

Gary Crowley and his wife, Mary, own Merlin Candies, Inc., a nearly 50-year-old business that makes hollow chocolate Easter rabbits—millions of them—and nothing else. Starting in early July of each year, their 6,000-square-foot plant and a nearby 8,000-square-foot warehouse begin filling up with boxed chocolate bunnies in cases of 30 or so each. The confections stack higher and higher in climate-controlled storerooms until January, when drug, discount, and grocery stores begin taking delivery of their Easter season orders.

Merlin's colorful rabbits (they come in chocolate, pink, purple, blue, yellow, peanut butter, and white) range in size from 3 1/2 ounces to 2 1/4 pounds. The Merlin chocolate recipe, concocted some 30 years ago, is actually blended by a major producer, then shipped to New Orleans in 10-pound slabs, 20 tons at a time. During much of the year, Crowley's three full-time employees handle the melting, tempering (a raising and lowering of the temperature to obtain proper consistency) and molding of the chocolate into the various bunny sizes. In the months just before Easter, however, Merlin's becomes a two-shift per day operation which employs more than 20 people.

SOURCE: Kathy Finn, "Merlin, the Hometown Chocolate Wizard," *New Orleans Magazine* (April 1990), p. 70.

In producing Merlin's chocolate bunnies, Gary Crowley is adamant about the recipe for the chocolate. He uses the same recipe that the original owners of Merlin's used in 1946. "When you buy a Hershey Bar or a bag of M&M's, you know what to expect," he said. "It's the same thing with our bunnies." Consistency of product can only occur if there are **standards** or benchmarks for both the materials and the process. Consistency and use of standards are important aspects of total quality management.

Standard

Additionally, performance can only be evaluated by comparing it against some predetermined measure or criterion. Without a predetermined measure of performance, there is no way to know what is expected. Without making a comparison between the actual result and the predetermined measure, there is no way to know if expectations were met and, thus, no way for managers to control processes. All predetermined measures of performance do not necessarily reflect exemplary achievement; some measures simply reflect the completion of a task.

For instance, Gary Crowley has determined that an experienced worker can decorate approximately 1,250 bunnies per day. He therefore defines labor success as this quantity multiplied by the number of decorators employed. Just before Easter, seasonal workers are hired who are not skilled in the bunny production process. These seasonal workers must undergo some on-the-job training and, during this period, are unable to produce at the typical rate. Thus, success for an unskilled decorator may be defined as 700 bunnies per day. In each case, a measure (or standard) of success has been defined against which actual results may be compared. Standards are norms used for planning and control purposes.

Organizations develop and use standards for almost all tasks. For example, charities set a standard for the amount of annual contributions to be raised; sales managers set standards against which employee business expenses are compared. This chapter focuses on standards for direct materials (DM) and direct labor (DL): how they are developed; how variances are calculated, why standard cost systems are used; and what information can be gained from detailed variance analysis.[1] The journal entries used in a standard cost system are also presented.

Because of the variety of production methods and information objectives existing in organizations, no single form of standard cost system is appropriate for all situations. Thus, many forms of standard cost systems are currently in use. Some systems use standard prices, but not standard quantities; other systems (especially in service businesses) use labor but not material standards. Traditional standard cost systems require price and quantity standards for both materials and labor. The traditional standard cost system is covered in this chapter.

The chapter illustrates the use of a single material and a single labor category. Appendix 1 expands the presentation by covering the mix and yield variances that may arise from the use of multiple materials or groups of labor. Appendix 2 provides information on how experience can change workers' efficiency and the effects of such learning curves on labor standards.

DEVELOPMENT OF A STANDARD COST SYSTEM

Standard cost system

Standard cost

Sales of American business products declined dramatically after World War I because of a reduction in government demand. In seeking a method to control costs and survive the economic slump, many companies instituted standard cost systems to provide managers with an effective means to review and evaluate cost data. Although usage was initiated by manufacturers, standard cost systems can also be used by service organizations.

In a **standard cost system**, both standard costs and actual costs are recorded in the accounting records. This dual recording provides an essential element of cost control: having norms against which actual operations can be compared. Standard cost systems make use of **standard costs**, which are the budgeted or estimated costs to manufacture a single unit of product or perform a single service. Standards are traditionally established for each component (material, labor, and overhead) of product cost.[2] Developing a standard cost involves judgment and practicality in identifying the material and labor types, quantities, and prices.

A primary objective in manufacturing a product is to minimize unit cost while simultaneously achieving certain quality specifications. Almost all products can be manufactured with a variety of inputs (materials, labor, and overhead) that would generate the same basic output. Even after the quality of the output is specified during the product design phase, there is still a wide spectrum of input factors that would achieve the quality objective. The input choices that are ultimately made will affect the standards that are set.

For example, How Sweet It Is (an illustrative candy company) determined that there were two alternative groupings of workers who could compose its production team: Team A, 2 skilled and 10 unskilled workers; and Team B, 5 skilled and 2 un-

[1] The use of direct materials and direct labor standards in job order and process costing systems is introduced in Chapters 7 and 8.
[2] The topic of overhead standards is covered in Chapter 12.

skilled workers. Each team could effectively perform the same quantity and quality of work, but would require a different number of hours and dollars of cost to do so. To operate in the most efficient (as well as effective) manner, company management would choose to have the work performed by the team having the lowest payroll cost.

Some possible input resource combinations are not necessarily practical or efficient. For instance, a work team might be composed entirely of craftspersons or skilled workers, but such a combination might not be cost-beneficial if there were a large differential in the wage rates of skilled and unskilled workers. Or, although it is possible to provide high-technology equipment to an unskilled labor population, to do so would not be an efficient use of resources, as indicated in the News Note "The Savings Isn't Worth the Cost."

Once management has established the desired quality of the output and determined the input resources to achieve that quality at a reasonable cost, quantity and price standards can be developed. Standards development should be a group endeavor. The group should be composed of representatives from the following areas: cost accounting, industrial engineering, personnel, data processing, purchasing, and management. It is especially important to involve managers and workers whose performance will be compared to the standards. This involvement helps ensure credibility of the standards and helps motivate personnel to operate as closely to the standards as possible. The discussion of the standard setting process begins with materials because they are normally introduced first in a production process.

Material Standards

The first step in developing material standards is to identify and list the specific direct material components used to manufacture the product. This list is often available on the product specification documents prepared by the engineering department prior to initial production. In the absence of such documentation, material specifications can be determined by observation in the production area, inquiry of production personnel, inspection of materials requisitions, and review of the cost accounts related to the product. It is essential that three things be known about the material inputs: what types of inputs are used; what quantity of inputs are used; and what quality of inputs are used.

In making quality decisions, managers should seek the advice of materials experts, engineers, cost accountants, marketing personnel, and sometimes suppliers. There

NEWS NOTE

Mars Inc.: Quality Candy Regardless of Cost

Forget the Japanese. Forget the Germans. The best lessons on management come from Mars.

No, not the planet. But the mutibillion-dollar, world-class company known as Mars Inc., a leader in candy, pet food, rice, and other products. Quality is an unrelenting obsession at Mars. One example of that obsession is a fear of "incremental degradation," a term used by Mars to describe what can happen by using cheaper ingredients. Rather than replace a high-priced ingredient with a cheaper one, even if taste tests show that the consumer would not notice a difference, Mars will forego the extra profits instead of risking an incremental degradation of the quality of its products.

SOURCE: Craig J. Cantoni, "Quality Control from Mars," *Wall Street Journal* (January 27, 1992), p. A10. Reprinted by permission of the *Wall Street Journal*, © 1992 Dow Jones & Company, Inc. All rights reserved worldwide.

are many cost-benefit trade-offs involved in making quality decisions. In most cases, as the materials quality rises, so does cost; decisions about material input components usually attempt to balance the interrelationships of cost, quality, and projected selling prices with company objectives, as indicated in the News Note on Mars Inc. The resulting trade-offs affect materials mix, materials yield, finished product quality and quantity, overall product cost, and product salability. Therefore, quantity and cost estimates become direct functions of quality decisions.

Given the quality selected for each component, physical quantity estimates can be made in terms of weight, size, volume, or other measures. These estimates can be based on results of engineering tests, opinions of managers and workers using the materials, past materials requisitions, and review of the cost accounts. Information about product material components, their specifications (including quality), and the quantities needed are compiled on a document called a **bill of materials**. Even a company that does not have a formal standard cost system is likely to develop a bill of materials for each of its products simply as a guide for production activity.

Exhibit 11–1 illustrates a bill of materials for a chocolate heart produced by How Sweet It Is. Some additional materials, such as the large packing boxes and sealing tape, are not shown on this bill of materials because these are period shipping costs rather than product costs.

When converting quantities on the bill of materials into costs, allowances are often made for normal waste of components.[3] For example, four ounces of chocolate (C-01) is considered the *minimum* quantity of material necessary to make one four-ounce bunny. In setting a standard for the chocolate, though, allowances may be made as follows:

Minimum of C-01 for one heart	4.00 ounces
Provision for material waste and spoilage	.01 ounce
Standard quantity of C-01 for one heart	4.01 ounces

There is limited material waste at How Sweet It Is. When the chocolate hearts are broken or spotted, they are placed in a large container and are remelted and reformed

Bill of materials

---

[3] While such allowances are often made, they do not allow for the most effective use of a standard cost system. Problems arising from their inclusion are discussed later in the chapter.

Product: _4 ounce decorated heart_   Revision Date: _8/1/93_
Product Number: _14_   Standard Lot Size: _10 cases_
    24 hearts per case

Component ID#	Quantity Required	Description	Comments
C-01	4.01 ounces	Milk chocolate	Blended to recipe specifications
S-06	1	Sugar flower	Dyed blue
R-33	6 inches	1/4" ribbon	Pink or yellow
B-14	1	Cardboard box	8"L X 5.5"W X 2.5"D with front cellophane window

at a later time. The majority of waste occurs because the machine dispensing the chocolate into the heart mold may be calibrated or set incorrectly. Thus, a four-ounce heart may have slightly more or less than four ounces of chocolate. Other minor material shortages may occur for various reasons, sometimes including employees being tempted to taste the product.

After the standard quantities for materials are developed, prices for each component must be determined. Prices should reflect factors such as desired component quality, reliability and physical proximity of the supplier, quantity discounts allowed, and freight and receiving costs. Although purchasing agents cannot always *control*

At Merlin Candies, chocolate bunnies are often broken when being removed from molds. Rework for these "defective" units is easy—the chocolate is simply remelted and remolded. Such rework must, however, be incorporated into the material standards and monitored as production occurs.

prices, these people are the most likely to *influence* prices given adequate lead time and resources. This influence is shown through the ability to know what suppliers are available and to choose those suppliers that provide the most appropriate material in the most reasonable time span at the most reasonable cost. The purchasing agent is also the person most likely to have expertise about the company's purchasing habits. Incorporating these types of information into the setting of price standards should allow a more thorough analysis by the purchasing agent at a later time as to the causes of any significant differences between actual and standard prices.

When all quantity and price information is available, component quantities are multiplied by unit prices to obtain the total cost of each component. (Remember, the *price paid* for the materials becomes the *cost* of the materials.) These totals are summed to determine the total standard materials cost of one unit of product. The standard cost of direct materials for one How Sweet It Is chocolate heart is shown in Exhibit 11–3 after the following discussion of labor standards.

Labor Standards

Development of labor standards requires the same basic procedures as those used for materials. Each production operation performed by either workers or machinery should be identified. These operations include such tasks as bending, reaching, lifting, moving materials, decorating, and packing. In specifying operations and movements, activities such as cleanup, setup, and rework need to be considered. While not strictly part of the production process, these actions may be necessary and will affect the time realistically needed to produce the units. All unnecessary movements by workers and of materials should be disregarded when time standards are set. As motion observations are made, the standards development team should evaluate the factory layout as to suitability for minimizing unnecessary motions.[4]

Quantitative information for each production operation must be obtained to develop a usable standard. In-house time and motion studies may be performed by the company; alternatively, times that have been developed from industrial engineering studies for various movements can be used.[5] A third way to set a time standard is to use the average time needed to manufacture a product during the past year. Such information can be calculated from employees' past time sheets. A problem with this method is that historical data may include past inefficiencies. To compensate for the problems of observed or historical data, management and supervisory personnel normally make subjective adjustments to the available data.

After the analysis of labor tasks is complete, an **operations flow** (or routing) **document** can be prepared that lists all operations necessary to make one unit of product (or perform a specific service). A simplified operations flow document is shown in Exhibit 11–2 for a chocolate heart produced by How Sweet It Is. Details of the process are as follows.

Approximately 1,500 pounds of 10-pound chocolate slabs are melted and tempered in water-jacketed vats at a single time. This quantity is necessary to maintain proper flow through the pumping system and to minimize the melting time. The vats are never completely emptied during processing. The liquid chocolate is then pumped into another tank and allowed to cool or "temper" slightly. Maintaining the proper temperature throughout the process is necessary to obtain a crystalline effect, which

---

[4] Plant layout and space utilization are covered in more depth in Chapter 18.
[5] In performing internal time and motion studies, observers need to be aware that employees may engage in "slow down" tactics when they are being clocked. The purpose of such tactics is to establish a longer time as the standard, which would make employees appear more efficient when actual results are measured. Or employees may slow down simply because they are being observed and want to be sure they are doing the job correctly.

EXHIBIT 11–2
How Sweet It Is
Operations Flow Document

Product: 4 ounce decorated heart   Revision Date: 8/1/93
Product Number: 14   Standard Lot Size: 10 cases
24 hearts per case

Operation ID#	Department	Description of Task
21	Melting	Move chocolate and place in tank
50	Melting	Melt chocolate
50	Tempering	Pump chocolate into tank to cool and temper
22	Molding	Pour chocolate into molds
50	Molding	Cool and allow hearts to harden
23	Molding	Remove hearts from molds
50	Finishing	Move hearts on conveyor
24	Finishing	Decorate hearts
25	Finishing	Package hearts

Note: All operations with ID# 50 require time, but no labor

makes the hearts shiny and prevents them from sticking to the molds once they have cooled. After processing, the chocolate is poured into molds that are clamped shut and placed in a refrigerated room. Over a period of 10 to 15 minutes, the chocolate, cools into the shape and detail of the mold. The molds are then transferred on a refrigerated conveyor belt to the decorating and packaging area. While the molds are being returned to the processing area on a heated conveyor belt to be refilled, workers decorate the almost-complete hearts with a sugar flower and ribbon.

When products are produced individually, the operations flow document shows the quantity of time necessary to produce each unit. In a flow process that produces goods in batches, such as manufacturing the chocolate hearts, individual times cannot be specified accurately. The time that it would take to make a single heart would not be 1/240 of the time that it would take to make the company's standard batch of 240 hearts because the melting and tempering are performed in mass quantities.

Labor rate standards should reflect the wages paid to employees who perform the various production tasks as well as the related employer costs such as fringe benefits and FICA (Social Security) and unemployment taxes. In the simplest situation, all personnel working in a given department would be paid the same wage rate; this situation could occur, for example, when wages are tied specifically to the job description or a labor contract. However, employees performing the same or similar tasks are often paid different wage rates, which means a weighted average rate must be computed and used as the standard. The differing rates could be caused by employment length or skill level.

The average rate is computed as the total wage cost per hour divided by the number of workers. As discussed earlier, a change in the membership composition of a labor team may affect the time needed to make a product. Thus, there will generally be trade-offs between rates and times for labor similar to those between price and quality for material. More skilled workers are typically paid higher rates, but may be able to perform tasks more rapidly than less skilled workers. Company managers need to decide on the labor team that achieves the optimal balance among quantity, quality, and cost considerations.

EXHIBIT 11–3

How Sweet It Is
Standard Cost Card

Product: _4 ounce decorated heart_
Product Number: _14_
Standard Lot Size: _10 cases (240 hearts)_

DIRECT MATERIALS

ID#	Unit Price	Total Quantity	Department Melting	Finishing	Total Cost
C-01	.25/oz.	962.4 oz.	240.60		240.60
S-06	.005/flower	240 flowers		1.20	1.20
R-33	.06/ft.	120 ft.		7.20	7.20
B-14	.20/box	240 boxes		48.00	48.00
Direct Materials Totals			240.60	56.40	297.00

DIRECT LABOR

ID#	Avg. Wage Rate/Minute	Total Minutes	Melting	Department Molding	Finishing	Total Cost
21	.07	10	.70			.70
22	.09	30		2.70		2.70
23	.10	120		12.00		12.00
24	.07	240			16.80	16.80
25	.07	160			11.20	11.20
Direct Labor Totals			.70	14.70	28.00	43.40

PRODUCTION OVERHEAD

This section is filled in from information about cost drivers (such as labor hours, machine hours, or number of setups) and their related predetermined overhead rates.

Standard cost card

After both the bill of materials and the operations flow document have been developed, a standard cost card is prepared. A **standard cost card** is a record of the direct material and direct labor standard quantities and costs needed to complete one unit (or one batch) of product. Exhibit 11–3 presents the standard cost card for a batch of 240 chocolate hearts produced by How Sweet It Is.[6] Labor costs per minute can be converted to hourly rates by multiplying the amounts shown by 60.

Standard cost card information is used during the period to assign costs to inventory accounts. In an actual cost system, actual material and labor costs are debited to Work in Process Inventory as production occurs. As will be illustrated by the journal entries later in the chapter, both actual and standard costs are recorded in a standard cost system, although it is the standard (rather than actual) costs of production that are debited to Work in Process Inventory.[7] Any difference between an actual and a standard cost is called a **variance**.

Variance

---

[6] As indicated in the exhibit, overhead standards are also shown on a standard cost card. Since overhead is discussed in Chapter 12, these standards are not detailed in this point.

[7] The standard cost of each cost element (direct materials, direct labor, variable overhead, and fixed overhead) is said to be *applied* to the goods produced. This terminology is the same as that used when overhead is assigned to inventory based on a predetermined rate.

A **total variance** is the difference between total actual cost incurred and total standard cost applied to the output produced during the period. This variance can be diagrammed as follows:

```
     Actual price of actual            Standard price of actual
        production inputs                production outputs
             └──────────────────┬──────────────────┘
                        Total Variance
```

Total variances can be computed for each production cost element and indicate differences between actual and expected production costs. However, total variances do not provide useful information for determining why such differences occurred. To help managers in their control objectives, total variances for materials and labor are each subdivided into price and usage components. The total variance diagram can be expanded to provide a general model indicating the two subvariances, one related to a price component and the other related to a usage component, as shown in Exhibit 11–4.

A price variance reflects the difference between what was actually paid for inputs and what should have been paid for inputs for the period. A usage variance shows the difference between the quantity of actual inputs and the quantity of standard inputs allowed for the actual output of the period. A quantity difference is multiplied by a standard price or rate to provide a monetary measure that can be recorded in the accounting records. Usage variances focus on the efficiency of results—the relationship of inputs to outputs. The price and usage subvariances for materials are known as the materials price and materials quantity variances.[8] The price and usage elements of the total labor variance are, respectively, the labor rate and labor efficiency variances.

Note that the middle column heading in the diagram is for inputs, while the far right heading is for outputs. This change reflects the fact that a specific quantity of production inputs will not necessarily produce the standard quantity of output. The far right column uses a measure of output known as the **standard quantity allowed.** This quantity measure translates the actual production output into the standard input quantity *that should have been needed* to achieve that output. The monetary amount shown in the right-hand column is computed as the standard quantity allowed times the standard price of the input resource.

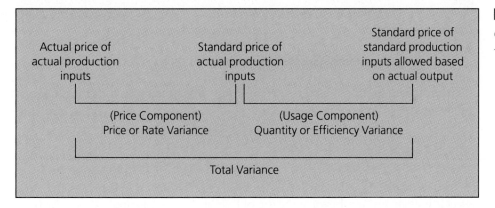

---

[8] Variances are often referred to by more than one name. For example, the materials quantity variance is also referred to as the materials usage variance.

EXHIBIT 11–5
Simplified Variance Model

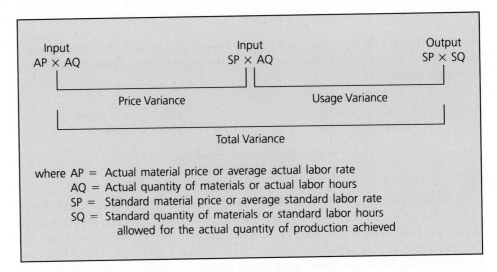

To illustrate the computation of the right-hand column, assume that the standard quantity of sugar needed to make 50 candy bars is one pound. The standard cost of a pound of sugar is $.30. During a period, 1,020 pounds of sugar are input to the production process and 50,000 candy bars are produced (output). The standard quantity of inputs allowed to produce the output achieved is only 1,000 pounds of sugar (50,000 bars ÷ 50 bars per pound). The far right column in the model would show 1,000 pounds times $.30 per pound or $300 as the standard price of actual production outputs.

If the variance calculation is for labor, quantity refers to time. For instance, assume that standard time to produce 50 candy bars is one-half hour and 50,000 candy bars are produced during the period. The standard quantity of time allowed for this production is 500 hours [(50,000 ÷ 50) × .5]. If the actual quantity of time used to make the 50,000 candy bars was 490 hours, the direct labor component of the production process was more efficient than expected.

The basic diagram can be simplified by using the abbreviated notations shown in Exhibit 11–5. This model moves from the *actual* price of *actual* input on the left to the *standard* price of *standard* input quantity on the right. The middle measure of input is a hybrid of *actual* quantity and *standard* price. The price variance portion of the total variance is measured as the actual input quantity multiplied by the difference between the actual and standard prices:

$$\text{Price Element} = (AP - SP)(AQ)$$

The usage variance portion of the total variance is determined by measuring the difference between actual and standard quantities at the standard price:

$$\text{Usage Element} = (AQ - SQ)(SP)$$

The following section illustrates actual variance computations for direct material and direct labor.

MATERIALS AND LABOR VARIANCES

The material and labor standards for the production of one lot of hearts by the How Sweet It Is company are shown at the top of Exhibit 11–6. For simplicity and because of the immaterial amounts, How Sweet It Is has decided to consider the flowers and ribbon shown on the bill of materials in Exhibit 11–1 as indirect materials and labor operations #21 and #22 from the operations flow document in Exhibit 11–2 as in-

Molding Department

Material standards for one lot (240) hearts:
    962.4 ounces of chocolate at $.25 per ounce
        (or $4 per pound) $240.60

Labor standards for one lot (240) hearts:
    Molding Department: 120 minutes for operation #23
        at $.10 per minute (or $6 per hour)   12.00

    Total Molding Department standard cost for 240 hearts $252.60

Actual data for October:
    Units produced—265 lots or 63,600 hearts
    Ounces of chocolate purchased—255,800
    Ounces of chocolate used—255,750
    Price per ounce of chocolate purchased—$.22
    Direct labor hours incurred in Molding Department—510
    Total direct labor cost in Molding Department—$3,075.30

EXHIBIT 11–6

**How Sweet It Is
Production and Cost Data
for October 1994**

direct labor. In addition, since labor operations #24 and #25 both occur in the Finishing Department and workers are paid the same wage rate, the labor standard for these two operations will be combined. These assumptions allow us to focus on the more significant monetary amounts related to the production process.

Also shown in Exhibit 11–6 are the actual quantity and cost data for October 1994 when hearts were produced. This standard and actual cost information is used to compute the material and labor variances for October. Variance computations must indicate whether the amount of the variance is unfavorable (U) or favorable (F). The information related to the chocolate and the Molding Department will be used in the following computations; the information related to the boxes and the Finishing Department would need to be considered along with the Molding Department computations.

Materials Variances

Using the model and inserting information concerning chocolate prices and quantities *used* in production provides the following computations:

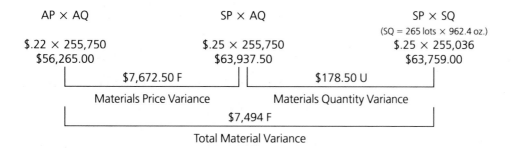

If the actual price/quantity amounts are larger than the standard price/quantity amounts, the variance is unfavorable (U); if the standard amounts are larger than the actuals, the variance is favorable (F).

The **materials price variance** indicates the amount the expenditure for materials was below (F) or above (U) the standard price for the quantity of materials. For How

Materials price variance

Sweet It Is, the actual price paid for chocolate was $.22, while the standard was $.25. The favorable materials price variance is $7,672.50. This variance can also be calculated as [($.22 − $.25)(255,750) = (−$.03)(255,750)= −$7,672.50]. The sign of the favorable variance is negative because the actual price is *less than* the standard.

The **materials quantity variance** indicates whether the actual quantity used was below (F) or above (U) the standard quantity allowed for the actual output. The difference between the actual quantity of material used and the standard quantity of material allowed for the goods produced during the period is multiplied by the standard price per unit of material. If the actual quantity used is less than the quantity allowed, the company has been more efficient than expected; if a greater quantity has been used than allowed, the company has been inefficient in its production activities. How Sweet It Is used 714 more ounces of chocolate than the standard allowed in producing the 63,600 hearts. This inefficient usage results in an unfavorable materials quantity variance [(255,750 − 255,036)($.25) = (714)($.25) = $178.50]. In this instance, the variance sign is positive because the actual quantity used is greater than the standard allowed.

The total material variance ($7,494 F) can be calculated by subtracting the total standard cost of outputs ($63,759) from the total actual cost of inputs ($56,265). Again, the negative result denotes a favorable variance. The total variance also represents the summation of the individual variances. Thus, an alternative computation for the total material variance is to add the price and quantity subvariances (−$7,672.50 + $178.50 = −$7,494 or favorable).

Point of Purchase Materials Variance Model

A total variance for a cost component is *generally* equal to the sum of the price subvariance and the usage subvariance. An exception to this rule occurs when the quantity of material purchased is not the same as the quantity of material placed into production. In such cases, the general model is altered slightly to provide more rapid information for management control purposes.

Because the materials price variance relates to the purchasing (not production) function, the point of purchase model calculates the materials price variance based on the quantity of materials *purchased* rather than the quantity of materials *used*. The variation in the model allows the materials price variance to be isolated or pinpointed as close to the variance source and as quickly as possible. The materials usage variance is still computed on the basis of the actual quantity of materials used in production.

As noted in Exhibit 11–6, How Sweet It Is purchased 255,800 ounces of chocolate during October. Using this information, rather than the 255,750 ounces used, the materials price variance would be calculated as:

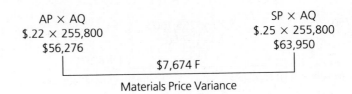

$$
\begin{array}{ccc}
AP \times AQ & & SP \times AQ \\
\$.22 \times 255,800 & & \$.25 \times 255,800 \\
\$56,276 & & \$63,950 \\
\end{array}
$$

$7,674 F

Materials Price Variance

This variance is also referred to as the materials price variance; however, this calculation is based on the quantity purchased rather than the quantity used as was done earlier. This $7,674 F materials price variance can also be calculated by multiplying the actual quantity purchased (255,800 ounces) by the difference between the actual price and the standard price or [($.22 − $.25)(255,800) = (−$.03)(255,800) = −$7,674 or favorable].

The materials quantity variance is still calculated as presented earlier because the actual quantity of chocolate used in production is not determined by the amount purchased. This change in the general model is shown below, using subscripts to indicate actual quantity purchased (p) and used (u).

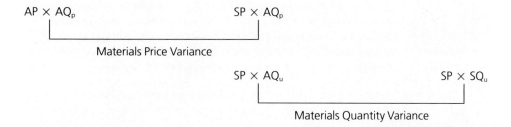

Because these two variances are computed using different bases, they should not be summed and, thus, no total material variance can be determined.

Labor Variances

The model for and computations of the labor variances for How Sweet It Is are as follows:

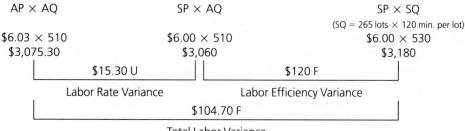

The **labor rate variance** shows the difference between the actual rate (or actual weighted average rate) paid to labor for the period and the standard rate for all hours actually worked during the period. The actual wage rate per hour was calculated by dividing total October labor cost for the Molding Department ($3,075.30) by the number of hours worked (510). The labor rate variance can also be computed as $[(\$6.03 - \$6.00)(510) = (\$.03)(510) = \$15.30\ U]$.

Labor rate variance

The comparison of the number of hours actually worked with the standard hours allowed for production achieved results in the **labor efficiency variance**. This difference is multiplied by the standard labor rate to establish a dollar value for the efficiency (F) or inefficiency (U) of the work force. The labor efficiency variance can also be calculated as $[(510 - 530)(\$6.00) = (-20)(\$6.00) = -\$120$ or favorable].

Labor efficiency variance

The total labor variance ($104.70 F) can be determined by taking the difference between the total actual labor cost ($3,075.30) and the total standard labor cost for the output achieved ($3,180.00). It may also be determined by adding the two labor subvariances $[\$15.30 + (-\$120) = -\$104.70$ or favorable).

The News Note "Separating Quality Problems" on page 436 provides a slightly different perspective on efficiency variances. It suggests that the efficiency variance is truly composed of two elements (quality problems and efficiency problems) that should be accounted for separately.

As the News Note points out, it is possible that reductions in labor time (and, thus, favorable efficiency variances) may be obtained by producing defective or poor qual-

Separating Quality Problems from Efficiency Problems

Historically, efficiency variances have been computed by multiplying excess inputs by the standard price. In recent years, this approach has been criticized for motivating managers to ignore quality concerns to avoid unfavorable efficiency variances. In other words, there is an incentive to produce a low-quality product by minimizing the amount of material used or the time spent in production.

[An approach could be taken that] separates the efficiency variance from the quality variance. Inputs consisting of conversion time or material used in defective units [would be] captured in the quality variance.

Separating the two variances allows production decision makers to evaluate the trade-offs between efficiency and quality. They can minimize production time to gain a favorable efficiency variance but this probably will increase the number of defective units and result in an unfavorable quality variance. Likewise, trying to minimize the number of defective units may result in investing more time and more material and therefore having an unfavorable efficiency variance.

SOURCE: Carole Cheatham, "Updating Standard Cost Systems," *Journal of Accountancy* (December 1990), pp. 59–60.

ity units. For example, workers in the Molding Department of How Sweet It Is are paid $6 per hour and can produce one lot of chocolate hearts in 2 hours (120 minutes). During October, 265 lots were made in 510 hours. The standard quantity of time allowed for production is 530 hours. The labor efficiency variance is $6 (510 − 530) or $120 F. However, assume that 7 of the lots produced were unacceptable because of defects. The quality variance would be computed as follows: 7 lots × 2 hours per lot × $6 per hour = $84 U.

STANDARD COST SYSTEM JOURNAL ENTRIES

Journal entries using the How Sweet It Is materials and labor information are given in Exhibit 11–7 for October 1994. This exhibit uses the 255,800 ounces purchased to account for the materials price variance. The following explanations apply to the numbered journal entries.

1. The debit to Raw Materials Inventory is for the standard price of the actual quantity of chocolate purchased. The credit to Accounts Payable is for the actual price of the actual quantity of chocolate purchased. The credit to the variance account reflects the favorable materials price variance.

2. The debit to Work in Process Inventory is for the standard price of the standard quantity of materials allowed, while the credit to Raw Materials Inventory is for the standard price of the actual quantity of materials used in production. The debit to the Materials Quantity Variance account reflects the overusage of materials valued at the standard price per ounce.

3. The debit to Work in Process Inventory is for the standard hours allowed to produce 63,600 chocolate hearts multiplied by the standard wage rate. The Wage Payable credit is for the actual amount of direct labor wages paid during the period. The debit to the rate variance account reflects the unfavorable rate variance. The efficiency variance credit reflects the less-than-standard hours allowed incurred by direct labor multiplied by the standard wage rate.

Note that all unfavorable variances have debit balances and favorable variances have credit balances. Unfavorable variances represent excess production costs; favorable variances represent savings in production costs. Standard production costs are shown in all inventory accounts (which have debit balances); therefore, it is reasonable that excess costs are also debits.

Although standard cost systems are useful for internal reporting, the accounting profession has maintained that actual costs are the proper basis for external financial statements. Standard costs are acceptable for financial statement purposes only if the statements produced using the standard costs are substantially equivalent to those that would have resulted from using an actual cost system. If standards are realistically achievable and updated annually, this equivalency should exist. The use of standard costs for financial statements should provide fairly conservative inventory valuations because the effects of excess prices and/or inefficient operations are eliminated.

If standard costs are used in the accounting records, but actual costs are to be used in the financial statements, standard cost information must be adjusted at year-end to approximate actual costs. The nature of the year-end adjusting entries depends on whether the variance amounts are insignificant or significant.

If variance amounts are small, standard costs are approximately equal to actual costs. All insignificant unfavorable variances are closed as debits to Cost of Goods Sold; favorable variances are credited to Cost of Goods Sold. Thus, unfavorable variances have a negative impact on operating income because of the higher-than-expected costs, while favorable variances have a positive effect on operating income because of the lower-than-expected costs. Although the year's entire production may not have been sold yet, this treatment of insignificant variances is based on the immateriality of the amounts involved.

In contrast, large variances are prorated at year-end among ending inventories and Cost of Goods Sold. This proration disposes of the variances and presents the financial statements in a manner that approximates the use of actual costing. Proration is based on the relative size of the account balances. Disposition of significant variances is similar to the disposition of large amounts of under- or overapplied overhead shown in Chapter 4.

To illustrate the disposition of significant variances, assume that there is a $10,000 unfavorable (debit) year-end balance in the Materials Purchase Price Variance ac-

(1) Raw Materials Inventory	63,950.00	
Materials Price Variance		7,674.00
Accounts Payable		56,276.00
To record the purchase of 255,800 ounces of chocolate at $.22 per ounce.		
(2) Work in Process Inventory	63,759.00	
Materials Quantity Variance	178.50	
Raw Materials Inventory		63,937.50
To record the issuance and usage of 255,750 ounces of chocolate to produce 63,600 hearts.		
(3) Work in Process Inventory	3,180.00	
Labor Rate Variance	15.30	
Labor Efficiency Variance		120.00
Wages Payable		3,075.30
To record the usage of 510 hours of direct labor time at a wage rate of $6.03 per hour to produce 63,600 hearts.		

■ **EXHIBIT 11–7**

How Sweet It Is Journal Entries for October 1994

count of How Sweet It Is. Other relevant year-end account balances are as follows:

Raw Materials Inventory	$ 21,630
Work in Process Inventory	12,360
Finished Goods Inventory	33,990
Cost of Goods Sold	241,020
Total of affected accounts	$309,000

The theoretically correct allocation of the material purchase price variance would use actual material cost in each account at year-end. However, as was mentioned in Chapter 4 with regard to overhead, after conversion has begun cost elements within account balances are commingled and tend to lose their separateness. For example, it would be difficult to determine the amount of direct materials cost within the Finished Goods Inventory account without retracing all the transfers of goods during the year. Thus, unless a significant misstatement would result, disposition of the variance can be based on the proportions of each account balance to the total, as shown below:

Raw Materials Inventory	7%	($ 21,630 ÷ $309,000)
Work in Process Inventory	4%	($ 12,360 ÷ $309,000)
Finished Goods Inventory	11%	($ 33,990 ÷ $309,000)
Cost of Goods Sold	78%	($241,020 ÷ $309,000)

Applying these percentages to the $10,000 materials price variance gives the amounts shown in the journal entry below to assign to the affected accounts:

Raw Materials Inventory ($10,000 × .07)	700	
Work in Process Inventory ($10,000 × .04)	400	
Finished Goods Inventory ($10,000 × .11)	1,100	
Cost of Goods Sold ($10,000 × .78)	7,800	
Materials Price Variance		10,000
To dispose of the materials price variance at year-end.		

All variances other than the materials price variance (regardless of whether it is computed on quantity purchased or quantity used) occur as part of the conversion process. Raw material *purchases* are not part of conversion, but raw materials *used* are. Therefore, the Materials Quantity Variance, as well as all other variances, are prorated only to Work in Process Inventory, Finished Goods Inventory, and Cost of Goods Sold.

The above discussion about standard setting, variance computations, and potentially necessary year-end adjustments indicate that a substantial commitment of time and effort is required to implement and use a standard cost system. Companies are willing to make such a commitment for a variety of reasons.

WHY STANDARD COST SYSTEMS ARE USED

"A standard cost system has three basic functions: collecting the actual costs of a manufacturing operation, determining the achievement of that manufacturing operation, and evaluating performance through the reporting of variances from standard."[9] These basic functions result in six distinct benefits of standard cost systems.

---

[9] Richard V. Calvasina and Eugene J. Calvasina, "Standard Costing Games That Managers Play," *Management Accounting* (March 1984), p. 49. Although the authors of the article only specified manufacturing operations, these same functions are equally applicable to service businesses.

Clerical Efficiency

A company using standard costs to trace the flow of costs through its accounting system usually discovers that less clerical time and effort are required than in an actual cost system. In an actual cost system, the accountant must continuously recalculate changing actual unit costs. In a standard cost system, unit costs are held constant for a period of time. Costs can be assigned to inventory and cost of goods sold accounts at predetermined amounts per unit regardless of actual conditions.

Motivation

Standards are a means of communicating management's expectations of efficiency to workers. Workers who are shown that the standards are achievable and who are informed of the rewards for consistent attainment of those standards are likely to be motivated to strive for accomplishment. The standards used must require a reasonable amount of effort on the workers' part. "Presumably, an easy standard will induce a minimal level of effort from the worker; a difficult standard will discourage the worker after he experiences repeated failures."[10]

Planning

Planning generally requires estimates of future costs. Managers can use currently available standard costs to estimate what future quantities and costs should be. These estimates should help in the determination of purchasing needs for materials and of staffing needs for labor that, in turn, will aid in planning for company cash flows. In addition, budget preparation is simplified if standard costs are available. A standard is, in fact, a budget for one unit of product. Standards are also used to provide the cost basis needed to analyze relationships among costs, volume of sales, and profit levels of the organization.

Controlling

The control process begins with the establishment of standards. Standards provide a basis against which actual costs can be measured and variances calculated. **Variance analysis** is the process of categorizing the nature (favorable or unfavorable) of the differences between standard and actual costs and seeking explanations for those differences. Managers analyze variances to monitor operations, take corrective action on problems, evaluate performance, and motivate workers to achieve standard production.

Variance analysis

In implementing the control function, managers are faced with managing one particular scarce resource—their time. They must distinguish between situations to ignore and those to investigate. To assist in making this distinction, managers establish upper and lower limits of acceptable deviations from standard. These limits are similar to tolerance limits used by engineers in the development of statistical process control charts. If variances are small and within the acceptable range, no managerial action is required. If an actual cost differs significantly from standard, the manager responsible for the cost is expected to determine the cause(s) of the variance. If the cause can be found and corrective action is possible, such action should be taken so that future operations will adhere more closely to established standards.

The setting of upper and lower limits of tolerance for deviations allows managers to implement the management by exception concept. This concept is illustrated in Exhibit 11–8. In the exhibit, the only significant deviation from standard occurs on Day 5, when the actual costs exceeded the upper limit of acceptable performance. An

---

[10] Chee W. Chow and William S. Waller, "Management Accounting and Organizational Control," in *Readings in Cost Accounting Budgeting and Control,* ed. William E. Thomas (Cincinnati, Ohio: South-Western Publishing Co., 1983), p. 239.

EXHIBIT 11–8

Illustration of Management by Exception Concept

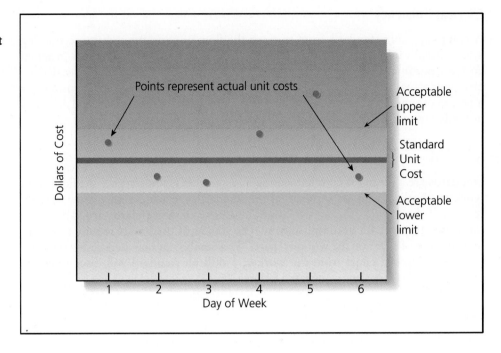

exception report should be generated on this date so that the manager will investigate the underlying causes of the variance.

Variances that are large enough to fall outside the ranges of acceptability often indicate trouble. However, variances themselves do not reveal the exact cause of the trouble or the person or group responsible. To determine variance causes, managers must skillfully and carefully investigate significant variances through observation, inspection, and inquiry. Such an investigation will involve the time and effort of people at the operating level as well as accounting personnel. Operations personnel should be alert in spotting variances as they occur and record the reasons for the variances to the extent it is possible to discern them. For example, operating personnel could readily detect and report causes such as machine downtime or material spoilage.

One important point needs to be made about the control uses of variances. An extremely favorable variance is not necessarily a good variance. Although the "favorable" designation may often equate to good, an extremely favorable variance could mean an error was made when the standard was set or that a related, offsetting unfavorable variance exists. For example, if low-quality material is purchased, a favorable price variance may exist, but additional quantities of the material may be used to overcome defective production. An unfavorable labor efficiency variance could also result because a longer time was spent on completing a job because a substantial number of defective units were produced as a result of using the inferior materials. Not only are the unfavorable variances incurred, but internal quality failure costs are also generated. Another common situation begins with labor rather than materials. Using lower-paid workers will result in a favorable rate variance, but may cause excessive usage of raw materials.

Alternatively, there may be a deliberate trade-off of variances, such as incurring an unfavorable labor rate variance because more skilled workers are used in exchange for a resulting favorable labor efficiency variance because fewer production hours were needed. Managers must constantly be aware that relationships exist and not analyze variances in isolation.

The time frame for which variance computations are made is being shortened, as is indicated in the News Note "When To Investigate Variances." Exhibit 11–9 provides the results of a limited survey conducted with controllers of manufacturing companies using standard cost systems. Monthly variance reporting is still the most com-

NEWS NOTE

When to Investigate Variances

Variance investigation policies [for materials and labor at large companies] are moving away from pure judgment and toward the use of structured or formalized exception procedures.

[One] explanation is that the results are being driven by manufacturing innovations that lead to shorter production runs and shorter product life cycles. In such an environment, monthly variance reports may be so untimely as to be virtually useless. In a flexible manufacturing environment, production runs can be extremely short—only days or perhaps even hours. To provide timely feedback in an environment where the nature of operations and the products being produced change rapidly, more accounts and greater reporting frequency are required.

[Another] explanation relates to the increasing globalization of markets rather than to the characteristics or individual operating policies of the firm. When competing internationally, companies face more competitors, are less likely to be the lowest-cost producers, and face more uncertainties than in domestic markets. . . . By reducing production cost surprises, intensified management accounting (in the frequency of reports and the details of variance composition) can compensate for these additional uncertainties.

SOURCE: Bruce R. Gaumnitz and Felix P. Kollaritsch, "Manufacturing Variances: Current Practice and Trends," *Journal of Cost Management* (Boston: Warren Gorham Lamont, Spring 1991), pp. 63–64.

mon, but the movement toward shorter reporting periods is obvious. As more companies integrate various world-class concepts such as total quality management and just-in-time production into their operations, there will be more frequent reporting of variances. Proper implementation of such concepts requires that managers be continuously aware of operating activities and recognize (and correct) problems as soon as they arise.

Decision Making

The availability of standard cost information facilitates many decisions. For example, managers can compare a standard cost with a quoted price to determine whether a

■ EXHIBIT 11–9
Time Period Covered by Variance Reports

	RAW MATERIALS				DIRECT LABOR			
	Currently		Five Years Ago		Currently		Five Years Ago	
	No.	%	No.	%	No.	%	No	%
Year	0	0	0	0	0	0	1	0.8
Quarter	3	2.5	4	3.3	2	1.7	2	1.7
Month	72	60.0	85	70.9	48	40.3	60	50.4
Week	16	13.3	16	13.3	32	26.9	32	26.9
Day	26	21.7	13	10.8	31	26.1	22	18.5
Hour or less	3	2.5	2	1.7	6	5.0	2	1.7
Total companies responding	120	100.0	120	100.0	119	100.0	119	100.0

SOURCE: Bruce R. Gaumnitz and Felix P. Kollaritsch, "Manufacturing Variances: Current Practice and Trends," *Journal of Cost Management* (Boston: Warren Gorham Lamont, Spring 1991), p. 60.

product or part should be manufactured in-house or purchased. Use of actual cost information in such a decision could be inappropriate because the actual cost may fluctuate from period to period. Also, in making a decision on a special price offering to purchasers, managers can use standard product cost to determine the lower limit of the price to offer. In a similar manner, if a company is bidding on contracts, it is essential to have some idea of estimated product costs. Bidding too low and receiving the contract could cause substantial operating income (and, possibly, cash flow) problems; bidding too high might be uncompetitive and cause the contract to be awarded to another company. Additionally, standard costs, when compared to selling prices and demand, can also be used to determine the contributions that different products make toward company profitability and, thus, which products to promote and sell most heavily.

Performance Evaluation

When top management receives summary variance reports highlighting the operating performance of subordinate managers, these reports are analyzed for both positive and negative information. Top management needs to know when costs were and were not controlled and by which managers. Such information allows top management to provide essential feedback to subordinates, to investigate areas of concern, and to make performance evaluations about who needs additional supervision, who should be replaced, and who should be promoted. For proper performance evaluations to be made, it is necessary that the responsibility for variances be traced to specific managers.[11]

VARIANCE RESPONSIBILITY

A well-designed system of variance analysis captures variances as early as possible, subject to management's cost-benefit assessments. The system should help managers determine who or what is responsible for the variance and who is best able to explain it. An early measurement and reporting system should allow managers to adjust operations and improve performance in areas where variances reflect poor performance. The longer the reporting of a variance is delayed, the more difficult it becomes to determine its cause. Materials price and labor rate variances are not as controllable at the production level as materials quantity and labor efficiency variances.

Materials Variances

Price standards tend to be more dependent on outside forces than are usage standards. Even so, some measures of control are still available to managers. The purchasing agent can influence the price paid for materials by purchasing materials in usable quantities that provide price discounts or by engaging in contractual arrangements such as long-term purchase contracts. Also, by virtue of being part of the team that originally sets the materials price standard, the purchasing agent is usually the individual to whom responsibility for material price variances is assigned.

Materials quantity variances can be determined during the production process. Materials are ordinarily requisitioned based on the number of units being produced multiplied by the standard quantity per unit. Excess materials requisition slips are filled out when additional materials are removed from inventory. The use of excess requisition slips allows control procedures to take place while production is underway rather than when production is completed. Monitoring requisition slips for significant excess material withdrawals alerts managers to identify causes for the ex-

---

[11] Performance evaluation is discussed in greater depth in Chapter 21 and 22.

Gary Crowley knows how many bunnies of a particular weight can be made from a melted 10-pound block of chocolate. Making certain that such production performance occurs requires close monitoring of materials quantity variances.

cesses and take timely corrective action. Such variances are usually considered the responsibility of the job or department supervisor.

Some production settings (such as food, chemical, and petroleum processing) involve a continuous flow process. In such cases, it may be neither practical nor reasonable to isolate materials quantity variances during the production process. In these situations, the materials quantity variance is more feasibly measured when production is complete and the total quantity of production is known. If the process involves continuous input of nondiscrete units, making timely measurements for relatively short time periods and reporting quantity variances after production is complete can still effectively assist management in controlling operations. Labor efficiency variances are also more appropriately measured at the end of production in these types of manufacturing activities.

There are exceptions to the normal assignment of responsibility for materials price and quantity variances. For example, assume the production supervisor asks the purchasing agent to acquire, without adequate lead time, additional quantities of materials. This request was necessitated because there has been excessive materials usage during the period. Such a spur-of-the-moment acquisition could result in paying a higher-than-standard price. Price variances from these types of causes should be assigned to production, not to purchasing. In contrast, assume the purchasing agent acquires inferior quality materials that result in excess usage and an unfavorable quantity variance. This variance should be assigned to purchasing rather than production. Such situations are more likely to be identified when shorter variance reporting periods are used because of the ability to view relationships among variances.

Labor Variances

Labor variances are commonly identified as a part of the payroll allocation process and are assigned to the job or departmental supervisor. Labor rate and labor efficiency variances both may be computed at the point of payroll allocation. Alternatively, labor efficiency variances may be identified during the production process because of the need for overtime or because of significant quality problems.

Like materials price standards, labor rate standards are often more reflective of external, rather than internal, conditions. Such conditions include changes in the minimal wage laws or labor contract renegotiations. A controllable internal condition that could contribute to a labor rate variance is the production supervisor's ability to influence the mix of direct labor personnel in work teams. The mix could affect the actual average labor rate paid. Such managerial influences keep labor rate variances from being considered uncontrollable.

Identifying rate variances at the point of payroll allocation assumes that production managers have responsibility for the rate variances because of their ability to influence the mix of labor used. As with materials variances, correlations may exist between labor variances. For example, excessive use of highly skilled, highly paid employees could cause an unfavorable labor rate variance, but a favorable labor efficiency variance.

As mentioned earlier, sometimes a common factor (such as the purchase of inferior materials) may influence both material and labor and cause a favorable materials price variance, an unfavorable materials usage variance, and an unfavorable labor efficiency variance. In such instances, accountability for the variances should be traced back and assigned to the person originally responsible for the decision—in this case, to the purchasing agent who decided to buy inferior materials.

The accounting and reporting process should highlight variance interrelationships to managers. The probability of detecting these interrelationships is improved, but not assured, by timely variance reporting. The ability to determine causes of variances is often proportional to how much time, effort, and money a company spends in gathering information about variances during the period. Managers must be willing and able to accumulate variance information regularly and consistently in order to evaluate the evidence, isolate the cause, and (if possible) influence performance to improve the process. If variances are ignored when they occur, it is often impossible or extremely costly to determine the relevant data later.

CONSIDERATIONS IN ESTABLISHING STANDARDS

When standards are established, appropriateness and attainability should be considered. Appropriateness, in relation to a standard, refers to the basis on which the standards are developed and how long they are expected to last. Attainability refers to management's belief about the degree of difficulty or rigor that should be incurred in achieving the standard.

Appropriateness

Although standards are developed from past and current information, they should reflect relevant technical and environmental factors expected during the time period in which the standards are to be applied. Consideration should be given to factors such as material quality, normal ordering quantities for materials, expected employee wage rates, degree of plant automation, facility layout, and mix of employee skills. Management should not think that, once standards are set, they will remain useful forever. Standards must evolve over the organization's life to reflect its changing methods and processes. Out-of-date standards produce variances that do not provide logical bases for planning, controlling, decision making, or evaluating performance. Current operating performance is not comparable to out-of-date standards.

To illustrate the above point, assume that How Sweet It Is management set price standards for chocolate in 1992 and did not change that standard for two years. By 1994, the price of cocoa beans and chocolate had declined drastically. The consistently favorable materials price variances for the chocolate should have been noticed and managers should have realized that the price variance was not relevant to evaluating the purchasing agent's performance, inventory valuation, or any product pricing decisions. The price reductions occurring since the standard was set have made the standard obsolete and its usage counterproductive.

Another example of the appropriateness of a standard relates to changes in plant layout. Assume that How Sweet It Is also set its labor time standards in 1992; in 1994, the company made major adjustments in the plant layout that resulted in significant reductions in the time needed by labor to perform production tasks. If the labor time standard were not reduced to reflect the productivity increases, labor efficiency variances would not be meaningful.

Attainability

Standards provide a target level of performance and can be set at various levels of rigor. The level of rigor invested in the standard affects motivation, and one reason for using standards is to motivate employees. Standards can be classified by their degree of rigor and, thus, their motivational value from easy to difficult, as follows: expected, practical, and ideal. Depending on the type of standard in effect, the acceptable ranges used to apply the management by exception principle will differ. This difference is especially notable on the unfavorable side.

Expected standards are those set at a level that reflects what is actually expected to occur in the future period. Such standards anticipate future waste and inefficiencies and allow for them. As such, expected standards are not of significant value for motivation, control, or performance evaluation. If a company uses expected standards, the ranges of acceptable variances should be extremely small (and, commonly, favorable) since the actual costs should conform closely to standards.

Expected standards

Standards that can be reached or slightly exceeded approximately 60 to 70 percent of the time with reasonable effort by workers are called **practical** (or currently attainable) **standards**. These standards allow for normal, unavoidable time problems or delays such as machine downtime and worker breaks. Practical standards represent an attainable challenge and traditionally have been thought to be the most effective at inducing the best worker performance and at determining the effectiveness and efficiency of workers at performing their tasks. Both favorable and unfavorable variances result from the use of such moderately rigorous standards.

Practical standards

Standards that provide for no inefficiency of *any* type are called **ideal** (or theoretical) **standards**. Ideal standards encompass the highest level of rigor and do not allow for normal operating delays or human limitations such as fatigue, boredom, or misunderstanding. Unless a plant is entirely automated (and then there is still the possibility of human or power failure), it is impossible for ideal standards to be attained. Most attempts to apply such standards result in discouraged and resentful workers who, ultimately, ignore the standards. Variances from ideal standards will always be unfavorable and traditionally have not been considered useful for constructive cost control or performance evaluation. Such a traditional perspective has, however, begun to change.

Ideal standards

In using variances from standards for control and performance evaluation purposes, many accountants (and, often, businesspeople in general) believe that an incorrect measurement is being used in many instances. For example, the chapter stated that material standards often include a factor for waste, and labor standards are commonly set at the practical level of attainment even though this level compensates for downtime and human error. Usage of standards that are not aimed at the highest possible (theoretical) level of attainment are now being questioned in a business environment concerned with world-class operations.

CHANGES IN STANDARDS USAGE

Use of Theoretical Standards

Recently there has been a significant amount of Japanese influence on American management philosophy and production techniques. Just-in-time (JIT) production systems and total quality management (TQM) concepts were both imported to this country as a result of an upsurge in Japanese productivity. These two world-class concepts are inherently based on a notable exception to the traditional disbelief in the use of ideals in standards development and use. Rather than including waste and inefficiency in the standards and then accepting additional waste and spoilage deviations under a management by exception principle, JIT and TQM both begin from the premises of zero defects, zero inefficiency, and zero downtime. Under such a system, ideal standards become expected standards and there is no (or only a minimal allowable) level of acceptable deviation from standard.

When the standard permits a deviation from the ideal, managers are allowing for less than perfectly efficient uses of resources. Setting standards at the tightest possible (ideal) level results in the most useful information for managerial purposes as well as the highest quality products and services at the lowest possible cost. If no inefficiencies are built into or tolerated in the system, deviations from standard should be minimized and overall organizational performance improved. Workers may, at first, resent the introduction of standards set at a "perfection" level, but it is in their and management's best long-run interest to have such standards. If theoretical standards are to be implemented, management must be prepared to go through the following four-step "migration" process.

First, teams should be established to determine where current problems lie and identify the causes of those problems. Second, if the causes relate to equipment, facility, or workers, management must be ready to invest plant and equipment items, equipment rearrangements, or worker training so that the standards are amenable to the operations. (Training is essential if workers are to perform at the high levels of efficiency demanded by theoretical standards.) If the causes are related to external sources (such as poor quality materials), management must be willing to change suppliers and/or pay higher prices for higher quality input. Third, since management has assigned the responsibility for quality to the workers, management must also empower workers with the authority to react to problems. "The key to quality initiatives is for employees to move beyond their natural resistance-to-change mode to a highly focused, strategic, and empowered mind-set. This shift unlocks employees' energy and creativity, and leads them to ask 'how can I do my job even better today?'"[12] And fourth, requiring people to work at their maximum potential demands recognition, meaning that management must provide rewards for achievement. The News Note "Reward Employees" discusses the steps in the quality program implemented by Rosco Manufacturing Company of Madison, South Dakota, a maker of road maintenance equipment.

Whether setting standards at the ideal level will become the norm of American companies cannot be determined at this time. However, we expect that the level of attainability for standards will move away from the practical and closer to the ideal. This conclusion is based on the fact that a company whose competitor produces goods based on the highest possible standards must also use such standards to compete on quality and to meet cost (and, thus, profit margin) objectives. Higher standards for efficiency automatically mean lower costs because of the elimination of non-value-added activities such as waste, idle time, and rework.

Price Variance Based on Purchases vs. on Usage

The price variance computation traditionally has been based more on purchases than on usage. This choice was made so as to calculate the variance as quickly as possible

---

[12] Sara Moulton, Ed Oakley, and Chuck Kremer, "How to Assure Your Quality Initiative Really Pays Off," *Management Accounting* (January 1993), p. 26.

NEWS NOTE

Reward Employees for Increased Productivity

At a time of increased competition and reduced demand in its market, Rosco's costs were high because productivity was not. The company turned itself around by helping its workers turn out higher-quality equipment more quickly and at a more competitive cost.

First, Rosco moved to South Dakota from Minneapolis, where it had occupied old buildings in a congested setting that frustrated efficiency—a street ran through the center of the property. Employees were briefed on various company objectives and asked for suggestions.

Technology was widely upgraded. Barriers to production were identified and eliminated. Obsolete fabrication and machining equipment was replaced.

Workers were now held accountable for the quality of equipment they made and their rate of production. All employees began pulling for the same objectives and sales per hour worked rose to $57 in the first half of 1990 from $28 in the first half of 1987. The labor content of goods sold dropped from 16.7 percent to 10.7 percent.

[To reward employees for their achievements,] Rosco pays an annual cash bonus if profits are adequate—as they were in 1991—and has set up a 401(k) retirement program to which it donates 15 percent of employee savings.

SOURCE: Connecticut Mutual Life Insurance Company and U.S. Chamber of Commerce, *Real-World Lessons for America's Small Businesses* (Nation's Business, 1992), pp. 60–61.

relative to the cost incurrence. While calculating the price variance for materials at the point of purchase allows managers to see the impact of buying decisions more rapidly, such information may not be most relevant in a just-in-time environment. Buying materials in quantities that are not needed for current production requires that the materials be stored and moved—both non-value-added activities. The trade-off in price savings would need to be measured against the additional costs to determine the cost-benefit relationship of such a purchase.

Additionally, computing a price variance based on purchases, rather than on usage, may reduce the probability of recognizing a relationship between a favorable materials price variance and an unfavorable materials usage variance. If the favorable price variance resulted from the purchase of low-quality materials, the effects of that purchase will not be known until the materials are actually used.

The determination of whether to use a materials price variance based on purchases or on usage is a management decision and should reflect the environment in which the company operates. Both variances could be computed and the information used at different times. If, however, a just-in-time inventory system is implemented by the manufacturer and materials variances are virtually eliminated, there is little need to compute the traditional material price and usage variances. Reasons for the elimination of materials variances are discussed more thoroughly in Chapter 18.

Decline in Direct Labor

As the proportion of product cost related to direct labor declines, the necessity for direct labor variance computations is minimized. Direct labor may simply become a small part of a conversion cost category, as noted in Chapter 2. Alternatively, the increase in automation often relegates labor to an indirect (rather than a direct) category because workers become machine overseers rather than product producers. The chapter suggested that the labor efficiency variance could contain a subvariance related to quality as well as one simply related to hours of effort. The News Note "Did the Employee or the Machine Create the Variance?" provides another alternative segmentation of the labor efficiency variance.

NEWS NOTE

Did the Employee or the Machine Create the Variance?

In an automated environment, the traditional labor efficiency variance should be divided into two new variances: an *employee labor efficiency variance* and a *machine labor efficiency variance*. In such an environment, employee efficiency has two different aspects. One aspect is directly related to the employee's skill and industriousness; the other is directly related to the equipment's state of readiness. Recognizing these aspects separately will allow the control system to direct management's attention to the real source of problems (the employee or the machine configuration).

Dividing the traditional labor efficiency variance into the two new variances requires the establishment of a *ratio standard* for employee labor hours to machine hours for each piece of equipment. The new variances also require two other items of information for each machine in the machine cluster:

1. Actual machine hours devoted by each machine to production in each accounting period; and

2. Actual hours devoted by the employee to each machine during the accounting period.

The new employee labor efficiency variance is calculated as: (Budgeted Employee Wages for Actual Hours) minus (Budgeted Employee Wages for Required Employee Hours) or (Standard Wage Rate × Actual Employee Hours) − (Standard Wage Rate × Actual Machine Hours × Ratio Standard). This variance indicates whether the employee devoted more (or fewer) hours to the machine than were required for the actual production.

The machine labor efficiency variance is calculated as: (Budgeted Employee Wages for Required Employee Hours) minus (Allowed Employee Labor Cost for Actual Production) or (Standard Wage Rate × Standard Machine Time Allowed for Actual Production × Ratio Standard). This variance reflects the additional (or reduced) costs of employee labor that was caused by the machine's having been operated more (or fewer) hours than were allowed based on the number of units produced.

SOURCE: Adapted from Alan S. Levitan and Sidney J. Baxendale, "Analyzing the Labor Efficiency Variance to Signal Process Engineering Problems," *Journal of Cost Management* (Boston: Warren Gorham Lamont, Summer 1992), pp. 63–72.

Adjusting Standards

Standards have traditionally been set after comprehensive investigation of prices and quantities for the various cost elements. These standards were often retained for multiple years, and they were almost always retained for at least one year. Currently, though, the business environment (which includes supplier prices, contractual relationships, technology, competition, product design, and manufacturing methods) changes so rapidly that a standard may no longer be useful for management control purposes throughout a year.

Company management needs to consider whether to incorporate rapid changes in the environment into the standards during the year in which *significant* changes occur. The two obvious choices are to ignore the changes or to reflect those changes in the standard. Ignoring the changes is a simplistic approach that allows the same type of cost to be recorded at the same amount all year. Thus, for example, any material purchased during the year would be recorded at the same standard cost regardless of when the purchase was made. This approach, while making recordkeeping easy, eliminates any opportunity to adequately control costs or evaluate performance. Additionally, such an approach could create large differentials between standard and actual costs, making standard costs unacceptable for external reporting.

Changing the standards to reflect the changes in prices or quantities would make some aspects of management control and performance evaluation more effective and others more difficult. For instance, budgets prepared using the original standards would need to be adjusted before appropriate actual comparisons could be made against them. Changing standards also creates a problem for recordkeeping and inventory valuation. At what standard cost should products be valued—the standard in effect when they were produced or the standard in effect when the financial statements are prepared? While production-point standards would be more closely related to actual costs, many of the benefits discussed earlier in the chapter might be undermined.

If possible, management may wish to consider combining these two choices in the accounting system. The original standards can be considered "frozen" for budget purposes and a revised budget prepared using the new current standards. The difference between these budgets would reflect variances related to business environment cost changes. These variances could be designated as uncontrollable (such as those related to changes in the market price of raw materials) or internally initiated (such as changes in standard labor time resulting from employee training or equipment rearrangement). Comparing the budget based on current standards with actual costs would provide variances that would more adequately reflect internally controllable causes, such as excess materials and/or labor time usage caused by inferior quality purchases.

R E V I S I T I N G

MERLIN CANDIES, INC.

Because of the seasonality of his business, Gary Crowley must rely heavily on good demand forecasts for product sales. Since Merlin's chocolate is a special recipe made by a supplier in Pennsylvania, orders for the company's raw material must be placed well in advance to ensure a steady supply of the type and quality of chocolate necessary for production.

The primary direct materials costs (for chocolate and boxes) are directly affected by the cost of, respectively, cocoa beans and cardboard. While the cost of beans has been declining because of ideal growing conditions in Africa and South America, the cost of the cardboard display boxes has steadily increased. In fact, the cost for boxes jumped 37 percent in 1989 over the previous year. The cellophane window for viewing the product requires the box to be specially produced, creating a high per unit cost. This cost is a factor over which cost control relative to standard is tightly practiced.

Most of Merlin's seasonal workers are paid the minimum wage for their hours of work. Thus, increases in the federally mandated wage scale serve to change the company's labor rate standard and the rate is one over which Gary Crowley has no control. Control over labor costs must be focused on worker efficiency, which is affected by adequate training.

CHAPTER SUMMARY

A standard cost is computed as a standard quantity multiplied by a standard price. In a true standard cost system, standards are derived for quantities and prices of each product component and for each product. Standards provide a degree of clerical efficiency, and assist management in their planning, controlling, decision making, and performance evaluation functions. Standards can also be used to motivate employees if the standards are seen as a goal of expected performance.

A standard cost card provides information about the components, processes, quantities, and costs that form the standard for a product. The materials and labor sections of the standard cost card are derived from the bill of materials and the operations flow document, respectively.

A variance is any difference between an actual and a standard cost. A total variance is composed of a price and a usage subvariance. The materials subvariances are the price and the quantity variances. The materials price variance can be computed on either the quantity of material purchased or the quantity of material used in production. This variance is computed as the quantity measure selected multiplied by the difference between the actual and standard prices. The materials quantity variance is the difference between the standard price of the actual quantity of material used and the standard price of the standard quantity of material allowed for the actual output.

The two labor subvariances are the rate and efficiency variances. The labor rate variance indicates the difference between the actual rate paid and the standard rate allowed for the actual hours worked during the period. The labor efficiency variance compares the number of hours actually worked against the standard number of hours allowed for the level of production achieved and multiplies this difference by the standard wage rate.

Actual costs are required for external reporting, although standard costs may be used if they approximate actual costs. If a standard costing system is used, adjusting entries may be necessary at the end of the period to convert from standard to approximate actual cost.

A standard cost system should allow management to identify significant variances as close to the time of occurrence as feasible and, if possible, to help determine the variance cause. Significant variances should be investigated to decide if corrective action is possible and practical. Guidelines for investigation should be developed using the management by exception principle.

Standards should be updated periodically so that they reflect actual economic conditions. Additionally, they should be set at a level to encourage high-quality production, promote cost control, and motivate workers toward production accomplishments.

APPENDIX 1

Mix and Yield Variances

The How Sweet It Is example in the chapter used only one type of material and one category of labor in the production of the company's product. Most companies, however, use a combination of many materials and various classifications of direct labor to produce goods. In such settings, the materials and labor variance computations presented in the chapter are insufficient.

When a company's product uses more than one material, a goal is to combine those materials in such a way as to produce the desired product quality in the most cost-beneficial manner. Sometimes, materials may be substituted for one another without affecting product quality. In other instances, only one specific material or type of material can be used. For example, a furniture manufacturer might use either oak or maple to build a couch frame and still have the same basic quality. A perfume manufacturer, however, may only be able to use a specific fragrance oil to achieve a desired scent.

Labor, like materials, can be combined in many different ways to make the same product. Some combinations will be less expensive than others; some will be more efficient than others. Again, all potential combinations may not be viable: unskilled laborers would not be able to properly cut Baccarat or Waterford crystal.

Management desires to achieve the most efficient use of labor inputs. As with materials, some amount of interchangeability among labor categories is assumed. Skilled labor is more likely to be substituted for unskilled because interchanging unskilled labor for skilled labor is often not feasible. However, it may not be cost effective to use highly skilled, highly paid workers to do tasks that require little or no training. A rate variance for direct labor is calculated in addition to the mix and yield variances.

Each possible combination of materials or labor is called a **mix**. Management's **Mix** standards development team sets standards for materials and labor mix based on experience, judgment, and experimentation. Mix standards are used to calculate mix and yield variances for materials and labor. An underlying assumption in product mix situations is that there is potential for substitution among the material and labor components. If this assumption is invalid, changing the mix cannot improve the yield and may even prove wasteful. In addition to mix and yield variances, price and rate variances are still computed for materials and labor.

Assume that How Sweet It Is begins making a 3.5-ounce chocolate-covered caramel and almond candy. The caramel and almonds are combined and it is possible, to some extent, to substitute one ingredient for the other. Regardless of the mix used, the quantity of chocolate covering is the same. This new candy is used to illustrate the computations of mix and yield variances.

A small amount of water is added to the mixture; water is considered an indirect material. The mixture is cooked and some shrinkage results during that process, indicating that more than 3.5 ounces of ingredients must be placed into production to yield one candy. The chocolate used is a different grade from that used to make the hearts discussed in the chapter and costs only $.19 per ounce. The company has two direct labor categories (A and B). There is a labor rate differential between these two categories. Exhibit 11–10 provides standard and actual information for the company for March 1994.

MATERIALS STANDARDS FOR ONE LOT (240 CANDIES):

Chocolate:	240 ounces at $.19 per ounce	$ 45.60
Caramel:	480 ounces at $.10 per ounce	48.00
Almonds:	240 ounces at $.15 per ounce	36.00
Total	960 ounces	$129.60

LABOR STANDARDS FOR ONE LOT (240 CANDIES):

Category A workers:	2 hours at $6.00 per hour	$12
Category B workers:	1 hour at $8.00 per hour	8
Total	3 hours	$20

ACTUAL PRODUCTION AND COST DATA FOR MONTH:

Production: 100 lots or 24,000 candies

Materials:

Chocolate:	Purchased and used	24,400 ounces at $.21 per ounce ($5,124)
Caramel:	Purchased and used	48,000 ounces at $.09 per ounce ($4,320)
Almonds:	Purchased and used	26,000 ounces at $.17 per ounce ($4,420)
Total		98,400 ounces

Labor:

Category A	203 hours at $5.90 per hour ($1,197.70)
Category B	98 hours at $8.10 per hour ($793.80)
Total	301 hours

■ **EXHIBIT 11–10**

How Sweet It Is Standard and Actual Information for March 1994

Materials Price, Mix, and Yield Variances

Materials mix variance

Materials yield variance

A materials price variance shows the dollar effect of paying prices that differ from the raw materials standard. The **materials mix variance** measures the effect of substituting a nonstandard mix of materials during the production process. The **materials yield variance** is the difference between the actual total quantity of input and the standard total quantity allowed based on output; this difference reflects standard mix and standard prices. The sum of the materials mix and yield variances equals a materials quantity variance similar to the one shown in the chapter; the difference between these two variances is that the sum of the mix and yield variances is attributable to multiple ingredients rather than to a single one. It is possible for a company to have a mix variance without experiencing a yield variance.

Yield

In the How Sweet It Is example, the standard mix of materials is 25 percent (240 ounces of 960 ounces per lot) chocolate, 50 percent (480 ounces of 960) caramel, and 25 percent almonds. The **yield** of a process is the quantity of output resulting from a specified input. For How Sweet It Is, the yield from 240 ounces of chocolate, 480 ounces of caramel, and 240 ounces of almonds (960 ounces of input) is one lot of 240 candies. (Again, the difference in weight is caused by shrinkage.) Computations for the price, mix, and yield variances are given below in a format similar to the one shown in the chapter:

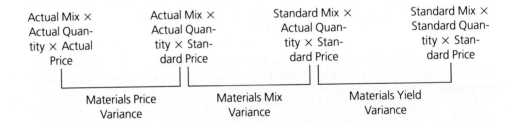

How Sweet It Is used 98,400 total ounces of ingredients to make 100 lots or 24,000 candies. The standard quantity necessary to produce this quantity of candies is 96,000 total ounces of ingredients (960 ounces per lot × 100 lots). The actual mix of chocolate, caramel, and almonds was 24.8 percent, 48.8 percent, and 26.4 percent, respectively:

Chocolate	(24,400 ounces out of 98,400) = 24.8%
Caramel	(48,000 ounces out of 98,400) = 48.8%
Almonds	(26,000 ounces out of 98,400) = 26.4%

Computations necessary for the materials variances are shown in Exhibit 11–11. These amounts are then used to compute the variances.

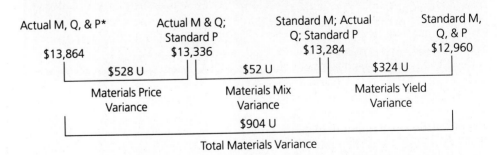

* M = mix, Q = quantity, and P = price

∎ EXHIBIT 11–11

**Computations for
How Sweet It Is
Materials Variances**

(1) Total actual data (mix, quantity, and prices):

Chocolate—24,400 ounces at $.21	$5,124	
Caramel—48,000 ounces at $.09	4,320	
Almonds—26,000 ounces at $.17	4,420	
Total actual materials cost		$13,864

(2) Actual mix and quantity; standard prices:

Chocolate—24,400 at $.19	$4,636	
Caramel—48,000 at $.10	4,800	
Almonds—26,000 ounces at $.15	3,900	$13,336

(3) Standard mix; actual quantity; standard prices:

Chocolate—25% X 98,400 ounces × $.19	$4,674	
Caramel—50% × 98,400 ounces × $.10	4,920	
Almonds—25% × 98,400 ounces × $.15	3,690	$13,284

(4) Total standard data (mix, quantity, and prices):

Chocolate—25% × 96,000 ounces × $.19	$4,560	
Caramel—50% × 96,000 ounces × $.10	4,800	
Almonds—25% × 96,000 ounces × $.15	3,600	$12,960

The above computations show a single price variance being calculated for materials. To be more useful to management, separate price variances can be calculated for each material used. For example, the material price variance for chocolate is $488 U ($5,124 − $4,636), for caramel $480 F ($4,320 − $4,800), and for almonds $520 U ($4,420 − $3,900). Also, the data indicate that the amounts of materials purchased and used during the period were the same. Had these quantities been different, the materials price variances could have been calculated on the quantities purchased, while the remaining variances would have been calculated on the quantities used in production.

How Sweet It Is paid less for the caramel than was expected, but more for the chocolate and almonds. The savings on the caramel was less than the added cost for the other ingredients. Less than the standard proportion of the least expensive ingredient (caramel) was used, so it is reasonable that there would be an unfavorable mix variance. The company also experienced an unfavorable yield because total ounces of material allowed for output (96,000) was less than actual total ounces of material used (98,400).

Labor Rate, Mix, and Yield Variances

The two labor categories used by How Sweet It Is are unskilled (A) and skilled (B). Each category is paid a different wage rate. When preparing the labor standards, the development team establishes the labor categories required to perform the various tasks and the amount of time each task is expected to take. During production, variances will occur if workers are not paid the standard rate, do not work in the standard mix on tasks, or do not perform those tasks in the standard time.

The labor rate variance is a measure of the cost of paying workers at other than standard rates. The **labor mix variance** is the financial effect associated with changing the proportionate amount of higher- or lower-paid workers in production. The **labor yield variance** reflects the monetary impact of using more or fewer total hours than the standard allowed. The sum of the labor mix and yield variances equals the labor efficiency variance. The diagram for computing labor rate, mix, and yield variances is as follows:

Labor mix variance

Labor yield variance

EXHIBIT 11–12

Computations for
How Sweet It Is
Labor Variances

(1) Total actual data (mix, hours, and rates):
    Category A—203 actual hours × $5.90
      per hour actual rate $1,197.70
    Category B—98 actual hours × $8.10
      per hour actual rate   793.80

    Total actual labor cost $1,991.50

(2) Actual mix and hours; standard rates:
    Category A—203 hours × $6.00 $1,218.00
    Category B—98 hours × $8.00   784.00 $2,002.00

(3) Actual hours; standard mix and rates:
    Category A—2/3 × 301 × $6.00 $1,204.00
    Category B—1/3 × 301 × $8.00   802.67 $2,006.67

(4) Total standard data (mix, hours, and rates):
    Category A—2/3 × 300 × $6.00 $1,200.00
    Category B—1/3 × 300 × $8.00   800.00 $2,000.00

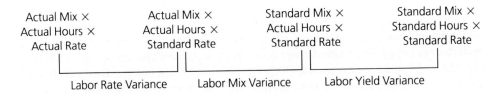

Standard rates are used to make both the mix and yield computations. For How Sweet It Is, the standard mix of A and B labor shown in Exhibit 11–10 is 2/3 and 1/3 (2 hours to 1 hour), respectively. The actual mix is 67.4% (A) and 32.6% (B) or 203 and 98, respectively, of 301 total hours. Exhibit 11–12 presents the labor computations for How Sweet It Is. Since standard hours to produce one lot of candies were two and one for categories A and B labor respectively, the standard hours allowed for the production of 100 lots of candies are 300 (200 of A and 100 of B). Using the amounts from Exhibit 11–12, the labor variances for How Sweet It Is are calculated in diagram form.

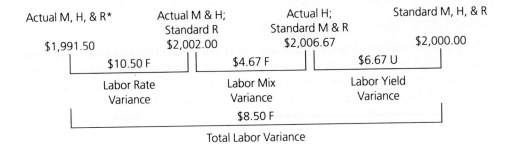

As with materials price variances, separate rate variances can be calculated for each class of labor. The labor rate variance for category A is $20.30 F ($1,197.70 − $1,218.00) and for category B is $9.80 U ($793.80 − $784.00).

---

* M = mix, H = hours, and R = rate

The company has saved $4.67 by using the actual mix of labor rather than the standard. A higher proportion of the less expensive class of labor (category A) than specified in the standard mix was used. One result of substituting a greater proportion of lower-paid workers seems to be that an unfavorable yield occurred because total actual hours (301) were greater than standard (300). Although this variance is extremely small, How Sweet It Is may wish to increase its efforts to stay with the standard mix so that costs from labor mix variances in the future do not rise out of control. These variances should all be evaluated within the context of maintaining an acceptable level of product quality.

Because there are trade-offs in mix and yield when component qualities and quantities are changed, management should observe the integrated nature of price, mix, and yield. The effects of changes of one element on the other two need to be considered for cost efficiency and output quality. If mix and yield can be increased by substituting less expensive resources *while still maintaining quality*, managers and product engineers should change the standards and the proportions of components. If costs are reduced but quality maintained, selling prices could also be reduced to gain a larger market share.

Learning Curves

APPENDIX 2

Part of the standards setting process is the determination of the quantity of labor necessary to achieve production levels. In making this determination, the company's standards development team should recognize the existence of learning curves. Learning curves are appropriate for any organization having repetitive labor tasks that require some degree of skill. A **learning curve** is a model that helps predict how labor time will decrease as people become more experienced at performing a task and are able to eliminate the inefficiencies associated with unfamiliarity. The learning curve model can be used for manufacturing, assembly, or office personnel although the degree of learning differs dramatically among occupations and tasks. For example, the learning curve for a person attempting to use a new computer program is much higher and lasts much longer than one for a person learning to assemble boxes in a warehouse.

Learning curve

In a learning curve situation, labor time is reduced in a distinct pattern as production is increased. Statistical studies show that the pattern is related to the doubling of the output level. The learning curve pattern indicates that, *as total production quantities double, the level of work time required per unit declines by a specified percentage*. The size of the learning curve percentage depends on the skills necessary to perform the task.

The How Sweet It Is example will be expanded and used to demonstrate the effects of learning curves on employee performance. Assume that the company decides to sell hand-decorated 16-ounce chocolate Easter eggs. The eggs are designed to open and have detailed scenes inside. A new employee, Jack, was hired. It took Jack three hours to decorate his first egg. How Sweet It Is asked other candy companies having experience in such detailed work about their learning curves. These companies told How Sweet It Is management that their employees experienced an 85 percent learning curve. Thus, the company can predict Jack's production output using the number of actual hours experienced in decorating the first egg. These predictions are shown in Exhibit 11–13 on page 456. Note that predictions are computed only for doubled production quantity levels.

The time shown in the "predicted average" column is an *average* for all the eggs that have been decorated at that point. It does not provide information on the actual time per egg for any egg except the first one. The second egg actually took Jack 2.1

■ EXHIBIT 11–13

How Sweet It Is
85% Learning Curve

TOTAL PRODUCTION QUANTITY	PREDICTED AVERAGE PRODUCTION HOURS PER UNIT (PREVIOUS TIME × 85%)	PREDICTED TOTAL PRODUCTION HOURS (TIME PER UNIT × PRODUCTION QUANTITY)
1	3.0000 (given)	3.0000
2	2.5500	5.1000
4	2.1675	8.6700
8	1.8424	14.7392
16	1.5660	25.0560

hours: the 5.10 total hours minus the 3.00 hours for the first egg. The next two eggs took 3.57 hours (8.67 − 5.10) or an average of 1.785 hours for each egg.

An important workplace application of learning curves relates to the installation of new computer applications. The time it takes for an employee to become proficient at various applications on alternative computer software programs must be considered when deciding which programs to purchase. A computer program that can show that users have a 70 percent learning curve is more cost effective than one having a 90 percent learning curve. The calculations supporting this conclusion are shown in Exhibit 11–14. If both programs can perform the same tasks with the same results, Computer Program 1 is more cost-beneficial in terms of labor time than Computer Program 2. The comparison assumes that each program has virtually the same level of difficulty to start.

Learning curves are applicable in developing labor time standards for efficiency and piece work. It must be recognized, however, that reductions in labor time are most noticeable when employees first begin performing a task. At some point, after some degree of learning has occurred, the learning curve becomes flat and only minimal improvements in performance are achieved. This point is referred to as the **steady state phase**. This point depends on the degree of complexity of the work and the original level of the learning curve.

Steady state phase

■ EXHIBIT 11–14

Comparison of 70% and 90% Learning Curves

First time to use computer application: 5 hours
Cost of employee per hour: $75

COMPUTER PROGRAM 1 (70% LEARNING CURVE):

# OF APPLICATIONS	CUMULATIVE AVERAGE UNIT TIME	TOTAL CUMULATIVE TIME	TOTAL COST
1	5.00 hours	5.0	$ 375
2	3.50	7.0	525
4	2.45	9.8	735
8	1.72	13.8	1,035

COMPUTER PROGRAM 2 (90% LEARNING CURVE):

# OF APPLICATIONS	CUMULATIVE AVERAGE UNIT TIME	TOTAL CUMULATIVE TIME	TOTAL COST
1	5.00 hours	5.0	$ 375
2	4.50	9.0	675
4	4.05	16.2	1,215
8	3.65	29.2	2,190

The most effective labor time standards are based on a time (per unit or per task) achieved at some point *after* start-up activities have begun and *before* the steady state phase occurs. If standards are set at the beginning of learning, they will rapidly become too easy to achieve and ineffectual for cost control. Cost estimates based on such standards would be significantly overstated for future jobs. Standards based on the steady state phase will be too tight and will result in unrealistic ideas about production time. Such a planning error would occur for two reasons: (1) all workers do not reach the steady state phase at the same time and (2) the labor force changes over time with new workers being added who are at the bottom of the learning curve. Standards set based on the steady state phase may also be poor motivators because they could be perceived by employees as being unattainable.

Additionally, the learning process can affect raw materials usage since waste and spoilage may be higher than normal early in the learning phase. The cost accountant should be aware of all the implications of learning curves when setting material usage and labor time standards and estimating job costs for new types of production or new operations involving repetitive actions. By acknowledging the effects of learning, more realistic cost estimates can be developed.

KEY TERMS

Bill of materials (p. 426)
Expected standards (p. 445)
Ideal standards (p. 445)
Labor efficiency variance (p. 435)
Labor mix variance (p. 453)
Labor rate variance (p. 435)
Labor yield variance (p. 453)
Learning curve (p. 455)
Materials mix variance (p. 452)
Materials price variance (p. 433)
Materials quantity variance (p. 434)
Materials yield variance (p. 452)
Mix (p. 451)

Operations flow document (p. 428)
Practical standards (p. 445)
Standard (p. 423)
Standard cost (p. 424)
Standard cost card (p. 430)
Standard cost system (p. 424)
Standard quantity allowed (p. 431)
Steady state phase (p. 456)
Total variance (p. 431)
Variance (p. 430)
Variance analysis (p. 439)
Yield (p. 452)

SOLUTION STRATEGIES

Actual Costs
Direct material: Actual price paid × Actual quantity purchased or used

$$\text{DM: AP} \times \text{AQ} = \text{AC}$$

Direct labor: Actual price (rate) paid × Actual quantity of hours worked

$$\text{DL: AP} \times \text{AQ} = \text{AC}$$

Standard Costs
Direct material: Standard price × Standard quantity allowed

$$\text{DM: SP} \times \text{SQ} = \text{SC}$$

Direct labor: Standard price (rate) × Standard quantity of hours allowed

$$\text{DL: SP} \times \text{SQ} = \text{SC}$$

Standard quantity allowed: Standard quantity of input (SQ) for the actual quantity of output achieved

Variances in Formula Format

$$\text{Materials price variance} = (AP \times AQ) - (SP \times AQ)$$
$$\text{Materials quantity variance} = (SP \times AQ) - (SP \times SQ)$$
$$\text{Labor rate variance} = (AP \times AQ) - (SP \times AQ)$$
$$\text{Labor efficiency variance} = (SP \times AQ) - (SP \times SQ)$$

Multiple Materials:

$$\text{Materials price variance} = (AM \times AQ \times AP) - (AM \times AQ \times SP)$$
$$\text{Materials mix variance} = (AM \times AQ \times SP) - (SM \times AQ \times SP)$$
$$\text{Materials yield variance} = (SM \times AQ \times SP) - (SM \times SQ \times SP)$$

Multiple labor categories:

$$\text{Labor rate variance} = (AM \times AQ \times AP) - (AM \times AQ \times SP)$$
$$\text{Labor mix variance} = (AM \times AQ \times SP) - (SM \times AQ \times SP)$$
$$\text{Labor yield variance} = (SM \times AQ \times SP) - (SM \times SQ \times SP)$$

Variances in Diagram Format

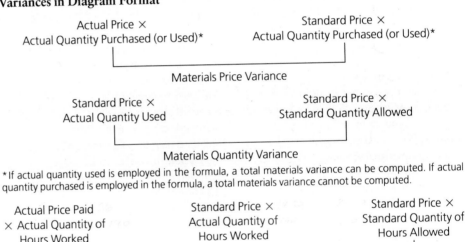

*If actual quantity used is employed in the formula, a total materials variance can be computed. If actual quantity purchased is employed in the formula, a total materials variance cannot be computed.

Multiple Materials

Multiple Labor Categories

Learning Curves

For multiple doublings of production quantities:

1. Determine time to produce first unit.

2. Double production quantity.

3. Multiply previous time by learning curve percentage to estimate average production time per unit produced.

4. Multiply average production time per unit times production quantity to estimate total production hours.

5. Repeat steps 2 through 4.

DEMONSTRATION PROBLEM

Talk About Tasty Confectioners makes special 5-pound chocolate cakes from a chocolate mix prepared for the company by its major chocolate supplier. The standard materials and labor costs are as follows:

Direct materials: 5 pounds @ $.80 $ 4.00
Direct labor: 1.5 hours @ $8.00   12.00

During May 1994, the company produced 200 cakes. Actual data for May 1994:

Direct materials purchased: 1,500 pounds @ $.78
Direct materials used: 1,100 pounds (all used from May's purchases)
Total labor cost: $2,397.60 for 296 hours

Required:

Calculate the following:

a. materials price variance based on purchases

b. materials price variance based on usage

c. materials quantity variance

d. labor rate variance

e. labor efficiency variance

Solution to Demonstration Problem

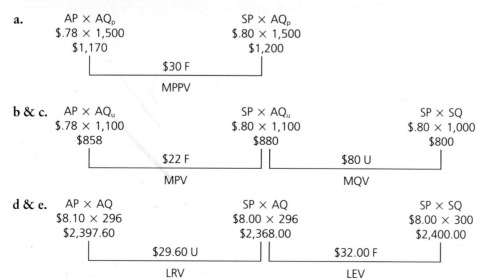

QUESTIONS

1. In a standard cost system, what is a standard? Why are standards used?

2. What is the difference between a standard cost system and an actual cost system?

3. The standards development team should be composed of what experts? Why are these people included?

4. Discuss the development of standards for materials. How is the quality standard established for materials?

5. What is a bill of materials and how is it used in a standard cost system?

6. What is a standard cost card? What information is contained on it?

7. The quantities shown in the bill of materials are not always the same quantities that are shown in the standard cost card. Why not?

8. How can the times shown on the operations flow document be determined?

9. What is a variance and what does it measure?

10. A total variance may be calculated for each cost component of a product. Into what two variances can this total be separated and to what does each relate?

11. Four materials variances may be calculated. What are they and what do they represent?

12. What are the two ways to compute the materials price variance?

13. What is meant by the term *standard hours allowed*? Does the term refer to inputs or outputs?

14. Which costs, actual or standard, are recorded in a standard costing system? Which are charged to the Work in Process Inventory account?

15. "Unfavorable variances will always have debit balances, while favorable variances will always have credit balances." Is this statement true or false? Why?

16. How are immaterial variances closed at the end of an accounting period? How are significant variances closed at the end of an accounting period? Why is there a difference in treatment?

17. In a business that routinely manufactures the same products or performs the same services, why would standards be helpful?

18. What is meant by the process of "management by exception?" How is a standard cost system helpful in such a process?

19. Discuss the three types of standards with regard to the level of rigor of attainment. Why are some companies currently adopting the most rigorous standard?

20. Why may traditional methods of setting standards lead to less than desirable material resource management and employee behavior?

21. *(Appendix 1)* What are the additional types of variances that can be computed for direct labor and direct material when some materials or labor inputs are substitutes for others?

22. *(Appendix 2)* Julia Cox is in the process of developing labor standards for the staff at the Chalmette Diagnostic Clinic. The staff will be performing six tests on each lab specimen received. She has asked you to explain learning curves and how they may assist her in setting her labor standards. How would you respond?

23. *(Direct material variances)* Leisure Furniture makes wrought iron table and chair sets. During April 1994, the purchasing agent bought 8,800 pounds of scrap iron at $.89 per pound. Each set requires a standard quantity of 69 pounds at a standard cost of $.85 per pound. During April, the company used 8,470 pounds and produced 125 sets.
   a. For April, compute the direct material price variance (based on the quantity purchased) and the direct material quantity variance.
   b. Identify the titles of individuals in the firm who would be responsible for each of the variances.

24. *(Direct material variances)* For July 1994, the Paper Planner Company's costs and amounts of paper consumed in the manufacture of its 1995 Executive Planner and Calendar were as follow:

Actual unit purchase price	$.157 per page
Standard quantity allowed for good production	165,000 pages
Actual quantity purchased during July	230,000 pages
Actual quantity used in July	140,000 pages
Standard unit price	$.1475 per page

   Calculate (a) the total cost of purchases for July, (b) the material price variance (based on quantity purchased), and (c) the material usage variance.

25. *(Direct material variances)* Radial Tire Company's direct material cost for January 1994 was as follows:

Actual quantity purchased	85,000 pounds
Actual unit price	$.29
Actual quantity used	70,000 pounds
Standard quantity allowed	80,000 pounds
Standard unit price	$.25

   a. Calculate the material price variance (based on quantity used) and the material quantity variance.
   b. Identify some potential explanations for the variances computed in part a.

26. *(Direct labor variances)* Prefab Construction Inc. builds standard prefabricated wooden frames for apartment walls. The standard quantity of direct labor is 3.5 hours for each frame. The average standard hourly wage of the crew of carpenters who make these frames is $14.50. During May 1994, the company produced 520 frames. Inspection of the payroll records revealed that the crew worked 1,950 hours and earned gross pay of $27,885. Determine the amounts of all direct labor variances.

27. *(Direct labor variances)* An analysis of budgets for Eastlake Awnings for 1994 revealed plans to build 575 awnings during September. Information regarding actual and standard direct labor costs for September 1994 follow:

Efficiency variance (unfavorable)	$2,200
Actual direct labor rate per hour	$10.50
Standard hours allowed for production	3,500
Standard direct labor rate per hour	$11.00

   a. Calculate (1) the actual hours worked during September, (2) the total payroll, and (3) the labor rate variance.
   b. If 7 direct labor hours are required, at standard, to make 1 awning, how many awnings were actually produced? Did the firm meet its budgeted level of production?

28. *(Direct labor variances)* In the audit of the cash account for a client, Mississippi Steel, the accounting firm of Larson and Associates set standards of 200 professional hours and an hourly rate of $24.50. The firm actually worked 190 hours auditing cash. The total professional labor variance for auditing cash was $40 unfavorable.
    a. Compute the professional labor efficiency variance.
    b. Compute the professional labor rate variance.
    c. Compute the total actual payroll.
    d. Offer a brief explanation that is consistent with the two variances.

29. *(Direct labor and direct material variances)* Wayne Glatz is the office manager for an environmental inspection company in Houston. The company handles certain types of investigations on possible environmental violations before the EPA is called. It has been determined that each job should take 20 hours for each of 3 inspectors who are paid $35 per hour. In addition, each job uses 1 gallon of XQ-7 test material, which costs $125 per gallon.

Wayne just received the report from the last job performed by the company and the following actual data were revealed:

5 workers; worked a total of 63 hours; received $33.50 per hour	$2,110.50
1.2 gallons of XQ-7 used; price paid per gallon, $110	132.00
Total cost of materials and labor for job	$2,242.50

    a. Compute the materials variances for the job.
    b. Compute the labor variances for the job.

30. *(Direct labor and direct material variances)* Lisa Scamponi Ltd. produces embroidered handbags. In December 1994, Ms. Scamponi, president of the company, received the following information from Antonio Buffa, the new controller, in regard to November production:

AQ Production during month, 1,200 handbags
AP Actual cost of material purchased and used, total $4,301.18
SQ Standard material allowed, 1/3 sq. yd. per handbag
Material quantity variance, $528 U
AQ Actual hours worked, 2,520
SQ Standard labor time per handbag, 2 hrs.
Labor rate variance, $630 F
SP Standard labor rate per hour, $7
SP Standard price per yard of material, $8

Ms. Scamponi asked Antonio to provide her with more specific information.
    a. Determine the material price variance and the labor efficiency variance.
    b. Determine the standard cost to produce one handbag.
    c. Determine the actual cost to produce one handbag.
    d. Offer an explanation for the difference between standard and actual cost. Make sure your explanation is consistent with the pattern of the variances.

31. *(Missing information)* For each of the independent cases below, fill in the missing figures.

	Case A	Case B	Case C	Case D
Units produced	800	?	240	1,500
Standard hours per unit	3	.8	?	?
Standard hours allowed	?	600	480	?
Standard rate per hour	$7	?	$9.50	$6
Actual hours worked	2,330	675	?	4,875
Actual labor cost	?	?	$4,560	$26,812.50
Labor rate variance	$466 F	$1,080 F	$228 U	?
Labor efficiency variance	?	$780 U	?	$2,250 U

32. *(Journal entries)* Thurston Custom Floors had the following balances in its trial balance at year-end, 1994:

	Debit	Credit
Direct Materials Inventory	$ 29,280	
Work in Process Inventory	43,920	
Finished Goods Inventory	73,200	
Cost of Goods Sold	585,600	
Materials Price Variance	7,250	
Materials Quantity Variance		$8,925
Labor Rate Variance		1,200
Labor Efficiency Variance	4,390	

Assume that the variances, taken together, are believed to be significant. Prepare the journal entries to dispose of the variances.

33. *(Appendix 1)* Hillshire Mixed Nuts produces 12-ounce cans of mixed nuts. The product consists of two materials—pecans and cashews. Standard and actual information is shown below.

Standard quantities and costs (12-oz. can):
Pecans—6 oz. at $3.00 per lb. $1.125
Cashews—6 oz. at $4.00 per lb.   1.50

Actual quantities and costs for February 1994 when production was 18,000, 12-oz. cans:
Pecans—7,425 lbs. at $2.90 per lb.
Cashews—6,638 lbs. at $4.25 per lb.

Determine the materials price, efficiency, mix, and yield variances.

34. *(Appendix 1)* Apex Mechanical Systems is a mechanical engineering firm. The firm employs both engineers and draftspeople. The engineers are paid an average hourly rate of $40 (at standard); the draftspeople are paid $20 per hour (at standard). For one project, the design of a canal lock with all mechanical systems, the standard was set at 750 hours of engineer time and 1,250 hours of draftsperson time. The actual hours worked for this project were

Engineers—1,000 hours at $42.50 per hour
Draftspeople—1,000 hours at $21.00 per hour

Determine the labor rate, mix, and yield variances for this project.

COMMUNICATION ACTIVITIES

35. *(Appendix 2)* Home Medical Services is a firm that has been experiencing financial difficulties. Its founder, Dr. Stephen Ross, has been studying the possibility of instituting a standard cost system. The firm's product is a basic physical examination that is administered in the client's home. Dr. Ross is aware that more experienced examiners (all employees are registered nurses) can conduct the basic exam in significantly less time than the firm's new hires. New hires typically require 60 minutes to complete their first exam. Dr. Ross is also aware of the learning curve concept, but has no idea how it affects his business, or its profitability. Dr. Ross has recently experienced significant employee turnover. Most of the employees who have quit have been with Dr. Ross for more than 2 years. Dr. Ross pays all employees a basic hourly wage of $25 plus fringe benefits.
   a. Assume that the administration of the health care exam is characterized by a 70% learning curve. Determine the average time required per exam to conduct 32 exams.

b. Alternatively, assume that the administration of a health care exam is characterized by a 90% learning curve. Determine the average time required per exam to conduct 32 exams.

c. Is it possible that Dr. Ross's employee turnover is related to the learning curve? Explain. Would the 70% or the 90% learning curve better explain the pattern in employee turnover?

36. *(Developing standard cost card and discussion)* The Frozen Fruitcup Company is a small producer of fruit-flavored frozen desserts. For many years, Frozen Fruitcup products have had strong regional sales on the basis of brand recognition; however, other companies have begun marketing similar products in the area, and price competition has become increasingly important. Tanya Morse, the company's controller, is planning to implement a standard cost system for Frozen Fruitcup and has gathered considerable information from her co-workers on production and material requirements for the company's products. Tanya believes that the use of standard costing will allow the firm to improve cost control and make better pricing decisions.

Frozen Fruitcup's most popular product is raspberry sherbet. The sherbet is produced in 10-gallon batches, and each batch requires six quarts of good raspberries. The fresh raspberries are sorted by hand before they enter the production process. Because of imperfections in the raspberries and normal spoilage, one quart of berries is discarded for every four quarts of acceptable berries. Three minutes is the standard direct labor time for the sorting that is required to obtain one quart of acceptable raspberries. The acceptable raspberries are then blended with the other ingredients; blending requires 12 minutes of direct labor time per batch. During blending, there is some loss of materials. After blending, the sherbet is packaged in quart containers. Morse has gathered the following pricing information.

Frozen Fruitcup purchases raspberries at a cost of $.80 per quart.
All other ingredients cost a total of $.45 per gallon.
Direct labor is paid at the rate of $9.00 per hour.
The total cost of material and labor required to package the sherbet is $.38 per quart.

a. Develop the standard cost for the direct cost components of a 10-gallon batch of raspberry sherbet. The standard cost should identify the
   1. standard quantity
   2. standard rate
   3. standard cost per batch for each direct cost component of a batch of raspberry sherbet
b. As part of the implementation of a standard cost system at the company, Tanya plans to train those responsible for maintaining the standards on how to use variance analysis. She is particularly concerned with the causes of unfavorable variances.
   1. Discuss the possible causes of unfavorable material price variances, and identify the individual(s) who should be held responsible for these variances.
   2. Discuss the possible causes of unfavorable labor efficiency variances, and identify the individual(s) who should be held responsible for these variances.

(CMA)

37. *(Appendix 1)* B&B Law Associates has three labor classes: secretaries, paralegals, and attorneys. The standard wage rates are shown in the standard cost system as follows: secretaries, $11.00 per hour; paralegals, $18.00 per hour; and attorneys, $44.00 per hour. B&B has established a standard of .5 hrs. of secretarial time and 2 hrs. of paralegal time for each hour of attorney time in probate cases. The actual direct labor hours worked on probate cases and the standard hours allowed

for the work accomplished for one month in 1994 were as follows:

	Actual DLHs	Standard Hours for Output Achieved
Secretarial	500	500
Paralegal	1,800	2,000
Attorney	1,100	1,000

a. Calculate the amount of the direct labor efficiency variance for the month and decompose the total into the following components:
   1. direct labor mix variance
   2. direct labor yield variance
b. Based on your answer in part a, did management use an efficient mix of labor? Explain.

(CMA adapted)

38. Some executives believe that it is extremely important to manage "by the numbers." This form of management requires that all employees with departmental or divisional responsibilities spend time understanding the company's operations and how they are reflected by the company's performance reports. Managers are then expected to apprise their employees of the need to be attuned to important signposts that can be detected in performance reports. One of the various numerical measurement systems used by companies is standard costs.

a. Discuss the characteristics that should be present in a standard cost system to encourage positive employee motivation.
b. Discuss how a standard cost system should be implemented to positively motivate employees.
c. The use of variance analysis often results in "management by exception." Discuss the meaning and behavioral implications of "management by exception."
d. Explain how employee behavior could be adversely affected when "actual to standard" comparisons are used as the basis for performance evaluation.

(CMA adapted)

39. *(Basic variances)* Louisiana Coastal Boat Company builds fishing boats and uses a standard cost system for prime costs only. The production of fishing boats requires three materials: fiberglass, paint, and a prepurchased trim package of oar locks, decals, and other ornaments. The standard costs and quantities for material and labor are given below.

PROBLEMS

Standards for 1 fishing boat

1,200 pounds of fiberglass @ $.80 per pound	$ 960
2 quarts gel coat paint @ $60.00 per gallon	30
1 trim package	165
40 hours of labor @ $12.00 per hour	480
Prime standard cost	$1,635

During July 1994, the company had the following actual data related to the production of 100 boats:

Material Purchased:
Fiberglass—130,000 pounds @ $.79 per pound
Paint—60 gallons @ $55.50 per gallon
Trim packages—100 @ $175 per package

Material Used:
Fiberglass—125,000 pounds
Paint—54 gallons
Trim packages—105

Direct Labor Used: 4,250 hours @ $11.50 per hour

Calculate the material and labor variances for Louisiana Coastal Boat Company for July 1994. Base the material price variance on the quantity of material purchased.

40. *(Variance calculation and journal entries)* St. Louis Video makes blank laser discs. Following are standard quantities and standard costs for materials and labor.

	Standard Quantity	Standard Cost
Material	1/4 pound	$2 per pound ($.50 per unit of output)
Labor	12 minutes	$8 per hour ($1.60 per unit of output)

During October 1994, 100,000 discs were produced. The purchasing agent bought 29,000 pounds of material during the month at $1.88 per pound. October payroll for the factory revealed direct labor cost of $165,240 on 20,400 direct labor hours. During the month, 24,800 pounds of raw material were used in production.

a. Compute material and labor variances. The material price variance should be based on the quantity of material purchased.

b. Assuming a perpetual inventory system, prepare general journal entries using standard material and labor costs for tracking inventory flows.

41. *(Incomplete data)* Georgia Surgical Supply manufactures latex surgical gloves. The company has determined that it takes 2.25 square feet of latex to manufacture one pair of gloves. The standard price for material is $.60 per square foot. Most processing is done by machine; the only labor required is for operators, who are paid $15.50 per hour. The machines can produce 400 pairs of gloves per hour.

During one week in May, Georgia Supply produced 20,000 pairs of gloves and experienced a $180 unfavorable material quantity variance. The company had purchased 2,000 more square feet of material than it used in production that week, producing a favorable price variance of $946. Based on 42 total actual labor hours to produce the gloves, an $18.80 favorable total labor variance was generated.

Determine the following amounts.

a. Standard quantity of material used
b. Actual quantity of material used
c. Actual quantity of material purchased
d. Actual price of material purchased
e. Standard hours allowed for production
f. Labor efficiency variance
g. Labor rate variance
h. Actual labor rate paid

42. *(Incomplete data)* Nevada Learning Aids makes wooden lap desks. A small fire on October 1 partially destroyed the books and records relating to September's production. The charred remains of the standard cost card appears below.

	Standard Quantity	Standard Price
Materials	5.0 board feet	
Direct labor		$12.50 per hour

From other fragments of records and several discussions with employees, you learn the following:

(1) The standard quantity of materials used in September was 4,000 board feet.
(2) The September payroll for direct labor was $19,220 based on 1,550 actual hours worked.

(3) The production supervisor distinctly remembered being held accountable for 50 more hours of direct labor than should have been worked. She was upset because top management failed to consider that she saved several hundred board feet of material by creative efforts that required extra time.

(4) The purchasing agent's files showed that 4,300 board feet had been purchased and consumed in September for $2.05 per board foot. She was proud of the fact that this price was $.05 below standard cost per foot.

a. How many units were produced during September?

b. Calculate all variances for direct materials and direct labor for September.

c. What is the standard number of hours allowed for the production of each unit?

d. Prepare general journal entries reflecting direct materials and direct labor activity and variances for September, assuming a standard cost, perpetual inventory system.

43. *(Basic variances)* Kustom Kards Inc. provides a unique service in the greeting card industry. The customer furnishes a description of the recipient of the card and the occasion for the card. The company then creates a greeting card for the customer's specific occasion. The card's message is developed with the specific recipient in mind. The company uses a standard cost system to track costs. Direct materials are so inconsequential that no separate standards exist for them; material costs are included with variable overhead. However, the company has two classes of labor, Verse Design and Art Design. Standards exist for both classes of labor. The following are the standards for one card:

Verse Design labor	4 hours @ $15 per hour	$ 60.00
Art Design labor	2 hours @ $12 per hour	24.00
Variable overhead	$5 per Verse Design labor hour	20.00
	$6 per Art Design labor hour	12.00
Fixed overhead	$3 per total labor hour	18.00
Total cost per unit		$134.00

Each greeting card sells for the exclusive price of $225.00. Standards are based on a normal capacity (per month) of 800 cards or the equivalent of 3,200 Verse Design labor hours and 1,600 Art Design labor hours. The relevant range is between 600 units and 1,000 units. Actual data for July 1994 are:

Verse Design labor: 3,000 hours @ $16.00 per hour
Art Design labor: 1,764 hours @ $13.00 per hour
Production: 840 cards

Calculate the following items.

a. Verse Design rate variance

b. Verse Design efficiency variance

c. Art Design rate variance

d. Art Design efficiency variance

e. Budgeted fixed overhead

44. *(Variance disposition)* Buzz's Glue Factory had the following variances at year-end 1994:

Materials price variance	$ 7,800 U
Materials quantity variance	8,300 F
Labor rate variance	1,750 F
Labor efficiency variance	12,300 U

In addition, the inventory and cost of goods sold account balances were as follows at December 31, 1994:

468

49. *(Appendix 2)* Spacetech Corp. has been a supplier to the Orion project since the program's inception. Two years ago Spacetech received a contract to produce 960 telecommunications devices to be used in space exploration. Funding for the project has been curtailed and Spacetech has received a contract modification decreasing the quantity of devices to be delivered to 240 units.

Direct material for each telecommunications device is $80,000 per unit. The direct labor is subject to a 95% learning curve. The average direct labor cost was estimated to be $50,000 per unit for the first lot of 30 units. This average direct labor cost figure and the 95% learning curve were used to develop the original bid for the contract. Variable manufacturing overhead was estimated to be 70% of direct labor cost. In calculating the original bid price, Spacetech added its regular markup of 35% on all variable manufacturing costs.

The learning curve of 95% has proven to be accurate over the first 60 units. Maximum efficiency is expected to be achieved with the production of 240 units.

a. Describe the theory underlying the use of learning curves.

b. Determine Spacetech's cumulative average cost of labor for producing the 240 units.

c. If Spacetech Corporation should be asked to produce additional telecommunication devices beyond the 240 units covered by the amended contract, calculate the unit price Spacetech should bid, employing the same markup that was used in the original bid. (Hint: Determine the average cost of labor of last 120 units.)

(CMA adapted)

CASES

50. NuLathe Co. produces a turbo engine component for jet aircraft manufacturers. A standard cost system has been used for years with good results. Unfortunately, NuLathe has recently experienced production problems. The source for its direct material went out of business. The new source produces a similar but higher quality material. The price per pound from the original source has averaged $7 while the price from the new source is $7.77. The use of the new material results in a reduction of scrap. This scrap reduction reduces the actual consumption of direct material from 1.25 to 1.00 pounds per unit. In addition, the direct labor is reduced from 24 to 22 minutes per unit because there is less scrap labor and machine setup time.

The direct material problem was occurring at the same time that labor negotiations resulted in an increase of over 14% in hourly direct labor costs. The average rate rose from $12.60 per hour to $14.40 per hour. Production of the main product requires a high level of labor skill. Because of a continuing shortage in that skill area, an interim wage agreement had to be signed.

NuLathe started using the new direct material on April 1, the same date that the new labor agreement went into effect. NuLathe has been using standards that were set at the beginning of the calendar year. The direct material and direct labor standards for the turbo engine component are as follows:

Direct material	1.2 pounds at $6.80 per pound	$ 8.16
Direct labor	20 minutes at $12.30 per DLH	4.10
Standard prime cost per unit		$12.26

Howard Foster, cost accounting supervisor, had been examining the following performance report that he had prepared at the close of business on April 30. Jane Keene, assistant controller, came into Foster's office and Foster said, "Jane, look at this performance report! Direct material price increased 11% and the labor rate increased over 14% during April. I expected greater variances, yet prime costs decreased over 5% from the $13.79 we experienced during the first quarter of this year. The proper message just isn't coming through."

"This has been an unusual period," said Keene. "With all the unforeseen changes, perhaps we should revise our standards based on current conditions and start over."

Foster replied, "I think we can retain the current standards but expand the variance analysis. We could calculate variances for the specific changes that have occurred to direct material and direct labor before we calculate the normal price and quantity variances. What I really think would be useful to management right now is to determine the impact the changes in direct material and direct labor had in reducing our prime costs per unit from $13.79 in the first quarter to $13.05 in April—a reduction of $.74."

Performance Report

Standard Cost Variance Analysis for April 1994

	Standard	Price Variance		Quantity Variance		Actual
DM	$ 8.16	($.97 × 1.0)	$.97 U	($6.80 × .2)	$1.36 F	$ 7.77
DL	4.10	[$2.10 × (22/60)]	.77 U	[$12.30 × (2/60)]	.41 U	5.28
	$12.26					$13.05

Comparison of 1994 Actual Costs

	1st Quarter Costs	April Costs	% Increase (Decrease)
DM	$ 8.75	$ 7.77	(11.2)%
DL	5.04	5.28	4.8 %
	$13.79	$13.05	(5.4)%

a. Discuss the advantages of (1) immediately revising the standards and (2) retaining the current standards and expanding the analysis of variances.

b. Prepare an analysis that reflects the impact of the new direct material and new labor contract on reducing NuLathe's prime costs per unit from $13.79 to $13.05. The analysis should show the changes in prime costs per unit that are due to (1) the use of new direct materials and (2) the new labor contract. This analysis should be in sufficient detail to identify the changes due to direct material price, direct labor rate, the effect of direct material quality on direct material usage, and the effect of direct material quality on direct labor usage.
(CMA adapted)

---

51. *In the mid-1940s, a young man named Donald Roy was working on a Ph.D. at the University of Chicago. As part of his dissertation project, Mr. Roy posed (anonymously) for eleven months as a radial-drill operator at a steel-processing plant. Workers in this plant were paid on a piece-rate basis (with a minimum hourly base pay of 85 cents) for all of the jobs (parts) they worked on. Some of the most interesting behaviors that Mr. Roy observed involved games the employees played based on their perceptions of the fairness of piece rates. If the employees perceived that the piece rates were set too low (required too much output per hour to exceed the base rate) they would engage in work slow-*

ETHICS AND QUALITY DISCUSSION

downs. Thus, they would receive the base rate pay of 85 cents per hour rather than the piece rate pay. The company's cost of components produced when employees engaged in slowdowns was consequently higher than the piece rate cost. The slowdown was essentially a way to express discontentment with the piece rate and implied to management a need to revise the piece rate pay. Communication among employees ensured that, with respect to a certain part, all employees participated in the slowdown. Other jobs were recognized by employees as "gravy jobs." On these jobs, the piece rates were sufficiently high to allow employees to easily exceed the base rate pay without exerting significant effort. On these jobs, employees carefully monitored each other so that no employee generated income substantially above the base rate of 85 cents per hour. The fear was that managers would revise the piece rate if employees generated too much hourly income from the piece rate pay.

[SOURCE: Donald Roy, "Quota Restriction and Goldbricking in a Machine Shop," *American Journal of Sociology*, March 1952, pp. 427–442. Published by the University of Chicago Press.]

a. Why would it be difficult in the environment described by Donald Roy to develop credible standards of performance?
b. Was the behavior of the employees ethical?
c. Is it ethical for managers to revise piece rate pay when it becomes obvious that standards can be easily met or beat?
d. How does honest communication between managers and workers help avoid the problems described by Donald Roy?

52. CoCo Company has just placed a classified ad to hire four people to work in the factory. The company needs individuals who can run specific robotic equipment and route products through processing. All factory space is on a single floor. Labor standards have been set for product manufacturing.

   Ten experienced people applied for the available jobs. One of the applicants for the jobs is Bill Williams. Bill is paralyzed and must use a wheelchair. He does have several years experience using the robotic equipment, but in order for him to use it, the controls must be placed on a special panel and lowered. Sam Snively, the personnel director, has interviewed Bill and has decided against hiring him because Sam does not believe Bill can work "up to the current labor standard."

   a. How, if at all, would hiring the physically disabled affect labor variances (both rate and hours) if the standards had been set based on the nondisabled?
   b. If a supervisor has decided to hire the physically disabled, how (if at all) should the supervisor's performance evaluations be affected?
   c. What are the ethical implications of hiring the physically disabled in preference to the nondisabled? What are the ethical implications of hiring the nondisabled in preference to the disabled?
   d. On what bases should Sam Snively make his decision to hire or not hire Bill Williams? Discuss what you believe to be the appropriate decision process.

53. *The chapter mentions that two trends in American industry are establishing higher standards (perhaps the ideal standard) as a benchmark for evaluating actual results, and adopting of just-in-time (JIT) production systems and total quality management (TQM).*

   There is a growing body of evidence to support the notion that successful adopters of JIT have higher quality production processes than nonadopters. One of the more interesting studies conducted to date examined supplier/consumer relationships among U.S. firms. The study found that the highest quality output was generated by the supplier firm when both the supplier firm and the consumer firm utilized JIT production techniques. The lowest quality output was generated in relationships where neither the supplier, nor the consumer, utilized JIT production techniques.

[SOURCE: M. Frank Barton, Surendra P. Agrawal, and L. Mason Rockwell, Jr., "Meeting the Challenge of Japanese Management Concepts," *Management Accounting*, September 1988, pp. 49–53. Reprinted from *Management Accounting*. Copyright by Institute of Management Accountants, Montvale, N.J.]

a. Why is lack of quality (e.g., substantial number of reworks) in the production process a less tolerable problem in JIT firms than other firms?

b. Based on your understanding of JIT, why is there a need for more communication between supplier and consumer firms when JIT production systems are used by one or both firms?

c. How could the communication mentioned in part b. lead to higher quality production?

d. Which would be of greater concern to a firm practicing JIT, an unfavorable direct material price variance or an unfavorable direct material efficiency variance (assume they are of equal magnitude)? Explain.

STANDARD COSTING FOR OVERHEAD

LEARNING OBJECTIVES

After completing this chapter, you should be able to answer these questions:

1. How are flexible budgets used by managers to plan and control overhead costs?
2. What are the differences between the one-, two-, three-, and four-variance approaches to overhead analysis?
3. How are overhead variances calculated and recorded?
4. How are variable and fixed overhead costs controlled?
5. How will standard costing be affected if companies use a single conversion element rather than the traditional labor and overhead elements?

INTRODUCING

SPRINGFIELD REMANUFACTURING COMPANY

The Springfield ReManufacturing Company (SRC) is an engine remanufacturer headquartered in Springfield, Missouri. Until 1983, SRC was a failing division of International Harvester. That year, Jack Stack and a group of employees initiated a leveraged buyout of the division. Mr. Stack became the chief executive officer of SRC and began a participative approach to management that is based on the concept of getting everyone involved in understanding accounting data or, as they prefer to say, "understanding the numbers."

Operating a profitable business is like winning at a team sport, says Mr. Stack. The employees (players) must work together as a unit (team), must perform [play according to a set of regulations (rules)], and must maintain financial records and statements (keep score).

"Knowing the rules" involves knowing and understanding the data contained in the financial statements. [In discussing the income statement], each line item is carefully explained. Care is taken to point out the relative significance of the various expenses. The primary focus is on cost of goods sold because this item alone usually consumes over 80% of each sales dollar at SRC.

The accounting department uses a standard costing system to assign costs to products. Employees learn SRC's standard cost system and how they can play a key role in developing standard costs. The initial standards are developed by the engineering department, but prior to implementation the employees who must attempt to meet the standards must approve them. Emphasis is placed on demonstrating the effect of variances from standard costs on the "bottom line" profitability. Variances from standard costs are monitored continually and provide frequent feedback to employees. Employees learn that they can produce favorable variances if they:

▌ Complete work faster than the standard labor [time allowed];

▌ Avoid scrapping too much raw material; and

▌ Use overhead items frugally.

SOURCE: Olen L. Greer, Stevan K. Olson, and Marty Callison, "The Key to Real Teamwork: Understanding the Numbers," *Management Accounting* (May 1992), pp. 39–41. Reprinted from *Management Accounting*. Copyright by Institute of Management Accountants, Montvale, N.J.

Like most companies that have a standard cost system, Springfield ReManufacturing Company computes variances for materials, labor, and overhead. The costs of materials and labor are fairly easy to identify because these elements can be acquired in specific, discrete quantities. Materials can be purchased by the pound or foot and employees can work one or more hours.

Most overhead costs, however, cannot be convincingly or reasonably divided into per unit or per hour amounts. For example, assume SRC pays $7,300 per year for insurance on its factory machinery. It is incorrect to state that insurance costs $20 per day because insurance rates differ depending on the policy's time frame. If the company canceled the policy after one day, that day's rate might be $50. Since it is relatively infeasible to know the exact cost per day for insurance, it is even less feasible to know the cost of insurance per unit of production or per hour of operation.

Further, overhead is composed of both variable and fixed costs which react differently to activity level changes. The differences make it difficult to determine overhead cost for one unit of output or other measure of activity. Fixed overhead per unit would be extremely high if only one unit were produced, but cost per unit declines as the quantity of output rises. These basic characteristics of overhead make variance analysis, cost control, and planning for overhead costs more difficult than for materials and labor.

Flexible budgets are helpful to managers when they are analyzing and controlling variations from expectations in a standard cost system. As indicated in the flexible budgets prepared in Chapter 4, each production activity level creates a different amount of total overhead cost. This chapter discusses the computation and analysis of variances from standard cost for overhead.

FLEXIBLE BUDGETS AND STANDARD OVERHEAD RATES

The assignment of actual overhead costs to production is usually untimely for making decisions and does not necessarily provide a stable cost per unit. To overcome these and other problems of using actual overhead for product costing, predetermined overhead application rates may be used. Managers need to estimate total overhead costs at various levels of activity to establish predetermined overhead rates. The estimated overhead costs are presented at different levels of activity in a flexible budget. Such a presentation requires that all costs be classified as either variable or fixed and, thus, mixed costs must be separated into their variable and fixed component.

The monthly flexible overhead budget formula and a partial flexible overhead budget for Hunter Corporation's Machining Department are given in Exhibit 12–1. A monthly presentation is used because Hunter's monthly costs are constant year-round. The department's activity base can be machine hours and its contemplated range of activity is between 10,000 and 15,000 machine hours. The cost accountant could have determined the fixed (a) and variable (b) costs using the high-low method or regression analysis. As discussed in Chapter 4, constructing a flexible budget is a good method of seeing any "steps" or unusual increases that exist for the categories of expected costs. In the case of Hunter Corporation, no fixed or mixed cost steps exist in the relevant range.

Flexible Budgets and Variable Overhead

Presenting variable overhead (VOH) components and costs in a flexible budget allows a predetermined VOH rate to be computed. Analysis of the flexible budget reveals the relevant range of activity as well as the variable rate per measure of activity. The relevant range of activity can be determined because, outside the limits of the relevant range, the variable cost per unit of activity will change. The variable rate can be calculated by dividing budgeted total variable overhead at *any* level of activity within the relevant range by that level of activity, since variable overhead is constant per unit of activity.

Flexible budgets can be prepared on either an input or output basis. An input basis focuses on successive levels of input activity, the standard number of units of output, and costs that should be produced and incurred at each level. Conversely, an output basis flexible budget focuses on the number of units produced, the standard levels of input activity, and costs that are required for such production. The technical relationship between input and output is called a **yield ratio**. To illustrate, assume that it takes 10 minutes of machine time to retool one engine valve. Each hour of machine time should yield six retooled valves, and the yield ratio of time to products can be stated as 1:6.

Yield ratio

(Formula Presentation Based on Machine Hours per Month)

	a = Fixed Cost	b = Variable Cost
Fixed Costs		
Supervision	$10,800	
Depreciation	4,900	
Insurance	500	
Total purely fixed	$16,200	
Variable Costs		
Indirect labor:		
Support workers		$ .50
Fringe benefits		.10
Indirect materials		.30
Machine setup		.04
Total purely variable		$ .94
Mixed Costs		
Power	1,200	.01
Maintenance	1,800	.09
Totals for Flexible Budget Formula	$19,200	$1.04

Flexible budget formula (where y = total manufacturing overhead): y = $19,200 + $1.04 per MH

	MACHINE HOURS					
	10,000	11,000	12,000	13,000	14,000	15,000
Fixed Costs						
Supervision	$10,800	$10,800	$10,800	$10,800	$10,800	$10,800
Depreciation	4,900	4,900	4,900	4,900	4,900	4,900
Insurance	500	500	500	500	500	500
Total	$16,200	$16,200	$16,200	$16,200	$16,200	$16,200
Variable Costs						
Indirect labor:						
Support workers	$ 5,000	$ 5,500	$ 6,000	$ 6,500	$ 7,000	$ 7,500
Fringe benefits	1,000	1,100	1,200	1,300	1,400	1,500
Indirect materials	3,000	3,300	3,600	3,900	4,200	4,500
Machine setup	400	440	480	520	560	600
Total	$ 9,400	$10,340	$11,280	$12,220	$13,160	$14,100
Mixed Costs						
Power ($1,200 + $.01 per MH)	$ 1,300	$ 1,310	$ 1,320	$ 1,330	$ 1,340	$ 1,350
Maintenance ($1,800 + $.09 per MH)	2,700	2,790	2,880	2,970	3,060	3,150
Total	$ 4,000	$ 4,100	$ 4,200	$ 4,300	$ 4,400	$ 4,500
Total Overhead	$29,600	$30,640	$31,680	$32,720	$33,760	$34,800
Total OH Cost per MH	$2.96	$2.79	$2.64	$2.52	$2.41	$2.32

EXHIBIT 12–1

Hunter Corporation's Machining Department Flexible Budget Information

Yield ratios also exist in relationship to variable costs. For example, assume that the indirect material cost to retool one valve is $.05. If $5 of indirect materials are placed into production, there should be an output yield of 100 valves. Thus, if a distinct yield ratio exists, the more materials that are input into the process, the more output should be achieved from the process.

Flexible Budgets and Fixed Overhead

Unless there are fixed cost "steps," fixed overhead (FOH) is constant in total at each successive level of activity on the flexible budget. Dividing a constant amount by each different activity level results in a different rate per unit of activity. For uniformity in product costing, a specific level of activity must be chosen to compute the standard fixed overhead application rate. The level of activity most often used to calculate the fixed overhead application rate is expected annual capacity.[1]

Flexible budgets can be prepared for fixed overhead even though the cost for each component is generally assumed to be constant throughout the relevant range of activity. No defined yield ratio exists between fixed overhead costs and production output as it does between variable overhead costs and output. Since most fixed overhead

---

[1] In Chapter 4, alternative capacity measures are defined and discussed in terms of reasonableness for computing predetermined fixed overhead rates. In most instances, using expected capacity to determine the FOH application rate will approximate actual costing. However, companies having wide fluctuations in capacity utilization may use normal capacity because expected capacity would cause significant variations in annual unit cost data. Any significant variances from actual costs must be prorated to the necessary accounts before external reports are prepared so that the financial statements amounts will approximate actual costs.

costs provide for the capacity to produce rather than for actual production, most fixed costs are incurred with or without production.

As discussed in the "Choosing the Capacity" News Note on page 478, selection of the capacity measure is an important issue. Although the standard application rate for variable overhead can be set using any level of activity within the relevant range, the standard application rate for fixed overhead can only be set after a particular level of capacity is specified. Once the standard overhead rates have been developed, they can be used to apply overhead to work in process. The amount applied reflects the standard measure of activity for the actual quantity of output produced. Comparisons of the standard and actual overhead quantities and costs provide information on the overhead variances.

When variable and fixed overhead are combined in a single account, the following formula is used to compute a combined overhead application rate:

$$\text{Combined OH Rate} = \frac{\text{Total Overhead Cost at Selected Capacity}}{\text{Selected Capacity Measure}}$$

COMBINED OVERHEAD RATE VARIANCES

The total overhead cost is the summation of both variable and fixed overhead and is shown on the flexible budget. A selected level of capacity is chosen because variable overhead changes *in total* with changes in the level of activity and, more importantly, because fixed overhead cost *per unit* changes with changes in the level of activity. Exhibit 12–1 provides calculations of the combined overhead rates at various capacity levels for Hunter Corporation's Machining Department.

Overhead variance computations are illustrated using the June 1994 information provided in Exhibit 12–2 for Hunter Corporation's Machining Department. The department expects to operate 12,000 machine hours each month and has chosen this level to compute the predetermined overhead rate. Thus, using the information given in Exhibit 12–1, the combined rate is $2.64 per machine hour. During June, the department retooled 72,600 valves, each one of which should have taken 10 minutes. Therefore, the standard quantity of time allowed for the actual production was 12,100 standard hours [(72,600 × 10 minutes) ÷ 60 minutes per hour)].

EXHIBIT 12–2
June 1994 Data for Hunter Corporation's Machining Department

STANDARD COST INFORMATION:
Each valve takes 10 machine minutes
Combined overhead rate—$2.64 per machine hour; computed as total budgeted overhead ($31,680) divided by expected monthly capacity of 12,000 machine hours

or

Variable overhead rate—$1.04 per machine hour (given in Exhibit 12–1)
Fixed overhead rate—$1.60 per machine hour; computed as total budgeted fixed overhead ($19,200) divided by expected monthly capacity of 12,000 machine hours

ACTUAL PRODUCTION AND COSTS FOR MONTH:
Production achieved—72,600 valves
Machine hours worked—12,178
Variable overhead costs—$12,800
Fixed overhead costs—$19,600

One-Variance Approach

Total overhead variance

When a combined rate is used, the **total overhead variance** is equal to the difference between total actual overhead and total standard overhead applied to production. The amount of applied overhead is determined by multiplying the combined rate by the standard input activity allowed for the actual production achieved. (If a measure other than direct labor hours or machine hours is used as the capacity measure, the applied overhead would be equal to the combined rate times that measure.) The one-variance model is diagrammed as follows:

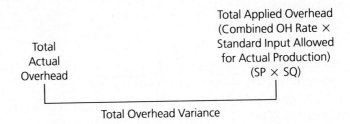

The Machining Department uses machine hours as the input measure for overhead application.[2] Overhead amounts are inserted into the model using the data from Exhibit 12–2:

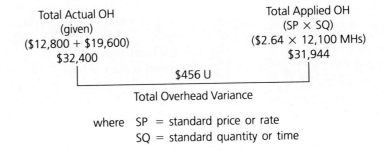

where SP = standard price or rate
SQ = standard quantity or time

Total actual overhead is $32,400 (actual VOH of $12,800 plus actual FOH of $19,600). As indicated previously, the standard quantity of time allowed for actual production is 12,100 machine hours. Thus, total applied overhead is $31,944 ($2.64 × 12,100 MHs). The total combined overhead variance is $456 unfavorable.

Like other total variances, the total overhead variance provides limited information to managers. The model is more appropriate and useful for variance analysis and control purposes if one or more additional measures are inserted.

Two-Variance Approach

Two-variance analysis is performed by inserting a middle column in the one-variance model as follows:

---

[2]Variance discussions in the chapter use machine hours as the measure of inputs. This measure is used and referred to in the models for illustrative purposes. There are alternative cost drivers (such as setup time, material costs, or number of parts) that may be more appropriately related to cost incurrence. If such drivers exist, better information will be achieved from their use.

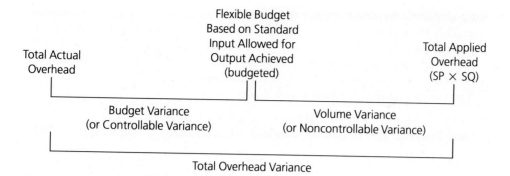

The middle column provides information on the expected total overhead cost based on the standard input allowed for the output produced. This amount represents total budgeted variable overhead at the standard hours allowed plus budgeted fixed overhead, which is constant across all activity levels in the relevant range.

The **budget variance** equals total actual overhead minus budgeted overhead based on the standard input allowed for this period's production. The budget variance of the two-variance approach is also referred to as the **controllable variance** because managers are somewhat able to control and influence this amount during the short run. The difference between total applied overhead and budgeted overhead based on the standard input allowed for the output achieved is the **volume variance**. As will be seen in the following discussion, the volume variance is related only to fixed overhead and is caused solely by producing at a level that differs from that used to compute the predetermined overhead rate.

Budget variance

Controllable variance

Volume variance

The budget amount for the middle column for the Machining Department is determined using the 12,100 standard hours allowed for the output achieved. At that level of hours, budgeted variable overhead is $12,584 ($1.04 × 12,100); budgeted fixed overhead is $19,200, the constant amount at any level of activity within the relevant range. Inserting these amounts into the model allows the budget and volume variances to be computed as follows:

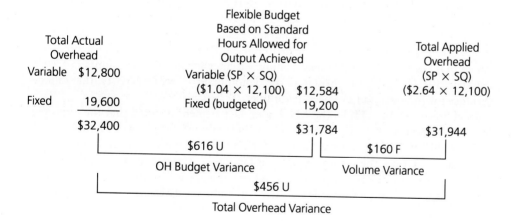

The budget variance can also be computed using the following formula:

Total Actual OH − Total Budgeted OH (based on standard hours allowed)

or

Total Actual OH − [(VOH rate × Standard Hours Allowed) + Budgeted FOH]

Since actual overhead was greater than budgeted overhead, the variance is unfavorable. This $616 U variance is the residual obtained by subtracting the volume variance from the total overhead variance. It results from all causes other than standard input quantity allowed not being equal to the activity level chosen for computing the fixed overhead portion of the combined application rate.

The volume variance formula is as follows:

$$\text{Total Budgeted OH (based on standard hours allowed)} - \text{Total Applied OH}$$

or

$$[(\text{VOH rate} \times \text{Standard Hours Allowed}) + \text{Budgeted FOH}] \\ - (\text{OH rate} \times \text{Standard Hours Allowed for the Production Achieved})$$

The amount of variable overhead is the same in the budgeted and applied columns of the model. In the budgeted column, the VOH amount is computed using the variable overhead rate ($1.04 per machine hour, given in both Exhibits 12–1 and 12–2) times the standard hours allowed for the production achieved. In the applied column, that same $1.04 per machine hour is included as part of the $2.64 per MH amount and, again, multiplied by the standard hours allowed.

The fixed overhead amounts, however, differ between the budgeted and the applied columns. At any level of activity in the relevant range, budgeted FOH for the Machining Department remains constant at $19,200 as shown in Exhibit 12–1. But the amount of FOH applied to production is related to the predetermined rate that was developed and the standard quantity of hours allowed for the actual production level. Exhibit 12–2 indicates that the fixed overhead portion of the total overhead rate is $1.60 ($19,200 ÷ 12,000 MHs) or ($2.64 total OH rate − $1.04 VOH rate). Muliplying $1.60 by 12,100 standard hours allowed gives $19,360 of FOH that was applied to production. Thus, the applied fixed overhead was $160 greater than the budgeted fixed overhead.

The reason the Machining Department's fixed overhead application rate is $1.60 per standard machine hour is that an expected capacity level of 12,000 MHs was chosen. Had any other capacity level been chosen, the rate would have differed, even though the total amount of budgeted fixed overhead ($19,200) would have remained the same. *If any level of capacity is used to apply FOH other than that used in determining the application rate, a volume variance will occur.* For example, if the department had chosen 12,100 MHs as the denominator level of activity to set the predetermined FOH rate, there would be no volume variance for June. If any number of MHs less than 12,100 had been chosen as the denominator level of activity, the volume variance for June would have been favorable.

In choosing 12,000 MHs, the Machining Department decided that the expected June 1994 capacity was 72,000 retooled valves. Actual output was 72,600 valves, which required 12,100 standard hours. Greater than expected capacity utilization took place and, thus, the volume variance is favorable. Management is usually aware, as production occurs, of the physical level of capacity utilization even if a volume variance is not reported. The volume variance, however, translates the physical measurement of under- or overutilization into a dollar amount.

An unfavorable volume variance indicates less than expected utilization of capacity. If available capacity is currently being utilized at a level below (or above) that which was anticipated, managers are expected to recognize that condition, investigate the reasons for it, and (if possible and desirable) initiate appropriate action. Managers can sometimes influence capacity utilization by modifying work schedules, taking measures to relieve any obstructions to or congestion of production activities, and carefully monitoring the movement of resources through the production process. Preferably, such actions should be taken before production rather than after it. Efforts

Many products—such as Pepsi—are currently produced in advance of orders because of the need for prompt and almost continual delivery. However, companies must be careful not to overproduce simply to produce a favorable volume variance.

made after production is completed may improve next period's operations, but will have no impact on past production.

Managers may see a need to adjust capacity utilization to conform to what was expected because of the relationship between production and sales volume. If capacity is underutilized (an unfavorable volume variance) and sales are backordered or going unfilled, managers should try to increase capacity utilization. If capacity is overutilized (a favorable volume variance) and inventory is stockpiling, managers should decrease capacity utilization.

Although utilization is controllable to some degree, the volume variance itself is the variance over which managers have the least influence and control, especially in the short run, which is why this variance is also called the **noncontrollable variance**. This lack of influence or control over the variance usually is not too important. What is important is whether managers exercise their ability to adjust and control capacity utilization properly. The degree of capacity utilization should always be viewed in relationship to inventory and sales. Managers must understand that underutilization of capacity is not always an undesirable condition. It is significantly more appropriate for managers to regulate production than to produce goods that will simply end up in inventory stockpiles. Unneeded inventory production, although it serves to utilize capacity, generates substantially more costs for materials, labor, and overhead (including storage and handling costs). The positive impact that such unneeded production will have on the fixed overhead volume variance is insignificant because, like the predetermined fixed overhead rate, this variance is of little or no value for managerial control purposes.

Noncontrollable variance

Three-Variance Approach

A slight modification of the two-variance analysis provides a three-variance analysis. Inserting an additional column between the left and middle columns of the two-variance model separates the budget variance into spending and efficiency variances. The new column represents the flexible budget based on the actual *input* level of activity.

The new model (and its relationship to the one- and two-variance models) is shown below.

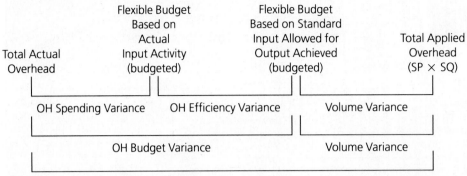

For the Machining Department, the newest column in the model has a value of $31,865 for June 1994. This amount results from computing budgeted variable overhead at 12,178 actual hours at $1.04 per hour or $12,665 (rounded) and adding the $19,200 constant amount of budgeted fixed overhead. The three-way variance computations are as follows:

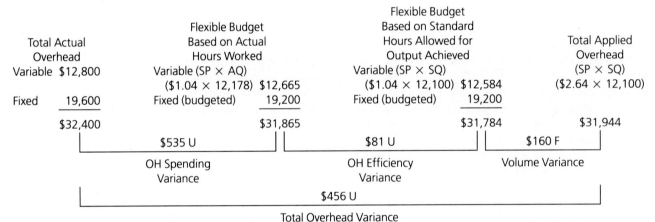

Overhead spending variance

The spending variance shown in the three-variance approach is a total **overhead spending variance**. It is equal to total actual overhead minus total budgeted overhead at the actual hours of activity. The formula for determining the overhead spending variance is:

$$\text{Total Actual OH} - \text{Total Budgeted OH (based on actual hours)}$$

or

$$\text{Total Actual OH} - [(\text{VOH rate} \times \text{Actual Hours}) + \text{Budgeted FOH}]$$

Overhead efficiency variance

The **overhead efficiency variance** is related solely to variable overhead and is the difference between total budgeted overhead at the actual input activity and total budgeted overhead at the standard input allowed (output activity). It measures, at standard cost, the approximate amount of variable overhead caused by using more or fewer inputs than is standard for the actual production. The overhead efficiency variance formula is:

Total Budgeted OH (based on actual hours)
    − Total Budgeted OH (based on standard hours allowed)

or

[(VOH rate × Actual Hours) + Budgeted FOH]
    − [(VOH rate × Standard Hours Allowed) + Budgeted FOH]

Note that the sum of the overhead spending ($535 U) and overhead efficiency ($81 U) variances of the three-variance analysis is equal to the budget ($616 U) variance of the two-variance analysis. The volume variance amount is the same as that calculated using the two-variance approach.

FOUR-VARIANCE APPROACH

The use of separate variable and fixed overhead application rates and accounts allows the computation of separate variances for each type of overhead. These separate computations provide managers with the greatest detail and, thus, the greatest flexibility for control and performance evaluation purposes. Using separate rates permits taking a four-variance approach for analyzing overhead.

As explained in Chapter 11, total variances can be divided into a price subvariance and a usage subvariance. The four-variance approach presents separate analyses for variable and fixed overhead and provides specific price and usage subvariances for both types of overhead. The different overhead subvariances are referred to as follows:

Variable overhead price subvariance   → Variable OH Spending Variance
Variable overhead usage subvariance   → Variable OH Efficiency Variance
Fixed overhead price subvariance   → Fixed OH Spending Variance
Fixed overhead usage subvariance   → Volume Variance

Computations of the variable overhead variances are presented first, followed by the fixed overhead variances.

Variable Overhead

The total variable overhead variance is the difference between the actual variable overhead costs incurred and the standard variable overhead cost applied to the period's production. The diagram below illustrates the computation of the total variable overhead variance.

Actual Variable   Variable Overhead
Overhead Cost   Applied to Production
                                       (SP × SQ)

Total Variable Overhead Variance
(Under- or Overapplied Overhead)

Actual variable overhead cost is the amount debited to the Variable Overhead account; applied variable overhead relates to the standard overhead application rate and the actual output achieved during the period. The applied variable overhead is debited to Work in Process Inventory and credited to Variable Overhead. The balance in the variable overhead account at year-end is the amount of under- or overapplied variable overhead.

The general variance analysis model can be used to subdivide the total variable overhead variance into its price and usage subvariances as shown below:

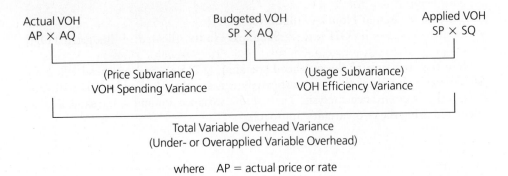

where   AP = actual price or rate

Variable overhead spending variance

The difference between actual variable overhead (AP × AQ) and budgeted variable overhead based on actual input (SP × AQ) is the **variable overhead spending variance**. This amount relates to the various components that comprise variable overhead. Variable overhead spending variances are often caused by price differences—paying higher or lower average actual variable overhead prices than the standard prices allow. Such fluctuations may occur because, over time, changes in variable overhead prices have not been reflected in the standard rate. As examples, average indirect labor wage rates, utility rates, or other variable prices may have changed since the predetermined variable overhead rate was computed. Managers usually have little control over prices charged by external parties and therefore should not be held accountable for variances arising because of such price changes. In such instances, the standard rates should be adjusted. However, if managers can influence prices through, for example, long-term purchase arrangements, such options should be investigated as to their long-term costs and benefits before a decision is made to change the standard.

Another possible cause of the VOH spending variance is unrelated to price. Waste and shrinkage associated with production resources (such as indirect materials) may have affected the variable overhead spending variance. For example, the fact that materials have deteriorated during storage or from lack of proper handling may only be recognized after the materials are placed into the production process. Such occurrences usually have little relationship to the input activity basis used, but they do affect the variable overhead spending variance. If waste or spoilage is the cause of the VOH spending variance, managers should be held accountable and be encouraged to implement more effective controls over the problems.

Variable overhead efficiency variance

The difference between budgeted VOH at actual input activity (SP × AQ) and budgeted VOH at standard input allowed (SP × SQ) is the **variable overhead efficiency variance**. The name of this variance is really a misnomer because it is unrelated to how efficiently variable overhead was used. The variance actually quantifies the effect of using more or less actual input than the standard allowed for the production achieved and reflects the degree of managerial control implemented (or needed) relative to the output obtained from the actual input. When actual input exceeds standard input allowed, production operations are considered to be inefficient. Excess input also indicates that a larger VOH budget is needed to support the additional input. If overhead is applied on the basis of direct labor (DL) hours, the signs (favorable or unfavorable) of the VOH and DL efficiency variances will be the same since the actual and standard hours compared in the two calculations are equal.

The VOH variance computations are made using the June 1994 data for Hunter Corporation's Machining Department. Using the information in Exhibits 12–1 and

12–2, the predetermined variable overhead rate is $1.04 per machine hour. Production and variable costs are interrelated; each hour of machine time allowed for production was expected to cost the Machining Department $1.04 in variable overhead. Thus, the VOH costs for the actual production should have been $12,584 ($1.04 × 12,100 standard hours). The total variable overhead variance is ($12,800 − $12,584) or $216; this amount is unfavorable or underapplied. A flexible budget prepared using actual hours worked (input) would show budgeted variable overhead of $12,665 ($1.04 per MH × 12,178 actual MHs, rounded). The variable overhead variances for the Machining Department are computed below using the input and output measures:

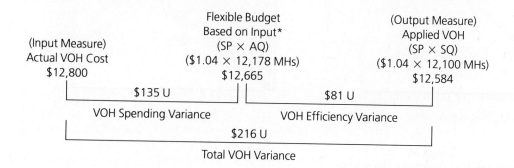

Actual variable overhead cost can have one of three relationships to the flexible budget amounts: (1) if actual is the same as the budget, there is no variance; (2) if actual is less than the budget there is a favorable variance; or (3) if actual is greater than the budget, there is an unfavorable variance. Exhibit 12–3 on page 488 graphically illustrates Hunter's Machining Department variable overhead variances and the input/output nature of the flexible budget. The y-axis in the graph represents dollars; the x-axis represents machine hours. Since variances are in dollars, they are read from the y-axis. The flexible budget lines in the exhibit represent the $1.04 variable overhead application rate multiplied by machine hours.

Graph I in Exhibit 12–3 shows the variable overhead spending variance. Actual cost of $12,800 (point a) exceeds budgeted cost of $12,665 (point b) at the actual level of input (12,178 MHs). Budgeted cost is computed as actual input hours multiplied by the VOH application rate. The difference between points a and b is $135 (range c), which represents the unfavorable variable overhead spending variance. Graph II in the exhibit presents the variable overhead efficiency variance that results from comparing actual input hours (point b) to standard hours allowed for actual production (point d) at the standard variable overhead application rate. The difference in the two points on the x-axis (hours) multiplied by the VOH application rate equals the difference in the two points on the y-axis (dollars). This difference (range e) represents the VOH efficiency variance.

Graph III is a combination of graphs I and II. In this situation, both variances are unfavorable and can be seen distinctly on Graph III. In other situations, one variance may be favorable and the other unfavorable, which would mean that one variance would partially or completely offset the other. Graphs under such conditions are less clear.

Fixed Overhead

The total fixed overhead (FOH) variance is the difference between actual fixed overhead costs incurred and standard fixed overhead cost applied to the period's pro-

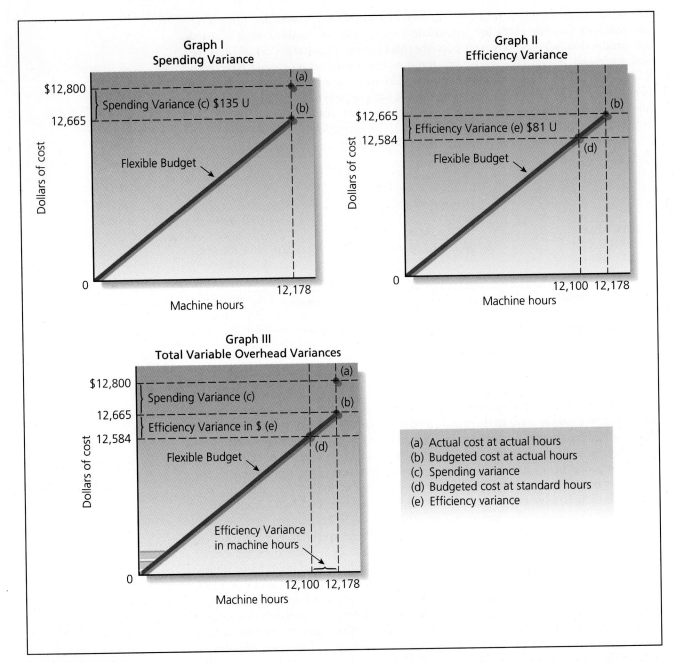

EXHIBIT 12–3

Hunter Corporation's Machining Department— Graphical Presentation of Variable Overhead Variances

duction. The following model shows the computation of the total fixed overhead variance.

Actual fixed overhead cost is the amount debited to Fixed Overhead. As with variable overhead, applied fixed overhead is related to the standard predetermined application rate and the standard hours allowed for the actual output of the period. Applied fixed overhead is debited to Work in Process Inventory and credited to Fixed Overhead. The difference between actual FOH and applied FOH is the total fixed overhead variance or the amount of under- or overapplied fixed overhead.

The total fixed overhead variance is divided into its price and usage subvariances by inserting *budgeted* fixed overhead as a middle column into the model.

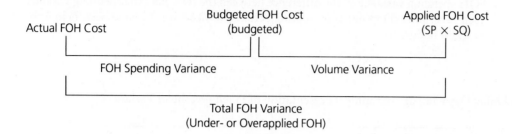

In the model, the left column is simply labeled "actual cost" and is not computed as a price times quantity measure because fixed overhead is generally acquired in lump sum amounts rather than on a per-unit input basis. The difference between actual and budgeted fixed overhead is the **fixed overhead spending variance**. This amount normally represents a weighted average price variance of the multiple components of FOH, although it can also reflect mismanagement of resources. The individual FOH components are detailed in the flexible budget and individual spending variances can be calculated for each component.

Fixed overhead spending variance

The fixed overhead volume variance is the difference between budgeted and applied fixed overhead. Budgeted fixed overhead is a constant amount throughout the relevant range; thus, *the middle column is a constant figure regardless of the actual quantity of input or the standard quantity of input allowed.* This concept is a key element in computing FOH variances. The budgeted amount of fixed overhead can also be presented analytically as the result of multiplying the standard FOH application rate by the expected capacity measure used to compute that standard rate.

Applied fixed overhead is equal to the FOH application rate multiplied by the standard input allowed for the production achieved. In regard to fixed overhead, the standard input allowed for the achieved production level measures capacity utilization for the period.

Inserting the data from Exhibit 12–2 for the Machining Department of Hunter Corporation into the model gives the following:

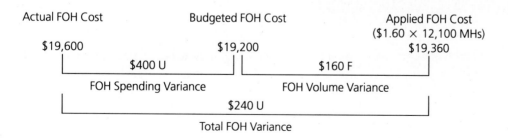

Since the actual fixed overhead for June 1994 was $19,600 and budgeted FOH was $19,200, the fixed overhead spending variance reflects this $400 unfavorable difference. Note that the $160 F volume variance is the same amount that was computed in both the two- and three-variance analysis approaches. The total fixed overhead variance of $240 is the unfavorable, underapplied balance in the fixed overhead account at year-end.

Exhibit 12–4 presents graphic illustrations of the fixed overhead variances. Graph I shows two lines: one represents budgeted FOH; the other represents possible amounts of applied fixed overhead. The budget line is constant ($19,200) at all levels of activity within the relevant range. The applied FOH cost line results from multiplying the FOH application rate times the standard hours allowed for each possible level of production. Graph II shows the June 1994 Machining Department actual (point a, $19,600) and budgeted (point b, $19,200) fixed overhead amounts and presents the FOH spending variance as the difference between the two. Had the spending variance been favorable, the point representing actual overhead would have been below the $19,200 budget line.

▌ EXHIBIT 12–4
Hunter Corporation's Machining Department—Graphical Presentation of Fixed Overhead Variances

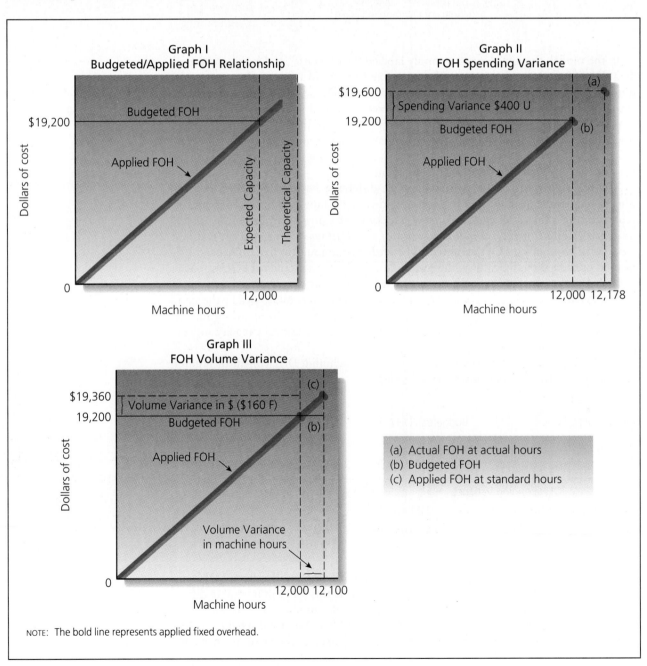

NOTE: The bold line represents applied fixed overhead.

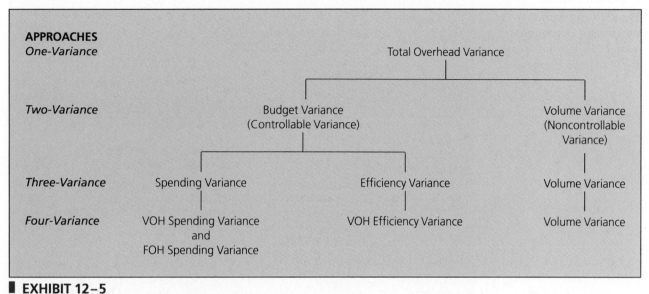

APPROACHES

One-Variance   Total Overhead Variance

Two-Variance   Budget Variance   Volume Variance
                                 (Controllable Variance)   (Noncontrollable
                                                                              Variance)

Three-Variance   Spending Variance   Efficiency Variance   Volume Variance

Four-Variance   VOH Spending Variance   VOH Efficiency Variance   Volume Variance
                              and
                       FOH Spending Variance

▌ **EXHIBIT 12–5**

Interrelationships of Overhead Variances

Graph III in Exhibit 12–4 shows the fixed overhead volume variance. This variance equals the difference between the number of hours used to determine the FOH application rate (12,000 MHs) and the number of standard hours allowed (12,100 MHs) for the production achieved multiplied by the $1.60 per hour FOH application rate. The volume variance occurs because, by using a machine hour application rate, the fixed overhead cost is treated as if it were variable even though it is not.

No combined graph is shown for Hunter's fixed overhead variances because the favorable volume variance would partially offset the unfavorable spending variance if the two were combined. This situation would be difficult to visualize on a two-dimensional graph.

Exhibit 12–5 summarizes the interrelationships of all of the overhead variances. Managers should select the variance approach that provides the most useful information and that conforms to the company's accounting system. If the accounting system does not distinguish between variable and fixed costs, a four-variance approach will be unworkable.

JOURNAL ENTRIES FOR OVERHEAD VARIANCES

During the period, overhead variances are shown as part of the individual Variable and Fixed Manufacturing Overhead accounts if separate rates are used or in a single Manufacturing Overhead account if a combined rate is used to apply overhead. For the remainder of this discussion, it is assumed that separate overhead accounts and rates are used. Actual costs incurred for the various overhead components are debited to the two manufacturing overhead accounts during the period. Overhead is applied to production based on the predetermined rates multiplied by the standard input allowed. Overhead application is recorded as a debit to Work in Process Inventory and as a credit to each of the manufacturing overhead accounts at completion of production or at the end of the period, whichever is earlier. The difference between actual debits and applied credits in each overhead account represents the total variable and fixed overhead variances and is also the under- or overapplied overhead of the period.

EXHIBIT 12-6

Hunter Corporation's
Machining Department
June 1994 Journal Entries
for Overhead Variances

During period:	Variable Manufacturing Overhead	12,800	
	Various accounts		12,800
	To record actual variable overhead costs incurred.		
During period:	Fixed Manufacturing Overhead	19,600	
	Various accounts		19,600
	To record actual fixed overhead costs incurred.		
Upon completion of production and/or at end of period:	Work in Process Inventory	31,944	
	Variable Manufacturing Overhead		12,584
	Fixed Manufacturing Overhead		19,360
	To apply overhead to production at $1.04 (variable) and $1.60 (fixed) per standard machine hour allowed (12,100) for retooling of 72,600 valves.		
Year-end:	VOH Spending Variance	135	
	VOH Efficiency Variance	81	
	Variable Manufacturing Overhead		216
	To close the variable overhead account.		
	FOH Spending Variance	400	
	FOH Volume Variance		160
	Fixed Manufacturing Overhead		240
	To close the fixed overhead account.		

The Variable Manufacturing and Fixed Manufacturing Overhead accounts are closed at year-end and the balances (under- or overapplied) are reclassified to the appropriate variance accounts. Using the four-variance approach, the journal entries for the Machining Department of Hunter Corporation are shown in Exhibit 12-6.

All manufacturing variances (materials, labor, and overhead) are considered together to determine the appropriate year-end disposition. If the combined impact of these variances is considered to be immaterial, the variances are closed to Cost of Goods Sold. If the total variance amount is significant, the overhead variances are prorated to Work in Process Inventory, Finished Goods Inventory, and Cost of Goods Sold in proportion to the relative size of those account balances. The proration process for overhead variances is the same as that presented in Chapter 11 for direct labor variances that were deemed to be significant.

COST CONTROL FOR OVERHEAD

Cost control focuses on the variances between actual overhead incurred for a period and the standard amount of overhead that should have been incurred based on actual output. The latter amount is the standard cost of overhead that is applied to Work in Process Inventory. The difference between actual and standard overhead cost is the amount of under- or overapplied overhead or the total overhead variance that must be explained. Analyzing overhead variances should help to indicate ways in which costs could be controlled. All significant variances (both favorable and unfavorable) need to be examined and communicated to the managers responsible for those costs so that discovery of causes can be made and appropriate action can be taken. Control purposes for variable and fixed overhead differ because of the types of costs that make up the two categories as well as the ability of managers to influence those costs.

Variable costs are incurred on an ongoing basis as production is in process and are directly related to that production. Because of this direct yield relationship to production activity, control of variable overhead is similar to control of materials and labor costs. Variable overhead is controlled in two ways: (1) keeping actual costs incurred in line with planned costs for the actual level of activity and (2) getting the planned output yield from the overhead resources placed into production.

Control of fixed overhead is distinctly different from that of variable overhead because fixed overhead may not necessarily be directly related to current production. Managers commit to many types of fixed costs in lump-sum amounts before production takes place to provide the capacity to produce. Once managers commit to a fixed cost, it becomes sunk regardless of whether actual production takes place. Thus, control of many fixed overhead costs must occur at the time of commitment on a transaction-by-transaction basis rather than at the time of production. Exceptions to this rule include costs of quality control, engineering, and supervisors' salaries, since these costs can often be decreased quickly if production is reduced.

To illustrate the concept of cost control for overhead costs, the variance computations shown for Hunter Corporation's Machining Department can be used. Regardless of the number of variances computed earlier in the chapter, the variances do not reflect the same individual cost components that were shown in Exhibit 12–1. These "summary" variance amounts would not provide management of the Machining Department with enough specific information to decide whether corrective action would be possible or desirable. Individual cost variances would need to be reviewed to determine the actual cause(s) of and responsibility for the several components of the total spending variance. To exercise any significant degree of control, managers must be provided more detailed information and, even then, they may have limited ability to control actual fixed overhead costs in the short run.

The best time to control fixed overhead is beforehand. Signing long-term lease agreements for facilities means that variances from budgeted costs shouldn't occur.

[Formula Presentation Based on
(1) Machine Hours and (2) Units of Production]

	FLEXIBLE BUDGET BASED ON MHs (INPUT)		FLEXIBLE BUDGET BASED ON UNITS PRODUCED (OUTPUT)	
	a = FC	b = VC	a = FC	b = VC
Variable Costs				
Indirect labor:				
Support workers		$ .50		$.083
Fringe benefits		.10		.017
Indirect materials		.30		.050
Machine setup		.04		.007
Power		.01		.002
Maintenance		.09		.015
Fixed Costs				
Supervision	$10,800		$10,800	
Depreciation	4,900		4,900	
Insurance	500		500	
Power	1,200		1,200	
Maintenance	1,800		1,800	
Totals	$19,200	$1.04	$19,200	$.174

During June 1994, actual production was 72,600 valves and actual machine hours were
12,178. Expected capacity for June is 12,000 machine hours. One valve requires 10
minutes of machine time.

Actual costs by cost component for June 1994 are:

Variable Costs		Fixed Costs	
Indirect labor:		Supervision	$10,800
Support workers	$ 6,100	Depreciation	4,900
Fringe benefits	1,280	Insurance	500
Indirect materials	3,700	Power	1,400
Machine setup	500	Maintenance	2,000
Power	110		
Maintenance	1,110	Total	$19,600
Total	$12,800		

Exhibit 12–7 presents two factory overhead flexible budgets; one is based on the
input measure (machine hours) and the other is based on the output measure (valves
retooled). Since it takes ten minutes to retool one unit of product, the variable cost
(b) values for output units are one-sixth of the variable cost values of input MHs.
These two flexible budgets provide the detail for useful cost analysis for each cost
component.

Using the Machining Department's bugeted and actual overhead cost information
(from Exhibits 12–1 and 12–7, respectively), a cost report (Exhibit 12–8) can be
produced that compares actual cost, estimated input cost, and estimated cost for actual output. First, the actual cost of each cost component is compared with its related
flexible budget amount based on the actual input that occurred. Next, the flexible
budget amounts based on input are compared to the costs allowed based on the actual
output.

The Machining Department cost report shown in Exhibit 12–8 is for a one-month period. Cost reports can be prepared just as easily for any other period of time for departments within a company. Each production department in multidepartment companies can be viewed as a center of responsibility for a specific manager. Weekly departmental cost reports (particularly for VOH costs) are more timely and useful for control purposes than are annual reports prepared for the entire company. Input and output flexible budgets prepared each week or month by each department provide useful bases against which to compare actual costs at each cost component level.

The Machining Department's fixed overhead costs are used to illustrate control over a spending variance. Of the individual fixed overhead costs, managers could, in the short run, probably influence the insurance charges by "shopping" for prices at the time the company negotiated insurance coverage. The remaining costs are less controllable in the short run. Supervisors' salaries are contractual obligations that were set at time of employment or salary review. Depreciation expense is based on the

▌EXHIBIT 12–8

Hunter Corporation's Machining Department Cost Reports on Variable and Fixed Overhead for the Month Ended June 30, 1994

	(1) Actual Cost	(2) Input Flexible Budget*	(3) Standard Cost Allowed Based on Production*	(4) Spending Variance Column (2) − (1)	(5) Efficiency Variance Column (3) − (2)	(6) Total Variance Column (3) − (1)
Variable Costs**						
Indirect labor:						
Support workers	$ 6,100	$ 6,089	$ 6,050	$ 11 U	$39 U	$ 50 U
Fringe benefits	1,280	1,218	1,210	62 U	8 U	70 U
Indirect materials	3,700	3,653	3,630	47 U	23 U	70 U
Machine setup	500	487	484	13 U	3 U	16 U
Power	110	122	121	12 F	1 U	11 F
Maintenance	1,110	1,096	1,089	14 U	7 U	21 U
Totals	$12,800	$12,665	$12,584	$135 U	$81 U	216 U

	(1) Actual Cost	(2) Fixed Cost Budget	(3) Standard Cost Allowed Based on Production	(4) Spending Variance Column (2) − (1)	(5) Volume Variance Column (3) − (2)	(6) Total Variance Column (3) − (1)
Fixed Costs						
Supervision	$10,800	$10,800	$10,890	$ 0	$ 90 F	$ 90 F
Depreciation	4,900	4,900	4,941	0	41 F	41 F
Insurance	500	500	504	0	4 F	4 F
Power	1,400	1,200	1,210	200 U	10 F	190 U
Maintenance	2,000	1,800	1,815	200 U	15 F	185 U
Totals	$19,600	$19,200	$19,360	$400 U	$160 F	$240 U

*Rounded to the nearest whole dollar. Some of these numbers were derived using a greater degree of precision than is indicated on Exhibit 12–7 so that the sum of the amounts will properly agree with the total of the budget category.
For variable costs, amounts in Column 3 are calculated by multiplying the number of units produced times the rate per unit (the **b value from the flexible budget based on output). For fixed costs, the amounts in Column 3 are calculated as follows: (1) divide each budgeted amount in Column 2 by the expected monthly capacity (12,000 MHs); (2) divide the result by six (because it takes one-sixth of a MH to produce 1 unit) to get a rate per unit of activity; and (3) multiply that rate by the number of units produced (72,600).

factory's historical cost, salvage, and expected life. The fixed portion of the power cost is related to a variety of factors including the firm's minimum power demand requirements. The fixed portion of the maintenance cost is related to the maintenance supervisor's salary and, like the other supervisory salary, can only be controlled at time of employment or salary review.

Because some overhead costs are not as susceptible as others to control and because there are a variety of recordkeeping techniques available to account for overhead, several methods have been presented to compute overhead variances. In addition, some companies may combine overhead with direct labor in setting standards and computing variances.

CONVERSION COST AS AN ELEMENT IN STANDARD COSTING

Conversion cost consists of both direct labor and manufacturing overhead. The traditional view of separating the elements of product cost into three categories (direct material, direct labor, and overhead) is appropriate in a labor-intensive production setting. However, in more highly automated factories, direct labor cost generally represents an extremely small part of total product cost. In such circumstances (and as discussed in Chapter 11), it is possible that one worker oversees a large number of machines and often deals with trouble-shooting machine malfunctions more than with converting raw materials into finished products. These new conditions mean that workers' wages are more closely associated with indirect, than direct, labor.

Many companies have responded to the condition of large overhead costs and small direct labor costs by adapting their standard cost systems to provide for only two elements of product cost: direct materials and conversion. In these situations, conversion costs are likely to be separated into their variable and fixed components. Conversion costs may also be separated into direct and indirect categories based on the ability to trace such costs to a machine rather than to a product. Overhead may be applied using a variety of cost drivers including machine hours, cost of materials, number of production runs, number of machine setups, or throughput time.

Variance analysis for conversion cost in automated plants normally focuses on the following: (1) spending variances for overhead costs; (2) efficiency variances for machinery and production costs rather than labor costs; and (3) volume variance for production. These types of analysis are similar to the traditional three-variance overhead approach. In an automated system, managers are likely to be able to better control not only the spending and efficiency variances, but also the volume variance. The idea of planned output is essential in a just-in-time system. Variance analysis under a conversion cost approach is illustrated in Exhibit 12–9. Regardless of the method by which variances are computed, it is essential that managers analyze those variances and use them for cost control purposes to the extent that such control can be exercised.

To illustrate, assume that Hunter Corporation's Machining Department is fully automated and direct labor is not needed. However, in this illustration, two highly trained employees monitor all processes by physical and computer observation. The $9,000 monthly salaries of these employees are considered indirect labor costs. Total monthly fixed overhead from Exhibit 12–1 was $19,200; with the new assumed salaries, this amount becomes $28,200. Variable factory overhead statistics remain unchanged from Exhibit 12–2.

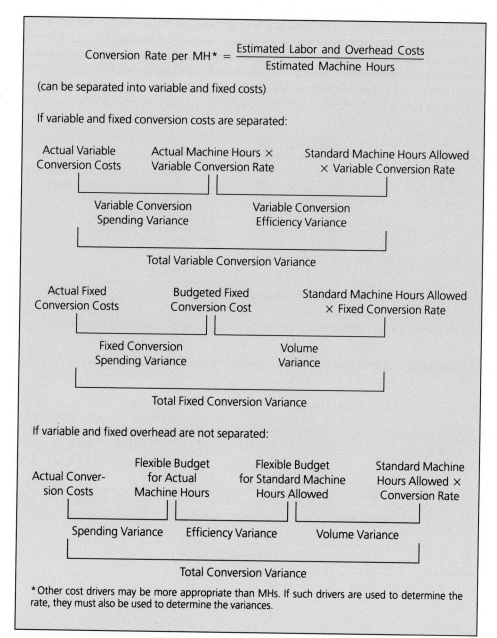

■ EXHIBIT 12–9
**Variances Under
Conversion Approach**

Using the variance model in Exhibit 12–9, the following analyses can be prepared for the conversion cost category:

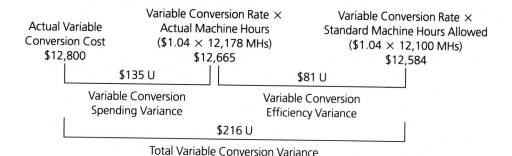

Because all direct labor is eliminated and no additional variable overhead is involved, the analysis of variable conversion costs shows the same computations as those to analyze variable overhead. On the other hand, the following analysis of fixed conversion costs reflects the newly assumed addition of $9,000 indirect labor salaries. The actual amount of indirect labor cost was $9,150; thus, the new actual amount of fixed conversion cost is the $19,600 (from Exhibit 12–2) plus the new $9,150.

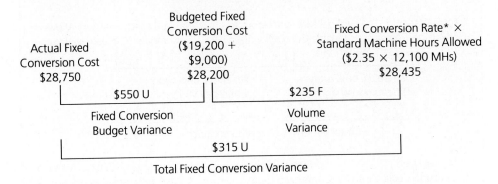

* Fixed Conversion Rate = ($28,200 budgeted fixed conversion cost ÷ 12,000 MHs) = $2.35

Combining variable and fixed conversion costs yields the following analysis:

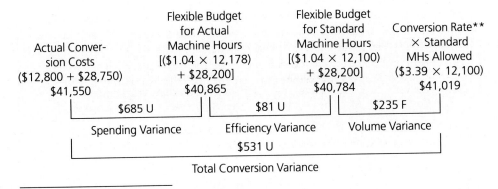

** Conversion Rate = ($1.04 + $2.35) = $3.39

R E V I S I T I N G

SPRINGFIELD REMANUFACTURING COMPANY

Once they learn the rules of the game and how to read the "scorecards," the employees become totally involved in SRC's "Great Game of Business." Employees must not only perform their assigned tasks in the factory, but they must continually monitor the variances over which they have control. In short, every employee is expected to follow the action and keep score. [In weekly meetings (huddles), information is shared among managers and employees on the week's activities and the income statement impacts of those activities.] By focusing on the accounting numbers in the huddles, management is able to identify problem areas, such as unfavorable cost variances. The team members discuss and plan adjustments (call new plays) to solve these problems. This is the heart of the great game of business as knowledge and creativity come together.

[Regardless of the number of variances reported, it is important that the information contained in those variances be analyzed and utilized as has been done at SRC.] The results [of the employees' accounting education program] have been nothing short of phenomenal. The company has grown from 199 employees to over 600 employees. Sales increased from $16 million in 1983 to over $70 million in 1991. SRC has never had a major layoff and now boasts the following customers: Sears; Chrysler; Deutz Allis Corporation; Dresser Construction and Mining Equipment; General Motors Corporation; and Mercedes Benz.

At SRC, the unique management accounting information system facilitates the collection, summarization, and distribution of timely, relevant accounting information to every employee for evaluation and decision making. [And much of that information focuses on standard cost variances.]

SOURCE: Olen L. Greer, Stevan K. Olson, and Marty Callison, "The Key to Real Teamwork: Understanding the Numbers," *Management Accounting* (May 1992), pp. 43–44. Reprinted from *Management Accounting.* Copyright by Institute of Management Accountants, Montvale, N.J.

CHAPTER SUMMARY

This chapter explains and illustrates the three primary uses of standard overhead costs: (1) to assign per unit costs to production for inventory valuation purposes, (2) to control the amount of overhead, and (3) to measure and evaluate the use of production capacity provided by fixed factory overhead costs.

Depending on the detail available in the accounting records, a variety of overhead variances may be computed. If a combined variable and fixed overhead rate is used, companies may use a one-, two-, or three-variance approach. The one-variance approach provides only a total overhead variance as the difference between actual and applied overhead. The two-variance approach provides information on a budget and a volume variance. The budget variance is calculated as total actual overhead minus total budgeted overhead at the standard input quantity allowed for the production achieved. The volume variance compares budgeted fixed overhead to applied fixed overhead. Fixed overhead is applied based on a predetermined rate using a selected measure of capacity. Any output capacity utilization actually achieved (measured in standard input quantity allowed), other than the level selected to determine the standard rate, will cause a fixed overhead volume variance to occur. The three-variance approach calculates an overhead spending variance, overhead efficiency variance, and a volume variance. The spending variance is the difference between total actual overhead and total budgeted overhead at the actual level of activity worked. The efficiency variance is the difference between total budgeted overhead at the actual activity level and total budgeted overhead at the standard input quantity allowed for the production achieved. The volume variance is computed in the same manner as it was using the two-variance approach.

If separate variable and fixed overhead accounts are kept (or if this information can be generated from the records available), two subvariances can be computed for each of the variable and fixed overhead cost categories. The subvariances for variable overhead are the VOH spending and VOH efficiency variances. The VOH spending variance is the difference between actual variable overhead cost and budgeted variable overhead based on the actual level of input. The VOH efficiency variance is the difference between budgeted variable overhead at actual activity level and variable overhead applied on the basis of standard input quantity allowed for the production achieved.

The fixed overhead subvariances are the FOH spending and volume variances. The fixed overhead spending variance is equal to actual fixed overhead minus budgeted fixed overhead. The volume variance is computed as it was using the two-variance approach.

Automated manufacturing systems will have an impact on variance computations. One definite impact is the reduction in or elimination of direct labor hours and costs for overhead application. Machine hours, production runs, and number of machine setups are examples of more appropriate activity measures than direct labor hours in an automated factory. Companies may also design their standard cost systems to use only two elements of production cost: direct materials and conversion. Variances for conversion under such a system focus on machine or production efficiency rather than on labor efficiency.

KEY TERMS

Budget variance (p. 481)
Controllable variance (p. 481)
Fixed overhead spending variance (p. 489)
Noncontrollable variance (p. 483)
Overhead efficiency variance (p. 484)
Overhead spending variance (p. 484)

Total overhead variance (p. 480)
Variable overhead efficiency variance (p. 486)
Variable overhead spending variance (p. 486)
Volume variance (p. 481)
Yield ratio (p. 476)

SOLUTION STRATEGIES

Variances in formula format
The following abbreviations are used below in addition to those from Chapter 11:

AQ = actual quantity of input measure
SQ = standard quantity of input measure
AVOH = actual variable overhead
AFOH = actual fixed overhead
BFOH = budgeted fixed overhead (remains at constant amount no matter what the level of activity as long as within the relevant range)
TAOH = total actual overhead

1-variance approach:
Total OH variance = TAOH − (Combined OH rate × SQ)

2-variance approach:
Budget variance = TAOH − [(VOH rate × SQ) + BFOH]
Volume variance = [(VOH rate × SQ) + BFOH] − [(VOH rate × SQ) + (FOH rate × SQ)] (This is equal to the fixed OH volume variance of the 4-variance approach)

3-variance approach:
Spending variance = TAOH − [(VOH rate × AQ) + BFOH]
Efficiency variance = [(VOH rate × AQ) + BFOH)] − [(VOH rate × SQ) + BFOH]
Volume variance = [(VOH rate × SQ) + BFOH] − [(VOH rate × SQ) + (FOH rate × SQ)] (This is equal to the fixed OH volume variance of the 4-variance approach.)

4-variance approach:
Variable OH spending variance = AVOH − (VOH rate × AQ)
Variable OH efficiency variance = (VOH rate × AQ) − (VOH rate × SQ)
Fixed OH spending variance = AFOH − BFOH
Fixed OH volume variance = BFOH − (FOH rate × SQ)

Variances in diagram format
Overhead 4-variance approach:

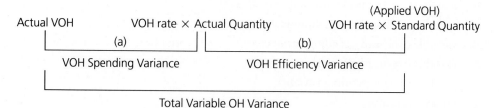

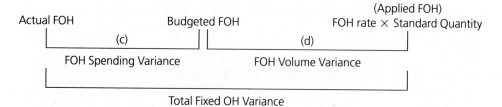

Overhead 1-, 2-, and 3-variance approaches:

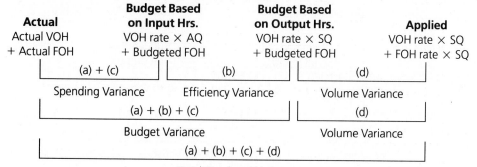

Sluggo Company makes high-performance racquetball rackets. The standard cost of a racket is:

Direct materials	.5 pounds @ $30	$15
Direct labor	4 hours @ $8	32
Variable factory overhead	$2 per DLH	8
Fixed factory overhead	$1 per DLH	4
Total		$59

DEMONSTRATION PROBLEM

The company had budgeted $112,000 of fixed factory overhead and 112,000 direct labor hours for 1994. The company actually produced 28,200 rackets and incurred 113,000 direct labor hours during the year. Actual costs and other manufacturing data related to overhead for the year were:

Variable factory overhead—$225,400
Fixed factory overhead—$123,800

Required:
Calculate the

a. total overhead variance
b. controllable and noncontrollable variances
c. spending, efficiency, and volume variances
d. variable overhead spending variance
e. variable overhead efficiency variance
f. fixed overhead spending variance
g. volume variance

Solution to Demonstration Problem

a. Total OH variance = TAOH − (Combined OH rate × SQ) = ($225,400 + $123,800) − ($3 × 112,800) = $349,200 − $338,400 = $10,800 U

b.

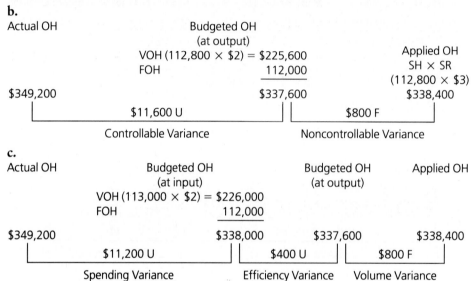

c.

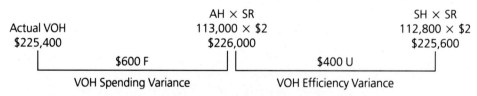

d & e. Variable overhead spending and efficiency variances

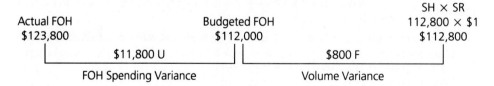

f & g. Fixed overhead spending and volume variances

Actual FOH	Budgeted FOH	SH × SR 112,800 × $1
$123,800	$112,000	$112,800

$11,800 U — FOH Spending Variance $800 F — Volume Variance

QUESTIONS

1. Why is it necessary to separate overhead costs into variable and fixed categories to prepare flexible budgets?

2. How does a flexible budget reveal "steps" in fixed costs that occur within the relevant range of operation?

3. Of what use is a flexible budget to a company that has already determined its expected level of activity for the upcoming period?

4. When using a flexible budget, what will occur to fixed cost per unit as production increases in the relevant range?

5. What is a yield ratio and how would you determine one for a pizza parlor?

6. Explain why the term "spending variance" may be somewhat misleading.

7. Why do managers care about the utilization of capacity? Are they controlling costs when they control utilization?

8. Why are the overhead spending and overhead efficiency variances said to be controllable? Is the volume variance controllable? Why or why not?

9. How are variances treated at the end of the period if they are considered to be material? Immaterial?

10. How are variances used by managers in their efforts to control costs?

11. Fixed overhead costs are generally incurred in lump-sum amounts. What implications does this have for control of fixed overhead?

12. Can combined overhead rates be used for control purposes? Are such rates more or less appropriate than separate overhead rates? Why or why not?

13. Which overhead variance approach (two-variance, three-variance, or four-variance) provides the most information for cost control purposes?

14. What are the two ways to control variable overhead costs? How is each used?

15. Can managers control fixed overhead on a per-unit basis? Explain.

16. Why are some companies replacing the two traditional cost categories of direct labor and manufacturing overhead with a "conversion cost" category?

17. How has automation affected standard costing? How has automation affected the computation of variances?

18. What are the three primary uses of a standard costing system?

---

 19. *(Calculation of flexible budget)* Eastland Technology Inc. has both variable and fixed overhead in its cost structure. In the past year, the company's cost structure was estimated to be $y = \$12,000 + \$14X$, where X represented machine hours. However, next year the company believes it will expand into a new relevant range. Fixed costs are expected to rise to $18,000 for any activity level above 5,000 machine hours, and the variable cost rate is expected to drop at the 6,000 unit volume by $2 per machine hour due to volume purchasing.
   a. Prepare a flexible budget for the 4,500, 5,500, and 6,500 machine hour levels.
   b. Calculate total overhead costs per machine hour at each level.
   c. If each unit of product requires 2 machine hours, compute the cost per unit if production is set at 4,000 units.

EXERCISES

20. *(Standard overhead application)* C&S Associates Ltd. uses a standard cost system. For March 1994, total overhead cost is budgeted at $200,000 based on the expected monthly capacity of 20,000 direct labor hours. Each tax return processed requires 4 standard direct labor hours. The following data are available for tax return preparations during March 1994:

Number of returns processed	4,800
Actual direct labor hours worked	19,000
Actual total overhead incurred	$199,500

   a. What amount should the company credit to the applied overhead account for March 1994?
   b. What is the total overhead variance?

21. *(Calculation of volume variance)* The Connection is a textile manufacturer of T-shirts and caps. Its fixed manufacturing overhead is budgeted at $20,000 per

month based on an expected annual capacity of 4,000 direct labor hours per month. For the year ended October 31, 1994, The Connection determined that 52,000 standard hours would be allowed for the output achieved. Calculate the volume variance for fixed overhead and explain its significance.

22. *(Computation of underapplied/overapplied overhead; variances)* Photocopier Service Company provides repairs and professional services to firms who use photocopiers. The company has determined its budgeted fixed monthly service overhead to be $20,000; the variable overhead component is $5 per technician labor hour. The company applies fixed overhead based on an expected monthly capacity of 10,000 technician labor hours. In October, the company consumed 10,500 technician labor hours. Total variable overhead incurred was $51,450 and total fixed overhead was $19,300.
    a. What was under- or overapplied variable overhead?
    b. What was under- or overapplied fixed overhead?
    c. What was the volume variance for October?
    d. What was the budget variance for the month?

23. *(Missing data, three-variance approach)* The flexible budget formula for total overhead for the Compass Division of Maritime Products Company is $360,000 + $8.00 per direct labor hour. The combined overhead rate is $20.00 per direct labor hour.

Actual total overhead for 1994	$580,000
Total overhead spending variance	$ 16,000 U
Volume variance	$ 24,000 U

    Calculate the overhead variances using the three-variance approach and determine
    a. the number of standard hours allowed.
    b. the actual hours of direct labor worked.

24. *(Computation of all variances)* The manager of the Automobile Registration Division of the state of Louisiana has determined that it typically takes 30 minutes for the department's employees to register a new car. The following predetermined overhead costs are applicable to Orleans Parish. Fixed overhead, computed on an estimated 4,000 direct labor hours, is $8 per DLH. Variable overhead is estimated at $3.00 per DLH.

    During July 1994, 7,600 cars were registered in Orleans Parish; this required 3,700 direct labor hours. The following overhead costs were incurred:

Variable overhead	$10,730
Fixed overhead	29,950

    a. Compute overhead variances using a 4-variance approach.
    b. Compute overhead variances using a 3-variance approach.
    c. Compute overhead variances using a 2-variance approach.

25. *(Calculation of variances)* Home Pesticide Manufacturing Company's overhead costs are as follows:

Standard overhead applied	$160,000
Budgeted overhead based on standard direct labor hours allowed for good output	$168,000
Budgeted overhead based on actual direct labor hours	$166,000
Actual total overhead	$192,000

    Calculate as many overhead variances as possible.

26. *(Calculation of predetermined overhead rate)* Phelps Mfg. expects the following abbreviated flexible budget for the upcoming year, 1994:

Direct Labor Hours

	10,000	11,000	12,000	13,000
Factory Costs:				
Variable overhead	$20,000	$22,000	$24,000	$26,000
Fixed overhead	16,500	16,500	16,500	16,500

The firm has set expected annual capacity at 11,000 direct labor hours. Two direct labor hours are required to make one unit of the company's product. The company expects to operate at 1/12 of the expected annual capacity each month.

a. Determine the separate rates for variable and fixed overhead per (1) direct labor hour and (2) product unit.

b. Determine the combined rate for factory overhead per (1) direct labor hour and (2) product unit.

27. *(Four-variance approach; journal entries)* Use the information from Exercise 26. During March 1994, the company produced 520 units. Phelps incurred $1,950 of variable overhead and $1,240 of fixed overhead that month and had 1,150 actual direct labor hours.

a. How much fixed factory overhead should be applied to Work in Process Inventory for March 1994? How much variable factory overhead should be applied to Work in Process Inventory for March 1994?

b. Using the four-variance approach, determine all four overhead variances for March 1994.

c. Prepare all journal entries for Phelps Mfg. for March 1994. Use the four-variance approach in part b to record variances.

28. *(Yield ratio; flexible budgets)* Yi's Yogurt produces yogurt and ice cream. The company has a yield ratio of 1:12, which means that for every hour of direct labor, 12 gallons of yogurt or ice cream can be produced. During July 1994, the company hired four new production workers who had no previous experience in operating the plant's machinery.

The cost accountant was reviewing July's production during August and found that 1,070 direct labor hours were worked and only 11,000 gallons of product were produced. The flexible budget cost formulas are as follows:

	Based on DLH		Based on gallons of product	
	Fixed	**Variable**	**Fixed**	**Variable**
Direct Labor		$12.00		$1.00
Indirect Materials		1.20		.10
Utilities	$ 900	.60	$ 900	.05
Depreciation	600		600	
Total	$1,500	$13.80	$1,500	$1.15

a. Compute the actual yield ratio for Yi's Yogurt.

b. Prepare flexible budgets based on both input and output measures and determine the cost of inefficiency for Yi's Yogurt in July.

29. *(Variances and cost control)* Tymbre Co. manufactures a product to which overhead is applied on a direct labor hour basis. Each unit of product requires 5 direct labor hours. Overhead is applied on a 40% variable and 60% fixed basis; the overhead application rate is $8 per hour. Standards are based on a normal monthly capacity of 2,500 direct labor hours.

During September 1994, Tymbre produced 505 units of product and incurred 2,450 direct labor hours. Actual overhead cost for the month was $19,300.

a. What were standard hours allowed for September?

b. What is total annual budgeted fixed overhead cost?

c. What is the controllable overhead variance?

d. What is the noncontrollable overhead variance?

30. *(Variances and conversion cost category)* Nebraska Corn Graders processes and grades seed corn for seed corn producers. Until recently, the company used a standard costing system and applied overhead to production based on direct labor hours. The company automated its facilities in March 1994 and revamped its accounting system to create new cost categories: direct materials (pesticides, fertilizers, etc.) and conversion costs. There is no direct labor category. Estimated variable conversion costs for April 1994 were $85,000, and estimated fixed conversion costs were $38,000; machine hours were estimated at 10,000 for April. Expected output for April was 5,000 bushels of processed seed corn. In April, the firm actually consumed 9,000 machine hours in processing 4,800 bushels of seed corn. The firm incurred conversion costs totaling $115,000; $75,000 of this amount was the variable cost.

a. Using the four-variance approach, compute the variances for conversion costs in April.

b. Evaluate the effectiveness of the firm in controlling costs in April.

COMMUNICATION ACTIVITIES

31. *(Calculation of four variances; journal entries)* Michele's Hattery utilizes a standard costing system. Data for October are presented below:

Standard Cost per Unit

(1 unit takes 1 hour)

Direct materials	$ 4.00
Direct labor	7.00
Variable overhead	2.00
Fixed overhead	4.00
Total	$17.00

The fixed overhead charge is based on an expected monthly capacity of 5,000 units, but due to a fire on the production floor, the company only produced 3,500 units. Actual variable overhead was $8,000 and actual fixed overhead was $19,000. The company recorded 4,000 direct labor hours for the month.

a. Prepare the journal entries for: (1) incurrence of actual overhead costs, (2) application of overhead, and (3) closing of variances (assume variances are immaterial).

b. Compute and compare the actual overhead cost per unit with the expected overhead cost per unit.

c. Calculate all overhead variances using the four-variance method.

d. Which variance computed in part a is the largest? Why?

32. *(Variances and cost control)* Hillsdale, Inc., planned to produce at the 4,000 unit level for its single type of product. Because of unexpected demand, the firm actually operated at the 4,400 unit level. The company's flexible budget appears as follows:

	3,000 units	4,000 units	5,000 units
Overhead Costs:			
Variable	$12,000	$16,000	$20,000
Fixed	8,000	8,000	8,000
Total	$20,000	$24,000	$28,000

Actual costs incurred in producing the 4,400 units:

Variable	$17,160
Fixed	8,200
Total	$25,360

The production manager was upset because the company planned to incur $24,000 of costs and actual costs were $25,360. Prepare a memo to the production manager regarding the following questions.

a. Was it correct to compare the $25,360 to the $24,000 for cost control purposes?

b. Analyze the costs and explain where the company did well and/or did poorly in controlling its costs.

33. What kind of dysfunctional behavior can be caused by production managers who attempt to show favorable variable and fixed overhead variances? Assume that the company uses a four-variance approach and address each variance individually, stressing the quality aspects of dysfunctional behavior.

PROBLEMS

34. *(Flexible budget)* The Big Dog wishes to determine its flexible budget formula to estimate costs at various activity levels. The only product sold by the business is an extra-large hot dog served on a bun with onions, relish, and cheese. The business is located in a rented building, has one employee, and pays for its own utilities. The company maintains an insurance policy for protection against product liability. The following information shows budgeted costs for a normal month.

At 1,200 hot dogs per month:

Ingredients	$1,440	variable
Rent	500	fixed
Employee wages (176 hours)	1,056	variable
Utilities (Electricity, phone, water)	120	variable
Insurance	100	fixed
Total cost	$3,216	

In June, the employee took a vacation and only worked 150 hours. Because of the reduced work period, the utilities' cost dropped to $86 and only 920 hot dogs were sold.

a. Determine the flexible budget formula for June for The Big Dog, if number of hours worked is specified as the best predictor of costs.

b. Determine the flexible budget formula for June if number of hot dogs sold is the best predictor of costs.

35. *(Flexible budget)* Sitting Duck Enterprises produces duck decoys for hunters. Each unit requires .5 direct labor hours. The relevant range of activity is between 6,000 and 9,000 direct labor hours. The following cost formulas were derived for the company after analyzing cost records:

Direct materials—$3.00 per unit
Direct labor—$6.50 per hour
Supervisor salaries—$15,000 per month
Other indirect labor—$5.00 per hour
Utilities—$3,700 plus $.25 per hour
Maintenance—$5,000 plus $.60 per hour
Indirect materials—$.20 per unit
Property taxes and insurance—$4,850 per month
Depreciation—$.35 per unit on a unit of production basis

a. Prepare a flexible budget for Sitting Duck for each 1,000 direct labor hours of activity within the relevant range. (*Hint:* Determine the number of units that can be produced at each level of activity.)
b. Determine the total cost formula for Sitting Duck.

36. *(Three-variance approach)* Modern Machete manufactures a line of chain saws that are marketed through a variety of department and sporting goods stores. The company uses a standard costing system with the following standard costs.

Materials:	motor	$65.00	
	chain	10.00	
	frame, etc.	45.00	$120.00
Direct labor: 2 hours @ $12.00			24.00
Overhead			16.00
Total cost			$160.00

The monthly overhead budget for the production department follows the flexible budget equation of total cost = $100,000 + $4.00 per machine hour. Expected capacity per month is 25,000 machine hours; fixed overhead is applied on this basis. At standard, two machine hours are required to produce one unit. The activity for November generated the following results:

Actual overhead	$189,750	
Actual machine hours	23,000	MHs
Units of production (in chain saws)	12,000	units

a. Compute the overhead variances using a 3-variance approach.
b. Analyze each variance and offer an explanation for its incurrence.

37. *(Three-variance approach)* Rubberflex is a material that is used as an outdoor surface for tennis courts, jogging and walking tracks, and basketball courts. This product is manufactured by Malaysia Rubber Co. The following data pertaining to the production of Rubberflex for 1994 have been obtained from company records:

Overhead budget formula: $400,000 + $8 per machine hour
Actual overhead for year: $1,889,000
Expected capacity for year: 200,000 machine hours
Actual machine hours worked: 198,000 machine hours
Standard hours allowed for year's production: 192,000 machine hours

a. Calculate the 3-variance analysis of overhead.
b. Was the company effective in controlling costs? Explain.

38. *(Multiple products; four-variance approach; journal entries)* Pine Valley Lumber Company produces three products (picnic tables, swings, and benches) and uses direct labor hours as its activity base. Standard hours allowed for each product are as follows:

Picnic table—10 standard direct labor hours
Swing—3 standard direct labor hours
Bench—12 standard direct labor hours

The standard variable overhead rate is $4 per direct labor hour; the standard fixed overhead application rate at expected annual capacity is $2 per direct labor hour. Expected capacity on a monthly basis is 3,000 direct labor hours.

Production for June 1994 was 100 picnic tables, 400 swings, and 60 benches. Actual direct labor hours incurred were 3,020. Actual variable overhead was $11,900, while actual fixed overhead was $6,100 for the month.

a. Prepare a variance analysis using the four-variance approach. (*Hint:* Convert the production of each type of product into standard hours allowed for all work accomplished for the month.)

b. Prepare journal entries for: (1) incurring overhead costs, (2) applying overhead costs, and (3) closing the variance accounts (assume *immaterial* variances).

c. Evaluate the effectiveness of managers in controlling costs.

39. *(Combined overhead rates; journal entries)* Life Bubble Inc. manufactures an inflatable life jacket. The industry regards this life jacket as revolutionary because it can be inflated to keep 70% of the wearer's body out of the water. Accordingly, the company is able to charge a premium price. The standard cost information for 1994 for the life jacket follows:

Each life jacket requires 3 hours of direct labor time to produce.
Variable overhead: $3 per direct labor hour
Fixed overhead: $2.50 per direct labor hour; calculated as total budgeted overhead divided by expected annual capacity of 50,000 direct labor hours

Production statistics for 1994 were:

Number of life jackets produced	21,000 units
Actual direct labor hours	62,200 hours
Variable overhead cost incurred	$189,710
Fixed overhead cost incurred	$132,200

a. Using a combined overhead rate, calculate variances according to the 2-variance approach.

b. Using a combined overhead rate, calculate variances according to the 3-variance approach.

c. Prepare journal entries for 1994 based on using one overhead control account and the 3-variance overhead analysis.

d. Post the amounts from the entries in part c to a factory overhead control T-account. Why is the ending balance in this account $0?

40. *(Comprehensive)* Rabar Corp. manufactures metal screen doors for commercial buildings. The company uses a standard costing system; its standard costs per screen door follow:

Direct materials:

Aluminum	4 sheets at $2	$ 8
Copper	3 sheets at $4	12
Direct labor	5 hours at $8	40
Variable overhead	5 hours at $3	15
Fixed overhead	5 hours at $2	10

Overhead rates were based on normal monthly capacity of 6,000 direct labor hours.

During November, 850 tools were produced. This was below normal levels due to the effects of a labor strike that occurred during union contract negotiations. Once the dispute was settled, the company scheduled overtime to try to catch up to regular production levels. The following costs were incurred in November:

Material:
Aluminum: 4,000 sheets purchased at $2; used 3,500 sheets
Copper: 3,000 sheets purchased at $4.20; used 2,600 sheets

Direct labor:
Regular time: 3,400 hours at $8.00 (precontract settlement)
          900 hours at $8.50 (postcontract settlement)
Overtime: 500 hours were worked during overtime, but the half-time overtime premium was included in the total variable overhead for November in accordance with company accounting policy.

b. The company has divided its responsibilities so that the Purchasing Department is responsible for the price at which materials and supplies are purchased. The Manufacturing Department is responsible for the quantities of materials used. Does this division of responsibilities solve the conflict between price and quantity variances? Explain your answer.

c. Prepare a report detailing the overhead budget variance. The report, which will be given to the Manufacturing Department manager, should display only that part of the variance that is the responsibility of the manager and should highlight the information in ways that would be useful to that manager in evaluating departmental performance and when considering corrective action.

d. Assume that the departmental manager performs the timekeeping function for this manufacturing department. From time to time analyses of overhead and direct labor variances have shown that the department manager has deliberately misclassified labor hours (i.e., listed direct labor hours as indirect labor hours and vice versa) so that only one of the two labor variances is unfavorable. It is not feasible economically to hire a separate timekeeper. What should the company do, if anything, to resolve this problem?

(CMA)

ETHICS AND QUALITY DISCUSSION

48. *One of the overhead costs incurred by the Jefferson Parish school system in its management of numerous schools is travel expenses for employees. For many years, some 200 employees received monthly mileage allotments without being required to document their expenses; additionally, the employees pay no taxes on the funds, which totaled about $200,000 annually. "Administrators who defend the policy said that the allotments are based on estimated mileage and that occasional checks are made to make sure the figures are correct."*

[SOURCE: Bill Walsh, "Jeff School Board's Travel Expense Plan Investigated by IRS," (*New Orleans*) *Times-Picayune* (January 19, 1993), pp. A-1, A-6.]

a. Why do you think the school does not require employees to document their travel expenses?

b. Do you believe that employees can be trusted not to inflate travel allotment needs? Why or why not?

c. From the taxability of income perspective, do you believe that the present system is a good one? Why or why not?

d. If you were a Jefferson Parish taxpayer, how would you feel about the system and why?

49. Tim Zeff is a plant manager who has done a good job of controlling some overhead costs during the current period and a poor job of controlling others. Tim's boss has asked him for a variance report for the period.

a. Discuss the ethics of using a two-variance approach to report the overhead variances rather than a three- or four-variance approach.

b. If Tim does not provide his boss with detailed information on the individual cost components and their related variances, can the boss judge Tim's performance during the period? Defend your answer.

50. *At a time when nearly 9 million people can't find jobs, other Americans are putting in the most overtime since the government started keeping records in the 1950s. With factory workers averaging 4.2 hours of overtime per week, the Bureau of Labor Statistics says more than a tenth of all work done in the nation's factories is performed on overtime.*

"If we could go back to the amount of overtime worked in 1982, we would create 3 million new jobs without increasing the federal deficit," said John Zalusky, an economist

at the AFL-CIO. He said many workers are putting in extra hours for pay against their wishes.

   One reason employers are going the overtime route, economists say, is that overtime pay doesn't cost much extra. Fringe benefits, representing as much as 40 percent of labor costs, are mostly covered by the first 40 hours worked. And the overtime hours generally are worked by employers' most skilled and productive people. Beyond that, using overtime avoids the cost of hiring and training new workers, finding space for them and dealing with the added paperwork. Because of all those factors, Zalusky calculates that paying a skilled worker time-and-a-half actually costs employers only about 3 percent extra.

[SOURCE: Mike Feinsliber, "Employers Paying Overtime Instead of Hiring," (*New Orleans*) *Times-Picayune* (March 18, 1993), p. C-2.]

a. How does overtime pay affect direct labor cost? Variable overhead?
b. Obviously, paying overtime to already employed workers makes better financial business sense than does hiring additional workers. If, however, workers would prefer not to work overtime but do so to maintain their jobs, how does overtime affect the ethical contract between employers and employees?
c. What effects might overtime have on job efficiency? On job effectiveness (such as quality of production)?
d. Would you be in favor of limiting allowable hours of overtime in order to have more individuals employed? Discuss from the standpoint of the government, the employer, a currently employed worker, and an unemployed individual.

ABSORPTION AND VARIABLE COSTING

LEARNING OBJECTIVES

After completing this chapter, you should be able to answer these questions:

1. What are the differences between absorption and variable costing?
2. How do changes in sales and/or production levels affect net income as computed under absorption and variable costing?
3. Can one accounting system provide both absorption and variable costing financial statements?
4. How can absorption costing information be converted to variable costing information? Variable to absorption?

INTRODUCING

THE GILLETTE COMPANY

In the mid-1980s, Gillette Co. engineers perfected the design of a new razor that would give a closer, smoother shave than any the company had ever made. Manufacturing it, however, was another thing. The new razor (Sensor—with flexible twin blades that adjust to the contours of the face—had 10 parts. Each part had to fit together just so, with a margin of error of only a few microns, or 25,000ths of an inch. Gillette assembly lines had to achieve this precision while running at speeds fast enough to make not just millions or tens of millions, but hundreds of millions of twin-blade cartridges a year. And, in a cutthroat market where a price difference of a few pennies can determine success or failure, Gillette had to make the shaving system at a low cost.

Because of its history, Gillette views manufacturing—especially in its razor and blade business—as a competitive tool. In the early 1900s, after Gillette introduced the first safety razor, executives recognized that they could be vulnerable to rivals. "A piece of steel [for making blades] was available to all our competitors at reasonable prices," notes Edward DeGraan, vice president of manufacturing and technical operations. Figuring out how to shape and strengthen the same piece of steel into a sharper, sturdier blade was a way to stay ahead of the pack. As a result, Gillette has long custom-designed—and jealously guarded—most of the manufacturing equipment for its razors and blades.

Making Sensor tested all of Gillette's manufacturing expertise. Existing laser-welding equipment couldn't work at the speeds necessary, or operate 24 hours a day, seven days a week. Gillette got board approval to spend $10 million to test a manufacturing system for Sensor, including a pilot manufacturing station with a company that specializes in laser welding. Today, the laser-welding equipment is the key to the Sensor assembly line.

SOURCE: Lawrence Ingrassia, "The Cutting Edge," *Wall Street Journal* (April 6, 1992), p. R6. Reprinted by permission of the *Wall Street Journal*, © 1992 Dow Jones & Company, Inc. All rights reserved worldwide.

If Gillette is to control its costs on millions of razors per year, company management must understand certain factors about those costs. First, the managers must understand the type of costing system in use by the company. Second, they must understand the valuation method being used for products. Third, they must understand the composition of product cost and which style of presentation the company is using for its reports.

Job order and process costing are two costing *systems* that allow costs to be accumulated in specific ways. Job order costing is appropriate for companies making products or performing services in conformity with customer specifications. Process costing is appropriate for manufacturers such as Gillette that are producing large quantities of homogeneous output.

Actual, normal, and standard costs are three methods of cost *valuation*. Actual costing uses actual direct materials, actual direct labor, and actual overhead costs to compute product or service cost; normal costing includes actual direct materials and actual direct labor costs, but uses predetermined overhead rates to apply overhead to

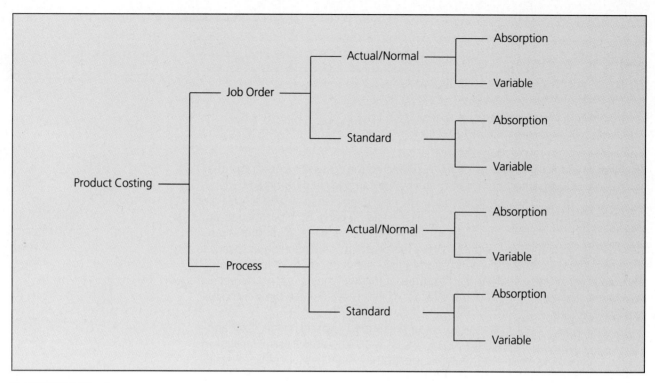

■ EXHIBIT 13–1

Product Costing Possibilities

production. Standard costing assigns direct materials, direct labor, and overhead to products or services using established per unit norms.

This chapter discusses the third and fourth dimensions of product costing: cost accumulation and cost presentation. The method of *accumulation* determines which manufacturing costs are recorded as part of product cost. While one method of cost accumulation may be appropriate for external reporting, that method is not necessarily appropriate for internal decision making. The *presentation* method focuses on how costs are shown on external financial statements or internal management reports. Accumulation and presentation procedures are accomplished using one of two methods: absorption costing or variable costing. Each method uses the same basic data, but they structure and process the data differently. Both methods may be used in job order or process costing and with actual, normal, or standard costs. Exhibit 13–1 depicts various product costing possibilities.

AN OVERVIEW OF THE TWO METHODS

Absorption costing

Functional classification

The traditional approach to product costing is **absorption costing,** which treats the costs of all manufacturing components (direct materials, direct labor, variable overhead, and fixed overhead) as inventoriable or product costs. This method has been used consistently in the previous chapters that dealt with product costing systems and valuation. In fact, the product cost definition given in Chapter 2 specifically fits the absorption costing method. Under absorption costing, costs incurred in the nonmanufacturing areas of the organization are considered period costs and are expensed in a manner that properly matches them with revenues. With regard to presentation, absorption costing presents expenses on an income statement according to their functional classifications. A **functional classification** is a group of costs that were all incurred for the same principal purpose. Functional classifications include categories such as cost of goods sold, selling expense, and general and administrative expense.[1] In contrast, **variable costing** is a cost accumulation method that includes only *variable* production costs (direct materials, direct labor, and variable overhead) as product or inventoriable costs. Under this method, fixed manufacturing overhead is treated as a period cost. Like absorption costing, variable costing treats costs incurred in the organization's selling and administrative areas as period costs. Variable costing income statements typically present expenses according to cost behavior (variable and fixed), although they may also present expenses by functional classifications within the behavioral categories.

Variable costing

This discussion indicates that there are two basic differences between absorption and variable costing. The first difference is the way fixed manufacturing overhead (FOH) is treated for product costing purposes. Under absorption costing, FOH is considered a product cost; under variable costing, it is considered a period cost. The second difference is in the presentation of costs on the income statement. Absorption costing classifies expired costs by function, while variable costing categorizes expired costs first by behavior and may further classify costs by function.

A brief initial example of the two methods for Forget-Me-Not Company is presented in Exhibit 13–2, using assumed data. The company incurs $40,000 of fixed

▌EXHIBIT 13–2

Comparison of Absorption and Variable Costing for Forget-Me-Not Company

Absorption Costing			**Variable Costing**		
Composition of Product Cost			Composition of Product Cost		
Direct materials	$2.00		Direct materials		$2.00
Direct labor	1.00		Direct labor		1.00
Variable manufacturing OH	.50		Variable manufacturing OH		.50
Fixed manufacturing OH	.40 ←*→				
Total product cost	$3.90		Total product cost		$3.50
Income Statement**			Income Statement***		
Sales (100,000 × $20)	$2,000,000		Sales (100,000 × $20)		$2,000,000
CGS (100,000 × $3.90)	390,000		Variable Expenses:		
			CGS (100,000 × $3.50)		350,000
Subtotal	$1,610,000		Subtotal		$1,650,000
Operating Expenses:			Fixed Expenses:		
Selling	$300,000		Manufacturing	$ 40,000*	
General & administrative	500,000	800,000	Selling	300,000	
			General & administrative	500,000	840,000
Income Before Income Taxes		$ 810,000	Income Before Income Taxes		$ 810,000

*Different treatment of fixed manufacturing overhead.
**Arranged according to functional expense categories.
***Arranged according to behavioral (variable and fixed) cost categories.

---

[1]Under FASB Statement 34, certain interest costs may be capitalized during a period of asset construction. If a company is capitalizing or has capitalized interest costs, these costs will not be shown on the income statement, but will become a part of fixed asset cost. The fixed asset cost is then depreciated as part of fixed overhead. Thus, while interest is typically considered a period cost, it may be included as fixed overhead and affect the overhead application rate.

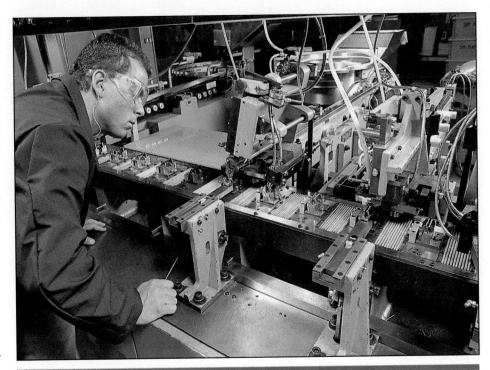

Depreciation on Gillette's production equipment creates a high fixed cost each period. Absorption costing allocates this cost on a per-unit basis to the razors produced; variable costing assigns it to the income statement as a period charge.

manufacturing overhead costs per period. During the period presented, production equals sales (100,000 units) for the firm's only product (travel kits), which sells for $20 per unit. Note that under absorption costing, fixed manufacturing overhead is a product cost ($.40 per travel kit), while the fixed manufacturing overhead ($40,000) is treated as a period expense under variable costing. The company's selling expenses are all fixed. Also observe that variable and fixed expenses are presented separately on the variable costing statement.

Absorption Costing

Full costing

Absorption costing is also known as **full costing** since all types of manufacturing costs are included as product cost. An organization incurs costs for direct materials (DM), direct labor (DL), and variable overhead (VOH) only when goods are produced or services are rendered. Since total DM, DL, and VOH costs increase with each additional product made or service rendered, these costs are considered product costs and are inventoried until the product or service is sold. Fixed manufacturing overhead (FOH) costs, however, may be incurred even when production or service facilities are idle. Although total FOH cost does not vary with units of production or level of service, this cost is incurred to provide the manufacturing capacity necessary for production to occur. Without the incurrence of fixed overhead (such as the depreciation on the specially-made Gillette machines), production could not take place. Thus, absorption costing considers FOH to be inventoriable.[2] Exhibit 13–3 depicts an absorption costing accounting model.

Major authoritative bodies of the accounting profession, such as the Financial Accounting Standards Board and Securities and Exchange Commission, apparently believe that absorption costing provides external parties with a more informative pic-

---

[2] There is significant controversy about the theoretical justification and practical application of absorption and variable costing. Without attempting to cover all the background issues surrounding these methods, a subsequent section of this chapter provides some insight into the cases made for both absorption and variable costing. Those who wish to understand the subject more thoroughly may refer to some of the articles listed in the selected bibliography in the Instructor's Manual to this text.

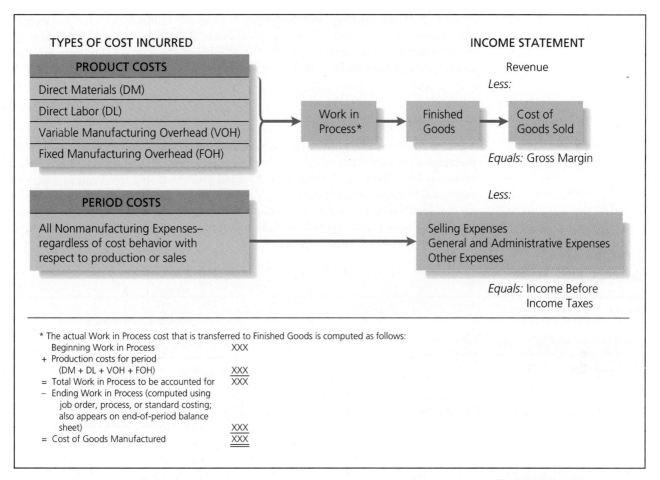

TYPES OF COST INCURRED

PRODUCT COSTS

Direct Materials (DM)

Direct Labor (DL)

Variable Manufacturing Overhead (VOH)

Fixed Manufacturing Overhead (FOH)

PERIOD COSTS

All Nonmanufacturing Expenses–
regardless of cost behavior with
respect to production or sales

INCOME STATEMENT

Revenue

Less:

Work in Process* → Finished Goods → Cost of Goods Sold

Equals: Gross Margin

Less:

Selling Expenses
General and Administrative Expenses
Other Expenses

Equals: Income Before Income Taxes

* The actual Work in Process cost that is transferred to Finished Goods is computed as follows:

Beginning Work in Process	XXX	
+ Production costs for period (DM + DL + VOH + FOH)	XXX	
= Total Work in Process to be accounted for	XXX	
− Ending Work in Process (computed using job order, process, or standard costing; also appears on end-of-period balance sheet)	XXX	
= Cost of Goods Manufactured	XXX	

EXHIBIT 13–3
Absorption Costing Model

ture of earnings than does variable costing. By specifying that absorption costing must be used to prepare external financial statements, the accounting profession has, in effect, disallowed the use of variable costing as a generally accepted inventory valuation method for external reporting purposes since the IRS began requiring absorption costing for tax purposes.[3]

On external absorption costing financial reports, Work in Process Inventory, Finished Goods Inventory, and Cost of Goods Sold include variable per-unit production costs as well as a per-unit allocation of fixed manufacturing overhead. Nonmanufacturing expenses are presented by functional account classifications indicating the reasons for the cost incurrence. The basic functional categories of nonmanufacturing expenses are: (1) selling, (2) general and administrative, and (3) other. Nonmanufacturing costs may vary in proportion to the sales level, be constant or fixed in amount, or be mixed or step costs.

Cost behavior (relative to changes in activity) is not observable from an absorption costing income statement or management report. However, cost behavior is extremely important for a variety of managerial activities including cost-volume-profit

---

[3]The Tax Reform Act of 1986 requires all manufacturers and many wholesalers and retailers to include many previously expensed indirect costs in inventory. This method is referred to as "super-full absorption" or uniform capitalization. The uniform capitalization rules require manufacturers to assign to inventory all costs that directly benefit or are incurred because of production, including some general and administrative costs. Wholesalers and retailers, which previously did not need to include any indirect costs in inventory, now must inventory costs for items such as off-site warehousing, purchasing agents' salaries, and repackaging. However, the material in this chapter is not intended to reflect "super-full absorption." This topic is discussed in more detail in the appendix to Chapter 6 on service department cost allocation.

analysis, relevant costing, and budgeting.[4] Although companies prepare external statements on an absorption costing basis, *internal* financial reports distinguishing costs by behavior are often prepared. The purpose of these internal reports is to facilitate management decision making and analysis.

Variable Costing

Direct costing

Variable costing is also known as **direct costing** and is depicted in Exhibit 13–4. This illustration indicates that variable costing only includes variable production costs as inventoriable. This costing method treats fixed manufacturing overhead as a period expense rather than as a product cost. Variable costing proponents believe this treatment is justified on the basis that product costs are, by definition, "costs of *production*" and, since fixed overhead will be incurred even if there is no production, it cannot be considered a production cost.

▌ **EXHIBIT 13–4**
Variable Costing Model

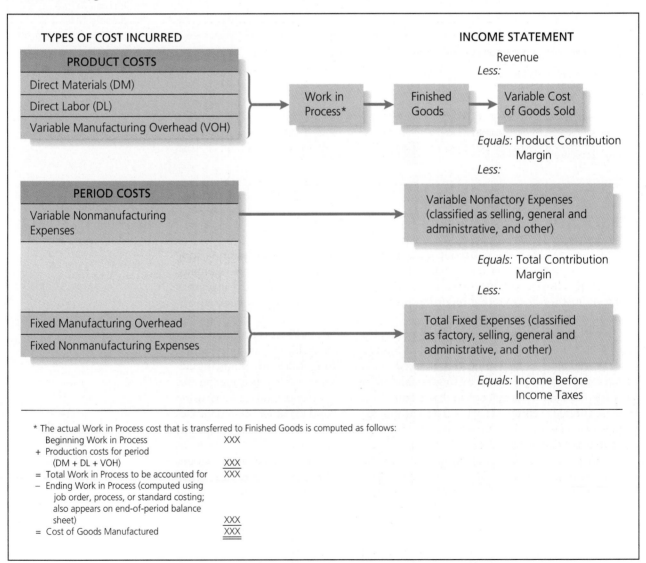

---

[4] Cost-volume profit analysis is discussed in the next chapter. Relevant costing is covered in Chapter 15 and budgeting is discussed in Chapter 16.

Variable costing allows costs to be separated by cost behavior on the income statement or internal management reports. Cost of Goods Sold, under variable costing, is more appropriately called Variable Cost of Goods Sold since it is composed *only* of variable production costs. Revenue minus variable cost of goods sold is called **product contribution margin** and indicates how much revenue is available to cover all period expenses and potentially to provide net income.

Variable, nonmanufacturing period expenses (such as a sales commission set at 10 percent of product selling price) are deducted from product contribution margin to determine the amount of **total contribution margin**. Total contribution margin is the difference between total revenues and total variable expenses. This amount indicates the dollar figure available to "contribute" to the coverage of all fixed expenses, both manufacturing and nonmanufacturing. After fixed expenses are covered, any remaining contribution margin provides income to the company. A variable costing income statement is also referred to as a contribution income statement.

The next section of the chapter provides a detailed illustration using both absorption and variable costing.

Product contribution margin

Total contribution margin

The Reeves Company makes a single product: the Sleek Shave disposable razor. Data for this product are used to compare absorption and variable costing procedures and presentations. The company employs standard costs for material, labor, and overhead.[5] Exhibit 13–5 gives the standard production costs per unit and the annual budgeted nonmanufacturing costs for Reeves Company. All standard and budgeted costs are assumed to remain constant over the three years 1994 through 1996 and, for simplicity, the company is assumed to have no Work in Process Inventory at the end of a period.

ABSORPTION AND VARIABLE COSTING ILLUSTRATIONS

▌ **EXHIBIT 13–5**
Reeves Company Basic Data

Standard variable cost per Sleek Shave unit:

Direct materials	$.05
Direct labor	.01
Variable manufacturing overhead	.03
Total	$.09

$$\text{FOH Application Rate} = \frac{\text{Estimated Annual Fixed Overhead Cost}}{\text{Estimated Annual Capacity}}$$

$$= \frac{\$1,500,000}{75,000,000} = \$.02 \text{ per unit}$$

Budgeted nonproduction costs:

Selling expenses = ($1,590,000 + $.002 per unit sold)
General and administrative expenses = ($2,350,000 + $.003 per unit sold)

---

[5] Actual costs can also be used under either absorption or variable costing. Standard costing was chosen for these illustrations because it makes the differences between the two methods more obvious. If actual costs had been used, production costs would vary each year and such variations would obscure the distinct differences caused by the use of one method, rather than the other, over a period time. Standard costs are also treated as constant over time to more clearly demonstrate the differences between absorption and variable costing and to reduce the complexity of the chapter explanations.

The company determines its standard fixed manufacturing overhead application rate by dividing estimated annual FOH by expected annual capacity. Total estimated annual fixed manufacturing overhead for Reeves is $1,500,000 and expected annual production is 75,000,000 units. These figures provide a standard FOH rate of $.02 per unit. Fixed manufacturing overhead is typically under- or overapplied at year-end when a standard, predetermined fixed overhead rate is used rather than actual FOH cost.

Under- or overapplication is caused by two factors that can work independently or simultaneously. These two factors are cost differences and utilization differences. If actual FOH cost differs from expected FOH cost, a fixed manufacturing overhead spending variance is created. If actual capacity utilization differs from expected utilization, a volume variance arises.[6] The *independent* effects of these differences are shown below:

Actual FOH Cost > Expected FOH Cost = Underapplied FOH
Actual FOH Cost < Expected FOH Cost = Overapplied FOH
Actual Utilization > Expected Utilization = Overapplied FOH
Actual Utilization < Expected Utilization = Underapplied FOH

In most cases, however, both costs and utilization differ from estimates. When this occurs, no generalizations can be made as to whether FOH will be under- or overapplied.

Assume that Reeves Company began operations in 1994. Production and sales information for the years 1994 through 1996 are shown below.

Year	Units Produced	Units Sold
1994	75,000,000	75,000,000
1995	74,000,000	72,000,000
1996	76,000,000	78,000,000
Totals	225,000,000	225,000,000

Since the company began operations in 1994, that year has a zero balance for beginning Finished Goods Inventory. The next year, 1995, also has a zero beginning inventory since all units produced in 1994 were also sold in 1994. In 1995 and 1996, production and sales quantities differ, which is a common situation because production frequently "leads" sales so that inventory can be stockpiled for a later period. The illustration purposefully has no beginning inventory and equal cumulative units of production and sales for the three years to demonstrate that, regardless of whether absorption or variable costing is used, the cumulative income before taxes will be the same ($9,539,900 in Exhibits 13–7 and 13–8) under these conditions.

Exhibit 13–6 provides the 1994–1996 budgeted and actual cost data for Reeves Company and computes the production variances for each of those years. Actual variable production costs for direct materials, direct labor, and variable overhead are combined for simplicity in the exhibit. Reeves Company accounting records would reflect the individual actual amounts of these production costs. Detailed variance analysis would be performed for control and decision making purposes. The managers responsible for the various costs would determine if the variances exceeded the tolerance limits allowed and, if so, investigate the causes for the variances. For illustrative purposes, all production variances are considered immaterial and are written off on the respective year's income statement rather than being allocated among Cost of Goods Sold and the various inventory accounts.

[6]These variances are covered in depth in Chapter 12.

[Unfavorable variances are presented without parentheses; favorable variances are shown in parentheses]

PRODUCTION VARIANCES:

	1994	1995	1996	Total
Expected capacity (units)	75,000,000	75,000,000	75,000,000	225,000,000
Actual production (units)	75,000,000	74,000,000	76,000,000	225,000,000
Under or (over) expected capacity	0	1,000,000	(1,000,000)	0
Application rate per unit	$.02	$.02	$.02	$.02
(1) Volume variances	$ 0	$ 20,000	$ (20,000)	$ 0
Budgeted FOH cost	$ 1,500,000	$ 1,500,000	$ 1,500,000	$ 4,500,000
Actual FOH cost	1,505,000	1,502,000	1,504,000	4,511,000
(2) FOH spending variances	$ 5,000	$ 2,000	$ 4,000	$ 11,000
Flexible budget for variable manufacturing costs (DM, DL, and VOH = $.09 per unit) based on actual units of production	$ 6,750,000	$ 6,660,000	$ 6,840,000	$ 20,250,000
Actual variable manufacturing costs	6,748,500	6,663,000	6,842,600	20,254,100
(3) Variable manufacturing cost variances	$ (1,500)	$ 3,000	$ 2,600	$ 4,100

▌ EXHIBIT 13–6

Reeves Company Actual and Budgeted Data and Computation of Variances

This illustration assumes for purposes of simplicity that actual and budget figures for nonmanufacturing costs are equal. In reality, each nonmanufacturing cost would be individually compared to the budget and the variance computed; if the variance were material, it would be investigated by the appropriate manager.

Exhibit 13–7 on page 526 presents absorption costing income statements for the Reeves Company for 1994–1996. The standard cost per unit is $.11. This amount is composed of the standard costs of direct materials, direct labor, and variable and fixed manufacturing overhead as shown at the bottom of the exhibit. Cost of goods manufactured is equal to the $.11 standard production cost per unit multiplied by the number of units produced that year. Ending inventory cost is calculated as the units in ending inventory multiplied by the $.11 standard cost per unit.

The volume variance for each year is shown in Exhibit 13–7 as an adjustment to Cost of Goods Sold. The write-off of an unfavorable volume variance in 1995 causes Cost of Goods Sold to increase, whereas a favorable volume variance in 1996 causes Cost of Goods Sold to be reduced. Gross margin is the difference between revenue and the adjusted Cost of Goods Sold.

The selling, general, and administrative costs shown in Exhibit 13–7 are grouped by functional areas. A portion of the selling, general, and administrative expenses varies each year, but what portion of those costs is variable and what portion is fixed is not apparent from the absorption costing income statement.

Exhibit 13–8 on page 527 provides the variable costing statements for Reeves Company for the years 1994–1996 using the same basic information. Under variable costing, the standard cost per unit is $.09 rather than $.11. This $.02 difference reflects the fact that fixed manufacturing overhead is included as a lump-sum period cost rather than being allocated on a per unit basis as part of product cost.

Note also that no volume variance is shown on the variable costing income statements. A volume variance arises only in absorption costing when actual production

	1994	1995	1996	Total
Units produced	75,000,000	74,000,000	76,000,000	225,000,000
Sales volume	75,000,000	72,000,000	78,000,000	225,000,000
Sales ($.21 per unit)	$15,750,000	$15,120,000	$16,380,000	$47,250,000
Cost of Goods Sold:				
Beginning inventory	$ 0	$ 0	$ 220,000	$ 0
Cost of goods manufactured	8,250,000	8,140,000	8,360,000	24,750,000
Cost of goods available	$ 8,250,000	$ 8,140,000	$ 8,580,000	$24,750,000
Ending inventory	0	220,000	0	0
Cost of goods sold	$ 8,250,000	$ 7,920,000	$ 8,580,000	$24,750,000
Volume variance [Exhibit 13–6(1)]	0	20,000	(20,000)	0
Total other manufacturing variances [Exhibit 13–6(2) and (3)]	3,500	5,000	6,600	15,100
Adjusted CGS	$ 8,253,500	$ 7,945,000	$ 8,566,600	$24,765,100
Gross Margin	$ 7,496,500	$ 7,175,000	$ 7,813,400	$22,484,900
Operating Expenses:				
Selling (planned and actual)	$ 1,740,000	$ 1,734,000	$ 1,746,000	$ 5,220,000
G & A (planned and actual)	2,575,000	2,566,000	2,584,000	7,725,000
Total	$ 4,315,000	$ 4,300,000	$ 4,330,000	$12,945,000
Income before Income Taxes	$ 3,181,500	$ 2,875,000	$ 3,483,400	$ 9,539,900

Absorption cost per unit of product includes:

Direct materials	$.05
Direct labor	.01
Variable manufacturing overhead	.03
Fixed manufacturing overhead	.02
Total unit cost	$.11

▌ EXHIBIT 13–7

Reeves Company Absorption Costing Comparative Income Statements

activity does not equal the activity level used in setting the application rate. Since no fixed overhead application rate exists under variable costing, no volume variance can occur.

Cost of goods manufactured (CGM) in Exhibit 13–8 equals the $.09 standard variable production cost multiplied by the number of units produced. Ending inventory is equal to the units *not* sold multiplied by the standard cost of $.09 per unit. Product contribution margin each year is a constant amount of $.12 multiplied by the number of units sold. The $.12 is the difference between the selling price of $.21 and the standard variable production cost of $.09. Since this per unit amount is constant, all years having equal sales volumes will also have equal amounts of product contribution margin.

Because of the emphasis on cost behavior, the next subtotal on a variable costing income statement is total unadjusted contribution margin. Variable selling, general, and adminstrative expenses are subtracted from product contribution margin to compute total unadjusted contribution margin. The unadjusted contribution margin per-

	1994	1995	1996	Total
Units produced	75,000,000	74,000,000	76,000,000	225,000,000
Sales volume	75,000,000	72,000,000	78,000,000	225,000,000
Sales ($.21 per unit)	$15,750,000	$15,120,000	$16,380,000	$47,250,000
Cost of Goods Sold:				
Beginning inventory	$ 0	$ 0	$ 180,000	$ 0
Cost of goods manufactured	6,750,000	6,660,000	6,840,000	20,250,000
Cost of goods available	$ 6,750,000	$ 6,660,000	$ 7,020,000	$20,250,000
Ending inventory	0	180,000	0	0
Variable cost of goods sold	$ 6,750,000	$ 6,480,000	$ 7,020,000	$20,250,000
Product contribution margin	$ 9,000,000	$ 8,640,000	$ 9,360,000	$27,000,000
Total nonmanufacturing variable expenses (Ex. 13–5; $.005 per unit)	375,000	360,000	390,000	1,125,000
Unadjusted contribution margin	$ 8,625,000	$ 8,280,000	$ 8,970,000	$25,875,000
Total variable cost variance [Exhibit 13–6(3)]	(1,500)	3,000	2,600	4,100
Adjusted contribution margin	$ 8,626,500	$ 8,277,000	$ 8,967,400	$25,870,900
Fixed expenses:				
Manufacturing OH (Exhibit 13–5)	$ 1,500,000	$ 1,500,000	$ 1,500,000	$ 4,500,000
Selling (Exhibit 13–5)	1,590,000	1,590,000	1,590,000	4,770,000
G & A (Exhibit 13–5)	2,350,000	2,350,000	2,350,000	7,050,000
Total fixed cost spending variance [Exhibit 13–6(2)]	5,000	2,000	4,000	11,000
Total fixed expenses	$ 5,445,000	$ 5,442,000	$ 5,444,000	$16,331,000
Income before Income Taxes	$ 3,181,500	$ 2,835,000	$ 3,523,400	$ 9,539,900

Variable cost per unit of product includes:

Direct materials	$.05
Direct labor	.01
Variable manufacturing overhead	.03
Total unit cost	$.09

▌ **EXHIBIT 13–8**

Reeves Company Variable Costing Comparative Income Statements

centage is equal to total unadjusted contribution margin divided by total sales. This percentage is constant at approximately 55 percent each year:

Sales price per unit		$.210		100.00%
Variable production costs per unit		.090		42.86%
Product contribution margin per unit		$.120		57.14%
Variable selling expenses per unit	$.002		.95%	
Variable G & A expenses per unit	.003	.005	1.43%	2.38%
Unadjusted contribution margin per unit		$.115		54.76%

Subtracting *variable* cost variances from the unadjusted contribution margin provides the adjusted contribution margin.

The section labeled Fixed Expenses represents the actual fixed expenses for each year. All fixed expenses and related unfavorable variances are deducted from the adjusted contribution margin to determine income before taxes for the year. (Favorable fixed cost variances would be added to the adjusted contribution margin.) The only fixed cost variance in this example is the FOH spending variance. As mentioned previously, a volume variance does not occur in variable costing because fixed costs are not assigned to the products.

The total amount of nonmanufacturing expenses for each year are shown as period costs on both sets of income statements. Under variable costing, these amounts are merely rearranged on the income statement into their separate variable and fixed amounts. For example, total 1994 selling expenses are shown in Exhibit 13–7 as a single amount of $1,740,000. In Exhibit 13–8, this amount is shown as $150,000 of variable selling expenses and $1,590,000 of fixed selling expenses. The variable selling expenses are included as part of the $375,000 total nonmanufacturing variable expenses. *Nonmanufacturing expenses are always period costs, no matter which costing method is used.*

Variable costing income statements are more useful internally for planning, controlling, and decision making than absorption costing statements. To carry out their functions, managers need to understand and be able to project how different costs will change in reaction to changes in activity levels. Variable costing, through its emphasis on cost behavior, provides that necessary information.

The income statements in Exhibits 13–7 and 13–8 show that absorption and variable costing tend to provide different income figures in some years. In comparing the two sets of statements, we see that the difference in income arises solely from what components are included in or excluded from product cost for each method.

COMPARISON OF THE TWO APPROACHES

Exhibit 13–9 compares yearly product cost flows for Reeves using absorption costing to those occurring under variable costing. The right-hand column of this exhibit indicates a single difference in product cost flows. That difference is caused by assigning fixed manufacturing overhead to products under absorption costing rather than to the period as is done under variable costing. The amount of fixed manufacturing overhead included as a product cost will ultimately affect the income statement when the products are sold. Product sales, however, may take place in a different time period from that in which the costs are actually incurred.

In 1994, the $1,500,000 difference between the $8,250,000 Cost of Goods Manufactured (CGM) under absorption and the $6,750,000 CGM under variable costing is equal to 75,000,000 units produced multiplied by the fixed manufacturing overhead application rate of $.02 per unit. Since all units produced in 1994 are also sold, this $1,500,000 differential is reflected on both methods' income statements in the same time period. Using absorption costing, this $1,500,000 is shown as part of Cost of Goods Sold. The $1,500,000 is expensed on the variable costing income statement as part of the fixed period expenses. Since the total fixed manufacturing overhead amount is shown on both 1994 income statements, there is no difference in income for that year. In a standard costing system in which standard costs are constant over time and in which production and sales volumes are equal, the income amounts under absorption costing and variable costing will be equal.

In years 1995 and 1996, there are differences under absorption and variable costing in the values of ending inventories as well as cost of goods manufactured; in 1996, differences exist in the values of beginning inventories and cost of goods manufactured. In both of these years, the fixed manufacturing overhead application rate mul-

	Units	Absorption Costing	Variable Costing	Fixed Cost Differential
1994				
BI	0	$ 0	$ 0	$ 0
CGM	75,000,000	8,250,000	6,750,000	1,500,000
CGA	75,000,000	$8,250,000	$6,750,000	$1,500,000
CGS	75,000,000	8,250,000	6,750,000	1,500,000
EI	0	$ 0	$ 0	$ 0
(Change from BI to EI) = (Fixed Cost Differential)				$ 0
1995				
BI	0	$ 0	$ 0	$ 0
CGM	74,000,000	8,140,000	6,660,000	1,480,000
CGA	74,000,000	$8,140,000	$6,660,000	$1,480,000
CGS	72,000,000	7,920,000	6,480,000	1,440,000
EI	2,000,000	$ 220,000	$ 180,000	$ 40,000
(Change from BI to EI) = (Fixed Cost Differential)				$ 40,000
1996				
BI	2,000,000	$ 220,000	$ 180,000	$ 40,000
CGM	76,000,000	8,360,000	6,840,000	1,520,000
CGA	78,000,000	$8,580,000	$7,020,000	$1,560,000
CGS	0	8,580,000	7,020,000	1,560,000
EI	0	$ 0	$ 0	$ 0
(Change from BI to EI) = (Fixed Cost Differential)				$ (40,000)

EXHIBIT 13–9

Reeves Company Comparison of Product Cost Flows

tiplied by the *change* in the number of units in inventory explains the differences in net income between the two methods. Whenever production and sales volumes differ and, thus, cause increases or decreases in inventory, income under the two methods will differ. If standard costs are used and remain constant over time, and if variances are expensed as immaterial, the amount of the difference can be computed as follows:

$$\begin{pmatrix}\text{Change in Number of}\\\text{Units in Inventory}\end{pmatrix} \times \begin{pmatrix}\text{Fixed Overhead}\\\text{Application Rate}\end{pmatrix} = \begin{pmatrix}\text{\$ Difference Between}\\\text{Absorption and Variable}\\\text{Costing Incomes}\end{pmatrix}$$

Using this formula for the Reeves Company data gives the following calculations:

Units in Ending Inventory	−	Units in Beginning Inventory	=	Change in # of Units	×	FOH Application Rate	=	Difference in Incomes
0	−	0	=	0	×	$.02	=	$ 0
2,000,000	−	0	=	+2,000,000	×	$.02	=	+$40,000
0	−	2,000,000	=	−2,000,000	×	$.02	=	−$40,000

If no beginning or ending inventories exist, cumulative total income under both methods will be identical. For the Reeves Company, over the three-year period, 225,000,000 Sleek Shave units are produced and 225,000,000 units are sold. Thus, all of the costs incurred (whether variable or fixed) are expensed in one year or another under both methods. The income difference in each year is solely caused by the timing of the expensing of fixed manufacturing overhead.

Whether absorption costing income is greater or less than variable costing income depends on the relationship of production to sales. In all cases, to determine the effects on net income, it must be assumed that variances from standard are immaterial and unit product costs are constant over time. Exhibit 13–10 shows the possible relationships between production and sales levels and the effects of these relationships on net income. These relationships are as follows:

▌ If production is equal to sales, absorption costing income will equal variable costing income.

▌ If production is greater than sales, absorption costing income is greater than variable costing income. This result occurs because some fixed manufacturing overhead cost is deferred as part of inventory cost on the balance sheet under absorption costing, while the total amount of fixed manufacturing overhead cost is expensed as a period cost under variable costing.

▌ If production is less than sales, income under absorption costing is less than income under variable costing. In this case, absorption costing expenses all of the current period fixed manufacturing overhead cost and releases some fixed manufacturing overhead cost from inventory where it had been deferred from a prior period.

▌ **EXHIBIT 13–10**

Production / Sales Relationships and Effects*

where P = Production and S = Sales
       AC = Absorption Costing and VC = Variable Costing

	Absorption vs. Variable Income Statement Income before Taxes	Absorption vs. Variable Balance Sheet Ending Inventory
P = S	AC = VC No difference from beginning inventory $FOH_{EI} - FOH_{BI} = 0$	No additional difference $FOH_{EI} = FOH_{BI}$
P > S (Stockpiling inventory)	AC > VC By amount of fixed OH in ending inventory minus fixed OH in beginning inventory $FOH_{EI} - FOH_{BI} = +$ amount	Ending inventory increased (by fixed OH in additional units because P > S) $FOH_{EI} > FOH_{BI}$
P < S (Selling off beginning inventory)	AC < VC By amount of fixed OH released from balance sheet beginning inventory $FOH_{EI} - FOH_{BI} = -$ amount	Ending inventory difference reduced (by fixed OH from BI charged to cost of goods sold) $FOH_{EI} < FOH_{BI}$

*The effects of the relationships presented here are based on two qualifying assumptions:
  (1) that unit costs are constant over time; and
  (2) that any fixed cost variances from standard are written off when incurred rather than being prorated to inventory balances.

NEWS NOTE

Income Manipulation Not Possible Under Variable Costing

Conceptually, variable costing has always given a more realistic income. Any "full" method of costing (absorption costing or activity-based costing) permits management to manipulate income by adjusting inventory. A company can increase income by producing more units and thus deferring more fixed costs of this period. In this way it even is possible for a company to report a profit when its sales are lower than the breakeven point. If planned income is more than sufficient in the current period, production could be reduced so that fewer fixed costs could be deferred. Accordingly, income can be reported higher or lower than in the previous period even if unit sales, prices, and costs are the same. Variable costing would eliminate this avenue for income manipulation. It is a purer system because costs are charged off as incurred.

SOURCE: Robert W. Koehler, "Triple-Threat Strategy," *Management Accounting* (October 1991), p. 34. Reprinted from *Management Accounting*. Copyright by Institute of Management Accountants, Montvale, N.J.

In the 1996 situation for Reeves Company, only current period fixed manufacturing overhead is shown on the variable costing income statement (Exhibit 13–8), so the additional amount released from beginning inventory makes absorption costing income lower (Exhibit 13–7). This process of deferring and releasing fixed overhead costs in and from inventory makes income manipulation possible under absorption costing, as discussed in the News Note on income manipulation. For this reason, some people believe that variable costing might be more useful for external purposes than absorption costing.

The basic differences between absorption and variable costing are in regard to the definition of product cost and the presentation of cost behavior on the income statement. These differences do affect the accounting process because information must be gathered and recorded somewhat differently under the two product costing methods.

EFFECTS OF COSTING METHODS ON ACCOUNTING RECORDS

Exhibit 13–11 provides four categories of differences between the absorption and variable costing methods: composition of product cost, structure of the chart of accounts, process of accumulating costs, and format of the income statement. Although these differences are divided into four categories, there are only two distinct differences between the methods. The major difference lies in the treatment of fixed manufacturing overhead for each method: FOH is a product cost for absorption costing and a period cost for variable costing. The second difference is that absorption costing does not focus on cost behavior, while variable costing does. This focus on cost behavior requires using a different chart of accounts, a different process of accumulating costs, and a different format for the income statement.

Even with their differences, the two costing methods have several underlying similarities. First, both methods use the same basic cost information. Second, the treatment of direct materials, direct labor, and variable manufacturing overhead is the same under absorption and variable costing; these costs are always considered product costs. Third, selling, general, and administrative expenses are considered period costs under both costing methods. Fourth, there are no differences between accounts other than Work in Process Inventory, Finished Goods Inventory, and the expense

ABSORPTION COSTING	VARIABLE COSTING
(1) Composition of Product Cost	
Fixed manufacturing overhead is attached to the units produced.	Fixed manufacturing overhead is recognized as a period cost (expense) when it is incurred.
(2) Structure of the Chart of Accounts	
Costs are classified according to functional categories (such as production, selling, general, and administrative).	Costs are classified according to both type of cost behavior (fixed or variable) and functional categories (manufacturing and nonmanufacturing). Mixed costs are separated into their fixed and variable components.
(3) Process of Accumulating Costs	
Costs are assigned to functional categories without the necessity of making prior analysis of behavior. All manufacturing costs are considered product costs. All nonmanufacturing costs are considered period costs.	Costs are classified and accumulated according to behavior on the basis of previous analysis. Only variable manufacturing costs are considered product costs. Fixed manufacturing costs are considered period costs. All nonmanufacturing costs are considered period costs.
(4) Format of the Income Statement	
Costs are presented on the income statement according to functional categories. This format highlights gross margin (as illustrated in Exhibit 13–3). The various functional categories present costs without regard to cost behavior. Nonmanufacturing period costs are deducted from gross margin to determine income before taxes.	Costs are presented on the income statement separately according to cost behavior. This format highlights contribution margin (as illustrated in Exhibit 13–4). Fixed manufacturing and nonmanufacturing costs are deducted from contribution margin to determine income before taxes. Costs may be further categorized by functional classifications.

▌ **EXHIBIT 13–11**

Differences Between Absorption and Variable Costing

accounts under the two methods. In short, the similarities outweigh the differences not only in number but also in importance.

Earlier in the chapter it was stated that absorption costing is used for external reporting and tax returns. However, managers might find absorption costing substantially less useful for the managerial functions of planning, controlling, and making decisions. Variable costing information provides managers with more useful information because costs are broken down and presented by cost behavior. To maintain two sets of accounting records would be both impractical and unnecessary. If only one system of records is to be maintained, the question becomes how to meet the needs of both external and internal users simultaneously.

Exhibit 13–12 presents a matrix that addresses the adjustments needed for statement presentation under the two accounting system possibilities. The accounting system that is implemented should be capable of providing external users with absorption costing statements and managers with financial information on product cost and cost behavior relative to production and sales levels.

Cell 1 depicts the use of an absorption costing accounting system and a desired absorption costing income statement presentation. In this instance, the system will automatically provide information in a functionally classified manner and no modification of the data is necessary to achieve the desired external presentation. Also, a "full" product cost is generated under this system because all manufacturing costs are classified as inventoriable.

Cell 3 indicates that using an absorption costing system, but desiring a variable costing income statement will necessitate certain information modifications. The variable costing income statement presents accounts according to cost behavior; to obtain this information, some analysis outside of the accounting system may be required. The amount of that analysis depends on the extent of data aggregation within the absorption-based system. In other words, obtaining a variable costing statement pre-

System of Cost Accumulation Employed

Desired Statement Presentation		Absorption Costing	Variable Costing
	Absorption Costing	(1) No modification of data needed.	(2) An adjusting entry is necessary to allocate fixed overhead cost to ending Work in Process Inventory, Finished Goods Inventory, and Cost of Goods Sold.
	Variable Costing	(3) Financial statements must be rebuilt according to cost behavior, perhaps requiring some analysis outside the accounting system.	(4) No modification of data needed.

sentation while using an absorption costing accounting system may require additional effort to analyze the behavior of the various costs. Most companies using absorption costing also require cost behavior information for internal purposes such as flexible budgeting. Therefore, much of the needed cost behavior information is often available. In fact, a coding system in the chart of accounts can readily classify an account as to its behavior.

Cells 2 and 4 assume that the cost accumulation system is based on the variable costing method. If a variable costing accounting system is employed and a variable costing income statement presentation is desired, no accounting difficulties are encountered since the information is already being accumulated in that format (Cell 4). However, absorption costing external financial statements will be necessary when a variable costing accumulation system is in use. In this case, a revised presentation can be developed using end-of-period working papers and working paper entries.

Assume that Reeves Company keeps its books on a variable costing basis. Exhibit 13–13 on page 534 provides the working paper entries necessary to convert the variable cost account balances to absorption costing account balances using the amounts from the exhibits indicated in the entries. These working paper revisions provide for the recognition of a fixed overhead volume variance and attach fixed manufacturing overhead to Finished Goods Inventory and Cost of Goods Sold based on, respectively, the number of units on hand or sold.

If a company had work in process on hand at the end of a period, adjusting entries would be required to attach fixed overhead to Work in Process Inventory, Finished Goods Inventory, and Cost of Goods Sold. The debits to the inventory and CGS accounts must reflect an allocation basis that approximates the results that would have been achieved had an absorption costing system been in use. Exhibit 13–14 on page 534 shows a simplified example of using a prorated allocation process and assumed amounts. If presenting expenses according to functional categories is important for income statement purposes, the fixed and variable elements of each functional category can be combined.

To summarize, it is possible to convert an absorption costing information gathering system to provide variable costing and cost behavior information and vice versa. An absorption costing chart of accounts can be modified to provide variable and fixed cost information if management so desires. A variable costing chart of accounts can

EXHIBIT 13–13

Reeves Company
Conversion from Variable
to Absorption Costing

12/31/94	Cost of Goods Sold (Exhibit 13–9)
	    Manufacturing Overhead
	    (Exhibit 13–5)
	To reclassify fixed manufacturing
	overhead costs.
		1,500,000	1,500,000

12/31/95	Finished Goods Inventory
	    (2,000,000 × $.02)
	    (Exhibit 13–9)
	Cost of Goods Sold
	    (72,000,000 × $.02)
	    (Exhibit 13–9)
	FOH Volume Variance (Exhibit 13–6)
	    Manufacturing Overhead
	    (Exhibit 13–5)
	To reclassify fixed manufacturing
	overhead costs.
		40,000
		
		1,440,000
		
		20,000
			
			1,500,000

12/31/96	Cost of Goods Sold
	    (78,000,000 × $.02)
	    (Exhibit 13–9)
	    FOH Volume Variance
	    (Exhibit 13–6)
	    Manufacturing Overhead
	    (Exhibit 13–5)
	    Retained Earnings
	To reclassify fixed manufacturing
	overhead costs.
		1,560,000	
			
			20,000
			
			1,500,000
			40,000

EXHIBIT 13–14

Converting from Variable to Absorption Costing*

Total fixed overhead = $420,000

Account balances at end of period under variable costing		% of all accounts needing to contain FOH under absorption costing	
Work in Process Inventory	$ 39,400	($ 39,400 ÷ $985,000) =	4%
Finished Goods Inventory	128,050	($128,050 ÷ $985,000) =	13%
Cost of Goods Sold	817,550	($817,550 ÷ $985,000) =	83%
Total	$985,000		100%

ADJUSTING ENTRY AT END OF PERIOD:

Work in Process Inventory ($420,000 × .04)	16,800	
Finished Goods Inventory ($420,000 × .13)	54,600	
Cost of Goods Sold ($420,000 × .83)	348,600	
Fixed Manufacturing Overhead Control		420,000

* This example assumes a homogeneous product and process. When this is not true, a more comprehensive approach to allocation should be employed.

be combined so that costs can be accumulated strictly according to functional areas. Product cost under either method can be adjusted to exclude or include fixed manufacturing overhead so as to convert from one cost accumulation process to the other. Maintaining accounting records using a variable costing system will more likely provide faster internal information for management and require less additional effort to convert to absorption costing external statements than maintaining accounting records using absorption and converting to variable costing.

THEORETICAL CONSIDERATIONS OF ABSORPTION AND VARIABLE COSTING

The basic underlying difference between absorption and variable costing is perceived by most accounting professionals to be a single issue regarding which production costs should be treated as assets (product costs) and which should be treated as expenses (period costs). Accounting literature defines *asset* as an expected future economic benefit and *product cost* as one that is incurred because of production activity. Thus, the relevant question for determining whether absorption or variable costing is more "appropriate" centers on which costs must be incurred to produce inventory and, thus, provide future economic benefits. A future economic benefit means that something has "service potential to the extent that (it averts) the necessity for incurring costs in the future."[7]

A basic proposition of absorption costing is that fixed manufacturing overhead costs are necessary production costs because they provide the basic capacity for productive activity. Products obviously cannot be produced without basic capacity; therefore the basic premise of absorption costing has theoretical merit and fixed manufacturing overhead should be included as part of product cost.

If the idea that fixed manufacturing overhead is a product cost is accepted, then the matching concept used in external reporting requires that period expenses (through Cost of Goods Sold) can only include that portion of fixed manufacturing overhead relating to the units sold during the period. Consequently, the remaining fixed overhead attaches to units that have not been sold and is carried as part of inventory cost until a future period when the sale of those units takes place.

In contrast, variable costing advocates do not consider fixed manufacturing overhead to be an asset or part of product cost. The premise underlying this philosophy is that fixed manufacturing overhead provides capacity *regardless* of whether production takes place. Fixed manufacturing overhead, then, is *not* caused by production and should not be inventoried. Since some fixed overhead costs must be incurred every period, proponents of variable costing view such overhead charges as a period rather than a product cost. Period costs are expensed when incurred and do not attach to the units produced.

Conclusions about the "rightness" or "wrongness" of absorption or variable costing depends on one's perspective and belief in what constitutes the cost of an asset. Each method has merit relative to the needs of different users of accounting information. The two basic parties interested in the output of accounting information systems are external users and internal users. Each group has different problems and needs and would prefer that information be generated in a manner most helpful to that group's particular objectives. In general, financial accounting focuses on the needs of external users of accounting information; cost and managerial accounting focus on the needs of internal or management users.

External financial readers make evaluations about an entity based on its global track record and use these evaluations in deciding whether to provide or withhold

---

[7]James M. Fremgen, "The Direct Costing Controversy—An Identification of the Issues," *Accounting Review* (January 1964), pp. 43–45.

capital to that entity. The accountant is seen by external readers primarily as a special type of historian who measures an entity's past conditions and performance and who reports these events in a consistent, standardized format. The use of absorption costing provides a long-run perspective in that product cost includes both variable costs and fixed costs.

In contrast, variable costing has long been actively endorsed by the Institute of Management Accountants for use internally by managers. Because variable costing provides information according to its current period behavior, proponents believe that it provides more useful internal cost information than does absorption costing.

Effective control of current costs is important because managers are held accountable for those costs. Attempts to control current costs are more effectively enhanced if reports present fixed costs in a lump-sum manner similar to the way in which the fixed costs are incurred—rather than having fixed costs presented on a per-unit basis. Furthermore, the magnitude of many fixed costs (for example, depreciation and management salaries) can only be influenced in the long run rather than the short run. Reporting fixed costs on a per-unit basis tends to contradict their actual behavior and, thus, may hinder a manager's ability to control those costs in the short run.

For short-run planning, controlling, and decision making, managers want information that is useful and relates to a specific task at hand. Since some managers are charged with finding the best current use of scarce resources within an organization, they seek to use decision models and information that clearly depict short-term relationships among independent and dependent variables. Because variable costing focuses on the relationship of costs to levels of activity, managers can more easily predict the immediate future consequences of present actions using variable costing information.

In contrast to the short-run perspective just discussed, many world-class companies are now taking a long-run perspective for planning, controlling, and decision making. This strategic cost management approach encourages managers to view all costs as variable in the long run. Costs currently viewed as variable generally are seen to vary with some measure of volume (or, as discussed in Chapter 5, they are unit- or

Does the periodic fixed depreciation charge for this tomato sorting equipment provide future economic benefit? Absorption costing says it does and, thus, depreciation should be allocated to products. Variable costing disagrees and assigns the cost to the income statement.

batch-level costs). Costs currently viewed as fixed are being reclassified as long-run variable costs and have often been found to vary (over some period of time) in relation to changes in some non-volume-related cost drivers.

Activity-based costing techniques (discussed in Chapter 5) suggest that costs should be accumulated over a product's life cycle rather than on a period-by-period basis and that organizational level costs not be allocated to products. Thus, a new, full-costing approach may be emerging that combines the best information of both absorption and variable costing: Products will have all true production-caused manufacturing costs attached to them (using a long-run perspective), but fixed costs (such as facility depreciation) that cannot be traced using some reasonable cost driver will be considered period expenses. Such an approach would permit management to engage in planning, controlling, and decision making for costs with a long-run perspective.

R E V I S I T I N G

THE GILLETTE COMPANY

How important is manufacturing technology to Gillette? In the shaving business, "we have more people in our R&D and engineering department designing the production equipment than the product," says Alfred M. Zeien, chairman and chief executive. Moreover, such attention has paid off: Gillette's razors and blades account for about one-third of the company's sales—but two-thirds of profits.

In a business of making lots of things that sell for very little, Gillette has honed the art of using technology to cut fractions of a cent from production costs year after year. "If we can take a couple of tenths of a cent off the cost of making a [blade] cartridge, it's worth it when you're making a billion," says DeGraan. In the just over two years it has been making Sensor, Gillette has cut unit costs by 30%, and its goal is to reduce costs a further 10% over the next two years.

[Gillette may be adamant about cutting costs, but the company is equally adamant about maintaining quality.] From start to finish, the Sensor goes through nearly 100 electronic or mechanical inspections as it moves from one station to another. By gathering and storing information in computers, the scanners can spot trends and raise red flags about things going wrong—even before they have gone wrong. This is essential to smooth operations at the plant, which makes 1.8 billion razors and blades a year with an average of seven parts each—or 34.5 million parts daily.

[Cost cutting is most likely to be in the areas of variable production overhead for two reasons. First, the company can have little impact on the amount of direct materials cost, except to the extent of negotiating long-range contracts; second, since the plant is almost fully automated, there is virtually no direct labor cost. Additionally, Gillette's fixed production costs for manufacturing equipment depreciation truly provide the "capacity to produce" because the equipment is specialized and distinct to the operation. While these costs can be allocated under absorption costing on a per-unit basis to the billions of razors produced each year, such an accounting technique provides Gillette's managers with little useful information for control purposes. Considering the fact that high-cost technology investments are one of the keys to Gillette's success, it is highly improbable that company managers, for example, would want to reduce the fixed cost of equipment depreciation per unit by buying less specialized equipment that would produce a lower quality product. Thus, absorption costing would obscure the variable cost information that is most appropriate to management's cost control and decision-making efforts.]

SOURCE: Lawrence Ingrassia, "The Cutting Edge," *Wall Street Journal* (April 6, 1992), p. R6. Reprinted by permission of the *Wall Street Journal*, © 1992 Dow Jones & Company, Inc. All rights reserved worldwide.

Absorption and variable costing are two product costing methods that differ in regard to product cost composition and income statement presentation. Under absorption costing, all manufacturing costs (both variable and fixed) are treated as product costs. The absorption costing income classifies nonmanufacturing costs according to functional areas rather than cost behavior.

Variable costing computes product cost as the sum of only the variable costs of production (direct materials, direct labor, and variable manufacturing overhead). Fixed manufacturing overhead charges are considered to be period costs and are expensed in the period in which they are incurred. The variable costing income statement classifies costs according to their behavior (variable or fixed). Variable costing is not considered an acceptable method of inventory valuation for preparing external reports or filing tax returns.

Absorption costing income differs from variable costing income for any period in which production and sales volumes differ. This difference reflects the amount of fixed manufacturing overhead that is either attached to, or released from, inventory in absorption costing as opposed to being immediately expensed in variable costing. Assuming that standard cost variances are immaterial and product cost is consistent over time, the following generalizations can be made:

1. If production is equal to sales, income under absorption costing is equal to income under variable costing because all fixed overhead is expensed in the period incurred.

2. If production is greater than sales, income under absorption costing is greater than income under variable costing because absorption costing attaches a per-unit fixed overhead cost to each unit produced but not sold during the period. This inventorying of fixed overhead is in contrast to the expensing of all fixed overhead incurred during the period under variable costing.

3. If production is less than sales, income under absorption costing is less than income under variable costing because some fixed overhead deferred in a previous period (due to units being produced but not sold) will be released from inventory as part of cost of goods sold. This release of fixed overhead means that there will be a greater amount of fixed overhead expensed on the absorption costing income statement than on the variable costing income statement.

Although absorption and variable costing are two distinct product costing methods, they definitely overlap. The objectives of both external and internal users can be accomplished by explicitly integrating cost behavior into the cost accounting system. Working paper entries can be made at the end of the period to convert one type of information to the other.

Each method takes a short-run viewpoint relative to costs and both absorption and variable costing have valid theoretical bases—each of which relates to the definition of an asset. Absorption costing proponents believe that fixed manufacturing overhead is definitely an inventoriable cost because it is typically related to having the capacity to produce. Variable costing proponents point to the fact that fixed manufacturing overhead costs are often incurred even if no production occurs to support their argument that such costs are period, rather than product, costs.

**SOLUTION
STRATEGIES**

1. Which method is being used (absorption or variable)?
   a. If absorption:
   - What is the fixed manufacturing overhead application rate?
   - What denominator capacity was used in determining the fixed manufacturing overhead application rate?
   - Is production equal to the denominator capacity used in determining the fixed manufacturing overhead application rate? If not, there is a fixed overhead volume variance that must be properly assigned to cost of goods sold and, possibly, inventories.
   - What is the cost per unit of product? (DM + DL + VOH + FOH)

   b. If variable:
   - What is the cost per unit of product? (DM + DL + VOH)
   - What is total fixed manufacturing overhead? Assign to income statement in total as a period expense.

2. What is the relationship of production to sales?
   a. Production = Sales
      Absorption costing income = Variable costing income
   b. Production > Sales
      Absorption costing income > Variable costing income
   c. Production < Sales
      Absorption costing income < Variable costing income

3. Dollar difference between absorption costing income and variable costing income = FOH application rate × Change in inventory units

4. Use dollar difference determined in part 3 to convert income and ending inventory values.

	From Absorption to Variable	From Variable to Absorption
No change in inventory	No adjustment	No adjustment
Increase in inventory	Subtract difference	Add difference
Decrease in inventory	Add difference	Subtract difference

**DEMONSTRATION
PROBLEM**

Plimsol Company's management is interested in seeing the company's absorption costing income statements for 1995 and 1996 (the first two years in operation) recast using variable costing. The company incurred total fixed manufacturing overhead of $80,000 each year and produced 25,000 and 20,000 units, respectively, each year.

The absorption costing statements based on FIFO costing follow.

	1995	1996
Net sales (a)	$300,000	$330,000
Cost of goods sold (b)	124,000	150,000
Gross margin	$176,000	$180,000
Operating expenses (c)	82,500	88,500
Net income	93,500	$ 91,500

(a) Net sales:

	1995	1996
20,000 units @ $15	$300,000	
22,000 units @ $15		$330,000

(b) Cost of goods sold:

	1995	1996
Beginning inventory	$ 0	$ 31,000
Cost of goods manufactured*	155,000	140,000
Goods available for sale	$155,000	$171,000
Ending inventory**	31,000	21,000
Cost of goods sold	$124,000	$150,000

(c) Analysis of operating expenses:

	1995	1996
Variable	$ 60,000	$ 66,000
Fixed	22,500	22,500
Total	$ 82,500	$ 88,500

* CGM

	1995	1996
25,000 units @ $6.20 (of which $3 is variable)	$155,000	
20,000 units @ $7.00 (of which $3 is variable)		$140,000

** EI

	1995	1996
5,000 units @ $6.20	$ 31,000	
3,000 units @ $7.00		$ 21,000

Required:

a. Recast the 1995 and 1996 income statements on a variable costing basis.

b. Reconcile net incomes for each year between absorption and variable costing.

Solution to Demonstration Problem

a.

	1995	1996
Net sales	$300,000	$330,000
Variable cost of goods sold	60,000	66,000
Product contribution margin	$240,000	$264,000
Variable operating expenses	60,000	66,000
Total contribution margin	$180,000	$198,000
Fixed costs:		
Manufacturing	$ 80,000	$ 80,000
Operating	22,500	22,500
Total fixed costs	$102,500	$102,500
Net income	$ 77,500	$ 95,500

b. Reconciliation 1995:

Absorption costing net income	$93,500
− Fixed manufacturing overhead in ending inventory ($3.20 × 5,000)	(16,000)
Variable costing net income	$77,500

Reconciliation 1996:

Absorption costing net income	$91,500
+ Fixed manufacturing overhead released from beginning inventory ($3.20 × 5,000)	16,000
− Fixed manufacturing overhead in ending inventory ($4.00 × 2,000)	(12,000)
Variable costing net income	$95,500

QUESTIONS

1. What are the four dimensions of product costing systems? Which of these dimensions are affected by the choice of variable versus absorption costing?

2. In what ways does absorption costing differ from variable costing?

3. What is the difference between absorption and variable costing in the treatment of fixed overhead?

4. What is a functional classification of costs? What is a behavioral classification of costs?

5. Which product costing alternative, variable or absorption, is generally required for external reporting? Why?

6. How do the income statement formats for variable and absorption costing differ?

7. If standard costs rather than actual costs are used to cost products, what types of variances can arise under absorption costing? Under variable costing? Why is there a difference?

8. Why does the variable costing approach provide more useful information for making internal decisions?

9. Why is income under absorption costing higher (lower) than under variable costing in years when production exceeds (is below) sales?

10. Can one accounting system produce both absorption and variable costing results? Explain.

11. If a company employs a variable costing system, how would a conversion be made to absorption costing information if there were both Work in Process and Finished Goods inventories? Only Finished Goods Inventory?

12. Given that most firms only maintain one set of books, which must generate both variable and absorption cost data, why is it advantageous to keep the books on a variable costing basis rather than an absorption costing basis?

13. Morgan Cyclery, a manufacturer with heavy investments in property, plant, and equipment, is presently using absorption costing for both external and internal reporting. The management of Morgan Cyclery is considering using variable costing for internal reporting purposes. What would be the rationale for using variable costing for internal reporting? Assuming that the quantity of ending inventory is higher than the quantity of beginning inventory, would operating income using variable costing be different from operating income using absorption costing? If so, would it be higher or lower? Discuss the rationale for your answer. *(CPA adapted)*

14. How does the emerging strategic cost management perspective blend the concepts of variable and absorption costing in the context of long-term decision making?

EXERCISES

15. *(Ending inventory valuation; absorption vs. variable costing)* Nogales Leather Products Co. produces leather purses. In July 1994, the company manufactured 25,000 purses. July sales were 23,400 purses. The cost per purse for the 25,000 purses produced was:

Direct material	$12.00
Direct labor	5.00
Variable overhead	3.50
Fixed overhead	4.50
Total	$25.00

There was no beginning inventory for July.
   a. What is the value of ending inventory using absorption costing?
   b. What is the value of ending inventory using variable costing?
   c. Which accounting method, variable or absorption, would have produced the higher net income for July?

16. *(Absorption vs. variable costing)* The data below were taken from records of the Super Clip Lawn Mower Company. The company uses variable costing. The data relate to the company's first year of operation.

Units produced:	20,000
Units sold:	17,500

Variable cost per unit:

Direct materials	$38
Direct labor	17
Variable overhead	7
Variable selling costs	12

Fixed costs:

Selling and administration	$750,000
Manufacturing	250,000

How much higher (or lower) would the company's first-year net income have been if the company had used absorption costing rather than variable costing? Show computations.

17. *(Production cost; absorption vs. variable costing)* The Clean-N-Brite Dish Soap Co. began business in 1994. Production for the year was 100,000 bottles of dish soap and sales were 98,000 bottles. Costs incurred during the year were:

Chemicals used	$28,000
Direct labor	13,000
Variable overhead	24,000
Fixed overhead	12,000
Variable selling expenses	5,000
Fixed selling and administrative expenses	14,000
Total actual costs	$96,000

   a. What was the actual production cost per bottle under variable costing? Under absorption costing?
   b. What was variable Cost of Goods Sold for 1994 under variable costing?
   c. What was Cost of Goods Sold for 1994 under absorption costing?
   d. What was the value of ending inventory under variable costing? Under absorption costing?
   e. How much fixed overhead was charged to expense in 1994 under variable costing? Under absorption costing?

18. *(Net income; absorption vs. variable costing)* Portaphone manufactures portable wireless telephones. Throughout 1994, unit variable cost remained constant and

fixed overhead was applied at the rate of $4 per unit. The net income using the variable costing method was $76,000 for July 1994. Beginning and ending inventories for July were 17,000 and 15,000 units, respectively.

a. Calculate net income under absorption costing assuming no variances.

b. Assume that the company's beginning and ending inventories were 15,000 and 18,000 units, respectively. Calculate net income under absorption costing.

19. *(Net income; absorption vs. variable costing)* The Dream Box produces a single product, a cedar storage chest, with the following per-unit production and selling costs:

Direct materials	$15
Direct labor	12
Variable overhead	3
Fixed overhead	5
Variable selling cost	2

Fixed overhead is applied to products based on an estimated 50,000 units to be produced each year. Fixed selling cost per year is $120,000 and the selling price per unit is $100.

a. What is product cost on an absorption costing basis?

b. What is product cost on a variable costing basis?

c. Assuming no beginning inventories exist, if the company produces 50,000 units this year and sells 40,000 units, what will be absorption costing net income? What will be variable costing net income?

20. *(Variable costing)* Automotive Electric Co., a maker of automotive distributor caps, had the following operating statistics for its first year in business, which ended December 31, 1994:

Sales (45,000 caps)	$360,000	
Production (75,000 caps)		

	Variable Costs	Fixed Costs
Production costs:		
Direct materials	$150,000	
Overhead	37,500	$56,250
Direct labor	225,000	
Nonproduction costs:		
Selling	90,000	40,000
Administrative		80,000
Financing		30,000

Prepare a variable costing income statement, ignoring income taxes.

21. *(Reconciliation of variable and absorption costing)* Use the information presented in Exercise 20.

a. Prepare an absorption costing income statement, ignoring income taxes.

b. Reconcile and explain the differences in the net incomes calculated under variable and absorption costing.

c. Assuming no Work in Process Inventory, what journal entry would be made to convert from a variable costing system to absorption costing information?

22. *(Standard costing; variable and absorption costing)* Southern Belle Co. manufactures women's stick deodorant. The company uses a standard costing system. Presented below are data pertaining to the company's operations for 1994.

Production for the year	180,000 units
Sales for the year (sales price per unit, $1.25)	195,000 units
Beginning 1994 inventory	35,000 units

COST PLANNING

COST-VOLUME-PROFIT ANALYSIS

LEARNING OBJECTIVES

After completing this chapter, you should be able to answer these questions:

1. Why and how is the breakeven point computed?
2. How do costs, revenues, and contribution margin interact with changes in an activity base (volume)?
3. How can cost-volume-profit (CVP) analysis be used by a company?
4. How does CVP analysis differ between single- and multi-product firms?
5. How are margin of safety and operating leverage concepts used in business?
6. What are the underlying assumptions of CVP analysis?
7. *(Appendix)* How are breakeven charts and profit-volume graphs constructed?

INTRODUCING

FRESH FROM TEXAS

"When you start in a business, you tend to do anything for volume without thinking how it's going to affect the bottom line." Now Jane and Bob Phipps, co-owners of Fresh From Texas, a San Antonio vegetable firm, know better.

[In 1987,] the Phippses were growing and distributing alfalfa sprouts and mung beans, and the markets were weakening. [They] had distributed tofu, or soybean curd, for another producer, and they were making good money on distribution alone. So they decided to try making the product themselves.

It took about three months to start processing tofu, Jane Phipps says. But the biggest blunder they committed, she says, was investing 10 percent of a year's gross into a product that was only 4 percent of sales. "We bought all the equipment without saying 'What percentage of our sales is tofu?' And, 'If sales increase, what percentage are they going to have to increase to justify [the investment]?' We've been losing money every month."

To offset the loss, they've balanced costs and volume elsewhere to increase profits. For example, before agreeing to supply items such as fresh, cut broccoli in bulk to a large grocery chain in 1989, the Phippses carefully analyzed all costs. They had five employees cut up a crate of broccoli, and the Phippses calculated their waste from cutting the broccoli heads into florets. They estimated the time spent bagging the products and multiplied that by the average wage rate to approximate labor costs. They also added up costs of product packaging, including artwork and printing of bags and shipping boxes. Finally, they calculated delivery costs.

All those little steps kept them from repeating their big tofu mistake. "In our market, the processing part of it is very competitive," Jane Phipps says, but "you have to quote a price where you can make a profit."

SOURCE: Bradford McKee, "Impressive Volume, But Does It Make Money?" *Nation's Business* (November 1991), p. 10. Excerpted by permission, *Nation's Business,* November 1991. Copyright U.S. Chamber of Commerce.

All businesses must be aware of the relationships among their product costs, selling prices, and volumes. Changing one of these essential ingredients in the income mix can affect the other amounts. For example, before increasing advertising expenditures, the owners of Fresh From Texas need to determine whether the projected increase in sales volume will generate enough contribution margin to offset the increased cost. Alternatively, as they did before adding broccoli florets to the Fresh From Texas product line, the Phippses needed to compare the additional product, labor, and overhead costs that would be incurred and analyze those costs in relation to the projected increased revenue. Such analysis allows future costs and revenues to be planned for and controlled as they occur.

Chapter 1 states that planning and controlling are two essential management functions. Planning emphasizes a goal orientation for the *future*, which means there is uncertainty or risk associated with this managerial function. Access to information related to the task or problem under consideration reduces uncertainty. In contrast, the function of control is performed *currently* by comparing actual performance to

559

preestablished plans. Such comparisons use information on company objectives and achievements.

This chapter focuses on understanding how costs, volume, and profits interact. Changes in one component (such as an increase in volume) will cause changes in other components (such as an increase in variable costs). Understanding these relationships can help in predicting future conditions (planning) and explaining, evaluating, and acting on past results (control). The cost-volume-profit model helps to link cost behavior and sales volume in a way that assists managers to plan and control.

DEFINITION AND USES OF CVP ANALYSIS

Cost-volume-profit analysis

Examining shifts in costs and volume and their resulting effects on profit is called **cost-volume-profit (CVP) analysis**. This analysis is applicable in all economic sectors, including manufacturing, wholesaling, retailing, and service industries. CVP can be used by managers to plan and control more effectively because it allows them to concentrate on the relationships among revenues, costs, volume changes, taxes, and profits. The CVP model can be expressed through a formula or, as graphically illustrated in the chapter appendix.

All costs, regardless of whether they are product, period, variable, or fixed, are considered in the CVP model. The analysis is usually performed on a company-wide basis. The same basic CVP model and calculations can be applied to a single- or multiproduct business.

Breakeven point

CVP analysis has wide-range applicability. It can be used to determine a company's **breakeven point** (BEP), which is that level of activity, in units or dollars, at which total revenues equal total costs. At breakeven, the company's revenues simply cover its costs; thus, the company incurs neither a profit nor a loss on operating activities. Companies, however, do not wish merely to "break even" on operations. The breakeven point is calculated merely to establish a point of reference. Knowing BEP, managers are better able to set sales goals that should generate income from operations rather than produce losses. CVP analysis can also be used to calculate the sales volume necessary to achieve a desired target profit. Target profit objectives may be stated as either a fixed or variable amount on a before- or after-tax basis. Since profit cannot be achieved until the breakeven point is reached, the starting point of CVP analysis is BEP.

THE BREAKEVEN POINT

Finding the breakeven point first requires an understanding of company revenues and costs. A short summary of revenue and cost assumptions is presented at this point to provide a foundation for CVP analysis. These assumptions, and some challenges to them, are discussed in more detail at the end of the chapter.

Relevant range: A primary assumption is that the company is operating within the relevant range of activity specified in determining the revenue and cost information used in each of the following assumptions.[1]

Revenue: Revenue per unit is assumed to remain constant; fluctuations in per unit revenue for factors such as quantity discounts are ignored. Thus, total revenue fluctuates in direct proportion to level of activity or volume.

Variable costs: On a per unit basis, variable costs are assumed to remain constant. Therefore, total variable costs fluctuate in direct proportion to level of activity or volume. Note that assumed variable cost behavior is the same as assumed revenue behavior. Variable

---

[1] Relevant range is the range of activity over which a variable cost per unit will remain constant and a fixed cost will remain fixed in total. Relevant range is discussed in Chapter 2.

production costs include direct materials, direct labor, and variable overhead; variable selling cost includes charges for items such as commissions and shipping. Variable administrative costs may exist in areas such as purchasing.

Fixed costs: Total fixed costs are assumed to remain constant and, as such, per unit fixed cost decreases as volume increases. (Fixed cost per unit would increase as volume decreases.) Fixed costs include both fixed manufacturing overhead and fixed selling and administrative expenses.

Mixed costs: Mixed costs must be separated into their variable and fixed elements before they can be used in CVP analysis. Any method (such as regression analysis) that validly separates these costs in relation to one or more predictors may be used. After being separated, the variable and fixed cost components of the mixed cost take on the assumed characteristics mentioned above.

An important amount in breakeven and CVP analysis is **contribution margin** (CM), which may be defined on either a per unit or total basis. Contribution margin per unit is the difference between the selling price per unit and the variable production, selling and administrative costs per unit. Unit contribution margin is constant because revenue and variable cost have been defined as remaining constant per unit. Total contribution margin is the difference between total revenues and total variable costs for all units sold. This amount fluctuates in direct proportion to sales volume. On either a per unit or total basis, contribution margin indicates the amount of revenue remaining after all variable costs have been covered.[2] This amount contributes to the coverage of fixed costs and the generation of profits.

Data needed to compute the breakeven point and perform CVP analysis are given in the income statement shown in Exhibit 14–1 for Short Sprouts, a small recently opened company that grows and sells alfalfa sprouts. The company sells its alfalfa sprouts exclusively by the pound and has a relevant range of 25,000 to 45,000 pounds per month. The company's production process is described as follows.

Alfalfa sprout seeds are purchased by the pound. The seeds are planted and, after five days, yield approximately ten pounds of sprouts per one pound of seed. The sprouts must be watered every three hours, 24 hours a day. The water provides nu-

Contribution margin

	Total	Per Unit	Percent
Sales (30,000 pounds)	$22,500	$.750	100%
Variable Costs:			
Production	$13,950	$.465	62%
Selling	900	.030	4%
Total Variable Cost	14,850	$.495	66%
Contribution Margin	$ 7,650	$.255	34%
Fixed Costs:			
Production	$ 2,000		
Selling and administrative	295		
Total Fixed Cost	2,295		
Income Before Income Taxes	$ 5,355		

▌ EXHIBIT 14–1
Short Sprouts Income Statement for the Month Ended September 30, 1994

_____

[2] Contribution margin refers to the total contribution margin discussed in Chapter 13 rather than product contribution margin. Product contribution margin is simply the difference between revenue and total variable *production* costs.

trients, but also serves an important cooling function. When sprouts are growing, they produce significant heat; so much so that, if the temperature were not constant, the sprouts would cook themselves before being harvested. When harvested, the sprouts are moved along a water conveyor system to a wash tank and then to a spin dryer before being packaged.[3] Because of this process, the company's variable water cost is quite high. Other variable costs, excluding seeds and water, are for direct labor to plant and harvest the seeds and package the sprouts, for plastic boxes for the sprouts, and for electricity. Fixed costs include depreciation and insurance on the building and equipment and supervision.

FORMULA APPROACH TO BREAKEVEN

The formula approach to breakeven analysis uses an algebraic equation to calculate the exact breakeven point. In this analysis, sales, rather than production, activity is the focus for the relevant range. The equation represents the variable costing income statement presented in Chapter 13 and shows the relationships among revenue, fixed cost, variable cost, volume, and profit as follows:

$$R(X) - VC(X) - FC = P$$

where   R = revenue (selling price) per unit
          X = number of units
       R(X) = total revenue
         VC = variable cost per unit
      VC(X) = total variable cost
         FC = total fixed cost
          P = profit

Since the above equation is simply a formula representation of an income statement, P can be set equal to zero so that the formula indicates a breakeven situation. At the point where P = $0, total revenues are equal to total costs and breakeven point (BEP) in units can be found by solving the equation for X.

$$R(X) - VC(X) - FC = \$0$$
$$R(X) - VC(X) = FC$$
$$(R - VC)(X) = FC$$
$$X = FC \div (R - VC)$$

Breakeven point volume is equal to total fixed cost divided by the revenue per unit minus the variable cost per unit. Using the operating statistics shown in Exhibit 14-1 for Short Sprouts ($.75 selling price per pound, $.495 variable cost per pound, and $2,295 of total fixed costs), breakeven point for the company is calculated as:

$$\$.75(X) - \$.495(X) - \$2,295 = \$0$$
$$\$.75(X) - \$.495(X) = \$2,295$$
$$(\$.75 - \$.495)(X) = \$2,295$$
$$X = \$2,295 \div (\$.75 - \$.495)$$
$$X = 9,000 \text{ pounds of alfalfa sprouts}$$

---

[3]Diana Sultenfuss, "Fresh From Texas Finds Greener Pastures in San Antonio," *San Antonio Light* (February 9, 1992), p. 3.

Revenue minus variable cost is contribution margin. Thus, the formula can be shortened by using the contribution margin to find BEP.

$$(R - VC)(X) = FC$$
$$(CM)(X) = FC$$
$$X = FC \div CM$$

where   CM = contribution margin per unit

Short Sprouts' contribution margin is $.255 per pound ($.75 − $.495). The calculation for BEP using the abbreviated formula is $2,295 ÷ $.255 or 9,000 pounds.

Breakeven point can be expressed either in units (or pounds, in the case of Short Sprouts) or dollars of revenue. One way to convert a unit breakeven point to dollars is to multiply units by the selling price per unit. For Short Sprouts, breakeven point in sales dollars is $6,750 (9,000 pounds × $.75 per pound).

Another method of computing breakeven point in sales dollars requires the computation of a **contribution margin** (CM) **ratio**. The CM ratio is calculated as contribution margin divided by revenue and indicates what proportion of revenue remains after variable costs have been covered. The CM ratio can be calculated using either per unit or total revenue minus variable cost information. Subtracting the CM ratio from 100 percent gives the **variable cost** (VC) **ratio**, which represents the variable cost proportion of each revenue dollar.

Contribution margin ratio

Variable cost ratio

The contribution margin ratio allows the breakeven point to be determined even if unit selling price and unit variable cost are not known. Dividing total fixed cost by CM ratio gives the breakeven point in sales dollars. The derivation of this formula is as follows:

$$Sales - [(VC\%)(Sales)] = FC$$
$$(1 - VC\%)Sales = FC$$
$$Sales = FC \div (1 - VC\%)$$

$$since\ (1 - VC\%) = CM\%$$

$$Sales = FC \div CM\%$$

where   VC% = the % relationship of variable cost to sales
            CM% = the % relationship of contribution margin to sales

Thus, the variable cost ratio plus the contribution margin ratio is equal to 100%.

The contribution margin ratio for Short Sprouts is given in Exhibit 14–1 as 34% ($.255 ÷ $.75). The company's computation of dollars of breakeven sales is $2,295 ÷ .34 or $6,750. The BEP in units can be determined by dividing the BEP in sales dollars by the unit selling price or $6,750 ÷ $.75 = 9,000 pounds.

The breakeven point provides a starting point for planning future operations. Managers want to earn operating profits rather than simply cover costs. Substituting an amount other than zero for the profit (P) term in the breakeven formula converts breakeven analysis to cost-volume-profit analysis.

USING COST-VOLUME-PROFIT ANALYSIS

CVP analysis requires the substitution of known amounts in the formula to determine an unknown amount. The formula mirrors the income statement when known amounts are used for selling price per unit, variable cost per unit, volume of units, and fixed costs to find the amount of profit generated under given conditions.

A more pervasive and significant application of CVP analysis is to set a desired target profit and focus on the relationships between it and known income statement amounts to find an unknown. A common unknown in such applications is volume because managers want to know what quantity of sales needs to be generated to produce a particular amount of profit. Sometimes, as indicated in the News Note "Customers Wouldn't Pay the Price," the volume answer that results from a specified selling price may prove to be unrealistic.

Selling price is not assumed to be as common an unknown as volume because selling price is often market-related and not a management decision variable. Additionally, since selling price and volume are often directly related and certain costs are considered fixed, managers may use CVP to determine how high variable cost may be and still allow the company to produce a desired amount of profit. Variable cost may be affected by modifying product specifications or material quality or by being more efficient or effective in the production, service, and/or distribution process(es).

Profits may be stated as either a fixed or variable amount and on either a before- or after-tax basis. The following examples continue the Short Sprouts example using different amounts of target profit.

Fixed Amount of Profit

Since contribution margin represents the amount of sales dollars remaining after variable costs are covered, each dollar of CM generated by product sales goes first to cover fixed costs and then to produce profits. *After the breakeven point is reached, each dollar of contribution margin is a dollar of profit.*

Before Taxes.   Profits are treated in the breakeven formula as additional costs to be covered. The inclusion of a target profit changes the formula from a breakeven to a CVP equation.

$$R(X) - VC(X) - FC = PBT$$
$$R(X) - VC(X) = FC + PBT$$
$$X = (FC + PBT) \div (R - VC)$$
$$or$$
$$X = (FC + PBT) \div CM$$

where   PBT = fixed amount of profit before taxes

Breaking even on any product (including bean sprouts) means that all variable and fixed costs have been covered by revenues. But breaking even isn't a company goal at Fresh From Texas—profits are!

NEWS NOTE

Customers Wouldn't Pay the Price

Looking back on the 1992 [TripleCast pay-per-view Summer Olympics] effort, executives at NBC and Cablevision readily concede they vastly overestimated viewer desire for tuning in to an overdose of the Olympic Games, about 1,080 hours (half of it live and unedited) on three cable channels over 15 days. They had first hoped for three million or more subscribing homes, then 2.8 million, then reduced that projection to perhaps two million homes by the time the Games began. Instead, they signed up only 250,000.

Viewers, used to decades of free network coverage, proved to be very reluctant to pay for Olympics programming. Many cable-TV executives also say that, given that reluctance, NBC sharply overpriced the package, charging $125 for the full 15 days and $29.95 a day for individual orders. Even after the price was cut by one-third, most viewers still refused to sign up.

Even if NBC and Cablevision had reached their goal of two million homes, they stood to run a loss on the pay-per-view project, depending on how the costs are accounted for. NBC assigned $100 million of its total $401 million in Olympics rights fees to the pay-per-view portion of its coverage. It also spent about $75 million in additional production and marketing costs for the cable venture.

At 250,000 homes, NBC would take in only about $31 million and it must give about a 40% portion to cable operators. That would push the total losses past $150 million; Cablevision's portion of that loss is believed to be limited to $50 million.

To reach their original financial goal of $150 million in gross revenues, NBC would have had to sign up 7.3 million subscribers for each daily package.

SOURCES: Mark Robichaux, "Pay-Per-View Games: Down But Not Out," *Wall Street Journal* (August 7, 1992), p. B1, B8; Mark Robichaux and Kevin Goldman, "Games on Cable Fail to Attract Late Subscribers," *Wall Street Journal* (July 29, 1992), p. B1, B3. Reprinted by permission of the *Wall Street Journal,* © 1992 Dow Jones & Company, Inc. All rights reserved worldwide.

Short Sprouts' management wants to produce a before-tax profit of $12,750. To do so, the company must sell 59,000 pounds of alfalfa sprouts that will generate $44,250 of revenue. These calculations are shown in Exhibit 14–2 on page 566.

After Taxes. Income taxes represent a significant influence on business decision making. Managers need to be aware of the effects of income tax in choosing a target profit amount. A company desiring to have a particular amount of net income must first determine the amount of income that must be earned on a before-tax basis, given the applicable tax rate. The CVP formulas that designate a fixed after-tax net income amount are:

$$PBT = PAT + [(TR)(PBT)] \text{ and}$$
$$R(X) - VC(X) - FC = PAT + [(TR)(PBT)]$$

where   PAT = fixed amount of profit after taxes
        PBT = fixed amount of profit before taxes
        TR = tax rate

PAT is further defined so that it can be integrated into the original CVP formula:

$$PAT = PBT - [(TR)(PBT)] \text{ or}$$
$$PBT = PAT \div (1 - TR)$$

Substituting into the formula,

$$R(X) - VC(X) = FC + PBT$$
$$(R - VC)(X) = FC + [PAT \div (1 - TR)]$$
$$CM(X) = FC + [PAT \div (1 - TR)]$$

■ **EXHIBIT 14–2**
**Short Sprouts CVP
Analysis—Fixed Amount
of Profit Before Taxes**

In units:

PBT desired = $12,750

$$R(X) - VC(X) = FC + PBT$$
$$CM(X) = FC + PBT$$
$$(\$.75 - \$.495)X = \$2,295 + \$12,750$$
$$\$.255X = \$15,045$$
$$X = \$15,045 \div \$.255 = 59,000 \text{ pounds}$$

In sales dollars:

$$Sales = (FC + PBT) \div CM \text{ ratio}$$
$$= \$15,045 \div .34 = \$44,250$$

Assume the managers at Short Sprouts want to earn $12,240 of profit after taxes and the company's marginal tax rate is 20 percent. The number of pounds of alfalfa sprouts and dollars of sales needed are calculated in Exhibit 14–3.

Variable Amount of Profit

Managers may wish to state profits as a variable amount so that, as units are sold or sales dollars increase, profits will increase at a constant rate. Variable amounts of profit may be stated on either a before- or after-tax basis. Profit on a variable basis can be stated either as a percent of revenues or a per unit profit. The CVP formula must be adjusted to recognize that profit (P) is related to volume of activity.

■ **EXHIBIT 14–3**
**Short Sprouts CVP
Analysis—Fixed Amount
of Profit After Taxes**

In units:

PAT desired = $12,240; tax rate = 20%

$$PBT = PAT \div (1 - TR)$$
$$PBT = \$12,240 \div (1 - .20)$$
$$= \$12,240 \div .80$$
$$= \$15,300 \text{ necessary profit before tax}$$

$$CM(X) = FC + PBT$$
$$\$.255X = \$2,295 + \$15,300$$
$$\$.255X = \$17,595$$
$$X = \$17,595 \div \$.255 = 69,000 \text{ pounds}$$

In sales dollars:

$$Sales = (FC + PBT) \div CM \text{ ratio}$$
$$= (\$2,295 + \$15,300) \div .34$$
$$= \$17,595 \div .34 = \$51,750$$

Before Taxes. This example assumes that the variable amount of profit is related to the number of units sold. The adjusted CVP formula for computing the necessary unit volume of sales to earn a specified variable amount of profit before taxes per unit is:

$$R(X) - VC(X) - FC = P_uBT(X)$$

where P_uBT = variable amount of profit per unit before taxes

Moving all the Xs to the same side of the equation and solving for X (volume) gives the following:

$$R(X) - VC(X) - P_uBT(X) = FC$$
$$CM(X) - P_uBT(X) = FC$$
$$X = FC \div (CM - P_uBT)$$

The variable profit is treated in the CVP formula as if it were an additional variable cost to be covered. This treatment effectively "adjusts" the original contribution margin and contribution margin ratio. When setting the desired profit as a percentage of selling price, the profit percentage cannot exceed the contribution margin ratio. If it does, an infeasible problem is created since the "adjusted" contribution margin is negative. In such a case, the variable cost percentage plus the desired profit percentage would exceed 100 percent of the selling price—such a condition cannot occur.

Assume that the president of Short Sprouts wants to know what level of sales (in pounds and dollars) would be required to earn a 16 percent before-tax profit on sales. The calculations shown in Exhibit 14–4 provide the answers to these questions.

▍EXHIBIT 14–4
Short Sprouts CVP Analysis—Variable Amount of Profit Before Taxes

In units:

P_uBT desired = 16% on sales revenues
P_uBT = .16($.75) = $.12

$$CM(X) - P_uBT(X) = FC$$
$$\$.255X - \$.12X = \$2,295$$
$$\$.135X = \$2,295$$
$$X = \$2,295 \div \$.135 = 17,000 \text{ pounds}$$

In sales dollars the following relationships exist:

	PER POUND	PERCENT
Selling price	$.750	100%
Variable costs	(.495)	(66%)
Variable profit	(.120)	(16%)
"Adjusted" contribution margin	$.135	18%

$$\text{Sales} = FC \div \text{"Adjusted" CM ratio*}$$
$$= \$2,295 \div .18 = \$12,750$$

*Note that it is not necessary to have per unit data; all computations can be made with percentage information only.

After Taxes. Adjustment to the CVP formula to determine variable profits on an after-tax basis involves stating profits in relation to both volume and the tax rate. The algebraic manipulations are shown below.

$$R(X) - VC(X) - FC = P_uAT(X) + [(TR)(P_uBT(X))]$$

where P_uAT = variable amount of profit per unit after taxes

P_uAT is further defined as that it can be integrated into the original CVP formula:

$$P_uAT(X) = P_uBT(X) - [(TR)(P_uBT(X))]$$
$$P_uAT(X) = P_uBT(X)[(1 - TR)]$$
$$P_uBT(X) = [P_uAT \div (1 - TR)](X)$$

where P_uBT = variable amount of profit needed per unit before taxes

Thus, the following relationship exists:

$$R(X) - VC(X) = FC + [P_uAT \div (1 - TR)](X)$$
$$R(X) - VC(X) = FC + P_uBT(X)$$
$$CM(X) = FC + P_uBT(X)$$
$$CM(X) - P_uBT(X) = FC$$
$$X = FC \div (CM - P_uBT)$$

Short Sprouts wishes to earn a profit after taxes of 16 percent on revenue and has a 20 percent tax rate. The necessary sales in units and dollars are computed in Exhibit 14–5.

EXHIBIT 14–5

Short Sprouts CVP Analysis—Variable Amount of Profit After Taxes

In units:

P_uAT desired = 16% of revenue = .16($.75) = $.12; tax rate = 20%
$P_uBT(X) = [$.12 \div (1 - .20)]X$
$P_uBT(X) = ($.12 \div .80)X = $.15X$ profit needed before tax

$$CM(X) - P_uBT(X) = FC$$
$$\$.255X - \$.15X = \$2,295$$
$$\$.105X = \$2,295$$
$$X = \$2,295 \div \$.105 = 21,857 \text{ pounds (rounded)}$$

In sales dollars:

	PER POUND	PERCENT
Selling price	$.750	100%
Variable costs	(.495)	(66%)
Variable profit before taxes	(.150)	(20%)
"Adjusted" contribution margin	$.105	14%

Sales = FC ÷ "Adjusted" CM ratio
= $2,295 ÷ .14 = $16,393*

*The slight difference between this amount and the revenue amount generated by multiplying 21,857 pounds by $.75 per pound revenue is due to rounding.

All the preceding illustrations of CVP analysis were made using a variation of the formula approach. Solutions were not accompanied by mathematical proofs. The income statement model is an effective means of developing and presenting solutions and/or proofs for solutions to CVP applications.

The income statement approach to CVP analysis allows accountants to prepare pro forma (budgeted) statements using available information. Income statements can be used to prove the accuracy of computations made using the formula approach to CVP analysis or the statements can be prepared merely to determine the impact of various sales levels on profit after taxes (net income). Since the formula and income statement approaches are based on the same relationships, each should be able to prove the other.[4] Exhibit 14–6 proves each of the computations made in Exhibits 14–2 through 14–5 for Short Sprouts.

THE INCOME STATEMENT APPROACH

The answers provided by breakeven or cost-volume-profit analysis are valid only in relation to specific selling prices and cost relationships. Changes that occur in the company's selling price or cost structure will cause a change in the breakeven point or in the sales needed to obtain a desired profit figure. However, the effects of revenue and cost changes on a company's breakeven point or sales volume can be determined through incremental analysis.

EXHIBIT 14–6

Short Sprouts Income Statement Approach to CVP—Proof of Computations

Previous computations:
Breakeven point: 9,000 pounds
Fixed profit ($12,750) before taxes: 59,000 pounds
Fixed profit ($12,240) after taxes: 69,000 pounds
Variable profit (16% on revenue) before taxes: 17,000 pounds
Variable profit (16% on revenue) after taxes: 21,857 pounds

R = $.75 per pound; VC = $.495 per pound; FC = $2,295;
tax rate = 20% for Exhibits 14–3 and 14–5

	BASIC DATA	EX. 14–2	EX. 14–3	EX. 14–4	EX. 14–5
Pounds of sprouts sold	9,000	59,000	69,000	17,000	21,857
Sales	$6,750	$44,250	$51,750	$12,750	$16,393
Total variable costs	4,455	29,205	34,155	8,415	10,819
Contribution margin	$2,295	$15,045	$17,595	$ 4,335	$ 5,574
Total fixed costs	2,295	2,295	2,295	2,295	2,295
Profit before taxes	$ 0	$12,750	$15,300	$ 2,040 *	$ 3,279
Taxes (20%)			3,060		656
Profit after taxes (NI)			$12,240		$ 2,623**

* Desired profit before taxes = 16% on revenue; .16 × $12,750 = $2,040
** Desired profit after taxes = 16% on revenue; .16 × $16,393 = $2,623

---

[4]The income statement approach can be readily adapted to computerized spreadsheets, which can be used to quickly obtain the results of many different combinations of the CVP factors.

INCREMENTAL ANALYSIS FOR SHORT-RUN CHANGES

The breakeven point may increase or decrease, depending on the particular changes that occur in the revenue and cost factors. Other things being equal, the breakeven point will increase if there is an increase in the total fixed cost or a decrease in the unit (or percentage) contribution margin. A decrease in contribution margin could arise because of a reduction in selling price, an increase in variable cost per unit, or a combination of the two. The breakeven point will decrease if there is a decrease in total fixed cost or an increase in unit (or percentage) contribution margin. A change in breakeven point will also cause a shift in total profits or losses at any level of activity.

Incremental analysis

Incremental analysis is a process focusing only on factors that change from one course of action or decision to another. As related to CVP situations, incremental analysis is based on changes occurring in revenues, costs, and/or volume. Following are some examples of changes that may occur in a company and the incremental computations that can be used to determine the effects of those changes on the break-even point or profits. In most situations, incremental analysis is sufficient to determine the feasibility of contemplated changes and a complete income statement need not be prepared.

The basic facts related to Short Sprouts presented earlier are continued; these facts are reiterated below:

Selling price		$.750
Variable cost per pound:		
Production	$.465	
Selling	.030	.495
Contribution margin per pound		$.255
Contribution margin ratio		34%
Fixed costs per month		$2,295
Breakeven point		9,000 pounds of sprouts

All of the following examples use before-tax information to simplify the computations. After-tax analysis would require the application of a $(1 - \text{tax rate})$ factor to all profit figures.

Case #1: The company wishes to earn a before-tax profit of $5,100. How many pounds of alfalfa sprouts does it need to sell?

The incremental analysis relative to this question addresses the pounds *above* the breakeven point that must be sold. Since each dollar of contribution margin after BEP is a dollar of profit, the incremental analysis focuses only on the profit desired:

$$\$5,100 \div \$.255 = 20,000 \text{ pounds above BEP}$$

Since the BEP has already been computed as 9,000 pounds, the company must sell 20,000 pounds above the BEP or a total of 29,000 pounds.

Case #2: Short Sprouts estimates that it can sell an additional 3,600 pounds of sprouts if it spends $765 more on advertising. Should the company incur this extra fixed cost?

The contribution margin from the additional pounds of sprouts must first cover the additional fixed cost before profits can be generated.

Increase in contribution margin (3,600 pounds × $.255 CM per pound)	$918
− Increase in fixed cost	(765)
= Net incremental benefit	$153

Since the net incremental benefit is $153, the advertising campaign would result in an additional $153 in profits and, thus, should be undertaken.

An alternative computation is to divide $765 by the $.255 contribution margin. The result indicates that 3,000 pounds would be required to cover the additional cost. Since the company expects to sell 3,600 pounds, the remaining 600 pounds would produce a $.255 profit per pound or $153.

Case #3: The company estimates that, if the selling price of each pound of alfalfa sprouts is reduced to $.70, an additional 2,000 pounds per month can be sold. Should the company take advantage of this opportunity? Current sales volume, given in Exhibit 14–1, is 30,000 pounds of sprouts.

If the selling price is reduced, the contribution margin per unit will decrease to $.205 per pound ($.70 SP − $.495 VC). Sales volume will increase to 32,000 pounds (30,000 + 2,000).

Total new contribution margin	
(32,000 pounds × $.205 CM per pound)	$ 6,560
− Total fixed costs (unchanged)	(2,295)
= New profit before taxes	$ 4,265
− Current profit before taxes	
(from Exhibit 14–1)	(5,355)
= Net incremental loss	$(1,090)

Since the company will have a lower before-tax profit than is currently being generated, the company should not reduce its selling price based on this computation. Short Sprouts should investigate the possibility that the reduction in price might, in the long run, increase demand to more than the additional 2,000 pounds per month and, thus, make the price reduction more profitable.

Case #4: Short Sprouts has an opportunity to sell 10,000 pounds of its alfalfa sprouts to an exclusive health food restaurant for $.60 per pound. The sprouts will be packaged and sold under the restaurant's own label. Packaging costs will increase by $.02 per pound, but no other variable selling costs will be incurred by the company. If the opportunity is accepted, a $200 commission will be paid to the salesperson calling on this restaurant. This sale will not interfere with current sales and is within the company's relevant range of activity. Should Short Sprouts make this sale?

The new total variable cost per pound is $.485 ($.495 total current variable costs + $.02 additional variable packaging cost − $.03 current variable selling costs). The $.60 selling price minus the $.485 new total variable cost provides a contribution margin of $.115 per pound of sprouts sold to the restaurant.

Total contribution margin provided by	
this sale (10,000 pounds × $.115 CM per pound)	$1,150
− Additional fixed cost (commission) related to this sale	(200)
= Net incremental benefit	$ 950

The total contribution margin generated by the sale is more than enough to cover the additional fixed cost. Thus, the sale produces a net incremental benefit to the firm in the form of increased profits and, therefore, should be made.

Similar to all proposals, this one should be evaluated on the basis of its long-range potential. Is the commission a one-time payment? Will sales to the restaurant continue for several years? Will such sales not affect regular business in the future? Is such a sale within the boundaries of the law?[5] If all these questions can be answered "yes," Short Sprouts should seriously consider this opportunity. In addition to the direct restaurant sales potential, referral business might also arise to increase sales.

The contribution margin or incremental approach will often be sufficient to decide on the monetary merits of proposed or necessary changes. In making decisions, however, management must also consider the qualitative and long-run effects of the changes. Additional considerations include production throughput, changes in future capacity requirements, ability to control quality, ability to make timely delivery, demographics, availability of raw materials, and price and quality of raw materials.

The above examples all assume a single product company, but most businesses do not produce and/or sell a single product. The next section of the chapter deals with the more realistic, multiproduct entity.

CVP ANALYSIS IN A MULTIPRODUCT ENVIRONMENT

Companies typically produce and sell a variety of products, some of which may be related (such as dolls and doll clothes or sheets, towels, and bedspreads). To perform CVP analysis in a multiproduct company, it is necessary to assume either a constant product sales mix or an average contribution margin ratio. The constant mix assumption can be referred to as the "bag" (or "basket") assumption. The analogy is that the sales mix represents a bag of products that are sold together. For example, whenever some of Product A is sold, a set amount of Products B and C are also sold. Use of an assumed constant mix allows the computation of a weighted average contribution margin ratio for the bag of products being sold. Without the assumption of a constant sales mix, breakeven point cannot be calculated nor can CVP analysis be used effectively.[6]

In a multiproduct company, the CM ratio is weighted on the quantities of each product included in the "bag" of products. This weighting process means that the contribution margin ratio of the product making up the largest proportion of the bag has the greatest impact on the average contribution margin of the product mix.

The Short Sprouts example is continued. Because of the success of the alfalfa sprouts, company management has decided to also produce tofu. The vice president of marketing estimates that, for every four pounds of sprouts sold, the company will sell one pound of tofu. Therefore, the "bag" of products has a 4:1 ratio. The company will incur an additional $1,230.60 per month in fixed costs related to plant assets (depreciation, insurance, and so forth) needed to support a higher relevant range of production. This new relevant range is specified as 45,000 to 60,000 pounds of product per year. Exhibit 14–7 provides relevant company information and shows the breakeven computations.

Any shift in the proportion of sales mix of products will change the weighted average contribution margin and, as such, the breakeven point. If the sales mix shifts toward products with lower contribution margins, there will be an increase in the BEP and a decrease in profits unless there is a corresponding increase in total revenues. A shift toward higher margin products without a corresponding decrease in revenues will cause a lower breakeven point and increased profits, as illustrated by

---

[5]The Robinson-Patman Act (discussed in Chapter 15) addresses the legal ways companies may price their goods for sale to different purchasers.
[6]Once the constant percentage contribution margin in a multiproduct firm is determined, all situations regarding profit points can be treated in the same manner as they were earlier in the chapter. It is necessary to remember, however, that the answers reflect the "bag" assumption.

EXHIBIT 14–7
Short Sprouts CVP Analysis—Multiple Products

	ALFALFA SPROUTS		TOFU	
Product Cost Information				
Selling price	$.750	100%	$1.00	100%
Total variable cost	.495	66%	.46	46%
Contribution margin	$.255	34%	$ .54	54%

Total Fixed Costs = $2,295 previous + $1,230.60 new = $3,525.60

	SPROUTS		TOFU	TOTAL	%
Number of pounds	4		1		
Revenue per pound	$.750		$1.00		
Total revenue per "bag"		$3.00		$1.00	$4.00	100%
Variable cost per pound	.495		.46		
Total variable per "bag"		1.98		.46	2.44	61%
Contribution margin per pound	$.255		$ .54		
Contribution margin per "bag"		$1.02		$ .54	$1.56	39%

BEP in units (where B = "bags" of products)

$$CM(B) = FC$$
$$\$1.56B = \$3,525.60$$
$$B = 2,260 \text{ ''bags'' to breakeven}$$

Note: Each "bag" consists of 4 pounds of alfalfa sprouts and 1 pound of tofu; therefore, it will take 9,040 pounds of sprouts and 2,260 pounds of tofu to break even, assuming the constant 4:1 sales mix.

BEP in sales dollars (where CM ratio = weighted average CM for "bag"):

$$B = FC \div CM \text{ ratio}$$
$$B = \$3,525.60 \div .39$$
$$B = \$9,040$$

Note: The breakeven sales dollars also represent the assumed constant sales mix of $3.00 of sales of sprouts to $1.00 of sales of tofu: a 75% to 25% ratio. Thus, the company must have $6,780 ($9,040 × 75%) in sprouts sales and $2,260 in tofu sales to break even.

Proof of above computations using the income statement approach:

	SPROUTS	TOFU	TOTAL
Sales	$6,780.00	$2,260.00	$9,040.00
Variable Costs	4,474.80	1,039.60	5,514.40
Contribution Margin	$2,305.20	$1,220.40	$3,525.60
Fixed Costs			3,525.60
Net Income			$ 0.00

the financial results shown in Exhibit 14–8. This exhibit assumes that Short Sprouts sells 2,260 "bags" of product, but the mix was not in the exact proportions assumed in the breakeven computation. Instead of a 4:1 ratio, the sales mix was 3.5:1.5

EXHIBIT 14–8

Short Sprouts Effects of Product Mix Shift

	SPROUTS	TOFU	TOTAL	%
Number of pounds	3.5	1.5		
Revenue per pound	$.750	$1.00		
Total revenue per "bag"	$2.6250	$1.50	$4.1250	100.0%
Variable cost per pound	.495	.46		
Total variable per "bag"	1.7325	.69	2.4225	58.7%
Contribution margin per pound	$.255	$ .54		
Contribution margin per "bag"	$ .8925	$ .81	$1.7025	41.3%

BEP in units (where B = "bag" or mix of products)

$$CM(B) = FC$$
$$\$1.7025B = \$3,525.60$$
$$B = 2,071 \text{ "bags" to breakeven (rounded)}$$

Actual results: 2,260 "bags" with a sales mix ratio of 3.5 pounds of sprouts to 1.5 pounds of tofu; thus, the company sold 7,910 pounds of sprouts and 3,390 pounds of tofu.

	7,910 POUNDS SPROUTS	3,390 POUNDS TOFU	TOTAL
Sales	$5,932.50	$3,390.00	$9,322.50
Variable Costs	3,915.45	1,559.40	5,474.85
Contribution Margin	$2,017.05	$1,830.60	$3,847.65
Fixed Costs			3,525.60
Net Income			$ 322.05

pounds of sprouts to tofu. Income of $322.05 was generated because the company sold a higher proportion of the tofu, which has a higher contribution margin than the sprouts.

MARGIN OF SAFETY

Margin of safety

When making decisions about various business opportunities and changes in sales mix, managers often consider the size of the company's **margin of safety.** The margin of safety is the excess of a company's budgeted or actual sales over its breakeven point. It is the amount that sales can drop before reaching the breakeven point and, thus, it provides a measure of the amount of "cushion" from losses.

EXHIBIT 14–9

Short Sprouts Margin of Safety

In units: 30,000 actual − 9,000 BEP = 21,000 pounds

In sales $: $22,500 actual − $6,750 BEP = $15,750

Percentage: 21,000 ÷ 30,000 = 70%
or
$15,750 ÷ $22,500 = 70%

The margin of safety can be expressed as units, dollars, or a percentage. The following formulas are applicable:

Margin of safety in units = Actual units − Breakeven units

Margin of safety in dollars = Actual sales \$ − Breakeven sales \$

$$\text{Margin of safety \%} = \frac{\text{Margin of safety in units or \$}}{\text{Actual sales in units or \$}}$$

The breakeven point for Short Sprouts (using the original, single product data) is 9,000 units or \$6,750 of sales. The income statement for the company presented in Exhibit 14–1 shows actual sales for the month ended September 30, 1994, of 30,000 pounds or \$22,500. The margin of safety for Short Sprouts is quite high, since it is operating far above its breakeven point (see Exhibit 14–9).

The margin of safety calculation allows management to determine how close to a danger level the company is operating and, as such, provides an indication of risk. The lower the margin of safety, the more carefully management must watch sales figures and control costs so that a net loss will not be generated. At low margins of safety, managers are less likely to take advantage of opportunities that, if incorrectly analyzed or forecasted, could send the company into a loss position.

OPERATING LEVERAGE

Operating leverage

Another measure that is closely related to the margin of safety and also provides useful management information is the company's degree of operating leverage. The relationship of a company's variable and fixed costs is reflected in its **operating leverage**. Typically, highly labor-intensive organizations, such as Burger King and Connecticut Mutual Life Insurance Company, have high variable costs and low fixed costs and, thus, have low operating leverage. (An exception to this rule is a sports team, which is highly labor-intensive, but the labor costs are fixed rather than variable.)

Conversely, organizations that are highly capital intensive (such as American Airlines) or automated (such as Allen-Bradley) have a cost structure that includes low variable and high fixed costs, providing high operating leverage. Because variable costs are low relative to selling prices, the contribution margin is high. However, the high level of fixed costs means that the breakeven point also tends to be high. If selling prices are predominantly set by the market, volume has the primary impact on profitability. As they become more automated, companies will face this type of cost structure and become more dependent on volume to add profits. In the News Note on postal rates and postal volume (on page 576), the plight of the United States Postal Service illustrates the significant impact of volume on profitability in a high-fixed-cost environment.

Companies with high operating leverage have high contribution margin ratios. While such companies have to establish fairly high sales volumes to initially cover fixed costs, once those costs are covered, each unit sold after breakeven produces large profits. Thus, a small increase in sales can have a major impact on a company's profits.

Degree of operating leverage

The **degree of operating leverage** (DOL) measures how a *percentage* change in sales from the current level will affect company profits. In other words, it indicates how sensitive the company is to sales volume increases and decreases. The computation providing the degree of operating leverage factor is:

$$\text{Degree of operating leverage} = \frac{\text{Contribution margin}}{\text{Profit before taxes}}$$

This calculation assumes that fixed costs do not increase when sales increase.

Assume that Short Sprouts is currently selling 20,000 pounds of alfalfa sprouts. Exhibit 14–10 provides the income statement that reflects this sales level. At this level of activity, the company has an operating leverage factor of 1.818. If the company increases sales by 20 percent, the change in profits is equal to the degree of operating leverage multiplied by the percentage change in sales or 36.36 percent. If sales decrease by the same 20 percent, there is a negative 36.36 percent impact on profits. Exhibit 14–10 confirms these computations.

The degree of operating leverage *decreases* the further a company moves from its breakeven point. Thus, when the margin of safety is small, the degree of operating

EXHIBIT 14–10

Short Sprouts Degree of Operating Leverage

	(20,000 POUNDS) CURRENT	(24,000 POUNDS) 20% INCREASE	(16,000 POUNDS) 20% DECREASE
Sales	$15,000	$18,000	$12,000
Variable costs	9,900	11,880	7,920
Contribution margin	$ 5,100	$ 6,120	$ 4,080
Fixed costs	2,295	2,295	2,295
Profit before taxes	$ 2,805	$ 3,825*	$ 1,785**

Degree of operating leverage:
Contribution margin ÷ Profit before taxes

($5,100 ÷ $2,805)	1.818		
($6,120 ÷ $3,825)		1.600	
($4,080 ÷ $1,785)			2.286

* Profit increase = $3,825 − $2,805 = $1,020 (or 36.36% of the original profit)
** Profit decrease = $1,785 − $2,805 = $(1,020) or (−36.36% of the original profit)

$$\text{Margin of Safety \%} = \frac{\text{Margin of safety in units}}{\text{Actual sales in units}} = \frac{20,000 - 9,000}{20,000} = .55$$

$$\text{Degree of Operating Leverage} = \frac{\text{Contribution Margin}}{\text{Profit before Taxes}} = \frac{\$5,100}{\$2,805} = 1.818$$

$$\text{Margin of Safety} = \frac{1}{\text{DOL}} = \frac{1}{1.818} = .55$$

$$\text{Degree of Operating Leverage} = \frac{1}{\text{MS\%}} = \frac{1}{.55} = 1.818$$

EXHIBIT 14–11
Short Sprouts Margin of Safety and Degree of Operating Leverage Relationship

leverage is large. In fact, at breakeven, the degree of operating leverage is infinite since any increase from zero is an infinite percentage change. If a company is operating close to the breakeven point, each percentage increase in sales can make a dramatic impact on net income. As the company moves away from breakeven sales, the margin of safety increases, but the degree of operating leverage declines.

The relationship between the margin of safety and degree of operating leverage is shown below:

Margin of safety % = 1 ÷ Degree of operating leverage
Degree of operating leverage = 1 ÷ Margin of safety %

This relationship is proved in Exhibit 14–11 using the 20,000-pound sales level information for Short Sprouts. Therefore, if one of the two measures is known, the other can be easily calculated.

UNDERLYING ASSUMPTIONS OF CVP ANALYSIS

CVP analysis is a short-run model that focuses on relationships among several items—selling price, variable costs, volume, fixed costs, and profits. This model is a useful planning tool that can provide information on the impact on profits when changes are made in the cost structure or in sales levels. However, the CVP model, like other human-made models, is an abstraction of reality and, as such, does not reveal all the forces at work. It reflects reality but does not duplicate it. Although limiting the accuracy of the results, several important but necessary assumptions are made in the CVP model. These assumptions are listed below.

1. All variable cost and revenue behavior patterns are constant per unit and linear within the relevant range.

2. Total contribution margin (total revenue − total variable costs) is linear within the relevant range and increases proportionally with output. This assumption follows directly from assumption 1.

3. Total fixed cost is a constant amount within the relevant range.

4. Mixed costs can be *accurately* separated into their fixed and variable elements. While accuracy of separation may be questioned, reliable estimates can be developed from the use of regression analysis or the high-low method (discussed in Chapter 4).

5. Sales and production are equal; thus, there is no material fluctuation in inventory levels. This assumption is necessary because of the allocation of fixed costs to inventory at potentially different rates each year. This assumption requires that variable costing information (Chapter 13) be available. Since both CVP and variable costing focus on cost behavior, they are distinctly compatible with one another.

Care must be taken to select only quality produce and to properly prepare and package it. Quality products can be priced higher and costs may actually decline because of reduced waste and spoilage.

6. There will be no capacity additions during the period under consideration. If such additions were made, fixed (and, possibly, variable) costs would change. Any changes in fixed or variable costs would violate assumptions 1 through 3.

7. In a multiproduct firm, the sales mix will remain constant. If this assumption were not made, no weighted average contribution margin could be computed for the company.

8. There is either no inflation or, if it can be forecasted, it is incorporated into the CVP model. This eliminates the possibility of cost changes.

9. Labor productivity, production technology, and market conditions will not change. If any of these changes occur, costs would change correspondingly and it is possible that selling prices would change. Such changes would invalidate assumptions 1 through 3.

These assumptions not only limit the volume of activity for which the calculations can be made, they also limit the time frame for the usefulness of the calculations to that period for which the specified revenue and cost amounts remain constant. Changes in either selling prices or costs will require that new computations be made for breakeven and product opportunity analyses.

The nine assumptions listed above are the traditional ones associated with cost-volume-profit analysis. An additional assumption must also be noted in regard to the distinction of variable and fixed costs. Accountants have generally assumed that cost behavior, once classified, remained constant over periods of time as long as operations remained within the relevant range. Thus, for example, once a cost was determined to be "fixed," it would be fixed next year, the year after, and ten years from now.

Long-term variable cost

It is more appropriate to regard fixed costs as, instead, **long-term variable costs.** Over the long run, through managerial decisions, companies can lay off supervisors and sell plant and equipment items. Fixed costs are not fixed forever. In fact, in many companies, overhead costs considered to be fixed "have been the most variable and rapidly increasing costs."[7] Part of this "misclassification" has been caused by improperly specifying the drivers of the costs. As companies become less focused on production and sales volume as cost drivers, they will begin to recognize that "fixed costs" only exist under a short-term reporting period perspective.

Such a reclassification simply means that the cost drivers of the long-term variable costs will have to be specified in the breakeven and CVP analysis. The formula will need to be expanded to include these additional drivers and more information and a longer time frame will be needed to make the calculations. No longer will sales volume necessarily be the overriding nonmonetary force in the computations.

These adjustments to the CVP formula will force managers to take a long-run, rather than a short-run, view of product opportunities. Such a perspective could produce better organizational decisions. As the time frame is extended, both the time value of money and life-cycle costing become necessary considerations. Additionally, the income statement becomes less useful for developing projects that will take several years to mature.

A long-run perspective is important in a variety of circumstances, such as when variable or fixed costs arise only in the first year that a product or service is provided to a customer. As the News Note on keeping customers indicates, differing current and future period costs are very important in various businesses. Failure to consider such changes in costs can provide a distorted picture on how profits are generated and, therefore, present an improper analysis of the relationships of costs, volume, and profits.

---

[7]Robin Cooper and Robert S. Kaplan, "How Cost Accounting Distorts Product Costs," *Management Accounting* (April 1988), p. 27.

QUALITY AND COSTS

One important long-run change that may create significant short-run costs is the implementation of a total quality management (TQM) program. A TQM program, as discussed in Chapter 3, generally causes prevention costs to increase. These costs probably will not be recouped in the short run by the decreases in appraisal and failure costs. However, in the long run, appraisal and failure costs should decline and the higher-quality goods produced might command higher selling prices and sell better than the lower-quality goods produced before the TQM program. Thus, the three primary factors in determining a company's profits (costs, price, and volume) are intimately related to a fourth factor: quality.

It would seem that the costs of ensuring quality should, in the long run, outweigh the costs of having poor quality. Implementation of the TQM program could cause higher variable costs (in the form of higher-quality materials) or fixed costs (for plant assets and training). Other costs (such as those attributable to rework, redesign, and product failure) should fall after a period of time. Higher variable costs will not necessarily result in a lower contribution margin because of the possibility of higher selling prices. Higher fixed costs may only be incurred for the short-run, returning to lower levels after the implementation program is completed.

Recall that CVP behavior patterns were required to be stable for the model to produce valid results. If the CVP component elements are sensitive to continuous quality improvement efforts, they must be reevaluated frequently enough to compensate for changes that have occurred. Updating the CVP factors and their relationships for the impact of quality initiatives will help ensure the measurement of longer-run valid results.

Although efforts to improve quality may take some time to produce noticeable results, it is widely believed that continuous quality improvement will increase sales volume and productivity, lower costs, and support management's ability to adjust product and service prices. As mentioned in the previous sections, when managers analyze breakeven computations or product opportunities, they should consider both quantitative and qualitative information. In addition, managers should consider the potential benefits generated by focusing their attention more on the long run and less on the short run.

REVISITING

FRESH FROM TEXAS

Bob and Jane Phipps learned early in their business careers about breakeven points. Before the couple opened Fresh From Texas, they lived in Bismarck, North Dakota. It was in this location that Bob Phipps and a colleague designed a device to turn sprouts while the plants were growing. The device was to be sold by mail-order. Breakeven point was 5,000 units and only about 300 were ever sold.

Then, the Phipps tried growing and selling sprouts from their home. Shortly afterwards, they recognized the limitations of the scarce population of North Dakota for such a business: "Unless we started force feeding sprouts to the entire state, we couldn't make a living from a total population of 650,000," Jane quips. They relocated the business in 1981 to San Antonio when they discovered that there was no supplier of fresh sprouts in Texas. Any of the very perishable product available at that time was shipped in from California.

Their previous experiences have served them well. Fresh From Texas now processes and packages over 30 products, employs over 50 people, covers a 12,000 square foot facility, and has its own fleet of distribution trucks. From being able to rinse their crop in their kitchen sink, the Phipps now produce more than 13 tons of sprouts a week.

Even the tofu fiasco was a blessing in disguise. After recognizing why the line was producing losses, Jane and Bob Phipps are much more careful about new products. Their most recent expansion has been into packaged spinach. Before making this move, however, they spent two years planning and learning how to purchase and package a spinach that could match the buyers' standards. To start production, Fresh From Texas had to purchase a complete system of spinach processing equipment. The new operation winds around a series of conveyor belts that begin with unloading, then to dry inspection, wash, wet inspection, spin dry, and packaging. The Phipps expect that the product line will significantly increase their current $3 million of annual sales.

CHAPTER SUMMARY

Management planning includes planning for price, volume, fixed and variable costs, contribution margins, and breakeven point. The interrelationships of these factors are studied when applying cost-volume-profit (CVP) analysis. Management should understand these interrelationships and combine them effectively and efficiently for company success.

The CVP model reflects linear relationships that can be used to calculate the level of sales volume necessary to achieve target profit objectives. CVP can also be used to compute breakeven point (BEP), at which total contribution margin is equal to total fixed costs. Contribution margin equals sales minus all variable costs. BEP can be calculated using a cost-volume-profit formula that reflects basic income statement relationships. The BEP will change if the company's selling price(s) or costs change.

Since most companies do not wish to operate at breakeven, CVP analysis extends the breakeven point computation through the introduction of profit. The sales necessary to generate a desired amount of profit are computed by adding the desired profit to fixed costs and dividing that total by contribution margin. Profit may be stated as a fixed or a variable amount on a before- or after-tax basis. After fixed costs are covered, each dollar of contribution margin generated by company sales will produce a dollar of before-tax profit.

In a multiproduct firm, all breakeven and cost-volume-profit analyses are performed using an assumed constant sales mix of products. This sales mix is referred to as the "bag" assumption. Use of the bag assumption requires the computation of a weighted average contribution margin (and, thus, contribution margin ratio) for the "bag" of products being sold by the company. Answers to breakeven or CVP computations are in units or dollars of "bags" of products; these bag amounts can be converted to individual products by using the sales mix relationship.

The margin of safety (MS) of a firm indicates how far (in units, sales dollars, or a percentage) a company is operating from its breakeven point. A company's degree of operating leverage (DOL) shows what percentage increase in profit would occur given a specified percentage increase in sales from the current level. The MS% is equal to $(1 \div \text{DOL})$ and the DOL is equal to $(1 \div \text{MS\%})$.

CVP analysis enhances a manager's ability to beneficially influence current operations and to predict future operations, thereby reducing the risk of uncertainty. The model is, however, based on several assumptions that limit its ability to reflect reality. Managers may also wish to begin viewing the CVP relationships more on a long-range basis than the currently held short-range viewpoint.

APPENDIX

Graphic Approaches to Breakeven

Solutions to breakeven problems are determined in the chapter using an algebraic formula. Sometimes, however, the cost accountant may wish to present information to managers in a more visual format, such as graphs. Exhibit 14–12 graphically presents each income statement item for Short Sprouts' original data (see Exhibit 14–1) to provide visual representations of the behavior of revenue, costs, and contribution margin.

While illustrating individual behaviors, the graphs presented in Exhibit 14–12 are not very useful for determining the relationships among the various income statement categories. A **breakeven chart** can be prepared to graph the relationships among revenue, volume, and the various costs. The breakeven point on a breakeven chart is located at the point where the total cost and total revenue lines cross.

There are two approaches to preparing breakeven charts: the traditional approach and the contemporary approach. A third graphical presentation, the profit-volume graph, is closely related to the breakeven chart.

Breakeven chart

█ **EXHIBIT 14–12**
Short Sprouts Graphical Presentation of Income Statement Items

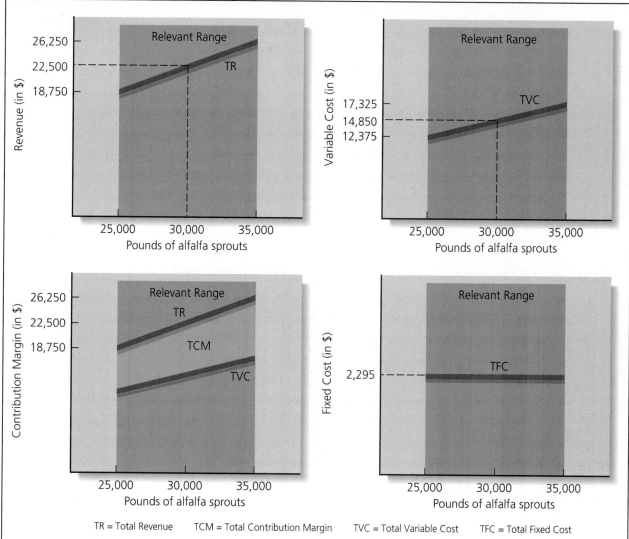

TR = Total Revenue   TCM = Total Contribution Margin   TVC = Total Variable Cost   TFC = Total Fixed Cost

NOTE: Linear functions are always assumed for total revenue, total variable cost, and total fixed cost. These functions are reflected in the basic assumptions given on pages 560–561.

Traditional Approach

The traditional approach to graphical breakeven analysis focuses on the relationships among revenues, costs, and profits (losses). This approach does *not* show contribution margin. A traditional breakeven chart for Short Sprouts is prepared as follows.

Step 1: Label each axis and graph the cost lines. The total fixed cost is drawn horizontal to the x-axis (volume). The variable cost line begins at the point where the total fixed cost line intersects the y-axis. The slope of the variable cost line is the per-unit variable cost. The resulting line represents total cost. The distance between the fixed cost and the total cost lines indicates total variable cost at each activity volume level.

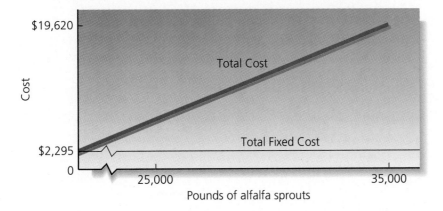

Step 2: Chart the revenue line, beginning at zero dollars. The breakeven point is located at the intersection of the revenue line and the total cost line. The vertical distance to the right of the BEP and between the revenue and total cost lines represents profits; the distance between the revenue and total cost lines to the left of the break-even point represents losses. If exact readings could be taken on the graph, the breakeven point for Short Sprouts, Inc. would be $6,750 of sales or 9,000 pounds of sprouts.

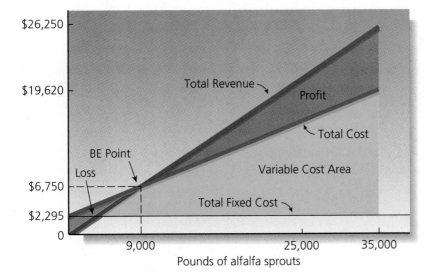

Contemporary Approach

The contribution margin provided by each level of sales volume is not apparent on the traditional breakeven chart. Since contribution margin is so important in CVP analysis, another graphical approach can be used. The contemporary approach specifically presents CM in the breakeven chart. The preparation of a contemporary breakeven chart is detailed in the following steps.

Step 1: The contemporary breakeven chart plots the variable cost first. The revenue line is plotted next and the contribution margin area is indicated.

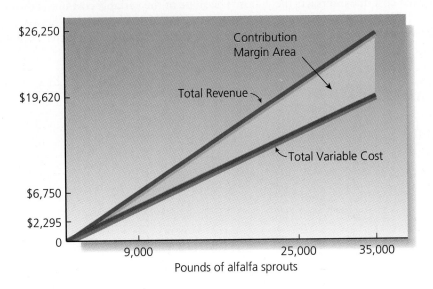

Step 2: Total cost is graphed by adding a line parallel to the total variable cost line. The distance between the total cost line and the variable cost line is the amount of fixed cost. The breakeven point is located where the revenue and total cost lines intersect. Breakeven for Short Sprouts is again shown at revenues of $6,750 and 9,000 pounds of sprouts.

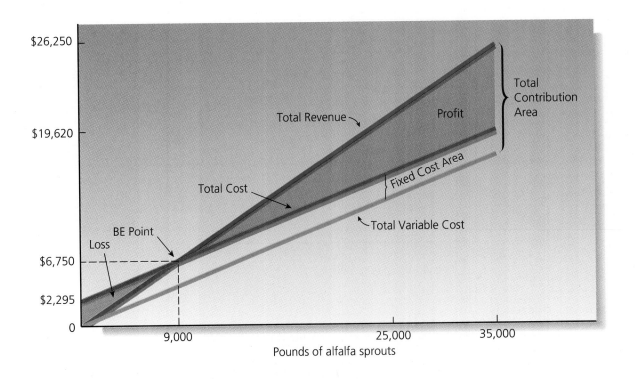

The contemporary graphic approach allows the following important observations to be made.

1. Contribution margin is created by the excess of revenues over variable costs. If variable costs are greater than revenues, no quantity of volume will ever allow a profit to be made.

2. Total contribution margin is always equal to total fixed cost plus profit or minus loss.

3. Before profits can be generated, contribution margin must exceed fixed costs.

Profit-Volume Graph

The **profit-volume** (PV) **graph** reflects the amount of profit or loss associated with each level of sales. The horizontal axis on the PV graph represents sales volume and the vertical axis represents dollars. Amounts shown above the horizontal axis are positive and represent profits; amounts shown below the horizontal axis are negative and represent losses.

Profit-volume graph

Two points are located on the graph: total fixed costs and breakeven point. Total fixed costs are shown on the vertical axis below the sales volume line as a negative amount. If no products were sold, fixed costs would still be incurred and a loss of the entire amount would result. The location of the breakeven point may be determined algebraically or by using a breakeven chart. Breakeven point in units is shown on the horizontal axis because there is zero profit/loss at that point. The last step in preparing the PV graph is to draw a profit line that passes between and extends through the two located points. Using this line, the amount of profit or loss for any sales volume can be read from the vertical axis. The profit line is really a contribution margin line and the slope of the line is determined by the unit contribution margin. The line shows that no profit is earned until the contribution margin covers the fixed costs.

The PV graph for Short Sprouts is shown in Exhibit 14–13. Total fixed costs are $2,295 and breakeven point is 9,000 pounds of alfalfa sprouts. The profit line reflects the original Exhibit 14–1 income statement data indicating profit of $5,355 at a sales level of 30,000 pounds.

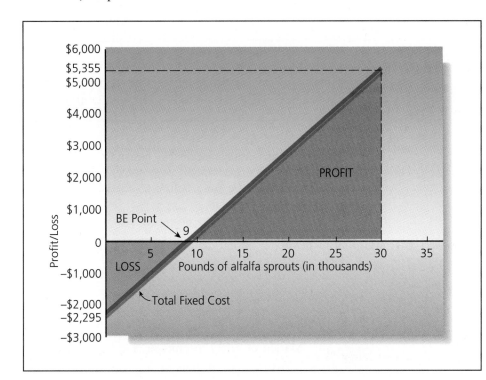

▌ EXHIBIT 14–13
Short Sprouts Profit-Volume Graph

The graphic approaches to breakeven provide detailed visual displays of breakeven point. They do not, however, provide a precise solution since exact points cannot be determined on a graph. A definitive computation of breakeven point can be found algebraically using the formula approach or a computer software application.

KEY TERMS

Breakeven chart (p. 582)

Breakeven point (p. 560)

Contribution margin (p. 561)

Contribution margin ratio (p. 563)

Cost-volume-profit analysis (p. 560)

Degree of operating leverage (p. 575)

Incremental analysis (p. 570)

Long-term variable cost (p. 578)

Margin of safety (p. 574)

Operating leverage (p. 575)

Profit-volume graph (p. 585)

Variable cost ratio (p. 563)

SOLUTION STRATEGIES

Cost-Volume-Profit

The basic equation for breakeven and CVP problems is:

$$\text{Total Revenue} - \text{Total Cost} = \text{Profit}$$

CVP problems can also be solved by using a numerator/denominator approach. All numerators and denominators and the types of problems each relate to are listed below. The formulas relate to both single- and multiproduct firms, but results for multiproduct firms are per bag and can be converted to units of individual products.

Problem Situation	Numerator	Denominator
Simple BEP in units	FC	CM
Simple BEP in dollars	FC	CM%
CVP with lump-sum profit in units	FC + P	CM
CVP with lump-sum profit in dollars	FC + P	CM%
CVP with variable profit in units	FC	CM − P_u
CVP with variable profit in dollars	FC	CM% − P_u%

where   FC = fixed cost

CM = contribution margin per unit

CM% = contribution margin percentage

P = total profit (on a before-tax basis)

P_u = profit per unit

P_u% = profit percentage per unit

To convert after-tax profit to before-tax profit, divide after-tax profit by (1 − tax rate).

Margin of Safety

Margin of safety in units = Actual units − Breakeven units

Margin of safety in dollars = Actual sales $ − Breakeven sales $

$$\text{Margin of safety \%} = \frac{\text{Margin of safety in units or \$}}{\text{Actual sales in units or \$}}$$

Degree of Operating Leverage

$$\text{Degree of operating leverage} = \frac{\text{Contribution margin}}{\text{Profit before taxes}}$$

$$\text{Predicted profit} = [1 + (\text{DOL} \times \text{Percent increase in sales})] \times \text{Current profit}$$

Doggy Deluxe makes a special automatic feeder for dogs. Each feeder sells for $25 and annual production and sales are 120,000 units. Costs for each feeder are as follows:

DEMONSTRATION PROBLEM

Direct materials	$ 6.00
Direct labor	3.00
Variable overhead	.80
Variable selling expenses	2.20
Total variable cost	$ 12.00
Total fixed overhead	$589,550

Required:

a. Calculate the unit contribution margin in dollars and the contribution margin ratio for the product.

b. Determine the breakeven point in number of feeders.

c. Calculate the dollar breakeven point using the contribution margin ratio.

d. Determine Doggy Deluxe's margin of safety in units, in sales dollars, and as a percentage.

e. Compute Doggy Deluxe's degree of operating leverage. If sales increase by 25 percent, by what percentage would before-tax income increase?

f. How many feeders must the company sell if it desires to earn $996,450 in before-tax profits?

g. If Doggy Deluxe wants to earn $657,800 after taxes and is subject to a 20 percent tax rate, how many units must be sold?

h. How many units would the company need to sell to breakeven if its fixed costs increased by $7,865? (Use original data.)

i. Doggy Deluxe has an offer to make a one-time sale of 4,000 feeders to a franchise network of dog kennels in England. This sale would not affect domestic sales or their costs, but the variable cost of the additional units will increase by $.60 for shipping and fixed costs will increase by $18,000. The selling price for each unit in this order would be $20. Based on quantitative measurement, should the company accept this offer?

Solution to Demonstration Problem

a. CM = Selling Price − Variable Cost = $25 − $12 = $13
   CM% = Contribution Margin ÷ Selling Price = $13 ÷ $25 = 52%

b. BEP = Fixed Cost ÷ CM = $589,550 ÷ $13 = 45,350 units

c. BEP = Fixed Cost ÷ CM% = $589,550 ÷ $.52 = $1,133,750
   (The answer is also equal to 45,350 units × $25 selling price per unit.)

d. Margin of Safety = Current Unit Sales − BEP in units
                    = 120,000 − 45,350 = 74,650 units
   Margin of Safety = Current Revenues − Breakeven Revenues
                    = (120,000 × $25) − $1,133,750 = $1,866,250
   Margin of Safety = 74,650 ÷ 120,000 = .6221 or 62.21%

e.   Current CM = 120,000 × $13 = $1,560,000
Current profit before tax = $1,560,000 − $589,550 = $970,450
Degree of operating leverage = $1,560,000 ÷ $970,450 = 1.608
Increase in income = 1.608 × 25% = 40.2%
Proof: 120,000 × 1.25 = 150,000 units; 150,000 × $13 = $1,950,000 CM;
$1,950,000 − $589,550 = $1,360,450 PBT; ($970,450 current PBT × 40.2%)
+ $970,450 = $1,360,571 (difference due to rounding)

f.   Target unit sales = (Fixed Cost + Desired Profit) ÷ CM
= ($589,550 + $996,450) ÷ $13 = 122,000 units

g.   Profit before tax = Profit after tax ÷ (1 − tax rate)
= $657,800 ÷ (1 − .20)
= $822,250
Target unit sales = (Fixed Cost + Desired Profit) ÷ CM
= $589,550 + $822,250) ÷ $13 = 108,600

h.   Additional units to breakeven = Increase in Fixed Costs ÷ CM
= $7,865 ÷ $13 = 605 units
New BEP in units = 45,350 + 605 = 45,955 units

i.   Additional CM for these units = $20.00 − $12.60 = $7.40; 4,000 × $7.40 =
$29,600. Because the additional CM exceeds the incremental fixed cost by

---

QUESTIONS

1. What is cost-volume-profit analysis?

2. What is the breakeven point? Why is calculating breakeven point the starting point for cost-volume-profit analysis?

3. For conducting CVP analysis, what are the important assumptions made with respect to variable costs, fixed costs, mixed costs, and revenues?

4. What is contribution margin and why does it fluctuate in direct proportion with sales volume?

5. Why is the formula for a variable costing income statement the basis for break-even or cost-volume-profit analysis?

6. If a product's fixed costs increase and its selling price and variable costs remain constant, what will happen to (a) contribution margin and (b) breakeven point?

7. How can contribution margin be used to calculate breakeven point in both units and dollars?

8. What is the contribution margin ratio? How is it used to calculate the breakeven point?

9. A company is in the 40% tax bracket. Why is desired profit after taxes divided by 60% to determine the needed before-tax profit amount?

10. What approach can an analyst use to "prove" the results she gets using the CVP equations? Of what value is this approach?

11. How is incremental analysis used in a CVP context?

12. What is meant by the "bag" or "basket" assumption and why is it necessary in a multiproduct firm? What additional assumption must be made in multiproduct CVP analysis that doesn't pertain to a single product CVP situation?

13. A multiproduct firm has a sales mix of 10 widgees to 3 squigees. Widgees have a contribution margin ratio of 45%, while squigees have a contribution margin ratio of 80%. If the sales mix changes to 8 widgees to 4 squigees, will the company have a higher or lower weighted average contribution margin ratio and a higher or lower breakeven point? Why?

14. What is operating leverage? How does it pertain to CVP analysis? What is the margin of safety? How does it apply to CVP analysis?

15. Elena's Frozen Yogurt's cost accountant has just informed the company president that the company is operating at a margin of safety of 5% with a degree of operating leverage of 62. Should the company president be pleased or upset? Why?

16. Cost-volume-profit analysis requires the use of certain assumptions. Why does the user need to keep these assumptions in mind when reflecting on the answers generated by CVP analysis?

17. "Since cost-volume-profit analysis is a quantitative tool, it is not necessary to consider qualitative factors when using it for decision-making." Is this statement true or false and why?

18. *(Appendix)* What are the purposes of a breakeven chart? What is the difference between the traditional approach and the contemporary approach to preparing a breakeven chart? Between a breakeven chart and a profit-volume graph?

19. *(Cost and revenue behavior)* The following financial data have been determined from analyzing the records of Vancouver Electric (a one-product firm):

EXERCISES

Contribution margin per unit:	$ 18
Variable costs per unit:	14
Annual fixed costs	275,000

How do each of the following measures change when product volume goes up by 1 unit at Vancouver Electric?
a. total revenue   b. total costs   c. profit before taxes

20. *(Breakeven point)* Mississippi Manufacturing has the following revenue and cost functions:

Revenue = $40 per unit
    Costs = $216,750 + $25 per unit

What is the breakeven point in units? In dollars?

21. *(Sales price computation)* Sportswear Inc. has developed a new pair of biker-type shorts. The company is planning to produce and sell 30,000 units of the new product; the annual fixed costs are $600,000 and the variable costs are 70% of the sales price. What would the selling price per unit have to be to realize a profit of $300,000?

22. *(Incremental sales)* Deep Wick Candle Co. has annual sales of $5,000,000 with variable expenses of 60% of sales and fixed expenses per month of $80,000. By how much will annual sales have to increase for Deep Wick Candle Co. to have pretax income equal to 30% of sales?

23. *(CVP, taxes)* Dr. K. Phillips is a dentist who charges (on average) $90 per patient hour for her services. She rents her office in Corpus Christi and incurs the following costs per month:

Office rent	$1,000
Secretary/receptionist/assistant	2,300
Utilities	400
Total fixed costs	$3,700

Dr. Phillips is required to acquire continuing education of 40 hours per year; she has budgeted this continuing education at an average cost of $800 per month.
    Due to the nature of her practice, variable costs are minimal, amounting only to $15 per patient hour.

a. How many patient hours does Dr. Phillips need to generate each month to break even?

b. Dr. Phillips wishes to develop a practice that will give her an after-tax income of $7,000 per month. She is in a 30% tax bracket. How many patient hours does she need to generate each month to produce this amount of income?

c. The doctor enjoys scuba diving and snow skiing. To pursue these hobbies, she wants to know if it would be possible for her to work 6-hour days and 4-day weeks and still earn the level of income she desires from part b above?

 24. *(CVP, taxes)* Henry Gonzalez has a small plant that makes playhouses. He sells them to local customers at $3,000 each. His costs are as follows:

Costs	Per Unit	Total
Direct materials	$1,400	
Direct labor	200	
Variable overhead	125	
Variable selling	75	
Fixed production overhead		$200,000
Fixed general, selling, and administrative		80,420

Henry is in a 35% tax bracket.

a. How many playhouses must he sell to earn $247,507 after taxes?

b. What level of revenue is needed to yield an after-tax income equal to 20% of sales?

25. *(CVP, margin of safety)* Harry Husker grows corn on his Nebraska farm. He currently sells his corn at the local market price of $2.25 per bushel. The variable cost associated with growing and selling a bushel of corn is $1.80. His annual fixed cost is $74,520.

a. What is Harry's breakeven point in sales dollars and bushels of corn? If Harry's farm covers 1,200 acres, how many bushels must he generate per acre to break even?

b. If the business is currently producing and selling 180,000 bushels, what is the margin of safety in bushels, dollars, and percentage?

26. *(CVP, operating leverage)* Susy's Salon is a nail sculpturing salon. A set of sculptured nails sells for $40. The variable and fixed costs of the business are as follows:

Variable costs:		
Materials	$ 4	
Labor—manicurist	6	$ 10

Fixed costs:		
Advertising	$ 50	
Rent	250	
Receptionist	600	
Utilities	150	$1,050

a. What is the breakeven point in units? In sales dollars?

b. If Susy Snyder, the owner, wishes to earn a before-tax profit of 40% of revenues, how many sets of nails will she need to sell in a month?

c. If Susy's Salon currently has 40 customers per month, what is the degree of operating leverage?

d. If the company can increase sales by 40% above the level in part c, what will be the increase in income? What will be the new level of income?

27. *(Operating leverage, margin of safety)* One of the products produced by Arizona Vineyards is the Texas Cooler. The selling price per package is $4.50 and variable cost of production is $2.70. Total fixed costs per year are $316,600. The company is currently selling 200,000 packages per year.
   a. What is the margin of safety in units?
   b. What is the degree of operating leverage?
   c. If the company can increase sales in units by 30%, what percentage increase will it experience in income? Prove your answer using the income statement approach.
   d. If the company increases advertising by $41,200, sales in units will increase by 15%. What will be the new breakeven point? The new degree of operating leverage?

28. *(Volume and pricing)* Clem Clunkhead, secretary of transportation of New Iberia, decided to institute tolls for persons using the ferry boats in that country. After the tolls had been in effect for 3 1/2 months, Astra Astute noticed that the country was incurring an average of $900 per day in expenses to collect $725 per day in tolls. The toll is $.25 per person.
   a. How many people are using the ferry boats per day?
   b. If all the expenses of collecting the tolls are fixed, how much would New Iberia have to charge each user in order to break even? To make a profit of $250 per day?
   c. Assume that 80% of the daily expenses of collecting the tolls are fixed and the remainder varies per user. If New Iberia raises the toll to $.30 per person, the Department of Transportation expects that volume will fall by 10%. Will the country be better or worse off than it is currently? By what amount?
   d. Assume that 80% of the daily expenses of collecting the tolls are fixed and the remainder varies with the number of users. If use will decline by 5% for every $.10 increase (from the current amount) in the toll, at what level of use and toll amount would New Iberia make a profit per day?
   e. Discuss the saying "We may be showing a loss, but we can make it up in volume."

29. *(Fixed costs and volume)* In late 1994, the Double Nugget, a Las Vegas casino, decided to sponsor a heavyweight boxing match. Revenue from the event was to come from gate receipts and television royalties. The casino hired promoter Donna Bradshaw to arrange the bout. Donna demanded a $12 million advance for arranging the fight; her contract with the casino indicates that the advance is to be offset by her 15% share of total revenues from the fight. However, if her share of the revenues is less than $12 million, she is not responsible for repaying any part of the advance. Other fixed costs budgeted for the bout include:

Advertising	$4,000,000
Fighters' salaries	7,000,000
Security	500,000

   Variable costs, other than Donna's fee, will run $.30 for each dollar of revenue.
   a. To justify the amount of the advance paid to Donna, how much revenue does the Double Nugget need to generate from the fight?
   b. Assume total revenues of $37,000,000 are generated from the fight. Compute the degree of operating leverage and margin of safety.

30. *(Miscellaneous)* Compute the answers to each of the following *independent* situations.
   a. Punk Corp. sells two products, S and T. The sales mix of these products is 2:4, respectively. S has a contribution margin of $10 per unit, while T has a contribution margin of $5 per unit. Fixed costs for the company are $90,000. What would be the total units of T sold at the breakeven point?

b. A company has a breakeven point of 2,000 units. At breakeven, variable costs are $3,200 and fixed costs are $800. If the company sells one unit over breakeven, what will be the pretax income of the company?

c. Candy Corp. sells boxed candy for $5 per box. The fixed costs of the company are $108,000. Variable costs amount to 40% of selling price. What amount of sales (in units) would be necessary for Candy Corp. to earn a 25% profit on sales?

d. Landry Industries has a breakeven point of 1,400 units. The company is currently selling 1,600 units for $65 each. What is the margin of safety for the company in units, sales dollars, and percentage?

31. (CVP, multiproduct) Sports Wholesalers Inc. purchases sports products from manufacturers and sells them to retailers. The Baseball Division handles both bats and gloves. Historically, the firm has averaged 3 bats sold for each glove sold. Each bat has a $4 contribution margin and each glove has a $5 contribution margin. The fixed costs of operating the Baseball Division are $200,000 per year. Each bat sells for $10 on average and each glove sells for $15 on average. The corporatewide tax rate for the company is 40%.

a. How much revenue is needed to break even? How many bats and gloves would this represent?

b. How much revenue is needed to earn a pretax profit of $90,000?

c. How much revenue is needed to earn an after-tax profit of $90,000?

d. If the Baseball Division earns the revenue determined in part b above, but in doing so sells 2 bats for each glove, what would the profit (or loss) be? Why is this amount not $90,000?

COMMUNICATION ACTIVITIES

32. A company is currently using breakeven analysis, but the president is uncertain as to the uses of this analytical tool.

a. Define breakeven point for the president and explain how it is computed.

b. Discuss the major uses of breakeven analysis.

(AICPA adapted)

33. (Appendix) Bud and Bill's Ice Cream Parlor, which specializes in making and selling old-fashioned, homemade ice cream, had the following income statement for 1994.

Sales (15,000 gallons @ $8)		$120,000
Variable Costs:		
Production (20,000 gallons @ $3)	$60,000	
Selling (20,000 gallons @ $.50)	10,000	70,000
Contribution Margin		$ 50,000
Fixed Costs:		
Production	$22,000	
General, Selling & Administrative	4,000	26,000
Income Before Taxes		$ 24,000
Income Taxes (40%)		9,600
Net Income		$ 14,400

a. Prepare a CVP graph, in the traditional manner, to reflect the relations among costs, revenues, profit, and volume.

b. Prepare a CVP graph, in the contemporary manner, to reflect the relations among costs, revenues, profit, and volume.
c. Prepare a profit-volume graph.
d. Prepare a short explanation for company management about each of the graphs.

PROBLEMS

34. *(CVP decision alternatives)* Freida O'lay owns a small travel agency. Her revenues are based on commissions earned as follows:

Airline bookings   10% commission
Rental car bookings   15% commission
Hotel bookings   20% commission

Monthly fixed costs include advertising ($1,200), rent ($800), utilities ($250), and other costs ($2,200). There are no variable costs.

During a normal month, Freida books the following items, which are subject to the above commission structure:

Airlines	$23,500
Cars	3,000
Hotels	7,000
Total	$33,500

Freida is concerned because her monthly income is so small.
a. What is Freida's normal monthly income?
b. Freida can increase her airline bookings by 40% with an increase in advertising of $600. Should she increase advertising?
c. Freida's friend Tim has asked her for a job in the travel agency. Tim has proposed that he be paid 40% of whatever additional commissions he can bring to the agency plus a salary of $300 per month. Freida has estimated Tim can generate the following additional bookings per month:

Airlines	$4,000
Cars	1,000
Hotels	4,000
Total	$9,000

Hiring Tim would also increase utility costs by $200 per month. Should Freida accept Tim's offer?
d. Freida hires Tim and in the first month Tim generates an additional $8,000 of bookings for the agency. The bookings, however, were all airline tickets. Was the decision to hire Tim a good one? Why or why not?

35. *(Single product CVP)* Fair Winds Co. manufactures portable hair dryers. The president, Red Murphy, is planning some changes and has enlisted your assistance to predict the potential effects. "Skinhead Red," as he is known around the plant, provides you with the following information:

Variable costs to produce each dryer:
Direct materials	$ 4.60
Direct labor	3.25
Variable production overhead	2.15
Total variable production cost	$10.00

Annual fixed production overhead	$300,000
Annual fixed selling costs	240,000
Annual fixed general and administrative costs	120,000

Nonproduction variable costs are as follows:

| Average variable selling costs per unit | $1.15 |
| Average variable general and administrative cost per unit | .75 |

The selling price is $23.50 per hair dryer and sales volume for the current year is expected to be 150,000 units.

Following are some changes about which Red has been thinking:

1. Engineers tell Red that if a radio headset were added to each unit at a cost of $3.60, the company's product would be so superior to the competitors' that business would increase 20%.
2. The sales manager tells Red that a $130,000 increase in advertising will increase sales by 15%.
3. Red's sales force believes that lowering the price by 5% will increase demand (in units) by 10%.
   a. Compute the breakeven point in units and dollars.
   b. Compute the margin of safety in (1) dollars and units and (2) percentage.
   c. Compute the effects on profit and dollar breakeven point of each of the independent propositions (ignore tax implications). For each, advise the president about the effects of the proposal.

36. *(Retail merchant CVP)* Dutton's Optical Shop has been in operation for several years. Analysis of the firm's recent financial statements and records reveal the following:

Average selling price per pair of glasses	$	70
Variable expenses per pair:		
Lenses and frames	$	28
Sales commission		12
Variable overhead		8
Annual fixed costs:		
Selling expenses		$18,000
General and administrative expenses		48,000

The company's effective tax rate is 40%. Sara Dutton, company president, has asked you to help her answer the following questions about the business.

a. What is the breakeven point in pairs of glasses? In dollars?
b. How much revenue must be generated to produce $80,000 of pretax earnings? How many pairs of glasses would this level of revenue represent?
c. How much revenue must be generated to produce $80,000 of after-tax earnings? How many pairs of glasses would this represent?
d. What amount of revenue would be necessary to yield an after-tax profit equal to 20% of revenue?
e. Ms. Dutton is considering adding a lens-grinding lab, which will save $6 per pair of glasses in lens cost, but will raise annual fixed costs by $8,000. She expects to sell 5,000 pairs of glasses. Should she make this investment?
f. A marketing consultant told Ms. Dutton that she could increase the number of glasses sold by 30% if she would lower the selling price by 10% and spend $20,000 on advertising. She has been selling 3,000 pairs of glasses. Should she make these two related changes?

37. *(Single product)* Child Safety Products, Inc. manufactures a rugged child safety seat for automobiles. For 1995, the firm projects sales of 20,000 units; variable manufacturing costs are $35 per unit and variable selling, general, and administrative costs are $10 per unit. Fixed costs will be incurred uniformly throughout the fiscal period and amount to $950,000. Each unit is to be sold for $60.
    a. Compute the breakeven point in dollars and units of product.
    b. Compute the number of units to be sold to earn income before taxes of $90,000 for the year.
    c. If the income tax rate is 60%, compute the number of units that must be sold to earn an after-tax profit of $150,000.
    d. If labor costs are 60% of the variable manufacturing costs and 40% of the total fixed costs, by how much would a 10% decrease in fixed labor cost and a 10% decrease in variable labor costs per unit decrease the breakeven point in dollars?

38. *(Multiproduct firm)* Big Apple Publishing produces and sells two book products: an encyclopedia set and a dictionary set. The company sells these book sets in a ratio of five dictionary sets to three encyclopedia sets. Selling prices for the encyclopedia and dictionary sets are, respectively, $1,200 and $240; respective variable costs are $480 and $160. The company's fixed costs are $1,800,000 per year. Compute the volume of sales of each type of book set needed to:
    a. break even.
    b. earn $400,000 of income before tax
    c. earn $400,000 of income after tax, assuming a 30% tax rate
    d. earn 12% on sales revenue in before-tax income
    e. earn 12% on sales revenue in after-tax income, assuming a 30% tax rate

39. *(Multiproduct)* Oklahoma Oil & Gas Co. wholesales three products: gasoline, engine oil, and grease. Gasoline is marketed to area gasoline retailers. Oil and grease are marketed through gasoline retailers, automobile repair shops, and department stores. Selling prices and variable costs for the three products in the most recent period were:

	Selling Price	Variable Cost
Gasoline	$.76 per gallon	$.68 per gallon
Oil	$.75 per quart	$.60 per quart
Grease	$6.00 per case	$4.50 per case

John Sooner, the marketing manager of the company, expects the products (gasoline, oil, and grease) to sell in the ratio of 40 to 2 to 1, respectively, in the coming month. Fixed costs for the firm are $120,000 monthly.
    a. What is the monthly breakeven point in units of gasoline, oil, and grease?
    b. If management wants to earn a monthly before-tax profit of $200,000, what quantity of each product must be sold?
    c. If management wants to earn an after-tax profit of $150,000 per month and the company has a 40% tax rate, how many units of each product must be sold?
    d. If management wants to earn a before-tax profit of 20% of revenues, how many gallons of gasoline must be sold?
    e. If management wants to earn an after-tax profit of 5% and the company has a 40% tax rate, how many cases of grease must be sold?

40. *(Comprehensive; multiproduct)* Alabama Flooring makes three types of flooring products: tile, carpet, and parquet. Cost analysis reveals the following costs (expressed on a per square yard basis) expected for the coming year:

	Tile	Carpet	Parquet
Direct materials	$5.20	$3.25	$8.80
Direct labor	1.80	.40	6.40
Variable overhead	1.00	.15	1.75
Variable selling expenses	.50	.25	2.00
Variable general and administrative expenses	.20	.10	.30

Fixed overhead	$760,000
Fixed selling expenses	240,000
Fixed general and administrative expenses	200,000

Per yard expected selling prices are: tile, $16.40; carpet, $8.00; and parquet, $25.00. In 1994, sales were as follows and the mix is expected to continue in 1995:

	Tile	Carpet	Parquet
Square yards	18,000	144,000	12,000

Review of recent tax returns reveals an expected tax rate of 40%.
a. Calculate the breakeven point for the coming year.
b. How many square yards of each product are expected to be sold at the breakeven point?
c. Assume that the company desires a pretax profit of $800,000. How many square yards of each type of product would need to be sold to generate this profit level? How much revenue would be required?
d. Assume that the company desires an after-tax profit of $680,000. Use the contribution margin percentage approach to determine the revenue needed.
e. If the company actually achieves the revenue determined in part d above, what is Alabama Flooring's margin of safety in (1) dollars and (2) percentage?

41. *(Comprehensive breakeven)* Chicago Healthcare Corp. (CHC) operates a general hospital, but rents space and beds to separately owned entities rendering specialized services such as pediatrics and physical therapy. CHC charges each separate entity for common services such as patients' meals and laundry, and for administrative services such as billings and collections. Space and bed rentals are fixed charges for the year (based on bed capacity).

   CHC charged the following costs to pediatrics for the year ended June 30, 1994:

	Patient Days (Variable)	Bed Capacity (Fixed)
Dietary	$ 600,000	-0-
Janitorial	-0-	$ 70,000
Laundry	300,000	
Laboratory	450,000	
Pharmacy	350,000	
Repairs and maintenance		30,000
General and administrative		1,300,000
Rent		1,500,000
Billing and collections	300,000	
Totals	$2,000,000	$2,900,000

During the year ended June 30, 1994, pediatrics charged each patient an average of $300 per day, had a capacity of 60 beds, and had revenue of $6,000,000 for 365 days.

In addition, pediatrics directly employed the following personnel at the specified annual salaries: supervising nurses, $25,000; nurses, $20,000; and aides, $9,000. CHC has the following minimum departmental personnel requirements based on total annual patient days:

Annual patient days	Aides	Nurses	Supervising Nurses
Up to 21,900	20	10	4
21,901 to 26,000	26	13	4
26,001 to 29,200	30	15	4

These staffing levels represent full-time equivalents. Pediatrics always employs only the minimum number of required full-time equivalent personnel. Salaries of supervising nurses, nurses, and aides are therefore fixed within ranges of annual patient days.

Pediatrics operated at 100% capacity for 90 days during the year ended June 30, 1994. It is estimated that during these 90 days the demand exceeded capacity by 20 patients. CHC has an additional 20 beds available for rent for the year ending June 30, 1995. Such additional rental would increase pediatrics' fixed charges based on bed capacity.

a. Calculate the minimum number of patient days required for pediatrics to break even for the year ending June 30, 1995, if the additional 20 beds are not rented. Patient demand is unknown, but assume that revenue per patient day, cost per patient day, cost per bed, and salary rates will remain the same as for the year ended June 30, 1994.

b. Assume that patient demand, revenue per patient day, cost per patient day, cost per bed, and salary rates for the year ending June 30, 1995, remain the same as for the year ended June 30, 1994. Prepare a schedule of increase in revenue and increase in costs for the year ending June 30, 1995, in order to determine the net increase or decrease in earnings from the additional 20 beds if pediatrics rents this extra capacity from CHC.

(AICPA adapted)

 42. *(Appendix)* The London Social Club (LSC) has provided you with the following monthly cost and fee information: monthly membership fee per member, £25; variable cost per member per month, £12; fixed cost per month, £1,800. Costs are extremely low because almost all services and supplies are provided by volunteers.

a. Prepare a traditional breakeven chart for the LSC.
b. Prepare a contemporary breakeven chart for the LSC.
c. Prepare a profit-volume graph for the LSC.
d. Indicate which of the above you would use in giving a speech to the membership in order to solicit volunteers to help with a fund raising project. Assume at this time there are only 120 members belonging to the LSC.

CASES

43. Linda McCartney owns the Holiday Litter Box, a luxury hotel for dogs and cats. The capacity is 40 pets: 20 dogs and 20 cats. Each pet has an air-conditioned room with a window overlooking a garden. Soft music is played continuously. Pets are awakened at 7 a.m., served breakfast at 8 a.m., fed snacks at 3:30 p.m.,

and receive dinner at 5 p.m. Hotel services also include airport pickup, daily bathing and grooming, night lighting in each suite, carpeted floors, and daily play visits by pet "babysitters."

Pet owners are interviewed about their pets' health care requirements, likes and dislikes, diet, and other needs. Reservations are essential and health must be documented by each pet's veterinarian. The costs of operating the pet hotel are substantial. The hotel's original cost was $85,000. Depreciation is $6,000 per year. Other costs of operating the hotel include:

Labor costs	$18,000 per year plus $.25 per animal per day
Utilities	$ 8,900 per year plus $.05 per animal per day
Miscellaneous costs	$ 4,000 per year plus $.30 per animal per day

In addition to these costs, costs are incurred for food and water for each pet. These costs are strictly variable and (on average) run $2.00 per day for dogs and $.75 per day for cats.

a. Assuming that the hotel is able to maintain an average annual occupancy of 75% in both the cat units and the dog units (based on a 360-day year), determine the minimum daily charge that must be assessed per animal day to generate $12,000 of income before taxes.

b. Assume that the price Linda charges cat owners is $10 per day and the price charged to dog owners is $12 per day. If the sales mix is 1 to 1 (one cat day of occupancy for each dog day of occupancy) compute:
   1. the breakeven point in total occupancy days.
   2. total occupancy days required to generate $20,000 of income before taxes.
   3. total occupancy days to generate $20,000 of after-tax income; Linda's personal tax rate is 35%.

c. Linda is considering adding an animal training service for guests to complement her other hotel services. Linda has estimated the costs of providing such a service would largely be fixed. Since all of the facilities already exist, Linda would merely need to hire a dog trainer. She estimates a dog trainer could be hired at a cost of $25,000 per year. If Linda decides to add this service, how much would her daily charges have to increase (assume equal dollar increases to cat and dog fees) to maintain the breakeven level you computed in part b?

44. Southern Airlines is a small local carrier in the Southeast. All seats are coach and the following data are available.

Number of seats per plane	120
Average load factor (percent of seats filled)	75%
Average full passenger fare	$70
Average variable cost per passenger	$30
Fixed operating costs per month	$1,200,000

a. What is breakeven point in passengers and revenues?
b. What is breakeven point in number of flights?
c. If Southern raises its average full passenger fare to $85, it is estimated that the load factor will decrease to 60%. What will be the breakeven point in number of flights?
d. The cost of fuel is a significant variable cost to any airline. If fuel charges increase by $8 per barrel, it is estimated that variable cost per passenger will rise to $40. In this case, what would be the new breakeven point in passengers and in number of flights? (Refer back to original data.)
e. Southern has experienced an increase in variable cost per passenger to $35 and an increase in total fixed costs to $1,500,000. The company has decided

to raise the average fare to $80. What number of passengers are needed to generate an after-tax profit of $400,000 if the tax rate is 40%?

f. (Use original data.) Southern is considering offering a discounted fare of $50, which the company feels would increase the load factor to 80%. Only the additional seats would be sold at the discounted fare. Additional monthly advertising costs would be $80,000. How much pretax income would the discounted fare provide Southern if the company has 40 flights per day, 30 days per month?

g. Southern has an opportunity to obtain a new route. The company feels it can sell seats at $75 on the route, but the load factor would be only 60%. The company would fly the route 15 times per month. The increase in fixed costs for additional crew, additional planes, landing fees, maintenance, etc., would total $100,000 per month. Variable cost per passenger would remain at $30.

1. Should the company obtain the route?
2. How many flights would Southern need to earn pretax income of $50,500 per month on this route?
3. If the load factor could be increased to 75%, how many flights would be needed to earn pretax income of $50,500 per month on this route?
4. What qualitative factors should be considered by Southern in making its decision about acquiring this route?

---

45. Jones Chemical Company's new president has learned that for the past four years, the company has been dumping its industrial waste into the local river and falsifying reports to authorities about the levels of suspected cancer-causing materials in that waste. His plant manager says that there is no proof that the waste causes cancer and there are only a few fishing villages within a hundred miles downriver. If the company has to treat the substance to neutralize its potentially injurious effects and then transport it to a legal dump site, the company's variable and fixed costs would rise to a level that might make the firm uncompetitive. If the company loses its competitive advantage, 10,000 local employees could become unemployed and the town's economy could collapse.

a. What kinds of variable and fixed costs can you think of that would increase (or decrease) if the waste were treated rather than dumped? How would these costs affect product contribution margin?
b. What are the ethical conflicts the president faces?
c. What rationalizations can you detect which have been devised by plant employees?
d. What options and suggestions can you offer the president?

46. Women often receive reports of positive Pap smears when, in actuality, the results are negative. Newspaper accounts detail an industry utilizing overworked, undersupervised, poorly paid technicians to perform Pap smear tests. Some labs allow workers to analyze up to four times as many specimens per year as experts recommend for accuracy. Workers may be paid $.45 to analyze a smear when patients are charged $35.

a. Discuss the cost-volume-profit relationships that exist in this case.
b. Discuss the ethics of the laboratories' owners who allow technicians to be paid piecework for such analysis work.
c. Discuss the ethics of the workers who rush through Pap smear analyses.

47. High quality raw materials are typically associated with high prices. Jane Phipps of Fresh From Texas, however, was quick to point out that such a situation does not exist in the vegetable market. "When floods or droughts occur in California, Texas, Florida, and Arizona, prices for inferior products skyrocket. On the other

ETHICS AND QUALITY DISCUSSION

hand, when the weather is great, produce is plentiful, the quality is great, and prices are low," she said.

If you were in the business of wholesaling produce to grocery stores, would you buy the low quality produce from the farms and package and resell it to your customers or would you refuse to handle the low quality produce because you have a reputation for high quality product to uphold? Discuss the pros and cons of each position before selecting the choice you would make.

48. *Recently, health professionals and others have taken notice of actions by pharmaceutical giant Eli Lilly & Co. to increase the volume of sales for its antidepressant drug, Prozac. Critics suggest the company has launched a major advertising program and sponsored other efforts to induce greater consumer demand for this prescription medication. At the heart of the issue is an expenditure of several million dollars by Lilly to sponsor ads that urge people who think that they might be depressed to see their doctor.*

   The American Psychological Association says such advertisements will encourage patients to see their primary-care physician, rather than a psychologist (who cannot prescribe medicine) to address their depression. Primary-care physicians would be more likely than mental health professionals to rely strictly on medication to treat depression. Critics suggest that Prozac is already overprescribed and that it is an appropriate treatment for only about 1/3 of its current users.

   Lilly has countered the criticism by suggesting that the ads it sponsored were not intended to promote its drug Prozac, but were instead intended to promote awareness of mental health.

   According to the Mental Health Association, the advertising campaign is expected to reach 93% of American adults.

   [SOURCE: Elyse Tanouye, "Critics See Self-Interest in Lilly's Funding of Ads Telling the Depressed to Get Help," *(New Orleans) Times-Picayune* (April 15, 1993), p. B1.]

   a. How could Lilly's advertising have been construed by critics as being intended to increase the volume of Prozac sales?
   b. Discuss the ethics of using advertising to generate demand for prescription drugs.
   c. Would the advertising be more or less ethical if it were directed at health care professionals rather than consumers? Discuss.
   d. Discuss whether advertising of medical products, including drugs, should be more strictly regulated by government agencies.

49. *When special event tickets (e.g., rock concert tickets) are purchased through Ticketmaster, a fee called "a convenience charge" is automatically added to the price of the tickets. For a recent U2 concert in Boston, concertgoers paid $30 for the ticket and an additional $4 or $5 for the convenience charge. In just four and a half hours, Ticketmaster sold 80,000 tickets for the U2 concert and collected around $320,000 in convenience charges. Although Ticketmaster's convenience charge is among the highest in the industry, the firm has grown to handle about $1 billion of ticket sales annually. Critics suggest Ticketmaster's high growth and high convenience charge are related. Specifically, critics suggest that a portion of the convenience charge collected by Ticketmaster has been used as a kickback to purchase future business from promoters.*

   Evidence indicates that Ticketmaster pays stadiums and clubs 18 to 22% of the convenience charge for the average event. Additional money is paid for advertising costs and cash bonuses. The Boston area's top indoor concert facility, the Worcester Centrum, reported average annual receipts over the past four years of $216,000 from Ticketmaster "ticket service income."

   Ticketmaster contends that it provides a high-quality service and receives reasonable compensation for that service. The company argues that "rebates" are a cost of doing business for all concessionaires. The firm likens its circumstance to that of hot dog and t-shirt vendors who pay the stadium for the right to market their products at an event.

   [SOURCE: Bruce Mohl, "Rising Ticket Fees Pad Concert Profits," *The Boston Globe* (September 20, 1992) pp. A1, A30, A31.]

a. Is the practice of adding a convenience charge to the advertised price of a ticket an ethical practice? Discuss both sides of the issue.

b. Discuss the rebate or kickback arrangement from both perspectives, then take a position on the issue and defend it.

c. Would the rebate or kickback arrangement be more ethical if patrons were informed of the amount of each convenience charge that was being returned to the promoter? Discuss.

RELEVANT COSTING

LEARNING OBJECTIVES

After completing this chapter, you should be able to answer these questions:

1. What factors are relevant in making decisions and why?
2. How do opportunity costs affect decision making?
3. How can management make the best use of a scarce resource?
4. How does sales mix pertain to relevant costing problems?
5. How are special prices set and when are they used?
6. How is segment margin used to determine whether a product line should be retained or eliminated?
7. *(Appendix)* How is a linear programming problem formulated?

HEWLETT-PACKARD

Hewlett-Packard Company (HP), headquartered in Palo Alto, California, is one of the 30 largest industrial companies in America and one of the top 15 American exporters. HP plants are located in 24 U.S. cities, mostly in California, Colorado, the Northeast, and the Pacific Northwest. The company has research and manufacturing facilities in Palo Alto, California; Tokyo, Japan; and Bristol, U.K.; it also has manufacturing facilities in the U.S., Europe, Latin America, Canada, and Asia Pacific. Slightly more than half of the company's business is generated outside the U.S., two-thirds of that in Europe. The company is conspicuously different from some of its major competitors, however, as indicated in the following *Wall Street Journal* article excerpt.

"What do International Business Machines Corp. and Digital Equipment Corp. have in common, other than making computers? Among high-tech manufacturers, they are among the most vertically integrated, capable of making almost every part of their products. And they are currently among the worst performers.

Both companies embraced the conventional wisdom of going it alone in the manufacturing process. Since the mid-1980s, many commentators have considered it a sign of weakness when a U.S. company relies on outsiders, especially Japanese or other Asian concerns, for critical parts manufacturing. They say the company risks losing its expertise to foreigners, employs fewer Americans, and could even be forced out of business if it turns into little more than an assembly line for others' components.

But now that reasoning is being stood on its head by the successes of rivals such as Hewlett-Packard.

Preparing to launch its first laser printer a decade ago, Hewlett-Packard had to decide whether to make all of it itself or turn to outside suppliers. Even though its researchers had already built a computer-driven laser printer from scratch, competitors were fast readying rival products. So HP bought the printer's laser engine from Canon Inc. of Japan. Then, Hewlett-Packard threw its resources into creating the software that links the printer to a computer and controls how the text and graphics look on paper.

Today, HP, with Canon's help, dominates the global laser-printer market. And its success suggests that high-tech companies that rely on others for crucial parts or manufacturing frequently rule fast-changing markets."

SOURCE: *Hewlett-Packard in Brief* (March 1992) and G. Pascal Zachary, "High-Tech Firms Find It's Good to Line Up Outside Contractors," *Wall Street Journal* (July 29, 1992), p. A1. Reprinted by permission of the *Wall Street Journal*, © 1992 Dow Jones & Company, Inc. All rights reserved worldwide.

Businesses have only limited resources at their disposal at any time. One of management's most important tasks is to allocate these resources to effectively and efficiently accomplish the company's goals and objectives. According to the *Wall Street Journal*, Hewlett-Packard chose to allocate a substantial portion of its resources to the perfection of differentiated software rather than in the production of laser-printer engines. In relying on Canon for its printer engines, HP managers made a "buy" choice in what is commonly referred to as a make-or-buy decision. This choice was the result of determining and comparing the costs of setting up engine manufacturing operations to the costs of purchasing the engines from Canon.

Accounting information can improve, but not perfect, management's understanding of the consequences of alternative resource allocations. To the extent that accounting information can reduce management's uncertainty about the economic facts, outcomes, and relationships involved in various courses of action, such information is valuable for decision-making purposes.

Relevant costing

As discussed in Chapter 14, many decisions can be made using incremental analysis. This chapter continues that discussion by introducing the topic of **relevant costing,** which allows managers to disregard extraneous information about economic alternatives and focus on a decision's relevant (or pertinent) facts. Relevant costing techniques are used in business decisions about replacing an asset, making or buying a product or part, allocating scarce resources, accepting specially priced orders, and determining the appropriate sales/production mix.

In making a choice from the various alternatives available, managers need to consider all the relevant costs and revenues associated with each alternative. Decision analysis can be based on changes in either cash flow or accounting income. Long-run decision analysis for capital budgeting generally uses cash flow as the decision criterion; this topic is covered in Chapters 19 and 20. Short-run decision analysis, the focus of this chapter, often uses accounting income although some past costs, such as depreciation on old assets, may be excluded. Regardless of whether the decision is short- or long-run, all decision making requires the following:

> relevant information at the point of decision; the knowledge of how to analyze that information at the point of decision; and enough time to do the analysis.
>
> In today's corporations, oceans of data drown most decision makers. Eliminating irrelevant information requires the knowledge of what is relevant, the knowledge of how to access and select appropriate data, and the knowledge of how best to prepare the data by sorting and summarizing it to facilitate analysis. This is the raw material of decision making.[1]

THE CONCEPT OF RELEVANCE

For information to be relevant, it must possess three characteristics. It must (1) be associated with the decision or question under consideration, (2) be important to a decision maker, and (3) have a connection to or bearing on some future endeavor.

Association with Decision

Information is relevant when it is logically related to a decision and can affect the decision-making process. In this regard, different costs exist that can be used for many different purposes. No single cost can be relevant in all decisions or to all managers. Cost accountants can assist managers in determining which costs are relevant to the objectives and decisions at hand. To be relevant, a cost must be a **differential cost,** which means that it varies in amount among the alternatives being considered. **Out-of-pocket** costs involve current or near-current cash expenditures and, if differential, these costs are also relevant costs.

Differential cost

Out-of-pocket cost

To the extent possible and practical, relevant costing compares the incremental revenues and incremental costs of alternative decisions. Incremental refers to an additional or extra amount associated with some action and, thus, **incremental revenue** is the additional revenue resulting from a contemplated sale or provision of a service.

Incremental revenue

An **incremental cost** is the additional cost of producing or selling the same contemplated good or service. If the costs between two alternatives differ, one will always be incrementally higher than the other. In this sense, an incremental cost is the same as a differential cost. Throughout the rest of the chapter, the term incremental is used instead of differential.

Incremental costs can be variable or fixed. Two general guidelines are that (1) most variable costs are relevant and (2) most fixed costs are not. The reasoning behind this guideline is that, as sales or production volume changes within the relevant range, total variable costs change but fixed costs do not. As with most generalizations, however, there are some exceptions in the decision-making process.

The difference between the incremental revenue and incremental cost of a particular alternative is either the positive or negative incremental benefit of that course of action. Management can compare the incremental benefits of alternatives to decide on the most profitable (or least costly) alternative or set of alternatives. Such a comparison may sound simple, but often it is not. The concept of relevance is an inherently individual determination and the quantity of information needed to make decisions is increasing as indicated in the following quote.

> Decision making in the 1990s will be more of an art and less of a science. Not only is the world growing more complex and uncertain at a faster and faster pace, but the old decision-making models are failing, and we can expect their failure to accelerate as well.
>
> If executives once imagined they could gather enough information to read the business environment like an open book, they have had to dim their hopes. The flow of information has swollen to such a flood that managers are in danger of drowning; extracting relevant data from the torrent is increasingly a daunting task.[2]

Some relevant factors, such as sales commissions or prime costs of production, are easily identified and quantified because they are integral parts of the accounting system. Other factors may be relevant and quantifiable, but are not part of the accounting system. Such factors cannot be overlooked simply because they may be more difficult to obtain or may require the use of estimates. For instance, **opportunity costs** represent the benefits foregone because one course of action is chosen over another. These costs are extremely important in decision making, but are not included in the accounting records.

An example of a relevant opportunity cost is the profit foregone from product sales. Assume that managers at Hewlett-Packard are considering dropping a product line and renting out the facilities in which that product line is currently being made. The company was selling 5,000 units annually with a contribution margin of $100 each. The rental income from the leased facilities is $250,000 and renting will cause fixed expenses to decline by $390,000. The opportunity cost of choosing to rent the facilities is the foregone profit on the discontinued product line of $500,000 (5,000 units × $100 contribution margin).

Incremental cost

Opportunity cost

Importance to Decision Maker

The need for specific information depends on how important that information is relative to the objectives that a manager wants or needs to achieve. Moreover, if all other factors are equal, more precise information is given greater weight in the decision-making process. However, if the information is extremely important but less precise, the manager must weigh importance against precision. The News Note "Quality, Health Risks, and Profits" illustrates both the need for qualitative information and the legal and ethical duties of managers to weigh important but imprecise qualitative information (risk to consumers and company) against company profits.

---

[2] Amitai Etzioni, "Humble Decision Making," *Harvard Business Review* (July–August 1989), p. 122.

Bearing on the Future

Information can be *based* on past or present data, but it can only be relevant if it pertains to a future decision. All managerial decisions are made to affect future events, so the information on which decisions are based should reflect future conditions. The future may be the short-run (two hours from now or next month) or the long-run (three years from now).

Future costs are the only costs that can be avoided, and the longer into the future a decision's time horizon, the more costs are controllable, avoidable, and relevant. *Only information that has a bearing on future events is relevant in decision making.* But people too often forget this basic characteristic and try to make decisions using inapplicable data. One common error is trying to use a previously purchased asset's acquisition cost or book value in current decision making. This error reflects the misconception that sunk costs are relevant costs.

SUNK COSTS

Sunk cost

Current costs (such as replacement or budgeted costs) are assumed to be accurate for the time period involved in a decision. As such, these costs represent relevant information and should be considered in the decision-making process. In contrast, costs incurred in the past for the acquisition of an asset or a resource are called **sunk costs** because they cannot be changed, no matter what future course of action is taken. Past expenditures are not recoverable, no matter what current circumstances exist.

	ORIGINAL SYSTEM (PURCHASED JAN. 2)	NEW SYSTEM (AVAILABLE JAN. 7)
Cost	$100,000	$80,000
Life in years	6	6
Salvage value	$ 0	$ 0
Current resale value	$ 64,000	Not applicable
Annual operating cost	$ 15,000	$10,000

EXHIBIT 15–1

Advanced Technology— Videoconferencing System Information

After an asset or resource is acquired, managers may find that it is no longer adequate for the intended purposes, does not perform to expectations, is technologically out of date, or is no longer marketable. They must then decide whether to keep or dispose of the old asset and, if disposed, whether to replace it. A current or future selling price may be obtained for a previously purchased asset, but that price is the result of current or future conditions and does not "recoup" a historical cost.

Asset-acquisition decisions (which are covered in depth in Chapters 19 and 20) provide an excellent introduction to the concept of relevant information. The following illustration makes some simplistic assumptions regarding asset acquisitions, but is used to demonstrate why sunk costs are not relevant costs.

Assume that Advanced Technology Corporation purchases a videoconferencing system for $100,000 on January 2, 1994. This system (referred to as the "original" system) is expected to have a useful life of six years and no salvage value. Five days later, on January 7, Elizabeth Weymann, a vice president for Advanced Technology, notices an advertisement for a similar system for $80,000. This "new" system also has an estimated life of six years and no salvage value; its features will allow it to perform as well as the original system and, in addition, it has larger video screens and will save $5,000 per year in operating costs over the original system. Upon investigation, Ms. Weymann discovers that the original system can be sold for only $64,000. The data on the original and new videoconferencing systems are shown in Exhibit 15–1.

Advanced Technology has two options: (1) use the original system or (2) sell the original system and buy the new system. Exhibit 15–2 presents the costs Ms. Wey-

EXHIBIT 15–2

Relevant Costs Related to Advanced Technology's Alternatives

Alternative (1): Use original system		
Operating cost over life of original system ($15,000 × 6 years)		$90,000
Alternative (2): Sell original system and buy new system		
Cost of new system	$80,000	
Resale value of original system	64,000	
Effective net outlay for new system	$16,000	
Operating cost over life of new system ($10,000 × 6 years)	60,000	
Total cost of new system		76,000
Benefit of purchasing new system		$14,000
The alternative, incremental calculation follows:		
Savings from operating the new system for 6 years ($5,000 × 6)		$30,000
Less effective incremental outlay for new system		16,000
Incremental benefit		$14,000

mann should consider in making her asset replacement decision—that is, the relevant costs. As shown in the computations in Exhibit 15–2, the $100,000 purchase price of the original system does not affect the decision process. This amount was "gone forever" when Advanced Technology bought the system. However, if the company sells the original system, it will be able to effectively reduce the net cash outlay for the new system to $16,000 because it will have $64,000 more money than it has currently. Using either system, Advanced Technology will spend money over the next six years for operating costs, but it will spend $30,000 less using the new system.

The common tendency is to initially assume that Advanced Technology should not purchase the new system because the company will show a $36,000 ($100,000 original cost − $64,000 resale value) loss as a current reduction of revenues on an asset that it has had for only five days. However, if Advanced Technology keeps the original system, that $36,000 will be deducted as depreciation expense from revenues over the system's life. Thus, the $36,000 loss or its equivalent in depreciation charges is the same in magnitude whether Advanced Technology retains the original system and operates it or disposes of it and buys the new one. This $36,000 cannot be avoided under either alternative; it will be either a loss or an expense. Since the amount is the same under both alternatives, it is not relevant to the decision process.

Ms. Weymann must resign herself to accept the past as a fact and make new choices given her set of *future* alternatives. The relevant factors in deciding whether to purchase the new system are:

1. cost of the new system ($80,000);
2. current resale value of the original system ($64,000); and
3. annual savings of the new system ($5,000) and number of years (6) such savings would be enjoyed.[3]

This example introduces the difference between relevant and irrelevant costs. The next section shows how the concepts of relevant costing, incremental revenues, and incremental costs are applied in making some common managerial decisions.

RELEVANT COSTS FOR SPECIFIC DECISIONS

Managers routinely make decisions on alternative courses of action that have been identified as feasible solutions to problems or feasible methods to use in the attainment of objectives. In doing so, managers weigh the costs and benefits of these alternatives and determine which course of action is best. Incremental revenues, costs, and benefits of all courses of action are measured from a base that corresponds to current conditions. This statement means that managers must provide for, in some way, the inclusion of any inherently nonquantifiable considerations. Inclusion can be made by attempting to quantify those items or by simply making instinctive value judgments about nonmonetary benefits and costs.

When evaluating alternative courses of action, managers should select the alternative that provides the highest incremental benefit to the company. In some instances, all alternatives result in incremental losses, and managers must choose the one that creates the smallest incremental loss. One alternative course of action often considered is the "change nothing" option.

Whereas other alternatives have certain incremental revenues and incremental costs associated with them, the "change nothing" alternative has a zero incremental benefit because it represents the current conditions from which all other alternatives

---

[3]In addition, two other factors that are not discussed are also important: the potential tax effects of the transactions and the time value of money. We have chosen to defer consideration of these items to Chapter 19 on capital budgeting. Because of the time value of money, both systems were assumed to have zero salvage values at the end of their lives—a fairly unrealistic assumption.

are measured. The "change nothing" alternative should be chosen only when it is perceived to be the best alternative solution. Often, the "change nothing" alternative is selected only because it is easier than making changes. At other times, managers "change nothing" because there is a lack of information, which is viewed by decision makers as causing the risk of making a change to be greater than the risk of continuing the current course of action. When this condition exists, the results achieved from the "change nothing" alternative (current results) are thought to be more advantageous than the potential incremental benefit of any other alternative.

There are some situations involving specific government regulations or mandates in which a "change nothing" alternative does not exist. For example, if a company were polluting river water and a duly-licensed governmental regulatory agency issued an injunction against it, the company (assuming it wishes to continue in business) would be forced to correct the pollution problem. The company could, of course, delay the installation of pollution control devices at the risk of fines or closure. Such fines would be incremental costs that would need to be considered; closure would create an opportunity cost amounting to the income that would have been generated from lost sales. Managers must make these types of decisions using a "now-versus-later" attitude and, as shown in the News Note on incremental benefits on page 610, may determine that "now" is better for two reasons: the potential benefits (both public relations and monetary) that may arise and the fact that the Clean Air Act provides for prison terms of up to 15 years and fines of up to $1 million for "knowing" or "intentional" felony offense violations.

A comprehensive evaluation of the monetary effects of all alternative courses of action is part of rational managerial behavior. The chosen course should be the one that will make the business better off in the future. The choices in numerous decisions, such as the HP make-or-buy one related to printer engines, can be evaluated using relevant costing techniques.

Make-or-Buy Decisions

A daily question faced by managers is whether the right components will be available at the right time to assure production. Additionally, the components must be of the

A firm that has been cited for polluting the environment does not really have a "change nothing" option relative to emissions. If the firm wants to continue operating, funds will need to be spent on pollution control devices.

appropriate quality and obtainable at a reasonable price. As mentioned at the beginning of the chapter, companies such as IBM and Digital Equipment assure themselves of component availability and quality by doing their own manufacturing. In some cases, this decision may be made because the company is interested in embarking on a vertical integration path, in which one division or subsidiary can serve as a supplier to others within the same company. Other companies, such as HP and Gateway 2000, believe that the better way is to purchase some or all components from others.

Make-or-buy decision

This type of **make-or-buy decision** should be made only after a proper analysis that compares manufacturing costs with purchasing costs and assesses the best uses of the available facilities. Consideration of a "make" option automatically implies that the company has the available capacity for that purpose or has considered the cost of obtaining the necessary capacity in the decision analysis. Relevant information for this type of decision includes both quantitative and qualitative factors.

Exhibit 15–3 presents some factors that should be considered in a make-or-buy decision. Several of the quantitative factors, such as incremental prime (direct material and direct labor) production cost per unit and purchase price quoted by the supplier, are known with a high degree of certainty. Other factors, such as the variable overhead per unit and the opportunity cost associated with production facilities, must be estimated. The qualitative factors should be evaluated by more than one individual so personal biases do not cloud valid business judgment.

Exhibit 15–4 provides information about a mirror produced by Advanced Technology Company and installed in the company's desktop scanners. The total cost to manufacture one mirror is $2.50. The company can purchase the mirror from a supplier for $2.41 per unit. Advanced Technology's cost accountant is preparing an analysis to determine if the company should make the mirrors or buy them from the outside supplier.

RELEVANT QUANTITATIVE FACTORS:
Incremental production costs for each unit
Unit cost of purchasing from outside supplier (price less any discounts available plus
    shipping, etc.)
Number of available suppliers
Quantity of production capacity available to manufacture components
Opportunity costs of using facilities for production rather than for other purposes
Quantity of space available for storage
Costs associated with carrying inventory
Increase in throughput generated by buying components

RELEVANT QUALITATIVE FACTORS:
Reliability of source(s) of supply
Ability to control quality of unit when purchased from outside
Nature of the work to be subcontracted (such as the importance of the part to the
    whole)
Impact on customers and markets
Future bargaining position with supplier(s)
Perceptions regarding possible future price changes
Perceptions about current product prices (are the prices appropriate or, in some cases
    with international suppliers, is product dumping involved?)

■ **EXHIBIT 15–3**

**Make-or-Buy
Considerations**

Production of each mirror requires a cost outlay of $2.20 per unit for materials, labor, and variable overhead. In addition, $.10 of the fixed overhead is considered direct product cost because it specifically relates to the manufacture of mirrors. This $.10 is an incremental cost since it could be avoided if mirrors were not produced. The remaining fixed overhead ($.20) is not relevant to the make-or-buy decision. This amount is a common cost incurred because of general production activity, unassociated with the cost object (the mirror). Therefore, since this portion of the fixed cost would continue under either alternative, it is not relevant.

The relevant cost for the "make" alternative is $2.30—the cost that would be avoided if the product were not made. This amount should be compared to the $2.41 cost quoted by the supplier under the "buy" alternative. Each amount is the incremental cost of, respectively, either production or purchase. All else being equal, management should choose to manufacture the mirrors rather than buy them, since $.11 will be saved on each mirror produced rather than purchased. Relevant costs are those costs that are pertinent and avoidable, regardless of whether they are variable

	PRESENT MANUFACTURING COST PER MIRROR	RELEVANT COST TO MANUFACTURE PER MIRROR
Direct materials	$ .80	$ .80
Direct labor	1.00	1.00
Variable factory overhead	.40	.40
Fixed factory overhead*	.30	.10
Total unit cost	$2.50	$2.30
Quoted price from supplier		$2.41

* Of the $.30 fixed factory overhead, only $.10 is actually caused by mirror production and could be avoided if the firm chooses not to produce mirrors. The remaining $.20 of fixed factory overhead is an allocated indirect (common) cost that would continue even if mirror production ceases.

■ **EXHIBIT 15–4**

**Advanced Technology—
Make-or-Buy Cost
Information**

or fixed. In a make-or-buy decision, variable production costs are relevant. Fixed production costs may be relevant if they can be avoided by discontinuing production.

The opportunity cost of the facilities being used by production is also relevant in a make-or-buy alternative. If a company chooses to buy a product rather than make it, an alternative purpose may exist for the facilities now being used for manufacturing. If a more profitable alternative is available, management should consider diverting the capacity to this alternative use.

Assume that Advanced Technology has an opportunity to rent the building now used to produce mirrors for $42,000 per year. If the company produces 300,000 mirrors annually, there is an opportunity cost of $.14 per unit ($42,000 ÷ 300,000 mirrors) from using rather than renting the building.

The opportunity cost is added to the production cost since the company is giving up this amount by choosing to make the mirrors. The giving up of inflows is as much a cost as the incurrence of an outflow. Exhibit 15–5 shows calculations relating to this decision on both a per unit and a total cost basis. Under either format, the comparison indicates that there is a $.03 per unit advantage to purchasing rather than producing.

Another opportunity cost associated with making is the ability to increase plant throughput by buying a product component. Assume that mirror production uses a resource that has been determined to be a bottleneck in the manufacturing plant. Management calculates that plant throughput can be increased by 2 percent per year on all products if the mirrors are bought rather than made. This increase in throughput would provide an estimated additional annual contribution margin (with no incremental fixed costs) of $1,800,000. Dividing this amount by the 300,000 mirrors currently being produced results in a $6 per-unit opportunity cost relating to making. When added to the production costs of $2.30, the true cost of manufacturing mirrors becomes $8.30 or approximately 344 percent of the cost of buying ($8.30 ÷ $2.41)!

Based on the information in Exhibit 15–5 (even without the inclusion of the throughput opportunity cost), Advanced Technology's cost accountant should inform company management that it is more economical to buy mirrors for $2.41 than to manufacture them. This analysis is the typical starting point of the decision process—determining whether an alternative satisfies the *quantitative* considerations of a problem. If it does, managers then use judgment to assess the decision's qualitative aspects.

▌EXHIBIT 15–5

Advanced Technology Company Opportunity Costs and Make-or-Buy Decision

	MAKE	BUY
PER UNIT:		
Direct production costs	$2.30	
Opportunity cost (revenue)	.14	
Purchase cost		$2.41
Cost per mirror	$2.44	$2.41

	MAKE	BUY	DIFFERENCE IN FAVOR OF PURCHASING
IN TOTAL:			
Revenue from renting capacity	$ 0	$ 42,000	$42,000
Cost for 300,000 mirrors	(690,000)	(723,000)	(33,000)
Net cost	$(690,000)	$(681,000)	$ 9,000*

*The $9,000 represents the net purchase benefit of $.03 per unit multiplied by the 300,000 units to be purchased during the year.

Assume that Advanced Technology's purchasing agent read in the newspaper that the supplier being considered was in poor financial condition and would probably file for bankruptcy. In this case, management would likely decide to continue producing rather than purchasing the mirrors from this supplier. In this instance, quantitative analysis supports the purchase of the units, but qualitative judgment suggests this would not be a wise course of action since the stability of the supplying source is questionable.

This additional consideration also indicates that there are many potential long-run effects of a theoretically short-run decision. If Advanced Technology had stopped mirror production and rented its facilities and the supplier had gone bankrupt, Advanced Technology could be faced with high start-up costs to revitalize its mirror production process. This was essentially the situation faced several years ago by Stoneyfield Farm, a New Hampshire–based yogurt company. Stoneyfield Farm subcontracted its yogurt production and one day found its supplier bankrupt, creating an inability to fill customer orders. It took Stoneyfield two years to acquire the necessary production capacity and regain market strength.

This long-run view was also expressed in Chapter 5 when it was suggested that the term "fixed cost" is really a misnomer. These costs should actually be referred to as long-run variable costs because, while they do not vary with volume in the short-run, they *do* vary in the long-run with non-volume-related cost drivers. As such, they are relevant for long-run decision making. For example, assume a part or product is manufactured (rather than purchased) and the company expects demand for that item to increase in the next few years. At that point, the company may be faced with a need to expand capacity and incur additional "fixed" capacity costs. These long-run costs would, in turn, theoretically cause product cost to increase because of the need to allocate the new overhead to production. To suggest that products made before capacity is added would cost less than those made afterward is a short-run view. The long-run viewpoint would consider both the current and "long-run" variable costs over the product life cycle to calculate the long-run cost.

Make-or-buy decisions are not confined to manufacturing entities. Many service organizations must also make these kinds of choices. For example, accounting and law firms must decide whether to prepare and present in-house continuing education programs or to outsource such programs to external organizations or consultants. Private schools must determine whether to have their own buses or use independent contractors. Doctors investigate the differences in cost, quality of results, and convenience to patients between having blood samples drawn and tested in the office or in a separate lab facility. These examples simply indicate that the term *make* in make-or-buy decisions does not necessarily require converting a raw material to a finished component. It can also mean the internal provision of a service, even one as significant as the internal audit function, as indicated in the News Note on internal auditing on page 614.

Make-or-buy decisions consider the opportunity costs of utilized facilities because those facilities are in limited supply. If capacity is occupied in one way, it cannot be used at the same time for another purpose. Limited capacity is only one type of scarce resource that managers need to consider when making decisions.

Scarce Resources Decisions

Managers are frequently confronted with the short-run problem of making the best use of **scarce resources** that are essential to production activity, but are available only in limited quantity. Scarce resources create constraints on producing goods or providing services and can include machine hours, skilled labor hours, raw materials, and (as mentioned above) production capacity. In the long-run, management may desire and be able to obtain a greater abundance of a scarce resource. For instance, additional machines could be purchased to increase availability of machine hours. However, in the short-run, management must make the most efficient use of the scarce resources it currently has.

Scarce resource

Is Internal Auditing Still an Internal Function?

Evaluating make-or-buy decisions for purchased parts and subassemblies has long been a routine function for management accountants. The practice of outsourcing corporate support services, especially commodity-type items such as payroll, security, and food service, also has become commonplace.

More recently, poor earnings brought about by global competition and also overcapacity in the banking and financial services industry has resulted in outsourcing of data processing, taxation, and legal services. Internal auditing is the latest subject for outsourcing evaluation.

Several years ago, Clark Equipment Company, a manufacturer with annual sales of $1.5 billion, successfully outsourced all of its internal auditing. New management decided to sell the function to the internal auditing management group. As a separate private corporation now numbering 75 persons, the group continues to provide internal auditing and other EDP or accounting-related management services to Clark as well as to a variety of other companies. Except for Clark, they provide expertise to supplement an existing in-house internal auditing function and avoid total outsourcing.

The outsourcing of internal auditing to CPA firms has begun to attract more attention recently. Contractual outsourcing services offered by CPA firms range from merely furnishing audit staff to work under the supervision of in-house internal auditing management or performing the internal audit of a foreign location to a total turnkey operation including contractual management of the entire internal auditing function. In explaining the advantages of total outsourcing, Arthur Andersen notes in its marketing brochure that outsourcing "is an effective way to manage cost without sacrificing quality."

SOURCE: Curtis C. Verschoor, "Evaluating Outsourcing of Internal Auditing," *Management Accounting* (February 1992), pp. 27–30. Reprinted from *Management Accounting*. Copyright by Institute of Management Accountants, Montvale, N.J.

Determining the best use of a scarce resource requires managerial recognition of company objectives. If the objective is to maximize company contribution margin and profits, a scarce resource is best used to produce and sell the product having the highest contribution margin *per unit of the scarce resource*. This strategy assumes that the company is faced with only one scarce resource.

Exhibit 15–6 presents information on two products being manufactured by Advanced Technology Company. The company's scarce resource is its access to machine time; only 1,000 machine hours are available per month to make either palmtop personal computers (PCs) or cellular telephones or some combination of both. Demand is unlimited for both products and there are no variable selling, general, or administrative costs related to either product.

The palmtop's $2,700 selling price minus its $1,800 variable cost provides a contribution margin of $900 per unit. The telephone's contribution margin per unit is $150 ($390 selling price minus $240 variable cost). Fixed overhead related to these two product lines totals $1,860,000 and is allocated to products for purposes of inventory valuation. Fixed overhead, however, does not change with production levels within the relevant range and, as such, is not relevant in a short-run scarce resource decision.

Since fixed overhead per unit is not relevant in the short-run, unit contribution margin rather than unit gross margin is the appropriate measure of profitability of the two products.[4] Unit contribution margin is multiplied by the quantity of output per

---

[4] Gross margin (or gross profit) is unit selling price minus total product cost per unit. Total product cost includes allocated fixed overhead.

■ EXHIBIT 15–6
Advanced Technology—
PC and Telephone
Product Information

	PALMTOP PC	CELLULAR TELEPHONE
Selling price per unit (a)	$2,700	$ 390
Variable production cost per unit:		
Direct materials	$ 950	$ 80
Direct labor	325	85
Variable overhead	525	75
Total variable production cost (b)	$1,800	$ 240
Unit contribution margin [(c) = (a) − (b)]	$ 900	$ 150
Times units of output per machine hour (d)	6	50
Contribution margin per machine hour [(c) x (d)]	$5,400	$7,500

unit of the scarce resource (in this case, machine hours) to obtain the contribution margin per unit of scarce resource. The last line in Exhibit 15–6 shows the $5,400 contribution margin per machine hour ($900 × 6) for the palmtop PCs compared to $7,500 for the cellular telephones ($150 × 50). Thus, it is more profitable for Advanced Technology to produce cellular telephones than palmtop PCs.

At first glance, it would appear that the palmtop PC would be the most profitable of the two products since its contribution margin per unit ($900) is significantly higher than that of the cellular telephone ($150). However, since one hour of machine time produces over eight times as many cellular telephones as palmtop PCs, a greater amount of contribution margin per hour of scarce resource is generated by the production of the phones. If these were the only two products made by Advanced Technology and the company wanted to achieve the highest possible profit, it would dedicate all machine time to the production of cellular telephones. Such a strategy would provide a total contribution margin of $7,500,000 per month, if all units produced were sold (1,000 MHs × $7,500 CM per MH).

When one limiting factor is involved, the outcome of a scarce resource decision will indicate that a single type of product should be manufactured and sold. Most situations, however, involve several limiting factors that compete with one another in the process of striving to attain business objectives. One method used to solve problems that have several limiting factors is **linear programming** (LP).[5]

Linear programming

In addition to considering the monetary effects related to scarce resource decisions, managers must remember that all factors cannot be readily quantified and the qualitative aspects of the situation must be evaluated in addition to the quantitative ones. For example, before choosing to produce only cellular telephones, Advanced Technology's managers would need to assess the potential damage to the firm's reputation and image if the company limited its product line to a single item. Such a choice severely restricts its customer base and is especially important if the currently manufactured products are competitively related. For example, if Hewlett-Packard began making only HP DeskJet 500 printers, all printer buyers might not believe that model was appropriate for their needs. These unfulfilled buyers would then be forced to purchase their printers from another company.

Concentrating on a single product can also create market saturation or company stagnation. There are some products, such as refrigerators and Rolex watches, that customers purchase infrequently or in single units. Making such a product limits the

[5]Linear programming techniques are useful in determining the appropriate amount of scarce resources to allocate to less profitable products. Linear programming techniques are discussed briefly in the appendix to the chapter and are covered in depth in most management science courses.

company's opportunity for repeat business. And, if the company concentrates on the wrong single product (such as buggy whips or Hula Hoops), that exclusionary choice can be the beginning of the end for the company.

In some cases, the revenues and expenses of a group of products must be considered as a set of decisions in allocating scarce resources. It is possible that multiple products may be complementary or that one product either is sold as part of a package with other products, cannot be used effectively without another, or will be the key to revenue generation in future periods. To illustrate these possibilities, consider the following products: Cross' well-known ballpoint pen and mechanical pencil sets; dining room tables and dining room chairs produced by Drexel Heritage Furniture; and the Barbie "family" of products made by Mattel, Inc. Would it be reasonable for Cross to make only pens, Drexel Heritage to make only tables, or Mattel to make only Barbie dolls and none of her related accessories (clothes, dream house, car, camper, and so forth)? Simply considering Mattel, company management would probably choose to manufacture Barbie dolls even if they produced zero contribution margin at the point of sale: sales of Barbie products produce close to $600 million per year for Mattel.

Thus, company management may decide that production and sale of some number of less profitable products is a necessary part of its product mix to maintain either customer satisfaction or sales of another product. Production mix translates on the revenue side into sales mix, which is addressed in the next section.

Sales Mix Decisions

Management is continuously striving to achieve a variety of company objectives such as company profit maximization, improvement of the company's relative market share, and generation of customer goodwill and loyalty. These objectives are accomplished by selling products or performing services. Regardless of whether the company is a retailer, manufacturer, or service organization, **sales mix** refers to "the relative combination of quantities of sales of the various products that make up the total sales of a company."[6] Some important factors affecting the appropriate sales mix of a company are product selling prices, sales force compensation, and advertising expenditures. A change in one or all of these factors may cause a company's sales mix to shift.

Information on Advanced Technology's calculator line are presented in Exhibit 15–7 and are used to illustrate the effects on sales mix of the three factors mentioned above. The product line includes economy, standard, and deluxe calculators, each having different features and aimed at a different market segment.

Sales Price Changes and Relative Profitability of Products.   Managers must continuously monitor the relative selling prices of company products, both in respect to each other as well as to competitors' prices. This process may provide information that causes management to change one or more selling prices. Factors that might influence price changes include fluctuations in demand or production/distribution cost, economic conditions, and competition. Any shift in the selling price of one product in a multiproduct firm will normally cause a change in sales mix of that firm because of the economic law of demand elasticity with respect to price.[7]

Advanced Technology management has set profit maximization as the primary corporate objective. Such a strategy does not necessarily mean selling the most units of the product with the highest selling prices and the fewest units of the product with

Sales mix

[6]Institute of Management Accountants (formerly National Association of Accountants), *Statements of Management Accounting: Management Accounting Terminology,* Number 2 (Montvale, N.J.: June 1, 1983), p. 94.
[7]The law of demand elasticity indicates how closely price and demand are related. Product demand is highly elastic if a small price reduction generates a large demand increase. If demand is less elastic, large price reductions are needed to bring about moderate sales volume increases. In contrast, a small price increase results in a large drop in demand if demand is highly elastic.

	ECONOMY	STANDARD	DELUXE
Unit selling price	$35	$80	$160
Variable production cost per unit:			
Direct materials	$ 3	$16	$ 58
Direct labor	1	10	30
Variable factory overhead	1	8	30
Total variable production cost	$ 5	$34	$118
Product contribution margin	$30	$46	$ 42
Less variable selling expense*	7	16	32
Contribution margin per unit**	$23	$30	$ 10

Total fixed costs:	
Production	$ 700,000
Selling and administrative	300,000
Total	$1,000,000

* The only variable selling expense is for sales commissions, which are always set at 20% of the selling price per unit.
** An equal number of any type of calculator can be made in one hour of machine time. Thus, the contribution margin per unit does not need to be converted to contribution margin per machine hour.

EXHIBIT 15–7
Advanced Technology—
Calculator Product
Information

the lowest selling price as possible. The product with the highest selling price per unit does not necessarily yield the highest contribution margin per unit or per unit of scarce resource. In Advanced Technology's case, the calculator with the highest selling price (the deluxe model) yields the lowest unit contribution margin of the three products. It is more profit-beneficial to sell one of the standard calculators than either the economy or deluxe models since one standard calculator provides the highest per unit contribution margin of all the company's products. Even unit sales of the economy calculators benefit the company more than sales of the deluxe because, although they have the lowest selling price per unit, their contribution margin is greater than that of the deluxe calculators.

If profit maximization is a company's goal, management should consider the sales volume and unit contribution margin of each product. Total company contribution margin is the sum of the contribution margins provided by all the products' sales. Exhibit 15–8 provides information on sales volumes and indicates the respective total contribution margins of the three types of calculators. Although economy calculators

	UNIT CONTRIBUTION MARGIN (FROM EXHIBIT 15–7)	CURRENT SALES VOLUME IN UNITS	INCOME STATEMENT INFORMATION
Economy calculators	$23	62,000	$1,426,000
Standard calculators	$30	43,000	1,290,000
Deluxe calculators	$10	38,000	380,000
Total contribution margin of product sales mix			$3,096,000
Fixed expenses (from Exhibit 15–7)			1,000,000
Product line income at present volume and sales mix			$2,096,000

EXHIBIT 15–8
Advanced Technology—
Relationship Between
Contribution Margin and
Sales Volume

EXHIBIT 15–9

Advanced Technology—
Relationship Between
Selling Price and Demand

	UNIT CONTRIBUTION MARGIN	NEW SALES VOLUME IN UNITS	INCOME STATEMENT INFORMATION
Economy calculators	$27*	50,000	$1,350,000
Standard calculators	$30	43,000	1,290,000
Deluxe calculators	$10	38,000	380,000
Total contribution margin of product sales mix			$3,020,000
Fixed expenses (from Exhibit 15–7)			1,000,000
Product line income at new volume and sales mix			$2,020,000

*New selling price of $40 minus [total variable production costs of $5 plus variable selling expense of $8 (20% of new selling price)].

do not have the highest contribution margin per unit, they do generate the largest total contribution margin in this product line for Advanced Technology because of their sales volume. To maximize profits from this product line, Advanced Technology management must maximize total contribution margin rather than per unit contribution margin.

A product's sales volume is almost always intricately related to its selling price. Generally, when the selling price of a product or service is increased and demand is elastic with respect to price, demand for that product decreases.[8] Thus, if Advanced Technology management, in an attempt to increase profits, raises the price of the economy calculators to $40, there should be some decline in demand. Consultation with the marketing research personnel indicates that such a price increase would cause demand for that product to drop from 62,000 to 50,000 calculators per period. Exhibit 15–9 shows the effect of this pricing decision on the calculator product line income of Advanced Technology.

Even though the contribution margin per unit of the economy calculators increased, the total dollar contribution margin generated by sales of that product declined because of the decrease in sales volume. This example assumed that customers did not switch their purchases from economy calculators to other Advanced Technology products when the price of the economy calculators was raised. Price increases normally cause customers to switch from a company's higher-priced products to its lower-priced products. Switching within the company was ignored in this instance because the economy calculators were the lowest-priced calculators sold by Advanced Technology. It is *unlikely* that customers would stop buying economy calculators because of a $5 price increase and begin buying standard calculators that would have cost twice as much—but that situation could occur. Customers might believe that the difference in quality between the economy and standard calculators is worth the $40 (rather than $45) price difference and make such a purchasing switch.

In making decisions to raise or lower prices, the relevant quantitative factors include: (1) prospective or new contribution margin per unit of product; (2) both short-term and long-term changes in product demand and production volume because of the price change; and (3) best use of the company's scarce resources. Some relevant qualitative factors involved in pricing decisions are: (1) impact of changes on customer goodwill toward the company; (2) customer loyalty toward company products; and (3) competitors' responses to the firm's new pricing structure.[9]

---

[8] Such a decline in demand generally would not occur when the product in question has no close substitutes or is not a major expenditure in consumers' budgets.

[9] In regard to this last item, consider what occurs when one airline raises or lowers its fares between cities. It typically does not take very long for all the other airlines flying that route to adjust their fares accordingly. Thus, any competitive advantage lasts only for a short time.

NEWS NOTE

Make Sure Your "Base Case" Is an Appropriate Comparison

Finance theory assumes that a project will be evaluated against its base case, that is, what will happen if the project is not carried out. Managers tend to explore fully the implications of adopting the project but usually spend less time considering the likely outcome of not making the investment. Yet unless the base case is realistic, the incremental cash flows— the difference between the "with" and the "without" scenarios— will mislead.

Often companies implicitly assume that the base case is simply a continuation of the status quo, but this assumption ignores market trends and competitor behavior. It also neglects the impact of changes the company might make anyway, like improving operations management.

Using the wrong base case is typical of product launches in which the new product will likely erode the market for the company's existing product line. Take Apple Computer's introduction of the Macintosh SE. The new PC had obvious implications for sales of earlier generation Macintoshes. To analyze the incremental cash flows arising from the new product, Apple would have needed to count the lost contribution from sales of its existing products as a cost of the launch.

Wrongly applied, however, this approach would equate the without case to the status quo: it would assume that without the SE, sales of existing Macintoshes would continue at their current level. In the competitive PC market, however, nothing stands still. Competitors like IBM would likely innovate and take share away from the earlier generation Macintoshes—which a more realistic base case would have reflected.

When deciding to make price changes for current products or introduce new products that will compete with and potentially affect current products' sales volumes, managers need to be certain that their assumptions about consumer behavior are rational. The News Note about "base case" discusses the concept of the rational "base case" scenario.

When pricing proposed new products, a long-run view of the product's life cycle should be taken. This view would include assumptions about consumer behavior, competitor behavior, pace of technology changes, government posture, environmental concerns, size of the potential market, and demographic changes. These considerations would affect product selling price estimates at the various stages in the product's life cycle. Then, as discussed in Chapter 5, these estimates would be averaged to obtain the starting point in the process of target costing.

Compensation Changes.   Many companies compensate their salespersons by paying a fixed rate of commission on gross sales dollars. Such a policy motivates salespeople to sell the highest-priced product rather than the product providing the highest contribution margin to the company. If the company has a profit-maximization objective, a commission policy of a percentage of sales will not be effective in achieving that objective.

Assume Advanced Technology currently has a commission policy of 20 percent of selling price. This commission structure encourages sales of the deluxe rather than the economy or standard calculators. The company is considering a new compensation structure for its sales force. The new structure would provide for a base salary to all salespeople, which would total $950,000 per period. In addition, the salespeople would be paid a 25 percent commission on product contribution margin (selling price minus total variable *production* costs). The per-unit product contribution margins of the calculators were given in Exhibit 15–7 as $30, $46, and $42, respectively, for economy, standard, and deluxe units. The new compensation policy should motivate sales personnel to sell more of the product that would produce the highest commission, which would correspondingly be the company's most profitable product.

Exhibit 15–10 compares Advanced Technology's total contribution margin using the original sales mix and commission structure (repeated from Exhibit 15–8) with total contribution margin provided under a newly assumed sales mix and the new salesperson compensation structure. The new structure is more profit-beneficial than the old because sales were shifted from the lower contribution margin calculators toward the more profitable standard calculators.

Fixed expenses would not be considered in setting compensation structures unless those expenses were incremental relative to the new policy or to changes in sales volumes. The new base salaries were an incremental cost of Advanced Technology's proposed compensation plan.

Advertising Budget Changes.   Another factor that may cause shifts in the sales mix involves either adjusting the advertising budgets respective to each company product or increasing the company's total advertising budget. This section continues using the original data for Advanced Technology and examines a proposed increase in the company's total advertising budget.

Advanced Technology's advertising manager, Alicia Daniels, has proposed doubling the advertising budget from $40,000 to $80,000 per year. Ms. Daniels thinks the increased advertising will result in the following additional unit sales during the coming year: economy, 5,000; standard, 3,000; and deluxe, 2,000.

▌ EXHIBIT 15–10

Advanced Technology—Impact of Change in Commission Structure

Old Policy—Commissions equal to 20% of selling price

	PRODUCT CONTRIBUTION MARGIN	–	COMMISSION	=	CONTRIBUTION MARGIN AFTER COMMISSION	×	OLD VOLUME	=	TOTAL CONTRIBUTION MARGIN
Economy	$30		(.2 × $ 35) or $ 7		$23		62,000		$1,426,000
Standard	46		(.2 × $ 80) or 16		30		43,000		1,290,000
Deluxe	42		(.2 × $160) or 32		10		38,000		380,000
Total contribution margin for product sales									$3,096,000

New Policy—Commissions equal to 25% of product contribution margin per unit and incremental base salaries of $950,000

	PRODUCT CONTRIBUTION MARGIN	–	COMMISSION	=	CONTRIBUTION MARGIN AFTER COMMISSION	×	OLD VOLUME	=	TOTAL CONTRIBUTION MARGIN
Economy	$30		(.25 × $30) or $ 7.50		$22.50		52,000		$1,170,000
Standard	46		(.25 × $46) or 11.50		34.50		49,000		1,690,500
Deluxe	42		(.25 × $42) or 10.50		31.50		42,000		1,323,000
Total contribution margin for product sales									$4,183,500
Less sales force base salaries									950,000
Contribution margin adjusted for sales force base salaries									$3,233,500

	ECONOMY	STANDARD	DELUXE	TOTAL
Increase in volume	5,000	3,000	2,000	10,000
Contribution margin per unit	× $23	× $30	× $10	
Incremental contribution margin	$115,000	$90,000	$20,000	$225,000
Incremental fixed cost of advertising				40,000
Incremental benefit of increased advertising expenditure				$185,000

EXHIBIT 15–11

Advanced Technology— Incremental Analysis of Increased Advertising Cost

If the company spends the additional $40,000 for advertising, will the additional 10,000 units of sales produce larger profits than Advanced Technology is currently experiencing on this product line? The original fixed costs as well the contribution margin generated by the old sales level are irrelevant to the decision. The relevant items are the increased sales revenue, increased variable costs, and increased fixed cost—the incremental effects of the change. The difference between incremental revenues and incremental variable costs is the incremental contribution margin from which the incremental fixed cost is subtracted to provide the incremental benefit (or loss) of the decision.[10]

Exhibit 15–11 shows the expected increase in contribution margin if the increased advertising expenditure is made. The $225,000 of additional contribution margin far exceeds the $40,000 incremental cost for advertising, so company management should definitely increase its advertising by $40,000.

Increased advertising may cause changes in the sales mix or in the number of units sold. Sales can also be affected by opportunities that allow companies to obtain business at a sales price that differs from the normal price.

Special Order Decisions

A **special order decision** requires that management compute a reasonable sales price for production or service jobs outside the company's normal realm of operations. Special order situations include jobs that require a bid, are taken during slack periods, or are made to a particular buyer's specifications. Typically, the sales price quoted on a special order job should be high enough to cover the job's variable and incremental fixed costs and to generate a profit. Moreover, as discussed in Chapter 5, overhead costs tend to rise with increases in product variety and product complexity. The increases are typically experienced in receiving, inspection, order processing, and inventory carrying costs. Activity-based costing techniques allow managers to more accurately determine these incremental costs and properly include them in analyzing special orders.

Sometimes companies depart from the above price-setting routine and "low-ball" bid jobs. A low-ball bid may cover only costs and produce no profit or may even be below cost. The rationale behind low-ball bids is to obtain the job and have the opportunity to introduce company products or services to a particular market segment. Special pricing of this nature may provide work for a period of time, but it cannot be continued over the long run. To remain in business, a company must set selling prices to cover total costs and provide a reasonable profit margin.[11]

Special order decision

---

[10]This same type of incremental analysis is shown in Chapter 14 in relation to CVP computations.
[11]An exception to this general rule may occur when a company produces related or complementary products. For instance, an electronics company may sell a video game at or below cost and allow the ancillary software program sales to be the primary source of profit.

Another type of special pricing job is that of private label orders in which the buyer's name (rather than the seller's) is used on the product. Companies may accept these jobs during slack periods to use available capacity more effectively. Fixed costs are typically not allocated to special-order, private label products. Some variable costs (such as sales commissions) may be reduced or eliminated by the very nature of the private label process. The prices on these special orders are typically set high enough to cover the actual variable costs and provide some coverage of ongoing fixed costs.

Special prices may also be justified when orders are unusual (because of the quantity, method of delivery, or packaging) or because the products are being tailor made to customer instructions. Lastly, special pricing may be used when goods are produced for a one-time job, such as an overseas order that will not affect domestic sales.

Assume that Advanced Technology has been given the opportunity to bid on a special order for 10,000 private label videodisc players for a major appliance company. Company management wants to obtain the order as long as the additional business will provide a satisfactory contribution to profit. Advanced Technology has machine and labor hours that are not currently being used, and raw materials can be obtained from the supplier. Also, the company has no immediate opportunity to use its currently unused capacity in another way, so an opportunity cost is not a factor.

Exhibit 15–12 presents information that management has gathered to determine a price to bid on the videodisc players. Direct materials, direct labor, and *variable* factory overhead costs are relevant to setting the bid price because these variable production costs will be incurred for each disc player produced. While all variable costs are normally relevant to a special pricing decision, the variable selling expense is irrelevant in this instance because no sales commission will be paid on this sale. Fixed manufacturing overhead and fixed selling and administrative expenses are not expected to increase because of this sale, so these expenses are not included in the pricing decision.

Using the available cost information, the relevant cost used to determine the bid price for each videodisc player is $24 (direct materials, direct labor, and variable overhead). This cost is the *minimum* price at which the company should sell one player. If the existing fixed costs have been covered by regular sales, any price set higher than $24 will provide the company some profit.

Assume that Advanced Technology's videodisc player line is currently experiencing a $10,000 net loss and that company managers want to set a bid price that would cover the net loss generated by other sales and create a $10,000 before-tax profit. In this case, Advanced Technology would spread the total $20,000 desired amount over the 10,000 special order videodisc players at $2 per player. This decision would give

■ EXHIBIT 15–12

Advanced Technology—
Videodisc Player Product
Information

	NORMAL COSTS	RELEVANT COSTS
Per unit cost for 1 videodisc player:		
Direct materials	$18	$18
Direct labor	4	4
Variable overhead	2	2
Variable selling expense (commission)	20	0
Total variable cost	$44	$24
Fixed factory overhead (allocated)	3	
Fixed selling & administrative expense	1	
Total cost per videodisc player	$48	

a bid price of $26 per player ($24 variable cost + $2). However, *any* price above the $24 variable cost will contribute toward reducing the $10,000 product line loss.

In setting the bid price, management must decide how much profit it would consider reasonable on the special order. As another example, assume Advanced Technology's usual selling price for a videodisc player is $70 and each sale provides a normal profit margin of $22 per player or 46 percent of the $48 total cost. Setting the bid price for the special order at $35 would cover the variable production costs of $24 and provide a normal 46 percent profit margin on the incremental unit cost. This computation illustrates a simplistic cost-plus approach to pricing, but ignores both product demand and market competition. Advanced Technology's bid price should also reflect these considerations. In addition, company management should consider the effect that the additional job will have on the activities engaged in by the company and whether these activities will create additional, unforeseen costs.

When setting a special order price, management must consider the qualitative issues as well as the quantitative ones. For instance, will setting a low bid price cause this customer (or others) to believe that a precedent has been established for future prices? Will the contribution margin on a bid, set low enough to acquire the job, earn a sufficient amount to justify the additional burdens placed on management or employees by this activity? Will the additional production activity require the use of bottleneck resources and reduce company throughput? How, if at all, will special order sales affect the company's normal sales? If the job is taking place during a period of low business activity (off-season or recession), is management willing to take the business at a lower contribution or profit margin simply to keep a trained work force employed?

A final management consideration in special pricing decisions is the **Robinson-Patman Act**, which prohibits companies from pricing the same product at different amounts when those amounts do not reflect related cost differences. Cost differences must result from actual variations in the cost to manufacture, sell, or distribute a product because of differing methods of production or quantities sold.

Robinson-Patman Act

Companies may, however, give **ad hoc discounts**, which are price concessions that relate to real (or imagined) competitive pressures rather than to location of the merchandising chain or volume purchased. Such discounts are not usually subject to detailed justification, since they are based on a competitive market environment. Ad hoc discounts do not require intensive justification under the law, but other types of discounts do since they may reflect some type of price discrimination.

Ad hoc discount

Prudent managers must understand the legalities of special pricing and the factors that allow for its implementation. For merchandise that is normally stocked, the only support for pricing differences is a difference in distribution costs.

In making pricing decisions, managers typically first analyze the market environment, including the degree of industry competition and competitors' prices. Then, managers normally consider full production cost in setting normal sales prices. Full production cost includes an allocated portion of fixed costs of the production process which, in a multiproduct environment, could mean common costs of production relating to more than one type of product. Allocations of common costs can distort the results of operations shown for individual products.

Product Line Decisions

Operating results of multiproduct environments are often presented in a disaggregated format indicating separate product lines within the organization or division. In reviewing these disaggregated statements, managers must distinguish relevant from irrelevant information as that information relates to the individual product lines. If all costs (variable *and* fixed) are allocated to product lines, a product line or segment may be perceived to be operating at a loss when actually it is not. Such perceptions may be caused by the commingling of relevant and irrelevant information on the statements.

EXHIBIT 15–13

Leyh Division of Advanced Technology Product Line Income Statements

	Scanners	Plotters	Printers	Total
Sales	$400,000	$600,000	$1,000,000	$2,000,000
Total direct variable expenses	140,000	240,000	450,000	830,000
Total contribution margin	$260,000	$360,000	$ 550,000	$1,170,000
Total fixed expenses	210,000	370,000	555,000	1,135,000
Net income (loss)	$ 50,000	$ (10,000)	$ (5,000)	$ 35,000
Fixed expenses are detailed below:				
(1) Avoidable fixed expenses	$120,000	$362,000	$ 230,000	$ 712,000
(2) Unavoidable fixed expenses	60,000	6,000	250,000	316,000
(3) Allocated common expenses	30,000	2,000	75,000	107,000
Total	$210,000	$370,000	$ 555,000	$1,135,000

Exhibit 15–13 presents basic earnings information for the Leyh Division of Advanced Technology, which manufactures three product lines: optic scanners, engineering plotters, and color printers. The format of the information given in the exhibit makes it appear that the plotter and printer lines are each operating at a net loss ($10,000 and $5,000, respectively). Managers reviewing such results might reason that the firm would be $15,000 more profitable if both products were eliminated. Such a conclusion may be premature because of the mixture of relevant and irrelevant information in the income statement presentation.

All fixed expenses have been allocated to the individual product lines in Exhibit 15–13. Such allocations are traditionally based on one or more measures of "presumed" equity, such as square footage of the manufacturing plant occupied by each product line, number of machine hours incurred for production of each product line, or number of employees directly associated with each product line. In all cases, however, allocations may force fixed expenses into specific product line operating results even though some of those expenses may not have actually been incurred for the benefit of the specific product line.

In Exhibit 15–14, the fixed expenses of the Leyh Division are segregated into three subcategories: (1) those that are avoidable if the particular product line is eliminated (these expenses may also be referred to as attributable expenses); (2) those that are directly associated with a particular product line but are unavoidable; and (3) those that are incurred for the company as a whole (common expenses) and that are allocated to the individual product lines. The latter two subcategories are irrelevant to the question of whether to eliminate a product line. An unavoidable expense will merely be shifted to another product line if the product line with which it is associated is eliminated. Common expenses will be incurred regardless of which product lines are eliminated. An example of a common cost is the insurance premium on a manufacturing facility that houses all product lines.

Segment margin

If both the plotter and color printer lines are eliminated, total company profit will decline by $318,000. This amount represents the combined lost **segment margin** of the two product lines—$320,000 positive for printers and $2,000 negative for plotters. Segment margin represents the excess of revenues over direct variable expenses and avoidable fixed expenses. It is the amount remaining to cover unavoidable direct fixed expenses and common expenses and then to provide profits.[12] The segment mar-

---

[12] It was assumed here that all common expenses are fixed expenses; this is not always the case. Some common costs could be variable, such as expenses of processing purchase orders or computer time-sharing expenses for payroll or other corporate functions.

	Scanners	Plotters	Printers	Total
Sales	$400,000	$600,000	$1,000,000	$2,000,000
Total direct variable expenses	140,000	240,000	450,000	830,000
Total contribution margin	$260,000	$360,000	$ 550,000	$1,170,000
(1) Avoidable fixed expenses	120,000	362,000	230,000	712,000
Segment margin	**$140,000**	**$(2,000)**	**$ 320,000**	**$ 458,000**
(2) Unavoidable direct fixed expenses (see Exhibit 15–13)	60,000	6,000	250,000	316,000
Total product line operating results	$ 80,000	$ (8,000)	$ 70,000	$ 142,000
(3) Common expenses	30,000	2,000	75,000	107,000
Net income (loss)	$ 50,000	$ (10,000)	$ (5,000)	$ 35,000

gin figure is the appropriate one on which to base the continuation or elimination decision since it measures the segment's contribution to the coverage of indirect and unavoidable expenses. The decrease in total income that would result with only one product line can be shown in the following alternative computations. With only one product line (scanners), Leyh would experience a total net loss of $283,000, computed as follows:

Current net income	$ 35,000
Increase in income due to elimination of plotter product line (segment margin)	2,000
Decrease in income due to elimination of color printer product line (segment margin)	(320,000)
New net income	$(283,000)

This new net income can also be proven by the following computation:

Segment margin of the scanner product line	$ 140,000
Minus all remaining unavoidable and allocated expenses shown in Exhibit 15–13 ($316,000 + $107,000)	423,000
Net loss with one product line	$(283,000)

Based on the information shown in Exhibit 15–14, the Leyh Division should eliminate the plotter product line because it is generating a negative segment margin and, therefore, is not even covering its own expenses. If the plotter line were eliminated, total company profit would increase by $2,000, the amount of the negative segment margin.

In classifying product line costs, managers should be aware that some costs may appear to be avoidable but actually are not. For example, the salary of a supervisor working directly with a product line appears to be an avoidable fixed cost if the product line is eliminated. However, if these individuals have significant experience, they are often retained and transferred to other areas of the company even if product lines are cut. Determinations such as these need to be made before costs can be appropriately classified in product line elimination decisions.

Depreciation on factory equipment used to manufacture a specific product is an irrelevant cost in product line decisions. But if the equipment can be sold, the selling price is relevant to the decision because it would increase the marginal benefit of the decision to discontinue the product line. Even if the equipment will be kept in service and be used to produce other products, the depreciation expense on it is unavoidable and irrelevant to the decision.

Before making spontaneous decisions to discontinue a product line, management should carefully consider what it would take to "turn the product line around" and the long-term ramifications of the elimination decision. For example, elimination of a product line shrinks market assortment, which may cause some customers to seek other suppliers that maintain a broader market assortment. On the other hand, the costs of maintaining too many product lines may lead to lower quality. As stated by James Wisner of Financial Services Corporation (Marietta, Georgia) before he decided to focus on specific core operations: "The company was not driven by excellence, but by diversity." Additionally, as in other relevant costing situations, a decision to eliminate a product line has qualitative as well as quantitative factors that must be analyzed.

Management's task is to effectively and efficiently allocate its finite stock of resources to accomplish its chosen set of objectives. A cost accountant needs to learn what uses will be made of the information requested by managers to make certain that the relevant information is provided in the appropriate form. In this way, managers will have a reliable quantitative basis on which to analyze problems, compare viable solutions, and choose the best course of action. Because management is a social rather than a natural science, there are no fundamental "truths" and few problems are susceptible to black-or-white solutions. Relevant costing is a process of making human approximations of the costs of alternative decision results.

Seiko makes a wide variety of watches and introduces new ones each year. Decisions on product line continuance must be made after considering the "right" margins—making certain that unavoidable and common costs aren't clouding the issue.

R E V I S I T I N G

HEWLETT-PACKARD

Relying on suppliers, of course, carries its own risks. "It's not a game for the naive player. It demands careful study," says Roger Levien, vice president of technology and market development for Xerox Corp., which has had a joint venture with Japan's Fuji Photo Film Co. for three decades. In fact, one major danger is that a supplier may wrest away control of a market from its corporate customer.

According to the WSJ, when Hewlett-Packard began selling laser printers, Canon, its engine supplier, was also peddling its own printers. In striking the engine deal, Hewlett-Packard sought to protect itself by denying Canon rights to the so-called PCL software that distinguishes Hewlett-Packard's printers. Denied the software, Canon can't easily clone Hewlett- Packard's printer and remains a relatively small player in laser printers.

Relying on an outsider's help for one product line doesn't preclude Hewlett-Packard from handling all the chief elements of another line. Thus, it sells a less expensive family of printers based on its own "ink-jet" technique. It makes the engines for them and even the replacement ink cartridges.

"It's dumb to make everything just in order to prove you can," says James Brian Quinn, a management professor at Dartmouth. "The key is to do something better than everyone else in the world." [Hewlett-Packard appears to have learned this lesson quite well.]

SOURCE: *Hewlett-Packard in Brief* (March 1992) and G. Pascal Zachary, "High-Tech Firms Find It's Good to Line Up Outside Contractors," *Wall Street Journal* (July 29, 1992), pp. A1, A5. Reprinted by permission of the *Wall Street Journal,* © 1992 Dow Jones & Company, Inc. All rights reserved worldwide.

CHAPTER SUMMARY

Relevant information is logically related and pertinent to a given decision. Relevant information may be both quantitative and qualitative. Variable costs are generally relevant to a decision; they are irrelevant only when they cannot be avoided under any possible alternative or when they do not differ between (among) alternatives. Direct avoidable fixed costs are also relevant to decision making. Sometimes costs give the illusion of being relevant when actually they are not. Examples of such irrelevant costs include sunk costs, arbitrarily allocated common costs, and nonincremental fixed costs that have been averaged on a per unit basis.

Relevant costing compares the incremental or additional revenues and/or costs associated with alternative decisions. Managers use relevant costing to determine the incremental benefits of decision alternatives. One option that provides zero incremental benefit to the company is to "change nothing."

Situations in which relevant costing is essential include asset replacements, make-or-buy decisions, scarce resource allocations, special price determinations, sales mix distributions, and retention or elimination of product lines. The following points are important to remember:

1. In an asset replacement decision, costs paid in the past are not relevant to decisions being made currently; ignore sunk costs.

2. In a make-or-buy decision, include the opportunity costs associated with the buy alternative; nonproduction potentially allows management an opportunity to make plant assets and personnel available for other purposes.

3. In a decision involving a single scarce resource, if the objective is to maximize company contribution margin and profits, production and sales should be focused toward the product with the highest contribution margin per unit of the scarce resource.

4. In a special order decision, the minimum selling price a company should charge to not lose money is the sum of all the incremental costs of production and sale of the order.

5. In a sales mix decision, changes in selling prices and advertising normally affect sales volume, thus changing the company's total contribution margin ratio. Also, tying sales commissions to contribution margin motivates salespeople to sell products that will most benefit the company's profit picture.

6. In a product line decision, product lines should be evaluated on their segment margins rather than on an income figure computed after deducting direct unavoidable fixed expenses and allocation of corporate common expenses.

Quantitative analysis is generally short-range in perspective. After analyzing the quantifiable factors associated with each alternative, a manager must assess the merit and potential risks of the qualitative factors involved to select the best possible course of action. Some of these qualitative factors (such as the community economic impact of closing a plant) may present long-range planning and policy implications. Other qualitative factors may be short-range in nature, such as competitor reactions. Managers must decide the relevance of individual factors based on experience, judgment, knowledge of theory, and use of logic.

APPENDIX

Linear Programming

Some factors restrict the immediate attainment of almost any objective. For example, assume that the objective of the board of directors at Cunningham Hospital is to help sick people in Zachary, Ohio, during the coming year. Factors restricting the attainment of that objective include number of beds in the hospital, size of the hospital staff, hours per week the staff is allowed to work, and number of charity patients the hospital can accept. Each factor reflects a limited or scarce resource and Cunningham Hospital must find a means of achieving its objective with its limited resources.

Managers are always concerned with allocating scarce resources among competing products. If a company has only one scarce resource, managers will schedule production or other measures of activity to maximize the use of the scarce resource. Most situations, however, involve several limiting factors that compete with one another during the process of striving to attain business objectives. Solving problems with several limiting factors requires the use of **mathematical programming**, which refers to a variety of techniques used to allocate limited resources among activities to achieve a specific goal or purpose. This appendix provides an introduction to linear programming, which is one form of mathematical programming.[13]

Mathematical programming

[13]This chapter discusses some basic linear programming concepts; it is not an all-inclusive presentation. Consult any standard management science text for an in-depth presentation of the subject.

Basics of Linear Programming

Linear programming (LP) is a method used to find the optimal allocation of scarce resources in a situation involving one objective and multiple limiting factors.[14] The objective and restrictions on achieving that objective must be stated as linear equations.[15] The equation that states the objective is called the **objective function;** it specifies whether the objective is to maximize or to minimize some measure of performance. For example, a company's objective could be to maximize contribution margin or to minimize product cost.

Objective function

A **constraint** is any type of restriction that hampers management's pursuit of the objective. Resource constraints involve limited availability of labor time, machine time, raw materials, space, or production capacity. Demand or marketing constraints restrict the quantity of product that can be sold during a time period. Technical product requirements can also be constraints. For example, management may be constrained in the production requirements for frozen meals by caloric or vitamin content. A final constraint in all LP problems is a **non-negativity constraint.** This constraint specifies that there cannot be negative values of physical quantities. Constraints, like the objective function, are specified in mathematical equations and represent the limits imposed on optimizing the objective function.

Constraint

Non-negativity constraint

Almost every allocation problem has a multiple number of **feasible solutions** that do not violate any of the problem constraints. Different solutions generally give different values for the objective function, although in some cases a problem may have several solutions that provide the same value for the objective function. Solutions may be generated that contain fractional values. If solutions for variables must be restricted to whole numbers, **integer programming** techniques must be used to add additional constraints to the problem. The **optimal solution** to a maximization or minimization goal is the one that provides the best answer to the allocation problem. Some LP problems may have more than one optimal solution.

Feasible solution

Integer programming
Optimal solution

Formulating an LP Problem

Two common situations for linear programming techniques are scheduling production and combining ingredients. Management's goal in determining production mix in a multiproduct environment is to find the mix of products that, when sold, will maximize the company's contribution margin (the goal). The goal in determining the mix of ingredients for a specific product is to find the mix providing the specified level of quality at the minimum variable cost.

Each LP problem contains a dependent variable, two or more independent (or decision) variables, and one or more constraints. A **decision variable** is an unknown item for which the problem is being solved. The first and most important step in solving linear programming problems is setting up the information in mathematical equation form. The objective function and each of the constraints must be identified. The objective function is frequently stated such that the solution will either maximize contribution margin or minimize variable costs. Basic objective function formats for maximization and minimization problems are shown below:

Decision variable

Maximization problem

$$\text{Objective function: MAX CM} = CM_1X_1 + CM_2X_2$$

---

[14]Finding the best allocation of resources when multiple goals exist is called goal programming. This topic is not addressed in this text.
[15]If the objective and/or restrictions cannot be expressed in linear equations, the technique of nonlinear programming must be used. No general method has been developed that can solve all types of nonlinear programming problems.

c. Qualitative factors include the following:

- Future control by MDE of quality, supply, cost, and price of the brain
- Supplier's long-run chances of being in business
- Existence and number of other suppliers
- Impact on customers and markets

QUESTIONS

1. Define a relevant cost. For a hospital considering the purchase of a new X-ray machine, what would be some of the relevant costs of the purchase decision? What would be an alternative to purchasing the X-ray machine?

2. What are the characteristics of a relevant cost? Why are future costs not always relevant? Are all relevant costs found in accounting records? Explain.

3. "A decision that has only incremental costs and no incremental revenues cannot be made using relevant costing techniques." Is this statement true or false and why?

4. Which are more important in decision making: quantitative or qualitative factors? Why? How can qualitative factors be explicitly considered in making a decision?

5. Can a particular cost be relevant for one purpose, but not for other purposes? Give three examples where this would be the case.

6. Are sunk costs ever relevant in decision making? If so, give one or more examples.

7. Kelly O'Riley, owner of Juanita's Mexican Cafe, is trying to decide whether to make tortillas or buy them from a supplier, Ricardo's Super Mercado. Kelly has come to you for advice. What factors would you tell her to consider in making her choice?

8. Discuss the relationship between the notion that "management's task is to allocate its finite stock of resources to accomplish its objectives" and the importance of defining and utilizing relevant costs. Why will the resource that is most scarce in an organization be likely to change from time to time?

9. Dr. Bob's Preppy Clothing Store sells a variety of men's clothing. The insignia pullover shirts provide the highest contribution margin of all the items in the store. Would it be feasible for Dr. Bob to carry only insignia shirts rather than the sales mix he currently maintains? Why or why not?

10. Suggest some possible alternatives to basing sales commissions on the sales revenue generated by each salesperson. What would be the benefits and drawbacks of your methods to the salesperson and to the company?

11. Why is the effect of a sales price change partly determined by the elasticity of demand for the product?

12. What is a special order decision? What are the typical circumstances that lead to the need to make such a decision?

13. What are the differences among avoidable fixed costs, sunk direct fixed costs, and common fixed costs? Which are relevant and which are irrelevant in the decision to keep or eliminate a particular product line?

14. Is segment margin or product line margin more important in product line decisions? Why?

15. *(Appendix)* Why is linear programming used in business organizations?

16. *(Appendix)* How is the objective function of a linear programming problem related to accounting information typically expressed?

17. *(Appendix)* Discuss non-negativity constraints in the linear programming model and why they do not need to be specified for every linear programming problem.

18. *(Appendix)* What is the difference between a feasible solution and an optimal solution?

19. *(Appendix)* "Resource constraints are always inequalities." Is this statement true or false? Why?

20. *(Appendix)* What is the difference between a slack variable and a surplus variable? Can each exist in the same linear programming problem? If so, discuss how; if not, discuss why.

21. *(Relevant costs)* Prior to the 1993 Super Bowl, the Bay Area Department Store ordered 25,000 T-shirts that read: San Francisco 49ers—1993 Super Bowl Champs. The company paid, on average, $10.50 for each of these custom T-shirts. With San Francisco losing to the Dallas Cowboys, the department store is now stuck with 15,000 of the T-shirts. (The first 10,000 T-shirts were sold prior to the Super Bowl at an average price of $18.50.) The company has learned from one of its suppliers that each shirt could be reworked at a cost of $4.00 per shirt (which involves removing the Super Bowl reference from each shirt). The company could then sell each shirt for $8.00. Alternatively, the company can sell the shirts for $2.00 each as scrap material.
    a. Which costs are sunk in this decision?
    b. What are the relevant costs of each decision alternative and what should the company do?

22. *(Asset replacement decision)* Managers at East Lake Fish Processors are trying to decide whether they should keep their old fish processing equipment or invest in new, more energy efficient equipment. Some data on both groups of equipment follow:

	Old Equipment	New Equipment
Original cost	$67,000	$99,000
Remaining life	5 years	5 years
Accumulated depreciation	$24,000	$ 0
Annual cash operating costs	$17,000	$ 4,000
Current salvage value	$22,000	NA
Salvage value in 5 years	$ 0	$ 0

    a. Identify any sunk costs listed above.
    b. Identify any irrelevant (nondifferential) future costs.
    c. Identify all costs relevant to the equipment replacement decision.
    d. What are the opportunity costs associated with the alternative of keeping the old machine?
    e. What is the incremental cost to purchase the new machine?

23. *(Asset replacement decision)* Bangor Tin Co. purchased a new material handling system on April 1, 1994, for $80,000. On May 15, 1994, a representative of a computerized manufacturing technology company demonstrated a new computerized material delivery system, priced at $140,000, that would save the company $12,000 annually in labor costs compared to the recently installed material handling system. Both systems should last ten years and have no salvage value at that time. Bangor Tin can get $40,000 for the system purchased on April 1. The output of both systems is of equal quality. Should the company keep and use the system just purchased or buy the new computerized system? Show computations to support your answer.

24. *(Make or buy)* Atlanta Appliance Company manufactures an electric toaster oven. The company's normal selling price is $40 per unit. Its costs per unit at full capacity of 200,000 units are as follows:

Direct materials	$14	(includes self-manufactured heating element, which is $5 per unit)
Direct labor	6	
Overhead (2/3 is fixed)	12	
Total	$32	

One-third of the overhead is avoidable relative to the ovens.

A key component in the production of toaster ovens is the heating element. Eastern Electric has offered to sell Atlanta Appliance Company as many heating elements as the company needs for its toaster oven production. The offering price is $10 per unit. If Atlanta Appliance Company accepts the offer, the facilities that are currently used to produce heating elements could be used to produce an additional 25,000 units of the toaster oven. What alternative is more desirable and by what amount? (Assume the company has been operating at its current capacity of 200,000 units.)

25. *(Make or buy)* Arizona Corporation manufactures a small part which is used in the production of its major product, a sun umbrella. The cost accountant and the purchasing manager have discussed the possibility of buying this part from New Mexico Industries. The following data are available:

Cost per unit to manufacture:

Direct materials	$10
Direct labor	7
Variable overhead	6
Fixed overhead—applied	9
Total cost	$32

Cost per unit to buy:

Purchase price (subject to 2% discount)	$28
Freight charges	1
Total cost	$29

a. If Arizona Corporation always takes advantage of purchase discounts, should the company make or buy the part? Explain. (Assume all production costs are avoidable if the part is purchased.)

b. If Arizona Corporation buys the part from New Mexico Industries, it has no alternative use of the equipment now used for this production. Thus, 40% of the fixed overhead will continue even if production of the part ceases. Will your answer to part a now differ? Why or why not?

26. *(Make or buy)* The Pneumatic Shoe Company manufactures various types of shoes for sports and recreational use. Several types of shoes require a built-in air pump. Presently, the company makes all the air pumps it requires for production. However, management is evaluating an offer from Surefoot Supply Co. to provide air pumps at a cost of $5 each. Pneumatic Shoe Company management has estimated that the variable production costs of the air pump amount to $4 per unit. The firm also estimates that it could avoid $30,000 per year in fixed costs if it purchased rather than produced the air pumps.

a. If Pneumatic Shoe Company requires 20,000 pumps per year, should it make them or buy them from Surefoot Supply?

b. If Pneumatic Shoe Company requires 50,000 pumps per year, should it make them or buy them?

c. Assuming all other factors are equal, at what level of production would the company be indifferent between making and buying the pumps?

27. *(Allocation of scarce resource)* Because of a labor strike in the plant of a major competitor, Georgia Electronics has found itself operating at peak capacity. The firm makes two electronic tools, timing lights and ohm meters. At this time, the company can sell as many of each product as it can make, but it takes twice as long in machine hours to make timing lights as it does to make ohm meters. The firm's machines can only be run 80,000 hours per month. Data on each product follow:

	Timing Lights	Ohm Meters
Sales	$25	$18
Variable costs	15	12
Contribution margin	$10	$ 6
Machine hours required	4	2

Fixed costs run $120,000 per month.
a. How many of each product should the company make? Explain your answer.
b. Might there be qualitative considerations in following your recommendation for part a above? Name several.

28. *(Allocation of scarce resources)* Merry Melodies manufactures holiday bells. The firm produces three types of bells: dings, dongs, and tingalings. Due to political turmoil in Bosnia, a critical raw material, bellinium, is in very short supply and is restricting the number of bells the firm can produce. For the coming year, the firm will only be able to purchase 30,000 pounds of bellinium (at a cost of $4 per pound). The firm needs to determine how to allocate the bellinium to maximize profits. The following information has been gathered for your consideration:

	Dings	Dongs	Tingalings
Sales price per unit	$15	$10	$4.00
Bellinium cost	5	4	2.00
Direct labor cost	6	3	1.00
Variable overhead cost	2	1	0.25
Sales demand in units	200,000	300,000	1,000,000

Fixed production costs total $100,000 per year, fixed selling costs are $38,000, and there are no variable selling costs.
a. How should Merry Melodies allocate the scarce bellinium?
b. Based on the optimal allocation, what is the company's projected contribution margin for the coming year?

29. *(Special order)* Cleveland Wire Company produces 14-gauge barbed wire, which is retailed through farm supply companies. Presently, the company has the capacity to produce 2,000 tons of wire per year. At this time, the firm is operating at 75% of annual capacity and, at this level of operations, the cost per ton of wire is as follows:

Direct materials	$140
Direct labor	40
Variable overhead	15
Fixed overhead	80
Total	$275

The average sales price for the output produced by the firm is $400 per ton. The firm has been approached by an English company about supplying 300 tons of wire for a new game preserve. The company has offered Cleveland Wire Comany additional revenues. The logic of top management is that one free service (the videotape presentations) is enough.

   a. Discuss the reasons behind offering each of the various services to patrons.

   b. What business and ethical issues are involved in eliminating the individual consultations?

   c. Discuss the reasons for and against eliminating the individual consultations from the standpoint of management and clients.

51. *In 1982, Ford Motor Co. officials went to the test track to evaluate a prototype of their new Bronco II, a sports utility vehicle. One of the officials was the head of automotive safety, another was his superior. These two officials, along with Ford's top lawyer, witnessed something that surely sent shivers up their spines—while rounding a corner, a front wheel of the Bronco II lifted off the ground; a clear indication of its instability.*

   The Ford Bronco II went into production in January 1983. As of early 1993, 260 people have died in Bronco IIs in accidents involving the vehicle flipping over. Also, more than 100 lawsuits relating to the Bronco II have been settled by Ford. Ford settled all but two of these lawsuits out of court. Of the two that went to court, Ford won one and lost one. Court testimony in the cases that went to trial revealed the following facts:

     1. Ford knew in 1981 that it could make the vehicle considerably more stable by switching to a wider chassis, but it didn't do so because that would have cost valuable time in getting the product to market; it was in a race with GM and GM's S-10 Blazer to get to market.

     2. Ford's safety changes following the test track incident were largely superficial.

     3. Ford's tests after the Bronco II was available to the market continued to indicate that the vehicle was prone to tip or roll over on sharp turns.

     4. More than 50 safety-related documents regarding early rollover tests and suggestions for design improvements were inadvertently destroyed by Ford.

[SOURCE: Milo Geyelin and Neal Templin, "Ford Attorneys Played Unusually Large Role in Bronco II's Launch," *Wall Street Journal* (January 5, 1993), pp. A1, A6. Reprinted by permission of the *Wall Street Journal*, © 1993 Dow Jones & Company, Inc. All rights reserved worldwide.]

   a. Discuss whether it was ethical of Ford Motor Co. to bring the Bronco II to market, given the company's knowledge about the vehicle's safety problems.

   b. In making the decision to bring the vehicle to market in 1983, rather than make safety design changes and bring it to market later, what relevant costs did Ford possibly overlook?

   c. What action could the head of automotive safety at Ford have taken to induce Ford to revise the design of the Bronco II before bringing it to market?

52. *In 1987 EEOC's [Equal Employment Opportunity Commission] local field office wrote me a letter saying they had reason to believe I didn't have enough women "food servers" and "busers." No woman had complained against me. So the EEOC advertised in the local paper to tell women whose job applications we had rejected—or even women who had just thought of applying—that they could be entitled to damages. Twenty-seven women became plaintiffs in a lawsuit against me. The EEOC interviewed me for hours to find out what kind of person I was. I told them in Sicily where I came from I learned to respect women. I supplied them with hundreds of pounds of paper. I had to hire someone full time for a year just to respond to EEOC demands. Six months ago I finally settled. I agreed to pay $150,000 damages and as jobs open up, to hire the women on the EEOC's list. Even if they don't know what spaghetti looks like! I have to advertise twice a year even if I have no openings, just to add possible female employees to my files. I also had to hire an EEOC-approved person to teach my staff how not to discriminate. I employ 12 food servers in these two restaurants. Gross sales, around $2 million. How much did it all cost me? Cash outlay, about $400,000.*

   What the government's done to me—devastating. I wouldn't wish it on my worst enemy.

       Thomas Maggiore
       Phoenix, Arizona

[SOURCE: Peter Brimelow and Leslie Spencer, "When Quotas Replace Merit, Everybody Suffers," *Forbes* (February 15, 1993), pp. 80–82ff. Adapted by permission of *FORBES* Magazine (1993). © Forbes Inc.]

a. Do you think Mr. Maggiore's cash outlay of $400,000 includes all of the costs he incurred because of the EEOC regulation? Try breaking down the various costs that he may have incurred into three categories: direct costs, indirect costs, and opportunity costs.

b. Are hiring policies based on quotas ethical? How do quota systems affect the economic viability of American firms?

c. If EEOC regulations are intended to right past wrongs, should EEOC guidelines apply differently to immigrant Americans than to second, third, and fourth generation Americans? (Consider, for example, that any immigrant who falls into a protected class qualifies for all U.S. quota programs just like an American whose great-great-great-grandfather was a slave.)

d. How can quota systems have an effect on the quality of American products?

THE MASTER BUDGET

LEARNING
OBJECTIVES

After completing this chapter, you should be able to answer these questions:

1. Why is budgeting important?
2. How are strategic and tactical planning related to budgeting?
3. What is the starting point of a master budget and why?
4. How are the various schedules in a master budget prepared?
5. How do the schedules of the master budget relate to one another?
6. Why is the cash budget so important in the master budgeting process?
7. *(Appendix)* What are the advantages and disadvantages of imposed budgets? Participatory budgets?
8. *(Appendix)* How does a budget manual facilitate the budgeting process?

MASCO CORPORATION

Masco Corporation, headquartered in Taylor, Michigan, is among the country's largest manufacturers of brand-name consumer products designed for the building and improvement of the home. Some of these include faucets (Delta and Peerless), kitchen and bath cabinets (Fieldston and KraftMaid), appliances (Thermador and Waste King), furniture (Henredon and Drexel Heritage), upholstery and other fabrics (Robert Allen Fabrics and Sunbury Textiles), and decorative accessories (mirrors by LaBarge and lamps by Balwin Brass and Maitland-Smith).

The company has invested significant resources in just-in-time business management programs designed to institutionalize a continuous improvement ethic in Masco's business units so that the company can deliver quality products to consumers when and where they want them. Key goals include increasing manufacturing efficiency, improving quality and customer responsiveness, reducing inventories for the company and its customers, and increasing profitability.

Utilizing miniaturized workstations, employing sophisticated equipment such as laser scanners, Masco companies are achieving greater throughput and higher manufacturing efficiencies as well as reducing work in process inventories to provide for more effective use of deployed capital.

Masco is confident that it has the resources, the know-how and the commitment necessary to achieve above-average sales growth and, as such, provides five-year sales growth and cash flow forecasts in each of its annual reports to stockholders.

Development of the company's forecasts required the use of rational and clearly defined assumptions about the business' operating environment. The underlying assumptions for the 1991 cash flow forecast include the following:

1. Average 2% annual real growth in GNP.

2. Average 4% annual inflation.

3. Present tax structure to continue.

4. No acquisitions or share repurchases.

5. No equity financing.

6. Average interest rate of 7% on bank debt and 5% on excess cash.

7. No change in currency exchange rates.

8. Cash dividend increasing at the rate of 7% annually.

9. Long-term debt to be refinanced.

SOURCE: Masco Corporation *1991 Annual Report*, pp. 10, 13, 37.

In virtually any endeavor, intelligent behavior involves visualizing the future, imagining what results one wishes to occur, and determining the activities and resources required to achieve those results. If the process is complex, the means of obtaining results should be written. Writing out complex plans is necessary because of the human tendency to forget and the difficulty of mentally processing many facts and relationships at the same time.

Planning is the cornerstone of effective management and effective planning requires that managers have "forecasts on a daunting range of variables: prices, costs, demand, events (such as new laws or regulations, entry of competitors, or the shortage of critical resources), the advent of new technology. Better forecasts translate into better decisions, improvements in customer service and quality, and reduced costs."[1] To provide sales growth and cash flow forecasts for the company, Masco management uses marketing analyses of expected economic conditions and combines those analyses with information on present financial status and desired future financial results. Masco must be quite satisfied with its forecasting abilities because such information, although not included in the typical annual report, is provided in the company's annual report.

Although financial planning is important even when future conditions will be roughly the same as current conditions, such planning is critical when conditions are expected to change. During the planning process, managers attempt to agree on company goals and objectives and how to achieve them. Typically, goals are stated as desired abstract achievements (such as "to become a market leader for a particular product"). Objectives are quantifiable for a period of time (such as "to have $1,000,000 in sales next year"). Achievement of a company's desired goals and objectives requires complex activities, uses diverse resources, and necessitates formalized planning.

Planning should include qualitative narratives of goals, objectives, and means of accomplishment. However, if plans were limited to qualitative narratives, a comparison of actual results to expectations would only allow generalizations, and no measurement of how well the organization met its specified objectives would be possible. The process of formalizing plans and translating qualitative narratives into a written, quantitative format is called **budgeting**. The end result of this process is a **budget**, which expresses an organization's commitment to planned activities and resource acquisition and use.

Budgeting
Budget

> A budget is more than a forecast. A forecast is a prediction of what may happen and sometimes contains prescriptions for dealing with future events. A budget, on the other hand, involves a commitment to a forecast to make an agreed-on outcome happen.[2]

This chapter covers the budgeting process and the detailed preparation of the master budget. While budgeting is important for everyone, the process becomes exceedingly complex in organizations that have significant pools of funds and resources.

THE BASIC BUDGETING PROCESS

Budgeting is an important part of the entire planning process of an organization. As with any other planning activity, budgeting helps provide a focused direction or a path chosen from many alternatives. Management generally indicates the direction chosen through some accounting measure of financial performance, such as net income, earnings per share, or sales level in dollars or units. Such accounting-based measures provide specific quantitative criteria against which future performance (also recorded in accounting terms) can be compared. Thus, budgets are a type of standard, and variances from budget can be computed. Budgets can also help identify potential problems of achieving the specified goals and objectives. By quantifying potential

---

[1] Larry P. Ritzman, "Making Better Business Forecasts," *Carroll Research Report* (Fall 1992), p. 2.
[2] Neil C. Churchill, "Budget Choice: Planning vs. Control," *Harvard Business Review* (July–August 1984), p. 150.

difficulties and making them visible, budgets can help stimulate managers to think of ways to overcome those potential difficulties before they become real.

A well-prepared budget can also be an effective device to communicate objectives, constraints, and expectations to personnel throughout an organization. Such communication promotes the understanding of exactly what is to be accomplished, how those accomplishments are to be achieved, and the manner in which resources are to be allocated. Determination of resource allocations is made, in part, from a process of obtaining information, justifying requests, and negotiating compromises. Participation in the budgeting process helps produce a spirit of cooperation, motivates employees, and instills a feeling of teamwork. Employee participation is needed to effectively integrate necessary information from various sources as well as to obtain individual managerial commitment to the resulting budget. (More is said later in the chapter and in the appendix about budget development and employee participation.) The budget indicates the resource constraints under which managers must operate for the upcoming budget period. Thus, the budget becomes the basis for controlling activities and resource usage. Most U.S. company managers make periodic budget-to-actual comparisons that allow managers to determine how well they are doing, assess the causes of any variances, and implement rational and realistic changes that can, among other benefits, create greater budgetary conformity.

Although budgets are typically expressed in financial terms, they must begin with nonquantitative factors. The budgeting and planning processes are concerned with all organizational resources—raw materials, inventory, supplies, personnel, and facilities—and can be viewed from a long-term or a short-term perspective.

Managers who plan on a long-range basis (five to ten years) are engaged in **strategic planning**. This process is generally performed only by top-level management with the assistance of several key staff members. The result of the process is a statement of long-range organizational goals and the strategies and policies that will help in the achievement of those goals. Strategic planning is not concerned with day-to-day operations, although the strategic plan is the foundation on which short-term planning is based.

Strategic planning

Planning combines people, ideas, and knowledge of the economic conditions in which the entity operates. The end result of the planning process is a set of budgets (the master budget) that provide a quantitative map of the upcoming period.

EXHIBIT 16–1

External Factors to Include in Strategic Plans

Organizational Characteristics
- Market share
- Quality of products
- Discretionary cash flow/gross capital investment

Market and Consumer Behavior
- Market segmentation
- Market size
- New market development
- Buyer loyalty

Industry Structure
- Rate of technological change in products or processes
- Degrees of product differentiation
- Industry price/cost structure
- Economies of scale

Supplier
- Major changes in availability of raw materials

Social, Economic and Political Factors
- GNP trend
- Interest rates
- Energy availability
- Government established and legally enforceable regulations

SOURCE: James F. Brown, Jr., "How U.S. Firms Conduct Strategic Planning," *Management Accounting* (February 1986), p. 55. Reprinted from *Management Accounting.* Copyright by Institute of Management Accountants, Montvale, N.J.

Key variable

Managers engaging in strategic planning should identify **key variables** or critical factors believed to be direct causes of the achievement or nonachievement of organizational goals and objectives. Key variables can be internal (under the control of management) or external (normally noncontrollable by managerment). Exhibit 16–1 provides the results of one study about the external factors considered to be the most critical in determining the strategic plans of manufacturing companies. One conclusion from the survey was that a "firm's long-term success is dependent on the integration of the forces in its environment into its own planning process so that the firm *influences* its own destiny instead of constantly *reacting* to environmental forces."[3]

After the key variables have been identified, information related to them can be gathered. Much of this information will be historical and qualitative and provides a useful starting point for **tactical planning** activities. This process determines the specific objectives and means by which strategic plans will be achieved. Although some tactical plans, such as corporate policy statements, exist for the long term and address repetitive situations, most tactical plans are short-term (one to eighteen months). Such short-term tactical plans are considered "single use" plans and have been developed to address a given set of circumstances or for a specific time frame.

Tactical planning

The annual budget is an example of a single use tactical plan. While a budget's focus is on a one-year period, shorter period (quarterly and monthly) plans should also be included for the budget to work effectively. A well-prepared budget translates a company's strategic and tactical plans into usable guides for periodic company ac-

---

[3] James F. Brown, Jr., "How U.S. Firms Conduct Strategic Planning," *Management Accounting* (February 1986), p. 55.

tivities. Exhibit 16–2 illustrates the relationships among strategic planning, tactical planning, and budgeting.

Both strategic and tactical planning require that information regarding the economy, environment, technological developments, and available resources be incorporated into the setting of goals and objectives. This information is used to adjust the previously gathered historical information for any changes in the key variables for the planning period. The planning process also demands that, as activity takes place and plans are implemented, a monitoring system be in place to provide feedback so that the control function can be operationalized.

Management reviews the budget prior to approving and implementing it to determine if the forecasted results are acceptable. The budget may indicate that the results expected from the planned activities do not achieve the desired objectives. In this case, planned activities are reconsidered and revised so that they will more effectively achieve the desired outcomes that were expressed during the tactical planning stage.

After a budget is accepted, it is implemented and is considered a standard against which performance can be measured. Managers operating under budget guidelines should be provided copies of all appropriate budgets. These managers should also be informed that their performance will be evaluated by comparing actual results to budgeted amounts. Such evaluations should generally be made by budget category for specific periods of time, such as one month.

Once the budget is implemented, the control phase begins, which includes making actual-to-budget comparisons, determining variances, investigating the causes of the variances, taking any necessary corrective action, and providing feedback to operating managers. Feedback (both positive and negative) is essential to the control process and must be provided in a timely manner to be useful.

The above discussion details the basic budgeting process performed by most U.S. companies. As with many other business practices, the budgeting process is unique to individual countries. For example, the News Note "Budgeting Purposes Are Not the Same Worldwide" indicates that the lengthy and highly specific budgeting process described for American companies differs dramatically in Japan.

■ **EXHIBIT 16–2**
Relationships Among Planning Processes

WHO?	WHAT?	HOW?	WHY?
Top management	Strategic planning	Statement of organizational mission, goals, and strategies; long range (5–10 years)	Establish a long-range vision of the organization and provide a sense of unity of and commitment to specified purposes
Top management and mid-management	Tactical planning	Statement of organizational plans; short range (1–18 months)	Provide direction for the achievement of strategic plans; state strategic plans in terms on which managers can act; furnish a basis against which results can be measured
Top management, mid-management, and operational management	Budgeting	Quantitative and monetary statements that coordinate company activities for a year or less	Allocate resources effectively and efficiently; indicate a commitment to objectives; provide a monetary control device

NEWS NOTE

Budgeting Purposes Are Not the Same Worldwide

Japanese planning and budgeting processes are very different from the typical American practice. Japanese companies develop a vision which is relatively permanent. They also develop a strategic plan which, again, is relatively brief and revised infrequently. More important, Japanese companies develop what they call a mid-term plan, which really is generated at only a very high level of the organization. It is relatively simple, containing such information as market share, sales, product costs, selling and administrative expenses, financing expenses, and inventory. It is revised periodically but never more than once a year.

The heart of Japanese companies' planning and budgeting is the six-month budget. Some companies tag onto it a rolling set of half-year projections that reach out several additional years. The six-month budget normally is prepared in no more than one month's time and often takes only two or three weeks.

The six-month budget is produced in a fashion similar to U.S. methods, with some top-down guidelines and a bottom-up estimate of achievable results. The finance and accounting staff plays a strong role in facilitation, working with senior management to communicate market realities and with line personnel to revise target costs. Even in the short two- to three-week cycle there may be several iterations of guideline delivery, budget preparation, and presentation.

The final budget is translated into target cost and productivity measures for the various groups. It is fair to say that the purpose to which Japanese companies put their plans and budgets is very different from U.S. companies. The primary purpose is to take a new look at the foreseeable future and to set short-run targets that are communicated clearly to the appropriate levels and groups of management so they can focus their efforts toward achieving them. Japanese companies spend virtually no time each month comparing actual results to budget and, more important, going through a lengthy, drawn-out process of explaining the causes of such variances. Rather, everyone is committed to achieving the targets that have been embodied into the six-month budgets.

Performance measurement and achievement of individual bonuses is another explanation for the different levels of detail generated by U.S. and Japanese companies in preparing annual budgets. In the United States, managers' bonuses and salaries are related directly to how well they achieve their individual plans. Japanese companies, on the other hand, place little emphasis on meeting budget when evaluating individual performance and therefore do not require as detailed a budget or plan.

SOURCE: Robert A. Howell and Michiharu Sakurai, "Management Accounting (and Other) Lessons from the Japanese," *Management Accounting* (December 1992), pp. 32–33. Reprinted from *Management Accounting*. Copyright by Institute of Management Accountants, Montvale, N.J.

Master budget

Regardless of the process by which a budget is developed (or the detail in which it is expressed), the budgeting process culminates in the preparation and use of the **master budget**. This budget is, in reality, a comprehensive *set* of budgets and budgetary schedules as well as the pro forma financial statements of an organization.

THE MASTER BUDGET

Operating budget

The master budget is composed of both operating and financial budgets as shown in Exhibit 16–3. An **operating budget** is expressed in both units and dollars. When an operating budget is related to revenues, the units are those expected to be sold and the dollars reflect selling prices. When an operating budget relates to cost items, the units are those expected to be consumed and the dollars reflect costs.

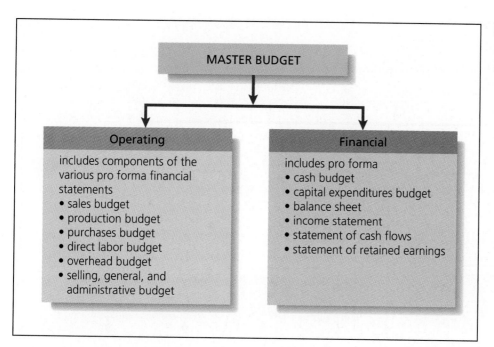

■ EXHIBIT 16–3
Components of a Master
Budget

Monetary details from the operating budgets are aggregated to prepare **financial budgets** indicating the funds to be generated or consumed during the budget period. Financial budgets include the company's cash and capital budgets as well as its projected or pro forma financial statements. These budgets are the ultimate focal points for the firm's top management.

Financial budget

The master budget is prepared for a specific period and is static rather than flexible. It is static in the sense that it is based on a single level of output demand.[4] The selection of this level of output is discussed in the News Note "Budget Targets" on page 662. Expressing the budget based on a single level of output is necessary to facilitate the many time-consuming financial arrangements that must be made before beginning operations for the budget period. Such arrangements include making certain that an adequate number of personnel are hired, needed production and/or storage space is available, and suppliers, prices, delivery schedules, and quality of resources are confirmed.

The sales demand level selected for use in the master budget preparation affects all other organizational components. Because of the budgetary interrelationships illustrated in Exhibit 16–4 (page 660), it is essential that all the departmental components interact in a coordinated manner. A budget developed by one department is often an essential ingredient in developing another department's budget.

The budgetary process shown in Exhibit 16–4 begins with the Sales Department's estimates of the types, quantities, and timing of demand for the company's products. The budget is typically prepared for an entire year and then subdivided into quarterly and monthly periods. A production manager combines sales estimates with additional information from the Purchasing, Personnel, Operations, and Capital Facilities departments; the combined information allows the production manager to specify the types, quantities, and timing of products to be manufactured and transferred to finished goods. The accounts receivable area uses sales estimates, in conjunction with estimated collection patterns, to determine the amounts and timing of cash receipts.

---

[4] Some companies engage in contingency planning that provides for multiple budgeting paths. Emerson Electric, for example, uses a technique they refer to as ABC budgeting in which the A budget applies to the most likely scenario, the B budget to a possible lower level of activity, and so on. As a result, company managers can react with previously considered plans in the event of business environment changes. [Charles F. Knight, "Emerson Electric: Consistent Profits, Consistently," *Harvard Business Review* (January–February 1992), p. 65.]

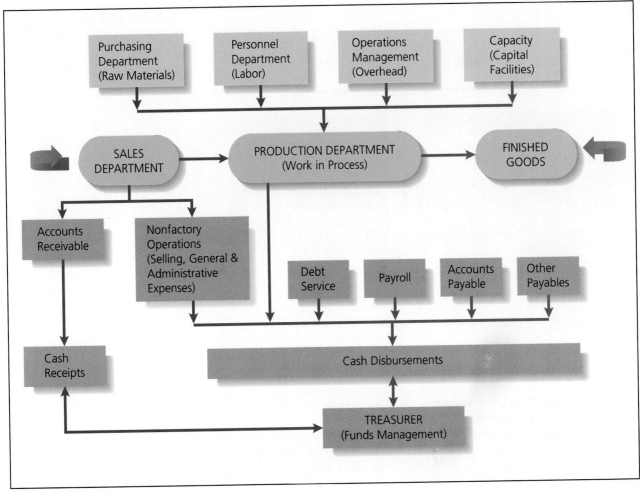

EXHIBIT 16–4

The Budgetary Process in a Manufacturing Organization

For the treasurer to properly manage the organization's flow of funds, the cash receipts information must be matched with cash disbursements information from all areas so that cash is available when, and in the quantity, it is needed.

Note that certain information must flow back into a department from which it began. For example, the Sales Department must receive finished goods information to know if goods are in stock (or can be produced to order) before selling products. In addition, the treasurer must *receive* continual informaton on cash receipts and disbursements as well as *provide* information to various organizational units on the availability of funds so that proper funds management can be maintained.

Assuming that top management allows lower-level managers to participate in the budgeting process, each department either prepares its own budget or provides information for inclusion in a budget. Exhibit 16–5 presents an overview of the sequence of preparation of component budgets of the master budget, indicates which departments are responsible for which budget's preparation, and illustrates how the budgets interface with one another. The master budget begins with the preparation of the sales budget that is based on expected demand. Production and cash flows are planned using the chosen level of sales, and ultimately pro forma financial statements are prepared. The flow of information is visible from Exhibit 16–5, but the quantitative and monetary implications are not. Therefore, the next section of the chapter is devoted to illustrating the preparation of a master budget.

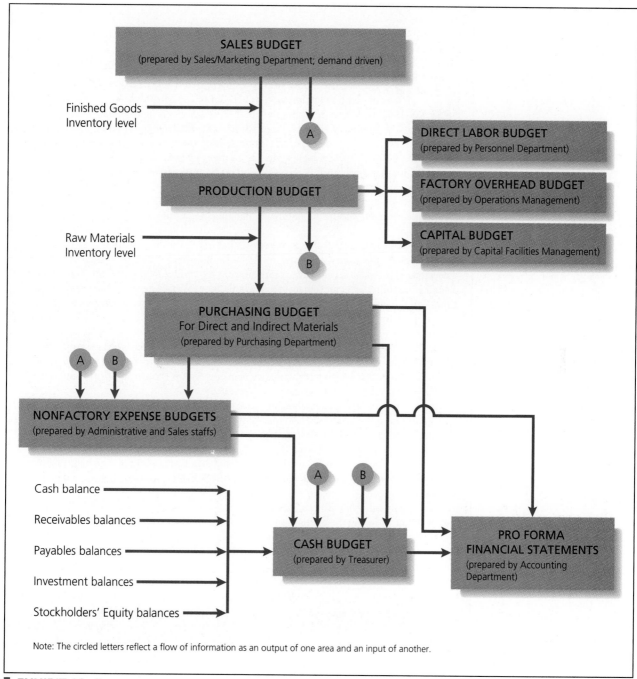

EXHIBIT 16–5

The Master Budget: An Overview

This illustration will use information for Import Designs, a small company that has been in business for several years. The company, which produces one style of rattan table with a glass top insert, is in the process of preparing its budget for 1995 and has estimated that total sales for the year will be 96,000 tables. While annual sales would be detailed on a monthly basis, the Import Designs illustration focuses only on the budgets for the first quarter of 1995. The process of developing the master budget is the same regardless of whether the time frame is one year or one quarter.

**THE MASTER
BUDGET
ILLUSTRATED**

NEWS NOTE   **Don't Make Budget Targets Too Easy or Too Difficult**

It is a basic axiom of management that budget targets should be set to be challenging but achievable. But to establish that target, management must first determine what "challenging but achievable" really means. Should profits be targeted at some easily obtainable goal, a realistic middle ground, or at a point so high that hope of attainment is slim?

There is no one right answer, given the number of purposes for which budgets are used: planning, coordination, control, motivation, and performance evaluation. Some may argue that planning purposes are served best with a best-guess budget, one that is as likely to be exceeded as missed. Others may propose that, for optimum motivation, budget targets should be highly challenging, with only a 25% to 40% chance of achievement.

There is one target-level choice, however, that serves the combination of purposes for which budgets are used quite well in the vast majority of organizational situations. Therefore, it provides an effective compromise. That choice is to set budget targets with a high probability of achievement—achievable by most managers 80% to 90% of the time—and then to supplement these targets with promises of extra incentives for performance exceeding the target level.

Only in a few organizational situations is it not desirable to set highly achievable profit budget targets. One exception is caused by organizational need. A company in grave difficulty may want to set less achievable budget targets as a signal to its managers that a certain higher level of performance is necessary for the corporation to survive or for the [organizational unit] to stave off divestment.

A second exception occurs when it is desirable to correct for [an organizational unit's] windfall gain. Sometimes when managers have been lucky in a prior period, perhaps earning large and mostly undeserved bonuses, a more challenging budget target can be set as an effective way of making compensation more fair across the multiyear period. Here, though, care must be taken to guard against unwarranted management turnover because current period expected compensation probably will fall below competitive market levels.

In virtually all other situations, it is desirable to set highly achievable profit budget targets while allowing the managers few excuses for not achieving the targets but providing them significant additional rewards for exceeding the targets. Setting targets that are highly achievable but not too easy takes considerable managerial skill. But when [upper-level managers] implement this combination of mechanisms effectively, they will ensure that all the purposes for which budgets are used are served well.

SOURCE: Kenneth A. Merchant, "How Challenging Should Profit Budget Targets Be?" *Management Accounting* (November 1990), pp. 46, 48. Reprinted from *Management Accounting*. Copyright by Institute of Management Accountants, Montvale, N.J.

The December 31, 1994, balance sheet presented in Exhibit 16–6 provides account balances needed to begin preparation of the master budget. The December 31, 1994, balances are really estimates rather than actual figures because the budget process for 1995 must begin significantly before December 31, 1994. The company's budgetary time schedule depends on many factors including its size and degree of forecasting sophistication. Assume that Import Designs begins its budgeting process in November 1994, when the sales forecast is received by management or the budget committee.

Sales Budget

The sales budget is prepared in both units and sales dollars. The selling price set for 1995 is $80 per rattan table, regardless of sales territory or customer. Monthly de-

ASSETS			LIABILITIES AND STOCKHOLDERS' EQUITY		
Current Assets			Current Liabilities		
Cash		$ 16,000	Accounts Payable		$228,000
Accounts Receivable	$128,520				
Less Allowance					
for Uncollectibles	(2,100)	126,420			
Inventories:					
Raw Materials	$155,040				
Finished Goods	135,000	290,040			
Total Current Assets		$432,460			
Plant Assets					
Property, Plant,			Stockholders' Equity		
and Equipment	$540,000		Common Stock	$300,000	
Less Accumulated			Retained Earnings	264,460	
Depreciation	(180,000)	360,000	Total Stockholders' Equity		564,460
			Total Liabilities and		
Total Assets		$792,460	Stockholders' Equity		$792,460

■ **EXHIBIT 16–6**

Import Designs' Balance Sheet (December 31, 1994)

mand and its related revenue impact for the first four months of 1995 are shown in Exhibit 16–7. Dollar sales figures are computed by multiplying sales quantities by product selling prices. April information is presented because some elements of the March budget require the following month's information.

The News Note on page 664 about budgeting for international sales indicates the importance of analyzing the characteristics associated with the market when preparing a sales budget. While such analysis is important domestically, for companies that have international operations such as Masco or Dawson/Berg, it is critical.

Production Budget

The production budget follows naturally from the sales budget and uses the information regarding the type, quantity, and timing of units to be sold. Sales information is used in conjunction with data on beginning and ending inventories so that managers can schedule necessary production. The following formula provides the computation for the units to be produced:

	JANUARY	FEBRUARY	MARCH	TOTAL FOR QUARTER	APRIL
Sales in units	5,000	8,000	10,000	23,000	11,000
Sales in dollars	$400,000	$640,000	$800,000	$1,840,000	$880,000

■ **EXHIBIT 16–7**

Import Designs' Sales Budget for the Three Months and Quarter Ending March 31, 1995

NEWS NOTE

There Are Many Complexities to Budgeting International Sales

Budgeting is impacted by conditions tied to a multinational's international business operations. Multinationals must be aware of and respond to the conditions of each market they service, including the level of economic development, degree of government price control, cost of sales in each market, product pricing decisons for each market (e.g., standard mark-up, market prices), available channels of distribution and promotion, and import/export controls.

Dawson/Berg Corporation is a multinational entity that does business in several areas of the world. In preparing its sales budget, the following analysis might occur:

Region/Country	Dominant and Distinctive Market Characteristics
Canada	U.S./Canada Free Trade Agreement
Denmark	Strong local competition
Eastern Europe	Recent democratization and uncertain trade regulations
European Community	EC92 economic integration
France	Price controls
Germany	New and uncertain situation caused by the reunification of the country
Japan	Complex distribution system
Pacific Rim	New area with many developing countries offering a growing consumer base
United States	Specific market penetration is desired in highly segmented market

[Factors requiring consideration may] arise from a specific nation's characteristics [or] from international forces. Whatever their origin, [t]he existence of these differences indicates that marketing strategies and the resulting sales budget cannot be transplanted merely from domestic operations to a foreign operation.

SOURCE: Paul V. Mannino and Ken Milani, "Budgeting for an International Business," *Management Accounting* (February 1992), p. 39. Reprinted from *Management Accounting.* Copyright by Institute of Management Accountants, Montvale, N.J.

Number of units to be sold (from sales budget)	XXX
+ Number of units desired in ending inventory	XXX
= Total units needed during period	XXX
− Number of units in beginning inventory	(XXX)
= Units to be produced	XXX

The number of units desired in ending inventory is determined and specified by company management. Desired ending inventory balance is generally a function of the quantity and timing of demand in the upcoming period as related to the capacity and speed of the firm to produce particular units. Frequently, management stipulates that ending inventory equal a given percentage of the next period's projected sales. Other alternatives include a constant amount of inventory, a build-up of inventory for future high-demand periods, or near-zero inventory under a just-in-time system. The decision about ending inventory levels results from the consideration of whether a firm wants to have constant production with varying inventory levels or variable production with constant inventory levels. Managers should consider the high costs of stockpiling inventory before making a decision about how much inventory to keep

	JANUARY	FEBRUARY	MARCH	TOTAL
Sales in units (from Exhibit 16–7)	5,000	8,000	10,000	23,000
+ Desired ending inventory	4,800	6,000	6,600	6,600
= Total needed	9,800	14,000	16,600	29,600
− Beginning inventory	3,000	4,800	6,000	3,000
= Units to be produced	6,800	9,200	10,600	26,600

■ EXHIBIT 16–8

Import Designs' Production Budget for the Three Months and Quarter Ending March 31, 1995

on hand, as indicated in the following discussion:

> Carrying excessive inventory or the wrong inventory can be extremely expensive. Costs of carrying inventory include storage, handling, obsolescence, insurance, taxes, shrinkage, damage, interest, and management time. Carrying costs can easily add 20 percent to 25 percent per year to the initial cost of inventory. Additionally, an inventory investment often consumes a major share of a company's cash and credit resources.[5]

Demand for Import Designs' products is extremely seasonal and the company's most active sales season is early spring and summer. The company has a policy for December through March that ending inventory be equal to 60 percent of the next month's sales. This policy allows the company to stockpile units for the busy season of the year. Implementing the ending inventory policy and using the sales information from Exhibit 16–7, the production budget shown in Exhibit 16–8 is prepared.

The beginning inventory balance shown for January is the number of units that were on hand on December 31, 1994. This inventory is 3,000 units, which represents 60 percent of January's estimated sales of 5,000 units. Desired ending inventory for March is 60 percent of April sales of 11,000 tables (given in Exhibit 16–7). Import Designs does not have any work in process inventory because all units placed into production are assumed to be fully completed each period.[6]

Purchases Budget

Direct materials are essential to production and must be purchased each period in sufficient quantities to meet production needs. In addition, the quantities of direct material purchased must be in conformity with the company's desired ending inventory policies. The management of Import Designs ties its policy for ending inventories of direct materials to its production needs for the following month. Because of occasional difficulty in obtaining the quality of materials needed, Import Designs' ending inventories of direct materials from December through March equal 60 percent of the quantities needed for the next month's production. Companies may have different direct materials policies for the direct materials associated with different products or for different seasons of the year. For example, if a direct material is consistently available in the quantity and quality desired, a company may maintain only a minimal ending inventory of that direct material. On the other hand, if direct materials tend to be difficult to obtain at certain times of the year (such as certain seafoods for preparation of frozen dinners), a company may stockpile those direct materials for use in future periods.

---

[5] Bill Moseley, "Boosting Profits and Efficiency: The Opportunities Are There," *(Grant Thornton) Tax & Business Adviser* (May/June 1992), p. 6.

[6] Most manufacturing entities do not produce only whole units during the period. Normally, partially completed beginning and ending work in process inventories will exist. These inventories create the need to use equivalent units of production when computing the production budget.

The purchases budget is first stated in whole units of finished products. It is subsequently converted to individual direct material component requirements and to dollar amounts. Production of an Import Designs' table requires two direct materials: 15 pounds of rattan and two 10-inch square pieces of glass. Unit materials costs have been estimated by the purchasing agent as follows: $2.00 per pound of rattan and $4 per piece of glass. Exhibit 16–9 shows Import Designs' purchases budget for the individual materials requirements and total purchases cost for each month of the first quarter of 1995. Note that beginning and ending inventory quantities are expressed first in terms of tables and then converted to the appropriate quantity measure (pounds or pieces of glass). Totals are not shown for the quarter because it is inappropriate to add heterogeneous inputs such as pounds of rattan and pieces of glass. The total budgeted cost of direct materials purchases for the quarter is $1,083,760 ($313,120 + $381,520 + $389,120).

Personnel Costs

Given expected production, the Engineering and Personnel Departments can work together to determine the necessary labor requirements for the factory, sales force, and office staff. Labor requirements are stated in total number of people, specific number of types of people (skilled laborers, salespeople, clerical personnel), and production hours needed for factory employees. Labor costs are computed from items such as union labor contracts, minimum wage laws, fringe benefit costs, payroll taxes, and

■ EXHIBIT 16–9

Import Designs'
Purchases Budget
for the Three Months
Ending March 31, 1995

	JANUARY	FEBRUARY	MARCH
Units to be produced (from Exhibit 16–8)	6,800	9,200	10,600
+ EI (60% of next month's production)*	5,520	6,360	6,000
= Total whole units needed	12,320	15,560	16,600
− Beginning inventory	4,080	5,520	6,360
= Tables for which purchases are required	8,240	10,040	10,240
Rattan			
Total tables	8,240	10,040	10,240
× Pounds needed per table	× 15	× 15	× 15
Total pounds to be purchased	123,600	150,600	153,600
× Price per pound	× $2	× $2	× $2
Total cost of rattan	$247,200	$301,200	$307,200
Glass			
Total tables	8,240	10,040	10,240
× Pieces needed per table	× 2	× 2	× 2
Total pieces to be purchased	16,480	20,080	20,480
× Price per piece	× $4	× $4	× $4
Total cost of glass	$ 65,920	$ 80,320	$ 81,920
Total material purchases:			
Total cost of rattan	$247,200	$301,200	$307,200
Total cost of glass	65,920	80,320	81,920
Total material purchases	$313,120	$381,520	$389,120

*April production is expected to be 10,000 units.

	JANUARY	FEBRUARY	MARCH	TOTAL
Units of production	6,800	9,200	10,600	26,600
× Standard hours allowed	.75	.75	.75	.75
Total hours allowed	5,100	6,900	7,950	19,950
× Average wage rate (including fringe benefits)	$ 5.40	$ 5.40	$ 5.40	$ 5.40
Direct labor cost	$27,540	$37,260	$42,930	$107,730

EXHIBIT 16–10

Import Designs' Direct Labor Budget for the Three Months and Quarter Ending March 31, 1995

bonus arrangements. The various personnel amounts will be shown, as appropriate, in either the direct labor budget, the manufacturing overhead budget, or the selling, general and administrative budget.

Direct Labor Budget

The management of Import Designs has reviewed the staffing requirements and has developed the direct labor cost estimates shown in Exhibit 16–10 for the first quarter of 1995. Factory direct labor costs are based on the standard hours of labor needed to produce the number of units shown in the production budget. The average wage rate shown in the exhibit includes both the basic direct labor payroll rate and the payroll taxes and fringe benefits related to direct labor (since these items usually add between 25 and 30 percent to the base labor cost). All compensation is paid in the month in which it is incurred.

Overhead Budget

Another production cost that management must estimate is overhead. Exhibit 16–11 presents Import Designs' monthly cost of each overhead item for the first quarter of

	Value of (fixed) a	Value of (variable) b	JANUARY	FEBRUARY	MARCH	TOTAL
Estimated machine hours (X) (assumed)			1,700	2,300	2,650	6,650
Factory overhead item:						
Depreciation	$1,500	$ —	$ 1,500	$ 1,500	$ 1,500	$ 4,500
Indirect materials	—	.10	170	230	265	665
Indirect labor	6,000	7.00	17,900	22,100	24,550	64,550
Machinery rent	700	—	700	700	700	2,100
Utilities	400	.50	1,250	1,550	1,725	4,525
Property taxes	200	—	200	200	200	600
Insurance	500	—	500	500	500	1,500
Maintenance	600	.80	1,960	2,440	2,720	7,120
Total cost (y)	$9,900	$8.40	$24,180	$29,220	$32,160	$85,560
Total cost net of depreciation			$22,680	$27,720	$30,660	$81,060

EXHIBIT 16–11

Import Designs' Factory Overhead Budget for the Three Months and Quarter Ending March 31, 1995

	Value of (fixed) a	Value of (variable) b	JANUARY	FEBRUARY	MARCH	TOTAL
Predicted Sales (from Exhibit 16–7)			$400,000	$640,000	$800,000	$1,840,000
SG&A items:						
Supplies	$ —	$.010	$ 4,000	$ 6,400	$ 8,000	$ 18,400
Depreciation	400	—	400	400	400	1,200
Utilities	200	.005	2,200	3,400	4,200	9,800
Miscellaneous	100	.001	500	740	900	2,140
Salaries and wages:						
Sales manager	4,000	—	4,000	4,000	4,000	12,000
Salespeople	2,000	.050	22,000	34,000	42,000	98,000
Gen. and admin.	20,000	—	20,000	20,000	20,000	60,000
Total cost (y)	$26,700	$.066	$53,100	$68,940	$79,500	$201,540
Total cost net of depreciation			$52,700	$68,540	$79,100	$200,340

▌ EXHIBIT 16–12

Import Designs' Selling, General, and Administrative Budget for the Three Months and Quarter Ending March 31, 1995

1995. The company has determined that machine hours are the best predictor of overhead costs.

In estimating overhead, all fixed and variable costs must be specified and mixed costs must be separated into their fixed (a) and variable (b) components. Each overhead amount shown is calculated using the $y = a + bX$ formula discussed in Chapter 4. For example, February maintenance cost is the fixed amount of $600 plus ($.80 times 2,300 estimated hours of machine time) or $600 + $1,840 = $2,440. Both total cost and cost net of depreciation are shown in the budget. The cost, net of depreciation, is the amount that is expected to be paid in cash during the month; this total is the one that will have an effect on the cash budget.

Selling, General, and Administrative (SG&A) Budget

Selling, general, and administrative expenses for each month can be predicted in the same manner as overhead costs. Exhibit 16–12 presents the first quarter 1995 SG&A budget for Import Designs. Note that sales figures rather than production levels are used as the measure of activity in preparing this budget. The company's sales force consists of a manager with a monthly salary of $4,000 and four salespeople who receive $500 per month plus a 5 percent commission on sales. The general and administrative staff are paid salaries totaling $20,000 per month.

Capital Budget

Capital budgeting

The budgets included in the master budget focus on the short-term or upcoming fiscal period. Managers, however, must also assess long-term needs in the area of plant and equipment purchases and budget for those expenditures in a process called **capital budgeting.** The capital budget is prepared separately from the master budget, but since expenditures are involved, capital budgeting does affect the master budgeting process.[7]

---

[7] Capital budgeting is discussed in depth in Chapters 19 and 20.

	JANUARY	FEBRUARY	MARCH	TOTAL
Acquisition of forklift	$10,000	$ 0	$0	$10,000
Cash payment for forklift	$ 0	$10,000	$0	$10,000

EXHIBIT 16–13

Import Designs' Capital Budget for the Three Months and Quarter Ending March 31, 1995

As shown in Exhibit 16–13, Import Designs' managers have decided that only one capital asset will be acquired in the first quarter of 1995. This asset, a forklift for moving raw materials from the warehouse to the production facilities, will be purchased and placed into service at the beginning of January at a cost of $10,000. Import Designs will pay for the equipment in February. Depreciation on the forklift was included in the overhead calculation in Exhibit 16–11. The old forklift (original cost of $15,000) will be fully depreciated by the end of 1994 and will be scrapped when the new equipment is purchased.

Cash Budget

After all the preceding budgets have been developed, a cash budget can be constructed. The cash budget may be the most important schedule prepared during the budgeting process because, without cash, a company cannot survive. "[O]f the 60,432 businesses that failed in 1990, more than 60% blamed their demise on economic factors linked to cash flow. And, according to a study by the accounting firm of BDO Seidman, 26% of small to medium-sized companies rank their inability to control their cash flow as problem No. 1."[8]

The following model can be used to summarize cash receipts and disbursements in a way that assists managers to devise appropriate financing measures to meet company needs.

Cash Budget Model

Beginning cash balance		XXX
+ Cash receipts (collections)		XXX
= Cash available for disbursements exclusive of financing		XXX
− Cash needed for disbursements (purchases, direct labor, overhead, SG&A, taxes, bonuses, etc.)		(XXX)
= Cash excess or deficiency (a)		XXX
− Minimum desired cash balance		(XXX)
= Cash (needed) or available for investment or repayment		XXX
Financing methods:		
± Borrowing (repayments)	XXX	
± Issue (reacquire) capital stock	XXX	
± Sell (acquire) investments or plant assets	XXX	
± Receive (pay) interest or dividends	XXX	
Total impact (+ or −) of planned financing (b)		XXX
= Ending cash balance (c), where [(c) = (a) ± (b)]		XXX

Cash Receipts and Accounts Receivable.   Once sales dollars have been determined, managers translate revenue information into actual cash receipts through the use of

[8]Shelly Branch, "Go With the Flow—Or Else," *Black Enterprise* (November 1991), p. 77.

an expected collection pattern. This expected pattern takes into consideration the actual collection patterns experienced in recent past periods and management's judgment about changes that could disturb current collection patterns. For example, changes that could weaken current collection patterns include recessionary conditions, increases in interest rates, less strict credit granting practices, or ineffective collection practices.

In specifying collection patterns, managers should recognize that different types of customers pay in different ways. Any sizeable, unique category of clientele should be segregated. For example, Wal-Mart typically pays its bills in 29 days, while Kmart generally takes 45.[9] And, at Mr. King (a furniture-and-more store in Birmingham, Alabama), most customers are high-risk—so collections may be slow and potential uncollectibles higher than at other furniture stores.

Import Designs has two different types of customers. The first type of customer is only allowed to purchase products for cash and never receives a discount. The other type of customer can purchase products on credit. Of the credit customers, wholesalers are allowed a 2 percent cash discount; retailers are not allowed the discount.

Import Designs has determined from historical data that the following collection pattern (diagrammed in Exhibit 16–14) is applicable to its customers. Of each month's sales, 40 percent will be for cash and 60 percent will be on credit. Thirty percent of the credit customers are allowed the discount and 70 percent are not. All customers allowed the discount pay in the month of the sale. Collections from the remaining credit customers are as follows: 10 percent in the month of sale, 60 percent in the month following the sale, and 29 percent collected in the second month following the sale. One percent of credit sales are uncollectible.

Using the sales budget, information on November and December 1994 sales, and the collection pattern, management can estimate cash receipts from sales during the first three months of 1995. Management must have November and December sales information because collections for credit sales extend over a maximum of three months, meaning that collection of some of the previous year's sales occur early in the current year. Import Designs' November and December sales were $240,000 and $260,000, respectively. Projected monthly collections in the first quarter of 1995 are shown in Exhibit 16–15. The individual calculations relate to the alternative collection patterns and corresponding percentages presented in Exhibit 16–14. All amounts have been rounded to the nearest dollar.

The amounts shown relating to November and December collections can be reconciled to the December 31, 1994, balance sheet (Exhibit 16–6) which indicated an

EXHIBIT 16–14
Import Designs' Collection Pattern for Sales

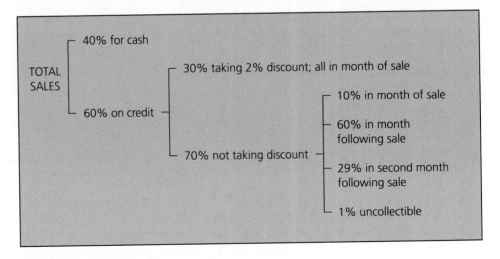

[9]George Stalk, Philip Evans, and Lawrence E. Shulman, "Competing on Capabilities: The New Rules of Corporate Strategy," *Harvard Business Review* (March–April, 1992), p. 63.

Accounts Receivable balance of $128,520. This amount appears in the collection schedule as follows:

January collections of November sales	$ 29,232
Estimated November bad debts	1,008
January collections of December sales	65,520
February collections of December sales	31,668
Estimated December bad debts	1,092
December 31, 1994, balance in Accounts Receivable	$128,520

January 1995 sales of $400,000 are used as an example of the collection calculations in Exhibit 16–15. The first line represents cash sales of 40 percent of total sales or $160,000. The next two lines represent the 60 percent of the customers who buy on credit. The first of these lines represents the 30 percent of the credit customers who take the discount, computed as follows:

Sales to credit customers (60% of $400,000)	$240,000
Sales to customers allowed discount (30% × $240,000)	$ 72,000
− Discount taken by customers (.02 × $72,000)	1,440
= Net collections from customers allowed discount	$ 70,560

From:	January	February	March	Total	Disc.	Uncoll.
November 1994 Sales:						
$240,000(60%)(70%)(29%)	$ 29,232			$ 29,232		
$240,000(60%)(70%)(1%)						$1,008
December 1994 Sales:						
$260,000(60%)(70%)(60%)	65,520			65,520		
$260,000(60%)(70%)(29%)		$ 31,668		31,668		
$260,000(60%)(70%)(1%)						1,092
January 1995 Sales:						
$400,000(40%)	160,000			160,000		
$400,000(60%)(30%)	70,560**N**			70,560	$1,440	
$400,000(60%)(70%)(10%)	16,800			16,800		
$400,000(60%)(70%)(60%)		100,800		100,800		
$400,000(60%)(70%)(29%)			$ 48,720	48,720		
$400,000(60%)(70%)(1%)						1,680
February 1995 Sales:						
$640,000(40%)		256,000		256,000		
$640,000(60%)(30%)		112,896**N**		112,896	2,304	
$640,000(60%)(70%)(10%)		26,880		26,880		
$640,000(60%)(70%)(60%)			161,280	161,280		
March 1995 Sales:						
$800,000(40%)			320,000	320,000		
$800,000(60%)(30%)			141,120**N**	141,120	2,880	
$800,000(60%)(70%)(10%)			33,600	33,600		
Totals	$342,112	$528,244	$704,720	$1,575,076	$6,624	$3,780

"**N**" stands for "Net of discount." To determine the gross amount, divide the net amount by .98 (i.e., 100% − 2%).

▌ EXHIBIT 16–15

Import Designs' Cash Collections—First Quarter 1995

The second of the two lines relates to the remaining (70 percent) of the credit customers who paid in the month of sale but were not allowed the discounts (10 percent). The remaining amounts in Exhibit 16–15 are computed in the same manner.

Once the schedule of cash collections is prepared, the balances of the Accounts Receivable, Allowance for Uncollectibles, and Sales Discounts accounts can be projected. These T-accounts for Import Designs are shown as follows. These amounts will be used later to prepare pro forma year-end 1995 financial statements. All sales are initially recorded as Accounts Receivable. Immediate cash collections are then deducted from the Accounts Receivable balance.

ACCOUNTS RECEIVABLE

12/31/94 Balance (Ex. 16–6)	128,520		
Jan. 1995 Sales (Ex. 16–7)	400,000	Collections in Jan. from beginning A/R ($29,232 + $65,520)	94,752
		Cash sales in Jan. (Ex. 16–15)	160,000
		Credit collections subject to discount (cash received, $70,560)	72,000
		Credit collections not subject to discount	16,800
Feb. 1995 Sales (Ex. 16–7)	640,000	Collections in Feb. from beginning A/R	31,668
		Cash sales in Feb. (Ex. 16–15)	256,000
		Collections in Feb. from Jan. sales	100,800
		Credit collections subject to discount (cash received, $112,896)	115,200
		Credit collections not subject to discount	26,880
March 1995 Sales (Ex. 16–7)	800,000	Cash sales in March (Ex. 16–15)	320,000
		Collections in March from Jan. sales	48,720
		Collections in March from Feb. sales	161,280
		Credit collections subject to discount (cash received, $141,120)	144,000
		Credit collections not subject to discount	33,600
3/31/95 Balance	386,820		

ALLOWANCE FOR UNCOLLECTIBLE ACCOUNTS

12/31/94 Balance (Ex. 16–6)	2,100
January estimate (Ex. 16–15)	1,680
February estimate [$640,000(60%)(70%)(1%)]	2,688
March estimate [$800,000(60%)(70%)(1%)]	3,360
3/31/95 Balance	9,828

SALES DISCOUNTS

Jan. discounts	1,440
Feb. discounts	2,304
March discounts	2,880
3/31/95 Balance	6,624

Note that the estimated uncollectible accounts from November 1994 through March 1995 have not been written off as of the end of the first quarter of 1995. Companies will continue to make collection efforts for a substantial period of time before the accounts are acknowledged as truly worthless. Thus, these receivables may remain on the books for six months or longer from the date of the sale. When the accounts are written off, the balances in the Accounts Receivable and the Allowance for Uncollectibles will both decrease; there will be no income statement impact relative to the write-off.

Cash Disbursements and Accounts Payable.   Using the purchases information from Exhibit 16–9, management can prepare an estimated cash disbursements schedule related to accounts payable. All purchases of raw materials are made on account by Import Designs. The company pays for 40 percent of each month's purchases in the month of purchase. These purchases are from suppliers who allow Import Designs a 2 percent discount for prompt payment. The remaining suppliers allow no cash discount for prompt payment, but require that credit payments be made within 30 days from the date of purchase. Thus, the other 60 percent of each month's purchases are paid in the month following the month of purchase.

Exhibit 16–16 on page 674 presents the cash disbursements information related to purchases for the first quarter of 1995. The December 31, 1994, Accounts Payable balance of $228,000 (Exhibit 16–6) represents 60 percent of December purchases of $380,000. All amounts have been rounded to whole dollars.

The accounts payable activity is summarized in the following T-account. The March 31 balance represents 60 percent of March purchases that will be paid during April.

ACCOUNTS PAYABLE

		12/31/94 Balance (Ex. 16–6)	228,000
Jan. payments for Dec. purchases (Ex. 16–9)	228,000	Jan. purchases (Ex. 16–9)	313,120
Jan. payments for Jan. purchases subject to discount (cash paid, $122,743)	125,248		
Feb. payments for Jan. purchases (Ex. 16–16)	187,872	Feb. purchases (Ex. 16–9)	381,520
Feb. payments for Feb. purchases subject to discount (cash paid, $149,556)	152,608		
March payments for Feb. purchases (Ex. 16–16)	228,912	March purchases (Ex. 16–9)	389,120
March payments for March purchase subject to discount (cash paid, $152,535)	155,648		
		3/31/95	233,472

PURCHASES DISCOUNTS

January discounts	2,505
February discounts	3,052
March discounts	3,113
3/31/95 Balance	8,670

Given the cash receipts and disbursements information for Import Designs, the cash budget model is used to formulate the cash budget shown in Exhibit 16–17. The company has established $16,000 as its desired minimum cash balance. There are two primary reasons for having a desired minimum cash balance: one is internal, the other is external. The first reason reflects the uncertainty associated with the budgeting process. Since managers do not have the ability to forecast with absolute precision, a "cushion" is maintained to protect the company from potential errors in forecasting collection and payment schedules. The second reason for a minimum cash balance is that it is required by the company's banks in relation to an open line of credit.

All borrowings by Import Designs take place in $100 increments at the beginning of a month and all repayments in $100 amounts at the end of a month. This borrowing/repayment schedule was mandated by Import Design's bank. To minimize interest costs, company management would, of course, have preferred not to borrow until the need for funds actually arose and would prefer to repay as quickly as it was able. The company probably agreed to these terms because of a longstanding relationship with the bank, in which Import Designs benefits by the bank's prompt approval of necessary company loans. For simplicity, it is assumed that any investments are also made in end-of-month $100 increments. Interest on company investments is credited (added) to the company's bank account at the end of each month.

Exhibit 16–17 indicates that Import Designs has a $95,551 inadequacy of disbursements over cash available in January. Such an inadequacy, however, does not include the need to also provide the specified $16,000 minimum balance. Therefore, the company must borrow $111,551 that month.

In February, Import Designs only had enough cash to meet its desired minimum cash balance, pay back some of January's borrowings with interest, and pay for the

■ EXHIBIT 16–16

Import Designs' Cash Disbursements—Accounts Payable for the Three Months Ending March 31, 1995

	JANUARY	FEBRUARY	MARCH	DISCOUNT
Payment for purchases of:				
December 1994	$228,000			
January 1995				
(from Exhibit 16–9)				
$313,120(.40)(.98)	122,743**N**			$2,505
$313,120(.60)		$187,872		
February 1995				
(from Exhibit 16–9)				
$381,520(.40)(.98)		149,556**N**		3,052
$381,520(.60)			$228,912	
March 1995 (from Exhibit 16–9)				
$389,120(.40)(.98)			152,535**N**	3,113
Total disbursements for A/P	$350,743	$337,428	$381,447	$8,670

"**N**" stands for "Net of discount." The total amount of gross purchases being paid for in the month of purchase is the sum of the net of discount payment plus the amount shown on the same line in the Discount column.

	JANUARY	FEBRUARY	MARCH	TOTAL
Beginning cash balance	$ 16,000	$ 16,049	$ 16,013	$ 16,000
Cash collections (Ex. 16–15)	342,112	528,244	704,720	1,575,076
Cash available exclusive of financing	$ 358,112	$544,293	$ 720,733	$1,591,076
Disbursements:				
Accounts payable (for purchases, Ex. 16–16)	$ 350,743	$337,428	$ 381,447	$1,069,618
Direct labor (Ex. 16–10)	27,540	37,260	42,930	107,730
Overhead (Ex. 16–11)*	22,680	27,720	30,660	81,060
SG&A expenses (Ex. 16–12)*	52,700	68,540	79,100	200,340
Total disbursements	$ 453,663	$470,948	$ 534,137	$1,458,748
Cash excess or (inadequacy)	$ (95,551)	$ 73,345	$ 186,596	$ 132,328
Minimum cash balance desired	16,000	16,000	16,000	16,000
Cash available or (needed)	$(111,551)	$ 57,345	$ 170,596	$ 116,328
Financing:				
Borrowings (repayments)	$ 111,600	$ (45,100)	$ (66,500)	$ 0***
Issue (reacquire) stock	0	0	0	0
Sell (acquire) investments	0	0	(103,400)	(103,400)
Sell (acquire) plant assets	0	(10,000)	0	(10,000)
Receive (pay) interest or dividends**	0	(2,232)	(665)	(2,897)
Total impact of planned financing	$ 111,600	$ (57,332)	$(170,565)	$ (116,297)
Ending cash balance	$ 16,049	$ 16,013	$ 16,031	$ 16,031

*These amounts are the net of depreciation figures.
**Interest is calculated assuming a 12% rate and that borrowings are made at the beginning of the month and repayments/investments are made at the end of the month ($111,600 X .12 X 2/12 = $ 2,232; $66,500 X .12 X 1/12 = $665).
***This is the net result of borrowings and repayments.

EXHIBIT 16–17
Import Designs' Cash Budget for the Three Months and Quarter Ending March 31, 1995

forklift. In March, there is enough excess cash available to pay off the debt and its related interest and make a $103,400 investment. Interest on borrowings is calculated at 12 percent in Exhibit 16–17. No interest is earned on the investment in the first quarter since the deposit is projected to be made at the end of March. The rate earned on deposits will typically be less than that paid on borrowings. Changes in the assumed interest rates will affect any future budget-to-actual comparisons.

Budgeted Financial Statements

The final step in the budgeting process is the development of budgeted (or pro forma) financial statements for the period. These financial statements reflect the results that will be achieved if the estimates and assumptions used for all previous budgets actually occur. Such statements allow management to determine if the predicted results are acceptable for the period. If the predicted results are not acceptable, management has the opportunity to change and adjust items prior to the beginning of the period.

For example, if expected net income is not considered to be a reasonable amount, management may wish to raise selling prices or find ways to decrease costs. Any specific changes considered by management may have related effects that must be included in the revised projections. For example, if selling prices are raised, volume may decrease. Alternatively, reductions in costs from using lower quality materials could have an effect on spoilage during production or cause a decline in demand. With the availability of the computer, such changes in assumptions and their resultant effects can be simulated quickly and easily.

Cost of Goods Manufactured Schedule.   Before an income statement can be drafted, management must prepare a schedule of cost of goods manufactured. This schedule is necessary to determine the cost of goods sold for use on the income statement. Using information from previous budgets, the management of Import Designs has prepared the budgeted cost of goods manufactured schedule shown in Exhibit 16–18. Since there were no beginning or ending work in process inventories, cost of goods manufactured is equal to the manufacturing costs of the period. Had work in process inventory existed, the computations would be more complex and involve the use of equivalent units of production.

Income Statement.   The projected income statement for Import Designs for the first quarter of 1995 is presented in Exhibit 16–19. This statement uses much of the information previously developed in determining the revenues and expenses for the period.

Balance Sheet.   Upon completion of the income statement, managers at Import Designs can prepare a March 31, 1995 balance sheet (Exhibit 16–20 on page 678). The letters in parentheses after each item in this exhibit indicate the calculations at the bottom of the page related to that account balance.

▌ EXHIBIT 16–18

Import Designs' Pro Forma Cost of Goods Manufactured Schedule for the First Quarter of 1995

Beginning work in process inventory		$ 0	
Cost of direct materials used:			
Beginning balance of DM (Ex. 16–6)	$ 155,040		
Net purchases (from Accounts Payable and Purchases Discounts pp. 673 and 674)		1,075,090	
Total direct materials available	$1,230,130		
Ending balance of DM (Note A)	(228,000)		
Cost of direct materials used	$1,002,130		
Direct labor (Ex. 16–10)	107,730		
Factory overhead (Ex. 16–11)	85,560		
Total costs to be accounted for		1,195,420	
Ending work in process inventory		0	
Cost of goods manufactured		$1,195,420	

Note A:	Rattan	Glass	Total
Ending balance (Ex. 16–9) in units	6,000	6,000	
Pounds/pieces per unit	× 15	× 2	
Total pounds/pieces	90,000	12,000	
Price per pound/piece	× $2	× $4	
Ending balance	$180,000	$48,000	$228,000

Sales (Ex. 16–7)		$1,840,000
Less: Sales discounts (p. 673)		6,624
Net sales		$1,833,376
Cost of goods sold:		
Finished goods—12/31/94 (Ex. 16–6)	$ 135,000	
Cost of goods manufactured (Ex. 16–18)	1,195,420	
Cost of goods available for sale	$1,330,420	
Finished goods—3/31/95 (Note A)	310,200	1,020,220
Gross margin		$ 813,156
Expenses:		
Bad debts expense (Note B)	$ 7,728	
SG&A expenses (Ex. 16–12)	201,540	
Interest expense (Ex. 16–17)	2,897	212,165
Income before income taxes		$ 600,991
Income taxes (assumed rate of 40%)		240,396
Net income		$ 360,595

Note A:

Beginning finished goods	3,000	
Production (Ex. 16–8)	26,600	
Units available for sale	29,600	
Sales (Ex. 16–7)	23,000	
Ending finished goods	6,600	
Costs per unit:		
Materials	$38	
Conversion (assumed)	9	× $47
Cost of ending inventory	$310,200	

Note B:

Total sales	$1,840,000	
× % credit sales	× .60	
Credit sales	$1,104,000	
× % not taking discount	× .70	
Potential bad debts	$ 772,800	
× % estimated uncollectible	× .01	
Estimated bad debts	$ 7,728	

Statement of Cash Flows.   The information found on the income statement, balance sheet, and cash budget is also used to prepare a Statement of Cash Flows (SCF). This statement can assist managers in judging the company's ability to handle fixed cash outflow commitments, adapt to adverse changes in business conditions, and undertake new commitments. Further, because the SCF identifies the relationships between net income and net cash flow from operations, it assists managers in judging the quality of the company's earnings.

Whereas the cash budget is essential to current cash management, the budgeted SCF gives managers a more global view of cash flows by rearranging them into three

ASSETS

Current Assets			
Cash (Exhibit 16–17)			$ 16,031
Accounts Receivable (p. 672)		$386,820	
Less Allowance for Uncollectibles (p. 672)		(9,828)	376,992
Inventory:			
Raw Materials (Exhibit 16–18, Note A)		$228,000	
Finished Goods (Exhibit 16–19, Note A)		310,200	538,200
Total current assets			$ 931,223
Investments (Exhibit 16–17)			103,400
Plant Assets			
Property, Plant, and Equipment (a)		$535,000	
Less Accumulated Depreciation (b)		(170,700)	364,300
Total Assets			$1,398,923

LIABILITIES AND STOCKHOLDERS' EQUITY

Current Liabilities			
Accounts Payable (p. 673)			$ 233,472
Income Taxes Payable (Exhibit 16–19)			240,396
Total current liabilities			$ 473,868
Stockholders' Equity			
Common Stock		$300,000	
Retained Earnings (c)		625,055	925,055
Total Liabilities and Stockholders' Equity			$1,398,923

(a) Beginning balance (Ex. 16–6)	$540,000
Scrapped fully depreciated asset	(15,000)
Purchased new forklift	10,000
Ending balance	$535,000
(b) Beginning balance (Ex. 16–6)	$180,000
Scrapped fully depreciated asset	(15,000)
Factory depreciation (Ex. 16–11)	4,500
SG&A depreciation (Ex. 16–12)	1,200
Ending balance	$170,700
(c) Beginning balance (Ex. 16–6)	$264,460
Net income (Ex. 16–21)	360,595
Ending balance	$625,055

distinct major activities (operating, investing, and financing). Such a rearrangement permits management to judge whether the specific anticipated flows are consistent with the company's strategic plans. In addition, the SCF incorporates a schedule or narrative about significant noncash transactions, such as an exchange of stock for land, that are disregarded in the cash budget.

It is acceptable for external reporting to present the operating section of the SCF on either a direct or an indirect basis. The direct basis uses pure cash flow information (cash collections and cash disbursements) for operating activities. The operating section for a SCF prepared on an indirect basis begins with net income and makes reconciling adjustments to arrive at cash flow from operations. Exhibit 16–21 provides a Statement of Cash Flows for Import Designs using the information from the cash budget in Exhibit 16–17; the second, indirect presentation of the operating section uses the information from the income statement in Exhibit 16–19 and the balance sheets in Exhibits 16–6 and 16–20.

It is interesting to note that Import Designs generates both a large cash flow from operations ($113,431) and a high net income per net sales dollar (20 percent). This strong showing by both measures suggests that Import Designs can expect to enjoy what is known as high quality of earnings. Both cash flow from operations and net income are necessary for long-run success in business. It appears that Import Designs' management is doing an effective job in pricing the company's product and an efficient job in controlling its costs.

EXHIBIT 16–21

Import Designs' Pro Forma Statement of Cash Flows for the First Quarter of 1995

Operating Activities:			
Cash collections			
From sales (Ex. 16–14 or 16–17)			$1,575,076
Cash payments			
For inventory:			
Direct materials (Ex. 16–17)	$1,069,618		
Direct labor (Ex. 16–17)	107,730		
Overhead (Ex. 16–17)	81,060	(1,258,408)	
For nonfactory costs:			
Salaries and wages (Ex. 16–12)	$ 170,000		
Supplies (Ex. 16–12)	18,400		
Other SG&A expenses (Ex. 16–12)	11,940		
Interest payments (Ex. 16–17)	2,897	(203,237)	
Net cash inflow from operating activities			$113,431
Investing Activities:			
Purchase of plant asset (Ex. 16–13)		$ (10,000)	
Short-term investment (Ex. 16–17)		(103,400)	
Net cash outflow from investing activities			(113,400)
Financing Activities:			
Issuance of short-term note payable (Ex. 16–17)		$ 111,600	
Repayment of short-term note payable (Ex. 16–17)		(111,600)	
Net cash outflow from financing activities			0
Net increase in cash			$ 31
Alternative (Indirect) Basis for Operating Activities:			
Net income			$360,595
+ Depreciation (Ex. 16–11 and Ex. 16–12)		$ 5,700	
− Increase in Accounts Receivable ($376,992 − $126,420)		(250,572)	
− Increase in Total Inventory ($538,200 − $290,040)		(248,160)	
+ Increase in Accounts Payable ($233,472 − $228,000)		5,472	
+ Increase in Taxes Payable ($240,396 − $0)		240,396	(247,164)
Net cash inflow from operating activities			$113,431

Tool Warehouse (Sevierville, Tennessee) accepts both cash and major credit cards in payment for purchases. Because the major cards deposit funds almost immediately to the store's account, there is little need to determine a collection pattern or estimate uncollectibles.

CONCLUDING COMMENTS

A well-prepared budget provides the following benefits:

1. a detailed path for managers to follow to achieve organizational goals;
2. an allocation of resources among departments;
3. a means by which managerial performance can be judged;
4. a device to allow employee participation and influence;
5. a means by which troublesome or hard-to-control cost areas can be noted;
6. a realization of the dynamic nature of departmental interrelationships;
7. improved planning and decision making;
8. "more timely responses to changing environmental conditions; and
9. an enhanced understanding of the factors important to the operations of the business".[10]

Because of its fundamental nature in the budgeting process, demand must be predicted as accurately and with as many details as possible. Sales forecasts should indicate type and quantity of products to be sold, geographic locations of the sales, types of buyers, and times when the sales are to be made. Such detail is necessary because different products require different production and distribution facilities; different customers have different credit terms and payment schedules; and different seasons or months may necessitate different shipping schedules or methods.

Estimated sales demand has a pervasive impact on the master budget. To arrive at a valid prediction, managers use as much information as is available and may combine several estimation approaches. Combining prediction methods provides managers with a means to confirm estimates and reduce uncertainty. Some ways of estimating future demand are (1) canvassing sales personnel for a subjective consensus;

---

[10] Gadis J. Dillon, "Getting the Most from Your Forecasting System," *Management Accounting* (April 1984), p. 32.

(2) making simple extrapolations of past trends; (3) using market research; and (4) employing statistical and other mathematical models.

Care should be taken to use realistic, rather than necessarily optimistic or pessimistic, forecasts of revenues and costs. Computer models can be developed that allow repetitive computer simulations to be run after changes are made to one or more factors. These simulations permit managers to review results that would be obtained under various circumstances.

The master budget is normally prepared on an annual basis and is detailed by quarters and months within those quarters. Some companies use a process of **continuous budgeting**, which means that an ongoing twelve-month budget is presented by successively adding a new budget month (twelve months into the future) as each current month expires. Such a process allows management to work, at any time, within the present one-month component of a full twelve-month annual budget. Continuous budgets make the planning process less sporadic. Rather than having managers "go into the budgeting period" at a specific time, they are continuously involved in planning and budgeting.

Continuous budgeting

If actual results occur that differ from plans, management must find the causes of the differences. Once the causes of the performance variations are known, management may wish to consider budget revisions. Arrangements usually cannot be made rapidly enough to revise the current month's budget. However, under certain circumstances and if they so desire, managers may be able to revise future months' budgets. If actual performance is substantially less than what was expected, the budget may or may not be adjusted, depending on the causes of the variances. If the causes are beyond the organization's control and are cost-related, management may decide to revise budget cost estimates upward to be more realistic. If the causes are internal (such as the sales staff simply not selling the product), management may leave the budget in its original form so that the lack of operational control is visible in the comparisons.

If actual performance is substantially better than expected, alterations may also be made to the budget, although management may decide not to alter the budget so that the positive performance is highlighted. Regardless of whether the budget is revised, managers should commend those responsible and communicate the effects of such performance to other related departments. For example, if the sales force has been very effective and has sold significantly higher quantities of product than expected (at the expected selling price), production and purchasing will need to be notified to increase the number of units manufactured and materials bought. The News Note "Develop a Good Budget Basis" on page 682 discusses why budget adjustments need to be made carefully.

When budgets are used for performance evaluation purposes, management often encounters the problem of **budget slack** being built into the budget. Budget slack is the intentional underestimation of revenues and/or overestimation of expenses. Slack can be incorporated into the budget during the participation process; slack is not often found in imposed budgets (which are discussed in the appendix to this chapter). Having slack in the budget allows subordinate managers to achieve their objectives with less effort than would be necessary if there were no slack. Having slack in the budget creates problems because of the significant interaction of the budget factors. If sales are understated, problems can arise in the production, purchasing, and personnel areas. One method that top management can use to try to reduce slack is tying actual performance to the budget through a bonus system. Operating managers are rewarded with large bonuses for budgeting relatively high performance levels and achieving those levels. If performance is set at a low or minimal level, achievement of that performance is either not rewarded or only minimally rewarded. Top management must be aware that budget slack has a tremendous negative impact on organizational effectiveness and efficiency.

Budget slack

Managers may also want to consider expanding their budgeting process to recognize the concepts of activities and cost drivers. Jeffrey A. Schmidt, a vice president in the management consulting firm of Towers Perrin, has suggested that management convert its traditional budget "into an activity budget, which discloses how much the company spends on specific tasks and the types of resources it devotes to them. An activity budget is created by mapping the line items in the conventional budget to a list of activities (responding to customer complaints, requisitioning new parts, etc.)."[11] Such a budget presentation would provide a focus on the costs of non-value-added activities and, hopefully, make managers more aware of why costs are being incurred and how much is being spent on non-value-added activities. Armed with such knowledge, managers could make more informed decisions about what activities to eliminate and why *seemingly* fixed costs continue to rise over time.

REVISITING

MASCO CORPORATION

Masco's stated corporate goal is "to build a unique company based on leadership in consumer products." From this goal, the company has identified a variety of strategies that encompass objectives in the following categories: to create value-added products; provide superior service; build positions of product leadership; and achieve

---

[11] Jeffrey A. Schmidt, "Is It Time to Replace Traditional Budgeting?" *Journal of Accountancy* (October 1992), p. 104.

above-average earnings per share growth. The goal, objectives, and strategies are translated during the budgeting process into tangible financial plans that serve as a benchmark of achievement.

At year-end, Masco managers are diligent about comparing the company's actual results to the forecast. If budgetary control is to be achieved, managers must understand where corporate activities went awry or, possibly, where budgetary assumptions were in error. For example, a 1990 annual report assumption related to the cash flow forecast was that interest rates on bank debt and excess cash would be eight and six percent, respectively. The downward spiral of interest rates during 1991 caused company management to reduce both of these interest rates in the preparation of the cash flow forecast for the 1991 annual report.

The letter to shareholders at the beginning of the Masco annual report discusses the causes of some of the differences between actual results and expectations. In 1991, top management reflected on the "severe and protracted recessions in our major markets" and to a strategic decision "not to sacrifice long-term growth and profit opportunities in order to achieve better short-term results."

Financial planning is a high priority at Masco Corporation and has helped the business change "from a small company generating a few million dollars in sales into a diversified [international] enterprise that currently manufactures and markets more than $3 billion of consumer products for the home and family."

SOURCE: Adapted from Masco Corporation *1991 Annual Report*, p. 6.

CHAPTER SUMMARY

Planning is the process of setting goals and objectives and translating them into activities and resources required for accomplishment within a specified time horizon. Budgeting is the quantifying of a company's financial plans and activities. Budgets facilitate communication, coordination, and teamwork.

A master budget is the comprehensive set of projections for a specific budget period, culminating in a set of pro forma financial statements. It is composed of operating and financial budgets and is usually detailed by quarters and months. Some companies prepare continuous budgets by successively adding a new budgetary month, twelve months into the future, as each current month expires.

Sales demand is the proper starting point for the master budget. Once sales demand is determined, the cost accountant forecasts revenues, production quantities and costs, and cash flows for the firm's activities for the upcoming period. These expectations reflect the firm's inflows and outflows of resources and are used in preparing the master budget.

When budgeting, it is important to remember that the various departments within an organization interact with each other and the budget for one department may form the basis of or have an effect on the budgets in other departments. Actual operating results can be compared to budget figures to measure how effectively and efficiently organizational goals were met. Variances can be calculated, and significant unfavorable differences dictate that managers either attempt to alter behavior of personnel or alter the budget if it appears to be unrealistic. Significant favorable differences most likely will not cause the budget to be adjusted, but rather will cause communication to affected departments on possible consequences (such as increased production needs indicated by a favorable difference in sales demand). Regardless of whether variances are unfavorable or favorable, feedback to operating personnel is an important part of the budget process.

APPENDIX

Purposes of Budgeting and the Budget Manual

Budgeting requires the integration of a complex set of facts and projections with human relationships and attitudes. Throughout the budgeting literature, it has been noted that "the appropriate budgetary system and its implementation techniques are dependent upon organizational structure, management strategies, corporate goals and objectives, leadership style of top management, and employee attitudes."[12] In other words, one system of budgeting is not right for all organizations.

Imposed vs. Participatory Budgets

Imposed budget
Participatory budget

The budgeting process can be represented by a continuum with **imposed budgets** on one end and **participatory budgets** on the other. Since the original goal of budgeting was monetary control, most budgets were imposed upon the individuals who had to work within those budgets. Imposed budgets are prepared by top management with little or no input from operating personnel. After the budget is developed, operating personnel are informed of the budget goals and constraints. Exhibit 16–22 indicates

■ EXHIBIT 16–22
Imposed Budgets

BEST TIMES TO USE?

- In start-up organizations
- In extremely small businesses
- In times of economic crises
- When operating managers lack budgetary skills or perspective
- When the organizational units require precise coordination of efforts

ADVANTAGES OF:

- Increase probability that organization's strategic plans are incorporated in planned activities
- Enhance coordination among divisional plans and objectives
- Utilize top management's knowledge of overall resource availability
- Reduce the possibility of input from inexperienced or uninformed lower-level employees
- Reduce the time frame for the budgeting process

DISADVANTAGES OF:

- May result in dissatisfaction, defensiveness, and low morale among individuals who must work under them
- Reduce the feeling of teamwork
- May limit the acceptance of the stated goals and objectives
- Limit the communication process among employees and management
- May create a view of the budget as a punitive device
- May result in unachievable budgets for international divisions if the local operating and political environment is not adequately considered
- May stifle initiative of lower-level managers

---

[12] Mary T. Soulier, "A Psychological Model of the Budgetary Process," *Woman CPA* (January 1980), p. 3.

that there are certain times when imposed budgets are effective and provide some distinct benefits; the disadvantages of imposed budgets are also listed.

At the other end of the continuum, a participatory budget is developed through a process of joint decision-making by top management and operating personnel. It was only in the last half century that the dissatisfaction caused by imposed budgets was first recognized and the idea of participation by various management levels was introduced. The degree to which lower-level operating management is allowed to participate in budget development usually depends on top management's awareness of and agreement with the advantages of the participation process.

From the standpoint of operational managers, participation could be viewed on a spectrum from having a right to merely comment on budgets before top management implements them to having the ultimate right to set budgets. Neither end of that spectrum is quite desirable. Simply commenting on the handed-down budget still reflects an imposed budgeting system, while each individual manager setting his or her own budget disregards the fact that cooperation and communication among areas is essential to the functioning of a cohesive organization.

The benefits and disadvantages of participatory budgets are listed in Exhibit 16–23 on page 686. One of the primary benefits of this type of budgeting process is that people who have participated in budget development are normally more committed to the budget's success than if the budget is imposed. Currently, most business budgets are prepared through a coordinated effort of input from operating personnel and revision by top management.

Cost accountants play a major role in the budgetary process. As members of management's staff, cost accountants assist top management by designing and communicating budgetary forms, procedures, and schedules for responsible personnel. Historical financial information is also provided by cost accountants so that participating managers can make effective projections. Cost accountants analyze, review, and summarize the projections and prepare budgeted financial statements for top management's consideration.

Budget Manuals

To be useful, a budget requires a substantial amount of time and effort by the persons who prepare it. This process can be improved by the availability of an organizational **budget manual**, which is a detailed set of documents that provides information and guidelines about the budgetary process. The manual should include the following:

Budget manual

1. statements of the budgetary purpose and its desired results;
2. a listing of specific budgetary activities to be performed;
3. a calendar of scheduled budgetary activities;
4. sample budgetary forms; and
5. original, revised, and approved budgets.

The statements of budgetary purpose and desired results communicate the reasons behind the process. These statements should flow from general to specific details. An example of a general statement of budgetary purpose is: "The Cash Budget provides a basis for planning, reviewing, and controlling cash flows from and for various activities; this budget is essential to the preparation of a Statement of Cash Flows." Specific statements could include references to minimum desired cash balances and periods of intense cash needs.

Budgetary activities should be listed by position rather than person because the responsibility for actions should be assigned to the individuals holding the designated positions at the time the budget is being prepared. The manual's activities section should indicate who has the final authority for revising and approving the budget.

■ EXHIBIT 16–23
Participatory Budgets

BEST TIMES TO USE?

■ In well-established organizations
■ In extremely large businesses
■ In times of economic affluence
■ When operating managers have strong budgetary skills and perspectives
■ When the organizational units are quite autonomous

ADVANTAGES OF:

■ Obtain information from those persons most familiar with the needs and constraints of organizational units
■ Integrate knowledge that is diffused among various levels of management
■ Lead to better morale and higher motivation
■ Provide a means to develop fiscal responsibility and budgetary skills of employees
■ Develop a high degree of acceptance of and commitment to organizational goals and objectives by operating management
■ Are generally more realistic
■ Allow organizational units to coordinate with one another
■ Allow subordinate managers to develop operational plans that conform to organizational goals and objectives
■ Include specific resource requirements
■ Blend overview of top management with operating details
■ Provide a social contract that expresses expectations of top management and subordinates

DISADVANTAGES OF:

■ Require significantly more time
■ May create a level of dissatisfaction with the process approximately equal to that occurring under imposed budgets if effects of managerial participation are negated by top management changes
■ May be unachievable because managers are ambivalent about participating or unqualified to participate
■ May motivate managers to introduce "slack" into the budget
■ May support "empire building" by subordinates
■ May start the process earlier in the year when there is more uncertainty about the future year

Budget approval may be delegated to a budget committee or reserved by one or several members of top management.

The calendar is essential to coordinate the budgetary process. It should indicate a timetable for all budget activities and be keyed directly to the activities list mentioned above. The timetable for the budget process is unique to each organization. The larger the organization, the more time that will be necessary to gather information, coordinate that information, identify weak points in the process or the budget itself, and take corrective action. The calendar should also indicate control points for the upcoming periods at which budget-to-actual comparisons are made and feedback is provided to managers responsible for operations.

Sample forms are extremely useful because they provide for consistent presentations of budget information from all individuals, which makes summarization of information easier and quicker. The sample forms should be easy-to-understand and may include standardized worksheets that allow managers to update historical information to arrive at budgetary figures. This section of the budget manual may also provide standard cost tables for items on which the organization has specific guidelines or policies. For example, in estimating employee fringe benefit costs, the company rule-of-thumb may be 25 percent of base salary. Or, if company policy states that each salesperson's per diem meal allowance is $30, meal expenses would be budgeted as estimated travel days multiplied by $30.

The final section of the budget manual contains the budgets generated during the budgeting process. Numerous budgets probably will be submitted and revised prior to actual budget implementation. It is helpful for future planning to understand this revision process and why changes were made. The final approved master budget is included in the budget manual as a control document.[13]

KEY TERMS

Budget (p. 654)
Budgeting (p. 654)
Budget manual (p. 685)
Budget slack (p. 681)
Capital budgeting (p. 668)
Continuous budgeting (p. 681)
Financial budget (p. 659)
Imposed budget (p. 684)
Key variable (p. 656)
Master budget (p. 658)
Operating budget (p. 658)
Participatory budget (p. 684)
Strategic planning (p. 655)
Tactical planning (p. 656)

SOLUTION STRATEGIES

Sales Budget
Units of sales
× Selling price per unit
= Dollars of sales

Production Budget
Units of sales
+ Units desired in ending inventory
− Units in beginning inventory
= Units to be produced

Purchases Budget
Units to be produced
+ Units desired
− Units in beginning inventory
= Units to be purchased

Direct Labor Budget
Units of production
× Standard time allowed per unit
= Standard labor time allowed
× Per hour direct labor cost
= Total direct labor cost

---

[13] In the event of changes in economic conditions or strategic plans, the "final" budget may be revised during the budget period.

financial targets have on the ethical behavior of the ministers and some board members of those churches?

c. Would there be certain instances in which pastors who exceeded their budgeted expenses should not be urged to cut those expenses? Discuss the rationale for your answer.

50. *Chambers Development Co.'s founder, John G. Rangos Sr., demanded results no matter where they came from. "Go find the rest of it," he told an executive in 1990 after the executive said profit would fall short of projections.*

The charade collapsed [on October 20, 1991] when an outside audit disclosed that in every year since Chambers went public in 1985, the company reported strong profits but actually lost money. Now, a chastened Chambers, once hailed on Wall Street as a waste-management star, has restated net income for each of the past seven years to reduce its reported profits by $362 million on an after-tax basis.

Mr. Rangos and his two sons hold a sizable equity stake in the company. Former and current managers describe Mr. Rangos as a man obsessed with making his garbage company a star and insistent on managers meeting his lofty profit goals.

[SOURCE: Gabriella Stern, "Audit Report Shows How Far Chambers Would Go for Profits," *Wall Street Journal* (October 21, 1992), p. A1. Reprinted by permission of the *Wall Street Journal*, © 1992 Dow Jones & Company, Inc. All rights reserved worldwide.]

a. Discuss whether it is more likely that Chambers Development used an imposed or participatory budgeting process. Explain the rationale for your answer.

b. How might it have been possible for managers to "find" additional profits? Why would such "found profits" not have been discovered by the auditors?

c. Why would the managers be willing to "find" the additional profits?

d. At some point should the ethics of the managers have outweighed the notion of budget performance responsibility? Why?

51. Many managers believe that, if all amounts in their budgets are not spent during a period, they will lose allocations in future periods and that little or no recognition will result from cost savings. The figure below indicates results of a survey of IMA members about the motivating factors behind budgeting issues.

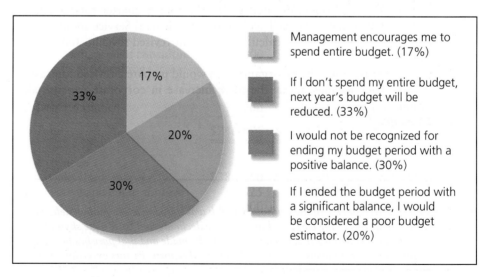

SOURCE: Gerald L. Finch and William Mihal, "Spend It or Lose It," *Management Accounting* (March 1989), p. 45. Reprinted from *Management Accounting*. Copyright by Institute of Management Accountants, Montvale, N.J.

Discuss the behavioral and ethical issues involved in a "spend it or lose it" attitude. Include in your discussion the issue of negotiating budget allocation requests prior to the beginning of the period.

COST CONTROL

PART

V

COST CONTROL FOR DISCRETIONARY COSTS

LEARNING OBJECTIVES

After completing this chapter, you should be able to answer these questions:

1. Why is cost consciousness important to all members of an organization?
2. How are costs determined to be committed or discretionary?
3. How are the benefits of expenditures for discretionary costs measured?
4. When are standards applicable to discretionary costs?
5. How does a budget help in the control of discretionary costs?
6. *(Appendix)* How is program budgeting used in not-for-profit entities?
7. *(Appendix)* Why is zero-base budgeting useful in cost control?

INTRODUCING

SOUTHWEST AIRLINES CO.

Structurally, Southwest is unique among major American airlines. Its competitors have built centralized empires—most of which are now distended and in danger of collapse. Wedded to the "hub-and-spoke" system, those carriers fly huge planes between major airports and link them with a galaxy of "feeder" flights from lesser sites. On paper, the hub-and-spoke concept makes sense, but in practice it ties up too many valuable assets at a handful of pressure points in the system.

Southwest's layout is more akin to a spiderweb, spun one strand at a time, flexible enough to disperse assets and dissipate stress. In airline jargon, Southwest is a "short-haul, point-to-point" carrier. It has no recognizable hub. It flies short distances nonstop, the average flight being 55 minutes. Southwest flights do not make connections with others, do not transfer baggage, do not serve meals, do not offer assigned seats. Southwest does not subscribe to expensive computerized reservation systems. It does relatively little business through travel agents because the margins on its fares are too thin. But by eschewing such services, the airline offers passengers rewards of more lasting value: frequent, reliable service and rock-bottom fares.

Since the U.S. airline industry was first deregulated in 1978, 169 airlines have failed, merged, or died before their first flight ever left the tarmac. Southwest, meanwhile, has been profitable in each of the past 18 years. In 1990 it was the only major U.S. carrier to show a net profit based solely on operations—while offering the lowest fares in the industry. Southwest's overall costs are the lowest of any major carrier (defined as one that brings in more than $1 billion in revenues), yet its work force is among the industry's best paid.

SOURCE: Edward O. Welles, "Captain Marvel," *INC.* (January 1992), p. 45. Reprinted with permission, *Inc.*, magazine (January 1992). Copyright 1992 by Goldhirsh Group, Inc., 38 Commmercial Wharf, Boston, MA 02110.

Because of its continual expansion and clearly unique policies, Southwest Airlines is an enigma in the airline industry. But because it can attain and sustain consistently reasonable levels of profitability, Southwest can be labeled a business success. It is traditionally agreed that, when costs are properly controlled, both income and efficiency will increase.

Previous chapters presented a variety of ways to control costs. For example, flexible budgets can be developed to monitor and control both product and period costs. Direct materials and direct labor cost control are typically tied to the development and implementation of a standard cost system. Use of a variable costing system tends to focus on the costs that are more susceptible to control by managers in the short run.

This chapter focuses on three major topics. First, the topic of cost control systems is discussed. A **cost control system** is a logical structure of formal and/or informal activities designed to analyze and evaluate how well expenditures are managed during a period. The next topic is control over **discretionary costs**, which are costs (such as

Cost control system

Discretionary cost

Committed fixed cost

advertising) that management sets each period at specified levels. Since the benefits provided by discretionary costs are often hard to measure, management may find these costs more difficult to control than **committed fixed costs**, which relate either to the long-term plant asset investments or to "permanent" organizational personnel. Third, methods of using budgets to help in cost control is discussed. The chapter appendix considers two alternative budgeting methods: program budgeting, which is often used in governmental and not-for-profit entities, and zero-base budgeting, which can be effective in some cost control programs.

COST CONTROL SYSTEMS

Cost consciousness

As indicated in Exhibit 17–1, an effective control system must perform at three points: before, during, and after an event. An "event" can be a period of time, the production of a product, or the performance of a service. The cost control process can also be diagrammed to include the **cost consciousness** concepts shown in Exhibit 17–2. Cost consciousness refers to a companywide employee attitude about cost understanding, cost containment, cost avoidance, and cost reduction.

Cost Understanding

Cost control is first exercised when the budget is prepared since a budget is a necessary tool for comparing expected and actual costs. However, a budget cannot be prepared without understanding why costs may change from one period to the next and cost control cannot be achieved without understanding why costs may differ from the budgeted amounts.

Costs may change from previous periods or differ from budget expectations for a variety of reasons. One major reason certain costs change is their underlying behavior. Total variable cost increases or decreases with increases or decreases in level of activity. Therefore, if the current period activity level differs from the activity level of a prior period or the level stated in the budget, total actual variable cost will differ from the prior period or the budget. A flexible budget can compensate for such differences by providing expected cost information at the actual level of activity. Flexible budgets allow cost accountants and managers to compare related budgeted and actual costs to determine whether total variable costs were properly controlled.

In addition to variable cost reactions to changes in activity levels, the following three factors can cause costs to differ from prior periods or the budget.

CONTROL POINT	REASON	COST CONTROL METHODS
Before an event	Preventive; reflects planning	Budgets; standards; policies concerning approval for deviations; expressions of quantitative and qualitative objectives
During an event	Corrective; ensures that the event is being pursued according to plans; management can correct problems as they occur	Periodic monitoring of ongoing activities; comparing activities and costs to budgets and standards; avoiding excessive expenditures
After an event	Diagnostic; guides future actions	Feedback; responsibility reports (discussed in Chapter 21); variance analysis

EXHIBIT 17–1

Functions of an Effective Cost Control System

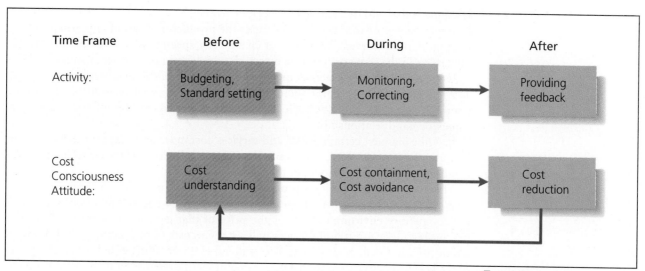

Time Frame	Before	During	After
Activity:	Budgeting, Standard setting	Monitoring, Correcting	Providing feedback
Cost Consciousness Attitude:	Cost understanding	Cost containment, Cost avoidance	Cost reduction

▌ **EXHIBIT 17–2**
Cost Control System

1. *Cost changes due to inflation/deflation.* Fluctuations in the value of the dollar are called general price level changes. When the general price level changes, the cost of goods and services that the dollar can purchase also changes. General price level changes affect almost all costs equally and in the same direction, if all other factors are constant.

2. *Cost changes due to supply/supplier cost adjustments.* The relationship between the availability of a good or service to the demand for that item affects its selling price.

Controlling costs was not of any importance when this castle was built. However, present economic conditions necessitate that almost all individuals and businesses be concerned with how costs can be controlled and what benefits are obtained by cost incurrence.

If supply is low and demand is high relative to the past, the selling price of the good or service increases and therefore increases the production costs of any firm purchasing that good or service. This type of change is a specific price level change, which may move in the same or opposite direction as a general price level change. To illustrate the dramatic effect such changes can create on profits, consider the fact that in 1990 each one cent per gallon increase in the price of jet fuel cost Southwest Airlines approximately $3.1 million. Such increases were caused, not by inflation, but by a supply/demand relationship.

In a like manner, certain goods and services cost more at certain times of the year because of use or demand. For example, it is generally less expensive to have an air conditioner serviced in the winter than in the summer.

The number of competitors producing a product or providing a service can also create a cost adjustment. As the number of suppliers of a good or service increases, the competitive environment causes the price of that good or service to fall. Firms purchasing these goods and services will see their costs of production fall. Likewise, a reduction in the number of suppliers will, all else remaining equal, cause the price of the goods or services to increase, causing upward pressure on the cost of production of any firm using these goods or services as inputs. A change in the number of *suppliers* is not the same as a change in the quantity of *supply*. If the supply of an item is large, one normally expects the price to be low, but if there is only one supplier, the price can remain high because of supplier control.

Specific price level changes may also be caused by advances in technology. As a general rule, as suppliers advance the technology of producing a good or performing a service, the cost of that good or service to the producing firm declines. Assuming competitive market conditions, such cost declines are often passed along to consumers of that product or service in the form of lower selling prices.

Correspondingly, when suppliers incur additional production or performance costs, they will typically pass those increases on to their customers as part of specific price level changes. As discussed in the accompanying News Note, airlines are facing this problem relative to the charges assessed them by airports.

Sometimes, cost increases are caused by increases in taxes or regulatory requirements. For example, airlines are continuously faced with more stringent noise-abatement, clean-air, and required maintenance legislation. Complying with these regulations increases costs for the airline company that must (1) be passed along in the form of ticket-price increases to maintain the same income level, (2) force decreases in other costs to maintain the same income level, or (3) cause a decline in net income.

3. *Cost changes due to quantity purchased.* Firms are normally given quantity discounts up to some maximum level when purchases are made in bulk. Therefore, a cost per unit may change because the lot sizes in which quantities are purchased differ from previous periods or from projections.

The preceding reasons indicate why costs change, but do not indicate what managers can do to contain the upward effects of the changes. Minimizing the upward trends means that costs are being controlled.

Cost Containment

Cost containment

To the extent possible, period-by-period increases in per unit variable and total fixed costs should be *minimized* through a process of **cost containment**. Cost containment is not possible for changes resulting from inflation, supply chain cost adjustments, tax and regulatory changes, and supply and demand adjustments. However, costs that rise because of reduced competition, seasonality, and quantities purchased are subject to cost containment activities. A company should look for ways to cap the upward changes in these costs. An example of a cost containment activity is given below for each type of controllable cost change.

NEWS NOTE

Airlines Face Increased Costs for Airport Construction

Stunned by continuous enormous losses, airlines are stepping up efforts to pressure the nation's airports to scale back or delay expansion projects in order to curb costs.

The airlines help finance airport projects through landing fees and terminal-space rental charges, which now total more than $3.5 billion a year, according to the Air Transport Association. Since 1982 such costs have climbed 76%, almost twice the rate of the consumer price index. That makes the charges one of the fastest growing items in airlines' budgets. A report by the Airports Association Council International found that U.S. airports will need [to spend] $60 billion between 1992 and 1997 for runways, terminals, and related facilities.

[For example, there are] plans to open Denver International, a new $2.7 billion airport, to replace Stapleton International Airport, even though Stapleton isn't being fully used. Airport officials say the airlines' cost-per-passenger will double to about $12 a passenger from the current $6 at Stapleton, but airlines' own estimates go as high as $20 a passenger. Denver officials point out that at least some of the projected increase in the airlines' costs at the new airport will be offset by what is expected to be a drastic reduction in flight delays. The savings from cutting delays should be substantial [because it is estimated] that a loaded airplane waiting to take off racks up $25 a minute in fuel and crew expenses.

SOURCE: Laurie McGinley, "Airlines Pressure Airports to Scale Back Expansion Plans in Bid to Reduce Costs," *Wall Street Journal* (September 25, 1992), pp. B1, B5. Reprinted by permission of the *Wall Street Journal*, © 1992 Dow Jones & Company, Inc. All rights reserved worldwide.

The purchasing agent of a company should be aware of new suppliers for needed goods and services and determine which, if any, of those suppliers can provide needed items in the quantity, quality, and time desired. Comparing costs and finding new sources of supply can increase buying power and reduce costs. If bids are used to select suppliers, the purchasing agent should remember that a bid is merely the first step in negotiating. While a low bid eliminates the supplier's competition from consideration, it is possible that additional negotiations between the purchasing agent and the supplier may result in a purchase cost even lower than the bid amount.

A company may circumvent seasonal cost changes by postponing or advancing purchases of goods and services. However, such purchasing changes should not mean buying irresponsibly or incurring excessive carrying costs. The concepts of economic order quantities, safety stock levels, and materials requirements planning as well as the just-in-time philosophy should be considered when making purchases. These concepts are discussed in the next chapter.

As to services, employees could repair rather than replace items that have seasonal cost changes. For example, maintenance workers might find that a broken heat pump can be repaired and used for the spring months so that it would not have to be replaced until summer when the purchase cost is lower.

The idea of buying in bulk is not new or unique, but it is not often applied on an extended basis for related companies or enterprises. In a corporation, one division could take the responsibility for obtaining a supplier contract for items (such as computer disks) that are necessary to all divisions. The savings resulting from buying in a quantity appropriate for all divisions could offset the additional costs of shipping or distributing the disks to the divisions. Even unrelated organizations can improve cost control by group purchasing of necessary items that do not directly enter into any product or service on which they may be competing. For example, several hospitals in an area could negotiate as one "entity" with a laundry to provide linen service. The result of this group negotiation is that all hospitals receive the best possible cost.

By flying only Boeing 737s, Southwest Airlines has a proven way to contain costs relative to its fleet of planes. Such standardization allows for cost containment in the areas of flight crew training and scheduling, maintenance simplification, and spare parts inventory size. In addition, cost containment is built on Southwest's average ground turnaround time of 15 minutes or less. If the company were to increase its ground time by even ten minutes per flight, the airline estimates it would have to buy an additional 16 aircraft at a cost of $25 million each.

Cost Avoidance

Cost avoidance

Cost containment can prove very effective if it can be implemented. In some instances, although cost containment may not be possible, **cost avoidance** might be. Cost avoidance means finding acceptable alternatives to high-cost items and/or not spending money for unnecessary goods or services.

For example, some business schools have joined forces to lower their expenditures on high-cost programs. Cleveland State, Kent State, Youngstown State and the University of Akron have decided to "create and collectively run a new school of international business. Alone, none of the institutions has sufficiently broad language and cultural expertise. More importantly, the four universities need each other to justify the school's $30 million projected price tag."[1]

Many hospitals are practicing cost avoidance with regard to orthopedic implants (such as those used in hip replacements). One survey found that over half the hospital respondents were using a consignment system for implants.

> Generally, consignment allows a hospital to have an implant device available for use, but it doesn't have to take title to the item—or pay for it—until it's actually been used in a procedure. As a result, a hospital doesn't have to tie up its money stocking implants [and it] avoids being saddled with implant systems that may become outdated or rendered useless if [an orthopedic] surgeon who prefers that system suddenly leaves the hospital.[2]

Although consigned implants may cost more per unit than purchased ones, hospitals employing this procedure believe that the additional cost is much less than the potential carrying costs or costs of obsolescence that are associated with buying the implants.

Cost Reduction

Cost reduction

Closely related to cost avoidance is cost reduction. **Cost reduction** refers to lowering current costs, especially those that may be in excess of what is necessary. For example, Chase Manhattan Bank, Hearst Corp., and the American Institute of CPAs employed cost reduction tactics when they moved their New York City locations to, respectively, Florida, North Carolina, and New Jersey because of high rents and high taxes.[3] Two cost reduction examples in the airline industry are as follows: one airline stopped putting spoons on economy-class trays and another trimmed the window for its lunch flights to those between noon and 1:30 p.m. rather than between 11:30 a.m. and 2:00 p.m.

---

[1] Gilbert Fuchsberg, "Business Schools Team Up with Rivals to Enrich Offerings But Keep Costs Down," *Wall Street Journal* (August 18, 1992), p. B8.
[2] Mary Wagner, "Common Buying Strategies Not Used to Acquire Implants," *Modern Healthcare* (March 23, 1992), p. 52.
[3] Stephen Kagann, "New York's Incentives, the Wrong Incentives," *Wall Street Journal* (October 6, 1992), p. A18.

NEWS NOTE

Energy Costs Are Candidates for Cost Reduction

All energy is not created equal. It will power your lights and run your shop floor, but from whom you buy it, how they ship it to you, and how you use it in your own operation can mean either big costs—or big opportunities for savings.

XENERGY, Inc., specializes in energy. Based in Burlington, Mass., the 320-person company advises manufacturers on how to buy energy—and buys it on their behalf—and then advises them how to use it to optimum advantage.

"If a manufacturer uses natural gas, simply changing how he buys this gas can cut his gas bills by 30 percent to 40 percent a year," says James Walker, vice president and director of XENERGY's industrial management services. "These savings require no purchases of equipment. You simply buy your gas more intelligently and start saving money immediately."

These savings are possible because of the ongoing deregulation of the natural gas industry. "In the old days, gas companies would bundle together the costs of the gas, its transport, and other costs into one price," says Walker. "Then they'd say to consumers, 'Here's the rate.'" But today, gas costs are "unbundled." Manufacturers now can buy their gas competitively from producers and other suppliers, not just from their local utilities. Consumers can buy their gas from one company and buy its transport from other companies. Consequently, the best deals for gas and its transport inevitably change as regulations and tariffs change. A gas pipeline that today has favorable rates for transportation will suddenly become too expensive. XENERGY responds by contracting to ship through another pipeline with more favorable rates or greater reliability. The utilities then distribute the gas to clients' facilities through the normal distribution networks. The customer sees no change in his physical equipment or in the quality of gas.

SOURCE: "Cutting Energy Costs Generates Bottom-Line Savings," (*Grant Thornton*) *Manufacturing Issues* (Spring 1992), pp. 5–6. Reprinted by permission from Grant Thornton's *Manufacturing Issues.* © Grant Thornton 1992.

Delta Air Lines views providing meals as a necessary part of its flight service, but implemented a cost reduction technique when management eliminated lettuce under the passenger meals' vegetables. The airline's president, W. Whitley Hawkins, said "an employee made the suggestion after noting that the large piece of lettuce looked nice, but few people ate it. Scrapping the lettuce, Hawkins said, will save Delta $1.4 million a year in labor and lettuce costs."[4]

Cost reduction can be easily practiced in regard to utility costs. Although it is not possible for a company to control the increase in utility rates nor to stop using electricity, employees can reduce some of the firm's energy costs by using sound energy conservation techniques or by using sound energy purchasing techniques. The News Note on energy costs indicates that even energy rates are not a given in today's deregulated environment.

Sometimes money must be spent to generate cost savings. Accountants may opt to use videotaped rather than live presentations to reduce the cost of continuing education programs. Some of the larger firms (such as Arthur Andersen) have their own in-house studios and staffs. Although the cost of producing a tape is high, the firms feel the cost is justified because many copies can be made and used by all the offices. Other firms bring in specialists to address their staffs rather than having the staff members attend external courses. "The firms consider the $1,000 or $1,200 fee for the speak-

---

[4]The Associated Press, "Lettuce Cut to Save $1.4 Million for Airline Seeking a Cheaper Way," *(New Orleans) Times-Picayune* (July 24, 1992), p. C-2.

ers' appearances well spent. As one practitioner calculated, the cost breaks down to $35 to $45 per attendee."[5] Other firms are even using satellite or two-way interactive television to provide continuing education hours to their employees.

Use of part-time rather than full-time employees is another cost reduction technique. When temporaries are used, companies do not have to pay payroll taxes, fringe benefits, or Social Security. Thus, although temporaries often cost more per hour than full timers, the total cost equation may be reduced. If the quantity of work in an area fluctuates substantially, part-time employees can be hired for peak periods. Businesses are also hiring temporaries to work on special projects, provide expertise in a specific area, or to fill in until the "right" full-time employee can be found for a particular position.

Strategic staffing

Companies are beginning to view their personnel needs from a **strategic staffing** perspective that basically requires a department to analyze its personnel needs by considering its long-term objectives and those of the overall company and determining a specific combination of permanent and temporary employees with the best skills to meet those needs. Using temporary workers provides a flexible staffing "cushion" that helps insulate the jobs of permanent, core employees. Airlines, for instance, often hire part-time ground personnel because of the "bunching" nature of the airline schedule (early morning, midday, and early evening flights). Use of these part-timers has dramatically reduced airline fringe benefit costs.

As discussed in Chapter 2, it is also possible for companies to reduce costs by outsourcing or using specialist external providers of services rather than maintaining internal departments. Data processing activities are a prime candidate for outsourcing. For example, in September 1989, Commercial Federal Savings and Loan Association hired Citicorp Information Resources on a six-year contract to do all its data processing. By March 1991, Commercial Federal had saved approximately $3 million on its data processing costs.[6] Southwest Airlines also outsources its data processing and, while most maintenance is performed in-house, major maintenance of engines and airframes is contracted to other companies. Another example of outsourcing involves The Claflin Company of Providence, Rhode Island. Claflin manages inventories for numerous hospitals and provides just-in-time deliveries of needed supplies.

When costs are reduced, care should be taken to determine that the reductions are not improper in some way, as in the situation involving the now-defunct Eastern Air Lines. Employees falsified records to cover nonperformance of maintanance requirements, reducing costs in the short run. Even if the airline had remained solvent, no customer would consider that methodology of cost reduction to be in the interest of quality service. The same observation would generally be made if companies decided to reduce costs by cutting their spending on worker safety equipment.

Managers may adopt the five-step method of implementing a cost control system shown in Exhibit 17–3. First, the type of costs incurred by an organization must be understood. Are the costs under consideration fixed or variable, product or period? What cost drivers affect those costs? Does management view the costs as committed or discretionary? Second, the need for cost consciousness must be communicated to all employees for the control process to be effective. Employees must be aware of which costs need to be better controlled and why cost control is important to both the company and to the employees themselves. Third, employees must be educated in cost control techniques, encouraged to provide ideas on how to control costs, and motivated by some type of incentives to embrace the concepts. The incentives may range from simple verbal recognition to monetary rewards to time off with pay. Managers must also be flexible enough to allow for changes from the current method of operation. Fourth, reports must be generated indicating actual results, budget-to-

---

[5] Bob Okell, "The Cost of CPE Comes Under Fire," *Accounting Today* (April 6, 1992), p. 3.
[6] Mel Mandell, "Corporate Computers: How Necessary?" *Across the Board* (March 1991), p. 51. Outsourcing activities are discussed in more depth in Chapter 15 on relevant costing.

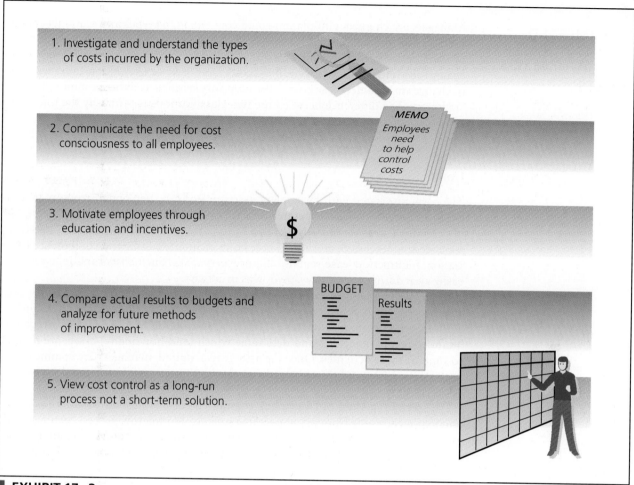

1. Investigate and understand the types of costs incurred by the organization.

2. Communicate the need for cost consciousness to all employees.

MEMO *Employees need to help control costs*

3. Motivate employees through education and incentives.

$

4. Compare actual results to budgets and analyze for future methods of improvement.

BUDGET   Results

5. View cost control as a long-run process not a short-term solution.

▌ EXHIBIT 17–3

Implementing a Cost Control System

actual comparisons, and variances. These reports must be evaluated by management as to why costs were or were not controlled in the past. Such analysis may provide insightful information about cost drivers so that the activities causing costs may be better controlled in the future. And last, the cost control system should be viewed as a long-run process, not a short-run solution. "To be successful, organizations must avoid the illusion of short-term, highly simplified cost-cutting procedures. Instead, they must carefully evaluate proposed solutions to insure that these are practical, workable, and measure changes based on realities, not illusions."[7]

Following these five steps will provide an atmosphere conducive to controlling costs to the fullest extent possible as well as deriving the most benefit from the costs that are incurred. Costs to be incurred should have been compared to the benefits expected to be achieved before cost incurrence took place. The costs should also have been incorporated into the budgeting system because costs cannot be controlled *after* they have been incurred. Future costs, on the other hand, may be controlled based on information learned about past costs. Cost control should not cease at the end of a fiscal period or because costs were reduced or controlled during the current period. However, distinct differences exist in the cost control system between committed and discretionary costs.

---

[7]Mark D. Lutchen, "Cost Cutting Illusions," *Today's CPA* (May/June 1989), p. 46.

COMMITTED VERSUS DISCRETIONARY COSTS

Managers are charged with planning and controlling the types and amounts of costs necessary to conduct business activities. The traditional cost classifications are those of variable or fixed. Variable costs are viewed as changing in direct response to changes in volume. Alternatively, fixed costs have been viewed as constant regardless of changes in volume; these costs have been subclassified as either committed or discretionary. The difference between the two classifications is primarily the time horizon for which management binds itself to the cost.

Committed Costs

The costs associated with basic plant assets or with the personnel structure that an organization must have to operate are known as committed fixed costs. The amount of committed costs is normally dictated by long-run management decisions involving some desired level of operations. These costs include facilities and equipment depreciation, multiperiod lease rentals, and property taxes. Such costs cannot be reduced easily even during temporary slowdowns in activity.

Control of committed costs is first provided during the capital budgeting evaluation process when expected benefits are compared to expected costs of investing in plant assets or human resources. Managers must decide on the activities needed to attain company objectives and determine which (and how many) assets are needed to support those activities. Once the assets are acquired, managers are committed to both the activities and the costs associated with those activities for some reasonable period of time.

The second method of controlling committed costs is through comparing actual and expected results from plant asset investments. During this process, managers review and evaluate the accuracy of their cost and revenue predictions relative to the investment. This comparison is called a postinvestment audit and is discussed in Chapter 19.

While company management is committed to these plant asset investments for some period of time, changes in circumstances may necessitate changes in the level of commitment. For example, Southwest Airlines had committed costs relative to its fleet of 139 jets in 1992. However, because it has grown consistently by at least 10 percent per year for the last five years, the company has decided to commit to another 34 new jets from 1995 through 1997.[8] Thus, it is important for Southwest's management to understand why "seemingly" fixed costs rise and, therefore, become long-run variable costs. The costs of the new, larger fleet will now become Southwest's committed fixed cost for upcoming years.

Discretionary Costs

In contrast, a discretionary cost is one "that a decision maker must periodically review to determine if it continues to be in accord with ongoing policies."[9] Discretionary fixed costs reflect managerial decisions to fund a particular activity at a specified amount *for a specified period of time.* The decision to fund an activity as discretionary is based on organizational policy or management preference. This statement means that there are no specific activities whose costs will, in all organizations, be considered discretionary costs.

---

[8]Bridget O'Brian, "Southwest Air Orders 34 737s for $1.2 Billion," *Wall Street Journal* (August 7, 1992), p. A2.
[9]Institute of Management Accountants (formerly National Association of Accountants), *Statements on Management Accounting: Management Accounting Terminology,* Number 2 (Montvale, N.J.: June 1, 1983), p. 35.

NEWS NOTE

Activity Reduction Equals Cost Reduction

With all their benefits, computers and copiers create great waste. A case in point was at a 2,000-person manufacturing company. Each month data processing produced 321 copies of 41 reports containing 140,000 pages and distributed these copies to 63 persons. After interviewing the recipients, it was found that only 2 copies of 9 reports were needed. The changes were made and, shortly, manufacturing removed 300+ filing cabinets, sold them, and freed up over 3,000 sq. ft. of floor space. The floor space was then used to store materials, saving $30,000 per year of rent for an outside warehouse. Giving up the warehouse eliminated the need for a driver and truck (operating costs about $4,000 per year) used to move goods to and from the warehouse. Two file clerks' and a printer operator's position were eliminated. Purchase orders for 42 new file cabinets were cancelled, as were appropriations for $38,000 in additional equipment. No one ever bothered to figure out how much was saved in computer paper or report folders. Because the cause was eliminated, a $100,000+ permanent cost reduction per year was achieved.

SOURCE: Adapted from Donald J. Byrum, "The Right Way to Control Period Expense," *Management Accounting* (September 1990), p. 53ff. Reprinted from *Management Accounting*. Copyright by Institute of Management Accountants, Montvale, N.J.

Discretionary costs have traditionally been seen as relating to activities that the company considers important, but somewhat optional. These activities are usually service oriented and include repairs and maintenance, advertising, research and development, and employee training. There is no "correct" or determinable amount at which to set funding for discretionary costs, such as there might be in regard to lease payments under a lease commitment. Managers believe that, in the event of short-run cash flow shortages or forecasted operating losses, reductions can be made in discretionary costs without impairing the long-range profitability or organizational capacity. For instance, companies shipping express mail may decide that package delivery can be equally effective by arriving the next afternoon or even the second day rather than before 10:30 a.m. the next day. In doing so, significant savings on shipping are provided.

Reducing discretionary costs typically requires focusing on the activities that are causing the costs to occur. As discussed in Chapter 4 on activity-based management, companies engage in both value-added and non-value-added activities. If it is possible to eliminate the non-value-added activities, the corresponding costs will also be reduced or eliminated. The News Note on activity reduction indicates the importance of analyzing discretionary cost activities (in this case producing computer reports) to uncover those that add no value, and identifying the amount of cost reduction resulting from elimination of such activities. Understanding the causes of discretionary costs can help in budgeting for them.

Before top management can address the issue of discretionary costs, company goals must be translated into specific objectives and policies that management believes will contribute to organizational success. Then management needs to budget the type and funding levels of discretionary activities that will accomplish those objectives. Budgets serve to officially communicate a manager's authority to spend up to a maximum allowable amount (**appropriation**) or rate for each budget item.

Discretionary costs are generally budgeted on the basis of four factors: the related activity's perceived significance to the achievement of objectives and goals; the up-

BUDGETING DISCRETIONARY COSTS

Appropriation

Public television stations typically offer special programming during their subscription drives. An increased number of subscribers would indicate the drive was, to some degree, effective. However, the station may never know whether the subscriptions resulted from the special programming or whether another technique would have been better.

coming period's expected level of operations; the cash flow and income expectations for the upcoming period; and managerial negotiations in the budgetary process. Management cannot know how much budgeted discretionary cost is the optimal amount for the activity involved. In regard to variable production costs, the common opinion is that "less is better" and that a lower variable production cost indicates efficiency. But because of the nature of discretionary cost activities, less is not necessarily better. For some discretionary costs, managers are expected to spend the full amount of their appropriations within the specified time frame. For other discretionary cost activities, the "less is better" adage is appropriate.

As an example of "less is *not* better," consider the cost of preventive maintenance. This cost can be viewed as discretionary, but reducing it could result in diminished quality, production breakdowns, or machine inefficiency. Although the benefits of maintenance expenditures cannot be precisely quantified, managers at the various airlines believe that incurring less maintenance cost than budgeted is not a positive type of cost control. In fact, spending (with supervisory approval) more than originally appropriated might be necessary or even commendable—assuming that positive results (such as a decline in customer complaints) were obtained. Such a perspective illustrates the earlier-mentioned perception that cost control should be a long-run process rather than a short-run concern.

Alternatively, spending less than budgeted on travel and entertainment (while achieving the desired results) would probably be considered positive performance, but requesting travel and entertainment funds in excess of budget appropriations might be considered irresponsible.

In developing discretionary cost budgets, top management often relies on the advice of specialists or project managers. Information from such specialists is an important input to the process because these people have more detailed knowledge of the specific discretionary cost area, the legitimate reasons for funding, and the potential benefits (at least qualitatively) to be derived from the expenditures. Top management should be aware, though, that specialists sometimes provide biased advice. To dissuade specialists from seeking excessive appropriations, a corporate officer with adequate technical knowledge of the service functions may be added to the administrative team. This officer would have the responsibility of working with the specialists in the planning and control of discretionary cost budgets.

Although management typically tends to be more generous in setting discretionary funding levels in strong economic climates and cutting back in weaker times, discretionary costs should be controlled at *all* times. Trying to control costs when the company faces an economic crisis is too late. This point is well illustrated by the fact that, in July 1991, Midway Airlines decided to stop painting its planes, which it estimated would save approximately $1.4 million per year.[10] The company had, though, been operating under Chapter 11 bankruptcy since March; the paint savings were never realized because the company went out of business in November 1991.

Based on the total amount budgeted for discretionary costs, management should fund activities in a manner commensurate with the level of operations projected for the period. However, if revenues, profits, or cash flows are reduced, funding amounts for discretionary expenditures should be evaluated not simply in reference to reduced operations, but relative to activity priorities. It may be possible to eliminate the funding for one or more discretionary activities altogether while maintaining other funding levels at the previously determined amounts. For instance, if a company experiences a downturn in demand for its product, the discretionary cost budget for advertising is often reduced—a potentially illogical reaction. Instead, it might be more appropriate to increase the advertising budget and reduce the corporate executives' travel budget.

Discretionary cost activities involve services that vary significantly in type and magnitude from day to day. The output quality of discretionary cost activities may also vary according to the tasks and skill levels of the persons performing the activities. Because of these two factors (varying service levels and quality), discretionary costs are generally not susceptible to the precise planning and control measurements that are available for variable production costs or to the cost-benefit evaluation techniques available for committed fixed costs.

Part of the difference in management attitude between committed and discretionary costs has to do with the ability to measure the benefits provided by those costs. Whereas benefits of committed fixed costs can be measured on a before and after basis (through the capital budgeting and postinvestment audit processes), the benefits from discretionary fixed costs are often not distinctly measurable in terms of money.

BENEFITS FROM DISCRETIONARY COST INCURRENCE

Because benefits from some activities traditionally classified as discretionary cannot be adequately measured, companies often assume that the benefits—and, thus, the activities—are unimportant. Many of the activities previously described as discretionary (repairs, maintenance, R&D, and employee training) are critical to a company's position in a world-class environment. These types of activities, in the long run, produce quality products and services; therefore, before reducing or eliminating expenditures in these areas, managers should attempt to more appropriately recognize and measure the benefits of activities through the use of surrogate, nonmonetary measures.

Although the benefits from discretionary cost expenditures are often not determinable in monetary amounts, the expenditures themselves can be significant. For example, in 1992, Merck & Co. increased the company's research and development budget 16 percent to $1.1 billion.[11] And, "Andersen Consulting spends more than $10 million per year on advertising, more than twice the annual spending of its five

[10] Brett Pulley, "Midway Airlines Will Discontinue Painting Aircraft," *Wall Street Journal* (July 12, 1991), p. A7.

[11] Elyse Tanouye, "Merck to Increase R&D Budget 16% to $1.1 Billion," *Wall Street Journal* (March 17, 1992), p. B12.

Discretionary Cost Activity	Surrogate Measure of Results
Preventive maintenance	• Reduction in number of equipment failures • Reduction in unplanned downtime • Reduction in frequency of production interruptions caused by preventable maintenance activities
Advertising	• Increase in unit sales in the two weeks after an advertising effort relative to the sales two weeks prior to the effort • Number of customers referring to the ad • Number of coupons clipped from the ad and redeemed
University admissions recruiting trip	• Number of students met who requested an application • Number of students from area visited who requested to have ACT/SAT scores sent to the university • Number of admissions that year from that area
Prevention and appraisal quality activities	• Reduction in number of customer complaints • Reduction in number of warranty claims • Reduction in number of product defects discovered by customers
Staffing law school indigent clinic	• Number of clients served • Number of cases effectively resolved • Number of cases won
Executive retreat	• Proportion of participants still there at end of retreat • Number of useful suggestions made • Values tabulated from an exit survey

▌ EXHIBIT 17–4

Nonmonetary Measures of Output from Discretionary Costs

major rivals combined."[12] Expenditures of this magnitude require that organizational management *believe* that some benefits are expected, even though measuring such benefits is difficult. Because of this difficulty, discretionary cost activities are often some of the first costs to be cut when profits are lagging—whether or not such a response is justifiable.

In making decisions to reduce or eliminate discretionary costs, the value of their outputs should be estimated using the nonmonetary, surrogate measures mentioned above. Devising such measures often requires substantial time and creativity. Exhibit 17–4 presents some useful surrogate measures for determining the effectiveness of various types of discretionary costs. Some of these measures are verifiable and can be gathered quickly and easily; others are abstract and require a longer time horizon before they can be obtained. The News Note about Motorola indicates why the measure of a discretionary cost must often be stated as a nonmonetary, rather than a monetary, one.

After the budget is established, some managers may view discretionary costs as being committed for that budget period. A manager who states that a particular ac-

---

[12]John Pickering and Rick Telberg, "The Efficiency Effect," *Accounting Today* (November 11, 1991), p. S16.

NEWS NOTE

The Amount of Money Spent Is Not the Proper Measure at Motorola

The first step to increasing white-collar productivity may be figuring out how to measure it. Motorola used to chart the productivity of its communications-sector employee recruiting department by the amount of money the recruiters spent to sign up each new hire. The goal was to spend less per hire each year. Yes, productivity went up steadily, but without regard to the quality of the people who were joining the company. Notes Bill Smith, a Motorola quality manager and VP: "If you hired an idiot for 39 cents you would meet your goal."

Motorola has completely revamped the way it calculates the effectiveness of its employees. In the office, as in the factory, the company emphasizes quality. The recruiting department is now measured by how well its recruits subsequently do at Motorola. Did they turn out to be well qualified for the job or did they need a lot of remedial training? Were they hired at the right salary or did they leave six months later for a higher-paying job at another company? Judged by such standards, the department decided to increase its spending per new hire.

SOURCE: Ronald Henkoff, "Make Your Office More Productive," *FORTUNE* (February 25, 1991), p. 76. © 1991 Time Inc. All rights reserved.

tivity's cost will not be reduced during a period has chosen to view the cost of that activity as a committed fixed cost. Such a viewpoint, however, does not change the underlying discretionary nature of the item. In such circumstances, top management must have a high degree of faith in the ability of lower-level management to perform the specified tasks in an efficient and effective manner.

MEASURING EFFICIENCY AND EFFECTIVENESS OF DISCRETIONARY COSTS

The amounts spent on discretionary activities reflect resources that are consumed by an activity that should provide some desired monetary or surrogate output. Comparing input costs and output results can help to determine if there is a reasonable cost-benefit relationship between the two. Managers can judge this cost-benefit relationship by how efficiently inputs (represented by costs) were used and how effectively those resources (again represented by costs) achieved their purposes. These relationships can be seen in the following model:

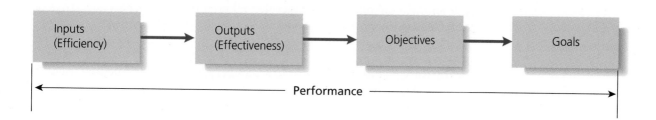

Efficiency

Measuring the degree to which a satisfactory relationship occurs when comparing outputs to inputs reflects the **efficiency** of the activity. Thus, efficiency is a yield concept and is usually measured by a ratio of output to input. For instance, one measure of airplane efficiency is miles flown per gallon of fuel consumed. The higher the number of miles per gallon, the greater the efficiency; fuel efficiency on short-haul flights was one reason the Boeing 737 was specifically chosen by Southwest Airlines.

Effectiveness

Comparing actual output results to desired results indicates the **effectiveness** of an activity or how well the objectives of the activity were achieved. When a valid output measure is available, efficiency and effectiveness can be determined as follows:

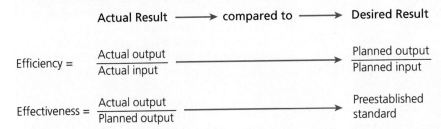

Actual Result ⟶ compared to ⟶ Desired Result

$$\text{Efficiency} = \frac{\text{Actual output}}{\text{Actual input}} \longrightarrow \frac{\text{Planned output}}{\text{Planned input}}$$

$$\text{Effectiveness} = \frac{\text{Actual output}}{\text{Planned output}} \longrightarrow \text{Preestablished standard}$$

A reasonable measure of efficiency can exist only when inputs and outputs can be matched in the same period and when there is a credible causal relationship between them. These two requirements make measuring the efficiency of discretionary costs very difficult. First, several years may pass before output occurs from some discretionary cost expenditures. Consider, for example, the length of time between making expenditures for research and development or a drug rehabilitation program and the time at which results of these types of expenditures are visible. Second, there is frequently a dubious cause-effect relationship between discretionary cost inputs and resulting outputs. For instance, assume that you clip out and use a cents-off coupon for Crest toothpaste from the Sunday paper. Can Procter & Gamble be certain that it was the advertising coupon that caused you to buy the product, or might you have purchased the toothpaste anyway?

Effectiveness, on the other hand, is determined for a particular period by comparing the results achieved with the results desired. Determination of an activity's effectiveness is unaffected by whether the designated output measure is stated in monetary or nonmonetary terms. But management can only subjectively attribute some or all of the effectiveness of the cost incurrence to the results. Subjectivity is required because the comparison of actual output to planned output is not indicative of a perfect causal relationship between activities and output results. *Measurement of effectiveness does not require the consideration of inputs, but measurement of efficiency does.*

Assume that last month Rural Airline Company increased its expenditures on customer service and, during that period, customer complaints dropped by 12 percent. The planned decrease in complaints was 15 percent. Although management was 80 percent effective (.12 ÷ .15) in achieving its goal of decreased customer dissatisfaction, that result was not necessarily related to the customer service program expenditures. It is possible that the decline in customer complaints was caused partially or entirely by other factors, such as use of better equipment, improved communication of flight information, or better weather that allowed flights to depart and arrive on schedule. Management, therefore, does not know for certain whether the customer service program was the most cost-efficient way in which to decrease customer complaints.

The efficiency relationship between discretionary costs and their desired results is inconclusive at best, and the effectiveness of such costs can only be inferred from the relationship of actual to desired output. Since many discretionary costs result in benefits that must be measured on a nondefinitive and nonmonetary basis, it is difficult to exercise control of these costs during activities or after they have begun. Therefore, planning for discretionary costs may be more important than subsequent control measures. Control after the planning stage is often relegated to monitoring discretionary expeditures to ensure conformity with budget classifications and preventing managers from overspending their budgeted amounts.

Managers should be aware that there are alternatives to the concept of "fixed" cost incurrences for certain types of discretionary cost activities. Some discretionary cost activities occur in a particular pattern and are repetitive enough to allow the development of standards. Such activities result in **engineered costs,** which are those that have been found to bear an observable and known relationship to a quantifiable activity base. An engineered cost can essentially be treated as a variable (rather than a fixed) cost.

CONTROLLING DISCRETIONARY COSTS

Engineered cost

Control Using Engineered Costs

Discretionary cost activities fitting into the engineered cost category are usually geared to a performance measure relative to work accomplished. For instance, the cost of an airline company-initiated preflight maintenance inspection (PMI) program in excess of government requirements may be considered an engineered cost. Taken as a whole, these preflight inspections are enough alike to develop a standard time for an average inspection. If an airline has access to preflight maintenance inspectors who can be paid on an hourly basis for only the hours they work, the company can determine how many inspectors to hire and can compare actual costs to a standard cost each month. The activity base of this engineered cost is the number of inspections. Budget appropriations for engineered costs are based on the static master budget level, but control can be exerted through the use of flexible budgets if the expected level of activity is not achieved.

Fly-High Airline is used to demonstrate how these PMI costs can be evaluated under both possible cost categories. Fly-High has found that its preflight program can be treated as an engineered cost. Company management, in a cost reduction effort, is willing to contract with part-time, highly qualified inspectors during peak-load times and retain only a minimal number of inspectors in the company's full-time labor force. The company and the inspectors are aware and agree that safety and the quality of inspections are never to be compromised. The company's cost accountant, through statistical analysis of past inspections, has found that inspections on all flights average slightly less than twenty minutes. Thus, each inspector should be able to perform approximately three inspections per hour. From this information, Fly-High's managers can obtain a fairly valid estimate of inspection costs for a particular activity level and, therefore, have a basis against which to compare actual costs.

In May, Fly-High predicts that 2,400 flights will be made; thus, 800 (2,400 ÷ 3 inspections per hour) inspection hours should be provided. If the standard hourly rate for inspectors is $15, the May budget would be $12,000. In May, 2,364 inspections are made at a cost of $11,533.59 for 783 actual hours. Using the generalized cost analysis model for variance analysis presented in Chapter 11, the following calculations can be made:

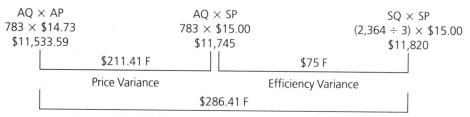

Total Maintenance Inspection Cost Variance

The price variance shows that Fly-High was able to negotiate a $.27 ($15.00 − $14.73) per hour more favorable average rate during May with its inspectors. The efficiency variance results from using five fewer hours than standard (788 − 783).

However, recall that the standard requires only three inspections per hour even though the average inspection is expected to take "slightly less" than 20 minutes. Thus, a favorable variance is not surprising. A "generous" standard was set by Fly-High to reinforce the importance of making high-quality inspections regardless of the time taken.

The preceding analysis is predicated on the company being willing and able to hire the exact number of inspection hours needed. If Fly-High Airline has to employ only full-time employees on a salary basis, analyzing inspection costs in the above manner is not very useful. In this instance, preventive maintenance inspections become a discretionary fixed cost and Fly-High may prefer the following type of fixed overhead variance analysis:

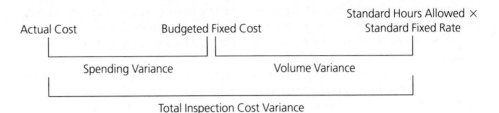

In this analysis, an assumption must be made about expected capacity to determine the application rate. Assume again that (1) $15 is the standard hourly rate, (2) three inspections per hour is the standard quantity of work for high-quality inspections, and (3) 2,364 inspections were made. The actual fixed payroll is $12,000 per month. The following variances can be computed:

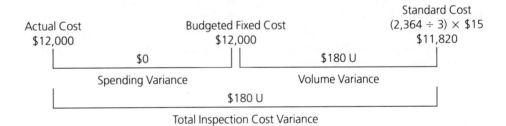

The method of variance analysis and thus cost control must be appropriate to the cost category and management information needs. But regardless of the variance levels or the explanations provided, managers should always consider whether the incurrence of the cost was sufficiently justified. For example, assume that $76,000 is spent on the salary of an additional systems analyst in the Systems Department. During the year, systems activities take place, but there is no measurable output such as systems modifications or a new system. Before determining that the discretionary cost expenditure was justified, top management should review the systems manager's activity reports for the analysts in the department. The discretionary expenditure would not be considered effective if the new analyst spent a significant portion of the period doing menial tasks. In other words, postincurrence audits of discretionary costs are important in determining the value of the expenditure.

Control Using the Budget

Once discretionary cost budget appropriations have been made, monetary control is effected through the use of budget-to-actual comparisons as is true with other costs in the budget. Actual results are compared to expected results and explanations should be provided for variances. Explanations for variances can often be found by recognizing cost consciousness attitudes. The following illustration involving two dis-

Revenues:		
Handling fees (250,000 × $1)		$250,000
Expenses:		
Employee training	$10,000	
Maintenance	25,000	
Utilities	1,310	
Wages and fringe benefits	78,000	
Salaries and fringe benefits	48,000	
Depreciation	30,000	192,310
Operating Income before Taxes		$ 57,690

EXHIBIT 17–5
Airline Bag Handlers Inc. Budget—First Quarter 1994

cretionary cost activities provides a budget-to-actual comparison that demonstrates employee cost consciousness.

Airline Bag Handlers Inc. (ABH) performs contract baggage handling for Fly-High and other small airlines. The company is located in a small building on the airport grounds and provides its own operating equipment. ABH has prepared the condensed budget shown in Exhibit 17–5 for the first quarter of 1994. Ms. Carolyn Williams, the controller for ABH, estimates 250,000 bags will be handled during that period.

ABH's management has chosen to fund employee training because of a belief that the training results in higher quality service which will benefit the company and its clients. Maintenance is also considered a discretionary cost; it is budgeted at $.10 per bag handled. Utility cost is variable and is budgeted at $1.20 for each hour that the firm operates. ABH operates twelve hours per day, seven days per week and there are thirteen weeks in the budget quarter. Wages are for the workers and security personnel, who are paid on an hourly basis. Salaries and fringe benefits are for management level personnel and, like depreciation, are fixed amounts.

Ms. Williams collected the revenue and expense data shown in Exhibit 17–6 during the first quarter of 1994. Because of the late arrival of some flights, ABH was asked to and did stay open two extra hours on ten different nights. Additional contracts were responsible for the majority of the increase in additional bags handled.

After reviewing the actual results, ABH's board of directors requested a budget-to-actual comparison from Ms. Williams and explanations for the cost variances. Because every cost was higher than budgeted, the board was of the opinion that costs had not been properly controlled. Ms. Williams' prepared the comparison presented in Exhibit 17–7 on page 728 and provided the following explanations for the variances. Each explanation is preceded by the related budget item number.

Revenues:		
Handling fees (286,000 × $1)		$286,000
Expenses:		
Employee training	$11,440	
Maintenance	28,100	
Utilities	1,668	
Wages and fringe benefits	89,782	
Salaries and fringe benefits	49,200	
Depreciation	32,000	212,190
Operating Income before Taxes		$ 73,810

EXHIBIT 17–6
Airline Bag Handlers Inc. Actual Results—First Quarter 1994

Program budgeting

nually). Thus, it is often extremely difficult to relate outputs to inputs. **Program budgeting** is an approach that relates resource inputs to service outputs.[14]

Program budgeting generally starts by defining objectives in terms of output results rather than in terms of quantity of input activities. For instance, an input measure of an executive development program would be the number of courses each person must complete by year-end. An output measure would state the objective in terms of expected improvement rates on executive annual performance evaluations. Once output results have been defined in some measurable terms, effectiveness can be measured.

The process of program budgeting requires a thorough analysis of the alternative activities that may achieve an organization's objectives. Such an analysis includes projecting both quantitative and qualitative costs and benefits for each alternative. Then, those alternatives are selected that, in the judgment of top management, yield a satisfactory result at a reasonable cost. These choices are translated into budget appropriations to be acted on by the manager(s) responsible for the related programs.

Program budgeting requires the use of detailed surrogate measures of output and necessitates answers to the following questions.

1. When should results be measured? Since many not-for-profit programs are effective only after some period of time, multiple measurements are necessary to determine effectiveness. When should these measures begin to be made and how often should they be made thereafter?

2. What results should be chosen as output measures? Many not-for-profit programs have multiple results. For example, the institution of reading programs for illiterate adults can reduce unemployment rates, overall crime statistics, welfare dollars provided, and so forth. Should a determination be made of which results are more important than others or should all results be given equal weight?

3. What program actually caused the result? There are questions about the legitimacy of cause-and-effect relationships when measuring the results of not-for-profit programs. For example, did an adult literacy program reduce the unemployment statistics or was that reduction more appropriately deemed a result of money spent for job placement programs?

4. Did the program actually affect the target population? An adult literacy program may be aimed at the unemployed. If the majority of persons who attended the program already had jobs, the program had no impact on the target group. However, the program could still be considered effective if the participants increased their job skills and employment levels.

Program budgeting is useful in government and not-for-profit organizations as well as for service activities in for-profit businesses. This process can help managers evaluate and control discretionary costs, avoid excessive cost expenditures, and make certain that expenditures are used for programs and activities that generate the most beneficial results.

Zero-Base Budgeting

Traditional budgeting is often limited in its usefulness as a cost control tool because poor budgeting techniques are used. For instance, many managers prepare budgets by beginning with the prior year's funding levels and treat these appropriations as

---

[14] Program and performance budgeting have often been used as interchangeable terms. The Municipal Finance Officers Association has suggested that the term *program budgeting* be used when dealing with one function regardless of the number of organizational units involved and *performance budgeting* be used when dealing with the inputs and outputs of a single organizational unit.

NEWS NOTE

Sounds Good, but Does It Work?

Zero-base budgeting (ZBB) is an excellent example of how a new practice can get adopted despite very little evidence as to its soundness, and how it fades away when companies generally find that it is not worthwhile.

In 1971, Governor Jimmy Carter [installed] ZBB in the State of Georgia. Not many people knew that shortly after the installation, "zero" became 80 percent of last year's expenditures; that the packages were in fact "increments" above the 80 percent, despite the criticism of incremental budgeting; that theoretically the governor should review 11,000 packages in order to arrive at a budget; and that there was very little agreement on how to arrive at priorities.

In 1973, when Governor Carter became President Carter, he ordered all government agencies to adopt ZBB. The idea was picked up by several companies and many government agencies. Before too long, it became apparent that the amount of paperwork required by ZBB was far more than could be handled in the time available during the budget preparation process. (One federal official estimated that the cost of the paper alone exceeded any conceivable savings that could be identified with ZBB.) ZBB as such thereupon faded away in practice.

SOURCE: Robert N. Anthony, *The Management Control Function* (Boston: Harvard Business School Press, 1988), pp. 184–185.

given and essential to operations. Decisions are then made about whether and by what percentage to incrementally raise existing appropriations. Such an approach has often resulted in what is known as the "creeping commitment syndrome" in which activities are funded without systematic annual regard for priorities or alternative means for accomplishing objectives.

Zero-base budgeting (ZBB) is a comprehensive budgeting process that systematically considers the priorities and alternatives for current and proposed activities in relation to organizational objectives. Annual justification of programs and activities is required to have managers rethink priorities within the context of agreed-upon objectives. ZBB does not necessarily mean that each operation is specified from a zero-cost base, since this would be unrealistic and extreme. However, ZBB requires that managers reevaluate all activities at the start of the budgeting process to make decisions about which activities should be continued, eliminated, or funded at a lower level. Some basic differences between traditional budgeting and zero-base budgeting are shown in Exhibit 17–8.

As indicated in the News Note "Sounds Good, but Does It Work?" ZBB is difficult to implement because of the significant effort needed to investigate the causes of prior

Zero-base budgeting

TRADITIONAL BUDGETING	ZERO-BASE BUDGETING
Starts with last year's funding appropriation	Starts with a minimal (or zero) figure for funding
Focuses on money	Focuses on goals and objectives
Does not systematically consider alternatives to current operations	Directly examines alternative approaches to achieve similar results
Produces a single level of appropriation for an activity	Produces alternative levels of funding based on fund availability and desired results

EXHIBIT 17–8

Differences Between Traditional Budgeting and Zero-Base Budgeting

costs and justify the purposes of budgeted costs. To be workable, it also requires a wholehearted commitment by the organization's personnel. Without the time, effort, and commitment, ZBB should not be attempted. With these ingredients, an organization can be more effective in planning and controlling costs.

KEY TERMS

Appropriation (p. 719)
Committed fixed cost (p. 710)
Cost avoidance (p. 714)
Cost consciousness (p. 710)
Cost containment (p. 712)
Cost control system (p. 709)
Cost reduction (p. 714)

Discretionary cost (p. 709)
Effectiveness (p. 724)
Efficiency (p. 723)
Engineered cost (p. 725)
Program budgeting (p. 732)
Strategic staffing (p. 716)
Zero-base budgeting (p. 733)

SOLUTION STRATEGIES

Determination of efficiency: Relationship of inputs to outputs

$$\text{Actual yield ratio} = \text{Actual output} \div \text{Actual input}$$
$$\text{Desired yield ratio} = \text{Planned output} \div \text{Planned input}$$

Determination of effectiveness: Actual output vs. desired output

Efficiency + Effectiveness = Performance

Cost variances: Actual costs compared to budgeted costs—allows management to compare absolute cost discrepancies from the original plan

Actual costs compared to budgeted costs at actual activity level—allows management to make determinations on the degree to which costs were controlled; makes use of a flexible budget

Variance analysis using standards for discretionary costs: Standards that allow for the computation of variances may be developed for routine, structured discretionary costs.

For discretionary costs that are susceptible to engineered cost treatment:

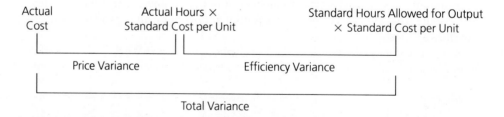

For discretionary costs that are managed as lump-sum fixed costs:

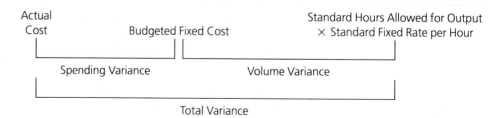

Carroll Manufacturing has just purchased a plastic extruding machine and ran the machine 35 hours during the first week. Management wants to know the efficiency and effectiveness of the machine. The production supervisor has provided you with the following statistics:

DEMONSTRATION PROBLEM

Planned output	50 pounds per hour
Power usage planned	100 kwh per running hour
Actual output	1,800 pounds
Actual power used	3,400 kwh

Required:

a. Calculate the planned output for 35 operating hours.

b. Calculate the degree of effectiveness of the machine in its first week.

c. Calculate planned efficiency for the machine.

d. Calculate the actual efficiency of the machine in its first week.

e. Comment on the machine's performance.

Solution to Demonstration Problem

a. Planned output: 35 hours X 50 lbs. = 1,750 lbs. of output

b. Degree of effectiveness: Actual output ÷ Planned output = 1,800 lbs. ÷ 1,750 lbs. = 103 percent

c. Planned efficiency: Planned input ÷ Planned output = 100 kwh ÷ 50 lbs. = 2 kwh per lb.

d. Actual efficiency: Actual input ÷ Actual output = 3,400 kwh ÷ 1,800 lbs. = 1.89 kwh per lb.

e. The performance of the machine is better than expected. The machine exceeded both effectiveness and efficiency expectations.

QUESTIONS

1. When is cost control for any specific organizational activity exercised?

2. What does cost consciousness entail?

3. What factors can cause costs to change? Which of these are subject to cost containment?

4. How are cost avoidance and cost reduction related? How do they differ?

5. Why are temporaries often currently employed in what used to be full-time labor positions?

6. Explain the difference between discretionary and committed costs. Could a cost be considered discretionary by one firm and committed by another? If so, discuss and give an example. If not, discuss why not.

7. How are committed costs controlled?

8. Why is it difficult to measure the output of activities funded by discretionary costs?

9. What issues does management need to consider when setting the budget appropriations for discretionary costs?

10. What are surrogate measures of output and how are they used in conjunction with discretionary costs?

11. What is efficiency? Explain why it is often difficult to measure the efficiency of discretionary costs.

12. What is effectiveness? Explain how effectiveness of discretionary cost activities can be measured.

13. Why does performance encompass the spectrum from organizational goals to inputs to outputs?

14. Discuss the differences between an engineered cost and a discretionary cost. Discuss any similarities between these two types of costs.

15. How can budget appropriations be used for controlling discretionary costs?

16. How are budgets used in controlling discretionary costs?

17. How does cost consciousness relate to variance analysis?

18. What approach would you take to investigate the control of engineered costs?

19. *(Appendix)* How is a "programmed budget" an improvement over a traditional budget?

20. *(Appendix)* What problems are encountered in using program budgeting?

21. *(Appendix)* How does zero-base budgeting differ from traditional budgeting?

22. *(Appendix)* How does zero-base budgeting assist in planning and controlling discretionary costs?

EXERCISES

23. *(Cost control activities)* An accounting firm hires some part-time clerical staff to work on specific audits. Some of the staff are employed for up to a year. The firm pays the employees $20 per hour. No fringe benefits are given during the year; however, at year-end, if the part-time employee has worked more than 1,600 hours for the firm, a bonus of $2,000 is paid to the employee.

    Assume that full-time clerical staff can be hired for $27,500 per year. Fringe benefit costs to the firm for each full-time employee amount to 20 percent of base salary.

    a. Does the firm's policy of hiring part-time clerical staff represent an example of cost containment, cost avoidance, or cost reduction? Explain.

    b. For a given clerical position, at what level of annual hours worked should the firm consider hiring full-time clerical staff rather than part-time?

24. *(Cost control activities)* Ms. Johnson has just been appointed as the new director of Youth Hot-Line, a not-for-profit organization that operates a phone bank for individuals experiencing emotional difficulties. The phones are staffed by qualified social workers and psychologists who are paid on an hourly basis. Ms. Johnson took the following actions in the first week at Youth Hot-Line. Indicate whether the actions represent cost understanding, cost containment, cost avoidance, or cost reduction. Some actions may have more than one implication; if they do, indicate the reason.

    a. Increased the budget appropriation for advertising of the Hot Line.

    b. Exchanged the more expensive pushbutton, cream-colored designer telephones for regular, pushbutton desk telephones.

    c. Eliminated the call-forwarding feature installed on all telephones since Youth Hot-Line will now be staffed 24 hours a day.

    d. Eliminated two paid clerical positions and replaced these individuals with volunteers.

    e. Ordered blank notepads for the counselors to keep by their phones; the old notepads (stock now depleted) had the Youth Hot-Line logo and address printed on them.

f. Negotiated a new contract with the telephone company; Youth Hot-Line will now pay a flat rate of $100 per month, regardless of the number of telephones installed by the Hot-Line. The previous contract charged the organization $10 for every telephone. At the time that contract was signed, Youth Hot-Line only had 10 telephones. With the increased staff, Ms. Johnson plans to install at least 5 additional telephones.

25. (*Committed versus discretionary costs*) Following is a list of committed and discretionary costs:

Advertising
Preventive maintenance
Executive training
Insurance—building
Depreciation—equipment
Quality control
Research and development
Secretarial pool
Marketing research
Property taxes
Interest expense
Salaries for EDP data conversion

a. Classify each of the above costs as *normally* being either committed (C) or discretionary (D).
b. Which of the above costs may be either committed or discretionary based on management philosophy?
c. For the expenses marked discretionary in part a, provide a monetary or non-monetary surrogate output measure. For each output measure, briefly discuss any objections that may be raised to it.

26. (*Committed versus discretionary costs*) Choose letter C (for committed cost) or D (for discretionary cost) to indicate which type of cost each of the sentences below best relates. Explain the rationale for your choice.

a. Control is first provided during the capital budgeting process.
b. Examples include advertising, research and development, and employee training.
c. This type of cost cannot be reduced even during temporary slowdowns in activity.
d. There is usually no "correct" amount at which to set funding levels.
e. Examples include depreciation, lease rentals, and property taxes.
f. This type of cost often provides benefits that are not monetarily measurable.
g. Temporary reductions can usually be made without impairing the firm's long-range capacity or profitability.
h. This cost is primarily affected by long-run decisions regarding desired capacity levels.
i. It is often difficult to ascribe outcomes as being closely correlated with this type of cost.
j. This cost usually relates to service-type activities.

27. (*Effectiveness measures*) The Accounting Department at State University has used funds during 1994 for the following purposes. Provide nonmonetary, surrogate measures that would help evaluate the effectiveness of the monies spent.

a. Hired an additional departmental secretary.
b. Sent various faculty members to seminars at which topical research areas in accounting were discussed.
c. Held continuing education programs for faculty.
d. Purchased a library of materials for teaching professional ethics.
e. Hired 3 additional graduate assistants to support the department's teaching missions.

28. *(Effectiveness and efficiency measures)* Big State University has formed a new out-of-state recruiting department. The mission of this newly formed department is to recruit top nonresident students. The department has been funded for 1994 at a level of $300,000. In justifying the budget, university administration set a goal for the department of recruiting 300 new nonresident students. By the end of 1994, the department had been credited with recruiting 325 new students. The department actually consumed $400,000 in its recruiting efforts.
a. How effective was the newly formed department? Show calculations.
b. How efficient was the department? Show calculations.

29. *(Effectiveness measures)* Each of the following discretionary activities is found in a high-tech manufacturing firm. The firm is wrestling with ideas as to how to evaluate the return on the costs incurred for each of the activities. For each of the five activities, briefly describe how the firm might evaluate the effectiveness of the expenditure.

1. research and development expenses
2. managerial training programs
3. advertising
4. factory safety education programs
5. corporate legal department

30. *(Variance analysis)* The manager of a lumber mill has been asked to explain to the company president why sales of scrap firewood were above budget by $1,400. He requests your help. Upon examination of budget documents, you discover that budgeted revenue from firewood was $25,000 based on expected sales of 1,250 cords of wood at $20 per cord. Further investigation reveals that 1,200 cords were actually sold at an average price of $22. Prepare an analysis of firewood sales and explain what happened.

31. *(Variance analysis)* Monique Lapeu markets French lessons on audiotapes. Each package of 15 audiotapes normally sells for $75. Ms. Lapeu sold 500 tape packages to schools, libraries, and specialty stores in 1993. She budgeted for a 10 percent increase in sales volume for 1994. At the end of 1994, she is disappointed that her actual revenue is only $35,000. She had sold 500 packages.
a. What was Ms. Lapeu's expected revenue for the current year?
b. Analyze why Ms. Lapeu did not achieve the expected revenue.

32. *(Variance analysis)* Heavy Metal Manufacturing is instituting a new quality control program. Management has estimated that each quality control inspector should be able to make an average of 12 inspections per hour. Retired factory supervisors are well suited to be quality control inspectors because they are experts concerning the products being made. Management has decided to staff the quality control program with these retirees and has set $9 as the standard hourly rate. During the first month of the new program, 6,280 inspections were made and the total pay to the inspectors was $4,982 for 515 hours of work.
a. Perform a variance analysis on the labor cost of the quality control program for management.
b. Assume that management could hire 2 full-time inspectors for a monthly salary of $2,500 each and hire part-timers for the overflow. Each full-time inspector would work 200 hours per month. How would total cost of this alternative compare to the cost of a 515-hour month at the standard rate of $9?

33. *(Matching)* Match each term on the left with the appropriate letter of its definition shown on the right.

1. Engineered cost
2. Zero-base budgeting
3. Discretionary cost
4. Committed cost

a. An attitude regarding cost understanding, cost containment, cost avoidance, and cost reduction
b. A cost incurred to provide physical or organizational capacity

5. Appropriation
6. Cost containment
7. Program budgeting
8. Cost consciousness
9. Efficiency

c. A measure of input-output yield
d. Any cost that bears an observable and known relationship to an activity base
e. An approach that relates resource inputs to service outputs
f. A maximum allowable expenditure
g. Reevaluation of activities to decide which should be eliminated or funded at a reduced level
h. A fixed cost incurred to fund an activity for a specified period of time
i. Unit variable costs and total fixed costs are not allowed to increase from prior periods

---

34. In the past few years, Able and Associates, an engineering firm, has been experiencing tremendous growth in its legal costs. Historically, independent law firms have performed all legal work for the firm. At present, the company is considering creating its own in-house legal department in an effort to gain better control of these costs. Discuss how each of the following might affect the decision to opt for in-house versus independent legal counsel.

1. efficiency of the legal activities
2. effectiveness of the legal activities
3. future volume of legal activities

35. Cost control in the Personnel Office of Big City Transit is evaluated based on engineered cost concepts. The office incurs both variable and fixed costs. The variable costs are largely driven by the amount of employee turnover in Big City Transit. For 1994, budgeted costs in the Personnel Office were:

| Fixed | $200,000 | |
| Variable | 400,000 | (based on projected turnover of 1,000 employees) |

For 1994, actual costs in the Personnel Office were:

| Fixed | $210,000 | |
| Variable | 450,000 | (actual turnover of 1,050 employees) |

Using traditional variance analysis, evaluate the control of fixed and variable costs in the Personnel Office of Big City Transit. Does this method of evaluation encourage the Personnel Office managers to hire low quality workers? Explain.

36. *The cost of "people" constitutes 75 percent to 80 percent of the total costs of operating a public accounting firm. In periods of economic contractions (such as the late 1980s and early 1990s), accounting firms have to look to cut labor costs to keep costs in line with decreasing revenues. Many firms have resorted to the restricted use of part-time employees who can be laid off during the slack periods in the year. Part-timers include college interns, and parents with young children who only want to work during the busy season. Firms have also resorted to the use of paraprofessionals, individuals with two-year degrees in business.*

[SOURCE: Don Istvan, "Cost Cutting: A Survival Plan," *Accounting Today* (November 11, 1991), p. 26.]

a. Discuss the use of part-timers and paraprofessionals from the perspective of controlling costs.
b. How could the use of part-timers and paraprofessionals impair the quality of work performed by public accounting firms?

COMMUNICATION ACTIVITIES

a. How does the depiction of cost control in the figure relate to the concept of activity-based management?

b. If the relation between cost and quality is as depicted in the figure, how does the quality level of the production process serve as a constraint on organizational profitability?

c. What does the figure suggest about the prospects of competing via a strategy of offering low-cost–low-quality products?

49. *In an effort to control costs, Medica, a Minneapolis health plan provider, has resorted to the use of committees in the drug prescription process. Plan doctors meet periodically and evaluate new drug treatments. By the process of a simple vote, new drugs are either accepted for use by plan doctors or are denied to plan doctors. Such an approach allows the plans to negotiate with the large pharmaceutical companies for quantity discounts and other concessions.*

Elsewhere, plans are enforcing the use of generic drugs over brand name drugs and others have adopted computer-technology to maintain real time controls over prescriptions of individual doctors.

[SOURCE: Ron Winslow, "Buyer's Market: Prescribing Decisions Increasingly Are Made By the Cost-Conscious," *Wall Street Journal* (September 25, 1992) pp. A1, A6. Reprinted by permission of the *Wall Street Journal*, © 1992 Dow Jones & Company, Inc. All rights reserved worldwide.]

a. Discuss the likely effectiveness of the above measures from the perspective of controlling costs.

b. Discuss the effect the above measures are likely to have on the quality of health care provided by the plans.

c. Are cost control efforts such as those discussed above ethical business practices in the medical industry? Discuss.

50. Mar-Pex Division of Sparta Corp. has been experiencing losses for several years. The division managers have determined that they are going to implement the following changes in order to improve the current year's profit picture: (1) cut advertising by 40 percent; (2) cut routine maintenance by 25 percent; (3) not replace any workers who leave through normal attrition; (4) eliminate all overtime; and (5) postpone the purchase of a new computerized packing system. These changes should provide an additional $750,000 in income and produce a bottom-line figure of a positive $300,000. The division will, however, experience some delays in shipping due to the reduction in workers and overtime and the lack of the packing system. Sparta Corp. has a management bonus policy for divisions with net income of greater than $250,000.

a. Are each of the above changes short- or long-term solutions to Mar-Pex's income difficulties?

b. What will be the long-term effects of each of the above changes?

c. What effects, if any, will each of the changes have on Mar-Pex's employees? Customers?

d. What do you think the motivation for the changes is? Discuss the ethical considerations involved.

51. After the oil shortages of the 1970s, Congress passed the 1978 Public Utility Regulatory Policies Act, which forced utilities to buy electricity at reasonable rates from "qualifying facilities" that use alternative energy sources. This act helped to create a new industry whose companies produce power from wind, water, garbage, cow manure, and used tires. For example, a Modesto, California plant will burn 40 million tires from the world's largest tire-disposal dump. In addition, the plant removes metal from steel-belted radials and then, to lower costs, sells the metal as scrap.

a. How can the major power companies use this act to help control costs? Can such purchases be justified by any or all of the cost consciousness ideas? If so, how?

b. If a large power company purchases energy from one of these "qualifying facilities," how or should the rate charged to consumers be affected? Justify your answer.

c. Discuss the business and ethical implications of a large power company being able to purchase a significant amount of megawatts of power from the independents without having to commit any of its own resources to the construction of power plants.

d. Discuss the ethical and environmental implications of utilizing trash as an energy source.

52. *The acquisition of new health-care technology by hospitals and other care providers is frequently based on a financial analysis of costs and benefits. Because the return on technology investments is influenced to a large extent by Medicare reimbursement policies, any change in Medicare reimbursement levels is likely to affect investment policies, and/or patient care policies in the medical industry.*

To illustrate, the typical U.S. dialysis patient receives about 10 hours of dialysis treatment a week. This amount may be contrasted with 12 hours for German patients, 14 hours for Japanese patients, and 18 hours for French patients. According to a recent study, many U.S. patients may be receiving an insufficient amount of time on dialysis machines. The five-year survival rate of U.S. dialysis patients is only 47% compared to an 87% survival rate in France.

Critics of U.S. health care suggest that the shorter treatment periods in the U.S. are due to a 44% drop in the Medicare reimbursement rate (in constant dollars) since 1983. By providing shorter treatment periods, hospitals can push more patients through the dialysis equipment, thereby reducing fixed costs, capital costs, and labor costs per patient.

[SOURCE: Ron Winslow, "Cost Control May Harm Dialysis Patients," *Wall Street Journal* (February 20, 1991), pp. B1, B4. Reprinted by permission of the *Wall Street Journal*, © 1991 Dow Jones & Company, Inc. All rights reserved worldwide.]

a. Discuss the ethical issues involved in medical professionals reducing the length of treatment for dialysis patients in response to a reduction in Medicare reimbursement rates.

b. How would medical professionals potentially respond to a new Medicare policy that required patients to receive, for example, 14 hours of dialysis treatment weekly?

c. Is it likely that Medicare officials could have predicted the response of the medical profession to a cut in Medicare reimbursement rates for dialysis treatment? If so, comment on the ethics of instituting reimbursement cuts.

18

CONTROL OF INVENTORY
AND PRODUCTION

LEARNING
OBJECTIVES

After completing this chapter, you should be able to answer these questions:

1. How are economic order quantity and reorder point determined and used?
2. Why do managers use ABC inventory control systems?
3. How does materials requirements planning differ from the economic order quantity model?
4. How do push and pull systems of production control work?
5. What is the just-in-time philosophy and how does it affect production?
6. How would the traditional cost accounting system change if a JIT inventory system were adopted?
7. *(Appendix)* Why does a company carry safety stock and how is the appropriate amount estimated?

INTRODUCING

ALLEN-BRADLEY CO. INC.

Allen-Bradley, a wholly-owned subsidiary of Rockwell International, is a leading worldwide manufacturer of industrial automation products and control devices that are used by manufacturing and process industries. While A-B has 28 manufacturing plants located around the world, it is the 45,000-square-foot facility at the company's headquarters in Milwaukee, Wisconsin that is quite revolutionary. In this plant, A-B uses computer-integrated manufacturing (CIM) technology to manufacture motor contactors with the highest quality and lowest cost in the world—600 per hour, with more than 1,000 variations, in lot sizes as small as one with only a few attendants overseeing the process.

"[The facility is] a CIM showcase that uses stockless production, advanced machine diagnostics and next-day shipping. It was developed not only to bring us into the factory-of-the-future manufacturing loop, but to prove that quality products can be produced at competitive prices when computers and advanced technologies are made the core of manufacturing," stated Larry Yost, senior vice president, Operations Group.

The next-day shipping feature creates an order-to-shipment capability. As a stockless production operation, the facility also minimizes material handling and warehousing needs. Once an order is placed, A-B's factory-in-a-factory automatically manufactures, tests, packages, and ships the product within 24 hours. When the design of the product and construction of the facility were planned, primary goals focused on lowering production costs by reducing the cost of materials, direct and indirect labor, scrap and rework, Yost explained.

The company's Total Quality Management System is incorporated in the facility's production process, too. With zero defects as a goal, the system depends on statistical quality control methods to maintain tolerance levels. There are more than 3,500 data collection points and 350 assembly test points checking each component and the final product as it progresses from station to station. Any component that doesn't meet predetermined quality parameters is rejected, as is a product if it doesn't meet final inspection standards. If a product is rejected, the system automatically starts to build a new one so the order is complete without delay.

SOURCE: "We're Reshaping the Way We Think and Work," *CIM Computer Integrated Manufacturing at Allen-Bradley* (June 1990), pp. 10, 12.

In recent years, some people have questioned whether some segments of American industry are as productive and efficient as their counterparts in Japan, Germany, or other parts of the world. Like Allen-Bradley, many U.S. companies are concentrating on ways to improve productivity and utilization of available technology. These efforts are often directed toward reducing the cost of producing and carrying inventory.

The amount spent on inventory may be the largest investment, other than plant assets, made by a company. Investment in inventory, though, provides no return until that inventory is sold. This chapter deals with ways for companies to minimize their monetary commitments to inventory. These techniques include economic order quantity (EOQ); materials requirements planning (MRP); the just-in-time (JIT) inventory philosophy and its accounting implications; and flexible manufacturing systems (FMS) and computer-integrated manufacturing (CIM). The appendix to this chapter covers the concepts of order point and safety stock.

BUYING AND CARRYING INVENTORY

In manufacturing organizations, one basic cost is for raw materials. While possibly not the *largest* production cost, raw materials purchases cause a continuous cash outflow each period. Similarly, retailers invest a significant proportion of their assets in merchandise purchased for sale to others. Profit margins in both types of organizations can benefit from reducing or minimizing inventory investment, assuming that demand for products could still be met. The term *inventory* is used in this section to refer to any of the following: raw materials, work in process, finished goods, indirect materials (supplies), or merchandise inventory.

Good inventory management relies largely on cost-minimization strategies. As indicated in Exhibit 18–1, there are three basic costs associated with inventory: (1)

EXHIBIT 18–1

Categories of Inventory Costs

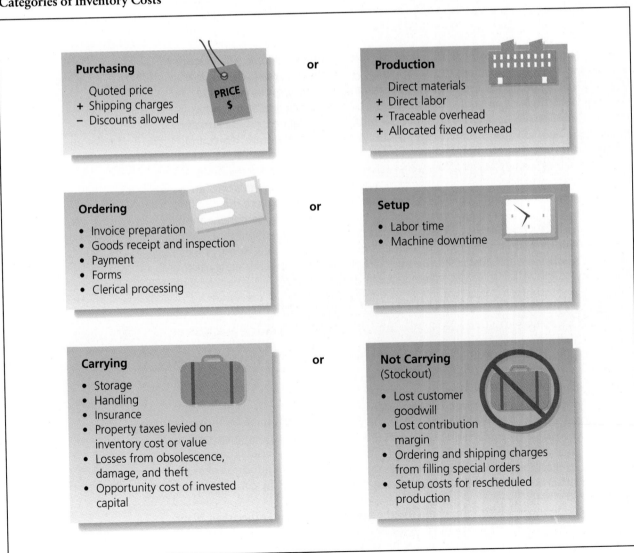

Purchasing
  Quoted price
+ Shipping charges
− Discounts allowed

PRICE $

or

Production
  Direct materials
+ Direct labor
+ Traceable overhead
+ Allocated fixed overhead

Ordering
• Invoice preparation
• Goods receipt and inspection
• Payment
• Forms
• Clerical processing

or

Setup
• Labor time
• Machine downtime

Carrying
• Storage
• Handling
• Insurance
• Property taxes levied on inventory cost or value
• Losses from obsolescence, damage, and theft
• Opportunity cost of invested capital

or

Not Carrying
(Stockout)
• Lost customer goodwill
• Lost contribution margin
• Ordering and shipping charges from filling special orders
• Setup costs for rescheduled production

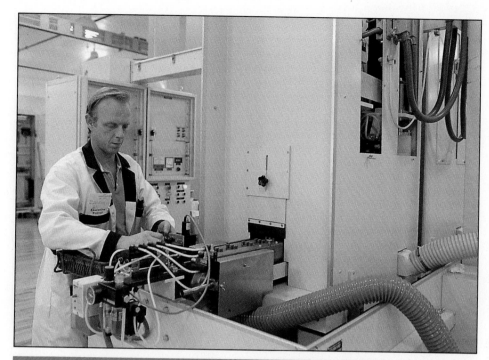

At Allen-Bradley, EMS1 team member Dennis Brost checks operation of a through-hole insertion machine on the production line. For products not requiring this operation, an overhead conveyor routes boards past the machine and on to the next process.

purchasing/production; (2) ordering; and (3) carrying/not carrying goods in stock. The **cost of purchasing** inventory is the quoted purchase price minus any discounts allowed plus shipping charges. For a manufacturer, production cost refers to the costs associated with purchasing direct materials, paying for direct labor, incurring traceable overhead, and absorbing allocated fixed manufacturing overhead. Purchasing/production cost is the amount to be recorded in the appropriate inventory account (Raw Materials Inventory, Work in Process Inventory, Finished Goods Inventory, or Merchandise Inventory).

Cost of purchasing

Unit cost commonly affects the degree of control maintained over an inventory item. As unit cost increases, internal controls (such as inventory access) are typically tightened and a perpetual inventory system is more often used. Recognition of the appropriate cost/benefit relationships may result in an **ABC analysis** of inventory, which separates inventory into three groups based on annual cost-to-volume usage.[1]

ABC analysis

Items having the highest value are referred to as A items; C items represent the lowest dollar volume usage. All other inventory items are designated as B items. Exhibit 18–2 on page 752 provides the results of a typical ABC inventory analysis—20 percent of the inventory items accounts for 80 percent of the cost; an additional 30 percent of the items, taken together with the first 20 percent, accounts for 90 percent of the cost; while the remaining 50 percent of the items accounts for the remaining 10 percent of the cost.

Once inventory is categorized as A, B or C, management can determine the best inventory control method for items in each category. A-type inventory should require a perpetual inventory system and would be likely candidates for just-in-time purchasing techniques that minimize the funds tied up in inventory investment. The highest control procedures would be assigned to these items. Such a treatment reflects the financial accounting concept of materiality.

Items falling into the C category may need only periodic inventory procedures and may use a two-bin or red-line system. Under a **two-bin system**, one container (or stack) of inventory is available for production needs. When production begins to use

Two-bin system

---

[1] ABC inventory analysis should not be confused with activity-based costing (also ABC), which is covered in depth in Chapter 5.

▌EXHIBIT 18–2
ABC Inventory Analysis

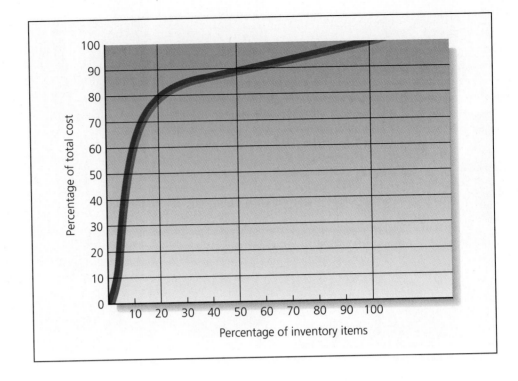

Red-line system

Ordering costs

Setup costs

Carrying costs

materials in the second bin, a purchase order is placed to refill the first bin. In a **red-line system**, a red line is painted on the inventory container at a point deemed to be the point at which to reorder. Both systems require that production needs and estimates of receipt-time from suppliers be fairly accurate. Having the additional container or stack of inventory on hand is considered to be reasonable based on the insignificant dollar amount of investment involved with C category items. The degree of control placed on C items will probably be minimal because of the lack of materiality of the inventory cost.

The type of inventory system (perpetual or periodic) and level of internal controls associated with items in the B category will depend on management's judgment. Such judgment will be based on cruciality of the item to the production process, quickness of response time of suppliers, and estimates of benefits to be gained by increased accounting or access controls. Technology, in the form of computers and bar coding, has made it easier and more cost-beneficial to institute additional controls over inventory.

Incremental, variable costs associated with preparing, receiving, and paying for an order are called **ordering costs** and include the cost of forms and a variety of clerical costs. Ordering costs are traditionally expensed as incurred by retailers and wholesalers, although under an activity-based costing system these costs could be traced to the ordered items as an additional direct cost. Retailers incur ordering costs for all their merchandise inventory. In manufacturing companies, ordering costs are incurred for raw material purchases. If the company intends to produce rather than order a part, direct and indirect **setup costs** (instead of ordering costs) would be created as equipment is readied for each new production run. Setup would necessitate costs for changing dies or drill heads, recalibrating machinery, and resetting tolerance limits for quality control apparatuses.

Inventory **carrying costs** are the variable costs of carrying one inventory unit in stock for one year. Carrying costs are incurred for storage, handling, insurance, property taxes based on inventory cost or value, and possible losses from obsolescence or damage. In addition, carrying cost should include an amount for opportunity cost. When a firm's capital is invested in inventory, that capital is unable to earn interest or dividends from alternative investments. Inventory is one of the many investments

NEWS NOTE

Boeing's Inventory Costs Were Flying High

The most obvious place for managers to find savings in Boeing's commercial aircraft operations [is in] its nearly $8 billion of inventory. Boeing turns over its stock a little more than twice a year, compared with ten times a year or higher for world-class manufacturers in other industries. By streamlining workflows and eliminating excesses, Boeing aims to shrink the time needed to manufacture a plane from more than a year to just six months by 1998. If inventories are cut in half as a result, *FORTUNE*'s estimate based on current production levels, that [change] would translate into an annual saving of $400 million in financing costs and as much as $600 million in storage, handling, and transportation.

The company used to rationalize its bulging warehouses by invoking the incredible complexity of its products; each 747 has more than three million parts, not counting fasteners. What's more, no two orders are exactly alike. Boeing prided itself on being able to satisfy each buyer. Explains Patrick Day, head of the plant that makes ducts for pneumatic, hydraulic, and fuel systems: "In the past, the idea was not to delay a $100 million plane for lack of a $2,000 part. It was just-in-case management instead of just-in-time."

[T]he inventory-cutting campaign, launched in 1990, has [by 1993] pared Boeing's [inventory] by some $700 million, or about 9%.

SOURCE: Shawn Tully, "Can Boeing Reinvent Itself?" *FORTUNE* (March 8, 1993), p. 68. © 1993 Time Inc. All rights reserved.

made by an organization and should be expected to earn the same rate of return as other investments. Carrying costs can be estimated using information from various budgets, special studies, or other analytical techniques and "can easily add 20 percent to 25 percent per year to the initial cost of inventory."[2] The accompanying News Note indicates the materiality of carrying costs for Boeing.

Although carrying inventory *in excess* of need generates costs, a fully depleted inventory can also generate costs. A **stockout** occurs when a company does not have inventory available upon request. The cost of having a stockout is not easily determinable, but some of the costs involved include lost customer goodwill, lost contribution margin from not being able to make a sale, additional ordering and shipping charges incurred from special orders, and possibly lost customers. For a manufacturer, another important stockout cost is incurred for production adjustments arising from not having inventory available. If a necessary raw material is not on hand, the production process must be rescheduled or stopped, which in turn may cause the incurrence of additional setup costs before resuming production.

All inventory-related costs must be evaluated when purchasing or production decisions are made. The costs of ordering and carrying inventory offset each other when estimating the **economic order quantity**.

Stockout

Economic order quantity

Companies making purchasing (rather than production) decisions often compute the economic order quantity (EOQ), which represents the least costly number of units to order. The EOQ indicates the optimal balance between ordering and carrying costs

ECONOMIC ORDER QUANTITY

[2] Bill Moseley, "Boosting Profits and Efficiency: The Opportunities Are There," (*Grant Thornton*) *Tax & Business Adviser* (May/June 1992), p. 6.

by mathematically equating total ordering costs to total carrying costs. Purchasing managers should first determine which supplier can offer the appropriate quality of goods at the best price in the most reliable manner. *After* the supplier is selected, the most economical inventory quantity to order—at a single time—is determined. The EOQ formula is:

$$EOQ = \sqrt{\frac{2QO}{C}}$$

where   EOQ = economic order quantity in units
       Q = estimated annual quantity used in units
            (can be found in the annual purchases budget)
       O = estimated cost of placing one order
       C = estimated cost to carry one unit in stock for one year

Note that unit purchase cost is not included in the EOQ formula. Purchase cost relates to the question of "from whom to buy," which is considered separately from the question of "how many to buy." Inventory unit purchase cost does not affect the other EOQ formula costs except to the extent that opportunity cost is calculated on the basis of investment.

Calculating EOQ Point

Casey-Glover (C-G) Inc. is a manufacturer of a variety of production control devices. Assume that the company purchases plastic housing covers from Calvin Plastics Company. The covers are essential for a motion sensor, one of C-G's products; therefore, it is critical that the housing covers be available at all times. C-G's purchasing manager has found several suppliers who can consistently provide the proper quality of covers at a cost of $.60 each. Exhibit 18–3 provides information for use in calculating economic order quantity and uses a flexible budget to show the total costs of purchasing 600,000 housing covers per year in various order sizes. This exhibit reflects the following traditional formula for determining total inventory costs:

[(Annual Demand × Order Cost) ÷ Order Quantity]
+ (Order Quantity × Carrying Cost) ÷ 2

= Total Inventory Cost

EXHIBIT 18–3

Yearly Costs of Purchasing Housing Covers

Annual quantity needed (Q) = 600,000
Cost of ordering (O)　　　 = $10.00 per order
Cost of carrying (C)　　　 = $.20 per unit

SIZE OF ORDER	4,000	5,000	6,000	7,000	8,000	9,000
Average inventory	2,000	2,500	3,000	3,500	4,000	4,500
Number of orders	150	120	100	85.71	75	66.67
Annual						
Ordering cost	$1,500	$1,200	$1,000	$ 857*	$ 750	$ 667*
Carrying cost	400	500	600	700	800	900
Total cost	$1,900	$1,700	$1,600	$1,557	$1,550	$1,567

*Rounded.

Order costs for C-G include the cost of purchase order forms and apportioned amounts for various clerical, telephone, and receiving department charges. Six cents of the $.20 per unit carrying cost is an opportunity cost, representing a foregone 10 percent rate of return on the $.60 per unit of funds invested in inventory. The remaining $.14 of carrying costs is for previously mentioned items such as storage, handling, and insurance.

Average inventory is one-half of the order size, because the EOQ model assumes that orders will be filled exactly when needed. Such a delivery schedule means that, before the order arrives, the inventory on hand is fully depleted. When the order arrives, inventory level is equal to the order size. Therefore, average inventory is half of any given order size or [(0 + order size) ÷ 2]. The number of times an order must be placed depends on how many units are ordered at a time. The total number of orders equals total annual quantity of units needed divided by the order size.

Exhibit 18–3 indicates that, as order size increases, the number of orders and the total annual ordering cost decline. However, at the same time, total annual cost of carrying inventory increases since more units are being held in inventory at any given point. Alternatively, smaller order sizes reduce carrying costs, but increase annual ordering costs. Total annual costs for Casey-Glover decline through an order size of 7,000 to 8,000 housing covers; then they begin to rise. These relationships are graphed in Exhibit 18–4.

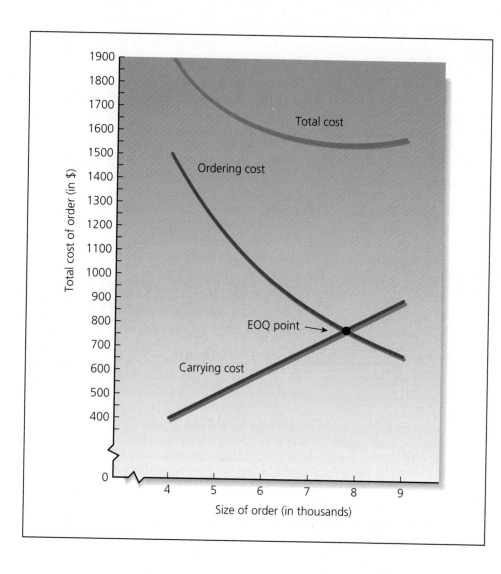

EXHIBIT 18–4
Casey-Glover Inc.—
Graphical Analysis of
Economic Order Quantity

Casey-Glover's most economical order size for housing covers is between 7,000 and 9,000 covers. This quantity range can be determined both from the amounts shown in Exhibit 18–3 and the graph in Exhibit 18–4. The precise economic order quantity of 7,746 units can be found using the EOQ formula:

$$EOQ = \sqrt{\frac{2(600,000)(10)}{.20}}$$

$$= \sqrt{\frac{12,000,000}{.20}}$$

$$= \sqrt{60,000,000}$$

$$= 7,746 \text{ (rounded)}$$

The total annual cost to place and carry orders of 7,746 units is $1,549.20, calculated as follows:

Average inventory (7,746 ÷ 2)	3,873	
Number of orders (600,000 ÷ 7,746)	77.46*	
Cost of ordering (77.46 × $10.00)		$ 774.60
Cost of carrying (3,873 × $.20)		774.60
Total cost (excluding $.60 per unit purchase cost)		$1,549.20

*This numerical result involves a partial (.46) order. In reality, a firm would order either 77 or 78 times. We have used the precise result of 77.46 orders to demonstrate the equality of total ordering costs and total carrying costs at the EOQ.

Note that, as mentioned previously, the total ordering costs and total carrying costs are equal at the EOQ point. While the mathematical proof of this equality is beyond the scope of this text, the equality relationship is nonetheless an important point of this technique.

Managers must remember when they use the EOQ formula that the formula contains *estimated* values. The estimate of ordering cost is often fairly precise, but the estimate of carrying cost is much more subjective. Carrying cost is often estimated as simply the direct financing cost of holding inventory. Such an estimate fails to include indirect costs such as additional space requirements and higher obsolescence. In most instances, though, small errors in estimating costs will not cause a major impact on total cost. Exhibit 18–5 illustrates the effect of a small error on the total assumed ordering and carrying costs of Casey-Glover.

Comparing the total cost ($1,549.20) of ordering the 7,746 unit economic order quantity with the total cost ($1,557 or $1,567, respectively, from Exhibit 18–3) of ordering 7,000 or 9,000 units shows that the total annual cost of ordering quantities immediately around the EOQ point does not vary significantly for Casey-Glover. There is only a $17.80 cost difference between ordering the economic order quantity and ordering 1,254 additional units. Because the cost of ordering quantities close to the EOQ level is not significantly different, management should consider the following questions before placing all orders at the EOQ level:

- Is storage space a limited resource? If so, it would be advantageous to order fewer units each time.
- How critical is the item to production? If it is extremely critical, it is more advantageous to order in larger quantities.
- What would be the effect of a stockout on customer goodwill? If this item is not critical to maintaining customer loyalty and positive image, smaller quantities may be more appropriate.

ORIGINAL ESTIMATES:
Annual quantity needed = 600,000
Cost of ordering = $10.00 per order
Cost of carrying = $.20 per unit
EOQ = 7,746 units

Assume that an error exists in the estimated ordering cost. The actual ordering cost is $11 per order. All other factors are appropriate. The actual cost of purchasing an EOQ of 7,746 units using the correct ordering cost of $11 is determined as follows:

Number of orders (600,000 ÷ 7,746) = 77.46
Average inventory (7,746 ÷ 2) = 3,873

Cost of ordering (77.46 × $11)	$ 852.06
Cost of carrying (3,873 × $.20)	774.60
Total actual cost of purchasing an EOQ of 7,746 units	$1,626.66

To recalculate both EOQ and total costs based on $11, the following results are obtainable:

$$EOQ = \sqrt{\frac{2QO}{C}} = \sqrt{\frac{2(600,000)(11)}{.20}} = 8,124 \text{ (rounded)}$$

Number of orders (600,000 ÷ 8,124) = 73.86
Average inventory (8,124 ÷ 2) = 4,062

Cost of ordering (73.86 × $11)	$ 812.46
Cost of carrying (4,062 × $.20)	812.40
Total cost	$1,624.86

Thus, an error of $1.00 in estimating the cost to place an order results in a total cost difference of only $1.80 ($1,626.66 − $1,624.86) over one year!

EXHIBIT 18-5

Estimation Error in EOQ Formula

- How critical is cash flow? If projected cash availability is limited or if the incremental cost of borrowing or holding cash is high, it is most appropriate to purchase in quantities as close to the EOQ as possible to minimize expenditures.

- Can units be ordered in the quantity indicated? The EOQ formula may indicate purchases in partial units or in unit quantities not provided by the supplier (who may only sell in 100-unit containers, for example). Quantities should be adjusted accordingly to the most economical purchase option.

At different times, answers to these questions may vary and managers may decide to place orders of varying quantities. But, to minimize costs associated with inventory, the actual quantity ordered should be close to the economic order quantity.

Economic Production Run

In a manufacturing company, managers are concerned with "how many units to produce" in addition to "how many units (of raw materials) to buy." The EOQ formula can be modified to calculate the appropriate number of units to manufacture in an **economic production run** (EPR). This estimate reflects the production quantity that minimizes the total costs of setting up a production run and carrying a unit in stock

Economic production run

for one year. The only change in the EOQ formula is that the terms of the equation are redefined as manufacturing rather than purchasing costs. The formula is:

$$EPR = \sqrt{\frac{2QS}{C}}$$

where   EPR = economic production run quantity
        Q = estimated annual quantity produced in units
        S = estimated cost of setting up a production run
        C = estimated cost of carrying one unit in stock for one year

Another product manufactured by Casey-Glover is a circuit board for bar code scanners. A total of 140,625 units of this product are produced each year. Setup cost for a scanner production run is $40 and the annual carrying cost for each scanner is $5. The economic production run quantity is:

$$EPR = \sqrt{\frac{2(140,625)(\$40)}{\$5}} = \sqrt{\frac{\$11,250,000}{\$5}} = 1,500 \text{ units}$$

Like the answer provided by the EOQ model, the cost differences among various run sizes around the EPR may not be significant. If such costs are insignificant, management would have a range of acceptable, economical production run quantities.

The critical point in using either an EOQ or EPR model is to properly identify costs. Identifying all the relevant inventory costs (especially carrying costs) is very difficult and some costs (such as facilities, operations, administration, and accounting) traditionally viewed as irrelevant fixed costs may, in actuality, be long-term relevant variable costs. The EOQ model also does not provide any direction for managers attempting to control all the separate costs that collectively comprise purchasing and carrying costs. By only considering tradeoffs between ordering and carrying costs, the EOQ model does not lead managers to consider inventory management alternatives that may simultaneously reduce both categories of costs.

Additionally, as companies significantly reduce the necessary setup time (and thus cost) for operations and move toward a "stockless" inventory policy, a more comprehensive cost perspective will indicate a substantially smaller cost per setup and a substantially larger annual carrying cost. For instance, if the setup and cost-to-carry information given above for Casey-Glover were reversed, the EPR would be only 187.5 units. Using either a new perspective of variable cost or minimizing setup costs will provide much lower economic order or production run quantities than indicated in the past.

Although the basic EOQ model determines what inventory quantity to order, it also ignores relationships among inventory items. For example, Casey-Glover might require four metal contactors and one plastic housing for each sensor produced. If the EOQs for contactors and housings were computed independently, this interrelationship might be overlooked. C-G might find that, when twelve thousand contactors were on hand, there were only two thousand housings. Computer techniques known as MRP or MRP II address this problem with the EOQ model by considering component interrelationships in the ordering process.

MATERIALS REQUIREMENTS PLANNING
Materials requirements planning

Materials requirements planning (MRP) is a computer-based information and simulation system for the ordering and/or production scheduling of items, the quantity demands of which are dependent on those of other items. This system was developed to answer the question of what items are needed, how many of them are needed, and when they are needed. A depiction of the interrelationships of the MRP system ele-

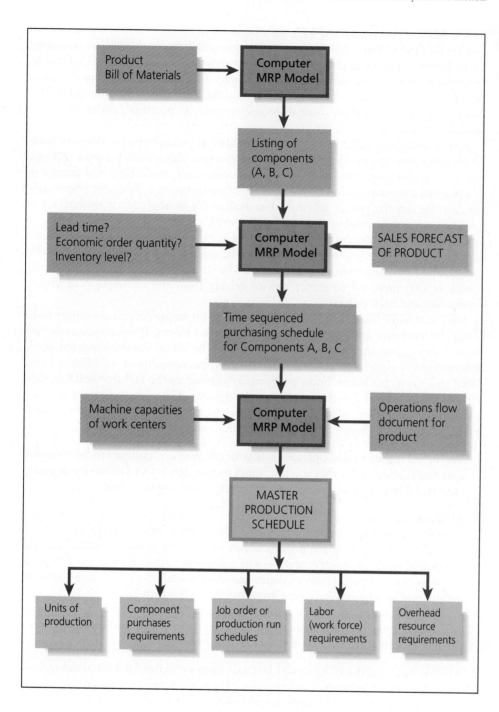

ments is shown in Exhibit 18–6. The MRP begins with a master production schedule (MPS) based on budgeted sales information. The MRP computer model then accesses the product's bill of materials to determine all the components needed for production. Quantities needed are compared to current inventory balances. If purchases are necessary, the model accesses information about component part interdependencies and supplier shipping times to determine the quantity and time to order, and ultimately generates a time-sequenced component purchases schedule. This schedule allows users to reduce inventory by eliminating the holding of unneeded parts. At J. R. Clarkson (Sparks, Nevada), for instance, MRP implementation reduced inventory by 30 percent.

The MPS is also integrated with the operations flow documents to project each work center's workload resulting from the master schedule. Workloads are compared to the center's capacity to determine whether meeting the master schedule is feasible. Potential bottlenecks are identified so that changes in input factors (such as the quantity of a particular component) can be made, and the MRP program is run again. This process is reiterated until the schedule compensates for all potential bottlenecks in the production system.

Manufacturing resource planning

A fully integrated MRP system, known as MRP II (**manufacturing resource planning**), plans production jobs using MRP and also provides a basis for both strategic and tactical planning. MRP II involves top management, marketing, and finance in determining the master production schedule. Manufacturing is primarily responsible for carrying out the master schedule, but availability of appropriate resources and sales support are essential to making the plan work.

Thousands of companies are currently using MRP and many have achieved significant benefits through lowering inventory levels, using labor and facilities more efficiently, and eliminating wasted activities in all facets of operations. In addition, companies report improved customer service arising from the elimination of erratic production and back orders.

MRP and MRP II are complex models that rely on strong technical support from computer hardware and software as well as detailed inputs. If these factors do not exist in an organization, the MRP models cannot be effectively implemented. And, although many positive effects can be shown by the adoption of an MRP system, MRP also has its problems. Some problems are caused by the fact that MRP models are based on several less-than-realistic assumptions. (These assumptions are not unique to MRP and can also cause difficulties when they are used in other decision-making situations.) These "problem" assumptions include the following:

1. The bill of materials and operations flow documents are assumed to be complete and totally accurate. If they are not, small inconsistencies or distortions in quantities or labor times may become cumulatively significant over time.

2. MRP assumes that there are no "bottleneck" operations in the factory even though most production processes include one or more operations that cannot be eliminated. (Remember, the process is run successively until the bottlenecks are eliminated on the computer model—which does not necessarily eliminate them in the workplace.) The best way to determine what bottlenecks exist is to go into the production facility and see where inventory is "stacking up."

   This assumption often provides unrealistic schedules of processing. MRP compensates for this lack of realism by building excess lead time and inventories into the model—creating additional costs for the company.

3. MRP is based on the EOQ model and uses fixed estimates for annual usage, carrying and ordering costs, and lead time. These estimates may be imprecise and actual cost factors may be quite volatile. While individually such errors may not make a significant difference in the EOQ/EPR/MRP models, the cumulative effect of such errors could be substantial.

4. Current inventory levels are assumed to be the amounts reflected by the accounting records. These records can be incorrect for a variety of reasons, such as shortages from theft, breakage, or human errors in counting or recording. In fact, a recent survey of manufacturing companies indicated that only 4.4 percent of the respondents had no inventory adjustments during the most recent year.[3]

---

[3] Il-Woon Kim and Arjan T. Sadhwani, "Is Your Inventory Really All There?" *Management Accounting* (July 1991), p. 37.

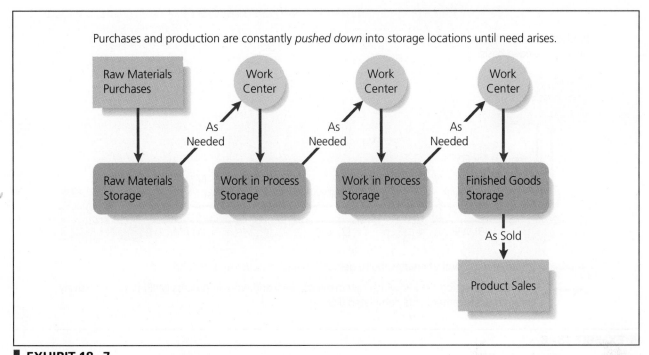

Purchases and production are constantly *pushed down* into storage locations until need arises.

EXHIBIT 18–7
Push System of Production Control

5. MRP assumes that the system will be in effect and used at all times. Managers, however, often use less formalized systems to achieve objectives and may not fully implement MRP.

The MRP models extend, but do not eliminate, the economic order quantity concept. EOQ indicates the most economical quantity to order at a time. MRP indicates which items of inventory to order at what point in time. Like EOQ, materials requirements planning models work in the traditional **push system** of production control. In such a system (illustrated in Exhibit 18–7), work centers may buy or produce inventory not currently needed because of lead time or economic order or production quantity requirements. This excess inventory is stored until it is needed by other work centers.

Push system

To reduce the costs of carrying inventory until future needs require it, many companies have begun to implement **pull systems** of production control (depicted in Exhibit 18–8 on page 762). In these systems, parts are delivered or produced only as they are needed by the work center for which they are intended. While some minimal storage must exist by necessity, work centers do not produce to compensate for lead times or to meet some economic production run model.

Pull system

Because the need for prompt and accurate communication between company and supplier is essential in a pull system, many companies are eliminating paper and telephone communication processes and relying instead on **electronic data interchange** (EDI). EDI refers to the computer-to-computer transfer of information in virtual real time using standardized formats developed by the American National Standards Institute. In addition to the cost savings obtained from reduced paperwork and data entry errors, EDI users experience more rapid transaction processing and response time than can occur using traditional communication channels. Such time reductions help companies in their implementation of pull systems, which are part of a just-in-time work environment.

Electronic data interchange

Product sales dictate total production. Purchases and production are *pulled* through the system on an as-needed basis.

Product Sales

(4)
FG

I
request for FG

II
request for WIP

III
request for WIP

IV
request for WIP

Work
Center

(3) WIP

Work
Center

(2) WIP

Work
Center

(1) RM

Raw Materials
Purchases

→ Information flow that creates (pulls) demand at each successive operation

← Physical production flow in which raw materials (RM) and work in process (WIP) flow successively through work centers until completed (FG)

▌ EXHIBIT 18–8

Pull System of Production Control

JUST-IN-TIME SYSTEMS

Just-in-time (JIT) is a philosophy about when to do something. The *when* is "as needed" and the *something* is a production, purchasing, or delivery activity. The JIT philosophy is applicable in all departments of all types of organizations. It has the following as its three primary goals:

1. elimination of any production process or operation that does not add value to the product/service;

2. continuous improvement in production/performance efficiency; and

3. reduction in the total cost of production/performance while increasing quality.

Note that these goals are totally consistent with and supportive of the total quality management program discussed in Chapter 3. The basic elements of the JIT philosophy are outlined in Exhibit 18–9.

Since JIT is most commonly discussed in regard to manufacturing or production activities, this is a logical starting point. Just-in-time manufacturing has many names including zero-inventory production systems (ZIPS) and Kanban (pronounced Kahn Bahn). (**Kanban** is Japanese for card. The manufacturing system originated in Japan because cards were used to indicate a work center's need for additional components.) A **just-in-time manufacturing system** (JIT) attempts to acquire components and produce inventory units only as they are needed, minimize product defects, and reduce lead/setup times for acquisition and production.

Production has traditionally been dictated by the need to smooth operating activity over a period of time. While allowing a company to maintain a steady workforce and continuous machine utilization, smooth production often creates products that must be stored until future sales arise. In addition, although smooth production works well with the EOQ concept, managers recognize that EOQ is based on estimates and therefore a stock of parts is maintained (as Boeing did) "just in case" they are needed. The discussion in the News Note on "The Big Box Theory" summarizes the traditional production situation.

Kanban

Just-in-time manufacturing system

■ **EXHIBIT 18–9**
Elements of a JIT
Philosophy

Quality is essential at all times; work to eliminate defects and scrap.

Employees often have the best knowledge of ways to improve operations; listen to them.

Employees generally have more talents than are being used; train them to be multi-skilled and increase their productivity.

Ways to improve operations are always available; constantly look for them, being certain to make fundamental changes rather than superficial ones.

Creative thinking doesn't cost anything; use it to find ways to reduce costs before making expenditures for additional resources.

Suppliers are essential to operations; establish and cultivate good relationships with them and use, if possible, long-term contracts.

Inventory is an asset that generates no revenue while it is held in stock. Thus, it can be viewed as a "liability"; eliminate it to the extent possible.

Storage space is directly related to inventories; eliminate it in response to the elimination of inventories.

Long lead times cause inventory buildup; keep lead times as short as possible by using frequent deliveries.

Thus, raw materials and work in process inventories historically have been maintained at levels that were considered sufficient to cover up for inefficiencies in acquisition and/or production. Exhibit 18–10 on page 764 depicts these inefficiencies or problems as "rocks" in a stream of "water" that represents inventory. The traditional philosophy is that the water level should be kept high enough for the rocks to be so deeply submerged that there will be "smooth sailing" in production activity. This technique is intended to avoid the original problems, but it creates a new one. By covering up the problems, the excess "water" adds to the difficulty of making corrections. The JIT manufacturing philosophy is to lower the water level, expose the rocks, and eliminate them to the extent possible. The shallower stream will then flow more smoothly and rapidly than the deep river.

NEWS NOTE

The Big Box Theory

You've heard of the "big bang theory," now hear about the "big box theory." The big box is our factory. We put costs into the box and out comes products. For too long we have been analyzing the individual costs within the box and forgetting about the number of products coming out. We played games like building inventory to lower our unit costs, but the product stayed in the box. We appeared to be very efficient in labor and machine utilization, but what good is it if the product stays in the box?

We also soon realized our box was not big enough to hold all the products we produced. So we built other boxes, called warehouses, to store them in. Most companies became very efficient at producing products with low unit costs. Unfortunately, the products sat in the warehouses.

While we were filling up the boxes with products we did not need, we were simultaneously missing our customer delivery promise dates. The factory was very efficient with long production runs but the wrong product was being produced.

SOURCE: John F. Towey, ed., "What is JIT and FMS?" *Management Accounting* (May 1988), p. 71. Reprinted from *Management Accounting*. Copyright by Institute of Management Accountants, Montvale, N.J.

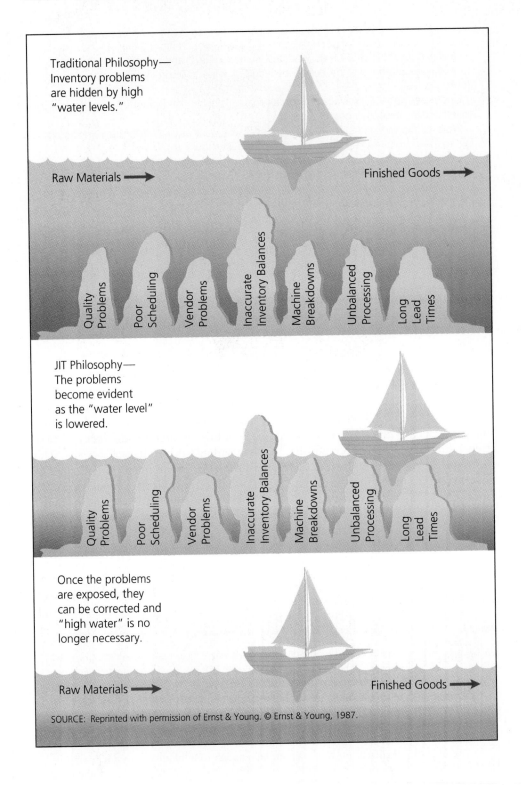

Traditional Philosophy—Inventory problems are hidden by high "water levels."

Raw Materials →   Finished Goods →

Quality Problems
Poor Scheduling
Vendor Problems
Inaccurate Inventory Balances
Machine Breakdowns
Unbalanced Processing
Long Lead Times

JIT Philosophy—The problems become evident as the "water level" is lowered.

Quality Problems
Poor Scheduling
Vendor Problems
Inaccurate Inventory Balances
Machine Breakdowns
Unbalanced Processing
Long Lead Times

Once the problems are exposed, they can be corrected and "high water" is no longer necessary.

Raw Materials →   Finished Goods →

SOURCE: Reprinted with permission of Ernst & Young. © Ernst & Young, 1987.

CHANGES NEEDED TO IMPLEMENT JIT MANUFACTURING

Implementation of a just-in-time system in a manufacturing firm does not occur overnight. It took Toyota over 20 years to develop the system and realize significant benefits from it. But JIT techniques are becoming better known and more easily implemented and, as indicated below, it is now possible for a company to have a system in place and be recognizing benefits in a fairly short period of time.

In a world where managers sweat bullets to grind out improvements of a percentage point or two, some numbers just don't look real. Coleman Co. of Wichita, Kansas, used to need two months of inventory to provide giant retailers like Wal-Mart and Kmart with a shipment of camping stoves or lanterns. [As of 1991,] it could make and ship a new order in a week. In 1989, the company offered 20 models of ice coolers in three color combinations; in 1991, it sold 140 models in 12 color combinations. Coleman cut inventory costs by $10 million, reduced scrap 60%, and raised productivity 35%. What on earth happened? In a word: speed. [In 1990, Coleman adopted a just-in-time inventory system.][4]

The most impressive benefits from JIT, though, are normally reached only after the system has been operational for five to ten years. Coleman President Bob Ring agrees; he thinks the company has not even scratched the surface of possible gains.

For just-in-time production to be effective, certain modifications must be made in purchasing, supplier relationships, distribution, product design, product processing, and plant layout. These topics are discussed below.

Purchasing Considerations

When applying JIT to purchasing, managers must first recognize that the lowest quoted *purchase* price is not necessarily the lowest cost. Suppliers should be screened to systematically consider other nonprice factors. If other costs such as the failure costs of poor quality (machine downtime, labor idle time, rework, and scrap) are considered, the lowest price could become the most expensive. Additionally, the vendor willing to quote the lowest prices may not be willing to make frequent small-quantity deliveries or sign a long-term contract.

Long-term contracts are being negotiated with suppliers and continuance of those contracts is based on delivery reliability. Vendors missing a certain number of scheduled deliveries by more than a specified number of hours are dismissed. Vendor agreements are made in which components are delivered "ready for use" without packaging, eliminating the need for the JIT manufacturer to unpack components; other agreements may specify that goods will be received from suppliers in modular form, so that less subassembly work is required in the assembly plant.

Suppliers may be requested to bar code raw materials purchases sent to a JIT company so that inventory management techniques are improved. Bar coding allows raw materials inventory records to be updated more quickly, raw materials to be selected from receiving more precisely, work in process to be tracked more closely, and finished goods shipments to be made more accurately. For example, Haggar Apparel's Dallas distribution center has an error rate of less than 0.01 percent because of the use of a bar code network.[5] Bar code technology is continually improving and one company, Symbol Technologies of Bohemia, New York, has developed a two-dimensional bar code that will allow storage of about two pages of text or 100 times the information currently available on a bar code. Bar codes will then be able to track products even more effectively and efficiently through the plant.

While bar codes on purchased goods will improve recordkeeping and inventory management, even that would not be necessary if the ideal JIT purchase quantity of one unit could be implemented. Such a quantity is typically not a feasible ordering level, although Allen-Bradley (and some other highly automated, flexible manufacturers) can produce in such a lot size. Thus, the closer a company can get to a lot size of one, the more effective the JIT system is. This reduction in ordering levels means more frequent orders and deliveries. Some automobile companies, for example, have some deliveries made every two hours! Thus, vendors chosen by the company should be located close to the company to minimize both shipping costs and delivery time. The ability to obtain suppliers close to the plant is easy in a country the size of Japan. Such an objective is not so readily accomplished in the United States where a plant

---

[4]Brian Dumaine, "Earning More By Moving Faster," *FORTUNE* (October 7, 1991), pp. 89–90, 94.
[5]Symbol Technologies, Inc., *1991 Annual Report*, p. 12.

can be located in New Jersey and a critical parts vendor in California. However, air express companies help to make just-in-time more practical.

Focused Factory Arrangements

Focused factory arrangements

Focused factory arrangements are often adopted to connect a vendor more closely to a JIT manufacturer's operations. Such an arrangement means that a vendor agrees to provide a limited number of products according to specifications or to perform a limited number of unique services to the JIT company. The supplier may be an internal division of the same organization or an external party. For example, in 1991, Bumper Works, in Danville, Illinois, was Toyota's only U.S. bumper supplier of lightweight pickup truck bumpers for trucks made in Japan.[6] Focused factory arrangements may also involve relocation or plant modernization by the vendor, and financial assistance from the JIT manufacturer may be available to recoup such investments. In addition, the vendor benefits from long-term supply contracts.

Major reliance on a single customer can be difficult, especially for small companies. A decline in the business of the primary customer or demands for lower prices can be disastrous for the focused factory. To maintain customers, some companies are submitting to vendor certification processes.

Vendor Certification

The optimal JIT situation would be to have only one vendor for any given item. Such an ideal, however, creates the risk of not having alternative sources (especially for critical parts) in the event of vendor production strikes, unfair pricing, or shipment delays. Thus, it is often more feasible and realistic to limit the number of vendors to a few that are selected and company-certified as to quality and reliability. The company then enters into long-term relationships with these suppliers, who become pseudo "partners" in the process. Vendor certification is becoming more and more popular. For example, Allen-Bradley has been named the preferred automation controls supplier to Ford's Automotive Components Group network of more than thirty manufacturing plants worldwide.

The vendor certification process requires substantial efforts on the purchasing company's part, such as obtaining information on the supplier's operating philosophy, costs, product quality, and service. People from various areas must decide on the factors by which the vendor will be rated; these factors are then weighted as to relative importance. Rapid feedback should be given to potential suppliers so that they can, if necessary, make changes prior to the start of the relationship or, alternatively, to understand why the relationship will not occur.

To illustrate the type of document necessary for such a rating process, Exhibit 18–11 provides Digital Equipment Corporation's vendor service rating form. This form does not consider factors such as supplier quality or delivery; these criteria are covered by different rating scales. Evaluations of new and infrequent suppliers are more difficult because of the lack of experience by which the purchasing company vendor analysis team can make informed judgments.

As discussed in the "Supplier Relationship" News Note on page 768, working with fewer vendors on a long-term basis provides the opportunity to develop better communications, ensure quality and service (including delivery), obtain quantity discounts, and reduce operating costs. "By forming partnerships with all members of the supply chain, we can eliminate redundancies in warehousing, packaging, labeling, transportation, inventories, etc., that will provide continuous savings instead of one-time inventory buy-backs or other current industry gimmicks and fads," says Fred

---

[6] Joseph B. White, "Japanese Auto Makers Help U.S. Suppliers Become More Efficient," *Wall Street Journal* (September 9, 1991), p. A.

| Characteristics of Vendor | Vendor | | |
Excellent = 5 points; Average = 4 points; Below average = 2 points	A	B	C

1. Personnel Capabilities:
  a. Caliber and availability of sales and technical personnel.
  b. Is management progressive?
  c. Technical knowledge of supervision.
  d. Cooperation on changes and problems.
  e. Technical field service availability.
  f. Labor relations.			

2. Facilities Capabilities:
  a. Capability for anticipated volume.
  b. Latest technology and equipment.
  c. Excess production capacity.
  d. Geographical location.
  e. Financial capacity to stand behind product failures.
  f. Investing capital in the organization.			

3. R&D Capabilities:
  a. New product development.
  b. Alerted for future needs?
  c. Does the vendor update the buyer with the latest techniques?			

4. Product Service Capability:
  a. Offers emergency assistance?
  b. Does vendor provide consultation for potential troubles?
  c. What type of warranty is furnished?
  d. Is the vendor willing to accept responsibility?
  e. What is the vendor's record for reliability in past dealings?			

Total service points			

SOURCE: Narenda S. Patel, "Source Surveillance and Vendor Evaluation Plan," *Quality Costs: Ideas and Applications*, A. Grimm, ed. (Milwaukee, Wis.: American Society for Quality Control, 1987).

EXHIBIT 18–11
Digital Equipment Corporation Vendor Service Rating

Ricker, a vice president at Owens & Minor, a Baylor University Medical Center (Dallas, Texas) certified supplier.[7]

Product Design

Products need to be designed to use the fewest number of parts and parts should be standardized to the greatest extent possible. For example, at Harley-Davidson, engines and their components were traditionally designed without regard for manufacturing efficiency. Harley was making two similar crankpins, one having an oil hole drilled at a 45-degree angle, and the other at a 48-degree angle. (A crankpin is a

---

[7]"Baylor University Medical Center Teams Up with O&M," *(Owens & Minor, Inc.) Community Post* (Fall 1991), p. 3.

NEWS NOTE

Supplier Relationships Improve Product Quality

Embracing supply-chain management means abandoning the way manufacturers and suppliers have typically related, says John Sutton, a senior manager with Grant Thornton's Minneapolis office. Instead of playing off one supplier against another, the manufacturer works closely, in complete trust, with only a chosen few. "You're trying to come up with a win-win situation for both the manufacturer and the supplier."

Time can be cut everywhere. Sutton cites the typical relationship of suppliers and customers. The supplier manufactures a part, inspects it, packs it, and sends it off to the customer with the accompanying paperwork.

The customer receives it, unpacks it, inspects it, and reviews the paperwork. This is double work, Sutton says. Both supplier and customer inspect the product, wrestle with packing material, and sort through invoices and purchase orders.

"If they viewed each other as extensions of themselves, none of this would be necessary," Sutton says. The customer would not have to inspect the product; he would know the quality was fine. Supplier and customer could use reusable containers for shipping instead of expensive disposable packing. The manufacturer produces a better product more quickly and the supplier develops a strong relationship with his customer and is encouraged to be cost-effective and quality conscious and may enjoy a steady stream of work.

SOURCE: "Speed Is Everything in Supply-Chain Management," (*Grant Thornton*) *Manufacturing Issues* (Summer 1992), pp. 3–4. Reprinted by permission from Grant Thornton's *Manufacturing Issues.* © Grant Thornton 1992.

cylindrical bar that attaches a connecting rod to a crank in an engine.) Repositioning the machines to make these different crankpins required about two hours. Engineers designed a common angle on both parts and common tools for drilling the holes, which cut changeover time for that process to three minutes.[8] Another company discovered that it used 29 different types of screws to manufacture a single product. Downtime was excessive because screwdrivers were continuously being passed among workers. Changing to all the same type screws significantly reduced production time.

Parts standardization does not have to mean identical products. To illustrate, the National Bicycle Industrial Co. of Kokubu, Japan, can produce 11,231,862 variations from only 18 models of racing, road, and mountain bikes.[9] Such differentiation can be substantially aided by flexible manufacturing systems and computer-integrated manufacturing, which are discussed in a later section of the chapter.

Products should be designed for the quality desired and should require only a minimal number of engineering changes after the design is released for production. Approximately 90 to 100 percent of all product costs are preestablished by the production team when the stage of product design is only 25 percent to 50 percent completed (see Exhibit 18–12). It is often helpful to have vendors' engineers participate in the design phase or simply to provide product specifications and allow the vendor company to draft the design for approval.

If costs are to be significantly affected, any design changes must be made early in the process. Each time an engineering change is made, one or more of the following problems occurs creating additional costs: the operations flow document must be reprinted; workers must relearn tasks; machine dies or setups must be changed; and parts currently ordered or in stock may be made obsolete. Regardless of whether a

---

[8] John Van, "Leaks No Longer Stain Harley-Davidson Name," *Chicago Tribune* (November 4, 1991), Section 1, p. 6.
[9] Susan Moffat, "Japan's New Personalized Production," *FORTUNE* (October 22, 1990), p. 132.

■ EXHIBIT 18–12
Development of Product
Cost Commitment

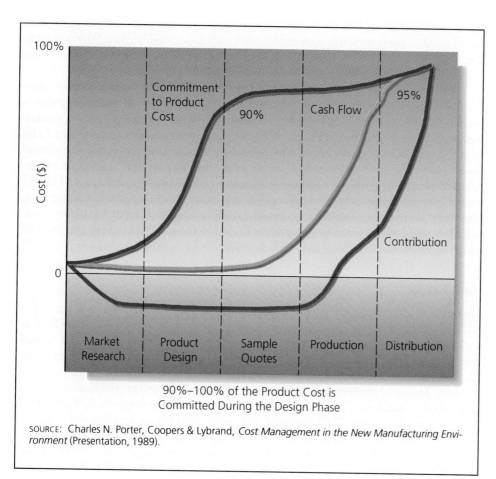

90%–100% of the Product Cost is
Committed During the Design Phase

SOURCE: Charles N. Porter, Coopers & Lybrand, *Cost Management in the New Manufacturing Environment* (Presentation, 1989).

company embraces JIT, time that is spent doing work that adds no value to the production process should be viewed as wasted. Effective activity analysis would eliminate such non-value-added work and its unnecessary cost.

From another point of view, good product design should address all concerns of the intended consumers, even the degree of recyclability of the product. For example, "BMW's plant is equipped to receive and take apart used-up models, remanufacture them, and then send them back into the marketplace."[10] Thus, companies are considering remanufacturing as part of their design and processing capabilities.

Product Processing

In the production processing stage, one primary JIT consideration is reduction of machine setup time. Reduction of setup time allows processing to shift between products more often and at a lower cost. The costs of reducing setup time are more than recovered by the savings derived from reducing downtime, WIP inventory, and materials handling as well as increasing safety, flexibility, and ease of operation.

Most companies implementing rapid tool-setting procedures have been able to obtain setup times of ten minutes or less. Such companies use a large number of low-cost setups rather than the traditional processing approach of a small number of more expensive setups. Under JIT, setup cost is considered almost purely variable rather than fixed, as it was in the traditional manufacturing environment. One way to reduce machine setup time is to have workers perform as many setup tasks as possible while the machine is on-line and running. All unnecessary movements by either work-

---

[10] Sandra Vandermerwe and Michael Oliff, "Corporate Challenges for an Age of Reconsumption," *Business Edge* (May 1992), p. 26.

ers or materials should be eliminated. Teams similar to pit-stop crews at auto races can be used to perform setup operations, with each team member handling a specialized task. Based on past results, it appears that with planning and education, setup times can be reduced by 50 percent or more.

Another essential part of product processing is the institution of high quality standards because JIT has the goal of zero defects. Under just-in-time systems, quality is determined on a continual basis rather than at quality control checkpoints. Continuous quality is achieved by first assuring vendor quality at point of purchase and also by having workers and machines (such as optical scanners or chutes for size dimensions) monitor quality while production is in process. Controlling quality on an ongoing basis can significantly reduce the costs of obtaining good quality. The JIT philosophy recognizes that it is less costly not to make mistakes than to correct them after they are made. Unfortunately, as mentioned in Chapters 3 and 11, quality control costs and costs of scrap are frequently buried in the standard cost of production, which often makes such costs hard to ascertain.

Plant Layout

Most manufacturing plants are still designed in conformity with functional areas. For a JIT system to work effectively, the physical plant must be conducive to the flow of goods and organization of workers, and to increasing the value added per square foot of plant space. Manufacturing plants should be designed to minimize material handling time and lead time from raw material input to completion of the finished product. This goal often means establishing linear or U-shaped production groupings of workers or machines, commonly referred to as **manufacturing cells**. A streamlined design allows for more visual controls to be instituted for such problems as excess inventory, production defects, equipment malfunctions, and out-of-place tools.

Exhibit 18–13 illustrates the flow of three products through a factory before and after the redesign of factory floor space. In the "before" diagram, processes were grouped together by function and products flowed helter-skelter through the plant depending on what type of processing needed to be performed. If the company uses JIT and a cellular design, substantial storage is eliminated because goods should only be ordered as needed. (All storage is not eliminated, since the company needs to maintain some minimal level of stock.) Products also flow through the plant more rapidly. Product 2 can utilize the same flow as Product 1, but skip the cell's grinding process.

Multiprocess handling

When plant layout is redesigned to incorporate manufacturing cells, an opportunity arises for workers to broaden their skills and deepen their involvement in the process because of **multiprocess handling**. Workers are trained to monitor numerous machines and thereby become more flexible and less bored because they are performing a variety of tasks rather than a single one. Being able to oversee an entire process may prompt employee suggestions on improvement techniques that would not have been visible had the employee been working on a single facet of the process.[11]

Autonomation

Highly automated equipment may run without direct labor involvement, but it will still require monitoring. For instance, some equipment stops automatically when a given situation arises. The "situation" may be positive (a specified quantity of production has been reached) or negative (a quality defect has been indicated). Toyota refers to the usage of such equipment in a factory environment as **autonomation** to distinguish it from automated factories in which the machinery is not programmed to stop when specified situations arise. Since machines "know" the certain conditions they are expected to sense, workers are able to oversee several machines concurrently. A worker's responsibility may be to monitor all those machines operating in a single manufacturing cell.

---

[11] The average American company receives about one suggestion per year from every seven employees. On the other hand, the Japanese companies of Mitsubishi, Canon, and Pioneer Electronic Corp. receive, respectively, an average of 100, 70, and 60 suggestions. [Lloyd Shearer, "Parade's Special Intelligence Report," *Parade Magazine* (May 19, 1991), p. 8.]

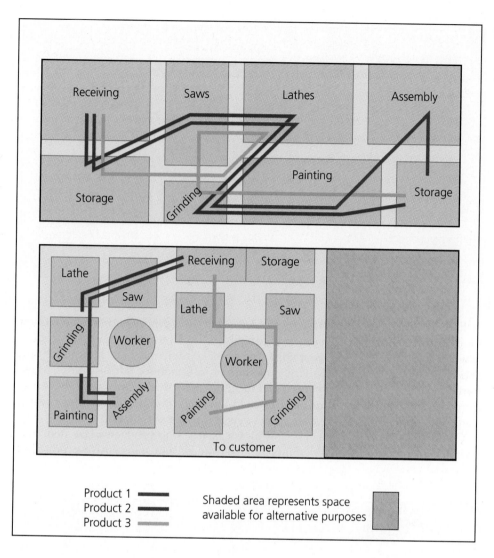

EXHIBIT 18–13
Factory Floor Space
Redesign

Automated equipment and cellular plant layout, coupled with computer hardware and software technology and new manufacturing systems and philosophies such as JIT and activity-based management, have allowed many manufacturers to change their basic manufacturing philosophy. Traditionally, most manufacturing firms employed long production runs to make thousands of identical models of the same products; this process was encouraged by the idea of economies of scale. After each run, the machines would be stopped and a slow and expensive setup would be made for the next massive production run to begin. Now, an entirely new generation of manufacturing processing known as flexible manufacturing systems (FMSs) is being developed.

As discussed in Chapter 1, an FMS is a network of robots and material conveyance devices monitored and controlled by computers that allows for rapid production and prompt responsiveness to changes in production needs. Two or more FMSs connected via a host computer and an information networking system are generally referred to as **computer-integrated manufacturing** (CIM). Exhibit 18–14 on page 772 contrasts the dimensions of a traditional manufacturing system with an FMS. While an FMS is typically associated with short-volume production runs, many companies (such as Cummins Engine) have also begun to use CIM for high-volume lines.

FLEXIBLE MANUFACTURING SYSTEMS AND COMPUTER-INTEGRATED MANUFACTURING

Computer-integrated manufacturing

■ EXHIBIT 18–14

Comparison of Traditional
Manufacturing and FMS

FACTOR	TRADITIONAL MANUFACTURING	FMS
Product variety	Few	Basically unlimited
Response time to market needs	Slow	Rapid
Worker tasks	Specialized	Diverse
Production runs	Long	Short
Lot sizes	Massive	Small
Performance rewards basis	Individual	Team
Setups	Slow and expensive	Fast and inexpensive
Product life cycle expectations	Long	Short
Work area control	Centralized	Decentralized
Technology	Labor-intensive	Technology-intensive
Information requirements	Batch-based	On-line, real-time
Worker knowledge of technology	Low to medium	Highly trained

FMSs are used in modular factories and are able to customize output upon request for customers. Customization can be accomplished because of the ability to introduce new products quickly, produce small lot sizes, make rapid machine and tool setups, and communicate and process large amounts of information. Information is transferred through an electronic network to the computers that control the robots performing most of the production activities. On-line, real-time production flow control using fiber optics and local area networks makes the system function.

Companies are able to quickly and inexpensively stop producing one item and start producing another. This ability to make quick and inexpensive production

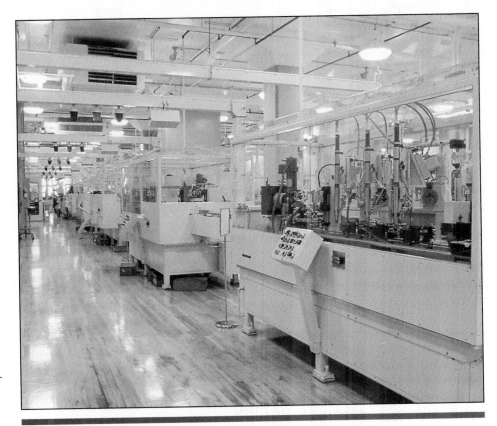

Just six attendants oversee operations in the $15 million factory in the Allen-Bradley company's Milwaukee headquarters location. The automated assembly line can produce 600 motor starters an hour, with up to 999 variations ensuring consistent quality. It utilizes minimal inventory, a stockless production concept.

NEWS NOTE   Flexible Systems Mean Frequent Changes

Flexibility is an explicit goal at Toshiba, whose $35.5 billion in sales in 1991 came from products as diverse as appliances and computers, light bulbs and power plants. Okay, so the slogan "synchronize production in proportion to customer demand" probably made a few hearts leap when Toshiba workers first heard it in 1985. The idea, explains Toshiba President Fumio Sato, is to push Toshiba's two dozen factories to adapt faster to markets. Says Sato: "Customers wanted choices. They wanted a washing machine or a TV set that was precisely right for their needs. We needed variety, not mass production.

Sato hammered home his theme in an almost nonstop series of factory visits. The key to variety: finding ways to make money from ever shorter production runs. Sato urged managers to reduce setup times, shrink lead time, and learn to make more products with the same equipment and people. He says: "Every time I go to a plant I tell the people, 'Smaller lot!'"

[Toshiba's computer factory in Ome is referred to as] an "intelligent works" because a snazzy computer network links office, engineering, and factory operations, providing just-in-time information as well as just-in-time parts. Ome workers assemble nine different word processors on the same line and, on an adjacent one, 20 varieties of laptop computers. Usually they make a batch of 20 before changing models, but Toshiba can afford lot sizes as small as ten.

Workers have been trained to make each model but don't need to rely on memory. A laptop at every post displays a drawing and instructions, which change when the model does. Product life-cycles for low-end computers are measured in months these days, so the flexible lines allow the company to guard against running short of a hot model or overproducing one whose sales have slowed.

When it comes to hardware for flexible manufacturing, the Japanese lead is, if anything, widening. Okuma Corp., which makes the world's broadest machine-tool product line, sells 14 flexible manufacturing systems in Japan for every one it exports to America. Though U.S. purchases of industrial robots are at record highs, Japan has already installed 390,000 to America's 45,000.

SOURCE: Thomas A. Stewart, "Brace for Japan's Hot New Strategy," *FORTUNE* (September 21, 1992), pp. 64, 74. © 1992 Time Inc. All rights reserved.

---

changes and to operate at great speed permits a company to build a large assortment of products and thereby offer its customers a wide variety of high-quality products while minimizing product costs. In effect, machines are able to make other machines and can do so with little human intervention. The system can operate in a "lights-out" environment and never tire. The News Note "Flexible Systems Mean Frequent Changes" discusses Toshiba's flexible manufacturing system in Ome, Japan.

The need for direct labor is diminished in such a technology-intensive environment. The workers who remain in a company employing an FMS must be more highly trained than in traditional systems and find themselves handling a greater variety of tasks than the narrowly specialized workers of earlier manufacturing eras. The manufacturing cells are managed by persons with greater authority and responsibility. This increase in control occurs because production and production scheduling changes happen so rapidly on the shop floor that an FMS relies on immediate decisions by persons who "live there" and have a grasp of the underlying facts and conditions.

The FMS works so fast that moving products along and out of the way of other products is sometimes a problem. Japan's Nissan Motor Company's new FMS facility on Kyushu Island is replacing the time-honored conveyor belt with a convoy of little yellow intelligent motor-driven dollies that "tote cars at variable speeds down the assembly line sending out a stream of computer-controlled signals to coach both robots and workers along the way."[12]

ACCOUNTING IMPLICATIONS OF JIT

There are significant accounting implications for companies adopting a just-in-time inventory and/or flexible manufacturing system. A primary accounting impact occurs in the area of variance analysis. Because it is primarily historical in nature, the main goal of a traditional standard cost accounting system is variance reporting. The reports allow the variances to be analyzed for cause and effect relationships to (hopefully) eliminate future similar problems.

Variances Under JIT

Variance reporting and analysis in JIT systems essentially disappears. Since most variances first appear in a *physical* (rather than financial) fashion, JIT mandates that variances be recognized on the spot so that causes can be ascertained and, if possible, promptly removed. JIT workers are trained and expected to monitor quality and efficiency continually *while production occurs* rather than just at the end of production. Therefore, the number and monetary significance of end-of-period variances being reported for managerial control should be limited.

Under a JIT system, long-term price agreements have been made with vendors, so material price variances should be minimal. The JIT accounting system should be designed so that purchase orders cannot be cut for an amount greater than the designated price without manager approval.[13] In this way, the variance amount and its cause are known in advance, providing an opportunity to eliminate the excess expenditure before it occurs. Calls can be made to the vendor to negotiate the price or other vendors can be contacted for quotes.

The ongoing use of specified vendors also provides the ability to control material quality. Since raw material quality is expected to be better controlled, little or no material usage variances should be caused by substandard materials. If usage standards are accurate, there should be virtually no favorable usage variance of materials during production. Unfavorable use of materials should be promptly detected because of ongoing machine and/or human observation of processing. When an unfavorable variance occurs, the JIT system is stopped and the error causing the unfavorable materials usage is corrected to minimize materials usage variances.

One type of usage variance is not caused by errors but by engineering changes (ENCs) made to the product specifications. A JIT system has two comparison standards: an annual standard and a current standard. Design modifications would change the current standard, but not the annual one. Such a procedure allows comparisons to be made that indicate the cost effects of having engineering changes implemented after a product has begun to be manufactured. A materials usage variance caused by an ENC is illustrated in Exhibit 18–15. In the illustration, the portion of the total usage variance caused by the engineering change ($9,600 U) is shown separately from that caused by inefficiency ($1,160 U). It is also possible to have ENC variances for labor, overhead and/or conversion.

Labor variances in a just-in-time system should be minimal if standard rates and times have been set appropriately. Labor time standards should be carefully evaluated after the implementation of a JIT production system. If the plant is not entirely auto-

---

[12] Clay Chandler and Joseph B. White, "It's Hello Dollies at Nissan's New 'Dream Factory,'" *Wall Street Journal* (July 6, 1992), p. 1.
[13] This same procedure can be implemented under a traditional standard cost system as well as under JIT. It is, however, less common to find in the traditional standard cost system, but it is a requirement under JIT.

■ EXHIBIT 18–15

Material Variances Under
a JIT System

Annual standard:	6 lbs. of product A @ $4.40	$26.40
	3 lbs. of product B @ $5.20	15.60
		$42.00
Current standard:	5 lbs. of product A @ $4.40	$22.00
	4 lbs. of product B @ $5.20	20.80
		$42.80

Production during month: 12,000 units

Usage during month:	60,500 lbs. of product A @ $4.40	$266,200
	47,800 lbs. of product B @ $5.20	248,560
	Total cost of materials used	$514,760

Materials usage variance:

12,000 × 5 × $4.40	$264,000
12,000 × 4 × $5.20	249,600
Materials cost at current standard	$513,600
Actual materials cost	514,760
Materials usage variance	$ 1,160 U

Engineering change variance for materials:

12,000 × 6 × $4.40	$316,800
12,000 × 3 × $5.20	187,200
Materials cost at annual standard	$504,000
Materials cost at current standard	513,600
ENC variance (materials)	$ 9,600 U

mated, redesigning the physical layout and minimizing any non-value-added labor activities should decrease the direct labor time component.

Another accounting change that may occur in a JIT system is the use of a "conversion" category for purposes of cost control rather than separate labor and overhead categories. This category becomes more useful as factories automate and reduce the direct labor cost component. A standard departmental or manufacturing cell conversion cost per unit of product (or per hour of production time per department) may be calculated rather than individual standards for labor and overhead. Denominators in each case would be practical capacity of either units or hours.[14] For example, if time were used as the base, the conversion cost for a day's production would be equal to the number of units produced multiplied by the standard number of production hours multiplied by the standard cost per hour. Variances would be determined by comparing actual cost to the designated standard.

In addition to minimizing and adjusting the variance calculations, a JIT system can have a major impact on inventory accounting. Companies employing JIT production processes would no longer need a separate raw materials inventory classification be-

[14]Practical capacity is the appropriate measure of activity since the goal of JIT is virtually continuous processing. In a highly automated plant, practical capacity would be set more closely to theoretical capacity than it is currently. It would still be impossible to set the denominator at the theoretical level because, even under a JIT system, there will be work stoppages for a variety of reasons.

cause materials would be acquired only when and as production occurs. Instead, they could use a Raw and In Process (RIP) Inventory account.

Backflush Costing

Throughput

The focus of accounting in a JIT system is on the plant's output (**throughput**) to the customer.[15] Since each sequential area is dependent on the previous area, any problems will quickly cause the system to stop the production process. Individual daily accounting for the costs of production will no longer be necessary because all costs should be at standard because variations will be observed and corrected almost immediately.

Additionally, fewer costs need to be allocated to products since more costs can be traced directly to their related output in a JIT system. Costs are incurred in specified cells on a per hour or per unit basis. Energy is a direct production cost in a comprehensive JIT system because there should be a minimum of downtime by machines or unplanned idle time for workers. Virtually the only costs still being allocated are costs associated with the structure (building depreciation, rent, taxes, and insurance) and machinery depreciation. The reduction of allocations provide more useful measures of cost control and performance evaluation than have been traditionally available.

Backflush costing

Backflush costing is a streamlined cost accounting method that speeds up, simplifies, and minimizes accounting effort in an environment that minimizes inventory balances, requires few allocations, uses standard costs, and has minimal variances from standard. During the period, this costing method records purchases of raw materials and accumulates actual conversion costs. Then, either at completion of production or upon the sale of goods, an entry is made to allocate the total costs incurred to cost of goods sold and to finished goods inventory using standard production costs.

The backflush costing system journal entries related to one of Casey-Glover's products are illustrated in Exhibit 18–16. The product's standard production cost is $129.50. The company has a long-term contract with its direct materials supplier to supply raw materials at $37.50 per unit, so there is no material price variance upon purchase. Casey-Glover's JIT inventory system has minimum inventories that basically remain constant from period to period. Beginning inventories for April are assumed to be zero.

Three alternatives are also possible for the Exhibit 18–16 entries. First, if Casey-Glover's production time were extremely short, it might not journalize raw material purchases until completion of production. In that case, the entry (in addition to recording actual conversion costs) would be:

Raw and In Process Inventory	15,000	
Finished Goods Inventory	2,590,000	
Accounts Payable		765,000
Conversion Costs		1,840,000

If goods were shipped immediately to customers upon completion, Casey-Glover could use a second alternative in which the entries to complete and sell would be combined:

Finished Goods Inventory	25,900	
Cost of Goods Sold	2,564,100	
Raw and In Process Inventory		750,000
Conversion Costs		1,840,000

The above entry would be made in addition to recording actual raw materials purchases and actual conversion costs.

---

[15] A company may wish to measure output of each manufacturing cell or work center rather than throughput. While this may indicate problems in a given area, it does not correlate with the JIT philosophy of the team approach, plantwide attitude, and total cost picture.

Cooper Lasers Inc.'s standard production cost per unit:

Direct materials	$ 37.50
Conversion	92.00
Total cost	$129.50

No beginning inventories exist.

Purchased $765,000 of direct materials in April:

Raw and In Process Inventory	765,000	
Accounts Payable		765,000

Purchased materials at standard cost under
a long-term agreement with supplier.

Incurred $1,843,500 of conversion costs in April:

Conversion Costs	1,843,500	
Various accounts		1,843,500

Record conversion costs. Various accounts include
wages payable for direct and indirect labor,
accumulated depreciation, supplies, etc.

Applied conversion costs to RIP:

Raw and In Process Inventory (20,000 × $92.00)	1,840,000	
Conversion Costs		1,840,000

Completed 20,000 units of production in April:

Finished Goods (20,000 × $129.50)	2,590,000	
Raw and In Process Inventory (20,000 × $129.50)		2,590,000

Sold 19,800 units on account in April for $210:

Cost of Goods Sold (19,800 × $129.50)	2,564,100	
Finished Goods		2,564,000
Accounts Receivable (19,800 × $210)	4,158,000	
Sales		4,158,000

Ending Inventories:

Raw and In Process ($2,605,000 − $2,590,000)	$15,000
Finished Goods ($2,590,000 − $2,564,100)	$25,900

In addition, there are underapplied conversion costs of $3,500 ($1,843,500 −
$1,840,000).

The third alternative reflects the ultimate JIT system, in which only one entry (other than recording actual conversion costs) is made. For Casey-Glover, this entry would be:

Raw and In Process Inventory		
(minimal overpurchases)	15,000	
Finished Goods Inventory (minimal overproduction)	25,900	
Cost of Goods Sold	2,564,100	
Accounts Payable		765,000
Conversion Costs		1,840,000

Inventory implementation of the just-in-time philosophy can cause significant cost reductions and productivity improvements. But, even within a single company, all inventory situations do not necessarily have to be on a just-in-time system. The costs and benefits of any inventory control system must be evaluated before management should install the system. The use of JIT, however, does allow workers as well as managers to concentrate on providing quality service to customers.

JIT IN NON-MANUFACTURING SITUATIONS

While a JIT manufacturing system can only be adopted by a company actually producing a product, other just-in-time systems can be employed by nonmanufacturers. An all-encompassing view of JIT covers a variety of policies and programs that are implemented to continuously improve the use of company human and mechanical resources. Thus, just-in-time is a type of management control system having a distinct underlying philosophy of which inventory minimization is only one element. In addition to being used by manufacturers, the JIT philosophy can be adopted within the purchasing and delivery departments of any organization involved with inventory, such as retailers, wholesalers, and distributors.

Many of the just-in-time techniques do not require a significant investment in new equipment but depend, instead, on the attitude of company management and the involvement of the organization's people and their willingness to work together and trust one another. People working under a JIT system must be open to change and question of established routines and procedures. All of an employee's talents, not just a limited few, should be used by the company. Creative abilities have sometimes been overlooked or neglected in the workplace. The "Five Whys" News Note discusses a valuable technique to enhance the creative thought process.

JIT emphasizes that there is always room for workplace improvement, whether in the area of floor space design, training and education, equipment and technology,

---

NEWS NOTE

"Five Whys" Approach to Problem Analysis

Rather than looking at problems as problems, it is more productive to consider problems as opportunities for improvement. Problems are the raw materials for improvement. Asking "Why?" five times is an attempt to challenge traditional thinking and accepted habits. The "five whys" approach gets to the root cause of a problem. Once the root cause is resolved, the problem will not occur again.

Here is an example of the use of the "five whys" approach:

Problem. A machine went down because of an electrical problem.

▮ Why did the machine go down? Because the fuse blew out.

▮ Why did the fuse blow out? Because the fuse was the wrong size.

▮ Why was the fuse the wrong size? Because the electrician made a mistake.

▮ Why did the electrician make a mistake? Because the supply room issued the wrong fuse.

▮ Why did the supply room issue the wrong fuse? Because the stocking bin for the fuses was mislabeled.

Solution. Relabel the stocking bin with the correct fuse size. Check all the other bins to assure accuracy.

As this example points out, the root cause of the machine's going down was a mislabeled bin in the supply room. Simple as it may seem, without repeatedly asking "Why?," the root cause of the problem might never have been discovered. Since the root cause was not identified, this problem would have occurred again sometime in the future. Asking a person "Why?" five times can cause conflict and be considered antagonistic; however, this is a risk that must be taken to prevent the recurrence of a problem.

SOURCE: Mark C. DeLuzio, "The Tools of Just-In-Time," *Journal of Cost Management* (Boston: Warren Gorham Lamont, Summer 1993), pp. 19–20.

■ **EXHIBIT 18–17**

Seven Steps to Implement
JIT

1. Determine how well products, materials, or services are delivered now.
2. Determine what customers consider superior service and set priorities accordingly.
3. Establish specific priorities for distribution (and possibly purchasing) functions to meet customer needs.
4. Collaborate with and educate managers and employees to refine objectives and to prepare for implementation of JIT.
5. Execute a pilot implementation project and evaluate its results.
6. Refine the JIT delivery program and execute it companywide.
7. Monitor progress, adjust objectives over time, and always strive for excellence.

SOURCE: Gene R. Tyndall, "Just-in-Time Logistics: Added Value for Manufacturing Cost Management," *Journal of Cost Management* (Boston: Warren Gorham Lamont, Spring 1989), pp. 57–59.

vendor relationships, or in any one of a multitude of other items. Managers and employees should be continuously alert to the possibilities for lowering costs while increasing quality and service. But JIT is more than a cost-cutting endeavor or a matter of reducing personnel; it requires good human resources management.

Exhibit 18–17 provides a seven-step action plan for implementing JIT in an organization. In many respects, JIT really requires management to act with common sense.

R E V I S I T I N G

ALLEN-BRADLEY CO., INC.

Building on the success of the Milwaukee World Contactor Facility, A-B's newest automated printed circuit board center—EMS1—sets the pace for computer-integrated manufacturing for the 21st century. Before plans were put to paper, the EMS1 project team toured several "best-in-class" electronics facilities, including [among others] AT&T, Digital Equipment Corporation, Hewlett-Packard Co., and Sony. According to the project team leader, "We learned quite a bit from these companies' successes and mistakes, and built on these benchmarks to create a truly magnificent facility." How magnificent? The companies A-B visited are now benchmarking EMS1. In addition, A-B customers not in the electronics business—such as Kraft, General Motors and Boeing—are visiting the facility to see how they can apply its manufacturing techniques in their own plants.

The most important requirements [of the EMS1 facility] are: unsurpassed quality, lot sizes as small as one, high-mix capabilities, one-day throughput, fast setup time, just-in-time stockless production and total computer-integrated manufacturing.

A-B's Manufacturing Resource Planning system receives an order and schedules the appropriate boards for production. Building based on a "rolling" forecast of future sales eliminates costly work-in-process inventory storage.

Depending on the end product's features and design, its printed circuit boards use between one and five different assembly processes. A conveyor system carries boards through each operation or, if an operation isn't needed, bypasses it using an overhead loop. Panels automatically are routed to the required process without manual intervention. At any time, as many as six different types of panels may be flowing through the center.

Latest production figures show a one-day circuit board throughput [and] output figures continue to grow. So far, product introduction time has been trimmed from

■ EXHIBIT 18–18

Casey-Glover Delayed Shipment and Impact on Production

	ORDER POINT DAY 1	DAY 2	DAY 3	DAY 4	DAY 5	DAY 6
Inventory	2,400					
Usage	(600)					
Inventory		1,800				
Usage		(600)				
Inventory			1,200			
Usage			(600)			
Inventory				600		
Usage				(600)		
Inventory					0	
Usage					**No production possible**	
Inventory arrives						7,500

units. Even with a safety stock of 400 units, the one-day shipping delay will cause Casey-Glover to stop production, as illustrated in Exhibit 18–18. The amounts shown on the lines labeled "Inventory" are as of 8:00 A.M. Thus, on Day 1, the purchasing agent for C-G orders 7,500 chips since the reorder point of 2,400 units has been reached. If the order had been received in the normal lead time, it would have arrived at 8:00 A.M. on Day 5. The fact that the order was delayed one day means that Casey-Glover has no chips on hand for Day 5 and, therefore, production is stopped.

Instead of estimating that only one factor can be out of the ordinary, the cost accountant can approximate the safety stock needed by using probabilities and weighing the cost of carrying safety stock against the cost of having a stockout. The cost of carrying safety stock is equal to the cost of carrying other units of inventory. This cost was estimated in computing economic order quantity. The cost of having a stockout is based on the concerns expressed earlier in the chapter—lost profits, lost customer goodwill, and production adjustments. As the safety stock increases, the probability of a stockout decreases. Stockout probability estimates can be based on historical data for usage and lead time. Such probabilities are related to each purchase order and it is possible to have a stockout before every order arrives.

Assume that Casey-Glover has estimated its stockout cost for computer chips to be $200 and the cost of carrying one chip in stock for one year is $1.00. The largest portion of the cost associated with carrying chips in stock is the opportunity cost of having funds invested in inventory rather than being used for another purpose. Computation of C-G's optimal safety stock of 400 to 800 units is shown in Exhibit 18–19.

Mathematical determination of economic order quantity and optimal quantity of safety stock helps a company control its investment in inventory. However, such models are only as valid as the estimates used in the formula. For example, projections of costs such as lost customer goodwill may be extremely difficult. In some cases, the degree of inaccuracy may not be important; in other cases, it may be critical.[16]

---

[16] Sensitivity analysis can indicate which estimates have the most significant impact on proper inventory planning. Sensitivity analysis is a means of determining the effect that a change in an independent variable will have on a dependent variable. One application of sensitivity analysis in relation to safety stock is the evaluation of the effects that a change in the rate of return expected on investments would have on the opportunity cost of carrying inventory and thus on the optimal size of inventory orders and safety stock.

Cost of stockout = $200 per occurrence
Cost of carrying safety stock = $1.00 per unit per year
Number of orders per year = 20

Size of Safety Stock	Probability of Stockout
50 units	65%
100 units	50%
200 units	30%
400 units	20%
800 units	10%
1,200 units	5%

COST OF CARRYING SAFETY STOCK

# of Units	×	Cost of Carrying	=	Total Cost
50		$1.00		$ 50
100		1.00		100
200		1.00		200
400		1.00		400
800		1.00		800
1,200		1.00		1,200

COST OF NOT CARRYING SAFETY STOCK

# of Units	Probability of Stockout	×	# of Purchase Orders per Year	=	Weighted Probability of Stockout	×	Cost of Stockout	=	Total Cost
50	65%		20		13		$200		$2,600
100	50%		20		10		200		2,000
200	30%		20		6		200		1,200
400	20%		20		4		200		800
800	10%		20		2		200		400
1,200	5%		20		1		200		200

Optimal safety stock will minimize the cost of carrying and not carrying safety stock units:

# of Units	Total Cost of Carrying	+	Total Cost of Not Carrying	=	Summation
50	$ 50		$2,600		$2,650
100	100		2,000		2,100
200	200		1,200		1,400
400	400		800		1,200*
800	800		400		1,200*
1,200	1,200		200		1,400

* Low point in summation of costs indicates an optimal safety stock in the range of 400 to 800 units.

the quantity of direct material to 100.4 yards per roll. The Accounting Department requires that the annual standard be continued for costing the In Process Inventory for the remainder of 1994. The effects of the engineering changes should be shown in two accounts: Materials Usage Engineering Change Variance and Machine Hours Engineering Change Variance.

5. Total production for the remainder of 1994 was 103,200 rolls of wire. Total conversion costs for the remaining 10 months of 1994 were $14,442,000. Of this amount, $4,000,000 was depreciation, $9,325,000 was paid in cash, and $1,117,000 was on account.

6. The standard amount of conversion cost is applied to the In Process Inventory for the remainder of the year.

(*Note:* Some of the journal entries for the following items are not explicitly covered in the chapter. This problem challenges students in the accounting effects of the implementation of a JIT system.)

a. Prepare entries for items 1, 2, 3, 5, and 6 above.

b. Determine the increase in materials cost due to the engineering change related to direct materials.

c. Prepare a journal entry to adjust Raw and In Process account for the engineering change cost found in part b.

d. Determine the reduction in conversion cost due to the engineering change related to machine time.

e. Prepare a journal entry to reclassify the actual conversion costs by the savings found in part d above.

f. Making the entry in part e raises conversion costs to what they would have been if the engineering change related to machine time had not been made. Are conversion costs under- or overapplied and by what amount?

g. Assume the reduction in machine time could not have been made without the corresponding increase in materials usage. Is the net effect of these engineering changes cost beneficial? Why?

49. *(Appendix)* Jenny Grant operates a health-food bakery that uses specially ground flour in its products. The bakery operates 360 days a year. Jenny finds that she seems to order either too much or too little flour and asks for your help. After some discussion you find she does not have any idea of when or how much to order. An examination of her records and Jenny's answers to further questions reveal the following information:

Annual usage of flour	14,000 pounds
Average number of days delay between initiating and receiving an order	12
Estimated cost per order	$ 8.00
Estimated annual cost of carrying a pound of flour in inventory	$ .25
Estimated cost of a stockout	$150.00

Pounds of flour in safety stock	Probability of stockout
33	70%
66	55%
99	40%
132	20%
165	10%
198	1%
231	.1%
264	.05%

a. Calculate the economic order quantity for flour.

b. Calculate the optimal safety stock (in pounds) for flour.

c. Calculate the appropriate order point.

50. *(Appendix)* Thurston Computer Systems acquires its CRTs from an external supplier to make microcomputers. Management is wondering what its safety stock should be and supplies the following information:

Cost of a stockout = $250 per occurrence
Cost of carrying safety stock = $16 per unit annually
Number of orders per year = 24

The following probabilities are associated with various safety stock sizes:

Size of safety stock	Probability of stockout
50 units	60%
100 units	35%
150 units	20%
200 units	10%
250 units	2%

   a. Calculate the cost of carrying the various safety stock sizes.
   b. Calculate the cost of not carrying the various safety stock sizes.
   c. Present the combined costs from parts a and b above and identify the size of safety stock that results in the lowest combined cost.

CASES

51. Chemcon Corp. sells various industrial supplies used for general-purpose cleaning. Approximately 85% of its sales are to not-for-profit and governmental institutions. These sales are on a contract basis with an average contract length of two years. Al Stanly, Chemcon's treasurer, wants to initiate a system that will maximize the amount of time Chemcon holds its cash in the form of marketable securities. Chemcon currently has $9 million of securities that have an expected annual earnings rate of 8%. Chemcon is expecting a cash drain over the next 12-month period. Monthly cash outflows are expected to be $2,650,000, but inflows are only expected to be $2,500,000. The cost of either buying or selling securities is $125 per transaction. Stanly has heard that the EOQ inventory model can be applied to cash management. Therefore, he has decided to employ this model to determine the optimal value of marketable securities to be sold to replenish Chemcon's cash balance.
   a. Use the EOQ model in the chapter to
      1. explain the costs Alan Stanly is attempting to balance in this situation.
      2. calculate the optimal dollar amount of marketable securities Stanly should sell when Chemcon needs to replenish its cash balance.
   b. Without prejudice to your solution in part a2, assume that the optimal dollar amount of marketable securities to be sold is $60,000.
      1. Calculate the average cash balance in Chemcon Corp.'s checking account that will be on hand during the course of the year.
      2. Determine the number of times during the year that Stanly will have to sell securities.
   c. Describe two different economic circumstances applicable to Chemcon Corp. that would render its use of the EOQ inventory model inappropriate as a cash management model.
   (CMA adapted)

52. The Smith Company manufactures various electronic assemblies that it sells primarily to computer manufacturers. Smith's reputation has been built on quality, timely delivery, and products that are consistently on the cutting edge of technology. Smith's business is fast-paced. The typical product has a short life; the product is in development for about a year and in the growth stage, with sometimes spectacular growth, for about a year. Each product then experiences a rapid decline in sales as new products become available.

Smith's competitive strategy requires a reliable stream of new products to be developed each year. This is the only way that the company can overcome the threat of product obsolescence. Although the products go through the first half of the product life cycle like products in other industries, they don't go through the second half of the product life cycle in a similar manner. Smith's products never reach the mature product or declining product stage. Toward the end of the growth stage, products just die as new ones are introduced.

a. In the competitive market facing Smith Company, what would be key considerations in production and inventory control?

b. How would the threat of immediate product obsolescence affect Smith's practices in purchasing product components and materials?

c. How would the threat of product obsolescence affect the EPR for a typical product produced by Smith Company?

(CMA adapted)

ETHICS AND QUALITY DISCUSSION

53. For nearly a decade since its forced divestiture, AT&T has been fighting to maintain market share and profitability in the telecommunications industry. In some cases, the quality of services offered by AT&T appears to be falling. Consider, for example, these facts.

- The company's market share of the corporate long distance market is estimated to have fallen from 80% in 1989 to 55% in 1993.

- AT&T's long distance network, after operating reliably for many decades, has failed four times in the past few years. One outage closed down air traffic control on the east coast and interrupted transaction processing on Wall Street. Three of the four failures were blamed on worker and management carelessness.

Some attribute AT&T's failures to its efforts to down-size and become more efficient and more profitable. Critics claim the down-sizing is affecting not only the firm's costs but the quality of its services. As a result of the cost cutting, the company has been slow in responding to customer service needs and has resorted to the use of independent contractors in some customer servicing roles.

[SOURCE: Adapted from John J. Keller, "Some AT&T Clients Gripe That Cost Cuts Are Hurting Service," *Wall Street Journal* (January 24, 1992), pp. A1, A4. Reprinted by permission of the *Wall Street Journal*, © 1992 Dow Jones & Company, Inc. All rights reserved worldwide.]

a. How would production control (or service control) at AT&T differ from production control in a typical factory?

b. In trying to improve the efficiency of its operations, is it possible that AT&T has lowered the quality of its operations? Explain.

c. Could the down-sizing and cost-cutting at AT&T create an endless downward spiral? Explain.

d. How could AT&T adopt a JIT service approach to improve its response time and the quality of its efforts in servicing its customers.

54. You are the owner of Wetzel Co., which provides a significant product component to the Guy Firm. The manager at Guy has asked you for a discount on the components you are providing. Since becoming a major supplier for Guy, your firm has spent $26,000,000 in plant layout changes, quality improvements, and equipment purchases in order to be able to provide the type of product and the delivery schedule requested by Guy. The only way in which you could provide the price break is to lower your quality control standards. The lowered quality control standards would save the company approximately $7,000,000 annually for the next 3 years.

a. Discuss your response to Guy Firm.

b. Is it ethical to make a product at lower than the best possible quality that you have already achieved? Why or why not?

DECISION MAKING

19 BASICS OF CAPITAL BUDGETING

LEARNING OBJECTIVES

After completing this chapter, you should be able to answer these questions:

1. Why do most capital budgeting methods focus on cash flows?
2. What is measured by the payback period?
3. How are the net present value and profitability index of a project measured?
4. Why would the internal rate of return be computed on a project?
5. What are the underlying assumptions and limitations of each capital project evaluation method?
6. Why may decisions to automate be more difficult to evaluate than other capital projects?
7. How and why should management conduct a postinvestment audit of a capital project?
8. *(Appendix 1)* How are present values calculated?
9. *(Appendix 2)* What are the advantages and disadvantages of the accounting rate of return?

INTRODUCING

SETON MEDICAL FACILITIES

In Austin, Texas, the Daughters of Charity Health Services operate three medical facilities in the area: Seton Medical Center, Seton East Community Health Center, and Seton Northwest Hospital. During the past decade, Seton has become the leading health care provider in the Austin area, delivering the most services to the largest number of people and, additionally, has been recognized as the image and quality pacesetter, according to patient comments and surveys.

Seton Medical Center has plans for a near $100 million facilities renovation and construction program that will begin in early 1993, with completion expected in late 1995. About 350,000 square feet of the existing hospital will be renovated and an additional 120,000 square feet will be added to the existing facility. This is the third addition to the Medical Center since it opened in 1975; the first was in 1975 and the second in 1983.

Some of the major changes include the following:

▌ Expansion of the Neonatal Intensive Care Unit;

▌ Expansion to house five new operating rooms and 18 new recovery rooms; and

▌ Creation of Outpatient Clinic Area that will include an eye lab/eye bank with laser treatment and Magnetic Resonance Imaging (MRI) services.

All of these changes were made in spite of the fact that, during the 1991 fiscal year, Seton provided more than $50 million in medical care and other health benefits for which payment was not received—or $970,000+ per week.

SOURCE: Seton *1991 Annual Report; Seton Medical Center Announces Major Reorientation* brochure (June 1992).

The renovation/expansion decision made by the management committee of Seton Medical Center is just one type of asset investment decision that is continuously made by managers. Choosing the assets in which an organization will invest is one of the most important business decisions. In almost every organization, investments must be made in some short-term working capital assets, such as merchandise inventory, supplies, or raw materials. But organizations must also invest in **capital assets** that are used to generate revenues or cost savings by providing distribution, service, or production capabilities for more than one year. A capital asset may be a tangible fixed asset (such as a piece of machinery or a building) or an intangible asset (such as a capital lease or a patent).

Capital asset

This chapter presents four analytical techniques for making capital asset investment decisions: payback period, net present value, profitability index, and internal rate of return. (The accounting rate of return is discussed in Appendix 2 of the chapter.) The complexities of acquiring automated equipment and the need for postinvestment audits are also covered.

Decisions to acquire long-term assets involve large commitments of capital. Managers typically find that the availability of projects that meet investment criteria exceeds the availability of resources. Making the most economically beneficial investments within resource constraints is critical to the organization's long-range financial and strategic well-being. The techniques discussed in this chapter are designed to enhance management's success in making decisions about significant long-term capital investments by minimizing the risks involved in the process.

Capital budgeting

Financial managers, assisted by cost accountants, are responsible for the **capital budgeting** process. Capital budgeting is "a process for evaluating proposed long-range projects or courses of future activity for an economic entity for the purpose of allocating limited resources to desirable projects."[1] The process includes planning for and preparing the capital budget as well as reviewing past investments to assess and enhance the effectiveness of the process. The capital budget presents planned annual expenditures for capital projects for the near term (tomorrow to five years from now) and summary information for the long term (six to ten years). As was shown in Chapter 16, capital expenditures shown for the next fiscal period are included in the capital budget of a firm's annual master budget.

Project

Capital budgeting involves comparing and evaluating alternative **projects** within a budgetary framework. A common type of project is the purchase, installation, and operation of a capital asset. Managers generally have a choice among several capital assets that can perform the same function. A manager's job is to select the best possible investment choices from the alternative projects and assets.

USE OF CASH FLOWS IN CAPITAL BUDGETING

Capital budgeting investment decisions can be made using a variety of techniques including payback period, net present value, profitability index, internal rate of return, and accounting rate of return. All but the last of these methods focus on the amounts and timing of **cash flows** (receipts or disbursements of cash). Cash receipts include the revenues from a capital project that have been earned and collected, savings generated by the project's reductions in existing operating costs, and any cash inflow from selling the asset at the end of its useful life. Cash disbursements include asset acquisition expenditures, additional working capital investments, and costs for project-related direct materials, direct labor, and overhead.

Cash flow

Any investment made by an organization is expected to earn some type of return in the form of interest, cash dividends, or operating income. Since interest and dividends are in the form of cash, accrual-based operating income must be converted to a cash basis for comparison purposes. Remember that accrual accounting records revenues when earned, not when cash is received, and records expenses when incurred regardless of whether a liability is created or cash is paid. Converting accounting income to cash flow information puts all investment returns on an equivalent basis.

Financing decision

Investment decision

Interest is a cash flow associated with debt financing choice and is not part of the project selection process. The funding of projects is a financing, not an investment, decision. A **financing decision** is a judgment regarding the method of raising capital to fund an acquisition. Financing is based on the entity's ability to issue and service debt and equity securities. On the other hand, an **investment decision** is a judgment about which assets to acquire to achieve an entity's stated objectives. Cash flows generated by the two types of decisions should not be combined. Company management must justify the acquisition and use of an asset *prior* to justifying the method of financing that asset.

---

[1] Institute of Management Accountants (formerly National Association of Accountants), *Statement on Management Accounting: Management Accounting Terminology*, Number 2 (Montvale, N.J.: NAA, June 1, 1983), p. 14.

Including receipts and disbursements, caused by financing, with other project cash flows conceals a project's true profitability because financing costs relate to the total entity. The assignment of financing costs to a specific project is often arbitrary and causes an inconsistency when projects that may be acquired from different financing sources are compared. In addition, including financing effects in an investment decision creates a problem in assigning responsibility. Investment decisions are typically made by divisional managers, or by top management after receiving input from divisional managers. Financing decisions are typically made by an organization's treasurer in conjunction with top management.

The cash flows used in this chapter to illustrate the various capital project evaluation methods are on a before-tax basis. Although a few organizations (such as Seton Medical Center) do not pay income taxes, most organizations must deal with the tax effects of proposed investments. If taxes are considered, depreciation is relevant to decision making because it is deductible for tax purposes and thus affects the amount of cash needed to pay taxes. However, depreciation expense is not a cash expenditure of the company. Further discussion of this topic is deferred until Chapter 20.

Cash flows from a capital project are received and paid at different times over the project's life. Some cash flows occur at the beginning of a period, some at the end, and some during the period. To simplify capital budgeting analysis, most analysts assume that all cash flows occur at a specific, single point in time—either at the beginning or end of the time period in which they actually occur. The following example illustrates how cash flows are treated in capital budgeting situations.

CASH FLOWS ILLUSTRATED

Assume that a variety of capital projects are being considered by Lima General Hospital, a small, not-for-profit regional care facility. Like Seton Medical and other hospitals worldwide, Lima General must consider capital investments in a variety of new technology equipment, such as the items discussed in the News Note "Machines Get Better, But More Expensive."

One acquisition being considered by the hospital is a new machine to develop X-rays. Basic *estimated* data about the asset and its acquisition appear in Exhibit

---

NEWS NOTE **Machines Get Better, But More Expensive**

Technology creep is as persistent as staph infections, and adds to [health care] expenses, not necessarily productivity. New instruments supplement rather than replace old ones and breed attendants and interpreters by the thousands. A new MRI costs about $2 million installed. A $200,000-a-year radiologist divines what the pictures mean. So hospitals charge up to $1,000 for an MRI scan. And while it takes crisp pictures of brains, spinal cords, and joints, the MRI is fuzzy on chests and abdomens, so it hasn't displaced the $1 million CAT (computerized axial tomography) scanner.

The latest in viewers is the PET (positron emission tomography) which can watch chemical changes take place within the body—helpful in identifying Parkinson's disease, for one. Because it requires its own cyclotron to produce a radioactive gas that the patient inhales (or a liquid injected into his vein), a PET rig takes a $5 million bite out of any hospital's budget.

SOURCE: Lee Smith, "A Cure for What Ails Medical Care," *FORTUNE* (July 1, 1991), p. 45. © 1991 Time Inc. All rights reserved.

Purchase price of new X-ray developer: $63,000 (terms 5% discount if paid by end of month)
Installation costs: $2,150
Sales price of old X-ray developer: $2,000
Life of new X-ray developer: 5 years
Salvage value at end of fifth year: $1,000
Maintenance required: $5,000 at the end of the 3rd year

Fee charged per X-ray developed: $18.00 (all collected in cash)
Expected number of x-rays to be developed each year: 3,600
Cash production cost per X-ray developed:

Direct materials	$ 4.80
Direct labor	5.20
Cash overhead (excludes depreciation)	3.00
Total cash cost	$13.00

Cash contribution margin per X-ray ($18 − $13): $5.00

CASH OUTFLOWS:

Cost of machine (now):

Purchase price of new developer	$63,000
Less discount (5%)	(3,150)
Cash cost of new developer	$59,850
Installation costs	2,150
Total cash cost of new developer	$62,000
Less sales price of old developer	(2,000)
Net cash outflow for new developer	$60,000

Cost of maintenance (end of 3rd year): $5,000

CASH INFLOWS:

Cash contribution margin per year: $18,000 (3,600 × $5.00)
Salvage value (end of 5th year): $1,000

19–1. First, the project cost is an estimate. Project cost includes purchase price, installation, and additional investments in working capital items such as inventory. While purchase price may be a known value, installation costs and working capital investments must be estimated. The amounts and timing of future cash flows are also estimated. Some future cash flows are obvious; others may not be. (For instance, companies installing computer systems find that the most expensive costs—supplies, support, training, maintenance, and opportunity costs—are not readily apparent. Some companies have estimated that the full cost of computer installations runs three to four times the cost of the hardware and software.)

This detailed information can be simplified to a net cash flow for each year: a net negative flow in the first year representing the initial expenditure for the acquisition, and a net positive flow for each of the remaining years of asset life representing the contribution margin earned each year less the maintenance cost in year three and plus the salvage value in year five. This net cash flow information for Lima General's machine acquisition can be illustrated through the use of a timeline.

Timeline

A **timeline** visually illustrates the points in time when cash flows are expected to be received or paid, making it a helpful tool for analyzing cash flows of a capital investment proposal. Cash inflows are shown as positive amounts on a timeline and cash outflows are shown as negative amounts.

The following timeline represents the cash flows from Lima General's potential purchase of the new X-ray developer. Although each individual cash flow can be shown on a timeline, it is much easier to use net cash flows. Thus, only two types of cash flows are shown below: the net negative flow for the acquisition and the net positive flow each year from product sales.

Time Point:	t0	t1	t2	t3	t4	t5
Cash Inflows:		+$18,000	+$18,000	+$18,000	+$18,000	+$18,000 + 1,000
Cash Outflows:	−$60,000			− 5,000		
Net Cash Flows:	−$60,000	+$18,000	+$18,000	+$13,000	+$18,000	+$19,000

On a timeline, the date of acquisition represents time point 0 because no time has passed from the point of acquisition. Each year after acquisition is represented as a full time period, and periods only serve to separate the timing of cash flows. Nothing is presumed to happen *during* a period. Thus, for example, cash flows each year from fees charged are shown as occurring at the end of, rather than during, the time period. A less conservative assumption would show the cash flows occurring at the beginning of the period.

PAYBACK PERIOD

The information on timing of net cash flows is an input to a simple and often-used capital budgeting technique called **payback period**. This method provides a measure of the time it will take a project's cash inflows to equal the original investment. At the end of the payback period, a company has recouped its investment.

Payback period

In one sense, payback period measures a dimension of project risk by focusing on timing of cash flows. The assumption is that the longer it takes to recover the initial investment, the greater is the project's risk because cash flows in the more distant future are more uncertain than current or relatively current cash flows. Another reason for concern about long payback periods relates to capital reinvestment. The faster capital is returned from an investment, the more rapidly it can be invested in other projects.

When the cash flows from a project are equal each period (an **annuity**), the payback period is determined as follows:

Annuity

$$\text{Payback period} = \frac{\text{Investment}}{\text{Annuity}}$$

Assume for a moment that the X-ray developer being considered by Lima General had no maintenance cost in the third year and no salvage value in the fifth year. The cash inflows from the project would have been an equal annuity of $18,000 each year ($5 contribution margin multiplied by 3,600 X-rays per year). In this case, the payback period would be equal to the $60,000 net investment cost divided by $18,000 or 3 1/3 years, or three years and four months.

The payback period for a project having unequal cash inflows is determined by accumulating cash flows until the original investment is recovered. Thus, using the actual information shown in Exhibit 19–1 and the timeline above, the X-ray devel-

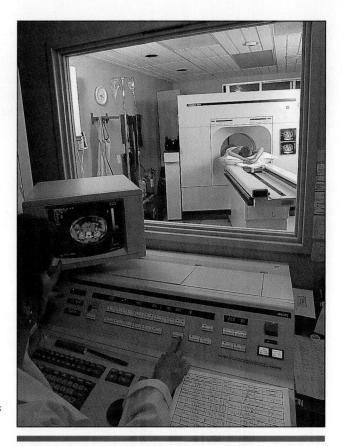

Computerized Axial Tomography (CAT) scan equipment requires a significant capital investment by a hospital. But its ability to provide extremely detailed pictures of body organs is invaluable in today's medical practice, regardless of the length of the payback period.

oper project's payback period must be calculated using a yearly cumulative total of inflows as follows:

Year	Amount	Cumulative Total
1	$18,000	$18,000
2	18,000	36,000
3	13,000	49,000
4	18,000	67,000
5	19,000	86,000

Since $49,000 will be received by the end of the third year, $11,000 more is needed to recover the original $60,000 investment. The $18,000 inflow in the fourth year is assumed to occur evenly throughout the year. Therefore, it should take approximately 61 percent ($11,000 ÷ $18,000) of the fourth year to cover the rest of the original investment, giving a payback period for this project of 3.61 years (or slightly more than three years and seven months).

Company management typically sets a maximum acceptable payback period as one of the evaluation techniques for capital projects. If Lima General has set five years as the longest acceptable payback period, this project would be acceptable under that criterion. Most companies, though, use payback period as only one way of judging an investment project. After being found acceptable in terms of payback period, a project is subjected to evaluation by another capital budgeting technique. This secondary evaluation is performed because the payback period method ignores three things: inflows occurring after the payback period has been reached; the company's desired rate of return; and the time value of money. These issues are incorporated into the decision process by using discounted future cash flow values.

Money has a time value associated with it; this value is created because interest is paid or received on money.[2] For example, the receipt of $1,000 today has greater value than the same sum received one year from today because that money be invested at an interest rate that will cause it to accumulate to more than $1,000 in one year. This fact encourages the use of discounted cash flow techniques in most capital budgeting situations.

Discounting future cash flows means reducing them to present value amounts by removing the portion representing interest, that could have been earned from the investment amount. This "imputed" amount of interest is based on two considerations: the time delay until the cash flow is received or paid and the rate of interest assumed. After discounting, all future values associated with a project are stated in a common base of current dollars, also known as their **present values**. Cash receipts and disbursements occurring at the beginning of a project are already stated in terms of their present values and do not need to be discounted.

As mentioned earlier, information on capital projects involves the use of estimates. It is extremely important to have the best possible estimates of current expenditures (such as initial project investment), since the full impact of these undiscounted dollars is used in the project evaluation process. Care should also be taken to include all potential future costs. To appropriately discount the cash flows, managers must estimate the rate of return on capital required by the company in addition to the project's cost and cash flow estimates. This rate of return is called the **discount rate** and it is used to determine the imputed interest portion of future cash receipts and expenditures. The discount rate should equal or exceed the company's **cost of capital** (COC), which is the weighted average rate for the costs of the various sources of funds (debt and stock) that comprise a firm's equity structure.[3] For example, if a company has a COC of 10 percent, it costs an average of 10 percent of each capital dollar to annually finance investment projects. To determine if a capital project is a worthwhile investment, this company should generally use a *minimum* rate of 10 percent to discount the project's future cash flows.

The rate of return for government securities (such as Treasury bills) can be seen as basically riskless. Thus, if a company were analyzing an investment with almost no risk, did not have to borrow funds to make the investment, and had no alternative investment possibilities, the T-bill rate could be used as the minimum rate of return rather than the cost of capital. However, as project risk increases and there is a need to borrow funds to make the investment, the minimum acceptable rate of return should also rise.

Some managers believe that the discount rate used for these higher-risk capital budgeting decisions should reflect the **opportunity cost of capital**. This COC rate is the highest rate of return that *could* be earned from the most attractive, alternative capital project available. Using the opportunity COC to discount project cash flows reflects the benefits that could have been realized from the foregone opportunity. Although use of the opportunity cost of capital has theoretical merit, its application would require that management calculate a rate of return on *all* available alternative projects. Since such a calculation generally is not feasible, most companies use the overall cost of capital as the discount rate.

A distinction must be made between cash flows representing a return *of* capital and those representing a return *on* capital. A **return of capital** simply means recovery of the original investment or the return of principal, while a **return on capital** repre-

DISCOUNTING FUTURE CASH FLOW VALUES

Discounting

Present value

Discount rate

Cost of capital

Opportunity cost of capital

Return of capital
Return on capital

---

[2] The time value of money and present value computations are covered in Appendix 1 of this chapter. These concepts are essential to understanding the rest of this chapter; be certain they are clear before continuing.
[3] All examples in this chapter use an *assumed* discount rate or cost of capital. Chapter 20 presents some basic computations used to find a cost of capital rate. More detailed computations are given in any principles of finance text.

sents income and equals the discount rate multiplied by the investment amount. The return on capital is computed for each period of the investment life. For a company to be better off by making an investment, a project must produce cash inflows that exceed the investment made. To determine if a project meets a company's desired rate of return, one of several discounted cash flow methods can be used.

DISCOUNTED CASH FLOW METHODS

Three basic discounted cash flow techniques are the net present value method, the profitability index, and the internal rate of return. Each of these methods is defined and illustrated in the following subsections.

Net Present Value Method

Net present value method

Net present value

The **net present value method** determines whether the rate of return on a project is equal to, higher than, or lower than the desired rate of return. Each cash flow from the project is discounted to its present value using the rate specified by the company as the desired rate of return. The total present value of all cash outflows of an investment project subtracted from the total present value of all cash inflows yields the **net present value** (NPV) of the project. Exhibit 19–2 presents net present value calculations, assuming the use of a 10 percent discount rate, for Lima General's prospective investment in the X-ray developer discussed in Exhibit 19–1.

The factors used to compute the net present value are obtained from the present value tables provided in Appendix A at the end of the text. Each lump-sum cash flow uses a factor from Table 1 (PV of $1) for 10 percent and the appropriate number of years designated for the cash flow. For example, maintenance cost shows a three-period factor; a five-period factor is used for salvage value. Contribution margin is a five-year annuity cash flow and Table 2 is used to obtain the necessary factor using 10 percent for five periods.

The net present value of this X-ray developer is a positive $5,098. The NPV represents the net cash benefit or net cash cost to a company acquiring and using the proposed asset. *If the NPV is zero, the actual rate of return on the project is equal to the desired rate of return. If the NPV is positive, the actual rate is greater than the desired rate. If the NPV is negative, the actual rate is less than the desired rate of return. Note that the exact rate of return is not indicated under the NPV method, but its relationship to the desired rate can be determined.* If all estimates about the investment are correct, the X-ray developer being considered by Lima General will provide a rate of return greater than 10 percent.

EXHIBIT 19–2

Lima General's Net Present Value Calculation for X-Ray Developer

NET PRESENT VALUE

Cost (present): − $60,000 × 1.0000	−$60,000	
Contribution margin (each year for 5 years):		
+$18,000 × 3.7908	+ 68,234	(factor from Table 2)
Repairs (at end of year 3): − $5,000 × .7513	− 3757	(factor from Table 1)
Salvage (at end of year 5): +$1,000 × .6209	+ 621	(factor from Table 1)
Net present value	+$ 5,098	

Using a 20% discount rate and factors from Tables 1 and 2 in Appendix A

NET PRESENT VALUE

Cost: −$60,000 × 1.0000	−$60,000
Contribution margin: +$18,000 × 2.9906 [20%; 5 years]	+ 53,831
Repairs: −$5,000 × .5787 [20%; year 3]	− 2,894
Salvage: +$1,000 × .4019 [20%; year 5]	+ 402
Net present value	−$ 8,661

For various other discount rates:

DISCOUNT RATE	NET PRESENT VALUE
2%	+$21,037
5%	+$14,396
8%	+$ 8,580
12%	+$ 1,894
18%	−$ 6,316

Had Lima General Hospital chosen any rate other than 10 percent and used that rate in conjunction with the same basic facts, a different net present value would have resulted. For example, if Lima General set 20 percent as the discount rate, a negative $8,661 NPV would have resulted for the project (see Exhibit 19–3). Net present values at other selected discount rates are also given in this exhibit. The computations for these values are made in a manner similar to those at 10 percent and 20 percent. (To indicate your understanding of the NPV method, you may want to prove these computations.)

The table in Exhibit 19–3 indicates the NPV is not a single, unique amount, but is a function of several factors. First, changing the discount rate while holding the amounts and timing of cash flows constant affects the NPV. Increasing the discount rate causes the NPV to decrease; decreasing the discount rate causes the NPV to increase. Second, changes in estimated amounts and/or timing of cash inflows and outflows also affect the net present value of a project. Effects of cash flow changes on the NPV depend on the nature of the changes themselves. For example, decreasing the estimate of cash outflows causes the NPV to increase; reducing the stream of cash inflows causes the NPV to decrease. When amounts and timing of cash flows change in conjunction with one another, the effects of the changes are determinable only with calculation. And, as indicated in the News Note on page 810, NPV analysis is also rendered more difficult when managers consider the concept of a "moving baseline."

Lima General can use a table such as the one in Exhibit 19–3 to compare various alternative investments. Assume that the hospital could invest $60,000 in another project. If this project earned exactly 20 percent, it would have an NPV of $0 at a discount rate of 20 percent. At a 20 percent rate, the X-ray developer has a negative NPV of $8,661. Comparing these two projects indicates that the alternative project is worth $8,661 more to Lima General than the X-ray developer. A third $60,000 project under consideration by Lima offers a 12 percent return. The table in Exhibit 19–3 indicates the X-ray developer has an NPV of $1,894 at a 12 percent discount rate and, thus, has $1,894 more present value than the third project.

A more complex example of net present value computations is found in another decision under consideration by Lima General. Assume that Lima's board of directors

HELICOPTER ALTERNATIVE #1:
Cost of helicopter: $4,000,000
Salvage value: $80,000 at end of 6 years
Annual operating cost: $500,000
20,000-hour flight-time maintenance: $8,000 at end of years 2, 4, and 6

HELICOPTER ALTERNATIVE #2:
Cost of helicopter: $3,550,000
Salvage value: $210,000 at end of 6 years
Annual operating cost: $675,000
20,000-hour flight-time maintenance: $20,000 at end of years 2 through 6

The helicopter is estimated to fly 700 flights per year. The average fee per flight is $2,200.

The following are timelines for each alternative (in thousands of dollars):

ALTERNATIVE #1*

Time Point	t0	t1	t2	t3	t4	t5	t6
Fees charged		+$1,540	+$1,540	+$1,540	+$1,540	+$1,540	+$1,540
Operating costs		− 500	− 500	− 500	− 500	− 500	− 500
Cost	− $4,000						
Maintenance			− 8		− 8		− 8
Salvage							+ 80

ALTERNATIVE #2*

Time Point	t0	t1	t2	t3	t4	t5	t6
Fees charged		+$1,540	+$1,540	+$1,540	+$1,540	+$1,540	+$1,540
Operating costs		− 675	− 675	− 675	− 675	− 675	− 675
Cost	− $3,550						
Maintenance			− 20	− 20	− 20	− 20	− 20
Salvage							+ 210

* Annuity amounts are listed first and non-annuity amounts are listed next.

▌ EXHIBIT 19–4

Lima General's Helicopter Acquisition

is trying to decide what type of helicopter to purchase for emergency medical services. Exhibit 19–4 provides necessary information to make the NPV computation for these alternative acquisition decisions. (Although revenues do not differ between the two alternatives, they are included in the exhibit to show that the project is cost-beneficial. If revenues were not included, the negative result of the net present value computations would make the project appear to be unacceptable.)

Lima General has determined that a discount rate of 12 percent is appropriate for this project because the risks associated with it are higher than those associated with the X-ray developer (evaluated in Exhibit 19–2 using a 10 percent discount rate). For example, there is higher potential legal liability related to helicopter usage; helicopter maintenance costs are subject to greater variation; and salvage value is less reliable because there is a limited resale market for this type of equipment. The difference in maintenance costs is related to the agreements with the sellers—not with the quantity, quality, or timing of the maintenance performed.

Because the purchase price, mileage maintenance, and salvage values are all lump-sum amounts, the present value factors are obtained from Table 1 in Appendix A, using a 12 percent rate and the appropriate number of periods. Revenues and annual operating costs are annuities and their present value factors are obtained from Table 2 in Appendix A. The NPV calculation is shown in Exhibit 19–5 and indicates that

Discount rate: 12%

ALTERNATIVE #1
Annuity cash flows for Years 1–6
    For fees (+$1,540,000 × 4.1114) (Table 2)   +$6,331,556
    For operating costs (−$500,000 × 4.1114) (Table 2)   (2,055,700)
Salvage value ($80,000 × .5066) (Table 1)   +   40,528
Purchase price ($4,000,000 × 1.0000)   (4,000,000)
Flight-time maintenance:
    Year 2 ($8,000 × .7972) (Table 1)   (6,378)
    Year 4 ($8,000 × .6355) (Table 1)   (5,084)
    Year 6 ($8,000 × .5066) (Table 1)   (4,053)

Net present value of Alternative #1   +$ 300,869

ALTERNATIVE #2
Annuity cash flows for Years 1–6
    For fees (+$1,540,000 × 4.1114) (Table 2)   +$6,331,556
    For operating costs (−$675,000 × 4.1114) (Table 2)   (2,775,195)
Salvage value ($210,000 × .5066) (Table 1)   +   106,386
Purchase price ($3,550,000 × 1.0000)   (3,550,000)
Flight-time maintenance:
    Year 2 ($20,000 × .7972) (Table 1)   (15,944)
    Year 3 ($20,000 × .7118) (Table 1)   (14,236)
    Year 4 ($20,000 × .6355) (Table 1)   (12,710)
    Year 5 ($20,000 × .5674) (Table 1)   (11,348)
    Year 6 ($20,000 × .5066) (Table 1)   (10,132)

Net present value of Alternative #2   +$ 48,377

the hospital is $252,492 ($300,869 − $48,377) better off by purchasing helicopter #1 rather than helicopter #2.

Before making a final decision, Lima General's board of directors should be apprised that many of the amounts used in the NPV computation are estimates of actual cash flows. Whether the decision to purchase helicopter #1 is ultimately deemed a wise or unwise choice will be affected by how closely the actual cash flows compare to the estimated cash flows.

Assume that Lima General buys and uses helicopter #1 for six years. Actual cash flows are as estimated except that the original purchase price was $4,250,000 and the helicopter's salvage value is only $10,000 at the end of the sixth year. Had these facts been properly estimated at the time of the acquisition decision, they would have affected helicopter #1's net present value, but not helicopter #2's. Exhibit 19–6 on page 810 shows that use of these actual cash flows would have created a $15,407 net present value for the purchasing alternative. The $48,377 NPV of helicopter #2, shown in Exhibit 19–5, would have been $32,970 greater, which means that the hospital would have been better off purchasing helicopter #2 rather than helicopter #1. An after-the-fact comparison of actual project information to expected information is called a **postinvestment audit**; this topic is discussed in a later section of the chapter.

Both the purchase and rental options for the helicopter had six-year lives. Such lifespan equality is essential when comparing similar alternative investments because the funds released from a shorter-lived project could be used for another investment that would generate additional revenues and cause additional costs. If the alternative projects' lives are not equal, they are treated for computational purposes as if they

Postinvestment audit

NEWS NOTE

Make Comparisons Using Realistic Scenarios

One major fallacy with [net present value] is encountered [when] net cash returns are estimated. The commonly used present value model evaluates cash flows against present industry and firm conditions and assumes that those conditions will remain constant throughout the projected life of the asset or project. Clearly this is not the case. If new equipment is not purchased, present equipment will not continue to produce at a constant level while requiring equivalent maintenance and repair costs. If innovative projects are not initiated by the firm, competitors will initiate similar projects that will change the competitive nature of the industry.

When companies compare numbers generated by net future cash flow with existing conditions, new technology sometimes seems to cost too much for the relatively small labor and material savings the technology affords. Often these projects appear to be associated with only minor improvements in cash flow. However, if a competitor invests in the new technology, the comparison cannot be made with the status quo. Instead, the company must assume that its own cash flow will decline. Indeed, financial justification does not prevent the forecasting of a loss of market share or a decline in profit margins as a result of falling behind in competitive techology.

The moving baseline concept evaluates investment decisions by comparing the financial outcome of equipment procurement with the financial impact of not investing. Various companies have identified several methods for evaluating noninvestment decisions. In practice, the noninvestment decision in each case results in decreased net present value due to deterioration of equipment or the inability to meet quality, delivery, or cost characteristics of competitors. The decreasing returns associated with the status quo operation invariably increase the value of new investment.

SOURCE: David H. Sinason, "A Dynamic Model for Present Value Capital Expenditure Analysis," *Journal of Cost Management* (Boston: Warren Gorham Lamont, Spring 1991), pp. 41–42.

were. For example, assume the life of helicopter #2 was only three years. An appropriate comparison of the two alternatives could have been made either by using only three years of cash flows on helicopter #1 or by assuming that another (or a different) helicopter #2 would be acquired at the end of the third year for three more years. If the latter assumption is made, appropriate estimates must be made relating to cash flows that may vary from the first three-year period. (The treatment of different project lives is covered in more depth in Chapter 20.)

■ **EXHIBIT 19–6**

Lima General's Actual Cash Flow Data on Helicopter #1 Acquisition

Discount rate: 12%	
Annuity cash flows for Years 1–6	
For fees (+$1,540,000 × 4.1114) (Table 2)	+$6,331,556
For operating costs (−$500,000 × 4.1114) (Table 2)	(2,055,700)
Salvage value ($10,000 × .5066) (Table 1)	+ 5,066
Purchase price ($4,250,000 × 1.0000)	(4,250,000)
Flight-time maintenance:	
Year 2 ($8,000 × .7972) (Table 1)	(6,378)
Year 4 ($8,000 × .6355) (Table 1)	(5,084)
Year 6 ($8,000 × .5066) (Table 1)	(4,053)
Net present value of purchase alternative	+$ 15,407

The net present value method, while not providing the actual rate of return on a project, provides information on how that rate compares to the desired rate. This information allows managers to eliminate from consideration any project producing a negative NPV because it would have an unacceptable rate of return. The NPV method can also be used to select the best project when choosing among investments that can perform the same task or achieve the same objective.

The net present value method should not, however, be used to compare independent investment projects not having the same original project investment. Such a comparison favors projects having higher net present values over those with lower net present values *without regard to the capital invested* in the project. As a simple example of this fact, assume that Lima General Hospital could spend $100,000 on Machine A or $20,000 on Machine B. Machine A's and B's net present values are $2,000 and $1,000, respectively. If only NPVs were compared, the hospital would conclude that Machine A was a "better" investment because it has a larger NPV. However, Machine A provides a cash flow return of only 2 percent ($2,000 ÷ $100,000) on the investment, while Machine B provides a 5 percent ($1,000 ÷ $20,000) cash flow return on its investment. Logically, organizations should invest in projects that produce the highest return *per investment dollar*. Comparisons of projects with uneven investments can be made by using a variation of the NPV method known as the profitability index.

Profitability Index

The **profitability index** (PI) is a ratio comparing the present value of a project's net cash inflows to the present value of the project's net investment. The PI is calculated as

Profitability index

$$PI = \frac{\text{Present Value of Net Cash Flows}}{\text{Present Value of Net Investment}}$$

The present value of net cash flows equals the PV of future cash inflows minus the PV of future cash outflows. The PV of net cash inflows represents an output measure of the project's worth, while the PV of the net investment represents an input measure of the project's cost. By relating these two measures, the profitability index gauges the efficiency of the firm's use of capital by indicating the cash benefit provided by the project. The higher the index, the more efficient is the capital investment.

The following information is used to illustrate the calculation and use of a profitability index. Lima General is considering purchasing two pieces of equipment: a CAT scanner for $1,440,000 and an X-ray machine for $850,000. Hospital administrators have computed the present values of the equipment by discounting all future expected cash flows at a rate of 15 percent. Present values of the expected net cash inflows are $1,800,000 for the CAT scanner and $1,160,000 for the X-ray machine. Dividing the PV of the net cash inflows by equipment cost gives the profitability index for each machine. Subtracting asset cost from the present value of the net cash inflows provides the NPV. Results of these computations are shown below.

	PV of Inflows	PV of Net Investment	Profitability Index	NPV
CAT scanner	$1,800,000	$1,440,000	1.25	$360,000
X-ray machine	1,160,000	850,000	1.36	310,000

Although the CAT scanner's net present value is higher, the profitability index indicates that the X-ray machine is a more efficient use of hospital capital.[4] The higher PI reflects a higher rate of return on the X-ray machine than on the CAT scanner. The higher a project's PI, the more profitable that project is per investment dollar.

If a capital project investment is made to provide a return on capital, the profitability index should be equal to or greater than 1.00. Sometimes, though, firms may make investment decisions on a least-cost basis. For example, assume Lima General's board of directors had determinined that all of the furniture in the hospital waiting rooms needed to be replaced. This decision might be made on a least-cost basis because waiting room furniture provides no cash inflows. In such decisions, profitability indices of the alternatives will be less than 1.00, but the project having the highest PI (the PI closest to 1.00) is still the best (in this case, least costly) investment.

Like the net present value method, the profitability index does not indicate the project's expected rate of return. However, another discounted cash flow method, the internal rate of return, is available. The internal rate of return is the expected rate of return to be earned on an investment.

Internal Rate of Return

Internal rate of return

A project's **internal rate of return** (IRR) is the discount rate that causes the present value of the net cash inflows to equal the cost of the project. It is the project's expected rate of return. If the IRR were used to determine the present value factors in a NPV computation, the NPV would be zero.

Consider the following formula to determine net present value:

$$NPV = -\text{Investment} + \text{PV of cash inflows} - \text{PV of}$$
$$\text{cash outflows other than the investment}$$

$$NPV = -\text{Investment} + \text{Cash inflows (PV factor)} - \text{Cash outflows (PV factor)}$$

Capital project information should include the amounts of the investment, cash inflows, and cash outflows. Thus, the only missing data in the above formula are the present value factors. When these factors are calculated, they can be found in the present value tables and the columns can be read upward to find the internal rate of return.

The internal rate of return is most easily computed for projects having equal annual net cash flows. When an annuity exists, the IRR formula can be restated as follows:

$$NPV = -\text{Net Investment} + \text{PV of annuity amount}$$

$$NPV = -\text{Net Investment} + (\text{Annuity amount} \times \text{PV factor})$$

The investment and annual cash flow amounts are known from the expected data, and net present value is known to be zero at the IRR. The IRR and its present value factor are unknown. To determine the internal rate of return, substitute known

---

[4] Two conditions must exist for the profitability index to provide better information than the net present value method. First, the decision to accept one project must require that the other project be rejected. On the surface, this situation does not exist for Lima General since a CAT scanner does not perform the same functions as an X-ray machine. Buying one machine would not automatically exclude buying the other. The second condition is that availability of funds for capital acquisitions is limited. If Lima General's total capital budget were $1,500,000, purchasing the CAT scanner would preclude purchasing the X-ray machine. However, purchasing the X-ray machine would leave $650,000 in the capital budget. The hospital could invest these funds in another capital asset if other alternative projects are available. In this case, the X-ray machine and any alternative projects must be considered as various "packaged" investments to determine the incremental benefits of each package. "Packaged" capital projects are discussed in more detail in the capital rationing section of Chapter 20.

amounts into the formula, rearrange terms, and solve for the unknown (the PV factor):

$$NPV = -\text{Net Investment} + (\text{Annuity} \times \text{PV Factor})$$

$$0 = -\text{Net Investment} + (\text{Annuity} \times \text{PV Factor})$$

$$\text{Net Investment} = (\text{Annuity} \times \text{PV Factor})$$

$$\text{Net Investment} \div \text{Annuity} = \text{PV Factor}$$

The solution yields a present value factor for the number of annuity periods of project life at the internal rate of return. Looking up this factor in the PV of an annuity table and reading the rate at the top of the column in which the factor is found provides the internal rate of return.

To illustrate an IRR computation for a project with a simple annuity, the "adjusted" information about Lima General's X-ray developer is used. In this case (as was the case with the first payback period computation), the information is similar to that presented in Exhibit 19–1, *except* that the third-year maintenance cost and fifth-year salvage value have been assumed away from this illustration. Thus, the investment project would have a $60,000 net investment cost, a five-year life, and annual net cash flows of $18,000. The NPV equation is solved for the present value factor.

$$NPV = -\text{Net Investment} + (\text{Annuity} \times \text{PV Factor})$$

$$0 = -\$60,000 + (\$18,000 \times \text{PV Factor})$$

$$+\$60,000 = (\$18,000 \times \text{PV Factor})$$

$$+\$60,000 \div \$18,000 = \text{PV Factor}$$

$$3.3333 = \text{PV Factor}$$

Note that *the present value factor needed to approximate the internal rate of return is equal to the payback period for a project returning only an annuity.*

The PV of an ordinary annuity table (Table 2, Appendix A) is examined to find the internal rate of return. A present value factor is a function of time and the discount rate. In the table, find the row representing the project's life (in this case, five periods). Look across the table in that row for the PV factor found upon solving the equation. On row 5, a factor of 3.3522 appears under the column headed 15 percent and a 3.3129 factor appears under 15.5 percent. Thus, the internal rate of return for this machine is between these two rates. Using interpolation, a computer program, or a programmable calculator show the IRR for this project to be 15.24 percent.[5]

Exhibit 19–7 on page 814 plots the net present values that result from discounting these simplified X-ray developer project data at various rates of return. For example, the NPV at 12 percent is $4,886 and the NPV at 18 percent is −$3,710. (These computations are not provided here, but can be performed by discounting the $18,000 annual cash flows and subtracting $60,000 of investment cost.)

The internal rate of return is located on the graph's horizontal axis at the point where the NPV equals zero (15.24 percent). Note that the graph reflects an inverse

---

[5] Interpolation is the process of finding a term between two other terms in a series. The interpolation process using the actual PV factor and the table factors gives the following computation:

Difference between factor at 15% and factor found: $3.3522 - 3.3333 = .0189$. Difference between factor found and factor at 15.5%: $3.3333 - 3.3129 = .0393$.

$$\text{Actual rate} = 15\% + [(.0189 \div .0393)(0.5)]$$
$$= 15\% + (.4809)(0.5)$$
$$= 15.24\%$$

EXHIBIT 19–7

Graph of NPVs and Rates
of Return for Simplified
X-Ray Developer Data

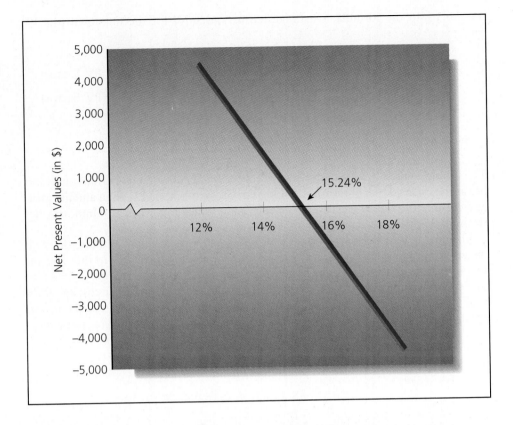

relationship between rates of returns and NPVs. Higher rates yield lower present values because, at the higher rates, fewer dollars need to be currently invested to obtain the same future value.

Manually finding the IRR of a project that produces unequal annual cash flows is more complex and requires an iterative trial and error process. An initial estimate is made of a rate believed to be close to the IRR, and the NPV is computed. If the resulting NPV is negative, a lower rate is estimated (because of the inverse relationship mentioned above) and the NPV is computed again. If the NPV is positive, a higher rate is tried. This process is continued until the net present value equals zero, at which time the internal rate of return has been found.

Exhibit 19–8 demonstrates the process of searching for the internal rate of return. This exhibit uses the actual (nonsimplified) data shown in Exhibit 19–1 for Lima General's potential X-ray developer purchase. Because a positive NPV resulted after discounting the cash flows at 10 percent, a first estimate is made that the IRR on this project is 12 percent. Exhibit 19–8 indicates that the NPV is still positive at this discount rate. A second estimate of 13.5 percent is made and this computation results in a negative NPV. A third attempt, using 13 percent, is made that produces a small positive net present value. Thus, the internal rate of return falls between 13 percent and 13.5 percent. Using interpolation, a computer program, or a programmable calculator shows the IRR for this project to be 13.3 percent.

The project's internal rate of return is then compared to management's preestablished **hurdle rate**, which is the rate of return specified as the lowest acceptable return on investment. Like the discount rate mentioned earlier, this rate should generally be at least equal to the cost of capital. In fact, the hurdle rate is commonly the discount rate used in computing net present value amounts. If a project's IRR is equal to or greater than the hurdle rate, the project is considered a viable investment. As indicated in the following passage, hurdle rates are no longer simply an American concept.

Hurdle rate

Basic cash flow information (repeated from Exhibit 19–1)

t0	t1	t2	t3	t4	t5
− $60,000	+ $18,000	+ $18,000	+ $18,000 − $ 5,000	+ $18,000	+ $18,000 + $ 1,000

If the initial IRR estimate is 12%, all present value factors are based on a 12% rate and the NPV calculation is:

NPV = − Net Investment + (PV of cash inflows) − (PV of cash outflows other than the net investment)

    = − $60,000 + ($18,000 × PV of an annuity factor for 5 periods) + ($1,000 × PV of $1 factor at end of 5 periods) − ($5,000 × PV of $1 factor at end of 3 periods)

    = − $60,000 + ($18,000 × 3.6048) + ($1,000 × .5674) − ($5,000 × .7118)

    = − $60,000 + $64,886 + $567 − $3,559

    = + $1,894

Since 12% yields a positive NPV, a higher rate should be tried. The present value factors for a 13.5% rate are attempted next:

NPV = − $60,000 + ($18,000 × 3.4747) + ($1,000 × .5309) − ($5,000 × .6839)

    = − $60,000 + $62,545 + $531 − $3,420

    = − $344

Since 13.5% yields a negative NPV, a lower rate should be tried. At 13%, the NPV is:

NPV = − $60,000 + ($18,000 × 3.5172) + ($1,000 × .5428) − ($5,000 × .6931)

    = − $60,000 + $63,310 + $543 − $3,466

    = + $387

Thus, the IRR is between 13% and 13.5%. Using a computer, the rate is determined to be 13.3%.

▌ EXHIBIT 19–8
Lima General's X-Ray Developer Internal Rate of Return—Unequal Cash Flows

Faced with higher capital costs, Japanese managers are beginning to embrace such previously little-known Western concepts as "hurdle rates" and "required rates of return." That's a big switch for executives who once concerned themselves only with market share. Says Tsunehiko Ishibashi, general manager of finance for Mitsubishi Kasei, a major petrochemical company: "As a result of the higher cost of capital, the profitability standards for new investments must be raised."[6]

The higher the internal rate of return, the more financially attractive the investment proposal is. In deciding among alternative investments, however, managers cannot look solely at the internal rates of return on projects. The rate does not reflect the dollars involved. An investor would normally rather have a 10 percent return on $1,000 than a 100 percent return on $10!

There are three drawbacks to using the internal rate of return. First, when uneven cash flows exist, there is the inconvenience of the iterative process. Second, there is the difficulty of finding the precise IRR on a project unless present value tables are available that provide factors for fractional interest rates. These two problems can be eliminated with the use of a computer or a programmable calculator. The last problem is that it is possible to find several rates of return that will make the net present value of the cash flows equal to zero. This phenomenon usually occurs when there are net cash inflows in some years and net cash outflows in other years of the investment project's life.

---

[6] John J. Curran, "Japan Tries to Cool Money Mania," *FORTUNE* (January 28, 1991), p. 66.

**CAPITAL
PROJECT
EVALUATION
ILLUSTRATION**

A final comprehensive example is used to illustrate all of the capital budgeting evaluation techniques, as applied to the same capital project. Lima General is considering purchasing a laparoscope for the hospital. There is a $400,000 cost for all the equipment related to this project that allows miniature TV cameras to monitor surgical and other internal processes. Expectations are for a ten-year life and salvage value of $30,000. The hospital currently has a similar piece of equipment that it will sell for $40,000 if the new equipment is acquired. A timeline representing expected cash flows (in thousands of dollars) from the technology purchase is shown below:

Time Point:	t0	t1	t2	t3	t4	t5	t6	t7	t8	t9	t10
Operating Flows:		+$40	+$47	+$70	+$70	+$70	+$85	+$80	+$80	+$45	+$30
Investment:	−$400										
Equipment Sale:	+$ 40										
Salvage Value:											+$30

Lima General's board of directors has the following policies regarding acceptability of capital projects: (1) the payback period cannot be longer than six years and (2) the rate of return must equal or exceed a discount rate of 10 percent.

Payback Period Computation

The payback period is determined by reviewing the cumulative total of the cash inflows and finding that point at which the original investment is recovered:

Point in Time	Cash Flows	Cumulative Total
1	+ 40,000	$ 40,000
2	+ 47,000	87,000
3	+ 70,000	157,000
4	+ 70,000	227,000
5	+ 70,000	297,000
6	+ 85,000	382,000
7	+ 80,000	462,000
8	+ 80,000	542,000
9	+ 45,000	587,000
10	+ 60,000	647,000

The above table shows that $297,000 of inflows have accumulated by the end of the fifth year. An additional $63,000 is needed to obtain the investment of $360,000. This amount is approximately 74 percent ($63,000 ÷ $85,000) of the sixth year inflows. Thus, the payback period is about five years and nine months. Since the Lima General management has a preestablished maximum payback period of six years, the project is acceptable.

Net Present Value Computation

Using cash flow information on the project and the present value factors from the 10 percent column in Table 1 (Appendix A), the NPV computation is:

Point in Time	Cash Flows	PV Factors (10%)	Present Values
0	− $360,000	1.0000	− $360,000
1	+ 40,000	.9091	+ $ 36,364
2	+ 47,000	.8265	+ 38,846
3	+ 70,000	.7513	+ 52,591
4	+ 70,000	.6830	+ 47,810
5	+ 70,000	.6209	+ 43,463
6	+ 85,000	.5645	+ 47,983
7	+ 80,000	.5132	+ 41,056
8	+ 80,000	.4665	+ 37,320
9	+ 45,000	.4241	+ 19,085
10	+ 60,000	.3855	+ 23,130

Subtotal of present values of net cash inflows   + $387,648

Total Net Present Value   + $ 27,648

Since the NPV is positive, the project's rate of return exceeds the firm's 10 percent established discount rate and is acceptable from this standpoint. The profitability index computation uses the present values of the cash outflows and inflows that were shown in the above table. The PV of the net outflow is $360,000, which represents the new equipment's cost ($400,000) minus the old equipment's sales price ($40,000). Both amounts are at their present values since they are paid/received at the current point in time. The present value of the cash inflows is $387,645.

The profitability index is 1.08 ($387,645 ÷ $360,000). Since the PI is greater than 1.00, the project can be said to be an efficient use of capital in that it yields more than the desired 10 percent rate of return.

Internal Rate of Return Computation

The internal rate of return must be calculated using an iterative process since the cash inflows are uneven. Because there is a $27,648 positive NPV at 10 percent, the IRR must be somewhat above that rate. An estimate is made and tested for a rate of return of 12 percent. (PV factors are from the 12 percent column in Table 1, Appendix A.)

Point in Time	Cash Flows	PV Factors (12%)	Present Values
0	− $360,000	1.0000	− $360,000
1	+ 40,000	.8929	+ $ 35,716
2	+ 47,000	.7972	+ 37,468
3	+ 70,000	.7118	+ 49,826
4	+ 70,000	.6355	+ 44,485
5	+ 70,000	.5674	+ 39,718
6	+ 85,000	.5066	+ 43,061
7	+ 80,000	.4524	+ 36,192
8	+ 80,000	.4039	+ 32,312
9	+ 45,000	.3606	+ 16,227
10	+ 60,000	.3220	+ 19,320

Subtotal of present values of net cash inflows   + $354,325

Total Net Present Value   − $ 5,675

Since the NPV is negative, the IRR is less than 12 percent. At a rate of 11.5 percent, the NPV is:

Point in Time	Cash Flows	PV Factors (11.5%)	Present Values
0	− $360,000	1.0000	− $360,000
1	+ 40,000	.8969	+ $ 35,876
2	+ 47,000	.8044	+ 37,807
3	+ 70,000	.7214	+ 50,498
4	+ 70,000	.6470	+ 45,290
5	+ 70,000	.5803	+ 40,621
6	+ 85,000	.5204	+ 44,234
7	+ 80,000	.4667	+ 37,336
8	+ 80,000	.4186	+ 33,488
9	+ 45,000	.3754	+ 16,893
10	+ 60,000	.3367	+ 20,202

Subtotal of present values of net cash inflows   + $362,245

Total Net Present Value   + $ 2,245

By using mathematical interpolation, a computer, or a programmable calculator, the actual rate is found to be approximately 11.6 percent. This IRR is acceptable because it is above the 10 percent discount rate desired by Lima General.

ASSUMPTIONS AND LIMITATIONS OF METHODS

Although each capital budgeting evaluation technique used in the Lima General example indicated that the laparoscope technology project was acceptable, it is possible that all evaluation methods will not provide the same results. Also, as summarized in Exhibit 19–9, each method has its own underlying assumptions and limitations on usefulness. To derive the most success from the capital budgeting process, managers should understand the basic similarities and differences of the various methods and use several techniques to evaluate a project.

All of the methods have two similar limitations. First, except to the extent that payback indicates the promptness of the investment recovery, none of these methods provide a mechanism to include management preferences in regard to the timing of cash flows. This limitation can be partially overcome by discounting cash flows further in the future at higher rates than those in earlier years, assuming that early cash flows are preferred. Second, all the methods use single, deterministic measures of cash flow amounts rather than probabilities. This limitation can be minimized through the use of probability estimates of cash flows. Such estimates can be input into a computer program to determine a distribution of answers for each method under various conditions of uncertainty.

Considering the various assumptions, benefits, and drawbacks of each of the capital budgeting techniques, the results given in the News Note "Comparing Techniques in the U.S., Korea, and Japan" on page 820 are interesting. These same techniques are used worldwide to evaluate the cost-benefit relationships provided by capital project investments.

ASSUMPTIONS	LIMITATIONS
Payback	
• Speed of investment recovery is the key consideration • Timing and size of cash flows are accurately predicted • Risk (uncertainty) is lower for a shorter payback project	• Ignores cash flows after payback • Basic method treats cash flows and project life as deterministic without explicit consideration of probabilities • Ignores time value of money • Cash flow pattern preferences are not explicitly recognized
Net Present Value	
• Discount rate used is valid • Timing and size of cash flows are accurately predicted • Life of project is accurately predicted • If the shorter-lived of two projects is selected, the proceeds of that project will continue to earn the discount rate of return through the theoretical completion of the longer-lived project	• Basic method treats cash flows and project life as deterministic without explicit consideration of probabilities • Alternative project rates of return are not known • Cash flow pattern preferences are not explicitly recognized • IRR on project is not reflected
Profitability Index	
• Same as NPV • Size of PV of net inflows relative to size of present value of investment measures efficient use of capital	• Same as NPV • Gives a relative answer but does not reflect dollars of NPV
Internal Rate of Return	
• Hurdle rate used is valid • Timing and size of cash flows are accurately predicted • Life of project is accurately predicted • If the shorter-lived of two projects is selected, the proceeds of that project will continue to earn the IRR through the theoretical completion of the longer-lived project	• Projects are ranked for funding using the IRR rather than dollar size • IRR does not reflect dollars of NPV • Basic method treats cash flows and project life as deterministic without explicit consideration of probabilities • Cash flow pattern preferences are not explicitly recognized • It is possible to calculate multiple rates of return on the same project
Accounting Rate of Return (Presented in Appendix 2 of this chapter)	
• Effect on company accounting earnings relative to average investment is key consideration • Size and timing of increase in company earnings, investment cost, project life, and salvage value can be accurately predicted	• Does not consider cash flows • Does not consider time value of money • Treats earnings, investment, and project life as deterministic without explicit consideration of probabilities

▌ **EXHIBIT 19–9**

Selected Assumptions and Limitations of Capital Budgeting Methods

One area of business investment in which uncertainty is extremely prevalent is that of high-technology equipment. Some of the most pressing investment decisions currently facing American companies are those related to the purchase of automated and robotic equipment. As of 1993, one estimate is that less than 15 percent of the factory

HIGH-TECH INVESTMENTS

NEWS NOTE

Comparing Techniques in the U.S., Korea, and Japan

In a recent survey, payback was found to be the most popular among the quantitative methods commonly used to justify long-term investments in the U.S., Japan, and Korea. As many as 86% of the Japanese, 75% of the Korean, and 71% of U.S. corporations surveyed use this naive approach as an important criterion in long-term investment decisions. While the payback method is theoretically inferior to discounted cash flow techniques, in an environment where technology changes rapidly and new products become obsolete quickly, corporations should look for investment opportunities that pay back within a short period of time. Corporations using payback period were asked about the number of years in which investments in advanced technology were expected to be recovered. The majority considered less than five years as the minimum payback period.

Approximately the same percentage of Korean and U.S. corporations use the three other quantitative methods: accounting rate of return, internal rate of return, and net present value. Surprisingly, not many Japanese corporations use discounted cash flow techniques. Only 20% of the Japanese sample corporations use the internal rate of return as an important criterion in making investment decisions, and only 28% use net present value.

Qualitative factors are also considered. For Korea, competing in the marketplace and operational performance improvements were at the top of the list of extremely important investment justifications—mentioned by 52% and 49%, respectively. The U.S. (43%) and Japan (41%) companies agreed on the assessment of marketplace competitiveness. Forty-six percent of the Japanese companies agreed with Korean ones that operational performance improvements were extremely important investment justifications. In the U.S., however, only 18% of the companies surveyed ranked it at that level.

SOURCE: Adapted from: Il-Woon Kim and Ja Song, "U.S., Korea, & Japan: Accounting Practices in Three Countries," *Management Accounting* (August 1990), pp. 26–27. Reprinted from *Management Accounting*. Copyright by Institute of Management Accountants, Montvale, N.J.

---

machinery in the United States is computer-controlled. The proportion is somewhat higher in Japan and the difference between the two countries is becoming wider.[7] Thus, in many instances, the decision is more a question of "how much" and "when" rather than "whether." High-technology equipment generally requires massive monetary investment and due consideration should be given to the tangible (such as increased throughput) and "intangible" (such as increased customer satisfaction with the quality of products) benefits generated by such equipment. In addition, management must consider the interdependent relationships arising from such investments, including significantly reduced labor costs, increased quality and quantity of production, shortened processing time, and increased utility and maintenance costs.

Possible Reasons for Noninvestment

Almost all businesses have now automated their office equipment and customer service activities. The 1990s will be the decade of substantially increased investment by manufacturers in factory automation. Some reasons for the slowness of companies to invest in automated equipment follow. First, many companies have wanted to minimize worker displacement and the corresponding increase in unemployment. A second concern has been morale problems for employees retaining their jobs after some degree of automation has occurred. These employees often feel guilty because they kept their jobs, and feel uneasy about learning new skills. Third, after some compa-

---

[7]Edmund Faltermayer, "Invest or Die," *FORTUNE* (February 22, 1993), p. 50.

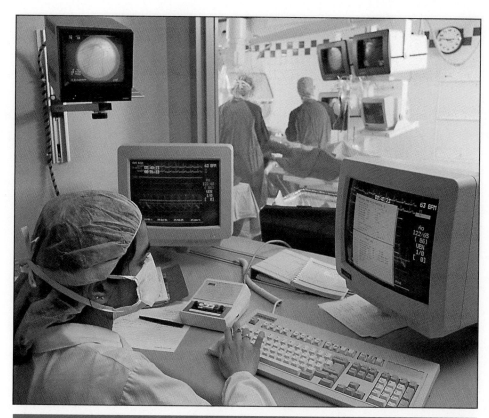

Investments in high-tech medical equipment may often need to be justified on a nonmonetary basis. Computers and scientific "wizardry" allow doctors to investigate (and sometimes solve) problems without invasive procedures— an important qualitative factor from the patient's perspective.

nies have installed automated equipment, management has found that the equipment often did not work correctly, was difficult to integrate with nonautomated equipment, did not do as good a job as had been done by humans, or the operators did not have the appropriate education and training to operate such equipment effectively. Fourth, many senior managers still view computerized equipment as "nonjustifiable" because they do not or will not recognize some of the less-tangible factors that add to its value as a competitive asset. But probably the most significant reason for not acquiring automated equipment is that it is often difficult, using traditional analyses, to justify the extensive capital investment required.

Consider the following example. Japan's Yamazaki Manufacturing Company spent $18 million to install a flexible manufacturing system (FMS). The number of machines went from 68 to 18; production floor space declined from 103,000 square feet to 30,000; average processing (throughput) time was reduced from 35 to 1.5 days. But the total savings after two years was only $6.9 million and $3.9 million of that amount came from a one-time inventory reduction. "Even if the system continued to produce annual labor savings of $1.5 million for 20 years, the project's return would be less than 10% per year."[8] Most American companies would not consider 10 percent a reasonable rate of return in spite of the huge savings in fixed assets and time. Additionally, the investment's payback period would extend far beyond the norms set by most firms.

Considerations in High-Tech Investment Analysis

Traditional capital budgeting analysis may need some modification to be useful to managers making automated equipment investment decisions. First, managers need

---

[8] Robert S. Kaplan, "Must CIM Be Justified by Faith Alone?" *Harvard Business Review* (March–April 1986), p. 87.

EXHIBIT 19–10

Basis of Justifying
Investments—Percentage
of Total Respondents

	QUALITATIVELY CONSIDERED ONLY	QUANTIFIED IN DOLLARS
Improved competitive position	70	18
Consistency with business strategy	70	8
Improved delivery and service	68	11
Improved product quality/reliability	65	27
Reduced product development time	61	7
Additional manufacturing capabilities/flexibility	59	23

SOURCE: Robert A. Howell, et al., *Management Accounting in the New Manufacturing Environment* (Montvale, N.J.: National Association of Accountants, now Institute of Management Accountants, 1987), p. 24.

to be very careful in setting the discount rate used to determine present value figures. One survey conducted in the late 1980s indicated that the cost of capital for most companies is only 9 to 12 percent.[9] Since that time, interest rates have fallen considerably, but management often still sets the discount or hurdle rate somewhere between 12 and 18 percent. Such high rates severely penalize capital investments (such as flexible manufacturing systems) that require high initial investments and may take quite a few years to achieve payback.

Second, weight needs to be given to both the quantitative and qualitative benefits to be provided by the capital expenditure. This point is appropriate for all investment decisions, but especially for high-tech ones. Qualitative benefits such as higher quality and more rapid delivery have typically been assigned a zero dollar value in making investment decisions. One qualitative benefit often overlooked is the improved competitive position that can result from higher product quality or shorter throughput time.

Exhibit 19–10 indicates the results of a survey showing various qualitative factors and the percentages of respondent companies that considered such factors in investment justification. Note that some respondents attempted to quantify these qualitative factors in their analyses. The following quote from a professor at England's University of Manchester Institute of Science and Technology discusses such quantification ideas:

> One of the biggest difficulties encountered [in investment justification is that] some of the benefits of advanced manufacturing technology are often considered intangible and—by implication—unquantifiable. But there is no such thing as an intangible benefit: Every benefit that can be identified can be redefined, quantified, and included in an investment appraisal.
>
> Quantifying every benefit is important because it overcomes the main excuse managers have for making investments without an evaluation. More importantly, if some benefits fail to be quantified, the project cannot be correctly reflected in the company's cost system.[10]

A third item of consideration in regard to high-tech investments is that such projects are not "free-standing." As discussed in the News Note "Projects Are Evaluated Better in 'Bundles,'" many high-tech investments are interrelated, integrated parts of a whole and should not be viewed as individual projects. When viewed in the entirety, the benefits of the "bundled" project are greater than those that would be achieved

[9] Allen H. Seed III and Randell G. Wagner, "Investment Justification of Factory Automation," *Cost Accounting for the 90s—Responding to Technological Change* (Montvale, N.J.: NAA, 1988), p. 88.
[10] P. L. Primrose, "Is Anything Really Wrong with Cost Management?" *Journal of Cost Management* (Boston: Warren Gorham Lamont, Spring 1992), p. 48.

| NEWS NOTE | Projects Are Evaluated Better in "Bundles" |

When Caterpillar embarked on its $1.5 billion worldwide plant modernization program, management realized that the traditional use of IRR or NPV on a project-by-project basis would be too narrow to analyze complex capital investments in synergistic manufacturing plants with just-in-time delivery schedules. To analyze the initial investments in these strategic projects and subsequently track their results, Caterpillar developed a concept called "bundling." At Caterpillar, a bundle is defined as a homogeneous segment of work or product that has common elements. The common elements of a bundle may be size of components, type of components, processes, or location.

A bundle may be a manufacturing process, a commodity, or a new product. A manufacturing bundle is a factory area or minifactory that could be managed on its own. Examples of manufacturing bundles at Caterpillar are a flexible machining and robotic welding system, an assembly line, an integrated heat treating system, and an integrated press shop. Examples of commodity bundles are gears or axles. An axle factory bundle might include gear line and integrated heat treat, wheel and drum line, axle machining line, and axle assembly area. A new product bundle would include all the R&D and new equipment required to produce a new product line.

Focusing on bundles rather than on individual machines or other components of bundles has two main advantages. First, cost and benefits can be identified more easily with bundles than with individual machines or other components in the bundles. For example, it is much easier to relate the benefits of lower work-in-process inventory or reduced throughput time to the axle factory bundle mentioned above than to individual machines in the bundle. Monitoring bundles avoids the arbitrary allocation of costs and benefits to individual components of bundles. Thus, the full impact of the related costs and benefits of capital projects is captured.

Second, bundle monitoring focuses on the strategic marketing and manufacturing goals of the firm. Top management is more interested in the performance of strategic bundles, such as an axle factory bundle, than in the performance of individual machines or other components within the bundle. Bundling encourages the proper evaluation of projects in the context of the total plant plan.

SOURCE: James A. Hendricks, Robert C. Bastian, and Thomas L. Sexton, "Bundle Monitoring of Strategic Projects," *Management Accounting* (February 1992), pp. 31–35. Reprinted from *Management Accounting*. Copyright by Institute of Management Accountants, Montvale, N.J.

from using the individual elements of the project. Exhibit 19–11 on page 824 indicates the potential synergistic benefits to be obtained from the installation of a computer-integrated manufacturing (CIM) system.

Finally, consideration should be given to the opportunity cost of *not* acquiring automated equipment. The opportunity cost of nonautomation refers to the competitive disadvantage a company will experience when its competitors acquire automated equipment and enjoy the substantive benefits mentioned earlier.

Illustration of High-Tech Investment Analysis

In making all capital budgeting decisions (including high-tech ones), all benefits and costs that can be quantified with a reasonable degree of accuracy should be. Managers may use probability analysis to attempt to quantify the qualitative benefits and then recalculate the project evaluation techniques to check for financial acceptability. Alternatively, management can simply make subjective evaluations of nonquantifiable items to make certain that those items are properly weighted in the decision model.

EXHIBIT 19–11

Potential Savings from a CIM

SAVINGS	FUNCTION
5% – 15%	Reduction in personnel costs
15% – 30%	Reduction in engineering design costs
30% – 60%	Reduction in overall lead time
40% – 60%	Reduction in work in process
40% – 70%	Gain in overall production
200% – 300%	Gain in capital equipment uptime
200% – 300%	Gain in product quality
300% – 3,500%	Gain in engineering productivity

SOURCE: Joel C. Polakoff, "Computer Integrated Manufacturing: A New Look at Cost Justifications," *Journal of Accountancy* (March 1990), p. 24.

For example, assume that Lima General is considering installing magnetic resonance imaging (MRI) equipment. Using the traditional capital budgeting models, the project is shown to be nonacceptable and it would take an additional $75,000 of cash inflow per year for the rate of return to be acceptable. However, it is known that some other medical facilities are installing MRI equipment that will meet the growing demand in the community for this type of diagnosis. A subjective decision can be made as to whether the qualitative benefits of the investment are worth that amount. If the answer is yes, the investment should be made; if not, the hospital should use its funds in another manner.[11]

Exhibit 19–12 illustrates an automated equipment acquisition decision. Reliable Medical Equipment Company is considering installing a CAD/CAM system for $580,000. The CAD portion of the system uses computers to develop and modify a product; CAM uses computers to plan, implement, and control product manufacturing. Reliable's management has set 10 percent as its discount rate and has a payback period of three-fourths of the life of the investment project. Based on these criteria, Part A of the exhibit indicates that the system would not be considered an acceptable acquisition. However, the marketing executive at Reliable estimates that the increase in customer goodwill because of the quickness with which design changes could be made can be valued at $40,000 per year. This amount is added to annual cash flow and a new NPV and payback period are computed as shown in Part B of the exhibit. By including the "value" of the qualitative benefit of goodwill, the CAD/CAM system meets Reliable's selection criteria. Part C of Exhibit 19–12 shows how to determine the minimum annual goodwill necessary to produce a net present value of zero. The $23,002 minimum is an indication that the $40,000 estimate could be off by $16,998 ($40,000 − $23,002) before the system would earn a negative NPV. As the News Note (page 826) on estimating the possibilities discusses, using such estimates in decision analysis is better than assuming away the traditionally "nonquantifiable" benefits.

Regardless of the type of investment project under consideration, the selection of and investment in a project should not end the capital budgeting process. At some point (or points), management should perform a postinvestment audit or review of the project.

---

[11]One survey indicated that upper-level managers may be placing more reliance on qualitative information and intuition than on analytical techniques. While they understand and know how to use such techniques, managers indicated that such tools were more important in making lower-level decisions. Managers are using more judgment "because they are unwilling to trust engineers or financial personnel to apply a concept like opportunity cost." Bernard A. Coda and Barry G. King, "Manufacturing Decision-Making Tools," *Journal of Cost Management* (Boston: Warren Gorham Lamont, Spring 1989), p. 30.

Cost: $580,000
Annual maintenance: $220,000
Life: 5 years

Efficiency: 3 times as efficient as manual design
Manual equivalent of system: 5 draftspeople
Annual salary per draftsperson: $70,000
Labor cost savings of system: $350,000 ($70,000 × 5)

PART A—TRADITIONAL CAPITAL BUDGETING TECHNIQUE

Annual net cash flows of system:
Maintenance   ($220,000)
Labor savings   +   350,000

Net cash flow   + $130,000

NPV @ 10% = − $87,196   [− $580,000 + ($130,000 × 3.7908)]
Payback period = 4.5 years   [$580,000 ÷ $130,000]

PART B—ADJUSTMENT FOR QUALITATIVE VALUE ADDED

Estimated value of customer goodwill from increased speed of design changes ($40,000
per year) raises "cash flow" to $170,000

NPV @ 10% = +$64,436
Payback period = 3.4 years

**PART C—MINIMUM GOODWILL NEEDED ANNUALLY TO PRODUCE A NPV
OF ZERO**

The minimum annual goodwill needed to cover the present value shortfall in Part A can
be found by equating the present value of the shortfall to an annuity payment multiplied
by the factor of the present value of an annuity of 5 payments at 10%:

3.7908 (Annuity amount) = $87,196
Annuity amount = $87,196 ÷ 3.7908 = $23,002

POSTINVESTMENT AUDIT

In a postinvestment audit of a capital project, information on actual project results is gathered and compared to expected results. This process provides a feedback or control feature both to the persons who submitted and those who approved the original project information. Comparisons should be made using the same technique or techniques as were originally used to determine project acceptance. Actual data should be extrapolated to future periods where such information would be appropriate. In cases where significant learning or training is necessary, startup costs of the first year may not be appropriate indicators of future costs. Such projects should be given a chance to stabilize before making the project audit.

As the size of the capital expenditure increases, a postinvestment audit becomes more crucial. Although an audit cannot change a past investment decision, it can pinpoint areas of project operations that are out of line with expectations for the purpose of correcting problems before they get out of hand. Secondly, an audit can provide feedback on the accuracy of the original estimates for project cash flows.

NEWS NOTE

Estimating the Possibilities Is Better Than Ignoring the Facts

Conceptually, there is no reason why the so-called "intangible benefits" (or "competitive advantages") of computerized automation (like quality, timeliness, and flexibility) should not be expressed in financial terms. Competitive and financial analyses must be considered two different tools that should be used together rather than as alternative tools.

If a strategic plan gives a company a sustainable competitive advantage, the plan must increase the company's profitability. If a strategic plan leads to a net present value greater than zero, this can occur only if some competitive advantages accrue from the project (perhaps because of cost reduction or improved quality).

It is by no means easy to determine the effect that improved quality or greater flexibility has on increasing the value of a company, but this should not prevent the use of rough estimates: It is always better to have useful (even if approximate) data than to have precise (but useless) information.

SOURCE: Giovanni Azzone and Umberto Bertelè, "Planning and Controlling Investments in Computer-Based Automation," *Journal of Cost Management* (Boston: Warren Gorham Lamont, Summer 1991), p. 28.

Sometimes project sponsors may be biased in favor of their own projects and provide overly optimistic forecasts of future revenues or cost savings. Individuals providing unrealistic estimates should be required to explain all major variances. Knowing that postinvestment audits will be made may cause project sponsors to be more careful to provide realistic cash flow forecasts for capital requests.

Performing a postinvestment audit is not an easy task. The actual information may not be in the same form as were the original estimates, and some project benefits may be difficult to quantify. Project returns fluctuate considerably over time, so results gathered at a single point may not be representative of the project. But, regardless of the difficulties involved, postinvestment audits provide management with information that can help to make better capital investment decisions in the future, as discussed in the News Note "Why Do Postinvestment Audits?" found on page 827.

R E V I S I T I N G

SETON MEDICAL FACILITIES

Historically, capital project investments were often made without significant justification. Projects were often approved if funds were available and the project sponsor prepared a reasonable and well-presented request. Now, however, organizations in all sectors of the economy—whether they are not-for-profit hospitals such as Seton Medical Center or profit-making enterprises such as General Motors—are becoming more cautious about their investments and are instituting more stringent evaluation policies for capital investments. Organizations are continuing to fund capital projects; they just seem to be doing so in a more careful and organized manner.

Seton Medical Center has worked to meet the needs of the Austin community for over 90 years. Seton believes that the renovation and expansion of its facilities will allow it to continue to provide excellent, cost-efficient service to patients in the Austin area. In making the determination of what areas to expand, Seton administrators recognized that "demand for traditional hospital services, measured by the

---

NEWS NOTE   ## Why Do Postinvestment Audits?

Larger, longer-term, and more uncertain returns heighten the importance of conducting postinvestment audits. These audits serve as an important control mechanism over the cash flows associated with investments in advanced automation. While an audit will have no direct impact on any investment decision, there are a number of substantive indirect benefits that warrant the effort. A postinvestment audit . . . provides valuable information that can be used to correct problems before the success of the investment is undermined and to provide management with feedback on how well the cash outlays and inflows associated with the investment were estimated.

[T]he postinvestment audit [should] include both an audit of the financial cash flows generated by the investment and the operating benefits forecasted. The financial expectations should be assessed against the actual cash flows. The operational expectations, such as the flexibility provided by the investment, are evaluated against the results achieved. The operating expectations often provide the most direct comparison of expected versus realized performance.

SOURCE: Robert A. Howell and Stephen R. Soucy, "Capital Investment in the New Manufacturing Environment," *Management Accounting* (November 1987), pp. 31–32. Reprinted from *Management Accounting*. Copyright by Institute of Management Accountants, Montvale, N.J.

---

number of regular medical/surgical beds, is not increasing [and, therefore, planned] no new capacity in that area."[12]

Because Seton is a not-for-profit, it was essential that hospital administrators analyze both the expected cash flows from each investment project as well as the intangible benefits to be generated by each project. If Seton is to remain focused on providing services to both revenue- and non-revenue-generating patients, all of the changing health care issues, resultant equipment needs, and qualitative effects must be considered before investments can be specified as "acceptable" or "unacceptable."

CHAPTER SUMMARY

Capital budgeting is concerned with evaluating long-range projects involving the acquisition, operation, and disposition of one or more capital assets. Commonly used capital budgeting evaluation techniques are payback period, net present value (NPV), profitability index (PI), and internal rate of return (IRR).

The payback period is the length of time needed for a firm to recoup its investment from the cash flows of a project. If a project's payback period is less than a preestablished maximum, the project is acceptable. This method ignores the time value of money and all cash flows beyond the payback period.

Net present value, profitability index, and internal rate of return are discounted cash flow methods. As such, these methods require management to discount the project's cash inflows and outflows using a desired rate of return. The minimum rate at which the discount rate should be set is the cost of capital. Managers may compensate for project risk by using a discount rate that is higher than the cost of capital.

---

[12] *Seton Medical Center Announces Major Reorientation* (June 1992), p. 1.

Under the NPV method, the total present value of the future cash flows is reduced by the current investment to derive the net present value. If the NPV is equal to or greater than zero, the project provides a rate of return equal to or greater than the discount rate. A positive NPV makes the project acceptable for investment.

The profitability index equals the present value of the net cash flows divided by the investment cost. The profitability index is considered an indicator of the company's efficiency in its use of capital. Revenue-producing projects should have a PI of 1.00 or more. For least-cost projects, the closer the PI is to 1.00, the more acceptable the project.

The internal rate of return method computes the rate of return expected on the investment project. The IRR is equal to the discount rate at which the net present value of all cash flows equals zero. If the internal rate of return of a project exceeds management's desired discount or hurdle rate, the project is acceptable.

Each capital project evaluation technique is based on certain assumptions and, therefore, has certain limitations. To compensate for these limitations, many managers subject capital projects to more than one evaluation technique.

High-technology equipment is often not justifiable under traditional capital budgeting evaluation techniques for three reasons. First, managers may use a discount rate that is significantly higher than the firm's true cost of capital. Second, a project's intangible benefits are often assigned a zero value in project evaluation. And third, since the time frame of the benefits provided by automated equipment is long, the payback period of such investments may exceed the established maximums. Managers should be aware of and compensate for these considerations when evaluating the purchase of high-technology equipment.

After a capital project is accepted and implemented, a postinvestment audit should be undertaken to compare actual with expected results. The audit will help managers identify and correct any problems that may exist, evaluate the accuracy of estimates used for the original investment decision, and help improve the forecasts of future investment projects.

APPENDIX 1

Time Value of Money

Future value

The time value of money can be discussed in relationship to either its future or present value. **Future value** (FV) refers to the amount to which one or more sums of money invested at a specified interest rate will grow over a specified number of time periods. Present value (PV) is the amount that one or more future cash flows are worth currently, given a specified rate of interest.[13] Thus, future and present values depend on three things: (1) amount of the cash flow; (2) rate of interest; and (3) timing of the cash flow. Only present values are discussed in this appendix since they are most relevant to the types of management decisions discussed in this text.

Future and present values are distinctly related. A present value is simply a future value discounted back the same number of periods at the same rate of interest. The rate of return used in present value computations is called the discount rate.

Simple interest
Compound interest

In computing future and present values, simple or compound interest may be used. **Simple interest** means that interest is earned only on the original investment or principal amount. **Compound interest** means that interest earned in prior periods is added to the original investment so that, in each successive period, interest is earned on both principal and interest. The time between each interest computation is called the **compounding period**

Compounding period. The more often interest is compounded, the higher the actual rate

---

[13] Interest can be earned or owed, received or paid. To simplify the discussion for definitional purposes, the topic of interest is only viewed from the inflow standpoint.

of interest being received is relative to the stated rate. The following discussion is based on the use of compound interest, since most transactions use this method.

Interest rates are typically stated in annual terms. To compensate for more frequent compounding periods, multiply the number of years by the number of compounding periods per year and divide the annual interest rate by the number of compounding periods per year.

Present Value of a Single Cash Flow

Assume that Fred Walker's bank pays interest at 10 percent per year compounded semiannually. Fred wants to have $13,401 in three years and wants to know what amount to invest now. The formula to solve for the present value is:

$$PV = \frac{FV}{(1 + i)^n}$$

where PV = present value of a future amount
       FV = future value of a current investment
        i = interest rate per compounding period
        n = number of compounding periods

Substituting known values into the formula gives the following:

$$PV = \$13,401 \left[\frac{1}{(1 + .05)^6} \right]$$

$$PV = \$13,401 \left[\frac{1}{1.3401} \right]$$

$$PV = \$10,000$$

Throughout the presentation on capital budgeting, many future value amounts need to be converted to present values. Rather than using the formula $[1 \div (1 + i)^n]$ to find PVs, a table of factors for the present value of $1 (Table 1) for a variety of "i" and "n" values is provided for ease of computation in Appendix A at the end of the text. Such factors are also available in programmable calculators, making the use of tables unnecessary.

Present Value of an Annuity

An annuity is a series of equal cash flows (either positive or negative) per period. In an **ordinary annuity**, the first cash flow is at the end of a period. In contrast, the cash flows from an **annuity due** occur at the beginning of a period.

To illustrate the computation of the present value of an annuity, consider the following situation. Mr. and Mrs. Clive Anderson are planning for their daughter Caty's college education. Caty will need $10,000 per year for the next four years. The Andersons want to know how much to invest currently at 8 percent so that Caty can withdraw $10,000 per year. The following diagram presents the situation:

Ordinary annuity
Annuity due

Time Point:	t0	t1	t2	t3	t4
Future Value:		$10,000	$10,000	$10,000	$10,000
Present Value:	?				

The present value of each single cash flow can be found using 8 percent factors in Table 1 as follows:

PV of first receipt:	$10,000 (.9259)	$ 9,259
PV of second receipt:	$10,000 (.8573)	8,573
PV of third receipt:	$10,000 (.7938)	7,938
PV of fourth receipt:	$10,000 (.7350)	7,350
		$33,120

The present value factor for an ordinary annuity can also be determined by adding the present value factors for all periods having a future cash flow. Table 2 in Appendix A provides present value of ordinary annuity factors for various interest rates and time periods. From this table, the factor of 3.3121 can be obtained and multiplied by $10,000 to yield approximately the same result as above. (The difference is caused by decimal-fraction rounding.)

Nested Annuities

Situations often exist in which an annuity is "nested" or surrounded by unequal flows. The present value of each cash flow could be found separately using the factors for the present value of $1 (Table 1). The alternative is to use Table 2 (PV of a $1 annuity), which is more direct, but does require a slight modification.

The Wheelwright Company has prepared the following information that illustrates a nested annuity. The project under consideration will require a $20,000 investment now and will return the amounts shown below for a ten-year period. Wheelwright's discount rate is 12 percent.

1/1/93 current investment
Returns at year-end: **($20,000)**

12/31/93	+$ 4,000
12/31/94	+ 5,000
12/31/95	+ 5,500
12/31/96	+ 6,000
12/31/97	+ 6,000
12/31/98	+ 6,000
12/31/99	+ 6,000
12/31/00	+ 6,000
12/31/01	+ 4,000
12/31/02	+ 9,000

A $6,000 annuity starts at the end of 1996 and ends in 2000. The present value of each annual cash flow, including the five annuity installments, could be computed separately by multiplying the cash flow amount by the present value factor for that period. Annual computations for the present value of the $6,000 annuity are as follows:

Year	Cash Flows	Present Value Factor	Present Value	
4	+$6,000	.6355	$3,813	
5	+$6,000	.5674	$3,404	
6	+$6,000	.5066	$3,040	Sum = $15,394
7	+$6,000	.4524	$2,714	
8	+$6,000	.4039	$2,423	

The above approach requires that five factors be extracted from the PV table and five multiplications be made. Alternatively, the five factors could be summed (2.5658) and multiplied by $6,000 to provide the same result.

However, because the situation involves an annuity, there is another method of making this computation. It is possible to use Table 2 (PV of an ordinary annuity of $1) to find the present value at a 12 percent rate. Since the $6,000 annuity stops at the end of year eight, find the PV factor for eight periods (4.9676). Because the annuity did not begin until after the end of the third period, subtract the PV factor for three periods (2.4018). This subtraction gives a factor of 2.5658, representing the PV of an ordinary annuity lasting for five periods between periods four through eight.

Accounting Rate of Return

The **accounting rate of return** (ARR) measures the rate of earnings obtained on the average capital investment over a project's life. This evaluation method is consistent with the accounting model and uses profits shown on accrual-based financial statements. It is the one evaluation technique that is *not* based on cash flows. The formula to compute the accounting rate of return is:

Accounting rate of return

$$ARR = \frac{\text{Average Annual Profits from the Project}}{\text{Average Investment in Project}}$$

Investment includes project cost as well as any other costs needed for working capital items (such as inventory) for project support. Investment cost, salvage value, and working capital released at the end of the project's life are summed and divided by two to obtain the average investment.[14]

To illustrate the ARR computation, information for a piece of equipment being considered by the Doctors' Clinic is available. Data on the potential investment are as follows:

Beginning investment:	
Initial cost of equipment	$80,000
Additional working capital needed for the project	20,000
Return at end of project:	
Salvage value of equipment at the end of 10 years	2,000
Working capital released at the end of 10 years	20,000
Return over life of project:	
Average incremental clinic profits after taxes	20,000

Solving the formula for the accounting rate of return gives:

$$ARR = \$20,000 \div [(\$100,000 + \$22,000) \div 2]$$

$$= \$20,000 \div \$61,000 = 32.8\%$$

The 32.8 percent ARR on this project can be compared with a preestablished hurdle rate set by management. This hurdle rate may not be the same as the desired discount rate since the data utilized in calculating the accounting rate of return are not cash flow information. Therefore, the ARR hurdle rate may be set higher than the discount rate because the discount rate automatically compensates for the time value of money. In addition, the 32.8 percent ARR for investment consideration by the Doctors' Clinic to see which projects have the highest accounting rates of return.

---

[14] Sometimes ARR is computed using initial cost rather than average investment as the denominator. Such a computation ignores the return of funds at the end of the project life and is less appropriate than the computation shown.

a. Compute the payback period for this investment.

b. Assume now that the annual cost savings would vary according to the following schedule:

Annual Cost Savings

Years 1–5	$ 50,000
Years 6–10	60,000
Years 11–15	115,000

Compute the payback period under the revised circumstances.

c. Compute the net cost savings to be realized over the life of the furnace under the conditions in part a and the conditions in part b.

d. Given your answers to part c, explain why the payback period differs between part a and part b.

28. *(Payback period)* The Hair Place is a successful styling salon in eastern Georgia. The firm is presently considering the addition of tanning booths to complement its other services. The firm estimates that the tanning booths would cost $95,000 and generate the following pattern of cash inflows:

Year	Amount
1	$11,000
2	18,000
3	22,000
4	31,000
5	39,000
6	21,000
7	20,000

If the firm requires a 5-year payback on its investments, should it acquire the tanning equipment? Explain.

 29. *(Net present value)* Boston Ceramics is considering the purchase of a kiln costing $850,000 to manufacture figurines created by a famous artist. The company has learned that the artist will allow no more than 100,000 of these art objects to be produced. Managers at Boston Ceramics are sure that the firm can sell the figurines at $100 each. The firm's controller estimates the following costs would be incurred to produce each figurine:

Direct labor	$24
Direct materials	10
Other out-of-pocket costs	6
Commissions and royalties	40
Total	$80

The firm's controller has also assembled the following schedule of production and cash sales and states that the production supervisor has confirmed the feasibility of the plan:

Year	Sales in Units
1	12,000
2	27,000
3	30,000
4	25,000
5	6,000

At the end of the 5 years, the kiln will have no salvage value.

Using a discount rate of 14%, determine the NPV of the kiln investment.

30. *(Net present value)* Samson Barbecue Co. is considering the installation of an automated material handling system. The initial cost of such a system would be $500,000. This system would generate labor cost savings over its ten-year life as follows:

Years	Annual Labor Cost Savings
1–2	$70,000
3–5	90,500
6–8	98,200
9–10	65,000

The system will have no salvage at the end of its ten-year life. The company uses a discount rate of 9%. What is the net present value of this potential investment?

31. *(Profitability index)* The Regional Transit Authority is considering replacing one of its current buses with a new one that will last 10 years, cost $120,000, and for which no salvage is expected. The RTA could "nurse" another 10 years out of the old bus, but maintenance costs are high. A $9,000 trade-in would be given on the old bus. The RTA uses a 10% required rate of return. Annual operating costs would be reduced each year by $13,000 if the new bus is acquired.
  a. Compute the profitability index.
  b. Should the RTA buy the new bus? Explain.

32. *(Multiple methods)* Jason's Flower Shop is considering buying a truck for $18,000 instead of continuing to pay a delivery service to deliver flowers to customers. The truck is expected to last 5 years and have a $2,000 salvage value. Annual operating savings are expected to be $6,000 for each of the first two years, $4,000 for each of the next two years, and $3,000 for the last year. The company's cost of capital is 7% and this rate was set as the discount rate.
  a. Calculate the payback period.
  b. Calculate the net present value.
  c. Calculate the profitability index.

33. *(Internal rate of return)* Florida Yacht Co. is considering the acquisition of a computerized mast extrusion system. A system is available for $210,000 that would save $37,167 annually for 10 years over current manual extrusion methods. No salvage value is expected on the machine at the end of its useful life. The firm's cost of capital and discount rate is 10%.
  a. Calculate the internal rate of return for the proposed machine.
  b. Based on your answer to part a, should the company purchase the machine?

34. *(Multiple methods)* Tick Tock Clock Co. is considering purchasing a robot to assemble its clocks. The robot will cost $700,000 and will produce annual labor and quality cost savings of $90,000. The robot is expected to last 12 years and have no salvage value.
  a. What is the payback period?
  b. If Tick Tock Clock Co.'s discount rate is 10%, what is the net present value?
  c. Using a 10% discount rate, what is the profitability index?
  d. What is the internal rate of return (to the nearest .5 percent)?

35. *(Profitability index, payback period)* The profitability index for a project under consideration by the Ustes Company is known to be 1.40. The investment cost is $200,000, the only cash inflow is an ordinary annuity with a 6 year life, and the firm uses a 10% discount rate. What is the project's payback period?

36. *(Net present value)* Arizona Jones is an industrial sleuth who has been engaged to discover the cost of capital of one of his employer's competitors. In talking to a salesperson who had recently called on the competitor, Arizona learned that the competitor's controller had estimated a $27,000 net present value on an

$80,000 machine sold to the company by the salesperson. Arizona also knows that the competitor uses the cost of capital as the discount rate in evaluating capital projects. The machine has a 4-year life and is expected to save its purchaser $35,600 annually in labor costs. Arizona Jones has asked for your assistance in estimating the competitor's cost of capital.

37. *(Missing data)* John Edwards has lost his paperwork concerning data on a project for which he had provided his company president a net present value analysis. All he could find was the last page of his report that indicated a net present value of $32,000, an original investment of $132,000, and a 4-year life. The president asks John to calculate the payback period on the project. John knows that the company uses a discount rate of 10%. Calculate the payback period.

38. *(Appendix 1)* You have just purchased a new car. Assume you financed 100% of the purchase cost on an installment credit plan. According to the credit agreement, you agreed to pay $350 per month for a period of 50 months. If the credit agreement was based on a monthly interest rate of 1%, what was the apparent cost of the car?

39. *(Appendix 1)* Use the tables in Appendix A to the text to determine the answers to the following questions.
   a. Edith Roundtree wishes to have $15,000 in 6 years. She can make an investment today that will earn 6% each year, compounded annually. What amount of investment should she make to achieve her goal?
   b. Lillith Bailey is going to receive $200,000 on her 30th birthday, 10 years from today. Lillith has the opportunity to invest money today in a government-backed security paying 6%, compounded semiannually. How much would she be willing to receive today instead of the $200,000 in 10 years?
   c. Demi Wingate has $45,000 today that she intends to use as a downpayment on a house. How much money did Demi invest 8 years ago in order to have $45,000 now, if her investment earned 7% compounded annually?
   d. Jim Tyson needs $10,000 a year for spending money. How much money does his dad need to deposit today in an investment that will earn 10%, compounded annually, in order to keep his son in spending money for 10 years?
   e. Pat Dawson is the host of a television game show that gives away thousands of dollars each day. A $50,000 prize on the show is an annuity paid to the winner in equal installments at the end of each year for 5 years. If the winner has an investment opportunity to earn 4% annually, what present amount would the winner take in exchange for the annuity?
   f. Jayne Howe is going to be paid modeling fees for the next 10 years as follows: year 1, $15,000; year 2, $25,000; year 3, $28,000; years 4–8, $50,000; year 9, $30,000, and year 10, $21,000. Jayne can invest her money at 6%, compounded annually. What is the present value of her future modeling fees?

40. *(Multiple methods, Appendix 2)* Minnesota Publishing Company is considering the purchase of a $200,000 page printer that is expected to last 6 years, have no salvage value, provide $70,000 in additional revenues, and generate $12,000 in additional labor and power costs annually. The company uses a 10% discount rate in evaluating capital projects. Assume that the company requires a maximum 5-year payback period and a minimum 15% accounting rate of return.
   a. Calculate the net present value.
   b. Calculate the internal rate of return (to the nearest .5 percent).
   c. Calculate the payback period.
   d. Calculate the accounting rate of return assuming that Minnesota Publishing Company uses straight-line depreciation.
   e. Under the criteria mentioned above, is the project acceptable?

41. Carolina Sound Systems manufactures radios and cassette players for use by U.S. auto makers. One of its main manufacturing processes involves attaching various radio components to the radio case. At present, this process is performed manually by a staff of 10 workers. The company is considering mechanizing this process with a robotic system. The machinery would cost $1,300,000 and would be operated by a single person. If this machine is purchased, it would have an estimated life of 10 years and a salvage value of $100,000 at the end of its life. Below are estimates of the annual labor savings as well as the additional costs associated with the operation of the new machine:

Annual labor cost savings (9 workers)	$250,000
Annual maintenance costs	14,000
Annual property taxes	8,000
Annual insurance costs	12,000

   a. Assuming the company's cost of capital is 9%, compute the NPV of the investment in the robotic machinery.
   b. Based on the NPV, should the company invest in the robotic machinery?
   c. Compute the profitability index for this potential investment.
   d. Write a memo to the company president discussing other factors the company should consider in evaluating this investment.

42. Dickson Inc. has formal policies and procedures to screen and ultimately approve capital projects. Proposed capital projects are classified as one of the following types:

   1. Expansion requiring new plant and equipment.
   2. Expansion by replacement of present equipment with more productive equipment.
   3. Replacement of old equipment with new equipment of similar quality.

   All expansion projects and replacement projects that will cost more than $50,000 must be submitted to the top management capital investment committee for approval. The investment committee evaluates proposed projects considering the costs and benefits outlined in the supporting proposal and the long-range effects on the company.
   The projected revenue and/or expense effects of the projects, once operational, are included in the proposal. Once a project is accepted, the committee approves an expenditure budget for the project from its inception until it becomes operational. The expenditures required each year for the expansions or replacements are also incorporated into Dickson's annual budget procedure. The budgeted revenue and/or cost effects of the projects, for the periods in which they become operational, are incorporated into the five-year forecast.
   Dickson Inc. does not have a procedure for evaluating projects once they have been implemented and become operational. The vice president of finance has recommended that Dickson establish a postcompletion audit program to evaluate its capital expenditure projects.

   a. Discuss the benefits a company could derive from a postcompletion audit program for capital expenditure projects.
   b. Discuss the practical difficulties in collecting and accumulating information that would be used to evaluate a capital project once it becomes operational.
   (CMA)

PROBLEMS

43. *(Timeline, payback, NPV)* Heartland Department Store is considering installing an elevator in its multistory retail facility to improve access for the elderly and physically disabled. The elevator would cost $80,000 and would last 8 years and have no salvage value at that time. Annual incremental operating costs on the new elevator are expected to be as follows:

Year	Amount
1	$4,700
2	5,800
3	5,800
4	5,800
5	6,300
6	6,300
7	7,500
8	8,500

The company's management estimates that annual revenues could be increased by $100,000 with the installation of the elevator. The firm's contribution margin is typically 20% of sales. The firm uses a 10% discount rate.

a. Construct a timeline for the purchase of the elevator.
b. Determine the payback period.
c. Calculate the net present value of the project.

44. *(NPV)* Canadian Auto Parts Ltd. is considering the purchase of a new robot for its brake shoe manufacturing process. "Bob" (the new robot) is expected to last 10 years and to be completely obsolete at the end of that time. The following timeline reflects the company's expectations about net inflows and net outflows (in thousands of dollars) of cash associated with acquisition and use of "Bob."

Time Point:	t0	t1	t2	t3	t4	t5	t6	t7	t8	t9	t10
Cash Flows:	−$180	+$50	+$52	+$55	+$55	+$10	+$20	+$20	+$20	+$10	+$10

The net inflow in year 5 is based on expected overhaul expenditures of $40,000 that will offset operating inflows of $50,000. The company's discount rate is 8%.

a. Determine the net present value of "Bob" to Canadian Auto Parts Ltd.
b. Upon questioning, the company president discovered that if the $40,000 overhaul expenditure were not incurred in period 5, the net inflows in the remaining years would be as follows: year 6, $20,000; year 7, $10,000; year 8, $5,000; and $0 for years 9 and 10. Should the overhaul expenditure be made? Show computations, using an incremental approach.
c. If the overhaul expenditure is not made, what is "Bob's" NPV?
d. What qualitative factors should be considered in purchasing this robot?

 45. *(Payback, IRR)* Joey's Tax Service prepares tax returns for individuals and small businesses in the Lexington, Kentucky area. Joey employs four people in his tax practice. Currently, all tax returns are prepared on a manual basis. Joey is considering purchasing a computer system that would allow the firm to service all of its existing clients with the use of only three employees. To evaluate the feasibility of the computerized system, Joey has gathered the following information:

Initial cost of the hardware and software	$50,000
Expected salvage value in 5 years	0
Annual depreciation	10,000
Annual labor savings	13,000
Expected life of the computer system	5 years

Joey has determined that he will invest in the computer system if its payback is less than 3.5 years and its IRR exceeds 8%.

a. Compute the payback period for this investment. Does the payback meet Joey's criterion? Explain.

b. Given the annual labor cost savings of $13,000, what is the maximum amount that Joey could pay for the computer system and still have it meet his payback criterion?

c. Compute the IRR for this project to the nearest .5 percent. Based on the computed IRR, is this project acceptable to Joey?

46. *(NPV)* Withers General Store is considering the acquisition of a small computer system. The store has been open for only 6 months and is on a fairly tight budget. Bill Withers, the owner, sees an advertisement for a computer system costing $2,225. This amount is considered a large expenditure for the store, but Bill feels that he can afford a cost of less than $3,000. He tells his wife Sandy about his decision and is surprised when she is not as excited about the purchase as he. She explains to him about additional costs involved with the purchase of a computer system and about the time value of money. Sandy presents the following estimates to Bill for the cost of a computer:

Zaire PC System with 2 disk drives (including sales tax)	$2,225
Monitor, printer, software, cables	1,485
Work station and related furniture	300
Working capital investment for supplies	200
Annual cost of service agreement	150
Annual cost of insurance	150
Annual cost of electricity	120
Annual labor savings (202.5 hours per year, $8 per hour)	1,620

Sandy estimates that the computer will be useful for 4 years. At that time, the computer can be sold for $200. The work station and other related furniture will have no salvage value.

a. Compute the total investment to be made in the computer system.

b. Compute the net cash inflow annuity for the four years.

c. Using a discount rate of 12%, determine the net present value of the system. Is the project acceptable?

d. Assume instead, that Sandy estimates 20 hours per month will be saved and that per hour cost of the savings is $8. Determine the net present value of the system using a 12% discount rate. Is the project acceptable?

e. If the discount rate is increased to 15%, will the project be acceptable under either the original information or the information in part d?

47. *(NPV)* Sally's is a limousine service operating in Baltimore. The owner is considering the purchase of 5 new white stretch limos at a cost of $75,000 each. Each limo will have a useful life of 5 years and a salvage value of $15,000. Estimated revenues and operating costs for each limo are as follows:

Rental fees:
First 2 years ($150 per hour; 20 hours per week for 52 weeks)
Next 3 years ($100 per hour; 15 hours per week for 52 weeks)

Operating costs:
Driver's annual salary, $12,000 (increases $1,000 each year)
Uniform, $200 (at the beginning of the first, third, and fifth years)
Annual insurance, $5,000 the first year; annual rate decreases for age are offset by annual increases in premium rates (paid at the beginning of each year)
Annual personalized license plate and inspection fees, $100 (paid at the beginning of each year)
Annual gas and oil, $36,850 (increases 10% each year of use)
Annual repairs and maintenance, $10,000 (increases 10% each year of use)
Major repairs at end of third year, $2,000
Tires at end of second and fourth years, $400

a. Determine the net cash flows for each year of the limousines investment.
b. Using a 14% discount rate, what is the net present value? Is the purchase acceptable?
c. Using a 16% discount rate, what is the net present value? Is the purchase acceptable?
d. What other factors should be considered by Sally's management before acquiring the limos, assuming a positive net present value?

48. *(Appendix 2, payback, NPV)* Nashville Wholesale is a growing business that is presently considering adding a new product line. The firm would be required by the manufacturer to incur setup costs of $400,000 to handle the new product line. Nashville Wholesale has estimated that the product line would have an expected life of 8 years. Following is a schedule of revenues and annual fixed operating expenses (including $50,000 of annual depreciation on the investment) associated with the new product line. Variable costs are estimated to average 65% of revenues. All revenues are collected as earned. All expenses shown, except for the included amount of straight-line depreciation, are paid in cash when incurred.

Year	Revenues	Fixed Expenses
1	$180,000	$90,000
2	200,000	$80,000
3	240,000	$80,000
4	320,000	$90,000
5	400,000	$80,000
6	400,000	$80,000
7	280,000	$80,000
8	170,000	$70,000

The company has a cost of capital of 12%. Management uses this rate in discounting cash flows when evaluating capital projects.
a. Calculate the accounting rate of return.
b. Calculate the payback period.
c. Calculate the net present value.

49. *(Comprehensive)* As of January 1, 1994, Johnson Metal Desk Company is considering a design change in its standard metal desk. The company has determined that the design change would reduce the number of metal screws required in production by 16 per desk. Installation of each screw requires 15 seconds of labor time. The average labor rate is $18 per hour and each screw costs $.05. The firm has estimated production and sales of the standard metal desk as follows over the remainder of the product's life cycle:

Year	Production and Sales Volume
1994	2,000
1995	3,500
1996	3,000
1997	2,000
1998	1,200

The company would be required to incur setup costs of an unknown amount in order to execute the design change. The company requires a 4-year payback period, uses a 12% discount rate, and depreciates all property (including setup costs) using the straight-line method.
a. Determine the annual cost savings associated with the design change.
b. Based on the 12% discount rate, what is the maximum amount the company could spend on the setup costs and still meet its required return? And still meet it required payback period?
c. Assuming the setup will cost $14,000, determine the net present value.

d. Based on your calculations in part c, determine the profitability index.

e. Based on a setup cost of $15,000, compute the accounting rate of return.

50. *(Comprehensive)* The management of Essen Manufacturing Company is evaluating a proposal to purchase a new drill press as a replacement for a less efficient piece of similar equipment that would then be sold. The cost of the new drill press including delivery and installation is $175,000. If the equipment is purchased, Essen will incur $5,000 of costs in removing the present equipment and revamping service facilities.

The present equipment has a book value of $100,000 and a remaining useful life of 10 years. Due to new technical improvements that have made the equipment outmoded, it presently has a resale value of only $40,000.

Management has provided you with the following comparative manufacturing cost tabulation:

	Present Equipment	New Equipment
Annual production in units	400,000	500,000
Revenue from each unit	$.30	$.30
Annual costs:		
Labor	$30,000	$25,000
Depreciation (10% of asset book value or cost)	10,000	17,500
Other cash operating costs	48,000	20,000

Management believes that if the present equipment is not replaced now, the company will have to wait 7 years before replacement is justified. The company uses a 15% discount or hurdle rate in evaluating capital projects and expects that all capital project investments recoup their costs within 5 years.

Both pieces of equipment are expected to have a negligible salvage value at the end of 10 years.

a. Determine the net present value of the new equipment.

b. Determine the payback period for the new equipment.

c. Determine the accounting rate of return for the new equipment.

d. Using an incremental approach, determine whether the company should keep the present equipment or purchase the new equipment?

(CPA adapted)

51. *(Postinvestment audit)* Ten years ago, based on an NPV analysis, California Hydraulics decided to add a new product line. The data used in the analysis was as follows:

Discount rate	12%
Life of product line	10 years
Annual sales increase:	
Years 1–4	$250,000
Years 5–8	350,000
Years 9–10	200,000
Annual fixed costs	$ 40,000
Contribution margin ratio	40%
Cost of production equipment	$250,000
Investment in working capital	20,000
Salvage value	0

As the product line was discontinued this year, corporate managers decided to conduct a postinvestment audit to assess the accuracy of their planning process. Accordingly, the actual cash flows generated from the product line were estimated to be as follows:

Actual investment:

Production equipment:	$240,000
Working capital	35,000
Total	$275,000

Actual sales:	
Years 1–4	$220,000
Years 5–8	400,000
Years 9–10	210,000
Actual fixed costs:	
Years 1–4	$ 30,000
Years 5–8	35,000
Years 9–10	50,000
Actual contribution margin ratio	35%
Actual salvage value	10,000
Return of working capital	35,000
Actual cost of capital	12%

a. Determine the projected NPV on the product line investment.

b. Determine the NPV of the project based on the postinvestment audit.

c. Identify the factors that are most responsible for the differences between the projected NPV and the postinvestment audit NPV.

52. *(Dealing with uncertainty)* The Arizona Sand & Gravel Company supplies materials to construction companies for building roads and bridges. The company has been searching for a location to "mine" gravel for a new major interstate road project. The owner of one location is willing to allow the company to mine all the gravel it needs for the road project, provided the firm reclaims the land (which essentially involves building a road and a small lake, and planting trees) after the road project is completed. The firm would also be required to post a $1,000,000 damage deposit which would be refunded (without interest) at the end of the reclamation. The road project is expected to last three years and the reclamation of the mining location would require an additional year. To evaluate the feasibility of this offer, the company has estimated cash expenses and cash income under a pessimistic and an optimistic scenario:

	Pessimistic	Optimistic
Costs to relocate mining equip.	$ 100,000	$ 100,000
Damage deposit	1,000,000	1,000,000
Year 1 gravel sales	2,000,000	2,200,000
Year 2 gravel sales	2,000,000	2,200,000
Year 3 gravel sales	3,000,000	3,500,000
Costs of reclamation (year 4)	500,000	350,000
Annual fixed cash expenses	400,000	400,000
Annual variable expenses	70% of sales	65% of sales

The annual fixed and variable expenses would be incurred only in years 1–3, when the mine is operational.

a. Assuming the company's cost of capital is 14%, compute the NPV under both the pessimistic and optimistic alternatives.

b. If the company estimates the probability of the pessimistic scenario occurring is 70% and the probability of the optimistic scenario occurring is 30%, what should the company do?

53. *(Capital budgeting decision related to JIT)* The management of Hirsch Electrical has decided to implement a just-in-time inventory control system and redesign the placement of equipment into manufacturing cells. The new layout in the company's 20,000-square-foot plant will cost $2,000,000 and will free 40% of the square footage of the plant. Hirsch Electrical has two possibilities for the newly released space:

1. The company can put in 3 additional manufacturing cells at a cost of $3,500,000 each. Each cell can produce 20,000 units per year and each unit provides a contribution margin of $54. These additional cells will each create cash fixed costs of $250,000 per year. The life of the equipment/cells is 10 years.

2. The company can rent out the released space for $900,000 for the first year. The tenant is an instrumental supplier of raw materials and agrees to sign a 10-year lease with 5% rent increases each year.

In either case, the new cell layout will increase the throughput of the company by 2,000 additional units per year.

a. Which if any of the above amounts are not relevant to the decision?

b. If the cost of capital of Hirsch Electrical is 10%, what is the present value of putting new manufacturing cells in the released space? What is the present value of the rental alternative?

c. Based on the calculations made in part b, which of the alternatives would be more cost-beneficial for Hirsch Electrical?

d. What problems, if any, do you see with the computations made in conjunction with the new manufacturing cell investments?

e. Referring to the original data and using a cost of capital of 10%, assume that the supplier company suggests that it locate close to Hirsch Electrical, but not in the released space. The supplier asks Hirsch's management for a $1,000,000 grant to relocate. The grant would not be repaid and would simply be considered by Hirsch as a front-end cost of future purchases from the supplier. In addition to the increase in throughput generated by redesigning the layout to manufacturing cells, the relocation of the supplier would increase throughput by another 8,000 units per year at the normal contribution margin. Should Hirsch invest the $1,000,000 in relocating the supplier, merely install 3 additional manufacturing cells, or rent the released space to the supplier?

54. Precision Instruments Inc. is considering the various benefits that may result from the shortening of its product cycle by changing from the company's present manual system to a computer-aided manufacturing (CAD/CAM) system. The proposed system can provide productive time equivalency close to the 20,000 hours currently available with the manual system. The incremental annual out-of-pocket costs of maintaining the manual system are $20 per hour.

The incremental annual out-of-pocket costs of maintaining the CAD/CAM system are estimated to be $200,000 with an initial investment of $580,000 in the proposed system. The estimated useful life of this system is six years. Precision Instruments requires a minimum rate of return of 20% on projects of this type. Full capacity will be utilized.

a. Compute the relevant annual cash flows related to the CAD/CAM project.

b. Based on the computation in part a above, compute the following:
   1. payback period
   2. internal rate of return (round to the nearest .5 percent)
   3. net present value
   4. profitability index

c. Based on the company's investment evaluation criterion, is the project acceptable? Explain.

(CMA)

ETHICS AND QUALITY DISCUSSION

55. In the U.S. companies generally respond to economic downturns by reducing spending on capital projects. A frequently observed strategy is to delay investment in new capital projects and products, and cut spending on research and development activities, advertising, and customer service activities.
    a. In economic downturns how can companies cut costs and activities without affecting quality or service?
    b. What are the likely effects of short-term cost cutting strategies such as those outlined above on long-term profitability and quality control?

56. Joe Johnson, the plant manager of the Cleveland plant of the Adams Tractor Company, has submitted a capital budgeting proposal for a new CAD/CAM system for his plant. He is really excited about the acquisition as it almost perfectly meets the plant's needs and he has received approval from the home office. However, he was reading the local newspaper this morning only to realize that his purchasing agent happens to be the sister of the vendor of the CAD/CAM system.

    The Adams Tractor Company has a strict policy that prohibits purchasing from relatives. If this relationship comes to light, the purchasing agent could be fired and Johnson would not get the system that is best, in his judgment, for his plant. Since the purchasing agent is married, her name is different from her brother's and it is unlikely that a connection will be made. Johnson is concerned about what to do—abide by the policy or acquire the necessary system at the reasonable price quoted by the vendor.
    a. Why would a company have a policy of this nature?
    b. What are the ethical conflicts in this situation?
    c. What are the potential risks for Johnson? For the company?
    d. What do you recommend and why?

57. The Fore Corp. has operations in over two dozen countries. Fore's headquarters is in Chicago, and company executives frequently travel to visit Fore's foreign and domestic operations.

    Fore owns two business jets with international range and six smaller aircraft for shorter flights. Company policy is to assign aircraft to trips based on cost minimization, but practice is to assign aircraft based on organizational rank of the traveler. Fore offers its aircraft for short-term lease or for charter by other organizations whenever Fore employees do not plan to use the aircraft. Fore surveys the market often to keep its lease and charter rates competitive.

    William Earle, Fore's vice president of Finance, claims that a third business jet can be justified financially. However, some people in the controller's office think the real reason for a third business jet is because people outranking Earle keep the two business jets busy. Thus, Earle usually must travel in the smaller aircraft.

    The third business jet would cost $11 million. A capital expenditure of this magnitude requires a formal proposal with projected cash flows and net present value computations using Fore's minimum required rate of return. If Fore's president and finance committee approve the proposal, it will be submitted to the full board. The board has final approval on capital expenditures exceeding $5 million and has established a policy of rejecting any discretionary proposal that has a negative net present value.

    Earle asked Rachel Arnett, assistant corporate controller and CMA, to prepare a proposal on a third business jet. Arnett gathered the following information:

    Acquisition cost of the jet, including instrumentation and interior furnishings.
    Operating cost of the jet for company use.

- Projected avoidable commercial airfare and other avoidable costs from company use of the plane.
- Projected value of executive time saved by using the third business jet.
- Projected contribution margin from incremental lease and charter activity.
- Estimated resale value of the jet.
- Estimated income tax effects of the proposal.

When Earle reviewed Arnett's completed proposal and saw the large negative net present value figure, he returned the proposal to Arnett and insisted she had made an error in her calculations.

Feeling some pressure, Arnett checked her computations and found no errors. However, Earle's message was clear. Arnett discarded her projections and estimates and replaced them with figures that had a remote chance of actually occurring but were more favorable to the proposal. For example, she used first-class airfares to refigure the avoidable commercial airfare costs, even though the company policy is to fly coach. She found revising the proposal to be distressing.

The revised proposal still had a negative net present value. Earle's anger was evident as he told Arnett to revise the proposal again, and to start with a $100,000 positive net present value and work backwards to compute supporting estimates and projections.

a. Explain whether Rachel Arnett's revision of the proposal was in violation of the Standards of Ethical Conduct for Management Accountants. (Refer to Exhibit 1–10.)

b. Was William Earle in violation of the Standards of Ethical Conduct for Management Accountants by telling Arnett specifically to revise the proposal? Explain your answer.

c. What elements of the projection and estimation process would be compromised in preparing an analysis for which a preconceived result is sought?

d. Identify specific controls over the capital budgeting process that Fore Corporation could implement to prevent unethical behavior on the part of the vice president of finance.

(CMA)

ADVANCED CAPITAL BUDGETING TOPICS

**LEARNING
OBJECTIVES**

After completing this chapter, you should be able to answer these questions:

1. How is the weighted average cost of capital computed and why is it important?
2. How do taxes and depreciation methods affect cash flows?
3. How do managers rank investment projects?
4. How is risk considered in capital budgeting analysis?
5. *(Appendix 1)* How can the risk of a capital project be measured on a statistical basis?
6. *(Appendix 2)* How are payback and the accounting rate of return linked?

LYONDELL PETROCHEMICAL COMPANY

Lyondell Petrochemical Company is a publicly held corporation, of which 49.96% of the outstanding common stock is held by Atlantic Richfield Company. Lyondell is an integrated manufacturer and marketer of petrochemicals and refined petroleum products, with manufacturing facilities in Houston, Channelview and Pasadena, Texas, and corporate headquarters in downtown Houston.

Lyondell's primary products are basic chemicals and refined products with no brand name recognition. Yet the products produced by the company are part of a multitude of consumer goods including fibers for clothing, ingredients in paint, medicines, carpet, recording tape, trash bags, and car dashboards.

Investment opportunities for existing businesses are evaluated by looking for projects that offer good long-term returns and prompt payback, typically less than three years. For acquisitions, joint ventures and similar opportunities, the company expects to achieve good overall profitability based on their integration with existing company businesses and their ability to enhance total returns to stockholders.

Capital expenditures were $43 million in 1991, $145 million in 1990 and $176 million in 1989. Various environmental laws and regulations impose substantial requirements upon the operations of the Company. The Company's policy is to be in compliance with such laws and regulations, which include the Comprehensive Environmental Response, Compensation and Recovery Act of 1980 (CERCLA), the Resource Conservation and Recovery Act (RCRA) and the Clear Air Act Amendments of 1990. The Company spent approximately 50 percent of its 1991 capital budget on environmentally related projects. The 1992 capital expenditures budget was set at $115 million, of which $75 million was for environmentally related projects. These environmental projects included a number of investments to significantly reduce benzene emissions; the first stage of construction of an on-site waste incinerator; initial work to install a wet gas scrubber on the Fluid Catalytic Cracking Unit (FCCU) at the Houston Refinery, completion of a vapor recovery project at the Channelview Complex, and initiation of a similar project at the Houston Refinery.

The 1992 capital budget also included several profit generating projects such as expansion of the product flexibility unit at the Channelview Complex that would more than double propylene capacity by 1993 and a four percent expansion of methanol capacity through a debottlenecking project. It also included a project to improve the operating performance of the FCCU at the Refinery and equipment modifications to the polypropylene plant to improve product quality, efficiency and flexibility.

SOURCE: Lyondell Petrochemical Company, *1991 Annual Report*, pp. cover, 4, and 24.

C hapter 19 presents the basic process and methods of making capital budgeting decisions, one of which is the payback method used by Lyondell. But Lyondell also considers legal requirements as well as "long-term returns" that encompass the impact of the time value of money. In making a decision about the discount rate to use in evaluating capital projects from a present value perspective,

Lyondell (like any other company) would consider its corporate cost of capital, which is the rate of return that must be earned on its various sources of capital. In addition, Lyondell management must determine the tax effects that capital projects will have since the company faces a 30+ percent marginal income tax rate as well as the risks of investing in different projects. These four advanced capital budgeting issues (cost of capital, income taxes, asset selection, and risk) provide a more comprehensive framework for making decisions concerning capital asset selection and investment and are discussed in this chapter and its appendixes.

WEIGHTED AVERAGE COST OF CAPITAL

Weighted average cost of capital

The net present value (NPV) and profitability index (PI) methods of evaluating capital projects require that a company specify a discount rate to be used in making present value computations. In addition, the internal rate of return (IRR) method uses a specified rate of return as a hurdle rate against which the IRR is compared for acceptability. In general, for projects bearing some degree of risk, the *minimum* rate of return specified for any of these three techniques should be the firm's weighted average cost of capital. This rate differs for each company and is computed based on the sources of capital used by a company. For example, Lyondell Petrochemical has debt and common stock equity; other companies may also have preferred stockholders. Although the method of financing a specific investment project does not affect the evaluation of that project, the mix of financing does affect the firm's cost of capital.

The **weighted average cost of capital** (COC) is "a composite of the cost of various sources of funds comprising a firm's capital structure. It is the minimum rate of return that must be earned on new investments [so as not to] . . . dilute the interests of the shareholder."[1] Each source of funds comprising a firm's capital structure (debt, preferred stock, and common stock equity) is analyzed to determine its cost of funds to the firm. Next, the percentage of the capital structure comprised by each funding source is found. The funding source's cost is multiplied by its capital structure percentage to derive its proportionate cost of capital. These results are summed to compute the weighted average cost of capital. Computations showing the costs of the various types of funds are shown next.

Cost of Components

Most firms have a variety of sources of funds composing their capital structures. Each source is issued for different reasons and requires a different method to compute its cost. Glover Company is used to illustrate the various cost of capital computations.

Debt. Debt includes long-term notes, bonds, and any portion of short-term debt expected to be refinanced in a manner that would make it appear to be permanent. Debt creates an interest cost that is tax deductible. Thus, the cost of debt is the after-tax cost of interest. The following formula indicates the computations for the cost of a new debt issuance:

$$k_d = YR(1 - TR)$$

where k_d = cost of debt
    YR = current yield (effective) rate[2]
    TR = tax rate

---

[1] "Institute of Management Accountants (formerly National Association of Accountants), *Statements on Management Accounting: Cost of Capital*, Number 4A (Montvale, N.J.: NAA, November 1, 1984), p. 1.
[2] The current yield rate is computed as the periodic interest payment divided by the *expected* market value of the debt. While the stated interest rate is used to compute the periodic cash flow interest payments, the current yield rate is more representative of the opportunity costs facing the firm considering new, current period debt issuances. If new debt is not being considered, the current yield rate should be computed using the current market price of the debt.

Glover Company is planning a $10,000,000 bond issue. The stated rate on the debt is 7 percent, but the bonds are expected to sell at a price that will yield a rate of 8 percent. The company is in a 40 percent tax bracket. The cost of Glover's contemplated debt issuance is:

$$k_d = .08 \ (1 - .40)$$
$$= .08 \ (.60)$$
$$= 4.8\%$$

Each $1 of interest expense reduces Glover's taxable income by $1, which in turn causes a $.40 reduction in tax expense. Therefore, the net effective cost of interest expense to Glover Company is 60 percent of the yield rate or 4.8 percent.

The cost of convertible debt is computed like other forms of debt, with one exception. If the debt's conversion price is close to the common stock's market price, the convertible debt should be treated as though it had been converted into common shares and the cost of capital computed accordingly.

Preferred Stock.   Preferred stock is considered a hybrid security that has characteristics of both bonds (debt) and common stock (equity). Generally, preferred dividend payments are fixed in terms of schedule and amount as are the interest payments on debt. However, since preferred dividends are not tax deductible and are paid from after-tax earnings, there is no tax adjustment when the cost of capital is computed for preferred stock. The calculation for the cost of preferred stock is:

$$k_p = D \div MP$$

where k_p = cost of preferred stock
         D = annual dividend amount
     MP = expected market price per share (or current market
                  price if no new preferred stock is to be issued)

In addition to the debt issue mentioned above, Glover Company is considering a $500,000 face value issuance of $100 par value, 9 percent preferred stock. The preferred stock is expected to sell for $115 per share. The cost of Glover's proposed preferred stock issuance is:

$$k_p = \$9 \div \$115$$
$$\approx 7.8\%$$

Glover would receive $115 for each share of preferred stock, but would only have to pay the 9 percent dividend on the $100 par value. Thus, the company has an approximately 7.8 percent effective dividend rate rather than the 9 percent dividend rate stated on each share.

Common Stock Equity.   The largest source of capital in most corporations is common stock equity, which refers to the common stock, paid-in capital, and retained earnings of a firm. One difficulty in determining the cost of common stock equity is that no specified interest or dividend payments are required for common stock. This lack of contractual payments means that a variety of possible methods have been developed to calculate the cost of common stock equity capital.

In theory, the cost of common stock equity is "the expected, required, or actual rate of return . . . which, if earned, will leave the market value of the stock unchanged."[3] Such a rate is difficult, if not impossible, to determine precisely, although an estimate can be made of it using the following **dividend growth method**. This method is based on the rate of return that stockholders expect to earn in the form of

Dividend growth method

---

[3] Institute of Management Accountants, "Cost of Capital," p. 7.

dividends on a company's common stock.[4] Dividends paid on common stock, like those paid on preferred stock, are not tax deductible by the company and therefore are not affected by the tax rate.

The dividend growth method computes the cost of common stock equity as follows:

$$k_c = (D \div MP) + g$$

where k_c = cost of common stock equity
  D = expected annual dividend amount
  MP = expected market price per share (or current market price if no new common stock is to be issued)
  g = expected average annual growth rate

Growth rate

The expected average annual **growth rate** is an estimate of the increase expected in dividends or in market value per share of stock. The growth rate is a function of a company's predicted earnings, dividend policy, and market price appreciation per share.

Assume that Glover Company expects to pay a $5 per share dividend on common stock this year. Current market price of the common stock is $60 per share, and the company's average annual growth rate of 4 percent is expected to continue indefinitely. Using the dividend growth model, the cost of Glover's common stock equity is computed as:

$$k_c = (\$5 \div \$60) + .04$$
$$= .08333 + .04$$
$$= 12.33\%$$

Optimal Mix of Capital

To determine a firm's total cost of capital, costs of the individual capital components are weighted in proportion to the entire equity base. A weighted average cost of capital can be computed for any mix of debt and equity. However, if market conditions remain stable, each firm should be able to compute its **optimal mix of capital**, which represents the combination of capital sources at which the lowest weighted average cost of capital is achieved. The COC determined for this optimal mix is the most reasonable rate to use for purposes of capital budgeting.

Optimal mix of capital

Using the previously computed capital costs (debt, 4.8 percent; preferred stock, 7.8 percent; and common stock equity, 12.33 percent) and the following information, the weighted average cost and optimal mix of capital for the Glover Company are determined in Exhibit 20–1.

▮ The 4.8 percent cost of debt is appropriate only for a capital structure that includes no more than 39 percent debt. Management recognizes that, as the level of company debt increases, debtholders require a higher rate of return because of increased risk. Glover's management has estimated that after-tax cost of debt will rise to 8 percent when debt composes between 40 percent and 59 percent of total capital, and to 12 percent if debt equals or exceeds 60 percent of total capital.

▮ Company management has established a policy that preferred stock cannot exceed 10 percent of total equity.

▮ The costs of preferred and common stock equity will remain constant at 7.8 percent and 12.33 percent, respectively, regardless of the proportion of other capital sources.

---

[4]Two other methods of determining cost of common stock equity are the historical rate of return and the earnings/price ratio. These methods are easier to compute than the dividend growth method, but they provide less reliable estimates of the true cost of equity. Therefore, we will use the dividend growth method for this COC computation.

FUNDING COMBINATION #	TYPE OF CAPITAL FUNDING SOURCE	% OF TOTAL CAPITAL	COST OF CAPITAL	WEIGHTED AVERAGE COST OF CAPITAL
1	Debt	0	4.80	0
	Preferred stock	0	7.80	0
	Common stock equity	100	12.33	12.330
				12.330
2	Debt	0	4.80	0
	Preferred stock	10	7.80	.780
	Common stock equity	90	12.33	11.097
				11.877
3	Debt	20	4.80	.960
	Preferred stock	10	7.80	.780
	Common stock equity	70	12.33	8.631
				10.371
4	Debt	30	4.80	1.440
	Preferred stock	10	7.80	.780
	Common stock equity	60	12.33	7.398
				9.618
5	Debt	40	8.00	3.200
	Preferred stock	10	7.80	.780
	Common stock equity	50	12.33	6.165
				10.145
6	Debt	59	8.00	4.720
	Preferred stock	10	7.80	.780
	Common stock equity	31	12.33	3.822
				9.322 ←——*
7	Debt	60	12.00	7.200
	Preferred stock	10	7.80	.780
	Common stock equity	30	12.33	3.699
				11.679

* Lowest weighted average cost and, therefore, the optimal mix of capital.

■ **EXHIBIT 20–1**

Glover Company Weighted Average Cost of Capital

■ Glover Company is not involved in international operations. Although international diversification provides a company with an expanded set of capital sources—possibly at significantly different capital costs than would be available domestically—those foreign capital sources are riskier. Such risk would need to be factored into any cost of capital computations.

The lowest weighted average cost of capital for Glover Company occurs in funding combination #6, in which debt is 59 percent, preferred stock is 10 percent, and common stock equity is 31 percent of total capital. At this mix, the weighted average COC is 9.322 percent. A change in proportions of capital sources in either direction from the optimal mix will raise the weighted average COC for the firm.

The weighted average cost of capital for the current capital structure may be computed on either past or current balance sheet values. Current values are preferable because they reflect amounts that are relevant to current decision making. Historical balance sheet data can be restated to the current market values for existing debt and equity. Such restatement allows the current cost of existing capital to be calculated. If the capital structure is expected to change, expected market values should be used to compute the costs of capital for any new capital sources (as indicated in the previous formulas).

Knowledge of the weighted average COC can assist managers in setting the discount or hurdle rate used in evaluating capital asset investments. Higher costs of capital will result in lower net present values and a greater likelihood that an investment project might be rejected. The cost of capital in the United States has for many years been the highest of the four leading industrialized economies (United States, Japan, Great Britain, and West Germany). As of 1989, the after-tax cost of capital in the U.S. was nearly 6 percent, compared to approximately 3 percent in Japan. Thus, "American companies can afford to wait just half as long as their Japanese competitors for capital investments to reach an acceptable level of profitability."[5]

Another rate of significance in the capital budgeting process is the marginal tax rate of the organization because this rate is used in assessing the acceptability of alternative capital projects.

THE EFFECT OF DEPRECIATION ON AFTER-TAX CASH FLOWS

Although Chapter 19 ignored income tax effects on the evaluation of capital projects, income taxes are an integral part of the business environment and decision-making process in our society. Tax planning is a central part of management planning and has a large impact on overall business profitability. Managers typically make decisions only after giving thorough recognition to how company taxes will be affected by those decisions. In evaluating capital projects, managers should use after-tax cash flows to determine project acceptability.

Note that depreciation expense is not a cash flow item. Although no funds are paid or received for it, depreciation on capital assets, like interest on debt, affects cash flow by reducing a company's tax obligation. Thus, depreciation provides a **tax shield** against the payment of taxes that, correspondingly, produces a **tax benefit** equal to the amount of the depreciation multiplied by the tax rate. The concepts of tax shield and tax benefit are shown on the income statements below. The tax rate is assumed to be 40 percent.

Tax shield (of depreciation)
Tax benefit (of depreciation)

No depreciation deduction		Depreciation deduction	
Income Statement		**Income Statement**	
Sales	$1,000,000	Sales	$1,000,000
Cost of goods sold	(350,000)	Cost of goods sold	(350,000)
Gross margin	$ 650,000	Gross margin	$ 650,000
Expenses other than depreciation	(150,000)	Expenses other than depreciation	(150,000)
Depreciation expense	0	Depreciation expense	(200,000)
Income before taxes	$ 500,000	Income before taxes	$ 300,000
Tax expense (40%)	(200,000)	Tax expense (40%)	(120,000)
Net income	$ 300,000	Net income	$ 180,000

---

[5]Louis S. Richman, "How Capital Costs Cripple America," *FORTUNE* (August 14, 1989), p. 51.

NEWS NOTE

The Complex World of MACRS

By depreciating assets as quickly as possible, manufacturers can save money on their income taxes. Careful attention to what can be depreciated and by how much pays off in real money.

Prior to the 1986 Tax Reform Act, assets were broadly classified as property with 3-year, 5-year, 10-year, or 19-year lives. Today, these four simple categories are gone. Under MACRS, assets are now classified into nearly 130 different categories, each with its own depreciable life of 3, 5, 7, 10, 15, 20, 27.5, or 31.5 years. Different methods of depreciation, such as straight-line or accelerated, will apply to the different classes of property.

For example, in a manufacturing plant, companies get a seven-year write-off on all their manufacturing equipment, such as assembly line equipment, robots, and machine presses. Companies can also claim seven-year depreciation on electrical, air-conditioning, or humidity-control systems specifically needed for the equipment to function. The key to identifying other seven-year assets is to look for items that can be removed if the occupant ever leaves the building.

[Analyzing the cost categories prior to construction or acquisition can help a company obtain the greatest depreciation benefit.] For example, if movable partitions are used between offices instead of fixed walls, the company can write off the partitions over a much shorter life. Fixed walls would be considered part of the real estate and be depreciable over 31.5 years.

SOURCE: Joseph Martini, "Cost-Segregation Studies: Saving Money Through Depreciation," *(Grant Thornton) Manufacturing Issues* (Winter 1990), pp. 14–15. Reprinted by permission from Grant Thornton's *Manufacturing Issues*. © 1990 Grant Thornton.

The tax shield is the depreciation expense amount of $200,000. The tax benefit is the $80,000 difference between $200,000 of tax expense on the first income statement and $120,000 of tax expense on the second income statement. The tax benefit is also equal to the 40 percent tax rate times the tax shield of $200,000. Since taxes are reduced by $80,000, less cash must be spent and, thus, the pattern of cash flows is improved.

Income tax laws regarding depreciation deductions are subject to annual revision. In making their analysis of capital investments, managers should use the most current tax regulations for depreciation to calculate cash flows from projects. Different depreciation methods may have significant impacts on after-tax cash flows. For a continuously profitable business, an accelerated method of depreciation (such as MACRS, the modified accelerated cost recovery system) will produce higher tax benefits in the early years of asset life than will the straight-line method. These higher tax benefits will translate into a higher net present value over the life of the investment project.

Changes in the availability of depreciation methods or in the length of an asset's depreciable life may dramatically affect projected after-tax cash flows. The changed cash flows will, in turn, affect the net present value, profitability index, and internal rate of return expected from the capital investment. Since capital projects are analyzed and evaluated before investments are made, managers should be aware of the inherent risk of tax law changes. "The Complex World of MACRS" News Note addresses such changes.

It is possible that assumptions made about the depreciation method or asset life may not be valid by the time an investment is actually made and an asset is placed into service. However, once purchased and placed into service, an asset can generally be depreciated using the method and tax life allowed when the asset was placed into service regardless of the tax law changes occurring after that time.

Changes may also occur in the tax rate structure. Rate changes may be relatively unpredictable. For example, the maximum federal corporate tax rate for many years was 46 percent; the Tax Reform Act of 1986 lowered this rate to 34 percent. A tax rate reduction lowers the tax benefit provided by depreciation because the cash flow impact is lessened. Tax rate changes (like asset tax-life changes) can cause the expected outcomes of the capital investment analysis to vary from the project's actual outcomes.

To illustrate such variations, assume that Glover Company is considering investing in a $100,000 petroleum storage tank. The tank has a 30-year economic life and would produce expected annual cash operating savings of $12,000. As indicated earlier, Glover Company's weighted average cost of capital is approximately 9 percent; this rate will be used as the discount rate for evaluating capital projects. Corporate assets are depreciated on a straight-line basis for tax purposes.[6]

In late 1993, prior to the tank purchase, Glover's cost accountant, Melanie Stringfellow, performed net present value analysis and also calculated the project's internal rate of return. The results of her calculations are shown in Exhibit 20–2 under Situation A. Note that depreciation is added back to income after taxes to obtain the amount of after-tax cash flow. *Even though depreciation is deductible for tax purposes, it is still a noncash outflow.* The present value amounts are obtained by multiplying the after-tax cash flows by the appropriate PV of annuity factors from Table 2 in Appendix A at the end of the text. Both evaluation techniques indicated the acceptability of the capital investment. At the time Ms. Stringfellow made her analysis, Glover's tax rate was 30 percent and the tax laws allowed a 15-year depreciable life on this property.

Early in 1994, Glover Company purchased the storage tank for $100,000. Immediately after the tank was purchased, Congress voted to change the tax laws related to this type of property. Exhibit 20–2 shows the different cash flows, net present values, and internal rates of return that result if the same project is subjected to either a 35 percent (Situation B) or 46 percent (Situation C) tax rate.

This example demonstrates that Glover will calculate a different NPV and IRR when a different tax rate is used. If the tax rate is raised either to 35 or 46 percent, the NPV and the IRR drop below that determined at a 30 percent tax rate. An increase in the tax rate makes the storage tank a less acceptable purchase, based on its net present value.

When a capital investment analyst considers the possibility that, in addition to the federal marginal tax rate of 34 percent, there may be state income taxes (and perhaps foreign income taxes), the appropriate tax rate can be in the range of 34 percent to 50 percent. When taxes are considered, depreciation expense affects not only NPV and IRR calculations, but also payback period and the accounting rate of return.

Understanding how depreciation and taxes affect the various capital budgeting techniques allows managers to make the most informed decisions about capital investments.[7] Well-informed managers are more likely to have confidence in capital investments made by the company if the substantial resource commitment required can be justified. That justification is partially achieved by considering whether a capital project fits into the long-range company plans.

---

[6] To simplify the presentation, we have elected to ignore a tax rule requirement called the half-year (or mid-quarter) convention. Under tax law, only a partial year's depreciation may be taken in the year an asset is placed into service. The slight difference that such a tax limitation would make on the amounts presented is immaterial for purposes of illustrating these capital budgeting concepts.

[7] These examples have all considered the investment project as a purchase. If a leasing option exists, the classification of the lease as operating or capital will affect the amounts deductible for tax purposes. A good illustration of this is provided in "The Lease vs. Purchase Decision," by Ralph L. Benke, Jr., and Charles P. Baril in *Management Accounting* (March 1990), pp. 42–46.

EXHIBIT 20-2
Glover Company Storage Tank Analyses

Initial investment	$100,000
Expected annual before-tax cash flows	12,000
Straight-line depreciation (15 years for tax purposes)	6,667
Expected economic life	30 years

Situation A: Tax rate of 30% (in effect when project was analyzed)
Situation B: Tax rate of 35%
Situation C: Tax rate of 46%

	SITUATIONS		
	A	**B**	**C**
Years 1–15:			
Before-tax cash flow	$12,000	$12,000	$12,000
Depreciation	(6,667)	(6,667)	(6,667)
Income before tax	$ 5,333	$ 5,333	$ 5,333
Tax	(1,600)	(1,867)	(2,453)
Net income	$ 3,733	$ 3,466	$ 2,880
Depreciation	6,667	6,667	6,667
Cash flow (after tax)	$10,400	$10,133	$ 9,547
Years 16–30:			
Before-tax cash flow	$12,000	$12,000	$12,000
Depreciation	0	0	0
Income before tax	$12,000	$12,000	$12,000
Tax	(3,600)	(4,200)	(5,520)
Net income (and cash flow after tax)	$ 8,400	$ 7,800	$ 6,480

Situation A—NPV calculations assuming a 9% discount rate:

PV @ 9% of $10,400 for years 1–15 (factor = 8.0607)		$ 83,831
PV @ 9% of $ 8,400 for years 16–30 (factor = 2.2130)*		18,589
		$102,420
	Cost	(100,000)
	NPV	$ 2,420

Situation B—NPV calculations assuming a 9% discount rate:

PV @ 9% of $10,133 for years 1–15 (factor = 8.0607)		$ 81,679
PV @ 9% of $ 7,800 for years 16–30 (factor = 2.2130)*		17,261
		$ 98,940
	Cost	(100,000)
	NPV	$ (1,060)

Situation C—NPV calculations assuming a 9% discount rate:

PV @ 9% of $9,547 for years 1–15 (factor = 8.0607)		$ 76,956
PV @ 9% of $6,480 for years 16–30 (factor = 2.2130)*		14,340
		$ 91,296
	Cost	(100,000)
	NPV	$ (8,704)

*Factor = Annuity factor for 30 years − Annuity factor for 15 years

THE INVESTMENT DECISION

Management must identify the best asset(s) for the firm to acquire to fulfill the company's goals and objectives. Making such an identification requires answers to the following four subhead questions.

Is the Activity Worthy of an Investment?

A company acquires assets when they have value in relation to specific activities in which the company is engaged. For example, Lyondell Petrochemical acquires an automated distillation system needed to analyze crude oil before purchase and processing by the company (the activity). Delta Air Lines acquires maintenance facilities because they are necessary to the reliable provision of its flight service (the activity). Before making decisions to acquire assets, company management must be certain that the activity for which the assets will be needed is worthy of an investment.

An activity's worth is measured by cost-benefit analysis. For most capital budgeting decisions, costs and benefits can be measured in monetary terms. If the dollars of benefits exceed the dollars of costs, then the activity is, to that extent, worthwhile. In some cases, though, benefits provided by capital projects are difficult to quantify. The "Determining the Drivers" News Note discusses overcoming such difficulties at a division of Lightolier Inc. during the analysis of a pollution prevention project to reduce the use of trichlorethylene (TCE), a reportable TURA (Toxics Use Reduction Act) chemical under Massachusetts law.

As noted in Chapter 19, though, difficulty in quantification is no reason to exclude benefits from capital budgeting analyses. In most instances, surrogate quantifiable measures can be obtained for hard-to-quantify benefits. For example, a company considering the installation of an employee fitness center might positively include the reduced per-day cost of absenteeism for unhealthy employees. Similarly, benefits from investments in day-care centers for employees' children may only be estimable based on the reduction in employee time off and turnover. At a minimum, managers should attempt to subjectively include such benefits in the analytical process.

In other circumstances, it may be known in advance that the monetary benefits of the capital project will not exceed the costs, but the project is essential for certain quality-of-life reasons. For example, a company may consider renovating the employee workplace with new carpet, furniture, paint, and artwork. The renovation would not make employees' work any easier or safer, but simply more comfortable. Such a project may be deemed "worthy" regardless of cost-benefit analysis.

Another example is a situation in which a rural hospital invests in a kidney dialysis machine even though there are only a limited number of kidney patients in the area. The hospital administrators may believe the goodwill generated by such an acquisition justifies the cost. If an activity is deemed worthwhile, the question of cost may become secondary.

Which Assets Can Be Used for the Activity?

The determination of available and suitable assets to conduct the intended activity is closely related to the evaluation of the activity's worth. Management must have an idea of how much the needed assets will cost to determine if the activity should be pursued. As shown in Exhibit 20–3 on page 860, management should gather the following specific monetary and nonmonetary information for each asset to make this determination: initial cost, estimated life, salvage value, raw material and labor requirements, operating costs (both fixed and variable), output capability, service availability and cost, maintenance expectations, and revenues to be generated (if any). As mentioned in the previous section, some of the information needed in a capital project analysis must employ surrogate, indirect measures. Management must have both quantitative and qualitative information on each asset to answer the next question.

NEWS NOTE

Determining the Drivers of Environmental Costs

The capital budgeting approval procedure at Lightolier is very formal, beginning with the development of project parameters and requirements, a request for proposal (RFP) and the in-house Project Appropriation Request Form (PAR). The PAR included financial analyses for the project's cash inflows and outflows, a qualitative assessment of the project's benefits, and a vendor spreadsheet containing base costs. Answers to questions about environmentally related indirect costs could not be collected from the cost accounting system because such costs were simply lumped in one or more overhead accounts. Thus, it became necessary to estimate the time and money spent on those costs in an alternative manner using the logic employed in activity-based costing. To deal with the indirect costs, questions about environmentally related activities were asked of the responsible personnel and the following sources for estimation were developed:

INDIRECT LABOR COSTS (ENVIRONMENTAL)

Activity	Cost Driver	Measurement	Source of Info
Spill/Leak Incident Reporting	Number of spills Number of incidents	labor hours ($ per week)	Engineer interview
Monitoring	Number of toxics Number of processes using toxics	labor hours ($ per week)	Engineer interview
Right to Know Training (in-house)	Number of sessions	labor hours ($ per year) training supplies ($ per session)	Engineer interview Engineering records
Permitting	Number of toxics used	labor hours ($ per week)	Engineer interview
	Number of gallons or pounds discharged	supplies fees ($ per chemical or $ per gallon)	Accounting records Regulatory agency document
Maintenance costs	Number of machines	labor hours ($ per week) spare parts, equipment ($ per item)	Equipment vendor Engineer interview

INDIRECT MATERIALS COST (ENVIRONMENTAL)

Items	Cost Driver	Measurement	Source of Info
TCE Disposal	Number of drums	$ per drum	Accounting records Engineering records
TURA Fees	Number of reportable chemicals	$ per chemical	TURA reporting form Engineering records
Protective Equipment	Number of employees Square footage protected	$ per employee	Engineering records Accounting records

Using the cost drivers, the company projected these environmental costs over the life of the project, adjusted them for inflation at the rate of 5 percent annually, and incorporated them into a discounted cash flow model. The 15 percent cost of capital was used as the discount rate for after-tax cash flows (assuming a 39 percent corporate tax rate).

SOURCE: Adapted with permission from Marlene R. Wittman, "Costing and Financial Analysis of a Pollution Prevention Project," *Environmental Finance* (V1N4, Winter 1991/92), pp. 433–452. Copyright 1992 by Executive Enterprises, Inc., 22 West 21st Street, New York, N.Y. 10010-6990. 212-645-7880. All rights reserved.

EXHIBIT 20–3
Capital Investment
Information

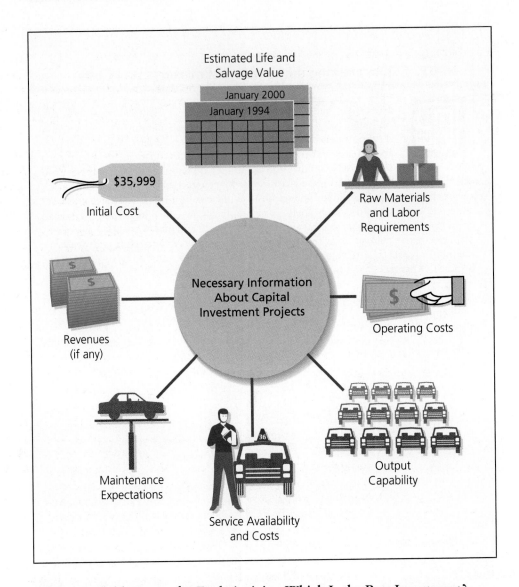

Of the Available Assets for Each Activity, Which Is the Best Investment?

Using all available information, management should select the best asset from the possible candidates and exclude all others from consideration. In most instances, a company has a standing committee to discuss, evaluate, and approve capital projects. In judging capital project acceptability, this committe should recognize that two types of capital budgeting decisions need to be made: screening and preference decisions. A **screening decision** indicates whether a capital project is desirable based on some previously established minimum criterion or criteria. If the project does not meet the minimum standard(s), it is excluded from further consideration. The second decision is a **preference decision** in which projects are ranked according to their impact on the achievement of company objectives.

Deciding which asset is the best investment requires the use of one or several of the evaluation techniques (payback period, net present value, profitability index, internal rate of return, and accounting rate of return) discussed in Chapter 19. Some techniques may be used to screen the projects as to acceptability; other techniques may be used to rank the projects in order of preferability. While different companies use different techniques for screening and ranking purposes, payback period is commonly used for screening decisions. The reasons for this choice are that payback focuses only on the short run and does not consider the time value of money. The remaining techniques may be used to screen or rank capital projects.

Screening decision

Preference decision

Of the "Best Investments" for All Worthwhile Activities, in Which Ones Should the Company Invest?

While many worthwhile investment activities exist, each company has limited resources to invest at any time and thus attempts to allocate its available resources in the most profitable manner. Therefore, after choosing the best asset for each activity, management must decide which activities and assets to fund. Investment activities may be classified as mutually exclusive, independent, or mutually inclusive.

Mutually exclusive projects perform the same basic task. One project will be chosen from such a group, causing all others to be excluded from further consideration because they would provide unneeded or redundant capability. The task of the new asset under consideration may be to replace a current asset by providing the same basic capabilities. If the company keeps the old asset, it will not buy the new one; if the new one is purchased, the old asset will be sold. Thus, the two assets are mutually exclusive. For example, if Lyondell Petrochemical decided to acquire a new corporate headquarters building in Corpus Christi, Texas, it would no longer need its downtown Houston headquarters. The Houston location would be sold to help finance the new location as well as to eliminate duplicate facilities.

Mutually exclusive projects

Alternatively, the new assets in the mutually exclusive group may each provide the company with new but similar capabilities. For instance, assume that Lyondell wanted to install a videoconferencing network for its various plant locations. Company managers would identify all technologically appropriate equipment, select one system, and eliminate all others since benefit can be obtained from only one system.

Other investments may be **independent projects** in that they have no specific bearing on one another. For example, the acquisition of an office microcomputer system is not related to the purchase of a factory machine. These project decisions are analyzed and accepted or rejected independently of one another. Although limited resources may preclude the acquisition of all acceptable projects, the projects themselves are not mutually exclusive.

Independent project

Management may be considering certain investments that are all related to a primary project, or are **mutually inclusive**. In a mutually inclusive situation, if the

Mutually inclusive projects

Upgrades to the fluid catalytic cracking unit comprised Lyondell's largest single capital project in 1992. This project was initiated because company managers determined that it was essential to meeting organizational goals and objectives.

FILAMENT PLANT TIMELINE

Time point:	0	1	2	3	4	5	6	7	8	9	10	11	12
Cash inflows:		+160	+160	+160	+160	+160	+160	+160	+160	+160	+160	+160	+160
Cash outflows:	(1,000)												

PV of ordinary annuity of $160,000 discounted
   at 9% for 12 periods ($160,000 × 7.1607) $1,145,712
Less cost (initial investment)   (1,000,000)

NPV $ 145,712

PI = $1,145,712 ÷ $1,000,000 = 1.15
IRR factor = $1,000,000 ÷ $160,000 = 6.2500 (annuity for 12 periods)

The IRR is approximately 11.81%; computer computations verify this finding.

TAPE MACHINE TIMELINE

Time point:	0	1	2	3	4	5	6	7	8	9	10	11	12
Cash inflows:		+20	+20	+20	+20	+20	+20	+20	+20	+20	+20	+20	+20
Cash outflows:	(100)												

PV of ordinary annuity of $20,000 discounted
   at 9% for 12 periods ($20,000 × 7.1607) $143,214
Less cost (initial investment)   (100,000)

NPV $ 43,214

PI = $143,214 ÷ $100,000 = 1.43
IRR factor = $100,000 ÷ $20,000 = 5.0000 (annuity for 12 periods)

The IRR is approximately 16.94%; computer computations verify this finding.

▮ EXHIBIT 20–5
Glover Company Multiple Projects; Conflicting Rankings

The timelines, NPV, and PI computations appear in Exhibit 20–5 for both projects. The amounts on the timelines are shown in thousands of dollars. The IRR is approximated from the present value of an annuity table (Table 2, Appendix A), and the actual rate can be found using a computer or programmable calculator.

The net present value model indicates that the better investment for Glover Company is the filament plant with a NPV of $145,712. However, using the profitability index or internal rate of return models, the tape machine would be selected because it has a higher PI and a higher IRR. Since these projects do not serve the same purpose, company management would most likely evaluate the selection based on priority needs rather than results of specific capital project evaluations.

Exhibit 20–6 provides net present value computations for the two projects to compute the Fisher rate. Using a programmable calculator, the Fisher rate for the two projects is found to be approximately 11.21 percent. At a weighted average cost of capital or discount rate below 11.21 percent, the filament plant yields the higher NPV. At a COC higher than 11.21 percent, the tape machine yields a higher NPV. At the point of indifference, the net present value for both projects is the same (approximately $28,572). This equivalency can be proven as follows.

NPV of Filament Plant = (PV factor)($160,000) − $1,000,000
NPV of Tape Machine = (PV factor)($20,000) − $100,000

WEIGHTED AVERAGE COST OF CAPITAL	NET PRESENT VALUE OF FILAMENT PLANT	NET PRESENT VALUE OF TAPE MACHINE
4%	$501,616	$87,702
6%	341,408	67,676
8%	205,776	50,722
10%	90,192	36,274
12%	(8,896)	23,888
14%	(94,352)	13,206
20%	(289,728)	(11,216)

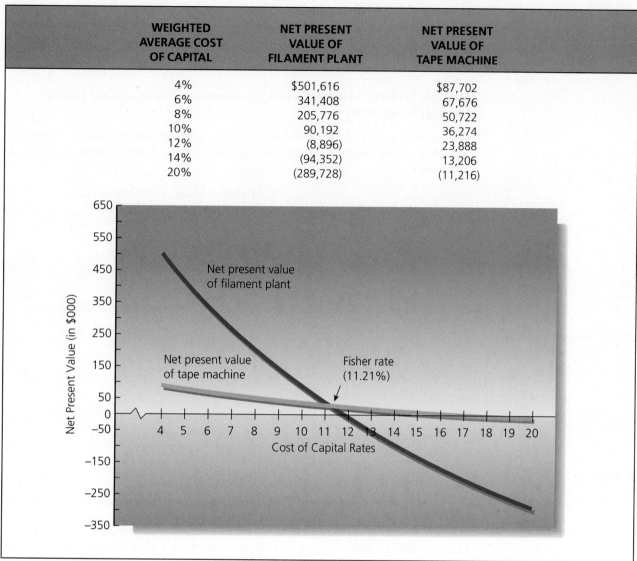

■ EXHIBIT 20–6

Glover Company's Filament Plant and Tape Machine NPVs Comparisons

At the Fisher rate, these two NPVs are equal, thus:

$$\text{(PV factor)}(\$160,000) - \$1,000,000 = \text{PV factor }(\$20,000) - \$100,000$$
$$\text{(PV factor)}(\$140,000) = \$900,000$$
$$\text{PV factor} = \$900,000 \div \$140,000$$
$$\text{PV factor} = 6.4286$$

Using this factor:

$$[6.4286(\$160,000) - \$1,000,000] = [6.4286(\$20,000) - \$100,000]$$
$$(\$1,028,576 - \$1,000,000) = (\$128,572 - \$100,000)$$
$$\$28,576 \approx \$28,572$$

(difference due to rounding of present value factors in the table)

From Table 2, the PV factors at 11 percent and 11.5 percent for 12 periods are, respectively, 6.4924 and 6.3406. Subtracting these factors gives a difference of .1518. The difference between the PV factor at the Fisher rate (6.4286) and the factor at

11 percent (6.4924) is .0638. Using interpolation, the Fisher rate is [11 percent + (.0638 ÷ .1518)(.5 percent)] or 11.21 percent. If management believes the true cost of capital could be above 11.21 percent, the tape machine would be considered over the filament plant.

Multiple Projects—Unequal Lives, Constant but Unequal Cash Flows, Unequal Investments

The second illustration of conflicting rankings uses data on two other investment opportunities for Glover Company, which has a weighted average cost of capital of 9 percent.

	Methanol Plant Debottlenecking Project	Polypropylene Plant Improvements
Investment	$1,200,000	$1,800,000
Annual after-tax cash flows	$ 436,000	$ 470,000
Asset life	5 years	8 years

The timelines (in thousands of dollars) for the two investments are as follows:

Debottlenecking Project (DP)

Time point:	0	1	2	3	4	5
Cash inflows:		+436	+436	+436	+436	+436
Cash outflow:	(1,200)					

Polypropylene Plant Improvements (PPI)

Time point:	0	1	2	3	4	5	6	7	8
Cash inflows:		+470	+470	+470	+470	+470	+470	+470	+470
Cash outflow:	(1,800)								

The net present value, profitability index, and internal rate of return are calculated for each investment, and the calculated results are shown in Exhibit 20–7. If the net present value or profitability index method is used, the PPI investment would be selected by Glover. If the internal rate of return method is used to choose between the two projects, the DP appears to be the better investment.

Although the IRR for the DP (24 percent) is higher than for the PPI (20 percent), rankings using the internal rate of return are misleading because of the reinvestment assumption. The IRR method assumes that the cash inflows of $436,000 each year from the DP will be reinvested at a rate of 24 percent; the $470,000 of cash flows from the PPI are assumed to be reinvested at 20 percent. Finding new investment projects that yield such high rates of return would be extremely difficult for any company. The NPV method, however, assumes reinvestment of the cash flows at the weighted average cost of capital of 9 percent, which is a more reasonable rate of return. The NPV computations show the PPI as the better investment.

When conflicting rankings exist between NPV and IRR, it is necessary to determine which of the projects should take precedence. (The difficulty of finding additional investment projects with IRRs of 24 percent and 20 percent is being ignored at this point). In Chapter 19, it was stated that proper comparison could be made only between projects with equal lives. The following method, however, gives the capital budgeting analyst a way to surmount this restriction.

For Glover's management to select the better investment, the difference in the annual cash flows between the DP and PPI investments must first be determined. The cash flow differences are then evaluated as if they resulted from a separate investment opportunity. Since the PPI investment requires a higher investment than the DP investment, the PPI is used as the comparison base. The investment opportunity result-

DEBOTTLENECKING PROJECT

PV of Inflows ($436,000 × 3.8897) $1,695,909
Less cost (initial investment)   (1,200,000)

NPV $ 495,909

PI = $1,695,909 ÷ $1,200,000 = 1.41

IRR factor = $1,200,000 ÷ $436,000 = 2.7523
By computer, IRR = 23.88%.

POLYPROPYLENE PLANT IMPROVEMENTS

PV of Inflows ($470,000 × 5.5348) $2,601,356
Less cost (initial investment)   (1,800,000)

NPV $ 801,356

PI = $2,601,356 ÷ $1,800,000 = 1.45
IRR factor = $1,800,000 ÷ $470,000 = 3.8298
By computer, IRR = 20.06%.

EXHIBIT 20–7
Glover Company's Debottlenecking and Polypropylene Plant Projects

ing from the cash flow differences is referred to here as Project (PPI—DP). If Project (PPI—DP) provides a positive net present value, the PPI investment is ranked higher than the DP. This higher ranking is assigned because the additional investment required for the PPI is more than compensated for by the additional cash flows. If Project (PPI—DP) shows a negative net present value, the DP is the better investment. The NPV calculation for Project (PPI—DP) is a positive amount as shown in Exhibit 20–8 using present value factors from Table 2, Appendix A.

EXHIBIT 20–8
Glover Company—Net Present Value of Project (PPI—DP)

	NET CASH FLOWS		
End of Period	DP	PPI	Difference Project (PPI—DP)
0	−$1,200,000	−$1,800,000	−$600,000
1	436,000	470,000	+ 34,000
2	436,000	470,000	+ 34,000
3	436,000	470,000	+ 34,000
4	436,000	470,000	+ 34,000
5	436,000	470,000	+ 34,000
6	0	470,000	+ 470,000
7	0	470,000	+ 470,000
8	0	470,000	+ 470,000

NPV of Project (PPI—DP):
  PV of net positive inflows of $34,000 discounted at 9%
    for years 1–5 ($34,000 × 3.8897) $132,250
  PV of net positive inflows of $470,000 discounted at 9%
    for years 6–8 ($470,000 × (5.5348 − 3.8897)   773,197

Total present value of net inflows $905,447
Less difference in original investment   (600,000)

    NPV of Project (PPI—DP)   +$305,447

Multiple Projects—Equal Lives, Equal Investments, Unequal Cash Flows

Glover Company's cost accountant, Melanie Stringfellow, has gathered the data on two additional projects. The company can invest in manual assembly production equipment for car dashboards. Workers would need little training and the firm would receive immediate returns from product sales. The other investment option is a special petroleum-based bacteria that has the capability to neutralize certain pollutants. The bacteria is self-reproducing and has a five-year maturation cycle. There will be an insufficient quantity of the bacteria to sell until Year 5. By that time, the company expects such advances in biotechnology that sales beyond Year 5 are highly uncertain and therefore are not considered. Glover's weighted average cost of capital of 9 percent is used as the discount rate. This set of projects illustrates another conflicting ranking situation. The relevant project data are as follows:

	Manual	Bacteria
Investment	$2,000,000	$2,000,000
Life	5 years	5 years
Net cash inflows		
Year 1	$ 730,000	$ 0
Year 2	730,000	0
Year 3	730,000	0
Year 4	730,000	0
Year 5	730,000	4,976,000

Using the same approach as presented in Exhibit 20–8, the following schedule computes a net present value for a "difference project" between the manual and bacteria projects:

End of Period	Manual	Bacteria	Difference Project (Manual—Bacteria)
0	$(2,000,000)	$(2,000,000)	$ 0
1	730,000	0	+730,000
2	730,000	0	+730,000
3	730,000	0	+730,000
4	730,000	0	+730,000
5	730,000	4,976,000	−4,246,000

PV of positive cash flows, discounted at 9% for years 1–4 ($730,000 × 3.2397)	$2,364,981
PV of negative cash flow, discounted at 9% for year 5 (−$4,246,000 × .6499)	(2,759,475)
NPV of difference project	$ (394,494)

Since the difference project considered the manual project first and the NPV of the difference project is negative, this computation indicates that the bacteria project is the preferred investment.

Exhibit 20–9 presents the net present value, profitability index, and internal rate of return computations for these projects. Purchase of the manual equipment has the higher IRR, but the bacteria project has a higher NPV and PI. The best selection depends on assumptions made about the future reinvestment rate applied to each of the $730,000 cash flows from the manual equipment.

The point of indifference between the two projects occurs when the $730,000 annuity can be discounted at a certain rate (the Fisher rate) and will equal $4,976,000

EXHIBIT 20-9

Glover Company—
Comparison of Manual
Equipment and Bacteria
Project

MANUAL EQUIPMENT

PV of ordinary annuity of $730,000 discounted at 9% for five periods ($730,000 × 3.8897)	$2,839,481
Less cost (initial investment)	(2,000,000)
NPV	$ 839,481

PI = $2,839,481 ÷ $2,000,000 = 1.42
IRR factor = $2,000,000 ÷ $730,000
= 2.74 (annuity for five periods)
By computer, the IRR is 24.1%.

BACTERIA PROJECT

PV of an amount of $4,976,000 discounted at 9% at the end of year 5 ($4,976,000 × .6499)	$3,233,902
Less cost (initial investment)	(2,000,000)
NPV	$1,233,902

PI = $3,233,902 ÷ $2,000,000 = 1.62
IRR factor = $2,000,000 ÷ $4,976,000
= .4019 (lump sum in five years)
By computer, the IRR is 20%.

discounted for five years at that same rate. That rate is 15.55 percent and is calculated by solving for a discount rate that causes the net present values of the two projects to be equal. If worked manually, repeated trials are used. A computer or programmable calculator can be used to find this rate quickly.

For reinvestment rates above 15.55 percent, the manual equipment is the superior investment because it would result in a higher net present value. For reinvestment rates below 15.55 percent, the bacteria project is the superior investment.

The preceding situations demonstrate that different capital budgeting evaluation methods often provide different rankings of projects. Because of this possibility, managers should select one primary evaluation method for capital projects. The critical question is whether higher cash flows or a higher rate of return is preferable. The answer is that higher present cash flows are *always* preferable to higher rates of return. The net present value method is considered theoretically superior to the internal rate of return in evaluating capital projects for two reasons. First, the reinvestment assumption of the IRR method is less likely to occur than that of the NPV method. Second, when a project has both positive and negative net annual cash flows during its life, there is the arithmetic possibility of calculating multiple internal rates of return for that project.

In addition, the net present value technique measures project results in dollars rather than rates, and monetary results are the objective of investment. To illustrate the problem that could occur by relying solely on the internal rate of return method, consider the following question: Would a manager rather receive a 100 percent return on a $1 investment or a 10 percent return on a $100 investment? The answer indicates the fallacy of focusing only on rates of return.

Although useful as a measure of evaluation under some circumstances, the profitability index is subject to the same concern as presented in the previous paragraph. Since monetary results *are* the objective of investments and the PI is expressed as a *rate* rather than as dollars, if used by itself it can lead to incorrect decisions. Taken together with other tools, however, the profitability index is a measure of capital efficiency and can assist decision makers in their investment analyses.

RANKING PROJECTS UNDER CAPITAL RATIONING

Capital rationing

Managers rank capital projects to select those projects providing the greatest return on company investment. A company often finds that it has more opportunity than money to invest in acceptable projects. In fact, most companies operate under some measure of **capital rationing**, which means that there is an upper dollar constraint on the amount of capital available to commit to capital asset acquisition.[9] When capital rationing exists, the selection of investment projects must fall within the capital budget limit. In these circumstances, the NPV model may not produce rankings that maximize the value added to the firm, since it does not consider differences in investment size.

Capital rationing is illustrated by the following situation. Assume that Glover Company has a capital budget of $7,500,000 and is considering all of the various investment projects discussed thus far in the chapter. These projects are reviewed in Exhibit 20–10.

By all quantitative measures except NPV, Project 1 should be eliminated if the firm has only $7,500,000 available in the capital budget. Its NPV is larger only than the tape machine project's NPV, but deleting the tape machine will not permit accepting any other project. The firm would need $8.1 million to complete all six projects and only $7.5 million is available; thus, it does not help to eliminate Project 2. On the other hand, Project 1 has the smallest NPV and return based on either the PI or IRR technique and should therefore be eliminated. Relatively speaking, Project 2 is of much less interest than Projects 3, 4, 5, and 6. Project 2 does, though, meet minimum quantitative standards, assuming that 9 percent is the hurdle rate by which to evaluate the IRR of a project.

Based on PIs, the attractiveness of the projects, in descending order, is: 6, 4, 2, 5, and 3. Based on IRRs, the preferences would be: 5, 3, 6, 4, and 2. Based on NPVs, the ranking would be: 6, 5, 4, 3, and 2.

Although managers should select one *primary* evaluation technique, the Glover Company example shows that capital project evaluation should not be performed using only one method. Evaluation tools should be used in conjunction with one another, not to the exclusion of one another. Each method provides valuable information. Even the nondiscounting technique of payback period can be helpful to management by indicating the quickness of return on investment.

In making their preference decisions, many company managers set ranking categories for projects such as those shown in Exhibit 20–11. Projects are first screened

EXHIBIT 20–10

Glover Company Potential Investment Projects

PROJECT	INITIAL PROJECT COST	PI	IRR	NPV
1. Filament plant	$1,000,000	1.15	12%	$ 145,712
2. Tape machine	100,000	1.43	17%	43,214
3. Debottlenecking project	1,200,000	1.41	24%	495,909
4. Polypropylene improvements	1,800,000	1.45	20%	801,356
5. Manual dashboard equipment	2,000,000	1.42	24%	839,481
6. Bacteria project	2,000,000	1.62	20%	1,233,902
Total cost of projects	$8,100,000			

---

[9] Many publicly traded companies have the luxury of being able to obtain additional capital through new issuances of debt or stock. This possibility may limit the degree to which they are subject to capital rationing but does not eliminate it. Nonpublicly traded companies operate under much more strict rationing of capital resources.

■ EXHIBIT 20–11

Ranking Categories for
Capital Projects

CATEGORY 1—REQUIRED BY LEGISLATION

This category would include items such as pollution control equipment that has been mandated by law. Most companies can ill afford the fines or penalties that can be assessed for lack of installation; however, these capital acquisitions may not appear to meet the company's minimum established economic criteria because of measurement difficulties.

CATEGORY 2—ESSENTIAL TO OPERATIONS

This category would include capital assets without which the primary functions of the organization could not continue. This category could include new purchases of capital assets or replacements of broken or no longer usable assets. For example, the purchase of a kiln for a ceramics manufacturer would fall into this category.

CATEGORY 3—NONESSENTIAL BUT INCOME GENERATING

This category would include capital assets that would improve operations of the organization by providing cost savings or supplements to revenue. Robots in an automobile manufacturer would be included in this group.

CATEGORY 4—OPTIONAL IMPROVEMENTS

Items in this category would be those that do not provide any cost savings or revenue increases but would make operations run more smoothly or make working conditions better. The purchase of computer hardware or software that is faster than that currently being used and the installation of a microwave oven in the employees' lounge would be included here.

CATEGORY 5—MISCELLANEOUS

This category exists for "pet projects" that might be requested. Such acquisitions may be more for the benefit of a single individual than for the organization as a whole, and may not even be related to organizational objectives. The installation of new carpeting in a manager's office could be an example of this group of investments. Items in this category normally will be chosen only when the organization has substantial, unencumbered resources at its disposal.

and placed in an appropriate category. Monetary resources are allocated to projects in a top-to-bottom fashion. In each category, projects are usually ranked through the use of net present value and profitability index techniques. Management's goal should be to select those projects that, within budget constraints, maximize net present value to the firm. It may be incorrect to select projects based solely on their internal rate of return rankings without consideration of the net present values.[10]

Regardless of the capital budgeting evaluation techniques used, managers must remember that the results provided are based on estimates of future events. The fact that estimates are involved indicates that risk is associated with the decision. All project estimates should be carefully understood and analyzed using sound management judgment and remembering, as indicated in the "Sell the Project" News Note on page 872, that capital project proposals are being advocated by proposers, who use different reasons under different conditions.

---

[10]If the set of projects is very large, the selection of projects may require the use of integer programming techniques, which are outside the scope of this text.

NEWS NOTE

"Sell" the Project Before Formal Consideration!

[A survey conducted at Scandinavia Corp. of Finland provided the following results regarding capital investment projects.] A capital investment, no matter how promising is not approved purely on the basis of its official proposal or calculations. People carry out selling capital investments by emphasizing economic, strategic, non-economic and production technology arguments. This means that by using such grounds a proposer attempts to convince his or her superior that the project is sound and worth implementing.

Strategic arguments are prevalent in situations characterized by a unit's good profitability, a large investment project, or an investment in standard technology. On the other hand, non-economic arguments are used when the project is not based on economic factors. Finally, production technology arguments are dominant when a unit's profitability is good and a project represents new technology in the company.

The findings also support the [idea that] efforts to sell the project to the decision-makers have been made before an official investment proposal is submitted. Moreover, the official proposal is presented after it is known that the investment will likely be accepted. In effect, so much has been discussed about the project in advance that the acceptance of the investment is insured before the project is even considered, for example, by the Executive Committee.

SOURCE: O. P. Lumijärvi, "Selling of Capital Investments," *Management Accounting Research* (September 1991), pp. 184–185.

COMPENSATING FOR RISK IN CAPITAL PROJECT EVALUATION

Risk

When choosing among multiple projects, it is important to consider the **risk** or uncertainty associated with projects. In accounting, risk reflects the possibility of differences between the expected and actual future returns from an investment. For example, the purchase of a $100,000, 10 percent treasury note would provide a virtually risk-free return each year of $10,000, since treasury notes are backed by the full faith and credit of the U.S. government. If the same $100,000 were used to purchase stock, the returns could range from −100 percent (losing the entire investment) to an abnormally high return. The potential for extreme variability would make the stock purchase a much more risky investment than the treasury note.

Managers considering a capital investment should understand and compensate for the degree of risk involved in that investment.[11] There are three approaches that a manager may use to compensate for risk: the judgmental method, the risk-adjusted discount rate method, and sensitivity analysis. These methods do not *eliminate* risk, but help managers understand and evaluate risk in the decision-making process.

Judgmental method (of risk adjustment)

The **judgmental method** of risk adjustment allows the decision makers to use logic and reasoning to decide whether a project provides an acceptable rate of return in relation to its risk. The decision maker is presented with all available information for each project, including the payback period, NPV, PI, and IRR. After reviewing the information, the decision maker chooses from among acceptable projects based on personal judgment of the risk-to-return relationship. The judgmental approach provides no *formal* process for adjusting data for the risk element.

Risk-adjusted discount rate method

A more formal method of taking risk into account requires making adjustments to the discount or hurdle rate. Under the **risk-adjusted discount rate method,** the deci-

[11] Information about the degree of risk is indicated by variability measures such as the standard deviation and the coefficient of variation. These measures and their use in capital project evaluations are discussed in the appendix to this chapter.

sion maker increases the rate used for discounting future cash flows to compensate for increased risk. As the discount rate is increased, the present values of the cash flows are reduced. Therefore, larger cash inflows are required to "cover" the investment and provide an acceptable rate of return. Changes in the discount rate should be reflective of the degree of cash flow variability and timing, other investment opportunities, and corporate objectives. If the internal rate of return is being used for project evaluation, the risk-adjusted discount rate method would increase the hurdle rate against which to compare the IRR.

Assume that the management of Glover Company is considering opening a new polymers production facility that will be operated for ten years and then be sold to employees. Estimates of the cost and annual cash flows for the facility are as follows:

Cost	$75,000,000
After-tax net cash flows	
Years 1–5	$10,000,000
Years 6–10	$15,000,000
Year 10	$30,000,000

Glover Company management typically uses its 9 percent weighted average cost of capital as the discount rate in evaluating capital projects under the NPV method. However, Don Dozier, a board member, feels that risk is created in this endeavor by two factors. First, potential environmental regulations related to the facility may cause variability in the projected annual cash flows. Second, the employees who have agreed to purchase the facility in ten years are relying on certain stock options and a promise from a local savings and loan for their financing. The stock's market value is related to factors outside the employees' control and the long-range financial health

Capital investments in Lyondell's world-class polymer laboratory are made in expectation of reasonable returns from the development of new resins with improved properties. But, like all investments in research and development, the risks related to the timing, quantity, and length of cash flows are high.

EXHIBIT 20-12

Glover Company Polymers Facility Project Evaluation

NPV using 9% discount rate
Cash flows, years 1–5 ($10,000,000 × 3.8897)	$38,897,000
Cash flows, years 6–10 ($15,000,000 × 2.5280)*	37,920,000
Cash flow, year 10 ($30,000,000 × .4224)	12,672,000
PV of total cash flows	$89,489,000
Less cost (initial investment)	(75,000,000)
Net present value of cash flows	$14,489,000

NPV using 14% discount rate
Cash flows, years 1–5 ($10,000,000 × 3.4331)	$34,331,000
Cash flows, years 6–10 ($15,000,000 × 1.7830)*	26,745,000
Cash flow, year 10 ($30,000,000 × .2697)	8,091,000
PV of total cash flows	$69,167,000
Less cost (initial investment)	(75,000,000)
Net present value of cash flows	$ (5,833,000)

*Factor = Annuity factor for 10 years − Annuity factor for 5 years

of the S&L industry as a whole is questionnable. Failure of projected market values to materialize or failure of the financial institution would mean that the employees could not afford to purchase the facility in ten years.

Mr. Dozier wants to compensate for these risk factors by using a 14 percent discount rate rather than the 9 percent cost of capital rate. Determination of the amount of adjustment to make to the discount rate (from 9 to 14 percent, for example) is commonly an arbitrary one. This fact means that, even though a formal process is used to compensate for risk, the process still involves a degree of judgment on the part of the project evaluators. Exhibit 20–12 presents the NPV computations using both discount rates. When the discount rate is adjusted upward, the NPV of the project is lowered and, in this case, shows the project to be unacceptable.

The same type of risk adjustment may be used for payback period or accounting rate of return. If the payback period method is being used, managers may choose to shorten the maximum payback period to compensate for increased risk. This adjustment assumes that cash flows occurring in the more distant future are more risky than those occurring in the near future. If the ARR method is used, managers may increase the preestablished acceptable rate against which the ARR is compared to compensate for risk. Another way in which risk can be included in the decision process is through the use of **sensitivity analysis**.

Sensitivity analysis

SENSITIVITY ANALYSIS

Sensitivity analysis is a process of determining the amount of change that must occur in a variable before a different decision would be made. In a capital budgeting situation, the variable under consideration could be the discount rate, annual net cash flows, or project life. Sensitivity analysis basically looks at the question of "what if" a variable is different than originally expected.

Except for the initial purchase price, all information used in capital budgeting is estimated. Using estimates suggests the possibility of errors, and sensitivity analysis identifies an "error range" for the various estimated values over which the project will still be acceptable. The following subsections consider how sensitivity analysis relates to the discount rate, cash flows, and life of the asset.

Range of the Discount Rate

A capital project providing a rate of return equal to or greater than the discount or hurdle rate is considered an acceptable investment. But returns from a project are not certain because, for instance, the cost of capital may increase because of increases in interest or dividend rates, respectively, on new issues of debt or preferred stock. Alternatively, common shareholders may believe they need a larger return on their investment, or the expected growth rate may rise.

Sensitivity analysis allows a company to determine what increases may take place in the estimated cost of capital and still have an acceptable project. The upper limit of increase in the discount rate is the project's internal rate of return. At the IRR, a project's net present value is zero; therefore, the present value of the cash flows equals the investment amount. As long as the IRR for a project is equal to or above the cost of capital, the project will be acceptable.

To illustrate the use of sensitivity analysis, the Glover Company Tape Machine project that was analyzed in Exhibit 20–5 using a 9 percent discount rate is reconsidered:

After-tax cash flows for 12 years discounted at 9% ($20,000 × 7.1607)	$143,214
Initial investment	(100,000)
NPV	$ 43,214

The project provides a positive net present value and, thus, is considered an acceptable investment candidate.

Glover Company management wants to know the highest discount rate that could be used and still have an acceptable project. To find the upper limit of the discount rate, the present value factor for an annuity of 12 periods at the unknown interest is computed as follows:

$$(\text{Cash flow})(\text{PV factor}) = \text{Investment}$$
$$(\$20,000)(\text{PV factor}) = \$100,000$$
$$\text{PV factor} = 5.0000$$

Looking across the row for 12 periods (the project life) in Table 2 of Appendix A, company management finds a factor of 4.9884 under the column headed 17 percent. Thus, the internal rate of return is approximately 17 percent. Using a computer or programmable calculator, the actual IRR is found to be 16.94 percent. As long as Glover's cost of capital is less than or equal to 16.94 percent, this project will remain acceptable. As the discount or weighted average cost of capital rate is increased toward the project's IRR, the project becomes marginally less desirable. These calculations assume that the cash flows and project life have been properly estimated.

Range of the Cash Flows

Another factor sensitive to changes in estimation is the investment's projected cash flows. The Glover Company data presented for the tape machine can be used to illustrate how to determine the acceptable range of cash flows. Company management wants to know how small the net cash inflows can be and still have the project remain desirable. This determination requires that the present value of the cash flows for 12 periods discounted at 9 percent be equal to or greater than the investment cost. The PV factor for 12 periods at 9 percent is 7.1607. The equation from the above section can be used to find the lowest acceptable annuity:

$$\text{(Cash flow)(PV factor)} = \text{Investment}$$
$$\text{(Cash flow)(7.1607)} = \$100{,}000$$
$$\text{Cash flow} = \$100{,}000 \div 7.1607$$
$$\text{Cash flow} = \$13{,}965$$

As long as the actual annual cash flows from this project do not fall below $13,965, the project will provide an acceptable rate of return. The following table presents the minimum annual cash flow amounts that would allow the project to be accepted at successively higher discount rates up to the project's internal rate of return:

Minimum Cash Flows	Discount Rates
$13,965	9.00%
15,403	11.00
16,898	13.00
18,448	15.00
19,999	16.94

As the table suggests, an overestimation of the amount of cash flows lowers the tolerance for error in the discount rate estimate. An underestimation of net cash inflows increases the tolerance for error in the discount rate. Because of the relationship between cash flow estimates and tolerance for error, managers are advised to use somewhat conservative initial estimates for all cash inflow variables and somewhat high initial estimates for all cash outflow variables.

Range of the Life of the Asset

Asset life is related to many factors, some of which, like the quantity and timing of maintenance on equipment, are controllable. Other factors, such as technological advances, are not controllable. An error in the estimated life will change the number of periods from which cash flows are to be expected. These changes could affect the accept/reject decision for a project.

The Glover Company example can be used to find the minimum length of time the cash flows must be received from the project to be acceptable. To find the solution, it is necessary to set the present value of the cash flows discounted at 9 percent equal to the investment. This computation will yield the PV factor for an unknown number of periods:

$$\text{(Cash flow)(PV factor)} = \text{Investment}$$
$$(\$20{,}000)\text{(PV factor)} = \$100{,}000$$
$$\text{PV factor} = 5.0000$$

Review the present value of an annuity table in Appendix A under the 9 percent interest column to find the 5.0000 factor. Reading down to the number of periods, the project life is almost seven years. By computer, the life is 6.94 years or six years and 11+ months. If the project cash flows were to stop at any point before 6 years and 11 months, the project would be unacceptable.

Sensitivity analysis does not reduce the uncertainty surrounding the estimate of each variable. It does, however, provide management with a sense of the tolerance for estimation errors by providing upper and lower ranges for selected variables. The above presentation simplistically focuses on single changes in each of the variables. If all factors change simultaneously, the above type of sensitivity analysis is not useful. More advanced treatments of sensitivity analysis, which allow for simultaneous ranging of all variables, can be found under the topic of simulation in an advanced mathematical modeling text.

R E V I S I T I N G

LYONDELL PETROCHEMICAL COMPANY

Lyondell Petrochemical states that it is committed to paying a secure and competitive dividend. Dividend changes are made after considering growth in earnings and cash flow, balanced against alternative investment opportunities. [Such a policy will affect the company's cost of capital and, therefore, its capital project analyses.]

[In addition to all of the capital spending in the last four years,] the Company estimates that it will spend $73 million more in 1993 in order to comply with applicable environmental laws and regulations. For periods beyond 1993, additional capital expenditures for environmental projects will be required but at lower levels than those proposed for 1992 and 1993, unless there are significant changes in applicable laws and regulations. Company management is quick to point out, however, that even though some of these projects are required under the law, some of them "also offer attractive returns."

[The company is not simply doing what is required in the way of capital spending on environmental projects.] Lyondell committed to a 55 percent reduction in air emissions by 1995 as part of the company's participation in the Environmental Protection Agency's Voluntary Reduction Program. Safety Process Assessment teams will continue to identify areas for future improvements in plant safety at Channelview, even though the company has one of the best performance records in the industry in regard to safety.

[Lastly, Lyondell's capital projects are part of an overall company plan that focuses on benefits to both the shareholders and the customers.] Lyondell has adopted the criteria of the Malcolm Baldrige National Quality Award process to benchmark progress throughout the organization and is also pursuing certification under ISO 9000, an important worldwide quality standard. The company will be making sizable environmental capital expenditures over the next two to three years to comply with expected regulations and is committed to continuous improvement in environmental performance.

SOURCE: Lyondell Petrochemical Company, *1991 Annual Report*, pp. 5, 15, and 24.

CHAPTER SUMMARY

The weighted average cost of capital is based on the optimal mix of debt and equity financing. It can be calculated by weighting each capital component (debt, preferred stock, and common shareholders' equity) by its proportion of total capital and summing the weighted rates of return for the different components. The weighted average COC should be used as the minimum discount rate under the net present value or profitability index method or as the minimum hurdle rate under the internal rate of return method.

Depreciation expense and changes in tax rates affect after-tax cash flows. The tax rates and allowable depreciation methods estimated when the investment is analyzed may not be the same as when the project is implemented. Such changes can cause a significant difference in the actual net present value and internal rate of return amounts from those originally estimated on the project.

Management should select investment projects that will help to achieve the organization's objectives and provide the maximum rate of return on capital resources utilized. The company must determine whether the activities in which it wishes to engage are worthy of an investment and which assets can be used for those activities.

Then decisions must be made about the best investment to accept from all the ones available. These decisions require that investment projects be ranked as to their desirability in relationship to one another.

Often the NPV, PI, and IRR computations will produce the same rankings of multiple investment projects. In some situations, however, the NPV, PI, and IRR methods produce different project rankings. The primary reason for differences is the underlying assumptions of each method regarding the reinvestment rate of cash flows released during the life of the project. The NPV and PI methods assume reinvestment at the discount rate, while the IRR method assumes reinvestment at the internal rate of return provided by the project. The assumption used for the NPV and PI methods is more probable of achievement than that of the IRR method.

Capital rationing indicates that management has imposed a spending limit in the capital budget. When capital rationing exists, the NPV model may provide the best first-cut ranking of projects in which the returns to the firm will be maximized. Projects can also be listed in descending order of their PI and IRR rates of return. Only projects having an IRR in excess of the weighted average cost of capital should be considered and then only to the extent of the budget. In addition, however, managers need to consider legal requirements as well as the goals and objectives of the firm when ranking projects. Categorization of projects (such as is shown in Exhibit 20–11) is a useful way to rank investments.

Different risks can be associated with each capital project. Risk is defined as uncertainty of the expected returns from an asset. Project risk can be assessed and imcluded in decision making judgmentally or, more formally, by calculating a risk-adjusted discount/hurdle rate. Sensitivity analysis can also be employed to compensate for risk by calculating a range for each of the variables (discount rate, cash flows, and life of project) in a capital budgeting problem. Sensitivity analysis assists management in determining the effect on project outcome of a range of change in the estimate of one or more of the critical variables in deriving the accept/reject conclusion about the project.

APPENDIX 1

Measurement of Risk

Risk is inherent in capital budgeting because most factors used in the decision process involve estimates of future occurrences. Capital budgeting risks include variations in estimated asset life, cash flow amounts, timing of cash flows, and expected salvage value of the property at the end of its life. In addition, changes in tax laws or in general economic conditions can render the original estimates obsolete. It is highly unlikely that predictions made before the capital asset's acquisition will occur precisely as forecasted. The best that can be hoped for is that the variability of any or all of the estimates will be minimal.

The life of a capital asset is treated in capital budgeting decisions as being an exact number of years. It would be more realistic to assume that the asset's life is a function of its specific application, level of maintenance performed, and changes in technology. Use of a variety of factors would provide a range of years for asset life rather than a specific period of time. For example, Glover Company management may know that automobiles used by the sales force each have an expected average life of three years. However, some autos last only two years, while others are still in use after four. Information about the range of life is useful to managers for planning purposes, but such information is difficult to integrate into the capital budgeting model. Thus, the naive but practical single point (deterministic) estimate of expected years is used.

As illustrated in the chapter, cash flows can be seriously affected by changes in depreciation methods or in tax rates. Capital budgeting analysis is most often performed using single point dollar estimates for annual cash flows and for salvage values. This practice disregards the inherent variability in the cash flows and, thus, the risk associated with a project. It would be more useful to prepare a probability distri-

■ EXHIBIT 20–13
Glover Company—
Probability Distribution

ECONOMIC CONDITIONS	PROBABILITY OF OCCURRENCE	CASH FLOWS	
		Project A	Project B
Rapid expansion	20%	$24,000	$30,000
Continued current	70%	20,000	20,000
Recession	10%	12,000	0

EXPECTED VALUE OF PROJECT A

	(1) Cash Flows	(2) Probability of Occurrence	(3) Expected Values (1) × (2)
Rapid expansion	$24,000	.20	$ 4,800
Continued current	20,000	.70	14,000
Recession	12,000	.10	1,200
Total expected value			$20,000

EXPECTED VALUE OF PROJECT B

	(1) Cash Flows	(2) Probability of Occurrence	(3) Expected Values (1) × (2)
Rapid expansion	$30,000	.20	$ 6,000
Continued current	20,000	.70	14,000
Recession	0	.10	0
Total expected value			$20,000

bution of the expected cash flows. A **probability distribution** is a range of possible values for which each value is assigned a likelihood of occurrence.

Glover Company's capital budgeting analysis for the tape machine can be used in conjunction with another project (a machine to produce compact disks) to illustrate the use of a probability distribution. Glover is comparing Project A (the tape machine) with Project B (the CD machine). Each project requires a $100,000 initial investment. Both projects are expected to produce annual after-tax cash flows of $20,000 for 12 years, assuming continued current economic conditions. The projects appear on the surface to be equally desirable. Discounting the cash flows at 9 percent yields an NPV of $43,214 for each project.

Ted DuCharm, Glover's chief financial officer, has estimated that the projects will have different annual cash flows if there is a change in economic conditions. DuCharm's cash flow projections under three economic conditions (rapid expansion, continued conditions, and recession) appear in Exhibit 20–13 with their related probabilities of occurrence.[12] The exhibit also presents each project's total expected value of the annual cash flows.

The **total expected value** of annual cash flows for a project is equal to the sum of individual cash flow amounts in a probability distribution multiplied by their related probabilities. The variability of the annual cash flows for Project A ranges from $1,200 to $14,000; the variability of Project B cash flows extends from $0 to $14,000. This wider range of possible cash flows makes Project B a more risky investment than Project A.

Probability distribution

Total expected value (for a project)

[12] In evaluating the Glover investment, analysis can focus on annual cash flows because all other factors are alike. In more complex project comparisons, analyses of additional factors (such as project life) and, ultimately, the NPV variability need to be considered.

Standard Deviation

Standard deviation

One measure used to determined the variability of a probability distribution is the **standard deviation,** the measure of variability of data around the average (or mean) value of a set of data. For example, assume that the average life of a holding tank used in the R&D area of Glover Company is 15 years. The standard deviation has been computed as three years. It has been mathematically determined that any population average plus or minus 1 standard deviation contains approximately 68 percent of the measurements in a normal distribution. In the case of Glover Company, this means that approximately 68 percent of all holding tanks (the population) used by the company will last between 12 and 18 years (that is, fifteen years $\pm$ the standard deviation of three years). If ± 2 standard deviations are considered, approximately 95 percent of all measurements are encompassed. When ± 3 standard deviations are used, 99 percent of all measurements are included. Therefore, 95 percent of all tanks used by Glover would last between 9 and 21 years, and virtually all tanks used would last between 6 and 24 years.

The standard deviation calculation uses expected values and the probabilities assigned to the expectations. The formula for the standard deviation (σ) is

$$\sigma = \sqrt{\sum_{i=1}^{n} [(R_i - \bar{R})^2 P_i]}$$

where   n = number of levels of possible cash flows in the probability distribution; number of economic conditions
   i = indication of the particular condition
   R_i = expected cash flow of condition i
   $\bar{R}$ = average for the cash flows
   P_i = probability for the expected cash flow of condition i

■ EXHIBIT 20–14

Glover Company Calculation of Standard Deviations

Data regarding Glover Company's evaluation of Projects A and B are used in Exhibit 20–14 to illustrate the calculation of the standard deviations for the projects. Using information from the columns, the standard deviations for each project are

	(1) R_i	(2) $\bar{R}$	(3) $(R_i - \bar{R})$	(4) $(R_i - \bar{R})^2$	(5) P_i	(6) $(R_i - \bar{R})^2(P_i)$
PROJECT A						
Rapid expansion	$24,000	$20,000	$ 4,000	$ 16,000,000	20%	$ 3,200,000
Continued current	20,000	20,000	0	0	70%	0
Recession	12,000	20,000	− 8,000	64,000,000	10%	6,400,000
						$\sigma^2 =$ $ 9,600,000
						$\sigma =$ $ 3,098.39
PROJECT B						
Rapid expansion	$30,000	$20,000	$10,000	$100,000,000	20%	$20,000,000
Continued current	20,000	20,000	0	0	70%	0
Recession	0	20,000	− 20,000	400,000,000	10%	40,000,000
						$\sigma^2 =$ $60,000,000
						$\sigma =$ $ 7,745.97

calculated. Project B has a much larger standard deviation than Project A. Since the standard deviation measures variability, the following statements are true: The higher the standard deviation, the higher the variability; the higher the variability of a project, the greater the risk. Thus, calculation of the standard deviation demonstrates that Project B is the more risky of the two projects being considered by Glover Company.

Coefficient of Variation

Situations may arise where one project has a substantially higher total expected value but the same standard deviation as another project. In these cases, it is reasonable to assume that the project with the lower expected value has the greater risk. The **coefficient of variation** is a useful measure of risk when the standard deviations are approximately the same size on two or more projects but the expected values are significantly different. The coefficient of variation (V) is calculated as

Coefficient of variation

$$V = \frac{\sigma}{\overline{R}}$$

$$\text{where} \quad \sigma = \text{expected standard deviation}$$
$$\overline{R} = \text{expected cash flow}$$

The smaller the value of the coefficient of variation, the lower the project's risk is relative to its expected value.

The projects under consideration by Glover Company do not need to be analyzed for risk using the coefficient of variation, because they had different standard deviations. However, using the data for those projects yields coefficients of variation as follows:

Project A	Project B
$\sigma = \$3,098.39$	$\sigma = \$7,745.97$
$\overline{R} = \$20,000$	$\overline{R} = \$20,000$
$V = \sigma \div \overline{R}$	$V = \sigma \div \overline{R}$
$V = \$3,098.30 \div \$20,000$	$V = \$7,745.97 \div \$20,000$
$V = .1549$	$V = .3873$

Project B, which has the higher coefficient of variation, is also the project with the greater risk.

As another example, suppose that the standard deviations for Projects M and N being considered by Glover Company are both determined to be $2,500. The average expected cash flow for Project M is $10,000, while it is $50,000 for Project N. Use of the standard deviation alone would have led to assuming that the risk was the same. By employing the coefficient of variation, it is determined that M has the higher coefficient of variation (as shown below) and, therefore, the greater relative risk.

Project M	Project N
$\sigma = \$2,500$	$\sigma = \$2,500$
$\overline{R} = \$10,000$	$\overline{R} = \$50,000$
$V = \sigma \div \overline{R}$	$V = \sigma \div \overline{R}$
$V = \$2,500 \div \$10,000$	$V = \$2,500 \div \$50,000$
$V = .25$	$V = .05$

Using standard deviations and coefficients of variation in analyzing capital budgeting projects can help managers assess the risk of a project. This assessment is useful to managers in making judgments about processes such as adjusting the discount rate used in making net present value and profitability index computations or developing a hurdle rate against which to measure the internal rate of return.

APPENDIX 2

Link Between Payback Period and Accounting Rate of Return

When taxes are included, payback period (the time necessary to recoup the initial investment) is computed as the original investment divided by annual after-tax cash flows. The accounting rate of return (ARR) is found by dividing annual after-tax net income from the investment by the amount of the investment. In other words, payback period focuses on cash-basis income; ARR focuses on accrual-basis income. Because most revenues and expenses except depreciation are cash-based, depreciation is usually a primary difference between accrual-based net income and the net cash inflow generated by a capital budgeting project. This difference is presented in the following simplified illustration using the previously presented income statement information for the Glover Company, assuming a 40 percent tax rate.

Accrual-based NI				Cash Flow	
Sales	$1,000,000	made on account	→ collected in cash	$1,000,000	
CGS	350,000	purchased on account	→ paid in cash	350,000	
GM	$ 650,000			$ 650,000	
Expenses other than depreciation	(150,000)	accrued	→ paid in cash	(150,000)	
Depreciation	(200,000)	accrued	→ never paid in cash	0	
Income before tax	$ 300,000		→ cash flow before tax	$ 500,000	
Taxes (40%)	(120,000)	accrued	→ paid in cash	(120,000)	
Net income	$ 180,000		Net cash flow	$ 380,000	

difference = $200,000 depreciation

In this case, the singular difference between accrual-based income and cash flow is depreciation. Any other noncash charges included in income (such as patent or goodwill amortization) would create the same basic effect. Thus, the relationship or "link" between a project's payback period and its accounting rate of return can be expressed by the following model:

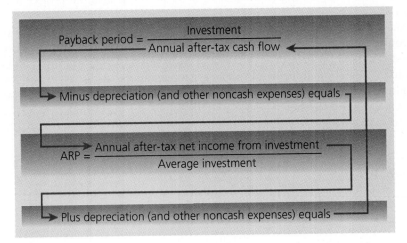

$$\text{Payback period} = \frac{\text{Investment}}{\text{Annual after-tax cash flow}}$$

Minus depreciation (and other noncash expenses) equals

$$\text{ARP} = \frac{\text{Annual after-tax net income from investment}}{\text{Average investment}}$$

Plus depreciation (and other noncash expenses) equals

This relationship is demonstrated using data for a capital project being investigated by the Glover Company—the purchase of three filters that will increase the flow of products through the pipelines at one of its chemical plants. The increased throughput will lower labor and energy costs, thus creating a positive cash flow. Data on the proposed purchase are:

Cost of filters (no salvage value) $150,000
Life for tax purposes   5 years
Depreciation method   straight-line
Annual net cash flows before tax $50,000
Tax rate   40%

Based on these data, annual after-tax net income and after-tax cash flow are calculated as follows:

Before-tax cash flow	$50,000	
Depreciation	(30,000)	
Income before tax	$20,000	
Tax	(8,000)	
Net income after tax	$12,000	(use as numerator in ARR)
Depreciation	30,000	(link between ARR and payback)
Cash flow after tax	$42,000	(use as denominator in payback)

Using this information, Glover's anticipated payback and ARR for the filters are calculated as follows:

Payback = $150,000 ÷ $42,000 = 3.57 years

less $30,000 depreciation

$$ARR = \$12,000 \div [(\$150,000 + \$0) \div 2]$$
$$= \$12,000 \div \$75,000$$
$$= 16\%$$

Capital rationing (p. 870)
Coefficient of variation (p. 881)
Dividend growth method (p. 851)
Fisher rate (p. 863)
Growth rate (p. 852)
Independent project (p. 861)
Judgmental method (of risk adjustment) (p. 872)
Mutually exclusive projects (p. 861)
Mutually inclusive projects (p. 861)
Optimal mix of capital (p. 852)
Preference decision (p. 860)

Probability distribution (p. 879)
Reinvestment assumption (p. 863)
Risk (p. 872)
Risk-adjusted discount rate method (p. 872)
Screening decision (p. 860)
Sensitivity analysis (p. 874)
Standard deviation (p. 880)
Tax benefit (of depreciation) (p. 854)
Tax shield (of depreciation) (p. 854)
Total expected value (for a project) (p. 879)
Weighted average cost of capital (p. 850)

KEY TERMS

Weighted average cost of capital

Equal to the summation of the costs of debt, preferred stock, and common shareholders' equity based on their proportion of the capital mix.

SOLUTION STRATEGIES

$$\text{Cost of debt } (k_d) = YR(1 - TR)$$
$$\text{Cost of preferred stock } (k_p) = D \div MP$$
$$\text{Cost of common stock equity } (k_c) = (D \div MP) + g$$

where   YR = yield rate
        TR = tax rate
        D = annual dividend amount
        MP = market price per share
        g = growth rate

Tax benefit of depreciation
Depreciation amount $\times$ tax rate

Standard Deviation (σ)

$$\sigma = \sqrt{\sum_{i=1}^{n} [(R_i - \bar{R})^2 P_i]}$$

where n = number of levels of possible cash flows
in the probability distribution
i = indication of the particular condition
R_i = expected cash flow of condition i
$\bar{R}$ = average for the cash flows
P_i = probability for the expected cash flow of condition i

Coefficient of Variation

$$V = \frac{\sigma}{R}$$

where σ = expected standard deviation
$\bar{R}$ = expected cash flow

Link between payback period and accounting rate of return

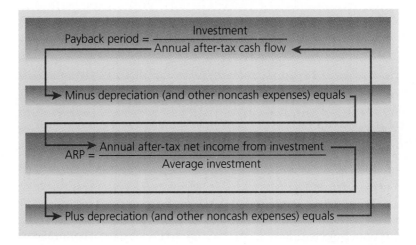

DEMONSTRATION PROBLEM

Earl Well Petroleum is considering two projects with the following statistics:

	Project A	Project B
Investment	$200,000	$200,000
Cost of capital	10%	10%
Annual after-tax cash flow	$ 50,000	
Annual before-tax cash flow		$ 70,000
Asset life	10 years	10 years
Tax rate for both projects = 35%		

Required:

a. Which project yields the larger net present value?

b. For Project A, what is the upper limit of the discount rate for which the project will be acceptable?

c. For Project A, how small can the annual cash flow be and have the project still be acceptable?

d. For Project A, what is the minimum length of time for which the project cash flows will be acceptable?

Solution to Demonstration Problem

a.   Annual after-tax cash flow for Project A $50,000 (given)

   Annual after tax cash flow for Project B
Before-tax cash flow	$70,000
Less depreciation ($200,000 ÷ 10 years)	(20,000)
Taxable income	$50,000
Income taxes (35%)	(17,500)
Income after taxes	$32,500
Plus depreciation	20,000
After-tax cash	$52,500

   Because the after-tax cash flow of Project B exceeds that of Project A, and because all other factors used to calculate NPV are the same for both projects, Project B will have the higher NPV.

b.
$$\text{(Cash flow)(PV factor)} = \text{Investment}$$
$$(\$50,000)(\text{PV factor}) = \$200,000$$
$$\text{PV factor} = \$200,000 \div \$50,000$$
$$\text{PV factor} = 4.0000$$

   This factor results in an IRR of slightly above 20%. A computer calculation shows 21%.

c.
$$\text{(Cash flow)(PV factor)} = \text{Investment}$$
$$\text{(Cash flow)}(6.1446) = \$200,000$$
$$\text{Cash flow} = \$200,000 \div 6.1446$$
$$\text{Cash flow} = \$32,549$$

d.
$$\text{(Cash flow)(PV factor)} = \text{Investment}$$
$$(\$50,000)(\text{PV factor}) = \$200,000$$
$$\text{PV factor} = \$200,000 \div \$50,000$$
$$\text{PV factor} = 4.0000$$

   Moving down the 10% column in Table 2 (Appendix A) shows that 4.0000 falls between 5 and 6 periods. A computer calculation shows 5.36 years.

QUESTIONS

1. Why do the costs of the various sources of capital funds differ from one another? Why do the relative costs change as the mix changes?

2. Why does taxation affect the cost of debt but not the cost of common or preferred equity?

3. Intrepid Inc. has 10 percent bonds and 8 percent preferred stock outstanding. The company's common stock has consistently paid a 3 percent dividend each year. The company has calculated its weighted average cost of capital as 7 percent, which is equal to [(10% + 8% + 3%) ÷ 3]. Is this computation of the weighted average COC correct? Why or why not?

4. Why should an issue of convertible debt whose conversion price is close to the market price of the related common stock be treated as though it had been converted into common stock for purposes of computing the cost of capital?

5. Why is the weighted average cost of capital at the optimal mix of capital considered the most reasonable to use for capital budgeting purposes?

6. Depreciation does not represent a cash flow. Why, then, is it given consideration in capital budgeting evaluation techniques that use discounted cash flows?

7. What is the difference between the tax shield of depreciation and the tax benefit of depreciation?

8. How do tax law changes regarding acceptable depreciation methods, asset lives, and tax rates affect cash flows?

9. Discuss management's process of analyzing investment projects with regard to the fulfillment of company goals and objectives.

10. A project deemed unsatisfactory from a monetary standpoint may be acceptable for investment. Give three examples of situations in which management would be willing to invest regardless of the outcome of the cost-benefit evaluation.

11. What is the difference between screening and preference decisions in capital budgeting?

12. What is the difference between mutually exclusive projects and mutually inclusive projects? Give two examples of each type.

13. Describe the basis and order of magnitude managers would use to rank projects for each of the following methods: net present value; profitability index; internal rate of return; payback period; and accounting rate of return.

14. When the weighted average cost of capital is less than the Fisher rate, why will the net present value and internal rate of return methods produce conflicting rankings? Discuss.

15. Why does the profitability index method sometimes give a different ranking from the net present value method when multiple projects are compared even though both methods use the same basic data?

16. Why should managers use several techniques to rank capital projects? Which technique should be used as the primary evaluator? Why?

17. Why does capital rationing exist, and how do managers deal with it in ranking capital projects?

18. Why is it a good idea for management to establish a set of categories to rank capital projects?

19. How is risk defined in capital budgeting analysis? List several aspects of a project in which risk is involved and how risk can affect the net present value of a project.

20. How can managers compensate for risk in capital budgeting analysis?

21. How is sensitivity analysis used in capital budgeting?

22. *(Appendix 1)* If both the standard deviation and the coefficient of variation measure risk, why are managers concerned with both measures?

23. *(Appendix 2)* Why is depreciation said to provide the primary link between cash flows and accounting income? What other items would provide the same type of linkage?

EXERCISES

24. *(Weighted average cost of capital)* Westover Chemical has the following current capital structure:

Component	Market Value	After-Tax Cost of Capital
Bonds	$1,000,000	5.5%
Preferred stock	500,000	9.0%
Common stock equity	5,000,000	12.0%

The company is planning to expand by $2,000,000. Funds for this expansion are to be raised 40% from debt and 60% from common stock. The after-tax cost of the capital components are expected to remain the same.

a. Determine the firm's weighted average cost of capital before and after expansion.

b. Why would the firm's weighted average cost of capital decline in the two calculations made in part a?

25. *(Weighted average cost of capital)* Expresso Financial Services Company provides the following table of data regarding the various components of capital and percentage costs associated with proportions of each:

	After-Tax Costs Associated with Respective Proportions									
	1–10%	11–20%	21–30%	31–40%	41–50%	51–60%	61–70%	71–80%	81–90%	91–100%
Bonds	6.0	6.0	7.2	7.2	8.0	8.0	12.0	12.0	14.0	N/A
Preferred stock	7.2	N/A	N/A	N/A	N/A	N/A	N/A	N/A	N/A	N/A
Common stock	N/A	10.0	10.0	10.0	10.0	10.0	10.0	10.0	10.0	10.0

Management has decided that it would limit the preferred stock component to 10% of the total capital structure.

a. Determine the optimal mix of capital and the weighted average cost of capital at that mix.

b. Why does the cost of debt financing rise as the portion of debt in the capital mix rises?

26. *(Weighted average cost of capital)* Cleveland Distillery has the following components in its corporate funding structure:

Bonds payable (12% stated rate)	$10,000,000
Premium on bonds payable	397,980
9%, $100 par preferred stock	2,000,000
Paid-in capital on preferred	100,000
$20 par common stock	8,500,000
Retained earnings	6,700,000

The bonds were originally issued ten years ago at $10,795,960 with a twenty-year life. Interest on the bonds is paid and amortized on an annual basis. The company uses straight-line amortization of bond discounts or premiums. The market yield of the bonds has not changed since the date of issue. The preferred stock was issued at $105 per share, and it is currently selling for $120. Common stockholders will receive a dividend of $3 next period. The most recent trading price of a common share is $45. Cleveland Distillery's management has promised a growth rate of 5% per year, and the tax rate for the company is 40%.

a. Determine the cost of capital for the bonds.

b. Determine the cost of capital for the preferred stock.

c. Determine the cost of capital for the common stock.

d. Determine the weighted average cost of capital using an assumed optimal capital mix as follows: bonds, 40%; preferred stock, 15%; and common stock, 45%.

27. *(Alternative depreciation methods, NPV)* Starkville Papermill Co. is considering an investment in a revolutionary new papermaking mill. The mill will cost $40,000,000, have a life of eight years, and generate annual net before-tax cash flows from operations of $7,400,000. The papermill will be worth $4,500,000 at the end of its eight-year estimated life. Starkville's tax rate is 34%, and its cost of capital is 8%. The selling price of the mill at the end of its life is taxable because the mill has been depreciated.

a. If Starkville Papermill uses straight-line depreciation on this project, is the project acceptable using the net present value method?

b. Assume the tax law allows the company to take accelerated depreciation on this asset in the following manner:

Years 1–2: 23% of cost
Years 3–8: 9% of cost

What is the net present value of the project? Is it acceptable? (*Hint:* Assume that a negative value for income before taxes will result in a tax benefit rather than a tax expense because the negative income will act as a tax shield against other company income.)

c. Recompute parts a and b, assuming the tax rate is increased to 40%.

28. *(Tax effects of asset sale)* Bellmore Corp. purchased a large drill three years ago. Now, the company is going to sell the drill press and acquire more advanced technology. Data relating to the drill press follow:

Market value now	$ 5,000,000
Original cost	12,000,000
Book value now, for tax purposes	4,000,000
Book value now, for financial accounting purposes	6,800,000
Corporate tax rate	40%

a. How much depreciation has been claimed on the drill press for tax purposes? For financial accounting purposes?

b. What will be the after-tax cash flow from the sale of this asset?

29. *(Project ranking)* Two independent potential capital projects are under evaluation by Ronsom Company. Project K costs $400,000, will last ten years, and provide an annual annuity of after-tax cash flows of $85,000. Project T will cost $600,000, last ten years, and provide an annual annuity of $110,000 in annual after-tax cash flows.

a. At what discount rate would management be indifferent between these two projects?

b. What is this indifference rate called?

c. If the firm's cost of capital is 10%, which project would be ranked higher?

30. *(Uncertain annual cash flow)* Tokyo Tire Masters Inc. is considering a ¥110,000 investment in a project that will provide an expected (but uncertain) annual after-tax cash flow of ¥40,000 for four years. If the cost of capital for Tokyo Tire Masters Inc. is 8%, how small could the annual cash flow be and still have the project be considered acceptable by management?

31. *(Uncertain project life)* Thurston Company is reviewing a project costing £160,000 that will return £56,000 annually for six years. The company's cost of capital is 10%. How few years could the project make an annual return of £56,000 and still be considered an acceptable project?

32. *(Uncertain cash flow, uncertain discount rate)* Quick Box Company is considering a capital project expected to cost $200,000, with annual net after-tax cash flows to be $32,500 for 12 years. The company uses a 10% cost of capital rate to discount cash flows in evaluating capital projects.

a. What is the lowest acceptable annual cash flow that would allow this project to be considered acceptable?

b. What is the maximum the company's cost of capital could be and still allow this project to be considered acceptable?

33. *(Appendix 1)* Assume that the following represent probabilities of the range of cash flows for potential projects 1 and 2:

Economic Condition	Probability	Cash Flows	
		Project 1	Project 2
Strong	.30	$7,000	$7,500
Moderate	.50	5,000	5,000
Weak	.20	2,000	1,250

For each project, calculate:

a. the expected value

b. the standard deviation

c. the coefficient of variation

34. *(Appendix 2)* Hillary Printing Company is evaluating the purchase of a state-of-the-art desktop publishing system that costs $54,000. The company purchasing agent advises the owner, Ms. Hillary, that the system will generate $16,000 of annual cash receipts for six years. At the end of that time, the system will have zero salvage value. The purchasing agent also estimates that cash operating costs will be $2,500 annually. The company's tax rate is expected to be 34% during the life of the asset, and the company uses straight-line depreciation.

   a. Determine the annual after-tax cash flows from the project.

   b. Determine the payback period for the project.

   c. Determine the accounting rate of return for the project.

35. *(Comprehensive including appendix 2)* Harraba Video Systems is an owner-operated company providing videotapings of weddings, parties, and other functions. Hassan Harraba, the owner, is considering the purchase of a $75,000 tape screening machine that will be used to edit the tapes. The machine has a life of five years and a salvage value of $0 for both financial accounting and tax purposes. The same method of depreciation will be used for accounting and tax purposes.

    Mr. Harraba expects that the new machine will generate an additional $22,000 per year in revenues because of reduced labor time and increased quality of tapes. The cost of capital and tax rate for Mr. Harraba are 9% and 36%, respectively.

   a. Determine the after-tax cash flows for the tape screening machine.

   b. Determine the net present value of the tape screening machine.

   c. Determine the accounting income of the tape screening machine.

   d. Determine the accounting rate of return and the payback period on an after-tax basis.

COMMUNICATION ACTIVITIES

36. The Jackson Ice Company is considering the purchase of a $500,000 ice machine. This machine will be used for two major purposes: to produce ice year-round for commercial sales and to produce "snow" during the winter for sale to companies and individuals. The net expected cash flow from operations is $190,000 per year for ten years. At that time, the machine will have a salvage value of $50,000.

    The company is also considering another investment project, a commercial cold storage locker. The locker will cost $850,000, have a useful life of ten years, and have a salvage value of $200,000. Expected before-tax cash flows from the locker are $200,000 for Years 1 and 2; $225,000 for Years 3 and 4; and $320,000 for Years 5 through 10.

    The cost of capital for Jackson Ice is 11%, and the tax rate is 35%. Jackson Ice uses straight-line depreciation for tax purposes. The salvage values of the equipment are taxable because both items have been fully depreciated at the end of their lives.

   a. Determine the net present value and the profitability index on an after-tax basis for each of the two projects.

   b. Determine the payback period using after-tax cash flows for each project.

   c. Using the information from parts a and b, rank the projects for the president of Jackson Ice. State any assumptions you made in determining your rankings.

   d. Is there any additional information you would like to know about these two projects? If so, discuss what it is and why it might be important to the decision.

37. *[American] companies caught up in retrenchment and restructuring have been short-changing research and capital investment. To fully appreciate America's chintzy ap-*

*proach to capital investment, it is necessary to look in Russian-doll fashion at succes-
sively more detailed statistics. Taking the big familiar macro number—plant and equipment expenditures as a percentage of GDP—the U.S. trails all major industrialized
economies, even easygoing Britain. Now subtract the plant figures, which include such
items as unneeded office buildings, and focus on equipment outlays. True, equipment
spending has advanced in inflation-adjusted terms since the late Seventies. But nearly all
the growth has been in information processing—computers and telecommunications
gear. A critical subset called industrial equipment, which includes the contraptions that
actually make stuff on the factory floor, has been flat. And purchases of metalworking
machinery, a doll within this doll, have trended downhill.*

*Keep in mind that these dismal numbers include outlays by foreign-owned companies
that have been spending heavily in the U.S.*

[SOURCE: Edmund Faltermayer, "Invest or Die," *FORTUNE* (February 22, 1993), pp. 42, 45. © 1993 Time Inc.
All rights reserved.]

a. One often-mentioned area of declining capital investment is that of research
and development. Provide some reasons for companies cutting back in such
an area. [*Hint:* Be sure to address the issue of time from R&D expenditures
to final results.]

b. In 1981, only one Japanese corporation was among the top ten patent recipients. By 1991, half of the ten top-ranked companies, including the first
three, were Japanese; General Electric had fallen from No. 1 to No. 6. Tie
part a together with this information and discuss the implications of such a
situation.

PROBLEMS

38. *(Cost of capital)* Helen's Custom Fashions Inc. has the following composition of
its capital structure:

Long-term debt (bonds)	30%
Preferred stock	15%
Common stock equity	55%
Total	100%

The before-tax interest on the bonds is 9%. The company's tax rate is 34%. The
per-share dividend amount on the preferred stock is $6, and the stock is currently
selling for $90 per share. Common stock is currently selling at $80, and its expected per-share dividend is $5. The company's expected annual growth rate is
2%. Calculate the following:
a. after-tax cost of the bonds
b. cost of the preferred stock
c. cost of common equity
d. weighted average cost of capital

39. *(NPV, PVI, IRR)* John Jones Company, which has a weighted average cost of
capital of 12%, is evaluating two mutually exclusive projects (A and B), which
have the following projections:

	Project A	Project B
Investment	$24,000	$40,000
After-tax cash flows	$ 6,400	$ 7,600
Asset life	6 years	10 years

a. Determine the net present value, present value index, and internal rate of
return for Projects A and B.
b. Using the answers to part a, which is the more acceptable project? Why?
c. What is the Fisher rate for the two projects?

40. *(NPV, different depreciation methods)* A staff accountant for Canada's Vancouver Dairy has been asked to evaluate a proposal to purchase a computerized milking machine that will cost C$52,000. The purchase would be made at the beginning of the fiscal year. The machine is expected to last eight years and to have no residual salvage value. The staff accountant has determined that the machine will save C$15,000 annually in labor costs. The firm's cost of capital is estimated to be 8%, and its tax rate is 35%.

   a. Using straight-line depreciation, calculate the net present value of the machine.

   b. Mr. Walker wants to know how much the net present value would differ if the sum-of-the-years' digits (SYD) method were used. Assume for this problem that the SYD method is acceptable for tax purposes in the fiscal year of the purchase. (Round all calculations to the nearest dollar.)

   c. Why is the net present value higher using SYD rather than SL depreciation?

   d. Referring to your answer in part a, how much margin for error is there in the NPV for miscalculation of the discount rate (estimated cost of capital)?

41. *(After-tax cash flows)* Hot Air Creations Inc. is considering the purchase of a computerized sewing machine to make hot-air balloons. The machine is expected to cost $425,000, have a useful life of five years, and have a zero salvage value at the end of its useful life. The IRS regulations permit the following depreciation patterns for this asset in the year it is placed into service:

Year	% Deductible	Year	% Deductible
1	15%	4	21%
2	22%	5	21%
3	21%		

The company's tax rate is 40%, and its cost of capital is 8%. The machine is expected to generate the following cash receipts and cash disbursements:

Year	Cash Receipts	Cash Disbursements
1	$160,000	$25,000
2	170,000	30,000
3	188,000	40,000
4	182,000	40,000
5	146,000	30,000

   a. Prepare a schedule presenting the after-tax operating cash flows.

   b. Determine the following on an after-tax basis: payback period, net present value, profitability index, and internal rate of return.

42. *(NPV)* Solomon Industries is considering the addition of a new product line. The expected life of the product line is 5 years. The new product line would require the following investment:

Equipment $800,000 (no salvage at end of life)
Working capital   200,000

The product line would generate the following expected net cash flows from product sales.

Year 1 $100,000
Year 2   200,000
Year 3   250,000
Year 4   600,000
Year 5   400,000

Solomon Industries' cost of capital is 10% and its income tax rate is 35%. All assets are depreciated according to the straight-line method.

   a. Compute the NPV of the potential product line investment.

   b. Based on the NPV, will the company invest in the new product line? Explain.

43. *(Cash flows, NPV)* Wyle Co. is considering a proposal to acquire new manufacturing equipment. The new equipment has the same capacity as the current equipment but will provide operating efficiencies in direct and indirect labor, direct material usage, indirect supplies, and power. Consequently, the savings in operating costs are estimated at $150,000 annually.

The new equipment will cost $300,000 and will be purchased at the beginning of the year when the project is started. The equipment dealer is certain that the equipment will be operational during the second quarter of the year in which it is installed. Therefore, 60% of the estimated annual savings can be obtained in the first year. Wyle will incur a one-time expense of $30,000 to transfer the production activities from the old equipment to the new equipment. No loss of sales will occur, however, because the plant is large enough to install the new equipment without disrupting operations of the current equipment. The equipment dealer states that most companies use a five-year life when depreciating this equipment.

The current equipment has been depreciated for tax purposes to a book value of $5,000. Management has reviewed the condition of the current equipment and has concluded that it can be used an additional five years. Wyle Co. would receive $5,000 net of removal costs if it elected to buy the new equipment and dispose of its current equipment at this time. This $5,000 is nontaxable because it is equal to the tax carrying value.

Wyle currently leases its manufacturing plant. The annual lease payments are $60,000. The lease, which will have four years remaining when the equipment installation would begin, is not renewable. Wyle would be required to remove any equipment in the plant at the end of the lease. The cost of equipment removal is expected to equal the salvage value of either the old or the new equipment at the time of removal.

The company uses the sum-of-the-years' digits depreciation method for tax purposes. A full-year's depreciation is taken in the first year an asset is put into use.

The company is subject to a 40% income tax rate and requires an after-tax return of at least 12% on an investment.

a. Calculate the annual incremental after-tax cash flows for Wyle Co.'s proposal to acquire the new manufacturing equipment.

b. Calculate the net present value of Wyle Co.'s proposal to acquire the new manufacturing equipment using the cash flows calculated in part a and indicate what action Wyle Co.'s management should take. Assume all recurring cash flows take place at the end of the year.

(CMA adapted)

44. *(Capital rationing)* Following are the capital projects being considered by the management of Big Time Movie Productions:

Project	Cost	Annual After-Tax Cash Flows	# of Years
Film studios	$18,000,000	$2,800,000	15
Cameras and equipment	3,200,000	800,000	8
Land investment	5,000,000	1,180,000	10
Motion picture #1	17,800,000	4,970,000	5
Motion picture #2	11,400,000	3,930,000	4
Motion picture #3	7,800,000	2,100,000	7
Corporate aircraft	2,400,000	770,000	5

Assume all projects have no salvage value and that the firm uses a discount rate of 12%. Company management has decided that only $20,000,000 can be spent in the current year for capital projects.

a. Determine the net present value, present value index, and internal rate of return for each of the seven projects.

b. Rank the seven projects according to each different method used in part a.

c. Indicate how you would suggest to the management of Big Time Movie Productions that the money be spent. What would be the total net present value of your selected investments?

45. *(Sensitivity analysis)* A 50-room motel is for sale in Memphis and is being considered by the Southern Comfort Motel Chain as an investment. The current owners indicate that the occupancy of the motel averages 80% each day of the year that the motel is open. The motel is open 300 days per year. Each room rents for $75 per day, and variable cash operating costs are $10 per day that the room is occupied. Fixed annual cash operating costs are $100,000.

An acquisition price of $2,000,000 is being offered by Southern Comfort. The chain plans on keeping the motel for fourteen years and then disposing of it. Since the market for motels is so difficult to predict in advance, Southern Comfort estimates the salvage value to be zero at the time of disposal. Depreciation will be taken on a straight-line basis for tax purposes. In making the following computations, assume that there will be no tax consequences of the sale in fourteen years. The chain's tax rate is estimated at 35% for all years.

a. Determine the net present value of the motel to Southern Comfort, assuming a cost of capital rate of 13%.

b. What is the highest level that the discount rate can be and still allow this project to be considered acceptable by Southern Comfort? If this discount rate exceeds the highest rate shown in the table (20%), simply state this fact and provide supporting computations and reasons.

c. How small can the net after-tax cash flows get and still allow the project to be considered acceptable by Southern Comfort, assuming a cost of capital rate of 13%?

d. What is the shortest number of years for which the net after-tax cash flows can be received and still have the project be considered acceptable?

e. Assume that the answer to part c is $217,425. If all costs remain as they are currently stated and the motel continues to stay open 300 days per year, approximately how many rooms would have to be rented each night to achieve this level of cash flows?

46. *(Appendix 1)* Oregon Electronic Systems is comparing two projects (M and N), each of which requires investments of $40,000, produces expected after-tax annual cash flows of $10,000, and will last nine years. Discounting the expected cash flows at 9%, the company's cost of capital, obviously yields the same net present value for each project.

Corporate president Bill Henson believes, however, that the levels of annual cash inflows each year will differ between the two projects depending upon economic conditions. He constructed the following schedule to reflect his assessment of cash flows under various conditions:

Economic Condition	Probability of Occurrence	Cash Flows From	
		Project M	Project N
Rapid expansion	15%	$20,000	$16,000
Continued current	60%	10,000	12,000
Recession	25%	4,000	1,600
Expected value		10,000	10,000

a. Calculate the standard deviation of the range of cash flows for each project.
b. Calculate the coefficient of variation for each project.
c. Discuss which project is more desirable and provide reasons for your choice.

47. *(Probabilities, appendix 1)* Texas Ship Co. is comparing the investment profiles of two projects. The first project is a shrimp boat that has a cost of $500,000 and provides net annual after-tax cash flows of $80,000. The life of the boat is ten years. The second project is an $850,000 yacht that can be rented to corporate

executives for meetings and parties. The yacht has a useful life of eight years and is expected to produce annual after-tax cash flows of $165,000. Texas Ship Co. uses a cost of capital rate of 11% to determine net present values.

a. Using an incremental approach, determine which of the two investments is the better choice for Texas Ship Co.

b. If the returns from the yacht are expected to be only $150,000 each year for eight years, which is the better project?

c. The probabilities for the differing returns exist on both projects. These probabilities are related to how well or how poorly the oil business does. If the oil business "booms," people will have more money, the yacht will be rented more often, and the selling price of shrimp will rise. Below are probabilities associated with changes in the oil business and how those changes will affect the returns from the projects:

Condition	Probability	Cash Flows Boat	Cash Flows Yacht
"Boom"	10%	$95,000	$185,000
Continued current	80%	80,000	165,000
"Depressed"	10%	70,000	120,000

What is the total expected value for each project?

d. Using the expected value from part c, compute the standard deviation and the coefficient of variation for the two projects.

CASE

48. Jersey Mfg. Co. is a relatively small manufacturing company with a total market value of approximately $100,000,000. The company has recently been experiencing profitability problems. As of now, the total value of the outstanding common shareholders' equity is $1,000,000 and the total value of outstanding debt claims is about $99,000,000 (the debt to equity ratio is therefore 99 to 1). The president of Jersey Mfg. Co., Ms. Tina Glass, has approached a private lender for a $20,000,000 loan to finance expansion. The expansion project involves the opening of another plant. According to Ms. Glass' data, the expansion project has an NPV of $2,000,000. Based on this data the lender has agreed to provide the funds.

Before Ms. Glass has an opportunity to invest in the project (*but after acquiring the lender's funds*), her friend, Marla MacGuire, suggests to Ms. Glass that she invest in an alternative project (a highly speculative R&D project), which also will require an initial investment of $20,000,000 and will have a useful life similar to the first project. Ms. MacGuire admits that there is a great deal of uncertainty about the NPV of this alternative project because the NPV of the project would be highly correlated with the future state of the economy. Based on her forecasts of the future state of the economy, Ms. MacGuire believes that the NPV of her project is $0. She arrived at this conclusion by determining the NPV of the project in each of the possible future states of the economy and multiplied each of those NPVs by its probability of occurring. Her computations follow:

State of the Economy	Resulting NPV	Probability	Expected Value
Great	$10,000,000	.5	$5,000,000
Fair	5,000,000	.4	2,000,000
Lousy	(70,000,000)	.1	(7,000,000)
		Overall expected NPV	$ 0

The NPV of the first project that Ms. Glass is considering (plant expansion) is not influenced by the state of the economy.

Assess *independently* the influence of each of the following factors on Ms. Glass' decision as to the project in which she will invest:
a. the debt to equity ratio of the company
b. the preference of the common shareholders of the company
c. the preference of the debtholders of the company
d. a management bonus plan based on a measure of corporate profit
e. the overall calculated NPV's: $2 million on the first project and $0 on the alternative project

---

ETHICS AND QUALITY DISCUSSION

49. *Conoco's new fitness center cost the company $3 million. Tenneco's two-story 100,000-square-foot facility in Houston cost $11 million. PepsiCo, Inc.'s $2 million fitness and health complex is located at its New York headquarters. [Since such programs are expensive] and intangible benefits can be hard to measure, how does a company know if it is in its best interest to establish and/or continue these programs? Is the company actually benefitting from having more healthy and fit employees, or is it simply incurring hefty expenses and low, if any, short-term returns on investments?*

[The following statistics indicate the benefits provided by such programs.]

1. *The average claim for nonexercising women at Tenneco was $1,535.83, more than double the $639.07 average claim for those who exercise. For men, the average claim for nonexercisers was $1,003.87, compared with $561.68 for those who exercise. The company also observed that a high proportion of excellent business performers also are the exercisers, while a great number of lower performers are nonexercisers. The reason may be that fitness requires discipline. Exercisers said that their "high" feeling from a good workout resulted in positive work attitude and fewer work frustrations.*

2. *Lockheed Missiles and Space Co. estimates that in five years it saved $1 million in life insurance costs through its wellness program. Absenteeism for exercisers was 60% lower than for nonexercisers. It also reports that turnover rate is 13% lower among regular exercisers.*

3. *Dallas school teachers who enrolled in a fitness program took an average of three fewer sick days per year, a savings of almost a half-million dollars a year in substitute teachers' pay.*

The evidence accumulated thus far strongly indicates that fitness programs pay off not only in monetary terms—such as savings in health insurance, life insurance, and sick pay—but also in intangible ways such as productivity, morale, retention, and recruiting.

[SOURCE: Otto H. Chang and Cynthia Boyle, "Fitness Programs: Hefty Expense or Wise Investment," *Management Accounting* (January 1989), pp. 45–47. Reprinted from *Management Accounting*. Copyright by Institute of Management Accountants, Montvale, N.J.]

a. As extensively as possible, describe the types of business costs and benefits that could be affected by exercise facilities.
b. How could an exercise facility affect the quality of a company's products?
c. Assume the benefits of exercise are consistent with those described above. Instead of providing exercise facilities for employees, would it be ethical for employers to hire only individuals who are actively involved with private exercise programs? Discuss.

50. Al Jones was reprimanded by the home office for recommending a pollution abatement project because the project did not meet the standard financial criterion of a 10% rate of return. However, Al had concluded that the $60,000 of equipment was necessary to prevent small amounts of arsenic from seeping into the city's water system.
a. Discuss the company requirement of a 10% rate of return on all projects.
b. What might be the ultimate consequence to Jones' company if it fails to prevent future arsenic seepage into the groundwater system?
c. How should (or can) Jones justify the purchase of the equipment to the home office?

RESPONSIBILITY ACCOUNTING AND TRANSFER PRICING IN DECENTRALIZED ORGANIZATIONS

LEARNING OBJECTIVES

After completing this chapter, you should be able to answer these questions:

1. Why is decentralization appropriate for some companies but not for others?
2. How are responsibility accounting and decentralization related?
3. What are the differences among the four types of responsibility centers?
4. Why are transfer prices for products used in organizations?
5. What are the advantages and disadvantages of each type of transfer price?
6. How can multinational companies use transfer prices?
7. *(Appendix)* How can coding systems be used in a responsibility accounting system?

INTRODUCING

UNILEVER

When Unilever was founded in 1930 as a Dutch-British company, it produced soap, processed foods, and a wide array of other consumer goods in many countries. These days, Unilever (producer of Lipton Tea and Lux Soap, among many other products) is often described as one of the foremost transnational companies. The very nature of our products requires proximity to local markets; economies of scale in certain functions justify a number of head-office departments; and the need to benefit from everybody's creativity and experience makes a sophisticated means of transferring information across our organization highly desirable. All of these factors lead to our present structure: a matrix of individual managers around the world who nonetheless share a common vision and understanding of corporate strategy.

In each of some 75 countries, we do business through one or more operating companies, with a total of about 500 companies in the Unilever group. In our case, "thinking transnationally" means an informal type of worldwide cooperation among self-sufficient units. Of course, there has to be a formal structure of some sort that encourages managers to think and act in the way corporate policy dictates.

The two companies that formed Unilever, Margarine Unie of the Netherlands and Lever Brothers of the United Kingdom, had a long tradition of expanding their businesses through both export and local production. Initially, local operations were almost exclusively managed by Dutch and British expatriates; however, even in the early days of Unilever, the new company started developing local managers and decentralizing the organization. Starting with the Indian subsidiary in 1942, Unilever put into place a management process that company insiders referred to as "ization." In other words, filling local executive and technical positions with Indian managers led to the "Indianization" of that subsidiary—along with "Australianization," "Brazilianization," and other examples of localization of management in various countries with Unilever operations.

Yet the head office also recognized the need for a common culture among its many scattered units and set up formal training programs aimed at the "Unileverization" of all its managers. [Thus,] the company's "ization" policy, as well as an increasing number of local competitors and the isolation of many of Unilever's operating companies during World War II, created a decentralized organization of self-sufficient subsidiaries.

SOURCE: Reprinted by permission of *Harvard Business Review*. An excerpt from "Inside Unilever: The Evolving Transnational Company," by Floris A. Maljers. *Harvard Business Review* (September-October 1992), pp. 46–49. Copyright © 1992 by the President and Fellows of Harvard College; all rights reserved.

An organization's structure evolves as its goals, technology, and employees change, and the progression is typically from highly centralized to highly decentralized. When the majority of authority is retained by top management, **centralization** exists. **Decentralization** refers to the downward delegation, by top management, of decision-making authority to subunit managers. Unilever recognized the need for decentralization early in its corporate development because the company's global operations demanded local managers who could most effectively use corporate resources.

Centralization
Decentralization

897

This chapter describes the degree to which top managers delegate authority to sub-ordinate managers and accounting methods (responsibility accounting and transfer pricing) that are appropriate in decentralized organizations. In addition, the appendix discusses a coding system that can be used to assign managerial responsibility in de-centralized organizations.

DECENTRALIZATION

The degree of centralization reflects a chain of command, authority and responsibility relationships, and decision-making capabilities and can be viewed as a continuum. In a completely centralized firm, a single individual (usually the company owner or president) performs all major decision making and retains full authority and respon-sibility for that organization's activities. Alternatively, a purely decentralized organi-zation would have virtually no central authority, and each subunit would act as a totally independent entity. Either end of the continuum represents a clearly undesir-able arrangement. In the totally centralized company, the single individual may have neither the expertise nor sufficient and timely information to make effective decisions in all areas. In the totally decentralized firm, subunits may act in ways that are incon-sistent with the total organization's goals. Each of these possibilities was recognized by Unilever and influenced the policy of the "Unileverization" of locally managed independent units with a common organizational culture.

Each organization tends to structure itself in light of the pure centralization versus pure decentralization factors presented in Exhibit 21–1. Most businesses are, to some extent, somewhere in the middle part of the continuum because of practical necessity. The combination of managers' personal characteristics, the nature of decisions re-quired for organizational growth, and the nature of organizational activities lead a company to find the appropriate degree of decentralization. Even traditionally highly centralized Asian firms, such as Lucky-Goldstar Group, a Korean company, are mak-ing the move toward decentralization as indicated in the following passage.

> Since [the organization's] start in 1947, . . . the founding Koo family dominated virtually every facet of decision-making. Inevitably, the group became too unwieldy for the Koo family to manage well. As sales from 31 separate companies hit the $25 billion mark,

EXHIBIT 21–1

Degree of Decentralization in an Organizational Structure

FACTOR	CONTINUUM		
	Pure Centralization	→	Pure Decentralization
Age of firm	Young	→	Mature
Size of firm	Small	→	Large
Stage of product development	Stable	→	Growth
Growth rate of firm	Slow	→	Rapid
Expected impact on profits of incorrect decisions	High	→	Low
Top management's confidence in subordinates	Low	→	High
Historical degree of control in firm	Tight	→	Moderate or loose

ADVANTAGES

■ Helps top management recognize and develop managerial talent

■ Allows managerial performance to be comparatively evaluated

■ Can often lead to greater job satisfaction

■ Makes the accomplishment of organizational goals and objectives easier

■ Allows the use of management by exception

DISADVANTAGES

■ May result in a lack of goal congruence or suboptimization

■ Requires more effective communication abilities

■ May create personnel difficulties upon introduction

■ Can be extremely expensive

■ **EXHIBIT 21–2**
Advantages and Disadvantages of Decentralization

quality slipped—and so did innovation. Critics said Chairman Koo Cha-Kyung's hierarchical decision-making style was at least in part to blame. Now, . . . , Koo is giving more decision-making authority to his front-line managers. "We are becoming more efficient in management, quicker in decision-making," says Byun Kyu-Chill, president of Lucky's trading arm.[1]

Decentralization does not necessarily mean that a unit manager has the authority to make all decisions concerning that unit. Top management selectively determines the types of authority to delegate and the types to withhold. For example, after Alcoa implemented a major reorganization program to decentralize in 1991, Chairman Paul H. O'Neill still views safety, environmental matters, quality, insurance, and information strategy to be "central resource" issues. He thinks that centralization is the most sensible and cost-effective method of handling those specific functions.[2]

As with any management technique, decentralization has advantages and disadvantages. These pros and cons are discussed in the following sections and are summarized in Exhibit 21–2.

Advantages of Decentralization

Decentralization has many personnel advantages. Decentralized units provide excellent settings for training personnel and for screening aspiring managers for promotion. Managers in decentralized units have the need and occasion to develop their leadership qualities, creative problem-solving abilities, and decision-making skills. Managers can be comparatively judged on their job performance and on the results of their units relative to those headed by other managers; such comparisons can encourage a healthy level of organizational competition. Decentralization also often leads to greater job satisfaction for managers because it provides for job enrichment and gives a feeling of increased importance to the organization.[3] Employees are given more challenging and responsible work, providing greater opportunities for advancement.

In addition to the personnel benefits, decentralization is generally more effective than centralization in accomplishing organizational goals and objectives. The decen-

---

[1] Laxmi Nakarmi, "At Lucky-Goldstar, the Koos Loosen the Reins," *Business Week* (February 18, 1991), p. 72.
[2] Paul H. O'Neill, *Remarks at Alcoa Organizational Meeting* (Pittsburgh Hilton Hotel, August 9, 1991), p. 5.
[3] Job enrichment refers to expanding a job to provide for personal achievement and recognition.

NEWS NOTE   Decentralization Spreads the "Power" Around

Listen to the new gospel of executive power: "The more you have, the less you should use," says Reuben Mark, CEO of Colgate-Palmolive. "You consolidate and build power by empowering others." Chief executives observe that major changes are under way in how power is deployed in U.S. corporations [and say that] you can't manage today's work force like yesterday's. The military command-and-control model went out with red meat. Your job is to set a strategic direction, get your people to agree, give them money and authority, and leave them alone.

Why give up on centralized control now, after hundreds, maybe thousands of years? In a sense, the cause of the change is change itself. In an environment rapidly altering due to intensified global competition and new technology, CEOs need to promote speed, flexibility, and decisiveness. When every customer demands special service, every sales rep has to have the power to offer it. He can't do that in what Raymond E. Miles (dean of the University of California business school) calls "the multi-multi-level organizations, which like great big thunderstorms suck everything up to the top." In a rapid-change world, leaders have to be free to think strategically, which often entails delegating operating authority.

Somewhat ironically, decentralization of power has also brought with it a renewed emphasis on formal planning. Variations on the old philosophies of management by objectives and management by exception flourish under the new regime. At Heinz, says senior vice president David Sculley, who oversees Weight Watchers, "We manage by exception generally"—using variances from projections to provide clues that something is going awry.

Smart CEOs of decentralized companies realize that they have to actively encourage communication among the different parts of the organization. The CEO must also take pains to see that all those independent operators running the company's different businesses have a care for the welfare of the whole.

If power is to be given to a new breed of mini-CEOs throughout the company, they must be trained and chosen more carefully than ever. They may even have to be men and women new to the organization. But when the empowering of subordinates works, the total power in the organization available to the CEO may well increase. More people find ways to use the personal kinds of power latent within them.

The idea behind sharing power more broadly is to move decisions and resources as close as possible to where action can be taken—not to spread power around, but to pinpoint it. The decisions that result are faster and cleaner, so more decisions can be made, more work done.

SOURCE: Thomas A. Stewart, "New Ways to Exercise Power," *FORTUNE* (November 6, 1989), p. 52ff. © 1989 Time Inc. All rights reserved.

---

tralized unit manager has more knowledge of the local operating environment, which means the following: (1) reduction of decision-making time; (2) minimization of difficulties that may result from attempting to communicate problems and instructions through an organizational chain of command; and (3) quicker perceptions of environmental changes than is possible for top management. Thus, the manager of a decentralized unit is both in closest contact with daily operations and charged with making decisions about those operations.

A decentralized structure also allows the management by exception principle to be implemented. Top management, when reviewing divisional reports, can address issues that are out of the ordinary rather than dealing with operations that are proceeding according to plans. The "Decentralization Spreads the Power" News Note expresses some opinions about the benefits of decentralization.

NEWS NOTE

Why Some Functions Should Be Home Office Functions

If decentralized management is increasingly popular among corporations, it also has its dark side. Consider this cautionary tale: KFC . . . kicked off a quality-improvement drive for its 2,000 company-owned restaurants [in 1990]. Instead, it got a bureaucratic mess [because] the chain's autonomous regional divisions failed to coordinate their efforts. "There was so much redundancy [that] the process became dysfunctional," says Edward A. Meager III, a vice president of the PepsiCo Inc. unit.

Facing the same problem, a growing number of U.S. companies are now reasserting central authority over a range of corporate activities. Bill Eaton, a senior vice president of Levi Strauss & Co., is replacing six separate order-processing computer systems with one system under centralized control. [M]any retailers complained that they had to deal with a plethora of different divisions—each with its own procedures—to buy the company's goods, Mr. Eaton says.

Companies still want to decentralize operations closest to customers because they "realize they must be more nimble in the marketplace," says Jim Down, who directs the Boston office of Mercer Management Consulting Inc. But at the same time, companies are consolidating less visible internal functions such as personnel, "where there can be massive economies of scale," says John J. Parkington [of] consultants Wyatt Co. in New York.

Indeed, saving money is a major motive for recentralizing, particularly in tough times. McDonnell Douglas Corp. cites reduced defense spending as the main reason for its recent consolidation of college-recruiting efforts. As many as five different recruiting teams, each from different units, used to visit the same schools. "We saw there was a great duplication of effort," says David Hutchins, a McDonnell Douglas employment manager.

Besides cost-cutting, another motive for centralization is the need for a companywide focal point. Avery Dennison Corp., an office supplies maker in Pasadena, Calif., has about 60 largely independent divisions. The company recently created a central office to spearhead a corporate drive to improve customer service [because] "each sector had a different slant on what was important" to customers.

SOURCE: Gilbert Fuchsberg, "Decentralized Management Can Have Its Drawbacks," *Wall Street Journal* (December 9, 1992), pp. B1, B8. Reprinted by permission of the *Wall Street Journal*, © 1992 Dow Jones & Company, Inc. All rights reserved worldwide.

Disadvantages of Decentralization

All aspects of decentralization are not positive. For instance, the authority and responsibility for making decisions may be divided among too many individuals. This division of authority and responsibility may result in a lack of **goal congruence** among the organizational units. (Goal congruence exists when personal goals of the decision maker, goals of the decision maker's unit, and goals of the broader organization are mutually supportive and consistent.) In a decentralized company, unit managers are essentially competing with each other since results of unit activities are compared. Because of this competition, unit managers may make decisions that positively affect their own units, but are detrimental to other organizational units or to the company. This process results in suboptimization, which is discussed later in the chapter. These difficulties may cause management to keep certain organizational functions at "headquarters" or recentralize some functions if they have been delegated to unit managers. The News Note regarding "Home Office Functions" discusses some companies' decisions to retain (or regain) central authority for certain organizational functions.

Goal congruence

A decentralized organization requires that more effective methods of communicating plans, activities, and achievements be established because decision making is removed from the central office. Top management has delegated the authority to make decisions to unit managers, but the responsibility for the ultimate effects of those decisions is retained by top management. Thus, to determine if those operations are progressing toward established goals, top management must maintain an awareness of operations at lower levels—something that may go unrecognized, as indicated in the following example about Daewoo, another Korean company.

> At Daewoo, day-to-day control was ceded by Chairman Kim Woo-Choong to the presidents of individual Daewoo companies. It didn't work.
>
> At Daewoo Shipbuilding, labor costs had risen tenfold over a decade and no attempt had been made to trim other expenses. Workers received free haircuts in the shipyard at a cost of $60 each a month, including lost hours. Kim personally took over Daewoo Shipbuilding for 18 months. Removing the barber shops saved $8 million a year. For bigger savings, Kim eliminated thousands of positions. From near-bankruptcy, the unit projected a $144 million profit for 1991.[4]

When top management attempts to introduce decentralization policies, some top managers may have difficulty relinquishing the control they previously held over the segments or may be unwilling or unable to delegate effectively. Reasons for this unwillingness or inability include the belief of managers that they can do the job better than anyone else, a lack of confidence in the lower-level managers' abilities, and a lack of ability to communicate directions and assignments to subordinates.

A final disadvantage of decentralization is that it may be extremely costly. In a large company, it is unlikely that all subordinate managers have equally good decision-making skills. Thus, companies must often incur a cost to train lower-level managers to make better decisions. There is the potential cost of poor decisions because decentralization requires managerial tolerance if and when subordinates make mistakes. The potentially adverse consequences of poor decisions by subordinates cause some top managers to resist a high degree of decentralization.

Decentralization also requires that a company develop and maintain a sophisticated planning and reporting system. With more organizations like Unilever having decentralized units worldwide, integrated ways to transfer information are extremely important. A manager at a Unilever office in Australia may need to work with a Unilever manager in India on a report for the home office in Rotterdam. In a company having operations spanning the globe, modems, fax machines, interactive computer networks, management information systems, and videoconferencing are no longer on capital budgeting "wish lists"; they are capital investment necessities. Frito Lay, for example, has installed a network that links all the senior staff and field managers at all levels nationwide and allows decisions to be made quickly from a well-informed perspective. The company refers to its system (shown in Exhibit 21–3) as "directed decentralization."

In a decentralized organization, top management delegates decision-making authority but retains ultimate responsibility for decision outcomes. Thus, a reporting system must be implemented to provide top management with information about, as **Responsibility accounting system** well as the ability to measure, the overall accountability of the subunits. This accounting and information reporting system is known as a **responsibility accounting system**.

[4]Laxmi Nakarmi, "At Daewoo, a 'Revolution' at the Top," *Business Week* (February 18, 1991), pp. 68–69.

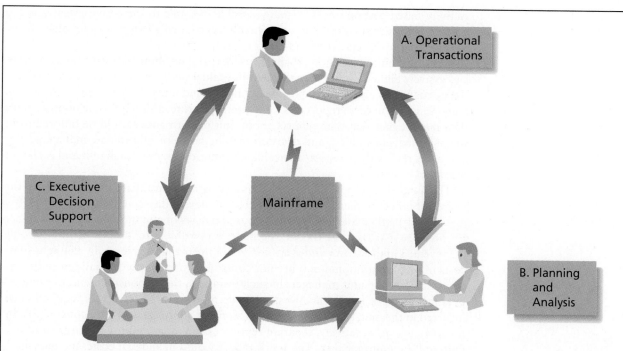

Frito Lay's system is built on a relational database. Any information entered into the system is immediately accessible to all users.

A.   A salesperson processes an order on his or her [laptop] computer. The purchasing, manufacturing, and logistics facilities are notified immediately and begin processing the order. Each successive transaction is entered as it occurs, that is, the company can track where the order is in manufacturing, when it left the plant, and when it will be delivered.

B.   At the same time, this information is available to the planning and analysis system. This allows the brand manager, the channel manager, and the area manager to spot trends in consumption. Competitive information from supermarket scanners is also fed into the mix, enabling managers to see their markets in wider perspective and to develop appropriate strategies to respond to market needs.

C.   This information, broader and more general in scope, becomes instantly available to top management. This allows managers to understand what is going on throughout the company, where the firm is losing market share, and why. This in turn allows the executive process to enter the picture sooner and with greater impact.

SOURCE: Charles S. Field, "Directed Decentralization: The Frito Lay story," *Financial Executive* (November/December 1990), p. 25. Reprinted with permission from *Financial Executive,* November/December 1990, copyright 1990 by Financial Executives Institute, 10 Madison Avenue, P.O. Box 1938, Morristown, N.J. 07962-1938. (201) 898-4600.

▌ **EXHIBIT 21–3**
Frito Lay's Directed Decentralization System

RESPONSIBILITY ACCOUNTING SYSTEMS

A responsibility accounting system is an important tool in making decentralization work effectively by providing information to top management about the performance of organizational subunits. As companies became more decentralized, responsibility accounting systems evolved from the increased need to communicate operating results through the managerial hierarchy. Responsibility accounting implies subordinate managers' acceptance of *communicated* authority from top management.

Responsibility accounting agrees with the concepts of standard costing and activity-based costing because each is implemented for a common basic purpose—that of control. Responsibility accounting focuses attention on organizational subunit performance and the effectiveness and efficiency of that unit's manager. Standard costing traces variances to the person (or machine) having responsibility for a particular variance (such as tracing the material purchase price variance to the purchasing agent).

Activity-based costing traces as many costs as possible to the activities causing the costs to be incurred rather than using highly aggregated allocation techniques. Thus, each technique reflects cause-and-effect relationships.

Responsibility reports

A responsibility accounting system produces **responsibility reports** that assist each successively higher level of management in evaluating the performances of its subordinate managers and their respective organizational units. Much of the information communicated in these reports is of a monetary nature, although some nonmonetary data may be included. The reports about unit performance should be tailored to fit the planning, controlling, and decision-making needs of subordinate managers. Top managers review these reports to evaluate the performance of each unit and each unit manager.

The number of responsibility reports issued for a decentralized unit depends on the degree of influence that unit's manager has on day-to-day operations and costs. If a manager strongly influences all operations and costs of a unit, one report will suffice for both the manager and the unit because responsibility reports should reflect only the revenues and/or costs *under the control* of the manager. Normally, though, some costs of an organizational unit are not controlled (or are only partially or indirectly controlled) by the unit manager. In such instances, the responsibility accounting report takes one of two forms. First, a single report can be issued showing all costs incurred in the unit, separately classified as either controllable or noncontrollable by the manager. Alternatively, separate reports can be prepared for the organizational unit and the unit manager. The unit's report would include all costs; the manager's would include only costs under his or her control.

Effectiveness

Efficiency

Responsibility accounting systems help to establish control procedures at the point of cost incurrence rather than allocating such costs in a potentially arbitrary manner to all units, managers, and/or products. Control procedures are implemented by managers for three reasons. First, managers attempt to cause actual operating results to conform to planned results; this conformity is known as **effectiveness**. Second, managers attempt to cause the standard output to be achieved at minimum possible input costs; this conformity is known as **efficiency**.

Third, managers need to ensure reasonable plant and equipment utilization, which is primarily affected by product or service demand. At higher volumes of activity or utilization, fixed capacity costs can be spread over more units, resulting in a lower unit cost. Reasonable utilization must be tied to demand, and thus does not mean producing simply for the sake of lowering fixed cost per unit if sales demand cannot support production. To illustrate this concept, consider that bank credit cards require huge front-end technology and marketing costs. Robert H. Burke, general manager of the Bank of New York's credit-card operation, says, "In effect, you're running a factory, and the more volume you can push through your fixed costs, the better the profits are."[5] BNY, though, selectively targets potential customers and does not send credit card applications to everyone in the United States.

A responsibility accounting system helps organizational unit managers in conducting the five basic control functions shown in Exhibit 21–4. First, a budget is prepared and used to officially communicate output expectations (sales, production, and so forth) and delegate authority to spend. Ideally, subunit managers negotiate budgets and standards for their units with top management for the coming year. The responsibility accounting system should be designed so that actual data are captured in conformity with budgetary accounts. Thus, during the year, the system can be used to record and summarize data for each organizational unit.

Operating reports comparing actual account balances with budgeted or standard amounts are prepared periodically and issued to unit and top managers for their review. However, because of day-to-day contact with operations, unit managers should

---

[5]Douglas R. Sease and Robert Guenther, "Big Banks Are Plagued by a Gradual Erosion of Key Profit Centers," *Wall Street Journal* (August 1, 1990), p. A14.

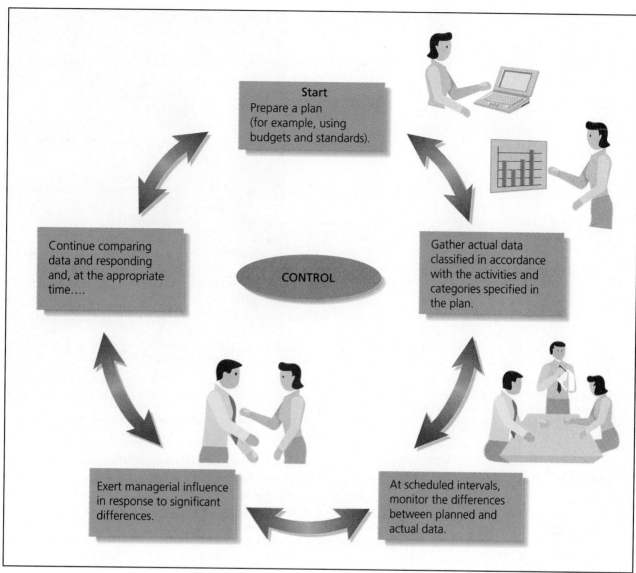

Basic Steps in a Control Process

have been aware of any significant variances *before* they were reported, identified the variance causes, and attempted to correct the causes of the problems. Top management, on the other hand, may not know about operational variances until responsibility reports are received. By the time top management receives the reports, the problems causing the variances should have been corrected, or subordinate managers should have explanations as to why the problems were not or could not have been resolved.

Responsibility reports for subordinate managers and their immediate supervisors normally compare actual results with flexible budget figures. These comparisons are more useful for control purposes since both operating results and flexible budget figures are based on achieved levels of activity. In contrast, top management may receive responsibility reports comparing actual performance to the master budget. Such a budget-to-actual comparison yields an overall performance evaluation, since the master budget reflects management's expectations about volume, mix, costs, and prices. This type of comparison is especially useful when accompanied by a supporting detailed variance analysis identifying the effect of sales volume differences on segment performance.

Areas of responsibility may be drawn by product lines or geographical location. If product lines are used, Unilever's top management must recognize in the responsibility reports that some costs may benefit more than one product line and that other costs may not be controllable by the product line manager.

Regardless of the type of comparison provided, responsibility reports reflect the upward flow of information from operational units to company top management and illustrate the broadening scope of responsibility. Managers receive detailed information on the performance of their immediate areas of control and summary information on all organizational units for which they are responsible. Summarizing results causes a pyramiding of information. Like the information received by the executives in the Frito-Lay exhibit, reports at the lowest level units are highly detailed, while more general information is reported at the top of the organization. Upper-level managers desiring more detail than provided in summary reports can obtain it by reviewing the responsibility reports prepared for their subordinates.

Exhibit 21–5 illustrates a set of performance reports for Beverages Division of Universal Foods, a Dutch conglomerate. All information is shown in home office currency, which is the guilder or Dutch florin (D.fl.); one D.fl. is equal to approximately $.55. The division's flexible budget is presented for comparative purposes. Data for the blending and bottling department are aggregated with data of the other departments under the production vice president's control. (These combined data are shown in the middle section of Exhibit 21–5.) In a like manner, the total costs of the production vice president's area of responsibility are combined with other costs for which the company president is responsible and are shown in the top section of Exhibit 21–5.

Variances are the responsibility of the manager under whose direct supervision they occur. Variances are individually itemized in performance reports at the lower levels so that the appropriate manager has the necessary details to take any required corrective action related to significant variances.[6] Under the management by exception principle, major deviations from expectations are highlighted under the subor-

---

[6] In practice, the variances presented in Exhibit 21–5 would be further separated into the portions representing price and quantity effects as is shown in Chapters 11 and 12 on standard costing.

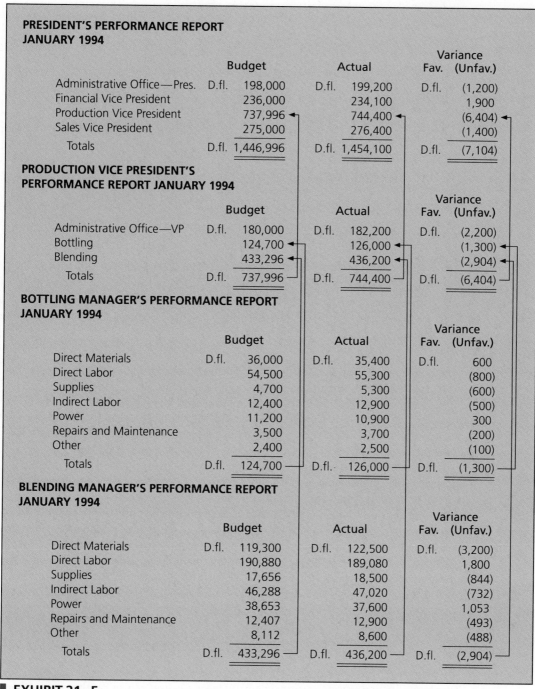

PRESIDENT'S PERFORMANCE REPORT
JANUARY 1994

	Budget	Actual	Variance Fav. (Unfav.)
Administrative Office—Pres.	D.fl. 198,000	D.fl. 199,200	D.fl. (1,200)
Financial Vice President	236,000	234,100	1,900
Production Vice President	737,996	744,400	(6,404)
Sales Vice President	275,000	276,400	(1,400)
Totals	D.fl. 1,446,996	D.fl. 1,454,100	D.fl. (7,104)

PRODUCTION VICE PRESIDENT'S
PERFORMANCE REPORT JANUARY 1994

	Budget	Actual	Variance Fav. (Unfav.)
Administrative Office—VP	D.fl. 180,000	D.fl. 182,200	D.fl. (2,200)
Bottling	124,700	126,000	(1,300)
Blending	433,296	436,200	(2,904)
Totals	D.fl. 737,996	D.fl. 744,400	D.fl. (6,404)

BOTTLING MANAGER'S PERFORMANCE REPORT
JANUARY 1994

	Budget	Actual	Variance Fav. (Unfav.)
Direct Materials	D.fl. 36,000	D.fl. 35,400	D.fl. 600
Direct Labor	54,500	55,300	(800)
Supplies	4,700	5,300	(600)
Indirect Labor	12,400	12,900	(500)
Power	11,200	10,900	300
Repairs and Maintenance	3,500	3,700	(200)
Other	2,400	2,500	(100)
Totals	D.fl. 124,700	D.fl. 126,000	D.fl. (1,300)

BLENDING MANAGER'S PERFORMANCE REPORT
JANUARY 1994

	Budget	Actual	Variance Fav. (Unfav.)
Direct Materials	D.fl. 119,300	D.fl. 122,500	D.fl. (3,200)
Direct Labor	190,880	189,080	1,800
Supplies	17,656	18,500	(844)
Indirect Labor	46,288	47,020	(732)
Power	38,653	37,600	1,053
Repairs and Maintenance	12,407	12,900	(493)
Other	8,112	8,600	(488)
Totals	D.fl. 433,296	D.fl. 436,200	D.fl. (2,904)

▌ EXHIBIT 21–5

Beverages Division of Universal Foods Performance Reports for Costs Incurred

dinate manager's reporting section to assist upper-level managers in making decisions about when to become involved in subordinates' operations. If no significant deviations exist, top management is free to devote its attention to other matters. In addition, such detailed variance analysis alerts operating managers to items that may need to be explained to superiors. For example, the items of direct materials and direct labor in Exhibit 21–5 on the blending manager's section of the report would probably be considered significant and require explanations to the production vice president.

■ EXHIBIT 21–6
Nonmonetary Information
for Responsibility Reports

■ Departmental/divisional throughput
■ Number of defects (by product, product line, supplier)
■ Number of orders backlogged (by date, quantity, cost, and selling price)
■ Number of customer complaints (by type and product); method of complaint resolution
■ Percentage of orders delivered on time
■ Manufacturing (or service) cycle efficiency
■ Percentage of reduction of non-value-added time from previous reporting period (broken down by idle time, storage time, quality control time)
■ Number of employee suggestions considered significant and practical
■ Number of employee suggestions implemented
■ Number of unplanned production interruptions
■ Number of schedule changes
■ Number of engineering change orders; percentage change from previous period
■ Number of safety violations; percentage change from previous period
■ Number of days of employee absences; percentage change from previous period

In addition to the monetary information shown in Exhibit 21–5, many responsibility accounting systems are now providing information on critical nonmonetary measures of the period's activity. Some examples of these types of information are shown in Exhibit 21–6. Many of these measures are equally useful for manufacturing and service organizations and can be used to judge performance in addition to basic financial measurements.

The performance reports of each management layer are reviewed and evaluated by each successive higher management layer. Managers are likely to be more careful and alert in controlling operations, knowing that the reports generated by the responsibility accounting system will reveal financial accomplishments and problems. Thus, in addition to providing a means for control, responsibility reports can motivate managers to influence operations in ways that will reflect positive performance.

The focus of responsibility accounting is on the managers who are responsible for a particular cost object. In the case of a decentralized company, the cost object is an organizational unit such as a division, department, or geographical region. The cost object under the control of a manager is called a **responsibility center**.

Responsibility center

TYPES OF RESPONSIBILITY CENTERS

Responsibility accounting systems identify, measure, and report on the performance of people controlling the activities of responsibility centers. Responsibility centers are classified according to their manager's scope of authority and type of financial responsibility. Companies may define their organizational units in various ways based on management accountability for one or more income-producing factors—costs, revenues, profits, and/or asset base. The four types of responsibility centers are illustrated in Exhibit 21–7 and discussed in the following sections.

Cost Centers

Cost center

A **cost center** manager has the authority only to incur costs and is specifically evaluated on the basis of how well costs are controlled. Revenues may not exist in a cost center because the unit does not engage in revenue-producing activity. Cost centers

Cost center—manager is responsible for cost containment.

Revenue center—manager is responsible for revenue generation.

Profit center—manager is responsible for net income of unit.

Investment center—manager is responsible for return on asset base.

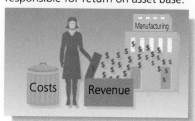

with no revenues are commonly the service and administrative departments discussed in Chapter 6. For example, the placement center in a university may be a cost center since it does not charge for the use of its services, but it does incur costs.

In other instances, revenues do exist for a cost center, but they are either not under the manager's control or are not effectively measurable. The first type of situation exists in a governmental agency that is provided a specific proration of sales tax dollars, but has no authority to levy or collect the related taxes. The second situation could exist in engineered and discretionary cost centers in which the outputs (revenues or benefits generated from the cost inputs) are not easily measured.[7] In these two types of situations, the revenues should not be included in the manager's responsibility accounting report.

In the traditional manufacturing environment, a standard costing system is generally used and variances are reported and analyzed. In such an environment, the highest priority in a cost center is often the minimization of unfavorable cost variances. Top management may often concentrate only on the unfavorable variances occurring in a cost center and ignore the efficient performance indicated by favorable variances. To illustrate this possibility, the January 1994 operating results for the Blending Department of the Beverage Division of Universal Foods are used. These data are shown in Exhibit 21–8 on page 910.

Anna Marie Hof is the manager of the Blending Department. During the month, the division produced 477,200 units of product at a cost of D.fl. .914. The standard production cost for these units is D.fl. .908. Top management's analysis of the responsibility report issued for the Blending Department for January might focus on the large unfavorable materials variance rather than on the large favorable variances for the direct labor and power production costs. Ms. Hof's job is to control costs and she did so relatively well when both favorable and unfavorable variances are reviewed. A considered evaluation by her superiors should recognize this fact.

Significant favorable variances should not be disregarded if the management by exception principle is applied appropriately. Using this principle, top management

---

[7]Engineered and discretionary costs are discussed in Chapter 17.

EXHIBIT 21–8

Blending Department's January 1994 Production Costs

Units produced: 477,200				
Standard cost per unit of production:				
Direct materials			D.fl.	.250
Direct labor				.400
Overhead				
Supplies	D.fl.	.037		
Indirect labor		.097		
Power		.081		
Repairs and maintenance		.026		
Other		.017		.258
Total			D.fl.	.908

	STANDARD COST ALLOWED	ACTUAL COST INCURRED	VARIANCE FAV. (UNFAV.)
Direct materials	D.fl. 119,300	D.fl. 122,500	D.fl. (3,200)
Direct labor	190,880	189,080	1,800
Supplies	17,656	18,500	(844)
Indirect labor	46,288	47,020	(732)
Power	38,653	37,600	1,053
Repairs and maintenance	12,407	12,900	(493)
Other	8,112	8,600	(488)
Total	D.fl. 433,296	D.fl. 436,200	D.fl. (2,904)

should investigate all variances (both favorable and unfavorable) that fall outside the range of acceptable deviations. The unfavorable materials variance in the Blending Department should be investigated further to find its cause. It is possible that substandard materials were purchased and caused excessive usage. If this is the case, the purchasing agent, not Ms. Hof, should be assigned the responsibility for the variance. Other possible causes for the unfavorable materials variance include increased materials prices, excess waste, or some combination of all causes. Only additional inquiry will determine if the variance could have been controlled by Ms. Hof.

The favorable direct labor variance should also be analyzed for causes. Ms. Hof may have used inexperienced personnel who were being paid lower rates. This might explain the favorable direct labor variance and, to some extent, the unfavorable direct materials variance (because of a lack of employee skill and possible overuse of materials). Alternatively, the people working in the Blending Department simply could have been very efficient this period.

Revenue Centers

Revenue center

A **revenue center** is strictly defined as an organizational unit for which a manager is accountable only for the generation of revenues and has no control over setting selling prices or budgeting costs. In many retail stores, the individual sales departments are considered independent units and managers are evaluated based on the total revenues generated by their departments. Departmental managers, however, may not be given the authority to change selling prices to affect volume and often they do not participate in the budgeting process. Thus, the departmental managers may have no impact on costs. In most instances, however, pure revenue centers do not exist. Managers of "revenue centers" are typically responsible not only for revenues, but are also involved in the planning and control over some (but not necessarily all) costs incurred in the center. A more appropriate term for this organizational unit is a "revenue and limited cost center."

For example, Hans Wilhoft is the German district sales manager for the Beverages Division of Universal Foods and is responsible for the sales revenues generated in his territory. In addition, he is also accountable for controlling the mileage and other travel-related expenses of his sales staff. Hans is not, however, able to influence the types of cars his sales staff obtain because cars are acquired on a fleetwide basis by top management.

Salaries, if directly traceable to the center, are often a cost responsibility of the "revenue center" manager. This situation reflects the traditional retail environment in which sales clerks are assigned to a specific department and are only allowed to check out customers wanting to purchase that department's merchandise. Most stores, however, have found such a checkout situation to be detrimental to business because customers were forced to wait for the appropriate clerk. Clerks in many stores are now allowed to assist all customers with all types of merchandise. Such a change in policy converts what was a traceable departmental cost into an indirect cost. Those stores carrying high-cost, high-selling-price merchandise normally retain the traditional system. Managers of such departments are thus able to trace sales salaries as a direct departmental cost.

Recall that revenue variances were presented in Chapter 17. That model will be expanded below to illustrate the effect of a mix different from budget in sales.

The following revenue statistics are presented for the American Candy Division of Universal Foods for May 1994:

Budget	Pounds	Unit Price	Revenue	Standard Mix		
Taffy	1,000	$1.80	$1,800	1,000 ÷ 2,700 =	37.0%
Bubble gum	500	.80	400	500 ÷ 2,700 =	18.5%
Jawbreakers	1,200	1.00	1,200	1,200 ÷ 2,700 =	44.5%
Totals	2,700		$3,400		100.0%

Actual	Pounds	Unit Price	Revenue
Taffy	1,100	$2.00	$2,200
Bubble gum	540	.70	378
Jawbreakers	1,180	1.10	1,298
Totals	2,820		$3,876

Using the revenue variance model and the information presented for American

Candy, variances can be determined as follows:

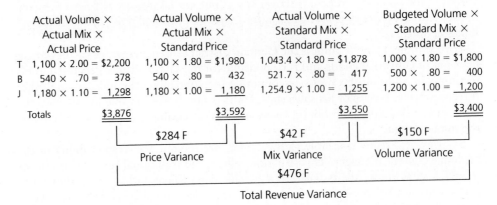

	Actual Volume × Actual Mix × Actual Price	Actual Volume × Actual Mix × Standard Price	Actual Volume × Standard Mix × Standard Price	Budgeted Volume × Standard Mix × Standard Price
T	1,100 × 2.00 = $2,200	1,100 × 1.80 = $1,980	1,043.4 × 1.80 = $1,878	1,000 × 1.80 = $1,800
B	540 × .70 = 378	540 × .80 = 432	521.7 × .80 = 417	500 × .80 = 400
J	1,180 × 1.10 = 1,298	1,180 × 1.00 = 1,180	1,254.9 × 1.00 = 1,255	1,200 × 1.00 = 1,200
Totals	$3,876	$3,592	$3,550	$3,400

$284 F
Price Variance

$42 F
Mix Variance

$150 F
Volume Variance

$476 F
Total Revenue Variance

Inspection of the results reveals that (1) prices increased (except for bubble gum), causing an overall favorable price variance; (2) the actual mix included more of the high-priced candy (taffy and jawbreakers) than the standard mix, causing an overall favorable mix variance; and (3) the total actual pounds (2,820) was greater than the budgeted total pounds (2,700), causing a favorable volume variance. The American Candy Division's manager would be commended for a good performance.

Profit Centers

Profit center

In a **profit center**, the manager is responsible for generating revenues and planning and controlling expenses related to current activity. (Expenses not under a profit center manager's control are those related to long-term investments in plant assets; such a situation creates a definitive need for separate evaluations of the subunit and the subunit's manager.) A profit center manager's goal is to maximize the center's net income. Profit centers should be independent organizational units whose managers have the ability to obtain resources at the most economical prices and to sell products at prices that will maximize revenue. If managers do not have complete authority to buy and sell at objectively determined costs and prices, it is difficult to make a meaningful evaluation of the profit center.

Profit centers are not always manufacturing divisions or branches of retail stores. Banks may view each department (checking and savings accounts, loans, and credit cards) as a profit center; trucking companies may view each 18-wheeler as a profit center; and a university may view certain educational divisions as profit centers (undergraduate education, non-degree-seeking night school, and the law school).

To illustrate the computations for a profit center, assume that Universal Foods uses 18-wheelers to deliver products in the United States and each truck is considered a profit center. The segment income statement's budgeted and actual results of the "Big Mack," a truck for which Doug Douglas is responsible, are shown in Exhibit 21–9. These comparisons can be used to explain to top management why the budgeted income was not reached. The profit center should be judged on the $43,400 of profit center income, but Doug Douglas should be judged on the controllable margin of $62,900. Because actual volume was greater than budgeted, it is natural that the comparison in Exhibit 21–9 would show unfavorable variances for all of the variable costs. A comparison of actual results to a flexible budget at the actual activity level would provide better information for assessing cost control in the profit center.

Investment Centers

Investment center

An **investment center** is an organizational unit in which the manager is responsible for generating revenues and planning and controlling expenses. In addition, the cen-

	BUDGET	ACTUAL	VARIANCE
Fees	$120,000	$124,000	$4,000 F
Cost of services rendered			
Direct labor	$ 3,000	$ 3,200	$ 200 U
Gas and oil	25,200	26,300	1,100 U
Variable overhead	5,200	5,800	600 U
Total	$ 33,400	$ 35,300	$1,900 U
Contribution margin	$ 86,600	$ 88,700	$2,100 F
Fixed overhead—controllable	25,600	25,800	200 U
Controllable segment margin	$ 61,000	$ 62,900	$1,900 F
Fixed overhead—not controllable by profit center manager	18,000	19,500	1,500 U
Profit center income	$ 43,000	$ 43,400	$ 400 F

EXHIBIT 21–9

Profit Center Comparisons for "Big Mack" for Month Ended June 30, 1994

ter's manager has the authority to acquire, use, and dispose of plant assets in a manner that seeks to earn the highest feasible rate of return on the center's asset base. Many investment centers are independent free-standing divisions or subsidiaries of a firm. This independence allows investment center managers the opportunity to make decisions about all matters affecting their organizational units and to be judged on the outcomes of those decisions.

Assume that the San Fran Sour Dough Plant of Universal Foods is an investment center headed by Teresa Cisneros. The 1994 income statement for the plant is as follows:

Sales	$860,000
Variable expenses	450,000
Contribution margin	$410,000
Fixed expenses	345,000
Net income	$ 65,000

Teresa has the authority to set selling prices, incur costs, and acquire and dispose of plant assets. The plant has an asset base of $740,000 and thus the rate of return on assets for the year was approximately 8.8 percent ($65,000 ÷ $740,000). This rate of return would be compared to the rates desired by Universal Foods' management and would also be compared to other investment centers in the company. Rate of return and other performance measures for responsibility centers are treated in greater depth in Chapter 22.

Because of their closeness to daily divisional activities, responsibility center managers should have more current and detailed knowledge about sales prices, costs, and other market information than top management does. If the responsibility centers are designated as profit or investment centers, their managers are encouraged, to the extent possible, to operate those subunits as separate economic entities that exist for the same basic organizational goals.

Regardless of the size, type of ownership, or product or service being sold, one basic goal for any business is to generate profits. For other organizations, such as a

Critical success factors

charity or governmental entity, the ultimate financial goal may be to break even. The ultimate goal will be achieved through the satisfaction of organizational **critical success factors**—those items that are so important that, without them, the organization would cease to exist. Most organizations would consider quality, customer service, efficiency, cost control, and responsiveness to change as five critical success factors. If all of these factors are managed properly, the organization should be financially successful; if they are not, sooner or later the organization will fail. All members of the organization—especially those in management—should work toward the same basic objectives if the critical success factors are to be satisfied. Losing sight of the organizational goal while working to achieve an independent responsibility center's conflicting goal results in **suboptimization**.

Suboptimization

SUBOPTIMIZATION

Suboptimization is a situation in which individual managers pursue goals and objectives that are in their own and/or their segments' particular interests rather than in the company's best interests. Because of their greater degree of flexibility in regard to financial decisions, it is essential that profit and investment center managers remember that their operations are integral parts of the entire corporate structure. Therefore, all actions taken should be in the best long-run interest of both the responsibility center and the organization. Unit managers should be aware of and accept the need for goal congruence throughout the entity.

For suboptimization to be limited or minimized, top management must be aware that it can occur and should develop ways to avoid it. A primary way managers can try to limit suboptimization is by communicating corporate goals to all organizational units, regardless of the types of responsibility centers. Exhibit 21–10 depicts other ways of limiting suboptimization as stairsteps to the achievement of corporate goals. These steps are not in a hierarchical order. If any steps are missing, the climb toward corporate goals and objectives becomes more difficult for divisional managers.

Each of the steps (except the bottom two) has either been discussed earlier in the text or in this chapter, or will be covered in Chapters 22 or 23. The concept of internal and operational auditing is briefly introduced at this point and should be covered in more depth in an auditing course. The remainder of this chapter deals with the topic of transfer pricing.

An internal and/or operational audit function is used to monitor and evaluate the effectiveness and efficiency of the various organizational units and programs. Part of the evaluation includes an assessment of subordinate managers' knowledge of company goals and objectives and of whether the managers are striving for and achieving those goals. Operational auditors are expected to act as a kind of management consultant team. Their expertise and abilities should be focused on recognizing suboptimal behavior. Rigorous and systematic monitoring by such a team can be highly advantageous to companies, especially large, decentralized ones.

To properly evaluate segments and their managers, it is necessary to have useful information about performance. When the various segments of a firm exchange goods or services among themselves, it is necessary to set a "price" for those goods or services so that the "selling" segment can measure its revenue and the "buying" segment can measure its costs. Such an internal price is known as a **transfer price**.

Transfer price

The steps of the Stairway to Achievement (from bottom to top):

Divisional Goals and Objectives

Use of internal and operational audit functions

Appropriate transfer prices between units

Ability to gather the appropriate information

Measurements made in appropriate time frame

Commitment to quality (not just quantity) of performance

Use of responsibility accounting system

Consideration of operating environment

Proper definitions of measurements

Multiple performance measurements

Long-range perspective on actions

Use of nonfinancial measurements

Goal congruence between units

Appropriate reward structure

Corporate Goals and Objectives

Stairway to Achievement

▋ EXHIBIT 21–10

Performance Measures to Limit Suboptimization

TRANSFER PRICING

Responsibility centers often provide goods or services to other company segments. Such transfers require that a price be established to account for the flow of these goods or services within the company. Transfer prices (or prices in a charge-back system) are *internal* charges established for the exchange of goods or services between organizational units of the same company. Although a variety of transfer prices may be used for internal reporting purposes, intercompany inventory transfers should be presented on an external balance sheet at the producing segment's actual cost. Internal transfers would be eliminated for external income statement purposes altogether.

Thus, if transfers are "sold" at an amount other than cost, any intersegment profit in inventory, expense, and/or revenue accounts must be eliminated.

Transfer prices may be established to promote goal congruence, make performance evaluation among segments more comparable, and/or "transform" a cost center into a profit center. The appropriate transfer price should be one that ensures optimal resource allocation and promotes operating efficiency. A number of different approaches are used to establish a transfer price for goods or services. The basic caveat is that intracompany transfers should be made only if they are in the best interest of the total organization. Within this context, the general rules[8] for choosing a transfer price are as follows:

▌ The maximum price should be no greater than the lowest market price at which the buying segment can acquire the goods or services externally.

▌ The minimum price should be no less than the sum of the selling segment's incremental costs associated with the goods or services plus the opportunity cost of the facilities used.

From the company's perspective, any transfer price set between these two limits is generally considered appropriate.

To illustrate the use of these rules, assume that a product is available from external suppliers at a price below the lower limit (selling division's incremental costs plus opportunity cost). The immediate short-run decision might be that the selling division is to stop production and allow the purchasing division to buy the product from the external suppliers. This decision may be reasonable since, compared to the external suppliers, the selling division does not appear to be cost efficient in its production activities. Stopping production would release the facilities for other, more profitable purposes. A longer-run solution may be to have the selling division improve its efficiency and reduce the internal cost of making the product. This solution could be implemented without stopping internal production, but possibly reducing it by making some external purchases until costs were under control.

After the transfer price range limits have been established, one criterion used to choose a price in the range is the ease by which the price can be determined. Managers should be able to understand the computation of a transfer price and to evaluate the impact of that transfer price on their responsibility centers' profits. The more complex the method used to set a transfer price, the less comfortable managers will be with both the method and the resulting price. In addition, from a cost standpoint, it takes more time and effort to administer and account for a complicated transfer pricing system than a simple one.

The difference between the upper and lower transfer price limits is the corporate "profit" (or savings) generated by producing internally rather than buying externally. The transfer price chosen acts to "divide the corporate profit" between the buying and selling segments. For external statements, it is irrelevant which segment shows the profits from transfers because such internal profit allocations are eliminated in preparing these statements. For internal reporting, though, this division of profits may be extremely important. Use of transfer prices affects the responsibility reports that are prepared, and top management may have established a subunit performance measurement system that is affected by such "profit" allocations.

Segment managers in a decentralized company often have competing vested interests if managerial performance is evaluated on a competitive basis. Such internal competition could lead to suboptimization because both buying and selling segment

---

[8]These rules are more difficult to implement when the selling division is in a "captive" relationship, in that it is not able to transfer its products to customers outside the corporate entity. Captive relationships often exist when the selling division was acquired or established in a company's move toward vertical integration. In such situations, opportunity cost must be estimated to provide the selling division an incentive to transfer products.

managers want to maximize their financial results in the responsibility accounting reports. The supplier-segment manager attempts to obtain the highest transfer (selling) price, while the buying-segment manager attempts to acquire the goods or services at the lowest transfer (purchase) price. Thus, transfer prices should be agreed on by the company's selling and buying segments.

Many top managers believe in giving subunit managers a considerable amount of autonomy to negotiate divisional transfer prices. Division managers are expected to make choices that will maximize the effectiveness and efficiency of their divisions as well as contribute to overall company performance.

Three traditional methods are used for determining transfer prices: cost-based prices, market-based prices, and negotiated prices. Following is a discussion of each method and its advantages and disadvantages. This discussion will use information on the Napoleon Company, an Australian subsidiary of Universal Foods. Napoleon Company is composed of two investment centers: a mustard-producing division (managed by Laura Sydney) and a bottle plant (managed by Paul Melbourne). The managers are attempting to establish a reasonable transfer price for jars in which to bottle the mustard. The Bottle Division data (shown in Exhibit 21–11 in Australian dollars) are used to illustrate various transfer pricing approaches. Note that the Bottle Division is capable of supplying all external and internal production needs.

Cost-Based Transfer Prices

A cost-based transfer price is, on the surface, an easily understood concept until one realizes the variations that can exist in the definition of the term *cost*. Different companies use different definitions of "cost" in conjunction with transfer pricing. These definitions range from variable production cost to absorption cost plus additional amounts for selling, general, and administrative costs (and, possibly, opportunity costs) of the selling unit. Another consideration in a cost-based transfer price is whether actual or standard cost is used. Actual costs may vary according to the season, production volume, and other factors, while standard costs can be specified in advance and are stable measures of efficient production cost. For these two reasons, standard costs provide a superior basis for transfer pricing. When standard costs are used, any variances from standard are borne by the selling segment because otherwise the selling division's efficiencies or inefficiencies are passed on to the buying division.

EXHIBIT 21–11
Napoleon Company Bottle Division

Standard unit production cost:		
Direct materials	A$.08	
Direct labor	.06	
Variable overhead	.10	
Variable selling and administrative	.04	
Total variable costs		A$.28
Fixed overhead*	A$.09	
Fixed selling and administrative*	.03	.12
Total cost		A$.40
Normal mark-up on variable cost (50%)		.14
List selling price		A$.54

Estimated annual production: 700,000 jars
Estimated sales to outside entities: 400,000 jars
Estimated intracompany transfers: 300,000 jars

*Fixed costs are allocated to all units produced based on estimated annual production.

Cost Alternative—Variable Cost.   Using the data provided in Exhibit 21–11, a variable cost transfer price for jars can be either A$.24 or A$.28. The difference depends on whether variable cost is defined as variable production cost or total variable cost. Even using A$.28 as the transfer price provides little incentive to Mr. Melbourne to sell to the mustard division. Fixed costs of the Bottle Division are not reduced by selling internally, but no contribution margin is being generated by the transfers to help cover these fixed costs. The low transfer prices could result in a poor financial showing for the Bottle Division that, in turn, could detrimentally affect Mr. Melbourne's performance evaluation.

Considering the total standard cost per unit of A$.40, a loss of A$.12 will result for Mr. Melbourne's division on each bottle sold internally at a transfer price of A$.28. If all sales and transfers occur as expected and there are no variances from standard costs, Mr. Melbourne's responsibility report will appear as follows:

Sales:		
External (400,000 × A$.54)	A$216,000	
Internal (300,000 × A$.28)	84,000	A$300,000
Costs:		
Total variable and fixed costs (700,000 × A$.40)		280,000
Net income		A$ 20,000

Had the Bottle Division been able to sell all its production externally, it would have shown a net income for the period of A$98,000:

Sales (700,000 × A$.54)	A$378,000
Costs (from above)	280,000
Net income	A$ 98,000

This A$78,000 difference can be reconciled as the 300,000 units multiplied by the A$.26 per unit (A$.54 − A$.28) "lost" revenue from making internal sales.

Assume, on the other hand, that the 400,000 units represented the total number of units that could be sold externally and the Bottle Division has no other opportunity to use the facilities. In this instance, the opportunity cost of the facilities used is zero and the division is no worse off by transferring the 300,000 jars internally than by sitting with idle capacity. Relating this situation to the general transfer pricing rules, the transfer price of A$.28 is at its lower limit.

Cost Alternative—Absorption Cost.   Transfer prices based on absorption cost (direct materials, direct labor, and variable and fixed overhead) at least provide a contribution toward covering the selling division's fixed production overhead. Such a transfer price does not produce the same amount of income that would be generated if the transferring division sold the goods externally, but it does provide for coverage of all production costs.

Absorption cost for a jar is A$.33 (A$.08 DM + A$.06 DL + A$.10 VOH + A$.09 FOH). The Bottle Division's income statement would appear as follows using absorption cost as the transfer price.

Sales:		
External (400,000 × A$.54)	A$216,000	
Internal (300,000 × A$.33)	99,000	A$315,000
Costs (shown previously)		280,000
Net income		A$ 35,000

Although the absorption cost transfer price provides a reasonable coverage of costs to the selling segment, that same cost could create a suboptimization problem because of the effects on the buying segment.

Suppose the Mustard Division of Napoleon Company can purchase jars externally from Glass Unlimited for A$.32 and that the externally purchased jars are of the same quality and specifications as those produced internally. If the transfer price is set at the absorption cost of A$.33, the Mustard Division may decide to purchase the jars from Glass Unlimited for A$.32. Purchasing at the lower price would give the buying unit's manager more favorable financial results than would making the acquisition internally. In such an instance, Napoleon Company is paying A$.32 for a product its Bottle Division can make for a variable cost of A$.28. Thus, although the buying segment manager *appears* to "save" A$.01 per jar, the *company* would be better off by A$12,000 if the jars were purchased internally rather than externally:

Unit cost to Mustard Division to purchase externally	A$.32
Unit cost to produce and deliver in Bottle Division (out-of-pocket costs)	.28
Net advantage of company to produce per unit	A$.04
Multiplied by number of units transferred	× 300,000
Total savings to produce internally	A$ 12,000

These facts assume that the Bottle Division does not have an opportunity cost of more than A$.04 per bottle for the use of the facilities devoted to the 300,000 units.

If, however, the Bottle Division can sell all the units it produces at list price, the division should do so. The Mustard Division could then purchase its jars from Glass Unlimited and Napoleon Company would be optimizing its resources. Computations to arrive at this conclusion are:

Bottle Division's additional contribution margin from outside sales (300,000 × A$.26)	A$78,000
Additional cost caused by Mustard Division's purchase from outside source (300,000 × A$.04)	(12,000)
Net incremental income to company	A$66,000

The company is better off by A$66,000 because the A$.26 contribution margin (A$.54 − A$.28) realized on each additional unit sale to outsiders is greater than the A$.04 difference between the A$.32 external purchase price paid by Mustard Division and the A$.28 incremental cost of the Bottle Division to produce the units.

Under the above circumstances, the general transfer pricing rules also would have yielded the decision not to make the internal transfer. The sum of the incremental cost to produce (A$.28) and the A$.26 opportunity cost of additional contribution on external sales is A$.54, which exceeds the upper limit of the A$.32 market price. Napoleon Company should not make the transfer as long as the Mustard Division can purchase the units externally for a price less than A$.54.

Cost Alternative—Modifications to Variable and/or Absorption Cost. Modifications can be made to minimize the definitional and motivational problems associated with cost-based transfer prices. When variable cost is used as a base, an additional amount can be added to cover some fixed costs and provide a measure of profit to the selling division. This adjustment is an example of a "cost-plus" arrangement. Some company managers think cost-plus arrangements are acceptable substitutes for market-based transfer prices, especially when market prices for comparable substitute products are unavailable.

Absorption cost can be modified by adding an amount equal to an average of the nonproduction costs associated with the product and/or an amount for profit to the selling division. In contrast, a transfer price could be set at less than absorption cost on the theory that there might be no other use for the idle capacity and the selling division should receive some benefit from partial coverage of its fixed factory overhead. Alternatively, absorption cost can be reduced by the estimated savings in production costs on internally transferred goods. For example, packaging may not be necessary or as expensive if the inventory is sold intracompany rather than externally.

Market-Based Transfer Prices

To eliminate the problems of defining "cost," some companies simply use a market price approach to setting transfer prices. Market price is believed to be an objective, arm's length measure of value that simulates the selling price that would be offered and paid if the subunits were independent, autonomous companies. If a selling division is operating efficiently relative to its competition, it should be able to show a profit when transferring products or services at market prices. In the same vein, an efficiently operating buying division should not be troubled by a market-based transfer price because that is what it would have to pay for the goods or services if the alternative of buying internally did not exist. Using such a system, the Bottle Division would transfer all jars to the Mustard Division at the A$.54 price charged to external purchasers.

Although this approach appears logical, several problems may exist with the use of market prices for intracompany transfers. First, transfers may involve products having no exact counterpart in the external market. Second, market price may not be entirely appropriate because of internal cost savings arising from reductions in bad debts and/or in packaging, advertising, or delivery expenditures. Third, difficulties can arise in setting a transfer price when the external market is depressed because of a temporary reduction in demand for the product. Should the current depressed price be used as the transfer price or should the expected long-run market price be used? Fourth, different prices are quoted and different discounts and credit terms are allowed to different buyers. Which market price is the "right" one to use?

Negotiated Transfer Prices

Negotiated transfer price

Because of the problems associated with both cost- and market-based prices, **negotiated transfer prices** are often set through a process of bargaining between the selling and purchasing unit managers. Such prices are typically below the normal market purchase price of the buying unit, but above the sum of the selling unit's incremental and opportunity costs. A negotiated price meeting these specifications falls within the range limits of the transfer pricing rules.

A negotiated transfer price for the Napoleon Company would be bounded on the top side by the Mustard Division's external buying price and on the bottom side by the A$.28 incremental variable costs of the Bottle Division. If some of the variable selling costs could be eliminated, the incremental cost would even be less. If the Bottle Division could not sell any additional jars externally nor downsize its facilities, there would be no opportunity cost involved. Otherwise, the amount of the opportunity cost would need to be determined and it could be as much as the A$.26 contribution margin (if all units could be sold externally).

Ability to negotiate a transfer price implies that segment managers have the autonomy to sell or buy products externally if internal negotiations fail. Because such extensive autonomy may lead to dysfunctional behavior and suboptimization, top management may provide a means of arbitrating a price in the event that the units cannot agree. This arbitration arrangement must be specified and agreed on in advance and be skillfully handled or the segment managers may perceive that their autonomy is being usurped by upper-level management.

To encourage cooperation between the transferring divisions, top management may consider joint divisional profits as one performance measurement for both the selling and buying unit managers. Another way to reduce difficulties in establishing a transfer price is simply to use a dual pricing approach.

Dual Pricing

Since a transfer price is used to satisfy internal managerial objectives, a **dual pricing arrangement** can be used to provide for different transfer prices for the selling and buying segments. Such an arrangement lets the selling division record the transfer of goods or services at a market or negotiated market price and the buying division to record the transfer at a cost-based amount.[9] Use of dual prices would provide a profit margin on the goods transferred and thus reflect a "profit" for the selling division. The arrangement would also provide a minimal cost to the buying division. Dual pricing eliminates the problem of having to divide the profits artificially between the selling and buying segments and allows managers to have the most relevant information for both decision making and performance evaluation.

Dual pricing arrangement

When dual pricing is used, the sum of the individual segment performances will not equal the companywide performance. The selling segment's recorded sales price is not equal to the buying segment's recorded purchase price for the same transaction. The difference is assigned to an internal reconciliation account used to adjust revenues and costs when company financial statements are prepared. Such a reconciliation is the same as would exist in preparing consolidated statements when sales are made between the consolidated entities at an amount other than cost.

Three distinct benefits can result from the use of dual transfer pricing. First, it "provides the selling department with an incentive to maximize profits while at the same time it provides the buying department with the relevant cost information for making short-run decisions."[10] Second, goal congruence may be enhanced because each manager is motivated to engage in intracompany transfers. In the selling division, internal transfers are reflected in an equitable manner to external sales; in the buying division, internal purchases would be at a cost lower than that for external purchases. Third, dual transfer prices should reduce potential managerial conflict arising through attempts to negotiate "equitable" transfer prices. (On the other hand, although reducing conflict, dual pricing could also eliminate some of the benefits of managerial competition, such as the understanding and cooperation resulting from negotiation and the opportunity for creative solutions to mutual problems.)

Using the information for the Bottle and Mustard Divisions of Napoleon Company, journal entries to record transfers under various transfer pricing systems are shown in Exhibit 21–12 on page 922.

Selecting a Transfer Pricing System

Setting a reasonable transfer price is not an easy task. Everyone involved in the process must be aware of the positive and negative aspects of each type of transfer price and be responsive to suggestions of change if the need is indicated. The determination of the type of transfer pricing system to use should reflect the organizational units' characteristics as well as corporate goals. No one method of setting a transfer price is best in all instances. Also, transfer prices are not permanent; they are frequently revised in relation to changes in costs, supply, demand, competitive forces, and other factors. Such cost adjustments allow a department "to stimulate consumption during

[9] Typically, the cost-based amount used by the buying division reflects only the variable costs of the selling division.
[10] Herbert S. Cassel, "The Transfer Pricing Dilemma—And a Dual Pricing Solution," *Journal of Accountancy* (September 1987), p. 172.

Assume that 1,000 jars are transferred from the Bottle Division to the Mustard Division:
Variable production cost (1,000 × A$.24) = A$240
Full production cost (1,000 × A$.40) = A$400
External selling price (1,000 × A$.54) = A$540

SITUATION	BOTTLE DIVISION (B)		MUSTARD DIVISION (M)	

Transfer at variable production cost	A/R—Division M 240
	   Intracompany Sales
	Intracompany CGS 400
	   Finished Goods
		240
		
		400
			Inventory 240
			   A/P—Division B
				240

Transfer at full production cost	A/R—Division M 400
	   Intracompany Sales
	Intracompany CGS 400
	   Finished Goods
		400
		
		400
			Inventory 400
			   A/P—Division B
				400

Transfer at external selling price	A/R—Division M 540
	   Intracompany Sales
	Intracompany CGS 400
	   Finished Goods
		540
		
		400
			Inventory 540
			   A/P—Division B
				540

Transfer at dual price of external selling price for selling division and full production cost for buying division	A/R—Division M 400
	Intracompany Sales
	  in Excess of As-
	  signed Costs 140
	  Intracompany Sales
	Intracompany CGS 400
	  Finished Goods
		
		540
		
		400
			Inventory 400
			   A/P—Division B
				400

NOTE: Entries for negotiated transfer prices would be similar to those at full production cost, except that the negotiated transfer price would be shown for the first entry for the selling division and the purchase entry for the buying division.

EXHIBIT 21–12

Journal Entries for Transfer Prices

its slack times and ration consumption during peak demand times, thus encouraging efficient use of resources."[11]

Regardless of what method is used, a thoughtfully set transfer price will provide the following advantages:

- an appropriate basis for the calculation and evaluation of segment performance;
- the rational acquisition or use of goods and services between corporate divisions;
- the flexibility to respond to changes in demand or market conditions; and
- a means of motivation to encourage and reward goal congruence by managers in decentralized operations.

TRANSFER PRICES FOR SERVICE DEPARTMENTS

The practice of setting prices for products transferred between one organizational segment and another is well established. Instituting transfer prices for services is a less common but effective technique for some types of service departments.

Setting Service Transfer Prices

Setting transfer prices for services requires that practical internal guidelines be developed to provide meaningful information for both the user and provider departments.

---

[11] Leon B. Hoshower and Robert P. Crum, "Controlling Service Center Costs," *Management Accounting* (November 1987), p. 45.

SERVICE ATTRIBUTE

Cost of Service	Commodity	Custom	Volume of Service
High			**High**
	Market-based	Negotiated	
	Hybrid	Cost-based	
Low			**Low**

Four pricing techniques were defined by one company based on the attribute, cost, and volume of the services.

Examples of high-cost commodity services (market-based)	Examples of high-cost custom services (negotiated)
• Warehousing • Transportation • Real estate management • Purchase order placement	• Executive recruiting • Internal MIS development • Contract management • Detailed engineering design • Advertising campaigns

Examples of low-cost commodity services (hybrid*)	Examples of low-cost custom services (cost-based)
• Facility maintenance • Equipment removal • Temporary clerical support	• Proposal evaluations • Vendor contract negotiations • Product evaluation (purchasing)

* Market-based transfer pricing is encouraged if the service is forecasted to attain significant growth in volume. At low volume, however, cost-based techniques are preferable. Hybrid transfer price is equivalent to a dual transfer price.

SOURCE: Daniel P. Keegan and Patrick D. Howard, "Making Transfer Prices Work for Services," *Journal of Accountancy* (March 1988), p. 100.

For an organization to be profitable, service department costs must be covered by revenue-producing areas. These costs can be allocated internally to user departments based on the direct, step, or algebraic methods shown in Chapter 6 or services can be "sold" to user departments using transfer prices. In either case, service department costs are included in the costs of revenue-producing departments so that those departments' sales can cover the service departments' costs. The decision as to the most useful information is at the discretion of top management.

Transfer prices for services can take the same forms as those for products: cost-based, market-based, negotiated, or dual. A Price Waterhouse survey on service transfer prices indicated that "[m]ost companies (72 percent) reported that transfer prices are negotiated between buyer and seller. This is especially true for services because value is often added by means that cannot be measured effectively—such as expertise, reliability, convenience and responsiveness."[12] The type of transfer price to use should depend on the cost and volume level of the service as well as whether comparable substitutes are available. Exhibit 21–13 presents an example of a model that can help determine the suitable transfer price for different types of services.

---

[12]Daniel P. Keegan and Patrick D. Howard, "Transfer Pricing for Services: A Price Waterhouse Survey," *Journal of Accountancy* (March 1988), p. 98.

	Revenue Departments	Service Departments
User Involvement	Suggestions of ways to improve services to benefit users	Promotes development of services more beneficial to users
Cost Consciousness	Relates to services used; restrict usage to those necessary and cost beneficial	Relates to cost of services provided; must justify transfer price established
Performance Evaluations	If control over amount of services used exists, costs can be included in making performance evaluations	Can make a service department a profit center rather than a cost center and this provides more performance evaluation measures

Advantages of Service Transfer Prices

A company should weigh the advantages and disadvantages of service transfer prices before instituting such a transfer policy. Transfer prices are useful when service departments provide distinct, measurable benefits to other areas or provide services having a specific cause-effect relationship. Transfer prices in these circumstances can provide certain organizational advantages in both the revenue-producing and service departments. These advantages (listed in Exhibit 21–14) are as follows. First, transfer prices can encourage more involvement between service departments and their users. Service departments are more likely to interact with users to determine the specific services that are needed and to eliminate or reduce services that are not cost-beneficial. If charged a transfer price, users may be more likely to suggest ways the service department could reduce costs and improve its performance, and thereby lower the transfer prices charged.

Second, using transfer prices for services should cause service department and user department managers to be more cost conscious and eliminate wasteful usage. If service departments incur excessive costs, a reasonable transfer price may not cover those costs or a high transfer price may not be justifiable to users. If user departments are charged for all services they receive, they may decide their service demands have been excessive. For example, if the MIS Department charged other departments for the number of reports received, managers would be less likely to request reports simply to be "on the receiving list," as sometimes occurs.

Lastly, transfer prices result in useful information for performance evaluations. Responsibility reports show a controllable service department cost relative to the actual services used by individual managers instead of noncontrollable allocated expense amounts. The use of transfer prices would also allow service departments to be established as profit rather than cost centers. However, while transfer prices are effective responsibility accounting tools, there are disadvantages to their use.

DISADVANTAGES OF TRANSFER PRICES

Transfer prices (whether for services or products) do have certain disadvantages. First, there can be (and most often is) disagreement among organizational unit managers as to how the transfer price should be set. Second, implementing transfer prices in the accounting system requires additional organizational costs and employee time. Third, transfer prices do not work equally well for all departments or divisions. For

Transfer prices may be used to charge one department for using the services of another department. Such prices should be reflective, in part, of both the cost of providing the service and the value of the service received.

example, service departments that do not provide measurable benefits or cannot show a distinct cause-effect relationship between cost behavior and service use by other departments should not attempt to use transfer prices. Fourth, the transfer price may cause dysfunctional behavior among organizational units or may induce certain services to be under- or overutilized. Last, there are quite complicated United States tax regulations regarding transfer prices in multinational companies.

Because of the differences in tax systems, customs duties, freight and insurance costs, import/export regulations, and foreign exchange controls, setting transfer prices for products and services becomes extremely difficult when the company is engaged in multinational operations. In addition, as shown in Exhibit 21–15 on page 926, the internal and external objectives of transfer pricing policies in multinational enterprises (MNEs) differ.

Because of these differences, there is no simple resolution to the determination of transfer prices in MNEs. Multinational companies may use one transfer price when a product is sent to or received from one country and a totally different transfer price for the same product when it is sent to or received from another. However, some guidelines on transfer pricing policies should be set by the company and be followed on a consistent basis. For example, a company should not price certain parent company services to host country subsidiaries in a manner that would send the majority of those costs to the subsidiary in the country with the highest tax rate *unless that method of pricing were reasonable and equitable to all subsidiaries.* The general test of reasonableness is that transfer prices should reflect an "arm's length" transaction.

Multinational transfer prices are now being carefully scrutinized by tax authorities in both the home and host countries because such prices determine which country taxes the income from the transfer. The United States Congress is concerned about both U.S. multinationals operating in low-tax countries and foreign companies operating in the U.S. In both situations, Congress believes that companies could avoid paying U.S. corporate income taxes because of misleading or inaccurate transfer pricing. Thus, the Internal Revenue Service (IRS) may be quick to investigate U.S.

TRANSFER PRICES IN MULTINATIONAL SETTINGS

■ **EXHIBIT 21–15**

Multinational Company Transfer Pricing Objectives

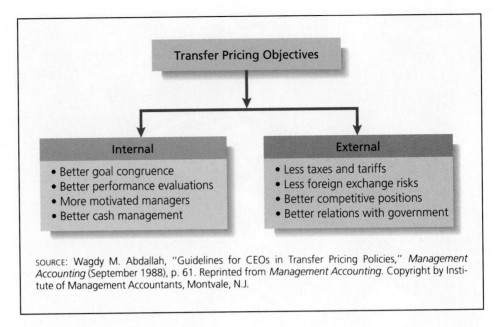

SOURCE: Wagdy M. Abdallah, "Guidelines for CEOs in Transfer Pricing Policies," *Management Accounting* (September 1988), p. 61. Reprinted from *Management Accounting*. Copyright by Institute of Management Accountants, Montvale, N.J.

subsidiaries that operate in low-tax areas (such as Ireland, Singapore, and Puerto Rico) and suddenly have unusually high profits. If foreign companies charge their U.S. subsidiaries higher prices than what they would charge subsidiaries in their home country, U.S. taxable income and thus the tax base will decline—which may also provoke an IRS review.

The determination of "reasonable" transfer prices has been improved because the IRS will now discuss and preapprove some advance pricing agreements. This process is extremely expensive, however, with a $500,000 minimum cost to receive an advance determination ruling which is valid for three years.[13] As discussed in the "Cost of Transfer Pricing Documentation" News Note, such a cost may be worthwhile considering the quantity of documentation required and potential penalties for lack of documentation. Additionally, the IRS can assess a 20 percent substantial valuation misstatement penalty if, after an audit, one of the following three conditions exists:

■ the transfer pricing adjustment exceeds $10 million;

■ the transfer price shown on the return is 200 percent or more of the amount determined to be the correct transfer price; or

■ the transfer price on the return is 50 percent or less of the correct transfer price.

This penalty can be doubled to 40 percent if there is a doubling of any of the conditions above.[14]

New IRS rules regarding multinational transfer prices became effective in late April 1993. These rules provide for five allocations for transfers of tangible property: comparable uncontrolled price method; resale price method; cost-plus method; comparable profits method; and other methods that are usable only if the standard methods are inapplicable. One of these methods will be superior to others under the "best methods rule." Factors that could be considered in determining the best method include: the completeness of the data used to apply each method; the degree of comparability between controlled and uncontrolled transactions; and the number, magnitude, and accuracy of the adjustments required to apply each method.

As mentioned in Chapter 1, transfers among nations are becoming easier through the institution of trade arrangements such as the European Economic Community

[13] Susan C. Borkowski, "Section 482, Revenue Procedure 91–22, and the Realities of Multinational Transfer Pricing," *International Tax Journal* (Spring 1992), p. 63.

[14] "Accuracy-Related Transfer Pricing Penalties," *Deloitte & Touche Review* (November 16, 1992).

NEWS NOTE

The Cost of Transfer Pricing Documentation Is High

The IRS's international division—which audits both US-owned and foreign-controlled companies—is increasingly becoming the pièce de résistance of the agency's efforts. The number one focus of IRS international tax cases concerns intercompany transfer pricing. Elsewhere in the world, tax experts say, concern is also on the rise about whether their jurisdiction is getting its fair share of tax money.

But no country is asserting itself as actively as the United States, where transfer pricing is at the heart of more than 50 lawsuits pending between the IRS and multinationals. The alleged tax deficiencies of these 50-odd companies amount to a staggering $16 billion.

The IRS had a tough break in its transfer-pricing case against Toyota. Suspecting that the car company was overpricing its automobiles in sales between its Japanese parent and US subsidiary, the agency demanded records detailing every conceivable factor that could influence transfer prices. These included costs of materials and labor and other expenses related to cars sold in both Japan and the United States. The agency also demanded marketing studies and the company's evaluations of the competition and its profit projections, as well as the profit margins of dealers and distributors.

That's not all. The IRS asked for voluminous data on taxes, rebates, discounts, freight, storage, advertising, promotion, selling expenses, warranties, commodity taxes, government regulations and currency exchange rates. The IRS wanted the information for each model and product made by Toyota Japan and sold in either Japan or the United States for each tax year at issue. Toyota balked at disclosing the information, forcing the US government into a lengthy court battle.

When it finally won the right to the records, however, the IRS suffered a Pyrrhic victory: Much of what it sought was no longer available. Eventually, the IRS and the Japanese carmaker reached an out-of-court settlement that was "in the hundreds of millions of dollars," according to one tax attorney.

Now record keeping and reporting rules require foreign-owned multinationals to disclose routinely the massive amounts of information that the IRS spent years seeking in the Toyota case. [And,] the IRS can impose penalties of $10,000 per violation for failing to produce a given document or request for data within 90 days of notice. If compliance is not forthcoming by the deadline, the agency can follow up every 30 days with a fine of $10,000 for each delinquency.

SOURCE: Paul Sweeney, "Getting Transfer Prices Right," *Global Finance* (October 1991), pp. 99–100. © Copyright 1991 *Global Finance* Magazine.

and the North American Free Trade Zone. These arrangements should help reduce the significance of transfer price manipulations through (among other features) the harmonization of tax structures and the reduction in import/export fees, tariffs, and capital movement restrictions.

To determine the effectiveness of their transfer pricing policies, multinational company managers should consider the following two questions:

(a) does the system achieve economic decisions that positively affect MNE performance, including international capital investment decisions, output level decisions for both intermediate and final products, and product pricing decisions for external customers? and
(b) do subsidiary managers feel that they are being fairly evaluated and rewarded for their divisional contributions to the MNE as a whole?[15]

---

[15] Wagdy M. Abdallah, "Guidelines for CEOs in Transfer Pricing Policies," *Management Accounting* (September 1988), p. 61.

If the answers to both of these questions are yes, then the company appears to have a transfer pricing system that appropriately coordinates the underlying considerations, minimizes the internal and external goal conflicts, and balances the short- and long-range perspectives of the multinational company.

R E V I S I T I N G

UNILEVER

Until the mid-1960s, the national management in every country where Unilever operated was fully responsible for the profits of all units in its territory. Product groups worked only in an advisory capacity, and their ability to affect how certain products were marketed or distributed basically depended on the attitude of the local manager.

In 1966, the company drastically reorganized responsibilities for all products, including those handled by the foods business, in its main European countries. Product groups became responsible for profits, while national managements worked in an advisory role—although in areas like industrial negotiations, local finance, and government relations, their advice usually determined decisions. In setting up the new profit-responsible groups, the head office created three separate food groups: an edible fats group, a frozen food and ice cream group, and a food and drinks group that took care of everything else—mainly soup, tea, and salad dressings.

Since the mid-1970s, however, the foods industry has become increasingly consumer-driven. Therefore, as time passed, the allocation of products to the three foods units started to hinder rather than help Unilever's progress. The market for low-calorie products, for example, has grown steadily since the 1970s. Yet, until 1988, our low-calorie spreads were the responsibility of the edible fats group, low-calorie soups belonged to food and drinks, and low-calorie frozen meals were part of the frozen food and ice cream group. By the late 1980s, it was clear we had to reconsider our organization of the business again. In this, as in all of Unilever's reorganizations historically, top management has tried to combine a decentralized structure (which has the advantage of providing deep understanding of local markets) with a degree of centralized control. In other words, we strive for unity in diversity.

The first step in our new reorganization was to create the necessary unity by forming a committee of three board directors, which we called the "Foods Executive." Located at our head office in Rotterdam, these three directors are now responsible collectively for all of Unilever's foods interests. In addition, control of the foods companies is now based on geography rather than the products they sell, with each of the directors responsible for profits in a group of countries.

In theory, we could have appointed one director with worldwide responsibility for foods. But at Unilever, the span of control would have been too broad for one person. It would have led to a second and perhaps a third layer of management, which we considered undesirable. However, the foods industry is still in considerable flux. The balance shifts continuously between centralized requirements (like research, finance, and packaging) and the need to stay close to local markets. Given that the market for foods—and all of Unilever's products, for that matter—may change in unpredictable ways, it's likely that we will reorganize again, adapting to a whole new set of trends or consumer needs in the future. Still, a transnational's structure and strategy must constantly adapt, regardless of the difficulties, in order to keep pace with the changing marketplace.

A decentralized organization is composed of operational units led by managers who have some degree of decision-making autonomy. The degree to which a company is decentralized depends on top management philosophy and on the ability of unit managers to perform independently. Decentralization provides managers the opportunity to develop leadership qualities, creative problem-solving abilities, and decision-making skills. It also lets the individual closest to the operational unit make decisions for that unit, thereby reducing the time spent in communicating and making decisions.

One disadvantage of decentralization is that responsibility may be spread too thinly throughout the organization. Competition can also result between the managers of decentralized units, which could lessen the organizational goal congruence. Some disruption may occur during a transition to decentralization because top managers resist delegating a portion of their authority to subordinates. Last, the costs of incorrect decisions made by the decentralized unit managers could be high.

Responsibility accounting systems are used to provide information on the revenues and/or costs under the control of unit managers. Responsibility reports reflect the upward flow of information from each decentralized unit to top management. Managers receive information regarding the activities under their immediate control as well as the control of their direct subordinates. The information is successively aggregated and the reports allow the application of the management by exception principle.

Responsibility centers are classified as cost, revenue, profit, or investment centers. Cost center and revenue center managers have control primarily only over, respectively, costs and revenues. Profit center managers are responsible for maximizing their segments' income. Investment center managers must generate revenues and control costs to produce a satisfactory return on the asset base under their influence. All responsibility center managers should perform their functions within the framework of organizational goal congruence, although there is a possibility of suboptimization of resources.

A transfer price is an intracompany charge for goods or services bought and sold between segments of a decentralized company. A transfer price for products is typically cost-based, market-based, or negotiated. The upper limit of a transfer price is the lowest market price at which the product can be acquired externally. The lower limit is the incremental cost of production plus the opportunity cost of the facilities used. A dual pricing system may also be used that assigns different transfer prices to the selling and buying units. Top management should promote a transfer pricing system that enhances goal congruence, provides segment autonomy, motivates managers to strive for segment effectiveness and efficiency, is practical, and is credible in measuring segment performance.

Setting transfer prices in multinational enterprises is a complex process because of the differences existing in tax structures, import/export regulations, customs duties, and other factors of the international subsidiaries and divisions. A valid transfer price for a multinational company is one that achieves economic benefit for the entire company and support from the domestic and international managers using the system.

Coding Design for Responsibility Accounting Systems

Coding journal entry information is essential in a computerized accounting system to properly retrieve and report information. This appendix illustrates an EDP coding system for expenditures in a responsibility accounting system. Expenditure entries are used in the illustration because they have the largest number of attributes that can be represented by codes.

The hierarchical block code is particularly useful in a responsibility system because it permits data to be readily retrieved and used in various ways. Each digit or set of digits represents a block of information about an attribute of the expenditure. Below is an illustrative nine-digit block code to classify and record expenditures in a CPA firm. The structure of this code flows from the general to the specific in a descending order from left to right.

Function	Activity	Subactivity	Organizational Unit	Character (Nature) of Expenditure	Type of Expenditure	Object of Expenditure
X	X	X	X	X	X	XXX

Each code block, except for the rightmost block, consists of a single digit. Each value represents either a unique meaning or an unassigned meaning. (Unassigned values can be subsequently assigned as new or unanticipated attributes are needed.) The meanings of each value are shown in Exhibit 21–16. Code specificity can be increased by adding digits; color-coded documents can be partially precoded for recurring transactions.

EXHIBIT 21–16

Coding System for CPA Firm Expenditures

BLOCK 1—FUNCTION
0—Auditing   1—Tax   2—Consulting   3—Accounting and Review
4—Other Client Services   5—Administration   6—Professional Development
7—Staff Meetings   8—Time Away   9—Other

BLOCK 2—ACTIVITY
0—Client Contact   1—Planning   2—Production
3—Staff Assistance and Consultation   4—Review   5—Research   6—Coordination
7—Clerical   8—Travel and Entertainment   9—Other

BLOCK 3—SUBACTIVITY
0—Information Gathering and Working Paper Preparation
1—Financial Statement Preparation   2—Tax Return Preparation
3—Other Report Preparation   4—Client Consultation and Advice   5—Testimony
6–9—Unassigned

BLOCK 4—ORGANIZATIONAL UNIT
0—Practice Management Department   1—EDP Department
2—Auditing and Accounting   3—Tax Department   4—MAS Department
5—College Recruiting   6–9—Unassigned

BLOCK 5—CHARACTER (NATURE) OF EXPENDITURE
0—Operating Activity   1—Investing Activity
2—Financing Activity   3–9—Unassigned

BLOCK 6—TYPE OF EXPENDITURE
0—Materials and Supplies   1—Professional Salaries and Wages
2—Clerical Salaries and Wages   3—EDP Costs   4—Travel and Entertainment
5—Capital Equipment   6—Library   7—Outside Consultants   8—General Overhead
9—Other

BLOCK 7—OBJECT OF EXPENDITURES (3 DIGITS)
000—999 Job Numbers (cross-referenced to clients, in-house jobs, and miscellaneous specified cost objects)

Using the information in Exhibit 21–16, the code number 010201237 can be interpreted as follows:

0—The function being recorded is auditing.
1—The activity to which the expenditure relates is planning.
0—The subactivity to which the expenditure relates is working paper preparation (e.g., the audit program).
2—The expenditure is made for the Auditing and Accounting Department.
0—The item is an operating activity.
1—The expenditure is to pay professional salaries and wages.
237—The job is auditing engagement #237.

In short, the code represents an expenditure for professional salaries and wages on audit job #237.

The same type of numerical hierarchical block code can be developed for expenditures in a manufacturing firm, as follows:

Function	Activity	Organizational Unit	Character (Nature) of Expenditure	Type of Expenditure	Behavior	Object of Expenditure
X	X	XX	X	X	X	XX

Organizational Unit and Object of Expenditure are the only blocks having multiple digits. Because there are more than ten organizational units and more than ten objects, these blocks use two digits that provide the capacity for 100 value designations. Meanings of the different values for each of the seven blocks comprising this code are shown in Exhibit 21–17.

When transactions are coded in the above manner, they can be retrieved, sorted, manipulated, and rearranged in many different ways to construct tailor-made responsibility accounting reports. This ability to reformat accounting data enhances the opportunity to refine responsibility reports according to the unique needs and desires of individual managers at various organizational levels. For example, assume top man-

■ **EXHIBIT 21–17**
Coding System for Manufacturing Firm Expenditures

BLOCK 1—FUNCTION
0—Manufacturing   1—Selling   2—Administration   3–9—Etc.

BLOCK 2—ACTIVITY
0—Production   1—Selling   2—Purchasing   3–9—Etc.

BLOCK 3—ORGANIZATIONAL UNIT (2 DIGITS)
00—Home Office   01—Assembly Department (Atlanta Plant)
02—Finishing Department (Atlanta Plant)   03–99—Etc.

BLOCK 4—CHARACTER (NATURE) OF EXPENDITURE
0—Operating Activity   1—Investing Activity   2—Financing Activity
3–9—Unassigned

BLOCK 5—TYPE OF EXPENDITURE
0—Direct Materials   1—Direct Labor   2—Overhead   3–9—Etc.

BLOCK 6—BEHAVIOR
0—Variable   1—Fixed   2—Mixed   3–9—Etc.

BLOCK 7—OBJECT OF EXPENDITURES (2 DIGITS)
00—Product 1   01—Product 2   02—Product 3   03–97—Etc.
98—Warehouse Inventory   99—Other

agement in a CPA firm needs a report on the amount of travel and entertainment cost for small, medium, and large clients. Use of computer software with a series of conditional "if" statements can retrieve such expenditures and construct the report. Such flexibility provides management with the ability to obtain a greater quantity and quality of information than was previously available.

KEY TERMS

Centralization (p. 897)
Cost center (p. 908)
Critical success factors (p. 914)
Decentralization (p. 897)
Dual pricing arrangement (p. 921)
Effectiveness (p. 904)
Efficiency (p. 904)
Goal congruence (p. 901)
Investment center (p. 912)

Negotiated transfer price (p. 920)
Profit center (p. 912)
Responsibility accounting system (p. 902)
Responsibility center (p. 908)
Responsibility reports (p. 904)
Revenue center (p. 910)
Suboptimization (p. 914)
Transfer price (p. 914)

SOLUTION STRATEGIES

Transfer Prices (Cost-Based, Market-Based, Negotiated, Dual)

Upper Limit: Lowest price available from external suppliers

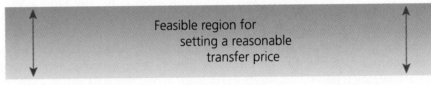

Feasible region for setting a reasonable transfer price

Lower Limit: Incremental costs of producing and selling the transfer goods or services plus the opportunity cost for the facilities used

DEMONSTRATION PROBLEM

Gordon Reisch Enterprises is a diversified company that has, among other segments, a segment that makes high-quality compact disc players and another segment that produces speakers. Costs for a pair of speakers produced by the Speaker Division are:

Direct materials	$22	
Direct labor	15	
Variable overhead	3	
Variable SG&A	2	
Total variable cost		$42
Fixed overhead*	$ 8	
Fixed SG&A	2	10
Total cost per pair		$52
Markup on total variable cost (33 1/3%)		14
List price to external customers		$66

*Fixed costs are allocated to all units produced based on estimated annual production.

- Estimated annual production: 400,000 pairs of speakers
- Estimated sales to outside entities: 300,000 pairs of speakers
- Estimated sales by the Speaker Division to the CD Player Division: 100,000 pairs of speakers

The managers of the two divisions are currently negotiating a transfer price.

Required:

a. Determine a transfer price based on variable product cost.

b. Determine a transfer price based on total variable cost plus markup.

c. Determine a transfer price based on full production cost.

d. Determine a transfer price based on total cost per pair.

e. Assume that the Speaker Division has no alternative use for the facilities that make the speakers for internal transfer. Also assume that the Player Division can buy equivalent speakers externally for $48. Calculate the upper and lower limits for which the transfer price should be set.

f. Compute a transfer price that divides the "profit" between the two divisions equally.

g. In contrast to the assumption in part e, assume that the Speaker Division can rent the facilities in which the 100,000 pairs of speakers are produced for $200,000. Determine the lower limit of the transfer price.

Solution to Demonstration Problem

a.

Direct materials	$22
Direct labor	15
Variable overhead	3
Transfer price	$40

b.

Total variable costs	$42
Markup	14
Transfer price	$56

c.

Variable production cost	$40
Fixed production cost	8
Transfer price	$48

d.

Total variable cost	$42
Total fixed cost	10
Transfer price	$52

e. Upper limit: Buyer's external purchase price = $48
   Lower limit: Total variable cost of Speaker Division = $42

f. (Lower limit + Upper limit) ÷ 2 = ($42 + $48) ÷ 2 = $45

g. $200,000 ÷ 100,000 pairs of speakers = $2 opportunity cost per pair
   Lower limit: Incremental cost of Speaker Division + Opportunity cost = $42 + $2 = $44

QUESTIONS

1. What is the distinction between a centralized organizational structure and a decentralized organizational structure? In what types of companies is decentralization appropriate and why?

2. "A company's operations are either centralized or decentralized." Discuss this statement.

3. Johnny Walker is the president and chief operating officer of Scottish Enterprises. Johnny founded the company and has led it to its prominent place in the electronics field. Scottish has manufacturing plants and outlets in 25 states, including Alaska and Hawaii. Johnny, however, is finding that he cannot "keep track" of things like he used to. Discuss the advantages and disadvantages of decentralizing the firm's decision-making activities among the various local and regional managers.

4. Even in a decentralized company, some functions may be best performed centrally. List several of these functions and the reasons you have for suggesting them.

5. Why is it suggested that decentralization has many costs associated with it? Describe some of the significant costs associated with decentralization.

6. How does decentralization affect accounting?

7. Why are responsibility reports prepared?

8. Is it appropriate for a single responsibility report to be prepared for a division of a major company? Why or why not?

9. Discuss the way in which a performance report consolidates information at each successively higher level of management.

10. Why might firms use both monetary and nonmonetary measures to evaluate the performance of subunit managers?

11. Discuss the differences among the various types of responsibility centers.

12. Why might salaries be included in the responsibility report of a revenue center manager?

13. What is suboptimization and what factors contribute to suboptimization in a decentrally organized firm?

14. What are transfer prices and why are they used by companies?

15. How or would transfer prices be used in each of the following types of responsibility centers: cost, revenue, profit, and investment?

16. How could the use of transfer prices improve goal congruence? Impair goal congruence?

17. What are the high and low limits of transfer prices and why do these limits exist?

18. A company is considering the use of a cost-based transfer price. What argument favors the use of standard rather than actual cost?

19. What problems may be encountered in attempting to implement a cost-based transfer pricing system?

20. What practical problems may impede the use of a market-based transfer price?

21. Why would the element of negotiation be "potentially both the most positive and the most negative aspect of negotiated transfer prices"?

22. What is dual pricing? What is the intended effect of dual pricing on the performance of each division affected by the dual price?

23. How can service departments use transfer prices and what advantages do transfer prices have over cost allocation methods?

24. "Activity-based costing for service departments is essentially the same as using transfer pricing for service departments." Is this statement true or false? Why?

25. What are some of the major disadvantages of using transfer pricing?

26. Explain why the determination of transfer prices may be more complex in a multinational setting than in a domestic setting.

27. (Appendix) How are coding systems useful in the preparation of detailed responsibility reports for management?

EXERCISES

28. (Decentralization advantages and disadvantages) Indicate which of the following is a potential advantage (a), disadvantage (d), or neither (n) of decentralization.
   a. Promotion of goal congruence
   b. Support of training in decision making
   c. Development of leadership qualities
   d. Complication of communication process
   e. Cost of developing the planning and reporting system
   f. Placement of decision maker closer to time and place of problem
   g. Speed of decisions
   h. Use of management-by-exception principle by top management

      i. Provision of greater job satisfaction
      j. Delegation of ultimate responsibility

29. *(Centralization versus decentralization)* For each situation below, indicate whether the firm would tend to be more centralized (c), tend to be more decentralized (d), or the tendency is indefinite (i).
    a. The firm's growth rate is rapid.
    b. The firm is small.
    c. The firm is in a growth stage of product development.
    d. Top management expects that incorrect subordinate management decisions could have a disastrous impact on company profits.
    e. The company was founded two years ago.
    f. Top management has a high level of confidence in subordinates' judgment and skills.
    g. Top management is proud of its record of tight control.
    h. Both d and f.
    i. Both c and g.
    j. Both a and b.

30. *(Matching)* Match each of the lettered items on the left with the number of the best matching item on the right.

    a. Cost center
    b. Investment center
    c. Profit center
    d. Revenue center
    e. Centralized organization
    f. Decentralized organization
    g. Dual pricing arrangement
    h. Goal congruence
    i. Suboptimization
    j. Transfer price

    1. Situation in which buying division is charged a price that differs from that credited to the selling division
    2. Structure in which most decisions are made by segment managers
    3. Situation in which decisions are made that are sometimes not in the best interest of whole firm
    4. Segment whose manager is responsible primarily for costs
    5. Segment whose manager is primarily responsible for revenues, expenses, and assets
    6. Segment whose manager is responsible for both revenues and expenses
    7. Segment whose manager is primarily responsible for revenues
    8. Structure in which most decisions are made by top management
    9. An internal exchange price
    10. Situation in which mutual support exists among goals of individual managers and the organization

31. *(Revenue variances)* The Marketing Department of Porcelain Connection is responsible for sales of two porcelain figurines. One is called "The Duke" and the other is called "The Country Wife." For July 1994, the Marketing Department's actual and budgeted sales were as follows:

	The Duke		**The Country Wife**	
	$	**units**	**$**	**units**
Budgeted sales	$20,000	2,000	$30,000	6,000
Actual sales	18,000	1,500	31,500	7,000

For July 1994, compute each of the following for the Marketing Department of Porcelain Connection:
    a. price variance   b. volume variance   c. mix variance

32. *(Revenue variances)* Consumer Leather Products Inc. manufactures two products: purses and baseball gloves. For 1994, the firm budgeted the following:

	Purses	Baseball Gloves
Sales	$800,000	$1,200,000
Unit sales price	$ 40	$ 30

At the end of 1994, managers were informed that total actual sales amounted to 70,000 units, and totaled $2,450,000. Baseball glove sales for the year amounted to 40,000 units at an average price of $35.

a. Compute the total revenue variance for 1994.
b. Compute the price variance for 1994.
c. Compute the mix variance for 1994.
d. Compute the volume variance for 1994.

33. *(Transfer pricing)* The Electronic Component Division, an autonomous segment of Belgium Motors, is considering what transfer price to set for transfers of computer chips to the company's Engine Division. The following data on production cost per computer chip have been gathered:

Direct materials	$1.40
Direct labor	3.95
Variable overhead	1.60
Fixed overhead	2.40
Total	$9.35

The Electronic Component Division sells the computer chips to external buyers for $21.50. Managers of the Engine Division have received external offers to provide the division comparable chips, ranging from $15 at one company to $23 at another.

a. Determine the upper and lower limits for the transfer price between the Electronic Component Division and the Engine Division.
b. If the Electronic Component Division is presently selling all the chips it can produce to external buyers, what is the minimum price it should set for transfers to the Engine Division?

34. *(Transfer pricing)* Midwest Steel Corporation is decentrally organized. One of its divisions, Bearing Division, manufactures large steel ball bearings for sale to other company divisions as well as to outside entities. Corporate management treats Bearing Division as a profit center. The normal selling price for a box of ball bearings is $12; costs for each box are shown below.

Direct material	$2.00
Direct labor	1.40
Variable overhead	.80
Fixed overhead (based on production of 700,000 boxes)	2.75
Variable selling expense	.50

Another division of Midwest Steel, Trailer Division, wants to purchase 25,000 boxes of ball bearings from Bearing Division during next year. No selling costs are incurred on internal sales.

a. If Bearing's manager can sell all the ball bearings it produces externally, what should the minimum transfer price be? Explain.
b. Assume that Bearing Division is experiencing a slight slowdown in external demand and will only be able to sell 600,000 boxes of ball bearings to outsiders next year at the $12 selling price. What should be the minimum selling price to the Trailer Division under these conditions? Explain.
c. Assume that Mr. Doyle, the manager of Trailer Division, offers to pay Bearing Division's production costs plus 25% for each box of ball bearings. He re-

ceives an invoice for $217,187.50 and he was planning on a cost of $131,250. How were these amounts determined? Did confusion exist? Explain.

35. *(Transfer pricing)* Two investment centers of Sacramento Household Technology Company are the Home Security Division and the Appliances Division. The Home Security Division manufactures an electronic heat sensor that can be sold externally and is also used by the Appliances Division in making microwave ovens. The following information is available about the heat sensor:

Total production annually—200,000 units; internal requirements are 150,000 units; all others are sold externally
List selling price—$25.60
Variable production costs—$12
Fixed overhead—$300,000; allocated on the basis of units of production
Variable selling costs—$3; includes $1 per unit in advertising cost
Fixed selling costs—$400,000

Determine the transfer price under each of the following methods:
a. Total variable cost
b. Full production cost
c. Total variable production cost plus necessary selling costs
d. Market price

36. *(Transfer pricing in service departments)* Indicate whether each of the following statements constitutes either a potential advantage (a), disadvantage (d), or neither (n) of using transfer prices for service department costs.
a. Can make a service department into a profit center.
b. May reduce goal congruence.
c. Can make users and providers more cost conscious.
d. May increase resource waste.
e. Can increase disagreements among departments.
f. Can put all service departments on an equal footing.
g. Can cause certain services to be under- or overutilized.
h. Can improve ability to evaluate performance.
i. Can increase communication about what additional services are needed and which may be reduced or eliminated.
j. Requires additional organizational data and employee time.

37. *(Transfer pricing for services)* The data processing operation of Thirston & Associates is in the process of developing a transfer price for its services. Capacity is defined as minutes of computer time. Expected capacity for next year (1995) is 350,000 minutes and full capacity is 450,000 minutes. Costs of the computer area for 1995 are expected to total $280,000.
a. What is the transfer price, based on expected capacity?
b. What is the transfer price, based on full capacity?
c. Assume the actual cost of operating the computer area in 1995 is $297,500. What is the total variance from budget of that department? What are some possible causes of that variance?

38. *(Appendix)* Use the 9-digit block code shown in Exhibit 21–16 to decode the following transaction number: 112301234.

---

39. Briefly indicate why you do or do not agree with each of the following statements.
a. Decentralization is always superior to centralization in an organization.
b. Noncontrollable costs should be reported on responsibility reports.

40. A multiple-division company is considering the effectiveness of its transfer pricing policies. One of the items under consideration is whether the transfer price should

COMMUNICATION ACTIVITIES

be based on variable production cost, absorption production cost, or external market price. Describe the circumstances in which each of these transfer prices would be most appropriate.

41. *(Cost center performance)* Bill Roach is the production supervisor at the Maine plant of Metalworks International. As plant production supervisor, Mr. Roach is evaluated based on his ability to meet standard production costs. At the Maine plant, the firm manufactures steel cattle panels (fence sections). The standard costs to produce a single cattle panel are given below:

Metal pipe	($.20 per foot)		$12.00
Paint	($10.00 per gallon)		2.00
Direct labor	($15.00 per hour)		3.00
Overhead			
Welding supplies		$ .90	
Utilities		1.10	
Indirect labor		.80	
Machine maintenance/repairs		.40	
Equipment depreciation		2.20	
Miscellaneous		.80	6.20
Total			$23.20

In October 1994, the Maine plant produced 35,000 cattle panels and incurred the following costs:

Metal pipe	($.25 per foot)		$507,500
Paint	($ 9.40 per gallon)		65,800
Direct labor	($14.90 per hour)		104,300
Overhead			
Welding supplies		$34,900	
Utilities		38,300	
Indirect labor		25,500	
Machine maintenance/repairs		21,200	
Equipment depreciation		77,000	
Miscellaneous		29,500	226,400
Total			$904,000

a. For October 1994, compute the variance for each production cost category in the Maine plant.

b. Based on the variances computed in part a, evaluate the performance of Bill Roach. Which variances might deserve closer scrutiny by top management? Explain.

42. *(Revenue center performance)* Daunita Weitz manages the marketing department at Minnesota Lighting Company. Daunita is evaluated based on her ability to meet budgeted revenues. For May 1994, Daunita's revenue budget was as follows:

	Price per Unit	Unit Sales
Floor lamps	$120	1,600
Hanging lamps	65	2,150
Ceiling fixtures	80	4,200

The actual sales generated by Ms. Weitz's marketing department in May were as follows:

	Price per Unit	Total Sales in Dollars
Floor lamps	$115	$195,500
Hanging lamps	70	141,400
Ceiling fixtures	75	311,250

a. Compute the revenue price variance.

b. Compute the revenue mix variance.

c. Compute the revenue volume variance.

d. Based on your answers to parts a–c, evaluate the performance of Ms. Weitz.

e. If Ms. Weitz is to be held accountable for meeting the revenue budget, why might it be advisable to also give her the authority to set the salesperson salary and commission structure?

43. Gold Finch Inc. manufactures small industrial tools and has an annual sales volume of approximately $3.5 million. Sales growth has been steady during the year and there is no evidence of cyclical demand. The company's market has expanded only in response to product innovation; therefore, R&D is very important to the company.

Cynthia Tatum, controller, has designed and implemented a new budget system. An annual budget has been prepared and divided into 12 equal segments to use for monthly performance evaluations. The vice president of operations was upset upon receiving the following responsibility report for the Machining Department for May 1994:

Machining Department—Responsibility Report
For the Month Ended May 31, 1994

	Budget	Actual	Variance
Volume in units	3,000	3,185	185 F
Variable manufacturing costs:			
Direct material	$24,000	$ 24,843	$ 843 U
Direct labor	27,750	29,302	1,552 U
Variable factory overhead	33,300	35,035	1,735 U
Total	$85,050	$ 89,180	$4,130 U
Fixed manufacturing costs:			
Indirect labor	$ 3,300	$ 3,334	$ 34 U
Depreciation	1,500	1,500	0
Taxes	300	300	0
Insurance	240	240	0
Other	930	1,027	97 U
Total	$ 6,270	$ 6,401	$ 131 U
Corporate costs:			
Research and development	$ 2,400	$ 3,728	$1,328 U
Selling and administration	3,600	4,075	475 U
Total	$ 6,000	$ 7,803	$1,803 U
Total Costs	$97,320	$103,384	$6,064 U

a. Identify the weaknesses in the responsibility report for the Machining Department.

b. Prepare a revised responsibility report for the Machining Department that reduces or eliminates the weaknesses indicated in part a.

c. Deviations in excess of 5% of budget are considered material and worthy of investigation. Should any of the variances of the Machining Department be investigated? Regardless of materiality, is there any area that the vice president of operations might wish to discuss with the manager of the Machining Department?

(CMA adapted)

PROBLEMS

44. *(Profit center performance)* Monica Haswell, the head of the accounting department at Big State U., has felt increasing pressure to raise external monies to compensate for dwindling state financial support. Accordingly, in early January 1995, she conceived the idea of offering a three-day accounting workshop on income taxation for local CPAs. She asked Mel Johnson, a tenured tax professor, to supervise the planning process for the seminar, which was to be held in late March 1995. In early February, Professor Johnson presented Haswell with the following budget plan:

Revenues ($400 per participant)		$40,000
Expenses:		
Speakers ($500 each)	$ 5,000	
Rent on facilities	3,600	
Advertising	2,100	
Meals and lodging	18,000	
Departmental overhead allocation	3,500	32,200
Profit		$ 7,800

Explanations of budget items: The facilities rent of $3,600 is a fixed rental, which is to be paid to a local hotel for use of its meeting rooms. The advertising is also a fixed budgeted cost. Meals expense is budgeted at $5 per person per meal (a total of 9 meals are to be provided for each participant); lodging is budgeted at the rate of $45 per participant per night. The departmental overhead includes a specific charge for supplies costing $10 for each participant as well as a general allocation of $2,500 for use of departmental secretarial resources.

After reviewing the budget, Haswell gave Johnson approval to proceed with the seminar.

a. Recast the above income statement in a segment income statement format.
b. Assume the actual financial results of the seminar were as follows:

Revenues (120 participants)		$38,500
Expenses:		
Speakers ($750 each)	$ 7,500	
Rent on facilities	4,200	
Advertising	2,900	
Meals and lodging	21,600	
Departmental overhead allocation	3,700	39,900
Loss		$ (1,400)

Explanation of actual results: Because signups were running below expectations, the seminar fee was reduced from $400 to $300 for late enrollees and advertising expense was increased. In budgeting for the speakers, Professor Johnson neglected to include airfare, which averaged $250 per speaker. After the fees were reduced and advertising increased, the number of participants grew and was larger than expected, a larger meeting room had to be rented from the local hotel.

Recast the actual results in a segment income format.

c. Compute variances between the budgeted segment income statement and the actual segment income statement. Identify and discuss the factors that are primarily responsible for the difference between the budgeted profit and the actual loss on the tax seminar.

45. *(Transfer prices)* In each of the following cases, the Electronic Division can sell all of its production of audio speakers to outside customers or it can sell some of them to the Hi Fi Division and the remainder to outside customers. Electronic Division's capacity for production of these speakers is 200,000 units annually. The data related to each independent case are presented below.

Electronic Division

	Case #1	Case #2
Production costs per unit:		
Direct materials	$30	$20
Direct labor	10	8
Variable overhead	3	2
Fixed overhead (based on capacity)	1	1
Other variable selling and delivery costs per unit*	6	4
Selling price to outside customers	75	60

*In either case, $1 of the selling expenses will not be incurred on intracompany transfers.

Hi Fi Division

Number of speakers needed annually	40,000	40,000
Current unit price being paid to outside supplier	$65	$52

a. For each case, determine the upper and lower limits for a transfer price for speakers.

b. For each case, determine a transfer price for Electronic Division that will provide a $10 contribution margin per unit.

c. Using the information developed for part b, determine a dual transfer price for Case #1 assuming that Hi Fi is to be able to acquire the speakers from Electronic at $10 below Hi Fi's purchase price from outsider suppliers.

46. *(Determining transfer price)* Two of the divisions of Greenline Industrial Equipment Company are the Engine Division and the Payloader Division. The Engine Division produces motors used by both the Payloader Division and a variety of external industrial customers.

For external sales, sales orders are generally produced in 50-unit lots. Using this typical lot size, a cost per motor is as follows:

Variable production costs	$1,050
Fixed manufacturing overhead	450
Variable selling expenses	150
Fixed selling expense	210
Fixed general and administrative expense	320
Total unit cost	$2,180

Engine Division normally earns a profit margin of 20% by setting the external selling price at $2,616. Because a significant number of sales are being made internally, Engine Division managers have decided that $2,616 is the appropriate price to use for all transfers to the Payloader Division.

When the managers in Payloader Division heard of this change in the transfer price, they became very upset since the change would have a major negative impact on Payloader's net income figures. Because of competition, Payloader has asked Engine Division to lower its transfer price; by reducing the transfer price, Engine's profit margin will be 15%. Payloader managers have asked Greenline if the Division can buy motors externally. Bud Hawkins, Greenline's president, has gathered the following price information in order to help the two divisional managers negotiate an equitable transfer price:

Current external sales price	$2,616
Total variable production cost plus a 20% profit margin ($1,050 × 1.2)	1,260
Total production cost plus a 20% profit margin ($1,500 × 1.2)	1,800
Bid price from external supplier (if motors are purchased in 50-unit lots)	2,320

facturing activity of the Aerospace Division is related to work performed for the government space program under negotiated contracts.

Klein Corp. headquarters provides general administrative support and computer services to each of the three operating divisions. The computer services are provided through a computer time-sharing arrangement. The central processing unit (CPU) is located in Kansas City and the divisions have remote terminals that are connected to the CPU by telephone lines. One standard from the Cost Accounting Standards Board provides that the cost of general administration may be allocated to negotiated defense contracts. Further, the standards provide that, in situations in which computer services are provided by corporate headquarters, the actual costs (fixed and variable) of operating the computer department may be allocated to the defense division based on a reasonable measure of computer usage.

The general managers of the three divisions are evaluated based on the before-tax performance of each division. The November 1994 performance evaluation reports (in millions of dollars) for each division are presented below.

	Aerospace Division	Ceramic Products Division	Glass Products Division
Sales	$23.0	$15.0	$55.0
Cost of goods sold	13.0	7.0	38.0
Gross profit	$10.0	$ 8.0	$17.0
Selling and administrative:			
Division selling and administration costs	$ 5.0	$ 5.0	$ 8.0
Corporate general administration costs	1.0	—	—
Corporate computing	1.0	—	—
Total	$ 7.0	$ 5.0	$ 8.0
Profit before taxes	$3.00	$3.00	$9.00

Without a charge for computing services, the operating divisions may not make the most cost-effective use of the Computer Systems Department's resources. Outline and discuss a method for charging the operating divisions for use of computer services that would promote cost consciousness by the operating divisions and operating efficiency by the Computer Systems Department. (CMA adapted)

ETHICS AND QUALITY DISCUSSION

56. Slick Corporation has decided to open a subsidiary in Germany. Bill Powell has been asked to go overseas and help in the startup of the subsidiary. Bill is still going to be responsible for his division in Lexington during the startup phase of the German plant. The Lexington Division manufactures the same products that the German Division will, although planned production costs for the German products are less. Bill's performance will be judged on the continued success of the Lexington plant as well as his abilities in getting the German plant on line. Bill was chosen for the assignment in part because of his knowledge of the language; Bill's wife is German and her family still lives there. When the German plant is on line, Bill and his family will return to Lexington.
    a. What impact will the fully operational German plant have on the performance of the Lexington plant?

   b. What conflicts will Bill face in regard to getting the German plant on-line? Do these conflicts relate to ethical or performance measurement problems? How can they be resolved?
   c. Was it reasonable of the company to ask Bill to take on the new position under these conditions?

57. A large American corporation participates in a highly competitive industry. To meet this competition and achieve profit goals the company has chosen the decentralized form of organization. Each manager of a decentralized center is measured on the basis of profit contribution, market penetration, and return on investment. Failure to meet the objectives established by corporate management for these measures is not accepted and usually results in demotion or dismissal of a center manager.

    An anonymous survey of managers in the company revealed that the managers felt pressure to compromise their personal ethical standards to achieve the corporate objectives. For example, at certain plant locations there was pressure to reduce quality control to a level that could not assure that all unsafe products would be rejected. Also, sales personnel were encouraged to use questionable sales tactics to obtain orders, including offering gifts and other incentives to purchasing agents.

    The chief executive officer is disturbed by the survey findings. In her opinion, such behavior cannot be condoned by the company. She concludes that the company should do something about this problem.
   a. Discuss what might be the causes for the ethical problems described.
   b. Outline a program that could be instituted by the company to help reduce the pressures on managers to compromise personal ethical standards in their work.
    (CMA)

58. The Gordon Company has several plants, one of which produces military equipment for the federal government. Many of the contracts are negotiated on a cost-plus basis. Some of the other plants have been only marginally profitable. The home office has engaged a consultant, Mr. Shifty, to meet with top management. Shifty observes that the company isn't using some of the more "creative" accounting techniques to shift costs toward the plant serving the federal government and away from the marginally profitable plants. He notes that "transfer pricing and service department allocations involve a lot of subjectivity and there is plenty of room to stack the deck and let the taxpayer foot the bill. Taxpayers will never know and even if the government suspects, it can't prove motive if we document the procedures with contrived business jargon." One of the staff stated that "this would be a way to get back some of those exorbitant income taxes we have had to pay all these years." The company president ended the meeting and asked for some time to consider the matter.
   a. What is the purpose of setting transfer prices and making service department allocations?
   b. Can or should transfer prices and service department allocations be used to shift income from one plant to another? If so, under what conditions?
   c. Do you think that what the consultant is suggesting is legal? Ethical? Has ever been done? Discuss your reasoning for each answer.

MEASURING ORGANIZATIONAL PERFORMANCE

LEARNING OBJECTIVES

After completing this chapter, you should be able to answer these questions:

1. Why is decentralization effective for some organizations but not others?
2. What is the relationship between decentralization and performance measurement?
3. What guidelines can be provided for the use of performance measures?
4. How can performance be measured for each type of responsibility center?
5. How may the Statement of Cash Flows be useful for performance measurement?
6. How are return on investment and residual income similar? How do they differ?
7. Of what value are nonfinancial performance measures to managers?
8. What difficulties are encountered in trying to measure performance for multinational firms?

INTRODUCING

J. I. CASE COMPANY

Jerome Increase Case founded his threshing machine business in Rochester, Wisconsin, in 1842. He moved the fledgling business to Racine, Wisconsin, in 1844 to take advantage of the city's abundant water supply. In 1869, the company expanded its product line with the introduction of its first steam engine. By 1886, J. I. Case Threshing Machine Company had become the world's largest manufacturer of steam engines. The company continued to innovate, experimenting with gasoline-powered agricultural tractors in the early 1890s and introducing luxury automobiles in 1910 and entering the construction equipment market in 1912.

J. I. Case Threshing Machine Company became J. I. Case Company in 1928 and, in 1970, became a wholly owned subsidiary of Tenneco Inc. In 1987, Tenneco acquired selected assets of the International Harvester agricultural equipment operations and merged these with J. I. Case, making Case the second-largest full-line manufacturer of farm equipment in the industry. Case is also a leading worldwide maker of light-to-medium-size construction equipment. Case employs 18,000 people worldwide, does business in 130 countries, and has more than 4,000 agricultural and construction equipment dealers and outlets around the world.

[The company's goal of achieving world-class manufacturing (WCM) status is evident from the fact that the organization's performance is measured by some tough standards.] Specific performance measurements will vary among organizations, depending upon the critical success factors established. However, the measurements can be broken down into five general categories in a WCM environment: quality, delivery, production process time, flexibility, and finance costs. Primary goals of WCM in each of these areas are:

▌ Quality—Do it right the first time; have zero defects.

▌ Delivery—Have 100% on-time deliveries.

▌ Production process time—Minimize it.

▌ Flexibility—Reduce setup time, downtime, materials handling; standardize parts.

▌ Finance—Reduce costs while retaining quality; measure progress improvements.

[While these measurements] have existed for years, they have not [typically] been recognized as reportable items.

SOURCE: J. I. Case *150th Anniversary Handout* (1992); used with permission, Case Corporation, Racine, Wisconsin and Michael R. Sellenheim, "Performance Measurement," *Management Accounting* (September 1991), pp. 50–53. Reprinted from *Management Accounting*. Copyright by Institute of Management Accountants, Montvale, N.J.

Regardless of the degree of centralization or decentralization in an organization, managerial performance will be judged by concerned parties such as higher level management, the board of directors, and stockholders. The performance measurements selected need to be appropriate for the type of responsibility center being evaluated. For example, profit center managers can be evaluated on a budget to actual income basis, but no "return on" measure could be used since those managers have no control over their asset bases.

Performance measures have traditionally highlighted one factor in the success equation—that of money. However, as noted in the J.I. Case introduction, financial measures do not necessarily indicate how well an organizational unit is performing in a customer-driven, global marketplace. To highlight the essential nature of items such as quality and lead time, many companies have chosen to supplement traditional financial performance measures with additional qualitative and nonmonetary quantitative measures. Thus, the success equation becomes multidimensional, rather than one dimensional. This chapter first covers the general concept of performance measurement and presents the traditional monetary measures of divisional profits (cash flows, return on investment, and residual income). Then, the more innovative performance measures needed in a world-class, customer-driven environment are discussed.

PERFORMANCE MEASURES

As indicated in previous chapters, people must have a benchmark against which their accomplishments can be measured in order to evaluate performance. The benchmark can be a monetary one (such as a standard cost or a budget appropriation) or a nonmonetary one (such as zero defects or a specified market share in an industry). Whatever measures are used (whether monetary or nonmonetary), four general rules relative to performance measurement should be established.

1. The measures should be established to assess progress toward organizational goals and objectives.

2. The persons being evaluated should be aware of the measurements to be used and have had some input in developing them.

3. The persons being evaluated should have the appropriate skills, equipment, information, and authority to be successful under the measurement system.

4. Feedback of accomplishment should be provided in a timely and useful manner.

Multiple Performance Measures

The first rule establishes the reason for using multiple performance measures, rather than a single one or measures of only a single type. Organizations have a variety of goals and objectives. A primary goal is, of course, to be financially able to continue to exist. If the organization is a profit-oriented one, this goal is satisfied by generating a net income amount considered by the owners to be satisfactory relative to the assets invested. That level of "satisfactory" earnings may change over time or differ based on the type of business. It is, therefore, necessary to have some relevant financial performance measures for the type of company or organizational unit being evaluated. It is equally necessary that any measures chosen reflect an understanding of accounting information and its potential for manipulation.

In addition to financial success, many companies are now establishing organizational goals of customer satisfaction, zero defects, minimal lead time to market, and social responsibility with regard to the environment. These goals cannot be measured directly by the periodic quantity of income generated. It seems reasonable, though, that companies which are not satisfying customers or are producing inferior goods, lagging in delivery, or polluting the environment will most likely lose market share. Should these companies continue such practices for the long-term, they will eventually be forced out of business. Thus, while the organization is in business, nonfinancial performance measures can be developed to indicate progress, or lack thereof, toward the achievement of these important critical success factors of a world-class company.

Exhibit 22–1 illustrates a "balanced scorecard" that considers all aspects of performance. The various company goals and suggested measures of performance are provided for an illustrative company in the semiconductor business.

▌ EXHIBIT 22–1
Illustrative "Balanced Scorecard"

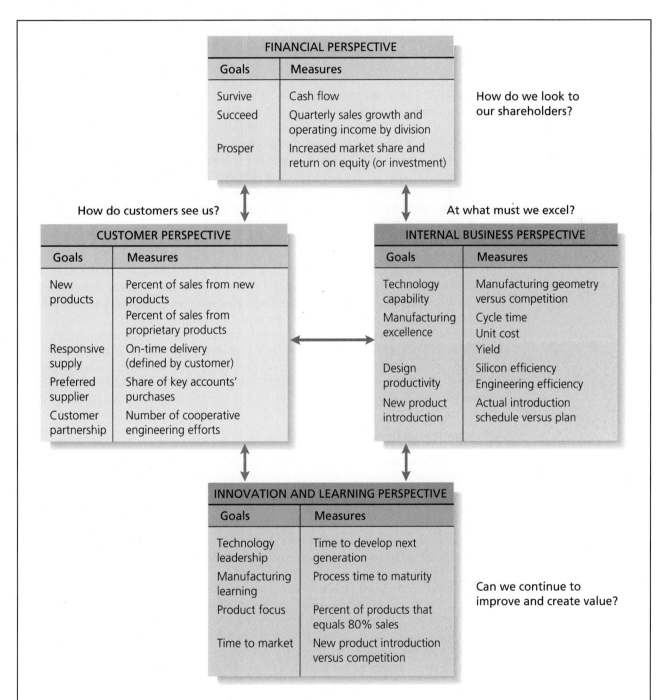

Awareness of and Participation in Performance Measures

Regardless of the number or types of measures chosen, top management must set high performance standards and communicate them to lower-level managers and employees. Additionally, the measures should promote harmonious operations between and among organizational units. This factor is important to minimize the effects of suboptimization (as discussed in the previous chapter) that might occur in a decentralized company.

People will normally act in accordance with how they are to be measured. Thus, it is essential that individuals know about and understand the performance measures to be used. This information is necessary so that managers can make a conscious choice to perform or not perform in a manner consistent with the measurement system. Withholding information about measures will not allow employees to perform at their highest level of potential, is frustrating for them, and does not allow for feelings of mutual respect and cooperation.

Assume your teacher told you to "Turn in the answer to Problem 7 and it will be graded." You work the problem and turn in *only* the answer, as requested. Your homework is returned and you receive two points out of a possible ten because the teacher's grading key assigned points for showing computations prior to the final answer. Do you believe your performance has been properly measured? Had you known that supporting computations were to be counted and you chose not to turn them in, would your performance have been properly measured? Thus, proper measurement is influenced by information about what is expected.

If actual-to-standard or actual-to-budget comparisons are to be used as performance measures, people are more likely to be committed to the process if they participated in setting the standards or the budget. Participation captures the interest and attention of those persons involved and results in a "social contract" between participants and evaluators. In this way, individuals demonstrate a mutual respect for each other's ability to contribute effectively to the development process. The participants who will be evaluated clearly understand and accept the reasonableness of the standards or budget and generally attempt to achieve the results so as to affirm that the plans were well founded. Employee involvement in a performance measurement system is so important that "management attempts to bolster productivity will plateau without employee support, which is the key to achieving maximum productivity."[1]

Appropriate Tools for Performance

Anyone who has accepted a job understands that there will be a performance measurement and evaluation process. Thus, it is first necessary that placement or personnel people put the right individuals in the available jobs. If placed in jobs for which they do not have the appropriate skills, candidates are usually destined to fail. Thus, the organization is responsible for making certain either that job skills exist or that they can be acquired through available training. Given job competence, people must then be given the necessary tools (equipment, information, and authority) to perform their jobs in a manner consistent with the measurement process. No matter where an employee is in the organizational hierarchy, there are certain job requirements. A carpenter must have a saw and a picture or idea of the product to be made; an accountant must have transaction information and/or source documents and a manual or electronic means by which to capture monetary changes; the company president must have the authority to obtain the needed resources to accomplish organizational objectives. Competent individuals having the necessary job "tools" can be held responsible for their performance. If the appropriate tools are unavailable, people cannot be presumed to be able to accomplish their tasks.

---

[1] Dan J. Seidner and Glenn Kieckhaefer, "Using Performance Measurement Systems to Create Gainsharing Programs," *(Grant Thornton) Manufacturing Issues* (Summer 1990), p. 8.

Need for Feedback

Managerial performance should be *monitored* (though not *evaluated*) on a continuous basis, and feedback should be provided. Thus, performance monitoring and feedback should be ongoing activities, while performance evaluation should take place at one or more specified and known points in time. Positive feedback motivates employees to future successes by encouraging them to continue favorable behaviors. Employees receiving negative feedback are made aware of problems and can attempt to change behaviors. Waiting to provide feedback until some delayed "measurement point" is reached allows employees no opportunity for early adjustment. As indicated by the survey data presented in Exhibit 22–2, some employees do not believe that the feedback they are receiving is of the highest quality.

Performance measurement has typically relied on information generated during the management control process. Exhibit 22–3 on page 956 provides a diagram of the basic management control process and indicates the point at which performance has traditionally been evaluated. Although this type of measurement system was easy to implement, it often focused on performance traits that were not the most conducive to sound competitive positions. Because of this, traditional performance measures are being supplemented with some additional ones.

The traditional focus of performance measurement at the managerial level was on financial aspects of operations and concentrated on monetary measures such as divi-

▌ EXHIBIT 22–2

Feedback and Performance Measurement

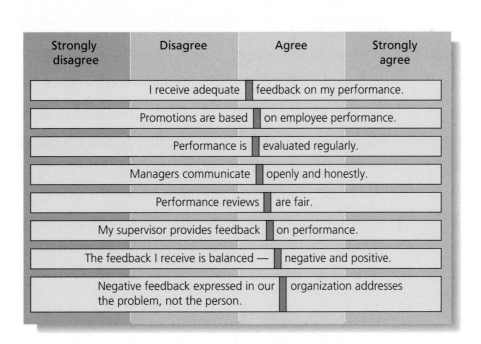

Strongly disagree	Disagree	Agree	Strongly agree
I receive adequate		feedback on my performance.	
Promotions are based		on employee performance.	
Performance is		evaluated regularly.	
Managers communicate		openly and honestly.	
Performance reviews		are fair.	
My supervisor provides feedback		on performance.	
The feedback I receive is balanced —		negative and positive.	
Negative feedback expressed in our organization addresses the problem, not the person.			

SOURCE: Ross Culbert Lavery & Russman Inc. (New York), compiled from company organizational audits, Perz Inc., Maumee, Ohio, 1992. Reprinted with permission, *Inc.* magazine, (September 1992). Copyright 1992 by Goldhirsh Group, Inc., 38 Commercial Wharf, Boston, MA 02110.

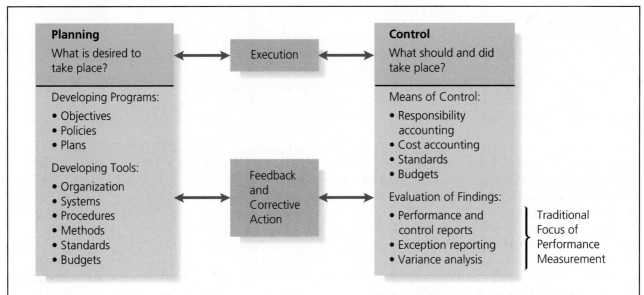

SOURCE: Patrick L. Romano, "Performance Measurement and Planning—Revisited," *Management Accounting* (January 1989), p. 62. Reprinted from *Management Accounting.* Copyright by Institute of Management Accountants, Montvale, N.J.

▌ EXHIBIT 22–3

Diagram of Management Control

sional profits, achievement of budget objectives, individual and total variances from budget or standard, and cash flow. Each of these measures provides different information that can be used to analyze the effectiveness and efficiency of managerial performances.

The type of responsibility center being evaluated affects the performance measure(s) used because people should only be evaluated using performance measures relating to their authority and responsibility. In a cost center, the primary financial performance measure is the materiality of the variances from budgeted costs. Performance in a pure revenue center can be primarily judged by comparing budgeted with actual revenues. These two responsibility centers are accountable for only one type of monetary object—costs and revenues, respectively. When a manager is responsible for only one monetary item, the financial measurements usable for performance evaluations are limited to those relevant to that single monetary item. However, as will be discussed later, nonmonetary performance measures are now being coupled with monetary measures to provide multidimensional views of responsibility center performance.

Profit and investment center managers are responsible for both revenues and expenses of those centers. Given this greater accountability, more financial performance measures can be used for these responsibility centers than the rather simplistic ones used by cost and revenue centers.

DIVISIONAL PROFITS

The segment margin of a profit or investment center is a frequently used measure of divisional performance.[2] This amount is compared with the center's budgeted income objective, and variances are computed to determine where objectives were exceeded or were not achieved.

One problem with the use of segment margin for measuring performance is that the individual components used to derive it (like any other accounting income-based

---

[2] The term segment margin is defined in Chapter 15 as segment sales minus (direct variable expenses and avoidable fixed expenses). Thus, the margin would not include allocated common costs.

Measuring the performance of the Colorado Springs Chorale and Symphony requires the use of a variety of tools. The organization may judge its success on financial measures of profits or return on investment. But just as—if not more—importantly, patrons will judge it on the nonfinancial tools of music and vocal quality, and popularity of the musical pieces played.

amount) are subject to manipulation. Segment margin manipulation can take many forms. For example:

▮ If the center is using a cost flow method other than FIFO, inventory purchases can be accelerated or deferred at the end of the period to change the CGS amount for the period.

▮ Replacement of workers who have resigned or been terminated can be deferred to minimize salary expense for the period.

▮ Routine maintenance can be delayed or eliminated to reduce expenses.

▮ If actual overhead is being allocated to inventory, an increase in production will cause cost per unit to decline.

▮ Recognition of sales transactions can be shifted between periods.

▮ Advertising expenses or other discretionary costs can be delayed.

▮ Depreciation methods may be changed.

All of the above tactics can be used to "cause" reported segment margin to conform to budget expectations, but such manipulations are normally not in the center's long-run best interest. Unfortunately, as indicated in the "Ethics of Income Manipulation" News Note on page 958, income manipulation seems to be part of a manager's job. Divisional segment margin (or profit) represents a short-term rather than a long-term objective. Most reward systems (promotions, pay raises, bonuses) are based on short-term performance. Short-run efficiency is important, but companies should not use the quarterly or annual segment margin as the only performance measure of a profit or investment center's manager. A year is often too short a time over which to judge managerial performance. The performance measurement period should coincide with the time it takes to evaluate the quality of the center manager's decisions.[3]

---

[3] Quality and financial benefits to the organization should be measured concurrently. The accounting system should be designed to capture both types of information (qualitative and quantitative) that can be used as valid predictors of long-term profitability. See Sue Y. Whitt and Jerry D. Whitt, "What Professional Services Firms Can Learn from Manufacturing," *Management Accounting* (November 1988), pp. 39–42.

NEWS NOTE

Ethics of Income Manipulation

Casual observers of the financial reporting process may assume that time, laws, regulation, and professional standards have restricted accounting practices to those which are moral, ethical, fair, and precise. But most managers and their accountants know otherwise—that managing short-term earnings can be part of a manager's job.

It seems many managers are convinced that if a practice is not explicitly prohibited or is only a slight deviation from rules, it is an ethical practice regardless of who might be affected either by the practice or the information that flows from it. This means that anyone who uses information on short-term earnings is vulnerable to misinterpretation, manipulation, or deliberate deception.

The essence of a moral or ethical approach to management is achieving a balance between individual interests and obligations to those who have a stake in what happens to the corporation (or what happens to a division or group within the corporation). These stakeholders include not only people who work in the firm, but customers, suppliers, creditors, shareholders, and investors as well.

Managers who take unproductive actions to boost short-term earnings may be acting totally within the laws and rules. Also they may be acting in the best interest of the corporation. But, if they fail to consider the adverse effects of their actions on other stakeholders, we may conclude that they are acting unethically.

SOURCE: William J. Bruns, Jr. and Kenneth A. Merchant, "The Dangerous Morality of Managing Earnings," *Management Accounting* (August 1990), pp. 22–23. Reprinted from *Management Accounting*. Copyright by Institute of Management Accountants, Montvale, N.J.

CASH FLOW

Managers who have authority over operating, investing, and financing activities know that, for their entities to succeed, two requirements must be met: (1) long-run profitability and (2) continuous liquidity. Since external financial statements use accrual-based figures, management's attention can become diverted from the size and direction of cash inflows and outflows. The Statement of Cash Flows (SCF) helps to correct this situation by providing information about the cash impacts of the three major categories of business activities (operating, investing, and financing). The SCF explains the change in the cash balance by reflecting the entity's sources and uses of cash. Such knowledge can assist in judging the entity's ability to meet current fixed cash outflow commitments, to adapt to adverse changes in business conditions, and to undertake new commitments. Further, because the cash flow statement identifies the relationships between segment margin (or net income) and net cash flow from operations, it assists managers in judging the quality of the entity's earnings.

While the cash budget presented in Chapter 16 is essential to current cash management, the budgeted SCF gives managers a more global view of cash flows by rearranging them by major activity. Such a rearrangement permits management to judge whether the anticipated flows are consistent with the entity's strategic plans, and thus provides an opportunity to evaluate performance. In addition, the cash budget disregards significant noncash transactions that are incorporated into a schedule or narrative on a Statement of Cash Flows. Since most noncash transactions ultimately result in cash flows, disclosure of noncash transactions provides a more complete picture of future operations and their potential effect on cash availability. Analysis of the SCF in conjunction with budgets and other financial reports provides information on cost reductions, collection policies, dividend payout, impact of capital projects on total cash flows, and liquidity position.

Like segment margins and income, cash flow can be manipulated and relates to the short run rather than the long run. As a measure of performance, cash flow suffers from some of the same problems as divisional profits because managers can defer inventory and equipment purchases or misassign collections among periods to enhance the appearance of cash flow. But adequate cash flow is a *necessity* for carrying on business activities. Inadequate cash flow may reflect poor judgment and decision making on the part of the profit or investment center manager. There are many useful financial ratios (such as the current ratio, acid test ratio, and number of days' collections in accounts receivable) that involve cash flow available to assist managers in the effective conduct of their functions. Two other financial measures often used to evaluate divisional performance in an investment center are return on investment and residual income.

RETURN ON INVESTMENT

The difference between a profit center and an investment center is that the investment center manager also has responsibility for assets under the center's control. Giving the manager responsibility for acquisition, use, and disposal of assets increases the number of financial performance measures available because another dimension of accountability is added. **Return on investment** (ROI) is a ratio relating income generated by the investment center to the resources (or the asset base) used to produce that income. The return on investment formula is:

Return on investment

$$\text{ROI} = \frac{\text{Income}}{\text{Assets Invested}}$$

Before ROI can be used effectively, both terms in the formula must be specifically defined. To do this, Exhibit 22–4 asks and answers several definitional questions about this ratio. Once definitions have been assigned to the terms, ROI can be used to evaluate individual investment centers as well as to make intracompany, intercompany, and multinational comparisons. However, managers making these comparisons must consider differences in the entities' characteristics and accounting methods.

Using segment margin rather than operating income is preferred in the ROI calculation because the investment center manager does not have control in the short run over unavoidable fixed expenses and allocated corporate costs. Therefore, unavoid-

QUESTION	PREFERRED ANSWER
Is income defined as segment or operating income?	Segment income
Is income on a before- or after-tax basis?	Before-tax
Should assets be defined as ▪ total assets utilized; ▪ total assets available for use; or ▪ net assets (equity)?	Total assets available for use
Should plant assets be included at ▪ original cost; ▪ depreciated book value; or ▪ current values?	Current values
Should beginning, ending, or average assets be used?	Average assets

▪ **EXHIBIT 22–4**
ROI Definitional Questions and Answers

EXHIBIT 22–5

Wong Equipment Corporation

	DES MOINES	VANCOUVER	TUCSON	TOTAL
Sales revenues	$ 6,400,000	$1,350,000	$ 860,000	$8,610,000
Direct costs:				
Variable	(2,240,000)	(621,000)	(344,000)	(3,205,000)
Fixed (avoidable)	(1,100,000)	(235,000)	(120,000)	(1,455,000)
Segment income	$ 3,060,000	$ 494,000	$ 396,000	$3,950,000
Unavoidable fixed and allocated costs	(744,000)	(156,000)	(100,000)	(1,000,000)
Operating income	$ 2,316,000	$ 338,000	$ 296,000	$2,950,000
Taxes (35%)	(810,600)	(118,300)	(103,600)	(1,032,500)
Net income	$ 1,505,400	$ 219,700	$ 192,400	$1,917,500
Current assets	$ 97,000	$ 66,250	$ 40,000	
Plant assets	12,358,000	9,220,000	975,000	
Total asset cost	$12,455,000	$9,286,250	$1,015,000	
Accumulated depreciation	(2,465,000)	(6,540,000)	(125,000)	
Asset book value	$ 9,990,000	$2,746,250	$ 890,000	
Liabilities	4,260,000	1,200,000	325,000	
Net assets	$ 5,730,000	$1,546,250	$ 565,000	
Proportion of total assets utilized	100%	92%	95%	
Current value of plant assets	$ 9,950,000	$2,360,000	$ 870,000	

NOTE: A summarized corporate balance sheet would not balance with the investment center balance sheets because of the existence of general corporate assets and liabilities.

able fixed expenses and allocated corporate costs should not be a part of the performance evaluation criteria.[4] The same logic applies to the exclusion of taxes (or corporate interest) from investment center income. Company tax rates are determined based on total company income. Investment centers might pay higher or lower rates if they were separate taxable entities.

Investment center managers may have a substantial number of assets that are not being used. Eliminating these assets from the ROI denominator provides no encouragement for the manager to dispose of duplicate or unnecessary assets. Thus, total assets available for use is preferable to total assets utilized. Disposition of idle assets provides the manager with additional cash flow that could be used for alternative projects. If the objective is to measure how well the segment is performing financially given the funds stockholders have provided for that segment, then net assets should be used to measure return on equity funds.

Use of the original cost of plant assets is more appropriate than net book value in determining the amount of assets invested. As assets age and net book value declines, an investment center earning the same income each year would show a continuously increasing return on investment solely because of the diminishing asset base. Such apparent increasing returns could cause managers to make erroneous assessments of

---

[4]When assets and costs cannot be directly traced and must be allocated to an investment center, ROI calculations may not carry the same credibility as when allocations are not necessary. ROI calculations for an entire company or its autonomous free-standing divisions are easier to make and are more meaningful than are ROI calculations for units requiring such allocations. Criticism of ROI comparisons may also arise when such comparisons are made among divisions of very unequal sizes or at different stages of growth and product development.

the manager's performance. The use of current plant asset values is, however, preferable to original costs. Current values measure the opportunity cost of using the assets. Such values, though, are more difficult to obtain and may be subject to low levels of assurance.

Regardless of which plant asset base is chosen for the ROI denominator, that value should be a periodic average. Since income is earned over a period rather than at a specific time, the averaging period for the denominator should be the same as that used to determine the ROI numerator.

Data for the Wong Equipment Corporation (Exhibit 22–5 on page 960) is used to illustrate return on investment computations. The company has divisions located in Des Moines, Vancouver, and Tucson, which are all operated as separate investment centers.

Return on investment computations (using a variety of bases) for the Wong Equipment Corporation investment centers are shown in Exhibit 22–6. This exhibit illustrates that ROI figures differ dramatically depending on the definitions used for the formula terms. Therefore, how the numerator and denominator in the ROI computation are to be determined must be precisely specified before making computations or comparisons.

The ROI formula can be restated to provide useful information about individual factors that compose the rate of return. This restatement indicates that ROI is affected by both profit margin and asset turnover. **Profit margin** is the ratio of income to sales and indicates what proportion of each sales dollar is *not* used for expenses and, thus, becomes profit. **Asset turnover** measures asset productivity and shows the number of sales dollars generated by each dollar of assets. The restatement of the ROI formula is referred to as the **Du Pont model** and is:

Profit margin

Asset turnover

Du Pont model

$$\text{ROI} = \text{Profit Margin} \times \text{Asset Turnover}$$
$$\text{ROI} = \frac{\text{Income}}{\text{Sales}} \times \frac{\text{Sales}}{\text{Assets}}$$

	DES MOINES	VANCOUVER	TUCSON
Operating Income	$ 2,316,000	$ 338,000	$ 296,000
Assets Utilized	$ 9,990,000	$2,526,550	$ 845,500
ROI	23.2%	13.4%	35.0%
Operating Income	$ 2,316,000	$ 338,000	$ 296,000
Asset Current Value	$ 9,950,000	$2,360,000	$ 870,000
ROI	23.3%	14.3%	34.0%
Segment Margin	$ 3,060,000	$ 494,000	$ 396,000
Total Asset Cost	$12,455,000	$9,286,250	$1,015,000
ROI	24.6%	5.3%	39.0%
Segment Margin	$ 3,060,000	$ 494,000	$ 396,000
Asset Book Value	$ 9,990,000	$2,746,250	$ 890,000
ROI	30.6%	18.0%	44.5%
Segment Margin	$ 3,060,000	$ 494,000	$ 396,000
Asset Current Value	$ 9,950,000	$2,360,000	$ 870,000
ROI	30.8%	20.9%	45.5%
Segment Margin	$ 3,060,000	$ 494,000	$ 396,000
Net Assets	$ 5,730,000	$1,546,250	$ 565,000
ROI	53.4%	31.9%	70.1%

▌ EXHIBIT 22–6

The Wong Equipment Corporation ROI Computations

DES MOINES INVESTMENT CENTER:

$$\text{ROI} = (\text{Income} \div \text{Sales}) \times (\text{Sales} \div \text{Assets})$$
$$= (\$3,060,000 \div \$6,400,000) \times (\$6,400,000 \div \$12,455,000)$$
$$= .479 \times .514 = 24.6\%$$

VANCOUVER INVESTMENT CENTER:

$$\text{ROI} = (\text{Income} \div \text{Sales}) \times (\text{Sales} \div \text{Assets})$$
$$= (\$494,000 \div \$1,350,000) \times (\$1,350,000 \div \$9,286,250)$$
$$= .366 \times .145 = 5.3\%$$

TUCSON INVESTMENT CENTER:

$$\text{ROI} = (\text{Income} \div \text{Sales}) \times (\text{Sales} \div \text{Assets})$$
$$= (\$396,000 \div \$860,000) \times (\$860,000 \div \$1,015,000)$$
$$= .460 \times .848 = 39.0\%$$

As with the original ROI formula, terms in the restated formula must be specifically defined before the formula is usable for comparative or evaluative purposes. The DuPont model provides refined information about an investment center's opportunities for improvement. Profit margin can be used to judge the center's operating leverage by indicating management's efficiency in regard to the relationship between sales and expenses. Asset turnover can be used to judge marketing leverage in regard to the effectiveness of asset use relative to revenue production.

Calculations showing the ROI components using the Wong Equipment Corporation information are given in Exhibit 22–7 and use segment margin and total historical cost asset valuation as the income and asset base definitions. Thus, these computations provide the same answers as those given in the third calculation of Exhibit 22–6.

The calculations indicate that the Tucson investment center has an extremely high asset turnover but, based on the proportions of accumulated depreciation to plant assets, it is also the center with the newest assets. The Vancouver center seems to have fairly old plant assets because the relationship of accumulated depreciation to historical cost (shown in Exhibit 22–5) is high. Perhaps because they are old, the Vancouver plant assets are not generating substantial sales dollars relative to the asset base. Vancouver's manager might consider purchasing more modern facilities to generate more sales dollars and greater profits. Such an acquisition could, however, cause ROI to decline, since the asset base would be increased. Rate of return computations encourage managers to retain and use old plant assets (especially when accumulated depreciation is excluded from the asset base) to keep ROIs high as long as those assets are effective in keeping revenues up and expenses down.

Whereas Des Moines enjoys the highest profit margin and a strong turnover, Tucson has the highest turnover. To some extent, rapid turnover rates indicate that inventory is not stockpiling. Thus, the Des Moines and Vancouver managers might investigate the reasons for Tucson's rapid throughput to determine if they can obtain the same level of performance.

ROI is affected by decisions involving sales prices, volume and mix of products sold, expenses, and capital asset acquisitions and dispositions. Return on investment might be increased through various management options including: (1) improving profit margins by raising sales prices without impairing demand; (2) decreasing expenses; and (3) decreasing dollars invested in assets, especially if those assets are no longer productive. Action should be taken only after considering all the interrelationships that determine ROI. A change in one of the component elements can affect many of the others. For instance, an increase in price could reduce sales volume if demand is elastic with respect to price.

Assessments about whether profit margin, asset turnover, and return on investment are favorable or unfavorable can only be made by comparing actual results for each component with some valid basis. Bases of comparison include expected results, prior results, or results of other similar entities. Many companies establish target rates of return either for the company or, alternatively, for the division based on the nature of the industry or market in which that division operates. Favorable results should promote rewards to investment center managers.

Unfavorable rates of return should be viewed as managerial opportunities for improvement. Factors used in the computation should be analyzed for more detailed information. For example, if asset turnover is slow, additional calculations can be made for inventory turnover, accounts receivable turnover, machine capacity level experienced, and other rate-of-utilization measures. This investigation should help to indicate to the manager the direction of the problem(s) involved, so that causes may be determined and adjustments made. Another measure related to return on investment is the amount of residual income of an investment center.

RESIDUAL INCOME

Residual income

An investment center's **residual income** (RI) is the profit earned that exceeds an amount "charged" for funds committed to the center. The amount charged for funds is equal to a specified rate of return multiplied by the asset base. Top management establishes a target minimum acceptable rate of return against which the investment center's ROI can be judged.[5] This target rate is comparable to an imputed rate of interest on the assets used by the division. The rate can be changed from period to period consistent with market rate fluctuations or to compensate for risk. The residual income computation is:

$$\text{Residual Income} = \text{Income} - (\text{Target Rate} \times \text{Asset Base})$$

The advantage of residual income over return on investment is that residual income is concerned with a dollar figure rather than a percentage. It would always be to a company's advantage to obtain new assets if they earned a dollar amount of return greater than the dollar amount required by the rate charged for the additional investment. Expansion (or additional investments in assets) could occur in an investment center as long as positive residual income is expected on the additional investment.

Continuing the Wong Equipment Corporation example, Exhibit 22–8 shows the calculation of residual income for each investment center. Wong Equipment has established 12 percent on total assets as the target rate of return on assets invested and has defined income as segment margin. The Des Moines and Tucson investment centers show positive residual income, which means that these responsibility centers are earning above what top management considers a reasonable charge for funds. The residual income computation for the Vancouver investment center indicates that income is being significantly underproduced relative to the asset investment. The divi-

---

[5]The target rate established for measuring residual income is similar to the discount rate used in capital budgeting (discussed in Chapter 20). For management to invest in a capital project, that project must earn at least a specified rate of return. In the same manner, the ROI of an investment center must be equal to or higher than the target rate used to compute residual income.

■ EXHIBIT 22-8
Wong Equipment Corporation Residual Income

Residual Income = Income − Target Rate(Asset Base)

Des Moines:
$3,060,000 − .12($12,455,000) = $3,060,000 − $1,494,600 = $1,565,400

Vancouver:
$494,000 − .12($9,286,250) = $494,000 − $1,114,350 = $(620,350)

Tucson:
$396,000 − .12($1,015,000) = $396,000 − $121,800 = $274,200

sion manager should be apprised of the situation so that he or she can take steps to discover the cause of and correct this unsatisfactory result.

When used to measure investment center performance, each of the above-mentioned financial measures of performance has certain limitations. For example, the limitations of divisional profit and cash flow are the potential for income and cash flow manipulation. Return on investment and residual income have similar limitations for a variety of reasons. These limitations and their causes are addressed in the following section.

LIMITATIONS OF RETURN ON INVESTMENT AND RESIDUAL INCOME

ROI and residual income have three primary limitations. The first limitation is, itself, a triple problem related to income. Income can be manipulated on a short-run basis. This possibility was explained earlier in the chapter in regard to the use of divisional segment margin as a performance measure. Income also depends on the accounting methods selected, for items such as inventory cost flow or depreciation. For perfectly valid ROI and RI comparisons to be made among investment centers, all centers must use the same accounting methods. Finally, income is based on accrual accounting, which does not consider the pattern of cash flows or the time value of money and, therefore, may not always provide the best basis for evaluating investment center performance.

The second limitation is also a triple problem related to the asset investment base on which both of these measures rely. Asset investment is difficult to measure properly and assign to center managers. Some expenditures have residual values beyond the accounting period, but are not capitalized (for example, research and development costs), and therefore create an understated asset base.[6] Also, assets included in the asset base might be the result of decisions made by previous investment center managers. Thus, current managers might be judged on investment decisions over which they have no control. Finally, "[w]hen fixed assets and inventory are not restated for [rising] price level changes after acquisition, net income is overstated and investment is understated. Thus managers who retain older, mostly depreciated assets [often] report much higher ROIs than managers who invest in new assets."[7]

The third limitation of these measures is a single, possibly critical problem. ROI and RI both focus attention on how well an investment center itself performs, rather than how well that center performs relative to companywide objectives. Such a focus can result in suboptimization of resources, meaning that the firm is not maximizing its operational effectiveness and efficiency.

---

[6] Life-cycle costing (discussed in Chapter 5) can help to eliminate this problem.
[7] Robert S. Kaplan, "Yesterday's Accounting Undermines Production," *Harvard Business Review* (July–August 1984), p. 99.

The Tucson Division of Wong Equipment is used to illustrate the effects of suboptimization. As indicated in Exhibit 22–5, the Tucson Division has income of $192,400 and an asset base of $1,015,000. ROI for the division is 19 percent ($192,400 ÷ $1,015,000). Assume that the Tucson Division has an opportunity to increase income by $48,000 from sales of a new plow. This venture requires an additional capital investment of $300,000. Thus, considered separately, this venture would result in a return on investment of 16 percent ($48,000 ÷ $300,000). If Tucson Division accepts this opportunity, divisional return on investment will fall, as shown below:

$$
\begin{aligned}
\text{ROI} &= (\text{Original income} + \text{New income}) \div (\text{Original assets} + \text{New assets}) \\
&= (\$192,400 + \$48,000) \div (\$1,015,000 + \$300,000) \\
&= \$240,400 \div \$1,315,000 \\
&= 18.3\%
\end{aligned}
$$

If top management evaluates investment centers' managers on the ROIs of their divisions, the Tucson Division manager will not accept this investment opportunity because it would cause the division's ROI to drop.

Remember, however, that Wong Equipment Corporation has established a target rate of return of 12 percent on investment dollars. The decision by the Tucson manager to reject the new opportunity suboptimizes the companywide returns. This venture should be accepted because it provides a return higher than the firm's target rate. Top management should be informed of such opportunities, made aware of the effects acceptance will have on divisional performance measurements, and be willing to reward such acceptance based on its impact on company performance.[8]

NONFINANCIAL PERFORMANCE MEASURES

Managerial performance can be evaluated using both qualitative and quantitative measures. Qualitative measures are often subjective; for example, a manager may be evaluated using simple low-to-high rankings on job skills, such as knowledge, quality of work, and need for supervision. The rankings can be given for an individual on a stand-alone basis, in relationship to other managers, or on a group or team basis. While such measures provide useful information, at some point and in some way, performance should also be compared to a quantifiable—but not necessarily financial—standard.

Selection of Nonfinancial Measures

Managers are generally more comfortable with and respond better to quantitative measures of performance because such measures provide a defined target at which to aim. Quantifiable performance measures are of two types: nonfinancial and financial. Nonfinancial measures "rely on data outside of a conventional financial or cost system, such as on-time delivery, manufacturing cycle time, set-up time, productivity for the total work force and various measures of quality."[9] According to the IMA's *Statement on Management Accounting 4D*, nonfinancial performance measures have two distinct advantages over financial performance measures:

---

[8] Capital budgeting techniques such as the internal rate of return and net present values (Chapters 19 and 20) can be used in conjunction with evaluating ROI. These techniques can indicate situations in which corporate performance will benefit to the perceived detriment of divisional performance.
[9] Peter R. Santori, "Manufacturing Performance in the 1990s: Measuring for Excellence," *Journal of Accountancy* (November 1987), p. 146.

▮ Nonfinancial indicators directly measure an entity's performance in the activities that create shareholder wealth, such as manufacturing and delivering quality goods and services and providing service for the customer.

▮ Because they measure productive activity directly, nonfinancial measures may better predict the direction of future cash flows. For example, the long-term financial viability of some industries rests largely on their ability to keep promises of improved product quality at a competitive price.[10]

The advantages provided by nonfinancial measures should be considered when establishing a performance measurement system. Choosing appropriate performance measures can significantly help a company focus on the activities that cause its costs to be incurred and, thereby, attempt to control those costs and improve processes.

Traditionally, managers have conducted performance evaluations based almost solely on financial results. But concentrating on financial results alone is analogous to a baseball player, in hopes of playing well, focusing solely on the scoreboard. Both the game score and financial measures reflect the *results of past decisions*. Success in playing baseball and in managing a business also requires that considerable attention be placed on actionable steps for effectively competing in the stadium, whether it is the baseball stadium or the global marketplace. The baseball player must focus on hitting, fielding, and pitching. The company must focus on performing well in activities such as customer service, product development, manufacturing, marketing, and delivery. Performance measurement for improving the conduct of these activities requires tracking statistical data about the actionable steps that entail the causes and occurrences that the activities involve.[11] Nevertheless, companies have historically disregarded nonfinancial measures.

The set of nonfinancial performance measures (NFPM) that could be used is quite large because it is limited only by the imagination. Notwithstanding this, using a very large number of NFPMs is counterproductive and wasteful. Management should strive to identify the firm's critical success factors and to choose a few qualitative attributes of each NFPM that managers desire to continuously improve.

Nonfinancial critical success factors could include quality, customer satisfaction, manufacturing efficiency and effectiveness, technical excellence, and rapid response to market demands. For each success factor chosen, management should select some short-run and long-run attribute measures to properly steer the company's activities aimed at both immediate and long-range success. A short-range success measure for quality is the number of customer complaints in the current period. A long-range success measure for quality is the number of patents obtained for quality improvements of the company's products.

Establishment of Comparison Bases

Once the NFPMs are selected, managers should establish acceptable performance levels to provide bases of comparison against which actual statistical data can be compared. These benchmark comparison bases can be developed internally (such as from another established world-class division) or determined from external sources (such as competitors, regardless of whether they are in the company's industry).

Managers need to agree to assign specific responsibility for performance and to be evaluated in each area in which a performance measurement is to be made. In this regard, a system of monitoring and reporting comparative performance levels should be established at appropriate intervals, as presented in Exhibit 22–9. The exhibit

---

[10] Institute of Management Accountants (formerly National Association of Accountants), *Statements on Management Accounting: Measuring Entity Performance*, Number 4D (Montvale, N.J.: NAA, January 3, 1986), p. 12.

[11] Joseph Fisher, "Use of Nonfinancial Peformance Measures," *Journal of Cost Management* (Spring 1992), p. 31.

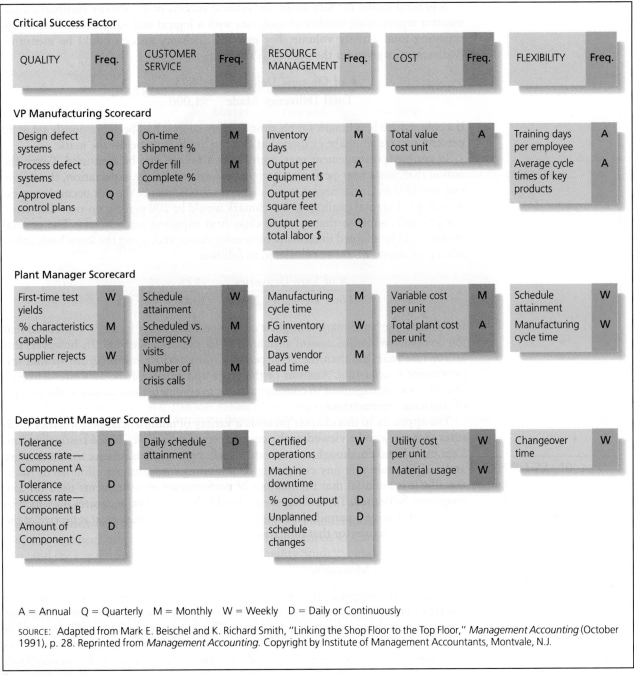

Critical Success Factor

QUALITY	Freq.	CUSTOMER SERVICE	Freq.	RESOURCE MANAGEMENT	Freq.	COST	Freq.	FLEXIBILITY	Freq.

VP Manufacturing Scorecard

QUALITY	Freq.	CUSTOMER SERVICE	Freq.	RESOURCE MANAGEMENT	Freq.	COST	Freq.	FLEXIBILITY	Freq.
Design defect systems	Q	On-time shipment %	M	Inventory days	M	Total value cost unit	A	Training days per employee	A
Process defect systems	Q	Order fill complete %	M	Output per equipment $	A			Average cycle times of key products	A
Approved control plans	Q			Output per square feet	A				
				Output per total labor $	Q				

Plant Manager Scorecard

QUALITY	Freq.	CUSTOMER SERVICE	Freq.	RESOURCE MANAGEMENT	Freq.	COST	Freq.	FLEXIBILITY	Freq.
First-time test yields	W	Schedule attainment	W	Manufacturing cycle time	M	Variable cost per unit	M	Schedule attainment	W
% characteristics capable	M	Scheduled vs. emergency visits	M	FG inventory days	W	Total plant cost per unit	A	Manufacturing cycle time	W
Supplier rejects	W	Number of crisis calls	M	Days vendor lead time	M				

Department Manager Scorecard

QUALITY	Freq.	CUSTOMER SERVICE	Freq.	RESOURCE MANAGEMENT	Freq.	COST	Freq.	FLEXIBILITY	Freq.
Tolerance success rate— Component A	D	Daily schedule attainment	D	Certified operations	W	Utility cost per unit	W	Changeover time	W
Tolerance success rate— Component B	D			Machine downtime	D	Material usage	W		
Amount of Component C	D			% good output	D				
				Unplanned schedule changes	D				

A = Annual   Q = Quarterly   M = Monthly   W = Weekly   D = Daily or Continuously

SOURCE: Adapted from Mark E. Beischel and K. Richard Smith, "Linking the Shop Floor to the Top Floor," *Management Accounting* (October 1991), p. 28. Reprinted from *Management Accounting*. Copyright by Institute of Management Accountants, Montvale, N.J.

▌ EXHIBIT 22–9

Performance Measurement Factors and Timetables

reflects a responsibility hierarchy of performance standards, with the broader issues addressed by higher levels of management and the more immediately actionable issues addressed by the lower management levels. Note also that the lower-level activities are monitored more frequently (continuously, daily, or weekly), while the upper-level measures are investigated less frequently (monthly, quarterly, and annually). Those measures utilized by middle management (in Exhibit 22–9, the Plant Manager) are intermediate linkages between the lower- and upper-level performance measures and require monitoring at intermediate points (weekly, monthly, and annually).

❙ EXHIBIT 22-11

Frequency of Use of Quality Information to Evaluate Business Performance

	Less than Annually or Not at All	Annually	Quarterly	Monthly or More Frequently
Canada	14%	7%	28%	51%
Germany	9%	24%	12%	55%
Japan	2%	10%	18%	70%
United States	18%	11%	16%	55%

SOURCE: Ernst & Young and American Quality Foundation, *International Quality Study* (1991), p. 16.

THROUGHPUT AS A NON-FINANCIAL PERFORMANCE MEASURE

Throughput
Synchronous management

One innovative, nonfinancial indicator of performance gaining wide acceptability is the concept of **throughput**. This term refers to the number of good units or quantity of services produced and *sold* by an organization within a time period. An important aspect of this definition is that the company must sell the units and not simply produce them for inventory stockpiles. Since a primary goal of a profit-oriented organization is to make money, inventory must be sold for that goal to be achieved. All endeavors helping an organization achieve its goal(s) are considered to be **synchronous management** techniques. "Synchronous management's strategic objective is to simultaneously increase throughput, while reducing inventory and operating expenses."[13]

One way to measure throughput is to view it as comprised of a set of component elements similar to the approach used earlier in regard to the rate of return. Just as the rate of return formula can be expanded to identify areas for improvement in profit margin or turnover, the throughput formula can be expanded to indicate productive capacity, productive processing time, and yield.[14]

$$\begin{array}{ccccc} \text{Productive} & & \text{Productive} & & \text{Process} \\ \text{capacity} & \times & \text{processing time} & \times & \text{yield} & = \text{Throughput} \end{array}$$

$$\frac{\text{Total Units}}{\text{Processing Time}} \times \frac{\text{Processing Time}}{\text{Total Time}} \times \frac{\text{Good Units}}{\text{Total Units}} = \frac{\text{Good Units}}{\text{Total Time}}$$

[13] Victor Lippa, "Measuring Performance with Synchronous Management," *Management Accounting* (February 1990), p. 54.

[14] These terms and formulas are based on the following article: Carole Cheatham, "Measuring and Improving Throughput," *Journal of Accountancy* (March 1990), pp. 89–91. One assumption that must be made in regard to this model is that the quantity labeled "throughput" is sold.

	QUALITATIVE	QUANTITATIVE	
		Nonfinancial	Financial
PERSONNEL	Acceptance of additional responsibility Increased job skills Need for supervision Interaction with upper- and lower-level employees	Proportion of direct to indirect labor (low or high depending on degree of automation) Diversity of ethnic background in hiring and promotion Hours of continuing professional education Scores on standardized examinations	Comparability of personnel pay levels with those of competitors Savings from using part-time personnel
MARKET	Addition of new product features Increased product durability Improved efficiency of product Improved effectiveness of product	Number of sales transactions Number of repeat customers Generation of new ideas Number of customer complaints Number of days to deliver an order Proportion of repeat business Number of new patents obtained Number of new (lost) customers	Increase in revenue from previous period Percent of total market revenues Revenue generated per advertising dollar
COSTS	Better traceability of costs Increased cost consciousness Better employee suggestions for cost reductions Increased usage of automated equipment for routine tasks	Time to design new products Number of engineering change orders issued for new products Proportion of product defects Number of different product parts Number of days of inventory in stock Length of process time Proportion of materials generated as scrap/waste Reduction in setup time since prior period	Reduction in production cost since prior period (individually for materials, labor, and overhead, and collectively) Reduction in distribution and scrap/waste cost since prior period Cost of engineering changes Variances from standard
RETURNS (profitability)	Customer satisfaction Product brand loyalty	Proportion of on-time deliveries Degree of accuracy in sales figures Frequency of customer willingness to accept an exchange rather than a refund	Increase in market price per share Return on investment Increase in net income Increase in cash flow

▌ **EXHIBIT 22–12**

Examples of Performance Measurements

The total units that could be produced based on available equipment during a period is called **productive capacity**. This measure assumes that all units that were started could have been completed and ignores downtime and spoiled units.

Productive capacity

The amount of total value added time from beginning to completion of production or service performance is called **productive processing time**. Value-added time indicates that activities took place that increased the product's worth to the customer. A useful performance measure in regard to value-added inventory production time is **dollar days**. A manager is "charged" with the inventory value multiplied by the time that inventory stays in an area. This total amount is then viewed by top management as though these funds had to be borrowed.

Productive processing time

Dollar days (of inventory)

To illustrate how the dollar days measure is calculated, assume that $12,000 of inventory enters Department 1 and stays there four days. Department 1 would be charged with $48,000 "dollar days" of inventory. Top management would view this

NEWS NOTE

Every Level of Management Is Judged By Someone

Performance measures represent management's expectations and reflect their philosophy of how people work. Some performance measures assume that people do not have to work together very much or very well.

Simple sales quotas do this. Efficiency measures do. Output-based incentives do. They tell people to just do *their* job and to worry little about long-term improvement, which is *someone else's* worry.

The goals of value-added manufacturing are *continuous improvement in* elimination of waste, reduction of lead times, increased quality, reduction in total cost, and people development. Performance measurement should, therefore, measure improvement on these dimensions. Not just acceptability, but *improvement*. Not routine performance, but *improvement* over the previous performance. Measure improvement trends and allow for such circumstances as new product introduction.

Performance measurements are the emblems of a management philosophy because people measure what they consider important. When the philosophy of management changes, the measurement systems change—or should change. However, changing measurement systems is more difficult than reworking a machine. Performance measurement is the basis of every system in a company: cost systems, planning systems, capital budgeting systems, personnel assignments, promotions, reorganizations, budget allocations—the mechanisms, built up over years, by which everything *runs*.

A truly accepted change in management philosophy knocks the props from under all this. Some of the most common roadblocks to progress are systems created to assist management in a previous incarnation and to which allegiance and deference are still committed. Major overhauls bring out the same emotions as if the perpetrators were to hold a rock concert in a cemetery. Performance measurement changes are only possible with strong leadership at the top of the company—and those leaders have to be careful if their performance is judged by a horde of impatient investors.

SOURCE: Robert W. Hall, *Attaining Manufacturing Excellence* (Homewood, Ill.: Dow Jones-Irwin, 1987), pp. 43–44.

$48,000 as a kind of "liability." The higher the dollar days assigned to a department, the greater the corporate cost because investment dollars are not generating a return. If the inventory remains in Department 1 because of a bottleneck, the manager is made more aware of the cost of having that bottleneck and is motivated to take actions to reduce the dollar days of cost assigned to the department. Measuring dollar days is also useful in nonmanufacturing areas. In the Marketing Department, for example, the concept could be used to encourage prompt sale of finished goods inventory; in Purchasing, dollar days could be used to encourage the use of just-in-time purchasing techniques.

Process yield

Production activities serve to produce both good and defective units. The proportion of good units resulting from activities is the **process yield**. This measure reflects the quality of the production process. Thus, if 10,000 units were produced during a period and 9,500 of those were good units, the company would have had a 95 percent process yield for the period.

Throughput can be increased by increasing the productive capacity, decreasing the unit processing time (which would increase the productive processing time), and/or increasing process yield. One useful way to measure performance is to determine how well the company's goal of making money is being met by having rapid and high-quality throughput.

Exhibit 22–13 provides the August 1994 throughput and related elements computations for the Des Moines Division of Wong Equipment Company. These calculations indicate that throughput for this division for the month was .332 units per hour (6,600 units ÷ 19,880 hours), meaning that the division produced and sold about one unit of product every three hours the plant operated during the month.

EXHIBIT 22–13
Throughput Measurement

Total units processed   7,000
Good units   6,600
Processing time   16,800 hours
Total time available   19,880 hours

Productive   Productive   Process
capacity $\times$ processing time $\times$ yield = Throughput

$$\frac{7,000}{16,800} \times \frac{16,800}{19,880} \times \frac{6,600}{7,000} = \frac{6,600}{19,880}$$
$$.417 \times .845 \times .943 = .332$$

Activity-based costing is concerned with reducing non-value-added activities as one way to increase throughput. In this manner, activity-based costing is influencing performance measurement, as discussed in the following section.

Traditional performance measurements in accounting are ingrained with factors that contribute to non-value-added activities. Materials standards are developed that include factors for waste, and labor standards are developed that include an estimate of idle time. Predetermined overhead rates are set using an estimate of expected capacity usage rather than full capacity usage. Inventories are produced to meet budget expectations rather than sales demand. Detailed treatments of how to account for spoiled and defective units are used. Exhibit 22–14 provides some traditional performance indicators and some potential suboptimizing results they may create.

ACTIVITY-BASED COSTING AND PERFORMANCE EVALUATION

EXHIBIT 22–14
Traditional Performance Measurements and Results

MEASUREMENT	ACTION	RESULT
Purchase price variance	Purchasing agent increases order quantity to get lower price and ignores quality and speed of delivery	Excess inventory; increased carrying cost; suppliers with the best quality and delivery are overlooked
Machine utilization percentage	Supervisor produces in excess of daily unit requirements to maximize machine utilization percentage	Excess inventory; wrong inventory
Scrap built into standard cost	Supervisor takes no action if there is no variance (from the lax standard)	Inflated standard; scrap threshold built in
Overhead rate based on expected capacity	Supervisor overproduces WIP or FG to have a favorable fixed overhead volume variance	Excess inventory; wrong inventory
Cost center reporting	Managers focus on cost centers instead of activities	Cost reduction opportunities are missed because common activities among cost centers are overlooked

SOURCE: Charles Porter, *Cost Management in the New Manufacturing Environment* (Coopers & Lybrand presentation, Directory XAT8803A).

Top management at Unilever's Rotterdam headquarters understands the need for divisional performance measures that recognize differences in economies, taxes, and accounting practices. Comparisons among the company's worldwide subunits may be more appropriate if nonfinancial measures (such as throughput and quality) are used rather than the traditional financial measures.

If companies are to move toward world-class operations, non-value-added (NVA) activities must be removed from performance evaluation measurements and value-added (VA) activities must be substituted. The adages "you get what you measure" and "measure what you want to get" are appropriate. Since companies are extremely concerned about the cost of quality (COQ) (and the non-value-added activities associated with lack of quality), measurements related to COQ such as those presented in Exhibit 22–15 should be developed.

▌ EXHIBIT 22–15
Cost of Quality Measurements

ELEMENT OF COQ	OPERATIONAL COST DRIVERS	MEASURE	VA OR NVA
▌ Prevention	▌ Investment in reducing overall COQ operations	$\dfrac{Prevention\ Cost^1}{Total\ COQ}$	VA
▌ Appraisal	▌ Setup frequency ▌ Tight tolerance operations ▌ Complex design	Number of inspections	NVA
▌ Internal failure	▌ Machine reliability ▌ Tooling age or condition ▌ Design error ▌ Operator error	Number of pieces rejected	NVA
▌ External failure	▌ Order entry errors ▌ Incorrect assembly instructions ▌ Product failure ▌ Operator error	Number of customer complaints	NVA

[1] Ideally, the formula should equal 1. Prevention costs are, by definition, all value-added costs. As non-value-added costs included in the denominator are eliminated, total COQ is composed of basically only value-added costs. Therefore, the formula ideally ends up equaling 1 (value-added costs ÷ value-added costs), which is the target measurement.

SOURCE: Michael R. Ostrenga, "Return on Investment Through the Cost of Quality," *Journal of Cost Management* (Boston: Warren Gorham Lamont, Summer 1991), p. 43.

For example, if a performance measurement is the cost of defective units produced during a period, the original assumption is that management is expecting defects to occur and will accept some stated or understood defect cost. Instead, if the performance measurement is zero defects, the assumption is that no defects are to occur. It would seem reasonable that managers would strive harder to eliminate defects under the second measurement than under the first.

Thus, "performance measurements must be externally focused. They . . . must be linked to and support the business goals. They must measure what is of value to the customer."[15] Some performance measurements, such as zero defects, are the same regardless of divisional locale. However, because multinational settings are more complex than domestic settings, they require some additional considerations in performance measurement and evaluation.

PERFORMANCE EVALUATION IN MULTINATIONAL SETTINGS

Many large, decentralized companies are heavily involved in overseas operations. In an attempt to measure and evaluate such operations, upper-level management often uses income as the overriding criterion in the evaluation of all subunits, regardless of their locales. Such a singular focus is generally not appropriate for domestic responsibility centers and is even less appropriate for multinational segments. This conclusion is valid regardless of whether the organization is Engelhard Corporation domiciled in the United States with operations in Germany, Korea, the Netherlands, and Italy, or ABB Asea Brown Boveri domiciled in Zurich with operations in Muncie (Indiana), Finland, Thailand, and Brazil.

Differences among cultures and economies are as important as differences in accounting standards and reporting practices when attempting comparisons of multinational organizational units. In Japan, for instance, a company president views shareholders as basically inconsequential. When the head of a large Japanese conglomerate was asked "whether stock-market movements would ever affect his business decisions, he answered in a single word: 'Never!'"[16] This type of attitude allows Japanese companies to concentrate on long-run rather than short-run business decisions. Such a concept is unheard of in the United States where top management is often removed by stockholders for making decisions that appear not to maximize shareholder value.

The dollar amount of investments in different countries necessary to create the same type of organizational unit may differ substantially. For example, because of the exchange rate and legal costs, it is significantly more expensive for a U.S. company to open a Japanese subsidiary than an Indonesian one. If performance is measured using a concept such as residual income, the Japanese unit would be placed at a distinct disadvantage because of its large investment base. On the other hand, the company may have believed that the possibility of future joint ventures with the Japanese was a primary corporate goal and justified the larger investment. One method of handling such a discrepancy in investment bases would be to assign a lower target rate to compute residual income for the Japanese subsidiary than for the Indonesian one. Such a differential would be appropriate because of the lower political, financial, and economic risks.

Income comparisons between multinational units may be invalid because of important differences in trade tariffs, income tax rates, currency fluctuations, and the

[15] Thomas O'Brien, "Measurements in the New Era of Manufacturing," proceedings from *Cost Accounting for the '90s: Responding to Technological Change* (Montvale, N.J.: National Association of Accountants, 1988), p. 72.

[16] Alan S. Blinder, "Doing It Their Way," *Business Edge* (October 1992), p. 27.

NEWS NOTE

What Is the IASC?

The International Accounting Standards Committee (IASC) was formed in 1973 and based in London. The members of the IASC are 105 professional accountancy bodies in about 80 countries. IASC is governed by a board of 14 members, representing 13 countries (Australia, Canada, France, Germany, Italy, Japan, Jordan, Korea, Netherlands, Norway/ Scandinavia, South Africa, United Kingdom, and the United States) and the International Association of Financial Analysts.

Three times a year the board meets for three or four days. In addition, the board meets at least twice a year with a broadly-based consultive group . . . which provides useful insights to both the technical and political dimensions of the standard-setting process. Due process procedures, in the form of exposure drafts, lengthy exposure periods and reconsideration upon review of comments received, add credibility to the work of the IASC.

Unfortunately, however, the diversity in accounting policies across countries, combined with a voting requirement of 11 favorable votes of the 14 members to issue a standard, has led to a total of 31 standards characterized by acceptable alternative practices. Only by acceptance of some alternatives (but with the elimination of others) could sufficient votes be garnered to issue a standard. Such standards, of course, are not the best, e.g., consider a standard for driving your car that said you could drive on either the right *or* the left side of the road. While alternatives within accounting standards may not lead to the same level of chaos, they surely fall short of optimum helpfulness. Thus, while IASC has made considerable progress and has eliminated a number of weak practices in the process, much remains to be done.

[In 1989, the IASC] embarked on a major project to eliminate about 80 percent of the alternatives in its existing standards. This would be accomplished by issuance of revised standards. The target date for the project's completion is set at the end of 1993. At that time, IASC standards will still contain eight to ten acceptable alternatives, a number many view as too large to achieve the desired level of efficiency. In all likelihood, a follow-up project will be undertaken to reduce those alternatives to four or five. . . . Should IASC standard use [ever] be mandated, financial experts around the world would find more comparable bases for their analytical efforts.

SOURCE: Excerpted from Arthur R. Wyatt, "Seeking Credibility in a Global Economy," *New Accountant* (Vol. 8 #1 September 1992), pp. 6, 51–52. Copyright © 1992 New DuBois Corporation.

possibility of restrictions on the transfer of goods or currency from a country. Income earned by a multinational unit may also be affected by conditions totally outside its control, such as protectionism of local companies, government aid in some countries, and varying wage rates because of differing standards of living, level of industrial development, and/or quantity of socialized services. If the multinational subunit adopts the local country's accounting practices, differences in international standards can make income comparisons among units arduous and inconvenient even after the statements are translated to a single currency basis.

The diverse economic, legal/political, and tax structures of countries have affected the development and practice of accounting. The International Accounting Standards Committee (discussed in the "IASC" News Note) is working to achieve harmonization of accounting standards. However, many of the standards issued to date by this organization reflect compromise positions, allow for a significant number of alternatives, and are accepted only through voluntary compliance. Last, within the constraints of moral and social responsibility, managers may be able to transfer goods between segments at prices that minimize profits or tariffs in locations where taxes

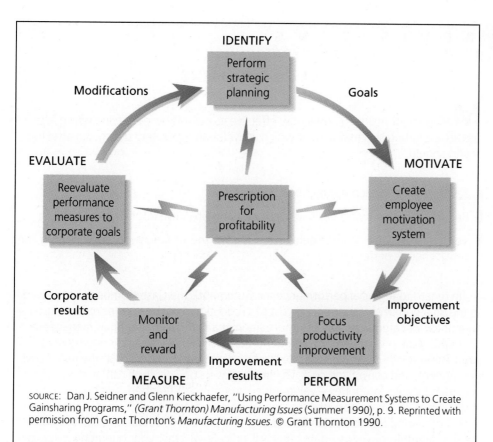

SOURCE: Dan J. Seidner and Glenn Kieckhaefer, "Using Performance Measurement Systems to Create Gainsharing Programs," *(Grant Thornton) Manufacturing Issues* (Summer 1990), p. 9. Reprinted with permission from Grant Thornton's *Manufacturing Issues.* © Grant Thornton 1990.

EXHIBIT 22–16

Performance Management System

are high by shifting profits or cost values to more advantageous climates from a tax or tariff perspective.

U.S. firms having multinational profit or investment centers (or subsidiaries) need to establish flexible systems of measuring profit performance for those units. Such systems should recognize that differences in sales volumes, accounting standards, economic conditions, and risk may be outside the control of an international subunit's manager. In such cases, qualitative factors may become significantly more useful. Performance evaluations can include measures such as market share increases, quality improvements (defect reductions), establishment of just-in-time inventory systems with the related reduction in working capital, and new product development. Use of measures that limit suboptimization of resources is vital to the proper management of both domestic and multinational responsibility centers.

In conclusion, companies need to make a variety of decisions regarding performance measurements. This package of decisions can be labeled a performance management system and is depicted in Exhibit 22–16. No one system is appropriate for all companies or, possibly, even all responsibility centers within the same company. The measurement of performance is the measurement of people. Since people are unique and have multiple facets, the performance management system must reflect those characteristics.

R E V I S I T I N G

J. I. CASE COMPANY

Management needs to know how effective its plant is by identifying which activities are operating successfully and which activities are operating poorly. An effective report should:

▌ Satisfy a specific need not met by other reports.

▌ Be prepared on a timely basis with relevant and objective information.

▌ Be understandable to the users and useful to the organization in measuring the organization's performance.

[In regard to financial performance measurement], the Case Company has moved in the direction of measuring total cost of production, but the current report structure does not categorize the cost information in a manner that enables management to measure the progress improvements in the operation. A recommended cost of production schedule would separate the firm's cost into material cost, the major cost component, and conversion cost. The firm's conversion cost then can be divided into two manageable categories—value-added and non-value-added. The goal is to minimize (eliminate where possible) the non-value-added activity in the production process. Comparing the non-value-added cost as a percent of value-added activity on a weekly, monthly, or year-to-date basis will indicate whether your operation is improving on eliminating non-value-added waste.

The criteria for a good performance measurement system must:

▌ Be driven by customer (user) requirements. The system must support the manufacturing [or service] strategy and critical success factors employed by management.

▌ Be flexible to change.

▌ Be simple and easy to understand. The "KIS" principle applies—"Keep It Simple."

▌ Be nonfinancial as well as financial.

▌ Provide for positive reinforcement.

The measurement system is not intended to be a tool to beat up on poor performance. It must be designed to support the WCM objective of "Kaizen"—the Japanese term meaning "continual improvement." It should focus on how the company is performing today and indicate where the organization needs to improve. When establishing reports geared toward world-class manufacturing, the old, traditional reports should be discarded once the new ones are in place. Otherwise, there may be a tendency to follow the old methods, and the effectiveness and benefits of the new measurements would be lost.

SOURCE: Michael R. Sellenheim, "Performance Measurement," *Management Accounting* (September 1991), pp. 50–53. Reprinted from *Management Accounting*. Copyright by Institute of Management Accountants, Montvale, N.J.

CHAPTER SUMMARY

Performance measures must be appropriate for the type of responsibility center under review and can be either financial or nonfinancial. These measures should assess progress toward goals and objectives and should be accepted by persons being evaluated. Persons to be evaluated should have the appropriate skills, equipment, information, and authority for accomplishment. Moreover, feedback on accomplishment should be provided in a timely and useful manner. Using multiple measures regarding the firm's critical success factors is more effective than using single measures. Those persons to be evaluated should participate in the development of the measures by which their performance will be evaluated. Divisional profits and cash flow are frequently used performance measures; however, care must be taken that these measures are not manipulated.

Two additional major financial measures of performance for investment centers are return on investment and residual income. Return on investment is net income divided by invested assets. Residual income is the amount of net income in excess of income calculated by using an imputed interest charge on the asset base. While both measures provide important information about the efficiency and effectiveness of managers, neither should be used alone nor without recognizing the limitations inherent in the measure. Financial measures should be coupled with nonfinancial measures to provide a more complete and useful picture of performance.

An innovative, nonfinancial measure of performance is throughput. Throughput refers to the goods or services started, finished, and sold by an organization. When throughput is increased, the company goal of making money is enhanced.

Performance measures of multinational units may be more difficult to establish than those of domestic units because of differences in taxes, tariffs, currency exchange rates, and transfer restrictions. Top management may wish to consider extending the use of qualitative performance measures because of such differences.

Performance Measurement Areas and Cost Drivers

APPENDIX

Exhibit 22–17 on pages 980–981 is from a joint study by the Institute of Management Accountants (formerly the National Association of Accountants) and the international public accounting firm of Coopers & Lybrand. The exhibit indicates some activity cost drivers that need to be measured to determine performance in the six specified areas.

KEY TERMS

Asset turnover (p. 961)
Dollar days (of inventory) (p. 971)
Du Pont model (p. 961)
Process yield (p. 972)
Productive capacity (p. 971)
Productive processing time (p. 971)

Profit margin (p. 961)
Residual income (p. 963)
Return on investment (p. 959)
Synchronous management (p. 970)
Throughput (p. 970)

EXHIBIT 22-17

Performance Measurements

PERFORMANCE MEASUREMENT AREA: DESIGN FOR MANUFACTURABILITY

Key Characteristics

Quantity and quality of
    engineering changes
Test results

Part standardization

Engineering cycle time

Product complexity

Cost Drivers/Measures

Number of engineering changes
Severity of engineering changes
First pass reject rate
Materials used versus design specification
Manufacturing skills required
Number of products
Percent common parts per product
Lead time to engineer (design) a finished product
Startup time from design to production
Number of components per finished product
Number of manufacturing operations per finished product
Number of tools required per finished product

PERFORMANCE MEASUREMENT AREA: ZERO DEFECTS

Key Characteristics

Product specification

Parts quality

Quality control checkpoints

Cost Drivers/Measures

Tolerances of critical components
Historical capability of process versus current performance
First pass reject rate versus test results
Units scrapped by cell
Cell downtime due to quality problems
Yield of finished product per raw material batch
Units reworked by cell
Sampling requirements for incoming materials
Time required for sample/test procedures
Production time loss due to quality control procedures/queues
Number of checkpoints
Effectiveness—number of returned units

PERFORMANCE MEASUREMENT AREA: MINIMIZE RAW AND IN PROCESS INVENTORY

Key Characteristics

Supplier performance

Component standardization

Market characteristics

Cost Drivers/Measures

Number and location of vendors
Number/frequency of deliveries
Lead time from order initiation to delivery
Flexibility in order quantity, delivery and variety
Complexity of components
Number of components to support total production
Demand variation
Forecast accuracy
Availability/accuracy of information

PERFORMANCE MEASUREMENT AREA: ZERO LEAD TIME

Key Characteristics	Cost Drivers/Measures
Velocity of units through cell	Actual production time
	Queue time between operations
	Move, setup, and inspection times
	Manufacturing cycle efficiency = value-added time ÷ total time
Quality of components	Scrap percent
	Rework percent
	Yield percent
Customer service levels	Late deliveries
	On-time deliveries
	Back orders
	Cancelled orders
Complexity of flow	Mix of products
	New product introductions
	Routing required per product

PERFORMANCE MEASUREMENT AREA: MINIMIZE PROCESS TIME

Key Characteristics	Cost Drivers/Measures
Product design	Number of components
▌ Complexity	Number of manufacturing procedures/steps
▌ Tolerance	Required tolerance versus matching optimum
▌ Materials	Maximum tolerance range per component
▌ Producibility	Packaging of component versus use configuration
	Quality of components
	Availability/ease of use
	Skills necessary to meet engineering requirements
Process capabilities and limitations	Information system capabilities
	Plant layout: optimum versus current
	Work rules: percent changed

PERFORMANCE MEASUREMENT AREA: OPTIMIZE PRODUCTION

Key Characteristics	Cost Drivers/Measures
Resource limitations	Bottleneck capacity level
	Setup time
	Lot size constraints
	Labor availability, qualifications, flexibility
	Material resources (e.g., availability, lead time, quality, proximity)
	Number of distribution centers
	Number of storerooms
Demand fluctuation	Volume variations (total units produced)
	Mix changes (number and magnitude)
	Schedule changes (number and magnitude)
Configuration of plant	Plant layout (e.g., move time, move distance, number of total moves)
Information processing constraints	Information accuracy and availability
	Data accuracy in planning execution (routing, bills, standards)

SOURCE: C.J. McNair, William Mosconi and Thomas Norris, *Meeting the Technology Challenge: Cost Accounting in a JIT Environment* (Montvale, N.J.: National Association of Accountants, now Institute of Management Accountants, 1988), pp. 199–210.

SOLUTION STRATEGIES

Performance Measurements for Responsibility Centers

■ Cost Center

    Budgeted costs
   − Actual costs

    Variances (consider materiality)

■ Revenue Center

    Budgeted revenues
   − Actual revenues

    Variances (consider materiality)

■ Profit Center

    Budgeted divisional profits
   − Actual divisional profits

    Variances (consider materiality)

    Cash inflows
   − Cash outflows

    Net cash flow (adequate to operations?)

■ Investment Center

    Budgeted investment center profits
   − Actual investment center profits

    Variances (consider materiality)

    Cash inflows
   − Cash outflows

    Net cash flow (adequate to operations?)

Return on Investment = Income ÷ Assets Invested (high enough rate?)

Du Pont model = Net Margin × Asset Turnover
= (Net Income ÷ Sales) × (Sales ÷ Average Total Assets)   (high enough rate?)

Residual Income = Income—(Target Rate × Asset Base)   (positive or negative? amount?)

Measuring Throughput

$$\text{Productive capacity} \times \text{Productive processing time} \times \text{Process yield} = \text{Throughput}$$

$$\frac{\text{Total Units}}{\text{Processing Time}} \times \frac{\text{Processing Time}}{\text{Total Time}} \times \frac{\text{Good Units}}{\text{Total Units}} = \frac{\text{Good Units}}{\text{Total Time}}$$

DEMONSTRATION PROBLEM

Jack Hunter Enterprises (JHE) compiled the following statistics for 1994 for its two subsidiary companies:

	Division J	Division H
Sales	$1,980,000	$2,500,000
Expenses	1,300,000	1,700,000
Average total asset base (AB)	5,400,000	7,600,000
Target rate of return required on AB (TR)	10%	10%
Total units processed	180,000	250,000
Good units	126,000	236,000
Total time (hours)	500,000	710,000
Processing time (hours)	425,000	600,000

Required:

a. Calculate the net margin percentage for each division.

b. Determine asset turnover for each division.

c. Compute the return on investment for each division.

d. Prove your answers to part c using one ratio for each division.

e. Calculate residual income (RI) for each division.

f. Calculate productive capacity (PC) for each division.

g. Calculate productive processing time (PPT) for each division.

h. Compute process yield (PY) for each division.

i. Determine throughput using one ratio for each division.

j. Prove your answer to part i using the results of parts f, g, and h.

Solution to Demonstration Problem

		Division J	Division H
a.	$\dfrac{\text{Segment Margin}}{\text{Sales}}$	$\dfrac{\$\ 680{,}000}{\$1{,}980{,}000}$	$\dfrac{\$\ 800{,}000}{\$2{,}500{,}000}$
		34.3%	32.0%
b.	$\dfrac{\text{Sales}}{\text{AB}}$	$\dfrac{\$1{,}980{,}000}{\$5{,}400{,}000}$	$\dfrac{\$2{,}500{,}000}{\$7{,}600{,}000}$
		.367 times	.329 times
c.	$\dfrac{\text{Segment Margin}}{\text{AB}}$	$\dfrac{\$\ 680{,}000}{\$5{,}400{,}000}$	$\dfrac{\$\ 800{,}000}{\$7{,}600{,}000}$
		12.6%	10.5%

d. ROI = Net Margin × Asset Turnover
Division J: .343 × .367 = 12.6%
Division H: .320 × .329 = 10.5%

e. RI = Income − (TR × AB)
Division J: $680,000 − (.10 × $5,400,000) = $140,000
Division H: $800,000 − (.10 × $7,600,000) = $ 40,000

		Division J	Division H
f.	$\dfrac{\text{Total Units}}{\text{Processing Time}}$	$\dfrac{180{,}000}{425{,}000}$	$\dfrac{250{,}000}{600{,}000}$
		.424	.447
g.	$\dfrac{\text{Processing Time}}{\text{Total Time}}$	$\dfrac{425{,}000}{500{,}000}$	$\dfrac{600{,}000}{710{,}000}$
		85.0%	84.5%
h.	$\dfrac{\text{Good Units}}{\text{Total Units}}$	$\dfrac{126{,}000}{180{,}000}$	$\dfrac{236{,}000}{250{,}000}$
		70.0%	94.4%
i.	$\dfrac{\text{Good Units}}{\text{Total Time}}$	$\dfrac{126{,}000}{500{,}000}$	$\dfrac{236{,}000}{710{,}000}$
		.252	.332

j. Throughput = PC × PPT × PY
Division J: .424 × .850 × .700 = .252
Division H: .417 × .845 × .944 = .333 (off due to rounding)

QUESTIONS

1. How should one decide on a basis for measuring the performance of a responsibility center?

2. Should performance measures be qualitative, quantitative, or both? Justify your answer.

3. Can the same quantitative measures of performance be used for all types of responsibility centers? If so, why; if not, why not?

4. How can feedback, both positive and negative, be used to improve managerial performance?

5. What is the traditional financial performance measure for a cost center? A revenue center? Why has each of these measures been used traditionally?

6. Why is managerial manipulation of accounting information an important concern in designing performance evaluation measures? Are internal or external measures more susceptible to manipulation? Explain.

7. How can cash flow be used as a performance measure? In what ways is cash flow a relatively stronger or weaker performance measure than accrual measures such as segment income?

8. Do the Statement of Cash Flows and the Cash Budget provide identical information on performance? Explain.

9. The president of Dolls, Inc. evaluates the performance of Ann and Andy, the divisional managers, on the basis of a variety of net income measures. Barbie, the controller, informs the president that such measures could be misleading. What are the major concerns in defining the "income" as used in the various measures?

10. What is the major difference between a profit center and an investment center? How does this difference create the need for different financial performance measures in an investment center and a profit center?

11. What is the most appropriate definition of the term *assets invested* in computing return on investment and why is it most appropriate?

12. How is it possible for an investment center's ROI to rise over time if assets are not replaced?

13. What is the Du Pont model? What are its component ratios? Why is each component important?

14. The senior managers of Jambino's Bakery Inc. were gathering for their monthly breakfast meeting when Mr. Jambino came in. Sara Fields, the cost accountant, was overheard to say, " . . . turnover looks good." Mr. Jambino, in a rather unpleasant mood that morning, turned to Sara and hollered, "Of course, the turnovers are good, but what does that have to do with the return this company should be making on its investment?" Sara calmly explained that she was discussing ROI. What kind of turnover was Sara discussing and how does it relate to ROI?

15. What is residual income and how is it used to measure divisional performance? How is it similar to, and different from, the return on investment measure?

16. Identify and discuss the major weaknesses associated with use of ROI and RI as performance measures.

17. Describe the circumstances in which use of ROI would be likely to create a suboptimization problem. Under what circumstances would use of this measure be less likely to create a suboptimization problem?

18. According to the NAA's (now IMA's) Statement 4D, what are the two distinct advantages of using nonfinancial performance measures?

19. What is a benchmark and what is its role in the use of nonfinancial performance measures?

20. Why is throughput defined on the basis of goods sold rather than goods produced?

21. How can activity-based costing concepts be used to design performance measures?

22. Why is the design of performance measures a more complex task in multinational companies than in single-country operations?

23. *(Appendix)* Birmingham Metalworks manufactures iron railings for ornamental fences. Recently, the company has become much more concerned about reducing the number of flaws in its completed products. Identify some performance measures that the company could use to monitor the effectiveness of its efforts to improve product quality.

EXERCISES

24. *(Return on investment)* Smithers Company has asked you to help its managers determine the ROI for the year just ended. You gather the following information: average assets invested, $2,400,000; revenues, $8,800,000; and expenses, $8,200,000.
    a. Calculate return on investment.
    b. Calculate profit margin.
    c. Calculate asset turnover.
    d. Using parts b and c, prove your answer to part a.

25. *(Return on investment)* Harriet Ketchum, a division manager of Eurotech, provides you with the following information regarding her division.

    Beginning of the year assets, $150,000
    End of the year assets, $194,000
    Revenues for year, $150,500
    Expenses for year, $122,500
    Variable expenses, 30% of total revenues; remaining expenses are fixed

    a. Compute the profit margin for the year.
    b. Compute average assets for the year.
    c. Compute asset turnover for the year.
    d. Compute return on investment for the year.
    e. If Harriet could increase revenues next year by 25% with an increase in advertising of $15,000 and no changes in asset investment, what would be her new rate of return?

26. *(Return on investment)* For the most recent fiscal year, the Home Division of U.S. Construction Company generated an asset turnover ratio of 6 and a profit margin (as measured by the segment margin) ratio of 3% on sales of $400,000. Compute
    a. average assets employed by Home Division.
    b. segment margin.
    c. ROI.

27. *(Residual income)* Last year, North Division management agreed to a 12% target ROI. The following data have been gathered for the division's operations for the year just ended: average total assets, $2,800,000; revenues, $7,500,000; and expenses, $7,140,000. What is the division's residual income? Did the division successfully meet the target ROI?

28. *(Residual income)* Global Services Company has two divisions, which are operated as investment centers. Information about these divisions is shown below.

	Division #1	Division #2
Sales	$2,400,000	$4,200,000
Total variable costs	600,000	2,870,000
Total fixed cost	1,400,000	500,000
Average assets invested	2,200,000	6,100,000

a. What is the residual income of each division if the "charge" on invested assets is 10%? Which division is doing a better job?
b. If the only change next year is that sales increase by 15%, what will be the residual income of each division? Which division would be doing a better job?
c. Why did the answers to the second questions in parts a and b differ?

29. *(Return on investment, residual income)* Legal Associates, Inc. has a target rate of return of 12% for its Corporate Law Division. For 1994, the Corporate Law Division generated gross fees of $4,000,000 on average assets of $2,000,000. The Corporate Law Division's variable costs were 35% of sales and fixed costs were $1,500,000. For 1994, compute the division's
   a. ROI   b. residual income   c. profit margin   d. asset turnover

30. *(Missing data)* Fill in the missing numbers in the following three independent cases.

	Case #1	Case #2	Case #3
Revenue	a	$450,000	k
Expenses	$100,000	f	l
Segment income	b	g	$ 20,000
Average total assets	$300,000	h	m
Asset turnover	c	4	2.5
Profit margin	d	8%	n
Achieved ROI	e	i	12%
Residual income	$ 15,000	$ 5,000	o
Target ROI	12%	j	14%

31. *(Missing data)* Three Rivers Dental Supply Company relies on a residual income measure to evaluate the performance of certain segment managers. The target rate of return for all segments is 12%. One segment, Tongue Depressors, generated segment income of $800,000 for the year just ended. For the same period, Tongue Depressors' residual income was $320,000. Compute
   a. the amount of average assets employed by Tongue Depressors.
   b. the ROI for Tongue Depressors.

32. *(Investment acquisition)* ABC Corp. has a target rate of return of 15%. C Division is analyzing a new investment that promises to generate an ROI of 25% and a residual income of $20,000.
   a. What is the acquisition cost of the investment C Division is considering?
   b. What is the estimated net income from the new project?

33. *(Throughput)* The Chocolate Bar Company has historically evaluated divisional performance on financial measures exclusively. Top managers have become increasingly concerned with this approach and are now actively seeking alternative measures that more accurately assess success in the activities that generate value for customers. One promising measure is throughput. To experiment with an annual throughput measure, management has gathered the following historical information on one of its larger operating divisions:

Units started into production	200,000
Total good units completed	130,000
Total hours of processing time	80,000
Total hours of divisional time	120,000

   a. What is the productive capacity of the division?
   b. What is the process yield of the division?
   c. What is the percentage productive processing time?
   d. What is the total throughput per hour?

34. *(Matching)* Match each of the lettered items on the left with the number of the best matching item on the right.

a. Asset turnover	**1.** Proportion of total time that is value-added time
b. Dollar days of inventory	
c. Throughput	**2.** Completed and sold output
d. Profit margin	**3.** An inventory control measure
e. Synchronous management	**4.** Proportion of total units that are good units
f. Productive processing time	**5.** Profit margin times asset turnover
g. Process yield	**6.** Total profit less target profit
h. Du Pont model	**7.** Ratio of income to sales
i. Productive capacity	**8.** Ratio of sales to assets
j. Residual income	**9.** All efforts that help managers achieve goals
	10. Total units that could be produced during a period

COMMUNICATION ACTIVITIES

35. You have been assigned the task of defining "income" and "assets" as they will be used to evaluate investment center performance in your firm, which is comprised of multiple investment centers. Explain how you will treat each of the following in your definitions:
   a. allocated corporate costs.
   b. corporate income taxes.
   c. salary of the investment center manager.
   d. idle assets under the control of the investment center manager.
   e. direct fixed costs of the investment center.
   f. current values or historical values for assets.

36. Below are a number of transactions affecting a specific division within a multiple-division company. For each independent transaction, indicate whether it would increase (IN), decrease (D), have no effect (N), or have an indeterminate (I) effect on the following measures: asset turnover, profit margin, ROI, and RI for the present fiscal year.
   a. The division writes down an inventory of obsolete finished goods. The journal entry is:

Cost of Goods Sold	$80,000	
Finished Goods Inventory		$80,000

   b. A special overseas order is accepted. Its sales price is well below the sales price on normal business but is greater than all costs traceable to this order.
   c. A piece of equipment is sold for $150,000. The equipment's original cost was $900,000. At the time of sale, the book value of the equipment is $180,000. The sale of the equipment has no effect on product sales.
   d. The division fires its R&D manager. The manager will not be replaced during the current fiscal year.

e. The company raises its target rate of return for this division from 10% to 12%.

f. At midyear, the division manager decides to increase scheduled annual production by 1,000 units. This decision has no effect on scheduled sales.

g. During the year, the division manager spends an additional $250,000 on advertising. Sales immediately increase thereafter.

h. The division manager replaces a labor-intensive operation with machine technology. This action has no effect on sales, but total annual operating expenses are expected to decline by 10%.

37. Training Services, Ltd. has two divisions operating in the management training field. One division, Domestic, operates strictly in the U.S.; the other division, Foreign, operates exclusively in the Pacific Rim countries. Both divisions are evaluated, in part, based on a measure of ROI. For the most recent year, Domestic's ROI was 14% and Foreign's ROI was 8%. One of the tasks of upper management is to evaluate the relative performance of the divisions so that an appropriate performance pay bonus can be determined for each manager. In evaluating relative performance, provide arguments as to why the determination of relative performance should

a. include a comparison of the ROI measures in the two divisions.

b. not include a comparison of ROI measures in the two divisions.

38. The Jackson Corporation is a large manufacturing company with several divisions. Each division is viewed as an investment center and has virtually complete autonomy for product development, marketing, and production.

Performance of division managers is evaluated periodically by senior management. Divisional return on investment (ROI) is the sole criterion used in performance evaluation under current corporate policy. Corporate management believes ROI is an adequate measure because it incorporates quantitative information from the divisional income statement and balance sheet in the analysis.

Some division managers complained that a single criterion for performance evaluation is insufficient and ineffective. These managers have compiled a list of criteria that they believe should be used in evaluating the division managers' performance. The criteria include profitability, market position, productivity, product leadership, personnel development, employee attitudes, public responsibility, and balance between short-range and long-range goals.

a. Discuss the shortcomings or possible inconsistencies of using ROI as the sole criterion to evaluate divisional management performance.

b. Discuss the advantages of using multiple criteria versus a single criterion to evaluate divisional management performance.

c. Discuss some ways in which each of the multiple criteria listed by the managers could be evaluated.

d. Describe the problems or disadvantages that can be associated with the implementation of the multiple performance criteria measurement system suggested to Jackson Corporation by its division managers.

(CMA)

PROBLEMS

39. *(Cash flow evaluation)* Keri Kash, the controller of Nevada Gaming Systems Inc., has become increasingly disillusioned with the company's system of evaluating the performance of profit centers and their managers. The present system focuses on a comparison of budgeted to actual income from operations. Ms. Kash's major concern with the current system is the ease with which the measure "income from operations" can be manipulated by profit center managers. The "basic business" of Nevada Gaming Systems Inc. is the design and production of slot machines and other gaming devices. Most sales are made on credit and most pur-

chases are made on account. The profit centers are organized according to product line. Below is a typical quarterly income statement for a profit center, Slot Machines, that appears in the responsibility report for the profit center:

Sales	$5,500,000
Cost of Goods Sold	4,500,000
Gross Profit	$1,000,000
Selling and Administrative Expenses	750,000
Income from Operations	$ 250,000

Ms. Kash has suggested to top management that the company replace the accrual income evaluation measure, "income from operations," with a measure called "cash flow from operations." Ms. Kash suggests that this measure will be less susceptible to manipulation by profit center managers. To defend her position, she compiles a cash flow income statement for the same profit center:

Cash receipts from customers	$4,400,000
Cash payments for production labor, materials, and overhead	(3,600,000)
Cash payments for selling and administrative activities	(700,000)
Cash flow from operations	$ 100,000

a. If Keri Kash is correct about profit center managers manipulating the income measure, where are manipulations probably taking place?
b. Is the proposed cash flow measure less subject to manipulation than the income measure? Explain.
c. Could manipulation be reduced if both the cash flow and income measures were used? Explain.
d. Do the cash and income measures reveal different information about profit center performance? Explain.
e. Could the existing income statement be used more effectively in evaluating performance? Explain.

40. *(Statement of Cash Flows)* The Portland Rubber Company controller prepared the following Statements of Cash Flows for the past three years and the budget for next year (1995):

				Budget
	1992	1993	1994	1995
Net Cash Flows from Operating Activities:				
Net income	$ 41,700	$ 39,200	$ 43,700	$ 45,100
Add net reconciling items	2,200	4,300	3,000	4,000
Total	$ 43,900	$ 43,500	$ 46,700	$ 49,100
Net Cash Flows from Investing Activities:				
Purchase of plant and equipment	$(18,700)		$(12,200)	$(4,600)
Sale (purchase) of investments	8,700	$ (3,600)	(12,600)	(15,800)
Other investing inflows	1,200	800	600	2,400
Total	$ (8,800)	$ (2,800)	$(24,200)	$(18,000)

Net Cash Flows from Financing Activities:				
Payment of notes payable	$(12,000)	$(24,000)	$(15,000)	$(7,000)
Payment of dividends	(20,000)	(7,000)	(13,300)	(20,000)
Total	$(32,000)	$(31,000)	$(28,300)	$(27,000)
Net Change in Cash	$ 3,100	$ 9,700	$ (5,800)	$ 4,100

After preparing the budgeted SCF for 1995, Joanna Jones, the company president, asked you to recompile it based on a separate set of facts. She is evaluating a proposal to purchase a local area network (LAN) computer system for the company at a total cost of $50,000. The proposal has been deemed to provide a satisfactory rate of return. However, she does not want to issue additional stock and she would prefer not to borrow any more money to finance the project.

Projecting the market value of the accumulated investments for the previous three years ($3,600 and $12,600) reveals an estimate that these investments could be liquidated for $18,400. Jones said the investments scheduled for 1995 did not need to be purchased and that dividends could be reduced to 40% of the budgeted amount. These changes are the only ones that will be made to the original forecast.

a. Evaluate the cash trends for the company over the past three years.

b. Giving effect to the changes above, prepare a revised 1995 budgeted Statement of Cash Flows and present the original and revised in a comparative format.

c. Based on the revised budgeted SCF, can the LAN computer system be purchased if Jones desires an increase in cash of at least $1,000?

d. Comment on the usefulness of the report prepared in part b to Joanna Jones.

41. *(Missing data, ROI)* Data for three similar companies for 1994 are as follows:

	Red Company	White Company	Blue Company
Average total assets	?	?	$ 600,000
Net operating income	$ 100,000	?	120,000
Sales	1,400,000	$440,000	1,400,000
Return on investment	5%	?	?
Margin on sales	?	10%	?
Asset turnover	?	1.8	?

a. Fill in the missing information.

b. Where needed, recommend how to improve the ROI for each company.

42. *(ROI)* California Mining Equipment, Inc. manufactures various pieces of equipment used in extraction industries. For 1994, the company's Conveyor System Division had the following performance targets:

Asset turnover	1.6
Profit margin	8%

The actual 1994 results for the division are summarized below:

Total assets at year end 1993	$4,800,000
Total assets at year end 1994	6,400,000
Sales	7,200,000
Operating expenses	6,400,000

a. For 1994, did the Conveyor System Division achieve its target objectives for ROI, asset turnover, and profit margin?

b. Where, as indicated by the performance measures, are the most likely areas to improve performance?

c. If California Mining Equipment, Inc. has an overall target return of 12.8%, what was the Conveyor System Division's residual income for 1994?

43. *(ROI, suboptimization)* Strategic Marketers Inc. has a two-division organizational structure and evaluates its managers using an ROI formula. For the forthcoming period, divisional estimates of relevant measures are:

	Division 1	Division 2	Total Company
Sales	$1,500,000	$6,000,000	$7,500,000
Expenses	1,350,000	5,250,000	6,600,000
Divisional assets	1,250,000	3,750,000	5,000,000

The managers of both operating divisions have the authority to make decisions regarding new investments. The manager of Division 1 is presently contemplating an investment in an additional asset that would generate an ROI of 14%, and the manager of Division #2 is considering an investment in an additional asset that would generate an ROI of 19%.

a. Compute the projected ROI for each division, disregarding the contemplated new investments.

b. Based on your answer in part a, which of the managers is likely to actually invest in the additional assets under consideration?

c. Are the outcomes of the investment decisions in part b likely to be consistent with overall corporate goals? Explain.

d. If Strategic Marketers Inc. evaluated the division managers' performance using a residual income measure with a target return of 17%, would the outcomes of the investment decisions be different from what you described in part b? Explain.

44. *(Adjusting income for ROI purposes)* Bobbie Daring manages a division of Harbor Resources Company. She is evaluated on the basis of return on investment and residual income. Near the end of November 1994, Bobbie was at home reviewing the division's financial information as well as some activities projected for the remainder of the year. The information Bobbie was reviewing follows.

1. Sales for 1994 are projected at 100,000 units. Each unit has a selling price of $30. Bobbie has received a purchase order from a new customer for 5,000 units. The purchase order states that the units should be shipped on Jan. 3, 1995, for arrival on Jan. 5.

2. The division had a beginning inventory for the year of 500 units, each costing $10. Purchases of 99,500 units have been made steadily throughout the year and the cost per unit has been constant at $10. Bobbie intends to make a purchase of 5,200 units before year-end. This purchase will leave her with a 200-unit balance in inventory after she makes the shipment to the new customer. Carrying costs for the units are quite high, but ordering costs are extremely low. The division uses a LIFO cost flow assumption for inventory.

3. Bobbie has just received a notice from her primary supplier that he is going out of business and is selling his remaining stock of 15,000 units for $9.00 each. Bobbie makes a note to herself to place her final order for the year from this supplier.

4. Shipping expenses are $.50 per unit sold.
5. Advertising is $5,000 per month. The advertising for the division is in newspapers and television spots. No advertising has been discussed for December; Bobbie intends to have the sales manager call the paper and TV station early next week.
6. Salaries are projected through the end of the year at $700,000, assuming that the position to be vacated by Bobbie's personnel manager is filled on December 1. The personnel manager's job pays $66,000 per year. Bobbie has an interview on Monday with an individual who appears to be a good candidate for the position.
7. Other general and administrative costs for the full year are estimated to total $590,000.
8. As Bobbie is preparing her pro forma income statement for the year, she receives a telephone call from the maintenance supervisor at the office. He informs Bobbie that electrical repairs to the office heating system are necessary, which will cost $10,000. She asks if the repairs are essential, to which the supervisor replies, "No, the office won't burn down if you don't make them, but they are advisable for energy efficiency and long-term operation of the system." Bobbie tells the supervisor to see her on Monday at 8:00 A.M.

Bobbie was fairly pleased with her pro forma results. While the results did provide the 13% rate of return on investment desired by Harbor Resources, the results did not reach the 16% rate needed for Bobbie to receive a bonus. Bobbie has an asset investment base of $4,500,000.

a. Prepare a 1994 pro forma income statement for Bobbie's division. Determine the amount of residual income for the division.
b. Bobbie's less-than-scrupulous sister, Ima, walked into the house at this time. When she heard that Bobbie was not going to receive a bonus, Ima said, "Here, let me take care of this for you." She proceeded to recompute the pro forma income statement and, based on her computation of $723,000 of income, Bobbie would be receiving her bonus. Prepare Ima's pro forma income statement.
c. What future difficulties might arise if Bobbie acts in a manner that will make Ima's pro forma income statement figures a reality?

45. *(Throughput)* Fernando Sanchez is concerned about the quantity of goods being produced by the Mexican Division of the Auto Products Company. The following production data are available for April 1995:

Total units	30,000
Total good units completed	26,400
Total hours of processing time	12,000
Total hours of departmental time	19,000

Determine each of the following for this department for the month of April.
a. What is the productive capacity?
b. What is the percentage productive processing time?
c. What is the productive yield?
d. What is the total throughput per hour?
e. If Fernando can eliminate 20% of the non-value-added time, how would throughput per hour for this data differ?
f. If Fernando can increase quality output to a yield of 94% and eliminate 20% of the non-value-added time, how would throughput per hour for this data differ?
g. How would Fernando determine how the non-value-added time was being spent in the department? What suggestions do you have for Fernando to decrease non-value-added time and increase yield?

h. If only 22,500 of the units produced in April had been sold, would your answers to any of the above questions differ? If so, how? If not, why not?

46. *(Dollar days of inventory)* Sidharta Bhutang is in charge of the U.S. Marketing Department of Indonesia Trading Company. Sidharta tends to purchase products in economic order quantities (EOQ) regardless of weekly variations in the sales budget. For example, one product has an EOQ of 2,000 units. This product costs $8.50 per unit. On average, this product sells out in about 5 weeks. The company controller has suggested that Sidharta talk to the supplier about buying the product on an arrangement that more nearly approximates a just-in-time basis. Under this arrangement, the product would be delivered twice a week in lots of 200 units.

   a. Determine, as of the beginning of each of the five-week use periods, the dollar days of inventory investment caused by Sidharta's EOQ purchases.

   b. Determine the quantity of dollar days of savings that would result if the just-in-time purchasing system were implemented and deliveries were made on Monday mornings and Wednesdays at noon.

   c. Why would the dollars days of inventory stockpiled in a plant be of concern to managers, since inventory is an asset?

47. *(Comprehensive, appendix)* The Texas Chili Company produces a variety of canned soups. The firm purchases all raw materials locally, cooks and processes the materials, and cans the soup in single-portion containers. The canned soup is distributed through several national wholesalers. On January 1, 1994, Janet Freemore was promoted to the production manager position in the Texas plant. While Ms. Freemore was given control over all production activities, she is not responsible for acquiring soup component materials. All production supervisors are evaluated based on their ability to meet certain standard costs. Only costs that are controllable by the production manager are included in the performance evaluation (all are variable). Standard costs for 1994 were set as follows for the Texas plant:

	Per Can of Soup
Direct labor	$0.03
Repairs	.05
Maintenance	.04
Indirect labor	.05
Power	.10

Actual 1994 costs were as follows for production of 12,000,000 cans of soup at the Texas plant:

Direct labor	$ 340,000
Repairs	590,000
Maintenance	476,000
Indirect labor	599,000
Power	1,170,000

   a. Prepare a performance report for Janet Freemore for 1994.

   b. Evaluate Ms. Freemore's performance based on your report.

   c. What performance dimensions are missing from Ms. Freemore's performance evaluation?

   d. Should additional performance measures (other than standard cost variances) be added to evaluate the production manager's performance? If so, identify the measures you would recommend.

CASES

48. The Notewon Corporation is a highly diversified company that grants its divisional executives a significant amount of authority in operating the divisions. Each division is responsible for its own sales, pricing, production, operating costs, and the management of accounts receivable, inventories, accounts payable, and facilities' usage. Cash is managed by corporate headquarters; all cash in excess of a division's normal operating needs is transferred periodically to corporate headquarters for redistribution or investment.

   The divisional executives are responsible for presenting requests to corporate management for investment projects. The proposals are analyzed and documented at corporate headquarters. The final decision to commit funds to acquire equipment, to expand existing facilities, or for other investment purposes rests with corporate management.

   The corporation evaluates the performance of division executives by the return-on-investment (ROI) measure. The asset base is composed of fixed assets employed plus working capital exclusive of cash.

   The ROI performance of a divisional executive is the most important appraisal factor for salary changes. In addition, the annual performance bonus is based on the ROI results with increases in ROI having a significant impact on the amount of the bonus.

   The Notewon Corporation adopted the ROI performance measure and related compensation procedures about 10 years ago. The corporation did so to increase divisional managers' awareness of the importance of the profit/asset relationship and to provide additional incentive to the divisional executives to seek investment opportunities.

   The corporation seems to have benefited from the program. ROI for the corporation as a whole increased during the first years of the program. Although ROI has continued to grow in each division, the corporate ROI has declined in recent years. The corporation has accumulated a sizeable amount of cash and short-term marketable securities in the past three years.

   Corporate management is concerned about the increase in short-term marketable securities. A recent article in a financial publication suggested that the use of ROI was overemphasized by some companies with results similar to those experienced by Notewon.

   a. Describe the specific actions division managers might have taken to cause the ROI to grow in each division but decline for the corporation. Illustrate your explanations with appropriate examples.

   b. Explain, using the concepts of goal congruence and motivation of divisional executives, how Notewon Corporation's overemphasis on the ROI measure might result in the recent decline in the corporation's return on investment and the increase in cash and short-term marketable securities.

   c. Discuss how divisional statements of cash flows might provide some additional useful information to divisional executives and corporate management.

   d. What changes could be made in Notewon Corporation's compensation policy to avoid the current problems? Explain your answer.

   (CMA adapted)

49. Terry Travers is the manufacturing supervisor of the Aurora Manufacturing Company, which produces a variety of plastic products. Some of these products are standard items that are listed in the company's catalog; others are made to customer specifications. Each month, Travers receives a performance report displaying the budget for the month, the actual activity for the period, and the variance between budget and actual. Part of Travers's annual performance evaluation

is based on his department's performance against budget. Aurora's purchasing manager, Bob Christensen, also receives monthly performance reports and is evaluated in part on the basis of these reports.

The most recent monthly reports had just been distributed, on the 21st of the month, when Travers met Christensen in the hallway outside their offices. Scowling, Travers began the conversation: "I see we have another set of monthly performance reports hand-delivered by that not very nice junior employee in the budget office. He seemed pleased to tell me that I was in trouble with my performance again."

Christensen: "I got the same treatment. All I ever hear about are the things I haven't done right. Now, I'll have to spend a lot of time reviewing the report and preparing explanations. The worst part is that the information is almost a month old, and we spend all this time on history."

Travers: "My biggest gripe is that our production activity varies a lot from month to month, but we're given an annual budget that's written in stone. Last month, we were shut down for three days when a strike delayed delivery of the basic ingredient used in our plastic formulation, and we had already exhausted our inventory. You know that, of course, since we asked you to call all over the country to find an alternate source of supply. When we got what we needed on a rush basis, we had to pay more than we normally do."

Christensen: "I expect problems like that to pop up from time to time—that's part of my job—but now we'll both have to take a careful look at the report to see where charges are reflected for that rush order. Every month, I spend more time making sure I should be charged for each item reported than I do making plans for my department's daily work. It's really frustrating to see charges for things I have no control over."

Travers: "The way we get information doesn't help, either. I don't get copies of the reports you get, yet a lot of what I do is affected by your department, and by most of the other departments we have. Why do the budget and accounting people assume that I should only be told about my operations even though the president regularly gives us pep talks about how we all need to work together as a team?"

Christensen: "I seem to get more reports than I need, and I am never getting asked to comment until top management calls me on the carpet about my department's shortcomings. Do you ever hear comments when your department shines?"

Travers: "I guess they don't have time to review the good news. One of my problems is that all the reports are in dollars and cents. I work with people, machines, and materials. I need information to help me solve this month's problems—not another report of the dollars expended last month or the month before."

a. Based on the conversation between Terry Travers and Bob Christensen, describe the likely motivation and behavior of these two employees resulting from the Aurora Manufacturing Company's performance reporting system.
b. When properly implemented, performance reporting systems should benefit both employees and companies.
   1. Describe the benefits that can be realized from using a performance reporting system.
   2. Based on the situation presented above, recommend ways for Aurora Manufacturing Company to improve its performance system so as to increase employee motivation.

(CMA *adapted*)

**ETHICS AND
QUALITY
DISCUSSION**

50. *A scheduled launch of the space shuttle* Columbia *was delayed from February 25, 1993, until the middle of March 1993. The problem—confusion over whether a correct engine part was installed. The part in question is a retainer that holds down seals around the turbine of the oxidizer pumps. In the event of a retainer breakage, pieces of retainer could fly into the turbine blades and cause an engine shutdown.*

   A NASA spokesperson indicated that two types of retainers exist and the newer type was to be installed in the space shuttle. However, workers mistakenly installed old retainers in some of NASA's 22 oxidizer pumps. Exactly how that happened is under investigation.

   [SOURCE: Marcia Dunn, "Inspection Problem Will Delay Columbia Flight," (New Orleans) *Times-Picayune* (February 11, 1993), p. A-8.]

   a. How is performance evaluation at NASA inherently different from performance evaluation in a for-profit business?
   b. Is there likely to be a link at NASA between the quality of the product (that is, the space shuttle) and performance evaluation of workers? Explain.
   c. For the space shuttle *Columbia,* what would be the most important performance indicators of quality?

51. Bailey Manufacturing has just initiated a formula bonus plan whereby plant managers are rewarded for various achievements. One of the current criteria for bonuses is the improvement of asset turnover. The plant manager of the Carson City plant told Horace Appleby, his young assistant, to meet him Saturday when the plant was closed. Without explanation, the plant manager specified certain raw materials to be loaded on one of the plant's dump trucks. When the truck was loaded, the plant manager and Horace drove to a secluded mountain road where, to Horace's astonishment, the plant manager flipped a switch and the truck dumped the raw materials down a steep ravine. The plant manager grinned and said that these were obsolete raw materials and the company would run more smoothly without them. For the next several weekends, Horace observed the plant manager doing the same thing. The following month, the plant manager was officially congratulated for improving asset turnover.
   a. How did the dumping improve asset turnover?
   b. What are the ethical problems in this case?
   c. What are Horace's options? Which should he choose and why?

52. Manhattan Electronics Corp. produces a variety of computer products. Recently the firm has revealed plans to expand into new office automation products. To realize the expansion plans, the firm will need to go to the stock market for additional capital in October of this year. Present plans call for raising $200,000,000 in new common equity. Historically, the firm's small notebook computer has been a significant contributor to corporate profits. However, a competitor has recently introduced a notebook model that has rendered Manhattan Electronic's notebook computer obsolete. At some point, the controller has informed the president, the inventory of notebooks needs to be "written down" to realizable value. Because Manhattan Electronics has a large inventory of the notebooks on hand, the write-down will have a very detrimental effect on both the balance sheet and income statement.

   The president, whose compensation is determined in part by corporate profits and in part by stock price, has suggested that the write-downs be deferred until the next fiscal year (next January). He argues that, by deferring the write-down, existing shareholders will realize more value from the shares to be sold in October because the stock market will not be informed of the pending write-downs.

a. What effect are the performance evaluation measures of the president likely to have on his decision to defer the write-down of the obsolete inventory?

b. Is the president's decision to defer the write-down of the inventory an ethical treatment of existing shareholders? Of the potential new shareholders?

c. If you were the controller of Manhattan Electronics, how would you respond to the president's decision to defer the write-down until after issuance of the new stock?

REWARDING PERFORMANCE

LEARNING OBJECTIVES

After completing this chapter, you should be able to answer these questions:

1. How are employee compensation and the concept of maximization of stockholder wealth related?
2. How can performance be rewarded?
3. Why is there a movement toward rewarding group as well as individual performance?
4. What are the potential positive and negative consequences of incentive pay programs?
5. Why do many financial incentive programs now involve shares of or options for common stock?
6. Of what importance are nonmonetary rewards in motivating managers?
7. How do taxes affect alternative compensation plans?
8. Why should ethics be considered in designing a compensation package?
9. What concerns need to be addressed in developing compensation packages for expatriates?

INTRODUCING

EATON CORPORATION

Eaton Corporation is based in Cleveland, Ohio. Eaton may not be a household name, and its products—including gears, engine valves, truck axles, and, at its Lincoln, Illinois plant, circuit breakers—aren't glamorous. But its success in raising productivity and cutting costs throws plenty of doubt on recent hand-wringing about unmotivated American workers and flaccid American corporations.

At its factory in Lincoln and another in Kearney, Nebraska, Eaton encourages workers to take thousands of small steps that incrementally improve the products they make and the processes used to make them. The penny-pinching extends to office workers, who haggle over utility rates, challenge local tax assessments, scrutinize inventory and eliminate paper work. Management shares extensive financial data with employees at the two plants to underscore the link between their performance and the factory's performance.

At 7:30 a.m., it's time for the morning quiz at Eaton's Lincoln factory. Ten union workers, each representing work teams, sit around a boardroom table. "What were our sales yesterday?" asks a supervisor at the head of the table. A worker, glancing at a computer printout, replies that they were $625,275. "And in the month?" From another worker comes the response: $6,172,666.

The staccato review continues on to other vital statistics: the cost of materials and supplies used the day before; the cost of labor, shipping and utilities.

The aim of the exercise isn't simply to help workers understand the bottom line but also to get their help in enhancing it. Out on the shop floor minutes later, Glen Naugle, a worker, tells plant manager William Kelly how sandblasting welding electrodes, rather than machining them, would save $5,126 a year. It's the 193rd time in the past year that Lincoln workers have formally presented their ideas on improving operations to managers.

The savings resulting from such suggestions total $1.4 million and helped Lincoln increase its 1992 first-quarter profit 30% from the previous year. [Valuable employee ideas can earn "Eaton bucks" that are exchangeable at the Eaton factory store for things like sporting goods.]

SOURCE: SOURCE: Thomas F. O'Boyle, "A Manufacturer Grows Efficient by Soliciting Ideas from Employees," *Wall Street Journal* (June 5, 1992), pp. A1, A5. Reprinted by permission of the *Wall Street Journal*, © 1992 Dow Jones & Company, Inc. All rights reserved worldwide.

When workers help to control costs and the bottom line increases, stockholders benefit through increased dividends or stock market prices. Throughout American business management literature, the expressed primary function of managers is to maximize stockholder value or stockholder wealth. Stockholders are granted this special attention because they (acting through the board of directors) have the unique power to hire, fire, and set compensation for top managers who, in turn, can hire, fire, and set compensation for workers.[1] On the

[1] We use the term employees to refer to all of the personnel of an organization. The terms workers and managers are used to identify mutually exclusive groups of employees.

other hand, workers and managers are naturally selfish to some degree and would prefer to maximize their own wealth rather than that of the stockholders. Consequently, the burden of motivating managers and employees to maximize stockholder wealth is clearly borne by the stockholders through their specifications of managerial pay and performance incentives and rewards.

Accounting frequently plays a primary role in defining expected performance, monitoring and measuring actual performance, and determining the quantity and quality of appropriate employee rewards. In Chapter 22, a variety of techniques to measure employee performance is discussed. This chapter explores the relationship of organizational plans, strategies, and performance to employee rewards as well as the tax and ethical implications of various compensation systems.

COMPENSATION STRATEGY

Compensation strategy

As noted in prior chapters, many changes (technological advances, globalization, quality orientation) have occurred in business in the recent past. These changes have created problems and opportunities in establishing responsibility and rewarding individuals for organizational performance. There are as many different compensation plans as there are organizations. A rational compensation plan ties its component elements (organizational goals, performance measurements, and employee rewards) together in a cohesive package. The relations and interactions among these elements are shown in Exhibit 23–1. In this model, the organizational strategic goals are determined by the board of directors (the governing body representing stockholder interests) and top management. From these strategic goals, the organization's critical success factors are identified and operational targets are defined. Operational targets, for example, could include specified annual net income, unit sales of a specific product, quality measures, customer service measures, or costs.

The board of directors and top management must also decide on a **compensation strategy** for the organization. This strategy should provide a foundation for the compensation plan by addressing the role compensation should play in the organization. It is also essential that the strategy be made known to everyone, from the board of directors to the lowest-level worker.

Financial incentives

The traditional American compensation strategy usually differentiates three basic employee groups, which are compensated differently. Top managers' compensation contains a salary element, but significant **financial incentives** or monetary rewards are provided for performance above targeted objectives. Usually these targeted objectives are specified in terms of some financial accounting measure such as companywide net income or earnings per share. Middle managers are given salaries with the opportunity for future raises based on some (again usually accounting-related) measure of performance such as segment income or divisional return on investment. Workers are paid wages (usually specified by union contract or tied to the minimum wage law) for the number of hours worked or production level achieved; current or year-end bonuses may arise when performance is above some specified quantitative measure. If provided, worker performance bonuses are usually fairly small in amount or percentage of wages. Significant incentive pay is usually limited to top management (and possibly the sales force)—regardless of the levels of the employees who may have contributed to increased profits.

This type of traditional compensation system provides little motivation for employees who are not top managers to improve organizational performance.

Compensation systems that reward sales growth or near-term accounting profits and personnel systems that reward managers for increasing the size of their organizations

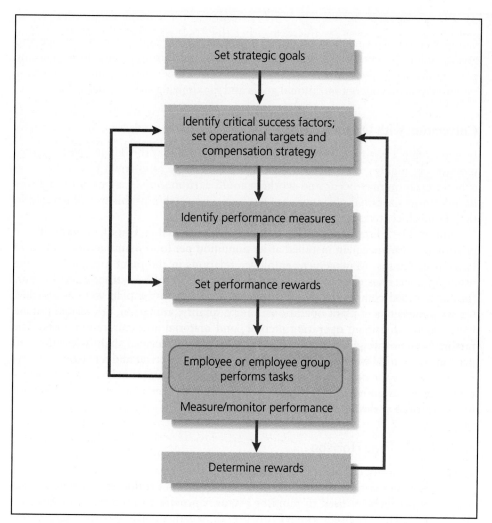

are a problem. Top executives should be rewarded in a way comparable with how share-holders are rewarded; line managers should be rewarded for managing the value drivers under their control. Incentive compensation should be a large part of any manager's compensation.[2]

In addition, in an era of cost-competitiveness, automatic cost-of-living adjustments and annual pay raises for lower-level employees are being reduced or eliminated. The trend is to tie compensation strategy more frequently to performance by providing incentive-based compensation systems (such as that discussed at Eaton Corporation) to all employees, regardless of organizational level or function. But the degree of change is slow: "While 98% of 270 large-company personnel managers surveyed by [the compensation consulting firm of] Towers Perrin say employee pay should reflect performance, only 48% say their systems achieve that goal."[3]

---

[2]David L. Wenner and Richard W. LeBer, "Managing for Shareholder Value—From Top to Bottom," *Harvard Business Review* (November–December 1989), pp. 64–65.
[3]Albert R. Karr, "Pay-for-Performance Plans Put a Premium on Long-Term Gains," *Wall Street Journal* (September 1, 1992), p. A1.

PAY-FOR-PERFORMANCE PLANS

Compensation plans need to encourage higher levels of employee performance and loyalty, while concurrently lowering overall costs and raising profits. Implementing plans of this nature would indicate a compensation strategy that encourages behavior essential to achieving organizational goals and maximizing stockholder value.

Correlation with Organizational Goals

In structuring a pay-for-performance plan, it is crucial that the defined performance measures be highly correlated with the organization's operational targets. Otherwise, suboptimization may occur and workers could earn incentive pay even though the broader organizational objectives are not achieved. Such a problem is illustrated in the "Bonus Incentives Go Awry" News Note.

Exhibit 23–2 lists the criteria employed by the Quaker Oats Company in the pay-for-performance plan installed at its nonunion pet food manufacturing plant in Lawrence, Kansas. Management-employee relations in the plant are good and the resulting open lines of communication were considered when structuring this performance-based plan. Performance measures included in the plan were established for six dimensions of plant operations: safety, quality, sanitation, designated critical factor focus, divisional operating income, and material and conversion costs. The factors were not weighted evenly; the financial factors received slightly less than 50 percent of the total weight. Although Quaker Oats has not yet had a reasonable time frame to assess the new pay plan's results, company managers believe that information sharing, awareness of bottom-line performance, coordination, and teamwork have improved at the plant.

Appropriate Time Horizon

A second important consideration in designing a performance-based system involves time. One recent criticism leveled at American businesses is that the measures (such as annual net income) used to monitor performance are focused on the short-run. Alternatively, the espoused primary function of American business is the maximization of shareholder wealth, which is inherently a long-run consideration. The message of this criticism is that short-run measures are not necessarily viable proxies for the long-run concept of wealth maximization. In particular, short-term profits may be garnered at the expense of long-term growth.

▌ EXHIBIT 23–2

Pay for Performance Plan at Quaker Oats

Criteria for performance-based pay plan:

1. Must link pay with divisional and plant performance
2. Must be fair in compensating employees
3. Must encourage employees to share information
4. Costs of the plan should be a reflection of the financial health of the business
5. Must be consistent with objectives of the plant and division
6. Must match the plant's culture
7. Should generate a stable amount of compensation
8. Must involve employees and foster communication

SOURCE: James P. Guthrie and Edward P. Cunningham, "Pay for Performance for Hourly Workers: The Quaker Oats Alternative," *Compensation and Benefits Review* (March–April, 1992), pp. 18–23. Reprinted by permission of publisher, from *Compensation and Benefits Review*, Mar/Apr 1992. © 1992 American Management Association, New York. All rights reserved.

NEWS NOTE

Bonus Incentives Go Awry

Installing a bonus plan requires careful consideration of the performance measures. If there are no clear proxies for the organizational objectives or targets, then any performance measures that trigger the payment of a bonus may not result in the achievement of the organization's objectives.

In testimony to this statement, compensation consultant Craig Schneier describes an experience by one of his clients who decided to pay the purchasing department employees bonuses if they kept the cost of purchases down:

"The problem was, to make that happen they were relying on second-tier sources and accepting poor-quality materials. The company was in the middle of a very big order, and the fasteners were lousy and ended up costing millions of dollars, while the [purchasing] department walked away with big bonuses."

SOURCE: Amanda Bennett, "Paying Workers to Meet Goals Spreads, But Gauging Performance Proves Tough," *Wall Street Journal* (September 10, 1991), pp. B1, B4. Reprinted by permission of the *Wall Street Journal,* © 1991 Dow Jones & Company, Inc. All rights reserved worldwide.

In responding to this criticism, pay-for-performance criteria should encourage workers to adopt a long-run perspective. Many financial incentives now involve shares of corporate common stock. When employees become stockholders in their employer company, they tend to develop the same perspective as other stockholders: long-run wealth maximization.

Consideration of Employee Age

Employee age is a third important factor in designing employee incentive plans. Younger employees, for natural reasons, may have a longer-term perspective than older employees who expect to retire from the firm in a few years. In designing employee incentives, this difference in perspective between younger and older employees should be given due regard.

To illustrate how age can affect decision processes, consider the case of Elaine Bermudez, a division manager evaluating two new projects. Each project would require an initial investment of $500,000. The projects promise to generate the following annual net returns:

Year	Project 1	Project 2
1	$ (250,000)	$ 300,000
2	(150,000)	200,000
3	0	0
4	300,000	(100,000)
5	600,000	(300,000)
6	500,000	(40,000)
Total	$1,000,000	$ 60,000

Assume that, based on the usual net present value criterion, Project 1 is acceptable and Project 2 is unacceptable. Consequently, Project 1 increases shareholder value and Project 2 decreases shareholder value. Further, assume that Elaine is evaluated, in part, based on the return on investment (ROI) generated by her division. If Elaine is two years from retirement, she would be reluctant to invest in Project 1 because she

NEWS NOTE   Pay-for-Performance at General Dynamics

[O]ne element of the plan is a gain-sharing provision that gives senior executives annual bonuses equal to their base salaries, under one condition: that General Dynamics Stock trades for 10 consecutive days at a price at least $10 a share above where it stood when the plan was adopted.... At least half of each bonus paid as a direct result of increasing shareholder value must remain in a General Dynamics account, the value of which we intend to link directly to the company's long-term performance until the individual participant reaches age 65.... Consequently, every manager who is part of gain-sharing has a continuing, tangible incentive to work to increase shareholder value over the long term.

The plan was adopted in February of 1991. On May 6, 1991, the stock price met the conditions specified above and managers split a pool of $5.1 million.

SOURCE: William A. Anders, "Hefty Bonuses for Hefty Gains," *Wall Street Journal* (May 20, 1991), p. A18. Reprinted by permission of the *Wall Street Journal*, © 1991 Dow Jones & Company, Inc. All rights reserved worldwide.

would never realize the positive ROI effects of this project. The positive benefits from Project 1 (or the negative effects of Project 2) would be realized by her successor. Elaine would be more enthusiastic about investing in Project 2 because, in the two years prior to her retirement, her division's ROI would be enhanced. A younger manager with a longer-term time perspective would likely find Project 1 acceptable and Project 2 unacceptable.

Balance Group and Individual Benefits

A fourth consideration in designing worker incentives is to balance the incentives provided for both groups (or teams) and individuals. In automated production systems, workers function more by indirectly monitoring and controlling machinery and are therefore less directly involved in hands-on production. Additionally, evolving organizational and managerial philosophies, such as total quality management and quality circles, have stressed group performance and the performance of work in teams.

Incentives for small groups and individuals are often virtual substitutes. As the group grows larger, incentives must be in place for both the group and the individual. Group incentives are necessary to encourage cooperation among workers. On the other hand, if *only* group incentives are offered, the incentive compensation system may be ineffective because the reward for individual effort goes to the group. The larger the group size, the smaller the individual's share of the group reward becomes. Eventually, individual workers will be encouraged to **shirk** or "free-ride" on the group. This situation occurs when individuals perceive their proportional shares of the group reward as insufficient to compensate for their efforts.

Shirking

Management Ownership

A final consideration in designing a performance reward system for upper management rewards is the degree of management ownership. Unlike managers at many small firms, managers of large firms often are not owners. When the managers and owners are different groups, a new set of issues emerges with respect to organizational performance. The two groups do not automatically have compatible interests with respect to the use of organizational resources. Consequently, incentive systems must be designed to align the interests of the two groups.

According to a survey by Hay Group, companies in which chief executives own a relatively large amount of company stock typically have greater stock-price performance.

INDUSTRY	AVERAGE PERCENT SHARES OWNED BY CEO	ANNUALIZED TOTAL RETURN TO SHAREHOLDERS (1989–1991)
Chemical		
High-ownership companies	.84	21.20%
Low-ownership companies	.63	– .40
Retail		
High-ownership companies	3.53	48.46%
Low-ownership companies	1.51	7.28
Pharmaceuticals		
High-ownership companies	1.21	57.00%
Low-ownership companies	.12	27.00
Insurance		
High-ownership companies	2.65	24.18%
Low-ownership companies	1.79	11.15

NOTES: Average percent shares of company owned is the number of shares owned by the chief executive, plus stock options exercisable within 60 days, as a percent of the shares outstanding of the company. The shareholder return is the annualized compound growth rate of a stock purchase, including dividends paid out as cash.

SOURCE: Hay Group, "The More You Own, the More You Earn," *Wall Street Journal* (April 21, 1993), p. R9. Reprinted by permission of the *Wall Street Journal,* © 1993 Dow Jones & Company, Inc. All rights reserved worldwide.

Many companies (including Eastman Kodak, Xerox, Union Carbide, and Hershey Foods) are beginning to either mandate or encourage top management stock ownership. As indicated in Exhibit 23–3, a recent survey found that chief executive stock ownership seems to enhance corporate profits. In the News Note on page 1004 entitled "Pay-for-Performance," William Anders, chairman of General Dynamics, describes the stock ownership plan instituted at the company in 1991.

Once the target objectives and compensation strategy are known, performance measures for individual employees or employee groups can be determined based on their required contribution to the operational plan. Performance measures should link the basic business strategies, directly or indirectly with individual actions. As discussed in the previous chapter, employee performance is typically measured relative to some designated set of financial and nonfinancial performance standards.

CONSIDERATIONS IN SETTING PERFORMANCE MEASURES

Degree of Control Over Performance Output

As companies shift from evaluating workers through observing their inputs to evaluating them based on their outputs, new problems for the pay/performance relationship are created. Earlier chapters stress the importance of evaluating managers and workers only on the basis of controllable factors. Most performance measures tend to capture results that are a function of both controllable and noncontrollable factors.

Actual performance is a function of worker effort, worker skill, and random effects. The random effects include performance measurement error, problems or effi-

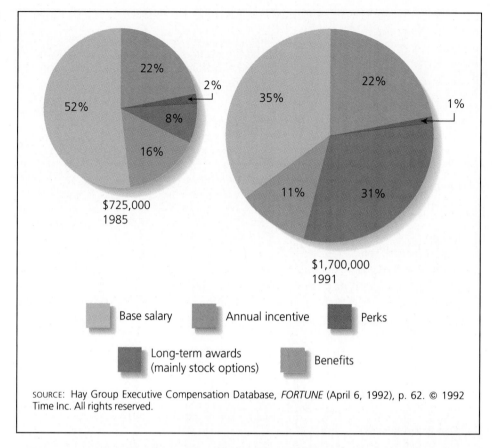

$725,000
1985

$1,700,000
1991

Base salary   Annual incentive   Perks

Long-term awards
(mainly stock options)   Benefits

SOURCE: Hay Group Executive Compensation Database, *FORTUNE* (April 6, 1992), p. 62. © 1992 Time Inc. All rights reserved.

ciencies created by co-workers or adjacent work stations, illness, and weather-related production problems. After the actual performance is measured, it is impossible (in many instances) to determine the contributions of the controllable and noncontrollable factors to the achieved performance. Consequently, the worker bears the risk of the outcome effects of both types of factors. Thus, in performance-based evaluations, determining the appropriate amount of compensation for workers is somewhat riskier than when fairly strict output measurements are used. Efforts should be made to identify performance measures that minimize the risk borne by the worker and are associated with noncontrollable factors.

At the basic worker level, performance measures should be specific and typically should have a short-run focus—usually on cost and/or quality control. At higher levels in the organizational hierarchy, increasingly more elements are related to the critical success factors under an individual's control and responsibility. Performance measures should, by necessity, become less specific, focus on a longer time horizon, and be more concerned with organizational longevity rather than short-run cost control or income. This type of thinking has resulted in shifts in pay incentives at the CEO level, as shown in Exhibit 23–4, which is based on information from 282 medium- to large-size companies.

Once the operational targets, compensation strategy, and performance measurements are determined, appropriate target rewards can be specified. These rewards should motivate individual employees to contribute in a manner congruent with the operational objectives and it is essential that employees be able to relate their performance to the reward structure.

Incentives Relative to Organizational Level

As with performance measures, an employee's organizational level and current compensation should affect the types of rewards chosen. Individuals at different levels of employment typically view monetary rewards differently because of the relationship of pay to standard of living. Relative pay scales are essential to recognizing the value of monetary rewards to different employees. At lower employee levels, more incentives should be monetary and short-term; at higher levels, more incentives should be nonmonetary and long-term. The system should, though, include some nonmonetary and long-term incentives for lower-level employees and some monetary and short-term incentives for top management. Such a two-facet compensation system provides lower-paid people with tangible rewards (more money) that directly enhance their lifestyles, and also provides rewards (such as stock options) that cause them to take a long-run "ownership" view of the organization. In turn, top managers, who are well paid by most standards, would receive more rewards (such as stock and stock options) that should cause them to be more concerned about the organization's long-term well-being rather than short-term personal gains.

Performance Plans and Feedback

As employees perform their required tasks, performance related to the measurement standards is monitored. Changes in the business environment have weakened the direct relationship between individual effort and organizational performance. Because many organizational tasks are currently being performed by teams rather than individuals, both types of effort and performance need to be monitored. For example, at Robbie Manufacturing (in Lenexa, Kansas), "shop-floor [employees working] as a team to achieve the company's overall goals may enable them to receive a percentage of their base compensation in bonus. However, if the team does well, but an individual does not, he or she will not receive a share of the bonus money."[4] Comparing the performance to the target(s) and to the compensation strategy will determine the reward to be provided.

The two feedback loops in the model shown in Exhibit 23–1 exist so that any problems identified in one period can be corrected in future periods. The first feedback loop relates to the monitoring and measurement of performance, which must be considered in setting targets for the following periods. The second feedback loop relates to the rewards given and the compensation strategy's effectiveness. Both loops are essential in the managerial planning process.

Since such great diversity can exist between organizational performance and employee rewards, a wide variety of pay plans also exists in businesses. The major types of compensatory arrangements for workers and managers are discussed next.

WORKER COMPENSATION

In addition to the recent competitive changes, organizational culture, local laws, union affiliation, and political considerations affect the choice of pay plan. For example, while the piece rate pay plan may work effectively for some U.S. businesses, such a compensation plan may not work at all in a Japanese plant. The Japanese work force is more attuned to the group and organization than to the individual. A plan that determines worker compensation based on individual performance would clash with the Japanese culture. And, as the "Risky" News Note on page 1008 indicates, installing a performance-based pay plan can be difficult if the plan's objectives are not clearly specified and/or if the organizational culture is not suited to such a plan.

The most basic of all reward plans consists of hourly, weekly, monthly, or other **periodic compensation**, which is based on spending time at work rather than on accomplishing tasks. Different workers may command different periodic pay rates/amounts because of seniority, skill, or educational level. However, this type of com-

Periodic compensation

---

[4]"Robbie Manufacturing Plans that Motivate," *(Grant Thornton) Manufacturing Issues* (Summer 1990), p. 5.

NEWS NOTE

The Risky Pay-for-Performance Plan

A survey by Hewitt and Associates indicates that 51% of American companies have performance-based pay plans for employees other than top management. However, implementing such plans can be difficult, as indicated by the experience of Du Pont.

[T]he (pay for performance) program required employees of its fibers business group to risk a percentage of pay for a potentially higher return if the unit's profits grew. For a while the program "changed the way a lot of people behaved and thought," says Patricia Beagle, a fashion marketing representative at Du Pont. "I found my secretary routing me through Godforsaken parts of the country" to save $300 on travel costs.

While the program initially saved costs and increased profits, the program was eventually dropped when the prospects seemed likely that a dip in sales and profits in the unit was going to occur and employees would suffer a resultant cut in their compensation.

SOURCE: Amanda Bennett, "Paying Workers to Meet Goals Spreads, But Gauging Performance Proves Tough," *Wall Street Journal* (September 10, 1991), pp. B1, B4. Reprinted by permission of the *Wall Street Journal*, © 1991 Dow Jones & Company, Inc. All rights reserved worldwide.

pensation provides no immediate link between performance and reward. The only motivational aspects of periodic compensation are the prospects for advancement to a higher periodic pay rate/amount, demotion to a lower pay rate/amount, or dismissal. Because this pay plan provides little incentive to achieve, worker performance is monitored by superiors rather than tracked by financial records. Organizational performance is ensured through oversight and instruction instead of the motivation of the performance/reward relationship.

Worker Pay and Performance Links

As discussed earlier, the competitive environment in many industries has undergone substantial changes that have, among other effects, led to companies using greater

Most line workers are compensated on an hourly or piece rate method. Tying their pay in some way to both their own and their company's performance provides an incentive to engage in greater cost and quality control.

automation and fewer labor-intensive technologies. Also, evolving management philosophies are now emphasizing the need for workers to perform in teams and groups. An interesting paradox has been created by these changes. First, workers are more detached from the production function and more involved with higher-technology tasks, so it is more difficult to control workers through direct oversight and supervision. These changes require firms to rely more on results-based evaluations even though identifying appropriate performance evaluation criteria is now more difficult because of the more indirect worker-production relationship. Nevertheless, the trend is to rely more on performance-based evaluation and less on direct supervision to control worker behavior.

One common performance-based pay plan is **merit pay**, in which a pay increment is earned after achieving a specific performance level. While merit pay typically represents a raise in the base pay that continues throughout the worker's tenure with the firm, some merit pay plans may expire at some future date, or be made contingent on a continuing high level of performance.

Merit pay

A variety of other performance-based pay plans exists. For some workers, the basic wage may be partly supplanted with a **contingent pay** plan. Contingent pay is not guaranteed like the basic wage, but is dependent on the achievement of some performance objective. The contingent pay plan adds a pay-for-performance dimension to the compensation package. The contingent pay can be a fixed amount or may vary with, for example, the level of achieved sales or profit. It can be paid in cash, stock, or some other form such as company product. Also, the plan can be structured to apply to group or individual performance. For a contingent pay plan to be successful, managers must have clear goals that they expect to achieve by implementing such a plan. Further, the organizational culture and environment must be supportive of the plan.

Contingent pay

At the extreme end of the performance-based pay incentive plans are **piece rate** payment arrangements wherein workers are paid a flat rate for each unit of work accomplished. Some alternatives may combine the piece rate with a basic hourly rate to guarantee workers a minimal return on their time and effort. Such combination-type piece rate plans serve to protect workers from poor judgments or errors in setting piece rates. The "Pay is Consistently Sizable" News Note on page 1010 provides a good example of what can happen when workers accept the concept of such a pay plan. From 1983 to 1990, Lincoln Electric paid its employees 50 to 75 percent bonuses and, "because of the way the profit sharing is calculated, a 50 percent bonus is actually equal to an employee's base wage. Consequently, the bonus doubles most people's incomes."[5]

Piece rate

Promoting Overall Success

A significant problem with piece rate payment plans is their failure to provide incentives for workers to consider overall organizational success. Alternative performance-based plans exist for this purpose, many of which have the expressed goal of getting common stock into the hands of employees. One popular arrangement is **profit sharing**, which provides incentive payments to employees. These current and/or deferred incentive payments are contingent on organizational performance and may be in the form of cash or stock. Allocation of the total profit sharing payment among individual employees is made on the basis of personal performance measurements, seniority, team performance, managerial judgment, and/or specified formulas.

Profit sharing

In addition to profit sharing arrangements, some firms pay employees a portion of their compensation in the form of stock options or stock appreciation rights. **Stock options** allow the holder to purchase shares of company common stock at specified terms. These terms usually relate to price and designate the future time frame during which the stock may be purchased. **Stock appreciation rights** allow employees to re-

Stock option

Stock appreciation rights

---

[5] "A Look at a Leader—and Its Followers," *Training* (January 1991), p. 30.

NEWS
NOTE   **The Pay is Consistently Sizable**

Thriving in America's rust belt is the Lincoln Electric Co. of Cleveland, Ohio. Unlike other American firms competing in the global market, Lincoln Electric has successfully maintained its dominance in the arc-welding industry as indicated by its 40% market share. Employing 3,000 non-union workers, this company has never laid off an employee, and voluntary employee turnover is rarely observed.

Lincoln Electric has achieved its success in a distinctly American way, by creating initiative in individual workers. Lincoln Electric's compensation system is based on a piece-rate pay plan. Employees are paid for the work they accomplish. If they accomplish nothing, they get paid nothing. However, workers that are creative and find more productive ways to accomplish their production tasks reap the benefits of their ingenuity. The benefits of this pay plan to both the company and its employees are enormous. The employees enjoy the highest compensation in the industry; it is not unusual for some production workers to make $50,000 or more annually. The benefits reaped by the stockholders include consistent year-to-year profitability and one of the lowest ratios of labor cost per sales dollar in the industry.

SOURCES: Kent R. Davies, "Is Individual Responsibility a Radical Idea in American Business?" *Training* (November 1988), pp. 63–65 and Arthur D. Sharplin, "Low-Cost Strategies to Improve Worker's Job Security," *Journal of Business Strategy* (Winter 1985), pp. 90–93.

ceive cash, stock, or a combination of cash and stock based on the difference between a specified amount per share of stock and the quoted market price per share at some future date. In each situation, the amount of compensation is not determinable with certainty at the date the incentive reward is received, but rather the options or rights will hopefully become more valuable as the price of the common stock rises.

Employee Stock Ownership Plan

Another popular profit sharing compensation program is the **Employee Stock Ownership Plan** (ESOP), in which investments are made in the securities of the employer.[6] An ESOP must conform to rules of the Internal Revenue Code, but offers both tax and incentive advantages. Under an ESOP arrangement, the employer makes tax-deductible payments of cash or stock to a trust fund. If cash is contributed, it is used by the trust to purchase shares of the employing company's stock. The trust beneficiaries are the employees and their wealth grows with both the employer contributions and advances in the per share price of the stock.

Nonfinancial Incentives

Besides various forms of monetary compensation, workers may also be motivated by nonfinancial factors. Although all employees value and require money to satisfy basic human needs, other human needs cannot necessarily be fulfilled with monetary wealth. Employees desire some compensation that is not monetary in nature, but satisfies the higher-order social needs of humans. For example, workers and managers typically will be more productive in environments in which they think their efforts are appreciated. Simple gestures such as compliments and small awards can be used by superiors to formally recognize contributions of subordinates. Allowing subordinates to participate in decisions affecting their own welfare and the welfare of the firm also contributes to making employment socially fulfilling. Such efforts provide assurance to employees that they are serving a productive role in the firm and that their superiors are attentive to, and appreciative of, employee contributions.

---

[6] For an explanation of some of the popular applications of ESOP plans, see "ESOP Power" by Ron J. Lint in *Management Accounting* (November 1992), pp. 38–41.

NEWS NOTE

Managerial Pay Under the Hay Plan

The new approach to pay is one effect of the profound organizational changes rippling through corporate America—downsizing, flatter management pyramids, greater emphasis on teamwork, quality, and customer service. Old compensation systems just don't fit this new world of work. Most managers have been getting paid largely according to how many people work for them, often with some variation based on how well they meet quantifiable goals.

The old [compensation] system was most prominently championed by the Hay Group consulting firm. The widely used Hay Plan, first employed in the 1950s and still in use at about 40% of the FORTUNE 500, rates each job according to know-how required, problem-solving capabilities needed, and accountability, or "answerability for action and the consequences thereof," as the manual puts it. The last category includes an analysis of a job's magnitude: How many workers do you control, and how big is your direct effect on the company's bottom line? The system also provides for instances where managers might be subjected to unsafe or particularly unpleasant working conditions. The result was a number of Hay points that determined a job's pay.

But what's the point, now that many corporations' aims include eliminating layers of management and pushing responsibility out of executives' offices and down to other workers? Instead, in leading-edge companies more managers are competing for raises based on less tangible criteria—leadership skills, flexibility, the ability to work well with others.

SOURCE: Kenneth Labich, "The New Pay Game . . . and How You Measure Up," *FORTUNE* (October 19, 1992), pp. 116–117. © 1992 Time Inc. All rights reserved.

Lastly, the concept of job security, which is so prevalent in Japanese companies, is a powerful incentive. For example, while A. T. Cross & Co. (makers of Cross pens and mechanical pencils) does offer a modest profit-sharing plan and comparable wages, CEO Brad Boss believes the company's high quality standards partially result from employee loyalty. "The company has never had a layoff. When new, more efficient production technology is introduced, workers are retained and generally promoted."[7]

MANAGERIAL COMPENSATION

In many respects, the preceding discussion of compensation is equally applicable to workers and managers. However, while workers have traditionally been paid for time and/or output, the majority of a manager's pay has traditionally been based on his/her job title or function and staff size, as indicated in the News Note entitled "Managerial Pay Under the Hay Plan."

Managers, though, are primary decision makers in organizations and are subject to less direct supervision; thus, they can be measured by some more unique compensation factors. Additionally, managers are more likely than workers to be evaluated and compensated based on the results they achieve and the contributions they make to the organization's strategic objectives. Frequently, top-level managerial compensation is directly linked to company stock price or to corporate earnings performance.

Prior chapters discuss various incentive-compatible ways to evaluate managerial performance. For example, Chapter 22 indicates that residual income and return on

[7]Louis S. Richman, "What America Makes Best," *FORTUNE* (The New American Century, 1991), p. 81.

EXHIBIT 23–5
Popular Perks

PERQUISITE OFFERED	COMPANY SALES OF LESS THAN $1M	COMPANY SALES OF $1–$5M
Company car allowance	40.3%	63.4%
Key-person insurance	30.3%	47.0%
Special parking	16.0%	14.9%
Luncheon clubs	14.3%	17.2%
Financial counseling/tax services	14.3%	17.2%
Employment contracts	13.4%	20.1%
Severance pay for execs	12.6%	17.2%
Country clubs	12.6%	19.4%
Deferred compensation	7.6%	5.2%

SOURCE: Ernst & Young, *1992 Executive Compensation Middle Market Survey of 649 Companies with Annual Sales of $50 Million or Less* (New York City). Reprinted with permission, *Inc.* magazine, (August 1992), p. 82. Copyright 1992 by Goldhirsh Group, Inc., 38 Commercial Wharf, Boston, MA 02110.

investment are two common financial performance measures for managers of decentralized operations. Other chapters discuss the roles of standard costing, variance analysis, budget-to-actual comparisons, and a variety of nonfinancial indicators as bases to assess the efficiency and effectiveness of managerial efforts. Managers will find improving these performance measures to be much more important when the reward structure is directly linked to them. "When many things are measured but only financial results are rewarded, it is obvious which measures will be regarded as most important."[8] Thus, the rewards to be provided in a performance-based compensation plan should be based on both monetary and nonmonetary as well as both short-term and long-term measures.

Perks

In addition to the monetary benefits, managers frequently are offered a variety of perquisites, or **perks**, for short. Perks are fringe benefits provided by the employer and include items such as vacations, free child care, free parking, personal assistants or private secretaries, health care, recreational memberships, an office with a view, or flexible work hours. Perks can be offered as an incidental benefit of the position or they can be offered as compensation for specific performance. Exhibit 23–5 indicates some popular perks and the proportion of a sample group of companies that offer them to managers.

The pay and performance relationships discussed earlier are not equally applicable to all types of organizations. The discussion that follows addresses the unique aspects of not-for-profit and governmental organizations.

NOT-FOR-PROFIT AND GOVERNMENTAL COMPENSATION

The prior discussion has assumed that employee performance and rewards would be determined under the oversight of a self-interested group of stockholders who are concerned about the effectiveness and efficiency of operations. The stockholders assume this oversight role because they are the residual claimants who are entitled to be paid only after all other involved parties have received their "compensation"—be it wages, salaries, or interest payments.

Not-for-profit and governmental organizations have no direct counterpart to stockholders. There is no single self-interested group that has the financial incentive to seek assurances that employees and managers perform their work effectively

---

[8] Robert G. Eccles and Philip J. Pyburn, "Creating a Comprehensive System to Measure Performance," *Management Accounting* (October 1992), p. 44.

and efficiently. This one distinct factor may partially account for the horror stories, detailing out-of-control purchasing practices in the Pentagon or some other governmental unit, that occasionally appear in the press. Although there is some link between pay and performance in not-for-profit and governmental agencies, this relationship typically is not as direct or strong as that existing in private companies.

The historical norm for public and not-for-profit organizations is time-based pay plans. There are several nonperformance advantages to the use of such plans, including the ease of predicting and budgeting costs and the avoidance of pay disputes. But as far back as 1988, federal government employees were expressing substantial dissatisfaction with their performance evaluation and reward system. "A poll of some 4,000 federal workers indicated that 70% of the workers regarded the pay as unfair, 74% felt that the bonus and merit pay system were unfair, and a whopping 90% supported innovation in pay plans that would more closely link pay and performance."[9] Such complaints are not unusual in many governmental and not-for-profit entities. The trend in these organizations has been to try to tighten the linkage between pay and performance so that the best and brightest employees do not leave the public sector.

Several experiments are ongoing, particularly in the federal government, to attract and retain the most qualified employees. The financial and nonfinancial incentives for producing quality products and services that are becoming an essential part of private industry compensation plans are also being considered for adoption in public sector agencies.

One of the experiments is the "Project Pacer Share."[10] This project involves 2,000 employees at McClellan Air Force Base in a five-year program that is designed to improve quality production services. The hope is that a management system will evolve that can be duplicated in other areas of the federal government. The project scope includes improvement in four areas: personnel policies, product and/or service quality, measurement of objectives, and quality of employee life. Some of the personnel changes that are being tested include a "gainsharing" plan that will provide cash bonuses to employees for increases in productivity, less reliance on annual reviews for performance evaluation, and more emphasis on employee training.

Whether employees work in the private sector, not-for-profits, or the government, the effects of income taxation should be considered when the compensation system is designed. The following section indicates that fringe benefits and certain other forms of compensation may be preferred to cash compensation because of the relative tax benefits.

TAX IMPLICATIONS OF COMPENSATION ELEMENTS

In recent years, individual tax rates have been as high as 50 percent and corporate tax rates have been as high as 46 percent of taxable income. Currently, tax rates for individuals and corporations are somewhat below these levels. But, because current tax rates are still significant, one important consideration is the tax consequences of the alternative rewards provided by compensation packages. Differences in tax treatments are important because they affect the amount of after-tax income received by the employee and the after-tax cost of the pay plan to the employer. There are three different tax treatments for employee compensation: full and immediate taxation, deferral of taxation, and exemption from taxation.[11] **Tax deferral** indicates taxation

Tax deferral

[9] Albert C. Hyde, "The New Environment for Compensation and Performance Evaluation in the Public Sector," *Public Personnel Management* (Winter 1988), pp. 351–358.
[10] Ronald Gilbert and Ardel E. Nelson, "The Pacer Share Demonstration Project: Implications for Organizational Management and Performance Evaluation," *Public Personnel Management* (Summer 1989), pp. 209–225.
[11] Myron S. Scholes and Mark A. Wolfson, *Taxes and Business Strategy: A Planning Approach* (Englewood Cliffs, N.J.: Prentice-Hall, 1992), p. 33.

Tax exemption

occurs at a future rather than current date. **Tax exemption** is the most desirable form of tax treatment because the amount is never subject to income taxation.

Most forms of compensation are fully and currently taxable to the employee and fully and currently deductible by the employer. For instance, wages represent income that is taxable to the employee when earned and tax deductible to the employer when incurred. The special, favorable tax treatments of deferral and exemption are provided under the tax code to encourage certain socially desirable behavior on the part of employers and employees.

For two reasons, the discussion of the tax aspects of compensation must center on the federal income tax and its effect on the employer and employee. First, while there are other taxes (such as payroll taxes, state income taxes, and unemployment taxes) that may be affected differentially by choices in reward structures, the impact of such taxes is rather minimal relative to the corporate and individual federal income taxes. Second, the impact of state income tax varies from state to state and thus is beyond the scope of this text.

Fringe Benefits

When analyzing the compensation plan, employers and employees must consider the entire package—not simply one element of the package. For the employer, compensation other than wages and salaries creates additional costs; for employees, such compensation creates additional benefits. Fringe benefits may range from employee health insurance to child care or physical fitness facilities to pension plans. However, different types of fringe benefits have different tax consequences.

Certain employee fringe benefits are not treated as taxable income to the employee, but are fully and currently deductible by the employer.[12] One important type of these fringe benefits is employer-provided accident and health insurance plans. Premiums on such plans can be deducted for tax purposes when paid by the employer, but the premium is not treated as taxable income to the employee. If each employee purchased the insurance individually, there would also be certain tax benefits. However, the tax treatment available when employees spend after-tax earnings for the services is not as preferable as the full exemption from taxation that occurs in an employer-provided plan.

Cafeteria plan

The importance of various fringe benefits is directly related to an individual employee's needs and wants, which is why some companies have instituted flexible fringe benefit programs called **cafeteria plans**. These plans contain a "menu" of fringe benefit options including cash compensation and nontaxable benefits alternatives. If the employee elects to receive cash in lieu of nontaxable fringe benefits, the cash is fully taxable. However, employees who elect fringe benefits such as health care, group term life insurance, or child care receive these benefits free of tax. Flexibility is the greatest benefit of cafeteria plans because employees, based on their perceptions of the benefits' value, choose which benefits to receive.

Deferred Compensation

Deferred compensation

Various forms of **deferred compensation** were identified earlier in this discussion. Deferred compensation represents pay related to current performance that will be received at a later time, typically after retirement. Among the diverse types of deferred compensation plans are profit sharing arrangements, pensions, and various stock-based plans (including the ESOP). Many of these plans receive substantially identical treatment under the tax rules. The employer is allowed a current deduction for payments made to the plan, but the employee is not taxed until distributions are received

---

[12] For more information on the taxation of fringe benefits, see the current edition of *West's Federal Taxation: Individual Income Taxes* by William H. Hoffman, James E. Smith, and Eugene Willis (St. Paul, Minn.).

from the plan. This treatment creates two significant tax benefits. First, there is no immediate taxable income created for the employee by the employer's contribution. Second, there is no taxation of earnings on the plan between the year of contribution and the year of distribution. In short, the employer's contributions and the earnings on these contributions are accorded tax-deferred treatment. When the employee reaches retirement and receives payments from the plan, all receipts are wholly taxable. At that time, the employee is frequently in a lower tax bracket and will have enjoyed tax-free growth in the contributions over his or her working career.

While the tax treatment to the employee of the various types of deferred compensation may not be significantly different, there are substantial differences in incentive effects. For example, the growth in the value of a pension plan may be largely unrelated to the employing corporation's stock performance. However, reward plans involving the employing company's stock have both a compensatory and an incentive element. Growth in the value of the deferred compensation depends both on current contribution amounts and the change in the stock's value. Hence, employees are motivated to be concerned with stock performance—which is typically tied to corporate earnings.

Because the self-serving motives of managers, workers, and stockholders frequently diverge, a proper reward structure needs to balance the interests of the three groups. Each group is entitled to an adequate return for the risks they bear and the contributions they make to the organization's success. Inevitably, ethical dilemmas will be encountered when opportunities arise for one of the three groups to gain advantage over one or both of the other groups. Exhibit 23–6 on page 1016 provides a summary of the pay elements and their relationships to the various concepts discussed in the chapter. The following section discusses some of the common pay circumstances in which ethical problems are encountered.

One of the phenomena that has accompanied corporate growth is the emergence of professional managers and the dispersion of organizational ownership. In the largest corporations, no individual or group may own a large enough portion of common stock to directly influence the efforts and decisions of professional managers. This circumstance gives top managers greater discretion in operating the business and may also allow them to feel insulated from stockholders and their desires. Some observers argue that this atmosphere of discretion/insulation may be used to the managers' benefit rather than to the stockholders'. There are a number of ethical issues to be resolved in the 1990s with regard to organizational governance and compensation of workers and managers.

ETHICAL CONSIDERATIONS OF COMPENSATION

Organizational Governance

It may be argued that laws protecting the rights of stockholders failed to evolve with the dispersion of corporate ownership in the U.S. Further, stockholder interests have become more diverse as institutional traders (such as pension funds) have moved into the capital markets along with individuals and industrial firms. Institutions historically have been passive investors and have not been diligent in voting their shares or monitoring managerial performance. Thus, professional managers have become less sensitive to stockholder concerns and have occasionally forgotten their primary duty is to act in good faith for the organization.

Role of Capital Markets

Under these circumstances, the capital markets have assumed an important role in ensuring that managements are disciplined in their use of corporate resources. For

	Link to Performance	Tied to Co. Objectives	Promotes Quality	Level of Motivation	Time Focus	Taxable to Employee*	Deductible by Employer*
Hourly wages/ Monthly salary	Little	No	No	Low	Short-term	Currently	Currently
Merit pay	Some	Possibly	Possibly	Medium	Short-term	Currenty	Currently
Contingent pay	High	Possibly	Possibly	Medium	Short-term	Currently	Currently
Piece rate	High	Possibly	No	High	Short-term	Currently	Currently
Profit sharing	Some	Yes	Yes	Medium	Depends	Depends	Currently
Stock options/ appreciation rights	High	Yes	Yes	Medium	Long-term	Deferred	Depends
ESOP	High	Yes	Yes	Medium	Long-term	Deferred	Currently
Perks	Some	Possibly	Possibly	Medium	Short-term	Exempt	Currently
Health insurance	Little	No	No	Low	Short-term	Exempt	Currently
Cafeteria plan	Little	Possibly	Possibly	Medium	Depends	Depends	Currently
Pensions	Some	Possibly	Possibly	Medium	Depends	Deferred	Currently

* Subject to proper compliance and to potential regulatory changes.

▌ EXHIBIT 23–6

Summary of Pay Plans

Takeover

Raiders

example, partly as a response to ineffective entrenched managements, the 1970s and 1980s were witness to many attempted and successful hostile **takeovers**. In a takeover action, an outside or inside investor acquires managerial control of the corporation. Control is achieved by acquiring enough common stock and stockholder votes to control the board of directors, and thereby control management. The adjective "hostile" (as opposed to "friendly") indicates that the takeover is not welcomed by management and frequently indicates that one objective of the takeover is to replace the management.

Raiders is a pejorative term used to describe firms or individuals who specialize in hostile takeovers. Raiders commonly identify firms as takeover targets when those firms are believed to be undervalued because managers are not acting in the stockholders' best interests. For example, managers of some conglomerates could increase stockholder value by selling pieces of the conglomerate that are not synergistic with other pieces.

NEWS NOTE

Banker's Golden Parachute—from the FDIC's Perspective

In the banking industry, the guarantor of customer deposits of last resort is the Federal Deposit Insurance Corporation (FDIC). In a failing institution, if the bank's capital is insufficient to cover the deposits of its customers, the FDIC is required to make recompense to depositors up to $100,000 per account. If a financially failing bank has a golden parachute arrangement in place, and the bank's capital is diverted to fund the golden parachute, the FDIC is, in effect, bearing the cost of the plan. Worse yet, the FDIC may be the entity that triggers the payment of the golden parachute benefits by threatening to take over the bank for its inadequate capitalization.

Two other aspects of this arrangement are bothersome. First, top managers may receive a large golden parachute payment which is essentially brought about by their mismanagement of bank assets. Secondly, in a failing bank the golden parachute payments may be borne by the FDIC and in turn be used by bank officers in defending themselves from FDIC legal actions for mismanagement.

In response to this view of golden parachutes, the FDIC has proposed rules which would proscribe the payment of golden parachutes to executives of failing banks.

SOURCE: Kenneth H. Bacon, "FDIC Seeks to Bar Golden Parachutes at Troubled Banks," *Wall Street Journal* (September 25, 1991), p A2. Reprinted by permission of the *Wall Street Journal*, © 1991 Dow Jones & Company, Inc. All rights reserved worldwide.

Takeovers can have either positive or negative effects on existing shareholders and employees, depending on the acquiring firm's objectives and the actions taken by the management of the target firm. A takeover can represent an attempt to steal value from the existing managers and workers; alternatively, it can represent an effective mechanism to revitalize an organization plagued by ineffective management. In either case, managers have often been permitted to include certain elements in their compensation packages that allow a retention of power in the face of a hostile takeover.

One compensation device that has helped discourage takeover attempts and protect managers is the **golden parachute**, which is a benefits package payable to incumbent managers if those managers are terminated following a successful hostile takeover (or in some cases a friendly merger). Both the ethical and incentive effects of golden parachutes are difficult to assess. Some proponents argue that golden parachutes serve stockholder interests because "top managers are free to devote their attention to serving the interests of existing stockholders in the face of a takeover threat."[13] The parachute is viewed as providing managers with financial protection that will keep them unbiased in their actions, regardless of the outcome.

Golden parachute

However, critics view the golden parachute as a means for entrenched managers to protect themselves in the event they are ousted. Proponents of this perspective are offended by the notion that managers who mismanage and create the conditions that originally attracted a takeover effort should profit by a takeover removing them for inept performance. The "Banker's" News Note provides the FDIC perspective on golden parachutes in the banking industry.

There are also taxation issues in regard to golden parachutes. When these devices were first introduced, corporations were allowed to deduct the payments as normal business expenses. Such deductibility was affected significantly by the 1984 Deficit Reduction Act, which added a 20 percent excise tax on parachutes in excess of three times a five-year average salary. While many companies have agreed to pay this tax as part of a manager's severance package, a corporate deduction is disallowed for the excess payment.

---

[13] Bob L. Sellers, "Bankers Discover the Golden Parachute," *Bankers Monthly* (June 1988), p. 54.

NEWS NOTE   **The Gap Between Pay and Performance of Top Management**

Herman Miller Inc. may be the only major company in America where workers hope the chief executive officer will get a huge raise.

The reason: His pay is directly linked to theirs. The big office furniture maker limits its chief executive's cash compensation—including salary and bonus—to 20 times the average paycheck—currently $28,000—earned by the company's factory hands.

Herman Miller's formula isn't unique. Ben & Jerry's Homemade, a Vermont-based ice cream maker, holds its chief executive's pay to seven times the average for its workers. But Ben & Jerry's is a young company that's steeped in counter-culture values. Herman Miller is a FORTUNE 500 company in deeply conservative western Michigan.

The simple, albeit radical, formula used at Herman Miller since 1984 is starting to draw attention. "We should follow this model, instead of the bad examples of the 1980s," says James O'Toole, executive director of the Leadership Institute at the University of Southern California. "The purpose of the corporation is much broader than meeting the needs of stock speculators or the power needs of top managers."

SOURCE: Jacqueline Mitchell, "Herman Miller Links Worker–CEO Pay," *Wall Street Journal* (May 7, 1992), pp. B1. Reprinted by permission of the *Wall Street Journal,* © 1992 Dow Jones & Company, Inc. All rights reserved worldwide.

Compensation Differentials

A major issue of discussion and contention involves perceptions of disparity between the pay of ordinary workers and top managers. Plato argued that no one should earn more than five times that earned by the lowest-paid worker. In the early 1900s, however, J. P. Morgan stated that the differential should be no more than twenty times. Exhibit 23–7 provides average total compensation (including cash pay, stock options, benefits, and perquisites) for four categories of employees in several countries. The exhibit also indicates that, in general, neither Plato's nor Morgan's compensation relationships are currently true in the United States. All other countries surveyed, however, are well within at least Morgan's guidelines. However, as discussed in the News Note entitled "The Gap Between Pay and Performance," there are some U.S. companies that do relate worker–CEO pay.

Salary differentials between workers and CEOs are often created by a type of self-fulfilling prophecy caused by the board of directors. It is the job of the board of directors to protect the interests of stockholders, but the composition of boards is usually split between outsiders and insiders. Insiders may be officers of the corporation and naturally identify more with the management group than the owners. Accordingly, they are sympathetic with the manager's position in stockholder/manager conflicts.

Often a company's board of directors will survey a group of similar organizations to determine the "average" compensation for an executive. If the company's executive appears to be underpaid, the board will increase his or her compensation. Therefore, the next time the survey is performed, the average will be increased—regardless of managerial performance. Such indiscreet consumption of organizational resources can cause common stock prices to decline and undermines the stockholder value maximization goal.

Thus, the greatest ethical dilemmas involve circumstances that pit the welfare of employees against those of stockholders or the welfare of managers against the welfare of workers. Only if there is a perception of equity across the contributions and entitlements of labor, management, and capital will the organization be capable of achieving the efficiency to compete in global markets.

Manufacturing Employee	White-Collar Employee	Manager	CEO
Germany $36,857	Britain $74,761	Italy $219,573	United States $717,237
Canada $34,935	France $62,279	France $190,354	France $479,772
Japan $34,263	Germany $59,916	Japan $185,437	Italy $463,009
Italy $31,537	Italy $58,263	Britain $162,190	Britain $439,441
France $30,019	United States $57,675	United States $159,575	Canada $416,066
United States $27,606	Canada $47,231	Germany $145,627	Germany $390,933
Britain $26,084	Japan $40,990	Canada $132,877	Japan $390,723

SOURCE: Amanda Bennett, "Managers' Incomes Aren't Worlds Apart," *Wall Street Journal* (October 12, 1992), p. B1. Reprinted by permission of the *Wall Street Journal,* © 1992 Dow Jones & Company, Inc. All rights reserved worldwide.

▌ **EXHIBIT 23–7**
Average Compensation Levels for Employees

As more companies engage in multinational operations, compensation systems must be developed that compensate **expatriate** employees and managers on a fair and equitable basis. Expatriates are parent company and third-country nationals assigned to a foreign subsidiary or foreign nationals assigned to the parent company. Relocating individuals in foreign countries requires consideration of compensation. A fair and reasonable compensation package in one locale may not be fair and reasonable in another. A recent survey of 45 multinationals indicated that every respondent considered differing pay levels, benefits, and perks as one of the biggest problems in developing an international work force.[14]

The compensation package paid to expatriates must reflect labor market factors, cost-of-living considerations, and currency fluctuations as well as considering tax consequences. Typically, an expatriate's base salary and fringe benefits should reflect what he or she would have been paid domestically. This base should then be adjusted for reasonable cost-of-living factors. These factors could be quite apparent (such as obtaining housing, education, and security needs similar to those that would have been obtained in the home country or compensating for a spouse's loss of employment) or they could be less obvious (such as a need to hire someone in the home country to care for an elderly relative or to handle real estate investments).

GLOBAL COMPENSATION

Expatriate

---

[14]Organizational Resources Counselors Inc., "Global Headaches," cited in *Wall Street Journal* (April 21, 1993), p. R5.

NEWS NOTE

How Am I Paid?

As more American companies emerge as global marketers and manufacturers, they are discovering a crying need for more sophisticated global compensation systems.

Some companies, for instance, are tying their peripatetic managers' pay to their own home countries, and some to the new countries where they reside. Still others struggle to come up with a truly global standard for pay—a task complicated by a host of factors ranging from fluctuating currencies to cultural differences in how pay is perceived. Europeans and Japanese, for example, often are leery of stock and stock options because such compensation tools aren't widely used outside the U.S.

At the root of the movement toward a global-style pay system is cost. Expatriate packages based on American salaries and needs increasingly are seen as too expensive for international managers. With salaries and standards of living varying drastically from country to country, companies must grapple with the issue of fairness. Employers want to find ways of making transfers attractive without paying people too much more—or too much less—than their new colleagues overseas.

Fairness, indeed, is a major issue in virtually every attempt at global pay programs—especially when two people doing the same job are on radically different pay standards based partly on their home-country pay. Yet plans that try to treat everyone equally also run into problems—[often because they are too complex to be understandable].

SOURCE: Amanda Bennett, "What's an Expatriate?" *Wall Street Journal* (April 21, 1993), p. R5. Reprinted by permission of the *Wall Street Journal*, © 1993 Dow Jones & Company, Inc. All rights reserved worldwide.

Because expatriates have a variety of monetary needs, these individuals may be paid in the currency of the country in which they reside, in their home currency, or a combination of both. Often, price-level adjustment clauses are built into the compensation system to counteract any local currency inflation or deflation. But, regardless of the currency makeup of the pay package, the fringe benefit related to retirement must be related to the home country and should be paid in that currency.

Income taxes are important in the compensation package of expatriates because they may pay taxes in the local country, home country, or both. Some countries (such as the United States and Great Britain) exempt expatriates from taxation on a specified amount of income earned in a foreign country. If a tax treaty exists and local taxes are paid on the balance of the nonexempt income of expatriates, such taxes may be credited against the expatriate's home nation income taxes.

As indicated in the "How Am I Paid" News Note, all of these issues are important in developing compensation packages for expatriates. But, regardless of how the package is ultimately determined, an ethical company will make certain that the system is as fair as possible to all employees involved and that it is cost-beneficial and not an administrative nightmare.

In conclusion, tying compensation to performance is essential because everyone in business recognizes that what gets measured and rewarded is what gets accomplished. Businesses must focus their reward structures to motivate employees to succeed at all activities that will create shareholder and personal value. In this highly competitive age, the new paradigm of success is to provide quality products and services at a reasonable price while generating a reasonable profit margin. Top management compensation has traditionally been tied to financial measures of performance; Exhibit 23–8 indicates that more and more companies are also beginning to tie that compensation to quality measures.

■ EXHIBIT 23–8
Relationship of Quality and Top Management Compensation

The following percentages of businesses indicate that quality is of primary importance as a criterion for top management compensation.

	Past (last 3 years)	Current	Future (next 3 years)
Canada	8%	15%	35%
Germany	2%	10%	39%
Japan	19%	20%	31%
United States	10%	19%	51%

SOURCE: Ernst & Young and American Quality Foundation, *International Quality Study* (1991), p. 15.

Transportation and child care costs in London are lower than in many large cities, but housing can be substantially more expensive. Costs affecting the standard of living must be reviewed in determining the appropriate compensation package to offer expatriates.

R E V I S I T I N G

EATON CORPORATION

Eaton is obsessive about costs because it has to be: Its chief customers, the automakers, are just as obsessive about their costs, and pay as little as possible for parts even in the best of times.

Some of Eaton's belt-tightening efforts are conventional. The four factories it closed in 1991 eliminated 807 workers, reducing its work force to 38,000 in 110 facilities around the world. But Eaton's experience shows that the best way to control costs is to get employees to understand how that can benefit them. [And, as] Eaton has learned, rewarding performance is essential. For years, the company paid incentives based solely on individual output: The more a worker produced, the more he or she earned. "It was one of our worst sins," Mr. Boatman says. "Incentive did nothing but build inventory and bad parts."

[In contrast to the output-based incentive pay that was in effect at Eaton's Lincoln plant, Eaton's Kearney plant pays bonuses] based on the entire plant's performance compared with the prior year. In the first quarter of 1992, for instance, Kearney topped the year-earlier profit and cost criteria by 7%—and workers got a quarterly bonus of 7%, or about $500 each. Kearney employees have earned a bonus every quarter since the system was introduced in 1986.

Workers also get a cumulative bonus of $25 for each year of perfect attendance. The system, which allows employees to offset sick days by foregoing vacation time, has promoted better attendance; 75% of the plant's 697 employees haven't missed one day of work for a year or longer. Absenteeism at Kearney runs 0.4%, compared with an average for all U.S. manufacturing of 1.7%.

At the unionized Lincoln plant, which for years was mired in labor-management animosity, Eaton rewarded 10% productivity gains last year by offering to relocate 70 low-wage jobs from Mexico. The union workers hired to fill them—initially at $6.31 an hour, about half the typical pay—have advanced up the salary scale as output within the special circuit-breaker department has accelerated.

There's noncash recognition as well. For example, the Kearney plant had a lunchtime barbecue to mark the first shift's 365th consecutive day without any injuries.

SOURCE: Thomas F. O'Boyle, "A Manufacturer Grows Efficient by Soliciting Ideas from Employees," *Wall Street Journal* (June 5, 1992), pp. A1, A5. Reprinted by permission of the *Wall Street Journal,* © 1992 Dow Jones & Company, Inc. All rights reserved worldwide.

CHAPTER SUMMARY

In American industry, corporate stockholders play a unique role. Stockholders do not receive benefits from their investments until all other parties have been paid for their contributions. For bearing this risk, stockholders have the right to establish the contributions to be made and rewards to be received by the corporation's employees.

Although maximizing stockholder value is the maintained objective of profit-oriented corporations, employees naturally are not concerned with stockholder welfare. Thus, employees must be provided incentives to motivate them to maximize their own wealth while concurrently maximizing that of the stockholders.

In the past, compensation was often based solely on individual performance and short-run financial results. Because of operational changes and shifts in managerial philosophies, performance measurements and their related rewards now encompass group success, nonfinancial performance attributes, and long-run considerations. Some of the rewards provide short-run satisfaction (merit pay and bonuses); others provide long-run satisfaction (common stock ownership).

Pay plans are available that involve current compensation, deferred compensation, and perks. Three important dimensions of pay plans are incentive effects, tax effects, and ethical considerations. Incentive effects vary from plan to plan. The periodic pay plan is the least effective in directly motivating employees to perform and provides the weakest link between performance and reward. At the other extreme, the piece rate pay plan provides a direct link between the work accomplished and the employee reward, as long as this plan encourages production quality, not just production quantity.

There has been some historical dissatisfaction with not-for-profit and governmental entity employees' compensation plans. Some of these organizations are now attempting to increase the connection between compensation and performance to encourage retention of high-quality employees in public sector careers.

Tax benefits also vary among reward structures. For the employee, rewards may be fully and currently taxable, tax deferred, or tax exempt. Although regular pay is generally fully and currently taxable, certain employer-provided fringe benefits are tax exempt to employees while providing current deductions for employers. Additionally, some elements of incentive compensation plans can be structured to defer taxation.

In designing reward structures, consideration should also be given to ethical questions. Three changes that have influenced the power structure in the corporate world are the rise of professional managers, dispersion of stock ownership, and extensive involvement of institutional investors in capital markets. Additionally, some top managers' compensation grossly exceeds pay to ordinary workers. Such excesses can be counterproductive, causing a demoralizing effect in the firm and, ultimately, the failure to succeed in the goal of maximizing long-term stockholder wealth. These situations create ethical issues that should be considered when establishing a compensation strategy that will ensure fairness, effectiveness, and efficiency in an organization.

KEY TERMS

Cafeteria plan (p. 1014)	Perks (p. 1012)
Compensation strategy (p. 1000)	Piece rate (p. 1009)
Contingent pay (p. 1009)	Profit sharing (p. 1009)
Deferred compensation (p. 1014)	Raiders (p. 1016)
Employee Stock Ownership Plan (p. 1010)	Shirking (p. 1004)
Expatriate (p. 1019)	Stock appreciation rights (p. 1009)
Financial incentives (p. 1000)	Stock option (p. 1009)
Golden parachute (p. 1017)	Takeover (p. 1016)
Merit pay (p. 1009)	Tax deferral (p. 1013)
Periodic compensation (p. 1007)	Tax exemption (p. 1014)

SOLUTION STRATEGIES

The design of an effective reward structure heavily depends on each organization's unique characteristics. It is impossible to design a generic incentive model that would be effective in a variety of firms. However, affirmative answers to the following questions provide guidance as to the applicability of a proposed incentive and reward plan for a particular organization.

1. Will the organizational objectives be achieved if the proposed compensation structure is implemented?

2. Is the proposed structure consistent with the organizational design, culture, and management philosophy?

3. Are there reasonable and objective performance measures that are good surrogates for the organizational objectives?

4. Are factors beyond employee/group control minimized under the performance measures of the proposed compensation structure?

5. Is there minimal ability of employees to manipulate the performance measurements tied to the proposed compensation structure?

6. In light of the interests of managers, workers, and stockholders, is the proposed reward structure fair and does it encourage and promote ethical behavior?

7. Is the proposed reward structure arranged to take advantage of potential employee/employer tax benefits?

8. Does the proposed reward structure promote harmony between employee groups?

9. Is there an adequate balance between individual and group incentives?

QUESTIONS

1. Why are common stockholders given such special attention by managers in American corporations?

2. Why would an effective compensation strategy treat top managers, middle managers, and other workers differently?

3. The trend in most businesses is away from automatic pay increases and toward more use of incentive compensation plans. Why has this trend developed?

4. If worker performance measures used in a pay-for-performance plan are not highly correlated with corporate goals, what is the likely result for the organization? For the workers?

5. How does the time perspective of a performance-based plan affect the selection of performance measures?

6. Why should worker age be taken into account in designing performance-based pay systems?

7. If a firm offers substantial group-level performance incentives, but no individual performance incentives, how might workers respond?

8. Why are performance-based worker evaluations more risky for workers than evaluations based on direct observation by superiors?

9. How is feedback used in a performance-based reward system?

10. Identify some important differences between periodic compensation and contingent compensation.

11. Why is piece rate pay the extreme form of a performance-based pay system?

12. Many pay structures involve both cash compensation and stock-based compensation. Why might owners and managers want employees to own the firm's common stock?

13. What are perks? What are the advantages associated with the use of perks in rewarding performance?

14. Why must reward structures in not-for-profit and governmental organizations be structured differently from those for profit-oriented firms?

15. Why must income taxation be taken into account in designing a reward system? What are the alternative tax treatments of the various compensation alternatives?

16. Why is flexibility the distinguishing characteristic of cafeteria plans? Why is flexibility important?

17. What are raiders? What positive role is served by raiders in capital markets?

18. What is a golden parachute? What are the alternative explanations for the existence of such plans?

19. What are some of the important fairness issues in designing reward structures? Why is the achievement of fairness in the reward structure important? Globally, where does the U.S. rank in the pay differential between the average worker and the CEO?

20. For global enterprises, what are the additional concerns in designing a reward system, relative to single-country operations?

21. *(Matching)* Match the numbered items on the left with the lettered items on the right.

1. Stock option	a. A right for the holder to purchase common shares
2. Merit pay	
3. Cafeteria plan	b. A menu of fringe benefit options
4. Deferred compensation	c. Employer-provided fringe benefits
5. Tax-exempt pay	d. An increase in pay earned through performance
6. Expatriate	
7. Profit sharing	e. Free-riding
8. Contingent pay	f. Pay that is not subject to tax
9. Perks	g. Pay that is dependent on performance
10. Shirking	h. Pay for current performance to be received in the future
	i. A specific type of contingent pay plan
	j. A foreign national assigned to the parent company

22. *(Characteristics of alternative pay plans)* For each of the following pay plan alternatives, indicate whether it provides a high (H) or low (L) level of motivation; whether the time focus is short-term (S) or long-term (L); and whether there is a strong (ST), weak (W), or moderate (M) link with employee performance.

a. Periodic pay plan
b. Cafeteria plan
c. Pension
d. Employee Stock Ownership Plan
e. Profit sharing
f. Merit pay
g. Contingent pay
h. Piece rate
i. Stock option
j. Perks

23. *(Pay plan and suboptimization)* Betty Jordan is a division manager of Long Island Marine. She is presently evaluating a potential revenue-generating investment that costs $1,000,000 and would increase divisional income before depreciation each year as follows:

Year 1	100,000	Year 4	800,000
Year 2	150,000	Year 5	800,000
Year 3	190,000		

The project would have a 5-year life with no salvage value. All assets are depreciated according to the straight-line method. Betty is evaluated and compensated based on the amount of pretax profit her division generates. More precisely, she receives an annual salary of $100,000 plus a bonus equal to 2% of divisional pretax profit. Before consideration of the above project, Betty anticipates that her division will generate $2,000,000 in divisional pretax profit.

a. Compute the effect of the new investment on the level of divisional pretax profits for years 1 through 5.

b. Determine the effect of the new project on Betty's compensation for each of the five years.

c. Based on your computations in part b, will Betty be hesitant to invest in the new project? Explain.

d. Will upper management view the new investment favorably? Explain.

24. *(Pay plan, age, and suboptimization)* Bama Beans Inc. has operations in 13 states. Bama Beans grows soybeans and processes the beans into soybean oil and soybean meal. These products are sold for various commercial uses. Operations in each state are under the control of an autonomous state manager whose performance is evaluated (in large part) based on the magnitude of annual profit. State managers typically receive an annual bonus equal to .5% of the net profits of that state's division. The manager of North Carolina operations is Benny DuMars. Benny has just turned 62 years old and has been with Bama Beans for 39 years. He would like to sell his division's existing bean crusher and purchase a new, technologically superior one. To evaluate the feasibility of such a move, the division controller prepared the information presented below. This information has created a tremendous dilemma for Benny.

Incremental cost of the new crusher	$2,000,000
Expected remaining life of the old crusher	5 years
Expected life of the new crusher	5 years
Expected effect of the new crusher on net profit for the next 5 years	

Year 1:	Decrease in operating costs	$ 600,000
	Loss on disposal of old crusher	1,500,000
	Net change in profit	$ (900,000)
Year 2:	Net increase in profit	400,000
Year 3:	Net increase in profit	400,000
Year 4:	Net increase in profit	510,000
Year 5:	Net increase in profit	600,000

a. Assume Benny expects to retire when he reaches age 65. Compute the total effect of purchasing the new crusher on Benny's divisional profit and his compensation over his remaining career with Bama Beans.

b. If Benny had just turned 60 rather than 62, what would be the compensation effect of purchasing the new crusher over his remaining career?

c. Is Benny's age likely to be an important factor in his decision regarding the purchase of the new crusher?

d. Would Benny's superiors prefer that he purchase the new crusher? Explain.

COMMUNICATION ACTIVITIES

25. Refer to the News Note entitled "Bonus Incentives Go Awry" on page 1003 in the chapter.

a. Using the plan-performance-reward model in Exhibit 23–1, identify where the company discussed in the News Note went awry in structuring the performance-based pay plan.

b. How can the company use the feedback received regarding the purchasing department's performance to improve the design of the pay plan?

c. How could the purchasing department's behavior be changed by combining the purchasing department with the production department for group-level performance evaluation purposes?

26. Gulfland Chemical Corp is a multinational firm that markets a variety of chemicals for industrial uses. One of the many autonomous divisions is the North America Petrochemical Division (NAPD). The manager of NAPD, Karyn Kravitz, was recently overheard discussing a vexing problem with her controller, William Michaels. The topic of discussion was whether the division should replace its existing chemical handling equipment with newer technology that is safer, more efficient, and cheaper to operate.

According to an analysis by Mr. Michaels, the cost savings over the life of the new technology would pay for the initial cost of the technology several times over. However, Ms. Kravitz remained reluctant to invest. Her most fundamental concern involved the disposition of the old processing equipment. Because the existing equipment has been in use for only two years, it has a very high book value relative to its current market value. To illustrate, Ms. Kravitz noted that if the new technology is not purchased, the division will anticipate a net income of $4,000,000 for the year. However, if the new technology is purchased, the old equipment will have to be sold, and Ms. Kravitz noted that the division can probably sell the equipment for $1.2 million. This equipment had an original cost of $8 million and $1.5 million in depreciation has been recorded. Thus a book loss of $5.3 million ($6.5M − $1.2M) would be recorded on the sale.

Ms. Kravitz's boss, Jim Heitz, is president of the Western Chemical Group, and his compensation is based almost exclusively on the amount of ROI generated by his group, which includes NAPD.

After thoroughly analyzing the facts, Ms. Kravitz concluded, "The people in the Western Chemical Group will swallow their dentures if we book a $5.3 million loss."

a. Why is Ms. Kravitz concerned about the book loss on disposal of the old technology in her division?

b. What are the weaknesses in the performance pay plan in place for Western Chemical Group that are apparently causing Ms. Kravitz to avoid an investment that meets all of the normal criteria of an acceptable investment (ignoring the ROI effect)?

27. *(Pay plans and goal congruence)* In 1994, the lead story in your college newspaper reports the details of the hiring of your new football coach. Your old football coach was fired for failing to win games and attract fans. In his last season his record was 1 win and 11 losses. The news story states the new coach's contract provides for a base salary of $100,000 per year plus an annual bonus computed as follows:

Win less than 5 games	$ 0
Win 5 games or more	25,000
Win 8 games or more	75,000
Win 8 games and conference championship	95,000
Win 8 games, win conference, get a bowl bid	150,000

There are essentially no other features or clauses in the coach's contract.

The first year after the new coach is hired, the football team wins 3 games and loses 8. The second year, the team wins 6 games and loses 5. The third year, the team wins 9 games and a conference championship and is invited to a prestigious bowl. Shortly after the bowl game, articles appear on the front page of several national sports publications announcing your college football program has been cited by the National Collegiate Athletic Association (NCAA) for 9 major rule violations including cash payoffs to players, playing academically ineligible players, illegal recruiting tactics, illegal involvement of alumni in recruiting, and more. All of the national news publications agree that your football program will be disbanded by the NCAA. One article also mentioned that over the past three years only 13% of senior football players managed to graduate on time. Additional speculation suggests the responsible parties including the coaching staff, athletic director, and college president will be dismissed by the board of trustees.

a. Compute the amount of compensation paid to the new coach in each of his first three years.

b. Did the performance measures in the coach's contract foster goal congruence? Explain.

c. Would the coach's actions possibly have been different if other performance measures were added to the compensation contract? Explain.

d. What performance measures should be considered for the next coach's contract, assuming the football program can be retained?

CASES

28. According to a recent news article, the chairman of HCA-Hospital Corp. of America, Thomas Frist, received $127 million in compensation for 1992. Of that amount, $125.9 million came from exercising stock options that had been received in 1989. According to the same article, many of the other HCA top managers also exercised substantial amounts of stock options in 1992. The stock options gave the officers the right to purchase the stock from the corporation for a price that was substantially below the market value.

One of the reasons cited by the managers for exercising the stock options in 1992 was an expectation that tax laws were going to change. Specifically, the managers expected two tax law changes to be enacted in 1993 or later years:

1. An increase in the tax rate on personal income.
2. A limit of $1,000,000 on the annual amount of compensation paid to top executives that would be deductible for tax purposes by corporations.

[SOURCE: Adapted from Helene Cooper, "HCA Chairman's 1992 Compensation Hit $127 Million Due to Stock Options," *Wall Street Journal* (March 24, 1993), p. B7. Reprinted by permission of the *Wall Street Journal*, © 1993 Dow Jones & Company, Inc. All rights reserved worldwide.]

a. Were the stock options exercised in 1992 compensation for job performance in 1992, or compensation for other years? Explain.
b. If the tax law changes expected by the managers were passed as anticipated, was exercising the stock options a wise move for the managers? For HCA? Explain.
c. For 1992, HCA's net income was $28.1 million. Given the level of compensation received by Mr. Frist for 1992, does Mr. Frist's pay appear to be equitable? Explain.
d. If Mr. Frist and the other top managers had not only exercised their stock options, but also sold their stock in 1992, how would this have affected their incentives?

29. Northstar Offroad Co. (NOC), a subsidiary of Allston Automotive, manufactures go-carts and other recreational vehicles. Family recreational centers that feature go-cart tracks, miniature golf, batting cages, and arcade games have increased in popularity. As a result, NOC has been receiving some pressure from Allston Automotive top management to diversify into some of these other recreational areas. Recreational Leasing Inc. (RLI), one of the largest firms that leases arcade games to family recreation centers, is looking for a friendly buyer. Allston Automotive management believes that RLI's assets could be acquired for an investment of $3.2 million and has strongly urged Bill Grieco, division manager of NOC, to consider acquiring RLI.

Grieco has reviewed RLI's financial statements with his controller, Marie Donnelly, and they believe that the acquisition may not be in the best interest of NOC. "If we decide not to do this, the Allston Automotive people are not going to be happy," said Grieco. "If we could convince them to base our bonuses on something other than return on investment, maybe this acquisition would look more attractive. How would we do if the bonuses were based on residual income using the company's 15% cost of capital?"

Allston Automotive has traditionally evaluated all of its divisions on the basis of return on investment, which is defined as the ratio of operating income to total assets; the desired rate of return for each division is 20%. The management team of any division reporting an annual increase in the return on investment is automatically eligible for a bonus. The management of divisions reporting a decline in the return on investment must provide convincing explanations for the decline to be eligible for a bonus, and this bonus is limited to 50% of the bonus paid to divisions reporting an increase.

Presented below are condensed financial statements for both NOC and RLI for the fiscal year ended May 31, 1994.

	NOC	RLI
Sales revenue	$10,500,000	
Leasing revenue		$2,800,000
Variable expenses	(7,000,000)	(1,000,000)
Fixed expenses	(1,500,000)	(1,200,000)
Operating income	$ 2,000,000	$ 600,000
Current assets	$ 2,300,000	$1,900,000
Long-term assets	5,700,000	1,100,000
Total assets	$ 8,000,000	$3,000,000
Current liabilities	$ 1,400,000	$ 850,000
Long-term liabilities	3,800,000	1,200,000
Shareholders' equity	2,800,000	950,000
Total liabilities and S.E.	$ 8,000,000	$3,000,000

a. Under the present bonus system how would the acquisition of RLI affect Mr. Grieco's bonus expectations?

b. If Mr. Grieco's suggestion to use residual income as the evaluation criterion is accepted, how would acquisition of RLI affect Mr. Grieco's bonus expectations?

c. Given the present bonus arrangement, is it fair for Allston Automotive management to expect Mr. Grieco to acquire RLI?

d. Is the present bonus system consistent with Allston Automotive's goal of expansion of NOC into new recreational products?

(CMA)

ETHICS AND QUALITY DISCUSSION

30. *In a survey published in 1990, 649 managers responded to a questionnaire and provided their opinion from an ethical perspective as to the acceptability of manipulating accounting earnings to achieve higher managerial compensation. One of the questions dealt with the acceptability of changing a sales practice to pull some of next year's sales into the current year so that reported current earnings could be pushed up. The results of the survey indicated about 43% of the respondents felt this practice was ethically acceptable, 44% felt the practice was ethically questionable, and 13% felt the practice was ethically unacceptable.*

   Other results of the survey indicate the managers felt large manipulations were more unethical than small manipulations, and income-increasing manipulations were more ethically unacceptable than income-decreasing manipulations.

   [SOURCE: William J. Bruns and Kenneth A. Merchant, "The Dangerous Morality of Managing Earnings," *Management Accounting* (August 1990), pp. 22–25. Reprinted from *Management Accounting.* Copyright by Institute of Management Accountants, Montvale, N.J.]

   a. If managers are able to manipulate earnings to change their pay, is this a signal of a weakness in the pay-for-performance plan? Explain.

   b. In your view, does the amount of a manipulation partly determine the extent to which the manipulation is ethically acceptable?

   c. Describe any circumstances in which you believe manipulations would be ethically acceptable.

31. General Dynamics is one of the many firms that has instituted bonus plans. Refer to the News Note entitled "Pay for Performance at General Dynamics" on page 1004 of the chapter.

a. Do you think it is possible that General Dynamics' managers could take actions between February 1991 and May 1991 that were so significant that share price would rise by $10? Explain.

b. As a shareholder, would you have been suspicious of the timing of the implementation of this plan? Explain.

c. In your view, is there any ethical problem with the implementation of the General Dynamics plan?

d. What factors, other than managerial actions, could have caused the stock price to rise?

32. During the recessionary times of the late 1980s and early 1990s, many companies turned to their workers for pay concessions in response to sagging profits. In other words, as profits declined, managers asked ordinary workers to make sacrifices in their compensation levels. However, the managers were not willing to participate in the workers' pain. For example:

While profits plunged 97% in 1989 for Commodore International Ltd., Chief Executive Irving Gould received a 40% pay hike. His salary was larger than the company's net income for the year. According to a survey of 325 large corporations in 1989, corporate profits fell 4.2% and executive cash compensation rose by 8%.

In 1989 at General Motors, Chairman Roger Smith's annual bonus fell by 7% to $1.4 million. Profits fell by 13%; worker bonuses dropped by 81%.

[SOURCE: Adapted from Carol Hymowitz, "More Employees, Shareholders Demand That Sacrifices in Pay Begin at the Top," *Wall Street Journal* (November 8, 1990), pp. B1, B5. Reprinted by permission of the *Wall Street Journal*, © 1990 Dow Jones & Company, Inc. All rights reserved worldwide.]

a. Based on the examples above and the data in Exhibit 23–7, do you perceive any equity problem or ethical problem in the relative pay treatments of ordinary workers and top managers?

b. Why do you think the pay gap between top managers and workers appears to be more pronounced in the U.S. than in other countries?

c. In the two examples above involving General Motors and Commodore, did the top managers act ethically in accepting the high level of pay, given the circumstances?

33. Stan Burkinshaw has worked for a major U.S. soft drink bottler for 22 years. At present, he is product line manager for two of the company's most popular soft drinks. With the recent events in Eastern Europe, the company has developed plans to open full service subsidiaries (production and marketing) in three of the former Eastern Bloc countries. Top management has approached Stan about managing the planned Russian subsidiary. Of the three planned installations, this subsidiary is intended to carry the largest volume of business.

As a product line manager, Stan earned $400,000 in 1993. Of this amount, about $250,000 was earned through bonuses based on achieved market share and other market factors. For 1993, Stan was the highest paid product line manager at the company.

Stan is 45 years old, married, and has three children who range in age from 12 to 16. His wife, Martha, is an executive with a major insurance company. She earns a salary of $275,000 annually. The family currently resides in Manhattan.

If Stan accepts the Russian position, the starting salary will be $250,000 plus an annual bonus based on the subsidiary's profits. However, the operation is not expected to achieve profitability until at least 1997.

a. Discuss the significant nonmonetary considerations that Stan and his family must factor in to his evaluation of this job opportunity.

b. In considering the Russian job opportunity, what are the ethical considerations that Stan must evaluate?

c. What are the ethical obligations of Stan's employer in extending this job offer to Stan? Is the offered salary of $250,000 a reasonable amount? Discuss.

PRESENT VALUE TABLES

TABLE 1   PRESENT VALUE OF $1

Period	1.00%	2.00%	3.00%	4.00%	5.00%	6.00%	7.00%	8.00%	9.00%	9.50%	10.00%	10.50%	11.00%
1	0.9901	0.9804	0.9709	0.9615	0.9524	0.9434	0.9346	0.9259	0.9174	0.9132	0.9091	0.9050	0.9009
2	0.9803	0.9612	0.9426	0.9246	0.9070	0.8900	0.8734	0.8573	0.8417	0.8340	0.8265	0.8190	0.8116
3	0.9706	0.9423	0.9151	0.8890	0.8638	0.8396	0.8163	0.7938	0.7722	0.7617	0.7513	0.7412	0.7312
4	0.9610	0.9239	0.8885	0.8548	0.8227	0.7921	0.7629	0.7350	0.7084	0.6956	0.6830	0.6707	0.6587
5	0.9515	0.9057	0.8626	0.8219	0.7835	0.7473	0.7130	0.6806	0.6499	0.6352	0.6209	0.6070	0.5935
6	0.9421	0.8880	0.8375	0.7903	0.7462	0.7050	0.6663	0.6302	0.5963	0.5801	0.5645	0.5493	0.5346
7	0.9327	0.8706	0.8131	0.7599	0.7107	0.6651	0.6228	0.5835	0.5470	0.5298	0.5132	0.4971	0.4817
8	0.9235	0.8535	0.7894	0.7307	0.6768	0.6274	0.5820	0.5403	0.5019	0.4838	0.4665	0.4499	0.4339
9	0.9143	0.8368	0.7664	0.7026	0.6446	0.5919	0.5439	0.5003	0.4604	0.4419	0.4241	0.4071	0.3909
10	0.9053	0.8204	0.7441	0.6756	0.6139	0.5584	0.5084	0.4632	0.4224	0.4035	0.3855	0.3685	0.3522
11	0.8963	0.8043	0.7224	0.6496	0.5847	0.5268	0.4751	0.4289	0.3875	0.3685	0.3505	0.3334	0.3173
12	0.8875	0.7885	0.7014	0.6246	0.5568	0.4970	0.4440	0.3971	0.3555	0.3365	0.3186	0.3018	0.2858
13	0.8787	0.7730	0.6810	0.6006	0.5303	0.4688	0.4150	0.3677	0.3262	0.3073	0.2897	0.2731	0.2575
14	0.8700	0.7579	0.6611	0.5775	0.5051	0.4423	0.3878	0.3405	0.2993	0.2807	0.2633	0.2471	0.2320
15	0.8614	0.7430	0.6419	0.5553	0.4810	0.4173	0.3625	0.3152	0.2745	0.2563	0.2394	0.2237	0.2090
16	0.8528	0.7285	0.6232	0.5339	0.4581	0.3937	0.3387	0.2919	0.2519	0.2341	0.2176	0.2024	0.1883
17	0.8444	0.7142	0.6050	0.5134	0.4363	0.3714	0.3166	0.2703	0.2311	0.2138	0.1978	0.1832	0.1696
18	0.8360	0.7002	0.5874	0.4936	0.4155	0.3503	0.2959	0.2503	0.2120	0.1952	0.1799	0.1658	0.1528
19	0.8277	0.6864	0.5703	0.4746	0.3957	0.3305	0.2765	0.2317	0.1945	0.1783	0.1635	0.1500	0.1377
20	0.8195	0.6730	0.5537	0.4564	0.3769	0.3118	0.2584	0.2146	0.1784	0.1628	0.1486	0.1358	0.1240
21	0.8114	0.6598	0.5376	0.4388	0.3589	0.2942	0.2415	0.1987	0.1637	0.1487	0.1351	0.1229	0.1117
22	0.8034	0.6468	0.5219	0.4220	0.3419	0.2775	0.2257	0.1839	0.1502	0.1358	0.1229	0.1112	0.1007
23	0.7954	0.6342	0.5067	0.4057	0.3256	0.2618	0.2110	0.1703	0.1378	0.1240	0.1117	0.1006	0.0907
24	0.7876	0.6217	0.4919	0.3901	0.3101	0.2470	0.1972	0.1577	0.1264	0.1133	0.1015	0.0911	0.0817
25	0.7798	0.6095	0.4776	0.3751	0.2953	0.2330	0.1843	0.1460	0.1160	0.1034	0.0923	0.0824	0.0736
26	0.7721	0.5976	0.4637	0.3607	0.2812	0.2198	0.1722	0.1352	0.1064	0.0945	0.0839	0.0746	0.0663
27	0.7644	0.5859	0.4502	0.3468	0.2679	0.2074	0.1609	0.1252	0.0976	0.0863	0.0763	0.0675	0.0597
28	0.7568	0.5744	0.4371	0.3335	0.2551	0.1956	0.1504	0.1159	0.0896	0.0788	0.0693	0.0611	0.0538
29	0.7493	0.5631	0.4244	0.3207	0.2430	0.1846	0.1406	0.1073	0.0822	0.0719	0.0630	0.0553	0.0485
30	0.7419	0.5521	0.4120	0.3083	0.2314	0.1741	0.1314	0.0994	0.0754	0.0657	0.0573	0.0500	0.0437
31	0.7346	0.5413	0.4000	0.2965	0.2204	0.1643	0.1228	0.0920	0.0692	0.0600	0.0521	0.0453	0.0394
32	0.7273	0.5306	0.3883	0.2851	0.2099	0.1550	0.1147	0.0852	0.0634	0.0058	0.0474	0.0410	0.0355
33	0.7201	0.5202	0.3770	0.2741	0.1999	0.1462	0.1072	0.0789	0.0582	0.0500	0.0431	0.0371	0.0319
34	0.7130	0.5100	0.3660	0.2636	0.1904	0.1379	0.1002	0.0731	0.0534	0.0457	0.0391	0.0336	0.0288
35	0.7059	0.5000	0.3554	0.2534	0.1813	0.1301	0.0937	0.0676	0.0490	0.0417	0.0356	0.0304	0.0259
36	0.6989	0.4902	0.3450	0.2437	0.1727	0.1227	0.0875	0.0626	0.0449	0.0381	0.0324	0.0275	0.0234
37	0.6920	0.4806	0.3350	0.2343	0.1644	0.1158	0.0818	0.0580	0.0412	0.0348	0.0294	0.0249	0.0210
38	0.6852	0.4712	0.3252	0.2253	0.1566	0.1092	0.0765	0.0537	0.0378	0.0318	0.0267	0.0225	0.0190
39	0.6784	0.4620	0.3158	0.2166	0.1492	0.1031	0.0715	0.0497	0.0347	0.0290	0.0243	0.0204	0.0171
40	0.6717	0.4529	0.3066	0.2083	0.1421	0.0972	0.0668	0.0460	0.0318	0.0265	0.0221	0.0184	0.0154
41	0.6650	0.4440	0.2976	0.2003	0.1353	0.0917	0.0624	0.0426	0.0292	0.0242	0.0201	0.0167	0.0139
42	0.6584	0.4353	0.2890	0.1926	0.1288	0.0865	0.0583	0.0395	0.0268	0.0221	0.0183	0.0151	0.0125
43	0.6519	0.4268	0.2805	0.1852	0.1227	0.0816	0.0545	0.0365	0.0246	0.0202	0.0166	0.0137	0.0113
44	0.6455	0.4184	0.2724	0.1781	0.1169	0.0770	0.0510	0.0338	0.0226	0.0184	0.0151	0.0124	0.0101
45	0.6391	0.4102	0.2644	0.1712	0.1113	0.0727	0.0476	0.0313	0.0207	0.0168	0.0137	0.0112	0.0091
46	0.6327	0.4022	0.2567	0.1646	0.1060	0.0685	0.0445	0.0290	0.0190	0.0154	0.0125	0.0101	0.0082
47	0.6265	0.3943	0.2493	0.1583	0.1010	0.0647	0.0416	0.0269	0.0174	0.0141	0.0113	0.0092	0.0074
48	0.6203	0.3865	-0.2420	0.1522	0.0961	0.0610	0.0389	0.0249	0.0160	0.0128	0.0103	0.0083	0.0067
49	0.6141	0.3790	0.2350	0.1463	0.0916	0.0576	0.0363	0.0230	0.0147	0.0117	0.0094	0.0075	0.0060
50	0.6080	0.3715	0.2281	0.1407	0.0872	0.0543	0.0340	0.0213	0.0135	0.0107	0.0085	0.0068	0.0054

11.50%	12.00%	12.50%	13.00%	13.50%	14.00%	14.50%	15.00%	15.50%	16.00%	17.00%	18.00%	19.00%	20.00%
0.8969	0.8929	0.8889	0.8850	0.8811	0.8772	0.8734	0.8696	0.8658	0.8621	0.8547	0.8475	0.8403	0.8333
0.8044	0.7972	0.7901	0.7832	0.7763	0.7695	0.7628	0.7561	0.7496	0.7432	0.7305	0.7182	0.7062	0.6944
0.7214	0.7118	0.7023	0.6931	0.6839	0.6750	0.6662	0.6575	0.6490	0.6407	0.6244	0.6086	0.5934	0.5787
0.6470	0.6355	0.6243	0.6133	0.6026	0.5921	0.5818	0.5718	0.5619	0.5523	0.5337	0.5158	0.4987	0.4823
0.5803	0.5674	0.5549	0.5428	0.5309	0.5194	0.5081	0.4972	0.4865	0.4761	0.4561	0.4371	0.4191	0.4019
0.5204	0.5066	0.4933	0.4803	0.4678	0.4556	0.4438	0.4323	0.4212	0.4104	0.3898	0.3704	0.3521	0.3349
0.4667	0.4524	0.4385	0.4251	0.4121	0.3996	0.3876	0.3759	0.3647	0.3538	0.3332	0.3139	0.2959	0.2791
0.4186	0.4039	0.3897	0.3762	0.3631	0.3506	0.3385	0.3269	0.3158	0.3050	0.2848	0.2660	0.2487	0.2326
0.3754	0.3606	0.3464	0.3329	0.3199	0.3075	0.2956	0.2843	0.2734	0.2630	0.2434	0.2255	0.2090	0.1938
0.3367	0.3220	0.3080	0.2946	0.2819	0.2697	0.2582	0.2472	0.2367	0.2267	0.2080	0.1911	0.1756	0.1615
0.3020	0.2875	0.2737	0.2607	0.2483	0.2366	0.2255	0.2149	0.2049	0.1954	0.1778	0.1619	0.1476	0.1346
0.2708	0.2567	0.2433	0.2307	0.2188	0.2076	0.1969	0.1869	0.1774	0.1685	0.1520	0.1372	0.1240	0.1122
0.2429	0.2292	0.2163	0.2042	0.1928	0.1821	0.1720	0.1625	0.1536	0.1452	0.1299	0.1163	0.1042	0.0935
0.2179	0.2046	0.1923	0.1807	0.1699	0.1597	0.1502	0.1413	0.1330	0.1252	0.1110	0.0986	0.0876	0.0779
0.1954	0.1827	0.1709	0.1599	0.1496	0.1401	0.1312	0.1229	0.1152	0.1079	0.0949	0.0835	0.0736	0.0649
0.1752	0.1631	0.1519	0.1415	0.1319	0.1229	0.1146	0.1069	0.0997	0.0930	0.0811	0.0708	0.0618	0.0541
0.1572	0.1456	0.1350	0.1252	0.1162	0.1078	0.1001	0.0929	0.0863	0.0802	0.0693	0.0600	0.0520	0.0451
0.1410	0.1300	0.1200	0.1108	0.1024	0.0946	0.0874	0.0808	0.0747	0.0691	0.0593	0.0508	0.0437	0.0376
0.1264	0.1161	0.1067	0.0981	0.0902	0.0830	0.0763	0.0703	0.0647	0.0596	0.0506	0.0431	0.0367	0.0313
0.1134	0.1037	0.0948	0.0868	0.0795	0.0728	0.0667	0.0611	0.0560	0.0514	0.0433	0.0365	0.0308	0.0261
0.1017	0.0926	0.0843	0.0768	0.0700	0.0638	0.0582	0.0531	0.0485	0.0443	0.0370	0.0309	0.0259	0.0217
0.0912	0.0826	0.0749	0.0680	0.0617	0.0560	0.0509	0.0462	0.0420	0.0382	0.0316	0.0262	0.0218	0.0181
0.0818	0.0738	0.0666	0.0601	0.0543	0.0491	0.0444	0.0402	0.0364	0.0329	0.0270	0.0222	0.0183	0.0151
0.0734	0.0659	0.0592	0.0532	0.0479	0.0431	0.0388	0.0349	0.0315	0.0284	0.0231	0.0188	0.0154	0.0126
0.0658	0.0588	0.0526	0.0471	0.0422	0.0378	0.0339	0.0304	0.0273	0.0245	0.0197	0.0160	0.0129	0.0105
0.0590	0.0525	0.0468	0.0417	0.0372	0.0332	0.0296	0.0264	0.0236	0.0211	0.0169	0.0135	0.0109	0.0087
0.0529	0.0469	0.0416	0.0369	0.0327	0.0291	0.0258	0.0230	0.0204	0.0182	0.0144	0.0115	0.0091	0.0073
0.0475	0.0419	0.0370	0.0326	0.0289	0.0255	0.0226	0.0200	0.0177	0.0157	0.0123	0.0097	0.0077	0.0061
0.0426	0.0374	0.0329	0.0289	0.0254	0.0224	0.0197	0.0174	0.0153	0.0135	0.0105	0.0082	0.0064	0.0051
0.0382	0.0334	0.0292	0.0256	0.0224	0.0196	0.0172	0.0151	0.0133	0.0117	0.0090	0.0070	0.0054	0.0042
0.0342	0.0298	0.0260	0.0226	0.0197	0.0172	0.0150	0.0131	0.0115	0.0100	0.0077	0.0059	0.0046	0.0035
0.0307	0.0266	0.0231	0.0200	0.0174	0.0151	0.0131	0.0114	0.0099	0.0087	0.0066	0.0050	0.0038	0.0029
0.0275	0.0238	0.0205	0.0177	0.0153	0.0133	0.0115	0.0099	0.0086	0.0075	0.0056	0.0043	0.0032	0.0024
0.0247	0.0212	0.0182	0.0157	0.0135	0.0116	0.0100	0.0088	0.0075	0.0064	0.0048	0.0036	0.0027	0.0020
0.0222	0.0189	0.0162	0.0139	0.0119	0.0102	0.0088	0.0075	0.0065	0.0056	0.0041	0.0031	0.0023	0.0017
0.0199	0.0169	0.0144	0.0123	0.0105	0.0089	0.0076	0.0065	0.0056	0.0048	0.0035	0.0026	0.0019	0.0014
0.0178	0.0151	0.0128	0.0109	0.0092	0.0078	0.0067	0.0057	0.0048	0.0041	0.0030	0.0022	0.0016	0.0012
0.0160	0.0135	0.0114	0.0096	0.0081	0.0069	0.0058	0.0049	0.0042	0.0036	0.0026	0.0019	0.0014	0.0010
0.0143	0.0120	0.0101	0.0085	0.0072	0.0060	0.0051	0.0043	0.0036	0.0031	0.0022	0.0016	0.0011	0.0008
0.0129	0.0108	0.0090	0.0075	0.0063	0.0053	0.0044	0.0037	0.0031	0.0026	0.0019	0.0013	0.0010	0.0007
0.0115	0.0096	0.0080	0.0067	0.0056	0.0046	0.0039	0.0033	0.0027	0.0023	0.0016	0.0011	0.0008	0.0006
0.0103	0.0086	0.0077	0.0059	0.0049	0.0041	0.0034	0.0028	0.0024	0.0020	0.0014	0.0010	0.0007	0.0005
0.0093	0.0077	0.0063	0.0052	0.0043	0.0036	0.0030	0.0025	0.0020	0.0017	0.0012	0.0008	0.0006	0.0004
0.0083	0.0068	0.0056	0.0046	0.0038	0.0031	0.0026	0.0021	0.0018	0.0015	0.0010	0.0007	0.0005	0.0003
0.0075	0.0061	0.0050	0.0041	0.0034	0.0028	0.0023	0.0019	0.0015	0.0013	0.0009	0.0006	0.0004	0.0003
0.0067	0.0054	0.0044	0.0036	0.0030	0.0024	0.0020	0.0016	0.0013	0.0011	0.0007	0.0005	0.0003	0.0002
0.0060	0.0049	0.0039	0.0032	0.0026	0.0021	0.0017	0.0014	0.0011	0.0009	0.0006	0.0004	0.0003	0.0002
0.0054	0.0043	0.0035	0.0028	0.0023	0.0019	0.0015	0.0012	0.0010	0.0008	0.0005	0.0004	0.0002	0.0002
0.0048	0.0039	0.0031	0.0025	0.0020	0.0016	0.0013	0.0011	0.0009	0.0007	0.0005	0.0003	0.0002	0.0001
0.0043	0.0035	0.0028	0.0022	0.0018	0.0014	0.0012	0.0009	0.0007	0.0006	0.0004	0.0003	0.0002	0.0001

TABLE 2   PRESENT VALUE OF AN ORDINARY ANNUITY OF $1

Period	1.00%	2.00%	3.00%	4.00%	5.00%	6.00%	7.00%	8.00%	9.00%	9.50%	10.00%	10.50%	11.00%
1	0.9901	0.9804	0.9709	0.9615	0.0524	0.9434	0.9346	0.9259	0.9174	0.9132	0.9091	0.9050	0.9009
2	1.9704	1.9416	1.9135	1.8861	1.8594	1.8334	1.8080	1.7833	1.7591	1.7473	1.7355	1.7240	1.7125
3	2.9410	2.8839	2.8286	2.7751	2.7233	2.6730	2.6243	2.5771	2.5313	2.5089	2.4869	2.4651	2.4437
4	3.9020	3.8077	3.7171	3.6299	3.5460	3.4651	3.3872	3.3121	3.2397	3.2045	3.1699	3.1359	3.1025
5	4.8534	4.7135	4.5797	4.4518	4.3295	4.2124	4.1002	3.9927	3.8897	3.8397	3.7908	3.7429	3.6959
6	5.7955	5.6014	5.4172	5.2421	5.0757	4.9173	4.7665	4.6229	4.4859	4.4198	4.3553	4.2922	4.2305
7	6.7282	6.4720	6.2303	6.0021	5.7864	5.5824	5.3893	5.2064	5.0330	4.9496	4.8684	4.7893	4.7122
8	7.6517	7.3255	7.0197	6.7327	6.4632	6.2098	5.9713	5.7466	5.5348	5.4334	5.3349	5.2392	5.1461
9	8.5660	8.1622	7.7861	7.4353	7.1078	6.8017	6.5152	6.2469	5.9953	5.8753	5.7590	5.6463	5.5371
10	9.4713	8.9826	8.5302	8.1109	7.7217	7.3601	7.0236	6.7101	6.4177	6.2788	6.1446	6.0148	5.8892
11	10.3676	9.7869	9.2526	8.7605	8.3064	7.8869	7.4987	7.1390	6.8052	6.6473	6.4951	6.3482	6.2065
12	11.2551	10.5753	9.9540	9.3851	8.8633	8.3838	7.9427	7.5361	7.1607	6.9838	6.8137	6.6500	6.4924
13	12.1337	11.3484	10.6350	9.9857	9.3936	8.8527	8.3577	7.9038	7.4869	7.2912	7.1034	6.9230	6.7499
14	13.0037	12.1063	11.2961	10.5631	9.8986	9.2950	8.7455	8.2442	7.7862	7.5719	7.3667	7.1702	6.9819
15	13.8651	12.8493	11.9379	11.1184	10.3797	9.7123	9.1079	8.5595	8.0607	7.8282	7.6061	7.3938	7.1909
16	14.7179	13.5777	12.5611	11.6523	10.8378	10.1059	9.4467	8.8514	8.3126	8.0623	7.8237	7.5962	7.3792
17	15.5623	14.2919	13.1661	12.1657	11.2741	10.4773	9.7632	9.1216	8.5436	8.2760	8.0216	7.7794	7.5488
18	16.3983	14.9920	13.7535	12.6593	11.6896	10.8276	10.0591	9.3719	8.7556	8.4713	8.2014	7.9452	7.7016
19	17.2260	15.6785	14.3238	13.1339	12.0853	11.1581	10.3356	9.6036	8.9501	8.6496	8.3649	8.0952	7.8393
20	18.0456	16.3514	14.8775	13.5903	12.4622	11.4699	10.5940	9.8182	9.1286	8.8124	8.5136	8.2309	7.9633
21	18.8570	17.0112	15.4150	14.0292	12.8212	11.7641	10.8355	10.0168	9.2922	8.9611	8.6487	8.3538	8.0751
22	19.6604	17.6581	15.9369	14.4511	13.1630	12.0416	11.0612	10.2007	9.4424	9.0969	8.7715	8.4649	8.1757
23	20.4558	18.2922	16.4436	14.8568	13.4886	12.3034	11.2722	10.3711	9.5802	9.2209	8.8832	8.5656	8.2664
24	21.2434	18.9139	16.9355	15.2470	13.7986	12.5504	11.4693	10.5288	9.7066	9.3342	8.9847	8.6566	8.3481
25	22.0232	19.5235	17.4132	15.6221	14.0939	12.7834	11.6536	10.6748	9.8226	9.4376	9.0770	8.7390	8.4217
26	22.7952	20.1210	17.8768	15.9828	14.3752	13.0032	11.8258	10.8100	9.9290	9.5320	9.1610	8.8136	8.4881
27	23.5596	20.7069	18.3270	16.3296	14.6430	13.2105	11.9867	10.9352	10.0266	9.6183	9.2372	8.8811	8.5478
28	24.3164	21.2813	18.7641	16.6631	14.8981	13.4062	12.1371	11.0511	10.1161	9.6971	9.3066	8.9422	8.6016
29	25.0658	21.8444	19.1885	16.9837	15.1411	13.5907	12.2777	11.1584	10.1983	9.7690	9.3696	8.9974	8.6501
30	25.8077	22.3965	19.6004	17.2920	15.3725	13.7648	12.4090	11.2578	10.2737	9.8347	9.4269	9.0474	8.6938
31	26.5423	22.9377	20.0004	17.5885	15.5928	13.9291	12.5318	11.3498	10.3428	9.8947	9.4790	9.0927	8.7332
32	27.2696	23.4683	20.3888	17.8736	15.8027	14.0840	12.6466	11.4350	10.4062	9.9495	9.5264	9.1337	8.7686
33	27.9897	23.9886	20.7658	18.1477	16.0026	14.2302	12.7538	11.5139	10.4664	9.9996	9.5694	9.1707	8.8005
34	28.7027	24.4986	21.1318	18.4112	16.1929	14.3681	12.8540	11.5869	10.5178	10.0453	9.6086	9.2043	8.8293
35	29.4086	24.9986	21.4872	18.6646	16.3742	14.4983	12.9477	11.6546	10.5668	10.0870	9.6442	9.2347	8.8552
36	30.1075	25.4888	21.8323	18.9083	16.5469	14.6210	13.0352	11.7172	10.6118	10.1251	9.6765	9.2621	8.8786
37	30.7995	25.9695	22.1672	19.1426	16.7113	14.7368	13.1170	11.7752	10.6530	10.1599	9.7059	9.2870	8.8996
38	31.4847	26.4406	22.4925	19.3679	16.8679	14.8460	13.1935	11.8289	10.6908	10.1917	9.7327	9.3095	8.9186
39	32.1630	26.9026	22.8082	19.5845	17.0170	14.9491	13.2649	11.8786	10.7255	10.2207	9.7570	9.3299	8.9357
40	32.8347	27.3555	23.1148	19.7928	17.1591	15.0463	13.3317	11.9246	10.7574	10.2473	9.7791	9.3483	8.9511
41	33.4997	27.7995	23.4124	19.9931	17.2944	15.1380	13.3941	11.9672	10.7866	10.2715	9.7991	9.3650	8.9649
42	34.1581	28.2348	23.7014	20.1856	17.4232	15.2245	13.4525	12.0067	10.8134	10.2936	9.8174	9.3801	8.9774
43	34.8100	28.6616	23.9819	20.3708	17.5459	15.3062	13.5070	12.0432	10.8380	10.3138	9.8340	9.3937	8.9887
44	35.4555	29.0800	24.2543	20.5488	17.6628	15.3832	13.5579	12.0771	10.8605	10.3322	9.8491	9.4061	8.9988
45	36.0945	29.4902	24.5187	20.7200	17.7741	15.4558	13.6055	12.1084	10.8812	10.3490	9.8628	9.4163	9.0079
46	36.7272	29.8923	24.7755	20.8847	17.8801	15.5244	13.6500	12.1374	10.9002	10.3644	9.8753	9.4274	9.0161
47	37.3537	30.2866	25.0247	21.0429	17.9810	15.5890	13.6916	12.1643	10.9176	10.3785	9.8866	9.4366	9.0236
48	37.9740	30.6731	25.2667	21.1951	18.0772	15.6500	13.7305	12.1891	10.9336	10.3913	9.8969	9.4449	9.0302
49	38.5881	31.0521	25.5017	21.3415	18.1687	15.7076	13.7668	12.2122	10.9482	10.4030	9.9063	9.4524	9.0362
50	39.1961	31.4236	25.7298	21.4822	18.2559	15.7619	13.8008	12.2335	10.9617	10.4137	9.9148	9.4591	9.0417

11.50%	12.00%	12.50%	13.00%	13.50%	14.00%	14.50%	15.00%	15.50%	16.00%	17.00%	18.00%	19.00%	20.00%
0.8969	0.8929	0.8889	0.8850	0.8811	0.8772	0.8734	0.8696	0.8658	0.8621	0.8547	0.8475	0.8403	0.8333
1.7012	1.6901	1.6790	1.6681	1.6573	1.6467	1.6361	1.6257	1.6154	1.6052	1.5852	1.5656	1.5465	1.5278
2.4226	2.4018	2.3813	2.3612	2.3413	2.3216	2.3023	2.2832	2.2644	2.2459	2.2096	2.1743	2.1399	2.1065
3.0696	3.0374	3.0056	2.9745	2.9438	2.9137	2.8841	2.8850	2.8263	2.7982	2.7432	2.6901	2.6386	2.5887
3.6499	3.6048	3.5606	3.5172	3.4747	3.4331	3.3922	3.3522	3.3129	3.2743	3.1994	3.1272	3.0576	2.9906
4.1703	4.1114	4.0538	3.9976	3.9425	3.8887	3.8360	3.7845	3.7341	3.6847	3.5892	3.4976	3.4098	3.3255
4.6370	4.5638	4.4923	4.4226	4.3546	4.2883	4.2236	4.1604	4.0988	4.0386	3.9224	3.8115	3.7057	3.6046
5.0556	4.9676	4.8821	4.7988	4.7177	4.6389	4.5621	4.4873	4.4145	4.3436	4.2072	4.0776	3.9544	3.8372
5.4311	5.3283	5.2285	5.1317	5.0377	4.9464	4.8577	4.7716	4.6879	4.6065	4.4506	4.3030	4.1633	4.0310
5.7678	5.6502	5.5364	5.4262	5.3195	5.2161	5.1159	5.0188	4.9246	4.8332	4.6586	4.4941	4.3389	4.1925
6.0698	5.9377	5.8102	5.6869	5.5679	5.4527	5.3414	5.2337	5.1295	5.0286	4.8364	4.6560	4.4865	4.3271
6.3406	6.1944	6.0535	5.9177	5.7867	5.6603	5.5383	5.4206	5.3069	5.1971	4.9884	4.7932	4.6105	4.4392
6.5835	6.4236	6.2698	6.1218	5.9794	5.8424	5.7103	5.5832	5.4606	5.3423	5.1183	4.9095	4.7147	4.5327
6.8013	6.6282	6.4620	6.3025	6.1493	6.0021	5.8606	5.7245	5.5936	5.4675	5.2293	5.0081	4.8023	4.6106
6.9967	6.8109	6.6329	6.4624	6.2989	6.1422	5.9918	5.8474	5.7087	5.5755	5.3242	5.0916	4.8759	4.6755
7.1719	6.9740	6.7848	6.6039	6.4308	6.2651	6.1063	5.9542	5.8084	5.6685	5.4053	5.1624	4.9377	4.7296
7.3291	7.1196	6.9198	6.7291	6.5469	6.3729	6.2064	6.0472	5.8947	5.7487	5.4746	5.2223	4.9897	4.7746
7.4700	7.2497	7.0398	6.8399	6.6493	6.4674	6.2938	6.1280	5.9695	5.8179	5.5339	5.2732	5.0333	4.8122
7.5964	7.3658	7.1465	6.9380	6.7395	6.5504	6.3701	6.1982	6.0342	5.8775	5.5845	5.3162	5.0700	4.8435
7.7098	7.4694	7.2414	7.0248	6.8189	6.6231	6.4368	6.2593	6.0902	5.9288	5.6278	5.3528	5.1009	4.8696
7.8115	7.5620	7.3257	7.1016	6.8889	6.6870	6.4950	6.3125	6.1387	5.9731	5.6648	5.3837	5.1268	4.8913
7.9027	7.6447	7.4006	7.1695	6.9506	6.7429	6.5459	6.3587	6.1807	6.0113	5.6964	5.4099	5.1486	4.9094
7.9845	7.7184	7.4672	7.2297	7.0049	6.7921	6.5903	6.3988	6.2170	6.0443	5.7234	5.4321	5.1669	4.9245
8.0578	7.7843	7.5264	7.2829	7.0528	6.8351	6.6291	6.4338	6.2485	6.0726	5.7465	5.4510	5.1822	4.9371
8.1236	7.8431	7.5790	7.3300	7.0950	6.8729	6.6629	6.4642	6.2758	6.0971	5.7662	5.4669	5.1952	4.9476
8.1826	7.8957	7.6258	7.3717	7.1321	6.9061	6.6925	6.4906	6.2994	6.1182	5.7831	5.4804	5.2060	4.9563
8.2355	7.9426	7.6674	7.4086	7.1649	6.9352	6.7184	6.5135	6.3198	6.1364	5.7975	5.4919	5.2151	4.9636
8.2830	7.9844	7.7043	7.4412	7.1937	6.9607	6.7409	6.5335	6.3375	6.1520	5.8099	5.5016	5.2228	4.9697
8.3255	8.0218	7.7372	7.4701	7.2191	6.9830	6.7606	6.5509	6.3528	6.1656	5.8204	5.5098	5.2292	4.9747
8.3637	8.0552	7.7664	7.4957	7.2415	7.0027	6.7779	6.5660	6.3661	6.1772	5.8294	5.5168	5.2347	4.9789
8.3980	8.0850	7.7923	7.5183	7.2613	7.0199	6.7929	6.5791	6.3776	6.1872	5.8371	5.5227	5.2392	4.9825
8.4287	8.1116	7.8154	7.5383	7.2786	7.0350	6.8060	6.5905	6.3875	6.1959	5.8437	5.5277	5.2430	4.9854
8.4562	8.1354	7.8359	7.5560	7.2940	7.0482	6.8175	6.6005	6.3961	6.2034	5.8493	5.5320	5.2463	4.9878
8.4809	8.1566	7.8542	7.5717	7.3075	7.0599	6.8275	6.6091	6.4035	6.2098	5.8541	5.5356	5.2490	4.9898
8.5030	8.1755	7.8704	7.5856	7.3193	7.0701	6.8362	6.6166	6.4100	6.2153	5.8582	5.5386	5.2512	4.9930
8.5229	8.1924	7.8848	7.5979	7.3298	7.0790	6.8439	6.6231	6.4156	6.2201	5.8617	5.5412	5.2531	4.9930
8.5407	8.2075	7.8976	7.6087	7.3390	7.0868	6.8505	6.6288	6.4204	6.2242	5.8647	5.5434	5.2547	4.9941
8.5567	8.2210	7.9090	7.6183	7.3472	7.0937	6.8564	6.6338	6.4246	6.2278	5.8673	5.5453	5.2561	4.9951
8.5710	8.2330	7.9191	7.6268	7.3543	7.0998	6.8615	6.6381	6.4282	6.2309	5.8695	5.5468	5.2572	4.9959
8.5839	8.2438	7.9281	7.6344	7.3607	7.1050	6.8659	6.6418	6.4314	6.2335	5.8713	5.5482	5.2582	4.9966
8.5954	8.2534	7.9361	7.6410	7.3662	7.1097	6.8698	6.6450	6.4341	6.2358	5.8729	5.5493	5.2590	4.9972
8.6058	8.2619	7.9432	7.6469	7.3711	7.1138	6.8732	6.6479	6.4364	6.2377	5.8743	5.5502	5.2596	4.9976
8.6150	8.2696	7.9495	7.6522	7.3754	7.1173	6.8761	6.6503	6.4385	6.2394	5.8755	5.5511	5.2602	4.9980
8.6233	8.2764	7.9551	7.6568	7.3792	7.1205	6.8787	6.6524	6.4402	6.2409	5.8765	5.5517	5.2607	4.9984
8.6308	8.2825	7.9601	7.6609	7.3826	7.1232	6.8810	6.6543	6.4418	6.2421	5.8773	5.5523	5.2611	4.9986
8.6375	8.2880	7.9645	7.6645	7.3855	7.1256	6.8830	6.6559	6.4431	6.2432	5.8781	5.5528	5.2614	4.9989
8.6435	8.2928	7.9685	7.6677	7.3881	7.1277	6.8847	6.6573	6.4442	6.2442	5.8787	5.5532	5.2617	4.9991
8.6489	8.2972	7.9720	7.6705	7.3904	7.1296	6.8862	6.6585	6.4452	6.2450	5.8792	5.5536	5.2619	4.9992
8.6537	8.3010	7.9751	7.6730	7.3925	7.1312	6.8875	6.6596	6.4461	6.2457	5.8797	5.5539	5.2621	4.9993
8.6580	8.3045	7.9779	7.6752	7.3942	7.1327	6.8886	6.6605	6.4468	6.2463	5.8801	5.5541	5.2623	4.9995

USING THE ETHICS DISCUSSION QUESTIONS

There are few more difficult issues facing business graduates or people in the business world today than those pertaining to ethical dilemmas. Some of these situations are specifically covered by professional codes of conduct; others reflect the differences among what is ethical, what is legal, and what is professionally accepted. Most traditional coverage of ethics in accounting courses focuses on the teachings of the various professional codes of ethics. While teaching about codes of ethics is important, it can be greatly enhanced by presenting cases involving questionable breaches of proper conduct in the myriad of everyday business transactions. By covering such situations, college faculty have an opportunity to make a significant contribution to their students' success and well-being in the area of day-to-day ethics.

The text provides a series of end of chapter situations that can be used to give the student practice in recognizing ethical issues and an opportunity to develop appropriate responses. Some of the questions address what appear to be fairly innocuous issues (price setting for a price bid); others address mainstream environmental and ethical matters (the handling of environmentally destructive waste materials). Both types of situations, however, have important underlying ethical conflicts and require a logical thought process to arrive at the most ethical solution rather than simply *rationalizing* any solution chosen. Students need to recognize that it may be easy to make an unethical decision when the stakes are not very high; however, when the stakes increase, the pattern of unethical decision making may already be in place. If the minor ethical decisions can be analyzed and resolved ethically, the major decisions are more likely to be addressed in a thoughtful and ethical manner.

It is important that students be prepared, while they are in school, for ethical conflicts with which they may be confronted in the workplace. An essential part of such preparation is obtaining the *ability* to recognize ethical problems before they become realities and learning how, when, and to whom to respond to such problems. The purpose of cost accounting is not to provide a philosophy lecture, but students should be made aware of at least some of the major existing ethical theories and problem-solving models before being asked to analyze and resolve ethical conflict situations. Thus, the following information may be useful to both the faculty member teaching this course as well as the students taking it.

Ethics can be viewed and taught at two levels: (1) as a set of general theories and (2) as a set of specific principles.

Ethical Theories

Viewing ethics as a set of general theories allows people to learn the background used in developing specific principles and, therefore, be able to develop their own principles or guidelines when confronted with unique situations in which the existing principles seem to have no relevance. This type of teaching is usually performed in philosophy courses, but some of the basic theories can be briefly defined and illustrated at this point.

Utilitarianism.   This theory holds that the primary method of determining what is right or ethical is the usefulness of an action or a policy in producing other actions or experiences that people value. It emphasizes the consequences that an action has on all the people directly and/or indirectly affected by that action. Utilitarianism reflects a societal viewpoint of the "greatest good for the greatest number." While this theory may provide extremely valid ethical decisions, it is highly unworkable in its theoretical state in practice. This model would require determining *all* possible solutions to a dilemma, determining *all* possible stakeholders for each solution, determining *all* the costs and benefits of *each* solution to *each* stakeholder, summing such costs and benefits, and choosing the decision that maximized the benefits of the most stakeholders. Thus, when utilitarianism is applied as a model of ethical decision making, certain shortcuts are normally taken, such as considering only certain types of stakeholders or solutions within a certain type of framework. When such shortcuts are taken, however, the decision maker should occasionally review them to make sure that such simplifications have not automatically ignored important constituencies, reference points, interests, or values. (Utilitarianism is a type of cost-benefit analysis.)

Categorical Imperatives.   This set of rules requires that a person act on the premise that whatever he or she does would become a universal law. Categorical imperatives form the basis of duties that are considered inherently right. Because actions are determined to be inherently right or wrong (regardless of the positive or negative consequences), the decision maker is responsible for behavior, not for consequences. Thus, the model emphasizes treating all persons equally and as the person acting would like to be treated. Additionally, the model emphasizes respect for individuals and their freedoms. (Categorical imperatives reflect a basic "Do unto others as you would have them do unto you" concept.)

The theory of rights asserts that people have some fundamental rights that must be respected in all types of decisions and is a variation of the duty-based analysis. Rights advocates suggest that there are liberty rights and welfare rights for all persons. Liberty rights basically have been embedded in the U.S. Constitution and include:

- the right of free consent (people should be treated only as they knowingly and willingly consent to be treated)
- the right to privacy (outside the work environment)
- the right to freedom of conscience
- the right to free speech
- the right to due process

Welfare rights reflect the rights of all people to some minimum standard of living; these rights typically have fallen into the realm of governmental or corporate social responsibilities.

The theory of justice requires that people make decisions based on equity, fairness, and impartiality. While the theory of justice requires that people who are similar must be treated in a similar manner, it allows people who are different in a *relevant* way to be treated differently. The relevant ways affecting when people can be treated differently cannot relate to arbitrary characteristics; the differences must be related to the task that is to be performed or differences in people's needs. In using the theory of justice, a decision maker must be careful to make certain that the characteristic(s) on which he or she is making the distinction is(are) relevant and not discriminatory.

(While these are not the only ethical theories that exist, they do provide a foundation from which to begin ethical discussions.)

Ethics as a Set of Principles

Teaching ethics as a set of specific principles provides individuals with a means to answer concrete, problem-oriented situations. This method is typically how ethics are treated in an auditing course or in discussions of codes of ethics.

It is important to point out to students the difference between ethics and legality. Ethics can be viewed as a nonjurisdictional system of moral rights. It represents the moral rights that people have regardless of where or when they live, whether these rights are recognized or not. Legality merely refers to what is permissible under the law in a particular society. Sometimes society may condone an act as legal because of the surrounding circumstances even though the act itself may be viewed as unethical. (For example, it is unethical to kill another human being, but society may make it legal to do so under certain situations.) Legitimizing a "wrong" act because of circumstances does not make that act any more moral.

In making ethical decisions, a person must first have the sensitivity to recognize that an ethical dilemma exists and exert the self-control to attempt to resolve it. This conflict may be at the personal, organizational, or societal level. All feasible alternatives should be considered along with their influencing factors such as values, laws, resource constraints, pressures, and cultural mores. *Once all ramifications are considered and the decision maker selects an alternative using whatever theories or processes he or she chooses, the decision maker must also be willing to accept the outcomes from and responsibility for that choice.* An individual acts as an autonomous agent when he or she acts on the basis of principles that have been consciously evaluated and accepted by the individual as the correct principles to direct behavior; individuals cannot be considered autonomous when they act based on principles that have been imposed from the outside (through peer pressure or by some authority) or that have been internalized as a matter of mere habit.

The making of ethical choices is not a science; it is subjective and cannot be resolved from a societal point of view. Different individuals will always have different viewpoints as to what is ethical and what is the proper decision for an ethical dilemma. The challenge is to create a means for students to foresee potential problems, recognize they have an obligation to derive internal and personal criteria by which to resolve such dilemmas, and accept personal, organizational, societal, and legal determinations as to the ethical or unethical nature of solutions chosen when (or if) those solutions are made public.

GLOSSARY

ABC see activity-based costing

ABC analysis a process of separating inventory items into three groups (A, B, and C) based on annual cost-to-volume usage

Abnormal loss a decline in units in excess of normal expectations during a production process

Abnormal spoilage spoilage in excess of the anticipated quantity or rate; is a period cost

Absorption costing a cost accumulation and reporting method that treats the costs of all manufacturing components (direct materials, direct labor, variable overhead, and fixed overhead) as inventoriable or product costs; is the traditional approach to product costing; must be used for external financial statements and tax returns

Accounting rate of return (ARR) the rate of earnings obtained on the average capital investment over the life of a capital project; computed as average annual profits divided by average investment; not based on cash flow

Accretion an increase in units or volume caused by the addition of materials or to factors inherent in the production process

Activity a repetitive action performed in fulfillment of business functions

Activity analysis the process of detailing the various repetitive actions that are performed in making a product or providing a service, classifying them as value-added and non-value-added and devising ways of minimizing or eliminating non-value-added activities

Activity center a segment of the production or service process for which management wants to separately report the costs of the activities performed

Activity-based costing (ABC) a process using multiple cost drivers to predict and allocate costs to products and services; an accounting system collecting financial and operational data on the basis of the underlying nature and extent of business activities; an accounting information and costing system that identifies the various activities performed in an organization, collects costs on the basis of the underlying nature and extent of those activities, and assigns costs to products and services based on consumption of those activities by the products and services

Activity-based management a discipline that focuses on the activities incurred during production/performance process as the way to improve the value received by a customer and the resulting profit achieved by providing this value

Actual cost system a valuation method that uses actual direct materials, direct labor, and overhead charges in determining the cost of Work in Process Inventory

Ad hoc discount a price concession made under competitive pressure (real or imagined) that does not relate to quantity purchased

Administrative department an organizational unit that performs management activities benefiting the entire organization; includes top management personnel and organization headquarters

Algebraic method a process of service department cost allocation that considers all interrelationships of the departments and reflects these relationships in simultaneous equations

Algorithm a logical step-by-step problem-solving technique (generally requiring the use of a computer) that continuously searches for an improved solution from the one previously computed until the best answer is determined

Allocate assign based on the use of a cost driver, a cost predictor or an arbitrary method

Allocation the systematic assignment of an amount to a recipient set of categories

Annuity a series of equal cash flows (either positive or negative) per period

Annuity due a series of equal cash flows being received or paid at the beginning of a period

Applied overhead the amount of overhead that has been assigned to Work in Process Inventory as a result of productive activity; credits for this amount are to an overhead account

Appraisal cost a quality control cost incurred for monitoring or inspection; compensates for mistakes not eliminated through prevention activities

Appropriation a budgeted maximum allowable expenditure

Approximated net realizable value at split-off allocation a method of allocating joint cost to joint products using a simulated net realizable value at the split-off point; approximated value is computed as final sales price minus incremental separate costs

Asset turnover a ratio measuring asset productivity and showing the number of sales dollars generated by each dollar of assets

Attribute-based costing (ABC II) an extension of activity-based costing using cost-benefit analysis (based on increased customer utility) to choose the product attribute enhancements that the company wants to integrate into a product

Authority the right (usually by virtue of position or rank) to use resources to accomplish a task or achieve an objective

Autonomation the use of equipment that has been programmed to sense certain conditions

Backflush costing a streamlined cost accounting method that speeds up, simplifies, and minimizes accounting effort in an environment that minimizes inventory balances, requires few allocations, uses standard costs, and has minimal variances from standard

Batch level cost a cost that is caused by a group of things made, handled, or processed at a single time

Benchmarking the process of investigating how others do something better so that the investigating company can imitate, and possibly improve upon, their techniques

Benefits-provided ranking a listing of service departments in an order that begins with the one providing the most service to all other corporate areas; the ranking ends with the service department providing service primarily to all the revenue-producing areas

Bill of materials a document that contains information about the product materials components and their specifications (including quality and quantities needed)

Bottleneck any object or facility whose processing speed is sufficiently slow to cause the other processing mechanisms in its network to experience idle time

Breakeven chart a graph that depicts the relationships among revenues, variable costs, fixed costs, and profits (or losses)

Breakeven point the level of activity, in units or dollars, at which total revenues equal total costs

Budget a financial plan for the future based on a single level of activity; the quantitative expression of a company's commitment to planned activities and resource acquisition and use

Budget manual a detailed set of documents that provide information and guidelines about the budgetary process

Budget slack an intentional underestimation of revenues and/or overestimation of expenses in a budgeting process for the purpose of including deviations that are likely to occur so that results will occur within budget limits

Budget variance the difference between total actual overhead and budgeted overhead based on standard hours allowed for the production achieved during the period; computed as part of two-variance overhead analysis; also referred to as the controllable variance

Budgeted cost a planned expenditure

Budgeting the process of formalizing plans and committing them to written, financial terms

Business process reengineering the process of combining information technology to create new and more effective business processes with a continuous improvement movement to lower costs, eliminate unnecessary work, upgrade customer service, and increase speed to market.

By-product an incidental output of a joint process; is salable, but the sales value of by-products is not substantial enough for management to justify undertaking the joint process; viewed as having a higher sales value than scrap

Cafeteria plan a "menu" of fringe benefit options that include cash or nontaxable benefits

Capacity a measure of production volume or some other activity base

Capital asset an asset used to generate revenues or cost savings by providing production, distribution, or service capabilities for more than one year

Capital budgeting a process of evaluating an economic entity's proposed long-range projects or courses of future activity for the purpose of allocating limited resources to desirable projects

Capital rationing a condition that exists when there is an upper-dollar constraint on the amount of capital available to commit to capital asset acquisition

Carrying costs the variable costs of carrying one unit of inventory in stock for one year; includes the opportunity cost of the capital invested in inventory

CASB see Cost Accounting Standards Board

Cash flow the receipt or disbursement of cash; when related to capital budgeting, cash flows arise from the purchase, operation, and disposition of a capital asset

Centralization a management style that exists when top management makes most decisions and controls most activities of the organizational units from the company's central headquarters

Certified Management Accountant a professional designation in the area of management accounting that recognizes the successful completion of an examination, acceptable work experience, and continuing education requirements

Charge-back system a system using transfer prices; see transfer price

Coefficient of correlation a measure of dispersion that indicates the degree of relative association existing between two variables

Coefficient of determination a measure of dispersion that indicates the "goodness of fit" of the actual observations to the least squares regression line; indicates what proportion of the total variation in y is explained by the regression model

Coefficient of variation a measure of risk used when the standard deviations for multiple projects are approximately the same but the expected values are significantly different

Committed cost a cost related either to the long-term investment in plant and equipment of a business or to the organizational personnel whom top management deem permanent; a cost that cannot be changed without long-run detriment to the organization

Common body of knowledge the minimum set of knowledge needed by a person to function effectively in a particular field

Compensation strategy a foundation for the compensation plan that addresses the role compensation should play in the organization

Compound interest a method of determining interest in which interest that was earned in prior periods is added to the original investment so that, in each successive period, interest is earned on both principal and interest

Compounding period the time between each interest computation

Computer-aided design a system using computer graphics for product designs

Computer-aided manufacturing the use of computers to control production processes through numerically controlled (NC) machines, robots, and automated assembly systems

Computer integrated manufacturing (CIM) the integration of two or more flexible manufacturing systems through the use of a host computer and an information networking system

Constraint a restriction inhibiting the achievement of an objective

Contingent pay pay that is dependent on the achievement of some performance objective

Continuous budgeting a process in which there is an ongoing twelve-month budget at all points in time during a budget period because a new budget month (twelve months into the future) is added as each current month expires

Continuous improvement an ongoing process of enhancing employee task performance, level of product quality, and level of company service through eliminating non-value-added activities to reduce lead time, making products (performing services) with zero defects, reducing product costs on an ongoing basis, and simplifying products and processes

Continuous spoilage spoilage that occurs uniformly throughout the production process

Contribution margin the difference between selling price and variable cost per unit, or in total for the level of activity; indicates the amount of each revenue dollar remaining after variable costs have been covered and going toward the coverage of fixed costs and the generation of profits

Contribution margin ratio the proportion of each revenue dollar remaining after variable costs have been covered; computed as contribution margin divided by sales

Control chart a graphical presentation of the results of a specified activity; indicates the upper and lower control limits and those results that are out of control

Controllable cost a cost over which a manager has the ability to authorize incurrence or directly influence magnitude

Controllable variance the budget variance of the two-variance approach to analyzing overhead variances

Controller the chief accountant (in a corporation) who is responsible for maintaining and reporting on both the cost and financial sets of accounts but does not handle or negotiate changes in actual resources

Controlling the process of exerting managerial influence on operations so that they conform to previously prepared plans

Conversion the process of transformation or change

Conversion cost the total of direct labor and overhead cost; the cost necessary to transform direct materials into a finished good or service

Correlation analysis an analytical technique that uses statistical measures of dispersion to reveal the strength of the relationship between variables

Cost the cash or cash equivalent value necessary to attain an objective such as acquiring goods and services used, complying with a contract, performing a function, or producing and distributing a product

Cost accounting a technique or method for determining the cost of a project, process, or thing through direct measurement, arbitrary assignment, or systematic and rational allocation

Cost Accounting Standards Board a body established by Congress in 1970 to promulgate cost accounting standards for defense contractors and federal agencies; disbanded in 1980 and reestablished in 1988; previously issued pronouncements still carry the weight of law for those organizations within its jurisdiction

Cost allocation the assignment, using some reasonable basis, of any indirect cost to one or more cost objects

Cost avoidance the practice of finding acceptable alternatives to high-cost items and/or not spending money for unnecessary goods or services

Cost-benefit analysis the analytical process of comparing the relative costs and benefits that result from a specific course of action (such as providing information or investing in a project)

Cost center a responsibility center in which the manager has the authority to incur costs and is evaluated on the basis of how well costs are controlled

Cost consciousness a companywide attitude about the topics of cost understanding, cost containment, cost avoidance, and cost reduction

Cost containment the practice of minimizing, to the extent possible, period-by-period increases in per-unit variable and total fixed costs

Cost control system a logical structure of formal and/or informal activities designed to analyze and evaluate how well expenditures are managed during a period

Cost driver a factor that has a direct cause-effect relationship to a cost; an activity creating a cost

Cost driver analysis the process of investigating, quantifying, and explaining the relationships of cost drivers and their related costs

Cost object anything to which costs attach or are related

Cost of capital the weighted average rate reflecting the costs of the various sources of funds that comprise a firm's debt and equity structure

Cost of goods manufactured the total cost of the goods completed and transferred to Finished Goods Inventory during the period

Cost of production report a process costing document that details all operating and cost information, shows the computation of cost per equivalent unit, and indicates cost assignment to goods produced during the period

Cost of purchasing the quoted purchase price of inventory, minus any discounts allowed, plus shipping charges

Cost-plus contract a contract in which the customer agrees to reimburse the producer for the cost of the job plus a specified profit margin over cost

Cost pool a collection of monetary amounts incurred either for the same purpose, at the same organizational level, or as a result of the occurrence of the same cost driver

Cost reduction the practice of lowering current costs, especially those that may be in excess of what is necessary

Cost tables databases providing information about the impact on product costs of using different input resources, manufacturing processes, and design specifications

Cost-volume-profit analysis a procedure that examines changes in costs and volume levels and the resulting effects on net income (profits)

Critical success factors those items (such quality, customer service, efficiency, cost control, and responsiveness to change) so important that, without them, the organization would cease to exist

CVP see cost-volume-profit analysis

Data bits of knowledge or facts that have not been summarized or categorized in a manner useful to a decision maker

Decentralization a management style that exists when top management grants subordinate managers a significant degree of autonomy and independence in operating and making decisions for their organizational units

Decision making the process of choosing among the alternative solutions available to a course of action or a problem situation

Decision variable an unknown item for which a linear programming problem is being solved

Defective unit a unit that has been rejected at a control inspection point for failure to meet appropriate standards of quality or designated product specifications; can be economically reworked and sold through normal distribution channels

Deferred compensation pay related to current performance that will be received at a later time, typically after retirement

Degree of operating leverage a factor that indicates how a percentage change in sales, from the existing or current level, will affect company profits; calculated as contribution margin divided by net income; is equal to (1 ÷ margin of safety percentage)

Dependent variable an unknown variable that is to be predicted using one or more independent variables

Differential cost a cost that differs in amount among the alternatives being considered

Direct cost a cost that is distinctly traceable to a particular cost object

Direct costing see variable costing

Direct labor the time spent by individuals who work specifically on manufacturing a product or performing a service; the cost of such time

Direct material a readily identifiable part of a product; the cost of such a part

Direct method a process of service department cost allocation that assigns service department costs directly to revenue-producing areas with only one set of intermediate cost pools or allocations

Discount rate the rate of return used to discount future cash flows to their present value amounts; should equal or exceed an organization's weighted average cost of capital

Discounting the process of reducing future cash flows to present value amounts

Discrete spoilage spoilage that occurs at a specific point in the production process

Discretionary cost a cost that is periodically reviewed by a decision maker in a process of determining whether it continues to be in accord with ongoing policies; a cost that arises from a management decision to fund an activity at a specified cost amount for a specified period of time, generally one year; a cost that can be reduced to zero in the short run if necessity so dictates

Dispersion the degree of variability or difference; is measured as the vertical distance of an actual point from the estimated regression line in least squares regression analysis

Distribution cost cost incurred to warehouse, transport, or deliver a product or service

Dividend growth method a method of computing the cost of common stock equity that indicates the rate of return that common shareholders expect to earn in the form of dividends on a company's common stock

Dollar days (of inventory) a measurement of the value of inventory for the time that inventory stays in an area

Du Pont model a model that indicates the return on investment as it is affected by profit margin and asset turnover

Dual pricing arrangement a transfer pricing system that allows a selling division to record the transfer of goods or services at one price (e.g., a market or negotiated market price) and a buying division to record the transfer at another price (e.g., a cost-based amount)

Economic order quantity (EOQ) an estimate of the number of units per order that will be the least costly and provide the optimal balance between the costs of ordering and the costs of carrying inventory

Economic production run (EPR) an estimate of the number of units to produce at one time that minimizes the total costs of setting up production runs and carrying inventory

Economically reworked when the incremental revenue from the sale of reworked defective units is greater than the incremental cost of the rework

Effectiveness a measure of how well an organization's goals and objectives are achieved; compares actual output results to desired results; determination of the successful accomplishment of an objective

Efficiency a measure of the degree to which tasks were performed to produce the best yield at the lowest cost from the resources available; the degree to which a satisfactory relationship occurs when comparing outputs to inputs

Electronic data interchange (EDI) the computer-to-computer transfer of information in virtual real time using standardized formats developed by the American National Standards Institute

Employee Stock Ownership Plan (ESOP) a profit-sharing

compensation program in which investments are made in the securities of the employer

Employee time sheet   a source document that indicates, for each employee, what jobs were worked on during the day and for what amount of time

Engineered cost   a cost that has been found to bear an observable and known relationship to a quantifiable activity base

Engineering change order   a business mandate that changes the way in which a product or service is manufactured or performed by modifying the design, parts, process, or even quality of the product or service

Equivalent units of production   an approximation of the number of whole units of output that could have been produced during a period from the actual effort expended during that period; used in process costing systems to assign costs to production

Expatriate   a parent company or third-country national assigned to a foreign subsidiary or a foreign national assigned to the parent company

Expected annual capacity   a short-run concept that represents the anticipated level of capacity to be used by the firm in the upcoming year

Expected standard   a standard set at a level that reflects what is actually expected to occur in the future period; anticipates future waste and inefficiencies and allows for them; is of limited value for control and performance evaluation purposes

Expired cost   an expense or a loss

Failure cost   a quality control cost associated with goods or services that have been found not to conform or perform to the required standards as well as all related costs (such as that of the complaint department); may be internal or external

Feasible region   the graphical space contained within and on all of the constraint lines in the graphical solution to a linear programming problem

Feasible solution   a solution to a linear programming problem that does not violate any problem constraints

FIFO method (of process costing)   the method of cost assignment that computes an average cost per equivalent unit of production for the current period; keeps beginning inventory units and costs separate from current period production and costs

Financial budget   a budget that aggregates monetary details from the operating budgets; includes the cash and capital budgets of a company as well as the pro forma financial statements

Financial incentives   monetary rewards provided for performance above targeted objectives

Financing decision   a judgment made regarding the method of raising funds that will be used to make acquisitions; is based on an entity's ability to issue and service debt and equity securities

Fisher rate   the rate of return that equates the present values of the cash flows of all the multiple projects being considered; the rate of indifference

Fixed cost   a cost that remains constant in total within a specified range of activity

Fixed overhead spending variance   the difference between the total actual fixed overhead and budgeted fixed overhead; computed as part of the four-variance overhead analysis

Fixed overhead volume variance   see volume variance

Flexible budget   a series of individual budgets that present costs according to their behavior at different levels of activity

Flexible manufacturing system   a production system in which a single factory manufactures numerous variations of products through the use of computer-controlled robots

Focused factory arrangements   an arrangement in which a vendor (which may be an external party or an internal corporate division) agrees to provide a limited number of products according to specifications or to perform a limited number of unique services to a company that is typically operating on a just-in-time system

Foreign Corrupt Practices Act   a law passed by Congress in 1977 that makes it illegal for a company to engage in various "questionable" foreign payments and makes it mandatory for a company to maintain accurate accounting records and a reasonable system of internal control

Full costing   see absorption costing

Functional classification   a separation of costs into groups based on the similar reason for their incurrence; includes cost of goods sold, and detailed selling, general, and administrative expenses

Future value   the amount to which one or more sums of money invested at a specified interest rate will grow over a specified number of time periods

Goals   desired abstract achievements

Goal congruence   a circumstance in which the personal and organizational goals of decision makers throughout a firm are consistent and mutually supportive

Golden parachute   a benefits package that is triggered by the termination of a manager's employment

Grade (of product or service)   the addition or removal of product or service characteristics to satisfy additional needs, especially price

Grapevine   the informal relationships and channels of communication that exist in an organization

Growth rate   an estimate of the increase expected in dividends (or in market value) per share of stock

High-low method   a technique used to determine the fixed and variable portions of a mixed cost; uses only the highest and lowest levels of activity and related costs within the relevant range

Historical cost   a cost incurred in the past; the recorded purchase price of an asset; a sunk cost

Hurdle rate   a preestablished rate of return against which other rates of return are measured; is usually the cost of capital rate when used in evaluating capital projects

Hybrid costing   a costing system combining some characteristics of both job order and process costing systems

Ideal capacity   see theoretical capacity

Ideal standard   a standard that provides for no inefficiencies of any type; impossible to attain on a continuous basis

Idle time   the amount of time spent in storing inventory or waiting at a production operation for processing

Imposed budget   a budget developed by top management with little or no input from operating personnel; operating personnel are then informed of the budget objectives and constraints

Incremental analysis   a process of evaluating changes that focuses only on the factors that differ from one course of action or decision to another

Incremental cost   the additional cost of producing or selling a contemplated quantity of output

Incremental revenue   the additional revenue resulting from a contemplated sale

Incremental separate costs   all costs that are incurred for each joint product between the split-off point and the point of sale

Independent project   an investment project that has no specific bearing on any other investment project

Independent variable   a variable that, when changed, will cause consistent, observable changes in another variable; a variable used as the basis of predicting the value of a dependent variable

Indirect cost   a cost that cannot be traced explicitly to a particular cost object; a common cost

Information   bits of knowledge or fact that have been carefully chosen from a body of data and arranged in a meaningful way

Input-output coefficients   numbers (prefaced as multipliers to unknown variables) that indicate the rate at which each decision variable uses up (or depletes) the scarce resource

Institute of Management Accountants (IMA)   an organization composed of individuals interested in the field of management accounting; was previously the National Association of Accountants; coordinates the Certified Management Accountant program through its affiliate organization (the Institute of Certified Management Accountants)

Inspection time   the time taken to perform quality control activities

Integer programming   a mathematical programming technique in which all solutions for variables must be restricted to whole numbers

Internal control   any measure used by management to protect assets, promote the accuracy of records, ensure adherence to company policies, or promote operational efficiency; the totality of all internal controls represents the internal control system

Internal rate of return (IRR)   the expected or actual rate of return from a project based on, respectively, the assumed or actual cash flows; the discount rate at which the net present value of the cash flows equals zero

Interpolation   the process of finding a term between two other terms in a series

Inventoriable cost   see product cost

Investment center   an organizational unit in which the manager is responsible for generating revenues and planning and controlling expenses and has the authority to acquire, dispose of, and use plant assets to earn the highest rate of return feasible on those assets within the confines and to the support of the organization's goals

Investment decision   a judgment about which assets will be acquired by an entity to achieve its stated objectives

ISO 9000   a comprehensive series of international quality standards that define the various design, material procurement, production, quality-control, and delivery requirements and procedures necessary to produce quality products and services

JIT   see just-in-time

Job   a single unit or group of units identifiable as being produced to distinct customer specifications

Job cost record   see job order cost sheet

Job enrichment   the process of expanding a job to provide for personal achievement and recognition

Job order cost sheet   a source document that provides virtually all the financial information about a particular job; the set of all job order cost sheets for uncompleted jobs composes the Work in Process Inventory subsidiary ledger

Job order costing   a system of product costing used by an entity that provides limited quantities of products or services unique to a customer's needs; focus of recordkeeping is on individual jobs

Joint cost   the total of all costs (direct materials, direct labor, and overhead) incurred in a joint process up to the split-off point

Joint process   a manufacturing process that simultaneously produces more than one product line

Joint products   the primary outputs of a joint process; each joint product individually has substantial revenue-generating ability

Judgmental method (of risk adjustment)   an informal method of adjusting for risk that allows the decision maker to use logic and reason to decide whether a project provides an acceptable rate of return

Just-in-time   a philosophy about when to do something; the when is "as needed" and the something is a production, purchasing, or delivery activity

Just-in-time manufacturing system (JIT)   a production system that attempts to acquire components and produce inventory only as needed, to minimize product defects, and to reduce lead/setup times for acquisition and production

Kanban   the Japanese word for card; the original name for a JIT system because of the use of cards that indicated a work center's need for additional components during a manufacturing process

Key variable   a critical factor that management believes will be a direct cause of the achievement or nonachievement of the organizational goals and objectives

Labor efficiency variance   the number of hours actually worked minus the standard hours allowed for the production achieved multiplied by the standard rate to establish a value for efficiency (favorable) or inefficiency (unfavorable) of the work force

Labor mix variance   (actual mix × actual hours × standard rate) minus (standard mix × actual hours × standard rate); presents the financial effect associated with changing the proportionate amount of higher or lower paid workers in production

Labor rate variance   the actual rate (or actual weighted average rate) paid to labor for the period minus the standard rate multiplied by all hours actually worked during the period; actual labor cost minus (actual hours times standard rate)

Labor yield variance   (standard mix × actual hours × standard rate) minus (standard mix × standard hours × standard rate); shows the monetary impact of using more or fewer total hours than the standard allowed

Lead time   the time between the placement of an order to the time the goods arrive for usage or are produced by the company

Learning curve   a model that helps predict how labor time will decrease as people become more experienced at performing a task and eliminate the inefficiencies associated with unfamiliarity

Least squares regression analysis   a statistical technique that investigates the association between dependent and independent variables; determines the line of "best fit" for a set of observations by minimizing the sum of the squares of the vertical deviations between actual points and the regression line; can be used to determine the fixed and variable portions of a mixed cost

Life cycle costing   the accumulation of costs for activities that occur over the entire life cycle of a product from inception to abandonment by the manufacturer and consumer

Line employee   an employee who is directly responsible for achieving the organization's goals and objectives

Linear programming   a method of mathematical programming used to solve a problem that involves an objective function and multiple limiting factors or constraints

Long-term variable cost   a cost that was traditionally viewed as a fixed cost

Loss   an expired cost that was unintentionally incurred; a cost that does not relate to the generation of revenues

Make-or-buy decision   a decision that compares the cost of internally manufacturing a component of a final product (or providing a service function) with the cost of purchasing it from outside suppliers or from another division of the company at a specified transfer price

Management accounting   a discipline that includes almost all manipulations of financial information for use by management in performing their organizational functions and in assuring the proper use and handling of an entity's resources; includes the discipline of cost accounting

Manufacturer   a company engaged in a high degree of conversion that results in a tangible output

Manufacturing cells   linear or U-shaped production groupings of workers or machines

Manufacturing cycle efficiency   a ratio resulting from dividing the actual production time by total lead time; reflects the proportion of lead time that is value-added

Manufacturing resource planning (MRP II)   a fully integrated materials requirement planning system that involves top management and provides a basis for both strategic and tactical planning

Maquiladora   a business (typically U.S.-owned on the Mexican side of the United States–Mexico border) that exists under a special trade agreement in which foreign companies import materials into Mexico duty-free for assembly, then export the goods back out of Mexico, and only pay duty on the value added to inventory in the process

Margin of safety   the excess of the budgeted or actual sales of a company over its breakeven point; can be calculated in units or dollars or as a percentage; is equal to (1 ÷ degree of operating leverage)

Master budget   the comprehensive set of all budgetary schedules and the pro forma financial statements of an organization

Materials mix variance   (actual mix × actual quantity × standard price) minus (standard mix × actual quantity × standard price); computes the monetary effect of substituting a nonstandard mix of materials

Materials price variance   total actual cost of materials purchased minus (actual quantity of materials × standard price); the amount of money spent below (favorable) or in excess (unfavorable) of the standard price for the quantity of materials purchased; can be calculated based on the actual quantity of materials purchased or the actual quantity used

Materials quantity variance   (actual quantity × standard price) minus (standard quantity allowed × standard price); the standard cost saved (favorable) or expended (unfavorable) due to the difference between the actual quantity of materials used and the standard quantity of materials allowed for the goods produced during the period

Materials requirements planning (MRP)   a computer-based information system that simulates the ordering and scheduling of demand-dependent inventories; a simulation of the parts fabrication and subassembly activities that are required, in an appropriate time sequence, to meet a production master schedule

Materials requisition form   a source document that indicates the types and quantities of materials to be placed into production or used in performing a service; causes materials and their costs to be released from the Raw Materials Inventory warehouse and sent to Work in Process Inventory

Materials yield variance   (standard mix × actual quantity × standard price) minus (standard mix × standard quantity × standard price); computes the difference between the actual total quantity of input and the standard total quantity allowed based on output and uses standard mix and standard prices to determine variance

Mathematical programming   a variety of techniques used to allocate limited resources among activities to achieve a specific objective

Matrix structure   an organizational structure in which functional departments and project teams exist simultaneously so that the resulting lines of authority resemble a grid

Merit pay   a pay increment earned by achieving a specific level of performance

Method of least squares   see least squares regression analysis

Method of neglect   a method of treating spoiled units in the equivalent units schedule as if they did not occur; used for continuous normal spoilage

Mix   any possible combination of materials or labor inputs

Mixed cost   a cost that has both a variable and a fixed component; changes with changes in activity, but not proportionately

Modified FIFO method (of process costing)   the method of cost assignment that uses FIFO to compute a cost per equivalent unit but, in transferring units from a department, the costs of the beginning inventory units and the units started and completed are combined and averaged

MRP   see materials requirements planning

MRP II   see manufacturing resource planning

Multiple regression   a statistical technique that uses two or more independent variables to predict a dependent variable

Multiprocess handling   the ability of a worker to monitor and operate several (or all) machines in a manufacturing cell or perform all steps of a specific task

Mutually exclusive projects   a set of proposed capital projects from which one is chosen, causing all the others to be rejected

Mutually inclusive projects   a set of capital projects that are all related and that must all be chosen if the primary project is chosen

National Association of Accountants (NAA)   see Institute of Management Accountants

Negotiated transfer price   an intracompany charge for goods or services set through a process of negotiation between the selling and purchasing unit managers

Net cost of normal spoilage   the cost of spoiled work less the estimated disposal value of that work

Net present value (NPV)   the difference between the present values of all cash inflows and outflows for an investment project

Net present value method   a process that uses the discounted cash flows of a project to determine whether the rate of return on that project is equal to, higher than, or lower than the desired rate of return

Net realizable value approach   a method of accounting for by-products or scrap that requires that the net realizable value of these products be treated as a reduction in the cost of the primary products; primary product cost may be reduced by decreasing either (1) cost of goods sold when the joint products are sold or (2) the joint process cost allocated to the joint products

Net realizable value at split-off allocation   a method of allocating joint cost to joint products that uses, as the proration base, sales value at split-off minus all costs necessary to prepare and dispose of the products; requires that all joint products be salable at split-off point

Noncontrollable variance   the fixed overhead volume variance; computed as part of the two-variance approach to overhead analysis

Non-negativity constraint   a restriction in a linear programming problem stating that negative values for physical quantities cannot exist in a solution

Non-value-added activity   an activity that increases the time spent on a product or service but that does not increase its worth or value to the customer

Normal capacity   the long-run (5–10 years) average production or service volume of a firm; takes into consideration cyclical and seasonal fluctuations

Normal cost system   a valuation method that uses actual costs of direct materials and direct labor in conjunction with a predetermined overhead rate or rates in determining the cost of Work in Process Inventory

Normal loss   an expected decline in units during the production process

Normal spoilage   spoilage that has been planned or foreseen; is a product cost

Objectives   desired quantifiable achievements for a period of time

Objective function   the linear mathematical equation that states the purpose of a linear programming problem

Operating budget   a budget expressed in both units and dollars

Operating leverage   the proportionate relationship between a company's variable and fixed costs

Operation costing system   a hybrid costing system applied to batches of goods having different direct materials, but similar processing activity; uses a job order feature to trace direct materials cost to output and a process costing feature to average labor and overhead over all productive activity

Operations flow document   a document listing all operations necessary to produce one unit of product (or perform a specific service) and the corresponding time allowed for each operation

Opportunity cost   a potential benefit that is foregone because one course of action is chosen over another

Opportunity cost of capital   the highest rate of return that could be earned by using capital for the most attractive alternative project(s) available

Optimal mix of capital the combination of capital sources at which the lowest weighted average cost of capital is achieved

Optimal solution the solution to a linear programming problem that provides the best answer to the objective function

Order point the level of inventory that triggers the placement of an order for additional units; is determined based on usage, lead time, and safety stock

Ordering costs the variable costs associated with preparing, receiving, and paying for an order

Ordinary annuity a series of equal cash flows being received or paid at the end of a period

Organization chart a depiction of the functions, divisions, and positions of the people/jobs in a company and how they are related; also indicates the lines of authority and responsibility

Organizational level cost a cost incurred to support the ongoing facility or operations

Outlier an abnormal or nonrepresentative point within a data set

Out-of-pocket cost a cost that is a current or near-current cash expenditure

Outside processing cost a cost for materials or labor that is performed by a person or company other than the actual manufacturer of the product

Outsource the use, by one company, of an external provider of a service or manufacturer of a component

Overapplied overhead the amount of overhead that remains at the end of the period when the applied overhead amount is greater than the actual overhead that was incurred

Overhead any factory or production cost that is indirect to the product or service; does not include direct materials or direct labor; any production cost that cannot be directly traced to the product

Overhead application rate see predetermined overhead rate

Overhead efficiency variance the difference between total budgeted overhead at actual hours and total budgeted overhead at standard hours allowed for the production achieved; computed as part of three-variance analysis; same as variable overhead efficiency variance

Overhead spending variance the difference between total actual overhead and total budgeted overhead at actual hours; computed as part of three-variance analysis; equal to the sum of the variable and fixed overhead spending variances

Pareto analysis a method of ranking the causes of variation in a process according to the impact on an objective

Participatory budget a budget that has been developed through a process of joint decision making by top management and operating personnel

Payback period the time it takes an investor to recoup an original investment through cash flows from a project

Perfection standard see ideal standard

Performance evaluation the process of determining the degree of success in accomplishing a task; equates to both effectiveness and efficiency

Period cost a cost other than one associated with making or acquiring inventory

Periodic compensation a pay plan based on the time spent on the task rather than the work accomplished

Perks fringe benefits provided by the employer

Physical measurement allocation a method of allocating a common cost to products that uses a common physical characteristic as the proration base

Piece rate a pay plan in which workers are paid a flat rate for each unit of work accomplished

Planning the process of creating the goals and objectives for an organization and developing a strategy for achieving them in a systematic manner

Postinvestment audit the process of gathering information on the actual results of a capital project and comparing them to the expected results

Practical capacity the physical production or service volume that a firm could achieve during normal working hours with consideration given to ongoing-expected operating interruptions

Practical standard a standard that can be reached or slightly exceeded with reasonable effort by workers; allows for normal, unavoidable time problems or delays and for worker breaks; believed to be most effective in inducing the best performance from workers, since such a standard represents an attainable challenge

Predetermined overhead rate an estimated constant charge per unit of activity used to assign overhead cost to production or services of the period; calculated by dividing total budgeted annual overhead by a selected measure of volume or activity; is also the standard overhead application rate

Predictor an activity measure that, when changed, is accompanied by consistent, observable changes in another item

Preference decision the second decision made in capital project evaluation in which projects are ranked according to their impact on the achievement of company objectives (see also screening decision)

Present value the amount that one or more future cash flows is worth currently, given a specified rate of interest

Present value index see profitability index

Prevention cost a cost incurred to improve quality by preventing defects from occurring

Prime cost the total cost of direct materials and direct labor for a product

Probability distribution a range of possible values for which each value has an assigned likelihood of occurrence

Process benchmarking benchmarking that focuses on practices and how the best-in-class companies achieved their results

Process costing a method of accumulating and assigning costs to units of production in companies producing large quantities of homogeneous products; accumulates costs by cost component in each production department and assigns costs to units using equivalent units of production

Process map a flowchart or diagram indicating every step that goes into making a product or providing a service

Process yield the proportion of good units that resulted from the activities expended

Product contribution margin the difference between selling price and variable cost of goods sold

Product cost a cost associated with making or acquiring inventory

Product (or process) level cost a cost that is caused by the development, production or acquisition of different items

Product life cycle a model depicting the stages through which a product class (not necessarily each product) passes

Product line margin see segment margin

Production (or service) time the actual time consumed performing the functions necessary to manufacture a product

Productive capacity the number of total units that could be produced during a period based on available equipment time

Productive processing time the proportion of total time that is value-added time; also known as manufacturing cycle efficiency

Profit center a responsibility center in which mangers are responsible for generating revenues and planning and controlling all expenses

Profit margin the ratio of income to sales

Profit sharing an incentive payment to employees that is contingent on organizational or individual performance

Profit-volume graph a visual representation of the amount of profit or loss associated with each level of sales

Profitability index (PI) a ratio that compares the present value of net cash flows to the present value of the net investment

Program budgeting an approach to budgeting that relates resource inputs to service outputs

Project the purchase, installation, and operation of a capital asset

Pull system a production system dictated by product sales and demand; a system in which parts are delivered or produced only as they are needed by the work center for which they are intended; requires only minimal storage facilities

Purchasing cost see cost of purchasing

Push system the traditional production system in which work centers may produce inventory that is not currently needed because of lead time or economic production/order requirements; requires that excess inventory be stored until needed

Quality all the characteristics of a product or service that make it able to meet the stated or implied needs of the person acquiring it; relates to both performance and value; the pride of workmanship; conformance to requirements

Quality assurance the process of determining that product or service quality conforms to designated specifications usually through an inspection process

Quality audit a review of product design activities (although not for individual products), manufacturing processes and controls, quality documentation and records, and management philosophy

Racketeer Influenced and Corrupt Organizations Act a law enacted by Congress in 1970 designed to discourage organized crime from investing profits from illegal activities in legitimate businesses

Raiders firms and individuals that specialize in taking over other firms

Realized value approach a method of accounting for by-products or scrap that does not recognize any value for these products until they are sold; the value recognized upon sale can be treated as other revenue or other income

Red-line system an inventory ordering system in which a red line is painted on the inventory container at a point deemed to be the reorder point

Regression line any line that goes through the means (or averages) of the set of observations for an independent and its dependent variables; mathematically, there is a line of "best fit," which is the least squares regression line

Reinvestment assumption an assumption made about the rates of return that will be earned by intermediate cash flows from a capital project; NPV and PI assume reinvestment at the discount rate; IRR assumes reinvestment at the IRR

Relevant cost a cost that is logically associated with a specific problem or decision

Relevant costing a process that compares, to the extent possible and practical, the incremental revenues and incremental costs of alternative decisions

Relevant range the specified range of activity over which a variable cost per unit remains constant or a fixed cost remains fixed in total; is generally assumed to be the normal operating range of the organization

Replacement cost an amount that a firm would pay to replace an asset or buy a new one that performs the same functions as an asset currently held

Residual income the profit earned by a responsibility center that exceeds an amount "charged" for funds committed to it

Responsibility the obligation to accomplish a task or achieve an objective

Responsibility accounting system an accounting information system for successively higher-level managers about the performance of segments or subunits under the control of each specific manager

Responsibility center a cost object under the control of a manager

Responsibility report a report that reflects the revenues and/or costs under the control of a particular unit manager

Results benchmarking benchmarking in which an end product or service is examined; the focus is on product/service specifications and performance results

Return of capital the recovery of the original investment (or principal) in a project

Return on capital income; is equal to the rate of return multiplied by the amount of the investment

Return on investment a ratio that relates income generated by the investment center to the resources (or asset base) used to produce that income

Revenue center a responsibility center for which a manager is accountable only for the generation of revenues and has no control over setting selling prices, or budgeting or incurring costs

Risk uncertainty; reflects the possibility of differences between the expected and actual future returns from an investment

Risk-adjusted discount rate method a formal method of adjusting for risk in which the decision maker increases the rate used for discounting the future cash flows to compensate for increased risk

Robinson-Patman Act a law that prohibits companies from pricing the same products at different amounts when those amounts do not reflect related cost differences

Rolling budget see continuous budgeting

Routing document see operations flow document

Safety stock a buffer level of inventory kept on hand by a company in the event of fluctuating usage or unusual delays in lead time

Sales mix the relative combination of quantities of sales of the various products that make up the total sales of a company

Sales value at split-off allocation a method of assigning joint cost to joint products that uses the relative sales values of the products at the split-off point as the proration basis; use of this method requires that all joint products are salable at split-off

Scarce resource a resource that is essential to production activity, but is available only in some limited quantity

Scattergraph a graph that plots all known activity observations and the associated costs; is used to separate mixed costs into their variable and fixed components and to examine patterns reflected by the plotted observations

Scrap an incidental output of a joint process; is salable but the sales value from scrap is not enough for management to justify undertaking the joint process; is viewed as having a lower sales value than a by-product; leftover materials that have a minimal but distinguishable disposal value

Screening decision the first decision made in evaluating capital projects that indicates whether a project is desirable based on some previously established minimum criterion or criteria (see also preference decision)

Segment margin the excess of revenues over direct variable expenses and avoidable fixed expenses for a particular segment

Sensitivity analysis a process of determining the amount of change that must occur in a variable before a different decision would be made

Service company an individual or firm engaged in a high or moderate degree of conversion that results in service output

Service department an organizational unit that provides one or more specific functional tasks for other internal units

Service time the actual time consumed performing the functions necessary to provide a service

Setup costs the direct or indirect costs of getting equipment ready for each new production run

Shirking the process of an individual free-riding on a group effort because the individual's share of the group reward is insufficient to compensate for his or her separate effort

Shrinkage a decrease in units arising from an inherent characteristic of the production process; includes decreases caused by evaporation, leakage, and oxidation

Simple interest a method of determining interest in which interest is earned on only the original investment (or principal) amount

Simple regression a statistical technique that uses only one independent variable to predict a dependent variable

Simplex method an iterative (sequential) algorithm used to solve multivariable, multiconstraint linear programming problems

Slack variable a variable used in a linear programming problem that represents the unused amount of a resource at any level of operation; associated with less-than-or-equal-to constraints

Special order decision a situation in which management must determine a sales price to charge for manufacturing or service jobs outside the company's normal production/service realm

Split-off point the point at which the outputs of a joint process are first identifiable or can be separated as individual products

Spoilage an occurrence in the production process that causes unacceptable units to be produced

Spoiled unit a unit that is rejected at a control inspection point for failure to meet appropriate standards of quality or designated product specifications; cannot be economically reworked to be brought up to standard

Staff employee an employee responsible for providing advice, guidance, and service to line personnel

Standard a model or budget against which actual results are compared and evaluated; a benchmark or norm used for planning and control purposes

Standard cost a budgeted or estimated cost to manufacture a single unit of product or perform a single service

Standard cost card a document that summarizes the direct materials, direct labor, and overhead standard quantities and prices needed to complete one unit of product

Standard cost system a valuation method that uses predetermined norms for direct materials, direct labor, and overhead to assign costs to the various inventory accounts and cost of goods sold

Standard deviation the measure of variability of data around the average (or mean) value of a set of data

Standard error of the estimate   a measure of dispersion that reflects the average difference between actual observations and expected results provided by a regression line

Standard overhead application rate   a predetermined overhead rate used in a standard cost system; can be a separate variable or fixed rate or a combined overhead rate

Standard quantity allowed   the quantity of input (in hours or some other cost driver measurement) required at standard for the output actually achieved for the period

Statements on Management Accounting   pronouncements developed and issued by the Management Accounting Practices Committee of the Institute of Management Accountants; application of these statements is through voluntary, not legal, compliance

Statistical process control (SPC)   the use of control techniques that are based on the theory that a process has natural variations in it over time, but uncommon variations are typically the points at which the process produces "errors," which can be defective goods or poor service

Steady-state phase   that point at which the learning curve becomes flat and only minimal improvements in performance are achieved

Step cost   a cost that increases in distinct amounts because of increased activity

Step method   a process of service department cost allocation that assigns service department costs to cost objects after considering the interrelationships of the service departments and revenue-producing departments

Stock appreciation rights   the right to receive cash, stock, or a combination of cash and stock based on the difference between a specified dollar amount per share of stock and the quoted market price per share at some future date

Stock option   a right allowing the holder to purchase shares of common stock during some future time frame and at a specified price

Stockout   the condition of not having inventory available upon need or request

Strategic planning   the process of developing a statement of long-range (5–10 years) goals for the organization and defining the strategies and policies that will help the organization achieve those goals

Strategic staffing   an approach to personnel management that requires a department to analyze its staffing needs by considering its long-term objectives and those of the overall company and determining a specific combination of permanent and temporary employees with the best skills to meet those needs

Strict FIFO method (of process costing)   the method of cost assignment that uses FIFO to compute a cost per equivalent unit and, in transferring units from a department, keeps the cost of the beginning units separate from the cost of the units started and completed during the current period

Suboptimization   a situation in which an individual manager pursues goals and objectives that are in his/her own and his/her segment's particular interests rather than in the best interests of the company

Substitute good   an item that can replace another item to satisfy the same wants or needs

Sunk cost   a cost incurred in the past and not relevant to any future courses of action; the historical or past cost associated with the acquisition of an asset or a resource

Surplus variable   a variable used in a linear programming problem that represents overachievement of a minimum requirement; associated with greater-than or equal-to constraints

Superfull absorption costing   see uniform capitalization rules

Synchronous management   the use of all techniques that help an organization achieve its goals

Tactical planning   the process of determining the specific means or objectives by which the strategic plans of the organization will be achieved; are short-range in nature (usually 1–18 months)

Takeover   the acquisition of managerial control of the corporation by an outside or inside investor; control is achieved by acquiring enough stock and stockholder votes to control the board of directors and management

Target costing   a method of determining what the cost of a product should be based on the product's estimated selling price less the desired profit

Tax benefit (of depreciation)   the amount of depreciation deductible for tax purposes multiplied by the tax rate; the reduction in taxes caused by the deductibility of depreciation

Tax-deferred income   current compensation that is taxed at a future date

Tax-exempt income   current compensation that is never taxed

Tax shield (of depreciation)   the amount of depreciation deductible for tax purposes; the amount of revenue shielded from taxes because of the depreciation deduction

Theoretical capacity   the estimated maximum production or service volume that a firm could achieve during a period

Theory of constraints   a method of analyzing the bottlenecks (constraints) that keep a system from achieving higher performance; states that production cannot take place at a rate faster than the slowest machine or person in the process

Throughput   the total completed and sold output of plant during a period

Timeline   a tool that visually illustrates the amounts and timing of all cash inflows and outflows; is used in analyzing cash flow from a capital project

Total contribution margin   see Contribution margin

Total cost to account for   the sum of the costs in beginning inventory and the costs of the current period

Total expected value (for a project)   the sum of the individual cash flows in a probability distribution multiplied by their related probabilities

Total overhead variance   the difference between total actual overhead and total applied overhead; the amount of under- or overapplied overhead

Total quality control (TQC) the implementation of all practices and policies designed to eliminate poor quality and variability in the production or service process; places the primary responsibility for quality at the source of the product or service

Total quality management (TQM) a structural system for creating organizationwide participation in planning and implementing a continuous improvement process that exceeds the expectations of the customer/client; the application of quality principles to all company endeavors; also known as total quality control

Total units to account for the sum of the beginning inventory units and units started during the current period

Total variance the difference between total actual cost incurred and total standard cost for the output produced during the period

Transfer price an internal charge established for the exchange of goods or services between organizational units of the same company

Transfer time the time consumed moving products or components from one place to another

Treasurer an individual (in a corporation) who handles the actual resources of the organization but who does not have access to the accounting records

Two-bin system an inventory ordering system in which two containers (or stacks) of raw materials or parts are available for use; when one container is depleted, the removal of materials from the second container begins and a purchase order is placed to refill the first container

Underapplied overhead the amount of overhead that remains at the end of the period when the applied overhead amount is less than the actual overhead that was incurred

Unexpired cost an asset

Uniform capitalization rules rules of the Tax Reform Act of 1986 that require entities to capitalize as product cost many costs that had previously been treated as period costs

Unit level cost a cost caused by the production or acquisition of a single unit of product or the delivery of a single unit of service

Units started and completed the difference between the number of units completed for the period and the units in beginning inventory; can also be computed as the number of units started during the period minus the units in ending inventory

Usage the quantity of inventory used or sold each day

Value the characteristic of meeting the highest number of customer needs at the lowest possible price

Value-added activity an activity that increases the worth of the product or service to the customer

Value chart a visual representation indicating the value-added and non-value-added activities and time spent in those activities from the beginning to the end of a process

Variable cost a cost that varies in total in direct proportion to changes in activity; is constant on a per unit basis

Variable cost ratio the proportion of each revenue dollar represented by variable costs; computed as variable costs divided by sales or as $(1 - \text{contribution margin ratio})$

Variable costing a cost accumulation and reporting method that includes only variable production costs (direct materials, direct labor, and variable overhead) as inventoriable or product costs; treats fixed overhead as a period cost; is not acceptable for external reporting and tax returns

Variable overhead efficiency variance the difference between budgeted variable overhead based on actual hours and variable overhead applied to production

Variable overhead spending variance the difference between total actual variable overhead and the budgeted amount of variable overhead based on actual hours

Variance a difference between an actual and a standard or budgeted cost; is favorable if actual is less than standard and is unfavorable if actual is greater than standard

Variance analysis the process of categorizing the nature (favorable or unfavorable) of the differences between standard and actual costs and determining the reasons for those differences

Vertex a corner produced by the intersection of lines on a graph

Volume variance a fixed overhead variance that represents the difference between budgeted fixed overhead and fixed overhead applied to production of the period; is also referred to as the noncontrollable variance

Waste a residual output of a production process that must be disposed of because it has no sales value

Weighted average cost of capital a composite of the cost of the various sources of funds that comprise a firm's capital structure; the minimum rate of return that must be earned on new investments so as not to dilute shareholder interests

Weighted average method (of process costing) the method of cost assignment that computes an average cost per equivalent unit of production for all units completed during the current period; combines beginning inventory units and costs with current production and costs, respectively, to compute the average

Yield the quantity of output that results from a specified input

Yield ratio the expected or actual relationship between input and output

Zero-base budgeting a comprehensive budgeting process that systematically considers the priorities and alternatives for current and proposed activities in relation to organization objectives; requires the rejustification of ongoing activities

AUTHOR INDEX

ORGANIZATION INDEX

SUBJECT INDEX

PHOTO CREDITS